State	Population (1000's in 2006)[c]	Per Capita Personal Income (2005)[d]	Bush Vote 2004 (%)[e]	Conservatism (rank)[f]
Alabama	4,599	$29,623	62.5	8
Alaska	670	$35,433	61.1	22
Arizona	6,166	$30,157	54.9	28
Arkansas	2,811	$26,641	54.4	6
California	36,458	$36,890	44.4	43
Colorado	4,753	$37,459	51.7	36
Connecticut	3,505	$47,519	43.9	47
Delaware	853	$37,084	45.8	42
Florida	18,090	$34,099	52.1	31
Georgia	9,364	$31,191	58.0	18
Hawaii	1,285	$34,468	45.3	48
Idaho	1,466	$28,398	68.4	12
Illinois	12,832	$36,264	44.5	40
Indiana	6,314	$31,150	59.9	16
Iowa	2,982	$31,795	49.9	23
Kansas	2,764	$32,948	62.0	10
Kentucky	4,206	$28,317	59.5	19
Louisiana	4,288	$24,582	56.7	7
Maine	1,322	$30,808	44.6	37
Maryland	5,616	$41,996	43.0	41
Massachusetts	6,437	$43,702	36.9	49
Michigan	10,096	$32,735	47.8	32
Minnesota	5,167	$37,322	48.0	38
Mississippi	2,911	$24,925	59.1	1
Missouri	5,843	$31,299	53.3	20
Montana	945	$28,906	59.1	17
Nebraska	1,768	$32,988	66.0	14
Nevada	2,496	$35,780	50.7	21
New Hampshire	1,315	$37,835	49.0	39
New Jersey	8,725	$43,822	46.2	45
New Mexico	1,955	$27,912	49.8	35
New York	19,306	$40,072	40.1	46
North Carolina	8,857	$31,029	56.1	15
North Dakota	636	$31,230	62.9	2
Ohio	11,478	$31,867	50.8	26
Oklahoma	3,579	$29,908	65.6	3
Oregon	3,701	$32,174	47.4	33
Pennsylvania	12,441	$34,848	48.5	30
Rhode Island	1,068	$35,219	38.7	43
South Carolina	4,321	$28,212	58.1	9
South Dakota	782	$32,642	59.9	4
Tennessee	6,039	$30,952	56.9	13
Texas	23,508	$32,604	61.1	10
Utah	2,550	$27,497	72.7	5
Vermont	624	$32,731	38.8	50
Virginia	7,643	$37,552	53.8	24
Washington	6,396	$35,234	45.6	34
West Virginia	1,818	$26,029	56.1	27
Wisconsin	5,557	$33,251	49.4	25
Wyoming	515	$37,270	69.0	29

Sources:

[c] Hovey, Kendra A., and Harold A. Hovey. 2007. *CQ's State Fact Finder 2007*. Washington, DC: CQ Press, 18.

[d] Hovey and Hovey 2007, 44.

[e] InfoPlease website (http://www.infoplease.com/ipa/A0922901.html).

[f] Adapted from: Erikson, Robert S., Gerald C. Wright, and John P. McIver. 2006. "Public Opinion in the States: A Quarter Century of Change and Stability." In *Public Opinion in State Politics*, ed. Jeffrey E. Cohen. Stanford, CA: Stanford University Press.

State and Local

POLITICS

Institutions and Reform

Todd Donovan
Western Washington University

Christopher Z. Mooney
University of Illinois at Springfield

Daniel A. Smith
University of Florida

WADSWORTH
CENGAGE Learning™

Australia • Brazil • Canada • Mexico • Singapore • Spain • United Kingdom • United States

WADSWORTH
CENGAGE Learning™

State and Local Politics:
Institutions & Reforms
First Edition
Todd Donovan, Christopher Z. Mooney,
Daniel Smith

Executive Editor: Carolyn Merrill

Senior Development Editor: Stacey Sims

Editorial Assistant: Katherine Hayes

Associate Development Project Manager:
Lee McCracken

Senior Marketing Manager: Trent Whatcott

Marketing Assistant: Aimee Lewis

Marketing Communications Manager:
Heather Baxley

Senior Content Project Manager: Josh Allen

Art Director: Linda Helcher

Manufacturing Manager: Barbara Britton

Permissions Editor: Roberta Broyer

Production Service: Pre-Press PMG

Photo Researcher: Sharon Donahue

Cover Designer: Beckmeyer Design

Cover Image: Elsa/Reportage/©Getty Images

For more information about our products, contact us at:
Cengage Learning Academic Resource Center, 1-800-423-0563

For permission to use material from this text or product, submit
a request online at **http://www.cengagerights.com**.
Any additional questions about permissions can be submitted
by e-mail to **cengagerights@cengage.com**.

Library of Congress Control Number:
2007942366
Student Edition:
ISBN-13: 978-0-495-09044-1
ISBN-10: 0-495-09044-1

Cengage Higher Education
10 Davis Drive
Belmont, CA 94002-3098
USA

Printed in Canada
1 2 3 4 5 6 7 11 10 09 08 07

To our families, with love: Deborah, Fiona, and Ian; Laura, Allison, and Charlie; and Brenda, Eliot, and Safi.

TODD DONOVAN (Ph.D. University of California, Riverside) is a professor of political science at Western Washington University where he teaches state and local politics, American politics, parties, campaigns and elections, comparative electoral systems, and introductory  research methods and statistics. His research interests include direct democracy, election systems and representation, political behavior, sub-national politics, and the political economy of local development. He has published extensively in academic journals, written a number of books on direct democracy, elections, institutions, and reform, and has received numerous grants and awards for his work. With Ken Hoover, he is the co-author of *The Elements of Social Scientific Thinking*, also with Wadsworth.

CHRISTOPHER Z. MOONEY (Ph.D. University of Wisconsin, Madison) is professor of political studies at the University of Illinois at Springfield, and research fellow at the Institute of Govern-  ment and Public Affairs at the University of Illinois. He is the founding editor of *State Politics and Policy Quarterly*, the official journal of the State Politics and Policy section of the American Political Science Association. He has published many books and articles on legislative politics, morality policy, and research methods. He can be heard each week as a regular panelist on State Week in Review, an NPR radio program broadcast state-wide in Illinois.

DANIEL A. SMITH (Ph.D. University of Wisconsin, Madison) is associate professor of political science at the University of Florida and the Interim Director of the M.A. Political Campaigning Program. He teaches courses on state and local politics,  political parties, interest groups, campaign finance, and direct democracy. He has published more than two dozen articles on direct democracy, political parties, interests groups, and campaign finance, as well as two books on the politics and processes of ballot initiatives. Smith, a former Fulbright Scholar, serves on the Board of Directors of the Ballot Initiative Strategy Center Foundation (BISCF) and is a Senior Research Fellow at the Initiative and Referendum Institute.

Studying State and Local Government

American state and local governments provide perhaps the best opportunity to study political phenomena in the world. They give political scientists a manageable number of cases similar enough in social structure, economics, politics, and government to make meaningful comparisons of them without becoming overwhelmed by extraneous variation. But they are also different enough from one another in theoretically and substantively important ways to allow us to test a wide range of questions concerning political behavior and policymaking central to our understanding of politics. For example, what is the best way to choose our leaders? How should we make public policy? What are the impacts of public policy on policy problems, people, businesses, the economy, or anything else? These and other fundamental questions can not only be explored more productively by studying the American states and communities, they can be explored *best* there.

The study of state and local government can be just as productive and interesting for *students* as it is for political scientists. But as we all know, an undergraduate state and local government class is usually not the highlight of a student's college career. It is often taught as a large service course required by a variety of majors—everything from education to journalism to social work—or as a social science general education course. Ironically, state and local governments will have a greater impact on most students for the duration of their lives than almost any other topic they study in a political science class. For example, teachers and social workers will be working for these governments, and many journalists will at least begin their careers by covering them. Even American college students not pursuing these majors will be deeply affected by the politics and government of the states and local communities. Laws, ordinances, and regulations about their driver's licenses, the clubs and restaurants where they work and play, landlord-renter relationships, and even the large state universities many of them attend are all in the bailiwick of these governments. Furthermore, college students tend to move more often than the average American, and in going from place to place for college, a new job, or just spring break, they are frequently exposed to the diversity of state and local government laws around the country—the differing speed limits, gambling laws, alcohol sales regulations, tax structures, and so forth. For the untrained person, these variations can be just confusing annoyances, but for those students who have taken a good state and local government class—and for those students who have read this book—the exposure to these variations are teachable moments. Such students are more likely both to notice and to understand these differences, making them better citizens in the process and for the long run.

Approach of the Book

We wrote this book with these teachable moments in mind, packing each chapter with lively and wide-ranging examples pulled from headlines across the nation to illuminate our points. From the outset, we have made every effort to engage, excite, and inform students about American state and local government and politics and to help them develop the critical thinking skills needed to make them better political scientists and better citizens.

Themes

To accomplish this task, we have integrated the following themes throughout the book.

Institutions Matter The central theoretical theme of this book is that institutions matter. The states and communities are especially well suited for testing and demonstrating this proposition. Furthermore, the institutions of state and local government matter, and we want students to understand why and how this is so. Throughout the book, we show countless ways in which state and local government affects students' lives, and the country in general, every day.

Reform Can Happen Reform is important. If institutions have consequences, then how and when they are changed is well worth considering, too. By focusing on reform, we excite students about the possibility of change and motivate their civic engagement. If reform can happen, then political science can be a dynamic and compelling pursuit.

Comparisons Help Us Understand the Political World This is our central methodological theme. We continually return to the questions of how politics and government differ among the states and communities and the causes and effects of this variation.

Approaches

Up-to-date Scholarship Since 1990, there has been a renaissance in political science scholarship using the states and communities to understand political processes and behavior. We have integrated the insights of this literature throughout the book so that students and instructors have access to the most current research available on the subject. We have meticulously documented our sources to assist students working on class assignments, as well as to help instructors wanting to keep abreast of this important and extensive literature.

Political Science Methods This is a *political science* textbook, not a government textbook.

We very self-consciously show students how to use the variation among the states and communities to develop and test hypotheses about political behavior and policymaking. Rather than simply describing how things are, we expose students to a multitude of differences among the states and communities and ask them to think about their causes and effects. In doing so, students will not only learn much about American states and communities, but they will also learn how to *think like political scientists*. That is a skill that will help them in any college course they take thereafter, as well as throughout the rest of their lives.

Three Unique Chapters on Direct Democracy, Land Use Policy, and Morality Policy These three subjects have been at the center of the most significant political battles in the country in recent years, have recently generated a great deal of high quality scholarship, and are sure to engage student interest. Direct democracy—which represents one of the major institutional differences between states—has been used by citizens to pass laws cutting taxes, increasing funding for public education, banning smoking in public places, prohibiting same-sex marriage, providing funding for stem cell research, and raising the minimum wage. Land use policy, including zoning regulations and eminent domain, is central to our understanding of the historical development, and current political landscape, of many American local governments. Morality policy—from teaching sex education in the public schools, to the regulation of alcohol, gambling, and pornography, to the permissibility of abortions and same-sex marriage—has long-inspired extraordinary political acts and has generated heated debate over the basic values that define our personal identities in the American states and communities.

Plan of the Book

We try to convince students that state and local politics have important consequences for their own lives. The book begins with an introduction to some of the major questions asked when we study state and local politics and a discussion of some of the methods we use to answer such questions. The second chapter places states and localities in the larger context of the American federal system.

Subsequent chapters introduce students to various state and local political institutions, with a particular emphasis on how different institutions, in different places, may produce different outcomes. Chapter 3 examines rules that affect elections and participation, and Chapter 4 covers the unique institutions of direct democracy. Chapter 5 covers political parties, and Chapter 6 examines interest groups. Chapters 7, 8, and 9 examine the core institutions of American state politics: legislatures, governors, and courts, respectively.

Chapter 10 is devoted to state and local fiscal politics, and serves as a segue to a series of chapters that explore how politics affect public policy. Although many of first ten chapters include treatments of state *and* local issues, Chapter 11 (municipal governments) and Chapter 12 (local land use) give particular attention to local politics and policy. The final three chapters are devoted to specific policy areas where states and local governments are particularly influential: morality policy (Chapter 13), social welfare and health (Chapter 14), and education (Chapter 15).

Special Features and Pedagogy

Boxed Features In order to emphasize further the themes of the book, we have developed boxed features for each chapter that highlight the effects of institutions, comparison, and reform. These boxes provide thought-provoking, concrete examples of the kinds of problems and issues faced at the state and local level, so that students understand how institutions and systems affect actual individuals in real-life situations.

- *Institutions Matter.* These boxes examine the way institutions influence outcomes and consider such topics as the impact the threat

of ballot initiative has in spurring legislative action on issues; the impact of federalism, home rule, and morality policy on decency standards in Utah and Nevada; and Alaska's use of the mixed primary system.

- *Comparisons Help Us Understand.* These boxes use comparative data from the states to test different hypotheses about the political process. For example, in Chapter 4, this feature examines the question of whether direct democracy or representative democracy results in better outcomes for minority groups; in Chapter 5, it describes the existence of factions of dissent within political parties; and in Chapter 13, it lays out variations in policies on same-sex marriage in a number of different states.

- *Reform Can Happen.* These boxes look at the different ways reforms may be implemented. In Chapter 4, for example, the feature looks at the impact of direct democracy in implementing medical marijuana legislation. Other chapters examine efforts to de-professionalize state legislatures by imposing term limits, the types of future reforms likely to inspire morality politics, and the role played by third party candidates to place reform issues on the public agenda.

Full-Color Design Vivid tables, maps, graphs, and photographs throughout the book provide the visual tools students need to process detailed comparative data on the states.

Endpapers The inside front and back cover of the book provide basic information on state and local governments for convenient reference.

Other Pedagogical Features Each chapter includes a full set of study aids including a chapter outline, a chapter opening vignette, a chapter summary, key terms, suggested readings, and an annotated list of websites. The chapter outlines list the major sections of the material presented so students can get a general sense of the topics to be covered. The opening vignettes introduce the chapter with a current example of an issue directly related to the material, so that students get a sense of how the principles and concepts presented play out in real-life situations. The summary provides a recap of the most important ideas of the chapter. The key terms and definitions provide an opportunity for students to check their mastery of the terminology, while the suggested readings and a list of annotated websites give students a starting point for further exploration and study.

Instructor Resources: The Instructor's Resource Manual CD-ROM contains:

- **A test bank in Microsoft Word and Exam-View® computerized testing,** created by the authors of the book, offers a large array of well-crafted multiple-choice and essay questions, along with their answers, page references, and learning objectives.
- **PowerPoint Lectures** bring together text-specific outlines, tables, figures, and photos from the book for each chapter.
- **An Instructor's Manual** with chapter summaries, learning objectives, discussion questions, suggestions for stimulating class activities and projects, and tips on integrating media into your class, including step-by-step instructions on how to create your own podcasts.
- **A Resource Integration Guide** outlines the rich collection of resources available to instructors and students within the chapter-by-chapter framework of the book, suggesting how and when each supplement can be used to optimize learning.

Student Resources:
- **A companion website for *State and Local Politics*** gives students access to tutorial quizzes and learning objectives and more.

This book represents the tangible expression of the work of dozens of people. Fortunately for us, we have the honor of putting our names on the spine. We would like to express our deepest gratitude to all those who offered countless hours of their valuable time to help us in our efforts on this project. First, some of the nation's top political scientists gave us detailed feedback on early drafts of the chapters in their areas of expertise: Thad Beyle (University of North Carolina at Chapel Hill), Chris Bonneau (University of Pittsburgh), Tom Carsey (University of North Carolina at Chapel Hill), Susan Clarke (University of Colorado-Boulder), Richard Clucas (Portland State University), Chris Cooper (Western Carolina University), Peter Eisinger (New York University), Margaret Ferguson (Indiana University at Indianapolis), Peter Francia (Eastern Carolina University), Don Haider-Markel (University of Kansas), Zoltan Hajnal (University of California, San Diego), Melinda Gann Hall (Michigan State University), Jennifer Jensen (SUNY-Binghamton), Lael Keiser (University of Missouri-Columbia), Gary Moncrief (Boise State University), Karen Mossberger (University of Illinois at Chicago), Dometrius Nelson (Texas Tech University), Adam Newmark (Appalachian State University), Steve Nicholson (University of California, Merced), Tony Nownes (University of Tennessee), Elizabeth Oldmixon (North Texas University), David Paul (Ohio State University-Newark), Marvin Overby (University of Missouri-Columbia), Eric Plutzer (Penn State University), Mark Rom (Georgetown University), Beth Rosenson (University of Florida), Richard Scher (University of Florida), Joe Soss (University of Wisconsin-Madison), Don Studlar (West Virginia University), Ray Tatalovich (Loyola University, Chicago), Bob Turner (Skidmore College), Craig Volden (Ohio State University), Carol Weissert (Florida State University), Dick Winters (Dartmouth College), Gerald Wright (Indiana University at Bloomington), and Joseph Zimmerman (SUNY-Albany).

We would also like to thank those scholars and teachers whom Wadsworth recruited to review the entire manuscript as it moved closer toward its final form:

Robert Alexander	Ohio Northern University
Ross C. Alexander	North Georgia College & State University
David Bartley	Indiana Wesleyan University
Jack M. Bernardo	County College of Morris
Scott E. Buchanan	Columbus State University
Thomas M. Carsey	University of North Carolina-Chapel Hill
Nelson Dometrius	Texas Tech University
Donald P. Haider-Markel	University of Kansas
Amy E. Hendricks	Brevard Community College
Paula M. Hoene	Walla Walla Community College Clarkston
Pressley Martin Johnson	University of California, Riverside
Andrew Karch	University of Texas at Austin
Christine Kelleher	Villanova University
Kenneth Kickham	University of Central Oklahoma
Junius Koonce	Edgecombe Community College
Dr. Adam Newmark	Appalachian State University

Anne Peterson	University of Washington, Bothell
Sherri Thompson Raney	Oklahoma Baptist University
John David Rausch, Jr.	West Texas A&M University
Scott Robinson	University of Texas at Dallas
David L. Schecter	California State University-Fresno
John A. Straayer	Colorado State U.
Paul Teske	UCDHSC, Graduate School of Public Affairs
Caroline Tolbert	University of Iowa
Susan Peterson Thomas	Kansas State University
Jeff Worsham	West Virginia University

We would like to send out special appreciation to three scholars who helped us by testing an early draft of the book in their state and local government courses, giving us thoughtful and detailed comments about the manuscript and their students' reactions to it: Caroline Tolbert (Kent State University and University of Iowa), Carolyn Cocca (SUNY-Old Westbury), and Richard Scher (University of Florida). For their invaluable (and frank) feedback, we also thank their students, including: Kathryn N. Domanico, Numan Imtiaz, Jason Von Buttgereit, Thomas Mastrocinque, and Michele Ricero, as well as many others who preferred to remain anonymous. Three scholars helped us by providing some of the data we have included herein: Tim Storey (National Conference of State Legislatures), Laura Langer (University of Arizona), and Barbara Van Dyke-Brown (University of Illinois at Springfield). Several of our own students helped us copyedit the manuscript and worked on the ancillaries, including Brian Bartoz (University of Illinois at Springfield) and Brittany Rouille, Leah Rose Cheli, and Aaron Retteen (University of Florida). We would also like to thank those wonderful people at Wadsworth who helped us turn the manuscript into this book and get it into your hands: Carolyn Merrill, executive editor; Stacey Sims; senior developmental editor; Rebecca Green, assistant editor; and Trent Whatcott, marketing manager. Finally, we would like to give a special thanks to Caroline Tolbert, not only for her extensive and valuable comments on the manuscript at various points in its development, but for her tremendous support, encouragement, and friendship from the beginning of this project to the end.

Brief Contents

Chapter 1   Introduction to State
            and Local Politics   2

Chapter 2   Federalism: State Politics
            within a Federal System   38

Chapter 3   Participation, Elections,
            and Representation   68

Chapter 4   State and Local Direct
            Democracy   98

Chapter 5   Political Parties   130

Chapter 6   Interest Groups   160

Chapter 7   State Legislatures   192

Chapter 8   Governors   242

Chapter 9   The Court System   282

Chapter 10 Fiscal Policy   318

Chapter 11 The Structure of
            Local Governments   350

Chapter 12 The Politics of Place   382

Chapter 13 Morality Policy   416

Chapter 14 Social Welfare and Health
            Care Policy   446

Chapter 15 Education Policy   478

Contents

Chapter 1 Introduction to State and Local Politics 2

What a Difference Your State Makes 3

Introduction 5

State and Local Government: Everywhere, All the Time 7

What Are Government, Politics, and Public Policy? 8

Institutions Matter 8 / Government 8 / Politics 9 / Public Policy 9

Differences in Government, Politics, and Public Policy across the Country 10

Differences in Government—Women in State Legislatures 11 / Differences In Politics: Voting, Party Labels, and State Governors 12 / Differences in Policy: Funding Higher Education 13 / Reform Can Happen 15

Other Differences across the States and Communities 15

History and Geography 15 / Social Forces 16 / Economic Characteristics 20

Reform and Political Institutions: The Rules of the Game Have Consequences 30

Why Do They Tax Dogs in West Virginia? Using the Comparative Method of Political Analysis 32

Thinking It Through 33

Summary 35

Chapter 2 Federalism: State Politics within A Federal System 38

Homeland Security or Unfunded Federal Mandate? 39

Introduction 40

What is Federalism? 40

Sovereignty and State Variation in a Federalist System 40 / Federalism and State Diversity 41 / Unitary Systems: Centralized Power 42 / Confederal Systems: Decentralized Power 43

Why Federalism? America's Founding 44

The Articles of Confederation 44 / The Federalists 45

The U.S. Constitution and the Historical Development of Federalism 45

Federal Powers under the U.S. Constitution 45 / Thinking It Through Internet Wine Sales 47 / State Powers under the U.S. Constitution 48 / Federalism Today 49

The Ebb and Flow (and Gradual Erosion) of Federalism 49

The Shifting Sands of Federalism 50 / John C. Calhoun's Compact Theory of Federalism 50 / Centralization and Devolution 51

Creeping Centralization: The Political Evolution of Federal Power 51

The New Deal, World War II, and Cooperative Federalism 51 / The Great Society and Coercive Federalism 52 / The Continued Expansion of Federal Powers during the 1970s 53 / New Federalism during Reagan Era 53 / The Political Expediency of Federalism 54 / Expanding National Power: Setting National Standards 54 / The Devolution Revolution? 55 / When Does the Federal Government Become Stronger? 56

Umpiring Federalism: The U.S. Supreme Court 55

Judicial Review of the Power of the Federal Government 56 / The Supreme Court and Dual Federalism 57 / The Civil War and National Unity 58 / Incorporating the Fourteenth Amendment in the States 58 / Establishing Minimum Standards for the States 59 / Expanding States' Rights 60 / Protecting the States from Lawsuits 61 / The States' Rights Legacy of the Rehnquist Court? 61

Federalism in an Age of Terror   62

9/11 and Federal Powers 62 / The War on Terror and State Militias 63 / Dishing Out Homeland Security Grants 64 / Crises and Opportunistic Federalism 65

Summary   66

Chapter 3   Participation, Elections, and Representation   68

Introductory Vignette   69

Introduction: Is All Politics Local?   71

Forms of Political Participation   71

Participation is Much More Than Voting 71 / Voting 73 / Contacting and Contributing 74 / Attending Meetings 74 / Interest Group Activity 74 / The Long, Slow Road to Voting Rights 75 / Grassroots Political Activity 75 / Social Movements and Protest 76 / Rioting 76 / How Many Citizens Participate? 77

Barriers to Participation at the State and Local Levels   77

Race- and Gender-Based Barriers 77 / Different Ways to Draw Districts 79 / Registration Barriers 80 / Districting Barriers 80 / Who is Ineligible? 81 / Should Noncitizens Vote? 81 / Where Are the Greatest Barriers? 82 / Party System Barriers 82 / Noncompetitive Elections 83 / The Effect of Place 84 / Personal Barriers 84

Breaking Down Barriers to Voter Participation   85

State-Level Reform Efforts 85 / Effects of Reforms on Voter Participation 85 / Interest Matters 86 / Increasing Citizen Engagement with Competitive Elections 86 / Experiments with Alternative Local Election Systems 86 / E-Government 87

Voter Choice in State and Local Elections   87

Effects of Voter Participation on Public Policy   87

High Voter Participation Election Rules 87 / Low Voter Participation Election Rules 88 / Public Policy and Public Opinion 88

Does Participation Make State and Local Policy More Representative?   89

Participation Bias 89 / Effects of Participation Bias 89

Elections and Representation   90

Number of Representatives per District 90 / Campaign Spending 91 / Representation of Parties 93 / Representation of Women 93 / Representation of Racial and Ethnic Minorities 93

Summary   95

Chapter 4   State and Local Direct Democracy   98

Governing by the Ballot   99

Introduction   100

Institutions of Direct Democracy   100

Referendum 100 / Initiative 101 / Recall 102

More Responsible *and* More Representative Government?   103

The Promise of Direct Democracy 103 / Defending Direct Democracy 103 / "The Gun Behind the Door" 105

Populist Origins of Direct Democracy   105

Adopting Direct Democracy during the Progressive Era 106 / The Ebb and Flow of Ballot Initiatives 106 / Direct Democracy and National Politics 107 / The Explosion Continues 107 / Initiating Medical Marijuana Laws 108

Differences across Initiative States   109

Using the Initiative 109 / Limits on Initiative Content 110 / Qualifying for the Ballot 111 / Amateurs or Professionals? 111 / Millionaires' Amusement? 113

The Financing of Direct Democracy Campaigns   113

An Initiative Industrial Complex? 113 / Direct Democracy Campaigns and the Supreme Court 114 / "Special Interests" and Initiative Campaigns 114 / Does Money Matter in Initiative Campaigns? 115

Dumber than Chimps? Voting on Ballot Questions   116

Does Direct Democracy Deceive Voters? 117 / The Role of the Media in Initiative Campaigns 117

Direct Democracy and Electoral Politics 118

Spillover Effects of Ballot Measures in Candidate Races 119 / Direct Democracy and Turnout in Elections 119 / Interest Groups, Initiatives, and Elections 120 / The Effects of Direct Democracy on Citizens 120 / Direct Democracy and Minorities 121 / Democracy and Minorities 122

The Effects of Direct Democracy on Public Policy 123

Long-Term Effects of Direct Democracy 123 / Majority Tyranny and Judicial Review 124

Assessments of Direct Democracy 124

Public Approval of Direct Democracy 125 / The Case For and against Direct Democracy 126 / The Future of American Direct Democracy 126

Summary 128

Chapter 5   Political Parties 130

Where's the Interparty Competition? 131

Introduction 132

Theorizing about Political Parties 132

Responsible Party Model 132 / Factions Within State Parties 133 / Functional Party Model 133 / Lingering Anti-Party Sentiments 134 / Why Parties? 134 /

Regulating Parties as Quasi-Public Entities 134

Primaries and Caucuses 135 / Alaska's Mixed Primary System 137 / Party Endorsements of Candidates 139 / Party Fusion 139 / Party Ballot Access 140 / Defending the Two-Party Duopoly 141 /

Party-in-the-Electorate 142

Partisan Identification 142 / Political Ideology 142 / Are a State's Partisan Identification and Political Ideology Related? 143 / Does Partisanship Affect Participation? 144

Party Organization 144

Parties in the "Party Era" 145 / The Urban Party Machine 146 / The Death and Rebirth of Party Organizations 146 / Measuring Party Organizational Strength 147 / State Party

Financing 147 / The Impact of the Bipartisan Campaign Reform Act of 2002 on State Party Organization 148

Party-in-Government 150

Party Competition in State Legislatures 150 / Party Control and Interparty Competition 152 / Increasing Interparty Competition 153 / Why Interparty Competition Matters 154

Parties Take the Initiative 155

Whither Third Parties? 155

Third Party Candidates Spoiling for a Fight 158

Summary 158

Chapter 6   Interest Groups 160

Representing the American Dream 161

Introduction 162

Understanding Interest Groups 162

Defining Interest Groups 163 / Types of Interest Groups 163 / Madison's *Federalist #10* 163 / Pluralist Theory 163 / Critiques of Pluralism 163

Interest Groups and Their Members 166

How Do Interest Groups Form? 166 / How Are Interest Groups Maintained? 167 / Who Joins Interest Groups? 167

Interest Group Techniques 167

Reform Can Happen 168 / Lobbying 168 / State Ethics Laws and Wayward Lobbyists 174 / Issue Advocacy 174 / Taking the Initiative for Animal Protection 178 / Electioneering 179 / Litigation 182

The Dynamics of State Interest Group Systems 183

The Advocacy Explosion 183 / Density and Diversity of State Interest Group Systems 184 / Interest Group Competition: Who's Got Clout? 187

Summary 190

Chapter 7   State Legislatures   192

Like Its State, a Legislature Changes Dramatically: Florida, 1968–2008 193

Introduction   195

State Legislatures: The Basics   195

State Legislative Elections   197

The Paradox of Competition in State Legislative Elections 198 / Party, Incumbency, and Voting Decisions in State Legislative Elections 198 / Variation in Two-Party Contestation in State Legislative Races 199 / State Legislative Redistricting 202 / Iowa's Nonpartisan Redistricting Institution 210 / The Paradox of Competition in State Legislative Elections Revisited 211

State Legislators: Who Are They?   211

Women in the State Legislature 211 / Racial and Ethnic Minorities in the State Legislature 213 / The Impact of Broader Representation 216

The Job of the State Legislature   218

Lawmaking 219 / The Legislature and the State Budget 222 / Overseeing the Executive Branch 224 / Representation 225

The Collective Action Problem   226

Committees 227 / Party Caucuses 227 / Legislative Leadership 229

State Legislative Reform   231

Legislative Professionalism 231 / Term Limits 233 / Other "De-Professionalization" Reforms in the State Legislatures 237

Summary   238

Chapter 8   Governors   242

Player: George Pataki, Governor of New York (1995–2007)   243

Introduction   245

Gubernatorial Elections   246

Voting for Governor 246 / Gubernatorial Campaign Costs 248 / Election Outcomes 250

Today's Governors: Who Are They?   251

Career Path 251 / Women and Minorities as Governor 254

The Powers of the Governor   257

Institutional Powers 258 / Wisconsin's Vanna White Veto 260 / Independently Elected Executives in the State Government 262 / Informal Powers 265

The Three Jobs of the Governor   271

Chief Policymaker: Charting the Course 271 / Chief Administrator: Managing the Bureaucracy 273 / Recent Patronage Appointment Scandals Demonstrate the Effectiveness of Civil Service Reforms 275 Intergovernmental Relations Manager— Working Well With Others 277

Summary   280

Chapter 9   The Court System   282

A Tale of Two Judges   283

Introduction   285

Two Essential Distinctions in the American Legal System   285

State Courts in the Federal System 285 / Criminal versus Civil Law 286

The Organization of State Court Systems   287

Trial Courts 287 / Teen Courts 296 / Intermediate Courts of Appeal 297 / Supreme Courts 298 / Contrasting State Court Organizational Structures 300

Policy Making in the Courts   303

Judicial Selection   304

Judicial Section Mechanisms 305 / Why Do States Select Their Judges Differently? 307 / What Difference Does Judicial Selection Mechanism Make? 310

Reform and the State Courts   314

The Battle Over Tort Reform in the States 315

Summary   316

Chapter 10   Fiscal Policy   318

Boom and Bust Budgeting   319

Introduction   320

Criteria for Evaluating Taxes   321

Where Does the Money Come From? Major Sources of Revenues   321

Income Tax 324 / Sales Tax 325 / Property

Tax 326 / State and local Sales Tax and the Internet 327

Other Revenue Sources 329

Selective Sales Taxes 330 / Direct Charges 331 / Estate Tax 331 / Lotteries 332/ Gambling 332 / Severance Taxes 332

Tax and Expenditure Limits 333

Effects of State Tax and Expenditure Limits 333 / Colorado's Tabor 334

Fiscal Federalism 334

General Funds versus Non-General Funds 335

Adding it All Up: Variation in State Revenue Packages 335

The Mix of State Revenues 336 / The Mix of Local Revenues 337 / This Rhode Island: A "Sin Tax" Revenue Model to Emulate? 338

Who Bears the Burden of State and Local Taxes? 339

When Do Taxes Go Up or Down? 340

What Are the Effects of Taxes? 340

The Growth of State Governments 341

Trends in State and Local Revenue 341

Where Does the Money Go? Government Spending 342

Social Services: Health Care 342 / Social Services: Aid to the Poor 343 / Education 343 / Pensions and Unemployment 344 / Transportation and Highways 344 / Government Administration and Debt Interest 345 / Public Safety, Police, and Prisons 345

Do State and Local Spending Actually Reflect What People Want? 345

Why is Spending Higher in Some States? 346

Budgeting 346

Deficits and Balanced Budget Requirements 346 / Borrowing 346 / Do Budgeting Rules Matter? 346 / Budget Surpluses 347 / Boom to Bust Budgeting 347

Summary 348

Chapter 11 The Structure of Local Governments 350

Who Is in Charge? Weak and Strong Mayors 351

Introduction 353

Forms of Local Government 353

Municipalities 353 / Counties 353 / Special Districts 354

The Rise of the Urban United States 354

Immigration 355 / The Need for Municipal Government 357 / Origins of Urban Party Machines 357

Urban Party Machines 359

Patronage 360 / Precinct-Based Politics 360 / District Elections, Large Councils 360 / Corruption 361

Who Benefited from the Machines? 362

Demise of the Machines 362 / **Tammany Hall and Boss Tweed** 363

The Urban Reform Movement 363

Who Were the Reformers? 364 / Many Different Reform Groups 364 / Changing the Design of Local Institutions 365 / Class Conflict and Institutional Reform 365 / How Did Local Institutions Change? 366 / **Sewer Socialism** 366 / A Menu of Reforms 367 / Municipal Reforms as a Continuum and Constant Process 376

Consequences of Municipal Reforms 377

Nonpolitical administration? 378 / Efficiency–Accountability Trade-Off? 378 / Barriers to Mass Participation 378 / Home Rule Charter 379 / Class and Racial Bias 379

Summary 379

Chapter 12 The Politics of Place 382

Competition over Growth and Development 383

Introduction 385

Land Use: The Key Power of American Counties and Cities 385

Local Governments and Demands for Public Services 385 / Land Use and Local

Revenues 386 / Location Decisions of
Businesses and Firms 386 / The Competitive
Local Environment 386

Metropolitan Fragmentation   387

What's a City? 389 / New Cities versus
Traditional Cities 390 / The Lakewood
Plan 390 / What do Cities Do? 393 / The
Power of Municipal Incorporation 394

**Race and the Rise
of the Suburbs**   394

**Regulating Land Use: Zoning
and Eminent Domain**   396

Zoning Powers 397 / Eminent Domain
399 / Much is at Stake 399 / Zoning
Controversy: Exclusion by Race and
Income 400

**The Enduring Role of Pro-Growth
Forces in Local Politics**   401

The Growth Machine 402 / The Rise of Slow-
Growth Politics 403 / Do Growth Controls
Work? 404 / Reasons for Sprawl 405

**Are We Better Off Without
Zoning?**   405

The Local Land Use Dilemma 407

**State and Regional Planning
Alternatives**   407

State Growth Management Laws 407 /
Regional Revenue Sharing 408

**Competition for Local Economic
Development**   408

The Logic of State and Local Economic
Development Policy 408 / How Does it
Work? 409 / Who Uses Local Economic
Development Policies? 410 / Effects of
Local Economic Development Policies 410 /
Competition for KIA Investment 411

**The Consequences of Metropolitan
Fragmentation**   412

The Isolation of the Poor in the United States'
Major Cities 413

**Regional and Metropolitan
Government?**   413

Summary   414

Chapter 13 Morality Policy   416

The Strange Politics of Morality

Policy   417

Introduction   418

What Is Morality Policy?   418

Federalism, Home Rule, and Mortality
Policy Variation   419

**The Politics of Morality Policy:
Issue Evolution**   421

Policy Equilibrium: Reflecting the Values of
the Majority 422 / Let the Politics Begin: The
Policy Shock 422 / Morality Policy Politics 422

**Examples of Morality Policy
Politics in the States and
Communities: Abortion Regulation
and Same-Sex Marriage**   427

Abortion Regulation 428 / Same-Sex
Marriage 435 /Same-Sex Marriage Laws in
the States 438 / Other Morality Policies: Now
and in the Future 433

Summary   433

**Chapter 14 Social Welfare and Health
Care Policy   446**

Running against Welfare   447

Introduction   448

America's Poor   448

Who are America's Poor? 448 / Where Are
America's Poor? 450

**Domestic Policy Making
in a Federal System**   451

Sharing Responsibility for Policy Making
452 / Paying for Programs 453 / Diffusion of
Policies 454 / Adoption of Policies 454

Social Welfare Policy   455

Social Security 456 / Unemployment
Compensation and Workers'
Compensation 456 / Public Assistance: From
AFDC to TANF 457 / Wisconsin's Welfare
Experiment 458 / Food Stamps 462 /
Housing Programs 463 / Minimum Wage
Laws 464 / Working at Minimum Wage 464 /
Undocumented Workers 465

Health Care Policy   467

Why do Americans Lack Health Insurance?
469 / Who Are the Uninsured? 469 /
Medicaid 469 / State Children's Health
Insurance Programs (SCHIPs) 474 /
Medicare 474 / Hammering Wal-Mart on

Health Care 475

Summary   476

Chapter 15   Education Policy   **478**

Who's Getting Schooled?   479

Introduction   481

**Issue Evolution of Education
Policy**   482

Public Education in Crisis 483 / Growth in
Public Education 484

**Organizational Control and
Responsiveness of Public
Schools**   484

Organizational Control of Public Schools
485 / School District Responsiveness 487

Financing Public Education   488

Comparing K-12 Public Education Finance
across the States 488 / Financing K-12
Public Education 490 / Financing Higher
Education 493

**Experimenting with Public
Education**   495

School Vouchers 495 / Washington, D.D.'s
School Voucher Experiment 495 / Education
Management Organizations 496 / "Baby
Blaines" and the Prohibition of Vouchers
497 / Charter Schools 497 / Homeschooling
498 / Initiating Education Policy 499

**The Federal Role in Public
Education**   500

The No Child Left Behind Act of 2002
(NCLB) 500 / Is NCLB Working? 501

Summary   503

1

Introduction to State and Local Politics

What a Difference Your State Makes

"Location, location, location"—this is no longer just the mantra of real estate agents. As you know all too well, where you live can have an enormous impact on how much money you pay for college tuition. Even besides the issues of in-state versus out-of-state tuition and public versus private school tuition (which, of course, affect a college student's tuition bill dramatically), students living in one state can pay a very different amount to go to a state college than those living in another state. For example, most Floridians pay almost nothing to attend the University of Florida, whereas Pennsylvanians pay more than $12,000 a year to go to Penn State. Why is there such an astounding difference here? Pennsylvania and Florida are both large states, with major urban centers and extensive rural areas; both states tout strong economies with a mix of industry and agriculture. Both Penn State and the University of Florida are flagship state universities ranking among the top 50 nationwide in undergraduate education.[1] So why are the costs of attending these universities so different?

The answer to this question can be found in decisions made by policy makers in Florida and Pennsylvania and in the institutions and policies these policy makers have established. In 1997, the Florida legislature created the Bright Futures scholarship program, which pays 100 percent of college tuition and fees for Florida high school graduates who earn at least a 3.5 grade point average (GPA) in high school and score over 1270 on the SAT. Those Florida students with lower scores get somewhat less tuition help, but it is still a considerable amount. Funded by the sales of lottery tickets, Florida's Bright Futures program costs the state almost $350 million a year—a sizable expenditure even for a big state. And even for in-state students who did not graduate from a Florida high school, college tuition in Florida is just over $3,000 per year, well below the national average for public universities.

Why did Florida policy makers establish this program to subsidize higher education so richly? They did so because Sunshine State lawmakers were worried about a "brain drain"—losing their top high school graduates to universities in other states. They feared that once gone, such students would not return to the state after college. Thus, Florida encourages its college-bound students to stay home by keeping tuition low. In addition, many of the Republican lawmakers—who controlled the state legislature—wanted to do away with need-based scholarships and replace them with merit-based ones like Bright Futures.[2] So Florida policy makers had both economic and ideological reasons for making higher education extremely cheap.

Why, then, is tuition so expensive at Penn State? The answer here also comes down to decisions made by state policy makers, but in Pennsylvania, these policy makers opted to subsidize

Introductory Vignette

Introduction

State and Local Government: Everywhere, All the Time

What Are *Government, Politics,* and *Public Policy?*

Differences in Government, Politics, and Public Policy across the Country

Other Differences across the States and Communities

Reform and Political Institutions: The Rules of the Game Have Consequences

Why Do They Tax Dogs in West Virginia? Using the Comparative Method of Political Analysis

Summary

private higher education more, and public higher education less, than do their counter-parts in Florida. Although Pennsylvania spends nearly as much money per resident on higher education as Florida does, it has cut funding to public higher education in recent years while increasing both direct and indirect funding for private colleges and universities. In fact, some argue that the increasing privatization of higher education in Pennsylvania has virtually eliminated the distinction between public and private universities, just as it has in certain other states, like Colorado and Vermont.[3] Such a public policy arises when policy makers see postsecondary education less as a public good that benefits the whole state and more as simply a private benefit for students who should, therefore, bear the brunt of its costs. Unlike Florida, Pennsylvania has many private colleges and universities for their high school graduates to choose from, so brain drain does not worry its policy makers. State appropriations now account for only about 20 percent of Penn State's total budget,[4] forcing it to rely heavily on tuition and fees to pay its bills. This, in turn, leads to the high costs that Penn State students must pay.

This comparison of tuition at Penn State and the University of Florida illustrates how state institutions and policies can have substantial effects on people's lives. Similarly, qualified high school graduates hoping to attend college in Florida and Pennsylvania have considerably different financial burdens placed upon them due to the decisions of their state policy makers. As a result, graduating high school students in these states may behave differently. College-bound students in Pennsylvania may be more likely to attend private colleges, whether in Pennsylvania or elsewhere, because there are few financial incentives for them to attend an in-state public institution. Some Pennsylvanian students may even decide not to attend college at all because tuition at in-state public schools is simply out of reach for them. On the other hand, high school students in Florida—especially those without wealthy parents—may decide to work harder for good grades so as to make that 3.5 GPA that gets them free tuition. In short, students with similar backgrounds, similar achievement in high school, similar financial situations, and similar goals and aspirations may behave quite differently simply because they live in states that have different sets of public policies and institutions.

Penn State (left) and the Universtiy of Florida (right) differ in many ways—besides those decided as a matter of public policy.

Introduction

We start our book with this story of college tuition and public policy because it demonstrates four important points about state and local government that we are going to focus on in every chapter. First, this vignette demonstrates one of the countless ways in which state and local governments are important to Americans. And these governments are not just important to things like "governance" and "the economy," concepts that may seem rather vague and general to you. No, these governments are also important to you personally, in dozens of ways every day, from the moment you wake up until you turn off your light to go to sleep. Even while you are sleeping, state and local governments are busy affecting the quality of your life and the choices you can make the next day, the next year, and for the rest of your life. In fact, state and local governments almost certainly have a far greater impact on your daily life than does the federal government—unless you happen to be a member of the U.S. armed forces. On virtually every page of this book, we will show in one way after another just how state and local governments affect you and everyone you know every day.

The second point that this opening vignette demonstrates is that **political institutions** matter. Political institutions are the rules, laws, and organizations through which and by which government functions. Institutions are enduring mechanisms that are designed to translate the principles and values of public policy into reality. They set up consequences for the choices of both policy makers and citizens, encouraging certain choices and discouraging others. For example, Florida's Bright Futures program is an institution that affects the choices of the state's high school graduates. In another example, the superintendent of Chicago Public Schools is appointed by the mayor, whereas Philadelphia's superintendent of schools is selected by an independently elected school board (see Chapter 15). Because of this, education policy in Chicago is probably more responsive to general citizen opinion, whereas in Philadelphia, teachers and their unions, school administrators, and other education professionals have greater input.[5] This is because education governance in an independent school board system is more obtuse and removed from the average citizen than in a mayoral system. In a perhaps more straightforward example, the initiative is an institution that allows citizens to vote directly on policy questions (Chapter 4). In the 1990s, 21 states adopted restrictions on how long state legislators could serve; that is, state legislative term limits (Chapter 7). Not coincidentally, 20 of these 21 states used the initiative to do this, and of the 24 states whose constitutions allow the initiative, 20 passed term limits. In other words, although citizens are eager to adopt term limits when their political institutions give them a chance to do so, state legislators are loath to restrict their own careers. In short, the institutions with which we organize government have important, complex, and not always intended consequences.

Reform is the third theme of this book, even if it is only implied in our opening vignette for this chapter. Political institutions are especially important because they are among the significant forces affecting people's lives that government can change most readily. That is, these institutions can be reformed by the actions of citizens and their government. There are many other social forces influencing individuals' lives that are too deeply rooted to allow for a quick government fix. A state or community's political culture, racial composition, and economy have major political and personal impacts, but the government cannot do much about these in the short term, even if it wanted to do so. But political institutions are relatively easy to change. For example, Florida's policy makers saw the brain-drain problem and reformed their higher education funding approach by establishing Bright Futures. Los Angeles has been considering reforming its educational governance institutions to be more like Chicago's system than Philadelphia's. And those 21 states[6] that adopted term limits in the 1990s engaged in significant institutional reform, the effects of which are only now becoming apparent. States and communities are constantly tinkering with institutional reforms, and throughout this book, we will discuss both the causes and effects of many of these.

Finally, this opening vignette demonstrates what is perhaps our most obvious point—that state and local governments differ from one another. They differ in how they are organized, the policies they pursue, the institutions they establish, and the effects they have on their citizens. And, thus, it matters in which state and city you live, whether as a student, a parent, a consumer, a businessperson, a retiree, or any other role in which you might find yourself throughout your life. For many people, this diversity can be baffling and, at times, frustrating. For example, upon reading of the difference between in-state tuition in Florida and Pennsylvania, you Penn State students might feel cheated, outraged, or at least annoyed. But other differences can be equally confusing and troublesome to other types of people. Why must truckers slow down from 70 miles per hour to 55 mph when they cross the border from Indiana to Illinois on I-72 at Danville? Why do people in Vancouver, Washington, pay no state income tax, while those just across the Columbia River in Portland, Oregon, pay no sales tax? Why do some states—and even some school districts in the same state—educate their children better than others? Why are rivers cleaner in some regions of the country than in others? And so on.

Although these questions may cause some people to scratch their heads or pound the table, students of politics and policy look at them as opportunities to better understand how people work together to help their communities survive and thrive. As such, the study of state and local politics and government not only raises important and interesting questions but also offers us an extraordinary means to answer them—the comparative method. If we want to know, for example, why some governments provide better services for the poor than

others do, we can identify state and local governments that provide for their impoverished residents differently and *compare* them on other characteristics to look for clues to explain this difference. Perhaps those governments that provide better services for their poor are wealthier, have more diverse economies, or have a more liberal political culture than those governments that provide the poor with fewer services. Even more interestingly, perhaps these causal factors have a more subtle and complex relationship than this.[7] With so many state and local governments in the United States (over 84,000 at last count)[8], political scientists have a vast and rich laboratory in which to study politics and policy, using the comparative method to tease out and demonstrate often quite intricate patterns of relationships.

Thinking more broadly, comparing state and local governments raises some of the most fundamental questions of governance that people have been grappling with for thousands of years. For example, what is the best way to select representatives to make public policy? What is the fairest way for governments to get the resources they need to produce public goods and services? And more generally, how can government best translate the wishes and values of its citizens into public policy? If we can answer such questions for American state and local governments, we can go a long way toward understanding how people behave and organize themselves politically anywhere in the world. At root, these questions speak to how human beings can develop political institutions and policies that best channel our energies and maximize our potential as a species.

In this chapter, we lay out our case for studying American state and local government, and we explain our approach to doing so. We hope that by the time you have finished this book, you will not be able to read the newspaper or watch the TV news without asking yourself why your government has done what it has done to deal with a particular problem, what other governments have done about that problem, why these governments have adopted these different approaches to solving that problem, and which approach is better. In this way, you will become an amateur political scientist and a better and more intellectually active citizen with the tools to understand politics and government at all levels more deeply.

State and Local Government: Everywhere, All the Time

It may be impossible to overstate the importance of state and local government in your life and the lives of all Americans. Just walk through your day and see how they affect you. Your alarm clock rings—the state government determines whether you will fall back or spring forward for daylight-saving time (residents of Arizona and Hawaii do not change their clocks).[9] You turn on the light—electricity is generated according to an extraordinarily complicated set of state and local regulations so that it is safe, affordable, and not unduly damaging to the environment. You may even be in one of those communities—like Springfield, Illinois, and Orlando, Florida—where the local government actually generates and sells its own electricity. You have breakfast—the organic milk on your cereal is regulated and inspected by state officials. You take a shower—the water is probably provided by your local public utility. You drive to school—the roads are built and maintained by state, county, and local employees, and they are made safe by police officers from these same governments. And if you are a student at a college or university run by a state or local government (as most American college students are), everything about your education is controlled by the state or local government and its employees, from the admissions requirements, the classes that are offered, the topics that are covered in each class, the degree requirements, your tuition, and who your professors are—even the fact that you have been assigned to read this book. State and local governments even have a great deal to say about what happens in private

schools and colleges, either through their various regulations or through the monetary incentives they set up for those schools.

Beyond the university, your life is affected by state and local governments in countless other ways. They make sure your life is safe by regulating restaurants, doctors, teachers, dentists, accountants, lawyers, and undertakers—and even hairstylists, fingernail salons, and tanning shops. Do you want to smoke a cigarette? State and local governments tax you heavily for the privilege and then tell you where and when you can do so. Do you want to use a gun? State and local governments closely regulate where and when you can buy that firearm and the ammunition for it and where and when you can shoot it. Do you want to go to a dance club? State and local laws regulate how loud the music can be, how much tax you pay on your food and beverage, who can serve you, and how late the club can stay open. Do you want to build a house or start a business? Buy insurance or drive a car? Get married or get divorced? Yes, these and many more of life's regular activities are regulated, assisted, deterred, modified, or monitored by state or local government.

You get the idea. State and local governments are deeply involved in your life every day, all day, whether you know it or not. Although this may sound like something out of George Orwell's *1984*, in fact, almost everything that these governments do consists of activities they have been asked to do by some group of citizens or businesses. We want government to do many things for us—to educate us; to build roads on which we can get to school and work; to make sure all the various industries and professions that we rely on are safe, reliable, and honest; and so forth. In a modern society, we need government to be involved in our lives both to encourage the things we want and need and to discourage those things that are unsafe or deemed undesirable by society. In the United States, state and local governments have been where we routinely have turned first for help throughout our history. The national government in Washington, D.C., is far away, both physically and psychologically, from most of us. State and local governments are literally as

INSTITUTIONS MATTER

Political institutions are the rules, laws, and organizations through which and by which governments function. Political institutions are established by human beings for a particular purpose and with a permanence that goes beyond the people who originally created them. They require or prohibit and encourage or discourage certain behavior. Because they are human-made, they can be changed when those with the necessary authority decide to do so. Political institutions can be large, complex, and well-known, like your state legislature and your university. Political institutions can also be relatively narrow and simple rules or laws that channel people and resources, like the type of primary election system your state chooses to use. Political institutions can be established through formal channels and backed by the force of law, like your state court system, or they can be processes and organizations developed voluntarily by people outside of government to engage in politics and influence policy making, like political parties and interest groups. Throughout this book, we discuss the various impacts that state and local political institutions have on politics and public policy in this country and on Americans' lives. In each chapter, we include a sidebar demonstrating these impacts.

close as the street in front of our house, the school down the block, and the cop on the corner. In fact, aside from international relations and defense (no small things, of course), the national government has very little to do with the public services you receive every day. State and local governments control virtually all domestic government policy in the United States. They are where the action is.

What Are *Government*, *Politics*, and *Public Policy*?

Before we get too far along, we want to clarify a few basic concepts that we will be discussing throughout this book: government, politics, and public policy. Although everyone has at least some idea of what these concepts are, we want to discuss them explicitly here so that we can have a common understanding as we move forward.

Government

Government is the authoritative apparatus by which people organize themselves to achieve

common goals; that is, goals that members of a group share with one another. People working together can do much more than they can do alone. Alone, nobody could build a dam, use stem cells to develop a cure for diabetes, or protect the environment from toxic waste dumping. Some common tasks can be accomplished by people working together voluntarily, usually out of an economic motivation. General Motors was organized to make cars so that its stockholders and workers could make a profit; United Airlines was organized to make money by flying people from place to place. But it is very difficult to gain immediate monetary benefit from building a dam, studying stem cells and diabetes, or monitoring the amount of waste that companies produce. Certainly, the community as a whole, and even some individuals, may benefit enormously from these things—towns are protected from floods, people are cured of disease, and the environment is improved. But no person or company would take the initiative to complete such projects alone because the benefits are widely dispersed, often noneconomic, and received over the very long term. In short, when people and firms cannot reap an immediate monetary profit, they rarely work together voluntarily—the Red Cross and Doctors without Borders notwithstanding.

These are the kind of tasks that government can do best: those with widely dispersed, long-term benefits where the potential for short-term, private profit is limited. By paying taxes, we collectively pitch in to undertake these tasks that help the community but that no one would or could do alone. Government, then, is the people who are hired and the institutions that are established to accomplish these common tasks that help us all.

Politics

Politics is the process by which we as a community determine what our government ought to do. Through politics, we decide which **public goods** our government should provide, how it should do so, who should benefit from these public goods, and who should bear the cost of providing them. Politics are the elections, the campaigns, the lobbying, the legislative process, and much else that we see day in and day out in our newspapers and on the TV news, all of them being actions that revolve around making these decisions. Candidates for political office present different ideas about what government ought to do. For example, in a given race for governor, both candidates say they want more money for education, but one says that the state should legalize gambling to do so, whereas the other one advocates raising the sales tax instead. One candidate wants to encourage industry to come into the state, whereas the other wants to control growth and help the environment. These candidates present their cases to the voters in their campaigns, and the voters decide between them based on which common goals the voters think that government should pursue and how they think the government ought to pursue those goals.

Politics also works in a less direct way when various groups of citizens and businesses contact or meet with mayors, governors, and state and local legislators to present arguments about which policies and goals government should undertake. These elected officials consider the values and testimony of these citizens and groups, weigh these against their own

Cory Booker in his successful 2006 campaign for mayor of Newark, NJ.

knowledge and judgment, and then make policy decisions. This is politics too, but it is a different kind than what you see in campaign commercials and debates on TV.

Public Policy

Finally, public policy is simply the decisions that government makes and the actions that government undertakes to accomplish these common goals. These are the institutions, laws, regulations, norms, and traditions that define what government officials do. Anything that government or government officials do routinely and officially is policy. And every policy has, at its root and no matter how hard it may sometimes be to discern, a role in accomplishing some common goal of the state, city, nation, or whatever **jurisdiction** that that government serves. For example, something as simple as police checking the speed limit of cars coming into a small town from the highway is public policy. What is the common goal that this policy is supposed to help accomplish? This policy helps ensure that the town's streets are safe for bicyclists, pedestrians, and other drivers.

Sometimes an action by a government worker may not seem like a public policy, and sometimes the common goal of a policy may be hard to figure out. For example, maybe all professors at a state university are required to give a final exam in every class. That is a public policy because it is a regulation established by a government official, such as the college dean or the university provost (who are both state workers). What is the common goal behind this policy? Perhaps it is meant to enhance students' education by (1) motivating them to study, (2) forcing professors to evaluate their students and thereby give them that motivation, and (3) forcing professors to teach well (because poor teaching may translate into poor performance on the exams). Each of these is in some way a public good that the university is charged with helping to produce.

You may disagree with a public policy either because you do not believe in the common goal or because you do not think that that policy will help reach that goal. For example, many state lotteries advertise on TV. That ad campaign represents a public policy, the goal of which is to generate money for the state to spend on other activities, like education and prisons. You might object to that policy either because you do not think that the government ought to encourage people to gamble or because you think that the ads are so poorly crafted that they will not persuade anyone to buy a lottery ticket. Public policy is constantly evolving and changing through the process of political reform as different common goals are pursued and different approaches to meeting those goals are tried.

Taken together, government, politics, and public policy are all about how different groups of people work to accomplish that which they could not accomplish alone. In this book, we explore how government, politics, and policy interact with the various social and economic conditions that exist in different parts of the United States to give us the marvelous mosaic of public life we find in the states and communities of this country.

Differences in Government, Politics, and Public Policy across the Country

American states and communities vary dramatically in a multitude of ways, including in their governments, politics, and public policy. Political scientists can use this variation to help explain why governments and people behave as they do in the political realm. You will read about many of these differences throughout this book, but here are three examples to whet your appetite.

State and local governments provide a wide variety of services for you, including fire protection, mass transit, and highways.

Differences in Government: Women in State Legislatures

Women are quite underrepresented in elective office in the United States, but as we discuss in various chapters of this book, women's representation in elective office both has improved dramatically in recent years and has great diversity across the state and local governments. For example, in 2007, almost a quarter of all state legislators in the Unites States were women, up from less than 5 percent in 1970. Yet, even today, women are considerably better represented in some legislatures than in others. As Figure 1.1 shows, in 12 states, women held over 30 percent of the legislative seats, whereas in other states, they held considerably fewer. In South Carolina, less than 10 percent of state legislators were women. Why is women's representation in state legislatures so different among the states?

One explanation for why women win legislative elections more frequently in some states than in others is simply the variation in the bias against women serving in elective office, a holdover from the prefeminist era (Chapter 7). For example, political scientists have shown that when a state's electorate and party leaders hold more traditional attitudes toward religion and gender roles, women are less well represented in its legislature.[10] And because these attitudes vary systematically

---

Figure 1.1

Women in the State Legislatures, 2007

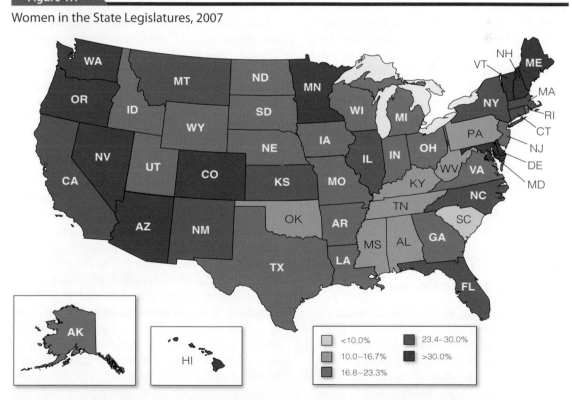

<10.0%	23.4–30.0%
10.0–16.7%	>30.0%
16.8–23.3%	

Notes: Each state is coded based on the percentage of women in both chambers of its 2007 legislature. In total, 23.5 percent of U.S. state legislators were women in 2007.

Source: Adapted from "Women in State Legislatures 2007," Center for American Women and Politics, Rutgers University, http://www.cawp.rutgers.edu/Facts/Officeholders/stleg.pdf.

among the states, so does women's representation in state legislatures. This explanation also helps account for the upward trend in women's representation since 1970, a period when women were just beginning to move into many nontraditional activities and professions in great numbers and attitudes toward women's role in society were changing quickly. Studies have also found that state legislatures that pay their members more money, have longer legislative sessions, and use electoral districts where only one member serves tend to have fewer women members.[11] One explanation for this pattern supports the bias against women theory, in that voters may be less likely to vote for women to fill those positions that are somehow more valuable (for example, they pay better and work longer). Another explanation for this pattern is that because seats in these more professionalized legislatures generate more electoral competition, and because women have shown a greater hesitancy to enter political races than men of equal qualifications,[12] women run for these seats less often. Whether women's greater reluctance to run for office is caused by some internalized social bias or something else remains to be explained. But note how studying the variation in women's representation in state legislatures not only helps us explain that intrinsically interesting phenomenon but also sheds light on the greater social forces surrounding women's role in American society.

Differences in Politics: Voting, Party Labels, and State Governors

Political parties in the United States are not nearly as ideological or as well-organized as those found in most other democracies, but they still serve as important labels for candidates for elective office (Chapter 5).[13] Stepping into the voting booth, voters usually know very little about what the numerous candidates on the ballot believe or even what their backgrounds and professional experiences are. But in most cases, they do know the political party that each candidate represents. In general elections, this allows voters to differentiate between the candidates and, thus, cast a meaningful (or at least nonrandom) vote. In this way, political party labels provide information for citizens to make voting decisions. This is very limited information, to be sure, but it is usually better than no information at all.

A party label is more useful in voting for races in which voters have less information about candidates; this includes many races for state and local office. In presidential elections, the party label is less useful because voters know a good deal about the candidates, everything from their military service to who their spouses and children are to their views on foreign policy. In state legislative elections, on the other hand, where most voters know virtually nothing about the candidates, voters typically cast their ballots based on their normal predisposition toward a candidate's party (Chapter 7).

Gubernatorial candidates fall in between presidential and state legislative candidates in terms of voter knowledge (Chapter 8). Although a state's governor holds a very important job and is typically the most visible public official in the state, many Americans still pay little attention to their governor. Thus, although the outcome of any gubernatorial race is influenced by the traditional party leanings of voters in the state, it is quite possible for a candidate of the state's minority party to win with a well-funded, well-run campaign and a personality and set of political positions that voters like. For example, all things being equal, a Republican gubernatorial candidate is disadvantaged in Democratic California, but with his celebrity status, large campaign war chest, and moderate political positions, Republican Arnold Schwarzenegger was elected governor of the Golden State in 2003. Gubernatorial candidates of a state's minority party are especially likely to win when the underlying values and ideology of the state's voters are less in line with those of the dominant party's national base. So, although the states of the Deep

South were solidly Democratic in congressional and state legislative elections for well over 100 years after the Civil War, they began electing Republican governors in the 1960s and 1970s, as that party's gubernatorial candidates articulated the party's conservative positions more clearly, showing that they fit well with the values of many Southern voters. And today, although Massachusetts is one of the most Democratic states in the country, it is not necessarily the most liberal, so it should not be too surprising that four of its last five governors have been Republicans. Some states have a history of thinking even more unconventionally about political parties, leading to the recent elections of independent or third-party governors in Minnesota, Connecticut, Alaska, and Maine—twice! Figure 1.2 shows the party affiliation of the governor of each state in 2007.

Differences in Public Policy: Funding Higher Education

Because government and politics vary so much across the country, it should be no surprise that the public policy that results from these also varies tremendously among the states and communities. For example, consider how states differ in their support of higher education, as we demonstrated with the Penn State–University of Florida tuition comparison at the beginning of this chapter. Figure 1.3 shows something of the state-to-state variation on a more general public policy—per capita spending on higher education.[14] Whereas New Hampshire spent only $87.74 per person on its colleges and universities in 2006, Wyoming was far more generous, spending $628.97 per person. The policy decisions that result in these funding levels affect people directly; for example, a

---

Figure 1.2

Governor's Party, 2008

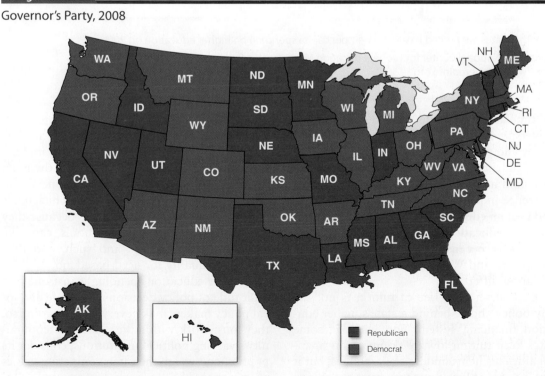

Source: National Governors Association, http://www.nga.org.

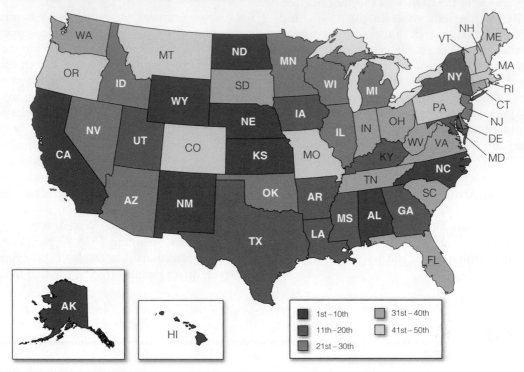

Figure 1.3

State per Capita Spending on Higher Education, 2006

Legend:
- 1st–10th
- 11th–20th
- 21st–30th
- 31st–40th
- 41st–50th

Note: The states are ranked based on their per capita spending on higher education on 2006.

Source: The National Center for Higher Education Management Systems' Information Center, http://www.higheredinfo.org.

full-time undergraduate state resident at the University of Wyoming paid as little as $2,700 in fees and tuition in 2006, whereas a comparable student at the University of New Hampshire paid more than $10,000. This enormous difference in tuition is not because students at UNH get an education that is four times better than the education that students at UW receive. It is because policy makers in New Hampshire and Wyoming value public higher education differently.

Of course, the price of tuition is not the only policy choice behind a state's higher education financing system. For example, some states keep tuition low by skimping on financial aid. This helps middle-class families, but it may mean that fewer poor students are able to

attend college. Alternatively, some states raise overall tuition but provide more aid for the most needy. This can put pressure on middle-class families' finances while helping the poor. Then again, some states give financial aid based more on merit than on need, which tends to benefit more well-off students because they can afford to attend better schools, can take SAT–ACT prep courses and such, and they would not qualify for need-based aid.

Higher education spending is just one of a multitude of policy decisions that state and local policy makers make every year. In doing so, they must work within their state's or community's varying political institutions, consider its politics, and weigh the often competing values of its citizens.

REFORM CAN HAPPEN

A *reform* is simply a change in something, but the word has the connotation of being both a positive and a purposeful change. Reform does not happen by accident; it is something that is done intentionally. Its positive connotation is such that those who advocate a particular change encourage others to think of that change as a "reform." After all, who can be against a reform? Thus, it is a word used in political advocacy to encourage agreement. Furthermore, *reform* connotes a relatively broad and systematic change. As such, we get *reform movements* that push for a variety of related changes. For example, in this book, you will read about reform movements to change campaign finance regulations, the selection of judges, and the professionalism of state legislatures. In each chapter, we include a sidebar that focuses on a reform movement—large or small—involving state or local government. These demonstrate that policy and institutions—even the oldest and most established—are human-made things that can be changed when either they are found to be deficient or people's goals and values change.

Other Differences across the States and Communities

As anyone knows who has ever traveled more than 20 miles from home, American states and communities differ from one another in many ways besides their governments, politics, and public policy. The United States is so incredibly heterogeneous in so many ways that its diversity in government, politics, and public policy is not only less noticeable but also perhaps even less significant than its diversity in other ways. In fact, the variation in the social, economic, and even geographical characteristics of this country goes a long way toward explaining some of the political and policy differences we find. In fact, in the 1960s and 1970s, at least one influential political scientist argued that these differences explained *all* the political and policy variation in the country.[15] But we argue that such a view goes too far. Throughout this book, we show how the choices that people and politicians make in setting up the institutions of government can affect the politics and policies we get, regardless of the socioeconomic forces at work. But we certainly do not argue that political

institutions are the only forces at work here. Just what are the other forces that affect our politics and policy so greatly? We do not have space to describe all the countless ways in which this country is diverse, but let us consider a few, many of which you will already be very familiar with. As we describe these characteristics, think about how they can help explain why different states and communities pursue different public policies and have different politics.

History and Geography

The roots of many differences among the American states and communities date many years back, some into prehistory. Even the very geography of the country—determined by millennia of glaciers, volcanoes, tectonic plate movements, and weather variations—affects our politics and policy. For example, tourists are attracted to the sunshine and beaches of Florida, so that state can rely heavily on the sales tax to funds its government because those tourists pay a large percentage of that tax. Likewise, Louisiana and Texas "export" some of their tax burden by taxing the extraction of oil and natural gas that lie beneath their ground. Perhaps most important, any area's geography strongly affects its economy, which in turn has a strong effect on its politics and public policy. The many rivers of New England gave that region the power needed to develop the first manufacturing economy in the country in the 19th century, which led to urban living, labor unions, and political machines. The climate and soil of the Southeast were especially suited for cotton and tobacco farming, which led to big plantations, slavery, Jim Crow laws, and conservative politics. Even within a single state, geographic variation can define politics and policy. For example, political conflict in Tennessee often splits those who live in its eastern mountains, those who live in the farming belt in the middle of the state, and those who live in the west along the Mississippi River. And many other states' internal politics are defined by conflict between their ocean coasts and inland areas or their mountainous and plains regions.

More recent history can also explain much of the variation in politics and policy around the country. During the Civil War, 11 states seceded from the country,[16] and the politics of these states still have certain unique qualities that can be traced all the way back to that war and its aftermath.[17] For example, a residual resentment for the depredations and humiliations of Union occupation during the Reconstruction era has instilled in these states a special antagonism for national government intervention into their affairs. And even though their citizens tend to be among the most conservative in the nation, the Democratic Party dominated politics in these states until quite recently simply because Abraham Lincoln was a Republican and his party was still held responsible for Reconstruction. Other historical events affect politics and policy in other places. Western states bear many marks of their years as frontier territory. For example, women are more likely to be elected to office in the West than in most states in the East (see Figure 1.1), in part because during their frontier days in the 19th and early 20th centuries, these states simply needed to attract women, and one way they did so was by empowering them politically. For example, Wyoming let women vote 50 years before the 19th Amendment to the U.S. Constitution gave them the vote throughout the country. Furthermore, women had to work just as hard as men in building a life on the frontier, making people in these states more supportive of women's rights quite early on.

Social Forces

States and communities also differ on a whole host of social characteristics that can affect their politics and policy. As a country of immigrants, an important set of social characteristics has to do with people's country of origin and how they are distributed around the United States. In the past, immigrants from the same place tended to use the same port of entry into the country and then stay near there, at least for a generation or two. This was especially true before the mid-20th century, when transportation became easier and more economical. As a result, for example, the big cities of the Northeast and Midwest still have many people of eastern and southern European descent whose ancestors arrived through those cities in the late 19th and early 20th centuries. The South has a higher percentage of African Americans than other parts of the country because it was largely to those states that their ancestors were brought by force before 1808 and enslaved until 1865. Many Latinos (or their ancestors) came to the United States from or through Mexico, so Texas, Arizona, and California have many Spanish-speaking residents within their borders. Cubans, Haitians, and others from the Caribbean basin often arrived through Miami, so Florida has many people with these ethnic backgrounds. The ancestors of Asian Americans arrived in the West, so Washington, Oregon, and California have many residents of Asian descent.

As generations passed, certain characteristic paths of migration within the United States developed, helping to shape the patterns of ethnic and racial settlement that we see today (Table 1.1). For example, as political oppression and the mechanization of agriculture forced many African Americans to leave the South in the early and mid-20th century, many of them moved north to work in the big manufacturing industries that developed in cities like Chicago, Detroit, and

| Table 1.1 |

State Racial and Ethnic Characteristics, 2005

State	% African American[a]	% Latino[b]	% Asian American[c]	% White (non-Latino)[d]	% Foreign Born[e]
AL	26.4	2.3	0.8	69.3	2.7
AK	3.7	5.1	4.6	66.5	5.4
AZ	3.6	28.3	2.2	60.4	14.5
AR	15.7	4.7	1.0	77.0	3.7
CA	6.7	35.2	12.2	43.8	27.2
CO	4.1	19.5	2.6	72.1	10.1
CT	10.1	10.9	3.2	75.4	12.5
DE	20.7	6.0	2.7	69.9	7.7
FL	15.7	19.5	2.1	62.1	18.5
GA	29.8	7.1	2.7	59.6	9.0
HI	2.3	8.0	41.5	23.5	17.2
ID	0.6	9.1	1.0	87.0	5.5
IL	15.1	14.3	4.1	65.8	13.6
IN	8.8	4.5	1.2	84.3	4.0
IA	2.3	3.7	1.4	91.5	3.6
KS	5.9	8.3	2.1	81.6	5.8
KY	7.5	2.0	0.9	88.6	2.4
LA	33.1	2.8	1.4	61.6	2.8
ME	0.8	1.0	0.8	96.0	3.0
MD	29.3	5.7	4.8	59.2	11.7
MA	6.9	7.9	4.7	80.3	14.4
MI	14.3	3.8	2.2	77.9	6.1
MN	4.3	3.6	3.4	86.3	6.3
MS	36.9	1.7	0.7	59.7	1.5
MO	11.5	2.7	1.3	82.9	3.4
MT	0.4	2.4	0.5	89.0	1.8
NE	4.3	7.1	1.6	85.4	5.6
NV	7.7	23.5	5.7	60.0	17.4
NH	1.0	2.2	1.7	94.1	5.7
NJ	14.5	15.2	7.2	63.2	19.5
NM	2.4	43.4	1.3	43.1	8.9
NY	17.4	16.1	6.7	60.9	21.4
NC	21.8	6.4	1.8	68.3	6.7
ND	0.8	1.6	0.7	90.8	2.0
OH	11.9	2.3	1.4	83.1	3.5
OK	7.7	6.6	1.5	72.5	4.5

State Racial and Ethnic Characteristics (continued)

State	% African American[a]	% Latino[b]	% Asian American[c]	% White (non-Latino)[d]	% Foreign Born[e]
OR	1.8	9.9	3.4	81.6	9.7
PA	10.6	4.1	2.2	82.6	5.0
RI	6.2	10.7	2.7	80.0	12.6
SC	29.2	3.3	1.1	65.5	4.2
SD	0.8	2.1	0.7	86.8	2.3
TN	16.8	3.0	1.2	77.9	3.8
TX	11.7	35.1	3.3	49.2	15.9
UT	1.0	10.9	1.9	83.5	7.9
VT	0.6	1.1	1.0	95.9	3.6
VA	19.9	6.0	4.6	68.2	9.9
WA	3.5	8.8	6.4	77.1	12.2
WV	3.2	0.9	0.6	94.4	1.1
WI	6.0	4.5	2.0	86.0	4.2
WY	0.9	6.7	0.6	88.6	2.3
US	12.7	14.4	4.3	67.0	12.4

Notes: These data are 2005 U.S. Census Bureau estimates.

Sources:

a. Hovey, Kendra A., and Harold A. Hovey. 2007. *CQ's state fact finder*. Washington, DC: CQ Press, 27.

b. Hovey, Kendra A., and Harold A. Hovey. 2007. *CQ's state fact finder*. Washington, DC: CQ Press, 30.

c. Hovey, Kendra A., and Harold A. Hovey. 2007. *CQ's state fact finder*. Washington, DC: CQ Press, 29.

d. Hovey, Kendra A., and Harold A. Hovey. 2007. *CQ's state fact finder*. Washington, DC: CQ Press, 31.

e. U.S. Census Bureau, American FactFinder, "Percent of People Who Are Foreign Born: 2005," http://factfinder.census.gov/servlet/GRTTable?_bm=y&-_box_head_nbr=R0501&-ds_name=ACS_2005_EST_G00_&-format=US-30.

New York, especially during the two World Wars. As a result, African Americans in the Northeast and Midwest are more concentrated in urban areas than are those in the South. More recently, Latinos, too, have moved north. But even though many Latinos are also attracted to the big cities, they are settling more frequently than blacks did in smaller towns and rural areas in the Midwest, where many have found jobs in food production industries. And in a unique settlement pattern, Arizona, Colorado, Utah, and even Arkansas have pockets of Americans of Japanese descent whose ancestors were forced there from the West Coast to live in concentration camps during World War II.

The pattern of a state's or community's racial and ethnic composition can affect its politics and policy. For example, despite their lower percentage of the population in the Midwest and Northeast, African Americans began to be elected to Congress and state legislatures far earlier there than in the South. This is because in these northern states, they were concentrated in the cities where they were able to dominate congressional and legislative districts more easily than in the South, where they were dispersed in rural areas. Of course, another important reason for the underrepresentation of blacks in political offices in the South until the end of the 20th century was the institutionalized racism in those states that used to deny blacks their rights to vote and participate in political activities. Another example of political and policy effects is that an influx of non-English-speaking immigrants has lead both to the implementation of English as a Second Language (ESL) programs in schools and to a political backlash against that influx, as reflected in such policies as requirements that only English be used in government offices.[18]

A state or community's general level of social diversity can also have a significant, if often subtle, impact on its choice of public policies.[19] One in-depth study found that homogeneous states (for example, Minnesota and Vermont) populated mainly by whites who do not identify with an ethnic group tend to be quite liberal on a range of health, education, and welfare policies, whereas states with a higher percentage of people from racial or ethnic minority groups (for example, Mississippi and Illinois) had much less generous social policies, even when accounting for population size and wealth.[20] But perhaps even more troubling, when the impact of these policies is broken down along racial and ethnic lines, members of minority groups living in

The states and communities in the US display a wide array of geographic, demographic, and economic differences.

largely homogeneously white states tended to do relatively worse than those minorities living in less socially homogeneous states. For example, whereas overall incarceration and child poverty rates are lower in Minnesota than in Mississippi, the incarceration and child poverty rates for African Americans are lower in Mississippi than Minnesota.[21] This suggests, perhaps, that pure interest group and voting politics, rather than enlightened liberalism or old-fashioned racism, are at the root of differences in how minorities are treated by public policy in this country. This is another example of how political scientists can study the states and communities to help us understand political behavior and policy making more generally.

The states and communities also differ along many other social characteristics that can have political consequences. Some places have more elderly people living in them than others, whether because of retirees moving there (for example, Florida and Arizona) or because of many of their younger people have moved away (for example, Iowa and West Virginia). What might be the political consequences of this? Older people tend to be both more politically active and wealthier. States and communities with many retirees need to spend more money on health care and other senior services, whereas places with fewer older people need to spend more on education but have a harder time generating the tax revenue to do so. Population density—the number of people per square mile of land—varies greatly not only between rural and urban areas within a state but also between states. Densely populated places tend to have more crime and poverty and greater diversity in income levels (that is, many rich people and many poor people). Furthermore, in cities and densely populated states (for example, New Jersey and Connecticut), transportation policy is all about mass transit, whereas in small towns and sparsely populated states (for example, Wyoming and Nebraska), transportation policy means highways. States and communities also differ in the extent to which people move in and out of them; that is, their mobility. In some places, people tend to stay put for generations,

whereas in others, those who have lived in their houses for five years are considered old-timers. What is the political consequence of differences in mobility? Voter turnout and political participation tend to be higher in places with low mobility because people feel more attached to the community and have more information about the candidates and issues. Table 1.2 contains data on how the states vary on these social factors. Each of these factors—and countless others—has many important political and policy consequences, some of which become apparent with only a little thought and some of which political scientists are still working to uncover.

Economic Characteristics

The geographic, historical, and social characteristics of a state or community help determine its economy; that is, the way that people there earn their living and the types of businesses and industries that exist there. But the economy can have significant independent effects on government, politics, and public policy as well. For example, the politics in places where most people earn their living by farming or in related agricultural industries are very different than the politics of places where most people work in factories. In a manufacturing economy, workers are more likely to belong to a union and people typically have more money to spend. Because many people must live relatively near the factories in which they work, places with manufacturing economies also tend to be more urban, which leads to certain characteristic political dynamics and policy outcomes. And in today's global economy, a manufacturing economy can also be less stable, with layoffs and rehirings happening frequently.

For example, Michigan's economy has long been dominated by the automobile manufacturing industry, so private sector unions play a more powerful role in its politics, and the state budget is subject to more radical swings than, say, Kansas, with its more agricultural economy.

On the other hand, people and businesses in agricultural economies need different things from

Table 1.2

State Social Characteristics

State	% Population 65 Years Old or Older[a]	Population Density Residents Per Square Mile[b]	Population Mobility[c] %
AL	13.2	89	26.6
AK	6.4	1	61.9
AZ	12.7	51	65.3
AR	13.8	53	36.1
CA	10.7	230	49.8
CO	9.8	44	58.9
CT	13.5	723	43.0
DE	13.1	425	51.7
FL	16.8	323	67.3
GA	9.6	152	42.2
HI	13.6	197	43.1
ID	11.4	17	52.8
IL	12.0	229	32.9
IN	12.4	174	30.7
IA	14.7	53	25.2
KS	13.0	33	40.5
KY	12.5	104	26.3
LA	11.7	104	20.6
ME	14.4	43	32.7
MD	11.4	569	50.7
MA	13.3	818	33.9
MI	12.3	178	24.6
MN	12.1	64	29.8
MS	12.2	62	25.7
MO	13.3	84	32.2
MT	13.7	6	43.9
NE	13.3	23	32.9
NV	11.2	21	78.7
NH	12.1	145	56.7
NJ	12.9	1,173	46.6
NM	12.1	16	48.5
NY	13.0	407	34.7
NC	12.1	175	37.0
ND	14.7	9	27.5
OH	13.3	280	25.3
OK	13.2	51	37.4

State Social Characteristics (continued)

State	% Population 65 Years Old or Older[a]	Population Density Residents Per Square Mile[b]	Population Mobility[c] %
OR	12.8	37	54.7
PA	15.3	277	22.3
RI	13.9	1,034	38.6
SC	12.4	139	36.0
SD	14.2	10	31.9
TN	12.5	143	35.3
TX	9.9	86	37.8
UT	8.7	29	37.1
VT	13.0	67	45.7
VA	11.4	188	48.1
WA	11.3	93	52.8
WV	15.3	75	25.8
WI	13.0	101	26.6
WY	12.1	5	57.5
US	12.4	83	40.5

Notes:
a. The percentage of a state's population that was 65 years old or older in 2005 based on U.S. Census Bureau estimates.
b. The number of residents per square mile of land in a state in 2005 based on U.S. Census Bureau estimates.
c. The percentage of a state's 2000 residents who were born outside that state based on the 2000 U.S. Census. A higher number means that the state's population is more mobile.

Sources:
a. Hovey, Kendra A., and Harold A. Hovey. 2007. *CQ's state fact finder.* Washington, DC: CQ Press, 24.
b. Hovey, Kendra A., and Harold A. Hovey. 2007. *CQ's state fact finder.* Washington, DC: CQ Press, 38.
c. Percentage born in the state of current residence. See U.S. Census Bureau, Population Reference Bureau, "Handout 1: State of Residence in 2000 by State of Birth," http://www.prb.org/LP/People_on_the_Move/LP6A1H1.pdf.

government than do those in manufacturing economies. For example, agriculture has had one major impact on public policy that you probably never had even given a thought to, although it has affected your life since you were five years old. Because the United States was almost entirely agricultural in the 19th century, when our public school institutions were developing, the traditional school calendar—with its three-month vacation in the summer—was developed so that kids would be available to work all day on the farm during the busy summer growing season.[22] Certainly, there is no educational reason why children need to take off three months in the summer. In fact, educational researchers now understand that such a long break actually has a negative impact on learning. Some American school districts have recently tried year-round schooling,[23] and it is commonly used in other industrialized countries. Not surprisingly, it is in states and communities where agriculture is still a significant part of the economy that the most opposition to year-round schooling persists. Table 1.3 shows how the states vary on the extent to which manufacturing and agriculture are important parts of their economies.

Table 1.3

State Economic Characteristics

State	Manufacturing Employment (%)[a]	Farm Income ($ per capita)[b]	Personal Income ($ per capita)[c]
AL	15.1	422	29,623
AK	4.5	11	35,433
AZ	6.9	189	30,157
AR	16.3	685	26,641
CA	10.2	252	36,890
CO	6.6	261	37,459
CT	11.5	54	47,519
DE	7.6	581	37,084
FL	4.9	181	34,099
GA	11.0	280	31,191
HI	2.5	81	34,468
ID	10.0	787	28,398
IL	11.3	83	36,264
IN	19.0	222	31,150
IA	15.5	1,162	31,795
KS	13.4	920	32,948
KY	13.9	499	28,317
LA	8.2	147	24,582
ME	9.4	136	30,808
MD	5.3	133	41,996
MA	9.4	20	43,702
MI	14.7	132	32,735
MN	12.5	596	37,322
MS	15.2	629	24,925
MO	10.9	267	31,299
MT	4.5	751	28,906
NE	10.8	1,535	32,988
NV	3.8	51	35,780
NH	11.8	45	37,835
NJ	7.8	32	43,822
NM	4.6	394	27,912
NY	6.5	58	40,072
NC	13.9	416	31,029
ND	7.4	2,011	31,230
OH	14.7	127	31,867
OK	9.6	406	29,908

State Economic Characteristics (continued)

State	Manufacturing Employment (%)[a]	Farm Income ($ per capita)[b]	Personal Income ($ per capita)[c]
OR	12.4	289	32,174
PA	11.5	139	34,848
RI	10.7	29	35,219
SC	13.2	172	28,212
SD	10.5	2,483	32,642
TN	14.5	150	30,952
TX	9.1	275	32,604
UT	10.0	133	27,497
VT	11.7	342	32,731
VA	7.9	133	37,552
WA	10.0	167	35,234
WV	8.1	30	26,029
WI	17.7	315	33,251
WY	3.7	589	37,270
US	10.4	250	34,455

Notes:
a. The percentage of the state's workforce employed in manufacturing in 2006 based on U.S. Bureau of Labor Statistics estimates.
b. The net farm income per capita (in dollars) in a state in 2005 based on U.S. Department of Agriculture estimates.
c. Per capita personal income in a state in 2005 based on the U.S. Department of Commerce's Bureau of Economic Analysis estimates.

Sources:
a. Hovey, Kendra A., and Harold A. Hovey. 2007. *CQ's state fact finder.* Washington, DC: CQ Press, 58.
b. Hovey, Kendra A., and Harold A. Hovey. 2007. *CQ's state fact finder.* Washington, DC: CQ Press, 65.
c. Hovey, Kendra A., and Harold A. Hovey. 2007. *CQ's state fact finder.* Washington, DC: CQ Press, 46.

Another economic characteristic of a state or community that has wide-ranging political effects is simply its wealth. Of course, states with more money can afford to pay for more and better services for their citizens. But less obviously, and ironically, wealthy places need to tax their citizens at a lower rate than poorer places. This is because their citizens have more wealth to tax, so doing so at a lower rate can yield plenty of revenue. For example, 10 percent of $100 is the same as 1 percent of $1,000. And to add insult to injury, wealthy states and communities may actually tax their residents less overall because well-off people need certain government services (like various social welfare programs, police and fire protection, and so forth) less than poor people. This is why people find that their property taxes sometimes go down when they move to the suburbs from the city, even though their schools and other services are sometimes better (Chapter 10). On the other hand, people with more money often demand better government services and are willing to pay for them. For instance, they may be willing to pay higher taxes for high schools that offer several foreign languages and have a swimming pool, whereas these may be luxuries that poor people simply cannot afford, no matter how much they may want them.

Besides differing in their total or average wealth, the states and communities also differ in how that wealth is distributed among the people who live there (Figure 1.4).[24] For example, consider two states, each of which has an average annual household income of $75,000. If every household in one state earns $75,000, whereas in the other state, half of all households make $25,000 and the other half make $125,000, the states have very different economies. This difference can manifest itself in politics and policy in a variety of ways. For example, all things being equal, the more diverse state may have more distinct political parties and more political conflict generally because the poor and rich each may find common cause within their own group and then align their groups squarely against one another. This may lead the diverse state to spend more on law enforcement and less on public education, among other things. In the state with a more homogeneous wealth distribution, the lack of distinct wealth groups will reduce conflicts of interest and, thereby, reduce political conflict. The tax structures of these states will also probably be very different because of both the political dynamics involved and the available resources.

These are just a few examples of various aspects of a state's or community's economy that can have significant effects on its government,

---

Figure 1.4

The Equality of Wealth Distribution in the States

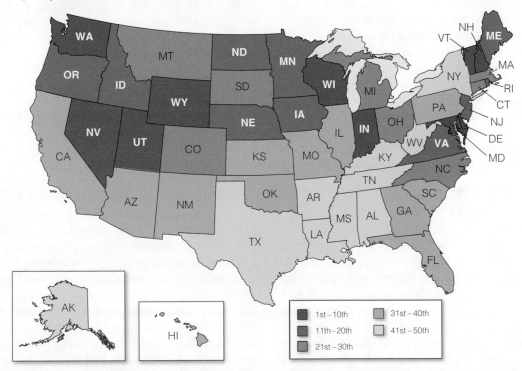

Legend:
- 1st–10th
- 11th–20th
- 21st–30th
- 31st–40th
- 41st–50th

Note: The states are ranked based on their distribution of wealth. A higher ranking means a more equal distribution of wealth in the state. That is, in high-ranking states (for example, Delaware, Indiana, and Washington), less difference in wealth exists between the richest and poorest people than in the low-ranking states (for example, Alabama, Alaska, and New York).

Source: Adapted from Langer, Laura. 1999. Measuring income distribution across space and time in the American states. *Social Science Quarterly* 80:55–67.

politics, and public policy. As you read through this book, you will see many more.

Our final set of potential explanations for the differences in the politics and policies of the states and communities may be precisely what most of us think *should* be determining these things in a democracy—the thoughts, ideas, and values of the people who live there. First, consider people's most deep-seated ideas and values about politics and, indeed, about other people, including their attitudes about the proper role of government, their religious values, what they think is socially and morally valuable and should be encouraged, and what they think is harmful and should be discouraged. These attitudes and beliefs do not change easily over time, either within a person or within a community. It is also true that these attitudes and beliefs are not evenly distributed around the country. Although Americans hold many attitudes and beliefs in common, there are some important differences in these from state to state and community to community in this country. And as most of us would hope, research has shown time and again that the basic political and social values of their residents closely parallel the policies that the states and communities adopt.[25]

The most common way Americans think about politics and policy is along a simple two-dimensional continuum of political ideology—liberal versus conservative. Although most Americans—and even political scientists—would be hard-pressed to define these terms explicitly, most of us have a general understanding about what they mean, and most people are willing to tell a political pollster whether they are more or less liberal or conservative. More important for our purposes, different parts of the country tend to be more or less liberal or conservative (see Figure 1.5). Political scientists Robert Erikson, Gerald Wright, and John McIver compiled hundreds of newspaper polls from around the country for several decades and documented the state-to-state variation in **political ideology**.[26] These researchers have also shown that this ideology has important political impacts. For one thing, those

places that tend to be conservative tend to vote Republican, and those that tend to be liberal tend to vote for Democrats, at least in recent years. Furthermore, those states that are more conservative and vote Republican tend to have policies that we associate with that ideology and that party, such as stricter abortion and gambling regulations, less spending on education and welfare, more punitive criminal laws, and more regressive taxes.[27] And we find a similar correlation between policy, party, and ideology in the more liberal and Democratic places around the country. Although this may not surprise you, it has only been relatively recently that scholars found real evidence that, in fact, in our democracy, citizens' ideologies are actually translated pretty accurately through political parties into public policy.[28]

Next, consider a place's political culture more specifically; that is, its residents' general attitudes about what government should be like and what it ought to do. A generation ago, political scientist Daniel Elazar made an observation about state political culture that scholars still use fruitfully today. Elazar argued that the United States has three dominant political cultures based on the values and attitudes of our original European settlers and the ways in which they migrated through the country.[29] As Figure 1.6 shows, the northern tier of states was populated more by reform-minded Protestants (starting with the Pilgrims of Plymouth Rock) who began in New England and then moved across the top of the country. These descendants of the Pilgrims were met in the rural areas of the upper Midwest by later-arriving, but like-minded, Scandinavians. These two groups of people tended to view government as a valuable tool with which to improve social conditions, and they felt that all citizens should participate in the political process in order to do so. Elazar called this set of attitudes a **moralistic political culture**, and we see strong remnants of it today in places like New Hampshire, Wisconsin, and Oregon.

In contrast, the southern tier of states was originally settled by wealthy planters and

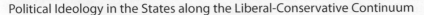

Figure 1.5

Political Ideology in the States along the Liberal-Conservative Continuum

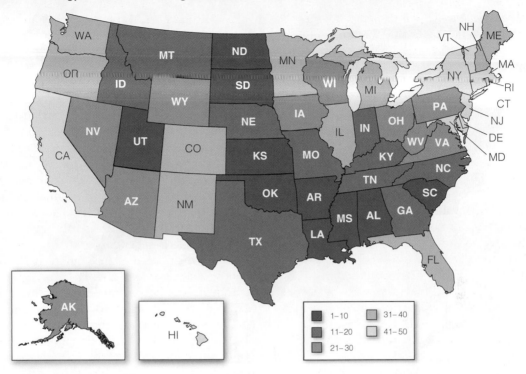

Note: These data consolidate and average hundreds of public opinion polls undertaken from 1996 to 2003. In this map, the darker the state, the more conservative are its residents.

Source: Adapted from Erikson, Robert S., Gerald C. Wright, and John P. McIver. 2006. Public opinion in the states: A quarter century of change and stability. In *Public opinion in state politics,* ed. Jeffrey E. Cohen. Stanford, CA: Stanford University Press.

noblemen from England and elsewhere, along with their African slaves and many white indentured servants. The plantation economy that evolved from this social structure led to a political culture where government was viewed as something that the social and economic elites could use to maintain and preserve the status quo—with them on top. Thus, it was thought that those in the lower classes (black or white) should not get involved in politics and government and not expect to get much from them. Elazar called this a **traditionalistic political culture,** and the politics of places like Mississippi, South Carolina, and Virginia continue to reflect this culture.

Finally, the mid-Atlantic seaboard states and the big cities of the Midwest tended to be settled by people who arrived with perhaps less money than the Southern planters but with a nonetheless strong commercial attitude, both about life in general and about government. These industrious people sought their fortunes through business and hard work, and they did not see any problem with government helping a person achieve his or her own personal economic goals. As a result, political machines arose in these areas to help immigrants adjust to American life, and a little political corruption was sometimes tolerated as the price for making government work. This culture still influences

---

Figure 1.6

Political Culture in the United States: Daniel Elazar's Classification

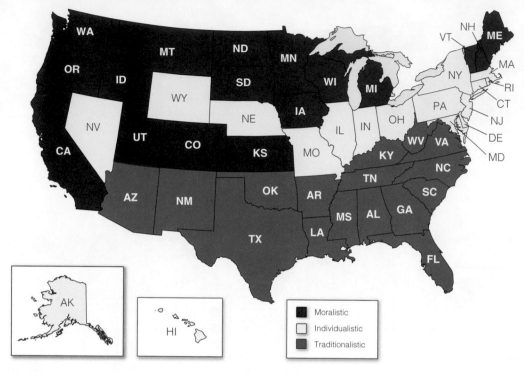

Moralistic
Individualistic
Traditionalistic

Notes: See the text for definitions of Elazar's categories of political culture.

Source: Elazar, Daniel J. 1984. *American federalism: A view from the states*. 3rd ed. New York: Harper and Row, 136–37.

politics and policy in New Jersey, Illinois, Ohio, and other places, and Elazar called it an **individualistic political culture.**

According to Elazar, as Americans moved westward (primarily) across the country in the 19th and 20th centuries, they took their political cultures with them, so that these cultures also diffused generally in an east-west pattern across the country. The impacts of this dimension of political culture have been wide-ranging. For example, places with a moralistic political culture make it easier for people to vote, places with an individualistic political culture have stronger and more competitive political parties, and places with a traditionalistic political culture spend less money on education and public services for their poor.

Lastly, consider people's opinions about specific public policies. Some people would like to spend more on education, whereas some would rather spend money on roads. Some people want to ban abortion, and some want to keep it legal. Some people want to see murderers executed, and some think that keeping them in prison for the rest of their lives is sufficient. Political scientist Barbara Norrander used a special poll conducted by the American National Election Studies in the 1990s to demonstrate that people's opinions on many policies vary systematically among the states.[31] She used questions about how much money people wanted to spend on things like AIDS research, national defense, and public schools to rate the states on their residents' policy opinions. Table 1.4 shows how

Table 1.4

"Should We Spend More Money on ...?" Ranking the States on Policy Preferences

State	Environmental Protection	Public Schools	AIDS Research	National Defense
AL	44	14	30	2
AK	37	36	41	39
AZ	18	21	33	16
AR	37	26	44	1
CA	30	17	18	31
CO	22	39	48	35
CT	8	26	3	39
DE	7	10	6	19
FL	4	17	30	10
GA	29	10	11	19
HI	10	1	24	13
ID	46	33	46	26
IL	8	9	16	47
IN	12	39	18	9
IA	35	28	48	43
KS	22	17	26	16
KY	42	20	12	10
LA	22	5	33	4
ME	33	39	3	39
MD	11	3	9	31
MA	4	10	3	47
MI	16	39	12	28
MN	4	30	18	42
MS	35	21	16	5
MO	34	10	18	19
MT	49	28	39	28
NE	40	47	46	19
NV	16	30	12	26
NH	18	39	24	31
NJ	2	33	18	44
NM	12	2	28	16
NY	27	36	7	28
NC	14	7	2	8
ND	48	48	28	35
OH	27	49	39	37
OK	46	14	42	10

"Should We Spend More Money on …?" Ranking the States on Policy Preferences (continued)

State	Environmental Protection	Public Schools	AIDS Research	National Defense
OR	44	46	18	50
PA	22	45	37	19
RI	1	5	1	37
SC	22	14	26	2
SD	40	33	33	25
TN	30	3	30	14
TX	20	30	44	7
UT	50	7	42	19
VT	3	36	8	49
VA	20	21	12	31
WA	15	21	9	45
WV	37	21	37	6
WI	30	50	33	45
WY	43	44	50	15

Note: The states are ranked from the most (1) to the least (50) public support for raising government spending in each of these policy areas. For example, these data show that Rhode Island (ranked first) is estimated to be the state with the highest percentage of residents who wanted to increase spending on the environment, whereas Utah (ranked 50th) was the state with the lowest percentage of residents who wanted to do so. States that have the same ranking on a given policy attitude were tied in their average response to spending on that policy. These data are from surveys taken from 1988 to 1992, but they are the most recent such data that we have on which to rank the states on the policy attitudes of their residents.

Source: Adapted from Norrander, Barbara. 2001. Measuring state public opinion with the Senate national election study. *State Politics and Policy Quarterly* 1:111–25. See this article for the original data.

the states rank on Norrander's public opinion ratings for four policies. Furthermore, Norrander's was another study that demonstrated that states' public policy choices are closely related to the attitudes of their residents.

Reform and Political Institutions: The Rules of the Game Have Consequences

Thus, the United States is a vast and diverse country. High-speed communications, the Internet, and low-cost travel have homogenized this country to a much greater extent than it used to be, but Nevada is still not Pennsylvania, and Chicago is still not Key West. And you have already seen how some of the very fundamental differences among people and places can go a long way toward explaining some of the differences we see in politics and policy around the country. But just as we as people are not prisoners of the basic characteristics of the conditions into which we were born (for example, our race, our parents' income, and where we live), people in the states and communities can make choices about the ways in which they organize themselves that can affect their politics and policy for good or ill. That is, we can establish the political institutions that we want, and these institutions can affect the way we live and how our government works.

Just as with their histories, social forces, economics, and political cultures, the differences among the political institutions of American states and local governments can help us better explain the variations we see in politics and public policy across the country. But perhaps more important, if we want to *change* our policies or politics, we need to concentrate on the aspects of civil society that we are able to change. For example, someone who wants to ban abortion cannot just suddenly make her state more conservative. Nor can someone who wants to spend more money on state universities easily make his state wealthier. But people can reform their state's political institutions to make it easier to achieve adoption of the policies that they desire. Therefore, political institutions take on a special importance in the study and explanation of the political differences among the states and communities.

A central theme of this book is that *politics and public policy are influenced by political institutions;* that is, by the rules that define how government works.[32] As everyone who has ever played a sport or a video game knows, a game's rules have a significant impact on who succeeds in it, and it is no different in government and politics. Political institutions can be thought of as sets of rules that define how the game of government and politics is played; the end product of the game is public policy. Some political institutions are at least somewhat familiar to everyone, such as the governor's office, the city council, and the state's Department of Motor Vehicles. These institutions have buildings and staff with official titles, some of whom even wear uniforms. These really look like institutions. But some political institutions exist simply as sets of rules without any kind of physical edifice. For example, there is no building that we can point to and say, "That is direct democracy," but direct democracy is a political institution that both is very important in some states and varies from state to state (Chapter 4). Political parties (Chapter 5) and interest groups (Chapter 6) are also institutions in this sense.

More important than any outward trappings, each political institution has its own elaborate set of rules; some of these rules are laws, some are official regulations, and some are merely procedures and customs. Such rules determine what powers the governor has, who can speak in the city council, and when you can be incarcerated by the sheriff's department. The rules of other political institutions determine how someone becomes a judge and what a court's jurisdiction is, who can vote in an election and how that election's winners are determined, and how your property tax rate is calculated and when you have to pay it. The rules that define and empower political institutions in U.S. states and communities are almost countless and incredibly diverse, even in a single state or community.

But just as important for our purposes, these rules can be quite different from jurisdiction to jurisdiction, even for parallel institutions. For example, the mayor's offices in Atlanta and Milwaukee are very different institutions because the rules that define their powers are very different. Judges in Alabama and California are selected in different ways, and their courts are organized differently. Rules can even vary within a single institution; for example, members of one chamber of the New Hampshire legislature have quite different powers and election rules than those of the other chamber. These differences in political institutions then cause a whole gamut of political and policy differences between these jurisdictions.

Those who work in and around politics and government understand very well the importance of institutions and institutional reform. State and local governments are constantly tinkering with their rules about elected officials' powers, how people can vote, who pays taxes, how property can be used, and every other government function and political activity you can think of. Rule changes—reforms—take up much of the time of policy makers and those trying to influence them. Throughout this book, we describe a wide range of political institutions and show how they affect who gets what from government and what happens when you change them.

Why Do They Tax Dogs in West Virginia? Using the Comparative Method of Political Analysis

As you have no doubt already noticed, another organizing theme of this book is our use of the **comparative method** of political analysis to *help explain patterns in politics and public policy*. We take advantage of the rich diversity found in the states and communities to pose general **hypotheses**, and test general theories, of political behavior and policy making. For example, many years ago, one of us wrote about how local governments tax dogs in West Virginia but not in New Jersey.[33] Why are these states' local government revenue policies distinctive in this way? Is it because West Virginia is not as wealthy as New Jersey and, therefore, simply needs more money? Is it because West Virginia is more rural and considers a dog to be an economic asset? Is it because of some difference in political culture or history? Other, perhaps more far-reaching, differences in government, politics, and public policy may already have occurred to you, and you may already have posed hypotheses to answer them. For example, why do Democrats usually win state legislative elections in Massachusetts, whereas Republicans tend to win them in Kansas? Are there social or economic reasons for this difference? Why do governors in 48 states serve four-year terms, whereas those in New Hampshire and Vermont have only two-year terms? Is there a historical explanation for this difference, or is it due to something special in the politics of these two neighboring states? Why does Texas execute a dozen or more murderers every year, while Wisconsin did not even execute serial killer Jeffrey Dahmer? Is this attributable to political culture or ideology?

The comparative method of explaining such differences is not complicated. First, we identify something we are interested in that varies in a general way from place to place, such as party success in state legislative elections, the length of gubernatorial terms, or the execution rate of convicted murderers. Second, we hypothesize what might have caused this variation. A *hypothesis* is a potential answer to a research question that is supported by a theoretical explanation.[34] For example, we might ask, "Why do some states tend to elect Democrats to their state legislatures, whereas others tend to elect Republicans?" We might then hypothesize that states where more people live in cities elect more Democrats and states where more people live in small towns and rural areas elect more Republicans. Why would we expect this relationship? What theory of political behavior is behind this hypothesis? Our theory might be that city dwellers demand more government services, such as mass transit, police protection, sewer and water, and so forth, and, therefore, these people tend to support the party that believes most strongly in the value of government—the Democrats. Finally, we could test this hypothesis, not just by looking at the states where we originally noticed this difference—Kansas and Massachusetts—but also by gathering data on state legislative partisanship and place of residence for all 50 states. If we find that the pattern holds—that rural states tend to have more Republicans in their state legislatures than do urban states—then our hypothesis and theory are supported.

Although this hypothesis and theory probably do not shock you, this story is a simple example of using the comparative method to suggest and then test an explanation for political differences among the states. And in doing so, we have not only explained this variation in state legislative partisanship, but we have also tested the general theory of political behavior that was behind the hypothesis—that people elect members of a political party whose philosophy of government fits with their own self-interest. This ability to use the states and communities to help make general statements about human political behavior is an important contribution to political science.

In this book, we are particularly interested in using the comparative method *to evaluate the effects of political institutions on politics and public policy*. Reformers who promote institutional change are essentially posing a hypothesis. For example, advocates of the initiative and referendum hypothesized that allowing people to vote directly on public policy would energize and educate them politically and lead to policy that was more in line with their values and beliefs than policy made through the traditional legislative process.[35] By using the comparative method, and by learning about research that has used the comparative method, you can see whether this and other tinkering with state and local government institutions have had the effects that these reformers had hypothesized. You can also see whether these reforms have had any of the unexpected and undesirable effects that those opposed to them had hypothesized or even if there were effects that no one predicted. At root, the comparative method not only allows us to develop and test theory about political behavior but also helps us assess which policies and institutions have the best outcomes so that they can be implemented in other states and communities.

And why does West Virginia authorize its counties to assess a tax on dogs? It comes down to a quirk of history. The state follows the old English tradition of taxing personal property, just as do Virginia and a few other states. In addition to taxing real estate, as most local governments do, these states tax things like cars, boats, livestock, and—sometimes—dogs. New Jersey developed its taxation system from different traditions. What lessons can we learn from this difference between these states? Perhaps that the reform of public policy is often slow and that history and inertia cannot be overlooked as explanations for sometimes odd political institutions and policies.

COMPARISONS HELP US UNDERSTAND

THINKING IT THROUGH

Now that you have been exposed to the comparative method of political analysis, it is your turn to give it a try. In Table 1.5, we show you how each of the states measure up on three characteristics: a political institution (the governor's institutional powers), a political trait (political corruption), and a public policy (cigarette tax). Try to explain why the states vary as they do on these factors. Think about the differences among the states that you are familiar with, and hypothesize which of these might be useful in explaining each of these three characteristics. Then, test your hypotheses by seeing if the states that are highest on your hypothesized causal factors are also high on the characteristic in the table you think caused it to vary. Then, check to see if the same states are lowest on each of these characteristics. Of course, because political phenomena are complex, there are many factors at work determining a state's value on any given characteristic, so the correlation between scores of your hypothesized cause and effect will never be perfect. But if you see a strong pattern, your explanation may have some validity. In each chapter, we include a sidebar that shows how the states and communities differ on a specific institution or policy, and we challenge you to use the comparative method to develop and test hypotheses about why these differences exist.

Table 1.5

Explain This.... Three State-Level Characteristics

State	Governors' Institutional Powers[a]	Political Corruption: Reporters' Perceptions (ranked from most to least corrupt)[c]	Cigarette Tax ($ per pack)[b]
AL	1	6	.425
AK	4	29	1.60
AZ	3	8	1.18
AR	2	21	.59
CA	3	27	.87
CO	4	45	.84
CT	5	12	1.51
DE	3	4	.55
FL	3	22	.339
GA	1	22	.37
HI	4	16	1.40
ID	2	37	.57
IL	5	10	.98
IN	2	16	.555
IA	4	39	.36
KS	4	38	.79
KY	3	7	.30
LA	3	2	.36
ME	4	44	2.00
MD	5	15	1.00
MA	4	N/A	1.51
MI	4	23	2.00
MN	5	41	1.23
MS	3	16	.18
MO	3	20	.17
MT	3	40	1.70
NE	3	34	.64
NV	2	22	.80
NH	2	N/A	.80
NJ	5	N/A	2.40
NM	3	3	.91
NY	5	16	1.50
NC	1	26	.35
ND	4	45	.44
OH	4	10	1.25
OK	2	4	1.03

Explain This.... Three State-Level Characteristics

State	Governors' Institutional Powers[a]	Political Corruption: Reporters' Perceptions (ranked from most to least corrupt)[c]	Cigarette Tax ($ per pack)[b]
OR	3	41	1.18
PA	4	13	1.35
RI	2	1	2.46
SC	2	22	.07
SD	4	45	.53
TN	4	28	.20
TX	2	29	.41
UT	4	14	.695
VT	2	41	1.19
VA	3	34	.30
WA	2	29	2.025
WV	4	8	.55
WI	4	36	.77
WY	3	29	.60

Notes:
a. A rating of each state's governor's office from least powerful (1) to most powerful (5) on characteristics including electoral considerations, appointment power, budget power, veto power, and party control.
b. State tax per pack of 20 cigarettes (in dollars) in 2006.
c. States are ranked from most corrupt (1) to least corrupt (47) based on a 1999 survey of statehouse reporters in each state. Three states (Massachusetts, New Hampshire, and New Jersey) were not ranked (N/A) lack of response to this survey.

Sources:
a. Adapted from Beyle, Thad. 2004. Governors. In *Politics in the American states,* ed. Virginia Gray and Russell L. Hanson 8th edition. Washington, DC: CQ Press, 212–13.
b. Illinois Commission on Government Forecasting and Accountability. 2006. *Illinois' cigarette tax, tobacco products tax, and tobacco settlement update.* Springfield: State of Illinois, 4.
c. Boylan, Richard T., and Cheryl X. Long. 2003. Measuring public corruption in the American states: A survey of state house reporters. *State Politics and Policy Quarterly* 3:420–38.

Summary

State and local governments are deeply and broadly important to your everyday life. All day, in dozens of different ways, these governments affect your pocketbook, your quality of life, your family, and your future. And the more you know about state and local government, the more control you can take over your own life.

Throughout this book, we build on the three themes we have laid out in this chapter:

- *Comparisons* among the states and communities
- The impact of *political institutions* on politics and public policy
- The potential to *reform* our policies and institutions

First, American states and communities differ from one another in myriad ways, including their histories, social structures, economics, values, politics, policies, and governments. We use the cause-effect relationships among these characteristics to understand our political world better. Second, we use the variation of political institutions around the country both to test and to demonstrate how the ways in which we choose to organize ourselves and our governments can have real impacts on politics and policies. And third, we examine the various efforts to reform our policies and institutions, considering why they have developed, what they have accomplished, and the impacts of their efforts.

Keywords

Comparative method

Hypothesis

Individualistic political culture

Jurisdiction

Moralistic political culture

Political ideology

Political institution

Public goods

Traditionalistic political culture

Suggested Readings

Berry, Mary Frances, and William D. Berry. 1990. State lottery adoptions as policy innovations: An event history analysis. *American Political Science Review* 84: 395–415.

Chi, Keon S., ed. 2008. *The book of the states* 2008. Lexington, KY: Council of State Governments.

Elazar, Daniel J. 1984. *American federalism: A view from the states*. 3rd ed. New York: Harper and Row.

Erikson, Robert S., Gerald C. Wright, and John P. McIver. 1993. *Statehouse democracy: Public opinion and policy in the American states*. New York: Cambridge University Press.

Gray, Virginia, and Russell L. Hanson, eds. 2008. *Politics in the American states: A comparative analysis*. 9th ed. Washington, DC: CQ Press.

Hovey, Kendra A., and Harold A. Hovey. 2008. *CQ's state fact finder 2008*. Washington, DC: CQ Press.

Johnson, Janet Buttolph, and H. T. Reynolds. 2008. *Political science research methods*. 6th ed. Washington, DC: CQ Press.

Key, V. O., Jr. 1949. *Southern politics: In the state and nation*. New York: Knopf.

Rosenthal, Alan. 1998. *The decline of representative democracy*. Washington, DC: CQ Press.

Web Sites

Council of State Governments (http://www.csg.org): The Council of State Governments is a not-for-profit association of state governments that does research, training, and advocacy for all branches of state government.

National League of Cities (http://www.citymayors.com/orgs/natleague.html): As the oldest organization representing municipal governments in the United States, the NLC works with 49 state municipal leagues to strengthen cities.

Stateline.org (http://www.stateline.org): Staffed entirely by professional journalists, Stateline.org was originally envisioned primarily as a resource for newsmen and newswomen who cover state government. Today, its audience is much broader, but it still offers journalistic stories on public policy in the states and communities, from both a single-state and comparative perspective. It is a not-for-profit organization funded by the Pew Research Center.

Statistical Abstract of the United States (http://www.census.gov/compendia/statab/): The U.S. government gathers an immense amount of information and data about U.S. states and communities and their residents. The *Statistical Abstract* is the U.S. Census Bureau's consolidation report of a wide range of these data.

2

Federalism: State Politics within a Federal System

Homeland Security or Unfunded Federal Mandate?

OUTLINE

Introductory Vignette

Introduction

What Is Federalism?

Why Federalism? America's Founding

The U.S. Constitution and the Historical Development of Federalism

The Ebb and Flow (and Gradual Erosion) of Federalism

Centralization and Devolution

Creeping Centralization: The Political Evolution of Federal Power

Umpiring Federalism: The U.S. Supreme Court

Federalism in an Age of Terror

Summary

Notice anything different about your new driver's license? Perhaps it has a digitized photograph, a hologram, a tamperproof casing, or a barcode on the backside? In January 2005, President George W. Bush signed into law the National Intelligence Reform Act. In addition to several other provisions that reorganized national security agencies in response to the 9/11 terrorist attacks, the law created national standards for the issuance of state driver's licenses. With the U.S. Department of Transportation overseeing the changes of what is known as the "Real ID" law, states are now required to develop "smart" driver's licenses that have a digital photograph or some other unique biometric identifier, such as a fingerprint or retinal-scan imprint. Although the law does not require states to immediately capture an applicant's biometrics, critics—including the Montana and Washington state legislatures, which have passed legislation refusing to comply with the law—claim that the law is an unfunded federal mandate and an intrusion of the federal government into an area traditionally regulated by the states.[1]

Minnesota high-tech driver's license

Introduction

Why does the U.S. Congress have the power to mandate how the states must issue their driver's licenses? Shouldn't this be a function retained by each of the 50 states? The Real ID law is but one of many examples of how Congress is able to expand its power into what traditionally has been the realm of state governments. The federal government's rapid response following the terrorist attacks of September 11, 2001, not only restructured the internal workings of the federal government but also altered the balance of power between the federal government and the states. Once again, the federal government—specifically Congress—exerted its power over the states, elevating the stature of the power-brokers operating in the national capital, Washington, D.C. As we shall see, the cycle of centralization and devolution of power between the federal government and the states is a hallmark of the American federal system.

In this chapter, we examine the dynamic relationship between the federal and state governments. The ambiguity in the demarcation of state and national (or *federal*) institutional powers inherent in the U.S. Constitution has defined the way Americans have thought about government and politics and how we have designed our government institutions. After defining *federalism* and placing the American federal system in a broader comparative context, we investigate the ambiguities inherent in the U.S. Constitution. In discussing the historical trajectory and evolution of American federalism, we discuss the roles Congress and the federal courts have played in delineating the relative powers of the national and state governments. We conclude by discussing how power has become more centralized in Washington following 9/11. What should become apparent in this story of American intergovernmental relations is the gradual, if at times punctuated, expansion of federal powers over the past century.

What Is Federalism?

The 50 American state governments constitute semisovereign political systems. Governmental powers in the United States are split geographically between national, state, and local governments. **Federalism** is the structural (or constitutional) relationship between a national government and its constitutive states. **Intergovernmental relations**, on the other hand, are the interactions among the federal government, state governments, and local governments. A federalist system of intergovernmental relations conjoins a national government with semiautonomous subnational governments, but allows each to retain, to some degree, its "own identity and distinctiveness."[2] Although maintaining separate and autonomous powers, each layer of government is responsible for providing for the social and economic welfare of the populations living within its jurisdiction.[3] As we discuss below, the structure of a federalist system is different from those of unitary and confederal systems of governance.

How does a federalist system work? In theory, federalism combines the unifying powers of the national government with the diversity of subnational governments. The American states are not mere administrative appendages or extensions of the national government. Rather, they have discrete powers that are derived from the federal Constitution as well as their own constitutions and laws. Each layer of government has some autonomy, but there is much overlap in the powers held by the national and state governments.[4] It may seem somewhat ironic, then, that although many countries—including Australia, Brazil, Canada, Germany, India, Italy, Mexico, Nigeria, Russia, Spain, and even Iraq—have adopted an American system of federalism, the term *federalism* is not mentioned in the U.S. Constitution.

Sovereignty and State Variation in a Federalist System

In theory, under federalism, states retain a broad swath of sovereign powers, subject to the will of their own citizens. "In establishing this system," writes the historian Samuel Beer, "the American people authorized and empowered two sets of governments: a general government for the whole, and state governments of the parts,"[5] Such is a system of **dual federalism**, whereby governmental functions are apportioned so that, in the words of Founding Father James Madison, the states are "no more subject within their respective spheres to the general authority than the general authority is subject to them within its own sphere"[6] (see Figure 2.1). Though sometimes pictured as a "layer cake," dual federalism does not necessarily imply that the national and state governments never encroach upon each other's territory. Rather, if a confectionary metaphor is to be used, the American system might be more aptly described as a "marble cake."[7]

Figure 2.1

Models of Federalism

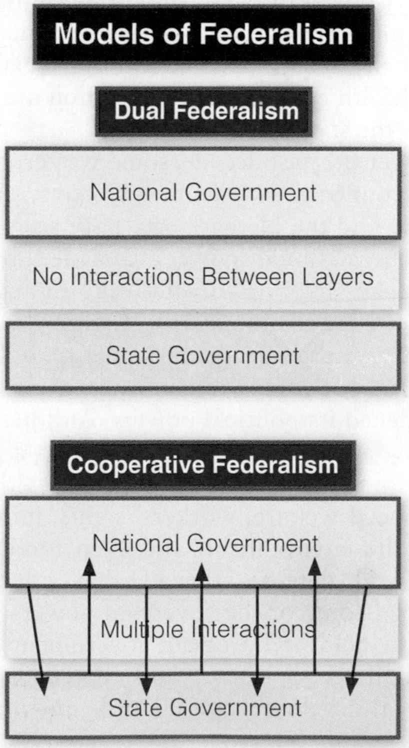

Models of Federalism

Dual Federalism

National Government

No Interactions Between Layers

State Government

Cooperative Federalism

National Government

Multiple Interactions

State Government

Federalism and State Diversity

Because the national government does not have monopoly power in the American system, decentralization leads to tremendous diversity in the kinds of constitutions and laws the states have adopted over time. As we discuss in Chapter 3, there are considerable institutional differences in state electoral systems. For instance, in nine states (Iowa, Idaho, Maine, Minnesota, Montana, New Hampshire, North Carolina, Wisconsin, and Wyoming), citizens may register to vote and cast a ballot on Election Day, provided they have a state-issued ID confirming their current place of residency. Citizens residing in other states may have to register as many as 30 days prior to an election if they wish to cast a ballot. The electoral systems of two states, Maine and Vermont, permit convicted felons doing time in prison to vote. However, in more than a dozen states, voting rights of convicted felons are taken away for life, even if a felon has completed the term of his or her sentence.[8] By some estimates, over 4 million citizens each year are disenfranchised because they are in prison, on parole, or on probation for a felony.

State institutions also are quite diverse. As we cover in Chapter 7, all but one state (Nebraska) has a bicameral (House and Senate), partisan state legislature. Since 1934, Nebraska has used a unicameral (single-chamber), nonpartisan legislature. In Chapter 4, we discuss how roughly half the states permit their citizens to propose statutes (laws) or constitutional amendments by collecting signatures and placing ballot initiatives before voters on Election Day.

And the constitutions of the states also vary considerably. Most state constitutions are longer than the U.S. Constitution, which has roughly 8,700 words (including its 27 amendments). State constitutions average 26,000 words; Alabama's weighs in at 310,000 words and has more than 700 amendments. Vermont's, by contrast, is shorter than the U.S. Constitution. A handful of states still have their original constitutions, including Massachusetts (1780),

Maine (1820), Wisconsin (1848), Minnesota (1858), Oregon (1859), Nevada (1864), Colorado (1876), Washington (1889), North Dakota (1889), South Dakota (1889), Wyoming (1890), Utah (1896), Oklahoma (1907), New Mexico (1912), Arizona (1912), Alaska (1959), and Hawaii (1959). Although Massachusetts still operates under its first constitution, hundreds of amendments have been added to it over the years. Georgia, by comparison, is on its 10th constitution, with citizens adopting the most recent one in 1983.[9] As we discuss in Chapter 8, some state constitutions permit their citizens to vote for an array of statewide elected officials, including the offices of lieutenant governor, attorney general, secretary of state, commissioner of education, secretary of education, and even secretary of agriculture; in other states, the governor appoints these cabinet-level offices.

Finally, as we discuss at some length in Chapters 13–15, public policies can differ widely across the states. In 36 states, for instance, convicted felons may face the death penalty. Texas alone has executed more than 380 prisoners since 1976. In other states, even those such as New York where the death penalty is on the books, not a single prisoner on death row has been executed over the past 30 years.[10] Whereas most states require residents to be at least 16 years of age to be eligible for a driver's license, teenagers in South Dakota may obtain one after turning 14. A handful of other states require their residents to take a driver's examination, including a road test, when they reach 80 years of age. In some states, the sale of alcohol (including wine and spirits) is permitted in grocery and convenience stories, whereas others ban the purchase of alcohol on Sundays. The diversity among the states is striking.

Unitary Systems: Centralized Power

In contrast to a federalist system of governance, some countries have *unitary* systems of governance, with all governmental power vested in the national government. As Figure 2.2 shows, a **unitary** system has a strong central government

that controls virtually all aspects of its constitutive subnational governments (be they regional, territorial, state, or local units). Unitary systems, such as those in France, Israel, the Philippines, Sweden, China, and Kenya, consolidate all constitutional authority in the national government. In a sense, subnational divisions of the country are mere administrative appendages of the national government; that is, policy is made at the national level, and the subnational units simply carry out that policy.

There is far less regional diversity in terms of subnational electoral systems, governance structure, and public policy in countries with unitary systems of governance. The central governments in unitary systems are simply able to control the policy making that takes place at the subnational levels of government. For example, between 1952 and 1975, Sweden's national parliament moved to eliminate 90 percent of all local governments.[11] In France, the national government in Paris makes most laws, which are then dutifully administered by the country's 22 provincial regions. By contrast, in the United States, policy decisions concerning criminal justice, public education, social welfare, health care, and transportation are often left to the states.

Over the past decade, some Western European countries with unitary systems, such as France and the Netherlands, have seen many of their national powers curtailed by the European Union (EU).[12] Driven originally by the need for economic consolidation so as to compete more effectively in the global marketplace with the United States, the EU has broadened its political powers. Although still lacking a formal constitution, across a plethora of policy domains—including health care and social welfare, workers' rights, immigration, the environment, and even foreign affairs and defense—the EU has effectively usurped some of the sovereign powers traditionally held by European governments.[13] As we shall see, in some ways the centralizing political development of the EU mirrors that of the United States.

Confederal Systems: Decentralized Power

In terms of a spectrum of the balance of power between national and subnational levels of government, a **confederal** system is located at the opposite pole from a unitary system. A confederacy, as Figure 2.2 shows, is a system of governance whereby the national government is subject to the control of subnational, autonomous governments. In a confederacy, the constituent subnational governments enter into a covenant with one another and derive the bulk of their sovereign powers not from the central government, but from their own constitutions.[14] As we discuss below, in the history of the United States there have been two confederacies: the Articles of Confederation (1781–89) and the Civil War–era Confederate States of America (1861–65).

Compared to both federalist and unitary systems of governance, the confederal form has come under criticism over the years for its apparent instability and ineffectualness. Yet, for over 500 years, Switzerland operated as a confederation, with its 23 autonomous cantons holding veto power over the policy decisions of the central government until 1847. The most prominent, and for some the most infamous, confederal governance structure in the world is headquartered in New York City—the United Nations (UN). Today, no purely confederal national government exists.

Despite the criticisms leveled at the UN's confederal structure, many countries with federal and unitary governments have decentralized power and authority to their subnational units. A 1999 study issued by the World Bank found that 76 percent of 127 countries in its study had at least some decentralized political systems (meaning they had at least one elected subnational level of government). The study also found a high correlation between fiscal and **political decentralization,** and found that countries with high gross national products were more likely to adopt both fiscal and political decentralization reforms.[15] Many of the decentralization efforts, which the World Bank and

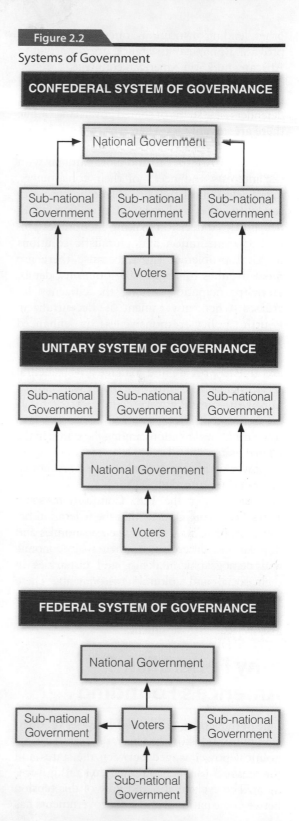

Figure 2.2

Systems of Government

other lending institutions often require when providing financial assistance, are occurring in African and Latin American countries.

Though wary of decentralizing authority to the point of becoming a confederal system, defenders of systems of shared governance argue there are advantages when governmental powers are devolved to subnational units. First, because they are closer to and more familiar with the interests and needs of their constituents, locally elected officials are able to better represent the wishes and needs of citizens. Second, decentralized decision making encourages policy experimentation and pluralistic solutions to local problems. Third, because there are more avenues for expressing opinions, democratic participation among the citizenry increases when government is decentralized. Fourth, policy responsiveness is enhanced when political authority is dispersed among subnational units. Finally, subnational units are able to provide and manage governmental services more efficiently than if they were carried out by the central government.

Yet, decentralizing political power can lead to asymmetrical relations among the states. In the United States, not all states have the same degree of power within the federalist system. Although all states are afforded the same protection and authority under the U.S. Constitution, some states have more clout within the federation because of the relative size of their economies and populations, differences in their socioeconomic and demographic makeup, and disparities in their social and cultural environments. These variations have led to differential power relations among the states, as well as between each state and the federal government.[16]

Why Federalism? America's Founding

One of the most fundamental struggles in American political history has been the turf battle for political power waged between the states and the national (or, as mentioned, federal) government. The cyclical ebb and flow of this tension between the national and state governments has been continuous for over two centuries, and is rooted in the founding of the country. As Martha Derthick writes, "American federalism was born in ambiguity, it institutionalizes ambiguity in our form of government, and changes in it tend to be ambiguous too."[17] The inherent, ambiguous tensions of the American federalist system can be traced back to the late 18th century. In developing a federalist system, the founders had no working model on which to draw.[18] So, why did the United States end up adopting a federalist system of governance?

The Articles of Confederation

The United States has not always had a federalist system. The American colonies were originally chartered as independent settlements, under the control of European colonial powers. Settlers identified themselves not as Americans, but as citizens of a colonial power. By the late 18th century, though, citizens of several of the original 13 colonies—frustrated by the dictates of the British Parliament and the monarchy of King George III—began challenging the consolidated power of Great Britain.[19] Rebellious leaders of the colonies convened in September 1774 to establish the First Continental Congress. Proposed jointly by the Massachusetts and Virginia legislatures, 12 of the 13 colonies sent delegates to Philadelphia for the proceedings; only Georgia did not immediately send representatives. The Continental Congress was weak, though, as the states retained the authority to reject or alter its wishes.

After the signing of the Declaration of Independence in 1776, it became apparent to many leaders of the fledging states that they needed a stronger central government, albeit one that would not undermine the sovereignty of the states. In 1777, the Second Continental Congress approved the **Articles of Confederation**, the country's first constitution, and sent it to the states for ratification.[20] As a confederal system, the document delimited the separation of powers between two layers of governments in an effort to make one nation out of 13 independent sovereign entities. Under the Articles, Congress was granted the authority to declare war and make peace, enter treaties and alliances, coin or borrow money, and regulate trade with Native Americans, but it could not levy requisite taxes or adequately enforce its commerce and trade regulations among the states. Members of the Continental Congress, who served one year terms and were chosen by their state legislatures, acted typically as delegates of their state legislatures. Beholden to the states, the federal government—which lacked an executive branch to enforce laws passed by Congress—was wholly reliant on the states for its operating expenses.

The Federalists

Many founders were appalled by the ineffectualness of the federal government under the Articles. General George Washington, for one, was "mortified beyond expression" that the federal government under the Articles was so emasculated that it could not even defend its citizens from relatively minor internal threats.[21] Tensions between rival sovereigns—the 13 states and Congress—were mounting. In May 1787, Congress called for a Constitutional Convention to amend the U.S. Constitution. Over that summer, delegates to the Constitutional Convention would decide to scrap the Articles, replacing them with a federalist system. In addition to restructuring the federal government's institutional design, the proposed constitution would alter the relationship between the federal government and the states, having each share power and the representation of their respective constituencies.[22]

Federalists who supported the new constitution argued in favor of a strong central government. But they made it clear that the central government's authority would be checked by the separation of powers among the legislative, executive, and judicial branches, as well as through the division of sovereignty between the states and the federal government.[23] Writing in 1788 under the pseudonym "Publius," James Madison, Alexander Hamilton, and John Jay authored a series of pamphlets that collectively became known as the *Federalist Papers*. As part of a public relations campaign to generate popular support for the ratification of the Constitution, the authors claimed the new constitution would provide for internal checks and balances in the fledgling nation and would structurally limit the supremacy of the national government by creating competitive (sometimes rival, sometimes cooperative) state governments.[24]

The U.S. Constitution and the Historical Development of Federalism

Following Congress' submission of the U.S. Constitution to the states in 1787 and its subsequent ratification, a vexing question continued to linger: which had more authority, the Union or the states?[25] Federalist sympathizers tried to downplay the power of the federal government in the proposed constitution. Temporally and territorially, of course, the states clearly preceded the Union. Yet, compared with the failed Articles, the U.S. Constitution laid out clear powers for the federal government. Figure 2.3 displays some of the basic powers held in principle by the national and state governments when the Constitution was first adopted. As we discuss later in the chapter, the division of powers between the states and the federal government today hardly resembles the allocation in the 1790s. The continual fluctuation in the relative authority of the states and the federal government has cumulated in a slow expansion of federal power over time.

Federal Powers under the U.S. Constitution

There are several provisions found in the U.S. Constitution that enhance the power of the federal government, and specifically the authority of Congress. The document grants Congress, the bicameral legislative arm of the national government, several explicit powers. These include the right to declare war; provide for the common defense; lay and collect taxes, duties, imposts, and excises; regulate commerce with foreign nations, among the several states, and with the Indian tribes; establish post offices and post roads;

Figure 2.3

Original Constitutional Powers of National and State Governments

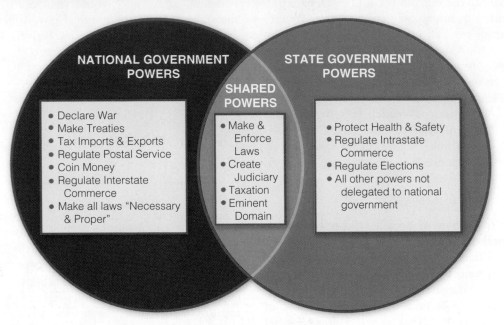

and provide for the general welfare of the United States. These "expressed" or "enumerated" powers of Congress, found in Article I, Section 8, Clauses 1–17 of the Constitution, especially the Commerce Clause, expand Congress' reach.

The National Supremacy Clause Article VI, Section 2, known as the **National Supremacy Clause**, stipulates that the U.S. Constitution and national laws and treaties "shall be the supreme law of the land … anything in the Constitution or Laws of any State to the Contrary notwithstanding." This means that the federal Constitution and federal laws trump any conflicting state constitutional provision or laws. Thus, when there is no clear delineation of which level of government is to have the dominant role in policy making, or when there is a conflict in national and state public policies, federal laws are superior to state laws.

States, for example, are not permitted to enter into treaties with American Indian tribal nations. Indian nations, which exist in 34 states, are *domestic dependent nations*, a term coined by the U.S. Supreme Court in its 1831 decision

Cherokee Nation v. Georgia. According to the high court's ruling in *Worcester v. Georgia*, which was handed down the following year, the national government has the authority to enter into agreements with sovereign Indian tribes. However, the federal government has occasionally granted states the power to negotiate certain compacts with the tribes located within their boundaries.

One of the most common negotiation areas between the states and Indian tribes has to do with casino gambling. Congress in 1988 passed the Indian Gaming Regulatory Act, which requires tribes to enter compacts with their state governments specifying the types of gaming that are permitted on reservation lands and any compensation that should be made to the state governments. In 2000, for example, California voters approved a constitutional amendment allowing Nevada-style gambling on Indian reservations; in return, more than 60 Indian tribes, which generate over $5 billion in gambling revenue each year, agreed to allow unions to organize in their casinos, provide more than $1 million in aid to nongaming tribes, and make quarterly payments to the state to offset gambling addiction programs and other costs associated with the increased economic development and social pressures stemming from gaming.[26]

The Commerce Clause The **Commerce Clause** is the third clause in Article I, Section 8 of the U.S. Constitution. The clause gives Congress the power "[t]o regulate Commerce with foreign Nations, and among the several States, and with the Indian Tribes." As we discuss at length below, Congress has interpreted the 16-word clause broadly, greatly expanding its legislative power to intervene in a wide number of facets of the national economy. Beginning in 1824, with its decision *Gibbons v. Ogden*, the U.S. Supreme Court has generally granted Congress broad powers to pass laws dealing with issues only indirectly related to interstate commerce, such as civil rights, environmental regulations, posses-

sion of firearms and drugs, and Internet transactions. Congress's broad definition of interstate commerce has even been used to regulate Internet sales, racial segregation in restaurants and hotels, and the production of subsistence wheat crops in Kansas. Today, with the increased interconnectivity of human activity, most economic activities extend beyond a state's borders and thus may fall prey to congressional regulations.

The Necessary and Proper Clause Unlike the Articles of Confederation, the Constitution also grants Congress wide discretion in its interpretation of its powers in Article I, Section 8. Clause 18 of Article I, Section 8, known as the **Necessary and Proper Clause** or the **Elastic Clause**, has been a key component in the centralization of power by Congress over time. The clause enables Congress to interpret and expand upon the 17 preceding substantive clauses in Article I,

COMPARISONS HELP US UNDERSTAND

THINKING IT THROUGH INTERNET WINE SALES

Have a thirst for a full-bodied Napa Valley Cabernet Sauvignon? How about a California-grown Pinot Noir, Merlot, or Chardonnay? Prior to 2005, if you were at least 21 years old and living in Wisconsin—or any of the other 28 states permitting direct shipments from California wine makers—your thirst could be readily quenched by ordering a bottle either by phone or over the Internet. Direct mailing of wine to consumers is big business, with the more than 3,200 wineries in the country accounting for more than $18 billion in annual sales. But if you were living in Michigan, New York, Florida, or five other states banning out-of-state shipments of wine, you were out of luck. In those eight states, you were permitted to order wine and have it delivered to your doorstep, but only if it was produced in-state. Thus, wine connoisseurs in Florida could ship directly to their homes all the Cabernet they wanted, but only if it was produced by wineries in the Sunshine State. California and other out-of-state wines had to be purchased from a licensed Florida distributor. In May 2005, in a 5–4 decision, the U.S. Supreme Court ruled in *Granholm v. Heald* that the Constitution prohibited such discriminatory regulation, as the "state regulation of alcohol is limited by the nondiscrimination principle of the Commerce Clause." Although the Twenty-First Amendment to the Constitution gives states tremendous leeway in regulating alcohol, "if a state chooses to allow direct shipments of wine," wrote Justice Anthony Kennedy in the majority opinion, "it must do so on evenhanded terms." The high court indicated that the states remain free to permit or ban the direct sale of wine to consumers, but it ruled that they may not give "preferential treatment" in direct sales to local wineries.[1] It remains to be seen whether the legislatures in the eight states that the Court ruled were engaging in economic protectionism, as well as the 13 other states that permitted reciprocal direct sales from out-of-state winemakers, will open up their direct sales, or shut them down completely as 15 other states have done.

Notes

1. Linda Greenhouse, "Supreme Court Lifts Ban on Wine Shipping," *New York Times*, 17 May 2005, p. A1.

Section 8. Congress' implied powers give the national legislative body authority to make all laws that shall be "necessary and proper for carrying into execution the foregoing powers."

The Full Faith and Credit Clause Enshrined in Article IV, Section 1, the **Full Faith and Credit Clause** stipulates that the states must mutually accept one another's public acts, records, and judicial proceedings. Congress is given the authority to oversee the manner and effect of the reciprocity among the states. Today, the Full Faith and Credit Clause has regained prominence in the controversy over the acceptance of gay marriage in Massachusetts. In 1996, Congress passed and President Bill Clinton signed into law the Defense of Marriage Act. The act gave states the power to not legally recognize marriages between gay and lesbian couples performed in another state. Still, some social conservatives contend that if the U.S. Constitution is not amended, gay rights activists may be able to use the clause to force states that have outlawed gay marriage to recognize legal same-sex marriages sanctioned in other states, such as in Massachusetts.

Privileges and Immunities Clauses: Article IV and the Fourteenth Amendment Article IV, Section 2 of the Constitution, the **Privileges and Immunities Clause**, ensures that residents of one state cannot be discriminated against by another state when it comes to fundamental matters, such as pursuing one's professional occupation, access to the courts, or equality in taxation.[27] Because of the Privileges and Immunities Clause, a state, for example, may not bar citizens from other states from practicing law in the state, assuming they pass the state's bar exam.

Section 2 of Article IV also includes a provision that was upheld by the U.S. Supreme Court's rather infamous 1857 decision *Dred Scott v. Sanford*. Before it was stricken by the Thirteenth Amendment in 1865, the third clause of Article IV permitted states to maintain the institution of slavery and required fugitive slaves who had fled to free states to be forcibly returned to their legal slaveholders. The clause continues to be invoked by states wishing to preserve states' rights. In 1978, the high court struck down the "Alaska Hire Law," which had restricted the occupational opportunities of nonresidents interested in working in the state's oil industry. The Court, though, continues to permit what some view as a discriminatory practice: allowing public universities to charge higher tuition for out-of-state students.

The Fourteenth Amendment, which we discuss in greater detail below, includes its own Privileges and Immunities Clause. The provision, ratified in 1868, was intended to bar discrimination by the states against their own citizens, most notably former slaves. The U.S. Supreme Court, however, greatly weakened the provision in what are known as the *Slaughterhouse Cases* (1873). The Court ruled that the Fourteenth Amendment's Privileges and Immunities Clause does not protect the privileges and immunities of a person's state citizenship, only his or her national citizenship. The decision has remained largely intact, despite the obvious fact that the post-Civil War amendments in the 1860s and 1870s were intended to end the discrimination of individuals, specifically newly freed slaves.

Although slavery, of course, is no longer legal, states nevertheless still engage in other forms of discrimination. All states, for example, only permit state residents to become governor. But in Florida, residents must also be citizens of the state for seven consecutive years before they are eligible to run for the office. Many Floridians were not aware of this residency requirement, which dates back to the late 19th century. This includes Lawton "Bud" Chiles III, the son of a former governor, who wanted to run for governor in 2006. After a few weeks on the campaign trail, the native Floridian was forced to drop out of the race after it was disclosed that he had lived for almost a decade in the Northeast before returning to the Sunshine State.

State Powers under the U.S. Constitution

Federalists such as Alexander Hamilton, James Madison, and their fellow delegates who supported a strong national government during the proceedings of the 1787 Constitutional

Convention in Philadelphia did not prevail on all fronts. Anti-Federalists, as they were known, expressed their discontent over the increased powers of the federal government. The Constitution was unfinished, they contended, as it failed to enshrine the rights of the states. "The Constitution *did* settle many questions, and it established a lasting structure of rules and principle," writes Herbert Storing. "But it did not settle *everything*; it did not finish the task of making the American polity."[28] With the ratification of the U.S. Constitution, the political dialogue was just beginning, as Anti-Federalist concerns and principles became central to the ongoing debate.

The Bill of Rights Joining Thomas Jefferson and George Mason of Virginia, James Madison would eventually moderate his strong defense of the national government, insisting too that a **Bill of Rights** be appended to the Constitution upon its ratification. In December 1791, three-quarters of the states ratified the first ten proposed amendments to the Constitution. A major goal of the Bill of Rights was to ensure the protection of individuals from the national government. But it also protects the autonomy of the states. The Ninth and Tenth Amendments guaranteed that states were not deprived by the federal government of any rights not explicitly expressed in the Constitution. As many people in the states quickly discovered, though, the Bill of Rights did not immediately prevent state governments from depriving their residents of rights.

The Tenth Amendment The Tenth Amendment explicitly limits the powers of national government vis-à-vis the states. Known also as the **Reserve Clause**, it gives the states broad authority, stipulating, "The powers not delegated to the United States by the Constitution, nor prohibited by it to the States, are reserved to the States respectively, or to the people." Because there is no mention in the U.S. Constitution of numerous substantive issues, such as those dealing with education, public health, the environment, or criminal justice, it was widely understood by the founders that these policy domains would be left to the states. Despite the centralization of power brought about by the ratification of the U.S. Constitution in 1788, the Bill of Rights infused the states with more sovereign powers. Because of the Tenth Amendment, in theory at least, the states are not administrative arms of the national government, but rather constituent parts that retain their autonomy from the central government.

Federalism Today

As discussed previously, there are numerous provisions in the U.S. Constitution granting authority to the national government. Through the various powers granted by the U.S. Constitution, Congress has often asserted its authority over the states, preempting state laws. **Federal preemption** occurs when the federal government takes regulatory action that overrides state laws. Advocates of federal preemption claim that it is necessary to create a uniformity of laws and regulations so as to avoid a confusing and inconsistent patchwork of standards across the states. But preemptive legislation by Congress has created an ongoing tussle between the federal government and the states.[29] According to one count, between 1789 and 2005, Congress passed 529 preemption statutes.[30] Since the mid-1990s alone, Congress has preempted, and thus partially or completely curtailed, state regulatory authority in numerous areas, including food safety, health care, telecommunications, international trade, and financial services. Critics of federal preemption claim that it leads to less flexibility in regulations and the delivery of public services, hurts the ability of states to experiment with and develop best practices, limits the ability of states to coordinate their economic development priorities with their regulatory policies, and diminishes the protections that states are able to craft for their citizens.[31]

The Ebb and Flow (and Gradual Erosion) of Federalism

In 1908, future President Woodrow Wilson wrote, "The question of the relations of the states and the federal government is the cardinal question" of the American political system.[32] The fluidity as well as the inherent tension existing between the national and subnational levels of government comprise the defining characteristic of American federalism. The ebb and flow between the states and the national government, which were codified by the ratification of the U.S. Constitution in 1788 and the Bill of Rights in 1791, are a recurrent theme in the study of American politics. Competition or even disharmony between the national and state levels of government, then, is to be expected, with disagreements between the two layers of government being interpreted as a healthy sign that the division of powers is working.[33]

The Shifting Sands of Federalism

Since the country's founding, the locus of political power in the United States has flowed from the federal government to the states and back again to the federal government. These tidal shifts, though, have not been equal in force. Although at any given moment the relative level of power between the states and the national government is refreshingly and predictably fluid,[34] with each wave the federal government has slowly eroded the sovereignty of the states. Many waves of federal encroachment on state power have been the result of crises—from the Civil War, to World War I, to the Depression and the New Deal, to the War on Poverty in the 1960s, to 9/11. In the aftermath of each of these tidal storms, the states did not become mere appendages of the national government, but they did successively lose ground to the federal government.

The reason for this constant shifting and gradual expansion of the power of the federal government stems from the fact that the authority of the federal and state government is not clearly demarcated in the U.S. Constitution. Because of the ambiguities of national and state powers, logical arguments have been made equally forcibly in defense of states' rights or for more centralized power. For example, at one extreme of the spectrum, Vice President John C. Calhoun of South Carolina in the mid-19th century advocated the

INSTITUTIONS MATTER

JOHN C. CALHOUN'S COMPACT THEORY OF FEDERALISM

States' rights under the dual federalist system were taken to their logical extreme by John C. Calhoun during the first half of the 19th century. Calhoun, who served as Vice President of the United States under the administrations of Presidents John Quincy Adams and Andrew Jackson, forcefully advanced what he called a *compact theory of federalism*. Interpreting the U.S. Constitution in the same vein as the Articles of Confederation, Calhoun argued the Constitution was confederal, binding together informally the several sovereign states. He contended that the enumerated powers of the federal government were severely circumscribed, being derived wholly from the powers of the states. Calhoun's defense of states' rights included the concept of **nullification**, which held that a state was justified in rejecting national legislation and could render federal laws void and unenforceable if it refused to accept them. If federal laws were to be enforceable, such as a protective tariff placed on imported goods that was passed by Congress in 1828, they would need *concurrent majorities*, whereby the laws were consented to by a majority of citizens at both the national and state levels. If citizens in a state took a national law to be objectionable, a state had the right to nullify the law, making it invalid within the state's borders. Calhoun went so far as to declare that states had the right to secede, removing themselves from the Union.[1]

Note

1. Irving Bartlett, *John C. Calhoun: A Biography* (New York: Norton, 1993); and John Niven, *John C. Calhoun and the Price of the Union* (Baton Rouge: Louisiana State University Press, 1988).

theory of **nullification**, arguing that the states held veto power over the actions of the federal government, which included the right to permit slavery and reject national trade agreements. At the other extreme, Alexander Hamilton argued that the United States had the right to establish a national bank that could assist the federal government in meeting its financial obligations, and that the national government could impose tariffs and duties to protect nascent industries that were central to the national interest. Over the long haul, Hamilton's view of a stronger, more centralized federal government has prevailed.

Centralization and Devolution

The American federal system continually cycles through periods of centralization and devolution. **Devolution** is the decentralization of power and authority from a central government to state or local governments; **centralization** reverses the flow, empowering a national governing authority with unitary control and authority. Writing in the 1830s, the French observer Alexis de Tocqueville noted that devolution not only had positive administrative effects but also had beneficial political effects, in that it enhanced the civic values and opportunities of citizens.[35]

In the American context, **centralization** and **devolution** are relative terms, denoting the distribution of power and the level of policy-making responsibility taken on by the national or state governments. Besides the role of the federal courts, the level of centralization or devolution present in the American federalist system is dependent on a host of outside factors. In times of war and national crises, such as the aftermath of 9/11, an increasing amount of power tends to become centralized in Washington, D.C. Centralization also occurs when people call to redistribute the nation's wealth in an effort to create greater equity in society, perceive a need to establish national standards or policy goals, and make efforts to create more efficiencies in the implementation of public policy. Power tends to flow back to the states when citizens clamor for public policies that are better tailored to fit their specific needs or when there is growing distrust of nationally elected officials. Although at times political power devolves to the states, rarely does it completely offset any preceding periods of centralization.

Creeping Centralization: The Political Evolution of Federal Power

Abetted by the power vested in Congress by the federal courts, the authority of the federal government relative to the states grew considerably during the late 19th and 20th centuries.[36] During the mid-19th century, Congress passed several laws that slowly expanded the power of the federal government. For example, in 1862 in the midst of the Civil War, the federal government cleared the way for westward expansion by passing the Pacific Railroad Act, giving charters to companies building a transcontinental railroad. That same year, Congress passed the Morrill Act, which provided territory to establish public schools and land grant universities, and the Homestead Act, which allowed citizens or persons intending to become citizens to acquire 160 acres of public land, and then purchase it after five years for a nominal fee.[37] Following the Civil War, with the Union Army's defeat of the Confederate Army, advocates of states' rights were momentarily silenced, setting the foundation for a stronger federal government and the development of a national grants-in-aid system. In 1913, with the ratification of the Sixteenth Amendment permitting the federal government to tax incomes, the powers of the federal government were dramatically enhanced.

The New Deal, World War II, and Cooperative Federalism

The relative sovereignty of the 50 states was altered during three notable high points of federal governmental power in the 20th century: the New Deal, World War II, and the Great Society programs of the 1960s.[38] Although there has been much rhetoric about the devolution of power to state and local governments, much of the political power initially grabbed by the federal government vis-à-vis the states during these time periods remains in Washington, D.C.

The New Deal programs of the 1930s advanced by the administration of President Franklin Delano Roosevelt forcefully inserted the administration of the federal government into the national economy as never before. In 1933, in an effort to mitigate the Great Depression, Congress passed the Agricultural Adjustment Act, which created educational programs and protected farmers by providing crop subsidies. The same year, Congress created the Civil Works Administration, which created public works jobs for millions of the unemployed, and also established the Civilian Conservation Corps, which sent a quarter of a million men to work camps around the country to help reforest and conserve the land. The Works Progress Administration, created by Congress in 1935, employed more than 8 million workers in construction and other jobs.[39] In 1936, Congress passed legislation creating a joint federal-state entitlement program, Aid to Families with Dependent Children (AFDC), which provided direct aid to families falling below the poverty line. Although these and other unprecedented incursions by Congress into policy areas previously controlled by the states were found to be constitutional, the U.S. Supreme Court struck down several other New Deal programs, including the National Recovery Administration and the Agricultural Adjustment Act, because of the congressional encroachment on the states.

The entry in 1941 of the United States into World War II gave rise to greater federal powers. In addition to asking Americans to make sacrifices for the war effort, the federal government commanded control of several aspects of the economy, rationing foodstuffs and consumer goods and even nationalizing some factories for wartime production. In addition to the dramatic increase in the number of military personnel, the number of civilian employees working in the federal bureaucracy skyrocketed, rising nearly fourfold to almost 4 million workers by 1945. At the same time, as we discuss in Chapter 10 when examining the fiscal effects of federalism, annual spending by the federal government rose tenfold during the war, from $9 billion to more than $98 billion. By the end of the war, political power rested squarely in the hands of the president and the U.S. Congress.

The efforts of the Roosevelt administration, with the blessing and support of the Democrat-controlled Congress, to insert the federal government into the economy by way of the states are often characterized as **cooperative federalism**.[40] In such an arrangement, responsibilities for virtually all functions of government are interdependent, shared between the federal, state, and local governments. National and subnational officials act primarily as colleagues, not adversaries.[41] Although traces of such interlevel cooperation existed prior to the New Deal, the collaboration between various layers of government blossomed during the 1930s, with the Congress utilizing **categorical grants** to entice the state governments to cooperate.

The Great Society and Coercive Federalism

In the 1960s, Congress further expanded the scope of the federal government by using **block grants** to spread a wide swath of programs across the nation. Following the assassination of President John F. Kennedy, President Lyndon B. Johnson urged Congress to create a "Great Society," one that would bring about many of the social and economic changes unrealized during his predecessor's truncated term in office. Many political observers questioned the ability, as well as the will, of many state officials to provide equal protection of the law and social services to all their citizens. Political scientist John Kincaid has characterized this period of expanding national growth and attendant federal programs, which some scholars date from 1960 to 1972, as **coercive federalism**.[42] With the federal government spearheading and funding several new programs in its war on poverty, some scholars have referred euphemistically to this period as **creative federalism**.[43] Congress sought to relieve growing social pressures found across the American states by expanding social welfare programs, including those intended to reduce urban and rural poverty and eradicate public school inequalities. In many instances, the federal government completely bypassed the states, funneling grant-in-aid directly to local governments.

In the 1960s, building on the U.S. Housing Act of 1937, Congress established an array of federal programs to aid citizens in policy areas traditionally left to the states. With the approval of the Economic Opportunity Act of 1964, Congress created an Office of Economic Opportunity that was in charge of administering numerous local antipoverty programs. The following year, Congress established the Department of Housing and Urban Development, which was charged with improving public housing and urban life. In addition, Congress passed the 1964 Civil Rights Act—which enforced the right to vote, extended federal protection against discrimination in public accommodations, and outlawed job discrimination—and the 1965 Voting Rights Act, which guaranteed the right to vote to African Americans. In the mid-1960s, Congress passed legislation creating Medicare, which created a national health insurance program for the elderly, and Medicaid, a joint federal-state–funded health care program for poor people. Each and every one of these programs increased the relative power of the federal government vis-à-vis the states.

The Continued Expansion of Federal Powers during the 1970s

Although many of the programs established during the Great Society era have been either mothballed or transferred in part by Congress to the states, many still exist. The list of programs created by the federal government during the 1960s and early 1970s is impressive and expansive. In each case, state sovereignty over these policy areas was slowly eroded. Created in the 1960s, the Head Start public education program continues to prepare disadvantaged poor children for their first years of school; similarly, the Food

Stamps program provides sustenance to those falling below the poverty line. Medicare and Medicaid, two of the largest domestic federal programs today, provide millions of Americans with medical insurance and health care. In addition to continuing to regulate auto emissions and the use of toxic chemicals, the Environmental Protection Agency, created by Congress in 1970, enforces the cleanup of hazardous waste, monitors the ozone layer, and enforces clean air and water laws.

In the early 1970s, the Nixon administration pushed for more block grants and changes to the way federal grants were administered. The president also pushed for **General Revenue Sharing (GRS)**, a grant-in-aid program whereby the federal government provides financial aid to subnational units, but does not prescribe how those units are to allocate the funding. Congress, however, abandoned the grant-in-aid scheme, as lawmakers were unable to claim credit for projects that the federal government paid for but were implemented by subnational officials.[44]

All of these social welfare programs have undergone restructuring since their creation. Yet, they are very much essential components of the social welfare system expanded by the federal government during the 1960s.[45] Indeed, Great Society programs have had lasting effects on reducing malnutrition, infant mortality, and inequality in obtaining medical services, as well as improving affordable housing, job training, and cleaning up the environment.[46]

New Federalism during the Reagan Era

In the 1980s, many scholars observed how power seemed to be devolving back to the states. They pointed to the rise of entrepreneurial activities of the American states, with the state governments taking on new responsibilities to energize their economies by creating new jobs and economic opportunities.[47] The creative, self-directed activities of state and local governments conformed to the dominant political ideology of the time, decentralization, advanced most prominently by Republican President Ronald Reagan. In his first inauguration in 1981, Reagan famously pronounced, "Government is not the solution to our problem; government is the problem." To many states' rights proponents, they had a champion in the White House.

During the Reagan years (1981–89), Congress aggressively consolidated categorical grants into block grants, cutting or eliminating entirely the funding of existing federal programs in the process. This wholesale transformation occurred despite the fact that the administration never outlined a clear set of principles regarding the proper delineation of federal and state powers. In 1982, the administration went so far as to propose what would become known as the "Big Swap," whereby the federal government would turn over to the states the responsibility to provide for education, social services, transportation, and cash public assistance programs, in exchange for taking over the provision of health services for the poor. To offset their increased costs, the states would receive a portion of the federal tax revenue. Congress rejected the proposal, as members were leery that the state and local governments would be unable to shoulder the financial costs of their new policy responsibilities.[48] As one longtime observer of American federalism noted, the Reagan administration's zeal to lessen the capacity of the federal government was not so much driven by devolution as by an "antigovernmental imperative" of "individualism."[49] Reagan and his top officials calculated that if federal dollars to states and localities were reduced, those governments would necessarily cut back on social programs. But rather than cutting programs, many state and local governments used their own funds to continue the programs. This was not the first time in American history that arguments over federalism were used to try to conceal or advance other political agendas.

The Political Expediency of Federalism

Despite Reagan's pronouncements that power should be devolved to the states, the federal government continued to exert its authority vis-à-vis the states during the 1980s and 1990s. It is often the case that federal officials will spout the devolution line, but when push comes to shove, they usually—if not always—back off.[50] Many actions taken by Congress in the 1980s were driven by political expediency as much as any ideological commitment to the Reagan doctrine of "New Federalism." Take, for instance, the passage of the Anti Drug Abuse Act of 1988, which came exactly four years after the passage of the Comprehensive Crime Control Act of 1984. The bills, which created mandatory sentences for federal crimes and revised bail and forfeiture procedures, came just a few weeks prior to the 1984 and 1988 general elections, respectively. Both pieces of legislation were largely the result of Democrats and Republicans trying to outbid each other to look tough on crime at election time.

With the Anti Drug Abuse Act of 1988, Congress felt it needed to respond to the tragic death of Boston Celtics first-round draft pick Len Bias. Bias was a collegiate star at the University of Maryland who died of a cocaine overdose. Then-speaker of the U.S. House of Representatives, Democrat Tip O'Neill from Boston, worked with Republican leaders to pass mandatory five-year federal sentences for possession of small amounts of illegal drugs favored by the poor (five grams of crack cocaine, 10 grams of methamphetamines or PCP) and of larger amounts favored by the wealthy (500 grams of powered cocaine). The law, which required employers receiving federal aid to provide a "drug-free workplace" or risk suspension or termination of a grant or contract, was adopted without hearings, debate, or expert testimony.

Expanding National Power: Setting National Standards

In the early 1990s, Congress passed numerous laws encroaching on the power of the states. In 1990, Republican President George H. W. Bush signed into law a bill (the Gun Free School Zones Act of 1990) passed by a Democratic-controlled Congress making the possession of guns in or near schools a federal crime. In 1994, President Clinton signed into law bills making domestic violence (the Violence against Women Act of 1994) and failure to run background checks before the sale of weapons (the Brady Bill of 1994) federal crimes. (Both laws were later struck down by the U.S. Supreme Court.) By 1994, Congress had created 50 new crimes that could be prosecuted in federal court, many with possible death sentences.[51] With its "Three Strikes You're Out" legislation, Congress federalized penalties for the possession of marijuana, created mandatory minimum sentence guidelines for federal judges, and allowed the death penalty for certain drug-related crimes. Prior to 1994, many of these crimes were prosecuted in state courts, at the discretion of state prosecutors. With all these laws, Democrats joined Republicans to ensure that their party would not be demonized come election time as being soft on crime.

The Devolution Revolution?

After Republicans took over the U.S. House and Senate in 1994, under the leadership of House Speaker Newt Gingrich, a more conservative Congress did try to tackle the centralization of power in Washington, D.C. Led by Gingrich, Republicans pushed forth their *Contract with America*, which, among other policy goals, called for devolution of power to the states. One of the only pieces of legislation packaged as part of the *Contract with America* to become law was the Unfunded Mandate Reform Act of 1995. In an effort to mitigate criticism among state and local government officials for the encroachment of the federal government on state powers, Congress agreed to restrict bills containing unfunded mandates. An **unfunded mandate** is a public policy that requires a subnational government to pay for an activity or project established by the federal government. Many state and local governments were upset with regulations handed down by Congress in the 1980s and 1990s with no money with which to implement the legislation. With its 1995 act, Congress must now include a cost estimate for

any program including a mandate costing state or local governments at least $50 million. In addition, any mandate costing state or local governments more than $50 million a year can be stopped by a point-of-order objection raised on either the House or Senate floor. A majority of the membership in either chamber is allowed to override the point of order and pass the mandate, but the objection affords the chamber an opportunity for debate.

Despite the flurry of rhetoric urging the decentralization of power to the states since the Republican Party took control of Congress in the mid-1990s, Congress has taken few concrete steps to actually transfer policy responsibilities to the states. As has been the case since the United States' founding, philosophical and ideological arguments over federalism have been trumped by quests for political power. Most notably, Congress passed legislation to "end welfare as we know it" by altering the long-standing joint federal-state social welfare entitlement program, AFDC. As we discuss in Chapter 14, the New Deal program was replaced by the Personal Responsibility and Work Opportunity Reconciliation Act (PRWORA), which created a block grant program, Temporary Assistance for Needy Families (TANF), signed into law by President Clinton in 1996. The new law required eligible recipients to work in exchange for time-limited assistance, but gave the states wide latitude in determining both the work requirements and levels of cash and in-kind assistance that recipients could receive.

Despite the rhetoric of devolution, the actions of Congress and the administration of George W. Bush have only increased the powers of the federal government in recent years. Following the complications of the 2000 presidential election, in 2002 Congress passed the Help America Vote Act, a grant-in-aid program that required the states to establish federal standards for voting. Earlier that same year, Congress passed the No Child Left Behind Act, which mandated that public schools make "adequate yearly progress" or risk losing federal support. In 2004 alone, the federal Department of Education placed more than

26,000 of the nation's 91,400 public schools on probation because they failed to make "adequate yearly progress." With each of these new laws, Congress has greatly expanded its reach into what are traditionally the domains of state or local government.

When Does the Federal Government Become Stronger?

There has been little systematic research investigating the distribution of political power between the American states and the federal government over time. Using a measure of the level of policy centralization between 1947 and 1998, one recent study finds that the authority of the national government in the United States has gradually increased since World War II, diminishing the power of the state governments. The authors do not find, however, any patterns of stable growth in federal authority during the five-decade period. Rather, the growth in the authority of the national government has come in fits and starts. More significantly, perhaps, efforts to devolve power to the states during the presidential administrations of Republicans Richard Nixon and Ronald Reagan—contrary to their rhetoric of devolving power to the states—did not lead to the states having increased policymaking authority.[52]

Umpiring Federalism: The U.S. Supreme Court

Given the inherent ambiguity in the interpretation and implementation of American federalism, who determines whether the state governments or the federal government has the constitutional authority to make laws? Soon after the founding of the United States, the federal courts assumed the role of adjudicating disputes between the federal and state governments. As umpire, the federal courts determine who is in the right when disputes between the national and subnational levels of government arise. In particular, the U.S. Supreme Court

serves as the ultimate arbiter of the tension existing between the federal government and the states, with the highest state courts deciding the constitutionality of state laws under state constitutions. However, as we witnessed in 2001 with the Supreme Court's controversial *Bush v. Gore* decision that tipped the presidential contest, its decisions on questions of federalism are not always consistent or grounded in historical precedence.[53] Table 2.1 provides a list of major U.S. Supreme Court decisions from 1992 to 2006 dealing with questions of federalism.

Judicial Review of the Power of the Federal Government

In 1819, 16 years after the U.S. Supreme Court ruled that it had the final word on determining whether laws were in conflict with the U.S. Constitution, the high court put the question of national government broadly usurping state power to the test in the case *McCulloch v. Maryland*. The State of Maryland had imposed a tax on transactions, including those of the Second Bank of the United States, on all banks that were not chartered in the state. The Supreme Court, under the direction of Chief Justice John Marshall, ruled that although it was not explicitly granted the right, Congress with its implied powers had the authority to establish a national bank. Under the Commerce Clause, found in Article I, Section 8 of the Constitution, the Court ruled that Congress had the power to lay and collect taxes, borrow money, and regulate commerce. Therefore, the Court ruled that the national bank was a "necessary and proper" outgrowth of the federal government's powers. Furthermore, the Court ruled that the State of Maryland had no constitutional authority to tax the national bank. The ruling, in tandem with *Gibbons v. Ogden* (1824), which permitted Congress to regulate interstate navigation, solidified the supremacy of the federal government over the state governments. In particular, the Court's rulings greatly empowered the federal government's hold over questions of dealing with interstate commerce.

Table 2.1

Major U.S. Supreme Court Rulings Dealing with Issues of Federalism

McCulloch v. Maryland (1819)	Court upholds the power of Congress to incorporate the Second Bank of the United States and upholds that the State of Maryland could not tax it.
Barron v. Baltimore (1833)	Court rules that the states are not limited by the Takings Clause of the Fifth Amendment, and that states may seize private property for public use.
Dred Scott v. Sanford (1857)	Court upholds the institution of slavery and rules that fugitive slaves who had fled to "free" states may be forcibly returned to their legal slaveholders.
Slaughterhouse Cases (1873)	Court rules that the Fourteenth Amendment prohibits states from infringing upon the rights of a person's national citizenship, but not his or her state citizenship.
Gitlow v. New York (1925)	Court rules that the Fourteenth Amendment incorporates the First Amendment's protection of freedom of speech, making it applicable to the states.
Garcia v. San Antonio Metropolitan Transit Authority (1985)	Court rules that federal wage and hour standards are applicable to employees of state and local governments.
United States v. Lopez (1995)	Court strikes down a federal law that prohibits possession of firearms near schools.
Seminole Tribe v. State of Florida (1996)	Court rules the Seminole Indians are not permitted to sue the State of Florida under a federal law, because Congress has only limited power to enact laws infringing upon state governmental entities.
Printz v. United States (1997)	Court strikes down federal law requiring mandatory background checks when purchasing firearms.
United States v. Morrison (2000)	Court strikes down federal Violence against Women Act because the law did not deal with an activity that substantially affected interstate commerce.
Bush v. Gore (2001)	Court rules that the Equal Protection Clause guarantees individuals that their ballots cannot be devalued later by arbitrary and disparate treatment, striking down the Florida recount because different standards were applied from county to county.
University of Alabama v. Garrett (2001)	Court rules that states have sovereign immunity from lawsuits filed in U.S. District court by their employees.
Nevada v. Hibbs (2003)	Court rules that state employees have the right to bring lawsuits against a state for violation of the Family and Medical Leave Act of 1993.
Tennessee v. Lane (2004)	Court upholds portions of the Americans with Disabilities Act of 1990, as it does not violate the 11th Amendment's sovereign immunity doctrine by allowing individuals to sue state governments if they denied services to people because of their disability.
Gonzales v. Raich (2005)	Court rules that federal law enforcement officials have the authority to enforce a congressional act prohibiting the cultivation and possession of marijuana, even for physician-approved uses.
Gonzales v. Oregon (2006)	Court upholds an Oregon law allowing physician-assisted suicide and limits the federal government's effort to punish doctors prescribing a lethal dose of drugs.

The Supreme Court and Dual Federalism

For much of American history, not all individuals have been protected equally by the U.S. Constitution's Bill of Rights. Irrespective of one's race, ethnicity, or creed, a person's civil liberties largely have depended on where that person resided. Although perhaps difficult to comprehend today, the civil liberties found in the first eight amendments to the U.S. Constitution did not automatically apply to all citizens. Rather, from the late 18th and into the 20th century (1789–1913), the United States was characterized by a system of **dual federalism**. In theory, under dual federalism, citizens are essentially governed by two separate legal spheres. Every eligible person is a citizen of the national government and, separately, a citizen of the state in which he or she resides.

In a series of early rulings, the U.S. Supreme Court interpreted the Bill of Rights as being applicable only to the actions of the federal government, not the states. In its 1833 decision *Barron v. Mayor and City Council of Baltimore*, the Court ruled that these federal civil liberties provided "security against the apprehended encroachments of the general government—not against those of local governments." The Court ruled that the Fifth Amendment to the U.S. Constitution—which limits the taking of private property for public use without just compensation—did not apply to the states, as "each state established a constitution for itself, and in that constitution, provided such limitations and restrictions on the powers of its particular government, as its judgment dictated."[54]

Unless specifically limited by their own state constitutions, states were not bound by the restrictions that the Bill of Rights placed on the federal government. Indeed, the states were not obliged to take positive (or affirmative) action to protect their citizens from governmental actions, even those of other citizens. For example, several states in the early 19th century had established official state religions; Congregationalism, for example, was Connecticut's official religion until 1818, and until 1833 every man in Massachusetts was required by state law to belong to a church. Other states limited the freedom of their citizens to openly criticize the government.

The Civil War and National Unity

Prior to the Civil War (1861–65), the American system of dual federalism permitted the states certain latitude to determine their own social and economic relations. In the mid-19th century, there were clear regional divisions in the United States. In addition to deep cultural differences, there were profound disagreements among the states on how to best manage and regulate the national economy, including most

notably the question of slavery. Undergirding these questions of human rights and the economy, though, was the ever-present issue of federalism, namely, states' rights.

The Civil War fundamentally changed American federalism. In early 1861, following the election of Republican Abraham Lincoln, seven Southern states seceded from the Union. In February, these states, led by South Carolina, created a new government, the Confederate States of America. The state governments seized property—including forts—of the federal government. Soon thereafter, in April 1861, the American Civil War began. Eventually, 11 Southern states would secede from the Union; by the end of the war, over 620,000 Union and Confederate soldiers were killed. With the end of the war came the opportunity for the victorious national government to reshape the contours of American federalism.

Incorporating the Fourteenth Amendment in the States

The end of the Civil War fundamentally altered the American system of dual federalism. Most notably, the ratification of the Fourteenth Amendment in 1868 provided for a single national citizenship. In part, the Fourteenth Amendment states,

> No State shall make or enforce any law which shall abridge the privileges or immunities of citizens of the US; nor shall any state deprive any person of life, liberty, or property without due process of law; nor deny to any person within its jurisdiction the equal protection of the laws.

In extending federal rights through the Due Process Clause and "Equal Protection of the Laws" Clause of the Fourteenth Amendment, the Supreme Court has slowly incorporated the Bill of Rights into the states. The **incorporation of the Bill of Rights** has been gradual, taking place through a series of U.S. Supreme Court decisions. For example, it was not until 1925, when the Court ruled in *Gitlow v. New York*, that the Fourteenth Amendment made the First Amendment's protection of freedom of speech applicable to the states. Subsequent rulings by the Court slowly began incorporating other amendments of the U.S. Constitution that protect the civil liberties of Americans into the states.[55] Although this process of incorporation was slow, many states adopted new state constitutions that provided greater rights than the federal Constitution.

Writing in the late 1800s, Lord James Bryce, a trenchant observer of American politics, was duly concerned about the system of American federalism. Bryce, the long-serving British ambassador to the United States, contended that the constitutionally prescribed dispersion of authority between the national and state governments weakened the ability of nationally elected officials to respond to internal and external threats to the nation, or changes in public opinion on domestic policy. For Bryce, the constitutional crisis over slavery that led to the Civil War was "the function of no one authority in particular to discover a remedy, as it would have been the function of a cabinet in Europe."[56]

Fortunately for Americans, Bryce noted, there were centrifugal forces that led toward increasing uniformity among the states, most notably national political parties that advanced coherent policy agendas, a transitory population, modern communications and transport, and a lack of significant physical boundaries between states. These forces, which were not bound by the federal structure, helped to homogenize differences among the states and allow for a more national trajectory in the historical development of federalism.

Establishing Minimum Standards for the States

Through a series of rulings during the 1950s and 1960s, the U.S. Supreme Court aggressively drew upon the Fourteenth Amendment to greatly expand the scope of powers held by Congress to enforce the amendment's guarantees. Under the guidance of Chief Justice Earl Warren, a former Republican governor of California who was appointed to the Court by President Dwight D. Eisenhower in 1953, the Court ruled that state and local governments were required to affirm the equal protection of their citizens. In the landmark decision *Brown v. Board of Education* (1954), the Court overturned the long-standing practice of "separate but equal" racial segregation of public schools. The Court also invalidated discriminatory electoral practices in several states with a series of decisions anchored by *Baker v. Carr* (1962), which granted the federal courts jurisdiction to hear reapportionment cases dealing with the malapportionment of legislative seats, and required that state legislatures be apportioned on the basis of population.[57]

The Court under Earl Warren, as well as his successor Chief Justice Warren Burger, also enshrined a broad array of due process rights afforded to individuals under the Fourteenth Amendment. In its 1963 decision *Gideon v. Wainwright*, the Court struck down a criminal procedural statute in Florida that criminal suspects did not have the right to consult with an attorney. In *Griswold v. Connecticut*, which the Court decided in 1965, the Warren Court struck down a Connecticut law that forbade married couples from using contraception after Estelle Griswold was arrested and convicted for distributing birth control products from her clinic. In its majority and concurrent decisions, the Court established the "right of privacy," found in the "penumbra" of the Ninth Amendment as well as that of the Fourteenth Amendment's Due Process Clause. In *Miranda v. Arizona* (1966), the Court ruled that when arresting a person, state and local police must inform a suspect of his or her Fifth and Sixth Amendment rights, and that a person has the right to remain silent and must be clearly informed of his or her right to consult an attorney during a subsequent interrogation prior to being charged with a crime. In its 1973 *Roe v. Wade* decision, the Court ruled that states, such as Texas where the case unfolded, were not permitted to criminalize or wholly thwart abortions, as such actions would violate a woman's right to privacy afforded to her under the Fourteenth Amendment, although in subsequent abortion-related decisions (as we discuss in detail in Chapter 13), such as *Webster v. Reproductive Health Services* (1989), the Court gave the states considerably more room to regulate the procedure.[58]

In each of these decisions, the high court established minimal standards—a floor—in terms of incorporating the protections of civil rights and liberties afforded by the federal Bill of Rights and Fourteenth Amendment. In this era of "new judicial federalism," the Court did not curtail the right of the states to go beyond these minimal standards. Indeed, many states have public policies—for example, minimum or living wage laws, environmental regulations, and antidiscrimination laws—that far exceed the standards set by the federal government.[59] Most notably, in 1985, the high court ruled in *Garcia v. San Antonio Metropolitan Transit Authority* that federal wage and hour standards (set by Congress in 1974) were applicable to employees of state and local governments. In other words, the Court agreed that Congress had the authority over the supposedly "sovereign" states regarding how much they had to pay their workers.[60]

Expanding States' Rights

With its ever-evolving interpretations of the Constitution, the U.S. Supreme Court recently has made decisions that have tried to return some authority back to the states. Leading the charge to rein in the powers of the federal government, former Chief Justice William H. Rehnquist, who died in 2005, took a much narrower view of the scope of the Fourteenth Amendment. In many of the Court's decisions under his watch (including *Garcia*), Rehnquist was in the minority, writing or joining dissents that were critical of the majority's failure to appreciate the restrictions on the powers of the federal government as covered by the Tenth Amendment. As chief justice, and with more conservative justices on the bench appointed by Republican Presidents Ronald Reagan and George H. W. Bush, Rehnquist steered the Court in a direction that helped to protect states' rights.

With Rehnquist at the helm of a deeply divided bench, the Supreme Court began to crack down on the national encroachment on state government prerogatives, especially those enhanced by an expansive reading of the Interstate Commerce Clause. In *United States v. Lopez* (1995), the Court found that Congress had overstepped its authority when in 1990 it passed the Gun-Free School Zones Act, which made it a federal crime to carry a firearm in a designated school zone. A high school senior, Alfonso Lopez Jr., was charged by the federal government after he brought a concealed handgun to school. Lopez was subsequently found guilty and sentenced to prison for six months. In its narrow 5–4 decision, the Court ruled that Congress did not have the authority to craft a criminal statute under the guise of regulating a supposed economic activity as permitted under the jurisdiction of the Commerce Clause. Rehnquist's majority opinion reasoned that because the activity did not directly affect interstate commerce (there was no evidence that the gun in question traveled across state lines), Congress did not have the authority to criminalize the possession of a gun in a school zone. It was the first decision in over 50 years in which the Court abrogated Congress's power to regulate an activity by using the Commerce Clause for cover.[61]

Two years later, in 1997, the high court ruled again to limit the reach of Congress. In *Printz v. United States*, the Court reaffirmed the principle that the Necessary and Proper Clause does not give Congress the power to compel local law enforcement agents, such as Montana's Ravalli County Sheriff Jay Printz, the plaintiff in the case, to conduct background checks on individuals wishing to buy a handgun. In a 5–4 decision, the Court ruled that Congress stretched the Necessary and Proper Clause too far when it passed the Brady Handgun Violence Prevention Act in 1993. The Court ruled that Congress could not use the Necessary and Proper Clause to regulate handgun sales. Then in 2000, the Court ruled in *United States v. Morrison* that the Violence against Women Act that Congress passed in 1994 was unconstitutional, as it did not deal with an activity that substantially affected interstate commerce. Time and again under the leadership of Rehnquist, the high court limited Congress's authority to invoke the Commerce Clause to regulate in areas that have only an insignificant connection with interstate commerce.[62]

Protecting the States from Lawsuits

Under Rehnquist, the Court also greatly expanded the rights of states by expanding their protection from lawsuits. According to the U.S. Constitution's Eleventh Amendment, ratified in 1795, the states have "sovereign immunity," meaning they have some protection from lawsuits brought by individuals.[63] In 1996 the U.S. Supreme Court ruled in *Seminole Tribe v. State of Florida* that the Seminole Indians were not permitted to sue the State of Florida for what the tribe alleged was the state's failure to negotiate in good faith new regulations for casino gaming activities as required by Congress's Indian Gaming Regulatory Act of 1988. The Court's 5–4 decision held that Congress did not have the authority under the Commerce Clause to trump the protections from lawsuits afforded the states under the Eleventh Amendment. In 2001, the high court gave states even greater protections when it ruled in *University of Alabama v. Garrett* that states had sovereign immunity from lawsuits filed in federal court by their employees. In its rulings, the Court has sent a message that federal powers could be limited, and that individuals are generally not permitted to sue state and local governments in federal court unless Congress specifically enacts legislation pursuant to its power to enforce "equal protection of the laws" under the Fourteenth Amendment.

The States' Rights Legacy of the Rehnquist Court?

Following a string of decisions granting more power to the federal government, Linda Greenhouse, the *New York Times*' celebrated chronicler of the Supreme Court, asked rhetorically, "Will the Rehnquist Court's federalism revolution outlast the Rehnquist Court?" Greenhouse asked if the Court's effort to protect states' rights was

more "a revolution of convenience" than driven by some deep ideological commitment.[64] With the appointment of John Roberts as the new chief justice in 2005, it appears that the effort to bolster states' rights has begun to fade.

Some cracks in the Court's bulwark to protect states' rights were already appearing in the waning days of the Rehnquist Court. A decade after Congress passed the Family and Medical Leave Act of 1993, which entitled eligible employees up to 12 weeks of unpaid leave for certain family and medical reasons, the Court ruled in *Nevada v. Hibbs* (2003) that state employees had the right to bring lawsuits against a state. Then in 2004, the Court again upheld portions of the Americans with Disabilities Act. The act, which was signed into law by Republican President George H. W. Bush in 1990, created a bevy of new regulations and standards for the treatment of people with disabilities. In *Tennessee v. Lane*, the Court ruled that the federal law did not violate the Eleventh Amendment's sovereign immunity doctrine. Rather, individuals were rightfully permitted to sue state governments if they were denied services because of their disabilities.

Prior to retiring from the bench in 2005, Chief Justice Rehnquist was on the losing side in the case *Gonzales v. Raich*, when the Court ruled that federal law enforcement officials have the authority to enforce a congressional act prohibiting the cultivation and possession of marijuana, even for physician-approved uses. Since the mid-1990s, 10 mostly Western states had passed statutory ballot initiatives permitting physicians to prescribe medical marijuana to patients to relieve their pain and suffering. The Court's majority allowed Congress to preempt state medical marijuana laws, meaning that the more than 100,000 patients receiving the herbal doses are now subject to federal arrest and prosecution. The chief justice was one of only three justices who voted in the minority, arguing that on grounds of states' rights, California should be allowed to regulate homegrown "medical marijuana." With the decision, some Supreme Court watchers, such as Michael Greve of the conservative-leaning American Enterprise Institute, now claim that "the federalism boomlet" that devolved responsibilities to the states "has fizzled," as "the court never reached a stable equilibrium" to enable decentralization to take hold for good.[65]

Yet in 2006, the newly constituted Roberts Court ruled 6–3 to uphold an Oregon law allowing physician-assisted suicide and to strike down the federal government's effort in 2001 to punish any doctor prescribing a lethal dose of a federally controlled drug in an effort to terminate a patient's life. The Court's majority in *Gonzales v. Oregon* found that the Department of Justice did not have the authority to use the 1971 Controlled Substances Act to override the Oregon law, which was passed via a citizen initiative in 1994, and then reaffirmed in a 1997 statewide referendum.[66] Rather, the Court ruled that the states—not the federal government—were responsible for the regulation of their own medical practices. The Court's ruling, with Roberts notably joining a dissenting opinion, provided the first evidence that the new leader of the high court was ready to retreat from Rehnquist's states' rights agenda, though some of his fellow justices were perhaps not yet ready to follow.[67]

Because of the inherent ambiguity in the U.S. Constitution, the Supreme Court has a tremendous amount of power in settling interpretive differences between the federal government and the state governments. In one sense, federalism is what five judges with lifetime tenure say it is, and the Court's interpretation evolves as its members come and go. As the recent spate of rulings on federalism suggests—with the Court deciding that Congress has the power to criminalize the cultivation of marijuana for medical use even though a state allows it, but that Congress does not have the power to criminalize the possession of a handgun near a school or prevent a state from allowing certain citizens to take their own lives—there is some truth to this somewhat cynical interpretation of how federalism plays out in practice. Whether this drastic or not, the American federalist system has been undoubtedly affected by the legal reasoning, political ideology, and personal preferences of the nine justices on the high court.

Federalism in an Age of Terror

As mentioned earlier, the national government's response to the terrorist attacks of September 11, 2001, as well as to subsequent threats to the security of the nation, has created a new set of challenges for the 87,000-plus local and 50 state governments. A hallmark of the "war on terror" waged by the administration of George W. Bush is the centralization of political power in Washington, D.C. Yet, much of the war on terror is being conducted on the ground at the state and local levels. As such, many state and local governments have been severely affected, and in some cases constrained, by the crush of new federal laws and administrative rulings stemming—however indirectly—from 9/11.

9/11 and Federal Powers

During the first term of George W. Bush, the Republican-controlled Congress passed numerous laws impinging on the authority of the states. The USA PATRIOT Act, passed in 2001 just 45 days after the 9/11 attacks, expanded the federal government's police powers, including the right to access medical and tax records, book purchases, and the borrowing of library books, as well as conduct secret home searches. President Bush even authorized the National Security Agency to monitor—without preclearance from a judge—phone calls and e-mails of U.S. citizens. In response, nearly 400 local governments and a handful of states passed resolutions denouncing the Patriot Act. Some of these nonbinding resolutions urge local law enforcement officials to refuse requests made by federal officials that may violate an individual's civil rights under the U.S. Constitution.[68]

Reverberations from 9/11 have also touched upon substantive policy areas that at first blush seem little to do with homeland security. Besides concerns voiced by civil libertarians that much of the new federal legislation has curtailed the civil liberties of American citizens, Congress passed legislation increasing federal control over state and local governments in a host of policy arenas. The federal crackdown on foreign threats has impinged directly on areas normally under the control of state and local governments, enabling the federal government to reign supreme over the states. Under the ever-expansive umbrella of homeland security, federal laws regulating public health care facilities, restricting the importation of prescription drugs, nationalizing K–12 education policies, and standardizing state driver's licenses have all encroached upon policy areas traditionally delegated to the states.

The War on Terror and State Militias

One of the areas greatly affected by the post-9/11 landscape concerns the National Guard. According to Article 1, Section 8 of the U.S. Constitution, the National Guard is commanded directly by governors during times of peace. Unlike federal troops, which may not enforce civilian laws unless authorized by Congress, the National Guard is permitted to enforce state laws. Immediately following 9/11, many governors called up members of the National Guard to protect potentially vulnerable airports, nuclear power plants, water treatment facilities, and bridges in their states. In the past, governors have activated the National Guard to deal with natural disasters and civil unrest in their states—providing flood relief to Iowa residents in 2001 and securing South Central Los Angeles in 1992 after rioters killed 55 people and destroyed more than $1 billion worth of property following the acquittal of police officers on trial for the beating of motorist Rodney King.[69]

Because of the war in Iraq, there are fewer National Guard troops available to governors to assist in emergency situations. Since September 2001, over 430,000 National Guardsmen and -women (along with other "reservists") have been "involuntarily activated"—that is, called into federal service by the Pentagon.[70] Because these erstwhile "weekend warriors" may serve up to two years of active duty overseas, governors have fewer troops to deploy when a natural disaster strikes. In September 2005, when Hurricane

National Guard helping Hurricane Katrina victims in New Orleans in 2005.

Mario Tama/Getty Images News

REFORM CAN HAPPEN

DISHING OUT HOMELAND SECURITY GRANTS

Calling the cut in federal aid to his city "very shortsighted," Washington, D.C., Mayor Anthony Williams decried the Department of Homeland Security's decision to reduce the amount of the antiterrorism money it sent to urban areas in 2006. New York City Mayor Michael Bloomberg was equally peeved about the millions his city wouldn't receive, saying, "When you stop a terrorist, they have a map of New York City in their pocket. They don't have a map of any of the other 46 or 45 places." In 2006 Congress cut appropriations for the Department of Homeland Security's Urban Area Security Initiative grant pro-

gram by $114 million, down to $711 million. The program is part of a $1.7 billion grant program run by the federal agency. Nearly 50 metropolitan areas were eligible for funding. Funding for homeland security initiatives in New York and Washington, D.C., was hardest hit, with both cities losing over 40 percent of funds from the previous year, whereas smaller cities, such as Sacramento, Louisville, Charlotte, Newark, and Jacksonville, in contrast, struck gold. New York City's funding, which dropped to $124 million down from $207 million the previous year, was particularly striking. The Department of Homeland Security justified the cuts by claiming that the city's grant application was faxed in late and that the city had "zero" national monuments or icons. Republican U.S. Representative Peter King was incredulous, calling the decision "indefensible" and "a knife in the back to New York." How could the Empire State Building, the headquarters of the United Nations, the Brooklyn Bridge, and Radio City Music Hall not make the cut? "As far as I'm concerned," the New York representative said, "the Department of Homeland Security and the administration have declared war on New York." King's criticism of the grant program had some merit. The State of New York in 2006 received $183.7 million, amounting to $2.78 per capita. In contrast, Wyoming received $14.83 per person in Homeland Security grant dollars.[1]

Note

1. Dan Eggen and Mary Beth Sheridan, "Anti-Terror Funding Cut in D.C. and New York," *Washington Post*, 1 June 2006, p. A1; and Eric Lipton, "Security Cuts for New York and Washington," *New York Times*, 1 June 2006, p. A16.

Katrina hit the northern Gulf of Mexico coast, search-and-rescue and disaster relief efforts were hampered in Alabama, Florida, Louisiana, and Mississippi due to the lack of National Guard troops available. Louisiana Governor Kathleen Blanco, a Democrat, was so disappointed by the slow response by the federal government that she initially refused a White House request to turn over control of the National Guard to the president. In response to the chaotic response in the aftermath of Hurricane Katrina, Congress in 2006 modified a 200-year-old law, the Insurrection Act of 1807, to empower the president to take control of National Guard troops not only to put down rebellions but also for natural disasters and other public emergencies.[71]

Crises and Opportunistic Federalism

The centralization of power in Washington, D.C., that followed 9/11 was not unexpected. After every other national crisis—the Civil War, the Great Depression, and World War II—the federal government has asserted greater authority over states and localities. For over 200 years, in the aftermath of a national tragedy the national government has tried to usurp political power, preempting the authority of subnational state and local governments.[72] The pattern simply reasserted itself after 9/11, as wave after wave of federal power has washed away much of the authority of the American states.

Due to the shock of 9/11 and the public outcry to secure the nation's homeland, President Bush increased the role of the federal government in the name of defending the homeland, and Congress obligingly followed his lead. Some, though, have questioned the increased role (and spending) of the federal government. For example, in 2005 the Republican-controlled

Congress appropriated $825 million in Urban Area Security Initiative grants to the nation's cities. Congress decreased the total amount it spent on the program in 2006, but many of the new grants to combat terrorism were disbursed to cities not typically considered high-risk areas, as Figure 2.4 documents. Ironically, many members of Congress, who once heralded the downsizing of the federal government when President Reagan was in office, eagerly supported increasing the powers and spending of the federal government, especially if those dollars were for homeland security programs or newly created federal jobs in their own states. Indeed, after a decade of downsizing the personnel of the federal bureaucracy, with more than 350,000 federal jobs cut during the eight years of the administration of President Clinton, the federal government created more than 100,000 new public sector jobs during Bush's first term in office.[73]

Republicans and Democrats both use centralization arguments when they advance their policy goals and political opportunism. Backlashes

---

Figure 2.4

Homeland Security Urban Security Initiative Grants, 2006

HOMELAND SECURITY LOSERS AND WINNERS

Urban Area Security Initiative grants, intended to provide additional money to high-risk areas, declined to $711 million in 2006 from $825 million last year. New York and Washington were among the biggest losers.

URBAN AREA	PERCENTAGE CHANGE, 2005-06	ACTUAL CHANGE (MILLIONS)	URBAN AREA	PERCENTAGE CHANGE, 2005-06	ACTUAL CHANGE (MILLIONS)
Phoenix	−60.8%	$ −6.1	Jersey City/Newark	+44.1%	$ +15.2
Denver	−49.8	−4.3	Louisville, Ky.	+41.2	+3.5
New Orleans	−49.8	−4.6	Charlotte, N.C.	+39.0	+3.5
Pittsburgh	−49.8	−4.8	Omaha	+38.3	+3.2
Buffalo	−48.8	−3.5	Atlanta	+29.6	+5.5
San Diego	−46.0	−6.8	Jacksonville, Fla.	+26.0	+2.4
Columbus, Ohio	−42.9	−3.3	Milwaukee	+25.9	+2.2
District of Columbia	−40.2	−31.0	St. Loius	+23.7	+2.2
New York City	−40.1	−83.1	Sacramento	+17.3	+1.3
Anaheim/Santa Ana, Calif.	−39.4	−7.8	Chicago	+13.8	+7.3

Note: Three cities received grants in 2006 that had not in 2005: Fort Lauderdale, Fla. ($10 million), Orlando ($9.4 million) and Memphis ($4.2 million)

Source: Department of Homeland Security   *The New York Times*

Source: New York Times, from Department of Homeland Security data, http://www.nytimes.com/2006/06/01/washington/01security.html.

against centralized policy making in the nation's capital—from the abandonment of the First Bank of the United States in 1811, to the collapse of Reconstruction in the 1870s, to the Great Society programs of the 1960s—are as predictable as the cycles of the moon. Indeed, there are growing indications that subnational resistance to contemporary federal policies and the co-optation of power by those inside the Beltway is already taking root. Somewhat

hypocritically, it is now the Democrats—who since the 1930s, and especially during the Great Society years of the 1960s, called on the federal government to override states' rights—who are leading the charge to downsize the federal government's reach in many policy realms, especially in areas concerning public education and homeland security. With the American federalist system, ideological visions of federalism are readily trumped by political considerations.

Summary

In his landmark dissent in *New State Ice Co. v. Liebmann* (1932), Louis Brandeis, an associate justice of the U.S. Supreme Court, coined the phrase "laboratories of democracy." Brandeis wrote, "It is one of the happy incidents of the federal system that a single courageous State may, if its citizens choose, serve as a laboratory; and try novel social and economic experiments without risk to the rest of the country." Many commentators have lauded Brandeis's minority ruling, as it highlights the genius of the United States' federal system. With the premium the system places on state and local experimentation as well as competition, in theory the responsibilities for policy making are often devolved to the states.

Despite the gradual erosion of authority caused by wave after wave of federal government power crashing on their shores, the states have retained much policy-making discretion. The states have been at the forefront of experimentation in education, social welfare, political economy, criminal justice, and regulatory policies, and are often in competition with one another in crafting and implementing public policies. As Justice Brandeis indicated, competition among the states, as well as between the states and the federal government, encourages policy experimentation and diffusion among the states.[74] In the American system, the states not only do battle with the federal government but also are perennially challenging one another over how to implement domestic public policies being handed down from Washington.

Since at least the turn of the 20th century to the present day, the states have had to struggle to maintain their autonomy from the federal government. In addition, states have had to go it alone when the federal government has opted not to become involved in making public policy. Recently, for example, California voters approved a $3 billion bond measure, placed on the ballot via an initiative, for stem cell research. The effort to fund such research was precipitated by cutbacks by the federal government to fund stem cell research. With the State of California functioning within a competitive market, taxpayers there are willing to finance research that will in all likelihood benefit the state's economy.

In this sense, the "quiet revolution" in the states, which Carl Van Horn observed in the 1980s, is still occurring.[75] However, as states have gradually become more powerful actors, increasing their state capacities and becoming more professionalized, so too has the federal government. State governments, with their ambiguous constitutional autonomy, continue to be relegated as semisovereign units in the system of American federalism. The following chapters compare many of the institutional differences found across the states and their localities.

Key Terms

Articles of Confederation

Bill of Rights

Block grants

Categorical grants

Centralization

Coercive federalism

Commerce Clause

Confederal system

Cooperative federalism

Decentralization

Devolution

Dual federalism

Federalism

Federal preemption

Full Faith and Credit Clause

General Revenue Sharing (GRS)

Incorporation of the Bill of Rights

Intergovernmental relations

National Supremacy Clause

Necessary and Proper Clause

Nullification

Privileges and Immunities Clause

Unfunded mandate

Unitary system

Suggested Readings

Beer, Samuel. *To make a nation: The rediscovery of American federalism.* Cambridge, MA: Harvard University Press, 1993.

Conlan, Timothy. *New federalism: Intergovernmental reform from Nixon to Reagan.* Washington, DC: Brookings Institution, 1988.

Elazar, Daniel. *American federalism: A view from the states.* 3rd ed. New York: Harper & Row, 1984.

Walker, David. *The rebirth of federalism.* Chatham, NJ: Chatham House, 1995.

Zimmerman, Joseph. *Contemporary American federalism.* Westport, CT: Praeger, 1992.

Web Sites

American Enterprise Institute (http://www.federalismproject.org): AEI's Federalism Project provides scholarly research on American federalism, as well as monitors recent developments.

Brookings Institution (http://www.brookings.edu): Brookings' Governance Studies Program provides numerous scholarly reports on the developments of American federalism.

Institute of Federalism (http://www.federalism.ch): An international research center based in Switzerland that focuses on questions of culture and federalism.

Publius (http://publius.oxfordjournals.org): *Publius: The Journal of Federalism* is the leading journal devoted to federalism, with scholarly articles examining the latest developments and trends on federalism and intergovernmental relations.

Urban Institute (http://www.urban.org/center/anf/index.cfm): UI's Assessing the New Federalism project examines federal programs that affect municipalities, documents how children and families are affected by these programs, and provides national survey data on the topic.

3

Participation, Elections, and Representation

Introductory Vignette

In 2006, the U.S. Congress was holding hearings on legislation that would have made it a crime for an immigrant to be present in the United States without proper documentation. Conservatives were calling for a law that would have made 12 million illegal immigrants felons, for tougher enforcement along the Canadian border, and for the construction of a wall along the border with Mexico. In December 2005, the Republican majority in the U.S. House passed a bill with some of these provisions, including a requirement that churches check the legal status of parishioners before helping them. The Senate was considering the bill in the spring of 2006.

At that same time, immigrant activists organized mass protests in 100 American cities in order to demonstrate opposition to the legislation and to pressure Congress to include an exemption that would allow undocumented workers to stay in the country. In Phoenix, Arizona, in a state that regularly votes Republican, 50,000 people attended a rally against the proposed immigration reforms in early April. Police estimated that the crowd stretched a mile long. A crowd of similar size gathered in Denver in March. Official estimates placed a massive crowd at a Los Angeles demonstration at well over 500,000 people on March 25. Many were wearing white as a sign of peace. Few demonstrations in American history have ever attracted as many people. On May 1, over 300,000

OUTLINE

Introduction: Is All Politics Local?

Forms of Political Participation

Barriers to Participation at the State and Local Levels

Breaking Down Barriers to Voter Participation

Voter Choice in State and Local Elections

Effects of Voter Participation on Public Policy

Does Participation Make State and Local Policy More Representative?

Elections and Representation

Summary

marched in Chicago. Hundreds of thousands more protested in other American cities as well.

By late May, Congress was backing away from the most restrictive immigration reform proposals. In June, the legislation was dead for the year. Immigration reform is a national issue, under the jurisdiction of the U.S. Congress. But in this instance, national policy was shaped not by voting but by people participating in local demonstrations—people who typically have little influence in our political system. As a man at one of the demonstrations noted, "The reason why they don't listen to many migrants is because they cannot vote. But hopefully that will change."[1] This chapter illustrates that there are different avenues for local political participation and that wealthier people are usually more likely to vote in state and local elections and contact state and local officials. We discuss some of the barriers to participation that the less affluent face and examine reforms designed to broaden the range of people participating in local politics.

Immigrants and their supporters prepare to march through downtown Seattle on a National Day of Action promoting the reform of U.S. immigration laws.

Introduction: Is All Politics Local?

Thomas Jefferson, who served as a legislator in colonial Virginia, suggested that a healthy democracy depends on having ordinary citizens engaged with local politics.[2] Jefferson's sentiments were shared by Alexis de Tocqueville, an early observer of American democracy. Jefferson and de Tocqueville stressed that people could best learn how to govern themselves and remain true citizens by participating in local politics.[3] Today, many perceive that access to elected officials in Washington, D.C., depends on large campaign contributions, whereas state and local officials are a short drive or bus ride away. One might assume that because state and local officials are fairly easy to contact, and because state and local politics are immediately accessible and visible to citizens, more people would participate in local than national politics. Clearly, political participation must be easier, and more common, closer to home.

By one key measure, the opposite is true. The average person is far more likely to vote in national elections than in his or her state and local contests. This chapter examines this paradox of participation: Despite the fact that state and local governments are closest to people, Americans participate more in national than state and local elections.[4] Despite many attempts to increase voter participation in the United States, turnout at state and local elections remains low. The decline in participation, furthermore, has been most dramatic in the United States' central cities.[5]

Forms of Political Participation

Citizens interact with their government in many ways—the most visible is electing their representatives and instructing them how to behave. Elections are by no means the only manner through which people participate

in the political process. Voting and elections are often given disproportionate attention because of their capacity to alter who controls government and to grant legitimacy on those who serve as elected officials. Low rates of participation in elections, then, may be a cause for concern. At some point, turnout at elections might be so low that the actions of elected officials lack legitimacy in the eyes of those who did not participate. But how low is too low? Most Americans over age 18 did not vote in recent presidential elections. Using this as a benchmark for "normal" levels of participation, the norm seems to be that most people don't participate.[6] As Table 3.1 illustrates, even fewer vote in "odd year" (that is, not during the year of a presidential election) state elections and even fewer in local elections.

Scholars and democratic theorists offer us limited guidance about how much public participation can shrink before the legitimacy of a democratic government evaporates. It seems clear, however, that fewer are participating now than in previous decades and that there are growing differences between those who do participate and those who do not.[7] If participating citizens were largely similar to non-participating citizens, low levels of political participation might not be such a worry. As we see below, however, there is clear evidence of **participation bias**—or differences between those citizens who participate and those who do not.[8]

Participation Is Much More Than Voting

Voting involves electing representatives, and in many places that use direct democracy (see Chapter 4), voting also involves public decisions to approve or reject policy proposals. There are many other ways, in addition to voting, that Americans are engaged politically. Some of these other forms of political participation may be seen as attempts to instruct elected officials how to act after elections are held. Indeed, all of

---

Table 3.1

Levels of Voter Participation in the United States in Different Races

Voting-Age Population Participating	%
2004 presidential race	55.2
2003 gubernatorial races	37.2 (CA, KY, and MS)
2006 congressional race	37.0
2000 California local races	30.0

Sources: Federal Election Commission; Zoltan Hanjal and Paul Lewis, "Municipal Institutions and Voter Turnout in Local Elections," *Urban Affairs Quarterly* 38, no. 5 (2003): 654–68; California, Kentucky, and Mississippi secretaries of state; and United States Elections Project, http://elections.gmu.edu.

---

what governments do—the laws, policies, rules, and regulations they pass—takes place between elections, after we have voted. People participate by joining groups, lobbying, contacting officials, attending meetings, and writing letters, among other activities.

Why Bother? The Stakes Are High Although most Americans do not usually vote in their state and local elections, political engagement at the local level is relatively impressive when compared with the public's engagement with national political campaigns and presidential elections. If public opinion surveys are to be believed, many (and occasionally most) adult Americans show up to vote in presidential elections once every four years, but they spend little time actively engaged working on national political issues. More Americans say that they spend their time working on issues that face their schools and their communities rather than spend time involved with high-profile presidential elections. This makes some sense, given the stakes. In the previous chapter, we discussed the scope of what state and local governments do. Most critically, state and local governments spend about 17 cents of every dollar generated by the American economy (far more than that spent by the federal government). The U.S. Supreme Court has given

states wide latitude over many areas of policy. Cities and counties control nearly all aspects of land use decisions, and state and local courts administer the vast majority of civil and criminal cases. Furthermore, over 95 percent of all elected positions in the United States are at the local level.

Participation at state and local levels, then, is likely to have a substantial impact on what government does. Americans are actually relatively optimistic about their ability to accomplish things at the local level. As Table 3.2 illustrates, nearly three-quarters believed that "people like you" can have a moderate or big impact in making their community a better place to live. Table 3.3 illustrates that although Americans are fairly cynical about politics generally, and many distrust government at any level, they are more trusting of their local governments and less likely to believe that they have "no say" at the local level compared to the national level.

Yet, the effect of political participation might be understood in terms of the cliché "The squeaky wheel gets the grease." That is, if we assume that governments respond mostly to those who participate, and less to those who do not, we can understand who gets what from government, at least in part, by considering who participates.

Who Participates? Who Does Not? Political participation in nearly all forms—voting, attending meetings, contacting public officials, and contributing to political candidates—is not behavior that is randomly distributed across

---

Table 3.2

Local Political Efficacy (N = 3,003)

Overall, How Much Impact Do You Think People Like You Can Have in Making Your Community a Better Place to Live?	%
No impact at all	4
A small impact	19
A moderate impact	42
A big impact	35

Source: Social Capital Benchmark Survey, 2000.

Table 3.3		

Public Trust and Efficacy in Local and National Government (N = 3,003)

Trust Local or National Government to Do What Is Right	Local (%)	National (%)
Always or most of the time	42	29
Some of the time	46	53
Hardly ever	11	18

Source: Social Capital Benchmark Survey, 2000.

People Like Me Have No Say in What Local or National Government Does[a]	Local (%)	National (%)
Agree	35	41
Disagree	62	50

[a] Question to respondents was as follows: "Do you agree or disagree that 'people like me have no say in what the [federal] government does' and 'People running my community don't really care much about what happens to me'?"

Sources: National Election Study, 2000; and Social Capital Benchmark Survey, 2000.

Table 3.4		

Levels of Local Participation in the United States (N = 3,003)

In the Last 12 Months, Did You	Overall (%)	Poor (%)	Wealthy (%)
Attend a public meeting to discuss school or town affairs?	45	31	63
Work on a community project?	38	23	60
Attend a PTA or school group meeting?	24	14	34
Participate in a neighborhood or homeowner association?	22	12	41
Participate in a group that took action for local reform?	18	9	30

Note: Poor = household income is $20,000 or less; wealthy = $100,000 or more.

In the Last 12 Months, Did You	Overall (%)	Rent (%)	Own (%)
Attend a public meeting to discuss school or town affairs?	45	36	49
Work on a community project?	38	28	42
Attend a PTA or school group meeting?	24	19	26
Participate in a neighborhood or homeowner association?	22	14	26
Participate in a group that took action for local reform?	18	15	19

Source: Social Capital Benchmark Survey, 2000.

the population. Depending upon the form of participation we are examining, there may be substantial differences between those who participate and those who do not. Consider the forms of participation listed in Table 3.4. There are striking differences across income groups. The wealthy tend to be overrepresented relative to average people and less wealthy people in several forms of local-level political participation. Most wealthy people say they go to public meetings and work on community projects. Most of the least affluent people do not. It is important to note that wealth itself and education alone are not what cause people to participate in politics. Education and wealth lower the costs of becoming engaged with politics. By *costs*, we mean such things as time and the difficulty of collecting and processing political information.

Voting

When we consider voting, there are clear differences between who votes and who does not.

One study found that although 55 percent of all American adults earned lower- to middle-level incomes, this majority group represented only 46 percent of voters in national elections, 43 percent of campaign hours volunteered, and just 16 percent of campaign dollars provided to candidates.[9] This participation gap between the affluent and less wealthy may even be greater in state and local elections that have lower levels of citizen participation. The voting population tends to overrepresent the affluent, older voters, people from white-collar professions, people with higher levels of education, and those who have jobs.[10] This said, voters are probably more representative of the general citizenry than other types of participants, such as campaign contributors and members of organized political groups.[11]

Voter turnout in local elections is also significantly higher in cities with a higher social status population and in places with more voters who are over 65 years old.[12] Public opinion surveys suggest that homeownership may have no impact on whether someone votes in national elections,[13] but the incentives to vote that come with homeownership—being concerned about property values and property taxes—are more likely to be felt in local elections. Records of actual votes cast in a nonpartisan Atlanta mayoral race, for example, demonstrated that homeowners are more likely to vote than renters. The stimulating effect of property tax issues on voter turnout was famously seen in California in 1978, where more people voted on a property tax cut measure (Proposition 13) than voted in the gubernatorial race on the same ballot.

As Table 3.4 illustrates, homeowners are more likely than renters to report many other forms of local political participation. With lower levels of participation, renters and the less affluent might be expected to have less influence in local politics relative to their share of the population.

Contacting and Contributing

The participation gap between rich and poor is even more striking when we look at the "activists"—people who donate their time and money to candidates and who contact government officials. Sixty percent of all reported "contacts" with public officials came from the top 45 percent of income earners.[14] Studies of people who contact local officials suggest that contacting increases with social status and income, although contacts based on needing help from the government may be related to having less income.[15] It's not just income alone

that causes contacting. Wealth corresponds with education, with political skills, and with **efficacy**—the sense that political involvement can actually make a difference.

Attending Meetings

State and local politics differ from national politics in that the actions of government are more accessible locally. Many aspects of state and local government require open public meetings that provide for public comment. Individual citizens and people representing organized groups may attend without having to bear substantial travel costs. Mandates that government provide open meetings do not necessarily ensure that officials give full consideration to all citizen comments.

Interest Group Activity

In addition to contributing to groups, citizens join and serve on boards of homeowners' associations, school groups, and many different voluntary political and social groups that work to shape their states and communities. An influential theory of interest group activity, **collective action theory,** predicts that groups seeking economic benefits from governments (such as tax breaks and public subsidies) are more likely to remain organized and well funded than groups seeking "public" benefits, such as parks and consumer protections.[16] Records detailing which political groups register to lobby the federal government are consistent with this theory. Nearly two-thirds of political action committees (PACs)—including those spending the most on **lobbying**—are affiliated with corporations, trade groups, professional associations, and the health care industry. Only 22 percent were "nonconnected" ideological and public interest groups, and 10 percent were labor groups.[17]

At the local level, the presence of organized suburban neighborhood associations may have an upper-status bias, reflecting that affluent suburbanites have resources to organize and work collectively to protect themselves (and their property values) from unwanted development.[18]

REFORM CAN HAPPEN

THE LONG, SLOW ROAD TO VOTING RIGHTS

The 15th Amendment to the U.S. Constitution, adopted in 1870, states that the right to vote shall not be denied on the basis of race, color, or previous condition of servitude. Despite this, it took decades to eliminate most race-based barriers to voting in the United States. By 1910, virtually all blacks were unable to vote in the former Confederate states. It wasn't until 1915, when the U.S. Supreme Court struck down the grandfather clause in an Oklahoma law in *Guinn v. United States,* that the Court began using the 15th Amendment to eliminate the major barriers that states used to disenfranchise blacks. By 1944, the Court ruled that Texas could not ban blacks from primary elections (in *Smith v. Allwright*). In 1960, the Court ruled that cities could not redraw boundaries to remove blacks from a city (*Gomillion v. Lightfoot*).

The Voting Rights Act of 1965 was a historic piece of legislation that provided a major expansion of access to voting for millions of Americans. One key feature of the act (Section 5) was taking control of elections away from local governments and granting authority over many voter registration and election procedures to the U.S. Department of Justice. Jurisdictions covered under Section 5 could not change any rules about voting until the attorney general or a federal court ruled that the change did not have a discriminatory effect.

Many barriers to voting still remained after the initial Voting Rights Act was passed. For example, the act had no provisions against the local poll tax. The U.S. Supreme Court ruled the poll tax unconstitutional in 1966 (*Harper v. Virginia Board of Elections*). Newly enfranchised blacks were denied influence in many jurisdictions by racial gerrymandering and at-large elections. The act was amended in 1975 and 1982 to address these issues and to expand protections against vote discrimination to Hispanics, Asians, and Native Americans. As Figure 3.2 illustrates, as of 2005, former Confederate states still have the most substantial regulations on voting and registration. States with larger black populations have significantly greater restrictions on voting and registration.[1]

NOTE

1. Shaun Bowler and Todd Donovan, "Barriers to Participation for Whom? Regulations on Voting and Uncompetitive Elections," in *Mobilizing Democracy,* eds. M. Levi, R. Johnson, and S. Stokes (New York: Russell Sage Foundation, forthcoming).

Survey data reported in Table 3.4 also show large differences across income groups in who gets involved with local political groups. Compared to those from households in the bottom one-fifth of all incomes, people in the top fifth of all incomes were twice as likely to be involved with Parent-Teacher Association (PTA) groups and other school groups. They were three times more likely to be involved with neighborhood groups and almost four times more likely to be involved with a local political reform group.

Group activity can have important effects on the policies that states and cities adopt. In the early part of the 20th century, the work of women's groups accelerated state adoption of "mothers' pension benefits"—a forerunner to federal Aid to Families with Dependent Children (AFDC).[19] When American women were largely shut out of the voting arena, middle-class and upper-status women formed a million-member General Federation of Women's Clubs that lobbied effectively for mothers' pensions and consumer protections.[20]

Grassroots Political Activity

Many interest groups function by collecting contributions from members to pay for the work of full-time staff. Groups with a broader base of support may rely on rank-and-file members or on the general public, to bring attention to their issue. As examples, neighborhood groups may attempt to pack city council hearings with residents worried about the impact of proposed developments, or to promote neighborhood interests. Crime and environmental degradation have prompted grassroots activism at the local level. Grassroots neighborhood groups also organize to fight poverty, promote quality housing, and resist urban renewal. Prominent figures supported by grassroots neighborhood groups have been elected mayor in cities such as Boston, Cleveland, Portland, and Santa Monica, California.

Social Movements and Protest

In addition to joining formal groups, people participate in larger, broad-based social movements. Social movements may comprise many loosely affiliated groups that share a common purpose of sustained, mass-based participation throughout a large number of communities in order to mobilize public opinion and change public policy. Formal channels of participation in social movements are sometimes difficult to define but may include the forms discussed above as well as lawful protest, public demonstrations, and peaceful civil disobedience.

The American Civil Rights Movement serves as a classic example of a broad, mass-based social movement working in many communities to change the nation's perceptions of racial segregation and voting rights abuses.

Rioting

Rioting is a rare, often spontaneous form of illegal action using physical violence. Rioting does not qualify as legitimate political participation, but it may reflect the failure of politics. Some consider rioting to be a political challenge to authority; others see it as an opportunistic attempt to loot and commit other crimes.[21] American cities have a history of riots fueled by racial animosity. Fatal white-on-black race riots were common in American cities in the

Peter Pettus/The Library of Congress

Participants in the 1965 civil rights march from Selma, Alabama, to Montgomery, the state capital. This march and others brought attention to barriers that kept blacks from voting. Participants were attacked and beaten by police before they reached Montgomery.

19th and early 20th centuries. In 1920, more than 300 African Americans were killed by whites in a single event in Tulsa, Oklahoma.[22]

Rioting occurred in hundreds of communities throughout the urban United States during the 1960s. Although the root causes of the 1960s rioting were traced to poverty, major riots were triggered by sudden, dramatic public events (such as a conflict with police or the murder of Dr. Martin Luther King Jr.). There is evidence that the participants in urban riots of the 1960s were fairly evenly distributed across income, educational, and occupational groups in their communities and that rioters were not simply jobless thugs and criminals.[23] The impetus for adopting antipoverty programs in the late 1960s can be traced, in part, to elected officials responding to widespread urban rioting.

Although much less common since the 1960s, sporadic rioting occurred in U.S. cities in the 1980s (Miami) and 1990s in response to conflicts with police in minority neighborhoods. In 1992, several days of widespread rioting caused at least 45 deaths, 2,000 injuries, and $1 billion in property damages in the greater Los Angeles area. The rioting began in response to a trial court acquitting police officers who had been charged with the 1991 beating of an African American motorist (Rodney King).

How Many Citizens Participate?

Records show low levels of voting at the state and local levels, yet many American adults are politically active at the local level. Between elections, these politically active citizens try to shape policy by attending meetings and testifying at public hearings. In 2000, 45 percent of Americans reported that they had attended at least one meeting in the last 12 months to discuss affairs related to their town or schools. Another 20 percent said they attended at least two such meetings in the previous year. Significant numbers also reported working on community projects and working with groups that promoted social and political change in their communities.[24] Political participation can also take forms such as circulating petitions, attend-ing protests, contacting elected officials, writing letters, and the like. Over 50,000,000 Americans belong to homeowners' associations, with over 1 million serving on boards and committees. Although these numbers are impressive, local political participation seems to be declining. By 1990, half as many people reported voting in local elections than did in 1967.[25]

Barriers to Participation at the State and Local Levels

As Figure 3.1 illustrates, there is substantial variation in voter participation across the 50 states, just as there is across American towns and cities. Minnesota and Maine lead the nation in the percentage of adults over 18 who voted in the 2004 presidential election, with over 70 percent of their **voting-age population** having participated. California, Texas, and Hawaii rank lowest, with less than half of the adults in these states voting. These vastly different participation rates are a result of many factors. States like Minnesota have far more people with traits known to correspond with interest in politics. A higher proportion of Minnesotans have college degrees and higher income levels than people in states like Texas. Maine and Minnesota also have far fewer noncitizens than Texas and California. Only U.S. citizens can vote in presidential elections, which means we should also think of voter turnout as a percentage of a state's **voting-eligible population**—that is, the proportion of citizens who vote who are not disenfranchised by felony convictions. States differ as to the rules they use to define which citizens are eligible to participate in elections, and they use different rules about when (or if) a person must register to vote prior to an election.

Race- and Gender-Based Barriers

States set many rules that affect who votes and who does not. Although the Fifteenth Amendment to the U.S. Constitution (1870) says that

Figure 3.1

Voter Participation in the 2004 Presidential Election, by State

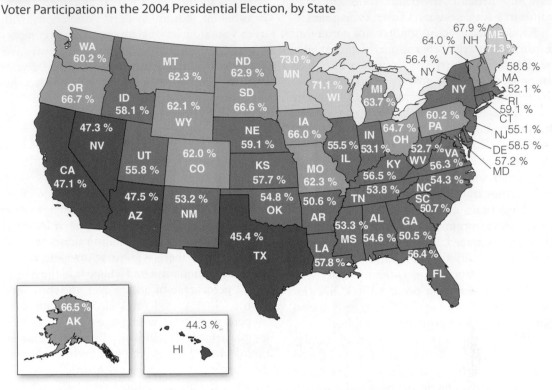

Percentage of all state residents 18 years of age or over voting in the November 2004 general election.

the right to vote cannot be denied "on account of race or color," the amendment was substantially meaningless for nearly a century. In the later half of the 19th century, many states erected substantial barriers to the voting process in order to prevent African Americans from voting. Some rules requiring that voters register far in advance of elections were often adopted in response to the perception that corrupt party machines (see Chapter 5) had their supporters "vote early, and vote often." Other barriers were racially motivated, such as **racial gerrymandering,** closing polling places, not allowing voters to register, implementing **literacy tests** and **poll taxes,** and establishing **grandfather clauses** that allowed whites to vote regardless of whether they paid a poll tax or passed a literacy test. Such rules were used to reverse the expansion of African American voting rights that occurred after the Civil War.[26]

Prior to 1920, states could also deny women the right to vote, and most did. Utah and Washington allowed women to vote briefly in the 1880s, and the Territory of Wyoming gave women the vote in 1869. Idaho (1896), Washington (1910), and California (1911) were the first states to extend voting rights to women. After the Nineteenth Amendment (1920) was adopted, women won the right to vote in any state, but racially motivated barriers to voting persisted.

Prior to the Civil Rights Movement and **Voting Rights Act of 1965,** local election officials had the discretion to apply these barriers selectively, in order to disenfranchise blacks but not whites.[27] In some places, blacks who attempted to register faced economic reprisals, physical violence, and even death. In 1964, for example, only 7 percent of blacks in Mississippi were registered to vote, compared to 70 percent of whites. In Alabama, 19 percent of blacks were registered in 1965, compared to 70 percent of whites.[28] At the time the Voting Rights Act was adopted, several southern states required people to pass subjective literacy tests in order to register, and four southern states required voters to pay a tax to vote in state elections.[29] The Voting Rights Act applied to states, counties, and cities that had low minority voter participation. It gave the federal government the authority to enforce the right to register and vote and allowed federal observers to monitor elections. It gave federal authorities the power to review and "pre-clear" any changes to voter registration and election rules in jurisdictions covered by the act in order to restore voting rights. It also ended literacy tests in six southern states

with low registration levels (Alabama, Georgia, Louisiana, Mississippi, Virginia, and much of North Carolina).

As late as 1970, 18 states still had literacy tests that prospective voters were required to pass in order to register (these were finally banned in 1975 due to their history of discriminatory application).[30] In 1972, the U.S. Supreme Court moved to end state laws requiring that a person reside in a jurisdiction at least one year prior to registering to vote. In 1975, the act was amended to apply to states and counties with low registration levels and large non-English-speaking populations (all of Alaska, Arizona, and Texas and many areas in other states). The act was also amended to give plaintiffs greater latitude to challenge election

INSTITUTIONS MATTER

DIFFERENT WAYS TO DRAW DISTRICTS

The practice of drawing electoral boundaries for a jurisdiction is known as *districting,* or *redistricting.* Because so many voters support whatever candidate their party nominates for an office, the location of boundaries for a district can have huge implications for which party wins the district. A district where 60 percent of the voters are Democrats will almost certainly elect a Democrat. Likewise, a district that is 60 percent Republican will almost certainly elect a Republican. People drawing boundaries for districts have knowledge of where each party's voters live.

This raises the question, then, about who should draw district boundaries. Although the process varies considerably from state to state, in most states, the legislature has the final say over what the boundaries for state legislative and congressional districts will look like. This means that a party having a majority in the legislature, with a sympathetic governor, can largely draw maps as it sees fit: it can maximize the number of districts that the majority party is likely to win or it can create "safe" seats for incumbents (or both). The majority party may also try to spread the opposition party's supporters thinly across as many districts as possible to dilute their power. If control of government is divided between both major parties, incumbents of both parties might see fit to agree that most districts should be safe for one or the other party.[1] These "bipartisan" plans may protect incumbents from having a serious threat in any re-election campaign.

Several states place control of drawing district maps in the hands of an appointed commission or with the courts. Commissions and courts may have partisan interests but not as strong as the partisan interests affecting legislators. One study of state districting plans found that elections were more competitive when districting plans were produced by courts and commissions than when produced by incumbent politicians.[2]

NOTES

1. Bruce Cain, "Assessing the Partisan Effects of Redistricting," *American Political Science Review* (1985): 320–33.
2. Jamie Carson and Michael Crespin, "The Effect of State Redistricting Methods on Electoral Competition in United States House Races," *State Politics and Policy Quarterly* (2004).

practices—including at-large plans—that can be shown to dilute minority representation.

Despite Civil War–era amendments to the U.S. Constitution extending voting rights regardless of race, it took well over a century for the U.S. Congress and the U.S. Supreme Court to strike down the most overt prohibitions on voting.[31] But the gap between white and black registration levels in southern states covered by the Voting Rights Act was nearly eliminated by 1988 as a result of the Voting Rights Act. This does not mean that all barriers were eliminated by the act. Some state and local governments responded to increased minority participation by changing how they conducted their elections in order to dilute the influence of minority voters. The act is still used to guard against such practices and was scheduled to be considered again by Congress in 2007. Whether racially motivated or not, as of 2005, state policies that made it difficult to register and vote were still more likely to be present in states with greater racial diversity.[32] Mississippi, Louisiana, and South Carolina—which have some of the highest proportions of black residents in the United States—had the longest requirements for pre-registration before elections (30 days in 2006). Polls were open for 14 or 15 hours in Connecticut, Rhode Island, Maine, and New Hampshire on Election Day in 2004 but for just 12 hours in racially diverse Florida, Georgia, Mississippi, South Carolina, and Texas.

Registration Barriers

Although many of the most egregious barriers to voting are now gone, there are still important differences in registration laws across the states. In 1995, the National Voter Registration Act (also called the "Motor Voter" Act) went into effect, requiring that states accept mail-in registrations for federal elections if postmarked 30 days prior to an election and requiring that public agencies provide voter registration forms. States continue to have discretion to allow voter registration on the same day of the election or to have waiting periods of up to 30 days. States also have the discretion to adopt laws that make it easier (or harder) to vote by mail. As of 2005, states with higher proportions of African American residents continued to have more barriers to registration and easy voting.[33]

Having registration offices open for shorter hours, and having closing dates for registration further from the election, can depress turnout.[34] Conversely, states that allow registration on the day of the election rank highest in voter participation. As of 2006, there were six states with Election Day registration at local polling places (Idaho, Maine, Minnesota, New Hampshire, Wisconsin, and Wyoming). North Dakota does not require voter registration, and Montana allows Election Day registration at a county clerk's office. In nearly every state, however, it is the citizen's responsibility to remember to register ahead of time and to seek out a public agency in order to do this. In many other nations with higher voter turnout, the government assumes the responsibility for finding citizens and making sure they are properly registered to vote (just as the U.S. Census Bureau attempts to find everyone once a decade).

Districting Barriers

A larger institutional barrier to voting may be found in the nature of American elections themselves. Elections for nearly every seat in the U.S. House of Representatives, most state legislatures, and many city and county councils are conducted in single-member districts under winner-take-all rules. This means that the single candidate winning the most votes represents a specific geographical area. Winner-take-all election rules tend to produce two-party systems. That is, because there is nothing to be won for candidates from parties that always place third or fourth, people fear wasting their vote on such parties, and only the largest parties survive.[35] Winner-take-all elections are the main reason that the U.S. Congress, every state legislature, and nearly every local partisan council are dominated by representatives of just one or two political parties.

Districts boundaries used to elect representatives must be redrawn on occasion, or **redistricted,** to account for shifts in population. Critics of the redistricting process note that incumbents can have too much influence over how their district lines are drawn, such that elected officials are picking their voters rather than voters picking the officials. Democrat incumbents have incentives to make sure that their districts' boundaries include as many loyal Democratic voters as possible, whereas Republican incumbents have incentives to pack their districts with as many Republican voters as possible.[36] In many states, partisan elected officials have near total control over how these districts are drawn. In other states, legislators pick "bipartisan" commissions to make district maps or have the courts settle the issues. Parties keep detailed records of block-by-block voting trends and use sophisticated computer mapping programs to design their preferred districts.

When elections are one-sided, there is less campaign activity. When elections are contested by just one major party, there may be no campaign. Without campaigns, voters are probably less likely to notice that an election is being held. Turnout decline in American elections since 1960 corresponds with a decline in competitive elections, as more districts are drawn to be safe for just one party or the other. Congressional and state legislative races are often uncontested by one of the major parties because they have no chance to win. In recent years, nearly one-third of all state legislative races have not been contested by one of the major parties.[37] When fewer races are contested, fewer candidates campaign, and fewer citizens are likely to be engaged by the election.[38]

Who Is Ineligible?

State governments set rules about who is eligible to vote in their state and local elections. They

COMPARISONS HELP US UNDERSTAND

SHOULD NONCITIZENS VOTE?

Although the U.S. Constitution stipulates that the right to vote in federal elections extends to citizens, this clause does not apply to state and local elections. States can determine if legal immigrant noncitizens are eligible to vote. An estimated 20 million legal immigrants work in the United States and pay taxes. They may also serve in the military, but they cannot vote. Historically, granting the right to vote to immigrants was seen as a method to get people engaged with politics. Advocates of voting rights for noncitizens note that America's noncitizens could vote in colonial times and in many U.S. states until an anti-immigrant backlash in the 1920s. Until 1926, 22 states and territories allowed immigrants to vote in local elections.[1]

Many nations, including Chile, Ireland, and New Zealand, allow noncitizens to vote in local elections.[2] A few places, such as Takoma Park, Maryland, do allow legal immigrants to vote in local elections. New York City and Chicago have recently allowed legal immigrants to vote in school board elections. In 2004, San Francisco voters rejected a proposal to allow noncitizens to vote in local elections, whereas voters in the Massachusetts cities of Amherst and Cambridge passed similar initiatives. Opponents, such as New York City mayor Michael Bloomberg, argue that if immigrants want the full rights of citizens, including voting rights, they should become citizens.

Notes

1. Alexandra Marks, "Should Noncitizens Vote?" *Christian Science Monitor,* 27 April 2004.
2. Ronald Hayduk, "Immigrant Voting Rights Receive More Attention," 2004, http://www.migrationinformation.org.

have the power to decide if certain groups of people may vote or not in state and local elections (federal law regulates who may vote in federal contests). Depending on the state, people found to be "mentally incompetent," convicted felons who served their time, people in prison, people on parole, and legal immigrant noncitizens may be banned from voting. Or depending on the state's laws, they may be permitted to vote.

California, Nevada, New Jersey, and Florida had more noncitizens per capita in 2005 than any other state. Noncitizens typically cannot vote. Florida, Texas, and Mississippi also have far more inmates, parolees, felons, and ex-felons than the average state and do not allow many of them to vote.[39] Felon voting bans were adopted by states in the late 1860s and 1870s as the 15th Amendment was extending voting rights to African Americans.[40] States with larger nonwhite prison populations were more likely to ban convicted felons from voting than states where more whites were in the prison population. States with more white prisoners in the 20th century were subsequently more likely to soften or repeal these laws than states with higher African-American prison populations.[41] Southern states have been significantly less likely to repeal laws that prevent ex-felons from ever voting again. One of the largest sources in the decline in voter turnout in recent years is the steep increase in the proportion of citizens who are losing their voting rights due to felony convictions, often for drug possession.[42]

Where Are the Greatest Barriers?

Figure 3.2 illustrates which states had the most barriers to voting and registration as of 2005. We identified 10 restrictions that states may place on voting and registration and then assigned a state one point for each restriction the state maintains. Restrictions include requiring that voters register at least 20 days in advance, not allowing polling place registration, not allowing parolees or felons to vote, having shorter than average polling place hours, allowing no early voting, placing restrictions on "no excuse" absentee voting, and other similar rules.

The state with the most of these restrictions on voting is Mississippi (scoring a perfect 10), followed by several other southern states, including Kentucky (9), Virginia and Alabama (8), and Maryland, Florida, Georgia, and Texas (7). Nevada, New York, and Pennsylvania also score high (7). North Dakota places the least restrictions on voting (1), followed by Vermont, Oregon, and Maine (2) as well as Utah (2.5), California (2.5), and New Hampshire (3). Other things being equal, states with more of these barriers had lower participation in the 2004 presidential election. On average, every three restrictions that a state maintains were associated with 2.4 percent less voter turnout. Rules requiring advance registration have particularly noticeable effects. Every 10 additional days that a state required for advance registration were associated with 2.5 percent less turnout in 2004.[43]

Party System Barriers

Local political party organizations traditionally played a large role in mobilizing voters and getting them to participate in politics. Local party "machines" once relied heavily on large numbers of loyal workers to get their supporters to the polls. Some party workers could be rewarded with municipal jobs in exchange for their work on behalf of the party's electoral efforts. Party workers checked the sign-in sheets at polling places to track who had not yet voted, tracked down those who had not yet voted, gave people rides to polling places, and called on neighbors to remind them to vote. It helped if local elections were contested under party labels and held in synch with high-profile national races. Party labels and local party organizations lowered the "cost" that voters faced when voting. Party labels—usually *Democrat* or *Republican*—told voters a lot about relatively unknown candidates seeking state and local offices.

Decades of antiparty reform laws passed by state legislatures have changed the role of parties in many states.[44] Civil service reforms make it difficult—if illegal—for parties to

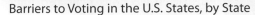

Figure 3.2

Barriers to Voting in the U.S. States, by State

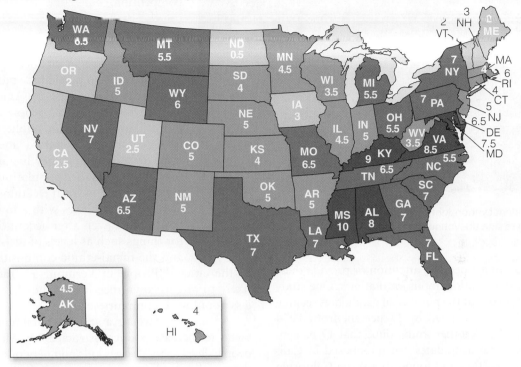

States are ranked on a scale of 0 to 10, with low scores representing few barriers to registration and voting and high scores representing more barriers. The index represents barriers such as long advance dates for registration, a prohibition on absentee voting, a prohibition on early voting, a restriction on parolees and felons voting, and shorter-than-average polling place hours.

reward their supporters with public sector jobs. Nowadays, nearly 75 percent of local elections are nonpartisan. Nearly all local elections (95 percent) in western states are nonpartisan, whereas most local contests in the northeastern states remain partisan.[45] Turnout remains higher today in local partisan elections. Many places also have their nonpartisan local elections in "off years," out of synch with higher profile contests—further depressing turnout.

Historians demonstrate that many of these antiparty reforms were adopted at the start of the 20th century to "depoliticize" local politics and insure that the influence of working-class people and racial and ethnic minorities would be diluted in favor of people who wanted to improve the business climate in their cities.[46] The

drop in party mobilization of voters has been found to be one of the largest factors behind low turnout in the United States.[47] With the decline of parties, Americans may now be less likely to have someone knock on their door to encourage them to vote. However, experiments in cities like Columbus, Ohio, and Raleigh, North Carolina, demonstrate that face-to-face visits with voters before a local election can increase participation by about 10 percent.[48] However, few organizations have the resources to mount large-scale, door-to-door canvassing drives.

Noncompetitive Elections

Local elections may be less competitive than in previous decades. This means elections have less

President Lyndon Johnson giving Dr. Martin Luther King Jr. a pen used to sign the Voting Rights Act of 1965.

ability to get people's attention or provide them with information about local affairs. One study estimated that the number of candidates seeking local office dropped by 15 percent from 1974 to 1994.[49] Another study found that 17 percent of mayoral candidates ran unopposed in California in 2003 and found that seven California cities cancelled their elections that year due to lack of competition.[50]

State laws determine how local elections will be conducted. In many local elections, candidates run **at large** (that is, citywide). At-large elections were another antiparty, **Progressive era** reform designed to weaken the influence of political parties and the lower-status voters, often recent immigrants, whom they relied upon for support. At-large elections were sold as a "good government" reform, in part, for their ability to get working-class ethnics, blacks, and Socialists off of city councils.[51] Because minorities and the poor are often concentrated in specific neighborhoods, and because most white voters usually vote for white candidates,[52] racial and ethnic minority candidates often have a better chance of being elected from small districts rather than at large when they run for a citywide office.[53] Districted contests facilitate the election of minority candidates, but if districts are drawn to be heavily homogeneous

(that is, safe for a minority group), districted elections may also limit competition.

The Effect of Place

People who live in smaller communities tend to participate more. Across a wide range of American towns and cities, people are more likely to contact public officials and attend board meetings, for example, if they live in a place with a smaller population.[54] Voter turnout in local elections is also higher in places with a lower population, even after accounting for things such as levels of income and the racial-ethnic composition of the cities.[55] People in Vermont are more likely to attend town meetings if they live in less populous communities.[56]

A sense of place, or a sense of community, seems to increase political participation. Many people develop the social skills and networks—the **social capital**—they use in political activity by volunteering with local service clubs and social, fraternal, and religious groups.[57] For example, by organizing a bake sale for a church, or an auction to raise money for a soccer team one might build social networks and learn fundraising skills that carry over to political activity. Where there is more social capital, then, there is likely to be more political participation. Social capital seems to coexist with trusting other people, and residents of smaller places tend to trust other people more than residents of larger places do.[58] A prominent investigation of social capital found that people in smaller places were much more likely to volunteer in their communities, to work on community projects, and to give to charity.[59]

Personal Barriers

When Americans are asked about the barriers to local participation, lack of information is the barrier most frequently cited as being a serious

Table 3.5

Public Attitudes as Barriers to Participation in Local Politics

Public Attitudes	%
Lack of information or don't know how to begin	35
Feel can't make a difference	26
Work schedule (too busy)	25
Poor transportation	20
Feel unwelcome	22
Safety concerns	28

Source: Social Capital Benchmark Survey, 2000.

impediment. As Table 3.5 illustrates, over one-third of Americans agree that not knowing where to begin, or not having enough information, is a serious barrier to becoming involved in local politics. People with no education beyond high school, African Americans, and Hispanics were significantly more likely to share these sentiments.[60] People who work in congested urban areas a few miles from their neighborhood polling places may also be less likely to vote.[61]

Breaking Down Barriers to Voter Participation

One of the ironies about low rates of political participation in the United States is that for the last several decades, serious efforts have been made to remove barriers to voting and political participation—but participation remains low. Congress passed the Voting Rights Act in 1965, empowering the federal government to take control of local voter registration agencies away from racist state and local governments. Federal antipoverty "community action" programs of the 1960s also included requirements for the "maximum feasible participation" of community residents in implementing the programs.[62] The participatory elements of community action programs were soon abandoned as being ineffective, but the Voting Rights Act had the dramatic effect of bringing voter participation rates among African Americans to levels equal with those of whites.[63]

Subsequent efforts to boost participation have been less effective. In the 1980s, political parties spent millions on Get Out the Vote (GOTV) drives. In the 1990s, Congress also passed the Motor Voter Act to make registration easier. MTV's Rock the Vote encouraged young people to register and vote. These efforts may have increased registrations, but they seem to have had little effect on getting newly registered voters to actually vote. The hotly contested Bush versus Kerry 2004 presidential race, in contrast, was associated with an increase in voting.

State-Level Reform Efforts

In the past decade, several states have also attempted to make it easier for people to vote. On the West Coast and in a few states in other areas, for example, many people now take advantage of less restrictive rules about absentee voting. These rules allow them to vote permanently by mail without having to provide any reason. Oregon adopted all-mail elections in 1998, and 34 of 39 counties in Washington held all elections by mail as of 2007. Texas and other states implemented "early voting" and set up polling places days before elections to make voting easier. Some states have experimented with Internet voting, particularly for overseas military personnel.

Effect of Reforms on Voter Participation

Despite these efforts, participation in American elections remains low compared to most other established democracies. There is some evidence that reforms such as voting by mail might slightly increase turnout, and liberal absentee laws were found to increase turnout among students.[64] Studies suggest that the increased turnout associated with making voting more convenient might exacerbate social bias in the electorate by increasing turnout among white, wealthy, and better-educated voters at a greater rate than turnout among minorities and the less affluent.[65]

Interest Matters

It probably comes as little surprise that participation in state and local politics is largely the domain of those who are most interested in politics. It may be less obvious that having an interest in politics often has a distinct class bias and that some reforms designed to increase turnout might, ironically, magnify this bias. Efforts to increase participation by making it easier to vote can increase turnout do not make elections any more interesting. As noted above, lack of information is the primary reason that people mention when citing barriers to participation—particularly the less affluent, the less educated, and racial and ethnic minorities. Competitive elections, increased campaign activity, and active political parties may increase interest and information about elections. Most current reform efforts focus on making it more convenient for people to vote. The people who take advantage of increased convenience tend to be people who already have some engagement with politics—those with education and higher incomes.[66]

Increasing Citizen Engagement with Competitive Elections

This is not to say that reforms can't increase participation across the board. Increased electoral competition, and more information about candidates and issues, may significantly increase participation in state and local politics. Partisan local elections, multiparty politics, and even "semiproportional" nonpartisan elections have each been shown to be associated with higher levels of participation.[67]

Eliminating partisan gerrymandering in the design of electoral districts might also help boost interest in state politics by making more state legislative contests competitive. In presidential, gubernatorial, congressional, and state legislative races, voter participation is greater in places where the vote gap between the winning and losing candidates narrows. People tend to participate more when elections are close than when they are uncompetitive. Some suggest that voters are more likely to calculate that their participation will be decisive in close races—causing turnout to increase.[68] We suggest that close, competitive elections increase participation, as these races generate more campaign activity and information. Others contend that close elections force party leaders and political groups to mobilize more voters.[69] However, if every district was drawn so that either party had a chance to win, a relatively small shift in votes in each district from one party to another could result in dramatic changes in how many seats a party holds in the legislature.

Experiments with Alternative Local Election Systems

Different types of local election systems can also encourage more candidates to run, which increases campaign activity and, as a result, increases participation. Unique experiments with "semiproportional" local election systems in Texas, Alabama, and a few other states demonstrated that **cumulative voting** systems offer minority candidates more opportunities to win than standard **at-large elections**. There are different forms of at-large elections. Under standard at-large elections, if there are five city council seats, each seat is elected separately by all voters in the city. Cities using standard at-large elections often narrow the field of candidates with a primary contest that determines the two candidates who will contest each position in the general election. The candidate with a majority wins, and if there is a cohesive city-wide majority, it sweeps every seat. This means minority-supported candidates have little chance to win. Cumulative voting modifies the at-large system by allowing voters to cast multiple votes for one or more candidates running citywide. This allows some candidates with less than a majority to win and causes minority candidates to run active campaigns. Cumulative voting has been found to increase campaign activity by local groups and increase turnout in local elections by about 5 percent.[70]

E-Government

City and state governments have also tried to stimulate citizen interest and participation by making it easier for people to follow government through electronic media from the convenience of their own homes. Many states and cities maintain public access cable TV stations to broadcast hearings and meetings and maintain ever-improving websites designed to make it easier to contact public officials.

Voter Choice in State and Local Elections

When people vote in partisan state and local elections, their decision-making process is somewhat similar to the process they use when voting in national elections. Voters who identify with a political party have a very strong inclination to pick candidates from their party. Party labels—Democrat, Republican, Libertarian, and so on—act as a cue as to the policies the candidate might pursue. If people know nothing about a candidate except the candidate's party label—as is often the case—the inclination to vote based on party labels may even be stronger because voters have little more to guide their choices. Voters also tend to give incumbents the benefit of the doubt and may also reward or punish candidates for state offices based on the health of the economy.[71] They may also be more likely to punish a governor for the health of the state economy than the national economy.[72] Despite these factors, a voter's party affiliation is the main thing driving voter choice in partisan contests.

If candidates must run for office without party labels on the ballot, however, the voter's decision-making process is different. In nonpartisan elections, which are quite common at the local level, voters may be more likely to rely on endorsements of *slating groups*. These groups mimic the role of parties by recruiting and publicizing candidates sympathetic to the goals of the group. Pro-business slating groups have been found to have important influence in low-turnout local elections.[73] In smaller communities, the absence of parties and slating groups may cause voters to look for familiar-sounding names (incumbents) or look for friends and neighbors who might be running.[74] Even in primary election contests in California (where all candidates are from the same party), candidates for less visible "down-ballot" offices collect more votes near their hometowns, where they are better known.[75]

Effects of Voter Participation on Public Policy

Levels of participation in state and local politics are affected by state laws that regulate voter registration, polling place hours, absentee voting rules, representation, and many other factors. As we have shown above, these rules can make it easier or harder to vote and can make elections more or less interesting by limiting or increasing electoral competition, information, and representation. It is important to stress that the effects of these rules are not neutral; many of them filter out minorities and the less affluent or increase participation by the wealthy. In this section, we consider how rules might affect who participates and how this affects who gets represented and who gets what from government.

First, one must consider how different the participating electorate could be under different institutional conditions, all of which can be changed by altering state laws. The first condition we describe below is a recipe for higher participation, and the second is a recipe for lower participation.

High Voter Participation Election Rules

Under one condition, state law could allow cities to have partisan local elections, with state and local contests held in conjunction with an "even year" general election. By holding state and local contests in synch with presidential contests, more people would probably vote in state and local races. New voters could be allowed to register at the polls and vote on the day of the election. If a state used highly competitive districts to elect its legislature, more candidates would campaign, further increasing interest. Ex-felons and legal immigrant noncitizens could be allowed to vote in state and local races. Some elections could also be awarded by proportional representation, further encouraging different candidates to campaign. It is unlikely these sorts of reforms would be adopted without massive public pressure, as incumbent politicians of both major parties typically resist changing the rules that existed when they were elected.[76]

Low Voter Participation Election Rules

Under a second condition, state law could require local elections to be nonpartisan—a rule that limits the information available to the voters. State and local contests could be allowed only in "odd years" when no important federal contests are on the ballot. Voters would have to register at least 30 days in advance, and only citizens without felony convictions could vote. State legislative districts could be gerrymandered to ensure that parties didn't have to compete against each other in a single district, and local council races could be by single-member districts, leaving many incumbents without opposition.

Our point is not that more voter participation is always better but that participation is, in part, a function of laws that are under state control. State legislatures can make it harder or easier for people to participate, and state laws can make elections more or less competitive. State laws affect not only who can vote but also if the elections will generate interest sufficient to stimulate the participation of a wide range of people. Rules thus shape the composition of

the electorate; that is, they determine who ends up making demands on government.

The scope of the differences between participants and nonparticipants is likely to vary across states and is due to state laws as well as the demographic profile of the state's residents. In California, for example, surveys estimate that 75 percent of likely voters in the 2004 election were white, yet only 49 percent of the state's adult population was white.[77] Part of these differences stems from lower participation rates among young voters and Latinos and the fact that many Latino citizens have not registered to vote. States with larger proportions of recent immigrants have similar gaps between participants and nonparticipants. An estimated 20 million legal, tax-paying immigrant noncitizens—1.3 million in New York City alone—are prohibited from voting in the United States. In a few communities, however, they are allowed to vote in local elections.[78]

Public Policy and Public Opinion

Representation means that elected officials, to some degree, produce laws and policies that their constituents want. Evidence from the 50 states demonstrates that citizens' preferences for public policy generally correspond with the policies that states adopt. States where more people identified themselves as liberals had more liberal public policies, and states where more people identified themselves as conservatives had more conservative policies.[79] Something must be working to connect public preferences to policy. Elected representatives may reflect the public in response to those citizens who participate in politics, and those who participate may be fairly representative of the public opinion of the state's larger population. That is, representatives may respond to pressure from voters and constituents and do what the voters want. Or politicians may simply anticipate what people want, regardless of whether people participate or not. This distinction presents an important question for democracy: does active political participation make the actions of government better represent what citizens want?

Put differently, does more participation—or less social bias in participation—make state and local policy more representative of public opinion?

Does Participation Make State and Local Policy More Representative?

It is possible for elected officials to be perfectly representative of the public, even if most people didn't participate in politics. This would require that representatives have a keen sense of what everyone wanted and strong incentives to give people what they want. More realistically, representatives may do things that reflect what the general public wants when there is more pressure on them to do so.

As examples, states with just one dominant political party (such as the U.S. South through most of the 20th century) had policies less representative of what the public probably wanted than states where two parties compete for voter support. Competition between parties is expected to force legislators to try to attract support by passing popular policies—including things that are popular with the poor.[80] **Primary election systems** that allow more people to participate also produce representatives who are more likely to share their constituents' opinions on policy.[81] States with direct democracy (Chapter 4) also adopt some public policies, such as death penalty laws as well as laws requiring parental notification for abortions, that are closer to the state's public opinion than policies adopted in states that lack the pressure of direct democracy.[82]

Participation Bias

As we illustrated earlier in this chapter, people who participate in politics are different than nonparticipants. But does this mean that nonparticipants want different things from their governments than participants do or that by responding mainly to those who participate, governments are not very representative of the general public? Scholars are divided on this question. A study of a national sample of public opinion in 1972 and another from 1988 found that voters and nonvoters had largely similar policy preferences.[83] These results have been used to support the idea that American governments are largely representative of all citizens, even those who do not vote. If government responds only (or mostly) to those who vote or contribute, participation bias (the overrepresentation of the wealthy) might mean that state and local policies are not representative of the population. Recent studies of national opinion have found that nonvoters are more liberal on social welfare issues than voters.[84]

Participation is relatively high in national elections, however. Far fewer vote in state and local contests. Given this fact, and given the increased information demands associated with state and local elections, it is possible that there are greater gaps in policy preferences between participants and nonparticipants in local elections than in national contests. If participants are different than nonparticipants, what are the policy consequences of this participation bias?

Effects of Participation Bias

Several scholars provide evidence that the turnout decline in American elections has produced an overrepresentation of upper-middle-class and upper-class people and an underrepresentation of lower- and middle-class citizens.[85] One way to assess if participation bias matters is to look at how differences in state policies across the 50 states correspond with differences in who participates.

Effects on State Policies The magnitude of this "class bias"—the overrepresentation of the wealthy—is larger in some states and smaller in others. A study of the 1980s found the inequality in participation was highest in Kentucky, New Mexico, Texas, Georgia, and

Arkansas. These are states with high minority populations—most with legacies of erecting barriers to voter participation (see Figure 3.2). States with the most balanced representation between the rich and poor were New Jersey, Minnesota, Louisiana, Illinois, and Nebraska.[86] The study found that state-level class bias in participation during the 1980s was strongly related to lower state welfare (AFDC) spending. States where the poor were underrepresented among participating voters spent less per person on welfare than states where the poor were better represented. A study of state spending from 1978 to 1990 found similar results, with welfare spending higher where there was higher lower-status-voter turnout.[87]

If bias in participation affects which candidates end up winning elections, then it may also affect what governments do. Despite claims by third-party presidential candidates Ralph Nader (in 2000) and George Wallace (in 1968) that there is no difference between the Democratic and Republican parties, there are clear policy differences at the state level related to which party has more control over the state government. Republican control at the state level means less Medicaid spending; Democrats spend more.[88] Republicans may tax less[89] and use a different mix of taxes and expenditures than Democrats[90] (see Chapter 10).

Elections and Representation

Elections can be thought of as a tool for translating votes into "seats." When a group or party has seats in a state legislature or on a city or county council, they have a form of representation. Election rules have a great effect on which parties or groups have representation. The rules used to conduct elections, like many things examined in this book, are not always (if ever) neutral. They can affect who wins and who loses, and who gets more seats—in short, who ends up being represented.

Number of Representatives per District

The number of representatives elected inside a district's boundaries can also affect who is represented in a legislature. Most states now elect their state legislators from single-member districts (SMDs)—but it hasn't always been this way. In single-member districts, the winning candidate is typically elected with a majority vote, but if three or more candidates divide up the vote enough, whoever has the most support—a simple plurality—wins. Some states have more than one representative per district (just as each U.S. state has two U.S. senators per statewide district or as Australian states elect six federal senators per statewide district). The number of representatives for a specific geographic area is referred to as **district magnitude.**

In the middle of the 20th century, about half of all American state legislative seats were elected by **multimember districts** (or MMDs), where two or more candidates are elected to represent each district.[91] Many of these older MMDs overrepresented rural areas. A series of U.S. Supreme Court rulings required that states apportion legislative districts equally according to population.[92] Since the 1950s, many states have abandoned their MMD systems, often as part of their plans to equally apportion districts by population. Those that now use MMDs can no longer give extra representation to rural areas.

There are important differences in how states use MMDs to elect their legislatures. In Washington and Idaho, lower house districts elect two representatives, but candidates run for two separate positions. These elections are largely identical to those held in SMDs because voters can't vote for more than one candidate per position. In Arizona, however, voters cast two votes to select two representatives from a single list of candidates who will represent their district. The top two candidates win. In Vermont, if there are three representatives per district, voters cast three votes across a single list, and the top three win. Illinois used three-member districts with a semiproportional representation system known as **cumulative voting** for decades, ending the system in 1980. In MMD systems such as those used in Arizona, Vermont, or Illinois (until 1980), candidates can win a seat with less than a majority and even with less than a plurality. The winning candidates are the first-, second-, and third-place finishers—depending on how many seats are elected from the district. New Jersey, North Dakota, and South Dakota also use MMDs to elect their lower house.

Effects of Multimember Districts on Minority Representation MMD elections can produce different patterns of representation than SMD elections. Some suggest that MMDs hurt the chances of minority candidates, especially in areas where minority vote strength is geographically concentrated—places where a heavily minority SMD might be drawn.[93] Others note that evidence showing MMDs giving advantages to white candidates is dated. Because MMDs allow candidates to win with a relatively low vote share, MMDs might help minority candidates get elected. Recent studies suggest these systems may have produced more racial and ethnic minority representation in state legislatures from 1980 to 2003 than found under SMDs. African Americans appeared particularly advantaged but Latinos less so.[94]

There is clear evidence that traditional "at-large" MMDs disadvantage minority candidates in local elections.[95] In these systems, candidates file for one position out of several in a district, and only the first-place candidate for each position can win a seat. In *Gingles v. Thornberg* (1986), the U.S. Supreme Court ruled that local MMD at-large elections may be an unconstitutional "dilution" of minority vote influence if the minority group is geographically compact and politically cohesive and there is a history of "bloc voting" by whites that leads to the defeat of minority candidates. If these conditions exist, a judge may order the jurisdiction to switch to SMD elections or some alternative that will allow the minority group to elect a representative of their choice. However, in *Shaw v. Reno* (1993),

a 5–4 Court decision also ruled that it would not tolerate district maps that maximize minority representation by drawing *majority-minority districts* based exclusively on where minority voters live.

District Type and Ideological Polarization
MMDs and SMDs may also create different representation of ideologies in state legislatures. Winner-take-all rules mean that just one candidate is ever elected for any position or just one representative per district (i.e., an SMD). One influential theory predicts that when only one candidate can win and most voters are centrists, all candidates seeking the office have incentives to take positions near the "center" of the political spectrum.[96] In contrast, when two or more candidates are elected to represent the same district, candidates may have incentives to position themselves closer to one or the other end of the ideological spectrum. If they can get elected with fewer votes by placing second or even third, they don't need to appeal to most voters in order to win. This means that candidates further from the ideological center may have more chances to win under MMD elections. There is evidence of more ideological extremism in the Arizona House, which is elected by MMDs, than in the Arizona Senate, which is elected by SMDs.[97] Another study found the same thing in Illinois when its house was elected by MMDs.[98]

Campaign Spending

Politicians campaign to tell voters about themselves (and their opponents). These campaigns cost money, and politicians spend a significant amount of their time raising campaign funds.[99] Money clearly matters at all levels of American politics: candidates who spend more in state and local races typically do better in elections than those who spend less.[100] Campaign spending may be particularly important for candidates challenging incumbents. Because challengers are less well-known than incumbents, challenger spending may produce more "bang for the buck" than incumbent spending.

Challenger spending disseminates information about a lesser-known candidate, so any dollar spent can increase information about the candidate. Incumbents may be so well-known prior to an election that their spending may have less effect on their vote share.[101]

Spending on campaigns transmits information to citizens—through TV, radio, direct mail, and other modes of advertising. Because the information is meant to cast candidates in a good light (and their opponents in a bad light), the quality of this information may be dubious. A survey of voters in one state found that 81 percent believed campaign advertising was "misleading." A slightly higher proportion of politicians in the state agreed.[102] Nonetheless, voters use the information they get from political ads. People are more likely to be aware of state-level elections as spending increases,[103] and spending may cause skeptical voters to seek out additional information. Spending may also cause increased media coverage. Although turnout in elections is mostly structured by larger socioeconomic and institutional forces already discussed in this chapter, higher levels of spending in state-level races can also increase voter turnout.[104] One study of spending in state legislative races concluded that for every dollar spent per eligible voter, turnout increased by 1.2 percent.[105]

Finance Regulations State laws also determine who can contribute to state and local candidates; how much individuals, groups, or political parties may give; and how contributions must be disclosed to the public. Some states, such as Massachusetts and Oregon, have a broad range of restrictions on contributions. Others, like Idaho, Texas, and Virginia, have minimal regulations.[106] Defenders of these regulations note that they give the public more information about who the candidates might be beholden to and that these rules limit the influence of money in politics. Critics argue that limits on spending might make it harder for lesser-known challengers to unseat incumbents and that spending limits may make elections less competitive. There is some evidence that these rules do reduce spending in state races and that they might also limit electoral competition if limits are set too low.[107]

Clean Money A handful of states provide full public financing for state legislative campaigns in exchange for candidates promising to reject all private contributions. Maine and Arizona became the first states to do this in 2000. Vermont, Massachusetts, New Mexico, and North Carolina have also adopted **clean money** programs, and other states, such as Minnesota, provide partial public funding of candidate campaigns in exchange for candidates limiting the total amount that they raise from private sources.

One major idea behind these **clean money** laws is to make sure candidates are not beholden to their donors. Advocates of publicly financed campaigns also hope it will broaden the pool of people who seek office and cut down the amount of time politicians spend raising money.

Hundreds of members of the California Nurses Association rally in Sacramento to promote the California Clean Money and Fair Elections Act, which would establish public financing for candidates who reject private contributions.

Jesse Ventura, a professional wrestler turned city mayor, was elected governor of Minnesota under the Reform Party banner with the help of public campaign funds. One study found that state legislative candidates do spend less time raising money in states with public financing of campaigns.[108]

Representation of Parties

Every American state is now—more or less— a two-party system: 99.9 percent of state legislative seats are held by Democrats or Republicans. There have been brief periods of **multiparty politics** in a few states and long periods of one-party rule in many southern states. These are exceptions, however, and not the rule. Nearly every partisan office in the United States is elected on a **winner-take-all** basis. Second-, third-, and lower-placing candidates win nothing. If a party rarely does better than second place in most contests, it will win few offices and likely disappear. The near total, oligopolistic control that Democrats and Republicans have over elected offices overstates the level of support these parties have among the public.[109] Winner-take-all election rules, combined with the ballot access laws discussed above, essentially predetermine that only two parties will ever be represented.

Despite this, third-party and independent candidates have had more success in state and local elections than in congressional and federal races over the last several decades. Since 1990, a few were elected as governor (Angus King in Maine, Jesse Ventura in Minnesota, and Lowell Weicker in Connecticut).[110] As of 2007, minor parties and independent candidates held just 19 seats in state legislatures (out of 7,382 positions in 50 states).[111] Almost half of these minor-party and independent candidates served in Vermont (which uses MMD elections and clean money for campaign finance). Minor-party and independent candidates have also won seats in Arizona and Massachusetts under clean money rules. Some of the remaining handful of candidates who are not affiliated with a major party are southern Democrats who defected from their party as their state's population grew more conservative.

Representation of Women

States differ substantially in terms of the number of women who are elected to office. As of 2007, 23.5 percent of state legislators were women— far more than in the U.S. Congress and double the levels of women in state legislatures back in 1981. Although this is still modest representation given that most of the population is female, the growth of representation of women in the past 25 years has important implications. A growing number of women in state-level posts means that the pool of women with elected experience who seek higher-level positions has grown.

In seven states (Maryland, Delaware, Arizona, Nevada, Vermont, and Washington), one-third of all state legislators were women as of 2005. States with the lowest rates of women representation were South Carolina (9 percent), Alabama (10 percent), and Kentucky (12 percent). Why do some states have three times more representation of women than others? Some have noted that three of the five states with the most women in their legislatures (Arizona, Vermont, and Washington) use MMD elections.[112] One problem with this logic, however, is that Washington does not use "pure" MMD elections; candidates actually run for individual positions, where the winner takes all. Other explanations for the differences in levels of women's representation emphasize the role of political parties and regional (or cultural) effects. Some parties have made greater efforts to recruit candidates to seek office.[113] There are clear regional differences. Women are less represented in the South and more represented in the West and New England.

Representation of Racial and Ethnic Minorities

African Americans, Latinos, Asians, and Native Americans are underrepresented in state legislatures relative to their share of U.S. population,

| Table 3.6 | | | | | |

Minority Representation in U.S. State Legislatures

	White (%)	African American (%)	Latino (%)	Asian or Pacific Islander (%)	Native American (%)
U.S. population	69	12	13	4	1
All state legislators	89	8	2	1	0.5

Source: Samantha Sanchez, "Money and Diversity in State Legislatures, 2003" (Institute on Money in State Politics, 2005).

as illustrated in Table 3.6. The pattern for minority representation at the local level is similar. Although 11 percent of all state legislative seats are held by minorities, some groups are better represented than others. Minority populations are not evenly distributed across the nation or within states such as Hawaii, California, and New Mexico, where various minority groups combine to form a majority of the state's population. This means that there are great differences across the United States in minority representation at the state and local levels.

Hawaii (67 percent "minority" legislators), California (27 percent), Texas (25 percent), Mississippi (25 percent), Alabama (25 percent), New Mexico (23 percent), and Louisiana (22 percent) have the highest levels of minority representation in their states' legislatures. States with few minorities, not surprisingly, elect few minorities. The Idaho legislature, for example, was 100 percent white in 2005. Yet, even relatively high levels of minority representation in places like California and New Mexico are deceptive. These states, along with Arizona, lead the nation in the gap between the proportion of state residents who are minority and the proportion of their representatives who are. In contrast, minorities in Mississippi and Alabama, although still underrepresented, are much more represented relative to their share of the population than minorities in California, Texas, and Arizona.[114]

Why are large populations of minorities better represented in some places than others? The answers are race and single-member districting. In state and local elections,

African Americans benefit from the use of **majority-minority districts** drawn with boundaries that ensure the district's population is heavily African American. This guarantees that the district will elect an African American, and it has led to near proportional representation of African Americans in many local elections. It also explains relatively high levels of minority representation in Deep South states, where African Americans are the predominant minority group.[115] In western and southwestern states, however, the largest minority group is Latino. Latinos turn out at lower rates than African Americans and are not as segregated as African Americans in the South.[116] Latinos, moreover, are a less ethnically cohesive group than African Americans. All of these factors combine to make it more difficult to design districts at the state or local level that are certain to produce Latino representation.[117] At the local level, Latinos win more seats via SMDs than they do under "at-large" arrangements,[118] but they may not win as many seats as African Americans.

Majority-minority districts present a paradox. They clearly increase the numbers of minorities holding state and local offices, and they offer people **descriptive representation;** that is, the ability to see people like themselves serving as their representative. When minority candidates win seats, moreover, they are able to affect the substance of public policy in ways that benefit their constituents and affect whether minorities are hired to implement policies approved by cities and school boards.[119] Descriptive representation of minorities at the local and congressional level may also increase minority trust and participation and reduce political alienation among minority citizens.[120]

Some suggest that there may be a trade-off between descriptive representation and the substantive representation of minority interests. By packing large proportions of a minority group into one safe district, the group may have less overall influence in a legislature than they may have had if they were a swing group electing representatives across a larger number of districts.[121] Almost 95 percent of minority state legislators were Democrats in 2005, so we might assume that people in these districts find their substantive policy interests advanced by Democrats more than Republicans. A majority-minority district can help elect a minority Democrat representative, but this may also weaken other Democrats' chances of winning in surrounding districts. The minority district gains descriptive Democratic representation locally, but Democrats may elect fewer seats statewide, making it more difficult to advance the substantive policy goals of minority voters in the majority-minority district. Another potential consequence of majority-minority districts is a loss of electoral competitiveness. Minority legislators are much more likely to run unopposed than white legislators.[122]

Summary

A healthy democracy depends, at least in part, on having citizens who are engaged with each other and with politics. Participation in local voluntary groups is one way that people learn the skills required to be citizens. As important as local democracy is, this chapter illustrates that there are substantial barriers to participation at the state and local levels. Elections are often designed to be uncompetitive, a situation that may only serve incumbents well. Nonpartisan races, uncompetitive elections, and other barriers may depress interest in state and local politics.

But this need not be the case. One theme of this book is that institutions matter and institutions can change. Race-based barriers to voting have been reduced substantially over the last 100 years. This is evidence that the rules can change and that political participation can become more inclusive.

Key Terms

At-large elections	Literacy tests	Primary election
Blanket primary	Lobbying	Progressive era
Clean money and public financing of campaigns	Majority-minority district	Racial gerrymandering
	Multimember district	Social capital
Closed primary	Multiparty politics	Voting-age population
Cumulative voting	Nonpartisan primary	Voting-eligible population
Descriptive representation	Open primary	Voting Right Act
District magnitude	Participation bias	Winners-take-all
Efficacy	Partisan primary	
Grandfather clause	Poll tax	

Suggested Readings

Berkman, Michael, and Eric Plutzer. 2006. *Ten thousand democracies: Politics and public opinion in America's school districts*. Washington, DC: Georgetown University Press.

Browning, Robert, D. Rodgers, and D. Tabb. 1984. *Protest is not enough: The struggle of blacks and Hispanics for equality in urban politics*. Berkeley: University of California Press.

Erikson, Robert, Gerald Wright, and John McIver. 1994. *Statehouse democracy: Public opinion and the American states*. New York: Cambridge University Press.

Gimple, James, J. Celeste Lay, and Jason Schuknecht. 2003. *Cultivating democracy: Civic environments and political socialization in America*. Washington, DC: Brookings Institution Press.

Oliver, J. Eric. 2001. *Democracy in suburbia*. Princeton, NJ: Princeton University Press.

Putnam, Robert. 2000. *Bowling alone: The collapse and revival of American community*. New York: Simon and Schuster.

Rosenthal, Alan. 1998. *The decline of representative democracy: Process, participation, and power in state legislatures*. Washington, DC: CQ Press.

Websites

The Immigrant Voting Project (http://www.immigrantvoting.org): The Immigrant Voting Project documents the practice of enfranchising noncitizens in local (municipal and school board) elections.

Center for Voting and Democracy (http://www.fairvote.org): The center promotes election systems that increase voter turnout, fair representation, inclusive policy, and meaningful choices. It conducts research, analysis, education, and organizing to ensure all Americans can exercise their right to vote and elect representatives who reflect our racial and political diversity.

Public Campaign (http://www.publicampaign.org): Public Campaign is a nonpartisan organization dedicated to reforming how elections are financed. It provides details on state and local efforts to promote publicly financed campaigns.

National Association of Secretaries of State (http://www.nass.org): The association offers information about election administration, voter participation, and electronic or e-government services administered by secretaries of state. It also has links to state-specific sites for voter registration and the location of local polling places.

Bowlingalone.com (http:www.bowlingalone.com): The site promotes a book on social capital by Robert Putnam. The site provides access to the public opinion data used in this chapter and information about how the United States can "civicly reinvent itself again."

4

State and Local Direct Democracy

Governing by the Ballot

OUTLINE

Introduction

Institutions of Direct Democracy

More Responsible and More Representative Government?

Populist Origins of Direct Democracy

Differences across Initiative States

The Financing of Direct Democracy Campaigns

Dumber than Chimps? Voting on Ballot Questions

Direct Democracy and Electoral Politics

The Effects of Direct Democracy on Public Policy

Assessments of Direct Democracy

Summary

Arnold Schwarzenegger might be remembered as the direct democracy governor. Schwarzenegger's first experience with statewide politics was as the public face and chief funding source behind a popular 2002 California ballot initiative that increased spending on after-school programs. His initiative, Proposition 49, was seen as an effort by the Hollywood actor to prepare for a future bid as a Republican gubernatorial candidate. Direct democracy soon paved the way to the governor's office for Schwarzenegger. Fiscal crisis and voter dissatisfaction in 2003 led to a recall of the incumbent governor, Gray Davis, and Schwarzenegger won a free-for-all special election that was part of the recall vote. As governor, he moved from campaigning for ballot initiatives to trying to govern with them. After being elected, Schwarzenegger promoted several ballot measures to advance policies that he could not push through the state legislature. At the height of his popularity, he weighed in on 10 measures on the November 2004 ballot, including some that determined the fate of his plans to deal with the budget crisis he inherited. The California Republican Party even mailed a 12-page, multicolored brochure entitled "Governor Arnold Schwarzenegger's Ballot Proposition Voter Guide" to millions of voters. Voters sided with the governor on nine of the 10 measures on which he voiced an official position.

Schwarzenegger later discovered that it can be difficult to govern by initiative. In 2005, he sponsored additional initiatives, asking the people to support his fiscal agenda after the Democratic-controlled legislature would not pass some of his key proposals. Schwarzenegger established ballot-measure committees to funnel interest-group contributions to his direct democracy battle, and called a special election in November 2005 for the sole purpose of letting voters have the final say on his policies. That time, voters rejected all four of the governor's proposals, including a measure to weaken the legislature's control over budgeting.[1] Schwarzenegger's style of "going to the people" illustrates how places with direct democracy can have different styles of politics than places that do not. As we will see in this chapter, direct democracy can have important effects on how citizens, groups, and elected officials are able to affect what government does.

Copyright California Republic Party

Governor Arnold Schwarzenegger's voter's guide. These were mailed to thousands of homes in 2005 with instructions on how to support his positions on ballot measures. All of the Governor's proposals were defeated.

Introduction

The link between citizens and their government can be quite different at the state and local levels than at the national level. State legislators and local governments regularly refer matters to voters for their approval; in fact, most states require that amendments to state constitutions ultimately be approved by voters. In nearly half the states, people can draft their own legislation and petition to have a public vote to approve or reject it. Additionally, many local governments, including those in states that do not allow the usage of direct democracy at the state level, permit the processes. Some of our biggest cities—including Baltimore, Columbus, Dallas, Denver, Detroit, Houston, Jacksonville, Los Angeles, Miami, Milwaukee, New York, Phoenix, Portland, San Antonio, San Diego, San Francisco, Seattle, and Washington, D.C.—permit citizens to propose charter amendments to be placed on the ballot for fellow citizens to either adopt or reject. In fact, a majority of Americans reside in cities and towns where they can vote directly on matters of public policy.[2] Processes of direct democracy can leave elected representatives with limited influence over public policy. It is difficult to understand state and local politics in much of the nation without considering the effects of direct democracy.

In many American states and communities, citizens have more ability to affect what their governments do than other people in almost any other political system in the world. Apart from areas in Switzerland, no other places with such freewheeling democratic arrangements exist. In its most extreme form, direct democracy gives people outside the corridors of power the potential to cut taxes, propose tax hikes or new spending programs, veto most laws passed by elected representatives, and even remove elected officials from office. This contrasts dramatically with how American citizens participate in national politics. Although the United States is one of the few advanced democracies to have never put a question of

national policy or constitutional design up for a public vote, these questions are commonly decided by voters at the state and local levels. Americans regularly decide on matters such as local school funding, land-use rules, social policy, or how much their state should borrow for specific long-term projects. The scope of direct democracy varies widely across the states and thus provides one of the key features distinguishing politics in some states and cities from those in other places.

In this chapter, we consider American direct democracy as a grand democratic experiment that allows us to consider, in effect, whether more democracy is "better." That is, does democratic politics work "better" when citizens are given more direct control over their government? As we shall see, no consensus exists among political observers, pundits, journalists, scholars, or politicians about these questions. We also illustrate that each state has a unique set of rules defining how direct democracy works, and these rules affect how much the process is used. Politics and policies can be fundamentally different in states with freewheeling forms of direct democracy.

Institutions of Direct Democracy

Three main features of direct democracy are the referendum, the initiative, and the recall. Almost every state uses some form of referendum. As Figure 4.1 reveals, 24 states have some form of a statewide initiative, 24 allow a statewide popular referendum (most of which also provide the initiative), and 18 states have provisions for the recall of state officials.

Referendum

A referendum is a public vote on a statute or a constitutional amendment that has already been considered by a state legislature or local government. The most widely used instrument of direct democracy in the American states

Figure 4.1

States with Statewide Initiative, Popular Referendum, and Recall

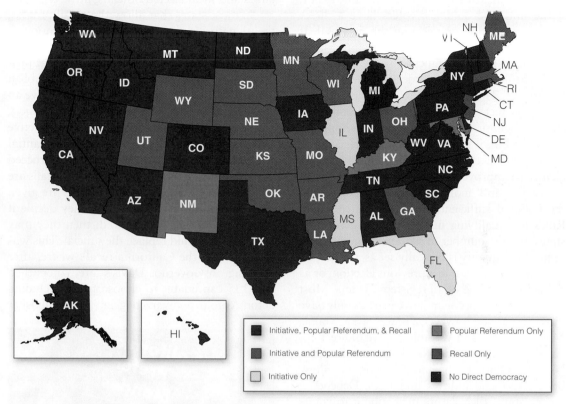

(and localities) is the **legislative referendum.** In the case of the legislative referendum, elected officials have control over the question that voters will consider, although legislators are often bound to place certain items on state ballots. Use of legislative referendums at the national level is quite widespread, with nearly every advanced democratic nation other than the United States using the process.[3] Every American state has some provision for a legislative referendum—particularly for state constitutional matters. Most state constitutions require that voters approve constitutional amendments via referendum, and some require that voters approve when a state issues debt. Legislators may also choose to defer to the wisdom of voters and allow them to have the final say over controversial issues, such as tax increases.

The **popular referendum,** by way of contrast, allows a person or group to file a petition to have a public vote on a bill that the legislature has already approved. Every state with the initiative process (except Florida, Illinois, and Mississippi) also allows citizens to propose popular referendums.[4] The popular referendum is effectively a public veto of a law. Proponents may qualify popular referendums for the ballot by collecting a certain percentage of signatures in a set amount of time following the passage of the legislation in question.

Initiative

The two types of initiative process in the United States are the direct initiative and indirect initiative. The **direct initiative** allows a person or group to file a proposed bill with a state office and then collect signatures from voters to qualify the measure for a spot on the state ballot. If the initiative qualifies, voters have a direct say on approving or rejecting the proposal. If voters approve the measure, it becomes law.[5] An **indirect initiative** functions as a petition to have the legislature consider a bill proposed by citizens. This is similar to the Swiss system. If the indirect initiative qualifies by collecting enough signatures, the legislature can adopt or reject the bill. If it is rejected by the legislature, it must be placed on the ballot to give voters a chance to approve or reject the proposal.

Direct and indirect initiatives appear on the ballot if sufficient signatures are collected. Rules for qualifying initiatives vary across the states, but the number of signatures on petitions required to qualify is typically set as a fixed percentage of votes cast in a previous election, or as a fixed percentage of all registered voters. Most states with any sort of initiative process only have direct initiatives; however, a few (Alaska, Maine, Massachusetts, and Wyoming) have indirect initiatives only. Five additional states (Michigan, Nevada, Ohio, Utah, and Washington) allow both direct and indirect initiatives. Depending on the state, a legislature may submit to voters an indirect initiative that it rejected, along with its own alternative proposal; alternatively, the legislature may simply take no action.

Recall

The **recall** allows a person or group to file a petition for a public vote to remove an elected official from office prior to when the official's term expires. The first place in the United States to adopt the recall was Los Angeles in 1903. Many cities and 18 states now have rules allowing for the recall of elected officials, although the process is rarely used at the state level. Only two governors have been recalled: Lynn Fraiser of North Dakota in 1921 and Gray Davis of California in 2003. A gubernatorial recall in Arizona came close to being successful, but before the process was completed, Governor Fife Symington was forced to resign in 1997 after being convicted

of bank fraud by a federal jury. There have been numerous successful recall efforts of state legislators and local elected officials, however.[6]

In most states that allow the recall process, the signature requirement for qualification is much greater than that required for initiative and referendum.[7] Some states require that proponents of either a state or local recall establish compelling grounds to have a vote to remove an elected official (such as criminal misconduct), whereas other states' rules are less restrictive or have no formal requirement that substantial misconduct be established in order to proceed with a recall. States also differ in how recalls are conducted. In some situations, voters are given two choices on one ballot: first, they decide if the official should be removed; then they may decide who should replace the official. This was the case with the California recall, where, after deciding on Governor Davis's fate, voters then had 135 candidates to choose from (including actor Arnold Schwarzenegger, porn publisher

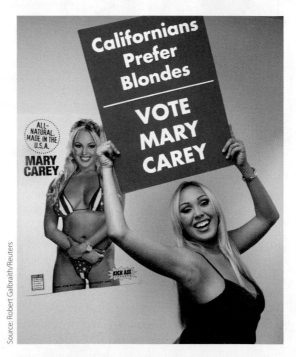

Source: Robert Galbraith/Reuters

In 2003, 135 people were listed on the special election ballot as candidates to replace Governor Gray Davis. This list included several actors, comedians, a prominent pornographer, and former adult film star Mary Carey.

Larry Flint, ex–child actor Gary Coleman, and at least two adult "entertainers," Angelyne and Mary Carey; see Figure 4.2). In other cases, voters are only asked the question about recall. In these cases, the office is left vacant until the next election, a replacement is appointed, or a special election is conducted later to fill the vacancy.

More Responsible *and* More Representative Government?

Part of the difficulty in assessing the merits and pitfalls of direct democracy lies in how we define what a "better" democratic system might look like. One way to consider this task is to ask if direct democracy in the states makes politics more responsible and more representative.[8] Early advocates of direct democracy claimed that it could do both.

The Promise of Direct Democracy

Direct democracy has its roots in the Populist and Progressive movements of the late 19th century and early 20th century, respectively. In the early 1900s, campaign contributions were largely unregulated, and bribery and graft were not uncommon in state legislatures. State and local elected officials were paid poorly, and, with few laws regulating political corruption, they were subject to influence by firms seeking favorable treatment from government. As one observer of the 1880s Oregon legislature noted, it consisted of "briefless lawyers, farmless farmers, business failures, bar-room loafers, Fourth-of-July orators [and] political thugs."[9] Many elected officials had little enthusiasm for social, economic, and political reforms that may have had widespread support among the general public.

To Populist and Progressive reformers of that era, representative government alone could not be trusted to serve the public interest. Their goal was to give the public greater influence over the behavior of elected officials. Reform-

ers were suspicious of the power that wealthy economic interests had over elected representatives. In this context, then, reformers argued that by giving people the ability to write their own laws and veto unpopular laws passed by legislators, public policy would be more *representative* of public opinion. Likewise, it was assumed, then, that elected officials would often work to protect powerful economic interests by doing such things as granting monopolies, giving away public resources, blocking health and safety regulations, and blocking anticorruption laws. If the public could use direct democracy as an end run around these elected officials, reformers assumed that public policy would become more *responsible*.

Defending Direct Democracy

Prior to being elected president in 1912, Woodrow Wilson offered a pragmatic defense of the instrumental use of the initiative. Wilson argued that if a state legislature was unable or unwilling to pass popular legislation, citizens could directly propose and adopt laws themselves to correct any legislative "sins of omission." Even indirectly, the mere threat of an initiative—the "gun behind the door," as Wilson called it—could pressure recalcitrant legislators to take action. For Wilson, direct legislation was not a radical solution; he foresaw the device being used sparingly. The initiative would serve as a stopgap mechanism—a benign tool that would "restore," not "destroy," representative government. The expedience of direct legislation, according to Wilson, could bring "our representatives back to the consciousness that what they are bound in duty and in mere policy to do is represent the sovereign people whom they profess to serve." As a prodding instrument, then, the initiative had the potential of directly or indirectly bringing forth substantive policy changes in the American states.[10]

This was, in part, the promise of direct democracy 100 years ago. In considering how direct democracy works in American states and communities today, it is important to consider the adoption of direct democracy in its historic

Figure 4.2

California Recall Ballot

A

003

OFFICIAL BALLOT

Statewide Special Election

Sonoma County

October 7, 2003

This ballot stub shall be removed and retained by the voter.

MARK YOUR CHOICE(S)
IN THIS MANNER ONLY: ▬
VOTING AREA ▶

I HAVE VOTED—HAVE YOU?

MARK YOUR CHOICE(S)
IN THIS MANNER ONLY: ▬
VOTING AREA ▶

Sample Ballot

STATE		
Shall GRAY DAVIS be recalled (removed) from the office of Governor?	Yes	
	No	
Candidates to succeed GRAY DAVIS as Governor if he is recalled. Vote for One		
KURT E. "TACHIKAZE" RIGHTMYER, Independent Middleweight Sumo Wrestler		
DANIEL W. RICHARDS, Republican Businessman		
KEVIN RICHTER, Republican Information Technology Manager		
REVA RENEE RENZ, Republican Small Business Owner		
SHARON RUSHFORD, Independent Businesswoman		
GEORGY RUSSELL, Democratic Software Engineer		
MICHAEL J. WOZNIAK, Democratic Retired Police Officer		
DANIEL WATTS, Green College Student		
NATHAN WHITECLOUD WALTON, Independent Student		
MAURICE WALKER, Green Real Estate Appraiser		
CHUCK WALKER, Republican Business Intelligence Analyst		
LINGEL H. WINTERS, Democratic Consumer Business Attorney		
C.T. WEBER, Peace and Freedom Labor Official/Analyst		
JIM WEIR, Democratic Community College Teacher		
BRYAN QUINN, Republican Businessman		
MICHAEL JACKSON, Republican Satellite Project Manager		
JOHN "JACK" MORTENSEN, Democratic Contractor/Businessman		
DARRYL L. MOBLEY, Independent Businessman/Entrepreneur		
JEFFREY L. MOCK, Republican Business Owner		
BRUCE MARGOLIN, Democratic Marijuana Legalization Attorney		
GINO MARTORANA, Republican Restaurant Owner		
PAUL MARIANO, Democratic Attorney		

49-A007R   **CONTINUED OTHER SIDE**   A

(CANDIDATES CONTINUED)	
ROBERT C. MANNHEIM, Democratic Retired Businessperson	
FRANK A. MACALUSO, JR., Democratic Physician/Medical Doctor	
PAUL "CHIP" MAILANDER, Democratic Golf Professional	
DENNIS DUGGAN MCMAHON, Republican Banker	
MIKE MCNEILLY, Republican Artist	
MIKE P. MCCARTHY, Independent Used Car Dealer	
BOB MCCLAIN, Independent Civil Engineer	
TOM MCCLINTOCK, Republican State Senator	
JONATHAN MILLER, Democratic Small Business Owner	
CARL A. MEHR, Republican Businessman	
SCOTT A. MEDNICK, Democratic Business Executive	
DORENE MUSILLI, Republican Parent/Educator/Businesswoman	
VAN VO, Republican Radio Producer/Businessman	
PAUL W. VANN, Republican Financial Planner	
JAMES M. VANDEVENTER, JR., Republican Salesman/Businessman	
BILL VAUGHN, Democratic Structural Engineer	
MARC VALDEZ, Democratic Air Pollution Scientist	
MOHAMMAD ARIF, Independent Businessman	
ANGELYNE, Independent Entertainer	
DOUGLAS ANDERSON, Republican Mortgage Broker	
IRIS ADAM, Natural Law Business Analyst	
BROOKE ADAMS, Independent Business Executive	
ALEX-ST. JAMES, Republican Public Policy Strategist	
JIM HOFFMANN, Republican Teacher	
KEN HAMIDI, Libertarian State Tax Officer	

49-A008R   **CONTINUED NEXT CARD**   A

INSTITUTIONS MATTER

"THE GUN BEHIND THE DOOR"

In 2006, state legislatures across the country were evidently feeling the "heat" being packed by various groups, as the threat of the citizen initiative impelled them into action. According to the Ballot Initiative Strategy Center (http://www.ballot.org; see above under "Websites"), a nonprofit group that tracks ballot initiatives, several state legislatures took up bills they had previously ignored (or opposed) because potential ballot issues resonated strongly with citizens.

In the spring of 2006, a citizens' group in Oregon collected signatures for an initiative to rein in the runaway interest rates that payday loan companies foist on borrowers. The measure was polling like gangbusters. It was so popular that the Oregon legislature decided to convene a special session in April to pass legislation nearly identical to the initiative. Not only that, but the sponsor of the bill was also the same woman who the previous year had killed legislation that would have accomplished the same ends—and all because of the threat of an initiative. In Michigan, the Republican-controlled legislature realized in March 2006 there was a good chance a popular minimum wage initiative would be on the November ballot. The GOP leadership, fearful of having their candidates running in an election with such a popular issue, wisely decided to push through the legislature a languishing Democratic bill to raise the state's minimum wage. Democratic governor Jennifer Granholm signed the bill into law. The initiative campaign, which was organized by organized labor, promptly shuttered its doors.

Using the initiative process as a lever to pry stubborn legislation out of the recesses of a legislature is nothing new. Woodrow Wilson argued in 1911 that it could be used by citizens to apply tacit pressure on capricious state legislatures, forcing them to abide by the will of the people. By way of analogy, Wilson understood the practice of citizen lawmaking as the "gun behind the door—for use only in case of emergency, but [a] mighty good persuader, nevertheless."[1]

NOTE

1. Ballot Initiative Strategy Center, "Oregon: Another Initiative 'Pays' Off," April 21, 2006. Available: http://ballotblog.typepad.com/ballotblog/2006/04/oregon_another_.html.

context. We assess how it might make politics more representative of public opinion and consider whether it makes policy more responsible. The latter quality, of course, is much more difficult to assess.

Populist Origins of Direct Democracy

Although states in New England have practice with town meeting forms of local government that provide for direct citizen voting on policy questions, direct democracy did not exist at the state level prior to the late 1890s. Eighteen of the 24 states that currently have the initiative process adopted it between 1898 and 1914. Many of the early initiatives reflected the agenda of groups that agitated for adoption of direct democracy. Issues such as suffrage, Prohibition, labor laws, and electoral reforms were common in the first decade that direct democracy was in use.

The initiative process at the state level was first adopted in South Dakota in 1898, but it was first used statewide in Oregon in 1904. Several political movements that included organized labor, disaffected farmers, proponents of the so-called single tax, Prohibitionists, and women's suffrage advocates pressed their states to adopt the initiative, recall, and referendum. These direct democracy tools were part of a larger set of reforms advocated by the **Populist Party** in the 1890s, including direct election of U.S. senators, direct election of the president, direct voter control candidate nominations, direct primary elections, and the income tax.

Although short-lived on the political scene, the Populists were one of the most influential third parties in American history. Their attack on the disproportionate influence of powerful economic interests (railroads, banks, mining firms, and monopolies) had great appeal to laborers, western farmers, and miners. Democrat William Jennings Bryan, who ran for president on the Populist ticket in some states in 1896, was soundly defeated, but he ran very strong in western states, sweeping Populist and "Fusion" Democrats into Congress and state legislatures. Bryan spent part of his career in the 1890s promoting direct democracy in states where Populists had political success.[11] States where Bryan had his greatest electoral appeal, as well as states where Socialist presidential candidate Eugene Debs ran strongest early in the 20th century, were most likely to amend their state constitutions to allow some forms of direct democracy by 1914.[12] Recall that Figure 4.1 illustrates how direct democracy is more common in the West, in part because Populists had greater political influence there and because some of these states were just forming their first constitutions when Populists and Progressives were most influential.

Adopting Direct Democracy during the Progressive Era

Whereas the Populists set the stage for U.S. direct democracy in the 1890s, most states actually adopted institutions of direct democracy during the Progressive era of the next two decades. Populists and Progressives differed in their critiques of American representative government. As such, the Populists' saw that common people were trustworthy and competent and that elected legislators were neither. The Populists' goal was to take power away from incumbent politicians, vested interests, and party machines and give it to voters. Progressives, on the other hand, were more sympathetic to the legislative process but wanted

to "liberate representative government from corrupt forces so that it might become an effective instrument for social reform."[13] The Progressive model aimed to use direct democracy to improve representative government rather than replace it. Early advocates of direct democracy envisioned a process that allowed regular citizens to resolve a particular grievance. But modern direct democracy may have evolved into a process where professional politicians and wealthy interests use initiatives and referendums to advance their own agendas.[14]

The Ebb and Flow of Ballot Initiatives

From the 1930s to the 1960s, as legislatures became more professional and anticorruption laws took hold, direct democracy was used less. It made a comeback, however, as groups again began to use the initiative process to promote public votes on policy questions. There was a steady increase in the number of ballot measures qualified in all states since the 1960s. After a decline in the 1940s and 1950s, use of initiatives reached a new peak in the 1990s, when there were nearly 400 initiatives on statewide ballots—far more than any other decade.[15] Annual use of initiatives remained relatively high by historic standards after 2000. It is important to remember that roughly 60 percent of all initiatives that qualify for state ballots are rejected by voters;[16] however, measures that pass can have a powerful effect on the design of state political institutions and on the political agenda.

Studies find a large degree of stability in terms of the subjects of ballot measures on which voters have been asked to decide over most of the last 100 years. The most common initiatives since 1980 have been governmental reform measures, such as term limits and campaign finance regulation (23 percent) and taxation questions (22 percent). Social and moral issues (17 percent) and environmental measures (11 percent) are the next most common questions.[17] Some attribute the revival of direct democracy in recent decades to a new generation of citizens who demand more say in politics but who are less interested in traditional forms of participation via representation by political parties.[18] Others note that the rise of initiative use in the United States corresponded with the proliferation of new interest groups[19] and with the maturation of a sophisticated industry of campaign professionals promoting the use of initiatives.[20]

Direct Democracy and National Politics

Battles over several state initiatives from the later decades of the 20th century have set the stage for major policy debates at the national level. Contemporary initiative efforts in the states sometimes become part of larger campaigns that shape the issues discussed by politicians in Washington and those trying to win election to federal office. Antitax initiatives from the late 1970s—most notably, California's **Proposition 13** in 1978—foreshadowed the enthusiasm for the Reagan-era federal tax cuts of the early 1980s.[21] Initiatives in California and Washington targeting affirmative action set the tone for national debate on the policy in the late 1990s. That same decade, voters in over a dozen states decided the fate of proposals to limit state legislative terms. Popular enthusiasm for term limits may have led some aspiring candidates for Congress to take positions in favor of short tenure in office (although several years later, many of those same members had less enthusiasm for limiting how long they should serve).

State initiatives and referendums proposing to ban gay marriage in 2004 had effects that spilled into the presidential election. Voters were more likely to evaluate George W. Bush and John Kerry in terms of the gay marriage issue if they lived in one of the 13 states where there was a gay marriage ban measure on the state's ballot.[22] Initiative activists with an eye on the national stage have gotten their proposals on the ballot in multiple states to promote their causes and set the national agenda.[23] As a result, measures backed by national groups advocating such things as increasing the minimum wage, eminent domain, school choice, nuclear freeze, term limits, the repeal of affirmative action, and tax cuts have each gotten their measures on the ballot in several different states.

Nonetheless, most of the initiatives and referendums to reach a state's ballot are homegrown proposals. This does not mean that most initiatives are the product of the "average" citizen who rallies the grassroots to challenge an established order. The initiative process is also used by a wide array of interest groups, by business groups, and by political parties. Ballot initiatives targeting the use of public services by illegal immigrants have been used by the Republican Party in attempts to mobilize supporters or drive a wedge through the rival party's base.[24] Democrats have made similar attempts to mobilize likely Democratic voters with minimum wage initiatives.[25] Incumbent politicians, candidates for office, and wealthy individuals also promote their pet causes with initiatives.[26] In states where expensive petition campaigns are required to qualify for the ballot, many of the same powerful interest groups that dominate legislative politics—trial lawyers, teachers' unions, nurses, insurance companies, and casinos and Indian tribes—also fund campaigns promoting and opposing initiatives.[27]

The Explosion Continues

In the 2006 general election, there were 74 initiatives and five popular referendums on the statewide ballots of 37 states.[28] On the ballots of all 50 states, there also were hundreds more local referendums and initiatives. Substantively, ballot propositions cover a remarkable range of issues; some of the issues involved are complex, whereas others are relatively straightforward. Some measures make national headlines; others remain obscure in terms of public or media attention. Voters have cast ballots dealing with issues as diverse as banning gay marriage, punishing negligent doctors, prohibiting the confinement of pregnant pigs, limit-

REFORM CAN HAPPEN

INITIATING MEDICAL MARIJUANA LAWS

Most Americans think that marijuana should be made legal for medical purposes. A 2005 Gallup Poll found 78 percent of Americans favored legalizing marijuana for medical use. Despite the popularity of medical marijuana, the federal government and nearly all the state legislatures have repeatedly rejected the policy.[1] Not to be stymied by their elected officials, citizens in 11 states (as well as those in the District of Columbia) have used ballot initiatives to pass laws allowing physicians to prescribe marijuana to patients suffering chronic pain.

Those sympathetic to direct democracy often suggest that elected officials are sometimes more responsive to lobbyists than public opinion. The initiative, they say, allows citizens to vote on laws that their state legislatures refuse to enact. Although ballot campaigns may be expensive, they claim that money cannot buy a ballot initiative victory at the polls. How can money buy a public policy that the citizens of a state don't want? On the other hand, critics of direct democracy suggest the legislative process is a better way to make policy because elected officials are more knowledgeable about complex issues. They claim that special interest money can buy public policy. Medical marijuana ballot initiatives are an example, they say. The successful measures do not reflect public opinion but instead are the brainchild of a few wealthy people who don't even live in their states. Indeed, in the past decade, George Soros, who earned billions in currency markets; George Zimmer, founder of the Men's Wearhouse clothing chain; and John Sperling, founder of the for-profit University of Phoenix, funneled millions of dollars to qualify medical marijuana initiatives in Alaska, Arizona, California, Montana, Oregon, and several other states. Much of the money was spent on collecting signatures to qualify for the ballot. Regardless of whether either interpretation is correct, direct democracy will continue to have important consequences on state politics and policy in the states permitting the plebiscitary process.

NOTE

1. Only three state legislatures (Hawaii, Rhode Island, and Vermont) have passed legislation making it legal for doctors to prescribe marijuana to their suffering patients. National Organization for the Reform of Marijuana Laws (NORML), from the web at http://www.norml.org/index.cfm?Group_ID=3391, accessed Jan. 4, 2006

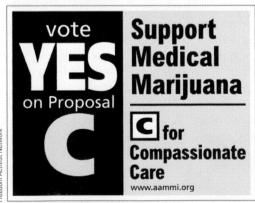

In 2004, 74 percent of Ann Arbor, Michigan, voters approved Proposal C, a ballot measure changing the city charter to allow use of marijuana for medical purposes. Voters in several states have approved similar ballot measures.

ing the taxation and spending powers of state governments, funding stem cell research, and ending affirmative action programs and social welfare benefits to illegal immigrants. In many states, virtually no subject matter is off limits.

Looking just at the November 2004 ballot, six states featured initiatives banning same-sex marriage, whereas another five had legislative referrals on the same topic. Four states had measures dealing with tort reform and medical malpractice, with voters in Florida and Nevada being faced with competing proposals authored by dueling doctors and trial lawyers. Floridians and Nevadans also voted to raise the minimum wage. Coloradoans approved a measure mandating utility companies to develop alternative energy sources and raised taxes on tobacco but rejected a proposal calling for the proportional allocation of electors for the Electoral College. Voters in Montana approved legalizing marijuana use for medicinal purposes. Californians voted on 16 statewide measures, including 11 initiatives and one popular referendum; one of the five initiated measures approved on Election Day was a proposition authorizing the state to issue $3 billion in state bonds over 10 years to finance embryonic stem cell research. As voters in Florida, Nebraska, and Oklahoma all voted to expand gambling operations in 2004, their counterparts in Michigan and California opted to rein in gambling operations by Native American tribes, and voters in Washington nixed the expansion of slot machines in current gaming establishments.[29]

Differences across Initiative States

States differ with regard to how directly democratic their direct democracy processes are in practice. In most of the United States, direct democracy is limited to legislative referendums used at both the state and local levels. Most western states that adopted the initiative early have rules that allow citizens to draft **constitutional initiatives** as well as **statutory**

initiatives. Statutory initiatives are more readily amended or repealed by the legislature in some states (such as Colorado, Maine, Idaho, and Missouri), whereas others require waiting periods, supermajorities, or both before a statutory initiative may be amended. California is the only state where the legislature may neither amend nor repeal an initiative statute.

In states where rules for direct democracy were put in place when Populists and Progressives were still influential (such as Arizona, California, Colorado, and Oregon), provisions for the initiative and popular referendum are more radically democratic than what exists in states that adopted the initiative process later in the 20th century. States that adopted the direct initiative and popular referendum in the early 1900s have rules that make it relatively easy to qualify for the ballot. Most early-adopting states have a relatively low threshold of signatures required to qualify initiatives as well as other requirements to qualify ballot measures.[30]

Using the Initiative

As Figure 4.3 reveals, Oregon and California—two early adopters—lead the pack in initiative use, with both states averaging 6.3 initiatives per each two-year election cycle. Over 300 initiatives have appeared on Oregon ballots since that state adopted direct democracy, with California having nearly as many. The six states with the most frequent use of initiatives (Arizona, California, Colorado, North Dakota, Oregon, and Washington) have averaged more than three initiatives per general election since the Progressive era.[31] Roughly 60 percent of all initiative activity has taken place in these six states.[32] Few states, however, look like California or Oregon in terms of the ease of qualifying initiatives for the ballot and the difficulty that legislatures face when it comes to amending voter-approved initiatives.

The handful of states that adopted direct democracy long after the demise of the Populists and Progressives have much more restrictive rules

Figure 4.3

Historic Statewide Initiative Use (year of adoption through 2006)

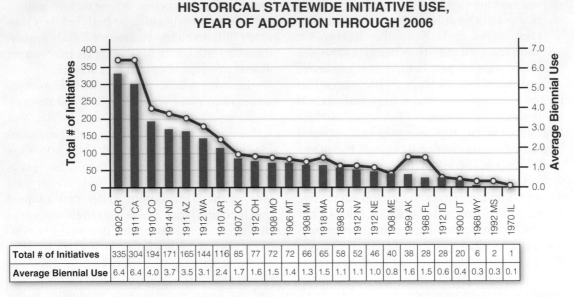

**HISTORICAL STATEWIDE INITIATIVE USE,
YEAR OF ADOPTION THROUGH 2006**

	1902 OR	1911 CA	1910 CO	1914 ND	1911 AZ	1912 WA	1910 AR	1907 OK	1912 OH	1908 MO	1906 MT	1908 MI	1918 MA	1898 SD	1912 NV	1912 NE	1908 ME	1959 AK	1968 FL	1912 ID	1900 UT	1968 WY	1992 MS	1970 IL
Total # of Initiatives	335	304	194	171	165	144	116	85	77	72	72	66	65	58	52	46	40	38	28	28	20	6	2	1
Average Biennial Use	6.4	6.4	4.0	3.7	3.5	3.1	2.4	1.7	1.6	1.5	1.4	1.3	1.5	1.1	1.1	1.0	0.8	1.6	1.5	0.6	0.4	0.3	0.3	0.1

Note: Bars represent the total number of initiatives that qualified in a state since adoption of direct democracy, with values plotted along the left-side axis. The line represents the average number of initiatives in a state every two years, with values plotted on the right-side axis.

on how it can be used. Alaska included the initiative in its constitution when it was admitted to the union (1959), but only Florida and Wyoming (1968), Illinois (1970), and Mississippi (1992) have adopted the initiative process since that time. Three of these states (Florida, Illinois, and Mississippi) only allow constitutional initiatives. Illinois and Mississippi place severe restrictions on the subject matter that may appear on the ballot, and both states have strict provisions for qualification. As such, initiatives are rarely used in these two states—only one initiative has ever appeared on the Illinois ballot, and only two have qualified in Mississippi.[33]

Limits on Initiative Content

Generally speaking, any topic is a potential initiative subject. A few states, however, prohibit measures dealing with the judiciary, bills of rights, or tax questions. The major constraints on initiatives are constitutionality and single-subject laws, both of which are typically evaluated by state courts after a measure has been approved by voters. Some states allow elected officials or courts to amend or revise the language of propositions without the proponent's consent. Of the 24 states, only six have much of a pre-election review at all. Four states—Colorado, Idaho, Montana, and Washington—have an advisory pre-election certification process.

Half of the initiative states have rules that limit initiatives to one subject. Most state courts have been fairly tolerant of individual proposals with sweeping breadth, as long as their component parts could be seen as reasonably germane to one subject. State legislatures originally adopted the **single-subject rule** to ban egregious attempts at building coalitions of supporters by rolling many attractive features into a single measure in the hope of expanding potential support for it. One famous yet unsuccessful initiative proposal from California linked the regulation of margarine, voting rights for Native Americans, gambling, fishing, mining, and apportionment of the state senate into a single initiative question.[34] This sort of "log-rolling" proposal is prohibited by single-subject laws. Only Florida's State Supreme Court has been known to regularly nullify initiatives on single-subject grounds, even after proponents have collected hundreds of thousands of valid signatures to qualify their measures for the ballot. The Florida State Supreme Court is also the only court to overtly declare that single-subject evaluations should be applied more rigorously to initiatives than legislative bills.[35] Since 2000, however, state courts in California, Colorado, Nevada, and Oregon have become more rigid in the application of their state's single-subject rule. At times, this has meant that a single initiative must be split into several questions that are put before voters simultaneously.[36]

Qualifying for the Ballot

Initiatives and referendums, when they qualify for the ballot, are usually placed on a ballot whenever the next regularly scheduled general election occurs. This means direct democracy votes typically occur in even-numbered years. Some states (including Maine, Ohio, and Washington) have initiative votes annually in November, and a few (such as California) place initiatives and referendums on general and primary ballots every two years, so voters decide on an array of initiatives and referendums at least twice a year in even years. California and a handful of other states also allow either the governor or the legislature to schedule special statewide elections in odd years for votes on initiatives and referendums.

States that allow the initiative have considerable variation regarding how easy it is for citizens to use the process. Most states share four basic steps.[37] First, the proposal is drafted by proponents. Next, it is forwarded to a state office that issues an official title and summary of the measure. Proponents may then circulate petitions—usually within a fixed time period, often 90 or 180 days—for voters to sign. Finally, the state verifies whether a valid number of signatures were collected. If so, the proposal is placed on the ballot.

Rules for qualification vary across direct democracy states. In some states, petitioners have less time than in others. Some states also require that a certain proportion of signatures be collected in specific geographical areas, such as congressional districts. States also differ in the proportion of voters' signatures required to qualify for the ballot. Differences in these rules, and in the population of a state, affect how costly it is to get on a ballot. The difficulty of collecting hundreds of thousands of signatures means that many proponents hire people to collect signatures. Qualification is more difficult, and more costly (see Table 4.1), when a higher proportion of signatures must be collected in a shorter time period.[38]

Amateurs or Professionals?

In many states, it is difficult to place a measure on the ballot unless professional petition firms are paid to collect some or all the signatures required for qualification. In large states like California and Florida, where roughly 600,000 valid signatures are required to qualify a constitutional amendment initiative, few measures reach the ballot without proponents resorting to hiring firms that use paid petition gatherers to collect signatures. Some of these signature-gathering firms will have their subcontactors carry multiple petitions for the various groups that have hired them to gather signatures. For instance, in Missouri in 2006, employees of National Voter Outreach, a paid signature-gathering firm based in Carson City, Nevada, were carrying petitions for three separate measures: a measure tightening the state's eminent domain law, a measure limiting the taxing and spending authority of the state, and a measure increasing the tax on cigarettes to pay for health care costs for people receiving Medicaid. In states that have fewer voters, it is easier to collect the required signatures. In Colorado, for example, less than 70,000 valid signatures are needed to qualify either a

Table 4.1

Ease of Qualifying Ballot Initiatives Index

State	Qualification Difficulty Index
Oregon	0
California	1
Colorado	1
North Dakota	1
Arkansas	2
Ohio	2
Michigan	2
South Dakota	2
Idaho	2
Arizona	3
Washington	3
Oklahoma	3
Montana	3
Missouri	3
Massachusetts	3
Utah	3
Nebraska	4
Maine	4
Nevada	4
Florida	4
Illinois	4
Alaska	5
Mississippi	5
Wyoming	6

Note: Higher scores indicate more difficulty; low scores are states with the easiest rules for qualification.

Source: Shaun Bowler and Todd Donovan, "Measuring the Effect of Direct Democracy on State Policy: Not All Initiatives Are Created Equal," *State Politics and Policy Quarterly* 4 (2004): 345–63.

statutory or constitutional amendment initiative. A hundred years ago, when there were far fewer people voting, fewer signatures were required to qualify a measure for the ballot, which may have helped to simplify the logistics of qualification.

Today, few citizen-based groups have the resources to collect signatures equal to 12, 8, or even 5 percent of a state's voting population. The use of paid signature-gatherers and professional campaign staff has been part of the process in some states since early in the 20th century.[39] In the early 1900s, paid petition-gatherers in some states were earning upwards of $0.03 a signature.[40] As the raw number of signatures required to qualify has increased, fewer voluntary, "grassroots" measures appear on state ballots.[41] In California, for example, volunteer petition campaigns are rarely successful. Those who wish to get a constitutional initiative amendment onto the ballot have to gather signatures equivalent to 8 percent of the number of votes for governor. This means gathering close to 1 million signatures in just 150 days, as a large percentage of signatures will surely be found to be invalid. Petition management firms in the state offer proponents a guarantee of qualification but at a price that runs close to $2 million for each initiative to be qualified. Paid signature gatherers in California have been known to earn up to $5 per valid signature, although the $1 to $2 range is more typical. In less populous states, the cost to qualify an initiative ranges anywhere between $50,000 and $400,000.

Champions of the Populist-Progressive vision of direct democracy have long argued that if the process is to combat the power of wealthy established interests, petition efforts should rely on volunteers only. In this spirit, several states passed laws banning the use of paid signature gathering. In the early 1900s, several states, including Ohio, South Dakota, and Washington, passed laws banning paid petition-gatherers. In the 1930s and 1940s, Oregon and Colorado also passed laws banning the practice, with Idaho and Nebraska following suit in the late 1980s.[42] The U.S. Supreme Court eventually overturned these laws in 1988, reasoning that the First Amendment protected paid petitioning, as it was a form of political speech.[43] This ruling, and the difficulties of qualifying measures, means that wealthy groups (unions, corporations, business organizations, professional associations, and trade groups) and wealthy individuals play a prominent, if not dominant, role in affecting what gets put to a public vote. Roughly a dozen states have responded by passing laws requiring circulators to disclose if they are being paid or not, and Oregon and North Dakota prohibit paid signature-gathers from being compensated on a per-signature basis, requiring them instead to be paid a fixed salary or an hourly wage.

Millionaires' Amusement?

Wealthy individuals, such as Microsoft cofounder Paul Allen, Hollywood actor-director Rob Reiner, billionaire financier George Soros, tech-industry businessman Ron Unz, and even actor Arnold Schwarzenegger (in his pre-governor, *Terminator* days), have all bankrolled the qualification of successful ballot initiatives. For his part, Allen convinced taxpayers to subsidize a new stadium for his then mediocre football team, the Seattle Seahawks, but Washington voters rejected the school reform initiative he funded. In 1998, Reiner sponsored an initiative to create early childhood development programs, and in 2006, he sponsored a tax on wealthy individuals to expand preschool education. In the 1990s, Soros, along with a couple of other wealthy individuals, helped finance nearly a dozen initiatives legalizing the medical use of marijuana. Unz used his money to bankroll measures to repeal bilingual education programs in California, Arizona, Colorado, and Massachusetts. In 2002, Schwarzenegger funded an initiative that bulked up spending on his state's after-school programs (and helped to burnish his image as a budding policy wonk).

The Financing of Direct Democracy Campaigns

The last election of the 20th century was a landmark year for direct democracy. In 1998, ballot committees spent nearly $400 million promoting and opposing ballot measures (both initiatives and referendums) in 44 states. Large and small states, regardless of the number of measures on their ballots, experienced high levels of expenditures on ballot measures. In California, the then record-setting 1998 elections gave further insight into how much spending on ballot measure campaigns could be involved. There were seven initiative measures on the state's November 1998 ballot. The secretary of state reported that $197 million was raised to qualify, support, and oppose ballot measures for that election in California alone, nearly half of all the campaign spending on direct democracy contests for that year nationally. The total was more than what the presidential candidates themselves spent nationally in the 2000 general election. The most expensive measure on the November 1998 ballot was Proposition 5, with some $92 million spent collectively to qualify, support, and oppose the successful initiative that legalized gambling on Native American reservations in California.[44]

An Initiative Industrial Complex?

The large sums of money spent on ballot measure campaigns gave rise to concerns about the presence of an "initiative industrial complex."[45] From this perspective, paid political consultants are seen not just as "guns for hire" but also as actors who create the demand for their services by advocating their own proposals for ballot measures. Their services include contracting petition work, polling, crafting TV ads, and purchasing airtime for the ads.

The public clearly has concerns about the campaign side of direct democracy. Despite being overwhelmingly in favor of the initiative process, people claim that initiative campaigns are misleading, that campaigns are too expensive, and that "special interests" dominate the process.[46] Writing in 2003, the *Los Angeles Times,* a longtime and persistent critic of the initiative process, editorialized, "Direct democracy is running amok" in California. Critics in other states agree, such as the former president of the Florida Senate, who has warned of the potential "Californication" of Florida resulting from the rash of expensive initiative campaigns.[47]

One critical question about direct democracy "is whether the process is driven . . . more by consultants than by citizens."[48] Some note that consulting and initiative marketing firms "sometimes test market issues for their feasibility . . . and then shop for a group to back them" and that petition firms may try to drum up business after pitching issues to potential sponsors.[49] However, few examples of this have occurred in California or elsewhere. The claim is likely overreaching, as one is hard-pressed to find evidence of this type of practice, save for a single campaign professional promoting a lottery initiative in 1988.[50]

Nonetheless, the amount of money spent on initiative politics can be staggering. In 2004, close to $400 million was spent on just 59 ballot initiative campaigns in 18 states.[51] In several states, more money was spent on ballot initiative campaigns than for all other races for political office combined. In 2004, Florida voters were presented dueling initiatives on regulating medical malpractice—one measure sponsored by doctors and the insurance industry and two sponsored by trial lawyers. The two industries spent over $33 million on the three initiatives, all of which passed. Nationally, the total expenditures in 2004 were double the amount spent on 117 ballot measures (both initiatives and referendums) on the ballot in 2002. Ballot measure committees squaring off in just four states—California, Florida, Michigan, and Oregon—spent more than $338 million, accounting for 85 percent of the total expenditures on ballot initiative campaigns in 2004. Nationally, proponents spent an average of $12.3 million to qualify and advance their initiatives in 2004, whereas groups opposing the measures spent slightly more than $6 million apiece.[52]

Direct Democracy Campaigns and the Supreme Court

These enormous expenditures are possible because the U.S. Supreme Court views initiative campaigns differently than candidate contests. The Court recognizes that large contributions *to candidates* may create either the appearance or the actuality that a candidate for office may become corrupted.[53] This ruling has allowed Congress and state legislatures some limited ability to regulate the size of contributions given to candidates. Contributions to initiative campaigns, in contrast, are seen as attempts at direct communication with voters rather than attempts to influence elected officials. In *Bellotti v. First National Bank of Boston*, the Court reasoned in 1978 that there was no possibility of corruption or appearance of corruption because a ballot measure can't provide any illicit political favors to a donor of a campaign. In its *Bellotti* decision, the Court reasoned that states thus have no compelling reason to limit the First Amendment right of donors contributing to initiative campaigns.[54] The 1978 decision was also the Court's first effort to explicitly extend free speech rights to corporations.[55] Put simply, no limits exist on what sources can be used, or the amount spent, in ballot initiative campaigns.

"Special Interests" and Initiative Campaigns

As noted above, one common critique of direct democracy is that well-financed campaigns trick voters into passing policies that they actually do not prefer. The argument that "special" interests dominate the initiative process is a plausible one. After all, if it can take up to $1 million to simply ensure a proposal gets on the ballot, playing initiative politics obviously requires significant resources. Ordinary citizens are likely to lack such funds, but established, well-funded groups are not so disadvantaged. Powerful special interests, the argument goes, can afford to get any issues they want onto the ballot, and once the initiative is on the ballot, they buy enough spin doctors, campaign managers, and TV ads to get voters to vote for things they do not want or for things that harm the public interest.[56]

We can assess this argument by breaking it into two questions: first, do "special" economic interests dominate the initiative process (as opposed to broad-based, citizen concerns);

and second, are voters readily swayed by expensive TV campaigns? One way to assess these questions is to ask whether narrowly focused economic interests (for example, banks, trade and industry groups, corporations, and professional associations) outspend other, broader-based kinds of citizens' groups. Another way is to ask whether these economic groups tend to win the initiative contests they finance.

Which Groups Dominate Direct Democracy?

One major study of the role that interest groups play in the initiative process defines *economic groups* as those whose members and donors are almost exclusively business firms and professional organizations rather than individual citizens. Examples include the Missouri Forest Products Association, the California Beer and Wine Wholesalers, the Washington Software Association, and businesses such as casino operators and tobacco giant Philip Morris.[57] This study of eight states found 68 percent of campaign contributions coming from such narrowly based economic groups. It also found that ballot measures with more financial backing from economic interests were more likely to fail.[58] A similar study found that wealthy economic interests in California regularly outspent broadly based "citizen" groups, and 80 percent of campaign spending by these economic groups was directed against citizen group proposals that threatened business interests. However, when economic interest groups spend in favor of their own initiatives, they usually lose.[59]

In short, most of the big money in direct democracy comes from "special" interests defending themselves or, as with the case of the malpractice initiatives in Florida, fighting each other. A battle over a 1988 automobile insurance regulation in California provides an extreme example: insurance companies and trial lawyers' groups spent over $82 million promoting four competing initiatives and spending heavily against a fifth proposal placed on the ballot by Ralph Nader's consumer group. Voters rejected all four well-financed initiatives but approved the fifth insurance measure (the one endorsed by consumer activist Nader).[60]

Record Expenditures In 2004, more than two-thirds of the nearly $400 million of ballot initiative expenditures was spent on just 10 campaigns. As Table 4.2 shows, initiative proponents and opponents in just three states (California, Florida, and Michigan) spent over $269 million to convince voters to support or reject measures on the ballot. In 2004, money more often than not equaled success. Proponents of seven of the most expensive initiatives were victorious on Election Day. On average, the proponents of these seven successful initiatives spent $4.67 million on their campaigns and outspent their opponents by nearly a three-to-one margin.

Over half of the total expenditures spent nationally on ballot initiatives (some $201 million) in 2004 were spent on 11 initiatives on California's November ballot. On average, proponents of the 11 California initiatives spent $12.3 million to qualify and promote their measures, roughly twice the amount spent by their opponents. Citizens ended up adopting five of the 11 ballot initiatives. Proponents spent an average of $3.39 per vote they received on Election Day; opponents spent only $0.69 per vote. Although the spending on ballot measures in California in 2004 dwarfed that of other states, total expenditures on ballot campaigns in Alaska, Montana, and Ohio all topped $3.00 a vote. In Montana, corporate backers of an ill-fated initiative that would have allowed cyanide to be used in mining operations spent over $20 per vote but netted only 42 percent of the vote. In contrast, spending on initiatives in Missouri averaged only $0.05 per vote and only $0.23 per vote in Oregon.[61]

Does Money Matter in Initiative Campaigns?

Money spent to defeat initiatives tends to be quite effective. Some research shows that a dollar spent by the "No" campaign has almost twice as much impact on the eventual vote share than a dollar spent by the "Yes" side.[62] Other studies suggest that spending by proponents is less effective or has no effect when compared to spending against ballot

Table 4.2

Top 10 Most Expensive Ballot Initiative Campaigns, 2006

State	Ballot No.	Title	Side	Expenditures
CA	68	Tribal Gaming Compact Renegotiation	Yes	$25,472,443
			No	**$47,415,763**
CA	71	Stem Cell Research	**Yes**	**$34,711,278**
			No	$624,973
CA	70	Tribal Gaming Compact	Yes	$29,972,493
			No	**$2,870,720**
FL	4	Expansion of Slot Machines	**Yes**	**$24,878,428**
MI	1	Voter Approval for Gambling	**Yes**	**$18,777,789**
CA	64	Unfair Business Competition Laws	**Yes**	**$19,479,094**
CA	67	Emergency and Medical Services	Yes	$6,144,544
			No	**$7,288,512**
FL	3	Tort Reform	**Yes**	**$2,862,167**
FL	7	Patients' Rights	**Yes**	**$8,362,721**
FL	8	Protection from Medical Malpractice†	**Yes**	**$8,362,721**

Note: **Bold** indicates winning side.

Source: Daniel A. Smith, "Money Talks: Ballot Initiative Spending in 2004," Ballot Initiative Strategy Center Foundation, Washington, D.C., May 2006, http://www.ballot.org.

measures. This may explain why narrow economic groups regularly defeat initiatives such as environmental regulations or consumer protections that enjoy substantial majority support in pre-election polls.[63] Despite this, measures supported by broad-based and grassroots citizens' groups pass at rates a bit higher than average.[64]

Although exceptions do exist, wealthy economic interests aren't usually successful at using initiatives to "buy" public policy, but they are often successful in blocking many proposals—such as health care requirements and environmental regulations—that directly affect them. Most initiatives that do pass can be seen as things, for better or worse, that tap into the preferences and concerns of the broader public, such as social and moral questions.[65] Many measures that pass, such as tougher criminal sentencing laws, animal protection laws regulating hunting, or even somewhat peculiar measures—such as a 1998 California initiative that banned the slaughter of horses for human consumption and a 2002 Florida initiative that amended the state's constitution to prohibit the confinement of gestating pigs in crates—pass despite having relatively little campaign spending by the proponents.

Dumber than Chimps? Voting on Ballot Questions

A voter's ability to make reasonably informed choices on ballot measures depends on what sort of information is available. Few suggest that voters study the details of the laws they are voting on. Rather than using exhaustive research, they decide on the basis of information shortcuts that are easily available.[66] Information about who is in favor or against a proposal may be the primary shortcut many people use.[67] Partisanship is one of the most reliable predictors of voting on ballot measures.[68] If, for example, voters see a prominent Democrat support a proposition, then loyal Democratic voters are likely to support the proposition and Republicans oppose it.

Where do voters find these cues to help them make informed decisions on ballot questions? In many states, an official state agency mails every registered voter a pamphlet that lists each ballot proposal and includes arguments for and against the proposition. Other sources include media coverage and paid ads. The availability of information shortcuts may explain why so few examples of initiatives pass that are later found to be unpopular with the voters who approved them.

Does Direct Democracy Deceive Voters?

Because voters may not know much about the subjects of ballot initiatives and may not have partisan cues when voting, there may be room for campaign ads to determine which initiatives voters approve. It is unclear, however, how much effect paid ads have on voter choices. Most people believe that initiative campaign ads are attempts to mislead.[69] Despite the expenditure of tremendous sums of money, voters claim to discount the usefulness of political ads. One survey found people had multiple sources of information to consider when deciding on initiatives, and most reported that they didn't rely much on information from paid ads. Most voters claimed that neutral information provided by the state, and information from the news media, was most important to them when figuring out how to vote on initiatives. When campaign consultants who worked on initiative campaigns were asked about the information voters relied on, they had a different sense

of which information was most important.[70] Table 4.3 displays results from surveys of voters and campaign consultants.

The Role of the Media in Initiative Campaigns

A survey of voters found that just 20 percent claimed to make use of TV ads. A followup question found that only 13 percent of this group thought the information in the ads was "very important" in affecting their decisions. In contrast, 85 percent of consultants saw TV and radio as "very important" information for voters. Consultants see TV and radio ads as the most influential, whereas voters themselves see ads as one of the least important sources of information. Similarly, consultants afford the advertising mailers produced by the campaigns a much larger degree of importance than do voters.

These differences between what voters say they use when deciding on ballot measures and what consultants think they use may come as little surprise. Most people probably have little wish to claim being dupes of advertising, whereas consultants believe in their own importance. Thus, if these responses contain bias, it is probably for voters to underestimate the effects of ads and for consultants to overestimate their effects. However disparate and inconsistent the results, they could be accurate: it may be that a relatively small group responds to information in TV ads, but these might be the voters who consultants are trying to reach with their ads.

Despite these differences in perceptions of information sources, some similarities emerge. Both consultants and voters, for example, recognize the importance of the news media. Voters see news media as more important than advertisements, and the consultants' evaluations of the importance of news are similarly high. Consultants and voters also have similar perceptions of the state-provided voter's guide in terms of importance. The voter's guide is seen by voters and consultants as an especially important piece of campaign information

Table 4.3

Importance of Sources of Information[a] for Ballot Initiative Campaigns

	Consultant's Views			Voter's Views		
	Very Important (%)	Important (%)	Not Important (%)	Very Important (%)	Important (%)	Not Important (%)
TV and radio ads	83	17	0	13	60	26
TV and radio news	72	28	0	34	56	10
Ballot pamphlet	64	31	5	69	30	1
Newspapers	41	59	0	50	47	3
Flyers and/or mailers	39	54	7	9	72	18
Word of mouth	35	37	28	34	53	13

[a] Values are the percentage responding that a source of information is very important, important, or not important at all.

Source: Shaun Bowler and Todd Donovan, "Do Voters Have a Cue? TV Ads as a Source of Information in Referendum Voting," *European Journal of Political Research* 41 (2002): 777–93.

provided to voters. This is consistent with our idea that it provides a convenient and easy source of endorsements.

TV ads may actually provide useful cues to voters. One study of initiative campaign TV ads from several states found the ads often provide cues, such as names of sponsors or opponents, as well as name prominent groups, newspapers, and politicians who have taken positions on the measure.[71] High levels of spending on initiative TV ads probably increase public awareness of initiatives and may increase public attention to campaign issues. This may explain higher levels of general knowledge about politics in states with prominent initiative campaigns.[72] Relatedly, another study found voters more likely to have heard about initiatives when more was spent on the campaigns and that more citizens voted on initiatives that had higher campaign spending.[73]

Direct Democracy and Electoral Politics

Initiative and referendum campaigns can alter a state's political context. Several examples of ballot measures affect the agenda and tone of candidate elections. In 1998, for example, Republican Party operatives in Colorado tried to link Democratic candidates to positions on state ballot initiatives that Republicans expected voters to find unpopular. Democrats did the same and ran campaign ads linking the Republican gubernatorial candidate to two anti-abortion measures. The Republican had been trying to distance himself from the social conservative.[74] During their 2004 Florida campaign, the rival U.S. Senate candidates attempted to craft their campaign themes to fit with initiatives on the state's ballot. Republican nominee Mel Martinez, for example, worked several ballot issues into his standard campaign speech and at candidate debates.[75] And in California, numerous candidates for governor, including Arnold Schwarzenegger, have sponsored initiatives to promote their candidacies.

Political party organizations also use initiatives to promote issues they hope will divide the opposing party's candidates and weaken the opposition's base of support. Major examples of **wedge issues** from the past decade are affirmative action and immigration initiatives. Republicans promoted a California initiative to restrict affirmative action and another measure restricting services to illegal immigrants, hoping that Democrats across the nation would be forced to adopt policy positions that would harm their chances for re-election. Republican governor Pete Wilson of California, as well as Democratic candidate John Van de Kamp, both raised money to put several policy questions on the ballot when they sought office.[76]

Anecdotes and academic studies also suggest that different ballot measures can mobilize different elements of the electorate at different times.[77] A classic example is the 1982 California gubernatorial election. The Democratic mayor of Los Angeles, Tom Bradley, led narrowly in polls conducted immediately prior to the November vote, but Bradley ended up losing to Republican George Deukmejian. In this case, polls may have had difficulty estimating how an initiative would shape the participating electorate. The same ballot included a highly contested gun control measure, Proposition 15, which the National Rife Association (NRA) opposed. The NRA spent over $5 million against the measure and rallied pro-gun voters to the polls.[78] Deukmejian, probably benefited from these voters being drawn to the polls.

Spillover Effects of Ballot Measures in Candidate Races

Direct democracy's effect on candidate races may be indirect. One prominent study found that various state and local ballot measures advocating a freeze on the development of nuclear weapons in 1982 affected how voters evaluated candidates in U.S. Senate elections, in some U.S. House races, and even in some gubernatorial contests. In places where voters were presented the nuclear freeze question, they were more likely to evaluate candidates in terms of the nuclear proliferation measure. There were similar effects with California's Proposition 187 in 1994, which restricted social services to illegal immigrants, and Proposition 209 in 1996, which ended affirmative action in the state. Both ballot questions shaped the issues voters used to evaluate candidates.[79]

One need only to point to the 2004 presidential election to understand the potential ramifications of ballot measures on candidate elections. Assessing George W. Bush's narrow victory in Ohio, which tipped the Electoral College balance in his favor, journalists and political analysts were quick to credit the mobilizing effects of Issue 1, a statewide anti-gay marriage measure on the ballot that year. *The New York Times* speculated that "state constitutional amendments banning same-sex marriage increased the turnout of socially conservative voters in many of the 11 states where the measures appeared on the ballot," with the measures appearing "to have acted like magnets for thousands of socially conservative voters in rural and suburban communities who might not otherwise have voted."[80] Although scholars have questioned the actual turnout effects of the statewide same-sex marriage ballot measures, the margin in Ohio was so close that if the initiative had even a minor effect on turning out pro-Bush voters, it may have been decisive.[81]

Direct Democracy and Turnout in Elections

As the 2004 Ohio example suggests, statewide ballot initiatives may affect politics by bringing voters to the polls. In 1978, more Californians cast votes for a critical antitax measure (Proposition 13) than cast votes for the governor's race on the same ballot. Studies of voting prior to the 1990s concluded that ballot measures did not affect voter turnout. Political scientist David Magleby concluded in 1984 that "turnout is not increased by direct legislation," although occasionally, a highly salient measure, such as California's Proposition 13 in 1978, "might encourage" higher turnout.[82]

Recent studies of initiative use, however, have produced evidence that initiatives can increase turnout by nearly 2 percent per initiative in midterm elections and nearly 1 percent in presidential elections, all else being equal.[83] Initiatives receiving substantial media attention have the greatest effect on turnout, particularly in "off-year" (non–presidential election year) state elections.[84] In municipal races, evidence has shown that at the local level, cities that use the initiative process have higher voter turnout than cities that don't allow their citizens to place measures directly on the ballot.[85]

Interest Groups, Initiatives, and Elections

Interest groups may use direct democracy to force the hands of legislative candidates running for office by placing measures on ballots to force them to take a position on their issues. Interest groups also use ballot initiatives to exploit wedge issues, drain campaign resources from potential opponents, and mobilize their voters.[86] California's anti–affirmative action measure, Proposition 209, was placed on the ballot by conservative groups who hoped that if the measure generated support from white Democratic voters, they might also consider breaking away from Democratic candidates who were opposed to the measure.

Pro-business interest groups, including Americans for Tax Reform, promoted "paycheck protection" ballot measures in Oregon and California to require individual union members to give their leaders prior approval for dues to be used for political purposes. A leader of Americans for Tax Reform envisioned that the issue would force organized labor to spend millions of dollars in campaign funds on efforts to defeat the measures—money that unions would not be able to contribute to Democratic candidates. They turned out to be right—unions spent some $24 million to narrowly defeat the measure in California.[87]

Groups also use initiatives to pass policies that they can't get through the legislature. Large membership interests, such as teachers' unions, have been successful in promoting initiatives designed to benefit their members. The California Teachers' Association, for example, sponsored the successful Proposition 98 in 1988, mandating that a fixed percentage of state general fund revenues support K–12 education. Washington's teacher's union recently promoted two successful initiatives: Initiative 728 mandated smaller class sizes, and Initiative 732 mandated pay raises for the state's public school teachers. Interest groups also use ballot initiatives to send signals to legislators, or to force legislators to come up with an alternative.

Some research suggests that the initiative process may actually stimulate greater interest group activity, increasing the number of broad-based interest groups in a state. Interest groups in initiative states tend to have more members than those in noninitiative states because the process provides potential groups with yet another incentive to become mobilized and engaged in the political process. States with the initiative, studies have found, have more registered citizens and nonprofit groups than those states without the process.[88]

The Effects of Direct Democracy on Citizens

The presence of highly visible initiatives and frequent voting on ballot measures may make people feel more as if they "have a say" in politics.[89] Evidence shows that people in states with initiatives have higher levels of political engagement and political participation than people in non-initiative states, although it is difficult to establish if this is due to the effects of direct democracy or due to something else that is unique to these states. One study found that people have higher levels of factual knowledge about politics in states where initiatives are used more frequently, perhaps because initiatives stimulate media attention and because voting on initiatives requires that they acquire information to make decisions.[90] Another found that people in initiative states are more likely to engage in political discussion, have greater political knowledge, and contribute to interest groups.[91] Some evidence indicates that frequent use of initiatives causes voters to feel more competent when participating in politics, more likely to think that they have a say, and more likely to think that public officials care about what they think.[92] Similar results have been found in Swiss cantons.[93]

Direct Democracy and Minorities

As noted above, one of the original concerns about direct democracy is the potential it has to allow a majority of voters to trample the rights of minorities. Many still worry that the process can be used to harm gays and lesbians as well as ethnic, linguistic, and religious minorities.[94] Those who worry about repressive majorities point to a series of anti-minority measures approved by voters. Initiatives to repeal affirmative action have appeared on state ballots in California, Michigan, and Washington as well as in Houston. Immigration has been a major issue on the ballot in both Arizona and California.[95] Proposals to repeal bilingual education were approved in Arizona, California, and Massachusetts (but rejected in Colorado). Initiatives declaring English an "official language" have been approved by voters in numerous states.[96] Scores of measures dealing with gay rights and gay marriage have appeared on state and local ballots,[97] and many cities hold referendums on whether to allow low-income housing.[98] This presents a critical question: does direct democracy harm minorities?

Evidence shows that the initiative process "is sometimes prone to produce laws that disadvantage relatively powerless minorities—and probably is more likely than legislatures to do so."[99] State and local ballot initiatives have been used to undo policies—such as school desegregation, protections against job and housing discrimination, and affirmative action—that minorities have secured from legislatures where they are included in the bargaining process. But most initiatives probably do not produce divisions between majorities of white voters and minority voters. Studies of support for ballot initiatives across different groups of voters show that minority voters were no more likely to support the losing side in an initiative contest than white voters. This may reflect that most initiatives do not pit the interests of racial and ethnic minorities against those of the majority or perhaps that minorities and whites have similar issues and concerns addressed by the initiative process. It is important to note, however, that on issues dealing with racial and ethnic matters, studies show that racial and ethnic minorities do end up more on the losing side of the popular vote.[100]

The issue of gay rights has been one of the more contentious areas of initiative politics where minority interests are frequently put to a vote. Majorities have, in some cases, voted to restrict the extension of some civil rights to gays and lesbians. Until recently, with the rash of anti-gay marriage amendments being placed on the ballot, voters in a number of states had refused to pass most measures that would deny gays and lesbians protections against discrimination. A 1992 anti-gay measure in Colorado, Amendment 2, which changed the state constitution to expressly prohibit local laws aimed at protecting gays and lesbians against discrimination, was a major exception.[101] The Colorado measure was eventually overturned by the U.S. Supreme Court in 1995 for being an unconstitutional denial of equal protection before the law.[102] Voters have been much less tolerant of granting equal rights to marriage. At least two dozen states have voted on whether to ban same-sex marriages, and voters in every state (except Arizona in 2006) have supported the ban.

The record of direct democracy for minority interests is a mixed bag then. Racial and ethnic minorities may agree with majority voters on most ballot measures, but there have been some critical initiatives where minority rights have been lost when put to a public vote. Yet, in nearly every instance where the initiative process has been used to limit minority rights to fair housing, desegregated schools, public services, and protections against discrimination, courts have stepped in to overturn initiatives and uphold minority rights.[103] But regardless of whether anti-minority ballot measures pass or fail, they may still have effects on people they target. By targeting a minority group with an initiative, for example, public attitudes about the group (or about policies

COMPARISONS HELP US UNDERSTAND

DEMOCRACY AND MINORITIES

Are minorities better off when policies are decided by representative democracy or directly by voters? History shows that both can produce anti-minority outcomes. State legislators have approved laws allowing slavery, racial segregation, laws excluding Chinese from owning land, the internment of Japanese in concentration camps during World War II, and laws advanced by the Ku Klux Klan designed to strip Catholics of their rights. None of these discriminatory laws needed direct democracy to flourish. But representative democracy, with its opportunities for minority representatives to participate while laws are being crafted, may have a better record of advancing civil rights.

In recent years, voters and legislators have been making decisions about the nature of rights that are extended to gays and lesbians. A recent study compared minority rights decisions produced by representative democracy to those produced by direct democracy.[1] It found that most civil rights bills affecting gays and lesbians in state legislatures were "pro-gay" (for example, banning job discrimination) and that slightly more pro-gay than anti-gay bills (for example, rules against being a foster parent) were approved by state legislators. With direct democracy, most civil rights proposals were anti-gay, and anti-gay measures were more likely to pass. Overall, representative democracy produced pro-gay outcomes 44 percent of the time, compared to 39 percent for direct democracy. The difference between outcomes across these institutions is subtle, because most pro- or anti–minority rights proposals failed. But the authors note that minority rights suffer more under direct democracy, especially when the policy is anti-minority in intent.

NOTE

1. Donald P. Haider-Markel, Alana Querze, and Kara Lindaman. 2007. "Win, Lose or Draw?" A Reexamination of Direct Democracy and Minority Rights." Political Research Quarterly. 60:304-14.

November 2006. Anti-gay marriage activists rally in front of Massachusetts State House demanding that the marriage question be put to a popular vote.

that benefit the group) can be changed, with mass opinion becoming less tolerant of the targeted minority group.[104]

The Effects of Direct Democracy on Public Policy

By this point, it should be clear that there are many reasons to expect that direct democracy can make a state's political environment and its public policies different than if there were no initiative process. When voters are allowed to make direct choices on policies, they sometimes make decisions that their elected representatives would not. An obvious example of this is term limits. Voters in many states have placed limits on time their representatives may serve. Absent the initiative process, elected representatives rarely, if ever, adopt such a policy.[105] It is unclear, though, whether or not direct democracy systematically makes policy more representative of what people want or if it leads to "better" public policy.

Some scholars and practitioners have proposed that the mere presence of the initiative process can affect public policy by changing how legislators behave. If legislators anticipate that there is a threat that someone might pass a law by initiative, legislators may have greater incentives to pass some version of the law so they can maintain influence over what the final law looks like.[106] Initiatives can also send signals about the sort of policies the public wants.[107] Several studies show that certain public policies—including abortion regulations, death penalty laws, some civil rights policies, and spending on some state programs—more closely match public opinion in states with initiatives than in states without initiatives.[108] As an example, states with liberal public opinion and initiatives may have relatively liberal abortion rules, whereas states with conservative opinions and initiatives may have conservative policies. Absent the initiative, policies may be less likely to reflect the state's opinion climate. Studies that examine a wide range of state policies, however, find no such effects; some initiatives may make policy more reflective of public opinion with some policies but not others.[109]

The biggest effects of direct democracy on policy may be in the realm of what Caroline Tolbert calls "governance policy,"—policies that set the rules about how government can function. Voters in initiative states can, and do, pass measures that amend rules that structure the political system itself. These include initiatives that may run counter to the interests of elected officials. States with the initiative process are more likely to have adopted term limits and tougher rules for adopting new taxes and increasing spending[110] and were quicker to adopt some campaign finance regulations.[111] Examples of tax limitation measures include California's Proposition 13 of 1978, Oregon's Measure 5 in 1990, and Colorado's Taxpayers Bill of Rights (TABOR) amendment of 1992. If given a chance via direct democracy, voters often place constraints on what their representatives can do, especially when it comes to fiscal matters.

Long-Term Effects of Direct Democracy

Direct democracy can alter state policy directly by providing an additional point of access for citizens and interest groups. Advocates of decriminalization of drugs, campaign finance reforms, physician-assisted suicide, and many other policies have successfully used direct democracy to do an "end run" around state legislatures that did not turn their ideas into policy. As noted above, some suggest this threat of the "gun behind the door" makes state policy more representative of state opinion. But what are the major long-term consequences of direct democracy on state policy?

In addition to promoting specific policy ideas, the initiative process allows those outside of the legislature, and those outside of the traditional corridors of power, the ability to permanently change rules that define institutions of government. As examples, initiatives have been used to rewrite state rules about how judges sentence criminals, how much a state may collect via existing taxes, and how much the legislature may spend in a given year. Initiatives have been used to change rules about future tax increases and have placed limits on how often legislators may run for re-election. As we note in Chapter 10, these tax and expenditure limits (TELs) adopted by direct democracy may have important long-run effects on state and local finances.

The long-term effect of policy passed by direct democracy is probably more consequential in states that allow constitutional initiatives. When initiatives constraining taxing and spending are embedded in a state's constitution, it is difficult for elected officials to amend budgeting rules. This complicates their budgeting tasks. This means that voters can place things in their constitution that limit property taxes, increase tobacco taxes, guarantee a certain share of general funds for education, or authorize teacher pay raises and smaller class sizes. Even statutory initiatives can complicate the task of crafting long-term budgets. A single ballot may present voters with choices about cutting some taxes, raising others, issuing bonds for specific projects, and increasing spending on specific programs. When legislatures pass their budgets, their choices about increasing spending or cutting taxes need not be linked to specific revenue sources and programs. Voters, deciding on individual initiatives, face no such constraints.

Despite all of this, there are reasons to expect that the long-range effects of direct democracy are not that dramatic. Once an initiative is approved by voters, proponents often do not have the resources or political clout to maintain pressure on legislators over time to ensure that their law is implemented as the proponents would like. Elected officials can eventually rewrite rules, amend what voters approved (in most states), or stall implementation. The end result may be that "the policy impact of most initiatives reflects a compromise between what electoral majorities and government actors want."[112] This means that governing is quite different in initiative states, yet direct democracy has not replaced the role of the legislature.

Majority Tyranny and Judicial Review

The potential effects of initiatives on policy are further muted when we consider judicial review. Initiatives, like any other law, must be consistent with the U.S. Constitution and state constitutions and must abide by a state's regulations on the initiative process, such as subject matter constraints. State and federal courts tend to treat initiative laws just like laws passed by legislatures, regardless of how popular they may have been with voters. Courts have been very willing to strike down voter-approved initiatives. One study of several states found that *most* state initiatives ended up being challenged in court, with 40 percent overturned in whole or in part.[113] People challenging voter-approved initiatives in court may increase their odds of success because they are able to "venue shop": they can file cases in different districts of either state or federal courts in order to find judges most likely to grant them a favorable ruling.

Assessments of Direct Democracy

When some of the most careful observers of American politics turn their attention to the process of direct democracy, their assessments of it are rather negative. Alan Rosenthal, a preeminent scholar of state legislatures, suggests that growing enthusiasm for direct democracy—in the form of growing use of opinion polls that influence representatives as well as use of initiative and referendum—has a corrosive effect on representative government. Rosenthal suggests that a demise of representative government has occurred in American states over recent decades, leaving legislators with less responsibility for government and leaving states more difficult to govern.[114] Some blame direct democracy for shattering the fiscal health of some states, then leaving elected officials to pick up the pieces. Initiatives are also blamed for promoting confrontational (and unconstitutional) policies that target minority groups, such as immigrants and gays and lesbians.

David Broder, one of the United States' most insightful journalists, echoes this sentiment. Broder spent weeks on the West Coast observing the initiative campaigns being waged in California in 1998. The nearly $200 million spent in California initiative campaigns was nearly as much as taxpayers spent on the public financing of the national presidential campaigns that year. Broder's experience in California led him to conclude that wealthy special interests and political parties were driving the process, spending millions to place their measures on ballots and then spending heavily on deceptive advertising to convince voters to approve their schemes.[115]

Public Approval of Direct Democracy

As Figure 4.4 reveals, the public remains quite supportive of the initiative process in states where it is used rather frequently. The public looks at direct democracy quite differently, and more positively, than many political observers and elected officials. Even voters who have experienced California's high-stakes, high-cost system of direct democracy remain supportive of the process. And as Figure 4.5 shows, Americans give widespread support to expanding direct democracy nationally. Over 70 percent of Americans surveyed said they favored having a national vote on important matters of policy.[116]

Surveys of elected officials find much less enthusiasm about direct democracy. For their part, legislators in direct democracy states would like to change things so that they have more say over what ends up going to a public vote and also have more ability to amend laws after voters approve them. Voters in these states, for their part, are unwilling to let their representatives have such discretion.[117] Recent proposals for expanding initiative use to additional states appear sensitive to critics of California's process and are less sweeping than the early 20th-century

Figure 4.4

Public Opinion about Direct Democracy in California and Washington

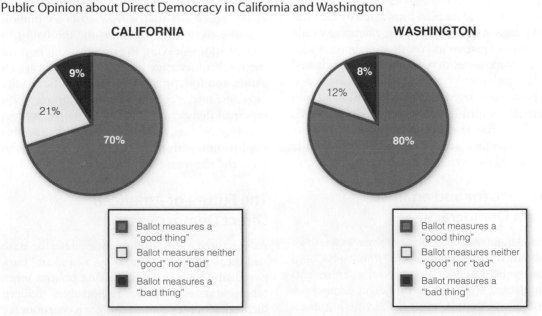

Source: Shaun Bowler, Todd Donovan, Max Neiman, and Johnny Peel, "Institutional Threat and Partisan Outcomes: Legislative Candidates' Attitudes toward Direct Democracy," *State Politics & Policy Quarterly* 1 (2001): 364–79.

Figure 4.5

Support for a National Referendum Process

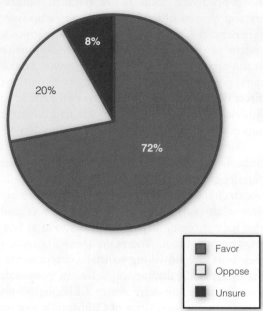

Source: Shaun Bowler and Todd Donovan, "Reasoning about Institutional Change: Winners, Losers and Support for Electoral Reform," *British Journal of Political Science* (forthcoming).

models. An initiative plan considered by the New Jersey legislature in 2002, for example, would limit subject matter and only permit petitions for statutory measures that would first be evaluated by the legislature.[118] In 2006, the Minnesota and Alabama state legislatures each considered bills to create a scaled-down version of the initiative, and the governor of Rhode Island asked voters in a November advisory referendum whether they would like to have the initiative process.

The Case for and against Direct Democracy

To its defenders, direct democracy was seen as a tool that would empower the "grassroots" and weaken the influence that special interests had over elected representatives. Direct democracy could "level the playing field" by giving more political value to individual voters, as opposed to those who finance political campaigns. Pro-

ponents of direct democracy also argued that the process can build better citizens. Participating in meaningful policy choice may lead citizens to seek out more information. Voting directly on policy might also encourage citizens to have more interest in politics and feel more engaged with their government.[119]

From the start, critics of direct democracy raised several objections to the process. It may be difficult, they claimed, for the average voter to understand the nuances of difficult public policy questions, as many people simply pay no attention to politics. Elected officials have time to deliberate about issues and reach compromises that might accommodate rival positions. Initiative proposals, in contrast, can be framed by a proponent as an all-or-nothing choice, which is then decided upon by a relatively ill-informed electorate. A more enduring critique focuses on the potential for tyranny of the majority. American representative government involves many checks and balances and veto points. Direct democracy, in contrast, allows voters to pass laws hostile to minority interests or pass laws repealing hard-fought victories that minorities achieved via representative government.[120] A modern criticism of the process is that it now costs $1 million or more to qualify measures for the ballot in a large state—leaving the process well beyond the reach of average citizens. Peter Schrag, an astute and longtime observer of politics in the Golden State, described in his scathing book on direct democracy how the initiative process encourages the "embracing and demagoguing [of] hot-button issues" by candidates who hope to "showcase" their credentials.[121]

The Future of American Direct Democracy

As we noted above, many critics describe state and local direct democracy as a kind of "faux populism."[122] Instead of making politics more representative or more responsible, modern direct democracy may no longer have room for regular, grassroots citizen activists. Criticism of modern direct democracy has led to the introduction of scores of proposals to reform the process. Each year, legislators in initiative states propose legislation to alter how the initiative process works. Few of these have been approved, but they illustrate how some elected officials view what the future of direct democracy should be.

Restricting the Use of the Initiative Process

Surveys of legislators reveal support for direct democracy as a concept, coupled with a desire to get elected representatives more involved with laws that voters might approve.[123] Many reform proposals introduced by state legislatures are designed to make it more difficult to qualify measures for the ballot.[124] These include proposals to raise the number of signatures required or shorten the time period to collect signatures. Other proposals of this sort include rules requiring that a certain proportion of signatures be collected across all regions of a state (counties or congressional districts) and rules making it more difficult to pay people to collect signatures. In the wake of California's recall of Governor Davis, there were also calls to make future use of recall petitions more difficult.

Serious barriers can prevent passing such reforms, even if these proposals were to enjoy majority support among legislators. Major structural rules governing direct democracy are embedded in state constitutions, and constitutional changes require voter approval. Public opinion surveys demonstrate that voters do not want to limit their control over the initiative process, so constitutional referendums proposing to do this are more than likely to be rejected. The courts have also rejected overt attempts to ban the use of paying people to collect signatures[125] and rejected rules requiring that signatures be collected across all of a state's counties, regardless of the population of counties.[126]

The popular appeal of direct democracy remains deeply rooted. Another problem with proposals to limit or reform direct democracy is that most do nothing about campaign spending levels. Rather than increasing the influence of "grassroots" citizens' groups, reforms that make it more difficult to qualify measures will probably increase any advantages that wealthy interests may already have. Tougher qualification barriers are likely to make it more difficult to organize volunteers to qualify measures and also increase the costs of paying petitioners to qualify something for the ballot. If it becomes more difficult or costly to collect signatures, the need to pay people to collect signatures is likely to increase.

Ballot Campaign Finance Reforms

Recognizing the high cost of qualifying initiative and referendum petitions, and how this may exclude some groups from the process but not others, one proposal suggested California should simply skip the petition process and allow someone to qualify a measure by paying a fee similar to what it would cost the proponent to collect signatures.[127] This would generate millions of dollars per initiative for a state and perhaps limit the number of initiatives to reach the ballot. Others have suggested that the problem is not too many initiatives—but initiative campaigns where one side has a huge spending advantage over the other.[128] Because the *Bellotti* decision means that ballot initiative campaign spending can't be limited, gross disparities in spending between proponents and opponents of an initiative can only be mitigated if public funds were used to maintain some minimum level of funding for both sides.

Expanding the Use of Direct Democracy

At the same time as many incumbent state legislators are attempting to limit use of direct democracy in their states, there have been proposals in noninitiative states to introduce the initiative and referendum. The most visible of these proposals come from governors rather than legislators. Past governors of Louisiana (Mike Foster), Minnesota (Jesse Ventura), New York (George Pataki), and Rhode Island (Donald Carcieri) have made public their support of the process. There have also been a few legislative attempts by minority parties in Minnesota, New Jersey, and Texas to introduce the process.[129] Surveys also demonstrate widespread public support for expanding the use of direct democracy to the national level (recall Figure 4.5). The idea of expanding the use of direct democracy is popular in states that already have it and in states that do not.

Despite this public enthusiasm and the support of some states' governors, voters have little reason to expect that direct democracy will expand to additional states in the near future.

This is due to the fact that state legislators largely control whether their state will change rules to allow direct democracy. Legislators are reluctant to adopt rules that weaken their control over the political agenda.[130] Absent the occurrence of another social movement pushing for major political reform similar to the Populist movement of the late 19th century, elected representatives are unlikely to adopt or expand direct democracy. Voters have probably even less reason to expect adoption of initiative, referendum, or recall at the national level.

Summary

Direct democracy is a curious American institution. It plays a large role in the politics of some states and communities but much less of a role in other places. The initiative, referendum, and recall were adopted in an era when overt corruption among state legislators and local elected officials was common. Rather than thwarting the political influence of wealthy interests, however, direct democracy may give powerful, established interests an additional tool they may use to shape public policy. It represents one of the major institutional differences between states like California and New York or between Arizona and Connecticut.

This chapter illustrates that direct democracy—specifically, the initiative process—has important effects where it is used. It may alter the issues voters use when evaluating candidates, and it changes the rules that affect how elected officials govern. We have also reviewed evidence that direct democracy may lead state policies to be more representative of what voters in a state prefer. In Chapter 10, furthermore, we see how direct democracy also affects state and local fiscal policy. In short, few similar institutions in the United States are associated with as many differences between the states. Whether direct democracy makes politics better is often left to the eye of the beholder.

Key Terms

Constitutional initiative	*Meyer v. Grant*	Recall
Direct initiative	Popular referendum	Single-subject rule
Indirect initiative	Populist Party	Statutory initiative
Legislative referendum	Proposition 13	Wedge issues

Suggested Readings

Bowler, Shaun, and Todd Donovan. 1998. *Demanding choices: Opinion, voting, and direct democracy.* Ann Arbor: University of Michigan Press.

Broder, David S. 2000. *Democracy derailed: Initiative campaigns and the power of money.* New York: Harcourt.

Ellis, Richard. 2002. *Democratic delusions: The initiative process in America.* Lawrence: University of Kansas Press.

Gerber, Elisabeth R. 1999. *The populist paradox: Interest group influence and the promise of direct legislation.* Princeton, NJ: Princeton University Press.

Magleby, David B. 1984. *Direct legislation: Voting on ballot propositions in the United States.* Baltimore: Johns Hopkins University Press.

Matsusaka, John. 2004. *For the many or the few: The initiative, public policy and American democracy.* Chicago: University of Chicago Press.

Nicholson, Stephen P. 2005. *Voting the agenda: Candidates, elections and ballot propositions.* Princeton, NJ: Princeton University Press.

Schrag, Peter. 1998. *Paradise lost: California's experience, America's future.* New York: New Press.

Smith, Daniel A. 1998. *Tax crusaders and the politics of direct democracy.* New York: Routledge.

Smith, Daniel A., and Caroline Tolbert. 2004. *Educated by initiative.* Ann Arbor: University of Michigan Press.

Websites

Ballot Initiative Strategy Center (http://www.ballot.org): In addition to coordinating a national strategy to use ballot initiatives to strengthen progressive politics across the states, BISC tracks initiatives circulating for qualification to statewide ballots.

Initiative and Referendum Institute (http://www.iandrinstitute.org): In addition to tracking initiatives and referendums on the ballot, the I&R Institute provides a historical database that dates back to 1904.

National Conference of State Legislatures (http://www.ncsl.org/programs/legman/elect/initiat.htm): Although generally critical of direct democracy, NCSL does an excellent job of tracking ballot initiatives and popular referendums and also provides a historical database.

Research and Documentation Centre on Direct Democracy (http://c2d.unige.ch): C2D, based in Geneva, Switzerland, provides an international online library and several direct democracy data sets.

5

Photo by Joe Burbank/Orlando Sentinel

Political Parties

Where's the Interparty Competition?

A descendant of pre-Civil War U.S. president Zachary Taylor, Senator Victor Crist represents portions of the Tampa metropolitan area. A Republican who previously served in the Florida House of Representatives for eight years, Crist was elected to the State Senate in 2000 and re-elected in 2004. His Senate District 12 has more than 300,000 registered voters, over 80 percent of whom are non-Hispanic whites. On paper, the district was one of the most competitive in the state, with 87,856 registered Republican voters, 88,417 registered Democratic voters, and 44,376 voters registered as independents or with third parties. In his most recent bid for re-election, Crist raised over $100,000, a princely sum considering he faced neither a primary election opponent nor a Democratic opponent in the general election.

As the contested 2000 presidential election made ever so clear, Florida is a battleground state. The Sunshine State has some 4.1 million registered Democrats and 3.7 million registered Republicans. Yet, due to the partisan way legislative districts are drawn in the state, little interparty competition develops when it comes to legislative elections. In 2006, only 6 of Florida's 20 Senate seats were contested by candidates from both major parties, and only 36 of the 120 House seats had both Republican and Democratic candidates.

The lack of interparty competition is not limited to Florida. Nationwide in 2006, over 30 percent of legislative contests had only one candidate on the ballot. Over two-thirds of the candidates running for the state legislature in South Carolina, Arkansas, and Georgia had no opposition.[1] National maps covered with red and blue states give a false impression of interparty competition in the states, as less party competition actually exists today in most states than when Zachary Taylor won the presidency in 1848.

OUTLINE

Introduction

Theorizing about Political Parties

Regulating Parties as Quasi-Public Entities

Party-in-the-Electorate

Party Organization

Party-in-Government

Parties Take the Initiative

Whither Third Parties?

Summary

Introduction

Political parties play a central role in the electoral process, governance, and policy making of the states. Two longtime observers of state politics, Sarah Morehouse and Malcolm Jewell, go so far as to say, "The single most important factor in state politics is the political party."[2] Not all parties at the state and local level, of course, are equally powerful. Parties come in all kinds of shapes, sizes, and political flavors, and their respective influence within a state varies widely. At their most rudimentary level, parties allow individuals to come together periodically to articulate a political viewpoint. Beyond aggregating and advancing citizen concerns, parties help to cultivate and nurture political leaders, mobilize citizens to vote, organize governments, and formulate public policy.[3] As rational actors, parties have a reflexive quality to their workings. Parties are shaped by other political institutions; in turn, they are able to shape and reform the political institutions under which they operate. In this chapter, we examine this dynamic, reflexive process by focusing on the functions and responsibilities of political parties.

Theorizing about Political Parties

Political parties serve multiple functions. Parties may be rightly understood as one of the principal agencies for "aggregating and mobilizing the interests of vast numbers of citizens, enhancing voters' capacity to hold public officials accountable, acting as agents of political socialization, and organizing the decision-making institutions of government."[4] Parties recruit candidates running for office, oversee the nominations of those candidates, and provide a durable link between citizens and their governments. Less clear is whether a party needs to be ideologically coherent or merely functional in order to truly be understood as a party.[5]

Responsible Party Model

Some scholars have viewed parties from a normative perspective, offering a prescriptive ideal of what parties ought to strive to become. According to this **responsible party model**, parties should be ideologically consistent, in that they should present to voters a clear platform and set of policies that are principled and distinctive. Voters are expected to choose a candidate based on whether or not they agree with the proposed programs and policies of that candidate's party. Once taking office, the candidate (and his or her party) is to be held responsible for implementing the party's program and policies. Edmund Burke, an Irish philosopher and a member of the British House of Commons, wrote in his 1770 political tract *Thoughts on the Present Discontents* that a "[p]arty is a body of men united, for promoting by their joint endeavors, the national interest, upon some particular principle in which they are all agreed."[6] For Burke, parties were distinguished by their unity and ideological purity (or lack thereof), their consistency, and their ability to provide for a "loyal opposition."[7]

Grounded in the belief that parties should promote the public's general interest, Burke's ideological definition of responsible parties seems at times far removed from the American context. Because of institutional constraints (as discussed in Chapter 3)—such as single-member, winner-take-all elections and direct and open primaries—the two major political parties tend to operate as "big tents," allowing considerable disagreement over their principles and policies in an effort to win elections. Still, the two major parties have retained ideological distinctiveness from one another since the 1850s.[8] Over the last 30 years, the Republican and Democratic parties at the national level increasingly seem to resemble European parties in terms of their internal coherence at both the mass and elite levels.[9]

Yet, if the Republican and Democratic parties strived to be ideologically pure and responsible, they would likely be relegated to the electoral sidelines, unable to build broad coalitions and be competitive. As we shall discuss later, third (or

COMPARISONS HELP US UNDERSTAND

FACTIONS WITHIN STATE PARTIES

All state parties have some internal divisions, although the internecine splits vary in degree. Some, such as those in California, Michigan, Minnesota, and Wisconsin, tend to be more ideologically consistent, paying considerable lip service to carrying out their party platforms once their members assume control of political office.[1] A great many state parties, though, are less ideologically coherent and have members who disagree widely on specific issues, be they social or economic. From Mississippi to Alaska, there are pro-choice and pro-life Democrats and Republicans who disagree fundamentally with other members of their respective parties on the issue of abortion. In socially conservative Utah, members of the Log Cabin Republicans support gay rights. Fiscally conservative "Blue Dog" Democrats in Louisiana and Mississippi support limited spending on welfare and lower taxes, and in Arkansas, "Yellow Dog Democrats" are such loyalists they will vote for a mangy yellow dog before voting for a Republican. In Colorado, California, Oregon, and Maine, there are sizeable numbers of Republicans who have libertarian streaks. These citizens readily vote in favor of ballot measures decriminalizing the use of marijuana for medicinal purposes, even though their Republican state parties officially oppose the policy.

Note

1. Sarah Morehouse and Malcolm Jewell, *State Politics, Parties, and Policy*, 2nd ed. (Boulder, Colo.: Rowman & Littlefield, 2003), 106. See also Richard Elling, "State Party Platforms and State Legislative Performance: A Comparative Analysis," *American Journal of Political Science* 23 (1979), 383–405.

minor) parties often have much more coherent and consistent principles and policies, but their candidates almost always fail to win office. Besides third parties, though, one would be hard-pressed to come up with examples of political parties in the American states that reflect Burke's normative ideal of responsible parties.

Functional Party Model

Whatever relevance Burke's ideological conception of party had for 18th-century England, it is clearly an inappropriate model for understanding the realities of American state parties. With the rarest of exceptions, American political parties (and their nominees) have not been known for their ideological purity. Although political parties have some established and agreed-upon principles and policies, these convictions may change over time. Indeed, it is sometimes the case that parties will pursue policies that run contrary to principles in order to *save* their

principles.[10] As we shall see, this should not necessarily be interpreted as the parties being hypocritical; rather, the parties, as rational actors, are being functionally responsible.

Instead of being ideologically coherent, it is quite rational at times for parties to try to broaden their coalitions in their search for the elusive median voter. After all, parties are self-interested organizations, striving to maximize votes for their candidates in order to win elections.[11] Emphasizing the pragmatic character of American parties, political scientist Leon Epstein offered a **functional party model,** defining parties as "any group, however loosely organized, seeking to elect governmental officeholders under a given label."[12] The functional definition captures the primary goal of parties in the United States: winning and maintaining control of political office. Although a party may be ideologically consistent and coherent, these are not prerequisites. From this perspective, the foremost goal of political parties at all levels—national, state, and local—is to wield political power.[13] As such, political parties are "institutions responding to changes and searching for roles."[14]

Lingering Anti-Party Sentiments

Writing over a half century ago, responsible party advocate E. E. Schattschneider argued that democratic governments could be governed by either special interests or parties, but he thought political parties were clearly superior political organizations. "Political parties created democracy," Schattschneider wrote with some hyperbole in 1942, and "democracy is unthinkable save in terms of parties."[15] Rule by parties, Schattschneider and other political scientists contend, allows for the public interest to prevail by encouraging the mobilization of majorities.[16]

Yet, although political parties are an essential component for democratic governance, they have been excoriated throughout American history. Many of the founders, for instance, viewed parties as nothing more than large factions driven by selfish motives that were destructive of the common good. In *Federalist Paper No. 10*, James Madison viewed political parties as majority factions that were evil and to be avoided if possible. Parties were not likely to promote the general interest; rather, they could be expected to promote the particular interests of a specific class of citizens. President George Washington had an even starker view of parties. In his farewell address in 1796, Washington chastised the growing "spirit of party," saying it would "distract" and "enfeeble the public administration."[17]

Why Parties?

As rational actors, political parties—regardless of their degree of ideological consistency or functional capacity—are essential for the exercise of democratic governance. Parties serve multiple functions, but nearly all of them are related to the individual ambition of politicians and the broader goal of obtaining and retaining political power.[18] In this sense, parties often

combine functional and responsible attributes. One of the main functions of parties is to regularize the "office-seeking ambition" of politicians. In other words, parties are essential players in the effort to increase the chances of a candidate winning office. Parties also function to help citizens overcome collective action barriers to mobilization. The American electoral system requires candidates for elective office to achieve broad-based electoral support in order to ensure they win a plurality of votes at the polls. Parties are the vehicles that can enable candidates to capture wide support. Finally, parties allow legislators to overcome collective action problems when voting on public policies. They help to routinize the decision making of governments, allowing officeholders to normalize the give-and-take of legislative policy making.

Regulating Parties as Quasi-Public Entities

Political parties are "quasi-public" entities, meaning that they are not only regulated by the states but also carry out official functions conferred upon them by the states. As such, they are more akin to public utilities than private associations.[19] Until the 1950s, for example, many Democratic parties in the South were permitted by state law to hold discriminatory "white-only" primaries that excluded blacks from participating in the party nomination process. These "Jim Crow" laws, which codified racial segregation far beyond electoral politics and were designed specifically to restrict black suffrage, included barriers to voting as poll taxes, literacy tests, and an array of complex voter registration laws.[20] In 1964 the 24th Amendment was ratified, outlawing the poll tax in federal elections. The next year, Congress enacted the Voting Rights Act, outlawing state election laws that discriminated against minorities, immigrants, and the poor.

Today, party registration law still vary greatly, including the openness of party primaries across the states and ballot access laws. Although federal law establishes that the voting age is 18 and over, that federal elections are held on the first Tuesday after the first Monday in November, that there may be no poll taxes or literacy tests to determine voter eligibility, and that all polling places must be accessible to people with disabilities, within these broad parameters, every state is permitted to establish its own set of laws that regulate voting and political party status.[21] As such, state regulations governing political parties differ considerably.

In a series of rulings, the U.S. Supreme Court provided broad contours of what is permissible when it comes to the rights of political parties and their members as well as the kinds of regulations the states may place on political parties.[22] In general, the high court has upheld the associational rights of the major parties, but it has also reaffirmed the rights of states to regulate state parties in the name of maintaining and preserving political stability.[23] Although hardly constitutive of a coherent jurisprudence, several important high court rulings concern the associational rights and state regulations of state political parties.[24]

Primaries and Caucuses

Parties have broad discretion in determining how candidates running on their party labels are to be nominated. By defining who may participate in their nomination process, the parties are essentially able to define who belongs as a party member. At the same time, state legislatures make the rules governing elections, including whether the state will have a primary election or a caucus in which the nominees running on party labels are determined. Primaries and caucuses are held weeks or months ahead of the general election to determine who will appear on the general election ballot. In a **direct primary** election, voters select one candidate affiliated with a political party for each elected office; the party nominees later face one another in a general election. In contrast to these partisan primaries, most local elections (as well as statewide elections in

Nebraska) are nonpartisan. In these contests, every voter receives the same primary ballot, voters do not have to be registered with a party to participate, and candidates' party affiliation is not listed on the ballot. The two candidates receiving the most votes win spots on the general election ballot. As discussed at greater length below, state laws and party rules regulate who may vote in primaries. Several types of direct primary elections are used: *closed, semiclosed, open, semiopen,* and *blanket.*

A few states use a **caucus,** or even a series of caucuses, to nominate candidates. At a caucus, party members informally meet, deliberate, and then cast votes for their preferred candidates. Party members not only discuss the candidates and the pressing issues but also elect delegates to the party's county conventions. These, in turn, elect delegates to the party's congressional and state conventions, which (in presidential election years) elect national convention delegates. In Iowa, for example, a caucus participant must be registered with a party as well as a resident of the precinct in which the caucus is being held (often in a school, a town hall, or even a private home). Iowa has no absentee voting, as the citizen must attend a caucus meeting to have his or her voice heard and counted. (Iowa allows all citizens to register, update their registration, and change their party registration on the night of a caucus.) Guests are permitted to attend a caucus, but they may not participate.

Closed and Open Primaries A **closed primary** system is one in which voters must register with a political party prior to Election Day and can only vote for candidates of the party for which they are registered. Independent or unaffiliated voters may not vote in a party's primary. In 1984, the Connecticut Republican Party challenged the state's closed primary system by adopting a party rule allowing independents—citizens not officially registered with any party—to participate in its party's primary elections. The Republican Party subsequently challenged the state's closed primary law in federal court, claiming that it barred individuals from entering into political association with the party. In *Tashjian v. Republican Party of Connecticut* (1986), the U.S. Supreme Court in a 5–4 decision ruled that a 1955 state law requiring voters who wished to participate in a party's primary to be a registered member of that party was unconstitutional.

Striking down the state's law as excessive, the court sided with the Republican Party, opening the way for the state to adopt an **open primary** system. In an open primary, voters are not required to register their party affiliation with the state and may freely and secretly choose the ballot of any party's primary in which they wish to vote. Some states use a **semiopen primary,** which permits registered voters to vote in any party's primary, although they must publicly declare on Election Day the party primary in which they choose to vote.

Despite the high court's 1984 *Tashjian* ruling requiring open primary systems if the state

parties so choose, many state parties have opted to keep their primaries closed. In 2005, the high court ruled in *Clingman v. Beaver* that Oklahoma's **semiclosed primary** law, which permits voting in a primary only by those who are registered with the party or who are registered as independents, was constitutional. In other words, Oklahoma may prohibit a voter who is registered with one party from voting in another party's primary.

Today, as Figure 5.1 displays, 26 states have closed or semiclosed primaries, 22 have open or semiopen systems, and two (Louisiana and Alaska) have a form of a blanket primary. A few states use a mix of open and closed primaries, as state parties have chosen for themselves different types of primary elections. It is not uncommon for states to change their primary systems. Up until 2007, West Virginia's Democratic primaries until recently

---

Figure 5.1

States with Closed Primaries, Open Primaries, and Nonpartisan Blanket Primaries

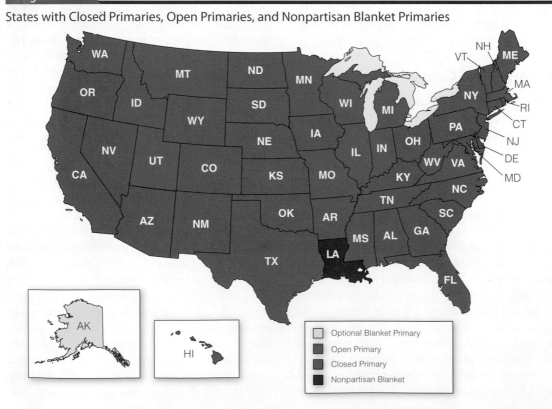

- ☐ Optional Blanket Primary
- ☐ Open Primary
- ☐ Closed Primary
- ■ Nonpartisan Blanket

INSTITUTIONS MATTER

ALASKA'S OPTIONAL BLANKET PRIMARY SYSTEM

The Alaska state legislature in 2001 adopted a restrictive closed primary system. In 2005, however, the Alaska Supreme Court invalidated the statute, ruling that only a blanket primary system would not contravene the state's constitutional guarantees of associational rights. As a result of the decision, Alaska now affords parties the option of holding the primary of their choosing. If two or more political parties decide to jointly hold a blanket primary, whereby the candidates from all the parties that have opted in will be on the ballot, they may do so. In contrast, a party may hold a closed primary. In 2006, as Figure 5.8 shows, the Democratic, Libertarian, Independence, and Green parties decided to hold a combined primary, allowing any registered voter (including Republicans) to vote for any of their candidates running for office. In contrast, the Alaska Republican Party opted to hold a semiclosed primary, allowing registered Republicans, as well as those who were registered as nonpartisans and those who were undeclared, to vote only for a slate of Republican candidates.

Figure 5.8

Alaska's 2006 Primary Election Ballot Choices

2006 Primary Election – Ballot Choices

There are three ballot types
Each Voter May Receive Only ONE Ballot Type

The party affiliation on the precinct register determines which candidate ballot a voter is eligible to vote.

Ballot Type	Political Party Candidates on Ballot	Who Can Vote This Ballot
Combined with **Ballot Measures**	Alaska Democratic Party Alaska Libertarian Party Alaskan Independence Party Green Party of Alaska	*Any registered voter* Party Affiliation Codes on Precinct Register: A – D – G – L – M – R – N – O – U – V
Republican with **Ballot Measures**	Alaska Republican Party	*Voters Registered as:* **Republican, Nonpartisan and Undeclared** Party Affiliation Codes on Precinct Register: R – U – N
Ballot Measures Only	No Candidates *This ballot is for voters who do not want to vote for any candidate*	*Any registered voter*

X01 (Rev. 5/30/06)

Source: Alaska Lieutenant Governor, http://www.gov.state.ak.us/ltgov/elections/forms/x01_06.pdf.

were closed, and Republican primaries were semiopen with independents allowed to cast ballots for GOP candidates. Now both parties have open primaries.

Blanket and Top-Two Primaries In 2000, the U.S. Supreme Court once again weighed in on the side of the associational rights of the major political parties. In *California Democratic Party v. Jones*, the high court struck down as unconstitutional a **top-two primary** system that had been approved by California voters in a 1996 ballot initiative. Modeled after Washington's old blanket primary system, which was created in 1935, California's proposed primary would have allowed all eligible voters, irrespective of their party affiliation, to vote in the primary for any candidate running on any party ticket. The triumphant candidates from each political party, including third-party candidates, would then square off in the general election. The Republican and Democratic state parties and two other minor parties argued that under the primary system—which replaced the state's closed primary system—the parties would lose control over their own nomination processes, which they claimed violated their First Amendment right of freedom of association. The Court struck down the state's blanket primary, ruling that California's law was "forcing political parties to associate with those who do not share their beliefs." After the ruling, the state legislature responded in 2000 by passing a modified closed primary system, permitting unaffiliated citizens to vote in a party's primary if the party so desired.

Citing the 2000 *Jones* decision as the controlling precedent, opponents of the blanket primary systems that were still in existence in Washington and Alaska immediately filed lawsuits asking the Court to invalidate their states' systems. In a series of rulings, the blanket primary systems in both states, which allowed voters to essentially split their primary ballots among candidates running on different party labels, were struck down. In Washington state, the legislature responded by passing a bill that created a top-two primary, whereby voters would be permitted to vote for any candidate in a primary election so long as the top two vote-getters advanced to the general election. Through a creative use of the veto pen, though, the outgoing Democratic governor Gary Locke scrapped the bill and replaced it with an open primary system.

Louisiana continues to use its unique **nonpartisan blanket primary** system. Louisiana's primaries are nonpartisan, with all candidates, regardless of their party, facing off in the same primary. A candidate wins the election outright if he or she wins more than 50 percent of the vote in the primary election. If no candidate wins a majority of votes in the primary, the top two candidates—irrespective of their party—then run against one another in the general election. Louisiana's primary system has enabled extremist candidates to qualify for the general election, even though they have combined for substantially less than 50 percent of the primary vote. In the 1991 gubernatorial election, Louisiana's blanket primary system received national attention when David Duke, the former head of the state's Ku Klux Klan and a Republican state legislator, qualified for the runoff election after a former governor (and the eventual general election winner), Edwin Edwards, failed to win 50 percent of the vote in the primary.

Presidential Party Nominations Numerous state legislatures have established special primary elections or caucuses in presidential election years in an effort to have more sway in determining who will be the parties' presidential nominees. States establish the date of their presidential caucuses or primaries, but the national parties ultimately determine whether the party delegates selected during these elections are valid.[25] For example, in 2007, the Florida legislature passed a law moving its presidential primary to January 29, 2008. The date conflicted with a Democratic National Committee's (DNC) rule that only four states—Iowa, New Hampshire, South Carolina, and Nevada—could hold binding presidential nominating contests prior to February 5. As a result, the DNC ruled that it would not recognize the results of Florida's Democratic early primary vote and would strip the state party of all its delegates to the 2008 Democratic National Convention in Denver. In the 2004 presidential campaign, twelve states were forced to eliminate their early presidential primaries due to partisan gamesmanship as well as budget cuts.[26]

The Effect of Primary Systems on Representation As should be evident, primaries vary with regard to how much voters are permitted to participate in the nomination process. The most restrictive form is the closed primary, where only previously registered party members may participate. New York, for example, requires a citizen to be registered with the state as a party member for a full year before being eligible to vote in a primary election. The semiclosed primary is not quite as restrictive, as independents are permitted to participate along with registered party members. With the open primary, any registered voter may vote in any party's primary on Election Day, although some require voters to temporarily declare a party on Election Day. Louisiana's nonpartisan blanket primary is the least restrictive system, with voters permitted to vote for any candidate running for office, irrespective of their party.

In theory, open primaries should encourage more participation among the electorate, as all voters, even independents (sometimes referred to as *unaffiliateds*), may cast a ballot in the election. The costs associated with voting are much less in blanket and open primary systems than in closed systems. Yet, analyses of voter turnout levels across states with open versus closed primary systems do not reveal any significant differences in rates, as the mobilization of citizens goes well beyond the particularized costs or benefits of an individual's decision to vote. Because open primaries diminish the control that parties and candidates have over who participates in the nomination process, parties and candidates may have less incentive to bolster turnout.[27]

Party Endorsements of Candidates

The U.S. Supreme Court has ruled that individuals are able to associate with a party of their choice. In *Eu v. San Francisco Democratic Committee* (1989), the Court struck down a California law that prohibited parties from officially endorsing or opposing candidates running in primary elections and forbade candidates running in primary elections from claiming that they were officially endorsed by their parties. The law also tightly regulated the internal governance of state parties, limiting the term of office for the state party central committee chair and requiring the chair to rotate between members living in northern and southern California. Members of the parties challenged the law in federal court on the grounds that it deprived them and the parties of their First Amendment rights, specifically the freedoms of speech and association. The court agreed, saying that the state legislature had no compelling state interest to burden the constitutional rights of the parties and their members. Despite the ruling, many state parties continue to abide by state regulations, satisfied with the status quo.[28] Roughly three-quarters of the states regulate the organizational structure of state parties, including how party leaders are to be selected and how their candidates are to be replaced should the need arise.

Party Fusion

States may prohibit the names of candidates running for political office from appearing more than once on a ballot, a practice known as **party fusion**. Fusion permits two or more parties to nominate the same candidate for office. The candidate's name appears on the ballot alongside the name of each party that cross-endorses him or her. In a 1997 ballot access case, *Timmons v. Twin Cities Area New Party*, the U.S. Supreme Court affirmed the regulatory power of state legislatures by affirming Minnesota's law banning fusion—the listing of a candidate on the ballot under two or more political parties. The court ruled 6–3 that the state's antifusion law was constitutional, as it did not severely burden the associational rights of the members of the New Party. In the words of the majority decision, the ruling upheld the right of the states to avoid "voter confusion," protect political stability in the state, and protect the integrity of the ballot by prohibiting candidates to be cross-listed as two or more parties' nominee for a given elective office. In his majority opinion, Chief Justice William Rehnquist concluded that state legislatures could choose to permit fusion but that "the Constitution does not require Minnesota, and the approximately 40 other States that do not permit fusion, to allow it."

During the late 19th century, party fusion was a regular feature of American electoral politics, especially in western and midwestern states. Issue-oriented third parties—such as the Greenback, Granger, Free Silver, and Populist parties—frequently cross-listed their candidates on the tickets of the weaker of the two major parties in the state. In the South, the Republican Party would occasionally temporarily fuse with third parties in an effort to derail the dominant Democratic Party.[29] Of the 10 states (Arkansas, Connecticut, Delaware, Idaho, Mississippi, New York, South Carolina, South Dakota, Utah, and Vermont) that allow party fusion, today parties in New York continue to use it with some frequency. The Conservative, Independence,

and Working Families parties in New York (see Figure 5.2) are usually not strong enough to have their candidates win when running against Republican or Democratic candidates. Instead, these minor parties routinely cross-endorse Republican or Democratic candidates running for office. If the cross-endorsed candidate wins, the minor party can claim that it had a hand in the victory—pointing to the votes cast for the candidate on its minor party label. Votes for the fused candidate also help the minor party retain its ballot access status.[30]

Party Ballot Access

States have been granted wide latitude by the U.S. Supreme Court to determine what parties and their candidates—from dog catchers to

---

Figure 5.2

New York Party Fusion Ballot, 2004

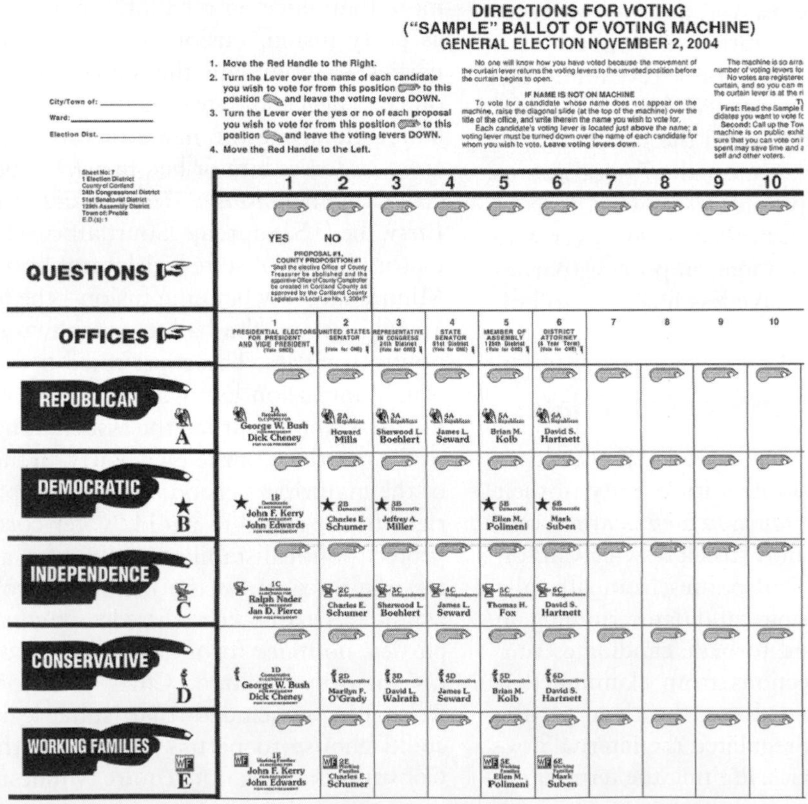

Source: Cortland County, New York, http://www.cortland-co.org/election/images/BallotSheets04/scan07.gif.

governors to the president—must do to qualify for the ballot. In some states, the rules are fairly restrictive; in others, they are less so. Democrats and Republicans are, by state law, usually given "major-party" status and are entitled to permanent space on the ballot. A minor party may have to collect a certain number of signatures or register some percentage of the state's voters with their minor party before being granted ballot access. Candidates wishing to run as independents in a general election or candidates running as the nominee of a new political party usually have to collect thousands of signatures in order to qualify for the ballot. In other states, candidates wishing to run for office need only pay a nominal filing fee. In Florida in 2000, 10 presidential candidates qualified for the election, which made designing the ballot layout (including Palm Beach County's infamous butterfly ballot) more complicated. In most states, parties typically retain their ballot access as long as one of their candidates collects a minimum percentage of votes cast in a state election.

During the 1950s, in the midst of the "Red Scare," many states made their ballot access laws more restrictive for third parties, as they feared members of the Communist Party might qualify for state ballots. The Supreme Court, in its 1968 decision *Williams v. Rhodes*, ruled that ballot access laws could be stricken if they were "invidiously discriminatory" and violated the 14th Amendment's Equal Protection Clause by giving the two major parties "a decided advantage over new parties." Three years later, though, the high court clarified that barriers to access for minor parties would have to be extremely high to be ruled unconstitutional. For example, the Court upheld state laws requiring third-party candidates to collect up to 5 percent of a state's registered voters—exceeding tens of thousands of signatures—to qualify for the ballot.[31]

Many states continue to have very onerous ballot qualification standards. Until 1939, for example, a Massachusetts law required only 1,000 signatures for a third-party candidate to qualify for the ballot. But the state legislature changed the law that year to require

third-party candidates to collect 3 percent of the previous gubernatorial vote—or more than 50,000 signatures. Although the legislature reduced the threshold to 2 percent of the last gubernatorial vote in 1973, only five third party candidates have qualified for the statewide ballot since the 1930s.[32] In the 1970s, Arkansas lawmakers required minor parties to collect signatures equal to 7 percent of votes cast in the last election in order to qualify for the ballot. The U.S. Supreme Court subsequently ruled the requirement could not exceed 5 percent. But it is still illegal in Arkansas for minor parties to nominate candidates by conventions. Not surprisingly, no third-party candidate for governor has ever reached the Arkansas ballot. In Virginia, candidates running as independents for statewide office are required to collect 10,000 signatures from registered voters to have their names placed on the ballot; at least 400 of those signatures must come from each of Virginia's congressional districts. In addition, three states (Nebraska, Oregon, and Texas) have primary screen-out laws. Citizens who vote in a partisan primary in these states are not permitted to sign a petition to qualify an independent candidate or a new party for the ballot. In West Virginia, registered Democrats and Republicans who sign petitions to qualify minor-party candidates on the ballot are prohibited from voting in their own parties' primaries.

Defending the Two-Party Duopoly

Despite some public sentiment in favor of shaking up the two-party system,[33] efforts by state lawmakers to keep new parties and independent candidates off the ballot have more often than not been upheld by the U.S. Supreme Court. Many of the high court's rulings have been tinged with strong normative overtones, with justices going out of their way to lavish praise upon the two-party system. Paying homage to the responsible party model, Justice Lewis Powell in his 1980 dissent in *Branti v. Finkel* celebrated how "[b]road based political parties supply an essential coherence and flexibility to the American political scene."

Similarly, Antonin Scalia opined in his dissent in *Rutan v. Republican Party of Illinois* (1990), "The stabilizing effects of such a [two-party] system are obvious." And Justice Sandra Day O'Connor wrote in her concurring opinion in *Davis v. Bandemer* (1986), "There can be little doubt that the emergence of a strong and stable two party system in this country has contributed enormously to sound and effective government." Because the Court has given wide discretion to the parties to regulate themselves and to the states to preserve order, states show considerable regulatory differences—from party nominations and pre-primary endorsements, to fusion, to ballot access. Each of these regulations has affected the strength of state parties and, in turn, has altered the representative nature of parties within the political process.[34]

Party-in-the-Electorate

Parties can be understood as tripartite social structures composed of three integrated components: party-in-the-electorate, party organization, and party-in-government.[35] Although somewhat limited and overly schematic, the three-pronged framework can serve as a heuristic, allowing us to isolate and appreciate the various dimensions of political parties.[36] We begin our discussion with *party-in-the-electorate,* which refers to ordinary citizens—eligible voters as well as nonvoters—who identify with and share some sense of loyalty to a particular party.

Partisan Identification

The strength of an individual's attachment to a political party is measured by **party identification** (PID). A person's PID usually forms early in adulthood, and is largely conditioned by one's family. Party identification is a genuine form of social identity that is affected in part by sociopsychological influences; a person is often initially drawn to a political party because of his or her sense of belonging and allegiance.[37] As people age, though, they often make retrospective and prospective cognitive evaluations (or *running tallies*) of how the parties are doing.[38] Because some people are continually adjusting their PID in response to political and economic change, evidence at the macro level reveals that the average PID in some states has been slowly changing.[39] For example, in the 1980s, many white Southerners who were ideologically conservative but still loyal to the Democratic Party began identifying more with the Republican Party. As a result, southern states began turning redder, as the party-in-the-electorate became more aligned with the GOP.

Political Ideology

Not all Democrats and Republicans have the same **political ideology** or a consistent and coherent belief system concerning the principles of political rule. When individual political ideologies are aggregated, political ideologies found across the states vary considerably. Cultural, economic, demographic, and sociological dissimilarities may lead states to have more liberal or more conservative electorates. Because national public opinion polls tend not to survey a representative number of respondents from all 50 states, there are relatively few direct measures of state-level political ideology. As such, scholars have tried to derive indirect measures of a state's political ideology by using election returns and interest groups' ratings of members of Congress from each state, by pooling data from newspaper public opinion polls, and by using data from national election surveys designed to study U.S. Senate races.[40] Regardless of the method, these studies show that southern states—such as Alabama, Arkansas, and Oklahoma—tend to be the most ideologically conservative, and northern states—such as Massachusetts, Maryland, and New York—tend to be the most liberal in the country.

Does a state's political ideology predict the kinds of public policies it adopts? Usually but not always. As discussed in Chapter 1, state policies tend to reflect the median ideological preferences of the states' citizens. However, Democratic-controlled legislatures, for example, tend to produce policies that are more conservative than their more liberal citizens.[41] The reason for this divergence between citizen ideology and public policy could be rational; parties often pursue public policies to win future elections rather than passing public policies that are reflective of their ideology.[42]

Are a State's Partisan Identification and Political Ideology Related?

A state's partisan identification leanings and its political ideology are not always *correlated,* or linked together. States populated with citizens having strong Republican ties—Utah, South Dakota, Idaho, and Kansas, for example—are not inhabited solely by citizens who are ideologically conservative. Some states with heavy Republican PID are actually less ideologically conservative than states with high percentages of Democratic identifiers. Likewise, several states with strong Democratic PID are considerably more ideologically conservative than states with high proportions of Republican identifiers. Only a functional understanding of political parties can accommodate the tremendous diversity of political ideology and partisanship found across the American states.

Disaggregating national-level surveys conducted between 1988 and 1992 to the state level, Barbara Norrander reported that a state's political ideology and PID were not always highly correlated. Using a scale of 1 to 5 (with lower scores indicating states that are more ideologically liberal and higher scores indicating those more ideologically conservative), she found that the mean ideological score across the states was 3.55, indicating the average state had a considerable conservative bent. Measuring a state's partisan identification with a scale of 0 to 6 (with lower scores signifying strong Democratic identification and higher scores signifying strong Republican identification), she found the mean score to be 2.95, indicating that the average state leaned Democratic. States more ideologically liberal are not necessarily more Democratic, and states more ideologically conservative are not necessarily more Re-

publican. Massachusetts, for instance, lived up to its reputation as being the most liberal state in the union according to Norrander's measure. However, seven states, including Oklahoma, a state ranked as the third-most conservative in the country, had stronger levels of Democratic PID than the Bay State. Two of the most conservative states—Arkansas and Alabama—did not even register in the top 30 of Republican-leaning states with respect to their PID.

From an institutional perspective, there are several reasons why a state's political ideology and partisanship are not always correlated. As mentioned in Chapter 3, states have differing registration laws, making it alternatively easier or more difficult for citizens to initially register with a political party or subsequently switch their party registration. Most states require voting-age citizens to register their party affiliation with the state at least 30 days prior to an election, although under the National Voter Registration Act passed by Congress in 1993, all states must allow voters to register to vote by mail and when applying for a driver's license. Nine states (Idaho, Iowa, Maine, Minnesota, Montana, New Hampshire, North Carolina, Wisconsin, and Wyoming) have same-day registration, allowing eligible citizens to register to vote on Election Day. North Dakota has no voter registration requirements; all voting-age citizens may cast ballots. These differences can affect partisan identification, irrespective of political ideology. Residents in states with strict registration laws, for example, might be more inclined to identify with a political party because they are required by state law to register with a party if they want to participate in the electoral process. Variations in state registration laws may also help to explain why the percentage of voters who are registered with a party in a state is not always a reliable indicator of the level of partisan identification within a state.

As we have seen, states also have different kinds of primary election laws. If a state has a closed primary, for example, only citizens who register with the state as members of the party may vote in primary elections when the party's nominee for political office is selected.

In states with closed primaries, as opposed to open primaries, citizens have a strong incentive to identify closely (and indeed register) with either the Democratic or Republican Party if they want to be full participants in the electoral process. As we detail later in the chapter, states also have varying levels of party competition. In states with low interparty competition, citizens may gravitate toward the more dominant of the two major parties in the state, shunning the perennial "loser" party. Finally, party organizational strength across the states varies considerably, which leads to differences in how state parties may be able to reach out to and mobilize the electorate.

Does Partisanship Affect Participation?

As we discussed in Chapter 3, some states and communities have higher turnout levels than others. From a party-in-the-electorate perspective, strong partisans—regardless of whether they are Republicans or Democrats—tend to vote more frequently than nonpartisans. But since the 1970s, turnout across all the states has steadily declined. Some scholars argue that this is due to a **partisan dealignment** in the electorate, as people increasingly consider themselves to be independents.[43] Others note that lower turnout is related to a decline in interparty competition,[44] with the parties achieving their policy objectives without mobilizing voters.[45] Several observers have suggested that the withering of the party-in-the-electorate is linked to the decline of state and local party organizations, as the parties have shifted away from mobilizing a broad array of voters, targeting instead only likely voters.[46]

Party Organization

Over the years, state and local party organizations have shown their adaptability by responding to changing regulatory and electoral conditions. In the early 1970s, state and local political parties—along with their national brethren—were often given up for dead because they were seen as dinosaurs of a bygone era. Today, most state and many local political parties are vibrant organizations, carrying out essential campaign activities, such as mobilizing voters and raising campaign funds in support of their candidates. *Party organization* refers to the network of elected and appointed party officials; paid staffers; national, state, and local committees; and volunteer workers.[47] Some political scientists have reduced the organizational role of parties to a single function—that of electing candidates. In today's "candidate-centered era," parties are designed primarily as "party-in-service" to candidates.[48]

The level of party organization across the 50 states varies considerably. State parties are typically composed of a state central committee, congressional district committees, county committees, and ward or precinct committees. The structure of state parties, though, can be far more complex. Figure 5.3 depicts the Byzantine organizational flowchart of the California Democratic Party. Each level of the state party has members who are either elected or appointed to their positions. Almost all party officials at the local level are volunteers, although most state parties now have permanent, paid staff at the central committee level.[49] Most state parties convene annual conventions that are attended by party delegates and the party's elected officials. Most states hold primaries to choose a party's nominee for the general election, but a few states use party conventions to vet and select party nominees.

At a minimum, if a party organization is to be successful, it must be able to overcome barriers to collective action. The organizational configuration a party selects, though, may be tight or loose. A functional definition of a political party accommodates variation in party organizations found across the country—from urban party machines, to well-financed and professionally staffed state party committees, to the underfinanced and disorganized bands of volunteers running some local party organizations. Recall that a functional definition

Figure 5.3

Organizational Structure of the California Democratic Party

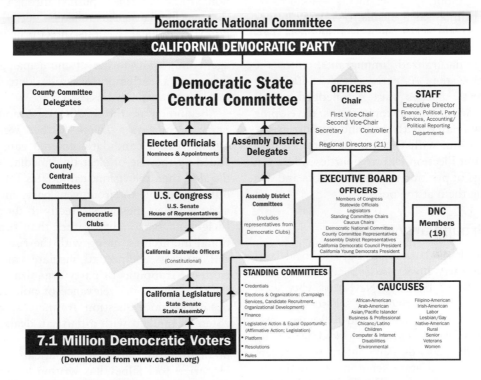

Source: California Democratic Party, http://www.kintera.org/site/pp.asp?c=fvLRK7O3E&b=33603.

of parties is not concerned with a party's organizational hierarchy but rather its preoccupation with contesting elections. As rational actors, then, state and local parties have been able to adapt their organizational structures to the changing regulatory and electoral environment, thereby ensuring their continued relevance.

Although there has been a shift over time to more candidate-centered campaigns in the American states, state parties have proven themselves to be quite resilient, mutating their structures to fit with the changing times.[50] Although state parties in the 50 states are nominally independent of one another and the national parties, there have been recent efforts to strengthen the ties between the national, state, and local parties as well as between the state parties.

Parties in the "Party Era"

During the mid-19th century, in the midst of the "Party era," state and local party organizations reigned supreme. They were far more powerful than the national parties. Forming coalitions to win elections, state and local parties responded to a rapidly expanding electorate. In New York in the 1820s, for example, the Democratic Party machine was known as the Albany Regency, which was controlled for a time by future U.S. President Martin Van Buren. The parties developed a **spoils system** whereby nonelective government positions were doled out to loyal supporters as **patronage appointments.** Through such appointments, state and especially local parties endeared themselves to their communities by offering jobs in the public sector in exchange for votes. The parties also garnished the pay of government workers and party supporters, requiring monthly "assessments"—akin to religious tithing—as a means for raising money for the party.[51] With such arrangements, parties helped to integrate citizens, many of them recently naturalized immigrants, into the political system. As early as the 1840s, state Democratic parties were full-fledged operations, holding annual conventions, developing their own party platforms, and mobilizing the party faithful with Get-out-the-Vote (GOTV) rallies. On Election Day, the parties were even in charge of printing their own ballots and distributing them at the polls.[52]

The Urban Party Machine

Working behind the scenes at the local level was the **party boss**. Bosses, such as William Marcy "Boss" Tweed of New York City, were often seen as unprincipled, self-serving, and corrupt. A chair maker and volunteer fireman, Boss Tweed gradually worked his way up through the party as a city alderman, U.S. representative, and state senator. Eventually, he came to rule Tammany Hall, the city's moniker for the Democratic Party political machine that emerged in the 1850s. In the 1860s and 1870s, under the guidance of Tweed, the party machine controlled virtually all the party's nominations for every office in not only the city but also the state. Quid pro quo financial arrangements were the norm, with the local party machine receiving payoffs from business interests in exchange for favorable legislation. Party bosses were handsomely compensated for their "honest graft." Tweed, for instance, was appointed as a director of the Erie Railroad in exchange for having the party push through legislation benefiting the company.

The Death and Rebirth of Party Organizations

For much of the 20th century, state and local political party organizations became a mere shadow of their former selves. During the Progressive Era, reformers intentionally weakened parties. In the late 1890s and early 1900s, nonpartisan reformers pushed through legislation—including the Australian (or secret) ballot, nonpartisan local elections, direct primaries for party nominations, and commission or manager-commission forms of municipal government—in an attempt to wrest control from local and state party bosses.

Beginning in the 1950s, state and local party organizations were further weakened by the rise of candidate-centered campaigns. Aided by the rise of electronic media, first radio and then television, candidates for public office were able to circumvent party machines and take their messages directly to the voters. Image and personality, rather than organizational hierarchies, along with the rise of special interests, helped to insulate candidates from the trappings of party organizations. By the late 1960s, the relevance of political parties came under question. An increase in nonvoters in tandem with a partisan dealignment in the electorate led some observers to write premature obituaries for political parties.[53] Historian Joel Silbey has written how parties today, when compared with their 19th-century predecessors, "can hardly be seen as the vigorous, robust, and meaningful players within the nation's political system that they once were."[54]

In the late 1970s, parties reemerged from their prolonged slumber. Many state and local party organizations—especially Republican state parties—began to strengthen themselves organizationally, expanding their bureaucratic and programmatic capacities. Research conducted during the 1970s and 1980s highlighted the institutionalization of state parties, depicting the integration of new party professionals and the bureaucratization of what were once often parochial, unsophisticated organizations. Most state parties during the period began to establish permanent headquarters and hire specialized staff to raise contributions and direct campaigns.[55] The parties transformed themselves from provincial party machines into service vendors ready to recruit,

Chris Livingston/Getty Images

Democratic National Committee chairman Howard Dean energizes Florida Democrats at the state party convention in 2006.

train, and support candidates in their run for office.[56] Although the labor-intensive parties of the 19th century are in the past, state and local party organizations have reinvigorated themselves as service providers. By the turn of the millennium, scholars generally agreed that state political parties were as strong and fiscally sound as they were anytime in recent history.[57]

Measuring Party Organizational Strength

There are several comparative studies of the 50 state organizations that measure party organizational strength. Unfortunately, none of these measures fully captures the organizational strength of state parties. In the 1980s, David Mayhew advanced a measure of traditional party organization (TPO) that classified state parties as being more or less conforming to a 19th-century ideal type of party control.[58] Mayhew's measure assessed the autonomy, durability, and hierarchy of the party organization, taking into consideration the degree to which it relied on material incentives to maintain and stimulate partisan loyalty and participation and to control the nominations and campaigns of their candidates. Sarah Morehouse argues that state party organizational strength varies considerably, but she finds states with stronger party systems tend to have greater legislative support for the agenda put forth by the governor.[59]

Unfortunately, the methodologies scholars have utilized to measure party organizational strength have varied widely, leading to some inconsistent findings.[60] Many of the studies gauging state party organization have measured the number of staff and other party assets. Party organizations, of course, are much more than their staff. They can also be understood as a complex web of political consultants and campaign specialists and elected officials in national, state, and local offices as well as their respective staff. A recent study finds that party organization strength influences the ideological tenor of the party, with more top-down, hierarchical structures being more moderate, and those with more open structures being more polarized.[61]

State Party Financing

As with any organization, the capacity and relative power of state party organizations are directly affected by their money-raising prowess. Considerable variation in state campaign finance laws exists across the states when it comes to restricting contributions and expenditures of political parties. A dozen states (Arkansas, Florida, Georgia, Idaho, Illinois, Maine, Missouri, Nebraska, New Mexico, Oregon, Utah, and Virginia) allow unlimited contributions from virtually any source to be made to state political parties. Roughly the same number have similarly lax contribution regulations, except that they prohibit donations from corporations and labor unions; eight other states prohibit contributions from corporate entities but allow union donations.[62] Alabama, for instance, allows individuals, political action committees (PACs), labor unions, and national party committees to contribute unlimited sums to the state political parties but limits corporations to donations of only $500 per election. Campaign finance laws in Arizona and Texas are similar to Alabama's, except that unions may not make contributions to state parties with money drawn from their own treasuries. Connecticut, on the other hand, allows individuals to contribute up to $5,000 per year to state parties, but it completely bans corporations and unions from making contributions from their treasuries, permitting them only to make limited PAC contributions.

Many of these state campaign finance regulations are new. Between 1990 and 2000, over 30 states adopted campaign finance laws that directly or indirectly affected state parties. Going through state legislatures, but also circumventing politicians who were the beneficiaries of lax campaign finance restrictions, good government public interest groups placed more than two dozen initiatives on statewide ballots dealing with campaign finance issues during the decade.

The capacity of state parties to raise campaign contributions ranges tremendously. The disparity across states in party fundraising has less to do with the organizational strength of the Democratic or Republican Party within a state and more to do with the kind of campaign finance laws that are on the books. Contribution levels are largely contingent on two factors: state campaign finance regulations and the competitiveness of state and federal elections. State parties raised a total of $723 million (combined federal and state accounts) in the 2003–04 election cycle. Table 5.1 provides the contribution and expenditures totals for the major state parties in all 50 states for the most recent election cycle. A handful of Democratic and Republican state parties raked in more than $20 million during the cycle, including the New Jersey, California, and Florida Democratic parties and the New York, Ohio, Pennsylvania, California, and Florida Repub-

lican parties. The Republican Party of Florida topped all other state parties in total receipts for the two-year period, with a haul of $50 million. Over half of the state parties went into debt during the cycle, with California Democrats and the Ohio GOP each spending over $10 million more than they raised.[63]

The Impact of the Bipartisan Campaign Reform Act of 2002 on State Party Organization

On December 10, 2003, the U.S. Supreme Court upheld the bulk of the Bipartisan Campaign Reform Act of 2002 (BCRA), also known as McCain-Feingold. In *McConnell v. Federal Election Commission*,[64] the Court let stand nearly all of BCRA's Title I, which banned parties from using **soft money** for "federal election activity."[65] In banning soft money—which before BCRA included six- and seven-figure contributions from individuals and the treasuries of companies and labor unions—the law not only altered the strategies and activities of the national political parties but also by extension those of state parties. With state parties no longer permitted to solicit soft money for use in federal campaigns or receive transfers of soft money from the national parties, some observers questioned whether state parties would be able to survive under BCRA.

Until the 2004 election cycle, many state parties were the beneficiaries of—and, in the eyes of some, dependent upon—soft money.[66] Under the Federal Elections Campaign Act of 1971 (FECA), the previous federal campaign finance regime, not only did state parties raise sizeable amounts of soft money for federal campaigns on their own, but they were also the beneficiaries of soft money transfers from the national parties to be used for electoral activities. In order to take advantage of financial incentives under FECA that permitted hard-soft dollar splits on coordinated spending between the national and state parties, the national parties often exchanged soft dollars that they raised for more valuable hard

Table 5.1

State Party Contributions and Expenditures, Combined State and Federal Accounts—2004 Election Cycle

State	Contributions		Expenditures	
	Democrats	Republicans	Democrats	Republicans
Alabama	$2,228,607	$1,150,753	$1,828,730	$2,062,699
Alaska	$4,266,936	$1,244,623	$4,747,438	$2,202,951
Arizona	$7,868,469	$5,847,710	$8,569,642	$3,855,934
Arkansas	$2,943,251	$1,637,127	$3,395,048	$1,444,130
California	$24,871,666	$29,493,501	$37,230,327	$28,517,361
Colorado	$5,740,980	$4,317,091	$5,127,778	$5,570,696
Connecticut	$1,688,552	$2,342,066	$1,939,843	$2,832,104
Delaware	$2,001,607	$1,651,491	$1,905,091	$1,582,113
Florida	$21,372,089	$50,920,376	$28,826,259	$39,999,847
Georgia	$6,228,851	$7,696,974	$6,147,029	$10,162,738
Hawaii	$1,038,010	$2,252,666	$1,120,111	$2,393,955
Idaho	$513,331	$747,980	$369,266	$638,171
Illinois	$12,267,926	$13,012,475	$12,627,788	$13,633,786
Indiana	$13,483,330	$12,968,497	$14,818,593	$13,625,773
Iowa	$11,653,703	$8,440,876	$7,821,188	$7,542,518
Kansas	$2,559,692	$618,137	$2,753,500	$756,729
Kentucky	$3,290,669	$5,955,769	$4,298,292	$6,663,057
Louisiana	$7,342,891	$4,158,138	$6,883,952	$4,313,624
Maine	$3,294,134	$2,829,943	$3,157,699	$3,071,361
Maryland	$1,346,095	$2,558,404	$1,758,031	$2,752,634
Massachusetts	$2,466,860	$5,044,456	$2,309,896	$5,358,005
Michigan	$16,038,229	$18,886,710	$11,451,416	$12,513,758
Minnesota	$10,857,185	$8,014,688	$12,050,827	$12,951,060
Mississippi	$450,550	$4,000,027	$593,053	$3,810,117
Missouri	$19,218,962	$17,969,958	$21,195,442	$18,019,525
Montana	$2,502,121	$984,479	$3,407,429	$1,167,296
Nebraska	$1,079,490	$1,369,485	$612,295	$1,147,048
New Hampshire	$4,882,164	$2,696,147	$5,645,423	$1,550,671
New Jersey	$28,347,364	$10,564,637	$22,890,214	$11,018,319
New Mexico	$3,878,665	$2,095,993	$3,415,008	$2,385,103
New York	$16,184,698	$22,870,163	$10,982,433	$17,394,286
North Carolina	$14,567,938	$3,109,030	$14,695,828	$5,256,104
North Dakota	$2,812,329	$668,196	$2,063,507	$1,907,874
Ohio	$15,964,691	$25,302,904	$19,429,790	$35,178,063
Oklahoma	$4,940,918	$2,433,460	$5,312,208	$3,212,378
Oregon	$7,434,057	$6,301,120	$7,691,021	$4,540,139

State	Contributions		Expenditures	
	Democrats	Republicans	Democrats	Republicans
Pennsylvania	$18,219,464	$26,163,070	$17,693,603	$22,958,551
Rhode Island	$257,139	$373,166	$435,943	$362,673
South Carolina	$3,022,456	$2,905,922	$2,962,866	$3,341,184
South Dakota	$2,524,836	$4,220,940	$2,282,389	$6,451,900
Tennessee	$6,645,989	$3,250,576	$8,362,960	$4,797,546
Texas	$3,863,263	$6,701,574	$4,002,354	$10,863,930
Utah	$721,803	$1,296,841	$925,775	$1,636,490
Vermont	$1,174,131	$446,210	$985,615	$563,407
Virginia	$6,500,605	$4,412,126	$5,440,565	$5,902,805
Washington	$17,350,707	$9,962,844	$18,203,345	$9,459,027
West Virginia	$1,823,046	$2,329,813	$1,931,433	$2,050,387
Wisconsin	$9,080,806	$8,458,743	$11,655,924	$6,881,854
Wyoming	$251,800	$1,486,756	$236,278	$1,164,552

Source: Center for Public Integrity, http://www.publicintegrity.org/partylines/default.aspx.

dollars raised by state parties. With BCRA's passage, there was good reason to anticipate dire consequences for state parties. Some observers thought the national parties would be able to offset their loss of outlawed soft dollars by raising more hard dollars, and others questioned whether state parties would be able to respond in the post-BCRA era.[67] Yet, BCRA's impact on state and local parties has been minimal, as most of them have been able to adapt to the changes in federal law.[68]

Party-in-Government

Party-in-government refers to candidates running for elective office as well as officeholders at the local, state, and national levels who are elected under the party label. With the exception of Nebraska (because of its nonpartisan, unicameral legislature), Republicans and Democrats dominate the governmental structure of every state. As we discuss in Chapter 7, political parties structure state government, especially state legislatures. Of course, because of winner-take-all elections and restrictive ballot access laws, the two-party dominance of state legislatures and statewide elected officials

exaggerates the level of popular support for the two parties in the electorate. Due to these structural barriers, it is difficult for citizens who are displeased with the two-party system to articulate their dissatisfaction with the status quo.[69]

Party Competition in State Legislatures

Although political parties may be inevitable, their mere existence is not sufficient to guarantee a democratic form of governance. Rather, competition between the parties is said to be essential for democracies to function. Competition forces the parties to become more internally cohesive and disciplined, giving citizens a real choice at the polls.[70] "Democracy," Schattschneider once claimed, "is not to be found in parties but between the parties."[71]

Aggregate election results suggest that competition in state legislatures among the two main political parties is at an all-time high. Going into the 2006 general election, out of the 7,382 state legislative seats, Democrats held exactly one more legislative seat than the Republicans. It's hard to get any closer than that.

Figure 5.4

Partisan Control of State Legislatures, 2007

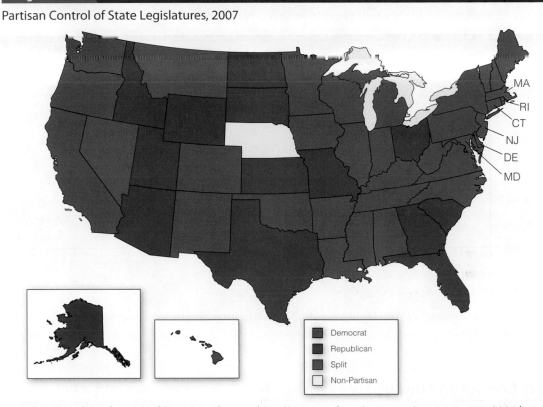

Source: National Conference of State Legislatures, http://www.ncsl.org/statevote/statevotemaps2006.htm#.

Figure 5.4 displays legislative party control in 2007 of the 49 states with partisan legislatures (Nebraska, with its nonpartisan legislature, is included). The map is somewhat deceptive, as states vary considerably with respect to the degree of party control. In addition, some states historically have had intense two-party competition, whereas others have had a tradition of single-party dominance. Many of the social and economic conditions as well as numerous institutional rules that helped to ensure one-party dominance have eroded or have been eliminated, making two-party competition more common throughout the country. This is particularly true in the South, as the Republican Party over the past 30 years has become more competitive, and even dominant, in some states. Today, two-party competition exists in every state, although to different degrees.

Between 1950 and 2000, a clear majority of legislative seats across the states were held by Democrats; by 2000, the partisan split in legislative seats had become dead, even between the parties. Figure 5.5 shows the overall trend over time in the number of legislative seats held by the two major parties between 1938 and 2006. Of the 5,411 state house seats in the 49 states (Nebraska does not have a house) in 2006, Democrats held 2,975 seats (55 percent), Republicans held 2,417 seats (44 percent), and independents and third parties held but 15 seats (with the balance being temporarily vacant). Of the 1,922 state senate seats (which excludes Nebraska's 49 nonpartisan seats), Democrats held a slim advantage of 1,010 seats (53 percent) to 907 seats (47 percent) for the Republicans, with just 3 seats held by independents and third-party candidates.[72]

Figure 5.5

Republican and Democratic Share of Legislative Seats, 1938–2000

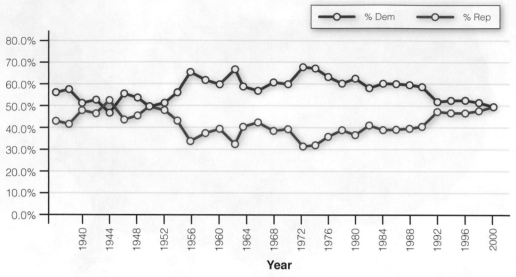

Source: National Conference of State Legislatures, http://www.ncsl.org/programs/legman/elect/demshare2000.htm.

Party Control and Interparty Competition

There are numerous ways to measure the party control and interparty competition of a state's party system. One of the most popular methods was first developed by Austin Ranney and has become known as the Ranney Index.[73] The index averages four measures of party competition: the proportion of the gubernatorial vote won, the proportions of the state senate and state house seats won, and the proportion of time (over a given period) the governorship and the two legislative chambers are controlled by a party. Ranney's measure of state party control ranges from 0 (complete Republican control) to 100 (complete Democratic control), and his measure of interparty competition ranges from 50 (no party competition) to 100 (a perfectly competitive two-party system).

Table 5.2 provides the party control and interparty competition figures over the period of 1980–2000 using the Ranney Index.

In terms of party control, 19 states over the 20-year period had solid Democratic control, and another 12 leaned Democratic. In contrast, there were only eight solidly Republican states, with another 10 that leaned Republican. The most Democratic state during this period—in terms of the control of the governor's office and the state legislature—was Maryland (with a score of 80.8), followed closely by Arkansas and Hawaii. Utah, with a score of 25.1, was by far the most Republican state, with South Dakota and Idaho also solidly in the hands of the GOP.

Ranney's interparty competition scores give us a sense of where the battles between the two major parties were taking place over this time period. The states with the highest scores—Delaware (98.5), followed closely by Wisconsin, Michigan, and New York—had intense interparty competition. Maryland, with a score of 69.2 and dominated by the Democratic Party, was by far the least competitive state over the time frame. Utah, with the strongest

Table 5.2

Ranney Indices of State Party Control and Two-Party Competition, 1980–2000

State	State Party Control, 1980–2000	State Two-Party Competition, 1980–2000
Utah	25.1	75.1
South Dakota	27.2	77.2
Idaho	30.8	80.8
Kansas	33.1	83.1
New Hampshire	33.5	83.5
Wyoming	35.0	85
Arizona	35.2	85.2
North Dakota	37.9	87.9
Colorado	40.9	94
Pennsylvania	43.9	93.9
Montana	44.1	94.1
Ohio	44.1	94.1
Indiana	44.2	94.2
New Jersey	45.7	95.7
Alaska	46.5	96.5
Iowa	46.9	96.9
Michigan	48.0	98
Illinois	48.3	98.3
Delaware	51.5	98.5
Wisconsin	52.0	98
New York	52.3	97.7
Vermont	53.9	96.1
Oregon	54.2	95.8
Maine	54.9	95.1
Connecticut	57.7	92.3
Nevada	57.7	92.3
Florida	57.7	92.3
Minnesota	59.2	90.8
Washington	59.4	90.6
California	59.5	90.5
Texas	60.7	89.3
Tennessee	61.6	88.4
New Mexico	62.1	87.9
Missouri	62.2	87.4
Virginia	62.2	87.8
South Carolina	62.6	*87.4*
Oklahoma	66.4	83.6
North Carolina	67.2	82.8
Alabama	72.6	77.4
Kentucky	72.9	77.1
Massachusetts	73.4	76.6
Rhode Island	74.9	75.1
West Virginia	75.4	74.6
Mississippi	75.8	74.2
Louisiana	76.5	73.5
Georgia	77.7	72.3
Hawaii	78.7	71.3
Arkansas	79.2	70.8
Maryland	80.8	69.2
Mean	55.6	86.7

Source: Sarah Morehouse and Malcolm Jewell, *State Politics, Parties, and Policy,* 2nd ed. (Boulder, Colo.: Rowman & Littlefield, 2003), Table 4.1.

Note: State party control ranges from 0 (complete Republican control) to 100 (complete Democratic control); interparty competition ranges from 50 (no party competition) to 100 (a perfectly competitive two-party system).

Republican Party control score of any state, interestingly had a higher interparty competition score (75.1) than seven states controlled by the Democrats.

Increasing Interparty Competition

Since the 1970s, across a range of indicators, there has been a gradual increase in interparty competition in the American states. Much of this increase has occurred in the South, where there has been a wholesale transformation of solid Democratic Party control giving way to the rise of the Republican Party. Between 1980 and 2000, Democratic Party control declined precipitously as the 20th century came to a close. When comparing the averages of the last five years with the first five years of the period, 40 states shifted from being less Democratic to being more Republican, and nearly all the states that were classified as Republican became even stronger under GOP control.[74] Figure 5.6 provides visual evidence of the level of interparty competition across the states.[75]

Why Interparty Competition Matters

State governments produce different kinds of public policies depending on the dynamics of party strength and interparty competition. Evidence shows that heightened interparty competition leads to public policies that are more representative of the whole population of a state rather than just the elites. In his classic work, *Southern Politics in the State and Nation,* V. O. Key argued that the lack of party competition in southern states from the 1880s

through the 1950s enabled the "haves" in society to run roughshod over the "have-nots," as the dominant Democratic Party had no fear of reprisal at the polls. Key argues that because they were unlikely to be defeated at the next election, the majority southern Democrats did not have to respond to the concerns and needs of all the people residing in their states. Others have formally tested Key's proposition that lack of party competition leads to worse redistributive policy outcomes, finding some support.[76] More recently, as interparty competition has increased across the country, scholars have found that increased party competition in a state tends to lead to the passage by state legislatures of more liberal public policies. Specifically, Democratic-controlled legislatures in states with tough electoral competition from Republicans tend to pass more liberal

Figure 5.6

Interparty Competition, 1999–2003

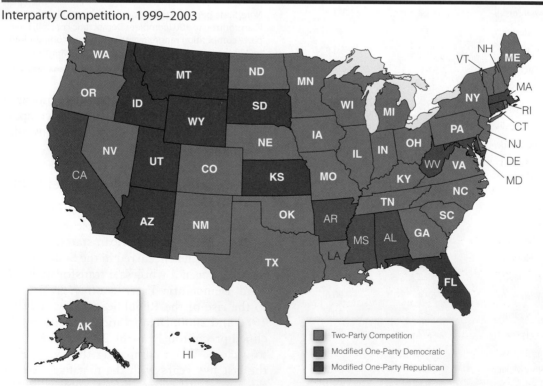

Legend:
- Two-Party Competition
- Modified One-Party Democratic
- Modified One-Party Republican

Source: John Bibby and Thomas Holbrook, "Parties and Elections," in *Politics in the American States,* 8th ed., eds. Virginia Gray and Russell Hanson (Washington, D.C.: CQ Press, 2004).

public policies, whereas the reverse holds for Republican-controlled state legislatures facing stiff Democratic electoral challenges.[77]

Evidence reveals that heightened interparty competition leads to greater levels of participation by citizens. General election voter turnout in the 11 southern states from 1960 to 1986 averaged less than 40 percent, well below the national average. With the decline of the Democratic Party's lock on state government and the advent of greater interparty competition, average turnout among these states increased to nearly 43 percent between 1990 and 1996. Comparing the two periods, Alabama had an 8 point increase, and Louisiana experienced a double-digit jump in turnout.[78]

Parties Take the Initiative

In the two dozen American states that permit it, direct democracy has traditionally been used by citizen groups to challenge the power of parties. In particular, the initiative, whereby citizens collect signatures to place a measure on the ballot for fellow citizens to consider, was used by anti-party forces during the Progressive Era to weaken the organizational autonomy of parties, most notably the control of parties over their candidate nominations. In the 1980s, though, state political parties began using the initiative process to help advance their candidates running for office. Although the mechanisms of direct democracy were originally intended to allow citizens to circumvent unresponsive state legislatures, the parties understand that placing ballot measures can help their candidates win office.

Ballot measures can help candidates distinguish themselves from their rivals, exploit wedge issues, drive up turnout, and raise and spend unlimited soft money. Ballot measures can also be used to drain the resources of opposing groups or parties.[79] For example, in 1996, the California Republican Party advocated the passage of Proposition 209, the California Civil Rights Initiative. Disavowing his long-standing support for affirmative action, Republican governor Pete Wilson helped rescue the floundering ballot initiative campaign to end affirmative action. The state Republican Party provided funding to the proponents of the measure with the hope that it would splinter Democratic support for President Bill Clinton's reelection bid. In a teleconference call with Newt Gingrich, Wilson claimed that Proposition 209 was "a partisan issue ... that works strongly to our advantage [and] has every bit the potential to make a critical difference" to defeat Clinton.[80] At Wilson's behest, the California Republican Party then contributed $997,034 to the Yes on Prop. 209 campaign, with the Senate Republican Majority Committee contributing an additional $90,000.[81]

Although party organizations are increasingly playing an important role in ballot campaigns when they have an opportunity to use an issue to their partisan advantage, parties do not ultimately control the direct democracy agenda. Compared to the amount of money contributed directly by corporations, unions, and even wealthy individuals, parties tend to be bit players. Parties rarely provide the majority of funding to campaigns for or against an initiative, and they rarely sponsor their own popular initiatives. Yet, directly and indirectly, parties have played a substantial role in funding some highly salient initiative campaigns, including ballot measures on term limits, paycheck protection, illegal immigration, affirmative action, and minimum wage.

Whither Third Parties?

Nearly every state is dominated by a two-party system. Over 99 percent of state legislative seats are held by either Democrats or Republicans, with third-party organizations in most states virtually nonexistent. Although some scholars point to the historical or cultural bias for having two dominant parties in the states, the primary reason for the two-party duopoly is institutional. There are many constraints that limit the possible success of third parties. Some of these barriers are constitutional, such as the single-member district electoral systems used in most states. Other hurdles are statutory, such as ballot access restrictions, which are often very onerous for third parties and their candidates.[82]

Third parties at the state and local levels have not always been weak. The adoption in most states of the *Australian ballot* (or *secret ballot*) in the late 19th century initially gave a boost to third parties. The Australian ballot placed governments—rather than the parties themselves—in charge of printing ballots and administrating elections, making voting a private rather than a public act. The secret ballot diminished the power of the party bosses, who could no longer directly monitor the vote choices of citizens and also made split-ticket voting possible. Furthermore, many states during this period switched from a **party-column ballot** (sometimes known as the *Indiana ballot*), which listed all the candidates running for separate offices by their political party and had the effect of strengthening the parties, to an **office-block ballot,** which made split-ticket voting easier, thereby weakening the major parties.[83] Today, 17 states still use party-column ballots, which encourage straight-party voting (see Figure 5.7). With the push of a single button, voters are able to support all the candidates running for office of a given party.[84]

Third parties, such as the Libertarian, Green, and Natural Law parties, have been hampered by both the direct primary system and ballot access laws adopted by the states. The direct primary system of nominating congressional and state officials has hurt the prowess of state-level third parties in the states. Because party bosses no longer overtly control the nomination processes of the two major parties, Republican and Democratic party dissidents are able to act as "outsiders" while remaining within the two parties. As such, the major parties are able to absorb dissidents and broader protest movements, which in the past often led to the rise of third parties.

Ballot access laws in the states ensure that the two major parties are guaranteed a place on the ballot, whereas minor parties—if they do not win a certain percentage of the vote in a previous election—are required to circu-

late petitions to gather signatures in order to qualify for the ballot. In some states, this barrier to access is relatively easy to overcome. Colorado lawmakers in 1998 made it easier for minor parties to win recognition as actual political parties and not just as political organizations; all a third party needs to be recognized is to have 1,000 registrants and run at least 10 candidates for statewide or legislative seats. If a minor party fails to meet this requirement, it must either collect 10,000 signatures on petitions or have one of its candidates win at least 5 percent of a statewide vote. Other states, such as Illinois, have much more stringent ballot access requirements for minor parties. Third-party candidates have three months to collect valid signatures from 5 percent of those who voted in the last election for the office for which they are running in order to qualify for the ballot.

Third parties and their candidates face a host of psychological barriers too. At the individual level, citizens who vote regularly (likely voters) tend to have a strong allegiance to one of the two major parties. In addition, citizens who are alienated from the political system, and who therefore might be likely suspects to vote for a third-party candidate, are much less likely to vote. Because of the winner-take-all nature of most state and local elections, third parties often have a difficult time convincing contributors to give them money. Because candidates running on third-party tickets have little chance of winning, the media tend not to cover them. It becomes a self-fulfilling prophecy that because their candidates rarely win, third parties have a difficult time recruiting qualified candidates to run on their ticket.

Every blue moon, of course, third-party candidates do win elective office at the state or local level. A study of voting patterns for presidential candidates found three factors have motivated citizens to vote for third-party candidates: majority party deterioration, an influx of new voters with weak allegiance to the two major parties, and, most importantly, attractive third-party candidates who present viable alternatives to major nominees.[85] The

Figure 5.7

Party-Column and Office-Block Ballots

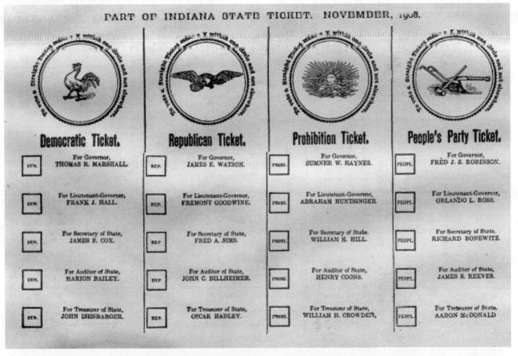

Source: Alex Peterman, *Elements of Civil Government*. New York: American Book Company, 1916, http://www.gutenberg.org/files/15018/15018-h/images/img-187.jpg and http://www.gutenberg.org/files/15018/15018-h/images/img-186.jpg.

REFORM CAN HAPPEN

THIRD-PARTY CANDIDATES SPOILING FOR A FIGHT

In 2006, voters in 27 of the 36 states with gubernatorial contests were able to cast a vote for a third-party candidate; in nine states, however, only Republican and Democratic gubernatorial candidates were on the ballot. Third-party and independent gubernatorial candidates not only face structural barriers such as ballot access restrictions but are also often excluded from public forums and debates, which can cost them valuable name recognition and fundraising opportunities. In 2006, Garrett Michael Hayes, the Libertarian Party's long-shot candidate for governor in Georgia, was permitted to join a debate with the Republican incumbent, Governor Sonny Perdue, and his Democratic challenger, Lieutenant Governor Mark Taylor. Hayes ended up winning less than 4 percent of the vote in the general election. Yet, his tally, paltry by most standards, was the most any minor-party gubernatorial candidate running in the state had earned since 1902, when the People's Party candidate won 6.4 percent of the vote in a two-man race. In 1998, former professional wrestler Jesse "The Body" Ventura, running as a Reform Party candidate, was invited to spar with the Democratic and Republican nominees in two televised debates. Ventura's solid performance in the debates gave his campaign a shot in the arm, especially among young voters, and he went on to win the election with 37 percent of the vote.

Minnesota Historical Society

same factors are often in place at the state level. Since 1930, eight third-party and independent candidates have been elected governor, including four since 1990 (Alaska independent Walter J. Hickel, Connecticut independent Lowell P. Weicker Jr., Maine independent Angus S. King Jr., and Minnesota Reform Party Jesse Ventura).

Summary

Regardless of whether they are understood as responsible or functional organizations, the two major political parties are essential players in state politics and governance. From primary systems to ballot access laws, parties help to structure the electoral and governing environments in states, which in turn affect the parties. The partisan identification and political ideology of a state's electorate, which are not always synonymous, help to shape the organization and the governance strategies of the parties. The strength of state parties is ever-shifting in terms of their electoral, organizational, and governance strength, with considerable differences across the states. As we shall see in the following chapter, the balance of power between political parties and interest groups varies across the states and even within states over time. Sometimes, it seems as though interest groups are subservient to parties; at other times, the relationship appears to be reversed.

Key Terms

Bipartisan Campaign Reform Act of 2002

Caucus

Closed primary

Direct primary

Functional party model

Nonpartisan blanket primary

Office-block ballot

Open primary

Partisan dealignment

Party boss

Party-column ballot

Party fusion

Party identification

Patronage appointments

Responsible party model

Semiclosed primary

Semiopen primary

Soft money

Spoils system

Top-two primary

Suggested Readings

Aldrich, John H. 1995. *Why parties?* The origin and transformation of party politics in America. Chicago: University of Chicago Press.

Bibby, John F., and Thomas M. Holbrook. 2004. Parties and elections. In *Politics in the American states: A comparative analysis*, 8th ed., eds. Virginia Gray and Russell L. Hanson. Washington, DC: CQ Press.

Cotter, Cornelius P., James L. Gibson, John F. Bibby, and Robert J. Huckshorn. 1984. *Party organizations in American politics*. New Brunswick, NJ: Eagleton Institute of Politics, Rutgers University.

Morehouse, Sarah, and Malcolm Jewell. 2003. *State politics, parties, and policy*, 2nd ed. Boulder, CO: Rowman & Littlefield.

Websites

Ballot Access News (http://www.ballot-access.org): A treasure trove of information on state ballot access laws, primary systems, and barriers to third parties.

Politics 1 (http://www.politics1.com/parties.htm): Provides background information and links to all the political parties that are active in the United States.

Project Vote-Smart (http://www.vote-smart.org): A nonprofit organization that provides a wealth of information on all candidates running for state and federal office.

Third Party News (http://www.thirdpartynews.net): Provides up-to-date links to recent media stories on third parties at the state and national levels.

6

AP Photo/Phil Coale

Interest Groups

Representing the American Dream

OUTLINE

Introduction

Understanding Interest Groups

Interest Groups and Their Members

Interest Group Techniques

The Dynamics of State Interest Group Systems

Summary

"We represent the American dream. That's why we win these things. It's about housing [but] the other stuff helps." The "other stuff," according to Mike Toalson, the chief lobbyist for the Home Builders Association of Virginia, is the extensive campaign contributions and gifts his group has lavished on members of the Virginia General Assembly. Over the past decade, his association, with its 5,400 dues-paying members and its powerful political action committee (PAC) known as Build-PAC, has pumped more than $1 million into the coffers of the 14 Senate incumbents who sit on the Local Government Committee and the 22 House members who sit on the Counties, Cities and Towns Committee. The association has been an equal-opportunity donor, contributing $715,000 to Republican and $650,000 to Democratic committee members. Democratic delegate Franklin Hall has raked in more than $145,000 from the home builders during his 30-plus-year career in the legislature. Several other members have received over $100,000 from building and construction PACs during their tenures in office. Only one member of the House committee—Republican delegate Robert Marshall, an ardent opponent of sprawl—has never taken a penny from the association.

Although limiting suburban sprawl was one of the key campaign planks of Democrat Timothy Kaine when he was elected governor in 2005, most observers of Virginia's legislature are doubtful that any new slow-growth bills will advance out of committee in the coming years. The contributions and lobbying prowess of the Home Builders Association have bought the group considerable access to key members of the Virginia General Assembly, virtually guaranteeing that bills limiting development or regulating sprawl will die in committee. Delegate Marshall, who sponsored the governor's slow-growth bills in 2006, refers somewhat ruefully to his own committee as "a funeral pyre for all those bills."[1]

Introduction

Interest groups are often portrayed in the media as detriments to the common good or general welfare. "The popular perception," according to one longtime observer of state politics, "is that interest groups are a cancer spreading unchecked throughout the body politic, making it gradually weaker, until they eventually kill it."[2] Yet, organized interests, like political parties, play an indispensable role in state politics. Documenting widespread voluntary organizations in the American states in the 1830s, French observer Alexis de Tocqueville noted, "In democratic countries knowledge of how to combine is the mother of all other forms of knowledge. . . . If men are to remain civilized or become civilized, the art of association must develop and improve."[3] Not only do voluntary associations—what we today call *interest groups*—help protect the interests of those who join them, but also, as Tocqueville pointed out, belonging to an organization cultivated the democratic values and capacities of individuals and enriched communities.

As we shall see, interest groups are essential components of the democratic process. They serve a basic function of aggregating different points of view and pushing policy agendas in the public sphere. By linking the public to elected officials, interest groups encourage individuals to participate in state and local affairs, allowing their voices to be heard. Without a collective voice, citizens would have relatively little direct power over their elected officials. Casting ballots, after all, happens infrequently, every two years or so. Most people have limited access to their elected officials; few have the cachet to be able to pick up a phone and talk directly to their governor or state legislator. If individuals are to be heard and represented by elected officials, they require a vehicle to collectively convey their concerns. As countervailing forces, interest groups can apply pressure on public officials, educating them about the issues. They can push for the creation of new public policies, urge the defeat of existing programs, or argue for the maintenance of the status quo. They can even serve as watchdogs, monitoring government programs and sounding a public alarm if they uncover inefficient or mismanaged programs or corruption.

Of course, interest groups do not always promote the values and desires of the public interest; regularly, they attempt to promote their own agendas and sway public officials. Some groups have more clout—some might say too much—in state and local politics, influencing who governs.[4] It will also become apparent to you that interest groups are not randomly distributed throughout society but reflect an inherent upper-class bias, with corporate interests and wealthier individuals having greater representation in state and community interest group systems.[5]

After defining *interest groups* and placing them within the broader framework of a pluralist system, we investigate in this chapter how interest groups are organized and maintained, what roles they play in state politics, and why states have different types of interest groups systems. How do interest groups form, and how are they able to sustain themselves? What types of activities, besides lobbying, do interest groups engage in? Why do some states have larger interest group systems than other states, and why are some interest group systems more diverse? Perhaps most importantly, we assess whether the structure of the interest group system is biased, which might make state and local governments less responsive to the public interest. As political institutions, then, interest groups are able to alter the political environment and public policies of states and communities.

Understanding Interest Groups

Some political observers warn that rule by special interests leads to government dominated by selfish, narrow, anti-majoritarian organizations.

Others argue that interest groups represent a broad swath of interests, leading to a counterbalancing of various issues and viewpoints. Regardless of which side is correct, interest groups try to aggregate a narrow set of preferences and concentrate them as specific demands. Exploiting the cracks of our federalist system and the separation of legislative, executive, and judicial powers existing at all governmental levels, interest groups have multiple points of entry into the political system when trying to shape public policies.

Defining Interest Groups

What are interest groups, and how do they differ from merely having an interest? As you might expect, interest groups come in all shapes and sizes, advancing a seemingly infinite number of political causes. Nearly every one of you will belong to at least one—if not several—interest groups during your lifetime. An **interest group** is a formally organized body of individuals, organizations, or enterprises that shares common goals and joins in a collective attempt to influence the electoral and policy-making processes. Simply put, an interest group is any organization that attempts to influence the electoral process or governmental policy making. Unlike political parties, interest groups do not nominate or run a slate of candidates for political office and do not take over the reins of government. Many interest groups are heavily involved in the electoral process; others focus on lobbying elected officials and policy makers.

If we are to adhere strictly to this definition, "farmers," for example, would not constitute an interest group. Because different farmers have different interests, they fail to meet the definitional standard of sharing common goals. For example, dairy farmers in Wisconsin have interests that are quite dissimilar from those of alfalfa, soybean, and corn growers in Iowa and Illinois or even other dairy farmers in California and Vermont. Wisconsin dairy farmers want to keep down the cost of the feed for their herd, prevent California milk producers from expanding their agribusiness operations, and ensure a fair milk-pricing system. Some may want to increase state and federal subsidies to set aside land for conservation easements protecting wetlands; limit price supports for small, organic dairies in Vermont; and even allow the injection of bovine growth hormone into their cows to increase milk production. Indeed, there are even several competing interest groups representing milk producers in Wisconsin, including the National Milk Producers Federation, the Dairy Farmers of America, the Wisconsin Dairy Business Association, and the State Dairyman's Association. Nationally, there are hundreds of organizations representing the interests of farmers, from the American Farm Bureau, to the Grange, to the Cattlemen's Association, to the National Pork Producers Council. It is important to keep in mind that an *interest* is categorically different from an *organization* or a *group*. Individuals may (and often do) share common concerns with one another without ever belonging to a group.

Types of Interest Groups

The universe of interest groups is not limited to *membership organizations*, or groups of like-minded individuals sharing common social, economic, or political goals joining together to advance them. Membership organizations bring together individuals—such as the myriad farmer organizations mentioned above—to pursue their collective goals. Some well-known membership organizations with an active presence in the states include the Chamber of Commerce, the Sierra Club, the National Rifle Association, the American Federation of Teachers, Common Cause, and the American Association for Justice (formerly known as the Association of Trial Lawyers of America).

In addition to membership organizations, the definition also includes associations. Associations do not have individuals as members; rather, their members are composed of individual businesses, unions, or even other associations from the public and private spheres. The

Texas Petroleum Marketers and Convenience Store Association, the Michigan Beer and Wine Wholesalers, and the Association of Washington Business are all examples of associations, which are also known as *peak associations*.

Finally, under this broad definition of interest groups, *enterprises*—from corporate and family-owned banks to hospitals to insurance companies to colleges and universities—are also included. Enterprises are not membership-based and do not have individuals as members. Employees of an enterprise are usually not involved or even consulted when it pursues a policy or electoral outcome. Publicly traded corporations, for example, do not need to obtain shareholder approval before pursuing political and electoral goals. As such, an enterprise is permitted to support issues and candidates that may be at odds with the preferences of its employees or shareholders.

Madison's *Federalist No. 10*

Interest groups are not new. Although the term did not become part of the political vernacular until the late 19th century, interest groups are rooted in the fabric of American political life and were heavily involved in the founding of the nation. Interest groups, or what Founder James Madison called "minority factions" in his classic essay, *Federalist Paper No. 10*, are inevitable in a free society. The causes of both majority and minority factions, Madison argued, are "sown into the nature of man." Although a "necessary evil," Madison realized that factions were essential to liberty. If citizens lacked the ability to form factions, they could potentially be tyrannized by government, squandering their fundamental liberties in the process. For Madison, the solution, then, was creating an institutional framework of checks and balances to control the baneful effects of factions.[6]

Pluralist Theory

An acceptance of minority factions—what today some might call *interest groups*—is central to the concept of pluralism. **Pluralism** assumes

that conflict is at the heart of politics and accepts that a diversity of interests will lead to consensual outcomes through the tug-and-pull of discussion and debate. In theory, the pluralist framework suggests that broad-based, public-regarding interests seeking the expansion or preservation of the **public good** are able to countervail and compete with private sector interests seeking narrow, concentrated benefits. Writing in 1951, David Truman expanded on Madison, arguing that humans are naturally predisposed to creating and participating in groups. Once formed, some groups not only exert power over other groups, keeping each other in check, but also are able to exert power over their own members. Because individuals have many, heterogeneous interests, most people belong to several groups. A stabilizing equilibrium among the competing interests gradually emerges over time, with various interests canceling out one another. Furthermore, even if a group has yet to form, there exist **potential interests** that are represented by the shared attitudes among individuals. These potential interests are adequately heard by elected officials, according to Truman, because they advance views that are widely held in society and reflect the attitudes of most citizens. Perhaps somewhat unbelievably, Truman went so far as to argue that individuals with few formal groups in the 1950s—such as African Americans working on plantations owned by white Southerners in the Mississippi Delta—were afforded representation by the pluralist interest group system, as established groups would represent the workers' interests on their behalf.[7]

Critiques of Pluralism

Pluralist theory is not without its critics. Over the years, scholars have pointed out that some of the assumptions regarding the formation of interest groups under the theory of pluralism are questionable. How innate and apparent for individuals is the "knowledge of how to combine," as Tocqueville observed, and is it as easy or natural as pluralists generally assume? Does everyone have an equal voice in the pluralist system? Do all potential interests eventually become heard? Do the various interests in a pluralist system really counterbalance one another?

Some critics of the Madisonian pluralist framework have focused on the transactions between interest organizations and their membership as well as government officials.[8] Among other things, these transactional theorists argue that a system of interest group competition, whether or not intended so, advantages economic interests, placing their narrow interests over those of the collective good. E. E. Schattschneider, for one, argued that powerful interest groups are able to privatize conflict so that other interests are limited in their ability to become involved in the policy-making process. The pressure group system contains an inherent bias, transactionalists such as Schattschneider claim, as it only represents interests that are organized. Public interests—those that are shared by and benefit the community because of the nonexclusive nature of the benefits being sought—are at a disadvantage when they go up against private interests that are exclusive and adverse to the rights of others.

Interest groups pressing for private gain, of course, try to rationalize their interests, calling them public interests ("What's good for GM is good for the country" was a common slogan in the 1950s), but public interests are often unorganized and cannot compete well against organized private interests. Contra Truman, Schattschneider did not think group organization is inherent, permanent, or inevitable; being an interest is not merely a stage of development in becoming a group. Rather, the pressure group system is limited to those groups that are private and that are organized. As a result, Schattschneider concluded, "The flaw in the pluralist heaven is that the heavenly chorus sings with a strong upper-class accent," in that the pluralist system has a **mobilization of bias** benefiting private, organized interests. The universe of interest groups, for Schattschneider, does not reflect all potential interests whose voices are not heard.[9]

Others have gone even further in their critiques of pluralism. Charles Lindblom contended that economic interest groups have a structural advantage in regard to politicians in market economies. For Lindblom, business has a "privileged position," in that its private decisions can hurt citizens and government officials with "automatic recoil" punishments. A business's decision to relocate or lay off workers can threaten the economic stability of a state or local government. If an automobile manufacturer in Michigan announces plans to move its operations to Mexico, the plant closing will likely increase unemployment in the community, prompt other businesses to also move, and discourage economic investment in the area. Using its threat of exit, business is able to indirectly limit the ability of governmental officials to regulate economic interests. Local and state officials are compelled to provide financial inducements—essentially, pay a ransom—to keep businesses from fleeing. Thus, for Lindblom, policy making is structurally constrained, or imprisoned, by the ability of certain interest groups to manipulate the market system.[10]

If critics such as Schattschneider and Lindblom are correct—that not all interests can be organized and some are structurally more advantaged than others—then it is questionable whether the pluralist system can effectively represent all interests equally. Interestingly, Madison himself had intimated in his *Federalist No. 10* essay that not all interests in society were equally represented nor were factions in society randomly distributed across the population. Madison noted that the "unequal distribution of property" has led to a persistent division in society: "Those who hold and those who are without property," Madison wrote, "have ever formed distinct interests in society."[11] These different classes of people would gravitate together, joining into factions to articulate their concerns. Because the distribution of interests participating in the interest group system is uneven and "far from isomorphic with the distribution of interests in society," for-profit and business organizations are likely to dominate.[12]

Interest Groups and Their Members

Why do people join interest groups, and how do they maintain themselves organizationally? Scholars have taken two very different approaches—one grounded in social dynamics and group theory and the other in micro-level economics—in an effort to gain some leverage on these questions.

How Do Interest Groups Form?

In the 1950s, Truman, who defended interest group pluralism, advanced what is known as **disturbance theory**. Focusing on macro-level shifts that cause groups to emerge in response to a change in the status quo, Truman argued that voluntary associations would form naturally out of the desire of humans to satisfy their needs. Various interests, including even potential interests, would galvanize collectively, according to Truman, when their common interests were marginalized or threatened. When macro-level societal or environmental disturbances in society occur—such as changes in demographic shifts, changes in the economy, advances in technology, or crises or societal disruptions, such as those resulting from plagues and disease, war, or even natural disasters like hurricanes or earthquakes—new patterns of interaction are created. With such occurrences, nascent groups will emerge in response to the change in the status quo. The resulting new groups help restore the larger "social equilibrium" of the interest group system. For Truman, then, it was rational for individuals to voluntarily join groups to further their own goals and interests.[13]

Other social scientists were not so sure about the natural proclivity of individuals to voluntarily join groups. For some, disturbance theory seemed too easy. Problematizing the logic of collective action, economist Mancur Olson turned his attention to micro-level, transactional reasons why an individual may—or may not—choose to join a group. Olson began by tackling the **free-rider problem;** that is, the assumption that individuals will try to benefit from public goods without paying for them. Contra Truman, Olson contended that there are many costs associated with an individual joining a group. If given a choice, rational actors would generally not join groups, choosing instead to benefit from the actions of the groups without bearing any of the attendant costs.[14]

Flipping many of the assumptions of pluralism on its head, Olson pointed out that individuals usually join groups for three reasons: peer pressure, coercion, or if they receive some type of selective benefit. By keeping itself small, a group can exert peer pressure on potential free-riders, embarrassing them to join the group. When small, it is easy for a group to determine who is benefiting from its actions without bearing the costs of membership. Individuals, too, have an easier way of calculating the costs and benefits of becoming a member when a group is small. People might also join groups when they are coerced to do so. For example: say you just graduated from law school and want to become a practicing attorney in the State of North Carolina. You first must pass the state bar exam. Once you do, you must pay annual dues to the North Carolina State Bar and complete mandatory continuing legal education course requirements every year.

For some, an important incentive to join a group is to receive a **selective benefit** that is only provided to members of the group. For example, some retirees join the American Association of Retired Persons (AARP) for the various benefits the association provides to its 30 million–plus members, such as discounts on group health insurance, lower rates on hotels and car rentals, or price-reduced tickets to the theater and the movies. Like Truman's macro-level perspective, Olson's rational choice micro-level framework does not provide a complete picture of group activity. Some people, of course, decide to join groups even if no overt peer pressure, coercion, or selective benefits exist. We do not necessarily think any worse of these people—call them altruistic if you will—but Olson's rational choice framework sees them largely as acting irrationally by not taking advantage of free-ridership.

How Are Interest Groups Maintained?

The theories advanced by Truman and Olson are still widely relied upon when explaining group membership, although they have been modified over the years. For example, some scholars have attempted to flesh out Olson's rational choice framework by adding to his subcategory of selective benefits additional reasons why people may join groups. Not only do groups provide material incentives to attract and retain members, but many also offer purposive and solidarity benefits to their prospective and current members.[15] The increase in the number of interest groups may also be due to the rise of *entrepreneurs*, people who drive dynamic political change by making personal sacrifices in order to get a group up and running. After all, selective benefits—whatever they may consist of—cannot be given to members of a group until the organization actually comes into existence. Furthermore, it may be the case that societal disturbances do not naturally beget new organizations.[16] Many of Truman's potential interests, especially those in the public interest, emerge and are maintained only because they are the beneficiaries of a generous patron. As government expands its reaches into various policy domains, many existing organizations, business enterprises, and foundations, and even some governmental agencies themselves, have used their wealth to create organizations to respond in kind. Rather than drawing from a membership base, private foundations such as the Ford, MacArthur, or Scaife foundations provide sustenance grants to groups that in turn advocate a progressive or conservative agenda.[17] Many of the groups that are beneficiaries of such largess do not have members. Instead, they are often centralized and oligarchic, focusing their energies on shaping the public debate in states and communities.

Who Joins Interest Groups?

As was certainly true during the founding, not all interests are equally represented in a state's interest group system. Individuals with higher incomes, those possessing more education, and those holding more professional jobs tend to belong to interest groups more than others. Drawing on survey data from more than 15,000 respondents from the late 1980s, a team of political scientists examined who was more likely to join groups. Beyond the obvious finding that not all individuals participate in interest groups at the same rates—some individuals have more resources (such as time and money) and more natural inclination to become engaged in civic life than others—they find that many people are never asked to participate in a group. Others are frequently recruited and mobilized to participate in interest groups. The study finds that an individual's education and income levels are the best predictors of who is recruited to join a group in political action. Groups, when trying to attract new members, tend to look to those with personal financial resources. Half of surveyed poor respondents said they never receive mass mailings soliciting them to join a group. In contrast, only 12 percent of wealthy respondents say they never receive solicitations in the mail. Agreeing with Schattschneider, the authors suggest that the structure of the interest group system possesses an inherent bias, as groups systematically direct their recruitment efforts toward wealthier, more educated individuals.[18]

Interest Group Techniques

In their concerted effort to represent their constituencies, interest groups use different tactics to shape public policies and elections. What do interest groups do, how do their techniques differ, and which groups are most active at the state and local levels? From classic insider techniques, such as lobbying policy makers, to outsider techniques, such as issue advocacy,

REFORM CAN HAPPEN

In 2005, both chambers of the New Mexico State Legislature passed with unanimous support a bill creating the New Mexico Housing Trust Fund (HTF). Democratic governor Bill Richardson signed the bill into law on April 4, 2005. The HTF, for which $10 million was appropriated from the state capital outlay fund, is run by the New Mexico Mortgage Finance Authority. The authority is providing competitive grants to state, local, and tribal organizations that are making investments in housing for persons of low and moderate income.

The establishment of the HTF was a huge victory for New Mexico's nonprofit community, which had lobbied tirelessly for the legislation. Joining forces in the Housing Trust Fund Coalition, which led the grassroots lobbying campaign, were over 150 organizations from New Mexico's nonprofit sector, including faith, labor, advocacy, and community groups. Some of the coalition members included the Community Action Agency of Southern New Mexico, the Enterprise Foundation, Jubilee Housing, the Lutheran Office of Governmental Ministry—New Mexico, the New Mexico Conference of Churches, the New Mexico Coalition to End Homelessness, the New Mexico Human Needs Coordinating Council, and the New Mexico Mortgage Finance Authority. The coalition's field campaign included phone calls, signed postcards, and letters mailed to state legislators as well as public presentations and testimony (including personal stories) given at legislative committee hearings. With the passage of the New Mexico Housing Trust Fund Act, the state joined 36 others that have created their own housing trust funds.[1]

Notes

1. New Mexico Human Needs Coordinating Council, "The State Housing Trust Fund," January 2007, http://www.hncc.org/issues/display.php?ID=22

electioneering, and litigation, interest groups are increasingly using multiple strategies to maximize their effectiveness.[19]

Although interest groups do not typically engage in every type of activity, there are many common patterns across the states and across interests. Table 6.1 details various insider and outsider techniques that some 301 state-level organizations surveyed in three states (California, South Carolina, and Wisconsin) used in the mid-1990s to shape public policy. Nearly all state-level interest organizations report using insider techniques, such as lobbying state legislators, testifying at legislative hearings, contacting government officials, helping to draft legislation, and meeting with government officials. Some outsider tactics are also reported, including grassroots campaigns to mobilize supporters, letter-writing campaigns, and having influential constituents contact elected officials. Less than half report they contribute money to candidates, and still fewer say they work on campaigns or

endorse candidates. Two of every five organizations claim they use litigation as a strategy, but only one in five runs issue ads or engages in protest activities.[20] Although activities of interest groups operating at the local level are similar, because many community-based groups lack necessary resources, they tend to use more reactive—as opposed to proactive—strategies when trying to influence public policy.[21]

Lobbying

Lobbying is an integral part of the state and local policy-making process, as it is the systematic effort to influence public policy by pressuring governmental officials to make decisions that comport with the interests of the group pursuing the desired action. The advocacy community in every state capital now consists of hundreds or even thousands of people being paid to alter public policy. The growth of the lobbying industry is indicative of its importance. As one

Table 6.1

Percentage of Interest Groups Using Various Insider and Outsider Techniques

Insider and Outsider Techniques	% of Groups Using Technique (n = 301)
Testifying at legislative hearings	99
Contacting government officials directly to present point of view	97
Alerting state legislators to the effects of a bill in their districts	94
Entering into coalitions with other groups	93
Having influential constituents contact legislator's office	92
Helping to draft legislation	88
Mounting grassroots lobbying efforts	86
Attempting to shape implementation of policies	85
Consulting with government officials to plan legislative strategy	84
Shaping government's agenda by raising new issues and calling attention to previously ignored problems	83
Inspiring letter-writing or telegram campaigns	83
Helping to draft regulations, rules, or guidelines	81
Engaging in informal contacts with officials	81
Serving on advisory commissions and boards	76
Talking to media	74
Making monetary contributions to candidates	45
Attempting to influence appointment to public office	42
Filing suit or otherwise engaging in litigation	40
Doing favors for officials who need assistance	36
Working on an election campaign	29
Endorsing candidates	24
Running advertisements in media about position	21
Engaging in protests or demonstrations	21

Source: Anthony Nownes and Patricia Freeman, "Interest Group Activity in the States," *Journal of Politics* 60 (1998): 86–112, table 2.

keen observer of state legislatures notes: "Any group that can be touched by state government cannot afford to be without representation. If groups do not realize the need for a lobbyist at the outset, they soon learn their lesson."[22] This was certainly the case regarding Native American tribes. Since the passage of the Indian Gaming Regulatory Act in 1988, which opened the way for casino-style gambling on tribal lands, the lobbying efforts of Indian tribes have skyrocketed, as they have used their newfound wealth to pursue traditional insider strategies.[23] As with other groups, the lobbying efforts of the tribes have helped ensure their collective voice is heard by state and local policy makers.

It should come as no surprise to you that lobbying is big business. In 2004, nearly $1 billion was spent on lobbying activities in the 42 states that require lobbying expenditure reports. In some states, lobbyists—not citizens—have become known sardonically as the "True Constituency."[24]

Lobbyists and lawmakers crowd the "Brass Rail" outside the Illinois House of Representatives chambers at the Illinois State Capitol in Springfield, Illinois. While angry citizens were pleading for legislative help in 2007 because of soaring electric rates, dozens of lobbyists, many with key connections to decision-makers, worked with Ameren and ComEd to fight a rate rollback and freeze.

What Do Lobbyists Do? Lobbyists try to influence policy making by marshaling information and communicating it to policy makers.[25] Lobbyists regularly monitor pending legislation, communicating directly with policy makers and their staff about the potential substantive and political impacts of policy choices. Lobbyists need to know not only how but also when to communicate information and to whom. In addition to meeting with policy makers, lobbyists provide information to officials about issues and give testimony before committee hearings. In states with less professional legislatures, elected officials often do not have the resources to stay informed on every issue, so they take cues from lobbyists. Lobbyists even help draft legislation.

In states with professional legislatures, lobbyists are still heavily relied upon by state legislators. When asked by a fellow state senator

during a committee hearing to explain a provision of a bill he was sponsoring, Majority Whip J. D. Alexander, with no sense of shame, beseeched a Florida Chamber of Commerce lobbyist to answer the question. Having the lobbyist answer the question made perfect sense to Alexander, as lawyers for the Florida Chamber of Commerce had drafted the legislation. Testimony provided by lobbyists, of course, is heavily biased, despite claims from lobbyists that they are simply providing impartial, objective information.

The general lobbying strategy of most interest groups is to use professional advocates, whether employed full time by the group or on a contractual basis, to meet with policy makers, help them with their policy and political concerns, and develop relationships with them beyond the immediate issue. To be effective, lobbyists need to consider the receptivity of policy makers to the sort of information the group the lobbyist represents wants to convey For a policy maker to accept a lobbyist's argument on an issue, the lobbyist—and the group or firm the lobbyist represents—must have not only access to but also credibility with lawmakers and policy makers. One surefire way lobbyists have traditionally enhanced the receptivity of public officials to their arguments has been by developing long-term working relationships with them.[26] The reputation of a lobbyist is a cherished resource and is essential for the lobbyist to gain access on behalf of the group he or she represents. Developing such a relationship enhances both the access and credibility of the group, making it more likely that the policy maker will believe and act upon the group's argument when it is presented to him or her.

Types of Lobbyists Lobbying may be conducted by in-house, contract, government, or voluntary lobbyists. Roughly 40 percent of all the lobbying done in state capitals is conducted by **in-house lobbyists,** with individuals who are employees of a membership group, association, or institution representing their own organization. The Kentucky Distillers' Association, the Montana Mining Association, the Texas Association of Business, the California Nations Indian Gaming Association, the Iowa Corn Growers Association, and the Nevada State AFL-CIO all use in-house lobbyists to maintain a foot in the doors of state lawmakers and policy makers. As part of their job, executive directors, public relations officers, and lawyers often serve as in-house lobbyists for their organizations. Most in-house lawyers have extensive experience working in the area in which they are doing the lobbying. According to one survey of interest group activity in the states, roughly 75 percent of in-house lobbyists are male.[27]

In contrast, **contract lobbyists** work either independently or for a lobbying firm. They typically work for multiple clients and charge their clients an hourly fee. Many contract lobbyists—who are predominantly male—are former legislators, elected or appointed state

officials, or staff. Contract lobbyist extraordinaire Frank L. "Pancho" Hays (who sold his Colorado lobbying firm Hays Hays and Wilson in 2003 but remains a registered lobbyist) was legendary in Denver for his self-effacing, ever-professional demeanor. The son of a former lieutenant governor, Hays represented business interests as diverse as the Denver Broncos professional football team, tobacco giant Philip Morris, the Wine and Spirits Wholesalers of Colorado, Colorado Ski Country USA, the Colorado Association of Realtors, and the Cherry Creek School District. Roughly 20 percent of the lobbying corps in state capitals is composed of contract lobbyists, depending on the professionalization of the state legislature.[28]

Lobbying done by government employees, who are sometimes referred to euphemistically as *governmental relations personnel* or *legislative liaisons,* is also quite common. Roughly 30 percent of all lobbyists in the states are government lobbyists, a figure that is difficult to exactly determine, as many states do not require government personnel to register when they lobby. Municipal, county, and regional governments as well as special districts, fire and police forces, and municipal and county hospitals and agencies all have business before the state. Similarly, state agencies, public colleges and universities, and other public utilities and corporations are affected by public policies. All of these public sector entities employee governmental relations personnel to advocate their vested interests in state capitals. Many, although still not half, of government lobbyists are female, who tend to be career bureaucrats or former legislative staff with extensive experience in dealing with the governmental agency they represent.[29]

Finally, about 10 percent of state lobbying communities are composed of individuals who give their time and expertise without compensation.[30] These individuals are known as *volunteers* or, in some instances, as *hobbyists.* Volunteer lobbyists tend to assist public interest groups—retirees helping out the League of Women Voters of Ohio or the Gray Panthers of

Metro Detroit, college students interning with Colorado Common Cause and Georgia Public Interest Research Group (GeorgiaPIRG), or high school students earning civic education credit that is part of a class requirement by putting in 10 hours a week working with Arizona Rock the Vote or the Maine chapter of Mothers Against Drunk Driving. Others are regular gadflies who like hanging around state legislatures and partaking in the action. As one public interest group jokes, volunteer lobbyists are the only ones left worthy of the name *lobbyists,* as contract and in-house lobbyists do not need to hang out in the lobbies anymore; their campaign contributions and influence enable them to be ushered directly in the front door of legislators' offices.[31]

The Rise of the Statehouse Lobbying Corps

In the 1980s, the number of firms and individuals registered to lobby state governments skyrocketed. By 1990, the average number of interest groups in a state registered to lobby a state legislature was 587, up from an average of only 196 in 1975. The total number of registered lobbyists also increased exponentially over the time period. In 1990, there were nearly 29,352 lobbyists registered in the 50 states, up from just 15,064 in 1980. Since that time, the number of groups registered to lobby and the number of lobbyists in the states have leveled off somewhat; in 1999, there were just under a total of 37,000 registered lobbyists.[32]

Today, state lawmakers are outnumbered by lobbyists on average by a ratio of five to one. In New York, there are nearly 4,000 lobbyists registered in Albany, enough for each lawmaker to have 18 lobbyists of his or her own. There are more than 10 registered lobbyists for each lawmaker in Colorado, Florida, Illinois, and Ohio. In contrast, only two states, Maine and New Hampshire, have more lawmakers than registered lobbyists.[33] Although the "old bulls"—large corporations—still tend to dominate the lobbying corps in state legislatures, much turnover occurs in the corridors of state capitols. The annual turnover of registered lobbyists working for businesses is actually higher than it is for those working for membership groups and associations.[34]

Regulating Lobbyists

State ethics laws and registration requirements for lobbyists have been on the books for years.[35] New York instituted the first comprehensive governmental ethics law in 1954. Since that time, states have passed a patchwork of ethics legislation, resulting in a "Byzantine array of public integrity rules and regulations that vary tremendously from state to state."[36] As Figure 6.1 reveals, 12 states only regulate legislative lobbying, 20 regulate the lobbying of both legislative and executive officials, and 18 regulate the lobbying of all government officials.

Every state requires lobbyists to register with a state regulatory agency or the state legislature, although limitations and disclosure requirements on lobbying activities vary considerably. Several states do not have a fee to register as a lobbyist; in Massachusetts, by way of contrast, the annual fee is $1,000. Thirty-seven states currently require lobbyists to report their expenditures, 24 have independent ethics commissions to launch investigations and enforce lobbying regulations, and 22 have a "cooling-off" period before government officials or legislators can become lobbyists. Another 38 states ban lobbyists from accepting payment that is contingent upon the defeat or enactment of a piece of legislation or administrative action and another four limit the practice. Several states, including Indiana, South Carolina, and Wisconsin, prohibit public employees from accepting "anything of value" that could be reasonably expected to influence a government employee's official action. In Wisconsin, this includes items as seemingly innocuous as a cup of coffee. Many states also ban gifts from lobbyists when the legislature is in session.

According to one scholarly composite index of state lobbying regulations, South Carolina had the toughest laws in 2003, followed by Arkansas, Maine, Texas, Washington, California, and Kentucky. North Dakota had by far the most lax lobbying requirements of any state in 2003, although Wyoming, Virginia, Oklahoma,

Figure 6.1

State Lobbying Laws

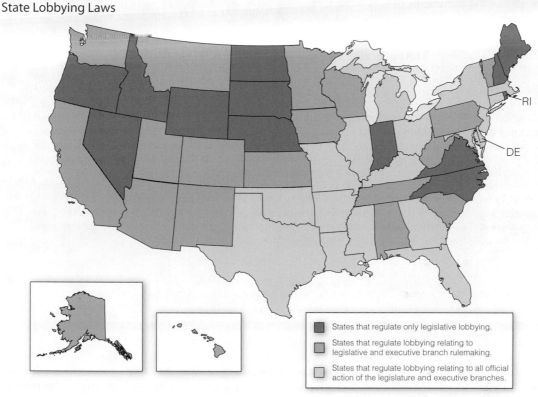

RI

DE

Alaska

Hawaii

■ States that regulate only legislative lobbying.

■ States that regulate lobbying relating to legislative and executive branch rulemaking.

□ States that regulate lobbying relating to all official action of the legislature and executive branches.

Source: Council on Governmental Ethics Laws

Source: State Legislatures, April 2005, http://www.ncsl.org/programs/pubs/slmag/2005/05SLApr_TandT.pdf.

North Carolina, Illinois, and Arizona were not too far behind. The stringency of South Carolina's laws increased dramatically in the early 1990s. In 1990, its lobbying laws had been among the least restrictive of any state. Kentucky also increased from one of the lower tiers of regulation to the top. On the other hand, Virginia, and to a lesser degree Indiana, which in the early 1990s had some of the most rigorous lobbying restrictions, now rank near the bottom of the index.[37]

For years, Alaska, California, Texas, and Washington have had some of the toughest and most comprehensive disclosure and monitoring regulations for lobbyists. Today, following the wake of recent scandals, states like Florida are going a step further in their lobbyist regulations, banning all gifts and travel provided by lobbyists and requiring lobbyists to submit detailed disclosure of all their spending. Others have recently taken smaller steps to revamp their relatively weak ethics laws.

New York, New Jersey, and Tennessee—after several lobbying scandals—have attempted to tighten rules for lobbyists. The first executive order of Jon Corzine, the multimillionaire Democratic governor of New Jersey who was elected in 2005, required all members of state boards and commissions to file financial disclosure forms. In Tennessee, where an FBI sting ensnared four state legislators taking bribes, the governor convened a special session in 2006 to deal with "a culture of corruption in Nashville." Saying he wanted to "get out in front of the curve and be actively addressing these issues," the governor, Democrat Phil

INSTITUTIONS MATTER

STATE ETHICS LAWS AND WAYWARD LOBBYISTS

In late 2005, lobbyist Linda Kowalski entered a plea bargain with the Connecticut Office of State Ethics, agreeing to pay a $25,000 fine and abiding to follow tighter disclosure requirements for her alleged ethics violations of filing false lobbying reports and exceeding limits on meals and gifts to legislators. Although Kowalski admitted no wrongdoing and maintained her innocence, she agreed to pay the fine and abide by the new restrictions. From 1998 to 2002, Kowalski worked as a contract lobbyist for the state's trash agency, the Connecticut Resources Recovery Authority. At the time, she also served for a while as a chief fundraiser for Governor John Rowland and the Republican Governors Association. In 2002, the trash agency was involved in negotiations with the now-defunct energy powerhouse Enron Corp. Kowalski allegedly exceeded lobbying expenditure limits when entertaining staffers of Rowland's office. A decade earlier, Kowalski had similarly run afoul of Connecticut's ethics laws. She had to pay a $50,000 civil penalty for illegal lobbying activities on behalf of the Connecticut Retail Merchants Association, which had provided meals and gifts of alcoholic beverages, tickets to sporting events, and golf outings to lawmakers in excess of the $50 annual limit.[1]

Note

1. Jon Lender, "Lobbyist Agrees to Pay Fine: Settlement Heads off Costly Ethics Case," *Hartford (Conn.) Courant,* 30 November 2005, p. B1.

Bredesen, asked the legislature to ban most gifts from lobbyists to elected officials and government employees, require disclosure of lobbyist expenditures, and create an independent ethics commission. In New York, the state Lobbying Commission is taking more cautious steps to rein in lobbyists: the state's long-standing $75 limit on lobbyists' gifts to lawmakers is now interpreted to apply to an entire year, as opposed to each event or meal.[38]

The relative effectiveness of lobbyists is conditioned by institutional constraints existing within a state. State lobbying restrictions on gifts to lawmakers and prohibitions on campaign finance activities by lobbyists can diminish the clout of lobbyists. Term limits on state legislators can affect the behavior and relative influence of lobbyists.[39] Term limits tend to weaken the long-standing ties and social networks that lobbyists work tirelessly to cultivate over time with government officials. Studies have shown that states with term limits have more lobbyists who report having to work harder to do their jobs. Yet, term-limited states also seem to have worse ethical behavior among lobbyists, which might be tied to lobbyists in these term-limited states wielding more influence in the legislative process than they do in states where incumbents may keep their office interminably.[40]

Issue Advocacy

Rather than having their lobbyists directly press lawmakers and public officials to take action that benefits their members, some interest groups use indirect tactics to influence the making of public policy. Although fewer interest groups report regularly engaging in outsider strategies rather than insider strategies, many groups do engage in issue advocacy. **Issue advocacy** is a form of political speech that mentions issues and the positions taken on those issues by elected officials or candidates but stops short of expressly advocating the support or defeat of those elected officials or candidates. Issue ads themselves may be articulated in any type of media—TV and

Sacramento Bee/Brian Baer, http://www.sacbee.com/content/politics/story/12956253p-13803679c¬tml.

Union members protesting Governor Arnold Schwarzenegger's budget cut, in Sacramento, California, 2005.

radio broadcasts, newspaper ads, billboards, placards, banners strung behind airplanes, handbills, and fliers—with some costing millions and other just a few dollars. Each state regulates issue advocacy differently, although most take their cues from the federal government's regulations. All are bounded by rulings handed down by the U.S. Supreme Court.

Issue Advocacy in Historical Perspective

Issue advocacy has been used by interest groups since the 19th century. In the late 19th century, party machines dominated state and local politics, and many citizen groups started to become more formally organized. Because their demands were not being fulfilled through two-party system politics, workers, farmers, and women were among the first interests to become organized at the subnational level. Industrial workers complained about being systematically denied fair working conditions

and the right to organize. Farmers and ranchers were upset with the high costs of transportation being charged by monopolistic railroad companies. Millions of women were upset with being denied the right to vote. Yet, these concerns were not making their way onto the agendas of the political parties. Tracing the development of interest organizations in California, Washington, and Wisconsin during the Progressive era, one scholar has shown how farmers, workers, and women—among other interests—were able to eventually organize themselves into interest groups, creating new political opportunities for representation.[41]

Today, a wide variety of interest groups engage in outsider issue advocacy strategies that often resemble the activities of the earliest interest groups. Although done with less frequency today than in the past, interest groups sometimes sponsor boycotts, sit-ins, rallies, mass rallies, and marches to give their issues visibility and engender public support. In May 2005, for instance, over 10,000 protestors congregated on the steps of the California state capitol building in Sacramento, donning T-shirts, carrying placards, and shouting the slogan "Schwarzenegger's got to go." With busloads of teachers, nurses, firefighters, prison guards, machinists, and hotel and service workers blanketing the capitol grounds, the protestors wanted to send Republican governor Arnold Schwarzenegger a clear message "that there are a lot of people who are really concerned about what he is doing to the state," as one elementary school teacher put it to a reporter. More specifically, the Alliance for a Better California, a broad coalition of unions, were protesting the governor's budget and proposed ballot measures, which included severe cuts in public education and health care and efforts to diminish the power of public sector unions.[42]

Earned Media When engaging in issue advocacy, interest groups try to frame issues to sway public opinion in a direction that may help place indirect pressure on policy makers. From authoring op-eds and running TV and newspaper ads pushing an issue, to blasting fax and e-mail press releases to the media, to mounting a grassroots letter-writing campaign, to engaging in more shocking protests and demonstrations, interest groups often take their influence to the proverbial (and sometimes literal) streets. By raising an issue outside of the legislative arena, organized interests are able to use **earned media**—generating newsworthy events or stories for the press to report on for free—to help mobilize public opinion in favor of or against a public policy. Interest groups hope that by communicating information and positions on policies to citizens directly, the resulting buzz concerning the issues will be indirectly relayed to policy makers, influencing their decisions.[43]

Grassroots and Astroturf Mobilization Mobilizing support for public policies at the grassroots level is another form of issue advocacy. Generating ground-level support from members of an organization, or more generally from supporters of an issue, helps a group apply pressure on legislators and other elected officials. When done well, it "demonstrates vocal and tangible support (or opposition) for a measure," says Alan Rosenthal, as "constituents tell legislators how the measure will affect them, instead of the lobbyist doing it."[44] Some lobbying firms also engage in what are more derisively known as **astroturf campaigns,** where constituencies are essentially manufactured by an interest group to give legislators the appearance that the electorate is up in arms about a certain policy. Corporations are increasingly using astroturf campaigns to influence public policy, as they can help expand the scope of conflict and give them the appearance that they have broader public support for their issue position.

Although nearly all interest groups engage in issue advocacy, groups use different tactics. Not surprisingly—as the anti-Schwarzenegger protest in California makes evident—labor unions at the state and local levels often engage in protest activities, drawing on their membership base to make their collective voice heard by elected officials, the media, and the general public. Public interest groups also engage in protest activities, relying on their legions of volunteers, whereas trade and professional organizations rarely engage in such demonstrations. Corporations, and to a lesser degree governmental groups, tend to be less likely to participate in grassroots lobbying efforts and letter-writing campaigns than unions, trade associations, and nonprofit citizen organizations. Governmental groups are much less likely to use these techniques as part of their issue advocacy strategy.[45]

Other groups, most notably liberal- and conservative-leaning public interest groups, associations, and labor unions, provide their members (and the broader general public) with information about incumbents and candidates running for office. These educational efforts—the groups do not actually endorse candidates—are nevertheless quite political.

Figure 6.2

Legislative Scorecard from New Yorkers Against Gun Violence

NEW YORKERS AGAINST GUN VIOLENCE	2004 STATE LEGISLATIVE SCORECARD
	www.nyagv.org

NEW YORK STATE SENATE   Votes/Positions

Bill #1 (S.397) Would make it easier to obtain a concealed carry gun permit. **(1998 Regular Session) Passed Senate 32-18**
NYAGV Position - OPPOSE

Bill #2 (S.8234) Nine measures, including: 1) ballistic imaging; 2) closed gun show loophole; 3) asault weapons ban; 4) safety locks; 5) increased penalties for criminal possession and sale; 6) age 21 for handgun permit/possession. **(Signed into law 2000) Passed Senate 39-20**
NYAGV Position - SUPPORT

Bill # 3 (S.3805) Increases criminal penalties for those who illegally possess or sell multiple guns. **(2003/2004) Passed Senate 60-0**
NYAGV Position - SUPPORT

Senator		Dist. #	Vote #1	Vote #2	Vote #3
LONG ISLAND					
LaValle	*Kenneth P.*	1	-	+	+
Flanagan	*John J.*	2	*	+(1)	+
Trunzo	*Caesar*	3	-	+	+
Johnson	*Owen H.*	4	-	+	+
Marcellino	*Carl*	5	-	+	+
Hannon	*Kemp*	6	-	+	+
Balboni	*Michael A.L.*	7	-	+	+
Fuschillo, Jr.	*Charles J.*	8	*	+	+
Skelos	*Dean G.*	9	-	+	+
NEW YORK CITY/WESTCHESTER					
Smith	**Ada L.**	10	Er	+	+
Padavan	**Frank**	11	+	+	+
Onorato	**George**	12	+	+	+
Sabini	**John**	13	*	*	+
Smith	**Malcolm**	14	*	+	+
Maltese	**Serphin R.**	15	-	-	+
Stavisky	**Toby Ann**	16	*	+	+
Dilan	**Martin M.**	17	*	*	+
Montgomery	**Velmanette**	18	+	er	+
Sampson	**John L.**	19	+	+	+
Andrews	**Carl**	20	*	*	+
Parker	**Kevin**	21	*	*	+
Golden	*Martin J.*	22	*	*	+
OPEN SEAT		23			
Marchi	*John J.*	24	-	+	+

Senator		Dist. #	#1	#2	#3
Connor	**Martin**	25	+	+	+
Krueger	**Liz**	26	*	*	+
Kruger	**Carl**	27	+	+	+
Mendez	**Olga A.**	28	er	+	+
Duane	**Thomas**	29	*	+	+
Paterson	**David**	30	+	+	+
Schneiderman	**Eric T.**	31	*	+	+
Diaz, Sr.	**Ruben**	32	*	*	+
Gonzalez, Jr.	**Efrain**	33	ab	+	er
OPEN SEAT		34			
Spano	*Nicholas A.*	35	-	+	+
Hassell-Thompson	**Ruth**	36	*	*	+
Oppenheimer	**Suzi**	37	+	+	+
UPSTATE					
Morahan	*Thomas*	38	*	+	+
Larkin, Jr.	*William J.*	39	-	-	+
Leibell	*Vincent L.*	40	ab	+	+
Saland	*Stephen M.*	41	-	-	+
Bonacic	*John J.*	42	*	-	+
Bruno	*Joseph L.*	43	-	+	+
Farley	*Hugh T.*	44	-	-	er
Little	*Elizabeth*	45	*	-(1)	+
Breslin	**Neil**	46	+	+	+
Meier	*Raymond A.*	47	-	-	+
Wright	*James W.*	48	-		+
Hoffmann	*Nancy Larraine*	49	-	-	+
DeFrancisco	*John*	50	-	-	+
Seward	*James L.*	51	-	-	+
Libous	*Thomas W.*	52	-	-	+
OPEN SEAT		53			
Nozzolio	*Michael F.*	54	ab	-	+
Alesi	*James S.*	55	-	-	+
Robach	*Joseph E.*	56	*	ab (1)	+
McGee	*Patricia K.*	57	*	-	+
Stachowski	**William T.**	58	-	-	+
Volker	*Dale M.*	59	-	-	+
Brown	*Byron*	60	*	*	+
Rath	*Mary Lou*	61	-	-	+
Maziarz	*George D.*	62	+	-	+

KEY

Party: Democrat (bold face)   Republican (italics)
VOTING: "+" supported NYAGV position
"-" opposed NYAGV position
er = excused   ab = absent   * = not a member at time of vote
FOOTNOTE
(1) Assembly member at time of vote

Source: New Yorkers against Gun Violence, http://www.nyagv.org/2004NYSSCORECARD.pdf.

Some groups produce scorecards reporting the voting records of incumbents. For example, New Yorkers against Gun Violence is a nonprofit advocacy group that publicizes the destructive effects of gun violence in New York and advocates gun legislation. The group regularly compiles and distributes a legislative voting scorecard detailing whether members of the legislature supported or opposed key bills dealing with guns, as Figure 6.2 shows.

Ballot Measures As discussed in Chapter 4, in many of the two dozen states that permit the process, ballot measures are increasingly becoming a way for interest groups to advance their causes. In these states, which tend to have more interest groups than states without the process, ballot measures serve as another issue advocacy weapon in the arsenal of politically active groups.[46] Although the costs of running a ballot campaign in some states can be substantial—in California, Florida, and even Colorado, ballot campaigns can reach more than $10 million—the resulting policy payoff may be worth it. By circumventing unresponsive legislatures, groups can take their issue directly to the citizens.

Historically, interest groups have turned to ballot measures when the usual legislative channels have been blocked by party bosses or rival interest groups. Although citizen-dominated interest groups have had more success than economic interest groups in passing favorable ballot measures, economic groups have not been shy to use the process.[47] Not always successful in their endeavors, vested economic interest groups still have played a major role in ballot campaigns since the turn of the 20th century.[48] In 1910, in South Dakota, for example, 12 propositions were placed on the ballot, including one by the railroad industry seeking to overturn a law requiring electric headlights for locomotives and another seeking to topple a law regulating embalming procedures of undertakers.[49]

COMPARISONS HELP US UNDERSTAND

TAKING THE INITIATIVE FOR ANIMAL PROTECTION

Why do some states prohibit some forms of hunting, while others allow it? During the 1990s, the Humane Society of the United States (HSUS) helped place 17 animal protection initiatives on the ballots of 11 states permitting the process. The measures dealt with an impressive array of animal protection issues—from prohibiting the use of steel-jaw leghold traps in Arizona, Colorado, and Massachusetts; to banning cockfighting in Arizona and Missouri; to barring the use of hounds and baiting in the hunting of bears in Colorado, Idaho, and Michigan; to ending trophy hunting of mountain lions in California and airborne hunting of wolves, foxes, lynx, and wolverines in Alaska; and to outlawing mourning dove hunting in Ohio.

As the largest animal protection membership association in the world, with more than 250 staff employed in nine regional offices, the Humane Society turned to the initiative process after having difficulty passing animal protection legislation in the states. According to Wayne Pacelle, president of the organization, many state legislatures are dominated by rural and agricultural interests. Frustrated by the unwillingness of some state legislatures to adopt animal protection laws, the interest group decided to circumvent intransigent state legislatures and use the initiative process to supplement its traditional insider lobbying approach. The decision to embark upon an outsider strategy was made easier by the fact that the group's membership was exploding. The organization was able to tap into its vast nationwide membership, which grew from roughly 1 million members in 1990 to over 7 million members in 2000. Members provided their labor as well as their financial resources during the qualifying and electoral stages of the ballot measure process. On Election Day, voters approved 12 and rejected five of the Humane Society's ballot measures, a 71 percent success rate.

In Oregon, in 1908, rival upstream and downstream fishing companies placed counterpropositions on the June primary ballot that tried to eradicate each other's means of fishing for salmon on the Columbia River.[50]

In the 2005 special election in California, over $262 million was spent by the various groups contesting eight ballot initiatives that were on the ballot.[51] The pharmaceutical industry's peak association, PhRMA, raked in over $80 million in its effort to defeat a progressive measure that would have reduced the cost of prescription drugs as well as to promote its own counterproposition preserving the status quo. Both measures ended up failing, which was a major victory for PhRMA. Other special interests also poured money into the ballot campaigns. Using a temporary dues increase on its 300,000-plus members, the California Teachers Association spent some $58 million in its successful effort to defeat ballot initiatives backed by Governor Schwarzenegger that targeted public sector unions and teacher tenure. All told, California unions and their out-of-state allies spent more than $120 million to defeat the governor's slate of propositions on the ballot. For their part, special interests backing Schwarzenegger's reform agenda contributed over $70 million to the sponsoring committees, including some $44 million to the governor's own ballot initiative committee, the California Recovery Team.[52]

Nonprofit groups have had some success using the initiative process to advance their issues. Spurned for years due to the grip of the tobacco and business lobbies in Tallahassee, a coalition of four prominent public health organizations—the American Cancer Society, the American Heart Association, the American Lung Association, and the Campaign for Tobacco-Free Kids—joined forces to place an initiative on Florida's 2002 statewide ballot. Their proposed constitutional amendment, Amendment 6, called for the prohibition of workplace smoking. The four nonprofits contributed 99 percent of the $5.854 million raised by the ballot committee, Smoke-Free for Health, Inc.[53] With public opinion polling numbers showing the public favored the measure by a three-to-one margin,

the tobacco and business associations decided not to aggressively oppose the measure. The measure passed easily, garnering 71 percent of the statewide vote and receiving a majority of votes in all of Florida's 67 counties.

Electioneering

Interest groups not only try to shape the public policy debate through their lobbying and issue advocacy. Organized interests can also actively participate in the electoral process in a variety of ways. Many become engaged in candidate campaigns in an effort to influence who will be elected and thus have a hand in making public policy. The practice of explicitly supporting candidates or political parties is known as **electioneering**. Working on campaigns or financing candidates and parties helps to solidify the relationships that interest groups have with winning candidates and the parties in control of the state legislatures. Not all electioneering comes in the form of financial contributions. Some interest groups provide candidates and political parties with nonmonetary, in-kind contributions. Such contributions include sharing data from public opinion polls, giving out membership lists for fundraising, and lending staff and field operations for support during the campaign. Other groups will publicly endorse their support or opposition for candidates. Of course, many groups give monetary contributions directly to candidates and political parties. For these groups, state laws vary considerably with regard to what kinds of contributions they are permitted to give, how much they may give, and to whom they may give.

Regulating Campaign Contributions Rulings by the U.S. Supreme Court have consistently struck down federal and state laws banning or limiting expenditures by interest groups that are made independently of candidates and parties, which are known as *independent expenditures*. However, the Court has given wide latitude to state legislatures to regulate and limit the amount of money that interest groups may give directly to candidates and political parties.[54] Countless municipal and county governments, and all but 13 states, have passed laws that place restrictions on the amount of campaign contributions that can be made by interest groups to candidates and political parties. The effort by states to limit spending in candidate campaigns has largely stemmed from the perception that special interests—predominantly corporations and business associations—have had undue influence in candidate races.

Similar to the regulation of elections, there exists a tremendous amount of variation across the states in the amount of regulation in the campaign finance activities of interest groups. Nineteen states prohibit corporations from making contributions to state parties and candidates from their general treasuries; another dozen states ban unions from contributing to campaigns using their general treasury funds. Eighteen states permit state parties to receive unlimited contributions from **political action committees (PACs),** legal entities that allow like-minded individuals who belong to a corporation, labor union, or virtually any other organization to pool their money and contribute directly to candidates and political parties.

PACs operating in Tennessee, for instance, may make unlimited contributions to parties, but they are limited in how much they can contribute to candidates ($7,500 per election to those running for statewide office). The Tennessee Registry of Election Finance is the regulatory body that is charged with overseeing and enforcing campaign finance activities in the state. The requirement that interest groups funnel their contributions through PACs is not universal. Thirteen states allow interest groups to give directly from their corporate or union treasuries to candidates. Eleven states, including Florida, Illinois, and Virginia, permit any type of interest group to make unlimited contributions to state political parties.[55]

PAC Contributions PAC contributions made to candidates running for office depend largely on the type and ideology of the interest group that controls the PAC. Some interest groups

give according to their principles; others have more pragmatic giving patterns. Liberal PACs affiliated with local and state chapters of unions such as the Service Employees International Union and the American Federation of Teachers as well as pro-choice groups, such as NARAL and Planned Parenthood, give nearly all their contributions to Democrats. Conservative PACs affiliated with single issues, such as the National Rifle Association (NRA) and state affiliates of the National Right to Life, give nearly exclusively to Republicans. In contrast, many corporate-controlled PACs are equal-opportunity givers, writing checks to both Republican and Democratic candidates— as long as they are incumbents. Rather than ideology, these pragmatic PACs use their campaign donations as a means to purchase continued access to lawmakers and policy makers. According to one study, the energy industry— primarily oil and gas companies and their peak associations—pumped more than $134.7 million into candidate committees and state parties between 1990 and 2004. Nearly 70 percent of those contributions went to incumbents, irrespective of their political party.[56]

In the 2004 election cycle, state-level candidates (running for governor, legislatures, and state supreme courts) raised over $1.4 billion for their campaigns, much of it coming from special interests through their PACs. The combined financial, insurance, and real estate sector gave the most to state legislative candidates, contributing more than $60 million (with roughly $37 million going to Republican candidates). The health sector contributed more than $45 million to both parties, with Republicans getting a slightly larger share. Organized labor and interest groups representing trial lawyers each gave more than $40 million to state-level candidates, with most of it going to Democrats. Single-issue groups, which usually are more ideological, contributed less than $10 million to candidates, with slightly more going to Democrats.[57]

Interest group contributions to Democratic and Republican party committees in the 2004 election cycle reveal similar patterns. Table 6.2

Table 6.2

Ten Top-Contributing Industries to State Party Committees, 2004

Sector	Democratic	Republican	Total
Lawyers and lobbyists	$17,994,946	$7,055,491	$25,050,437
Real estate	$7,476,160	$13,411,317	$20,887,477
Public sector unions	$15,203,765	$2,953,606	$18,157,371
General trade unions	$14,094,523	$1,002,604	$15,097,127
Insurance	$2,631,211	$7,552,733	$10,183,943
Health professionals	$2,769,111	$5,055,840	$7,824,950
Retail sales	$984,884	$5,934,597	$6,919,481
General contractors	$2,003,226	$4,268,974	$6,272,199
Securities and investment	$2,082,896	$3,684,684	$5,767,581
Tribal governments	$3,324,530	$2,095,275	$5,419,805
Totals	$68,565,252	$53,015,121	$121,580,371

Source: Institute on Money in State Politics, *State Elections Overview, 2004,* December 2005, http://www.followthemoney.org/press/Reports/200601041.pdf.

details the contributions, totaling over $121 million, made by interest groups to state political parties in the 2004 election cycle, broken down by industry sector. The contributions (which come largely from PACs and, where permitted, direct contributions from corporate and labor treasuries) give a sense of which kinds of interest groups are contributing to which state parties. It is clear from the table that some industries give much more to one political party, whereas others give to both equally. Not surprisingly, trade unions, public sector unions, and groups representing trial lawyers and lobbyists tend to give disproportionately to Democrats. Republican state parties receive the bulk of contributions made by real estate interests, the insurance industry and health professionals, general contractors, and retail sales corporations and associations.[58] For example, RPAC, the PAC for the National Association of Realtors, raised $12.6 million for state and local candidates, with roughly 40 percent of its 1.2 million members making voluntary PAC donations.[59]

Some single-issue, ideological organizations make extensive PAC contributions to state-level candidates and state party committees. Over three two-year election cycles (1997–2002), the NRA's PAC, the copacetic-sounding Political Victory Fund, contributed more than $3.35 million to candidates running in all but three states (Alaska, Massachusetts, and New Hampshire). In the 2002 election cycle, the NRA contributed a total of $1.1 million, with over half of the money going to state legislative candidates. The total amount that cycle was nearly double what the NRA spent on state-level campaigns four years earlier.[60] The NRA also gave nearly $1 million over the six-year period to 82 state party and legislative caucus committees in 36 states. Topping the recipient list, the NRA gave the Republican Party of Florida a total of $205,000 during the period.

Money, it is often said, is like water. It is hydraulic, leveling itself and circumventing any barriers placed in its way. It can swamp the democratic process. A survey conducted in 2002 of some 1,300 interest groups operating in 38 states found that state contribution limits affect the contribution strategies that groups make. States with laws severely restricting interest group contributions to candidates tend to increase their spending in other electioneering areas. Interest groups operating in those

Library of Congress, http://www.loc.gov/exhibits/brown/images/brf0098s.jpg.

Lawyers for the NAACP (Thurgood Marshall, center) confer at the U.S. Supreme Court prior to oral arguments for *Brown v. Board of Education* (1954).

states tend to increase their expenditures on issue advertising and independent expenditures on behalf of candidates.[61]

Litigation

Some interest groups turn their attention to state and federal courts when doing battle. As interpreters of laws and constitutions, courts are important venues for interest groups if they have been stymied by policy makers or administrators charged with implementing a law. One survey of state organizations finds that roughly half of all interest groups report that they either often or sometimes use *litigation,* or legal action, as a tactic.[62] For some groups, a lawsuit may be easier, less expensive, and more effective than paying lobbyists to advance their cause through the legislative process. This might be especially true for groups with small memberships, little political influence in the state or community, or less than stellar reputations.

When pursuing a litigation strategy, interest groups tend to use one of two tactics. Some groups will seek out laws that they view as unconstitutional and file what is known as a *test case* on behalf of an aggrieved individual. One of the best-known test cases is *Brown v. Board of Education of Topeka* (1954). The National Association for the Advancement of Colored

People (NAACP) had filed a suit on behalf of the parents of an eight-year-old elementary student, Linda Brown, who was forced to attend an all-black school in Kansas even though an all-white elementary school was only a few blocks from her home. In 1954, the U.S. Supreme Court struck down the practice of racial segregation in public schools ("separate but equal"). The court ruled that the 14th Amendment of the U.S. Constitution prohibited states from denying equal protection of the laws to persons within their jurisdiction.[63] Following the success of *Brown,* many other liberal organizations turned to the courts in the 1950s and 1960s, as many judges were seen as more progressive on social issues than were many state and local governments. In addition to civil rights associations like the NAACP, consumer rights advocacy organizations, women's and pro-choice groups, and environmental organizations all used lawsuits—especially pursued in federal courts—to advance their causes.

Beginning in the 1970s, many conservative groups started pushing lawsuits to advance their agendas, in part because they had more sympathizers sitting on the federal and state benches. Perhaps most notably, the National Right to Life Committee, founded in 1973 following the U.S. Supreme Court's *Roe v. Wade* ruling legalizing abortion, has relied on litigation as a key strategy to challenge state statutes protection a woman's right to an abortion. The increase in litigation by interest groups has been well-documented: between 1953 and 1993, the number of U.S. Supreme Court cases drawing interest group attention increased from just 13 percent to 92 percent of all cases.[64]

When an interest group is not an immediate party in a lawsuit, its lawyers may choose to file an amicus curiae brief (*amicus curiae* is Latin for "friend of the court"). These written briefs, which are usually filed on appeal of a case in either state or federal court, offer supplemental legal arguments that attempt to influence the reasoning of the court. To file an *amicus,* as they are often referred to, an interest group must first obtain the permission of one of the parties involved in the case. It is increasingly the case that lawyers for multiple interest groups will file friend-of-the-court briefs for a single case. For instance, in 1972, the U.S. Supreme Court case ruled in *Wisconsin v. Yoder* that children of the Old Order Amish faith were permitted to stop going to school after they turned 16 because attendance conflicted with their religious beliefs. Prior to the Court's judgment, several religious denominations filed briefs supporting the students, including the National Council of Churches of Christ in the United States, the General Conference of Seventh Day Adventists, the American Jewish Congress, the Synagogue Council of America, the National Jewish Commission on Law and Public Affairs, and the Mennonite Central Committee. Although not always prevailing, lawsuits filed by interest groups can deliver results that are otherwise unattainable in other political arenas.[65]

The Dynamics of State Interest Group Systems

How do state interest group systems evolve over time, how are they comparatively different from one another, and which groups tend to hold the upper hand in a state's system? As studies on the dynamics of state interest group systems make evident, the concern voiced by critics of pluralist theory—that the system is biased in favor of economic interests—appears to be supported by empirical data.

The Advocacy Explosion

Paralleling the trend in Washington, D.C., the number and types of interest groups in the American states greatly expanded during the 1960s and 1970s.[66] In part, the so-called advocacy explosion was due to the rapid increase in the number of public interest groups that grew out of the social movements for civil rights, women's rights, consumer protection, environmentalism, and protests against the Vietnam War. The rise in the number and types of interest groups was also partly in response

to the increased power and involvement in the economy of federal and state governments.

Many of the emergent groups were markedly different from federated interest groups of a bygone era. The new groups relied more on members writing checks than participating in mass demonstrations.[67] There was also a marked decline in the number of members belonging to older federated civic associations, such as the Rotary Club, the Lions Club, the Kiwanis Club, the League of Women's Voters, and the National Parent-Teacher Association. These groups, like the Women's Christian Temperance Union in the 19th century, combined social and ritual activities, elected their leaders, held regular meetings of the membership, and had members who came from different economic backgrounds. Somewhat ironically, the progressive groups that emerged out of the 1960s had an upper-class bias. These new public interest groups were structurally different than those of the past, essentially "organizations without members." They were fairly oligarchic, were more centralized and professionalized, and fostered a "doing for, not doing with" mentality.[68]

The rise of public interest groups in the American states and communities in the 1970s was not limited to newfangled nonprofit public interest groups pushing postmaterialist values. The rise of liberal-leaning citizen groups in the 1960s and 1970s helped to fuel a conservative backlash. During the 1970s and 1980s, conservative public interest groups, such as the Eagle Forum, with over 30 state chapters; the Moral Majority; and the Christian Coalition established themselves as key political actors in many of the states. As countervailing forces, these economic and social groups continue to serve as foils to the liberal and progressive groups that emerged out of the social changes begotten from the 1960s.

There was a simultaneous backlash in the business community. In response to the strengthened public interest lobby as well as to the prowess of organized labor which had reached its zenith of influence in the 1950s, businesses began forming their own peak associations.[69] Today, corporate and business interests dominate the universe of state interest group systems. According to the most recent survey of interest groups registered in the states, enterprises comprise nearly three-fifths of all registered groups, with associations accounting for an additional 22 percent. Membership-based groups only account for 19 percent of all registered interest groups, down from 31 percent of all groups in 1980.[70]

The number of professional associations registered in the states, particularly ones representing business and trade interests, also rose in the 1970s and 1980s. The sharp rise was fueled in part by the surge in the number of white-collar jobs and women entering the workforce. By one count, the number of professional associations nationally increased from just 6,500 national organizations in 1958 to more than 23,000 by 1990.[71] Whereas some of these professional associations are well-established and have active chapters in the states, others such as the Montana Bed and Breakfast Association, the Mid-Atlantic Alpaca Association, and the Oregon State Beekeeper's Association are relatively new.

Density and Diversity of State Interest Group Systems

The explosion of interest groups has not been consistent across all states, policy domains, or types of interests represented in a state's interest group system. The states have considerable variation in terms of the composition of interest groups. Interest group power, in turn, is not distributed evenly across the systems. So, why are state interest group systems different from one another?

Following the pluralist logic that groups emerge when a disturbance in the status quo occurs, the number and types of interest groups will grow as a society becomes more complex. There are considerable differences in the size, strength, and dynamics of state economies. As a state's economy grows, so does the number of interest groups operating in that state.[72] States with the largest economies invariably have the most interest groups. In 1997, for instance,

Texas and California both had over 2,000 interest groups with registered lobbyists, Illinois had over 1,500, and Pennsylvania, Minnesota, New York, Ohio, Missouri, Florida, Michigan, and Massachusetts all had more than 1,000. At the other end of the spectrum, five states—Rhode Island, Wyoming, New Hampshire, Delaware, and Hawaii—all had less than 300 interest groups with registered lobbyists.

As competition for resources among registered organizations in the states increases, however, interest group systems gradually become denser and the expansion rate of the system slows down.[73] A state's **interest group system density** refers to the number of functioning groups relative to the size of the state's economy. Wealthier states tend to have more interest groups, in part because governments are able to attract new businesses by increasing their expenditures. In states with fairly dense interest group systems, the relative power of each group is lessened. A state's **interest group system diversity**, in contrast, refers to the spread of groups across various social and economic realms. Interest group diversity is positively related to a state's economic diversity.[74] Table 6.3 lists the percentage of interest groups in the 50 states that are for-profit, nonprofit, membership, associations, and industry in 1997.

The states show a tremendous amount of diversity in terms of the kinds of interest groups that have representation. As you can see in Table 6.3, in some states, such as New Mexico, California, Montana, and Wyoming, nearly one out of every three interest groups with a registered lobbyist is a nonprofit organization. In New Jersey, by way of contrast, only 14 percent of all groups are in the nonprofit sector. The Dakotas, followed closely by Montana, lead the way with the highest percentage of membership organizations, with roughly 30 percent of their interest group systems composed of groups with individuals as members. Less than 14 percent of all groups are membership-based in Pennsylvania and New Jersey, with Texas having the fewest, at only 11.7 percent. Texas is the state with the highest percentage (71.5 percent) of interest groups

Table 6.3

Percentage of Interest Groups That Are For-Profit, Nonprofit, Membership, Associations, and Enterprises, 1997

State	For-Profit (%)	Nonprofit (%)	Membership (%)	Associations (%)	Institutions (%)
Texas	82.1	16.0	11.7	16.7	71.5
New Jersey	81.8	14.0	12.0	18.3	68.5
Hawaii	80.7	16.7	21.9	25.5	52.6
Arkansas	80.3	17.8	17.5	19.7	61.9
Pennsylvania	79.3	18.6	13.8	17.8	67.8
Oklahoma	78.9	19.3	21.3	21.4	57.0
Tennessee	78.1	20.9	20.9	23.4	55.4
South Carolina	77.7	22.3	21.2	28.4	50.4
Idaho	77.6	22.0	23.3	29.7	47.0
Louisiana	77.2	19.7	18.0	18.8	63.1
Vermont	76.8	22.4	18.3	28.9	52.6
Massachusetts	76.7	21.2	17.5	19.8	62.6
Connecticut	76.7	23.3	21.7	24.8	53.5
Maine	76.4	23.6	22.4	29.5	48.1
Delaware	76.3	23.8	22.5	22.1	55.4
Kentucky	75.9	23.6	21.2	27.3	51.6
Utah	75.6	19.2	17.3	15.8	65.2
Maryland	75.0	23.2	19.0	24.3	56.4
New Hampshire	74.9	24.3	21.7	26.6	51.7
Mississippi	73.8	26.2	22.5	27.8	49.3
Georgia	73.5	23.4	19.1	19.1	61.0
West Virginia	73.4	24.7	21.8	26.3	51.9
Illinois	73.3	23.8	16.6	19.2	64.0
North Dakota	73.3	25.5	30.5	26.2	42.6
Virginia	73.1	25.5	22.1	25.1	52.6
New York	72.8	25.9	19.6	25.4	54.6
Washington	72.6	27.4	25.9	27.8	46.3
North Carolina	72.3	26.6	24.6	31.6	42.6
Kansas	72.2	26.3	25.6	26.1	48.2
Wisconsin	72.1	27.9	21.7	29.1	39.1
Alaska	71.9	26.8	21.2	22.5	55.3
Missouri	71.9	29.3	16.3	19.5	67.5
Alabama	71.5	27.8	17.9	18.3	63.1
Nebraska	71.2	26.9	26.4	28.4	45.2
Nevada	71.1	25.6	21.2	18.1	59.6
Indiana	71.0	28.5	22.5	25.1	52.4
Ohio	70.8	26.7	15.6	20.4	64.0

Percentage of Interest Groups That Are For-Profit, Nonprofit, Membership, Associations, and Enterprises, 1997 (continued)

State	For-Profit (%)	Nonprofit (%)	Membership (%)	Associations (%)	Institutions (%)
Michigan	70.8	27.4	17.0	21.3	53.8
Rhode Island	69.9	29.7	28.4	25.7	45.6
South Dakota	69.8	28.6	29.8	28.3	40.0
Iowa	69.2	30.1	24.2	24.4	50.9
Colorado	68.8	29.6	21.5	22.7	55.3
Oregon	68.0	31.3	24.2	28.6	47.1
Minnesota	67.5	31.5	22.5	26.8	50.5
Florida	67.3	31.3	18.7	21.4	59.7
Arizona	66.6	30.8	16.6	16.7	66.5
Montana	66.3	32.4	29.0	29.4	41.4
Wyoming	66.1	31.0	28.5	21.2	48.2
California	61.6	37.2	19.3	21.4	58.8
New Mexico	60.3	37.5	21.9	20.3	57.2

Source: Virginia Gray and David Lowery, "The Institutionalization of State Communities of Organized Interests," *Political Research Quarterly* 54 (2001): 265-84.

that are enterprises; in Wisconsin, less than 40 percent of all groups with a registered lobbyist are enterprises. At 31.6 percent, North Carolina has the highest percentage of associations, with Idaho a close second; the percentage in Utah, by contrast, is roughly half that amount.

Several factors seem to contribute to the density and diversity of a state's interest group system. States with more competition among the parties also tend to have denser interest group systems, as the lack of single-party rule perhaps exacerbates policy uncertainty and, thus, more intergroup competition. The legislatures of states with denser interest group systems tend to be less productive, as measured by the proportion of all bills introduced that are passed. Interestingly, states that have the initiative process also tend to have an increased number and a greater diversity of active interest groups. One study finds that states that allow the initiative process had on average 17 percent more interest groups between 1975 and 1990, after controlling for other factors that might lead to interest group growth, than states without the process.[75]

A parallel study finds that actual initiative use by a state leads to a general increase in the number of membership groups, associations, and not-for-profit organizations that have registered lobbyists in the state, indicating that the institution of direct democracy can increase the aggregate size as well as the diversity of state-level interest groups.[76] Finally, states with more diverse interest group systems tend to adopt more public policies that are more distributive and progressive.[77]

In states with dense and diverse interest group systems, it is difficult for a single interest to dictate the overall policy agenda of state government. But even in these states with more diversified economies, interest groups are often able to carve space for themselves within a policy domain that is central to their policy objectives, where they become a dominant force. The number of participants in these policy niches tends to be limited in scope, with the vested interests holding considerable influence. In ensuring its survival, a successful interest group is able to stake out its own niche within a given policy domain.

The maximum size of a state's interest group system ultimately depends on the broad parameters of a state's economic and political resources. From this perspective, a state's interest group system is largely driven by its internal economic resources and is constrained by environmental factors. Interest group system stabilization, thus, is set sooner in states with smaller economic capacities.[78] As occurs with biological ecosystems, though, there appears to be a saturation point for state interest group systems. When such a saturation point is reached, the density and diversity of interest groups begin to slow. The competition among interest groups for scarce resources, in this case government grants and programs, intensifies. In turn, as the interest group system stabilizes, it becomes increasingly difficult for the system to support more groups in competition with one another. In terms of turnover of groups within state interest group systems, a recent study finds that for-profit organizations are no more persistent than nonprofit organizations, and enterprises are actually less likely to persist year-in and year-out when compared to membership groups and associations.[79]

Interest Group Competition: Who's Got Clout?

Today, most states and many communities have much more diversified economies than they did a half century ago. This economic change has led to a robust competition among a variety of private and public sector interest groups that battle over the making of public policy. Yet, as Lindblom suggested, private economic interests dominate pluralist interest group systems. For example, the oil industry remains king in Alaska and Louisiana, the agriculture lobby reins supreme in Iowa and South Dakota, ranching interests continue to be a strong force in Nebraska, and the tourism industry holds an upper hand in Florida, Nevada, and Hawaii. Although the company town, communities literally built by firms to house their employees, disappeared from the local landscape long ago,[80] some towns—Bentonville, Arkansas, the

corporate headquarters of Wal-Mart, comes to mind—are still dominated by a single industry.

An interest group's *clout,* or relative influence, is largely determined by its own internal resources, but it is bounded by external conditions. Internal resources include a group's political, organizational, and managerial skills as well as its finances, the size and geographical distribution of its membership, its political cohesiveness, and its long-term relations with public officials. A group's policy goals are also conditioned by external factors, such as the political climate of the state or community, including partisan identification, political culture, issues and events, and public opinion. Although it is difficult, if not impossible, to precisely measure a group's "clout," these internal and external factors affect the ability of an interest organization to wield influence and power within a state or community. When lacking in clout, some groups opt to team up with other organizations to build coalitions. Rather than acting independently and going it alone, it sometimes makes strategic sense for an organization to form alliances with other like-minded groups, especially if competition increases among groups in the system.[81]

Most Influential Interests in the 50 States

Is it possible to rank the most powerful interests in the 50 states? Drawing on data collected by researchers in all 50 states, Table 6.4 categorizes interest organizations by their effectiveness, listing the 20 most influential interests in the states in 2002 (with comparison rankings from 1985). The table reveals how some sectors of interest organizations are influential interests across many states, whereas others are only effective in a few states. General business organizations, most notably the Chamber of Commerce, and teachers' associations, such as the American Federation of Teachers and the National Education Association, are powerful interest groups in all 50 states today, just as they were in 1985. Interest groups representing energy utilities, insurance companies, hospitals, lawyers, and manufacturers are also forces to be reckoned with in

Table 6.4

The 20 Most Influential Interests in the 50 States (2002 and 1985)

2002 Ranking (1985 ranking)	Interest Organization	Number of States in Which Interest Ranked Among		
		Most Effective	Somewhat Effective	Less or Not Effective
1 (2)	General business organizations (state Chamber of Commerce, for example)	40	12	5
2 (1)	Schoolteachers' organizations (National Education Association and American Federation of Teachers)	37	12	2
3 (6)	Utility companies and associations (electric, gas, water, and telephone and telecommunications)	24	26	6
4 (13)	Insurance: general and medical (companies and associations)	21	19	15
5 (17)	Hospital and nursing homes associations	21	18	13
6 (8)	Lawyers (predominantly trial lawyers and state bar associations)	22	15	15
7 (4)	Manufacturers (companies and associations)	18	20	19
8 (9)	General local government organizations (municipal leagues, county organizations, and elected officials)	18	17	17
9 (11)	Physicians and state medical associations	17	16	19
10 (10)	General farm organizations (state Farm Bureau)	16	16	18
11 (3)	Bankers' associations	15	15	22
12 (5)	Traditional labor associations (predominantly the AFL-CIO)	13	16	22
13 (19)	Universities and colleges (institutions and employees)	13	13	26
14 (12)	State and local government employees (other than teachers)	11	15	26
15 (22)	Contractors, builders, and developers	13	11	26
16 (14)	Realtors' associations	13	10	27
17 (16)	K–12 education interests (other than teachers)	9	12	29
18 (15)	Individual traditional labor unions (Teamsters, United Automobile Workers, and other unions)	8	14	29
19 (27)	Truckers and private transport interests (excluding railroads)	9	11	31
20 (35)	Sportsmen, hunting, and fishing (including anti–gun control groups)	9	10	32

Source: Clive Thomas and Ronald Hrebenar, "Interest Groups in the States," in *Politics in the American States,* 8th ed., eds. Virginia Gray and Russell Hanson (Washington, D.C.: CQ Press, 2004).

most states. Although liquor, wine, and beer interests are not nearly as powerful, they have a presence in all 50 states. The brewer Anheuser-Busch, for instance, maintains active lobbies in all the states because alcohol policy is largely regulated by the states. On the other hand, groups representing senior citizens, forest products, mining companies, and tobacco companies have a strong presence in only a handful of states.

Overall, the relative power of interest groups across the 50 states has remained fairly constant over time. Table 6.4 reveals little change between 1985 and 2002 in terms of the relative strength and weakness of interest organizations. In addition to the aforementioned economic interests, groups representing physicians, general farm organizations, and realtors have retained their strength through the years. Although minimal, some change has occurred across some of the sectors: hospital and nursing home associations, the insurance industry, gaming, and hunting and fishing interests have all become relatively stronger (including the venerable NRA), whereas energy corporations and their associations, banks, and other financial enterprises have become weaker players.

Despite some flux in the relative strength of the different sectors represented in state interest group systems, economic groups remain powerful players in most states, just as they were back in the 1950s when the first survey

Table 6.5

Classification of the Overall Impact of Interest Groups, 2002

Dominant	Dominant/ Complementary	Complementary	Complementary/ Subordinate
Alabama	Arkansas	Colorado	Delaware
Florida	Arizona	Connecticut	Minnesota
Louisiana	Alaska	Indiana	Rhode Island
New Mexico	California	Maine	South Dakota
Nevada	Georgia	Maryland	Vermont
South Carolina	Hawaii	Massachusetts	
West Virginia	Idaho	Michigan	
	Illinois	Missouri	
	Iowa	New Hampshire	
	Kansas	New Jersey	
	Kentucky	New York	
	Mississippi	North Carolina	
	Montana	North Dakota	
	Nebraska	Pennsylvania	
	Ohio	Utah	
	Oklahoma	Washington	
	Oregon	Wisconsin	
	Tennessee		
	Texas		
	Virginia		
	Wyoming		

Source: Clive Thomas and Ronald Hrebenar, "Interest Groups in the States," in Politics in the American States, 8th ed., ed. Virginia Gray and Russell Hanson (Washington, D.C.: CQ Press, 2004).

of interest groups was conducted.[82] This has led some observers, following the pioneering work of Schattschneider and Lindblom, to again ask whether a corporate bias in the interest group systems of the states exists. One recent study—which finds that 77 percent of the total universe of state interest groups is made up of for-profit organizations—seems to confirm Schattschneider's prediction that private interest organizations will dominate the interest group system.[83] Yet, the dominance of business interests is not hegemonic. Business interests do not control all policy niches. As state economies increase in size, business interests tend to fragment to some degree.[84] As interest group systems become more and more crowded and complex, it is possible that powerful groups—including business associations and firms—may lose their "clout."[85]

Relative Impact of Interest Groups Interest group strength can also be measured with a fivefold typology that assesses the overall impact of interest groups relative to other actors (most notably political parties) in a state's political system. Last updated in 2002, a survey of the 50 states reveals that the power of interest groups compared to other actors can be considered *dominant* in 7 states, *dominant/complementary* in 21 states, *complementary* in 17 states, *complementary/subordinate* in 5 states, and *subordinate* in no states.[86] Table 6.5 provides the overall impact of interest groups in the 50 states. The number of states found in each category today has changed since the survey was first conducted in the early 1980s; three-fifths of the states are still classified in the same category as they were in 1985, with the remainder shifting categories. Slightly less than half of the states today are categorized as *dominant/complementary*. Why are interest group systems in some states more dominant than others? Although it's difficult to precisely answer this question, states with less robust economies tend to have political systems with more dominant interest groups. Conversely, in states with larger economies, interest groups were weaker or more complementary relative to other actors, such as parties.[87]

Summary

Despite some concerns over the undue influence of economic interests, voluntary associations since Madison's time have played a vital role in American states and communities. Like political parties, interest groups are political institutions that operate as rational actors. Some interest groups employ lobbyists to place pressure on public officials. Others use issue advocacy, electioneering, and litigation to advance their collective goals. Whatever their tactic, interest groups are constantly fighting to shape the political terrain, molding it to reflect their image. Although pluralist theory suggests all interests have an equal chance to be heard in the public sphere, there are many barriers to collective action. Because economic and political resources are not distributed evenly across society, some interests are more easily articulated and aggregated than others. As such, not all societal interests are equally represented in states and communities by organized interests nor are they all heard by elected officials and policy makers. It should come as no surprise, then, that in a country with a market-oriented political economy, state and local interest group systems tend to favor economic interests.

Key Terms

Astroturf campaign	Interest group	Pluralism
Contract lobbyist	Interest group system density	Political action committee (PAC)
Disturbance theory	Interest group system diversity	Potential interest
Earned media		Public good
Electioneering	Issue advocacy	Selective benefit
Free-rider problem	Lobbying	Watchdog
In-house lobbyist	Mobilization of bias	

Suggested Readings

Alexander, Robert. 2005. *The classics of interest group behavior*. Boston: Thomson Wadsworth.

Baumgartner, Frank, and Beth L. Leech. 1998. *Basic interests: The importance of groups in politics and in political science*. Princeton, NJ: Princeton University Press.

Berry, Jeffrey. 1999. *The new liberalism: The rising power of citizen groups*. Washington, DC: Brookings Institution Press.

Gray, Virginia, and David Lowery. 1996. *The population ecology of interest representation: Lobbying communities in the American states*. Ann Arbor: University of Michigan Press.

Nownes, Anthony, and Patricia Freeman. 1998. "Interest group activity in the states." *Journal of Politics* 60 (1): 86–112.

Olson, Mancur. 1965. *The logic of collective action*. Cambridge, MA: Harvard University Press.

Rosenthal, Alan. 2001. *The third house: Lobbyists and lobbying in the states*. Washington, DC: CQ Press.

Schattschneider, E. E. 1960. *The semisovereign people*. New York: Holt, Rinehart & Winston.

Truman, David B. 1951. *The governmental process*. New York: Alfred A. Knopf.

Websites

American League of Lobbyists (http://www.alldc.org): The American League of Lobbyists is an association devoted to enhancing the professionalism, competence, and ethical standards of lobbyists.

Common Cause (http://www.commoncause.org): Founded in 1970 and with chapters in all 50 states, Common Cause is a nonpartisan, nonprofit advocacy organization that strives to hold elected leaders accountable to the public interest.

Political Advocacy Groups: A Directory of United States Lobbyists (http://www. csuchico.edu/~kcfount/index.html): An index by issue area of over 400 interest groups in the United States, with hypertext links.

Project VoteSmart (http://www.vote-smart.org/issue_group.php): Project VoteSmart, a nonprofit, nonpartisan organization, provides a compilation of interest organizations that can searched by subject or by state.

7

Jon Arnold Images/Danita Delimont

State Legislatures

Like Its State, a Legislature Changes Dramatically: Florida, 1968–2008

OUTLINE

Introductory Vignette

Introduction

State Legislatures: The Basics

State Legislative Elections

State Legislators: Who Are They?

The Job of the State Legislature

The Collective Action Problem

State Legislative Reform

Summary

In the 1960s, Florida was a rural, Deep South state with an agricultural economy. With fewer than 6 million residents, it was the 26th largest state. Its capital was Tallahassee, a sleepy little town in the panhandle. As in the rest of the Deep South, conservative Democrats dominated Florida's legislature, controlling 91 percent of the seats in the House and 95 percent in the Senate. Service in the Florida Legislature was a part-time job because it met only once every two years for 60 days.[1] Legislators received an annual salary of only $2,400—small even in those days. In fact, legislators were paid less than the capitol janitors.[2] Most legislators had no office, just their desk on the floor of the chamber. A legislator's district office was usually his or her kitchen table at home. In 1968, only two of the 156 state legislators were not white (they were African Americans) and only four were women.[3] Most legislators served only a few terms and then returned to private life, thankful to be finished with this onerous public service.

By 2008, things had changed dramatically in Florida and its legislature. Florida is now the fourth-largest state in the nation, with over 17 million people; it will soon pass New York for the third spot. This population explosion was caused by immigration: from the north, retirees and young people, and from the south, people from Central and South America and the Caribbean, all looking for good weather and opportunity. Florida's economy is much more diverse and vibrant, with tourism, high tech, and international trade joining agriculture in fueling the state's boom.

Florida's legislature has also been transformed, responding to the economic and social changes in the state. It now meets every year, and although it is still limited to only 60 official session days each year, its committees meet year-round and throughout the state. Every legislator has an office in Tallahassee and in his or her district. In addition, every legislator has at least three personal staff. Many more staff are assigned to the committees, party leaders, and committee chairs. Something that has not changed much is that legislators are not well paid; rank-and-file members earn $29,916 per year, plus expenses.[4] Most legislators support themselves with another job. This means that legislators are often lawyers, real estate salespeople, or insurance agents or in other types of business that allow flexible schedules.

Among the most dramatic changes in the Florida Legislature are the characteristics of its members. Reflecting the changes everywhere in the Deep South, Florida's legislature is now dominated by Republicans, who constitute 65 percent of each chamber.

Florida's legislators also now look a lot more like Floridians overall than they did in the 1960s, with 21 percent of them being women, 16 percent being African American, and 12 percent being Latino. In fact, 18 percent of Florida's senators are Jewish;[5] no Southern legislature would have come near this in the 1960s.

Florida has also made some major institutional changes in its legislature since 1966. Florida now redraws its legislative districts every 10 years. In a reform designed to rationalize lawmaking, the legislature slashed the number of its committees by more than half. But perhaps most significantly, in 1992, Floridians enacted state legislative term limits, forcing legislators to step aside after only eight years of service. Back in the 1960s, many Florida legislators voluntarily stepped aside every election, tired of the long drives to Tallahassee and the low pay. But there was always a cadre of long-serving lawmakers who provided continuity and stability to the body. With term limits, when each new session begins, no legislator has more than six years of experience in the chamber.

Introduction

State legislatures provide a vital link between a state's citizens and its government—they are the "guts of democracy," as one longtime observer of them once wrote.[6] State legislators are closer to the people they represent than any other state or federal elected official. The state legislator's job is not glamorous and it is not well paid, but it is essential in converting the wishes and needs of a state's citizens into public policy.

Because the job of the state legislature is so difficult and so important, the states have constantly tinkered with these institutions to improve their performance. And as the Florida story demonstrates, these bodies have undergone particularly radical change in the past generation. A prime motivator of this period of reform was the set of U.S. Supreme Court decisions in the 1960s mandating that the states redraw their legislative districts every 10 years. Regular redistricting has stirred the political pot, leading to changes large and small in every state. In addition to this redistricting revolution, two other major reform movements have swept the country: the legislative professionalism movement of the 1970s and 1980s and the term limits movement of the 1990s. Each wave of reform was motivated by the optimistic assumption that institutional change can improve legislative performance. But determining what constitutes good legislative performance and deciding upon the best way to achieve it have been matters of continuing debate.[7]

Other changes in the state legislatures have not been matters of institutional reform. Dramatic social changes in the 1960s and 1970s allowed a much broader array of citizens to participate in the American political system, and these changes were reflected first and to the greatest extent in the state legislatures. It is now common for women and members of minority racial and ethnic groups not only to serve in state legislatures but also to hold the highest leadership positions there. It is not even surprising anymore to find legislators who are openly homosexual. And because state legislatures are a prime political training ground for many of those in higher office,[8] the demographic changes of our national leaders today were foreshadowed in the states. Long before Nancy Pelosi was speaker of the U.S. House of Representatives, Vera Katz was speaker of the Oregon House; 32 other women have also led a state legislative chamber to date.[9] And before presidential candidate Barack Obama was a U.S. senator from Illinois, Emil Jones was the president of the Illinois State Senate (where he was Obama's mentor); seven other African Americans have also led a state legislative chamber.

In this chapter, we consider state legislators and legislatures and their role in state government, reflecting on the dramatic changes in these bodies in recent decades. What does the legislature do, and how does it do it? Who are state legislators? How do they get into office, and how do they behave once there? We discuss states' attempts to improve their legislatures' performance through institutional reform. As clearly as anywhere in government, institutional reform in the state legislature has affected politics and policy—but not always in the ways that reformers intended.

State Legislatures: The Basics

As lawmaking institutions, state legislatures are quite similar to one another and to the U.S. Congress. Forty-nine state legislatures have a **bicameral** structure, with two independent chambers (the **unicameral** Nebraska Legislature has only a senate); a bill must pass through both chambers in exactly the same form to become law. One chamber is called the *Senate*, and the other chamber is usually called the *House of Representatives*, although some states use other names, such as the House of Delegates in Virginia and the Assembly in California. Houses have more members than do senates, typically about two or three times as many, and so, they have smaller districts. Senators are most commonly elected to four-year terms from

Table 7.1

State Legislatures, Terms, Seats, and Multimember Districts (MMDs)

State	Name of Both Chambers Together	Senate			Name of Other Chamber			
		Length of Term	Number of Seats	% MMDs[a]		Length of Term	Number of Seats	%MMDs[a]
AL	Legislature	4	35	0	House*	4	105	0
AK	Legislature	4	20	0	House*	2	40	0
AZ	Legislature	2	30	0	House*	2	60	100
AR	General Assembly	4	35	0	House*	2	100	0
CA	Legislature	4	40	0	Assembly	2	80	0
CO	General Assembly	4	35	0	House*	2	65	0
CT	General Assembly	2	36	0	House*	2	151	0
DE	General Assembly	4	21	0	House*	2	41	0
FL	Legislature	4	40	0	House*	2	120	0
GA	General Assembly	2	56	0	House*	2	180	0
HI	Legislature	4	25	0	House*	2	51	0
ID	Legislature	2	35	0	House*	2	70	0
IL	General Assembly	4	59	0	House*	2	118	0
IN	General Assembly	4	50	0	House*	2	100	0
IA	General Assembly	4	50	0	House*	2	100	0
KS	Legislature	4	40	0	House*	2	125	0
KY	General Assembly	4	38	0	House*	2	100	0
LA	Legislature	4	39	0	House*	4	105	0
ME	Legislature	2	35	0	House*	2	151	0
MD	General Assembly	4	47	0	House of Delegates	4	141	67
MA	General Court	2	40	0	House*	2	160	0
MI	Legislature	4	38	0	House*	2	110	0
MN	Legislature	4	67	0	House*	2	134	0
MS	Legislature	4	52	0	House*	4	122	0
MO	General Assembly	4	34	0	House*	2	163	0
MT	Legislature	4	50	0	House*	2	100	0
NE	Legislature	4	49	0	**	**	**	**
NV	Legislature	4	21	11	Assembly	2	42	0
NH	General Court	2	24	0	House*	2	400	88
NJ	Legislature	4	40	0	General Assembly	2	80	100
NM	Legislature	4	42	0	House*	2	70	0
NY	Legislature	2	62	0	Assembly	2	150	0
NC	General Assembly	2	50	0	House*	2	120	0

State Legislatures, Terms, Seats, and Multimember Districts (MMDs) (continued)

State	Name of Both Chambers Together	Senate			Name of Other Chamber	Length of Term	Number of Seats	%MMDs[a]
		Length of Term	Number of Seats	% MMDs[a]				
ND	Legislative Assembly	4	47	0	House*	4	94	100
OH	General Assembly	4	33	0	House*	2	99	0
OK	Legislature	4	48	0	House*	2	101	0
OR	Legislative Assembly	4	30	0	House*	2	60	0
PA	General Assembly	4	50	0	House*	2	203	0
RI	General Assembly	2	38	0	House*	2	75	0
SC	General Assembly	4	46	0	House*	2	124	0
SD	Legislature	2	35	0	House*	2	70	100
TN	General Assembly	4	33	0	House*	2	99	0
TX	Legislature	4	31	0	House*	2	150	0
UT	Legislature	4	29	0	House*	2	75	0
VT	General Assembly	2	30	77	House*	2	150	39
VA	General Assembly	4	40	0	House of Delegates	2	100	0
WA	Legislature	4	49	0	House*	2	98	100
WV	Legislature	4	34	100	House of Delegates	2	100	40
WI	Legislature	4	33	0	Assembly	2	99	0
WY	Legislature	4	30	0	House*	2	60	0

Sources: Council of State Governments, *The Book of the States 2006,* vol. 38 (Lexington, KY: Council of State Governments, 2006); and the National Conference of State Legislatures, http://www.ncsl.org.

[a] This is the percentage of districts that have more than one member serving in them.

* House of Representatives.

** Nebraska's unicameral legislature only has a senate.

single-member districts (SMDs); that is, districts from which they are the only senator; house members are usually called *representatives*, and they are usually elected to two-year terms from SMDs. But in 12 states, senators have two-year terms, and in five states, representatives have four-year terms. Some legislators (about 13 percent of them nationwide) are elected from districts with more than one more member serving in them, like members of the U.S. Senate (two of whom serve each state). These are called multimember districts (MMDs). Table 7.1 lists how the different state legislatures vary on these characteristics. MMDs used to be more common in state legislatures because they reduced the difficulty of drawing districts (because fewer districts needed to be drawn). But MMDs are now used less often because they seem to diminish the representation of racial minorities.[10]

State Legislative Elections

There are 7,382 men and women serving in the 50 state legislatures, with the number in each chamber ranging from 20 (the Alaska State Senate) to 400 (the New Hampshire House of Representatives). Each of these legislators was elected to his or her seat.[11] So, to understand state legislatures and state legislators, you must first understand state legislative elections.

The Paradox of Competition in State Legislative Elections

Political competition is the lifeblood of a healthy representative democracy. When any candidate could win an election, each one works hard to appeal to voters. The resulting energetic campaign activity raises voters' interest in, and understanding of, the race, the office being contested, and the candidates. Elected officials who anticipate a close race in the next election pay close attention to what their constituents want them to do in office, and they make every effort both to serve and represent them well. When a race is not competitive—that is, when one candidate has no hope of winning—neither the voters nor the candidates take much interest in it. Elected officials who feel safe in office have little electoral incentive to do anything special for their constituents. Of course, elected officials serve their districts for other, less selfish reasons, but the fear of losing the next election is a strong institutional motivation for politicians.

Are state legislative elections competitive? Recent election results answer this question with a paradox. In the aggregate, state legislative elections appear to be extremely competitive, but at the district level, they seem to not be at all competitive. As you saw in Chapter 5, recent elections have yielded remarkably similar numbers of Democratic and Republican state legislators overall nationwide. Before the Democrats picked up 322 seats in their big wins in the 2006 midterm elections, they had a mere one-seat advantage out of 7,382. This looks like pretty close competition. But in individual state legislative races, there is precious little political competition at all. Many state legislative races are routinely won by 10 or 20 percent.[12] In fact, in the last two general elections, 35 percent of the winners of these races did not even have an opponent in the general election.[13]

If state legislative elections overall reflect the close competition between the political parties that we have seen in recent presidential elections and in Congress, why are the races for most individual state legislative seats so uncompetitive? The answer has to do with (1) how people vote in state legislative elections and (2) the way state legislative districts are drawn. That is, we can explain this paradox by looking at voting and how our electoral institutions translate these votes into state legislative seats.

Party, Incumbency, and Voting Decisions in State Legislative Elections

First, consider the nature of state legislative elections. About 87 percent of state legislators run for office in SMDs. The size of these districts varies dramatically from state to state based on the number of seats in a chamber and, most important, the number of people living in the state. For example, California's senate districts have about 887,000 people in them, whereas New Hampshire's house districts have only about 3,220 people. The average state legislature has house districts with about 55,000 people and senate districts with about 150,000 people. Thus, compared to members of the U.S. House of Representatives, who each represent about 650,000 constituents, most state legislators have quite small districts. And because Americans tend to live near those who are like themselves racially, socially, and economically, these small districts are often relatively homogeneous. That is, whereas a congressional district may stretch hundreds of miles and encompass farms, small towns, suburbs, and cities, a state legislative district may cover as little as a few square miles in a heavily populated urban district or many counties that are sparsely populated with farmers and small-town folks. So, state legislative districts tend to have small and homogeneous populations, which contributes greatly to the lack of competition in them.

Explaining state legislative elections also requires the recognition that they are not at the forefront of most voters' minds when they step into the voting booth on Election Day. Even

COMPARISONS HELP US UNDERSTAND

VARIATION IN TWO-PARTY CONTESTATION IN STATE LEGISLATIVE RACES

Most state legislative races are not very competitive, but over one-third of general election races for the state legislature do not even have both a Democratic and Republican candidate. This means that the nominee of the one party with a candidate wins the election by default. This is an extreme lack of competition. Furthermore, the rate of this lack of contestation varies considerably from state to state. For example, in the 2006 general election, although 97 percent of the races for seats in the Michigan Legislature had both a Democrat and Republican running, the same was true in only 25 percent of the races for the South Carolina General Assembly. Table 7.2 shows the percentage of races in each state with two-party contestation in the 2006 general election. Can you explain this wide variation in state legislative contestation and competition? Think about why people vote as they do in these elections and why a person might decide to run in one. Also, think about the institutional factors that might encourage or discourage such competition. For example, political scientist Peverill Squire found that the incentives offered to legislators in professionalized legislatures made seats there more attractive, causing more people to run for them, resulting in more competition in those legislatures.[1] And advocates of legislative term limits argued that the reform would increase competition.[2] Develop your own hypothesis and test it against the data in Table 7.2 and data in other tables and figures in this and other chapters.

Notes

1. See Peverill Squire, "Uncontested Seats in State Legislative Elections," *Legislative Studies Quarterly* 25 (2000): 131–46; see also Richard G. Niemi, Lynda W. Powell, William D. Berry, Thomas M. Carsey, and James M. Snyder Jr., "Competition in State Legislative Elections, 1992–2002," in *The Marketplace of Democracy*, eds. Michael P. McDonald and John Samples (Washington, D.C.: Brookings Institution, 2006); and Robert E. Hogan, "Institutional and District-Level Sources of Competition in State Legislative Elections," *Social Science Quarterly* 84 (2003): 543–60, for more discussion of the factors that affect competition in state legislative elections.
2. John H. Fund, "Term Limitation: An Idea Whose Time Has Come," in *Limiting Legislative Terms*, eds. Gerald Benjamin and Michael J. Malbin (Washington, D.C.: Congressional Quarterly Press, 1992); Mark P. Petracca, "The Poison of Professional Politics," *Policy Analysis*, online ed., 151 (1991); and George F. Will, *Restoration: Congress, Term Limits, and the Recovery of Deliberative Democracy* (New York: Free Press, 1993).

though state government affects people's lives in profound ways every day, few people know much about the legislature, so they do not spend much time pondering these races.[14] State legislative candidates work hard and spend tens of thousands of dollars to communicate their messages to voters, but their campaigns are typically overshadowed by candidates "up the ticket" for Congress, governor, and president. People have a limited attention span for politics, and state legislative races are not nearly as relevant to most people as are those other races.

In particular, two important factors work against voters getting information about state legislative races. First, these districts usually do not include an entire **media market**, so advertising on TV and radio is uneconomical.[15]

For example, a candidate for one of the 23 state house seats in the New Orleans media market who buys a TV ad would be wasting 22/23 of every dollar spent because that fraction of the audience would be outside of his or her district and, thus, unable to vote for the candidate even if they wanted to. Some state legislative candidates have been trying to deal with this problem by using cable TV to tailor their audience in a much more fine-tuned way; this reduces the amount of TV advertising "waste," but it usually does not eliminate it. Second, state legislative races fare little better on TV news coverage. A recent study estimated that even during the peak of the general election campaign, the average 30-minute local news broadcast devoted only about 36 seconds

Table 7.2

Partisan Contestation in State Legislative Races in the 2006 General Election (arranged from most to fewest combined races contested)

State	Combined % Races Contested*	% House Races Contested*	% Senate Races Contested*
MI	97	95	100
ME	96	95	97
MN	96	96	94
OH	92	91	100
CA	88	91	75
MT	84	83	88
OR	84	82	93
HI	83	90	54
ND	83	81	87
SD	82	83	80
CO	81	78	89
NH	80	79	92
UT	75	71	94
WV	74	75	71
WA	72	70	79
NY	70	71	69
AK	68	65	80
PA	68	67	72
IN	67	66	72
CT	66	62	83
MD	66	67	66
WI	66	65	76
MO	64	63	76
AZ	62	57	73
IA	62	64	52
KS	62	62	No election
DE	56	59	45
FL	56	56	60
ID	56	53	63
OK	55	49	75
VT	55	51	77
NV	53	57	36
IL	52	48	64
AL	51	46	66
NC	49	46	56

Partisan Contestation in State Legislative Races in the 2006 General Election (arranged from most to fewest combined races contested) (continued)

State	Combined % Races Contested[II]	% House Races Contested*	% Senate Races Contested[II]
RI	49	47	53
TN	47	44	59
TX	46	47	44
KY	44	44	42
NM	40	40	No election
WY	35	32	47
GA	28	24	41
AR	27	29	18
MA	27	26	32
SC	25	25	No election
U.S. average	62	62	67

Note: Louisiana, Mississippi, New Jersey, and Virginia held no state legislative races in 2006. The state senates in Kansas, New Mexico, and South Carolina held no elections in 2006. Nebraska's legislature is excluded because it is nonpartisan.

* The percentage of those seats up for election that had both a Democrat and a Republican running in the general election.

Source: John McGlennon and Cory Kaufman, "Expanding the Playing Field: Competition Rises for State Legislative Seats in 2006," report from the Thomas Jefferson Program in Public Policy (Williamsburg, VA: College of William and Mary, 2006).

to election coverage.[16] And these 36 seconds include information on congressional, statewide, and local races—state legislative races are lucky to even get a mention. Furthermore, state legislators rarely get any news coverage during the course of their regular lawmaking duties, and this coverage has even been shrinking in recent years.[17] Because Americans tend to get their political information from mass media advertisements and news, the absence of state legislators and state legislative races from them makes these races virtually invisible for most voters.

So, how do Americans decide for whom to vote in a state legislative election? Surprisingly, little research has been done on this question,[18] but much can be surmised from what we know about these races and American voters. In short, most people probably choose a state legislative candidate right inside the voting booth itself. Voters step into the booth with a pretty good idea about how they will vote in the more visible races, like those for president and governor, but they typically have given little thought to their state legislative vote.

Regardless of the lack of information about the state legislative candidates that they bring into the voting booth, voters always[19] have one important piece of information on which to base their vote—the candidates' party affiliation, as written on the ballot. In conjunction with voters' own party leanings, the candidate's party likely determines most votes in state legislative races. All else being equal, why not vote for the candidate of the party with which you typically agree? And because state legislative districts are so small, they tend to be more politically homogeneous than, say, congressional districts or the state as a whole. Thus, the size and homogeneity of state legislative districts and the invisibility of these races to most voters certainly contribute to the scarcity of two-party competition in state legislative elections.

In addition to this party affiliation **voting cue,** simply recognizing a state legislative candidate's name can influence a voter's decision. If a voter recognizes one of the names on the ballot, he or she will usually be more likely to vote for that candidate. Why might a voter be more likely to have heard about one candidate than another? Incumbency is the biggest reason. The current state legislator—the **incumbent**—has campaigned before, has gotten his or her name in the newspapers for legislative accomplishments, has perhaps been seen by the voter in a parade or at a meeting of a group, or has sent newsletters about his or her service to the voter for the past two years or more. Thus, the voter is most likely to have heard of the incumbent, and this information is likely to have been positive because it has largely been controlled by the incumbent himself or herself. Thus, all things being equal, name recognition usually works to the incumbent's advantage in the voting booth.

Campaigns can also increase name recognition; in fact, that is largely what they are designed to do. State legislative campaigns have traditionally been pretty down-home affairs, being run from a kitchen table and a home computer, with a small group of the candidate's friends and neighbors going door to door, distributing campaign brochures, putting up yard signs, and so forth.[20] Candidates can also increase their name recognition among voters by earning the endorsements of newspapers and interest groups that are important to voters in their districts.[21] And the more the average candidate spends on the campaign, the more votes he or she will likely receive.[22] Of course, the effects of incumbency and campaign spending are intertwined; interest groups may try to gain access to legislators by making campaign contributions to them. Thus, incumbents' electoral chances are improved both by the name recognition they earn from serving in the legislature and by having more money to spend on their campaigns than their challengers.

The results of state legislative elections confirm this line of thinking—incumbent state legislators who run for re-election win overwhelmingly, especially where legislators are well paid and have plenty of staff.[23] In these states, legislators have both the incentive and the resources to enhance their positive name recognition by providing various services for their constituents, bringing home special projects for their districts, and reflecting their constituents' preferences closely in policy making. Incumbents are sometimes challenged successfully, even in their party's primary, but the defeat of a state legislative incumbent is so rare as to be newsworthy. However, voters' lack of information about state legislative candidates—even incumbents—means that one bad piece of information may be enough to turn even a long-term legislator out of office. For example, after Pennsylvania lawmakers voted themselves a pay raise in 2005, the state's media wrote stories about various perks of office that these legislators enjoyed, such as generous pension benefits, lobbyist wining and dining, tickets to Steelers and Eagles games, and so forth. So, in 2006, Pennsylvania voters finally noticed their state legislators—and threw them out in record numbers, including some key leaders.[24]

Thus, state legislative races are typically determined by incumbency and the partisan alignment of the district. The partisan alignment of a district changes very slowly, when it changes at all, and the futility of taking on an incumbent leads most potential challengers to seek their political fortunes elsewhere. This certainly helps explain the dearth of district-level competition in state legislative races these days, but it is not the whole story. Next, we consider an institutional factor that helps us complete our explanation—the mechanisms by which state legislative districts are drawn.

State Legislative Redistricting

Each state legislator is elected from a specific, legally defined subsection of the state; that is, his or her legislative district. Established by law, the boundaries of these districts are incredibly detailed, specifying exactly which streets each district's lines run down and defining in which senate and house district every square foot of the state lies. Precisely where each of these lines runs is determined as a matter of public policy based on certain criteria, some of which are also established by law and others of which are simply desirable. Because of these criteria, districts are generally not just shaped by geographic features (like rivers or mountain ranges) nor can they neatly follow other political boundaries (like county or city lines). Furthermore, the U.S. Supreme Court requires that these districts be redrawn every 10 years to reflect changes in a state's population. How these districts are drawn and who draws them have a lot to do with explaining the lack of political competition in state legislative districts today.

"One Person, One Vote" Before the early 1960s, states rarely redrew their legislative district boundaries. **Redistricting** causes political conflict because which areas and people are in which districts has a major effect on elections. For state legislators, their districts define exactly who can vote for (and against) them and what interests they need to represent in the state capitol. Changing district boundaries means shifting some of a legislator's former constituents to a new district and bringing in new people to take their place. Although legislators might not mind doing this if those who moved out voted against them and those moving in were going to vote for them, a legislator can never be certain that this will be the case. More important, legislators invest considerable time and effort building favorable name recognition among their constituents through campaigns, newsletters, personal favors, professional service, and the like.[25] The loss of any constituent, regardless of party, through redistricting represents the loss of that investment. As a result, legislators generally favor the status quo in anything concerning their elections—the current arrangements got them elected, so why change things? Thus, it is much easier for states to let their legislative districts remain as they are. And before the 1960s, they did so, sometimes for many decades.

The problem with this status quo bias in legislative districting was that although the district boundaries remained the same, the states' populations were constantly shifting, sometimes dramatically so. In particular, people moved from the country, where most

people lived in 1900, to the cities, where most people lived in 1960. Because of this shift in population, districts that were equal in population in 1900 were very unequal by 1960, when some states' legislative districts suffered from extreme **malapportionment;** that is, the unequal representation of people living in different districts. For example, Connecticut's and Florida's districts were so malapportioned that a party that controlled districts containing as little as 12 percent of the state's population could have had a majority of the seats in their state houses.[26] Because people were moving from the country to the city, this malapportionment gave rural areas more state legislative representation and power than their population warranted, and it gave urban and suburban areas much less of it.[27]

But in a series of decisions beginning in 1962, the Supreme Court ruled that having districts of unequal population in the same legislative chamber[28] violated the Equal Protection Clause of the 14th Amendment and was, therefore, unconstitutional.[29] The Court established the principle of one person, one vote,[30] whereby everyone's vote in a state should be equal. Without legislative districts of equal population, the value of a person's vote in a smaller district is worth more than that of a person in a larger district. For example, a person in a sparsely populated rural house district of 5,000 people would have three times the influence in an election and, therefore in the legislature, as a person in a more densely populated urban house district of 15,000 people— 1/5,000 versus 1/15,000. Responding to these Supreme Court decisions, the states spent the rest of the 1960s undertaking the politically wrenching task of completely redrawing their state legislative (and congressional) districts so that they would be equal in population based on the 1960 U.S. Census. This process had such a wide-ranging effect on politics in the United States that it was called the **reapportionment revolution.**[31]

Each state had to establish a regular process for legislative redistricting. Most of these processes involved the state legislature in some way, but in some states, the courts had to step in to draw the map when the legislature failed to do so. For example, the failure of Illinois's legislature and governor to agree on a set of legislative district maps led to that state's infamous "bed sheet ballot" in the 1964 general election, a 33-inch ballot on which every voter in the state had to choose between 236 candidates for 177 state house seats.[32] But by the end of the 1960s, every state had redrawn its legislative districts equally. The result was a shift in power from the rural areas of the states to the urban and suburban areas, reflecting the end of the malapportionment bias under which many legislatures had long suffered.[33]

Drawing New Districts Of course, because Americans are highly mobile, districts with equal populations today will not remain equal for long. To maintain the one person, one vote standard, the Supreme Court's rulings mean that states must go through the redistricting process after the national census at the beginning of each decade to adjust their legislative districts to the population shifts that occurred since the previous census. But if redistricting in the 1960s was like a Category 4 hurricane, the regular decennial redistricting is only like a Category 1 in most states. Yes, it is a major political battle in every state every decade, but policy makers have come to accept and expect redistricting, and they have developed the processes and skills required to do so. And the changes that are made each decade are not nearly as large as those that were required in the 1960s, when policy makers had to adjust for generations of neglect and malapportionment.

An exception to this was the Texas redistricting wars in the early 2000s. Republican Congressman Tom DeLay, the majority leader in the U.S. House of Representatives, did not like the districts that the Democrats in the Texas state legislature drew for the Texas congressional delegation after the 2000 U.S. Census (recall that the states draw both congressional districts and districts for the state legislature). After the Republicans took control of the Texas

legislature in the 2002 election, DeLay had a novel idea—why not re-redistrict? That is, he convinced the legislature to draw a new set of congressional districts that would be favorable to Republicans. After heated political battles that included the spectacle of Democratic state legislators fleeing the state (twice) to deprive the legislature of the quorum necessary to pass the plan, the Republicans adopted districts that were successful in increasing the party's numbers in the U.S. House.[34] Before DeLay's maneuver, no one had tried to redistrict more than once a decade, and opponents of the plan fought it all the way to the U.S. Supreme Court. In 2006, in *League of United Latin American Citizens v. Perry*,[35] the Court decided that states could redraw their congressional (and, by extension, state legislative) districts whenever they wanted to, as long as they did so at least once a decade. Although it remains to be seen how many states will take advantage of this opportunity, the political toll[36] of such extraordinary redistricting makes it unlikely that it will occur very often, especially for state legislative districts.

Most states take one of two approaches to state legislative and congressional redistricting, adopting their new maps through the regular legislative process or through a nonpartisan or bipartisan commission process.[37] Using either method, the questions are (1) where exactly to put the district lines and (2) which criteria should be used to make these decisions? These are the practical questions that face state policy makers in every state every 10 years (at least), and the answer to them will have a major influence on politics and policy in the state for the next decade.

Two criteria must always be met by any redistricting plan:

- Each district must be geographically **contiguous** (all of its area must be connected by land—except for islands).
- All districts must be almost equal in population as of the most recent census.[38]

No map that defines districts that fail to meet these criteria will hold up to a court challenge.

But beyond these two legal absolutes, a variety of criteria have been used to determine a "good" legislative map, but no single criterion is universally accepted or legally required in every state. Some argue that legislative districts should be compact, or follow local government boundaries, or reflect "communities of interest"; that is, groups of people with common racial, ethnic, or economic interests.[39] State legislators themselves would like to have their own districts full of voters from their own party so that they can win re-election easily. Political parties would like to see their partisans spread around more evenly so as to establish a modest majority in as many districts as possible, thereby winning more seats.[40]

Racial and ethnic representation has long been an important consideration in legislative redistricting. Multimember districts were once used to dilute minority voters' power, but this use of MMDs was banned by the federal Voting Rights Act of 1965.[41] In the 1980s, the Supreme Court seemed to encourage drawing "majority-minority" districts; that is, packing enough of those of a given race or ethnicity—generally, African Americans or Latinos—into a district so as to elect one of their own.[42] But in the 1990s, the Court appeared to change its mind, holding that race could not be the primary consideration in drawing a district.[43] Race continues to be a consideration for redistricters because (1) it is illegal to draw maps deliberately to disenfranchise minority voters; (2) partisanship and race are closely intertwined in the United States, and it is legal to draw maps for partisan advantage;[44] and (3) all things being equal, many people believe that fairness in the representation of minorities is an important redistricting criterion. Include in this mix the likelihood that the Supreme Court may at any time rule again on this subject, and you can see that race and legislative redistricting will likely be linked for the foreseeable future.

So just how do the states decide on the specific boundaries for their state legislative districts? Three broad factors shape this decision-making process:

- The conflicts of interest among those drawing the maps (in most cases, state legislators and political parties)
- The general public's lack of interest in, and knowledge about, the redistricting process
- The lack of clear criteria for redistricting

Because state legislators and the political parties are the only ones who care very much about these maps, and because there are so few specific legally enforceable guidelines for redistricters to follow, the interests of legislators and parties tend to dominate the process in most states.

The state legislative districts that result from these forces have at least two characteristics.[45] First, they tend to be electorally safe for many, if not most, of the current incumbents and their parties, especially when the maps have to be approved through the legislative process. The price of a legislator's vote for a plan may be having a favorable district drawn for him or her. Such **incumbent-protection districts** have lopsided partisan balances and incorporate as much of an incumbent's previous district as possible. Although it is easy to tell where a legislator's former constituents live, it is harder to know the partisanship of citizens who could potentially be included in a new district. This information is typically divined by redistricters from the results of previous elections and voter registration rolls. The effect of such districts is often to freeze the political status quo, with incumbent legislators being even more difficult to defeat than normal and the overall balance of the parties' seats in the state legislature being stabilized. This tendency toward protecting the status quo is especially strong when both parties have a hand in the process, whether due to **divided government** or by the parties being represented on a redistricting commission.

The second effect of these redistricting forces is that when one party controls the redistricting process, whether by having unified government or controlling the redistricting commission, that party will try to draw districts that improve its chances of winning seats in the state legislature. This is done by spreading out some of its opponent's voters at less than a majority in many districts—so-called **cracking** of voters—and **packing** many of the others into a few seats so as to "waste" their votes over 50 percent. Such machinations often require boundaries that are irregular, if not downright tortured, as redistricters draw district boundaries searching for just the right balance of partisan votes. This is called political **gerrymandering**, after the 19th-century Massachusetts political boss and U.S. vice president Elbridge Gerry. Because the districts Gerry drew to maximize his party's advantage were so weirdly shaped, a political cartoonist thought that one looked like a salamander; thus, the name *gerrymander.* But with today's detailed census and voting databases and computerized geographic information systems (GIS), redistricters now outdo even Gerry in their creativity in pursuing political advantage.

Ohio's current state legislative map provides a good example of the effect of partisan gerrymandering.[46] As is well-known from recent presidential elections, Ohio's electorate is split virtually 50–50 between the parties. What's more, 2006 was a terrible year for the GOP in the Buckeye State. A major financial scandal and a retiring governor with the lowest poll ratings in the country led the party to landslide losses in the races for governor, U.S. senator, secretary of state, treasurer, and attorney general for the first time in over 10 years.[47] But Republicans controlled redistricting in Ohio in 2001, and their effective cracking and packing of voters in legislative districts allowed the party to emerge from the election with a 7 percentage point advantage in the Ohio House and a whopping 27 percentage point advantage in the Ohio Senate (see Table 7.3). And Republicans are not the only ones

Table 7.3

Partisan Distribution of State Legislative Seats, 2008

State	Senate			House		
	% Democrat	% Republican	% Other	% Democrat	% Republican	% Other
AL	65.7	34.3	0	59.0	40.1	0
AK	45.0	55.0	0	42.5	57.5	0
AZ	43.3	56.7	0	46.7	53.3	0
AR	77.1	22.9	0	75.0	25.0	0
CA	62.5	37.5	0	60.0	40.0	0
CO	57.1	42.9	0	60.0	40.0	0
CT	66.7	33.3	0	70.9	29.1	0
DE	61.9	38.1	0	43.9	56.1	0
FL	35.0	65.0	0	34.2	65.8	0
GA	39.3	60.7	0	41.1	58.9	0
HI	80.0	20.0	0	84.3	15.7	0
ID	20.0	80.0	0	27.1	72.9	0
IL	62.7	37.3	0	55.9	44.1	0
IN	34.0	66.0	0	51.0	49.0	0
IA	60.0	40.0	0	54.0	45.0	0
KS	25.0	75.0	0	37.6	62.4	0
KY	42.1	55.3	2.6	63.0	37.0	0
LA	61.5	38.5	0	59.0	39.0	1.0

Partisan Distribution of State Legislative Seats, 2008 (continued)

State	Senate			House		
	% Democrat	% Republican	% Other	% Democrat	% Republican	% Other
ME	51.4	48.6	0	58.9	39.7	1.3
MD	70.2	29.8	0	75.2	24.8	0
MA	87.5	12.5	0	88.1	11.9	0
MI	44.7	55.3	0	52.7	47.3	0
MN	65.7	34.3	0	63.4	36.6	0
MS	53.8	46.2	0	60.7	39.3	0
MO	38.2	61.8	0	43.6	56.4	0
MT	52.0	48.0	0	49.0	50.0	1.0
NE	*	*	100.0	*	*	*
NV	47.6	52.4	0	64.3	35.7	0
NH	58.3	41.7	0	59.8	40.3	0
NJ	57.5	42.5	0	60.0	40.0	0
NM	57.1	42.9	0	60.0	40.0	0
NY	45.2	54.8	0	72.0	28.0	0
NC	62.0	38.0	0	56.7	43.3	0
ND	44.7	55.3	0	35.1	64.9	0
OH	36.4	63.6	0	46.5	53.5	0
OK	50.0	50.0	0	43.6	56.4	0
OR	56.7	36.7	6.7	51.7	48.3	0
PA	42.0	58.0	0	50.2	49.8	0
RI	86.8	13.2	0	80.0	20.0	0
SC	43.5	56.5	0	41.1	58.9	0
SD	42.9	57.1	0	28.6	71.4	0
TN	48.5	51.5	0	53.5	46.5	0
TX	35.5	64.5	0	46.0	54.0	0
UT	27.6	72.4	0	26.7	73.3	0
VT	76.7	23.3	0	62.0	32.7	5.3
VA	52.5	47.5	0	44.0	54.0	2.0
WA	65.3	34.7	0	64.3	35.7	0
WV	67.6	32.4	0	72.0	28.0	0
WI	54.5	45.5	0	47.5	52.5	0
WY	23.3	76.7	0	28.3	71.7	0
US average	51.3	46.0	2.6	55.1	44.6	0.3

Source: National Conference of State Legislatures, http://www.ncsl.org/statevote/partycomptable2007.htm.

Note: These figures were correct as of 15 January 2007. Updated by the authors.

* Nebraska's unicameral legislature is nonpartisan.

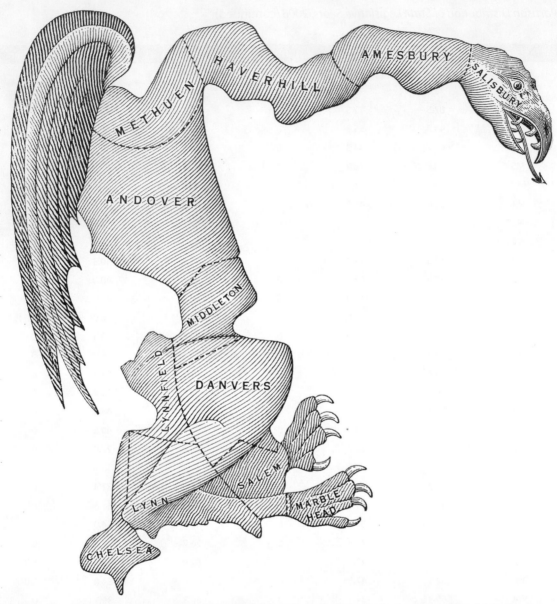

Elbridge Gerry's legislative district map was satirized in 19th-century Massachusetts for a tortured attempt to gain political advantage. But compare this cartoon map to today's Texas State Senate District 17. What sort of monster could you make out of this example of a partisan gerrymander?[1] The Texas Senate 17th consists of about one quarter of the city of Port Arthur (in Jefferson County), linked by marshland, Galveston Bay, and some lightly populated portions of Galveston Island and Bend and Bazoria counties to the west side of Houston. Analysts argued that the breakup of Jefferson County between districts in this way caused the defeat of a Democratic senator—not surprisingly, Republicans controlled this redistricting.

[1]Layla Copelin, "Redistricting Drama Heading to the Courtroom after State Board's Contentious Vote, Challenges to Maps Move Forward," *Austin (Tex.) American-Statesman,* 26 July 2001, p. A1.

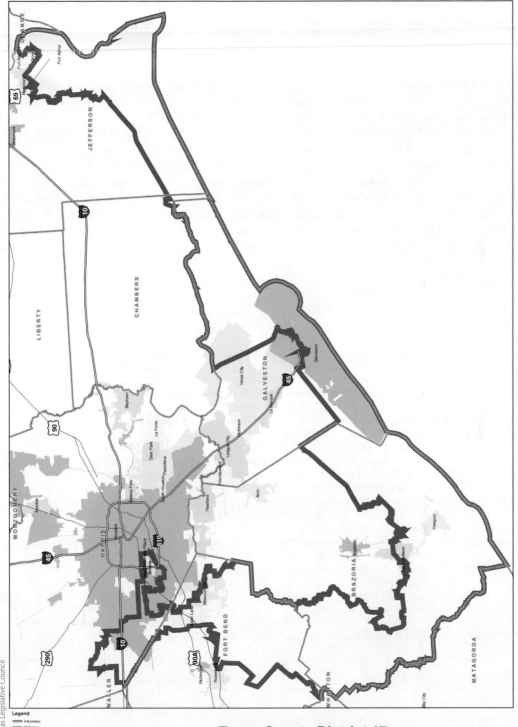

Legend
Interstates
Highways
Counties

Texas Senate District 17

who indulge in partisan gerrymandering. California Democrats gerrymandered a 10 percentage point voter advantage (based on the 2004 presidential election) into a 20 (Assembly) and 25 (Senate) percentage point advantage in the legislature. Political gerrymandering (among other things) also yielded a bizarre partisan distribution in the New York legislature, with the Senate Republicans holding a 9 percentage point majority while the Assembly Democrats hold a 44 percentage point majority.

Sometimes, a successful political gerrymander requires shaving the district support of individual majority party legislators too close for their own comfort, causing a revolt. Thus, even where one party controls the entire redis-

tricting process rather than pushing gerrymandering to its extreme, redistricters typically compromise between the interests of individual legislators and those of the party. This leads to many electorally secure districts along with some effort toward partisan advantage, especially in districts where no incumbent is seeking re-election.[48]

Furthermore, some states have constitutional provisions or statutes that limit gerrymandering in some way. For example, 21 states require that county or municipal boundaries be followed to the greatest extent possible while meeting the one person, one vote standard.[49] Nineteen states require that districts be compact, and 10 require that old districts be preserved as much as

INSTITUTIONS MATTER

IOWA'S NONPARTISAN REDISTRICTING INSTITUTION

Iowa has a unique redistricting system that seems to purge legislative redistricting of political gerrymandering and incumbent protection.[1] In the Hawkeye State, a group of nonpartisan legislative staff are assigned to divide the state into districts for their state house and senate and congressional districts based almost solely on simple population data (rather than the detailed demographic and political data used elsewhere), with an eye toward not splitting political units (like cities and counties) between different districts, when possible. By law, these redistricters are not even allowed to know (or at least consider) where incumbent legislators live. The Iowa General Assembly must officially approve the district maps drawn in this way, and legislators can ask the staffers to go back and redraw the plan, if they wish. But usually, the staffers' first or second plan is passed into law, largely due to public and media pressure in Iowa that the process should be nonpartisan. The result is that Iowa has legislative and congressional districts that are more competitive for both incumbents and parties than other states.

Although many other states have nonpartisan or bipartisan redistricting commissions, the maps they produce tend to be biased toward either partisan advantage or incumbent protection,[2] although they are a bit more competitive than those adopted strictly through the legislative process.[3] There has been a flurry of redistricting reform proposals in recent years, but even where voters have been offered new redistricting institutions in initiatives, such as in California and Ohio in 2005, they have been rejected. The problem is that these reform efforts have often been viewed, rightly or wrongly, as partisan power grabs.[4] Given that redistricting has such a direct impact on the interests of those politicians who have the responsibility for accomplishing it, can an institution be adopted in the other 49 states that takes the politics out of it? The prospects are not promising.

Notes

1. Alan Greenblatt, "Monster Maps: Has Devious District-Making Killed Electoral Competition?" *Governing* 19, no. 1 (2005): 46–50.
2. Michael P. McDonald, "A Comparative Analysis of Redistricting Institutions in the United States, 2001–02," *State Politics and Politics Quarterly* 4 (2004): 371–95.
3. Jamie L. Carson and Michael H. Crespin, "The Effect of State Redistricting Methods on Electoral Competition in United States House of Representatives Races," *State Politics and Policy Quarterly* 4 (2004): 455–69.
4. Sam Hirsch and Thomas E. Mann, "For Election Reform, A Heartening Defeat," *New York Times*, online ed., 11 November 2005; and Jill Sanders, "Setting Political Boundaries Done in Variety of Ways across the Country," *Sacramento Bee*, online ed., 3 November 2005.

possible. Because these provisions are subjective (for example, "as much as possible" is certainly debatable), politically motivated redistricters are not completely thwarted. But these provisions give those arguing—whether in court or the legislature—against egregious political gerrymandering more ammunition for their cases.

The Paradox of Competition in State Legislative Elections Revisited

The result of this sort of voting behavior and redistricting for state legislative elections is the paradox we introduced above—close competition between the parties in the aggregate (or at least a good reflection of the state or national electorate's partisan balance) but very little competition in individual legislative races. State legislative districts that tend to be homogeneous due to their relatively small size and Americans' increasingly segregated living patterns are further homogenized and manipulated during the redistricting process, resulting in near certainty about which party will win each seat in the general election.[50] Incumbents' advantages in name recognition and campaign spending stifle competition even in party primaries. Magnifying this tendency in the most recent round of redistricting has been the great improvement in computer technology that allows districts to be drawn with extreme precision. Although redistricters cannot predict future population shifts, they have greater skill, more sophisticated technology, and more detailed data to pursue their goals than ever before. For example, in California's 2004 general election, of the 153 congressional and state legislative seats up for election, *none* of them changed parties—and this is in a state with state legislative term limits that are supposed to decrease the dominance of incumbents in elections.

State Legislators: Who Are They?

Soon after these 7,382 state legislators have won their individual elections, they meet in their respective state capitols to begin work. These people make big decisions about public policy and the allocation of state government resources that affect your life every day, so who they are makes a difference. Although any generalization about these thousands of unique individuals glosses over a lot, it is useful to take a look at them in broad strokes to begin to understand who they are and how well the legislature represents the citizens of the states.

The average state legislator is a 53-year-old white man, in business or a lawyer, who is married and has lived in the same area most of his life.[51] Thus, like most political elites in this country, state legislators do not represent the diversity of the American population. Non-Latino whites make up only about 70 percent of our population, about half of us are women, and most of us are not lawyers or businessmen.[52] But if we look past the averages, and especially if we look at changes in state legislatures in recent years, we see a demographic picture for state legislatures that is much richer than that of any other set of state or federal elected officials.

Women in the State Legislature

First, consider the representation of women in state legislatures. No woman had served in a state legislature until 1894, when three women were elected in Colorado. In the following 80 years, women made some progress but not much. In 1971, at the beginning of the modern women's movement in this country, still only 4.5 percent of state legislators were women. But over the following three decades, women made steady gains. By 2008, they constituted 23.5 percent of state legislators (Figure 7.1). So, although women are still underrepresented in state legislatures, they have made great strides. Indeed, this influx of women was one of the most dramatic changes in these bodies in the 20th century. And just as important for women's political power in the legislative process, more of them are assuming leadership positions in state legislatures.[53] Women continue to gravitate toward committees in the areas of health, education, and social welfare, but they now also receive their fair representation on

---

Figure 7.1

Percentage of All State Legislators Who Were Women, 1971–2007

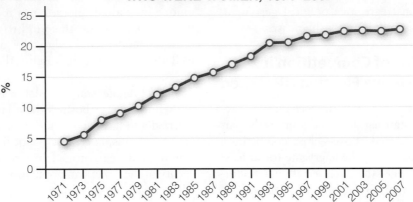

**PERCENTAGE OF ALL STATE LEGISLATORS
WHO WERE WOMEN, 1971–2007**

Source: Center for American Women and Politics, "Women in State Legislatures 2007," Rutgers University, http://www.cawp.rutgers.edu/Facts/Officeholders/stleg.pdf.

the powerful fiscal committees in state legislatures.[54] And although it was not until the 1980s that the first women assumed the top leadership positions of house speaker and senate president, as of 2006, 33 women from 17 states had done so.[55]

There are two caveats to this general picture of increased women's representation in state legislatures. First, after 28 years of steady increases, the overall percentage of women in state legislatures stayed remarkably constant at about 22 percent from 1999 to 2007.[56] Second, women are not represented equally well in all states. As Table 7.4 shows, the percentage of women in state legislatures varies dramatically, from 43.3 percent in the Arizona Senate to only 2.2 percent in the South Carolina House. States in the West and the Northeast tend to have more women legislators, and those in the Southeast tend to have fewer (except for North Carolina and Florida).

Why has women's representation in state legislatures increased so dramatically since the 1970s, why has this progress slowed in recent years, and why is there such variation in wom-

en's representation across the states? Scholars have identified several factors that are associated with a legislature having more women, and this can give us some insight into these questions. For example, state legislatures with lower pay and shorter sessions, and those that use MMDs, tend to have more women.[57] The standard explanation for these findings has to do with a bias against women serving in elected office, a carryover from the prefeminist period. Seats in full-time, high-pay legislatures and single-member districts may seem more important, leading to more competition for them and the tendency to fill them with men. Supporting this explanation is the finding that when a state's electorate and party leaders hold more traditional attitudes toward religion and gender roles, women are more poorly represented in its legislature.[58] This explanation fits with the upward trend in women's representation in the last quarter of the 20th century, a time when women were moving in greater numbers into many nontraditional activities and professions and when attitudes toward their role in society were changing quickly. There is

| Table 7.4 |

Women State Legislators, 2007–08 (arranged from highest to lowest % of women in both chambers)

State	Both Chambers (%)	Senate (%)	House (%)
VT	37.2	33.3	38.0
NH	36.3	41.7	36.0
MN	34.8	40.3	32.1
AZ	34.4	43.3	30.0
CO	34.0	31.4	35.4
MD	33.0	23.4	36.2
HI	32.9	28.0	35.3
WA	32.7	40.8	28.6
OR	31.1	30.0	31.7
DE	30.6	33.3	29.3
ME	30.6	34.3	29.8
NV	30.2	28.6	31.0
NM	29.5	26.2	31.4
KS	29.1	32.5	28.0
CA	28.3	25.0	30.0
CT	28.3	22.2	29.8
IL	27.7	22.0	30.5
MT	25.3	16.0	30.0
NC	24.7	16.0	28.3
MA	24.5	30.0	23.1
FL	23.8	27.5	22.5
NY	23.6	17.7	26.0
WY	23.3	13.3	28.3
ID	22.9	14.3	27.1
IA	22.7	12.0	28.0
WI	22.7	24.2	22.2
AK	21.7	15.0	25.0
AR	20.7	17.1	22.0
NE	20.4	20.4	N/A
TX	20.4	12.9	22.0
MI	19.6	23.7	18.2
GA	19.5	14.3	21.1
RI	19.5	18.4	20.0
MO	19.3	20.6	19.0
NJ	19.2	17.5	20.0
IN	18.7	26.0	15.0
ND	17.7	12.8	20.2
LA	17.4	17.9	17.1
OH	17.4	21.2	16.2
UT	17.3	10.3	20.0
SD	17.1	14.3	18.6
VA	17.1	20.0	16.0
TN	15.9	21.2	14.0
PA	14.6	20.0	13.3
WV	14.2	5.9	17.0
MS	13.8	9.6	15.6
AL	12.9	11.4	13.3
OK	12.8	14.6	11.9
KY	12.3	13.2	12.0
SC	8.8	2.2	11.3
U.S. average	23.5	21.4	24.2

Source: Center for American Women and Politics, "Women in State Legislatures 2007," Rutgers University, http://www.cawp.rutgers.edu/Facts/Officeholders/stleg.pdf.

Note: These figures were correct as of 15 January 2007.

evidence that women's continuing underrepresentation in state legislatures is also affected by their greater hesitancy to enter political races that they likely could win.[59]

Racial and Ethnic Minorities in the State Legislature

The state legislative representation of members of racial and ethnic minorities has also improved greatly in recent decades but for different reasons than the improvement in women's representation. In 1969, there were only 172 African-American state legislators (about 2 percent), but this increased to 438 by 1991 and 607 by 2003 (the last year data are available), or 8.2 percent of all legislators.[60] Thus, the proportion of African Americans in state legislatures now better represents their proportion in the population (12.8 percent) than does the proportion of women in state legislatures. On the other hand, there were 140 Latino state legislators in 2003 (1.8 percent), far less than

Latinos' 13.7 percent share of the population. In 2003, there were also 72 Asian-American legislators and 36 Native-American legislators.

Why has the representation of racial and ethnic minorities in state legislatures improved in recent decades? First, the **Voting Rights Act (VRA) of 1965** had a lot to do with it, especially in the South, which includes the states with the largest proportion of blacks. By getting rid of MMDs that diluted African-American voting power, encouraging districts to be drawn with a majority of blacks where possible, and banning practices that discouraged blacks from voting, the VRA helped increase the number of black state legislators in the states of the old Confederacy from only three in 1965 to 176 as early as 1985.[61] Efforts to draw black majority-minority districts in the 1980s and 1990s helped increase their representation to legislatures outside the South as well. Latino representation has been helped by these events to some degree, but the biggest reason for their increased success in state legislative races in recent years has simply been their increasing numbers in the United States. However, Latinos are currently the most underrepresented racial or ethnic group, probably due to their historical lack of political participation.[62]

As with women, the percentage of racial and ethnic minorities in state legislative chambers varies dramatically across the states, from none to as much as 41 percent (the New Mexico House) for Latinos and 29 percent (the Mississippi House) for African Americans, according to the most recent data available. But unlike women, much of this cross-state variation is easy to explain. In large part, the percentage of blacks or Latinos in a state's legislature is a function of their percentage in the state's population, as Table 7.5 shows. With the VRA and the sensitivity to fair racial and ethnic representation that the courts have shown since the 1970s, this should not be surprising. However, although there may be more legislators belonging to racial and ethnic minorities in states where more people belong to racial and ethnic minorities, their level of representation—the ratio of their proportion in the legislature to their proportion in the population—is more difficult to explain.

As Figure 7.2 shows, some sparsely populated states with very few minorities living in them, like West Virginia, Idaho, and Maine, tend to have very poor representation ratios because if voting follows racial lines, there is not the critical mass to elect even one minority person. On the other end, large states with substantial numbers of minorities, like Florida, Illinois, and California, have better representation. But some states do not follow this pattern. For example, Utah, Oregon, and Nevada do very well on state legislative minority representation, whereas Delaware, Kentucky, and Virginia do not. And interestingly, whereas African Americans and Latinos are poorly represented in the Oklahoma Legislature, Native Americans are actually a little overrepresented; in 2008, 14 percent of Oklahoma legislators were Native American, whereas only 12 percent of Oklahomans were of that heritage.[63] Why do these states have these unusual patterns of representation? Political scientists have yet to explain it.

There is considerable debate about the effects of drawing state legislative districts that are purposely homogeneous on race or ethnicity; that is, majority-minority districts. On one hand, assuming voting along racial or ethnic lines, this may lead to proportional minority representation in the state legislature. But on the other hand, some argue that the political and policy interests of members of these minority groups would be better served by having some influence in more districts, regardless of the race of the legislator. For example, by packing African-American voters (who predominantly vote Democratic) into fewer districts to ensure that some black legislators are elected, Republicans may gain seats in other districts that have been stripped of Democratic voters.[64] This raises a potential conflict between policy representation (based on voters' policy needs and desires) and descriptive representation (based on voters' demographic characteristics).[65]

Table 7.5

African-American and Latino State Legislators

State	African Americans as % of State Population (2005)	% African-American State Legislators (2006)		Latinos as % of State Population (2005)	% Latino State Legislators (2007)	
		Senate	House		Senate	House
AL	26.0	22.9	24.8	2.0	0.0	0.0
AK	4.0	5.0	0.0	5.0	0.0	0.0
AZ	4.0	0.0	1.7	29.0	20.0	18.3
AR	16.0	8.6	12.0	5.0	0.0	0.0
CA	7.0	5.0	5.0	35.0	45.0	12.5
CO	4.0	5.7	4.6	19.0	5.7	6.2
CT	10.0	8.3	6.6	11.0	0.0	4.0
DE	21.0	4.8	7.3	6.0	0.0	2.4
FL	16.0	17.5	14.2	19.0	7.5	11.7
GA	30.0	19.6	21.1	7.0	0.0	1.7
HI	2.0	0.0	2.0	8.0	4.0	0.0
ID	1.0	0.0	0.0	9.0	0.0	1.4
IL	15.0	15.3	16.9	14.0	5.1	6.8
IN	9.0	8.0	8.0	5.0	0.0	1.0
IA	2.0	0.0	3.0	4.0	0.0	0.0
KS	6.0	5.0	4.0	8.0	0.0	3.2
KY	8.0	2.6	5.0	2.0	0.0	0.0
LA	33.0	23.1	21.9	3.0	0.0	0.0
ME	1.0	0.0	0.0	1.0	0.0	0.0
MD	29.0	21.3	22.7	6.0	2.1	2.1
MA	7.0	2.5	3.8	8.0	2.5	1.9
MI	14.0	13.2	12.7	4.0	2.6	1.8
MN	4.0	0.0	1.5	4.0	1.5	1.5
MS	37.0	21.2	28.7	2.0	0.0	0.0
MO	12.0	8.8	10.4	3.0	0.0	0.6
MT	0.0	0.0	0.0	2.0	0.0	1.0
NE	4.0	2.0	N/A	7.0	2.0	N/A
NV	8.0	14.3	9.5	24.0	4.8	4.8
NH	1.0	0.0	1.0	2.0	0.0	0.5
NJ	14.0	12.5	13.8	15.0	0.0	5.0
NM	2.0	0.0	2.9	43.0	33.3	42.9
NY	17.0	12.9	14.7	16.0	6.5	8.7
NC	22.0	14.0	15.8	6.0	2.0	0.8
ND	1.0	0.0	0.0	2.0	0.0	0.0
OH	12.0	12.1	14.1	2.0	0.0	0.0

African-American and Latino State Legislators (continued)

State	African Americans as % of State Population (2005)	% African-American State Legislators (2006)		Latinos as % of State Population (2005)	% Latino State Legislators (2007)	
		Senate	House		Senate	House
OK	8.0	4.2	3.0	7.0	0.0	0.0
OR	2.0	10.0	0.0	10.0	0.0	1.7
PA	11.0	8.0	7.4	4.0	0.0	0.5
RI	6.0	2.6	4.0	11.0	2.6	2.7
SC	29.0	17.4	20.2	3.0	0.0	0.8
SD	1.0	0.0	0.0	2.0	0.0	0.0
TN	17.0	9.1	16.2	3.0	0.0	1.0
TX	12.0	6.5	9.3	35.0	16.1	20.7
UT	1.0	0.0	1.3	11.0	3.4	1.3
VT	1.0	0.0	0.7	1.0	0.0	0.0
VA	20.0	12.5	11.0	6.0	0.0	1.0
WA	4.0	2.0	2.0	9.0	2.0	2.0
WV	3.0	0.0	2.0	1.0	0.0	0.0
WI	6.0	6.1	6.1	4.0	0.0	1.0
WY	1.0	0.0	0.0	7.0	0.0	3.3
U.S. average	13.0	7.7	8.5	14.0	3.3	3.2

Note: The columns show the percentage of members in each chamber who were African American (2006) or Latino (2007) and the state population percentages for 2005. These are the most recent data available for each of these characteristics.

Sources: Joint Center for Political and Economic Studies, "Black Elected Officials Roster: 2006 Black State Legislators"; Evan Bacalao, research associate, National Association of Latino Elected and Appointed Officials; and U.S. Census Bureau, *The Statistical Abstract of the United States,* http://www.census.gov/statab/www/ranks.html.

* Nebraska's unicameral legislature only has a senate.

The Impact of Broader Representation

What difference does this recent improvement in African-American, Latino, and women's state legislative representation make in state public policy or governance? Scholars have begun to explore this difficult question by assessing the degree to which these sorts of state legislators differ from white male legislators. For example, we know that African-American and women legislators tend to be more interested than their white male colleagues in education and social welfare policy and (for females) in health care policy as well.[66] These preferences are illustrated by differences in the type of committees these legislators serve on, the bills they introduce, and the way they vote on legislation. Political scientists have recently found evidence that as these groups become better represented in state legislatures, their preferences are reflected better in public policy,[67] although this is not always the case.[68]

African-American state legislators are more likely to have started their political careers outside of government, such as in social movement groups, churches, or unions, whereas white legislators are more likely to have started in local government positions.[69] Black legislators are also more likely to have a pessimistic view of race relations than whites, even feeling that black interests and they themselves are given short shrift in the state legislature.

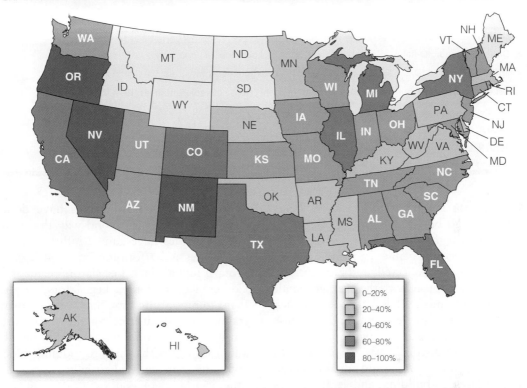

FIGURE 7.2

THE GAP IN RACIAL AND ETHNIC MINORITY REPRESENTATION IN STATE LEGISLATURES

Legend:
- 0–20%
- 20–40%
- 40–60%
- 60–80%
- 80–100%

Note: We measure a state's gap in racial and ethnic legislative representation as the ratio of the percentage of African Americans and Latinos in a state's population to their percentage in its state legislature. Therefore, a 100 percent score for a state indicates that the percentages of these groups in the state's population and legislature are equal. On the other hand, a 50 percent score indicates that their percentages in the state legislature are half that of their percentage in the state's population. For example, if 10 percent of a state's population was African American or Latino, but only 5 percent of its legislature were members of one of these racial or ethnic groups, that state would score 50 percent on this measure. Thus the lighter the color for a state, the greater is the representation gap.

Source: Joint Center for Political and Economic Studies, "Black Elected Officials Roster: 2006 Black State Legislators"; Evan Bacalao, research associate, National Association of Latino Elected and Appointed Officials; and U.S. Census Bureau, *The Statistical Abstract of the United States*, http://www.census.gov/statab/www/ranks.html.

Indeed, they may have good reason to feel this way. One study of attitudes in and around the North Carolina statehouse[70] supports this belief, showing that, all things being equal, lobbyists and white legislators there have less respect for African-American legislators than their white colleagues—although, interestingly, journalists' attitudes were not racially biased in this way.

The differences between women and men state legislators were fairly stark in the 1970s and 1980s, when women were first making inroads at the statehouse. Aside from their having a somewhat different policy agenda than men, female legislators tended to be older, have fewer children, be unmarried or divorced, be social workers or teachers rather than lawyers, and be less politically ambitious.[71] But as the novelty of women serving in elected office has worn off in recent years, these differences between the sexes in the statehouse have

Table 7.6

African-American Leaders of Majority Parties in State Legislative Chambers

- **Emil Jones Jr.** (D-Chicago), president of the Illinois Senate (2003–present)
- **Herbert Wesson** (D-Los Angeles), speaker of the California Assembly (2002–04)
- **Daniel T. Blue Jr.** (D-Raleigh), speaker of the North Carolina House of Representatives (1991–94)
- **Willie L. Brown Jr.** (D-San Francisco), speaker of the California Assembly (1981–95)
- **K. Leroy Irvis** (D-Pittsburgh), speaker of the Pennsylvania House of Representatives (1977–79 and 1983–89)
- **S. Howard Woodson Jr.** (D-Trenton), speaker of the New Jersey Assembly (1974–75)
- **Cecil A. Partee** (D-Chicago), president of the Illinois Senate (1971–73 and 1975–77)
- **John R. Lynch** (R-Natchez), speaker of the Mississippi House of Representatives (1871–73)

vanished, with female state legislators being just as likely to be young, with children, and married as their male colleagues. On the other hand, the ideological gender gap among Americans generally—is reflected, and even intensified, in the statehouse, with the average female legislator being more liberal on social issues, the environment, gun control, and abortion regulation, regardless of her party or the characteristics of her district.[72] Women also engage in more constituent service and are more cooperative, consensus-building, and egalitarian in the legislative process.[73]

Of course, for any underrepresented group, achieving its political goals requires more than just gaining a few seats in a legislative chamber. As we shall see, real policy making requires majorities in the legislative process. So, how can a minority group ever hope to influence policy? There are two important ways this can be done. First, women and minorities can influence the legislative process better when they gain leadership positions, whether as committee chairs or in party or chamber positions.[74] These positions have been filled increasingly by women and minorities in recent years, largely in proportion to their numbers in their chambers.[75] On the other hand, women have been more successful in attaining the top jobs in their chambers than members of minority groups. For example, whereas 36 women have served as a senate president or speaker of a house,

only eight African Americans have done so (see Table 7.6). The second way that women and minorities have gained influence in state legislatures is by forming informal legislative groups, like a Black Legislators' Caucus or a Conference of Women Legislators, to pursue their common interests. Such groups provide training and mentoring for new legislators, a sense of group cohesion among its members, and a vehicle with which to mobilize blocs of votes that can be used to gain support from other legislators on issues central to the group's agendas.[76]

The Job of the State Legislature

The state legislature has four basic duties:
- To establish and revise the state's laws and constitution
- To determine how the state will get and spend money
- To oversee the activities of the executive branch as it implements the state's laws
- To represent the interests of the state's citizens before the state government

Although there is some overlap in these duties, it is useful to discuss them separately, especially when considering the impacts of institutions on how well they are accomplished.

Lawmaking

The state legislature's primary function is to consider the public problems of the state and make or modify state law to address them. This is a huge job and one that is at the core of any state government action. The state legal code consists of thousands of laws touching on every facet of life and business, and every one of these laws has been passed by the legislature.[77] Everything that a state or local government official does must ultimately be authorized by the legislature. In each legislative session, lawmakers consider issues including everything from abortion and the new birth technologies to capital punishment and the right to die. Gay rights, education from preschool to the Ph.D., prisons and homeland security, public health and driver's licenses, road building, and coal mine regulation—all these and much more are considered in depth in a state legislature each year. The number of formal proposals annually for new laws or amendments to current law is immense. The Michigan Legislature has a representative workload. In its 2005–06 legislative session, members of the Michigan House and Senate considered 4,227 bills and passed 681 of these into law. These new laws took up over 1,500 pages in the *Michigan Compiled Laws*.[78] By any standard, state legislators' lawmaking job is large and important, and they take it seriously.

The process by which a state legislature makes law is complex and difficult (Figure 7.3)—and for a good reason. Americans tend to be suspicious of government, so we establish institutions to maximize the chances that every government decision is well thought through. Mark Twain once said, "No man's life, liberty, or property is safe while the legislature is in session";[79] like all good jokes, this one has a large grain of truth. To reduce the risk of unwise or dangerous state government action, the legislative process has been made slow and difficult. In fact, on average, only about 20 percent of proposed laws, or **bills,** that a state legislature considers actually become law.[80] The process

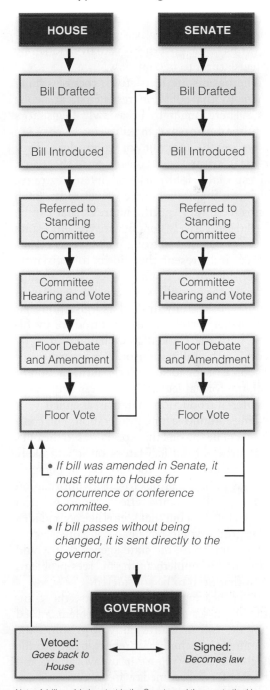

Figure 7.3

Simplified Version of How a Bill Becomes a Law in the Typical State Legislature

Note: A bill could also start in the Senate and then go to the House.

is set up so that the legislature will make reasoned, well-informed, sober decisions about
how the state should ban, require, tax, or encourage something. In the end, a bill must pass
both chambers of the legislature by at least a
majority vote and then be signed by the governor (or have the governor's veto overridden by
the legislature) to become law.

The basic state legislative process is quite
similar to that of Congress. First, someone
says, "There ought to be a law!" Legislators
are in the business of making law, so they are
always on the lookout for good ideas. They
get ideas from their constituents, the news,
and especially lobbyists and interest groups,
which are the main source of bill ideas. Such
groups have very specific interests that can be
affected—positively or negatively—by state
policy, so they have strong incentive to get organized and present their ideas to legislators
for consideration. Lobbyists for these groups
routinely approach sympathetic legislators
with proposals fully drafted as legislation that
a lawmaker merely needs to introduce by filing it with the clerk of the chamber, thereby
becoming the **bill's sponsor.** But regardless of
the source of the idea, with the introduction of
a bill, the formal legislative process begins.

After introduction, a bill is assigned to a
standing committee for consideration. This committee will be the one that specializes in the bill's
policy area, so the legislators on it will likely
have some expertise in the subject. The committee holds public hearings to gather information
about the bill's potential effects and its political
support. Often, a bill that seems like a good idea
to one group would have bad consequences for
others. Sometimes, the state agency that would
be assigned to implement the bill sees problems
with it that need to be considered.

After hearing these arguments, the committee discusses the bill. If the problems raised
about the bill are sufficiently worrisome, the
committee will simply not report it back to the
full chamber (or report it unfavorably), and
the bill will not become law in the current legislative session. In this way, standing committees

serve the important function of screening out
bad, weak, or politically unpalatable bills. The
main reason the legislature splits itself up into
these committees is to do the initial screening of
bills, as we discuss later. There is no reason to
waste the full chamber's time considering bills
that have obvious problems. But state legislative standing committees are weaker than their
congressional counterparts, so they are much
less likely to screen out bills before they get to
the floor.[81] In fact, in many states, if a sponsor
really wants to get his or her bill passed in committee, he or she can do so. And about a quarter
of state legislative chambers require that their
committees report all bills assigned to them to
the full chamber, whether favorably or not.[82]

Of course, not all bills are bad ideas—far
from it. But even if the committee agrees with
the general idea behind a bill, the hearings often point out its specific weaknesses. In such
cases, the committee will **amend** the bill, typically with the sponsor's permission. Finally, if
the committee is convinced of the amended
bill's merit, it will vote to report it to the full
chamber for further consideration.

At this point in the process, in most chambers (especially in houses), the majority party
leader (whether the speaker of the house, president of the senate, or some other title) has a
critical opportunity to affect the bill's fate, particularly if he or she opposes the bill. Standing committees report far more bills than their
full chambers can reasonably consider, and one
of the majority party leader's important functions is to manage this bottleneck by selecting
which bills will be considered on the **chamber
floor.**[83] A number of factors go into a leader's
decision about which bills the chamber will
consider. First, these leaders typically prefer
bills that will pass on the floor. Uncontroversial
bills waste less of the chamber's precious floor
time, and they are less likely to cause controversy with the public, which might threaten the
party's majority in the next election. Second,
and less commonly, the majority leader will
use this **gatekeeping** power to kill bills he or
she does not want to see debated on the floor,

whether for policy or political reasons. Perhaps the debate would expose rifts among legislators of his or her own party or perhaps voting on the bill would be politically damaging for some majority party legislators facing tough re-election campaigns. Third, and probably least frequently, the majority party or its leader has a policy agenda that would be helped by killing or advancing a particular bill, and the leader uses his or her gatekeeping power to do so.

On the floor of the full chamber, legislators first consider amending the bill. Various legislators, especially the bill's sponsor and members of the committee that reviewed it, may speak to describe to the chamber both the bill's intent and its political support and opposition (if any). Sometimes, suggestions for modifications are offered, with the floor typically deferring to the wishes of the bill's sponsor and committee members about these proposed amendments. To reduce controversy and increase the chances of passing the bill, sponsors usually agree to most amendments, unless they think that they would undermine the original intent of the bill.

Finally, the chamber votes on the bill, and a majority vote typically passes it in that chamber.[84] Why does a legislator vote aye or nay on a bill? First, remember that the goal of the legislative process up to the floor vote is to screen out bills that are flawed or lack political support. Thus, most bills that survive to the chamber floor not only pass there but also pass by wide margins. So, a legislator's typical default floor vote is aye; in other words, legislators need a reason to vote *against* a bill on the floor rather than for it. So, why might a legislator vote nay on a particular bill? Certainly, if he or she knows something special about that bill, perhaps by having followed its discussion in committee or having heard from a constituent about it, that information will factor into his or her vote. But this is unusual. Each year, lawmakers must vote on hundreds of often very technical and arcane bills on a wide range of topics, so they usually know little about any particular bill when they vote on it. But the

institutions of the legislative process are such that rational decisions can be made by the legislature as a body even if each individual legislator does not personally make a well-informed decision on each bill.

The most common reason why legislators vote against a bill is if it somehow hurts their district and, thereby, hurts their re-election chances. Legislators pay close attention to their districts' interests and scrupulously weigh the impact of bills against those interests. But either most bills have no direct impact on the district or the legislator does not know what those impacts might be because the bill is too complex or the legislator is not familiar with its subject. In such cases, legislators typically take cues from how their colleagues are voting.[85] A large electronic "tote board" at the front of most state legislative chambers tells everyone how each legislator has voted during a **roll call.** Legislators first look to the votes of members of their own party, especially those on the committee that considered the bill. If all their co-partisans are voting one way on a bill, they likely will vote that way too. Likewise, legislators consider the votes of those from similar districts and those near their own districts. If they have no other information about the bill, voting with their colleagues who are similarly positioned is a good way to avoid casting a vote that may hurt their district and come back to haunt them in a future campaign. Legislative leaders may advise their co-partisans about how to vote in line with their districts' interests, even if that means sometimes voting against the party's position. As we will see, a central responsibility of party leaders is to get members of their party re-elected. Rarely is a party's leadership so desperate for a vote that they will encourage—or even allow—a legislator to vote against his or her district. And a party leader who insists on many such votes will not likely be the leader for long.

If a bill manages to pass all of these hurdles successfully in its chamber of origin, it is sent over to the other chamber, where the entire process is repeated—introduction, committee evaluation, and floor consideration and voting. As in its chamber of origin, if the bill fails to pass any of the hurdles in the second chamber, it dies for the session. Even if the bill does pass the other chamber, it may be amended during the process. Recall that a bill must pass both chambers in identical form before it can become law. Therefore, if the bill is amended in even the smallest way in the second chamber, the different versions must be reconciled and then voted on again in each chamber. This may be done by one chamber simply accepting the version of the other chamber, or if neither chamber acquiesces, a temporary **conference committee** may be convened to craft a bill that will gain support in both chambers.

Conference committee members typically are appointed by the leaders of each party in each chamber and include the bill's primary sponsor in each chamber and the leaders of the standing committees that heard the bill. The conference committee can also be another opportunity for the majority party leaders to influence the bill by forming a committee that reflects the leaders' views. Regardless of its composition, if the conference committee can reach a compromise on the bill, they report it out to both chambers (they often do not reach agreement, thus killing the bill). On the chamber floor, legislators can vote only aye or nay on a conference committee bill, with no amendments being allowed. But even more often than with regular bills voted on the floor, conference committee bills usually pass. Too much effort has been put into them by this point in the process for them to fail.

Once both chambers pass the bill in identical form, it is sent to the governor. If the governor approves of the bill, he or she signs it, and the process is complete—the bill becomes state law on its effective date, as specified in the bill. But if the governor does not approve of the bill, he or she may **veto** it, sending it back to the legislature for further consideration. As you will read about in the next chapter, governors' veto powers vary significantly among the states, with many governors having a much more powerful

veto than that of the president. For example, some governors have the **line-item veto,** so they can veto only part of a bill while letting the rest become law, and other governors have the **amendatory veto,** so they can send the bill back to the legislature requesting specific changes. But regardless of the type of veto used, the legislature always has the opportunity for the last word by **overriding** the governor's veto, usually through a **supermajority** vote on the bill in each chamber. But a governor's vetoes are very hard to override and not just because an override requires more votes than normal. Governors do not veto bills lightly or often, so when they do, they take them seriously and often use considerable political resources to make sure they are not overridden.[86]

Most bills of any significance do not pass the first time they are introduced. Legislators are wary of major policy change; they ask themselves, "If this is such a good idea, why has no one thought of it before?" Lawmakers know that changes in the law can have unpredictable effects, so they move cautiously, and the bias is toward the status quo. In most state legislatures, standing committees give legislation its closest scrutiny. A major bill needs to come back again and again, sometimes for several years, as the bill's advocates and other people and groups affected by it modify and craft it, finally coming to a compromise on which they can all agree. Legislators do not like to choose sides between opponents and proponents on an issue. Rather, legislators want these people to work out their differences and develop a proposal that everyone can accept, even if no one is completely happy with it. The legislative process is designed to be one of deliberation and compromise, and to the extent that it is, the state and its citizens benefit.

The Legislature and the State Budget

We'll talk in more detail about the state budget in Chapter 10, but here let's consider the legislature's role in the process. Legislative budget making is a special case of lawmaking. Since the English Magna Carta, a central power of legislatures in Anglo-American democracies has been their control over the purse strings of government.[87] The legislature must authorize all state—and, indirectly, all local—taxes and expenditures, and all state taxes and expenditures are summarized in the state budget. In 30 states, the legislature must approve a budget every year; 20 states have a two-year budget cycle.[88] The budget is proposed by the governor at the beginning of the legislative session, usually with much fanfare, a major address, and masses of supporting documentation (see Chapter 8). The legislature then deals with the budget as it does any other bill—through committee and floor discussion, voting, and bicameral reconciliation.[89]

But the budget bill is far more important than any other bill the legislature considers each year. In fact, the budget may be more important than all the other bills a legislature considers combined. The state budget affects every aspect of state and local government, so all the people, businesses, groups, and government agencies that are affected by government in the state have a stake in it—this means virtually everyone in the state. Because they are perhaps most directly affected by the budget, the governor and members of the executive branch have a special interest in it, so they do their best to work closely with the legislative leaders and budget committees to craft a budget bill that fits their preferences.

Because of its importance, the budget bill gets special attention from the legislature and especially from the legislative leaders. The committees reviewing the budget (which have names like the Budget Committee, Ways and Means Committee, and Finance Committee) are among the most important in the legislature, attracting the most experienced legislators and those most closely connected to legislative leaders. These committees have far more staff than other committees, and these staffers are among the most experienced and best educated. State legislatures hire highly trained, nonpartisan economists to do sophisticated financial analysis of projected expenditures and revenues.[90] Without this technical capacity, lawmakers would be at the mercy of the governor and his or her economists, as typically was the case until recent years. Such economic analysis and information are especially crucial to the budget debate because, unlike the federal government, states must balance their budgets each year. That is, the budget bill must not propose that the state spend any more money than it plans to take in.

Although it is worked on throughout the legislative session, the budget bill is usually one of the last items passed. The two chambers' budget committees work continuously, independently, and simultaneously to scrutinize and amend the governor's proposal.[91] The budget bill can be hundreds of pages long, listing in excruciating detail the proposed expenditures and revenues for the upcoming fiscal year, so considerable effort goes into its analysis. Typically, as the session begins to wind down, the legislative leaders and the governor (or their representatives) meet privately to hammer out the final budgetary details. Legislative leaders meet with their colleagues to find out what they want from the budget and to keep them informed about how negotiations are going. Legislators may want particular items for their districts, such as a bridge to be repaired or a new playground built for a school. Legislative leaders and the governor can use this sort of **pork barrel** project to round up the votes they need to pass the entire budget bill. The governor and legislative leaders have the institutional responsibility to see to it that the entire state government is funded and continues to function; **rank-and-file legislators** may have more parochial interests. With its importance, conflicting interests, and complexity, it should not be surprising that the budget is often passed in the middle of the night on the last day of the session, when deals are finalized under the pressure of a looming constitutional or statutory deadline to pass the budget.

Overseeing the Executive Branch

Although it is neither as formal, nor as time-consuming, nor as well publicized as law-making, another important duty of the state legislature is to oversee the executive branch's **implementation** of the laws and policies it makes. The legislature acts like the board of directors of a very large corporation (the state bureaucracy). It sets general policy, empowers executive officials and workers to execute this policy, and then checks up now and then to make sure that those officials and workers are executing law and policy as the legislature intended.

The most obvious way for the legislature to control policy implementation by an agency is to specify very clearly what the agency is supposed to do on the subject involved in its original legislation. The more detailed the legislation, the less discretion an agency has in implementing the policy and, therefore, the more likely that **legislative intent** will be followed. For example, if the legislature passes a law that states simply, "The Department of Natural Resources (DNR) shall regulate deer hunting," the agency has enormous discretion to determine the regulations it deems necessary and desirable to regulate hunting. Such regulations may turn out to be completely at odds with what legislators actually had in mind when they passed the bill. Maybe the DNR decides to regulate deer hunting by banning it outright, whereas the rural legislators who championed the bill really wanted regulation that would promote hunting. Had these legislators been more specific in the legislation, they probably would have gotten the regulations they wanted from the DNR. Indeed, legislators write very specific legislative language when they want to force a recalcitrant agency or a governor into implementing legislation a certain way.[92]

But most of the time, there are far too many details and uncertainties in running an agency or enforcing a law for legislators to anticipate when they pass legislation. So, they give agencies great leeway to make the multitude of specific, but important, policy decisions to fill in these details. Arguably, these decisions are best made by those with specialized training and experience, such as those who run the executive agencies. For example, who would you rather see set the exact dates or kill limits for deer hunting: generalist state legislators or professional wildlife managers in the DNR? Furthermore, these detailed decisions can often be made only after seeing how a new law actually works in practice.

The legislature can also check up on an agency to make sure that it is implementing policy according to legislative intent. Such **ex post oversight** can be done through either *fire alarm* or *police patrol* activities.[93] Fire alarm oversight occurs in response to a problem that has been pointed out to a legislator. This commonly occurs as a result of legislators' **casework** for their constituents, helping them with problems they have with state government. Although most constituent concerns are not caused by an agency violating legislative intent, casework can sometimes call attention to systematic problems with an agency that need to be addressed by the legislature. But probably more effective control occurs due to the fact that agency officials simply know that the citizens with whom they work *could* complain to their state legislators. This gives these officials an incentive to do a conscientious job of implementing the policy and providing good public service every day. Another important source of fire alarm oversight is the media. When reporters uncover problems in state government, lawmakers notice, holding hearings to investigate problems and changing policy as required.

State legislatures also have more systematic, ongoing methods of overseeing their executive branches, more like police patrols than fire alarms. For example, legislators use their annual or biennial budget bill hearings to hold directors accountable for their agencies' performance. Experienced and influential budget committee members often specialize in certain agencies' budgets so that, year after year, they learn the ins and outs of those agencies and can question these officials using their in-depth knowledge. Another form of police patrol oversight occurs in **administrative rules review committees,** bodies of the legislature that review the myriad rules that agencies issue each year in implementing policy. These rules and budget reviews can be more or less rigorous, depending on the institutional arrangements of a state.[94] But as with casework, when agency officials know they have to face these committees, they have a stronger incentive to follow legislative intent. Finally, most state auditors are employed by the legislature to conduct financial and program evaluations of state agencies, both routinely and in response to legislative requests. Requested audits are often instigated by crises or scandals. In some states, the auditor is a powerful institutional tool of legislative oversight.[95]

But in general, state legislatures do not oversee the executive branch very well or very often, for a number of reasons. First, the state executive branch is large and complex; by comparison, the state legislature is very small. Even the best-staffed legislatures in the largest states do not have enough resources to examine closely what every state agency is doing all the time. In many states, oversight is only a hit-and-miss activity, at best. But even if they had the resources, legislators simply have very little incentive to invest their time and energy in effective executive branch oversight. Legislators are far more interested in lawmaking. Regardless of the relative impact of the two activities on a state's government and citizens, most legislators probably get more electoral and professional payoff from introducing bills that their districts favor, even if those bills fail, than from spending countless hours trying to understand the intricacies of an executive agency and how well it is following legislative intent. On the other hand, lawmakers can gain some political points from helping constituents with their problems with executive agencies, which encourages legislative oversight at least in professionalized legislatures.[96]

Representation

The third major duty of the state legislature is to represent the state's citizens to state government.[97] Legislators are the closest state government policy-making officials to the people in the sense that their districts are relatively small and scattered throughout the state in proportion to the population, they spend most of their time in these districts, and they must face re-election frequently. All this makes representing their districts as natural and reflexive to legislators as breathing, and they do it in a variety of ways.

First, legislators introduce bills that are intended to benefit people and businesses in their districts, and they vote on bills with a sharp eye on the wishes and values of their constituents. Sure, sometimes a legislator's personal political ideology and even his or her party allegiances will affect how he or she votes on bills,[98] but it is the interests of the district—or at least how the legislator perceives the interests of the district—that drive most legislative policy making. Even legislative party leaders help legislators represent their districts this way, even if this means voting against the overall party position on a particular bill. These leaders know that voting against the district's interests imperils a member's re-election chances, and that threatens the party's influence in the legislature. For example, a Democratic state senator from a rural part of Georgia is certainly not going to vote for a gun control bill that her party is supporting. Whereas gun control is seen as a law enforcement and public safety issue to Georgia Democrats from Atlanta and other urban areas of the state, it is seen as a threat to hunting and the traditional way of life for her rural constituents. Indeed, the Democratic Party leader in the Senate will probably urge her to vote against this bill because it might threaten her re-election chances. The result of legislators' close attention to their districts is that despite all the forces that influence state public policy—especially those of interest groups, which you read about in Chapter 6—a state's overall public policy follows the general ideology and values of its citizens remarkably closely.[99]

In addition to this direct, district-based representation in policy making, state legislators also represent their constituents' interests in a variety of other ways. For example, casework is a way of representing the interests of their constituents by acting as ombudsmen for those struggling with the state bureaucracy. Legislators also represent their constituents by seeking out pork barrel projects—specific public construction and economic development projects for their districts.[100] Even conservative legislators who have a basic ideological opposition to government spending try to win such projects for their districts. Legislators believe that "bringing home the bacon" helps their electoral chances, and legislative leaders shower the districts of their co-partisans at risk of losing the next election with such "worthy projects."[101]

Finally, out of a broader sense of responsibility, some legislators also think of themselves as representing certain classes of people, whether they live in their districts or not. This may be because a legislator has an interest in a certain business or profession, such as when a legislator who is a farmer or a pharmacist watches out for these interests in the state legislature. But this broader representational sense is most consciously felt by legislators who are women or members of a racial or ethnic minority group. These legislators often assume the responsibility to watch out for other members of their group, regardless of where they live in the state.[102]

The Collective Action Problem

These four basic jobs that we assign to our state legislatures—lawmaking, budget making, oversight of the executive branch, and representation—are difficult under the best of circumstances, but our state constitutions make them even harder to accomplish by establishing an unwieldy and complex institutional legislative structure. Think about it. A state legislature consists of dozens and dozens of people from all around the state, each with different interests, ambitions, and goals, converging on the statehouse for perhaps only a few months out of the year to deal with hundreds of very complex problems. Formally, every one of these people has an equal say in any final decision of the body, and none of them can be fired or expelled by anyone in the group.[103] Two parallel sets of people (senators and house members) are working at the same time on the same problems, and they must agree completely with one another in the end. All their deliberation and decision making occur in public view (or at least with the media paying attention), and all the people making these decisions are on very short-term contracts—contracts that most of them would like to see renewed. The final kicker is that although they must work together to accomplish their jobs, they are held accountable in elections only as individuals. If you have ever worked on a group project for a class, you know just how tricky this last arrangement can be.

Clearly, such an institution is not one that is likely to generate quiet, careful deliberation and quick, clear decisions. In fact, under such conditions, it is surprising that *anything* ever gets done. Political scientists and economists call this a **collective action problem**—how to get a group of people to work together to accomplish a common goal.[104] You see these difficulties everywhere, from a sorority trying to run a fundraiser to an international airline trying to move people around the world. Different organizations solve the problem in different ways. In a small group, like a sorority, it may be done by informal consensus-building. In a large business, like an airline, it is usually done by setting up institutions, such as a command-and-control organizational structure and a division of the work among different units, such as sales, accounting, and customer service. Because of its unique constitutional arrangements, a state legislature must use a variety of techniques—both institutions and informal norms—to overcome its collective action problem and get its jobs done. The process that results is complex and rarely pretty, but it can work. Of course, there is always room for improvement, and states are continually tinkering with their legislative institutions to improve their performance.

The basic strategy that legislatures use to solve their collective action problem is to use institutions to divide their members on two dimensions along which state policy varies—policy type and policy preference—and then assign leaders the responsibility of organizing individual members in these subgroups. Legislatures use three important state legislative institutions to organize themselves in this way—committees, party caucuses, and legislative leaders. By dividing up policy problems among their standing committees, making sure that both parties are represented on these committees and at all other stages of the process, and assigning leadership responsibilities to some of its members, state legislatures go a long way toward dealing with the collective action problem and getting their jobs done for the state.

Committees

Legislatures must address a vast range of public issues, everything from preventing birth defects to cemetery regulation, and they must have information and expertise on all these issues so that nothing gets forgotten and good decisions can be made on any problem that arises. Like Congress, state legislatures divide themselves into standing committees to do this.[105] A committee specializes in one area of policy—say, agriculture or transportation—so its members gain special knowledge and experience on it through hearings, the review of bills, and discussions with other committee members, lobbyists, staff, and interested citizens. When voting on a bill on the chamber floor, legislators typically look to members of the bill's committee for guidance because these are the legislature's

in-house experts on the subject. Each committee has members of both parties, so different political perspectives and policy preferences are represented in the preliminary review of bills and a variety of members are available to help noncommittee members later in the process.

On the other hand, in comparison with the standing committees of the U.S. House of Representatives, state legislative committees typically have much less control over legislation, especially relative to the chamber leaders.[106] Whereas committees in the U.S. House are the primary center of policy-making activity, in state legislatures, much of this activity also occurs in party caucuses, in leaders' offices, and on the chamber floor. State legislative committees are controlled by the party caucuses and chamber leaders much more so than are their congressional counterparts, and the seniority norm that determines the chairs and membership of congressional committees does not typically exist in state legislatures. For this reason, state legislative committees are much less stable than those in Congress, forming and disbanding from session to session and with their members changing committee assignments frequently. **Committees' jurisdictions** are less well defined and less stable in the states. For all these reasons, committees in most state legislatures are weaker than those in Congress.

Party Caucuses

In addition to developing some expertise in all the policy areas that state government handles, legislatures also try to ensure that most major points of view are considered in the discussion of every policy. Without the representation of these views in the proportion that they are found in the state, the legislature loses legitimacy as a policy-making institution. State legislatures represent these policy positions by organizing themselves along the most obvious characteristic of American electoral politics—the two-party system. Because Democrats and Republicans have basic differences in their inclinations toward most of the areas of policy that state policy makers consider, organizing the legislature by party also organizes it by policy preference, even if in an imperfect way.

The importance of party as an organizing principle in state legislatures cannot be overstated. Besides those in Nebraska's nonpartisan **unicameral** body, over 99 percent of state legislators are elected as either a Democrat or Republican.[107] The two **party caucuses** in each chamber meet frequently to discuss strategy and policy; in some chambers, all the most crucial policy decisions are made in the majority party caucus rather than in committee or on the floor. Members of each party usually sit together on the chamber floor, with members of the other party on "the other side of the aisle," literally. Although members of the same party do not always agree on policy—far from it, in some chambers—a legislator's party affiliation is the single most important predictor of how he or she will vote on bills, even more important than his or her general political ideology.[108] This similarity in roll call voting is the result of shared policy preferences, a sense of common cause against the other party in the chamber, and legislators' use of their co-partisans as voting cues.

To understand why any state legislature acts as it does, you have to know the party distribution in its chambers. The party that has a majority of members in a chamber is said to "control" that chamber—and for good reason. Because a majority must vote in favor of a bill in committee and on the floor for it to pass, the party with the majority of members—if those members vote together—can pretty much do anything it wishes. As a long-time staffer in the West Virginia Legislature once told one of the authors, "If the majority wants to paint its chamber polka dot, you'd better buy the paint because we're going to paint it polka dot." In fact, the majority party can have influence far out of proportion to its representation in the chamber. For example, a cohesive party with 51 percent of the seats may wield virtual control over policy making even though it has only maybe one or two more members than the minority party. Because of this inordinate power, gaining a majority in a chamber is the holy grail of state legislative parties.

On the other hand, sometimes a legislative majority party is not cohesive. Most systematically, and perhaps surprisingly, the larger the majority, the less party members tend to stick together and the less overt power the party can exert over legislative decision making.[109] When the parties' percentages in a chamber are close—say, the 52 percent to 48 percent Democratic majority in the Montana Senate following the 2006 election—the majority party must work extremely hard to maintain control over legislation and, indeed, to maintain their majority in the next election. The minority party smells success just a few votes away, so it scrambles to gain whatever advantage it can, whether to win passage of legislation or to position bills and votes to use as campaign issues in the next election. On the other hand, minority parties facing a lopsided partisan split—say, Idaho Senate Democrats' 20 percent to 80 percent minority—know that the only way they will ever manage to pass a bill is with the help of many majority party members, so they try hard to avoid partisan conflict. Because majority party members are not threatened by the minority in such chambers, they do not mind working with them from time to time.

In fact, when the majority party does not have a large minority threatening its power, it often crumbles in factions, making legislative conflict less along partisan lines than along regional, ethnic, or economic lines.[110] In such legislatures, parties are not a relevant organizing principle, making the collective action problem more difficult to overcome. For decades, this was the case in many southern state legislatures, where Democrats regularly held 70–90 percent majorities. But since the 1980s and 1990s, Republicans have successfully challenged for control of these bodies, making party an important consideration and increasing these legislatures' effectiveness.[111]

Legislative Leadership

Finally, once they have organized themselves along party and policy lines, legislators select from among themselves various leaders, both for their parties and committees, whose responsibility it is to move the group along toward making some collective decisions. The fundamental problem of collective action in the state legislature—as opposed to collective action in a corporation or the executive branch of government—is that all the members of the legislature are constitutionally equal, and no one member is responsible for achieving its common goal. To address this, legislators select various leaders and give them powers that rank-and-file legislators do not have, along with the responsibility to accomplish group tasks.

The two basic types of leaders parallel the two methods of organizing a state legislative chamber: committee chairs and party leaders. Committee chairs call committee meetings, schedule which legislation is to be heard and voted upon, and have what can often be significant procedural powers to organize and structure committee hearings and votes. Committee chairs are typically, but not always, members of the majority party. The corresponding leadership position of the minority party spokesperson or vice chair is usually established for each committee, but this leader has far less control of the committee's activities than the chair. Given that committees are less powerful in most state legislatures than in Congress, committee chairs are less powerful and important in the states as well.

On the other hand, party leaders are usually much more important in state legislatures than in Congress. State legislative party leadership is focused on a single office for each party in each chamber. The leader of the majority party in a chamber is the most powerful person in that chamber, serving as the presiding officer in all 50 of the state houses of representatives (usually called the speaker of the House) and in 24 state senates (usually called the president

of the senate).[112] The lieutenant governor presides over the senate floor proceedings in 26 states, but in most of these, the real power still rests in the hands of the majority party's leader (who is usually called the president pro tempore, in these cases). Minority party leaders are important players in the legislative process, but most have far fewer powers and responsibilities than the majority leaders. There are also several subsidiary leadership positions in each chamber that as a group make up the party leader's team.

The power and importance of state legislative party caucus leaders are suggested by the informal names they sometimes acquire as a group, like the "Four Tops" in Illinois and the "Big Five" in California (including the governor).[113] Most important, state legislative majority party leaders have an especially strong hand in the legislative process.[114] For example, these leaders usually appoint committee chairs and members, so they have substantial control over the output and proceedings of those bodies. Committee chairs and the subsidiary party leadership positions that the top leaders control usually receive extra pay as well as boosts in their power and prestige, making these positions very attractive and those holding them beholden to the leader who appointed them. As presiding officer over the proceedings on his or her chamber floor, a majority party leader can have considerable influence on which bills get passed. Party leaders also often negotiate among themselves and with the governor, representing their caucuses on important bills, especially the budget. Party leaders may also control much of the legislature's staff, and they may even allot offices and parking spaces. In short, party leaders, especially majority party leaders, can dominate state legislatures in ways they cannot do in Congress.

On the other hand, state legislative party leaders cannot just do whatever they wish. They are elected by their caucuses, and if they fail to help their co-partisans meet their goals, they will not be re-elected to their position in the next legislative session.[115]

But the overthrow of a powerful leader is rare, not because they are powerful but because most leaders work hard to help the members of their caucuses meet their goals. Traditionally, this has meant helping legislators overcome the collective action problem to achieve their policy-making goals. That is, these leaders are accountable to their caucus for the policy output of the legislature. They are the ones who make sure the system runs smoothly so that members can pass the legislation that is important to them and their constituents. Without strong leadership taking collective responsibility for the output of the chamber, very little would ever get done.

Legislative party leaders also spend considerable time and effort helping their caucus members get re-elected. They do this in a variety of ways, from making sure they do not cast votes on legislation that will be used against them by an election opponent to helping them pass bills that they can tout in their own election campaigns, supporting projects like new roads and parks for their districts, training new members about constituent service and media relations, and even working to draw legislative districts in ways that advantage members of their caucuses (see "State Legislative Redistricting," above). But in recent years, many legislative leaders have gone beyond these traditional approaches and begun to take an active role in their caucus members' actual campaigns.[116] Given the importance of a majority in the legislative process, these leaders focus especially on gaining or maintaining a chamber majority. By doing so, they help their caucus members meet both their re-election and policy goals because it is easier for majority party members to pass their legislation.

The basic electoral strategy for state legislative party leaders to gain or maintain a chamber majority is as follows:

1. Leverage their powerful positions in the legislature to attract lots of campaign contributions.
2. Hire and train top-flight campaign personnel.
3. Identify those districts in their chamber that are likely to have close races in the general election due to the lack of an incumbent and/or changing demographics.
4. Inundate these few targeted competitive races with massive campaign resources in an effort to swing them to their party.

These leaders are in a unique position to pursue this **targeting electoral strategy**. Their extra influence over the legislative process can attract plenty of campaign contributions from groups anxious to influence policy. They can take a statewide perspective by both learning where the competitive seats are and making the hard decisions about which candidates would benefit from extra campaign help and which would not, whether because they are sure winners or sure losers. By gathering money and campaign expertise from around the state and using it in only a few targeted districts, these leaders can concentrate the party's resources efficiently.

Because the leaders of both parties in a chamber typically use this targeting strategy and are more or less equally adept at it, legislative campaign activity is very uneven in a state. As we have seen, most general election state legislative races are blowouts, with a minimal amount of campaign activity and spending. But a handful of races scattered around the state will become intense campaign battles, with perhaps 10 times the amount of campaign funds spent as in nontargeted races, lots of TV and radio ads, out-of-town campaign managers and workers, and so forth. In fact, targeted state legislative races can become proxy battlegrounds for the parties statewide. These campaigns are usually run completely by the legislative leaders' campaign experts, with the candidates themselves becoming something of an afterthought. But few of these candidates complain (at least very loudly) when this happens because the leader is helping them win their race.

In summary, state legislators solve the collective action problem established by the formal legislative institutions in their states' constitutions by establishing their own institutions: standing committees, party caucuses, and committee and party leaders. Without such institutions, state legislatures would not be able to accomplish any of their four jobs. This is an example of how institutional arrangements can cause a problem for a political actor (in this case, the legislature) and how the establishment of other institutions can help that actor overcome those problems.

State Legislative Reform

The states have continually tried to improve their legislatures by tinkering with their institutions, rules, and processes. Sometimes, these reforms are dramatic, affecting the very foundations of these bodies. Not surprisingly, major institutional reforms are usually controversial, with serious debate over just what a state legislature should be. Interestingly, the two most significant waves of state legislative reform in the past 40 years were driven by seemingly contradictory ideas about just this question.[117] Some argued that a legislature should have sufficient resources to be a strong force in state government. These people advocated **legislative professionalism**, and the major institutional changes in state legislatures in the 1970s and 1980s reflected this value. Other reformers focused more on who state legislators were than on the institution, arguing that legislators ought to be as much like the average citizen as possible. Such "citizen-legislators" would provide a counterweight to those in the state capital whose pro-government biases could distort public policy. The most significant reform that these people advocated was state legislative **term limits**, which have begun to take effect this decade after many states adopted them in the 1990s.

What were the goals of the advocates of these reforms? What were these reforms supposed to do? What impacts, intended and unintended, have these reforms actually had on state politics and policy? Although the answers to these questions are not straightforward, we explore them in this chapter's final section.

Legislative Professionalism

In the 1950s and 1960s, a consensus developed among scholars, journalists, and good government advocates that state legislatures were simply not up to the task of governing modern state governments.[118] After World War II, state governments took great strides in their responsibilities and administrative capacity, with growing and increasingly urban populations and rising state and local government employment and spending. But state legislatures' capacity for sound planning, decision making, and analysis had not expanded along with their responsibilities. Indeed, the facilities and institutions of state legislatures in 1965 looked much more like those of 1865 than those of today. Legislative sessions typically lasted only a month or two, with many legislatures meeting only every other year. Most legislators had no office, with only a desk on the chamber floor to call their own. Staff was minimal; a legislator might share a secretary with 10 colleagues, and that secretary would be employed only during the short legislative session. In 1971, a think tank, the Citizens Conference on State Legislatures (CCSL), published a detailed and influential study derisively titled *The Sometime Governments*.[119] This book graded each state legislature on a range of criteria, primarily having to do with institutional operations, effectiveness, and efficiency. In the final analysis, the CCSL found just about every state legislature sorely lacking on most of these criteria.

With Congress as a model, these reformers and researchers argued that state legislatures lacked three things: time, staff, and pay. Legislatures needed longer, yearly sessions to be able to deal effectively with all the policy problems facing the states. They needed more staff to provide information and expertise for their policy deliberations and to give them independence from their traditional sources of policy information—interest groups and executive agencies. And legislators needed to be paid better so that lawmaking could be less of a hobby and more of a profession. Without a salary that allowed them to support their families, legislators needed another full-time job—or to be independently wealthy, supported by someone else, or retired, each of which has its biases. Such moonlighting could distract legislators from their duties at the statehouse and cause conflicts of interest in working on legislation.[120]

Given the very unusual combination of a consensus about what needed to be done, media pressure to do it, and expanding state budgets that allowed them to be able to afford to do it, the states adopted various legislative professionalism reforms extensively in the 1970s and 1980s. Of course, not every state professionalized its legislature completely—far from it. But all states progressed along the professionalism continuum to some degree. States with larger, more urban, growing, and diverse populations, like Illinois, Massachusetts, and especially California, professionalized their legislatures sooner and more thoroughly than those smaller, more rural, and more homogeneous states, like New Hampshire, Wyoming, and Arkansas, who retain their **citizen legislatures** even today.[121] In other words, the states that needed the extra help in dealing with their public problems tended to get that help, at least in part, by beefing up the capacity of their legislatures. Figure 7.4 breaks down today's state legislatures into three categories according to

Figure 7.4

State Legislative Professionalism

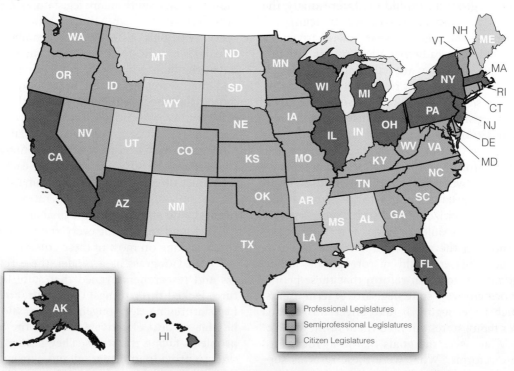

Note: Legislative professionalism is measured based on legislative salary, session length, and staffing, all compared to the U.S. Congress, using 2003 data.

Source: Modified from Peverill Squire, "Measuring Legislative Professionalism," *State Politics and Policy Quarterly* 7 (2007): 211–227.

their level of professionalism based on session length, members' salaries, and number of staff.[122]

The Impact of State Legislative Professionalism

Have these professionalized legislatures lived up to the reformers' expectations? Although they certainly have been better able to "perform [their] role in the policymaking process with an expertise, seriousness, and effort comparable to that of other actors in the process,"[123] state legislative professionalism has had some unexpected—and not universally praised—side effects. Political scientist Alan Rosenthal, who was a leader in the professionalization movement in the 1960s, has more recently criticized the reforms for promoting careerism among legislators, weakening legislative leadership, politicizing staff and the legislative process generally, polarizing the parties in the legislature, and reducing civility in these bodies.[124] That is quite an indictment for reforms that were once so universally advocated.

Other scholars have identified a variety of other effects of state legislative professionalism, many of whose value is open to debate. Political scientist Morris Fiorina argues that professionalism increased the number of Democrats in state legislatures because they are more likely than Republicans to be attracted by the relatively modest salaries even the professionalized bodies offer and the activist approach to government they encourage.[125] From this line of argument, some drew the hypothesis that professionalized legislatures spent more than nonprofessional legislatures, and one early study appeared to support this proposition.[126] But a more recent study by Neil Malhorta shows that this is not the case—when controlling for the public problems in each state, professional legislatures spend no more than citizen legislatures.[127] On the electoral side, whereas William Berry, Michael Berkman, and Stuart Schneiderman demonstrate that incumbents in professional legislatures are especially safe in their re-election bids,[128] Squire finds that these legislatures have fewer uncontested races, suggesting increased competition.[129]

Regarding constituency contact and representation, Cherie Maestas finds that professional legislatures attract more ambitious lawmakers who are especially attentive to the needs of their constituents.[130] Interestingly, Squire shows that although citizens do, in fact, have more contact with their legislators in states with professional legislatures, they are also less satisfied with their legislature as an institution.[131] So, although legislative professionalism has largely fulfilled the reformers' hopes of leading to a more active, influential, and co-equal legislative branch of state government, it has also had some peripheral effects that need to be considered when judging the reform.

Term Limits

In the late 1980s and early 1990s, certain reformers began arguing that ordinary Americans, not professional politicians, ought to serve in state legislatures and Congress, contending that such citizen-legislators would bring some common sense to government.[132] Libertarian and Republican activists tapped into Americans' mistrust of government, a deep-rooted political value stretching back to Thomas Jefferson and other thinkers of the American Revolution. In particular, these reformers focused on the lack of competition in legislative elections and the high rate of incumbent re-election. Their remedy? Specific and reasonably short restrictions on the number of times a legislator could be re-elected: term limits.

Term limits was a very popular reform among voters. From 1990 to 2000, 21 states enacted the reform for their state legislators, and some of these states also did so for their congresspeople.[133] This is an extraordinarily swift set of reform adoptions, especially for such a significant change of an institution that most people do not think about much. And the way this reform was adopted in these states is quite telling. Nineteen of these 21 states adopted their limits with an initiative, usually with the help of a national campaign by U.S. Term Limits, an organization run by an energetic policy entrepreneur named Paul Jacob.[134]

On the other hand, of the states that allow initiatives, only two (North Dakota and Mississippi) voted against having term limits.[135] Furthermore, only two state legislatures (Utah and Louisiana) limited their own terms through regular legislation—and Utah lawmakers did so under the imminent threat of an initiative with even more severe limits than they themselves passed.

We see a similar pattern at the national level. Term limits were part of the Republican Party's 1994 Contract with America, the set of campaign promises that helped them break the Democrats' 40-year grip on the U.S. House of Representatives. But during the 12-year period of mainly Republican control after 1994, Congress never limited its own members' terms. In fact, many of those who favored term limits as insurgent candidates in 1994 became much less enamored of them as their congressional careers progressed, continuing to serve even after their own self-imposed limits. Clearly, it is far easier to convince voters than legislators of the wisdom of legislative term limits. But this is not only because legislators just want to keep their jobs, although that is surely part of it. As we shall see, there are legitimate policy reasons for opposing term limits, just as there are legitimate reasons for supporting them.

Legislative term limits are not uniform among the states that have them, varying in two important respects (see Table 7.7). First, states limit their legislators to different numbers of terms. The lower chambers of Arkansas, California, and Michigan are the most limited in this respect, with their members being allowed to serve only three two-year terms. At the other extreme, Louisiana, Nevada, and Oklahoma

---

Table 7.7

State Legislative Term Limits

State	Year Enacted	House		Senate		Lifetime or Consecutive Term Ban?
		Limit (years)	Year of First Impact	Limit (years)	Year of First Impact	
Maine	1993	8	1996	8	1996	Consecutive
California	1990	6	1996	8	1998	Lifetime
Colorado	1990	8	1998	8	1998	Consecutive
Arkansas	1992	6	1998	8	2000	Lifetime
Michigan	1992	6	1998	8	2002	Lifetime
Florida	1992	8	2000	8	2000	Consecutive
Ohio	1992	8	2000	8	2000	Consecutive
South Dakota	1992	8	2000	8	2000	Consecutive
Montana	1992	8	2000	8	2000	Consecutive
Arizona	1992	8	2000	8	2000	Consecutive
Missouri	1992	8	2002	8	2002	Lifetime
Oklahoma	1990	12	2004	12	2004	Lifetime
Nebraska	2000	n/a	n/a	8	2006	Consecutive
Louisiana	1995	12	2007	12	2007	Consecutive
Nevada	1996	12	2010	12	2010	Lifetime

Source: National Conference of State Legislatures, http://www.ncsl.org/programs/legman/about/states.htm.

allow their legislators to serve for 12 consecutive years. The second way term limits vary is whether the limit represents a lifetime ban or just a restriction on consecutive terms, allowing incumbents to sit out a term or two after they reach their limit and then run again. Taking these two factors together, Arkansas, California, and Michigan have the most restrictive term limits, with short limits and a lifetime ban. On the other hand, Louisiana's 12-year limit on only consecutive terms probably does not impede the ambitions of Bayou State politicians very much.

The Impact of State Legislative Term Limits

Term limits go straight to the heart of the most basic forces that political scientists believe shape legislatures and legislative behavior: incumbent security, the influence of seniority, legislative and leadership apprenticeship, and, most importantly, legislators' drive to be re-elected. It should not be surprising, then, that scholars have spent considerable effort assessing term limits' effects, both because of the potential importance of these effects on policy and politics and as a way of testing legislative theory. Indeed, some of the most extensive collaborative research efforts ever undertaken by state politics scholars have been marshaled recently to assess the impacts of term limits.[136]

The predictions that term limits' advocates and detractors made about the reform's potential effects during the battles over its adoption in the 1990s were usually vague and often contradictory. Proponents argued that term limits would purge state legislatures of career politicians, providing more opportunity for average citizens to serve.[137] These citizen-legislators would not worry about re-election and, therefore, would be better able to vote their own consciences on legislation and avoid the narrow focus on their individual districts and pork barrel politics. Furthermore, the power of lobbyists and interest groups would be reduced because their leverage over lawmakers would be decreased, since it was it largely derived from campaign contributions, which would be less important to citizen-legislators.

On the other hand, critics of term limits argued that the desire to be re-elected encouraged legislators to represent their constituents well, so under term limits, representation would suffer.[138] But perhaps most worrisome to critics, term limits would strip legislatures of vital institutional knowledge of both policy and process. By purging the legislature of its "old heads," those senior members who knew how state government worked and had a deep, long-term understanding of policy problems, term limits would reduce the quality of legislation and subvert the legislature's influence relative to that of other actors in the process, such as interest groups, the governor, executive agencies, and even their own staff.

Unfortunately, because it has not been that long since the first state legislators actually reached their maximum number of terms and were forced from office, it is too early to make authoritative statements about the effects of term limits. Also, term limits have been struck down by four state supreme courts (see Table 7.8), typically because they restrict a person's right to vote for whom he or she wishes, and in controversial moves, the Utah and Idaho state legislatures actually repealed their own term limits.[139] But even so, we are already beginning to see some important changes in the politics of the 15 states where term limits are still in effect—but not all of these changes were the ones predicted by either their opponents or proponents.

First, consider how this reform has influenced elections. Reformers thought that term limits would increase competition in state legislative elections by eliminating incumbents from many legislative races, and one early study gave these reformers hope that this was true.[140] But several researchers have shown more recently that competition and campaign spending are probably no different under term limits, and that, in fact, competition may even decrease because more incumbents run unopposed under term limits.[141] Potential candidates simply wait for their incumbent's limit to be reached, at which time they all join in the fray for the

| Table 7.8 | | | |

Term Limits Repeals

State	Year Enacted	Year Repealed	Repealed by
Idaho	1994	2002	State legislature
Massachusetts	1994	1997	State supreme court
Oregon	1992	2002	State supreme court
Utah	1994	2003	State legislature
Washington	1992	1998	State supreme court
Wyoming	1992	2004	State supreme court

Source: National Conference of State Legislatures, http://www.ncsl.org/programs/legman/about/states.htm.

open seat. We also see a steady stream of state house members running for state senate seats whenever they come open, so that term-limited senates may soon be made up almost entirely of former house members.[142] This may increase the legislative expertise and experience of state senators relative to state representatives, potentially leading senates to gain policymaking ascendancy over houses. Term limits also seem to have stirred the political pot for other offices, with termed-out legislators running more frequently for local offices and Congress and local officials running for legislative seats opened up by term limits.[143]

Contrary to reformers' hopes, term limits have made few changes in the demographic makeup of state legislatures, although they may have accelerated ongoing trends toward better representation for women and minorities by forcing some long-serving white, male incumbents from their seats.[144] On the other hand, **legislative turnover** has increased in most states with term limits, bringing in the new blood reformers predicted.[145] But perhaps more significantly, the first wave of limits purged cadres of legislative old heads from many chambers.[146] Especially in citizen-legislatures that were term limited, like in Arkansas, where staff and legislative sessions are very restricted, these senior members had been able to counterbalance the power and knowledge of interest groups and executive agencies through their deep and extensive knowledge of state politics and policy.[147] So, as term limits got rid of these "entrenched

incumbents," as reformers had hoped, they also deprived the legislature of an important resource, as opponents feared. Furthermore, there is also good reason to believe that term-limited legislators are more partisan and less knowledgeable about policy and the legislative process than non-term-limited legislators.[148]

Term-limited legislators tend to be less focused on their districts, more concerned with statewide issues, and more willing to vote their own minds on legislation.[149] They also spend less time campaigning and raising money. These are all results that reformers would applaud. On the other hand, term-limited legislators do not appear to spend any more time studying and developing legislation than their non-term-limited counterparts. So, what are they doing with their time? It appears that term-limited legislators need to put in extra effort during the beginning and end of their legislative careers on activities with which non-term-limited legislators are not as concerned. In California, political scientist Renee Van Vechten explains this with her "2-2-2 Rule": "The first two years they're learning. The next two years they're legislating. The final two years they're looking for a job."[150] The shorter the limits on terms, the greater the proportion of a legislator's career is spent gearing up and winding down.

Because term limits disrupt relationships among legislators,[151] reduce their understanding of the rules of the legislature and their appreciation for its institutions, and make them in a hurry to make their mark,[152] they have

REFORM CAN HAPPEN

OTHER "DE-PROFESSIONALIZATION" REFORMS IN THE STATE LEGISLATURES

In addition to state legislative term limits, the states have considered a variety of other reforms to "de-professionalize" their legislatures or, more often, to keep them from changing from citizen legislatures into full-time bodies. For example:

- Colorado voters have approved two constitutional amendments that establish rigid limits on its legislature's power and discretion in policy making. First, in 1988, the state's voters approved the GAVEL ("give a vote to every legislator") initiative, which requires a committee hearing and a full legislative vote on every bill introduced in the legislature. Although this reform prevents committee chairs and legislative party leaders from biasing legislation unduly, it also significantly reduces committees' ability to screen out unmeritorious bills and make the legislative process effective and efficient. Second, in 1992, Colorado voters approved the TABOR ("taxpayers' bill of rights") initiative, which severely restricts the legislature's ability to control the purse strings of state government through tax increases and shifting policy priorities in the budget.[1]

- In recent sessions, some members of the Alaska Legislature have worked to decrease from 121 to 90 the maximum number of days that that body could meet each year. A sponsor of the bill argued, "Less time, less bills. Less bills means less chance of passing bad legislation."[2] This is not the first time Alaskans have debated legislative de-professionalization; in 1984, the state amended its constitution to impose the current 121-day limit on its previously unlimited legislature. In 1999, Nevada also restricted its legislative session length, imposing a maximum of 120 days through an initiative.

- The California initiative that imposed state legislative term limits also mandated a variety of other de-professionalization provisions, including a severe cutback in its expenditures for legislative operations, cuts in legislative staff, and the elimination of the state legislative pension program.[3] To date, no other state has so severely cut back on its legislative staff, but California has long been a leader in state legislative reform—from professionalism to term limits—so other legislatures may follow.

Notes

1. Ronald K. Snell, "Nuts and Bolts of TABOR," State Legislatures (January 2005): 24–5.
2. Hal Spence, "Lawmakers Tout Shorter Sessions," (Kenai, Alaska) Peninsula Clarion, online ed., 5 June 2005.
3. Thad Kousser, *Term Limits and the Dismantling of State Legislative Professionalism* (New York: Cambridge University Press, 2005).

---

caused the legislative process itself to be messier, more chaotic, more partisan, more rancorous, more confrontational, and less predictable than without term limits.[153] Although you might think that this does not sound good, some term limits supporters are so suspicious of government that they actually welcome this legislative gridlock as a way of keeping the state from making new inroads into people's lives.[154]

From an institutional perspective, term limits have reduced the influence of the legislature on state policy relative to the governor, executive agencies, and legislative staff, just as

its critics predicted.[155] This shift in power is especially noticeable in technical and ongoing areas of policy, like the state budget, where a deep understanding of policy history and state government is vital.[156] Term limits may also weaken legislative leaders, something both hoped for by term limits' proponents and feared by their opponents.[157] Throwing out strong leaders opens up the legislature to more voices, but it restricts its ability to speak with a powerful voice when negotiating with the governor and other outsiders. On the other hand, a major study in Michigan has suggested that term limits may actually increase legislative party leaders' control of the chamber because they are the center of decision-making power and policy information.[158] It is not yet clear what impact term limits will have on the overall influence of interest groups in the legislative process, but it appears that more lobbyists are working harder in term-limited legislatures and that their influence is more evenly distributed than previously.[159] There is also evidence that the lack of institutional memory among term-limited legislators has led to more lobbyists trying to deceive legislators and other unethical behavior.[160]

Thus, term limits have had a variety of significant impacts on those state legislatures subject to them. Are term limits good or bad?

The jury is still out, and more time must pass before we can fully understand their effects. But beyond simply needing better information about the impacts of term limits, different people may apply different value judgments to its impacts. For example, is it good or bad that state legislatures have less influence on public policy, relative to governors and executive agencies? Should we be concerned or pleased that legislators are more partisan and less attentive to their districts in term-limited legislatures? Will legislators with less experience lead to better or worse public policy? These are values questions that need to be discussed by citizens and policy makers as term limits become part of the political landscape of many states.

Summary

State constitutions charge their legislatures with difficult responsibilities—to set the state's public policy, to guard its purse strings, to oversee the executive branch, and to represent its citizens' values and interests before the government. But these constitutions also make it very difficult for legislatures to do these jobs well by setting up a bicameral process, by having lawmakers equal in power and elected frequently, and by just making it difficult to pass laws in general. Over the years, state legislatures have developed a variety of processes and institutions to help them overcome these obstacles and accomplish their mission. Standing committees, political parties, and legislative leaders all help legislatures solve their collective action problem. Never content with these arrangements, reformers continually argue about, and regularly implement, institutional changes in state legislatures to improve their performance.

This brings us back to the questions we raised at the beginning of this chapter: what constitutes good legislative performance, and what is the best way to achieve it? As you have seen, these questions cannot be answered easily. At its root, the answer to the first question must be based on our political values. Should legislatures engage in the technical evaluation of policy problems and quiet, fact-based debate and compromise or should they be a forum for the clear exchange of divergent views, ending with a majority vote to decide any conflicts? Do we value efficiency, fairness, effectiveness, or deliberation? Do we perhaps value all of them? Is there an inherent conflict between some of these values? Should we encourage public participation in the legislative process even if it slows down decision making? Is the efficiency that strong legislative leadership gives us beneficial even if it means that some views are ignored in the process? Should the opinion of the majority always decide policy no matter how badly it hurts the minority? These are questions for citizens and politicians to decide in the public arena. In some respects, the two major legislative reform movements of recent years reflect the tension between these values. The professionalism movement was an attempt to bring more efficiency and rational decision making into lawmaking, whereas the term limits movement was an attempt to link the legislature more closely to the people of the state.

Once these values are decided, political scientists can assess whether they are being reflected in a state's governmental institutions and in its public policy. We have done some of this in this chapter. But given the ongoing changes in, and differences among, the states, their continual tinkering with their legislative institutions, and especially the conflicting values that may be used to evaluate a legislature, no institutional design is going to be ideal. However, we should be encouraged by the fact that state policy makers care enough about our legislatures to continue working to improve them. As citizens, we must be vigilant to see that our values are indeed reflected in this, our closest political institution—the state legislature.

Key Terms

Administrative rules review committee

Amend

Amendatory veto

Bicameral

Bill

Bill sponsor

Casework

Chamber floor

Citizen-legislature

Collective action problem

Committee jurisdiction

Conference committee

Contiguous

Cracking

Divided government

Ex post oversight

Gatekeeping

Gerrymander

Implementation

Incumbent

Incumbent-protection district

Legislative intent

Legislative professionalism

Legislative turnover

Line-item veto

Malapportionment

Media market

Multimember district (MMD)

Override

Packing

Party caucus

Pork barrel

Rank-and-file legislator

Reapportionment revolution

Redistricting

Roll call

Single-member district (SMD)

Standing committee

Supermajority

Targeting electoral strategy

Term limits

Two-party contestation

Unicameral

Voting cue

Voting Rights Act of 1965

Suggested Readings

Camissa, Anne Marie, and Beth Reingold. 2004. Women in state legislatures and state legislative research: Beyond sameness and difference. *State Politics and Policy Quarterly* 4:181–210.

Hamm, Keith E., and Gary F. Moncrief. 2004. Legislative politics in the states. *In Politics in the American states*, eds. Virginia Gray and Russell L. Hanson. 8th ed. Washington, DC: CQ Press.

Haynie, Kerry L. 2001. *African American legislators in the American states.* New York: Columbia University Press.

Kousser, Thad. 2005. *Term limits and the dismantling of state legislative professionalism.* New York: Cambridge University Press.

McDonald, Michael P., guest ed. 2004. Special issue: Electoral redistricting. *State Politics and Policy Quarterly* 4:369–490.

Moncrief, Gary F., Peverill Squire, and Malcolm E. Jewell. 2001. *Who runs for the legislature?* Upper Saddle River, NJ: Prentice Hall.

Neal, Tommy. 2005. *Learning the game: How the legislative process works.* Denver, CO: National Conference of State Legislatures.

Rosenthal, Alan. 2004. *Heavy lifting: The job of the American legislature.* Washington, DC: CQ Press.

Rosenthal, Cindy Simon. 1998. *When women lead: Integrative leadership in state legislatures.* New York: Oxford University Press.

Squire, Peverill, and Keith E. Hamm. 2005. *101 chambers: Congress, state legislatures, and the future of state legislative studies.* Columbus: Ohio State University Press.

Wright, Ralph G. 2005. *Inside the statehouse: Lessons from the speaker.* Washington, DC: CQ Press.

Websites

American Legislative Exchange Council (http://www.alec.org): ALEC is a national association of conservative state legislators whose goal is to advance the Jeffersonian principles of free markets, limited government, federalism, and individual liberty.

Center for American Women and Politics (http://www.cawp.rutgers.edu): The CAWP is a unit of Rutgers University that conducts research and training about and for women in elective office in the United States. Women in state legislatures are a major focus of the CAWP.

National Black Caucus of State Legislators (http://www.nbcsl.org): The NBCSL is a bipartisan national organization that conducts research and training designed to enhance the effectiveness of its members: African-American state legislators.

National Conference of State Legislatures (http://www.ncsl.org): The NCSL is a national, bipartisan organization that provides state legislators and their staff with research, technical assistance, and opportunities to exchange ideas on the most pressing state issues.

Progressive States Network (http://www.progressivestates.org): The PSN is a liberal organization website that conducts and publishes research, tracks state legislation, and coordinates and networks like-minded policy makers and citizens.

8

AP Photo/Lindsey Bauman

Governors

Player: George Pataki, Governor of New York (1995–2007)

OUTLINE

Introductory Vignette

Introduction

Gubernatorial Elections

Today's Governors: Who Are They?

The Powers of the Governor

The Three Jobs of the Governor

Summary

On July 27, 2005, at his office in Albany, New York Governor George Pataki formally announced that he would not seek an unprecedented fourth term in 2006.[1] Just like much that the Empire State Republican did as governor, this announcement had major repercussions around the state and even around the nation.

An upstart state senator who unexpectedly brought down Democratic icon and three-term governor Mario Cuomo in 1994, Pataki used New York's powerful governorship to wrestle with some of the most difficult policy and political problems in the country. With his strong budget and veto powers, Pataki took a firm hand in setting the legislature's agenda, cutting taxes and higher education funding, and advocating the cleanup of the Hudson River, tough-on-crime laws, and incentives for nanotechnology, among other things. Appointing strong leaders to key positions helped him gain control of the sprawling New York state government and implement his policy initiatives effectively. Intense political and policy debate focused on the World Trade Center and the Port Authority throughout his tenure as governor, first as he fought successfully to privatize them and later as he dealt with the September 11, 2001, attacks and their aftermath. And like other governors, he was also forced to deal with changes in national policy that had huge impacts on the state, especially the 1996 welfare reforms and the 2001 No Child Left Behind Act.

Pataki also had political challenges. As a Republican in one of the most Democratic states in the country, he could not afford to move in the conservative direction that has been successful for so many Republicans elsewhere during the 1990s and 2000s. He had to walk a fine political line to achieve his goals. For instance, although he cut taxes and worked to re-enact the death penalty in New York, he also supported abortion rights, gun control, and—sometimes—public employee unions in their contract negotiations with the state. He took heat for some of these positions from his political right; billionaire Thomas Golisano spent millions of dollars running against him three times as the candidate of the conservative Independence Party, a third party with well-established ties to the New York GOP.

But in 2005, as Pataki announced his intention to step down as governor, there was little time to look back on his long tenure in the office. Candidates to replace him in this important job were already swinging into action. The race for governor of New York in 2006 saw some of the best-known political figures in the country either vying for the job themselves or working hard for someone else's candidacy. Candidates included billionaires and millionaires, a son-in-law of a former president (Edward Cox, who is married to Richard Nixon's daughter), a former governor of Massachusetts and ambassador to Mexico (William Weld), and the best-known state attorney general in the country—the eventual winner, Eliot Spitzer.[2]

And as he made his retirement announcement, Pataki was also looking to his own future. Throughout American history, governors' offices have been fertile ground for presidential timber; New York itself has supplied the country with four governors-turned-presidents, more than any other state (Van Buren, Cleveland, and two Roosevelts). Just about every New York governor in the 20th century had been a serious, even if unsuccessful, presidential candidate. Pataki demonstrated his interest in a presidential run by paying multiple visits to the early presidential primary and caucus states. In his last State of the State speech, he even touted the use of ethanol—important in corn-growing Iowa, the home of the first presidential caucus.[3] In the end, his presidential aspirations fizzled, but 2008 finds him in another important position—as one of the U.S.'s three representatives to the U.N.'s General Assembly.

Mario Tama/Getty Images News

George Pataki, governor of New York (1995–2007), at Ground Zero in New York City, flanked by West Virginia Governor Bob Wise (2001–2005) (right) and Washington State Governor Gary Locke (1997–2005) (left).

Introduction

The governor is the single most visible and powerful person in state government, even better known than most states' two U.S. senators.[4] As the official **head of state** (like the president of the United States or the queen of England), the governor symbolizes the state to people, business leaders, and leaders of other governments, both in and out of the state and in and out of the country. So, when Governor Tim Kaine visited the campus of Virginia Tech just after the April 2007 shooting rampage, he demonstrated the sympathy of all Virginians for the plight of those affected, just as governor Kathleen Sebelius's visit to Greensburg the following month showed the compassion of Kansans for that tornado-ravaged town (see chapter-opening photo).[5] And on a more positive note, when Delaware governor Ruth Ann Minner flew to Europe to promote economic development in her state with the German minister of economics and the Italian Chamber of Commerce, she was singing the praises of the workers and business opportunities in her home state.[6] Governors also meet with schoolchildren and Olympic athletes, business and community leaders, delegations of foreign dignitaries, and many others, showing these people their states' concern for and interest in them and those people they represent.

Also, like the president, a governor is the state's chief executive officer and chief policy maker, taking a major role in formulating, enacting, and implementing a wide range of public policy. Given the size and complexity of modern state governments, few administrative jobs in the world compare to being the governor of even the smallest state. Only a few countries are as big and complex as California or New York, and even medium-sized states, like Louisiana and South Carolina, are about the size of smaller, but important, countries, such as Ireland and Israel. And certainly few corporations match any of the states in terms of their annual budget, number of employees, and scope of activities.

Thus, being governor is a big job with big responsibilities, and we recognize successful governors accordingly. Indeed, more presidents have been governor than any other type of office or position. In 47 of the 54 presidential elections in U.S. history, at least one of the major party candidates for president or vice president had been a governor; often, more than one governor was on the ticket.[7] Other important positions are regularly filled by former governors too, including key federal-level cabinet positions, seats in the U.S. Senate, and top executive positions in business, education, and the arts.

But American governors have not always been as powerful as they are today. In fact, out of fear of tyranny and the memory of severe royal governors, when the original 13 colonies set up their state governments, they made their governors very weak indeed. An important scholar of early state governors argued that one such governor "had just enough power to sign the receipt for his salary."[8]

But as the states grew in population and their governments expanded and became more complex, Americans soon realized that their governors needed to be more than just symbolic leaders or simple bureaucrats. Because of the office's pivotal role in state government, the institution of the governorship has been the focus of large and small reforms since the beginning of our nation. These reforms have reflected the political values held most deeply by Americans at different points in history and in different parts of the country.[9] As a result, the 50 governors' offices are extremely diverse in their duties and powers, and these differences have important impacts on policy and governance in the 50 states. Following the central themes of this book, we focus on the governor's office as an institution, describing and comparing those attributes that are largely a function of state law and constitutional provision rather than the personality of the person temporarily in the position. Of course, because a governor's personality has a major effect on how, and how well, he or she does the job, we will not ignore this aspect of governors entirely.

In this chapter, we look at how today's governors are elected, what kinds of people win those races, and the institutional and informal powers of the office. Then, we bring all this together by discussing how three governors use their powers to accomplish three of a governor's main jobs—chief policy maker, chief administrator, and intergovernmental relations manager.

Gubernatorial Elections

In general, gubernatorial races are the most important elections on a state's political calendar, often drawing even more interest in a state than presidential elections. All but two states now hold gubernatorial elections every four years (New Hampshire's and Vermont's governors still serve two-year terms), with 34 of these being held in the even-numbered year in which no presidential election is held (for example, 2006, 2010, and 2014).[10] Nine states elect their governors to four-year terms during presidential election years, and five states hold their gubernatorial elections in odd-numbered years (see Figure 8.1). Thirty-five states limit their governors to two consecutive terms, Virginia is the last state to limit its governors to one term. Although 14 other states have no formal term limits on governors, a two-term limit is the informal norm in most of them—recent 12-plus-year careers of governors in Illinois, Wisconsin, and New York notwithstanding.

Voting for Governor

When a citizen enters the booth to vote in a race for governor, how does he or she decide which lever to pull, hole to punch, or spot to touch on the screen? Recall our discussion of voting in state legislative races, and think how that might apply to voting for governor. First, voters have much more specific information about gubernatorial candidates than they do about state legislative candidates. Because the race is run statewide, gubernatorial candidates can advertise on television and radio more cost-effectively than those running for the legisla-

ture. Campaigning also has economies of scale, so that a gubernatorial candidate can transmit more sophisticated messages across the state more frequently. But more importantly, political parties, interest groups, and the general public all recognize the governor's office as a uniquely important position in the state. As a result, that gubernatorial candidates can raise more money to get their messages out to the public, groups will make their preferences in the race widely known, and voters will simply spend more time and energy paying attention to the race than they do for lower-level offices.

Because of these factors, voters will have more information about the candidates when voting for governor than when voting for state legislator. We know that voters actually retain information from these gubernatorial campaigns because voters know more about candidates after a hard-fought race than when the race is less competitive and less interesting.[11] Furthermore, gubernatorial races are closely covered in the print media, even if more of that coverage is about which candidate is leading in the polls than about campaign issues.[12]

But what information actually influences how people vote in gubernatorial elections? First, not surprisingly, voters are most likely to vote to re-elect popular incumbent governors. For example, Pennsylvania governor Ed Rendell (a former mayor of Philadelphia) was so popular that he was able to raise taxes significantly and still easily beat a popular Pittsburgh Steelers NFL Hall of Famer for re-election in 2006. Interestingly, an incumbent governor's popularity can rub off on the candidate of his or her's party even if the incumbent is not running for re-election.[13] Second, voters hold incumbent governors accountable for the state's economy, especially its unemployment rate.[14] Yet, the effect of a state's economy on gubernatorial voting appears to be highly nuanced, suggesting that voters are quite sophisticated in making their decisions. For example, evidence reveals that voters hold a gubernatorial candidate accountable for the state's economy only when that candidate's party controls both the legislature and the governor's office[15] and voters

Figure 8.1

Gubernatorial Election Cycles[a]

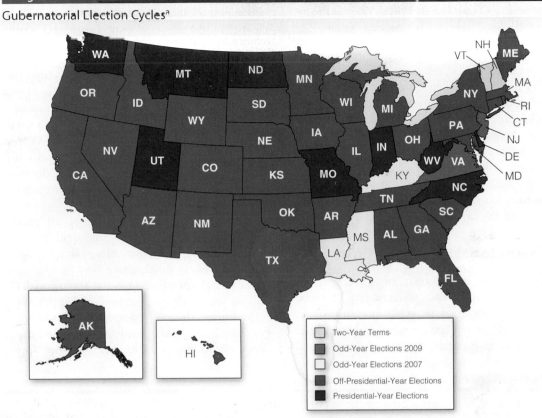

Two-Year Terms
Odd-Year Elections 2009
Odd-Year Elections 2007
Off-Presidential-Year Elections
Presidential-Year Elections

[a] Election cycle coding as follows:

Two-Year: Every even-numbered year (for example, 2008, 2010, and 2012)

Odd-Year Elections 2009: Every fourth odd-numbered year, with the next election being held in 2009 (for example, 2009, 2013, and 2017)

Odd-Year Elections 2007: Every fourth odd-numbered year, with the last election being held in 2007 (for example, 2007, 2011, and 2015)

Off-Presidential-Year Elections: Even-numbered years when no presidential election is held (for example, 2006, 2010, and 2014)

Presidential-Year Elections: Years when presidential elections are held (for example, 2008, 2012, and 2016)

hold the governor accountable for the economy only in election years, when the campaigns make getting this information relatively easy.[16]

On the other hand, most Americans do not base their votes entirely on their understanding of the candidates and issues, even in gubernatorial elections.[17] Politics and elections are low on the list of most people's priorities, behind family, jobs, friends, and maybe even their favorite sports team. So, like for other offices, voters often use shortcuts when they vote for governor—shortcuts that allow them to make a reasoned voting choice without working too hard at it. The most important of these shortcuts is political party; people tend to vote for the gubernatorial candidate to whose party they feel closest. And unlike a candidate's record of achievements and policy positions, in practice, he or she has little control over his or her party affiliation.

Other factors affect gubernatorial voting that candidates have even less control over. In particular, national-level forces, such as the country's economy and the party of the president (relative to the party of the gubernatorial candidate), can influence people's votes for governor.[18] Indeed, the 41 gubernatorial races held in nonpresidential election years are sometimes seen as midterm referendums on a president's performance.[19] But as gubernatorial campaigns become more costly, more sophisticated, and more personality-based, the link between gubernatorial voting and presidential approval will probably continue to weaken, with people voting more on party, the issues, and the candidates in the race.[20]

Gubernatorial Campaign Costs

The growing importance of governors in American politics and government and the growing importance of state government in our federal system have caused gubernatorial campaigns to become increasingly costly and competitive over the past 25 years. Candidates know that people base their votes, at least in part, on the information they have about the candidates, so they campaign hard to get favorable information about themselves (and, often, unfavorable information about their opponents) to voters.[21] All this campaigning costs a lot of money. Indeed, the costs of running a serious gubernatorial campaign in even a small state have skyrocketed. Figure 8.2 shows that the combined cost of all gubernatorial campaigns in four-year cycles more than doubled between 1977 and 2004, even controlling for inflation.[22]

Furthermore, the spending of all candidates in both primary and general election campaigns for governor varies dramatically. For example, in 2002, there was $155.8 million in total spending in New York and $1.7 million in total spending in Nebraska. Not surprisingly, this variation is not random.[23] For one thing, gubernatorial races are more expensive in larger states because more voters

---

Figure 8.2

The Rising Cost of Gubernatorial Elections (1977–2004)

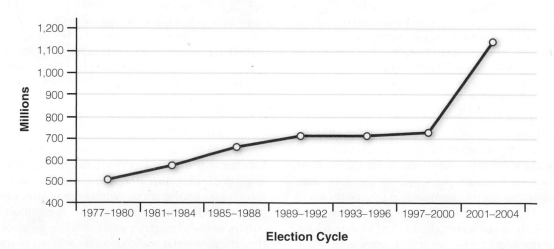

GUBERNATORIAL CAMPAIGN SPENDING

Note: Dollars are adjusted for inflation, with 2004 as the base year.

Source: Thad Beyle, "Gubernatorial Elections, Campaign Costs and Powers," in *The Book of the States 2006,* vol. 38 (Lexington, Ky.: Council of State Governments, 2006).

need to be persuaded there. But other factors can also cause gubernatorial campaign costs to increase. In general, the more uncertain the outcome of an election, the more likely candidates will work very hard to win it. Gubernatorial candidates running against a popular incumbent or in a state where their party is in the minority have little chance of winning, so not only will they have less incentive to work hard personally, but interest groups and other contributors will also be less inclined to "invest" in their lost cause. A sure winner also has little incentive to work hard and spend exorbitantly. So, when competition is closest, when no incumbent is running, and when the partisan balance is even, gubernatorial campaign spending is the highest. For example, in 2002, the tough-fought, open-seat race that Rendell won in Pennsylvania saw total spending of $69.2 million, whereas across the border in Ohio, a very similar state politically, the incumbent governor won easily in a race where only $15.4 million was spent.

An institutional factor that might affect campaign spending is **campaign finance regulation**. Some states have very low limits on the amount of money an individual can contribute to a candidate, bans on union and corporation contributions, and onerous reporting requirements. Some states even entice gubernatorial candidates to limit their overall spending by offering them some public financing. Perhaps the 2002 Pennsylvania gubernatorial race was so expensive because that state had fewer restrictions on campaign contributions than did Ohio. Campaign finance reformers would like to think so.[24] On the other hand, research has found little evidence that these regulations actually hold down spending in gubernatorial races; voluntary limits on spending can reduce overall spending but only if public financing is large enough to be meaningful.[25]

But why have gubernatorial campaigns overall become so much more expensive in recent years? It is an issue of both supply and demand. On the supply side, the importance of the governor's office and state government

in general has made a wide range of interest groups and businesses more than willing to contribute money to candidates who they think will pursue their interests once in office. Groups may even donate money to two or more candidates in an election so that they will be more likely to have access to the governor, regardless of who wins. Gubernatorial candidates even tap hit up groups, businesses, and individuals outside of their state for contributions. For example, California governor Arnold Schwarzenegger raised millions in campaign fundraisers in 2005.[26] Ironically, Illinois governor Rod Blagojevich raised millions at fundraisers in California that same year. Even national party groups are getting involved in some races in a big way. In 2006, the Republican Governors Association and the Democratic Governors Association contributed close to $50 million to candidates in close races around the country.[27]

There have also been more **self-financing candidates** in governor's races recently, just as there have been in congressional races.[28] A multimillionaire may worry little about spending $5–10 million or more in pursuit of a challenging opportunity for public service. In New Jersey in 2005, two such men spent a total of over $70 million in the governor's race.[29] Of the six candidates in Illinois's 2006 gubernatorial primaries, four were millionaires. In California, it costs so much to run for governor that one political scientist quipped, "[T]he rich and famous only need apply."[30] Yet, even the super-rich Schwarzenegger had to solicit contributions; he could not afford the $75 million it cost to re-elect him in 2006.[31]

So, the money is available to gubernatorial candidates—at least to those who look viable—but why do they need so much of it? The demand side of the gubernatorial campaign finance equation has to do with the nature of modern American political campaigns. First, the importance of the governor's office attracts many highly qualified and well-financed candidates. Gubernatorial races routinely attract popular U.S. senators, congresspersons, big-city mayors, and other elected statewide officials as well as successful and well-heeled businesspeople and even celebrities, like NBA Hall of Famer Charles Barkley and actor–movie producer Rob Reiner. Such candidates have the knowledge, desire, and money to employ the most up-to-date tools of modern campaigning, including hiring campaign professionals, doing extensive polling, and—most important and expensive—producing slick television ads and running them heavily on stations throughout the state.[32]

Another contributing factor in gubernatorial candidates' insatiable need for campaign funds is the demise of the state political party as a vehicle for campaigning in the general election.[33] Parties almost never get involved in gubernatorial primary elections, which means that candidates have to develop and fund their own campaigns from the start. So, once they win the primary, they are understandably reluctant to hand over control of their successful campaigns to others. This means that campaigns tend to be custom-made, but this personalized approach to running a campaign costs more because the campaign organizations have to be reinvented each election, and the professional campaign consultants who travel from state to state and campaign to campaign to run them are more expensive than simply tapping into the expertise of homegrown party officials.

The final reason that the demand for gubernatorial campaign spending has grown so dramatically is simply that campaigns are longer and more competitive these days. As soon as the votes are counted in one election, potential candidates for the next contest begin jockeying for favor with the media, interest groups, and potential donors. This is especially the case in those 36 states with gubernatorial term limits, where open races occur at least every two cycles, but it is true in any state even when an incumbent is likely to run. For example, at least as early as 18 months before the 2006 election, incumbent governors in Texas, Illinois, and California were raising millions of dollars for their re-election campaigns as well as attracting visible and highly qualified

opponents, several of whom were already running television ads.

Election Outcomes

So, once the smoke clears and the votes have been counted, what can we say about the outcomes of gubernatorial elections? To begin to answer this, remember what we know about voting and campaigns. Because party matters a great deal in voters' decision making, it should not be surprising that the candidate from the dominant party in a state is the most likely to win. But given the high profile of gubernatorial elections and their candidates and the millions of dollars that are spent on their campaigns, the competition between major party gubernatorial candidates in the general election has become closer than ever in most states.[34] In fact, the minority party candidate often wins the governor's race. We saw this clearly in the 1970s and 1980s in the states of the old Confederacy, which since the Civil War had been the most reliably Democratic region of the country. Following the success of Republican presidential candidates here in the 1950s and 1960s, some of these states began electing Republican governors. When voters have enough candidate-specific information, they can overcome even generations-old tendencies and vote for the candidate whose political views are most in line with their own. Recently, personality-driven campaigns have led to gubernatorial wins for Republicans in such strongly Democratic states as Massachusetts, California, and New York and for Democrats in the Republican-dominated states of Virginia, Kansas, and Wyoming. Thus, almost no state's governorship is safe for one party or the other anymore, and competition for these offices is intense.[35]

This intense competition can also be seen in the rate of incumbent governor re-election. From 1970 to 2005, of the 286 incumbent governors seeking re-election, 74 percent were successful.[36] Although that may sound like a high re-election rate, when compared to the much higher rates for state legislators, members of

Congress, and even U.S. senators (whose prestige of office and constituency parallel the governors'), we see that incumbent governors are quite vulnerable. Much of this vulnerability is due to the fact that as chief executives, they are held accountable for the state's problems and their own actions to a much greater degree than are, for example, legislators.[37] In fact, the only major office with a worse re-election rate in recent years is that other chief executive of a large and complex government—the president of the United States.

Today's Governors: Who Are They?

Who are the people who win these expensive and competitive elections and serve as governor in the states today? Although each governor has his or her own personal history, experiences, and background, we can make some generalizations about them. First, as a group, they are a long way from the political hacks, the so-called "**goodtime Charlies**," who often occupied governors' mansions before the 1960s.[38] Today's governors are younger and better educated than those in years gone by, they have been highly successful in their chosen fields before becoming governor, and they often move on to important and powerful careers after being governor. Governors fight hard to win their jobs, and while in office, they energetically pursue their vision of the state and its government. To better understand who today's governors are, let's consider both their career paths and what is perhaps the most striking trend in American governors today: the rise of the woman governor.

Career Path

Where governors come from can tell us a lot about their interests and values. Where governors go tells us not only about these people but also about the skills they learn in office and the esteem in which that office is held.

The Rise to Governor What does the résumé of today's typical governor look like? Because the governorship is the top political job in a state, governors often have considerable and progressive experience in state and local government. Governors typically start out their careers in the local or state legislature or in law enforcement, often as a local prosecutor. They are usually college educated and frequently have a graduate degree, especially a law degree. These are people who are interested in politics, policy, and government from an early age, and their careers reflect this. Governors typically rise through local or state legislative or administrative office fairly quickly, as their skills are recognized and their ambition propels them.

Political scientist Thad Beyle surveyed the 40 governors first elected from 2002 to 2005 about their most recent job prior to becoming governor,[39] and this can give us a feel for the progressive nature of the state political career ladder (see Table 8.1). The most common job these people last had before becoming governor was a statewide elected office, like lieutenant governor or secretary of state. Statewide officials are elected by the same voters that they have to face in a gubernatorial race, and they have already served that constituency and raised their name recognition among it. In 2006, attorneys general Eliot Spitzer and Charlie Crist were elected governors of New York and Florida, respectively. The next most common former job among the governors Beyle surveyed was member of the U.S. Congress. This indicates that the governor's office is seen as a step above a seat in Congress (especially the House) on the political career ladder today. Why else would a person give up a safe seat in that notoriously stable body to fight tooth and nail for the more competitive—and much more difficult—position of governor? In 2006, Nevada's Jim Gibbons and Ohio's Ted Strickland took this route to the governor's mansion.

Some governors last served as state legislators, such as Minnesota's Tim Pawlenty and Oklahoma's Brad Henry. But this number is smaller than it used to be, again demonstrating that the governor's office has become both

Table 8.1

Governors' Most Recent Former Jobs (2002–05)

Most Recent Job	Number of Governors
Elected Statewide Office	
Lieutenant governor	4
Attorney general	4
Secretary of state	2
Treasurer	1
Insurance commissioner	1
Congress	
Senate	8
House	2
Other Jobs	
Business	6
State legislature	5
Mayor	3
Criminal justic e	2
Other	2
Total	40

Source: Thad Beyle's survey of governors newly elected from 2002 to 2005, in Thad Beyle, "Gubernatorial Elections, Campaign Costs and Powers," in *The Book of the States 2006*, vol. 38 (Lexington, Ky.: Council of State Governments, 2006).

more attractive and filled by more experienced people than in years gone by. Six of Beyle's governors had most recently been in business, like California's Schwarzenegger, and another three had been mayor, like Pennsylvania's Rendell. Two of these governors worked in the criminal justice system, one as a state supreme court justice (Oregon's Ted Kulongoski) and the other as a U.S. attorney (Wyoming's Dave Freudenthal). The last two governors in this survey came to office through unique routes, with Indiana's Mitch Daniels having last served in the Bush administration as director of the Office of Management and Budget and Mississippi's Haley Barbour having last served as the Republican Party National chairman.

The power and prestige of the governor's office not only attract those moving up the political ladder but also hold considerable cachet for those who have been successful outside of government. Some such outsiders have sought and gained governorships throughout our history. For example, on his way to the White House, Woodrow Wilson moved from the presidency of Princeton University to New Jersey's governor's mansion in 1911. But in recent years, more highly successful people are taking their first step into politics by running for high political office, especially the governor's office, which appears to many to be quite like that of a manager in private business. Governors George W. (Texas) and Jeb (Florida) Bush each went straight from private business into the governor's mansion. California's Schwarzenegger and Minnesota's Jesse Ventura were in the entertainment industry before becoming governor (although Ventura had also served a stint as the mayor of a small Minneapolis suburb). Massachusetts's Mitt Romney went from private business to the governor's office, just as his father (George) had done in Michigan in the 1960s. Another political neophyte who became governor in the 1960s was California's Ronald Reagan. Besides these well-known examples, many others with a lower profile have moved straight from the private sector to the governor's office, including Rhode Island's Don Carcieri and North Dakota's John Hoeven.

Less experienced governors face pros and cons when taking over the governor's office free of the political and governmental experience and baggage that most governors bring, and these are hashed out on the campaign trail whenever one of these **outsider gubernatorial candidates** runs. Governors experienced in government better understand its nuances and how to get things done. On the other hand, outsider governors may bring fresh ideas and are not locked into standard operating procedures and old political relationships. In general, it is just harder for voters to predict how, and how well, such candidates would act as governor should they be elected. As a result, such candidates are more of a gamble than those with extensive governmental experience.

Furthermore, because these outsider governors may never have been forced to think seriously about their public ethics before, they can sometimes inadvertently commit acts that, although in the private sector would cause no problem, can be politically embarrassing when committed by a public official. For example, California's Schwarzenegger was criticized for retaining a lucrative contract with a weightlifting magazine that advertises nutritional supplements while at the same time making policy decisions about steroid use,[40] and Minnesota's Ventura came under fire for serving as a television commentator for the short-lived XFL football league while in office.[41] These situations raise issues both of **conflict of interest** and of the propriety of a governor moonlighting. A few outsider governors have even gotten into legal trouble for their activities before or during their terms of office. For example, two recent outsider governors in Arizona, Evan Mecham and Fife Symington, were removed from office or forced to resign due to legal action. Of course, politically experienced governors are not immune to such problems—witness the recent resignations amid allegations of impropriety of experienced politicians New Jersey governor Jim McGreevey and Connecticut governor John Rowland.[42]

Beyond the Governor's Mansion If the governor's office is the pinnacle of a state's political ladder, what can a governor do for an encore? This is an especially important question for those many governors in recent years who have been elected to office in their 40s and even their 30s and have faced a long postgovernorship life. Most former governors today continue to do what former governors have always done—move into private business and make a lot of money. Many former governors put together a portfolio of business activities that can include legal work, lobbying, public speaking, university teaching, corporate board service, and public relations work. Former governors can make considerable money in these lines of work, cashing in on the years of experience and many contacts made in state

government. And who can blame them? Being a state governor is an extremely difficult job, and governors make nowhere near the salary of a CEO of a Fortune 100 company, which would be a comparable job in the private sector.

But many of today's former governors continue to work in the public realm, sometimes in addition to their private ventures. Former governors serve on various top-level public commissions and boards at both the state and national levels. For example, three of the 10 members of the national commission investigating the 9/11 terrorist attacks were former governors, including its chair, former New Jersey governor Thomas Kean. Kean also held another public position that former governors sometimes fill—president of a university (Drew University, in Kean's case). As mentioned earlier, former governors often serve on presidents' cabinets and as ambassadors; President Bush, a former governor himself, has used them extensively in these ways. Having proven themselves to be able administrators and adept at handling the press and interest groups, former governors can make excellent cabinet secretaries. Presidents also use former governors symbolically, as when President Bush showed his support for midwestern farmers by appointing Nebraska governor Mike Johanns to be secretary of agriculture. Several former governors have also served on the U.S. Supreme Court, although none has done so since California governor Earl Warren became chief justice in 1953. Two former governors, Virginia's L. Douglas Wilder and California's Jerry Brown, have recently taken unusual postgubernatorial jobs—as mayors of troubled cities in their states. Former governor Roy Romer of Colorado may have taken on one of the most difficult jobs of all—superintendent of the distressed Los Angeles School District.

Of course, if the governor's office is the pinnacle of the political career ladder in a state, the presidency is the national pinnacle. The fact that the job of a governor is more like that of the president than any other job in the country makes the nation's governors a natural talent pool for future presidents. This has been true throughout U.S. history, as 17 of our 43 presidents (40 percent) were former governors (see Table 8.2). Indeed, as of 2008, former governors had served as president for 108 of the nation's 220-year history under the U.S. Constitution—almost 50 percent of the time.

The longest time in which a former governor did not serve as president was the 32 years between the death of Franklin Roosevelt (1945) and the inauguration of former Georgia governor Jimmy Carter (1977). During this period, every president except former Army general Dwight Eisenhower came from Congress, having made his political name in the House or the Senate.[43] Perhaps not coincidentally, this period was also the nadir of state and gubernatorial prestige and competence and a time when Congress was heavily involved in domestic policy initiatives that made good fodder for

presidential campaigns. But since the states and governorships were revitalized, former governors have dominated the White House like no other time in U.S. history. Since 1976, a former governor has occupied the Oval Office in all but four years. Only President George H. W. Bush had not been a governor—but two of his sons were.

Of course, only a small percentage of former governors actually become president, but just as important is the idea that a governor *could* become president. Just as used to be the case for the U.S. Senate, the nation's governors' offices are thought of as being filled with "presidential timber" by the media, the political parties, up-and-coming politicians, and, just as importantly, governors themselves. This burnishes the image of both the governor's office and specific governors, which in turn attracts higher-quality candidates to governors' races and gives sitting governors more informal persuasive power, both within and outside of their states. Simply being mentioned as a potential presidential candidate makes people pay closer attention to what a governor says, even though governors sometimes take flak for neglecting their home state in the pursuit of their presidential ambitions.[44] And a governor's presidential aspirations may even be good for a state, as a governor strives to perform well to gain favorable publicity. For example, the performance of Massachusetts's Romney in managing Boston's "Big Dig" highway reconstruction was seen by many as having implications for his 2008 presidential bid, giving him great incentive to do the job well.[45]

Women and Minorities as Governor

Until quite recently, governors were almost exclusively white men. Given the social, economic, and political dominance of white males in American society, this should not be surprising. American women were not even allowed to vote in this country until fewer than 100 years ago, and racial minorities were effectively disenfranchised in the areas where most of them lived until even more recently. But in the past

Table 8.2

Presidents Who Were Former Governors

President	Governor of State
Thomas Jefferson	Virginia
James Monroe	Virginia
Andrew Jackson	Florida (territory)
Martin Van Buren	New York
William Henry Harrison	Indiana (territory)
James K. Polk	Tennessee
Andrew Johnson	Tennessee
Rutherford B. Hayes	Ohio
Grover Cleveland	New York
William McKinley	Ohio
Theodore Roosevelt	New York
Calvin Coolidge	Massachusetts
Franklin D. Roosevelt	New York
Jimmy Carter	Georgia
Ronald Reagan	California
William J. Clinton	Arkansas
George W. Bush	Texas

two decades, progress has been made in electing governors who are more representative of the sex and race of all Americans,[46] just as progress has been made in electing more representative state legislatures, as we discussed in Chapter 7.

The most significant recent development in the demographics of American governors has been the election of women to the post. Prior to 1974, only three women had ever served as governor, and these were spouses of former governors who could not run again due to term limits, were banned from office for official malfeasance, or had died. These governors were elected as obvious surrogates for their husbands, with one running under the slogan "Two governors for the price of one," and another using the slogan "Let George [her husband] do it."[47]

In 1974, Connecticut's Ella Grasso, a former state legislator, Connecticut secretary of state, and U.S. congressperson, became the first woman elected governor on her own merits.[48] Soon after Grasso's historic election victory, Washington State elected Dixy Lee Ray to its governorship in 1977. Three more women were elected to governorships in the 1980s and six more in the 1990s. This pace has continued to pick up in the 2000s, with 10 women being elected governor in the first seven years of the 21st century. Indeed, six women were elected or re-elected in 2006—fully 17 percent of those winning gubernatorial elections that year. In addition to those women who have been elected governor since 1982, seven women have succeeded to the governorship when the elected governor died, resigned, or was impeached. These succeeding women governors served anywhere from several days to three years. Jane Dee Hull of Arizona and Jodi Rell of Connecticut succeeded to their governorships and were later elected in their own rights.

Twenty-nine women have served as governor (see Table 8.3). Most of these women have been Democrats, but the balance is not too

Table 8.3

Women Governors

Name	State	Party	Dates of Service
Wives of Former Governors			
Nellie Taylor Ross	Wyoming	D	1925–27
Miriam "Ma" Ferguson	Texas	D	1925–27, 1933–35
Lurleen Wallace	Alabama	D	1967–68[a]
Elected in Their Own Right			
Ella Grasso	Connecticut	D	1975–80[b]
Dixy Lee Ray	Washington	D	1977–81
Martha Layne Collins	Kentucky	D	1983–87
Madeleine M. Kunin	Vermont	D	1985–91
Kay A. Orr	Nebraska	R	1987–91
Joan Finney	Kansas	D	1991–95
Barbara Roberts	Oregon	D	1991–95
Ann Richards	Texas	D	1991–95
Christine Todd Whitman	New Jersey	R	1994–2001
Jeanne Shaheen	New Hampshire	D	1997–2003
Jane Dee Hull[c]	Arizona	R	1997–2003
Judy Martz	Montana	R	2001–05

Women Governors (continued)

Name	State	Party	Dates of Service
Elected in Their Own Right			
Ruth Ann Minner	Delaware	D	2001–
Linda Lingle	Hawaii	R	2002–
Janet Napolitano	Arizona	D	2003–
Kathleen Sebelius	Kansas	D	2003–
Jennifer Granholm	Michigan	D	2003–
Kathleen Blanco	Louisiana	D	2004–08
M. Jodi Rell[d]	Connecticut	R	2004–
Christine Gregoire	Washington	D	2005–
Sarah Palin	Alaska	R	2007–
Successors			
Vesta M. Roy	New Hampshire	R	1982–83
Rose Mofford	Arizona	D	1988–91
Jane Dee Hull[c]	Arizona	R	1997–2003
Nancy P. Hollister	Ohio	R	1998–99
Jane Swift	Massachusetts	R	2001–03
Olene Walker	Utah	R	2003–05
M. Jodi Rell	Connecticut	R	2004–

a. Died in office.

b. Resigned for health reasons.

c. Jane Dee Hull succeeded to office upon the resignation of Fife Symington in 1997 and then was elected to a full term in her own right in 1998.

d. M. Jodi Rell succeeded to office upon the resignation of John Rowland in 2004 and then was elected to a full term in her own right in 2006.

Source: Susan J. Carroll, "Women in State Government: Historical Overview and Current Trends," in *The State of the States,* vol. 36 (Lexington, Ky.: Council of State Governments, 2004); updated by the authors.

---

lopsided (18 Democrats and 11 Republicans). Perhaps more important, the states that have elected these women represent the country very broadly. Indeed, 22 of the 50 states have had a woman governor; Texas, Washington, Arizona, Connecticut, and Kansas have elected more than one. Big states (Michigan and Texas) as well as small states (New Hampshire and Hawaii) have elected women governors, as have states at various points on the ideological, demographic, and economic spectrums. For example, could Delaware, Louisiana, and Hawaii be less alike? Clearly, the rise of women governors is not a regional, partisan, or ideological phenomenon. Women are even winning in states where their political party tends to be the perennial minority, like Republican governors Linda Lingle (Hawaii) and Rell (Connecticut) in Democratic states and Democrats Kathleen Sebelius (Kansas) and Janet Napolitano (Arizona) in Republican states. All this is a hopeful sign for improved women's representation in the governor's mansion, as is the fact that women are being elected at an increasing rate in the last few elections. As women continue to serve as governors, Americans will become used to seeing women in powerful executive positions in government, which will help candidates to be judged more on their qualifications than their sex. This will level the playing field for female candidates and improve sexual representation in all public offices. And when Americans elect their first woman president or vice president, she will have these governors to thank for helping pave the way.

Better racial and ethnic gubernatorial representation has been much harder for the states to achieve than better sexual representation. But some nonwhites have been elected in recent years, especially in those states with higher proportions of nonwhites than the nation as a whole. Hawaii, with its polyethnic population where whites are in the minority, has elected three Asian-American governors. New Mexico has the country's highest proportion of Latino's, and it has elected three Latino governors recently, including its current governor, former Clinton cabinet secretary Bill Richardson. New Mexico's neighbor, Arizona, also elected a Latino governor, as has Florida. Latinos make up a large percentage of voters in both these states. In 1990, Virginia's Wilder became the first African American to be elected a state governor.[49] Although 20 percent of Virginia's population is African American, the seven other states with higher proportions of black residents have never elected an African-American governor.

Recently, three nonwhite men were elected governor in states where members of their racial groups make up only a small proportion of voters. In 1996, Washington State's Gary Locke was the first Asian American to be elected governor of a mainland state. Although Washington's Asian-American population is the fifth largest in the nation, at only about 6 percent, this is still a low number. In 2006, Deval Patrick was elected governor of Massachusetts, a state whose population is only about 7 percent African American. In 2007, Bobby Jindal was elected Louisiana's governor; Jindal's parents emigrated from Punjab, India, making him the first governor of Indian descent. Thus, although racial and ethnic minorities have been much underrepresented in the ranks of the nation's governors, the recent successes of Patrick, Jindal, and Locke in states where people of their own race are in the distinct minority suggests that more governors of color may be elected in the coming years.

The Powers of the Governor

Once in office, what does a governor do, and how does he or she do it? The answer to this question is not so clear-cut as it may seem for officials of the other two branches of state government. Legislators pass laws, and judges interpret and enforce laws by deciding on cases, but what do governors do exactly? We see them in the media giving speeches, meeting with various officials and schoolchildren from around the state, visiting disaster areas, and so forth, and we are vaguely aware that they somehow run state government, but what does that mean?

Governors have three basic jobs—helping set public policy for the state, directing the state government bureaucracy, and acting as the point person for relations with people and governments outside of state government, including the state's local governments, other state governments, the national government, businesses, and even foreign countries. How do governors accomplish these three jobs? In order to understand this fully, we must first look at the powers available to a governor.

As with presidential power, gubernatorial power is largely the power to persuade.[50] One way or the other, most of the people governors need to help them govern the state can choose to ignore or even work against the governor's goals if they want to do so. But governors have a variety of tools—both institutional and informal—that, when used skillfully, can make them a more effective "persuader." In this section, we describe these tools, or **gubernatorial powers**, and how they can be useful to a governor. We also describe how some of these powers vary among the states and over time and how this translates into important variations in gubernatorial control of state government. Once we have an understanding of these individual powers, in the following section, we provide examples of how three governors have put them together to accomplish each of a governor's three main jobs.

Institutional Powers

First, consider the institutional powers that states give their governors, largely through their constitutions and statutes. These are powers that a state's policy makers have consciously decided to give to their governors. In recent decades, the states have increased their governors' powers in each of these areas, but significant variation remains in the institutional powers granted to states' governors.

Budget-Making Authority As you will see in Chapter 10, the budget is one of the most concrete expressions of a state's policy. Almost everything a state does, from providing needy children with health care to housing prisoners to building and maintaining roads, requires spending money, and the budget plans and authorizes all the state's spending. Although the budget must pass the state legislature each year[51] through the regular legislative process, all but a few states give the governor special powers to influence the budget process that they do not have in regular lawmaking.

In the early years of the republic, state government was small and simple and so was its budget. Then, state budgets tended to be written piecemeal in various legislative committees based on each agency's spending needs. But as state government grew in complexity and size, it became evident that such a haphazard budgeting process allowed for overlap, mismanagement, and fraud. One of the most enduring reforms of the **Progressive Era** was the **unified executive budget,** a system of state budget-making where the governor is given the responsibility to assess the state's spending needs and develop a single budget proposal for the legislature to consider. Developing a unified executive budget may seem more like an administrative pain in the neck than an important political power, especially because the legislature can make virtually any modifications in the proposal that it wants to, but this authority to propose the budget is widely seen by administrators, legislators, interest groups, and political scientists as probably the governor's most important power.[52]

Why is developing the budget such an important gubernatorial tool? It comes down to logistics. As hundreds of pages of very small type outlining exactly how the state will spend its money for the entire year, the budget is extremely large, complex, and technical. The governor has a large budget office staff and perhaps hundreds of other people in the offices throughout the executive branch helping him or her put this document together for the better part of a year. The legislature has only two or three months and very limited staff to review the proposal, and at the same time, they are also taking care of thousands of other pieces of legislation. The result of this imbalance is that the legislature only can review the budget around the edges, with most of the governor's proposal usually being adopted. Beyond the power to propose a state's budget, most governors also have special veto powers for spending bills (see below) and the ability to estimate revenue for the coming year (which can sometimes allow the governor to justify cuts or expansions in spending, as desired). All this adds up to real power for the governor over anyone or any group that wants to determine state government spending—which is just about everyone involved in state policy making.

On the other hand, special fees and taxes that are **earmarked** in statutes for particular purposes can limit governors' budget-making power by reducing the discretion with which they can target spending. For example, gasoline taxes that are earmarked for building new roads cannot be used to buy textbooks or even fund mass transit. A governor's control over the budget is reduced in proportion to the amount of the state's revenue that is designated for some predetermined purpose.

Veto As discussed in Chapter 7, a governor's only institutional role in the state legislative process is at the end, when, after both chambers have passed a bill in identical form, the governor chooses whether to sign it into law or to veto it in some fashion, sending it back to the legislature for further consideration. Legislatures have the opportunity to **override** a veto by voting again in favor of the bill in both chambers, but usually by a **supermajority** vote. Given the difficulty of mustering a supermajority on a controversial measure (and a bill is controversial by definition if it has been vetoed by the governor), and given the other powers and respect accorded a governor, vetoes are very difficult to override.[53] For example, during his 14-year tenure in Wisconsin in the 1980s and 1990s, Republican governor Tommy Thompson made 1,937 legislative vetoes, and the Democrat-controlled Wisconsin Legislature failed to override any of them.[54]

Governors in different states have different levels of veto power. All governors can execute a **full veto**[55] on bills—the same veto power that the president has. But in most states, a governor's veto power is even stronger than that of the president, at least on **appropriations bills**. First, 43 governors have **line-item veto power** on appropriations bills; that is, the ability to veto a single expenditure item (literally, a line in a budget bill) while letting the rest of the bill pass into law.[56] This way, the legislature cannot hold the budget hostage for a single spending item that the governor thinks is unnecessary (say, a bridge or a new fire truck for a town) or else stop the whole budget from passing. The line-item veto allows the governor to remove such items surgically from the budget. Presidents have long coveted this power,[57] but the U.S. Constitution grants them only the full veto.[58]

Twelve states also grant their governors a second kind of enhanced veto for appropriations bills: a **reduction veto**. A reduction veto allows the governor to reduce the amount that is authorized to be spent on a budget item. This way, governors avoid the all-or-nothing choice of the line-item veto on each project, allowing them simply to scale back what they see as excessive spending on a useful project. Six states give their governors even greater power with the **amendatory veto,** which allows them to send a budget item or even a whole bill back to the legislature with a message that asks for a specific change.[59] Then, either the legislature can override the veto by passing the original bill or item with a supermajority vote or it can pass the governor's suggested language with a simple majority vote. Because it is often much easier to generate a simple majority to agree with the governor than to generate a supermajority to oppose him or her, this is a powerful tool. Finally, Wisconsin gives its governor the ability to veto individual letters and digits in appropriations bills, making this the most powerful veto of all (see Sidebar 8.1).

The reason these states give governors special veto powers on spending bills to help reduce state spending. In particular, these special vetoes are said to allow the governor to cut out pork barrel projects. Although legislators have incentives to pass such district-level largesse and inflate the state budget, governors, with their statewide perspective, may be less prone to do so. But although this institutional tool makes sense in theory, there is little evidence shows that these special vetoes do in fact reduce state spending.[60]

On the other hand, the veto is a very powerful weapon for the governor, and these special vetoes certainly enhance this power. And the veto is useful to a governor in more ways than one. Of course, the full veto allows governors to stop legislation that they do not wish to become law, and the special vetoes allow them to reduce or eliminate specific spending. But these blunt effects of the veto are really only the last resort of governors who cannot get their way in a more subtle fashion. Because the process of passing a bill can be difficult, as you saw in Chapter 7, legislators do not want their bills vetoed. Therefore, vetoes may have their greatest effect through their *threat* rather than their actual use. If a legislator knows that the governor disapproves of a bill or a project, the existence of a strong veto power will give that lawmaker great incentive

INSTITUTIONS MATTER

WISCONSIN'S VANNA WHITE VETO

Legislatures at both the national and state level in the United States have almost always been bicam- Wisconsin gives its governor a unique veto power, allowing the vetoing of individual words, letters, and even punctuation marks in appropriations bills. Some call this variant of the line-item veto the *Vanna White veto,* after the game show personality who constructs words one letter at a time.[1] A governor whose party is in the minority in the legislature, but where the other party does not have a **veto-proof majority,** can use this power to change the meaning of legislation, at least according to those who do not like the outcomes. The photo below demonstrates how effective this power can be. With these vetoes in the 2005 budget bill, Democratic governor Jim Doyle gave the Wisconsin sec- retary of administration the "unprecedented" power to shift money around in the state's funds, thus greatly enhancing the governor's budgetary authority. These vetoes (among 139 Doyle made in this bill alone) were challenged in court by Republican lawmakers (who had a majority in the legislature) who argued that this power creates an unconstitutional encroachment on legislative prerogatives. Perhaps this is true. But the Wisconsin Supreme Court has repeatedly upheld the constitutionality of the Vanna White veto when both Democratic and Republican governors have ably used it.[2]

Cited segments of 2005 Assembly Bill 100:

SECTION 9255. **Appropriation changes; other.**

(1) STATE AGENCY APPROPRIATION LAPSES TO THE GEN- ERAL FUND.

Vetoed In Part (b) *Prohibited appropriation lapses and transfers.* The secretary of administration may not lapse or transfer

Vetoed In Part moneys to the general fund from any appropriation account specified in paragraph if the lapse or transfer would violate a condition imposed by the federal

government on the expenditure of the moneys or if the lapse or transfer would violate the federal or state constitution. **Vetoed In Part**

(2) TRANSFER FROM GENERAL FUND TO TAXPAYER PROTECTION FUND. There is transferred $36,000,000 from the general fund to the taxpayer protection fund . **Vetoed In Part** **Vetoed In Part**

Wisconsin's "Vanna White" Veto. On this section of Wisconsin's 2005 budget bill, note how Governor Jim Doyle has completely changed the meaning of these paragraphs with the Vanna White veto (the grayed-out words have been vetoed). As passed by the legislature, the bill said that the secretary of administration could *not* transfer these funds to the general fund; with the veto, the secretary is authorized to do exactly that.

Notes

1. Steven Walters, "Vetoes Strike at Spending Power," *Milwaukee (Wisc.) Journal-Sentinel,* 30 July 2005, p. A1.
2. Mike Nichols, "See, It's Easy to Abuse This Veto," *Milwaukee (Wisc.) Journal-Sentinel,* 30 July 2005, p. B1.

to work with the governor prior to its passage and modify it as necessary to win a guberna- torial signature. Even more subtly, a governor can threaten to veto a legislator's pet bill as leverage to get help on an unrelated piece of legislation. Indeed, when a governor actually has to use the veto, it may be an indication of weakness. In practice, governors typically use the veto quite sparingly, unless they are faced with a legislature with a majority of the other party—which is why Thompson used it so of- ten in Wisconsin.

Appointment Power The states vary in the power they give their governors to make ap- pointments to positions in government. These include appointments to judgeships and various boards and commissions, but the most important powers of appointment tend to be those to posts in the executive branch. Governors who can appoint their people to many or most of the policy-making and upper-management positions in the executive branch can control better the bureaucracy and policy implementation.[61] This helps a governor get policies administered as he or she wants them to be, and it forces those who want something from a particular agency to come to the governor (or the governor's appointee) to get it. The power to appoint more people also allows governors to reward their supporters by giving them positions of prestige and power. Such appointments can also be bargaining chips for a governor in dealing with state legislators or others in the policy-making process. In short, a governor who controls many jobs in state government is more powerful than one whose appointment power is more limited.

Governors' appointment powers vary in two important ways. First, some states allow for the direct and independent election of various top-level executive branch officials, including the lieutenant governor, attorney general, secretary of state, and treasurer, among others (see Sidebar). When these officials are elected independently, not only can governors not order them around directly, but they may also actually be rivals for power. Sometimes, these executives are from the other party and bent on working against the governor as a precursor to their own gubernatorial runs.[62] Remember that many governors held one of these independently elected executive positions themselves before moving up to the governorship.

A second way that gubernatorial appointment powers vary among the states is how far up a state's **civil service system** reaches into the managerial positions of the bureaucracy. At one time, governors gained political power from handing out as many as 20,000 of **patronage jobs** to political supporters and their families. Although no one begrudges a governor the power to appoint the top managers of

state government so that he or she can hold the bureaucracy accountable and set public policy, many of these positions clearly had no policy-making power, such as workers on road construction crews and driver's license examiners. Although a state legislator might not be persuaded to vote for a governor's bill by the offer of a road crew job, he or she might be happy to get one of these jobs for a constituent or supporter. States with extensive civil service systems hire more workers through merit testing, giving governors less power over the bureaucracy and fewer political bargaining chips. But the lack of independently elected statewide executives and the ability to hire and fire top agency managers without the approval of the state legislature are the most important facets of this gubernatorial power.

Tenure Potential A governor is more powerful if those with whom he or she deals in the political process believe that he or she may be around for a long time. Governors who will soon be leaving office have less both to threaten and to offer those with whom they negotiate. State bureaucrats, interest groups, and legislators (at least where no legislative term limits are in place) may be able to wait out a governor who will soon be replaced, giving them little incentive to compromise.

Governors' institutional tenure potential varies in two ways: term length and term limits.[63] One of the major institutional reforms of the 1960s and 1970s for governors was the lengthening of their terms. In 1960, many states elected their governors to two-year terms; today, only Vermont and New Hampshire do. Governors elsewhere serve four-year terms. Gubernatorial term limits make a governor a **lame duck** as soon as he or she has won the last election allowed. Although term limits have been a feature of some governorships for many years, the legislative term limits movement also affected some governorships. Fourteen of the 21 states that passed legislative term limits in the 1990s enacted

COMPARISONS HELP US UNDERSTAND

Independently Elected Executives in the State Government

As a remnant of **Jacksonian democracy,** all but three states (Maine, New Hampshire, and New Jersey) elect statewide executive branch officials in addition to their governor. Unlike the federal government, to which we elect only the president and vice president, most states' executive branches have more than one independently elected executive, and some have many—North Dakota takes the prize by electing 11 statewide executives besides its governor. The powers and scope of control of these officials vary greatly among the states, even for officials with the same title. For example, in most states, the secretary of state is a minor official whose main job is to oversee elections, but in Illinois, the secretary of state is second only to the governor in political power and the size and scope of government operations that he or she controls. In Table 8.4, we list these independently elected executives, the number of states that elect each, and their typical duties (but remember that these duties can vary greatly from state to state). Why do you think the states vary so greatly on this important institutional characteristic of their executive branches? What factors do you think could explain the variation in the number of independently elected executives in each state?

Table 8.4

Independently Elected Executives in the State Government

Title	Number of States Electing It	Typical Duties (may vary from state to state)
Governor	50	Chief executive officer for state government
Lieutenant governor	42	Next in line to succeed the governor; other duties as assigned by the governor
Attorney general	42	Chief legal officer of the state; represents the state in legal action
Secretary of state	35	Oversees the administration of elections; other various record-keeping functions
Treasurer	34	Banks and invests the state's funds
Auditor	18	Evaluates state government spending and performance
Education commissioner	15	Head of the state department of education
Comptroller	13	Controls the disbursement of state funds
Agriculture commissioner	9	Head of the state department of agriculture
Insurance commissioner	6	Regulates the insurance industry
Labor commissioner	5	Head of the state department of labor

Source: Data developed from *The Book of the States 2006,* vol. 38 (Lexington, Ky.: Council of State Governments, 2006), table 4.9.

gubernatorial term limits at the same time. Currently, 34 states limit their governors to two four-year terms, whereas 14 states have no limits.[64] Governors of Utah can serve up to three four-year terms, and those of Virginia can serve only a single four-year term.[65]

Gubernatorial Staff A governor's personal staff can be considered an institutional power.[66] Although staffing varies more from governor to

governor in a given state than do other institutional powers, it still must be approved in a state's budget, and as such, it is statutory. These staff can include press spokespeople, legislative liaisons, and deputy governors to coordinate policy areas that spread out over a variety of agencies, such as education or drug enforcement. Unlike cabinet secretaries and other managerial appointees, these staff are solely responsible to the governor and should have no mixed loyalties. They have no agencies or interest groups to appease, and their appointments are not typically subject to legislative approval. These staff serve as additional eyes, ears, feet, and hands for the governor, greatly extending his or her reach and information-gathering ability. And because the staff serve solely at the governor's discretion, and because their fate is inextricably linked to that of the governor, a good staff acts simply as a proxy for the governor. The flipside of this is that when these staff generate controversy, whether because of ethical issues or concern over how high their salaries are (reaching upwards from $100,000 annually for top gubernatorial staff), this controversy reflects directly on the governor.

The number of staff that a governor has varies dramatically across states, from a dozen close aides and secretaries to an extended office of well over 100 staffers in a variety of roles. In general, governors' staffs are much larger today than they were even 20 years ago, and they are largest in more populous states.[67] In some states, the budget office is housed in the governor's office and considered part of the governor's staff. This unit has the primary responsibility for developing the governor's budget proposal and monitoring the budget's execution throughout the fiscal year. As governors have gained more control over the budget, these offices have been increasingly shifted to the governors' direct control rather than being an independent unit. Indeed, for many governors, the state budget office now acts as one of the main tools for controlling the bureaucracy and guiding policy, much the same way that presidents now use the federal Office of Management and Budget.[68]

Instruments to Set the Legislative Agenda

Most governors have two institutional powers that give them some influence over the legislature's policy agenda. First, at the beginning of each legislative session, most governors give a **State of the State address** to the legislature, much like the president's annual State of the Union address. This major address is an opportunity for governors to identify what they think are the most important problems for

their legislatures to tackle that session and to offer a list of proposals for the legislature to consider.[69] Of course, the legislature is not bound to follow the agenda the governor lays out in his or her speech, but traditionally, the governor's proposals receive serious consideration. Indeed, legislators will complain of a lack of leadership if the governor's proposals are not clear in the State of the State speech.

The other institution that lets governors set the legislative agenda is their power to call the state legislature into **special session** after it has adjourned its regular session. Just the threat of a special session can be a potent weapon in part-time legislatures because it would require these members to sacrifice extra time from their regular jobs. Such legislators may quickly give in to the governor's legislative demands to avoid this overtime work, for which they do not receive extra pay.[70]

More important than simply assembling legislators in a special session, most governors are empowered to set a limited agenda for that session, in effect forcing legislators to consider a specific issue. For example, in 2006, Governor Rick Perry ordered the Texas Legislature into special session to deal with public school financing issues, and California's Schwarzenegger called a special session to deal with prison overcrowding.[71] Calling a special session not only shows the legislature that the governor really cares about an issue but also puts the media spotlight on the legislature's deliberations, increasing pressure on it to act. Although the governor may force the legislature into special session on a particular issue, the governor cannot force the legislature to pass anything. A recalcitrant legislature can simply adjourn a special session without taking any action. Occasionally, a battle royal ensues as the governor keeps calling the legislature into special session and the legislature keeps adjourning without acting; in 1999, this happened in Illinois over the budget.[72] But this sort of brouhaha is rare because the media, the public, and rank-and-file legislators quickly get fed up with the spectacle and the expense, giving both legislators and the governor the incentive to settle their differences.

Executive Orders Governors, like presidents, can make executive orders, which are official pronouncements mandating certain government actions.[73] Such orders are public written documents, typically filed with the secretary of state or some other official for public access. Executive orders have the force of law, but their scope is usually limited. The power of governors to make executive orders varies on whether they are authorized by statute, constitution, or simply tradition, by the areas of policy in which a governor is authorized to make such orders, and whether these orders can be reviewed by the legislature or are subject to any other restrictions.[74] Governors are typically authorized to make executive orders in four policy areas: to reorganize or control the bureaucracy; to call out the National Guard to respond to emergencies or crises; to set up commissions to study particularly vexing policy problems; or to respond to federal rules, regulations, and initiatives. The stronger the legal basis for these executive orders, the broader the scope of their power, and the fewer restrictions or less oversight of them, the more potent a tool they become a governor.

In 2006, New Jersey governor Jon Corzine used an executive order as a powerful and effective weapon in his fight with his state legislature over a tax increase.[75] Faced with a budget deficit, the speaker of the assembly wanted to cut expenses, whereas the governor wanted to raise the sales tax one cent. In a game of political chicken, the start of the fiscal year arrived on July 1 with no agreement, no budget, and, therefore, no money to pay state workers. Corzine upped the ante by issuing an executive order that closed down all nonessential[76] state government services—parks, beaches, driver's license testing stations, bureaucratic agencies, and so forth. Even Atlantic City's casinos were closed down because the required state inspectors were laid off. For 10 days, the shutdown went on—even over the important Fourth of July holiday. Finally, the governor got his way (with perhaps at least a little compromising), and he rescinded the order. States where governors have a weaker executive order power might have seen a different outcome.

Formal Powers: Comparing the States
Political scientist Beyle has studied gubernatorial power for over 40 years, documenting how it has increased over that time across the country.[77] Figure 8.3 shows how today's governorships differ on an index that Beyle developed. Even though all state governors are stronger today than in the past, this map demonstrates that the institutional powers of different states' governors vary a great deal. Although most governorships fall into the middle range, 12 of them are either quite strong or quite weak compared to these institutions in the other states. This map also gives some hints about what types of states tend to develop weaker or stronger gubernatorial institutions.

First, the states of the South tend to have weaker governorships, probably a legacy of the reaction to the strong **Reconstruction** governors in the post–Civil War era. Second, more populous and more urban states tend to have more powerful governorships, whereas smaller, rural states tend to have weaker ones. This might be a case of states arming their governors with just the level of power they need to deal with the forces at work in their states. Governors in large or urban states must contend with both more diverse public problems and a broader range of actors in the policymaking arena, such as big-city mayors, strong unions, major industries and corporations, and so forth. Perhaps these governors need greater institutional power just to do their jobs as well as those governors with less institutional power do in the small, rural states where they are big fish in a small pond. Finally, and although it is not obvious in this map, those states with more liberal citizens tend to have stronger governorships. Perhaps liberals appreciate strong, active government, whereas conservatives prefer weaker, limited government. On the other hand, the causal effect may also run the other way. One study has found that regardless of the ideology of a state's citizens, its political party tendencies or its economic and demographic characteristics, states with stronger governors tend to have more liberal policies.[78]

Figure 8.3

Governors' Institutional Powers: Beyle's Index

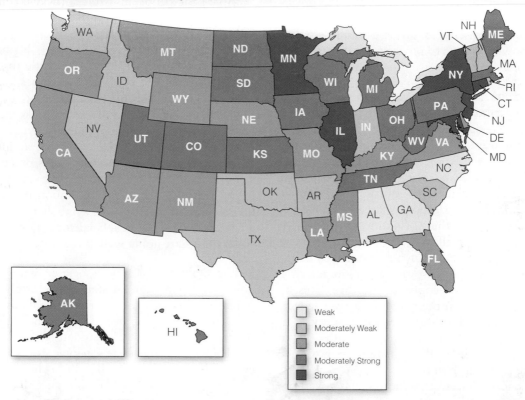

Note: This is a modification of Beyle's index of governors' institutional power based on appointments, independently elected executives, tenure potential, the state budget, and the veto.

Source: Thad Beyle, "Governors," in *Politics in the American States,* 8th ed., eds. Virginia Gray and Russell L. Hanson (Washington, D.C.: CQ Press, 2004).

Informal Powers

In addition to the institutional powers that states give their governors as a matter of policy, the circumstances of the office, the state, and the incumbent himself or herself also provide a governor with more or less effective tools for running the state. These informal powers are not as obvious as the institutional powers, and their potency can vary among states, among governors within a state, and even over the term of a single governor. Some informal powers are hard to compare systematically. For example, some governors are just more charismatic or intelligent than others. But several important

dimensions of a governor's informal power are comparable across the states and across time and are based on the office itself rather than the person holding it. Of course, just as with the institutional powers, the effectiveness of these informal powers in helping governors manage a state and achieve their policy agendas depends in large part on the skills of the governor in using them. But unlike the institutional powers, informal powers can often be a double-edged sword, either helping or hurting a governor, depending on circumstances and the governor's skill.

The first three of these informal powers we discuss are largely things that affect governors'

political capital; that is, their perceived political power in the eyes of state legislators, interest groups, or whomever else the governor wants to influence. The last two informal powers we discuss involve a governor's political power relative to other actors in the state's political process.

Head of State The governor is a state's symbolic head of state, just as (as mentioned above) the queen of England is for her country and the president is for the United States as a whole.[79] That is, the governor represents the state to people both within and outside of the state. As head of state, governors gain political capital by undertaking largely ceremonial duties that get them around the state in a positive way, such as when Florida governor Charlie Crist visits a town devastated by a hurricane. Although Crist might be more effective in helping these people rebuild their lives by spending time on the telephone to the federal authorities and insurance companies, a visit to the disaster site conveys the sympathy of the entire state—as well as earning the governor some political capital.

Another facet of the power that governors gain from being head of state is the fact that, today, Americans look for executive leadership from our government. We look to the governor, the president, and the mayor when we want government to act, rather than the state legislature, the Congress, or the city council. Governors can benefit from this attitude by stepping into the role forthrightly, pursuing an active policy agenda in the legislature and taking a strong hand with the executive agencies. Although other state government officials may chafe under such an "imperial" governor, like the general public, they, too, expect the governor to lead and will complain if such leadership does not materialize. Indeed, one study found that even in a highly partisan legislature, bills the governor advocated were regularly supported even by members of the opposite party—except during election years.[80]

Certainly, the expectation of gubernatorial leadership can backfire on the governor if things do not go well. A governor who is not a strong and visible leader may lose influence with the people and state officials. Some argued that this was in part what led to California governor Gray Davis's recall in 2003.[81] Furthermore, governors are often blamed for state actions, even if they had little to do with them. A clear example of this goes back to the 1950s and 1960s, when many states implemented their first sales tax. Shopkeepers upset with the tax would often ring up the price of an item at the cash register, adding, "And a penny for the governor." This practice went on for many years after the sales tax was introduced and the governor responsible for it was out of office.[82] Thus, symbolizing state government is most beneficial for a governor when things are going well in the state.

Public Opinion Closely associated with the power of being head of state is the effect of public opinion on a governor's informal power. Governors have long used the argument that their statewide electoral mandate gives them the backing of the state's people for whatever they wanted to do. But since the recent advent of state-level public opinion polling, a governor's support among the people can be assessed more finely and followed as it changes throughout the term.[83] A governor riding high in the polls will be quick to point out this fact to obstinate legislators or bureaucrats. Legislators, in particular, are much more susceptible to a popular governor's request because they have to face the voters themselves. And although the chance to have a well-liked governor appear with a legislator in his or her district may entice that lawmaker to be more compliant with that governor's wishes, no legislator wants to be associated with an unpopular governor.

Governors understand the importance of public opinion, and they do what they can to keep their ratings high. They monitor the ratings closely through their own internal office polls (sometimes run through their campaign offices to avoid any suggestion of impropriety), and they appear at popular, nonpolitical functions, like the state fair and ribbon-cutting ceremonies for new highways, among other events. Some governors go even further, such as when California's Schwarzenegger bought television ads and executed a public image "makeover" after his poll numbers began to drop in his first term.[84] On the other hand, if a governor's efforts to improve his or her public approval ratings are too obvious, they can backfire, such as when Illinois's Blagojevich ordered some state workers to write letters to the editors of various newspapers supporting one of his programs.[85] When this was made public, it probably hurt Blagojevich's image more than it helped it. Table 8.5 gives a snapshot of public opinion toward governors in the middle of the last major campaign, August 2006. You can see a wide range of these governors' net approval ratings; that is, the difference between the percentage of those who approve of a governor's job performance and the percentage of those who disapprove. Clearly, Blagojevich needed all the help he could get here.

Some of a governor's popularity is beyond his or her control. Governors of large states tend to have lower ratings, whereas governors of less populated states tend to be more popular, as you can see in Table 8.5. Larger states tend to have more, larger, and more complex public problems than other states, and that makes the job of governor more difficult. Furthermore, as in elections, the national economy is an important influence on gubernatorial popularity.[86] On the other hand, the state economy is also a factor here, especially the state's economy relative to that of other states,[87] and governors probably have at least some control over this. A governor's perceived success—or lack thereof—in handling a major state crisis can affect his or her popularity. West Virginia's Joe Manchin is near the top of Table 8.5, in part due to his handling of a coal mining disaster, whereas Louisiana's Kathleen Blanco is near the bottom of the list, in part due to the Hurricane Katrina debacle. Governors' own actions—or those of their appointees—can also affect their popularity if they result in scandals. The scandals surrounding Ohio's Bob Taft go a long way in explaining his abysmal popularity in August 2006. Only 17 percent of Ohioans approved of his actions, whereas 79 percent disapproved. Taft's woes played no small role in the Democratic landslide in the Ohio elections in November 2006.

Mass Media Attention Governors can also work to affect their popularity through the skillful use of the mass media. In fact, the governor's office is especially well-positioned to gain political capital from the effective use of print, broadcast, and even on-line media, and the special attention they get from the mass media relative to other state policy makers is one of their primary informal powers.

Governors attract media attention for a variety of reasons but mainly because it is just easier to report and understand state government by focusing on the governor. First, the governor is a single, authoritative news source. Who speaks authoritatively for the legislature, the courts, or the bureaucracy? No one. Who appears more reliable and unbiased to talk about a given issue: the governor or an interest group spokesperson? Certainly, important, thoughtful, and honest people work in all those other institutions, but in none is there a single, recognizable news source that a reporter can go to time and again for the final word on that institution's position on an issue. And the governor is clearly an important and well-known person whose actions are significant to a lot of people. As we noted at the start of the chapter, more people know who the governor is than any other public official in every state.[88]

Keep in mind that news organizations are in business to attract readers, viewers, or listeners. It is easier to do this when discussing a familiar person than a more obscure official—like the state speaker of the house—who, although important, would need to be introduced to the media consumer before getting to the heart of the story. Americans' attention span for political news is short, especially for news about state politics.[89] As a chief executive, the governor is easier to understand than the legislature—both for media consumers and for reporters. The

Table 8.5

A Snapshot of Gubernatorial Popularity (August 2006)

Rank	State	Governor	Governor's Party	Approval (%)	Disap-proval (%)	Net Approval (%)
1	North Dakota	Hoeven, John	R	78	16	62
2	Montana	Schweitzer, Brian	D	76	18	58
2	Utah	Huntsman, Jon	R	76	18	58
4	New Hampshire	Lynch, John	D	72	20	52
5	West Virginia	Manchin, Joe	D	72	24	48
6	Connecticut	Rell, Jodi	R	70	25	45
7	Oklahoma	Henry, Brad	D	69	25	44
8	Wyoming	Freudenthal, Dave	D	66	27	39
9	Hawaii	Lingle, Linda	R	66	28	38
10	Nebraska	Heineman, Dave	R	65	30	35
11	New Mexico	Richardson, Bill	D	65	32	33
12	Kansas	Sebelius, Kathleen	D	63	32	31
13	Georgia	Perdue, Sonny	R	63	33	30
14	Alabama	Riley, Bob	R	62	35	27
14	South Dakota	Rounds, Mike	R	62	35	27
16	Vermont	Douglas, Jim	R	60	34	26
16	Virginia	Kaine, Tim	D	59	33	26
18	Idaho	Risch, Jim	R	53	32	21
18	Arizona	Napolitano, Janet	D	59	38	21
20	Pennsylvania	Rendell, Edward	D	58	38	20
20	Tennessee	Bredesen, Phil	D	57	37	20
22	North Carolina	Easley, Michael	D	56	38	18
22	Arkansas	Huckabee, Mike	R	57	39	18
24	Minnesota	Pawlenty, Tim	R	56	42	14
25	Nevada	Guinn, Kenny	R	53	40	13
26	Colorado	Owens, Bill	R	53	41	12
27	Florida	Bush, Jeb	R	54	44	10
28	Maryland	Ehrlich, Robert	R	52	43	9
29	Iowa	Vilsack, Tom	D	52	44	8
30	Mississippi	Barbour, Haley	R	51	44	7
31	South Carolina	Sanford, Mark	R	51	45	6
31	Washington	Gregoire, Christine	D	51	45	6
33	Rhode Island	Carcieri, Don	R	49	46	3
34	Wisconsin	Doyle, Jim	D	48	48	0
35	Massachusetts	Romney, Mitt	R	48	49	−1
36	Oregon	Kulongoski, Ted	D	44	47	−3
37	New Jersey	Corzine, Jon	D	45	50	−5

A Snapshot of Gubernatorial Popularity (August 2006) (continued)

Rank	State	Governor	Governor's Party	Approval (%)	Disapproval (%)	Net Approval (%)
38	Maine	Baldacci, John	D	45	51	6
39	Illinois	Blagojevich, Rod	D	44	52	−8
40	California	Schwarzenegger, Arnold	R	44	53	−9
40	Delaware	Minner, Ruth	D	42	51	−9
40	Texas	Perry, Rick	R	43	52	−9
43	Michigan	Granholm, Jennifer	D	43	53	−10
44	New York	Pataki, George	R	42	54	−12
45	Missouri	Blunt, Matt	R	40	54	−14
45	Louisiana	Blanco, Kathleen	D	42	56	−14
47	Indiana	Daniels, Mitch	R	39	54	−15
48	Kentucky	Fletcher, Ernie	R	24	73	−49
49	Alaska	Murkowski, Frank	R	19	76	−57
50	Ohio	Taft, Bob	R	17	79	−62

Note: Governors are listed in descending order of net approval, where net approval (seventh column) is the percentage of respondents approving of the job a governor is doing (fifth column) minus the percentage of respondents disapproving (sixth column). These results are from the most recent survey done in each state before August 22, 2006.

Source: Survey USA, http://www.surveyusa.com/50state2006/50stategovernor060822net.htm.

governor is like the boss of the state or the parent of the family; this is a role with which people are familiar, even if it does distort reality. Legislatures are complex, mysterious, and unfamiliar, so it is harder to write a relatively short, understandable news story about them. Legislators, especially legislative leaders, also try to work with the media, but they are generally less successful because they have a less media-friendly institution to explain.

It is also no accident that governors' power and prestige rose in the 1960s and 1970s just as television became the main source of political news for Americans.[90] Governors are particularly attractive for television news, where stories are much shorter than in newspapers and rely more on pictures. A governor speaking at a press conference or giving a speech makes pretty good television; a governor touring a disaster site or visiting a state facility or cutting a ribbon on a new highway is even better. The state legislature in session makes bad television (except as a background shot while the reporter speaks); legislative negotiations and discussions are even worse.

Governors work hard to make the reporters' job easy for them. They hire professional media relations staff (many of whom are former statehouse reporters themselves) to develop effective press releases and manufacture television-friendly media events at times convenient for news deadlines. Some governors even send out prepackaged video clips of themselves making brief comments on current issues. This allows those television stations without the resources to have their own statehouse reporter—which is most stations these days—to air footage that looks like their own reporter actually interviewed the governor. Of course, governors are not likely to send out footage that makes them look bad, so although they are helping the station get good video for the nightly news, the governors also present themselves in a very good light without fear of any tough questions from reporters. This can only help a governor's popularity. On the other hand, it raises serious questions about the quality and ethics of journalism about state government.

Partisan Balance in the State Legislature

A governor's informal power also depends on the partisan balance in the state legislature. Legislators who are in the governor's party are thought of, and often think of themselves, as loyal lieutenants of the governor. In particular, an important job of the legislative leaders of the governor's party is to marshal the party's members behind the governor's bills.[91] Therefore, governors who have a majority in both legislative chambers—a situation known as **unified government**—can get their bills passed if the party sticks together. But ironically, governors with the most lopsided legislative majorities often have the hardest time leading their legislative co-partisans, as that venerable scholar of state politics, V. O. Key Jr., documented in the Democrat-dominated state legislatures in the South in the 1940s.[92] Sometimes, a governor of the other party can work with a legislative majority better because the expectations of their cooperation are more realistic. For example, Democratic Governor Mark Warner surprised observers by being able to work with the Republican majority in the Virginia General Assembly to solve their recent fiscal problems.[93]

But **divided government** typically makes it more difficult for a governor to pass his or her legislative agenda. In such cases, not only does the legislative majority have basic ideological differences with the governor, but the party also has an electoral incentive at least to offer alternative positions on key issues, if not to sabotage the governor's efforts actively. Of course, when the legislature and the governor are at loggerheads publicly, the governor's advantage with the media really helps in the battle over public opinion but only if the governor uses the media cleverly. Furthermore, sometimes the legislature can work against the governor so subtly that the public does not recognize its obstructionism. Divided government has become much more common in recent decades, encouraged by legislative professionalism and the personalization of gubernatorial campaigns.[94]

Big Government and Rivals for Power

Finally, governors gain informal power to the extent that they (1) preside over a large and powerful state government and (2) have few other heavyweight political actors in the state. If state government is powerful and important, the person who runs it—the governor—must be dealt with in any policy discussion. Similarly, governors from large states are seen as somehow more important, newsworthy, or powerful than those in smaller states. For example, governors of New York, California, and Ohio are far more likely to be mentioned in the press as potential presidential contenders than governors of North Dakota, Hawaii, and Utah—although the candidacies of Arkansas's Bill Clinton, Vermont's Howard Dean, and New Mexico's Bill Richardson may belie this generalization. Also, governors who have less competition for political attention and power in their state, such as from large urban centers, major corporations, or a large federal government presence, are the biggest fish in the pond and, therefore, are more powerful. For example, the governor of Maryland must contend with a major city dominating its state and with the federal government, for which many of its residents work. As such, the mayor of Baltimore and even the president are rivals for the governor's power and prestige. The governor of Maine, on the other hand, lacking such competition, can dominate state politics more easily.

Unfortunately for governors, these two factors are usually inversely related with one another—large states have both big state governments and many competing power centers, balancing off these forces of gubernatorial influence in most states. For example, New York governors run a massive and diverse operation, but they must also contend with the political power and influence of the mayor of New York City, the many Fortune 500 corporations headquartered there, and so forth. On the other hand, governors of Wyoming have a relatively small government to run, but because it is the biggest operation in the state, they gain significant informal clout by doing so.

The Three Jobs of the Governor

Today's governor has three basic jobs: chief policy maker, chief administrator, and intergovernmental relations manager. Each of these is a demanding and complicated task that requires all of a governor's institutional and informal powers as well as his or her personal knowledge, skills, and abilities. In this section, we bring together what you have learned about gubernatorial powers to demonstrate how three current governors have tackled these jobs.

Chief Policy Maker: Charting the Course

The first American states wanted their governors to be mere administrators, simply following the orders of the all-important state legislatures. But over time, fear of a strong governor declined and Americans grew disenchanted with legislature-driven government. As a result, governors gained considerable power and responsibility. Today's governors are expected to set the course of state government by taking the lead in policy making. This is not to say that governors are dictators; they certainly are not. But the governor sets the tone in state policy making, and all other people involved in the process look to him or her for guidance.

Political scientist Nelson Dometrius describes gubernatorial policy making as having four stages: agenda setting, policy development, enactment, and implementation.[95] We'll discuss policy implementation in the next section, but we take up the first three here. These three stages take place primarily, but not exclusively, in and around the legislative process. Although, in theory, the legislature is the main policy-making branch of the government, in practice, today's legislature takes its lead on most big issues from the governor.[96]

Setting the **policy agenda** means defining for the legislature, other relevant policy makers, and the general public which public problems are most important. The state could address countless problems at any given time, but because its resources are limited, policy makers must choose carefully which problems are most pressing and where the state can do the most good. Every state capital is swarming with people and organizations trying to get policy makers to address their pet problem, everything from regulating or subsidizing new birth technologies to banning or instituting the death penalty. The person who can define which are the most important issues has tremendous power.[97] Wise governors use their powers judiciously to do just that.

Once the most important public problems have been identified, the potential solutions to these problems also need to be prioritized. Every public problem has many potential solutions. These are not all likely to work equally well and neither are they equally feasible, either economically or politically. The governor has a large staff of analysts, in addition to the entire state executive branch, to develop, weigh, and modify the various alternatives.

Finally, decisions ultimately must be made about which solution the state will try for a given problem on the agenda. As you saw in Chapter 7, the state legislative process is complex and requires strong leadership to pass the laws that determine state policy. Even though the governor has only a small formal role in the legislative process (in signing or vetoing a bill), and legislators are very concerned about broaching the constitutional boundaries between the branches,[98] all those in and around the process expect the governor to engage informally in the process at all stages. And because governors care about which policies are enacted, they routinely get actively involved in the legislative process. California governor Arnold Schwarzenegger was deeply involved in the legislative process when he tried to influence changes in the state's legislative redistricting policy.

Governor Arnold Schwarzenegger and Legislative Redistricting Reform Republican movie star–businessman Arnold Schwarzenegger became governor of California in 2003 after winning the extraordinary recall

election that ousted Gray Davis. During the campaign, Schwarzenegger ran as a reform candidate—a breath of fresh air who would solve all of California's very serious problems (including the biggest state budget deficit in national history and electricity blackouts around the state).[99] As an outsider candidate with no political baggage and lots of money and popular appeal, Schwarzenegger won over an electorate fed up with the status quo, sweeping to victory in one of the most raucous and unusual gubernatorial elections in the nation's history.

Arriving in Sacramento with very high approval ratings, Schwarzenegger dove right into policy-making. After some initial legislative successes, he ended his first full year in office (2004) frustrated by the Democrat-controlled state legislature and his lack of experience in working with such an institution. So, he decided to make 2005 his "Year of Reform" for California, setting his agenda explicitly in his State of the State speech kicking off the legislative session in January, proposing a wide range of institutional and legal changes. He followed this speech with a series of personal appearances around the state to gather support. Using his advantages with the media and his position as head of state to the utmost, he pressured the legislature by appealing directly to their constituents. Although his popularity had ebbed somewhat from its lofty post-election heights, it was still in the 60 percent approval range, and he used this to try to steamroll the legislature into passing his proposals.

At the top of Schwarzenegger's reform agenda was a plan to change legislative redistricting procedures: that is, the way congressional and state legislative maps were drawn in the state. California used the regular legislative process to redistrict, but Schwarzenegger argued that this caused a conflict of interest for legislators, eliminating political competition as they drew districts to protect themselves and their parties. Schwarzenegger proposed that a panel of three retired judges draw the maps instead. Along with legislative redistricting reform, Schwarzenegger's agenda included calling for limits on state government spending,

tenure restrictions and performance pay for public school teachers, cutbacks in the state workers' pension plan, and a variety of other reforms, large and small.

Unfortunately for Schwarzenegger, he made a fundamental mistake in setting his Year of Reform agenda—he simply asked for too much. The speaker of the California Assembly likened Schwarzenegger's agenda to "dropping a hand grenade on the Legislature."[100] Governors have more success in the legislature when they restrict the size of their agendas, focusing only on a few top priorities.[101] And not only did Schwarzenegger set a large agenda, he also set a controversial one. Each of these reforms was opposed by powerful interest groups, and because Schwarzenegger linked his ideas into a reform package, their opponents joined forces to fight them all together. So, for example, although teachers' and other public employees' unions had no direct interest in legislative redistricting, they made common cause with legislators who opposed it in exchange for their opposition to other reforms the unions opposed. Schwarzenegger himself helped solidify this coalition with unfortunate off-the-cuff comments to the news media, such as when he outraged a nurses' union by suggesting that he was "kicking their butts" in the legislature.[102]

Schwarzenegger's personal popularity, use of the media, head-of-state role were not enough to overcome his problems with a divided government and a too-large, too-controversial agenda, and his redistricting plan, the centerpiece of his reform agenda, bogged down in the legislature. In 2004, the popular, newly elected governor had played roughly with the legislature, vetoing hundreds of bills and using all of his budget powers to get what he wanted. Legislators remembered this, making them even less willing to work with him in his Year of Reform. So, in March 2005, Schwarzenegger again pulled off the gloves, this time threatening to go directly to the people with an initiative if the legislature refused to adopt his redistricting plan. This was an especially potent threat, given that the governor himself had recently gained office through his predecessor's recall, another direct democracy mechanism. Over the next three months, as he continued to work with legislative leaders on a compromise redistricting plan, the threat of the initiative hung in the air.

Schwarzenegger wanted his plan in place quickly so that new districts could be drawn for the 2006 legislative election. This was the businessman talking—let's just get it done. But even though they were sympathetic to the political need for change in the redistricting process, legislative leaders held out for a compromise that would reform redistricting for the next scheduled round after the 2010 U.S. Census. Finally, after a failure to agree on a plan with legislators, on June 13, Schwarzenegger issued an executive order calling for a special election in November to vote on, among other things, his Proposition 77 redistricting initiative.

The development of Schwarzenegger's redistricting plan was relatively simple, given the nature of the issue. But during the campaign, the exact content of Proposition 77 became an issue. Although Schwarzenegger's staff spent months tinkering with the proposal, the final version that was certified by the California secretary of state's office had what was referred to as a "clerical error," making it different from the version that was on the petitions circulated for the measure. This discrepancy caused a minor uproar during the campaign, including a lawsuit brought by the proposal's opponents to get it tossed from the ballot. Although the Schwarzenegger team won the case in the California Supreme Court, it distracted them from their main job at that time—working on the initiative campaign. Schwarzenegger himself also spent most of the summer of 2005 negotiating with legislative leaders in hopes of arriving at a compromise before the last day the secretary of state would allow the proposition to be pulled from the ballot (August 18).

While Schwarzenegger and his staff were distracted, Proposition 77's opponents were focused on campaigning. The coalition against this and his three other reform propositions spent tens of millions of dollars on TV ads during the summer of 2005, while Schwarzenegger failed to get his campaign off the ground. The governor had pegged these propositions' success to his personal prestige, and as his opponents' TV ads attacked him directly, his popularity ratings plummeted into the 30–40 percent range. By the time Schwarzenegger's campaign got under way in the fall, it was too late. Proposition 77 was defeated at the ballot box by a 3 to 2 margin.

Even though Schwarzenegger failed to reform the way California draws its legislative districts—and even though Schwarzenegger is not exactly a typical governor—his story illustrates many of the ways that governors can use their powers in their role as chief policy maker. He used his popularity, his staff, his position as head of state, an executive order, and his State of the State speech to force the legislature at least to consider his reform. But his problems with divided government, missteps with the media, declining popularity, and lack of governmental experience were just insurmountable. But as is so often the case in policy making, his reform may only have been temporarily defeated. Only a few months after Proposition 77's ignominious defeat, the California Senate again worked on a legislative redistricting bill in the spring of 2006 legislative session. And Schwarzenegger seemed to learn from his political mistakes. By the end of 2006, he had changed his image, moved toward the center of the political spectrum, and won re-election handily.[103] Whether he tries again to reform the state's districting process depends on whether he and his advisors decide that his first pass at the reform was defeated due to bad political decisions and low political capital or simply due to the time not being right for the reform in California.

Chief Administrator: Managing the Bureaucracy

The original job of the governor was strictly to implement the laws passed by the state legislature by supervising various agencies staffed by nonpolitical workers. In the beginning of the republic, these duties and workers were few. But as the nation and its needs for public services grew, so did the responsibilities of the executive branch of state government. Today, state and local governments comprise the largest employer in each state. Almost 16 million people work for state and local governments nationwide, including over a million each in California, New York, and Texas.[104] Even the states with the fewest state and local employees —Vermont, Wyoming, and the Dakotas—each have over 40,000 of them. All but a small percentage of these workers serve in the executive branches. As these executive agencies have grown, so has the importance of the governor's job of managing them.

The **bureaucracy** of the executive branch is the quiet giant of government. Although the media often report about the courts, the legislature, and the governor, it is the bureaucracy that carries out the important day-to-day jobs of government, from teaching our children and college students, to testing new drivers for their licenses, to guarding prisoners, to caring for patients in public hospitals, and so much more. And in the process of doing this work, bureaucrats—those who work in the executive branch, including your professors, if you are attending a state university—control a lot of public policy, both formally and informally.

Formally, high-level administrators write **administrative rules** to implement state law. By necessity, legislation is written in general language. Legislators have neither the time nor the expertise to go into detail about, say, how a school curriculum ought to be written or how deer hunting ought to be regulated. The agencies charged by the legislature with carrying out these general policies use their staff and expertise to write these detailed rules and regulations.

Informally, bureaucrats, even **street-level bureaucrats,** make decisions every day that have the power of the state behind them.[105] When a police officer chooses between giving you a warning or writing you a ticket when he catches you driving five miles per hour over the speed limit, that matters a lot to you personally.

When police officers as a group make similar decisions, they are setting public policy for the state at the street level.

The speed limit serves as a good example of how the bureaucracy helps set policy, both formally and informally. First, the legislature charges the Department of Transportation (DOT) with setting speed limits on public roads throughout the state. Next, the DOT sets the limit at 65 miles per hour on a specific stretch of highway by writing an administrative rule. Finally, the police implement a speed limit in practice of, perhaps, 72 miles per hour on that stretch of highway; that is, they do not charge anyone with speeding until they go faster than 72. Of course, if you do not want a ticket, you should not go faster than the posted speed limit because you never know for sure what the informal limit is on a particular stretch of road.

Given the importance of the bureaucracy in setting and implementing policy and the governor's historic role as chief executive, it should not be surprising that most governors spend a good deal of time trying to impose their will on their executive branch. This is no small task; the state bureaucracy is a mammoth operation, and the governor is but one person, perhaps with several dozen staff. Most state workers are far removed from the governor, doing their jobs as they have always done them and watching governors come and go. Furthermore, government workers hold a strong ethic that they are experts in their fields and that they should be allowed to do their jobs without undue political influence from above. This value of **neutral competence** is strong in government service, with roots in the Progressive Era civil service reforms. On the other hand, elected officials appreciate **political accountability** in the bureaucracy so that the "will of the people"—or, more accurately, the will of the elected official in question—is reflected in policy implementation. Although recent research suggests that a mix of gubernatorial appointees and merit-based employees in a state agency workforce enhances its efficiency,[106] the tension between these two values pervades the relationship between governors and the bureaucracy.[107]

Not surprisingly, governors appreciate political accountability in the bureaucracy, but bureaucratic neutral competence helps governors tremendously by making the huge ship of state run smoothly on a daily basis. Judicious management of the state bureaucracy can give governors enormous impact on public policy, and many of their powers are useful in doing so. Sometimes, governors just need to communicate their preferences clearly; often, bureaucrats are happy to do what the governor wants, as long as they know what that is and if it fits with their professional norms. Such communication can occur through the governor's staff interacting with agency officials, gubernatorial appointments to policy-making and management

REFORM CAN HAPPEN

RECENT PATRONAGE APPOINTMENT SCANDALS DEMONSTRATE THE EFFECTIVENESS OF CIVIL SERVICE REFORMS

The power of governors to hire and fire state workers has varied through U.S. history as the temptation to hire friends and political supporters has been tempered by reforms and legal investigations. After the election of President Andrew Jackson in 1828, executive branches at all levels were staffed through the unrepentant use of political appointees, with the justification being that more representative government would result. But after the turn of the 20th century, the Progressives, a reform movement with the goal of making government service more efficient and effective, advocated establishing civil service systems and making qualifications and talent the central criteria for hiring government workers.[1] Indeed, even in states like Illinois, where patronage hiring had been the norm long into the 20th century, over 90 percent of state and local employees are now hired through a civil service system. Furthermore, these reforms have penetrated legal thinking so thoroughly that in recent years, the U.S. Supreme Court has held that no government worker can be hired or fired based on political affiliation unless he or she is in a policy-making position.[2]

But when one party holds a governor's office for a long time, the state's bureaucracy can become permeated with members of that party, through patronage appointments and changes in the state personnel system that transform patronage positions into civil service positions. So, when a party takes over the governor's mansion after a long absence, the governor may feel frustrated by merit-based hiring standards, wanting not only to help his or her supporters by giving them jobs but also to gain control of an unfriendly bureaucracy by filling it with more sympathetic workers. However, in doing so, overzealous governors may run afoul of state civil service regulations and cause their administrations to become embroiled in legal scandal. This has happened recently with Republican governors Robert Ehrlich of Maryland and Ernie Fletcher of Kentucky and Democratic governor Rod Blagojevich of Illinois.[3] Fletcher was actually indicted for such activities, but the charges were dropped before he lost his re-election bid in 2007.[4] These cases show that even when a politician shows a strong tendency to help political supporters with patronage jobs, rigorous enforcement can make the civil service reforms effective in keeping political influence out of hiring for government jobs where politics should be irrelevant.

Notes

1. Richard Hofstadter, *The Age of Reform: From Bryan to FDR* (New York: Knopf, 1956); Alan Ehrenhalt, "The Unconstitutional Governor," *Governing* (May 2006): 11–12; Glyndon G. Van Deusen, *The Jacksonian Era, 1828–1848* (New York: Harper, 1958); and Nelson C. Dometrius, "Governors: Their Heritage and Future," in *American State and Local Politics,* eds. Ronald E. Weber and Paul Brace (New York: Chatham House, 1999).
2. *Rutan v. Republican Party of Illinois* 497 U.S. 62 (1990); and *Elrod v. Burns* 427 U.S. 347 (1976).
3. Eric Kelderman, "Gov's Hiring under Fire," *Stateline.org,* online ed., 2 June 2006; and Alan Ehrenhalt, "The Patronage Trap," *Governing* (December 2005): 6–9.
4. Ryna Alessi and Jack Brammer, "Deal Drops Charges against Fletcher," *Lexington (Ky.) Herald-Leader,* online ed., 24 August 2006.

positions in the agency, and executive orders, among other gubernatorial powers. But sometimes, a governor has strong policy preferences that are at odds with the norms and preferences of bureaucrats. In such circumstances, a governor must work harder to manage the bureaucracy. Such was the case with Governor Rod Blagojevich and the Illinois State Board of Education in 2004.

Governor Rod Blagojevich and the Illinois State Board of Education

At the beginning of 2004, a year after becoming the first Democratic governor in Illinois since 1976, Rod Blagojevich was flying high.[108] He had strong poll numbers and a solid Democratic majority in both chambers of the General Assembly. These allowed him to pass most of his legislative agenda the previous year. But his top priorities were in education policy, and in this area, the state Board of Education (BOE) stood in his way.

The 1970 Illinois Constitution established the BOE as an independent agency, overseen by nine board members appointed by the governor on a staggered basis so that no governor could appoint a majority in a single term. The director of the agency, the state superintendent of education, was also appointed for a long term, yielding some degree of independence from the current governor. This arrangement reflected the belief of members of the 1970 constitutional convention that education policy should be above politics and that neutral competence, rather than political accountability, should be the dominant value in implementing it.

In 2003, the BOE and superintendent had frustrated and embarrassed Blagojevich by, among other things, refusing to cancel a contract for its Washington lobbyist, criticizing the governor's education proposals and budget, and submitting its own budget request to the legislature that far exceeded what the governor wanted to spend. So, in 2004, Blagojevich decided to make every effort to get control of the BOE and the implementation of state education policy. To do this, he tried an approach that many governors have

Blagojevich Brings out the State Board of Education's Regulations. During his 2004 State of the State speech, Illinois Governor Rod Blagojevich uses the State Board of Education's "2,800 pages of rules" as a prop to symbolize bureaucratic intransigence. Note that this speech was covered statewide on TV—an important tool for earning the political capital that can be useful when dealing with state agencies.

tried lately—bureaucratic reorganization.[109] Bureaucratic reorganization involves rearranging the lines of authority and duties of various offices and departments. Governors often justify such changes as an effort to increase an agency's efficiency, but usually, at least part of the goal is to change power relationships to allow the governor more control over it. This is what Blagojevich was up to in 2004. But unlike many reorganizations that can proceed simply by executive order, the arrangements that Blagojevich wanted to change were written into the state's constitution, so he had to go through the legislature to get the job done.

Blagojevich began his campaign to get control of the BOE with his State of the State speech, just as Schwarzenegger began his redistricting reform campaign in California. But Blagojevich's 2004 speech was unprecedented in its focus and intensity. Blagojevich devoted virtually his entire 90-minute speech to lambasting the BOE. He dubbed it a "Soviet-style bureaucracy" that stymied education in the state with red tape and top-heavy spending on administration rather than on teachers and schoolbooks. He slammed several large books onto the podium, saying that they were the "2,800 pages rules and regulations" under which the BOE forced schools to work. He proposed a plan to shift almost all of the BOE's functions to an agency directly under the governor's control (which is how the state education authority is organized in many states), with the governor appointing the top administrators of that department. The board would be left as a small education policy "think tank" with little policy-making power.

Throughout the spring legislative session, the governor fought to pass his BOE reorganization bill. He and his staff spent a good deal of time working with the media making his case to the public, and he tried to leverage the fact that he had unified party government by counting on the votes of Democrats in the legislature. He used his budgetary powers to entice the BOE to drop its opposition to the plan by linking a $2.2 billion school construction program to it. And he had tenure potential in his favor; as a popular governor early in his first term, all those involved knew that they may well have to work with him for a long time.

But critics argued that this reorganization was simply an unconstitutional power grab. The BOE itself worked with the media and the legislature to fight Blagojevich's plan, and various influential education interest groups mobilized to support the BOE. The board had allies in the legislature, as such independent boards often do. For years, the legislature's education committees had worked closely with the BOE and the teachers' and school administrators' organizations that opposed the reorganization. But most important, the speaker of the Illinois House of Representatives, Michael Madigan, opposed the plan on constitutional grounds. Madigan had special moral authority here—as a young man, he had been a delegate at the 1970 constitutional convention that established the BOE.

Near the end of the legislative session, the governor and the speaker worked out a compromise that both gave Blagojevich the power over education policy that he wanted and passed constitutional muster with Madigan. The new arrangement kept the BOE intact, but it let new governors choose five of the nine board members and the superintendent upon taking office and the other four board members two years later. And it also allowed Blagojevich to appoint an entirely new board and superintendent immediately, which he did. So, although Blagojevich did not get the exact organizational arrangement that he wanted, he did get what he ultimately desired—control over state education policy.

For example, after these institutional changes, the BOE always followed the governor's lead in its budget requests. And at the other end of the spectrum, when he was unable to pass a highly visible junk food ban for schools in the legislature, he simply had his newly compliant board order such a ban. The downside for the governor of all this was that with full responsibility for education policy, only he was left to blame for problems in the area. For example, in 2006, when major foul-ups with contracts caused standardized testing for schoolchildren across the state to be delayed, the governor had to take the heat himself.

Intergovernmental Relations Manager: Working Well with Others

Since the modern age of state governors began in the 1960s, an increasingly important job for these chief executives has been acting as the point person for relationships between their states and other governments, including local governments, other state governments, the national government, and even foreign governments and Indian tribal governments.[110] Today's global economy and fast communication and transportation mean that people, businesses, and governments interact with one another constantly and repeatedly, as we discussed in Chapter 2. Commerce, social problems, and crime move freely across state borders, as they do, perhaps a little less freely, across international borders. Four states border Mexico, 10 border Canada, 16 others have ocean coastlines, and every state has at least one international airport. As the central coordinating figure in state government, governors have by necessity taken on the role of intergovernmental relations (IGR) manager.[111]

Many of these IGR interactions are financial, especially with so many federal grants coming to the states and state and federal grants going to local governments. This net of financial transactions has drawn the three levels of American government so close that it is often hard to tell where one leaves off and another begins. For example, a state government employee might award a contract to a construction company to spend federal money to build a city street. As this example suggests, private firms are also a very important part of this mix of relationships.

Governors play an important role in coordinating these financial relationships, but their IGR duties go far beyond this. As head of state, a governor works with representatives of other governments in negotiations over mutual and competing interests in much the same way that the president does this in international relations.[112] But given the complexity of the relationships and the number of other governments with which governors must deal, their job may be even more difficult in this respect than that of the president (although the stakes are undoubtedly not as high). The gubernatorial job of IGR manager is made more difficult by the fact that it is both newer and less well-defined than the job of either chief policy maker or chief administrator. Therefore, governors must use their powers creatively to be successful IGR managers. Arizona governor Janet Napolitano certainly found this to be true when she wrestled with international border security in her role as IGR manager.

Governor Janet Napolitano and International Border Security International borders appear to have a clarity and precision that belie the fact that much is vague and subjective in borderland regions, where societies, norms, and rules intermingle.[113] In such areas, governors' institutional powers are less important in IGR management than their informal powers and relationship-building skills. Arizona's governor Janet Napolitano has found this to be the case in her management of one of the most complex and important policy issues facing her state—international border security.[114]

The U.S.-Mexico border is the epicenter of some of the knottiest social, political, and policy problems in the United States today—illegal immigration, drug trafficking, and homeland security. And because they all arise from people and goods crossing governmental borders, they are also IGR problems. Furthermore, no state can deal with these problems by itself; the problem in any given state is affected by the actions of the federal government, the Mexican government, its local governments, and other state governments. Within each state, local governments and their schools, law enforcement agencies, public hospitals, and the like bear the brunt of many of these problems. The federal government runs the Border Patrol and

Governors and Intergovernmental Relations on the U.S.—Mexican Border. Arizona's governor Janet Napolitano (front), backed by other U.S. and Mexican border state governors, at a conference on their common policy problems.

has official responsibility for international border checkpoints and security. Governors have little official authority over any of these political actors, so they must use informal methods to deal with public problems regarding border security.

With her state's 350 miles of highly porous international border, these problems are high on Napolitano's policy agenda, and almost all her work on them has involved IGR. Divided government has hampered her ability to pass legislation to facilitate her efforts. But because the issue of border security splits opinion in the Republican Party so badly,[115] the legislature has not been able to pass legislation that causes too much trouble for Democrat Napolitano, who has successfully vetoed several high-profile border security bills that she did not like.

Napolitano has worked with the federal government on border issues in a variety of ways, although sometimes not very cooperatively. A former U.S. attorney, Napolitano is a tough negotiator and familiar with Washington. After unsuccessfully negotiating with the U.S. Department of Homeland Security for various resources for Arizona during her first two years in office, in February 2005, she used her budget powers to send the federal government a bill for $118 million for the costs of imprisoning illegal immigrants who had been convicted of crimes in Arizona. She argued that these people were the federal government's responsibility because it had a duty to secure the international borders. Even though this move was largely symbolic—the bill was never paid—she showed skill in using the media and her position as head of state to draw national attention to the issue. Another such move was her executive order later in 2005 declaring a state of emergency on the border, following a series of violent incidents there. This declaration not only again drew national media attention but also made millions of state and federal dollars available to her to pay for more security. Napolitano also sent National Guard troops to the border four months before President Bush ordered them there in 2006. The National Guard serves both the state and federal governments as well as often helping local governments, so its use always involves the governor's IGR role.

Napolitano has also worked closely with other governors in her efforts to solve Arizona's border security problems. Her 2005 state emergency declaration was done in coordination with New Mexico governor Bill Richardson making the same declaration in his state, giving the announcement more publicity value—two governors are better than one. We do not know whether Napolitano and Richardson tried to get Texas governor Rick Perry and California's Schwarzenegger (the other two U.S. governors of states on the Mexico border) to join them in the declaration, but partisan politics may have been at play. Republicans Perry and Schwarzenegger likely are not as inclined to embarrass President Bush as are Democrats Napolitano and Richardson. Also in 2005, Napolitano served as the vice chair of the Western Governors Association. At the WGA's annual conference, after a closed-door, governors-only discussion of the issue—out of earshot of the media—she and Utah governor Jon Huntsman pushed through a resolution calling on the federal government to be tougher on border security. In 2006–07, Napolitano served as president of the **National Governors Conference,** where she worked to get that organization to lobby for more federal border help.

Napolitano also worked on the issue with her counterparts in the six Mexican states that border the United States. These Mexican governors are just as concerned with the public problems at the border as officials in the United States because they must deal with the effects of organized crime, violence, and drug and immigrant trafficking on their side of the border too. The governors of Arizona, New Mexico, Texas, and California, along with these Mexican governors, belong to the Border Governors Association, an organization that deals with issues these states have in common. In 2005, Napolitano and Governor Eduardo Bours of Sonora (the Mexican state bordering Arizona) made an official agreement to coordinate their border security strategies, especially in sharing information and conducting joint law enforcement exercises and operations. Such cross-border intergovernmental cooperation has become increasingly frequent and effective in recent years.[116]

Finally, Napolitano has also worked closely with local government officials in Arizona on border security issues, mostly in informal ways. For example, her office staff have been working with the counties on the border to apply for federal aid to help cover the school, social services, and law enforcement costs caused by illegal immigration and drug smuggling. And as part of her efforts to assess the impact of illegal immigration on Arizona, school districts were ordered to reveal how many children of illegal immigrants they enrolled.

Summary

Today's American governors are among the most powerful and important public officials in the country. The 50 governors are an impressive bunch, with future cabinet secretaries, ambassadors, and perhaps even presidents among them. They are also a diverse bunch; perhaps the first nonwhite or female president is sitting today behind a governor's desk. The states provide their governors with more powerful offices than ever before, and their informal powers can be tremendous, if used skillfully. And to get their jobs done, governors need all these powers. Next to the president, the job of state governor is probably the most difficult in the country. Governors are responsible for leading the reform of policy and its implementation within their states, and they must interact with other governments—from the smallest town in their state to the governments of other nations—to serve their states' needs. We have seen three examples of how governors have faced important problems in their states, and we have seen that even with all their power and prestige, they do not always succeed. But as the 21st century begins, it is clear that there is not a more challenging place for an ambitious and talented person wishing to serve the public than the office of state governor.

Key Terms

Administrative rules	Gubernatorial powers	Political accountability
Amendatory veto	Head of state	Political capital
Appropriations bill	Injunction	Progressives
Bureaucracy	Jacksonian democracy	Reconstruction
Campaign finance regulations	Lame duck	Reduction veto
Civil service system	Line-item veto	Self-financing candidates
Commutation	National Governors Conference	Special session
Conflict of interest	Neutral competence	State of the State address
Divided government	Outsider gubernatorial candidates	Stay of execution
Earmark	Override	Street-level bureaucrats
Executive budget	Pardon	Supermajority
Full veto	Patronage job	Unified government
Good-time Charlie	Policy agenda	Veto-proof majority

Suggested Readings

Beyle, Thad. 2004. Governors. In *Politics in the American states,* 8th ed., eds. Virginia Gray and Russell L. Hanson. Washington, DC: CQ Press.

Bowling, Cynthia J., and Margaret R. Ferguson. 2001. Divided government, legislative gridlock and policy differences: Evidence from the fifty states. *Journal of Politics* 63:182–206.

Carsey, Thomas M. 2000. *Campaign dynamics: The race for governor.* Ann Arbor: University of Michigan Press.

Dometrius, Nelson C. 1999. Governors: Their heritage and future. In *American state and local politics,* eds. Ronald E. Weber and Paul Brace. New York: Chatham House.

Ferguson, Margaret R. 2003. Chief executive success in the legislative arena. *State Politics and Policy Quarterly* 3:158–82.

———, ed. 2006. *The executive branch of state government: People, process, and politics.* Santa Barbara, CA: ABC-CLIO.

Morehouse, Sarah McCally. 1998. *The governor as party leader: Campaigning and governing.* Ann Arbor: University of Michigan Press.

Niemi, Richard G., Thad Beyle, and Lee Sigelman, eds. 2002. Special issue: Approval ratings of public officials in the American states: Causes and effects. *State Politics and Policy Quarterly* 2:213–316.

Ransone, Coleman B., Jr. 1956. *The office of the governor in the United States.* Tuscaloosa: University of Alabama Press.

Sabato, Larry. 1983. *Goodbye to good-time Charlie: The American governorship transformed,* 2nd ed. Washington, DC: Congressional Quarterly Press.

Websites

Border Governors Association (http://www.bordergovernorsassociation.org): The BGA holds an annual meeting of the four U.S. governors whose states border the Mexican border and their six counterparts in Mexico. It also conducts research and holds bimonthly discussion groups among gubernatorial staff.

Center the American Women and Politics (http://www.rci.rutgers.edu/~cawp/): The CAWP is a research center at Rutgers University in New Jersey that compiles information about women in government and politics. The center also studies and monitors the status and prospects of those women. The CAWP is a great source of data and information about women public officials of all types in the United States, including woman governors.

National Governors Association (http://www.nga.org/portal/site/nga): The NGA is a bipartisan organization of the nation's governors, which shares best practices, conducts research, holds conferences, and lobbies Congress and the president for the common interests of the states and the governors. The NGA website has lots of information on individual governors and links to their sites.

9

AP Photo/Tony Dejak

The Court System

OUTLINE

Introductory Vignette

Introduction

Two Essential Distinctions in the American Legal System

The Organization of State Court Systems

Policy Making in the Courts

Judicial Selection

Reform and the State Courts

Summary

A Tale of Two Judges

Consider Lloyd Karmeier, Illinois Supreme Court justice from the 5th District, which covers the bottom third of the state. In 2004, after spending almost $1.5 million in the most expensive state supreme court race in U.S. history, Justice Karmeier won a 10-year position on Illinois's highest bench. Seven to eight weeks during the year, he travels to Springfield to hear oral arguments about cases with his six supreme court colleagues. The rest of the year, he works out of a large and well-appointed suite of offices in his district, where he is assisted by four attorneys and a receptionist. In addition to these people who work exclusively for Karmeier, the Illinois Supreme Court has dozens of legal and secretarial staff in Springfield whom he can use as needed. In his district office, Karmeier's daily routine largely consists of long hours studying legal documents and writing opinions about some of the most profound and significant legal issues of the day, including the death penalty, police powers, and the constitutionality of laws passed by the Illinois General Assembly. By law, he is not allowed to hold any other employment, but that's OK—he earns over $175,000 annually.

Now, consider Renee' Hardin-Tammons. In 2003, she was appointed by the county executive to be a judge on the St. Louis County Municipal Court, North Division, just across the Mississippi River from Justice Karmeier's district. Judge Hardin-Tammons presides over her municipal court on Monday and Wednesday evenings, sharing the duties with another judge who presides on Thursday—the court is closed Tuesday and Friday. The municipal court deals mainly with traffic violations, property ordinance violations (on the last week of the month), and minor criminal cases (on the second week of the month). Hardin-Tammons shares the services of the few clerks who handle all the court's paperwork, and she shares her small office with another judge. Because she only comes into the office on the evenings she holds court, Hardin-Tammons also practices law privately, focusing on traffic and criminal law. And she needs to—she makes only $32,000 for being a municipal court judge.

To some extent, the differences between these two judges' jobs can be attributed to the different stages at which they find themselves in their careers. Hardin-Tammons may well reach the Missouri State Supreme Court some day, and Karmeier had to work his way up to his lofty position. But this short sketch hints at some of the great diversity within the American state court systems. Some judges are elected in high-profile races, and some are appointed. Some lawyers follow the track of prestigious legal and political positions to high-level judgeships; others toil in the public sector quietly, attaining less visible positions that provide little pay or prestige—although their work is vitally important to those who have cases before them. Although all courts resolve conflict, some judges deal with conflicts of legal theory with broad implications, whereas some deal with conflicts as simple and down to earth as whether a person ran a red light.

Even the physical setting of a state supreme court (above) differs greatly from that of a local trial court (below).

Introduction

In this chapter, we both describe the wide variety of courts and judicial activity in the states and consider what the effects of these differences are. State court systems are very complex, and not many people have a clear view of even their own state's system. But understanding state courts and how they work can have a significant impact on your life—especially when it's your turn to have your day in court.

Ironically, some people think they know a good deal about the legal system, when, in fact, their beliefs are often mistaken. Courtroom and law enforcement dramas have long been among the most-watched shows on TV, and now we can even see the "real" criminal justice system in action on *Cops, Judge Brown,* and the like. There's even a whole cable network devoted to courtroom reality shows and dramas. But perceptions of the judicial system formed by watching TV often do more to distort our view of this important branch of government than to enlighten us. For example, dramatic trials are far less common than tedious negotiations; rather than sensational murder trials, the vast majority of criminal cases are for minor offenses, such as drug possession, simple assault, or drunk and disorderly conduct. Despite the extensive media coverage of the U.S. Supreme Court, state courts handle far more cases than federal courts. In fact, the state supreme courts together handle 100 times more cases than the U.S. Supreme Court does. And urban legends and the occasional news story of multimillion dollar jury awards for overly hot coffee or whiplash notwithstanding, most lawsuits result in either no or a modest amount of money being awarded to the injured party.

The application of law through the judicial system has been an aspect of government that has concerned people deeply since time immemorial because those who interpret and enforce the law—judges and the police—literally have life and death power over us. Not surprisingly, then, the American states have spent considerable energy over the years trying to figure out how to get their judicial systems right. Because of this, the three themes of this book—institutions, reform, and comparison—become thoroughly intermingled when discussing the courts. Because getting their courts right has always been a top priority, the states have continually tinkered with their judicial institutions. The history of these reforms reflects the history of Americans' values. But because it seems to be so much harder to get our judicial institutions right—or because the social conditions surrounding the courts change more often—and because the courts must do so many different jobs, far more institutional variation exists within and among states' judicial branches than among either their executive or legislative branches. In this chapter, we explore both the causes and effects of this institutional variation in an attempt to understand our state court systems.

Two Essential Distinctions in the American Legal System

We begin our discussion of the state courts by presenting two sets of basic distinctions in American law: state versus federal courts and criminal versus civil law. Much of the complexity of the state court systems can be clarified by understanding these distinctions.

State Courts in the Federal System

As with everything else in American government and politics, the administration of justice is complicated by federalism. But although most people can easily distinguish between their state legislature and Congress and between their governor and the president, the distinction between federal and state courts can be less obvious, even for well-educated people.

In every state, a parallel set of federal and state court systems has developed. Each state is covered by state and federal trial and supreme courts, and most states and the federal system have intermediate appeals courts. The court system that a case goes into depends primarily on the nature of the crime or conflict involved. Basically, if the crime or conflict is about a federal law, the case goes into the federal court system; if it is about a state law, it goes into the state court system. And so, which laws are state laws and which are federal laws? This is somewhat idiosyncratic, depending on which laws Congress and the state legislatures decided to pass over the years, but some generalities can be made.

Most important, understand that by far, most cases are handled in state courts under state or local law. For example, in a typical recent year, whereas 80,424 criminal cases went through federal court, fully 5,287,438 went through the state courts.[1] In other words, 98.5 percent of these cases went through state courts. Most of the crimes you have heard of— like assault, murder, and robbery—as well as almost all traffic infractions, are violations of state laws or local ordinances. Federal crimes typically involve federal officials (like assassinating the president), interstate activity (like taking a stolen car across a state border), or activities that were outlawed by Congress for some historical reason (like bank robbery and kidnapping). And for civil cases (which we discuss in the next section), like lawsuits for injuries and family law cases (like divorce and child custody), the proportion of state versus federal cases is even more lopsided.

Sometimes, it is not obvious whether state or federal law is at issue in a case, such as in April 1995 when Terry Nichols and Timothy McVeigh were arrested for killing 168 people in the bombing of the Alfred P. Murrah Federal Office Building in Oklahoma City. Murder is against Oklahoma law, but killing federal officers in the performance of their duty is also against federal law, and eight such officers died in the blast. Because of the greater resources available to the federal government and because

it would be less complex to try McVeigh and Nichols for eight murders rather than 168, state officials let federal prosecutors try them first in the federal system. McVeigh was convicted of murder by the federal government and sentenced to death, and his execution on June 11, 2001, made Oklahoma's case against him moot. But Nichols was sentenced by the federal court only to life in prison, so Oklahoma officials were able to prosecute him for those other murders under state law. Remember, federal prosecutors convicted neither Nichols nor McVeigh of the murder of the vast majority of the bombing's victims. In 2004, Nichols was found guilty of 160 murders in Oklahoma state court. But because the jury was deadlocked over the penalty he should receive, Nichols was again sentenced to life in prison rather than to death. So, were the time and expense that Oklahoma went through to try Nichols wasted? Perhaps, in terms of the practical punishment he received. But his conviction did give a measure of satisfaction to both the relatives of the 160 victims—someone was finally convicted of those murders—and to the citizens of Oklahoma because someone had been convicted of the violation of their state law.

Criminal versus Civil Law

The second legal distinction that you need to bear in mind when thinking about state court systems is that between criminal and civil law.[2] Criminal cases involve the government prosecuting a person for violating a specific criminal statute, whether this involves doing something that is prohibited (e.g., stealing a car) or failing to do something that is required (e.g., having car insurance). Criminal cases are initiated by government prosecutors. In state court systems, head prosecutors are typically elected at the county level and called the *district attorney* or *state's attorney,* but other names are used, and some of these top prosecutors are appointed by the governor or other executive official. These top prosecutors supervise an office of sometimes dozens of assistant prosecutors,

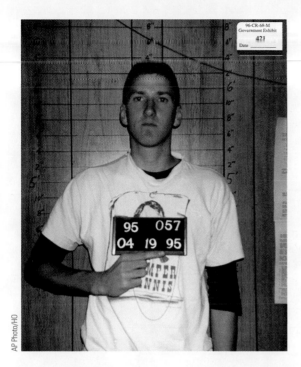

When Timothy McVeigh was arrested for blowing up the Alfred P. Murrah Federal Office Building in Oklahoma City in 1995 state officials allowed federal prosecutors to try him first. Because he was convicted under federal law and executed on June 11, 2001, he was never tried in Oklahoma state courts. His accomplice, Terry Nichols, was tried and convicted in both federal and state courts, receiving the death penalty in neither.

depending on the size of the **jurisdiction.** Their job is to follow up on the criminal investigations of the police, deciding whether cases are worth bringing to trial, negotiating with defense attorneys, and acting as the people's lawyer in cases that go to trial.

On the other hand, civil law cases involve noncriminal disputes between people, corporations, or even the government. A civil case may arise out of a dispute over a contract, where one party to the contract feels that another party has not lived up to his or her obligations under it or where one party claims to have been injured (either bodily or monetarily) by another party, such as in an automobile accident. Civil cases are brought by the party that feels he or she has been injured (the plaintiff) against the party that allegedly has done the injury (the defendant). The case is all about the plaintiff trying to get the defendant to make the injury right, usually by giving the plaintiff a certain amount of money. Lawyers in civil cases make arguments based on case law, or **common law,** a traditional system of law about disputes over contracts and injuries that has evolved case by case over the last 500 years or so, first in England and then in the United States.

The Organization of State Court Systems

The states organize their courts in a variety of ways, and these institutional differences can affect the efficiency, and perhaps even the fairness, of the administration of justice. But generally, state court systems have the same basic hierarchical structure, with each level having its unique role in the process. Figure 9.1 shows this generic state court system structure. To oversimplify, **trial courts** establish the facts of a case and apply the law, **intermediate courts of appeal** judge any questions of fairness about the trial, and the **supreme court** decides whether a law or legal procedure is allowable under the state's constitution. The pyramidal structure of Figure 9.1 reflects not only the fact that these courts' authority flows hierarchically but also that the number of cases handled by these courts drops dramatically as you move up the pyramid.

Trial Courts

If you have ever seen *Law & Order, Judge Judy,* or virtually any other courtroom drama or reality court show, you have been watching a trial court. TV shows focus on trial courts because this is really the only level of court that could possibly make for good drama. The proceedings of intermediate courts of appeal and supreme courts are exciting only to those involved in the cases themselves and to legal

Figure 9.1

A Generic State Court System Structure

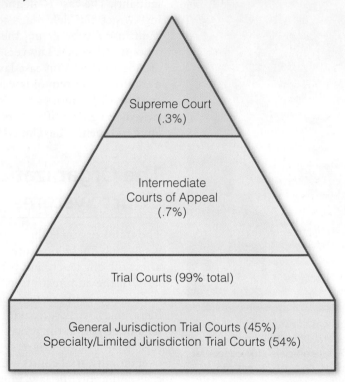

Note: The figures given are the percentage of cases in all state court systems that are disposed of in each type of court. This caseload data is for 2002, the most recent year for which these data are available.
Source: Shauna M. Strickland, *State Court Caseload Statistics, 2003* (Williamsburg, Va.: National Center for State Courts, 2004).

scholars. But it is also appropriate that trial courts get the most public attention because the vast majority of cases begin and end there. Indeed, virtually every case starts in a trial court, and only about 1 percent[3] of cases get any further than this.

Whether a case is civil or criminal, trial courts have two basic functions: (1) to establish the facts of the case and (2) to apply the relevant law to these facts, whether this is common law or criminal statute. As straightforward as this may sound, this process contains considerable room for judgment—and for error.

Procedures and Decision Making The fundamental job of any court is to resolve disputes between parties and to back this resolution with the authority of the state. Trial courts

are the first step toward such a resolution. To this end, the first thing a trial court must do is determine the facts of the case, which are typically in dispute. For example, a prosecutor alleges that Bryan Kaneski stole a specific Nikon camera from the 2003 Toyota Camry with Kentucky license plate number 715-H93 on May 16. By pleading not guilty, Bryan disputes this claim of fact—he did not take that camera from that car on that day. Did DeQuardo's Restaurant serve Maria Butsch tainted pizza that made her sick on June 2, as she alleges? If the owner of DeQuardo's disputes this claim of fact, they may go to court to get a definitive resolution of this civil dispute.

The trial courts resolve criminal and civil disputes between two parties through **adversarial argument** and **adjudication** by a neutral third party. These disputes are usually about the facts of the case, but they may also be about whether a certain statute or case law applies. Both sides of the dispute make their best argument in court, usually with the help of a trial lawyer who understands the legal system. Each side makes its case through legal and logical analysis, by questioning witnesses who may have relevant information, and by presenting any documents and physical evidence that might support their story. This process will sound familiar to viewers of courtroom dramas, but unlike on TV, real trials have almost no surprises because both sides not only should know in advance what their witnesses will say, but they also usually know who the opposition's witnesses are and what they will say.

This adversarial approach to judicial decision making requires that both sides do their best to sharpen their arguments and counter those of the opposition. The idea is that through this competitive process, both sides will make their best case before the neutral third party who will resolve the conflict by deciding which version of the facts and the law to accept. So, who is this neutral third party? A trial court has two possibilities. First, a **jury** may make the decision. Trial juries consist of about a dozen citizens, selected randomly, often from voter registration lists. Their job is to listen to both parties' arguments about the law, the facts, and the presiding judge's instructions. The jury then renders a verdict—an authoritative decision—about the dispute. In a jury trial, the judge is just there to make sure that the trial is conducted fairly and in accordance with the relevant rules and laws. Of course, the judge can have considerable impact on the jury's verdict in how he or she runs the trial, decides on procedural questions, and instructs the jury before its deliberations. But the final decision making on the dispute, in terms of both the facts and the application of the law, is done by the jury.

Table 9.1

Names of the States' Supreme, Intermediate Appeals, and Trial Courts

State	Supreme Court	Intermediate Courts of Appeal	Trial Courts of General Jurisdiction	Trial Courts of Limited Jurisdiction
AL	Supreme Court	Court of Criminal Appeals Court of Civil Appeals	Circuit Court	Probate Court Municipal Court District Court
AK	Supreme Court	Court of Appeals	Superior Court	District Court
AZ	Supreme Court	Court of Appeals	Superior Court	Municipal Court Justice of the Peace Court Tax Court
AR	Supreme Court	Court of Appeals	Circuit Court	City Court District Court
CA	Supreme Court	Courts of Appeal	Superior Court	*
CO	Supreme Court	Court of Appeals	District Court	County Court Municipal Court Denver Probate Court Denver Juvenile Court Water Court
CT	Supreme Court	Appellate Court	Superior Court	Probate Court
DE	Supreme Court	*	Superior Court	Court of Common Pleas Family Court Justice of the Peace Court Alderman's Court Chancery Court

Names of the States' Supreme, Intermediate Appeals, and Trial Courts (continued)

State	Supreme Court	Intermediate Courts of Appeal	Trial Courts of General Jurisdiction	Trial Courts of Limited Jurisdiction
FL	Supreme Court	District Courts of Appeal	Circuit Court	County Court
GA	Supreme Court	Court of Appeals	Superior Court	Civil Court County Recorder's Court Municipal Court State Court Juvenile Court Magistrate Court Probate Court City Court of Atlanta
HI	Supreme Court	Intermediate Court of Appeals	Circuit Court	District Court Family Court
ID	Supreme Court	Court of Appeals	District Court	Magistrates Division
IL	Supreme Court	Appellate Court	Circuit Court	*
IN	Supreme Court	Court of Appeals Tax Court	Superior Court Circuit Court	County Court City Court Town Court Probate Court Small Claims Court of Marion County
IA	Supreme Court	Court of Appeals	District Court	*
KS	Supreme Court	Court of Appeals	District Court	Municipal Court
KY	Supreme Court	Court of Appeals	Circuit Court	District Court
LA	Supreme Court	Courts of Appeal	District Court	Justice of the Peace Court Mayor's Court City and Parish Courts Juvenile Court Family Court
ME	Supreme Judicial Court Sitting as Law Court	*	Superior Court	District Court Probate Court
MD	Court of Appeals	Court of Special Appeals	Circuit Court	District Court Orphan's Court
MA	Supreme Judicial Court	Appeals Court	Superior Court	District Court Boston Municipal Court Juvenile Court Housing Court Land Court Probate and Family Court
MI	Supreme Court	Court of Appeals	Circuit Court Court of Claims	District Court Probate Court Municipal Court
MN	Supreme Court	Court of Appeals	District Court	*
MS	Supreme Court	Court of Appeals	Circuit Court	Chancery Court County Court Justice Court Municipal Court

Names of the States' Supreme, Intermediate Appeals, and Trial Courts (continued)

State	Supreme Court	Intermediate Courts of Appeal	Trial Courts of General Jurisdiction	Trial Courts of Limited Jurisdiction
MO	Supreme Court	Court of Appeals	Circuit Court	Municipal Court
MT	Supreme Court	*	District Court	Justice of the Peace Court Municipal Court City Court Water Court Workers' Compensation Court
NE	Supreme Court	Court of Appeals	District Court	Workers' Compensation Court County Court Separate Juvenile Court
NV	Supreme Court	*	District Court	Municipal Court Justice Court
NH	Supreme Court	*	Superior Court	District Court Probate Court
NJ	Supreme Court	Appellate Division of Superior Court	Superior Court	Tax Court Municipal Court
NM	Supreme Court	Court of Appeals	District Court	Magistrate Court Municipal Court Probate Court Bernalillo County Metropolitan Court
NY	Court of Appeals	Appellate Division of Supreme Court Appellate Terms of Supreme Court	Supreme Court County Court	Court of Claims Surrogates' Court Family Court District Court City Court Civil Court of the City of New York Criminal Court of the City of New York Town and Village Justice Court
NC	Supreme Court	Court of Appeals	Superior Court	District Court
ND	Supreme Court	*	District Court	Municipal Court
OH	Supreme Court	Courts of Appeal	Court of Common Pleas	Municipal Court County Court Mayors Court Court of Claims
OK	Supreme Court Court of Criminal Appeals	Court of Civil Appeals	District Court	Court of Tax Review Municipal Court Not of Record Municipal Criminal Court of Record
OR	Supreme Court	Court of Appeals	Circuit Court	County Court Justice Court Municipal Court Tax Court
PA	Supreme Court	Superior Court Commonwealth Court	Court of Common Pleas	Philadelphia Municipal Court Philadelphia Traffic Court District Justice Court Pittsburgh City Magistrates

Names of the States' Supreme, Intermediate Appeals, and Trial Courts (continued)

State	Supreme Court	Intermediate Courts of Appeal	Trial Courts of General Jurisdiction	Trial Courts of Limited Jurisdiction
RI	Supreme Court	*	Superior Court	Workers' Compensation Court District Court Traffic Tribunal Municipal Court Family Court Probate Court
SC	Supreme Court	Court of Appeals	Circuit Court	Magistrate Court Municipal Court Family Court Probate Court
SD	Supreme Court	*	Circuit Court	*
TN	Supreme Court	Court of Appeals Court of Criminal Appeals	Circuit Court Criminal Court	Juvenile Court Municipal Court General Sessions Court Probate Court Chancery Court
TX	Supreme Court Court of Criminal Appeals	Courts of Appeals	District Court Criminal District Court	County Court at Law Justice of the Peace Court Constitutional County Court Municipal Court Probate Court
UT	Supreme Court	Court of Appeals	District Court	Juvenile Court Justice Court
VT	Supreme Court	*	Superior Court District Court	Environmental Court Probate Court Vermont Judicial Bureau Family Court
VA	Supreme Court	Court of Appeals	Circuit Court	District Court
WA	Supreme Court	Court of Appeals	Superior Court	Municipal Court District Court
WV	Supreme Court of Appeals	*	Circuit Court	Magistrate Court Municipal Court Family Court
WI	Supreme Court	Court of Appeals	Circuit Court	Municipal Court
WY	Supreme Court	*	District Court	Justice of the Peace Court Municipal Court Circuit Court

* State has no court of this type.
Source: Council of State Governments, *The Book of the States 2005* (Lexington, Ky.: Council of State Governments, 2005), 311–12; and the National Center for State Courts, http://www.ncsconline.org/D_Research/Ct_Struct/Index.html.

Juries can be unpredictable. Unlike judges, who have extensive legal training and experience, juries represent a cross-section of the community. For good or ill, they may make decisions and be swayed by factors other than a strict interpretation of the law. We have all read media reports of **runaway juries** awarding seemingly outrageous sums in lawsuits or freeing "obviously guilty" defendants.[4] Trial lawyers may appeal to jury members' emotions rather than the law or facts in arguing that, for example, a doctor's neglect led to a child's death or disability.

Where juries are unduly generous in civil suit awards, defendants can appeal to a higher court for a new trial, arguing that the original trial was unfair. But in criminal cases, any potential bias of jury verdicts can be corrected only in one direction. Suppose that a defendant is particularly unappealing to a jury (due to his appearance, the crime he is accused of, or something else), resulting in the jury being biased against him. Two factors limit the harm that this bias can do to the defendant. First, the legislature typically sets a range of allowable sentences for a given crime. So, for example, no matter how much a jury dislikes a defendant, if he is convicted of a simple burglary, by law, they probably cannot sentence him to 40 years in prison. Second, if a defendant feels that his trial was unfair, he can appeal the decision to a higher court in the hopes of gaining a new trial, one that would be more fair.

On the other hand, if the jury is biased in favor of the defendant, the trial might result in **jury nullification,** where the jury acquits the defendant (or convicts him on a lesser charge) despite strong evidence that he did in fact commit the crime.[5] Sometimes, this is a case of "home cooking," where a jury refuses to convict a local person of a charge brought by state officials. Perhaps the most famously egregious case of jury nullification was the acquittal of Roy Bryant and J. W. Milam of the 1955 murder of Emmett Till, an African-American teenager whom these racists accused of whistling at a white woman in pre–civil rights era Mississippi. Even though the facts clearly showed that these men committed the murder, the all-white jury acquitted them. This sort of jury bias cannot be corrected in our judicial system because of a constitutional ban on **double jeopardy;** that is, being tried again for a crime for which you have already been acquitted. Indeed, after their acquittal, this immunity allowed Bryant and Milam to sell the story of

Bettmann/Corbis

The jury nullification acquittal of the racist murderers of Emmett Till in Mississippi in 1955 led to a massive public funeral (above) and helped spark the Civil Rights Movement.

how they murdered Till to a national magazine—shocking the nation and energizing the civil rights movement.[6]

Despite the potential for an appeal to a higher court in some circumstances, the fact that a successful trial ends in an authoritative decision on the dispute makes the parties in the case very nervous. Think about it. Suppose a person ran their car into yours, causing $2,000 worth of damage, and you took him to court to get this money. The trial might result in you getting all that $2,000 or getting nothing. And criminal defendants walk into the courtroom to hear a decision that could send them to prison for years or release them immediately. The magnitude of these consequences and the uncertainty of the outcomes lead most parties in a dispute to try to minimize the unpredictability of a trial as much as possible. This leads to two common characteristics of state court trials.

First, despite what you see on TV, by far most trials do not use juries but rather are **bench trials,** at which a single judge not only runs the trial but also makes the final decision on the facts and the law. Judges are far more predictable than juries because their experience and education usually cause them to follow standard legal practice and interpretation closely. Also, where discretion is possible, experienced trial court judges have long records that the parties in the case can review to assess how they are likely to rule. Although the assignment of judges to cases is typically done by a neutral court administrator, lawyers may have some influence and so will try to get the judge most sympathetic to their arguments.

The second result of the fear of trial uncertainty is that the vast majority of legal disputes are settled between the parties before they even get to trial. By one estimate, only 1 percent of disputes filed in trial courts are decided at trial,[7] and a vast and unknown number of civil disputes get settled before they even get formally filed. In criminal cases, the uncertainty of conviction and sentencing frequently encourages the defense and prosecution to agree on a **plea bargain,** a reduction in charges or sentence in exchange for a guilty plea from the defendant. For example, a prosecutor with shaky evidence of drunk driving might allow the defendant to plead guilty to reckless driving, a crime that carries far less penalty and social stigma. In this way, plea bargaining assures the prosecutor a conviction while it allows the defendant to avoid the possibility of a more severe sentence.

Plea bargaining has advantages and disadvantages.[8] On the positive side, it is an efficient way to administer justice. If all the cases filed in state trial courts had to be settled with a full trial (especially a jury trial), the cost to the state would be astronomical and the already slow progress of cases through the courts would grind to a halt. At the same time, completely innocent people charged with a crime may be intimidated into pleading guilty to a reduced charge by the potential of a long sentence. This pressure may be especially difficult to withstand for defendants who cannot afford to hire a skilled lawyer or who are poor and poorly educated. Plea bargaining may also leave victims of crime feeling that they have not received justice. In both these ways, the efficiency of plea bargaining may come at the expense of fairness in the trial courts.

Uncertainty in trial courts also influences how civil cases are handled, whether it is a dispute between a renter and a landlord over fixing a toilet or a dispute between Wal-Mart and a local property developer over the plumbing in one of its stores. Not every disagreement is settled in court nor should it be. Going to court is expensive, time-consuming, and uncertain, so much of the time, just the threat of a lawsuit gives the parties enough incentive to work out a deal. In difficult disputes, this can turn into a game of chicken, with both sides putting off a settlement until the very last minute. In fact, many civil suits are settled "on the courthouse steps," with the parties resolving the dispute privately just as they are ready to walk into the courtroom.

Like with plea bargaining, these **out-of-court settlements** increase the efficiency of the civil justice system, but they also have their downside. Most obviously, this process benefits those with more experience in the judicial system and more resources—especially money.[9] So, landlords are more likely to negotiate a good deal for themselves than renters, and Wal-Mart will probably get a better deal than a local property developer. But beyond this, some argue that the prevalence of out-of-court settlements has encouraged unscrupulous people to abuse the civil law system by suing big companies and wealthy individuals for damages that never occurred.[10] A company may settle such a case even if it is in the right simply because of trial uncertainty, the cost of defending itself in court, and the potential for the bad publicity that the suit might bring. On the other hand, trial lawyers, victims' rights groups, and consumer groups argue that civil lawsuits are an important check on the rich and powerful, keeping them accountable for damages their actions may cause to even the poorest person. In this sense, this system offers an avenue for average citizens to fight big companies and institutions—and even the government.[11]

Although juries add considerable uncertainty to judicial decision making, trial court judges are certainly not just legal robots who make decisions mechanically. A case would probably never even get to court if it did not involve some uncertainty about the facts or the law. Strong professional norms restrain judges from imposing personal preference or bias on their decisions, but political scientists have found some evidence that the backgrounds and values of judges can sometimes influence their judgments. For example, one study found that trial court judges hand out somewhat longer prison sentences as they get closer to their re-election dates.[12] Judges appear to be concerned with appearing "soft on crime" just before they face the voters. Other studies have found that female judges give longer sentences to rapists and that evangelical Protestant judges are more conservative in death penalty, obscenity, and gender discrimination cases.[13] Although judges probably do not let these factors bias their decisions on purpose, unconscious bias may creep in when ambiguity about the facts and law gives a judge some discretion in a case.

It should be clear by now that trial courts have a very different approach to decision making than the legislative or executive branches. First, the format of trial court decision making is formal and consistent across courts, unlike that of governors or legislators. Second, governors and legislators are able to consider a variety of points of view, whereas in trial courts, the only information a judge can consider comes through the formal, adversarial process. In fact, any attempt by either party in the case to communicate with the judge or jury outside of the formal trial procedures is not only inappropriate, it is also illegal. Third, like all courts, trial courts are passive decision makers. That is, whereas a governor or legislator can identify a public problem and propose a solution for it, judges can make decisions only about questions that are brought to them. Finally, judges decide on specific disputes about specific facts and law in specific cases. Legislatures (and, to a large degree, governors) make policy decisions that apply equally to all people and organizations of the same type. Although state courts—especially supreme courts—can make broader policy (as we will see later), the main focus of judicial decision making is always on the individual case at hand.

Courts of Limited Jurisdiction All states have trial courts of **general jurisdiction;** that is, courts where virtually any type of legal case can be tried, criminal or civil. But 40 states also have various trial courts of **limited jurisdiction** specializing in a particular type of case. These courts are an institutional way to increase the efficiency of the trial court system.

Some courts of limited jurisdiction simply handle minor matters, such as traffic offenses. Traffic court personnel spend most of their time processing violations and assessing fines, with only the occasional dispute over a ticket. On the civil side, **small claims courts** handle suits claiming damages of up to, say, $5,000 or $10,000, depending on the state. For example, landlord–tenant disputes typically go to small claims courts. Small claims court proceedings can be pretty informal, often with the parties presenting their own arguments—without lawyers—to an **adjudicator.** The filing fee for bringing such a suit is kept low (perhaps $20), making these courts accessible to the average person. But the relatively small amounts of money involved and the informality of the proceedings do not mean that traffic and small claims courts can be treated lightly. Their decisions have the force of law just as do those of any other trial court.

Many states also have **problem-solving courts**—courts of limited jurisdiction that specialize in technical, but widely litigated, areas of the law. These courts are established to resolve disputes on these subjects fairly and expeditiously. For example, the states have used family courts to deal with divorce and child custody issues, probate courts to deal with wills and estates, and tax courts. Colorado even has Water Courts to settle disputes over that precious commodity in that arid state.

INSTITUTIONS MATTER

TEEN COURTS

Juvenile offenders have always been difficult for the state court systems to handle. In particular, first-time offenses for younger teens are typically minor and impulsive, like smashing a store window on a dare or shoplifting a six-pack of beer. Ending up in the regular (adult) criminal justice system for such offenses can often be more harmful than helpful, for both the teenaged offender and society, traumatizing the teen or indoctrinating him or her into the culture of crime. Traditional juvenile court systems have tried to address the special needs of these young people, but they often fail.

In the 1990s, many states and local governments around the country established a new set of institutions to help these offenders—teen courts.[1] Teen courts allow first-time offenders the chance to keep their criminal records clear by pleading guilty to the crime and submitting themselves to the judgment of a jury of their peers—a panel of trained teens who volunteer to participate in the program. Typically, the members of the teen jury are not from the same town or neighborhood as the offender, allowing for anonymity for both the offender and the panel. The panel members listen to the story of the offense and the offender's explanation of the crime and its circumstances and then it suggests a "sentence." This sentence may consist of community service—like working with younger kids or helping the aged with chores—fines or restitution, or such tasks as writing an essay about the crime or an apology letter to the victim. Studies of teen courts suggest that this innovative institution can not only work to reduce the recidivism rate of youthful offenders but also encourage civic engagement by both offenders and those teens serving on the sentencing boards.

Notes

1. Madelyn M. Herman, "Teen Courts: A Juvenile Diversion Program," Knowledge and Information Services, National Centre for State Courts, 2002, http://www.ncsconline.org/WC/Publications/KIS_JuvJus_Trends02_TeenPub.pdf.

Recently, some states have added two new types of problem-solving courts: **drug courts** and **mental health courts.** Criminal cases involving drug-related offenses or offenses committed by drug abusers are among the most common cases facing trial courts today. Because of the special nature of drug addiction and the very high **recidivism** rate of these offenders, these courts focus as much on drug and alcohol treatment as on punishment, often using the threat of jail time to motivate offenders to participate in treatment programs.[14] In 1997, Florida established the first mental health courts.[15] Modeled on drug courts, mental health courts hear misdemeanor and minor felony cases involving crimes allegedly committed by mentally ill people. Their judgments emphasize court-supervised treatment, diverting mentally ill people from the corrections system and into the mental health system.

Courts of limited jurisdiction are used heavily in the states that have them, where fully two-thirds of trial court cases are filed in them. In fact, among the states are over 13,000 of these courts, as compared to just over 2,000 trial courts of general jurisdiction.[16] If a party in a case is not satisfied with the decision of a court of limited jurisdiction, he or she can often appeal to a trial court of general jurisdiction for a new trial. But relative to the number of cases that these courts handle, this is done infrequently, indicating that they are indeed useful in expediting the fair administration of justice in the states.

Intermediate Courts of Appeal

Trial courts establish the facts of a case and apply the law to those facts. But we have all heard about those who have lost in court "appealing" their decision. What does that mean?

First, it is important to understand that a person cannot appeal a trial court decision simply because he or she lost the case. Perhaps surprisingly, the legitimate grounds for an appeal in civil or criminal law have nothing to do with the facts of the case. An appeals court never deals with questions of facts; these are determined by the trial court.

A case can be appealed based only on questions about either the fairness of the trial or the constitutionality of the law involved. Most state court systems have two levels of appellate courts: the intermediate courts of appeal and the supreme court. In general, intermediate courts of appeal decide questions about the trial's fairness, whereas supreme courts consider questions of constitutionality.

The Role of the Intermediate Courts of Appeal Intermediate courts of appeal (ICAs) have jurisdiction over those cases that are appealed from trial courts with general jurisdiction. In essence, ICAs act as a check to ensure that trials are carried out fairly. Without such oversight, trial judges could act arbitrarily and tyrannically, something that the nation's founders feared. The Fifth Amendment to the U.S. Constitution gives us the right to a fair trial, and the ability to appeal a trial court's decision to a higher court plays a large part in maintaining that right.

Originally, the oversight of trial courts was one of the main jobs of state supreme courts. But by the mid-20th century, as their populations and economies grew, many states' supreme courts became overloaded with relatively routine appeals, denying them the time they needed to consider the deeper issues of law raised only occasionally by certain important cases.

ICAs are an institutional reform designed to relieve this burden on state supreme courts. ICAs decide on appeals that do not raise general points of law, allowing the supreme courts to consider only the most significant cases. Thus, ICAs' jurisdiction consists primarily of mandatory appeals; that is, appeals that they must consider. The supreme court, then, can pick and choose the cases it wants to hear, as we will discuss later. In 1957, only 13 states had ICAs; today, 40 states do. Those 10 states without ICAs tend to be small or rural states with less complex economies (Delaware, Maine, Montana, Nevada, New Hampshire, Rhode Island, South Dakota, Vermont, West Virginia, and Wyoming).

By relieving the supreme courts of the burden of routine appeals, ICAs help insure that the state court system provides fair, timely, and consistent decisions.[17] They promote fairness by reviewing trials where proper procedures may not have been followed. They promote timeliness by eliminating the backlog that an overworked supreme court can generate. They promote consistency by ensuring that trial judges and juries around the state apply legal procedures and law the same way.

Procedures and Decision Making Judicial procedures and decision making in ICAs differ markedly from those in trial courts. First, all appeals are heard only by judges, never by a jury, but typically, they are heard by more than one judge, perhaps three to five of them. No witnesses testify, and no physical evidence is presented. Witnesses and evidence are used in trials to determine the facts of the case, but these case facts are not relevant in an appeal. Instead, the defense and plaintiff or prosecution simply offer arguments about the trial's fairness. These arguments are made in **legal briefs**—documents in which the parties point out what they see as the problems with the trial and respond to the arguments made in the other party's brief. The primary evidence at an appeal is the **trial transcript,** the official record of events in the trial. Typically, the parties to the case do not even attend ICA hearings, whereas they almost always attend the trial. Only their lawyers appear before the ICA to represent their interests, and these are usually specialists in legal appeals, not the same lawyers who argued the trial. Indeed, for some appeals, legal arguments are made completely through their legal briefs, with no public hearing whatsoever.

ICAs also differ from trial courts in their decision making. First, after hearing or reading both sides' arguments, the panel of judges votes on the appeal, with the majority determining the verdict. Typically, the panel hearing the appeal does not consist of all the state's ICA judges. The judges are divided, usually geographically, into panels of three or five judges to cover their large caseloads more efficiently. Only for certain especially important or controversial cases will a state's ICA sit **en banc;** that is, as a whole.

Appeals court judges are also more likely than trial court judges to write formal justifications for their decisions. Given the high volume and often routine nature of their cases, trial court judges try to move cases through their courts as quickly as possible. The legal issues involved in appeals often require more explanation, and the smaller caseloads of appeals court judges give them the time it takes to write up such explanations.

Finally, decisions handed down by trial courts and those handed down by ICAs have a fundamental, important difference. In trial court, case facts are determined and decisions involve the application of law. That is, people can be found guilty and sentenced to jail in criminal cases, and fault can be assigned and judgments awarded in civil cases. But in ICAs, the judges' decision is about the original trial itself—was it fair or not? If the ICA holds that the trial was fair or, more specifically, if it fails to accept the exact arguments of unfairness brought in the appeal, the decision of the trial court stands. On the other hand, if the ICA decides to accept the argument that the trial was flawed, it can either order the lower court to correct the sentence (in a criminal case) or judgment (in a civil case) or overturn the entire decision, necessitating a completely new trial. But often, after a trial court verdict has been overturned on appeal, the prosecutor or the party to the lawsuit that won the original trial decides not to pursue a new trial. For example, the appeals court may decide that the camera in the defendant's possession on the night of the robbery cannot be used as evidence in his trial because the police found it with an illegal search. Without that piece of evidence, the prosecutor may decide that she cannot win a second trial and so she drops the case. But that is a decision made by the prosecutor—ICAs only make decisions about the procedures of the trial, not the facts of a case or its verdict.

Supreme Courts

Shirley Abrahamson, the current chief justice of the Wisconsin Supreme Court, once quoted a 19th-century journalist who wrote that "things were so quiet on the Wisconsin State Supreme Court that you could hear the justices' arteries clog."[18] Abrahamson was making the point that state supreme courts were once quiet backwaters of legal esoterica, but that is certainly not true today. In the 21st century, state supreme courts regularly make decisions that have momentous impacts on their states' residents, businesses, and local governments. Indeed, on all matters of a state's law, its supreme court is the final arbiter.[19] This is why these courts are also called **courts of last resort.** And in most states, the supreme court also runs the state's entire court system and regulates the state's legal profession. As such, the supreme court dominates a state's entire legal system.

Jurisdiction   If trial courts have **original jurisdiction** over the vast majority of cases in the state legal system and ICAs handle the mandatory appeals from these trial courts on issues of procedural fairness, what cases do supreme courts handle? In part, this depends on whether a state has ICAs. In the 10 states that do not have them, the supreme courts' **dockets** are made up largely of the same sort of routine, mandatory appeals that occupy the time of ICAs. But in states with the three-tiered system shown in Figure 9.1, supreme courts have significant discretion over which cases they hear, which makes them very important actors in state government and policy.

In the 40 states with ICAs, the state supreme courts handle three types of cases. First, they hear cases about the balance of power in state government at the highest levels. In particular, when the state legislature and the governor have a conflict over their powers under the state constitution, they can bring suit directly in the supreme court.[20] These interbranch conflicts usually do not involve disputes of fact, so no trial is needed. Rather, the conflicts are over the interpretation of the state constitution, so the supreme court can be asked directly to make an authoritative interpretation of that document.

State supreme courts are also required to hear appeals of certain criminal convictions in some states. Most commonly, trials resulting in a death sentence must be reviewed by the supreme court regardless of the facts of the case, what happened in the trial, or even the defendant's wishes. Because the death penalty is irreversible, these states want to be sure that those who are executed have every possible opportunity for a fair trial. The states vary with respect to which other cases their supreme courts are required to hear on appeal and the percentage of the supreme court's docket such cases account for. For example, one study found that as much as 17 percent of Georgia's state supreme court docket consists of these mandatory appeals, whereas south of its border, in Florida, mandatory appeals account for only about 2 percent of the docket.[21]

Finally, and perhaps most significantly, a state supreme court also hears those appeals of trial court and ICA decisions that it "chooses" to hear, at its discretion, because of these cases' potential implications for public policy and state law. In this respect, state supreme courts are much like the U.S. Supreme Court. If a party in a case does not feel that the trial was fair, and if the ICA decision went against him or her or if the case involves a dispute over the constitutionality of a state law, that party may **petition** the supreme court to hear the case, something called a **writ of certiorari,** writ of review, or certification for appeal. Most of these petitions are denied; in fact, nationwide, supreme courts grant only about 7 percent of these requests of certiorari.[22] In states with ICAs, this leads to a sort of inversion of the types of cases these courts hear. Whereas about 85 percent of the cases that ICAs hear involve mandatory appeals, about 70 percent of state supreme courts' caseloads involve cases that they have granted a hearing at their discretion.[23]

As the ultimate authority on a state's law,[24] the supreme court has a duty to clarify and guide the interpretation of that law for all courts in the state's system. Supreme courts do this by selecting their discretionary cases carefully. Trial courts and ICAs follow the lead of their supreme court closely in interpreting state statutes and case law both because of judicial norms and because supreme courts can overturn lower court decisions. So, supreme courts choose to review those cases that will help them clarify and guide the interpretation of state law. This means, first, that they choose to review cases that are representative of general classes of cases so that their decisions can be used as **precedents** by the lower courts for similar cases. A supreme court is less interested in cases that have unique features; it wants to hear cases so that its decisions can be used as examples for lower courts facing similar cases.

In particular, supreme courts like to hear cases that raise *ambiguous legal questions that are common to a class of cases*. This ambiguity is often manifested in inconsistency in trial court and ICA decisions. Without clear guidance on a point of law raised in cases facing them, lower court judges will simply use their own best legal judgment when making decisions. But if judges' judgments vary, decisions for similar cases will vary from judge to judge. Because the consistent administration of justice is one of the hallmarks of a fair legal system, and because the state supreme court has the responsibility to maintain a fair legal system in the state, it agrees to hear cases that allow it to clear up these ambiguities.

An area of state law may be ambiguous at a given time for at least two reasons. First, new statutes often need to be interpreted by the supreme court to help judges, the police, lawyers, and the public understand what exactly they mean in practice. For example, in the past few

COMPARISONS HELP US UNDERSTAND

CONTRASTING STATE COURT ORGANIZATIONAL STRUCTURES

Within the general parameters outlined in this chapter, each state court system is organized in its own unique way. For example, compare the court systems of California and New York (Figure 9.2). California has a very simple structure, with only one type of court at each of the three levels—trial courts, intermediate courts of appeal, and supreme court. California does not even use any trial courts of limited jurisdiction. Contrast this with New York's very complex system. Figuring out which type of court a case should go to and the paths that appeals can take is far more difficult in New York than in California, making the system less understandable to the average person. Why are states' systems so different from one another? Typically, the more recently a court system has been overhauled, the simpler it is. As time goes by, complications get tacked onto a system for various reasons that are often idiosyncratic. What might be other reasons why one type of state would establish a more complex court system than another type of state? To view different states' court structures, go to the National Center for State Courts' Web Site at http://www.ncsconline.org.

years, several states have banned "aggressive driving" in response to the deaths, injuries, and property damage caused by road rage.[25] These statutes are the result of the legislative process, so they typically do not define "aggressive driving" clearly, leaving it up to police officers and trial court judges to decide whether a person's specific behavior in a case violates the law. If conflict over, or inconsistency in, how these officials interpret these laws arises, a representative aggressive driving case will make its way to the state's supreme court for clarification.

Legal ambiguity can also be caused by changes in society, the economy, or even technology. For example, suppose that statutory and case law in a state have traditionally given child visitation rights to, and required child support payments from, noncustodial parents in divorce cases.[26] But what if a nonmarried, live-in couple has a child and one of the partners moves out? Should that person get visitation rights and pay child support? Maybe this is so similar to the traditional divorce situation that trial judges (probably in family court) would all agree that traditional divorce case law applies. But what if a couple had a child but never lived together and simply stopped being romantically involved? Can the divorce analogy be applied here for child custody and support purposes?

What about a couple (married or not) who has a child using a sperm donor? Is the man entitled to visitation rights after a breakup? What if a lesbian couple has a child through sperm donation? Does the divorce analogy apply here?

As the facts in these cases move farther from those in established case law, the legal questions become more ambiguous and court decisions become less consistent. By hearing a representative case of this type, a supreme court can make a definitive legal interpretation, thus bringing consistency and fairness to the administration of justice in the state.

Procedures and Decision Making State supreme court decision making is more like that of ICAs than trial courts. State supreme courts hear cases with no juries, witnesses, or physical evidence and with only lawyers making oral arguments and filing elaborate legal briefs that detail the parties' arguments. Supreme courts are made up of multiple judges (typically called *justices*), but unlike ICAs, supreme courts decide almost all cases en banc. Decisions are made with a majority vote; supreme courts have an odd number of justices (usually five to nine) to avoid ties.

Because a supreme court's decisions serve as precedents for its lower courts, they are usually

Figure 9.2

Comparing Simple and Complex State Court System Structures

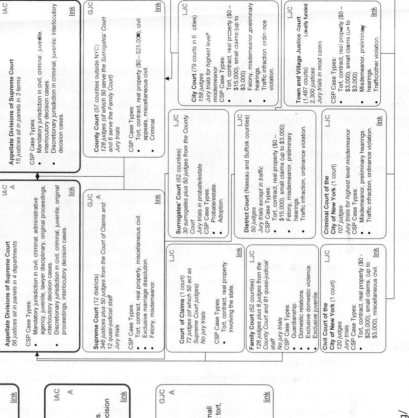

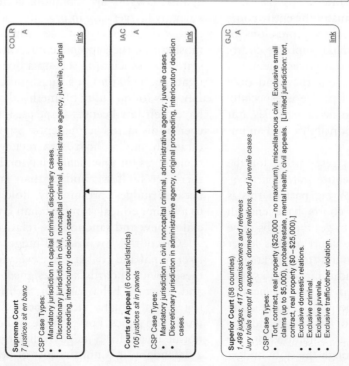

Source: National Center for State Courts, http://www.ncsconline.org/
D_Research/Ct_Struct/Index.html.

supported by elaborate written opinions explaining their legal reasoning, especially for their discretionary cases. But because supreme court justices have sharp legal minds and strong opinions, disagreement among them inevitably arises from time to time. When one or more justices dissents from a case's majority opinion, he or she can write a dissenting opinion. A dissenting opinion can establish the arguments for future legal debate on a point of law, perhaps even signaling that the court might change its mind in the future if it has a personnel change. The prevalence of dissenting opinions on state court decisions varies from state to state, largely due to variations in court institutions and rules. For example, published dissents are more common in states where justices are elected and ICAs exist, and they are less common where justices are constrained by rules of seniority and deference to the chief justice.[27]

The Administrative Duties of the State Supreme Court In addition to making authoritative decisions on state law, most state supreme courts also administer the entire court system and regulate the legal professions in their state. These duties make supreme courts much more influential in state government and policy than they would be if they had only judicial powers. The chief justice is especially involved in these administrative activities, but the entire court has a responsibility and an important role to play here.

The supreme court is responsible for the smooth operation of the entire state court system as an organization. A big part of this is ensuring that the lower courts have enough judges in the right places to get their jobs done properly. So, the supreme court assigns lower court judges to specific courts (to the extent it has discretion on this), and it hires and assigns temporary judges as needed. But more generally, the supreme court is responsible for the many mundane tasks required of any large and far-flung bureaucracy, such as administering the court system's budget through the state budget process, running its personnel system, buying and distributing supplies, and so forth. In addition to judges, a state's courts employ hundreds of law enforcement officers and clerical workers, such as bailiffs and court reporters. Juries have to be summoned, organized, and paid; courthouses have to be cleaned; and paperwork must be completed and filed, and all this requires staff. Each supreme court employs a **director of state courts** to do most of this day-to-day administrative work. A court director is a major state administrator, on the same level as a secretary of a cabinet-level state executive agency.

The state supreme court also regulates the legal and judicial professions in most states. In harmony with state statutes and often in collaboration with the state bar association, the court establishes professional and ethical standards for a state's lawyers and judges, runs training courses for new judges, and regulates the bar examinations that prospective lawyers must pass before being allowed to practice law in the state. The supreme court also establishes procedures for investigating and sanctioning judges and lawyers accused of unethical conduct. Charges of impropriety or incompetence against lawyers are common, largely because so many lawyers are in practice and they often deal with expensive and sensitive disputes. In most states, the supreme court, often with the state bar association, sets up a board to investigate such charges in a quasi-judicial process. Lawyers found guilty of unethical conduct can have their law licenses suspended, be fined, or even be disbarred permanently. Supreme courts establish similar boards to review and sanction judges for unethical behavior. But because there are far fewer judges than lawyers, and because judges, presumably, hold themselves to a higher ethical standard than lawyers, judicial review and sanction are relatively rare.

Of course, lawyers and judges are subject to criminal and civil law like everyone else. But these review boards are designed to evaluate and sanction behavior that, although maybe not illegal, might violate professional standards and ethics. For example, although it may not be illegal for a judge to direct profanity at a defendant, it is not the sort of behavior that is conducive to the proper administration of justice, and so, a judicial review board could punish a judge for it.

Policy Making in the Courts

In high school civics class, you learned that the legislative branch makes policy, the executive branch implements it, and the judicial branch interprets it. But as we have already seen, whereas the legislative branch certainly does make policy, the executive branch (especially the governor) does too. What about the state judicial branch? Does it make policy too? In the narrowest sense that legislatures and governors establish statutes and official rules and regulations, no, judges do not make policy. But if we think of policy making a little more broadly, the state judicial branch—especially the supreme court—is very much involved in policy making.

Although the advisability and propriety of judicial policy making are debated,[28] the nature of law and the role the supreme court plays in the state legal system make it almost inevitable. In writing law, legislators cannot consider every eventuality, so statutes often have gray areas where they are not specific. In fact, legislators sometimes intentionally write bills ambiguously to help them through the legislative process—ambiguous wording allows different legislators to believe different things about a bill and, therefore, support it for different reasons. But the courts must enforce laws in specific cases based on specific factual circumstances. To do so, judges have to decide exactly what the words of a law mean. And because they have the power to make the definitive interpretation of state law, supreme courts have the clearest judicial policy-making power. Of course, this power is limited to ambiguously written statutes and rules, the decisions can be overturned if the legislature amends the law to make its intentions clearer, and the decisions can be made only on points of law that are brought before them in specific cases. But in fact, the definitive interpretation of state law by the supreme court frequently has a significant impact on public policy.

One way to look for judicial policy making is by identifying those factors that affect supreme court justices' votes on cases. Certainly, the facts of a case and legal precedent ought to have a tremendous impact on judicial decision making; if not, our entire system of justice would be illegitimate. Fortunately, many studies have shown that case facts and existing legal decisions play the dominant role in the decisions of state supreme court justices. But *dominant* is not *exclusive*. These same studies show that several other factors can also affect supreme court justices' voting on cases.[29] First, the ideology of both a justice and the state's population can affect judicial decision making on issues where an ideological divergence of opinion is clear. For example, conservative justices as well as justices in conservative states are more likely to vote to uphold death penalty sentences than liberal justices or justices in liberal states. The influence of ideology is especially pronounced in those states where these justices are elected.[30] Other studies have shown that a justice's political party,[31] gender,[32] and even religion[33] may sometimes influence his or her voting. Because these factors influence judicial decision making systematically, over and above the effect of case facts and law, it is reasonable to say that the state supreme court is in the business of policy making.

But if justices' votes are affected systematically by things that are irrelevant to the case at hand—like their party or gender—is not this the very definition of biased judicial decision making? Perhaps. But after all, judges are human, not legal machinery. They bring a lifetime of personal and professional experience to the bench, and perhaps it should not be surprising that these color their thinking once they put on their robes. These biases may be small, and justices may do their best to eliminate them, but they do exist. In particular, these influences come into play when state supreme court justices interpret statutes and case law in ambiguous areas of law; that is, when they are effectively helping make public policy.

In addition to interpreting state law, state supreme courts can affect public policy through **judicial review.** Like the U.S. Supreme Court, the state supreme courts have the power to judge whether a statute violates the state's constitution and, if so, to nullify that law.[34]

Especially since the 1970s, state supreme courts have been very active in using judicial review to influence policy, although their propensity to do so varies over time and among the states. One study reviewed over 3,000 judicial review cases heard by the 50 state supreme courts and found that almost 20 percent of the laws involved were overturned.[35] Another study found that the Washington State Supreme Court invalidated one out of every four laws it reviewed.[36] The influence of these decisions goes well beyond those directly involved in the case being reviewed; these decisions apply to everyone potentially affected by that law. The state legislature can initiate a change in the state constitution to reverse such a nullification, but this process is much more difficult than simply amending a statute. This gives considerable staying power to this sort of court-made constitutional law.

Finally, we can see indirect evidence of the importance of judicial policy making in the actions of interest groups and others with a stake in state policy. These groups understand that the state supreme court makes policy, but it is difficult for anyone who is not a party to a case to influence judicial policy making. Unlike legislatures and governors, judges cannot be lobbied directly. Such lobbying violates judicial norms and is typically illegal. But recently, groups have been increasingly active in trying to influence state supreme court justices through *amicus curiae*—or "friend of the court"—briefs.[37] Amicus briefs give those not party to a case an official and legal route by which to present their legal arguments to a court. Further evidence of interest group attention to the courts is that in those states where judges are elected, groups have been increasing their pursuit of indirect influence on judicial policy making through campaign contributions to judicial candidates who support their legal philosophy.[38] Both these activities show that interest groups recognize the influence of the courts in state policy making.

On the other hand, several factors work against the courts having a strong policy-making role in state government. Perhaps most importantly, the judicial branch has little policy-making legitimacy in popular American political culture. Judges' values are not supposed to enter into their decisions; they are just supposed to apply the law to the facts of the case. But, by definition, policy making is the application of values to a decision. Likewise, judges are supposed to evaluate each case individually, but policy making is about setting general rules. So, to admit to making policy, a judge would be violating professional norms and our cultural standards. Furthermore, unlike legislatures and governors, courts are passive decision makers. They do not seek out issues on which to make decisions; they simply decide on those cases brought before them. So, even if judges wanted to make policy, their agenda would be set to a much greater degree by events and outsiders than are the policy agendas of legislatures or governors.

Thus, although the nature of the job forces state judges—especially those on the supreme courts—to influence public policy, cultural and professional norms make at least the acknowledgment of that influence difficult. Indeed, if you ask a judge, even a state supreme court justice, if the courts make policy, he or she will likely deny it vehemently. It was not until recent decades that political scientists started studying whether even U.S. Supreme Court justices made decisions based on criteria other than case facts and the law.[39] But the evidence that the courts have substantial influence on policy makes it important even for those of us who never become directly involved in the court system to care about its institutions and performance.

Judicial Selection

Unlike almost any other type of American public official, state judges are selected in a variety of ways. Whereas all governors and state legislators are elected and all federal judges are appointed by the president, depending on the state and the level of the court, state judges may gain their judicial robes in any of five ways: appointment by the governor or state legislature, partisan or nonpartisan election, and a hybrid of election and appointment known as the **Merit Plan.** This variety of judicial selection mechanisms demonstrates Americans' evolving attitudes and ambivalence about the role of judges in the political process. It also offers political scientists a unique opportunity to examine how the method by which officials gain office affects their behavior in office.

Judicial Selection Mechanisms

Table 9.2 shows the ways the states select their judges. Some states use different selection methods for different courts; Indiana has the most diverse system, using three of the five selection mechanisms for its trial courts alone. Also note that the states' judicial selection systems vary idiosyncratically in many subtle ways. For example, in Illinois, Pennsylvania, and New Mexico (supreme court only), judges are initially elected in partisan elections, but if they wish to serve a second term, they face only a **retention** election. But although classifying judicial selection methods can be a little tricky, important distinctions can be drawn. We describe the five methods as they are most commonly used.

Legislative Appointment In the post-Revolutionary War era under the earliest state

Table 9.2

Judicial Selection Mechanisms in the States

State	Legislative Appointment	Gubernatorial Appointment	Partisan Election	Nonpartisan Election	Merit Plan
AL			X		
AK					X
AZ				T (small counties)	SC, ICA, T (large counties)
AR				X	
CA				T	SC, ICA
CO					X
CT					X
DE					X
FL				T	SC, ICA
GA				X	
HI		X			
ID				X	
IL			X*		
IN			T (some)	T (some)	SC, ICA, T (some)
IA					X
KS				T (some)	SC, ICA, T (some)
KY			X		
LA				X	
ME		X			
MD					X
MA					X
MI				X**	

Judicial Selection Mechanisms in the States (continued)

State	Legislative Appointment	Gubernatorial Appointment	Partisan Election	Nonpartisan Election	Merit Plan
MN				X	
MS				X	
MO			T (some)		SC, ICA, T (some)
MT				X	
NE					X
NV				X	
NH					X
NJ		X			
NM			SC*		ICA, T
NY			T		SC, ICA
NC				X	
ND				X	
OH				X**	
OK				T	SC, ICA
OR				X	
PA			X*		
RI					X
SC	X				
SD				T	SC
TN			T		SC, ICA
TX			X		
UT					X
VT					X
VA	X				
WA				X	
WV			X		
WI				X	
WY					X

Note: X = judges for all courts selected with this mechanism; SC = supreme court; ICA = intermediate courts of appeal; T = trial courts.

* Illinois, New Mexico (supreme court), and Pennsylvania elect their judges to their first terms through partisan elections, after which incumbent judges need only face a retention election when their terms expire.

** Michigan and Ohio select nominees for judicial elections in a partisan way (in conventions in Michigan and through primaries in Ohio), but by law, the general election ballot for judicial candidates has no partisan affiliations.

Source: Council of State Governments, *The Book of the States 2006* (Lexington, Ky.: Council of State Governments, 2006), 251–54; see the source for details.

constitutions, most states' judges were appointed by their legislatures, reflecting the faith that the founders had in those representative assemblies. Today, only South Carolina and Virginia continue to select their judges this way. In these states, a legislative committee or commission screens candidates and reports its findings to the full legislature for a vote. These judges are appointed for a fixed term and subject to reappointment by the legislature.

Gubernatorial Appointment Three states—Hawaii, Maine, and New Jersey—continue to use the second-oldest method of selecting judges: gubernatorial appointment. In these states, the governor has almost unfettered discretion in appointing judges to a fixed term (with the caveats that judges can serve only until age 70 in New Jersey, and legislative approval is needed for appointees in Maine and New Jersey).

Partisan Elections In 12 states, judges for at least some state courts are elected on partisan ballots. Just like governors and state legislators, those wishing to become a judge in these states must run for a party's nomination in a primary election (or gain the nomination in a convention) and then face an opponent from the other party in a general election. Among the six states that use partisan elections for only some of their judges, all but New Mexico use them for trial courts, using other methods for judges for their supreme court and ICAs.

Nonpartisan Elections The second-most common method of state judicial selection today is nonpartisan election, with 21 states using this method for at least some of their judges. These elections are typically not held during the November general election, but rather, in the spring, often coinciding with nonpartisan municipal elections.

The Merit Plan The Merit Plan (also called the Missouri Plan, after the first state to adopt it) is the most widely used judicial selection mechanism. Twenty-four states use some variant of this approach for at least some of their courts. The Merit Plan has three steps. First, a nominating commission is formed to recruit and evaluate potential judges. The composition of this commission varies from state to state, but it generally includes representatives of key government institutions (such as the state legislature, the governor, and the state supreme court) and the legal establishment (perhaps through the state bar association). For a specific judicial vacancy, the commission identifies a small number of qualified candidates (usually three) and sends their names to the governor. Next, the governor appoints one of the nominees to the vacancy for a short term, usually one to three years. Finally, once the new judge has served this initial probationary term, he or she faces the voters in a **retention election.** That is, the question on the ballot is not which of two or more candidates the voter prefers but, rather, whether this judge should be allowed to have another (usually much longer) term (that is, voters choose between *yes* or *no*). This probationary term and retention election are the unique features of the Merit Plan.

All this variation in how the states select their judges raises two questions: (1) why don't all states select their judges the same way, as they do with most of their other government officials; and (2) what effect does the method of judicial selection have on the administration of justice? We turn to these questions next.

Why Do States Select Their Judges Differently?

Since the founding of the republic, Americans have debated the best way to select their state judges. The key to explaining the current variation in judicial selection mechanisms lies in the evolution of Americans' values about our courts.[40] We establish institutions for selecting a class of public officials based on the functions that we believe these officials should perform and the values that we hold about these functions. The current variation in state judicial selection roughly follows the historic and geographic variation in Americans' beliefs about the proper role of the judiciary.

Our expectations for judges have never been as clear or as universally accepted as our expectations for most other officials. Some have debated the proper role of legislators and governors, for example, about whether they should use their own judgment or follow their constituents' values in making policy decisions. But no doubt exists about how governors and legislators act, and about how they are rewarded for acting, when these two roles conflict, at least on major issues. Books are written about the political courage of politicians who stand for what is right against what is popular, not because we value such behavior so much (although we do value it sometimes), but because it is so rare. When push comes to shove, we want our legislators and governors to reflect our preferences, and we elect them directly to ensure that they do so.

We are less certain about the proper role of judges in our representative democracy. For example, consider how you think judges should make decisions. Legal culture and norms hold that their decisions should be based only on the law and the facts of the case—this is the fair administration of justice that we prize. But what about when the fair administration of justice conflicts with public opinion? Such conflicts are more common than you might think. For example, an angry mob might want to lynch a person who they think got a too-lenient sentence for a particularly heinous crime. Most Americans would agree that the judge was right to ignore the wishes of this community and apply the law as passed by the state legislature. But what about when a law is passed by a state legislature or through a voter initiative that conflicts with the fundamental rules of governance or human rights set out in the state's constitution? Should a state supreme court override the current will of the people (the statute) in favor of the constitution, which represents the will of the people at a previous time? In the federal court system, judges are appointed for life so that they can protect constitutional rights and values against the heat of current popular opinion. They have done this to protect the rights of minorities of all types, from African Americans trying to vote in the South in the 1950s and 1960s to the Ku Klux Klan and neo-Nazi groups trying to hold rallies more recently.[41] Is this the proper role of the courts?

Even if you agree that the judiciary should protect certain basic rights against popular opinion, consider other legal situations where the law and the facts are not clear-cut, giving a judge room for interpretation. To what extent should judges decide such cases (many of which exist) using their professional judgment based on their years of legal training and experience, and to what extent should they reflect the values and preferences of the communities they serve? Furthermore, consider this question: is there a difference between the ability of the general public to understand the job of a judge, on one hand, versus that of a governor or legislator, on the other, such that we can trust the average voter to know who would make a good governor or legislator but not who would make a good judge?

Many different answers to these questions are backed by good arguments, and this debate is reflected in the states' judicial selection institutions.[42] As we have seen, the earliest state legislatures embodied what was seen as the only legitimate source of political power—the people. The British had used the colonial courts as instruments of royal oppression, and so, the founders were suspicious of them. Thus, the first state governments subordinated the courts to the legislature by giving the latter the power to appoint judges. As state legislatures fell out of favor in the early 19th century, states embraced executive leadership, and this included giving governors the power to appoint judges. Thus, in keeping with the strongly elitist tone of early American democracy, state judges were almost all appointed for the first half-century of the country.

With the rise of Jacksonian democracy in pre–Civil War America, the states began electing many more of their state officials directly, and this included judges. In 1832, Mississippi became the first state to elect its judges, and by the turn of the 20th century, about 80 percent of the states did likewise. Like all officials in this era, judges were elected in partisan elections, with the idea being that the party label would give voters an indication of the candidates' values and preferences. In this way, judges would reflect voters' values in the same way that legislators or governors would.

By the early 20th century, the good-government reformers of the Progressive Era pushed for nonpartisan judicial elections. These reformers valued judges who would decide cases fairly and impartially based on the law and the facts of the case. They felt that partisanship and political ideology should have nothing to do with judicial decision making, so it made no sense to select judges using those criteria. Nonpartisan elections would force voters to select judges on more job-related criteria, like their training and experience. North Dakota established the first nonpartisan elections for state judges in 1910, and by 1952, 15 other states had done so.

Finally, in 1940, Missouri adopted the first Merit Plan, a hybrid of appointment and election. The values reflected by this institution are also a hybrid. The first part of this hybrid is the notion that judicial selection is best made by experts (the selection committee and the governor) because the job is highly technical and voters know little about it. But the retention election reflects the democratic impulse to give voters a way to evaluate their judges once in office. In this way, the Merit Plan is a scientific

Figure 9.3

Method of Selection of the State Supreme Court Justices

Sources: Council of State Governments, *The Book of the States 2006* (Lexington, Ky.: Council of State Governments, 2006), 251–54; see the source for details.

management approach to good government; that is, it is about appointing a qualified person to the post based on technical merit and then letting voters evaluate that person based on his or her subsequent performance on the job.

Thus, the diversity among the states in judicial selection mechanisms reflects the diversity in values about the role of judges over time and around the country (see Figure 9.3). New states adopted the institution that reflected the values in vogue at the time of their statehood. For example, from 1846 to 1900, every state admitted to the union initially elected its judges on a partisan ballot.[43] Likewise, when states made major changes to their constitutions, they tended to adopt the mechanism that better reflected the existing values about the judiciary. For example, in recent decades, Rhode Island (legislative appointment), Delaware and New Hampshire (gubernatorial appointment), New York and Tennessee (partisan election), and South Dakota (nonpartisan election) all changed to the Merit Plan, whereas Mississippi, Arkansas, and North Carolina all changed from partisan to nonpartisan elections since 1992.

Why have some states retained their older systems of judicial selection? This can often be explained simply by inertia and the difficulty of changing a state's constitution. For example, Article VI, Section 7, of the Virginia state constitution requires judges to be selected by the legislature, and this has not been changed since the constitution was adopted in 1776. In other states, even when the opportunity to change their selection mechanism arose, it was not taken because the existing system reflected the values of the state well. For example, even though Illinois adopted a completely new constitution in 1970, it continued to elect its judges on a partisan basis due to the highly partisan and individualistic political culture of the state.

What Difference Does a Judicial Selection Mechanism Make?

The current interstate variation in judicial selection has given political scientists a unique opportunity to assess the impact of these mechanisms and the impact of institutions more generally. Before reviewing the results of recent research on this question, let's consider what effects we might expect based on the arguments of reformers and critics.

The original elite appointment system for judges has been criticized for reducing the independence of the courts and shifting political and policy-making power to the appointing institution, whether it is the governor or legislature. One of the central principles of the American system of government is the separation of powers among the three branches, and elite appointment seems to some to upset that balance.[44] In addition, appointments may also influence the type of person who rises to the bench. For example, in South Carolina, one of only two states still using legislative appointment, almost all judges are former state lawmakers.

Judicial elections also have their critics, with the American Bar Association being perhaps the most prominent among them.[45] Given the widespread use of judicial elections and the extensive debate over their reform over the past 100 years, these arguments are more extensive and multifaceted than those for the elite appointment system.

First, judicial elections are criticized for being low-turnout, low-information affairs.[46] Very few voters know anything about candidates for state judgeships, especially those below the supreme court level. And without such information, voters cannot very well form and express a coherent preference about who should be a judge. In such a situation, people tend either to vote less often or to fall back on voting cues that may be weakly related to their preferences, completely irrelevant, or even misleading. In partisan elections, a candidate's party may provide some very imperfect information about his or her political values and policy preferences but not about his or her fairness and judicial competence. And in nonpartisan elections and primaries, voters do not even have this limited information. The result can sometimes be problematic. For example, because he happened to have the same name as a popular state senator, an inexperienced lawyer on the verge of disbarment for a string of bad debts was once elected to the Texas Supreme Court. Luckily, the mistake was short-lived—eight months after his election, the judge quit the court and fled the country to escape federal charges related to hiring a hit man![47]

One of the reasons that voters know so little about judicial candidates is their professional norm against campaigning on anything other than basic résumé data. In essence, judicial candidates have traditionally been able to tell voters only where they went to law school and what jobs they have held. This information may be useful to voters who are very familiar with the legal profession, but it does not help most of us. For example, few voters would be able to rank the qualifications of two judicial candidates knowing only that one attended the College of William and Mary School of Law and served as a clerk in the U.S. Circuit Court of Appeals and the other attended the John Marshall School of Law and was a partner in Fouts, Hicks, and Taylor, LLC. The legal profession frowns on judicial candidates offering the sort of information that we routinely get from candidates for other offices—their opinions on the important issues on which they might be called to decide. For example, although no self-respecting judicial candidate would run a TV ad that said "Mike Pyle for Judge—No More Coddling Criminals," we would not be surprised to see a state legislative candidate run such an ad—in fact, we would expect it.

The reason for the judicial profession's norm against policy-oriented information in judicial campaigns is its parallel value that judges should administer the law based only on the specific facts and the established law involved in each case. How would you like to be on trial on a charge of drunk and disorderly conduct—guilty or not—before the newly elected Judge Pyle fresh off his "law-and-order" election campaign? Or suppose you were suing a negligent doctor for botching a surgical procedure. Would you want to face a judge who gave campaign speeches against "excessive lawsuit settlements"? In their campaigns, these judges proudly declared their values and promised to inject them into their judicial decisions. Governors and legislators are expected to have opinions on public policy and discuss these in their election campaigns; judges are expected to be unbiased.

Another important criticism of judicial elections arises from their recent dramatic increases in campaign spending, especially in supreme court races.[48] Reformers are most troubled not so much simply by the great amounts of money being spent in these races but how and why these candidates receive their campaign contributions. The lawyers and law firms that face these judicial candidates once they are elected have long been their major donors. And recently, interest groups have begun actively financing state supreme court races—and even some ICA races—because of the broad judicial issues that are decided there.[49] Some groups have even been airing independent TV ads for the judicial candidates they favor, raising further worries because these groups may not feel constrained by judicial norms about the content of these commercials. Another new twist with interest groups is that some have begun targeting sitting judges whose opinions they do not like, especially those who rule as unconstitutional the initiatives they just worked so hard to encourage voters to pass.[50]

But what really disturbs observers of state judicial elections about skyrocketing campaign spending and contributions is the potential for **conflict of interest,** especially when one side in a case is represented by a contributor and the other side is not.[51] For example, recently, just after a West Virginia Supreme Court justice was elected with the help of millions of dollars in campaign ads from those associated with Massey Energy, he sat in judgment on that coal company's appeal of a $50 million settlement; a similar case also just happened in Illinois with State Farm Insurance.[52] Like legislators who claim that campaign contributions do not affect their roll call votes, judges protest that this money causes "no bias or prejudice,"[53] but recent research suggests otherwise.[54] One way to avoid even the appearance of such bias is for a judge who has received contributions from a party to a case to **recuse** him or herself from deciding on it.

But even if no explicit quid pro quo on a case—which would be bribery and patently illegal—is apparent, is it possible that a judge might develop an unconscious bias on a class of cases based on his or her campaign support? Furthermore, wouldn't we even expect interest groups to support candidates who have a particular point of view, thereby trying to stack the judiciary in their favor? This happens all the time in legislative and gubernatorial races, so why might it be more problematic in judicial elections? And even if judicial decisions are in no way affected by campaign contributions, could just the appearance of such bias damage the public's opinion about the courts? These important questions raise concerns about the wisdom of electing judges.

To address these fears, states have regulated judicial elections much more heavily than they have legislative and gubernatorial races. For example, some states have enacted professional norms into law through restrictions on the policy statements that judicial candidates can make. But starting in 2002, the federal courts have struck down many of these regulations, ruling that they violate the candidates' First Amendment right to free speech.[55] One case even struck down restrictions on candidates in Minnesota's nonpartisan elections in regard to soliciting campaign funds from political parties, calling into question the very legitimacy of nonpartisan elections.[56] In the coming years, it will be interesting to see whether professional norms alone will prevail in the absence of statutory regulations or whether judicial campaigns will simply become more like those for other offices. In a creative attempt to entice candidates into accepting voluntary restrictions, North Carolina has recently tried public financing of judicial elections, but it remains to be seen if the funding for their program will be significant enough to lure candidates away from interest groups' contributions.[57] A few state supreme courts

have also established committees to monitor campaign conduct, but the committees do not have the power to punish candidates, only to scold them.[58] If states' efforts fail to keep the lid on competitive judicial elections, reformers' campaigns to adopt the Merit Plan may pick up steam.

Indeed, after considering the arguments against judicial election and elite appointment, the Merit Plan may sound like a great idea. After all, who could argue against picking judges based on *merit*? And this hybrid of expert evaluation and voter double-checking through a retention election has been the most frequently selected format among the states that changed their judicial selection mechanism since World War II. Most would agree that judges need certain technical expertise and training; not just anyone can be a judge. On the other hand, going back to Thomas Jefferson, Americans have strongly believed, in their political thought, that the average citizen could serve well as a legislator, and even the executive skills needed of a governor are probably more evenly distributed in the population than those skills needed to be a judge. Furthermore, the average person probably cannot determine who has the specialized skills a judge needs. Would you want your doctor or car mechanic to be selected by a popular vote or would you rather have them picked (or at least certified) by experts in their fields? The Merit Plan also reduces the temptation in appointment systems for judicial selection to be made on criteria other than pure technical merit, such as political party or returning a political favor.

On the other hand, you have to be careful not to take labels like *Merit Plan* at face value. What exactly does *merit* mean in this context? The answer is that Merit Plans define merit based on the values of a state's legal establishment. Old, established law firms, the state bar association, and their political allies tend to dominate Merit Plan nomination committees. These people know—and really care about—the difference between the John Marshall School of Law and the College of William and Mary School of Law. So, they may well be the best people to evaluate judicial merit. But the social hierarchy of the legal profession suggests that there may be some differences in the types of lawyers who are selected to be judges through the Merit Plan and through, for example, a nonpartisan election. Consider the "See a Lawyer for 10 Bucks" guy who advertises on afternoon TV and city buses. He is not likely to win a judgeship through the Merit Plan because the legal establishment does not likely think highly of him. But he might have a pretty good chance of getting elected to a judgeship—assuming he wants to give up his lucrative personal injury law practice—due to the name recognition that his advertisements have generated, his money, and his self-promotional talent. Given that the background, values, and clients of establishment lawyers might be quite different than those of lawyers who advertise on buses, consider who gains and loses by having these different sets of values reflected in judicial decision making.

So far, we have considered reformers' arguments about the effects of these different judicial selection systems, but what has objective research told us about them? Recently, many scholars have worked on this issue, focusing mostly on state supreme courts. Some of these studies have scrutinized potential effects that reformers never even considered. For example, one study found that the length of a justice's service is not related to the judicial selection mechanism,[59] and other studies have found conflicting evidence about the impact of selection mechanism on public opinion of a state's supreme court.[60] But a series of studies has allowed us to draw some general conclusions about two important hypothesized impacts of judicial selection mechanism—the type of person who becomes a judge and the decisions made by judges once they are on the bench.

In considering the effect of the selection mechanism on who becomes a judge, as of yet, scholars have studied only judges' most obvious demographic characteristics. To a far greater degree than even other public officials, state judges are overwhelmingly middle-aged, middle-class, white, and male. Again compared to other types of officials, their educational and professional experiences are pretty homogeneous—but this is not surprising because they are all in the same profession. Despite this homogeneity, political scientists have found that elections tend to reduce the level of racial and ethnic diversity among judges, whereas Merit Plans and appointment systems tend to increase it.[61] Why might this be so? First, because elections are decided on a majority rule principle, if people tend to vote for those of their own racial or ethnic group (of course, a questionable assumption), only candidates from majority groups will win. On the other hand, with an appointment system or Merit Plan, the appointing officials may look at the totality of the bench and seek diversity purposefully, whether out of the normative belief that this is the right thing to do or as a way of rewarding various constituencies. But if this is so, why do we find that women judicial candidates do worse in election systems, even though they constitute a slight majority in most states?[62] This may be attributed to a lingering gender bias in the electorate, something that affects elections for almost all offices.

Because of the judicial selection's importance for the administration of justice and for public policy, political scientists studying it have focused most on its impact on judicial decision making. The general conclusion drawn from these studies is that judicial selection does not have major impacts on judicial decision making.[63] This is good—judges' decisions should be driven by the law and the facts in the cases before them, to the extent possible. This norm that judges should be impartial arbiters of justice appears largely to override any institutional differences in selection mechanism. But political scientists have found some minor impacts of the selection mechanism on judicial decision making, primarily differences between elected judges on one hand and appointed and Merit Plan judges on the other. That is, when a judge has discretion in his or her decision, elected judges tend to be different in the following ways, especially at the supreme court level.

First, as democratic theory suggests, elected judges' decisions tend to reflect the ideology and values of their state's citizens, especially on issues that are in the public eye, such as the death penalty.[64] This effect is stronger for competitive elections than for retention elections.[65] Moreover, elected judges tend to adjust their decisions as elections approach, both reflecting their state's ideology more closely[66] and issuing harsher criminal sentences.[67] This suggests that elections give judges, like governors and legislators, the incentive to reflect their constituents' values in carrying out their public duties. Elections also lead to more plea bargaining, fewer trials,[68] and fewer dissenting opinions on controversial issues decided by supreme courts.[69] These suggest an effort by incumbent judges to reduce conflict, which might help their re-election chances.

Judges elected on partisan ballots tend to vote in ways that reflect their partisanship,[70] and in civil cases, they all tend to grant higher awards to injured parties than judges selected through other systems.[71] Furthermore, partisan election results are influenced more by the actual behavior of the incumbent judge running for re-election than are nonpartisan and retention elections, which are more influenced by social and political events. This is the opposite of what Progressive Era and Merit Plan reformers argued would be the case.[72]

Thus, although a state's judicial selection mechanism affects the type of judges selected and the decisions these judges make, we can offer no definitive answer about which method is the best. This is not only because we do not completely understand the effects of these different mechanisms but also, just as important, because of the ambiguity in the values Americans hold about the role of the courts in state government and about judges' behavior. Until we can agree more closely on these values, the debate over judicial selection and the successive waves of reform that this debate spawns will likely continue.

Reform and the State Courts

The history of American state courts has been a history of institutional experimentation and reform. From partisan and nonpartisan elections to the Merit Plan, from intermediate courts of appeal to family and drug courts, from directors of state courts to boards to review attorney and judicial misconduct, the states have been trying to get the administration of justice right since the beginning of the republic. As we have discussed, this is an especially difficult task because of the lack of a clear vision about what we want from our courts. Certainly, we want fair and impartial adjudication of cases based on the facts and law, but we also value democracy, and as such, we want our courts to reflect the basic principles that our citizens hold dear. We also want the courts to guard the basic rights of minorities because besides being the right thing to do, we know that each of us will be in the minority sometimes, and we want our rights protected then.

Fulfilling all these needs is a tall order for the courts, so it should be no surprise that they never get them exactly right. Consider a few new reforms that have been touted recently and how they speak to the values we want our courts to reflect:

- CourTools—CourTools are a set of 10 performance measures developed by the National Center for State Courts in an effort to make courts more user-friendly and efficient.[73] Aimed at evaluating court systems, rather than specific judges, CourTools use both objective court data and surveys of those who have participated in court activities, whether as parties to a case, jurors, witnesses, or family members.

- Court-stripping—*Court-stripping* refers to laws designed to change the jurisdiction of a type of case so as to improve the chances of preferred court decisions by those making the laws.[74] Before Democrats took control

REFORM CAN HAPPEN

THE BATTLE OVER TORT REFORM IN THE STATES

Bringing a civil suit against someone we feel has injured us is an old way of settling disputes in the English American tradition of common law. Such an injury is known as a **tort.** The parties in tort suits can be people, corporations, or government entities. But some argue that tort actions are sometimes abused, whether through excessive awards for damages or outright fraud. We read stories and hear urban legends about million-dollar settlements for silly things like too-hot coffee in a Styrofoam cup and cases like the lady who claimed to have found a finger in her chili at a Wendy's restaurant a couple of years ago,[1] where criminals simply try to use lawsuits to rob others. But in many situations, a person has been hurt by another person or organization and, through no fault of his or her own, is made to suffer, sometimes for a lifetime. How can fraud and frivolous lawsuits be combated while maintaining a system where even the least well-off can fairly fight a large corporation or powerful person who has hurt them?

Today, a heated debate continues in the states about this question. Business groups, medical groups (because doctors are the target of many such lawsuits), and their political allies (often Republicans) have led the fight for *tort reform,* laws that limit the right to sue or the amount that can be awarded in a lawsuit. Trial lawyers, consumer and victims' rights groups, and their political allies (often Democrats) oppose tort reform, arguing that the ability to sue for damages not only compensates those who have suffered such damages but also encourages manufacturers and other businesses to avoid inflicting damage in the first place.

Social scientists are now researching the impacts—intended and unintended—of tort reform,[2] even as politicians debate their desirability and legal scholars debate their constitutionality.[3] Even President Bush has gotten into the debate, working with the Republican-led Congress in 2005 to limit **class action lawsuits,** an effective way for plaintiffs to pool their resources to sue large and powerful defendants.[4] The debate and research on tort reform are likely to continue for some time, and this cyclical issue will likely remain on the political agenda in the states, off and on, for the foreseeable future.

Notes

1. "The Week," National Review, online ed., 6 June 2005.
2. C. M. Sharkey, "Unintened Consequences of Medical Malpractice Damages Caps," New York University Law Review 80 (2005): 391–512; and Fred J. Hellinger and William E. Encinosa, "The Impact of State Laws Limiting Damage Awards on Health Care Expenditures," American Journal of Public Health 96 (2006): 1375–81.
3. J. C. P. Goldberg, "The Constitutional Status of Tort Law: Due Process and the Right to a Law for the Redress of Wrongs," Yale Law Journal 115 (2005): 524–627.
4. Joseph Kay, "Bush Signs Bipartisan Bill to Curb Class Action Lawsuits," World Socialist Web Site, online ed., 22 February 2006.

of Congress in 2007, much court-stripping involved shifting the jurisdiction of cases, like class action lawsuits, right-to-life decisions, and same-sex marriage questions, from state courts to the federal courts.

- Judicial Accountability Initiative Laws (JAIL)—Advocated by the group Jail-4Judges, JAIL would abolish the immunity against civil lawsuits held by judges, juries, and others working in the court systems and establish special boards to review court actions that someone thinks are too lenient, too harsh, or just plain wrong—what JAIL advocates call "black-collar crime."[75] But in its first initiative vote, in South Dakota's 2006 general election, JAIL earned only a 10.8 percent "yes" vote. It seems as though this is a reform whose time has not yet come.

Summary

The states' court systems are both complex and diverse, and the central themes of this book—the importance of institutions, reform, and comparison—become thoroughly intermingled when discussing them. Because the courts can have such a fundamental and direct impact on a person's life, and because we have such mixed expectations for them, Americans have continuously reformed their judicial institutions, leading to the wide variation we see in them across the states today. But through this complexity, we can both discern clear patterns and use the variation to understand how the states' institutions of justice work.

State courts settle civil and criminal legal disputes among people, corporations, and government entities. These courts work as a self-contained system within each state, working parallel to, rather than in competition with or as inferior to, the federal court system. Trial courts, intermediate courts of appeal (ICAs), and supreme courts each have an important and unique role in administering justice in a state, with the supreme court being the final arbiter of the constitutionality and meaning of state law. Although their explicit job is "merely" to interpret and apply the law in specific disputes, in doing so, the courts have an important impact on state public policy. Unlike most other American public officials, state judges gain their positions through a variety of methods, including partisan and nonpartisan election, appointment by the governor or legislature, and the Merit Plan. Although scholars have found some significant impacts on the ways in which judges are selected, little evidence exists that judges selected in different ways behave radically differently from one another on the bench.

Key Terms

Adjudication

Adjudicator

Adversarial argument

Bench trial

Class action lawsuit

Common law

Conflict of interest

Court of last resort

Defendant

Director of state courts

Docket

Double jeopardy

Drug courts

General jurisdiction

Intermediate courts of appeal

Judicial review

Jurisdiction

Jury

Legal brief

Limited jurisdiction

Mental health courts

Merit Plan

Original jurisdiction

Out-of-court settlement

Petition

Plaintiff

Plea bargaining

Problem-solving courts

Recidivism

Recuse

Retention election

Runaway jury

Small claims courts

Supreme court

Tort

Trial court

Trial transcript

Writ of certiorari

Suggested Readings

Baum, Lawrence. 2001. *American courts: Process and policy.* 5th ed. Boston: Houghton Mifflin.

Bonneau, Chris W. 2004. Patterns of campaign spending and electoral competition in state supreme court elections. *Justice System Journal* 25:21–38.

Brace, Paul, and Melinda Gann Hall. 1997. The interplay of preferences, case facts, context, and structure in the politics of judicial choice. *Journal of Politics* 59:1206–31.

Galanter, Marc. 1974. Why the "haves" come out ahead: Speculations on the limits of legal change. *Law & Society Review* 9:95–160.

Glick, Henry R. 2004. Courts: Politics and the judicial process. In *Politics in the American states,* eds. Virginia Gray and Russell L. Hanson. 8th ed. Washington, DC: CQ Press.

Hall, Melinda Gann. 2001. State supreme courts in American democracy: Probing the myths of judicial reform. *American Political Science Review* 95:315–30.

Langer, Laura. 1999. *Judicial review in state supreme courts: A comparative study.* Albany: State University of New York Press.

Sheldon, Charles H., and Linda S. Maule. 1997. *Choosing justice: The recruitment of state and federal judges.* Pullman: Washington State University Press.

Tarr, G. Alan, and Mary Cornelia Aldis Porter. 1988. *State supreme courts in state and nation.* New Haven, CT: Yale University Press.

Websites

American Bar Association (http://www.abanet.org): The ABA is the largest professional association of lawyers in the United States, whose activities include accrediting law schools, training lawyers and judges, and advocating for changes in the law and legal system that it feels are necessary.

American Prosecutors Research Institute (http://www.ndaa.org/apri/index.html): The APRI is the research, development, and technical assistance unit of the National District Attorneys Association, the professional association of these local officials.

Justice at Stake Campaign (http://www.justiceatstake.org): Justice at Stake is a national, nonpartisan, not-for-profit organization that does research and advocacy work to improve the impartiality and fairness of American courts.

National Center for State Courts (http://www.ncsconline.org): The NCSC is a professional association for judges that provides them with training, conducts research about law and legal systems, and advocates for judges' interests in the political system.

10

(Crist) AP Photo/Phil Coale

Fiscal Policy

Boom and Bust Budgeting

Economic boom and bust can have dramatic effects on state and local budgets. California provides one example. The 1990s boom in technology sector stocks created many instant millionaires in California. It also propelled state tax revenues higher as these new millionaires paid income and capital gains taxes. Increased economic activity associated with the tech boom meant the state collected more revenues while tax rates remained fixed. There was so much new money that the state spent lavishly. Elementary class sizes were reduced, college tuition was frozen, teachers were paid more, public employee pension plans became more generous, and more children were covered by state health care programs. Some taxes were cut.

The "dot-com" bubble burst when many firms failed to become profitable. Businesses closed, tech jobs were eliminated, businesses cut investments, spending declined, and profits plunged. As a result, there was little stock profit to tax. Tax revenues started to dry up in 2002, and the state soon faced a $38 billion dollar deficit—more than an average state budget. The state faced tough choices: raise college tuition, cut spending, raise taxes, borrow money—or all of the above. California's boom and bust experience is an extreme case, but it is not unique. Although the federal government can ride out economic cycles with deficit spending, states generally need to have a balanced budget. Unlike their federal counterparts, state and local elected officials have less room to hide from tough choices associated with budgeting. This chapter examines how and when states make choices about taxing and spending and what some of the consequences of these choices might be.

OUTLINE

Introductory Vignette

Introduction

Criteria for Evaluating Taxes

Where Does the Money Come From? Major Sources of Revenues

Other Revenue Sources

Tax and Expenditure Limits

Fiscal Federalism

General Funds versus Non-General Funds

Adding It All Up: Variation in State Revenue Packages

Who Bears the Burden of State and Local Taxes?

When Do Taxes Go Up or Down?

What Are the Effects of Taxes?

The Growth of State Governments

Where Does the Money Go? Government Spending

Do State and Local Spending Actually Reflect What People Want?

Budgeting

Summary

Introduction

State and local governments provide people with a wide array of services—literally from birth to death. States, counties, and cities run hospitals and health care systems, child care programs, elementary education, and colleges and universities. They provide for public safety by enforcing building codes, inspecting restaurants, maintaining drinking water systems, and operating police and fire-fighting services. Some jurisdictions even run cemeteries.

One of the most difficult tasks of governing is generating the revenue required to fund the wide range of public services that people expect and demand and then balancing limited revenues with those demands for services and programs. Matters are complicated by the fact that people do not agree on what the government's spending priorities should be and by disagreement over which taxes should be used to fund government. Fiscal politics involves policies and decisions relating to raising and spending public money. Fiscal policy—or budgeting—is how state and local elected officials figure out who gets what from government, at whose expense.

People generally do not like to pay taxes, but a fundamental trait of a sovereign government is that it has some ability to coerce citizens to pay their taxes. For example, it is very difficult, and typically illegal, to avoid paying taxes that you owe. Whether a tax applies to your income or the purchase of this book, the federal, state, county, or city governments that have the power to tax also have the power to penalize you if you are found to have avoided a tax you owed.

To some observers, the tax and spending powers of government are feared because they see governments as predatory **leviathans,** always seeking and finding new funding sources and collecting ever more revenue.[1] The leviathan theory of government proposes that politicians tax and spend without regard to how much citizens are actually willing to pay. The word *leviathan* refers to government as an ever growing, predatory giant. But fiscal politics and policy aren't so simple. In democratic societies, governments at any level are in a weak position to simply rely on coercion or duplicity to collect the revenues they need. Voters are not easily tricked into paying taxes they don't like, and history shows that this nation was founded after a revolution against taxes that people found unreasonable. Some taxes are more unpopular than others (few taxes can be called popular), and some levels of taxation are not realistic. As we shall see in this chapter, perceptions of unreasonable taxation can still lead to public revolts that affect what state and local governments can do. In Chapter 12, we also see that taxation may affect whether businesses and people leave one place to locate in another.

Although government is constrained in regard to raising revenues, nearly all elected officials have a spending program they will fight to defend—largely in response to demands from their constituents. For elected representatives, the act of budgeting involves balancing demands for expensive government programs against practical limits on how much revenue a government can or should raise. Budgeting is an attempt to deal with scarcity: there's never enough money to fund every possible government program that people might want. As we shall see, states and communities deal with scarcity in different ways, and their ability to balance demands for programs against limits on resources depends on many factors. Demands for government spending vary widely across places due to differences in state populations. More children, for example, may mean more demand for education; more elderly may mean more spending on health care. Demand may never overlap with public willingness to pay because some people may be willing to support taxes to pay for services that assist them, but they may be reluctant to support funds for public goods and services they don't use.

Criteria for Evaluating Taxes

The public's willingness to pay a particular tax (or a fee or charge) is one criterion we will use in this chapter when evaluating the revenue sources that state and local governments use. Willingness to pay, as we show below, may be a function of how visible a tax is. We also focus on additional features of taxes that are of interest to political scientists, economists, and, perhaps most importantly, government officials. As we examine different taxes, we see they differ in terms of **tax equity**—or who bears the burden of paying them. When a tax is **progressive**, the wealthier people pay a larger proportion of their total income to cover the tax than the less affluent pay of theirs, whereas when the tax is **regressive**, the poor pay a larger proportion of their income than the wealthy do to cover the tax.

Some governments may also be positioned to use taxes that are exportable. Exportable taxes are those mostly paid by people from other places (such as hotel taxes and taxes on natural resources, such as oil). Taxes also differ in their **elasticity**; that is, in how stable (or volatile) revenues from the tax are in times of economic boom and bust. Furthermore, some taxes may be "neutral" in their ability to alter the economic behavior of people and businesses. Others may create odd incentives that distort behavior. All these factors enter into the politics of which taxes governments use to fund public services.

Options for revenues also vary widely due to the economic structure of a state or community, institutional differences, and differences in popular support for taxation. Options for revenues that are available in California and New York, such as increasing the state personal income tax, are not available in, say, Florida or Texas. California and New York have established income taxes and have rather liberal public preferences for government spending. Florida and Texas, in contrast, have voters who may be less sympathetic to public spending, and neither state has adopted a personal income tax. States also vary considerably on what can be taxed. Alaska can rely heavily on revenue from oil extraction, whereas Ohio cannot.

Where Does the Money Come From? Major Sources of Revenues

State and local governments spend about 17 cents of every dollar generated by the American economy, more than what is spent by the federal government. This reflects that states spend the money they collect in taxes, in charges, and fees and that states also spend billions of dollars that the federal government collects each year that is transferred to the states.

Each level of government competes for revenue—sometimes applying the same kind of taxes to the same sources. This is why in some places, you may pay a state income tax in addition to your federal income tax or a local sales tax on top of your state's sales tax. However, the American fiscal environment has evolved such that the national government, the states, and local governments each have one particular revenue source, respectively, that they tend to rely upon for much of the resources they raise by taxation.

States vary in terms of how much revenue they raise and how they raise it. This makes it difficult to clearly define which states have the highest taxes. It depends on how we rank the states. The first two columns in Table 10.1 rank states according to how much they tax residents relative to the amount of income in the state per person. Ranked this way, Vermont, Maine, and New York tax the most and Alaska and New Hampshire the least.

The third column ranks states according to the total state and local taxes collected per resident (rather than as a function of state income). This illustrates how states compare in terms of the total dollars they collect per person. Had we ranked states

A paycheck lists the multiple jurisdictions that tax a person working in New York.

this way, Alaska and Wyoming would top the list, while South Dakota and Mississippi would be last. These rankings are affected by the state's level of wealth and the size of its population. But they also reflect the political and economic circumstances that shape the mix of taxes used in a state. New York has wealth to tap and relatively high taxes. Alaska and Wyoming are less affluent, but both generate tremendous revenues from resource taxes relative to the size of their populations.

The final column in Table 10.1 ranks states according to their level of per capita personal in-come, from the wealthiest (Connecticut) to the least affluent (Mississippi). Some states that are below average on this measure of wealth (for example, Maine and Louisiana) nonetheless rank relatively high on how much revenue they collect as a percentage of per capita income. Conversely, some affluent states (such as Virginia and Delaware) rank fairly low on taxes as a percentage of income. Again, this reflects political and economic circumstances in these states. Voters in Maine may be more receptive to higher taxes than Virginians. Delaware is uniquely situated to collect a substantial proportion of revenue from the unusually large number of businesses

Table 10.1

State and Local Taxes as a Percent of State Income, 2007

	State and local revenue as % of per capita income	States ranked by revenue as % of per capita income	States ranked by total revenues per capita	States ranked by per capita income
	2007	2007	2005	2000
Vermont	14.1%	1	12	25
Maine	14.0%	2	14	34
New York	13.8%	3	3	8
Rhode Island	12.7%	4	13	17
Ohio	12.4%	5	21	22
Hawaii	12.4%	6	9	19
Wisconsin	12.3%	7	19	20
Connecticut	12.2%	8	4	1
Nebraska	11.9%	9	15	33
New Jersey	11.6%	10	6	2
Minnesota	11.5%	11	10	10
California	11.5%	12	8	13
Arkansas	11.3%	13	47	48
Michigan	11.2%	14	22	15
Kansas	11.2%	15	31	26
Washington	11.1%	16	17	12
Louisiana	11.0%	17	32	47
Iowa	11.0%	18	28	31
North Carolina	11.0%	19	37	28
Kentucky	10.9%	20	46	40
West Virginia	10.9%	21	33	49
Illinois	10.8%	22	25	11
Maryland	10.8%	23	11	4
Pennsylvania	10.8%	24	23	24
Indiana	10.7%	25	27	27
South Carolina	10.7%	26	34	37
Utah	10.7%	27	35	39
Massachusetts	10.6%	28	7	3
Mississippi	10.5%	29	50	50
Colorado	10.4%	30	20	5
Arizona	10.3%	31	45	29
Georgia	10.3%	32	43	21

Table 10.1				
State and Local Taxes as a Percent of State Income, 2007 (continued)				
	2007	2007	2005	2000
Virginia	10.2%	33	18	6
Missouri	10.1%	34	42	30
Idaho	10.1%	35	40	41
Nevada	10.1%	36	16	16
Oregon	10.0%	37	30	23
Florida	10.0%	38	26	18
North Dakota	9.9%	39	24	42
New Mexico	9.8%	40	29	45
Montana	9.7%	41	38	46
Wyoming	9.5%	42	2	36
Texas	9.3%	43	39	32
South Dakota	9.0%	44	49	44
Oklahoma	9.0%	45	44	43
Alabama	8.8%	46	41	38
Delaware	8.8%	47	5	9
Tennessee	8.5%	48	4	35
New Hampshire	8.0%	49	36	7
Alaska	6.6%	50	1	14

Source: Tax Foundation (2007); Tax Policy Center (2005) US Census (2000).

incorporated there. Delaware thus collects a great deal of revenue per capita but not much relative to its overall level of wealth per capita. Mississippi and Louisiana, in contrast, tax relatively high relative to their limited wealth, but those taxes generate much less revenue per capita than lower taxes do in affluent Delaware.

Below, we consider the various tools that state and local governments use to raise revenues and the political issues associated with some of these.

Income Tax

The first state began collecting income taxes in 1911, prior to the constitutional amendment that granted the federal government the power to tax income. The most recent state to adopt an income tax was Connecticut in 1991. Today, most of the revenue collected in the United States as income tax goes to fund the federal government. For most states, however, income taxes are a major part of their mix of revenue sources. Nearly all states (41) tax personal income, and two more states (Tennessee and New Hampshire) tax just personal income from investments. In addition, Alaska and Florida tax corporate income. This means that Wyoming, Washington, Nevada, Texas, and South Dakota are the only states that lack taxation of personal or corporate income.[2] A handful of states allow local governments to levy an income tax.

A few of states have **flat rates** for their income tax, but most state income tax systems place people into one of several brackets defined by how much they earn. Tax rates increase for each bracket, with people in the highest income brackets paying the highest tax rate. Even for people in the top brackets, state income tax rates are far lower than those levied by the federal government. An average state has about five brackets, with the tax rate for people in the lowest income bracket averaging about 2.6 percent, and the rate for people in the highest bracket averaging about 6.5 percent. Montana (11 percent), Vermont (9.5 percent), and California (9.3 percent) have the highest rates for top income brackets.[3] The proportion of all states' total personal income collected in state income taxes has increased steadily since the 1960s.[4]

Evaluating the Income Tax Supporters of the income tax note several features they find attractive. Advocacy groups note that states making use of an income tax have the most progressive revenue systems overall, whereas the poor pay a much larger proportion of their income in state and local taxes than the wealthy in states that lack an income tax (such as Washington, Florida, and Texas).[5] Income taxes are relatively easy for governments to collect (through payroll deduction), and revenues collected tend to be more stable in times of economic downturns when compared to sales taxes. Public opinion polls illustrate that voters find state income taxes more politically acceptable than federal taxes and property taxes, at least in states where the income tax already exists.[6] One study of the political consequences of adopting income taxes found that the party in control of the legislature that adopted the tax was usually re-elected. When voters did punish politicians for adopting a state income tax, Republicans were much more likely to suffer than Democrats.[7] This may be due to the fact that Republican voters expect more fiscal prudence from Republicans than Democratic voters expect from Democrats.

Critics point out that income is already taxed by the federal government, and that inflation can drive people who get **cost of living raises (COLAs)** into higher tax brackets even though their real earning power does not increase. Income taxes may also distort the incentives that people have to work. And by taxing income that people save, it creates disincentives for savings, which makes less money available for investment and economic growth.

Sales Tax

If you travel overseas, you might find that you pay a form of a national sales tax—also known as a consumption tax, value-added tax, or goods and services tax. These are taxes on what people spend rather than on what they earn. In the United States, taxation on the sale of goods and services is largely the domain of states and local governments. States began taxing the purchase of goods during the Great Depression of the 1930s. At the time, federal social programs were in their infancy and states were searching for resources to deal with massive unemployment and poverty.

Mississippi first adopted the sales tax in 1932, and another 11 states had adopted it by 1933.[8] Today all but five states (Oregon, Alaska, Montana, New Hampshire, and Delaware) have a sales tax. About half of all tax revenue collected by state governments comes from the sales tax, with Mississippi, Tennessee, and Rhode Island having the highest rates (7.0 percent). In addition, nearly all states grant their local governments the power to levy an additional increment on top of the state rate. This is the reason why you might pay a different rate as you move from one county to the next inside a state. When local sales taxes are considered, residents in parts of several high-sales-tax states pay over 9 percent in state and local sales tax on their purchases (for example, Alabama, Arkansas, Oklahoma, and Tennessee).

Evaluating the Sales Tax One of the most noteworthy features of the sales tax is its relative political acceptability. Surveys of opinion demonstrate that when compared to other major revenue sources, state sales taxes are the most popular (or usually the least disliked). Taxes are collected at the point of sale on individual purchases, so they may not be as noticeable to the taxpayer as lump sum payments that can come due with property taxes and income taxes. For local governments, sales tax revenue can be particularly attractive because it offers the opportunity to get folks from out of town to bear some of the costs of funding services. As a tax on consumption, sales taxes may also create fewer distortions in people's incentives to work, save, and invest than an income tax does.

Susan Hansen's study suggests that most state governments that adopted a state sales tax between 1911 and 1977 survived the next election, but that they faced a slightly greater threat of defeat than governments that adopted the income tax. Again, Republican governments that adopted the tax were at a greater risk of defeat than Democratic governments.[9]

The sales tax has two clear weaknesses, however. The first is the elasticity or stability of it as a revenue source. The total amount collected depends on how much people are spending on "big-ticket" consumer goods. When the economy cools, and consumer confidence wanes, the demand for things such as new cars, boats, TVs, computers, and construction materials declines—and so does sales tax revenue. This problem is magnified when the sales tax applies only to goods and not to services.

The second issue is equity. People who earn less usually spend all their income, which means the sales tax applies to most of what they earn. People who earn more are able to save and invest some of what they earn, and the sales tax does not apply to that portion of their income. This means the poor pay much more of their overall income to sales taxes than the rich. It also means that states that rely heavily on sales taxes have the most regressive tax systems. Many states offset the regressive nature of this tax by exempting basic items such as food and medicine from the tax. The definition of basic needs is a political question and must be defined by the legislature. The California legislature's attempt to apply the sales tax to "non-essential luxury foods" (snacks) in California set various lobbyists scrambling to defend their particular products as essential, basic foods. They eventually launched a successful initiative (Proposition 163) to amend the state constitution in 1992 (the Don't Tax Food and Water Campaign) to prohibit the state from applying the sales tax to things like candy and bottled water.

Due to growing exemptions and shifts in the nature of the economy, the base of what the sales tax applies to has been eroding over time. Over the past several decades, spending has shifted from goods to services (lawyers, health care, advertising, consulting), and purchases are moving from the physical storefront to the virtual store online. Services are not always covered by state sales taxes (in part due to successful lobbying efforts by the affected groups), and states have particular difficulty collecting taxes from sales made via the Internet. As the base of the tax erodes, states are under pressure to raise sales taxes on the remaining items subject to the tax.[10] And if more exemptions are made for "basic" necessities, the remaining base of the sales tax becomes more dependent on big-ticket purchases, making revenues even more volatile.[11] Sales taxes may also distort behavior by creating incentives for people to travel to make purchases where taxes are lower or by encouraging them to shop online in order to avoid paying any sales tax.

Property Tax

The property tax predates the income and sales taxes as the traditional source of public revenue and continues to serve as the primary revenue source for local governments. Some states collect state property taxes, but for most states, the property tax contributes less than 2 percent to total state taxes collected. However, property taxes are the main source of revenues for local governments. Property taxes are typically levied as a flat rate proportion (1 percent), for example, multiplied by the assessed value of property. These rates are often referred to as *mill levies*. A 1 percent mill levy is the same as saying the tax is $1 per $1,000 in assessed value of property, or the property value multiplied by .01. The amount one pays in tax is determined as much by the value of the property as by the tax rate. Most homeowners pay the same rate on residential property, with those having more valuable homes paying a higher tax amount overall. For example, a home assessed at $276,000 in Clark County, Washington, is subject to a 1.618 percent annual county property tax (or 0.00161 mill), a 2.766 percent state property

INSTITUTIONS MATTER

STATE AND LOCAL SALES TAX AND THE INTERNET

Traditional sales tax rules evolved in an era where goods were mostly sold to local people from local businesses. But what happens to the sales tax when more people make purchases via the Internet from businesses in other states? If the vendor has a physical presence in your state (such as a shop or warehouse), it must charge sales tax for your state and local governments. If no "bricks and mortar" presence exists, however, it is not required to collect the tax. Some worry that this gives online retailers a major advantage over local businesses. As the Internet became a common shopping destination, many large retailers like Wal-Mart, Target, Toys "R" Us, and Barnes and Noble that have physical stores in nearly every state avoid charging sales taxes by setting up separate legal dot-com entities that are, at least on paper, distinct from their traditional stores. The large online retailers argue that the old rules were obsolete and that it was too complicated to collected taxes for 50 states and thousands of local governments.

In theory, the *buyer* is supposed to pay the tax to the state if the online seller doesn't collect it. Given the difficulty of administering and monitoring Internet sales, states focused enforcement on a few "big-ticket" items, such as cars, and left large-volume sales areas, such as clothing, books, and music, untaxed. Sites like Travelocity.com also allow people who book rooms online to avoid paying local hotel taxes because rooms are purchased online. States may lose $38 billion annually in sales tax revenue by 2011 as retailers shift sales to the Internet—with some states losing nearly 10 percent of their total tax collections.[1] States have banded together to pressure retailers to voluntarily charge sales tax, and in February 2003, some large retailers (Walmart.com and ToysRUs.com) began to do so. However, absent federal legislation, states cannot force online retailers to pay the tax. Since 2003, the high-tech industry has lobbied successfully in Washington, D.C., against giving states power to enforce their sales tax collections for purchases made online.[2] A large coalition of states have responded by crafting new rules—a "streamlined" Internet sales tax with uniform rules in order to make it easier for retailers to collect sales taxes from online sales.

Notes

1. Donald Bruce and William F. Fox, "State and Local Sales Tax Revenue Losses from E-Commerce: Updated Estimates" (Chattanooga: University of Tennessee, Center for Business and Economic Research, 2001).
2. Brian Krebs, "Internet Sales Tax Effort on Hold Now," *Washington Post,* December 17, 2003, http://www.washingtonpost.com/wp-dyn/articles/A5949-2003Dec16.html.

tax (0.00276 mill), and various other property taxes. It would owe $446 a year in county property tax and $763 per year in state property tax (most state property tax rates are much lower than this).[12] All property taxes are usually collected on a single bill or two bills that arrive six months apart. This means that taxpayers are likely to be highly attentive to the total dollar amount they pay in property taxes (compared to what they pay in sales taxes—imagine if you received one large bill each year for all that you owed in sales taxes rather than paying it at each individual purchase). Depending on where the property is located, the bill may include taxes for the county, the city, the school districts, the state, and other special service districts (that is, library districts, port districts, and water districts).

In the first half of the 20th century, property taxes accounted for nearly all of municipal revenues. Today, the local government revenue mix is quite different. Because cities, counties, and towns now use a wider range of taxes and fees to raise revenue while also receiving funds from the national government and their state governments, property taxes now contribute

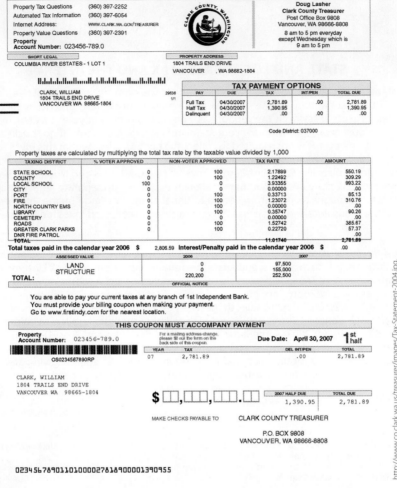

CLARK COUNTY TREASURER 2007 REAL PROPERTY STATEMENT

Property Tax Questions	(360) 397-2252
Automated Tax Information	(360) 397-6054
Internet Address:	WWW.CLARK.WA.GOV/TREASURER
Property Value Questions	(360) 397-2391
Property Account Number:	023456-789.0

Doug Lasher
Clark County Treasurer
Post Office Box 9808
Vancouver, WA 98666-8808

8 am to 5 pm everyday
except Wednesday which is
9 am to 5 pm

SHORT LEGAL	PROPERTY ADDRESS
COLUMBIA RIVER ESTATES - 1 LOT 1	1804 TRAILS END DRIVE
	VANCOUVER , WA 98682-1804

CLARK, WILLIAM
1804 TRAILS END DRIVE
VANCOUVER WA 98665-1804   29638   1/1

TAX PAYMENT OPTIONS

PAY	DUE	TAX	INT/PEN	TOTAL DUE
Full Tax	04/30/2007	2,781.89	.00	2,781.89
Half Tax	04/30/2007	1,390.95		1,390.95
Delinquent	04/30/2007	.00	.00	.00

Code District: 037000

Property taxes are calculated by multiplying the total tax rate by the taxable value divided by 1,000

TAXING DISTRICT	% VOTER APPROVED	NON-VOTER APPROVED	TAX RATE	AMOUNT
STATE SCHOOL		100	2.17899	550.19
COUNTY	0	100	1.22492	309.29
LOCAL SCHOOL	100	0	3.93355	993.22
CITY	0	0	0.00000	.00
PORT	0	100	0.33713	85.13
FIRE	0	100	1.23072	310.76
NORTH COUNTRY EMS	0	100	0.00000	.00
LIBRARY	0	100	0.35747	90.26
CEMETERY	0	0	0.00000	.00
ROADS	0	100	1.52742	385.67
GREATER CLARK PARKS	0	100	0.22720	57.37
DNR FIRE PATROL				.00
TOTAL			**11.01740**	**2,781.89**

Total taxes paid in the calendar year 2006 $ 2,806.59   Interest/Penalty paid in the calendar year 2006 $ .00

ASSESSED VALUE	2006	2007
LAND	0	97,500
STRUCTURE	0	155,000
TOTAL:	220,200	252,500

OFFICIAL NOTICE

You are able to pay your current taxes at any branch of 1st Independent Bank.
You must provide your billing coupon when making your payment.
Go to www.firstindy.com for the nearest location.

THIS COUPON MUST ACCOMPANY PAYMENT

Property Account Number: 023456-789.0

OS0234567890RP

For a mailing address change,
please fill out the form on the
back side of this coupon.

Due Date: April 30, 2007   **1st half**

YEAR	TAX	DEL INT/PEN	TOTAL
07	2,781.89	.00	2,781.89

CLARK, WILLIAM
1804 TRAILS END DRIVE
VANCOUVER WA 98665-1804

$ ☐☐,☐☐☐,☐☐☐.☐☐

2007 HALF DUE	TOTAL DUE
1,390.95	2,781.89

MAKE CHECKS PAYABLE TO   CLARK COUNTY TREASURER

P.O. BOX 9808
VANCOUVER, WA 98666-8808

0234 5678901101000027818900001390955

Property tax bills require a large lump sum payment. This example lists all the different local governments that tax a single property.

less overall to local budgets. Nonetheless, it is still the primary source of revenue for local governments. At the end of the 20th century, property taxes still generated 79 percent of all *local* tax revenues.[13] Cities, counties, school districts, and special districts (see Chapter 12) each levy their own property taxes.

The Property Tax Evaluated One traditional rationale for the property tax is that it taxes people who benefit the most from local public services. Property values are increased by public services, such as fire, police protection, and quality schools, so property taxes target people who benefit from these services. Historically, real property (land, homes, and farms) was the place where most Americans held their wealth. When fewer people owned property and fewer people invested their wealth in stocks and bonds, the wealthy had a greater share of their assets in real property. This made a tax on property relatively progressive.

In the contemporary era, however, homeownership is no longer something reserved for the wealthy. About two-thirds of American families now own a home. Moreover, for most middle-class families a home, is their primary investment and thus represents most of their wealth. In contrast, the wealthiest people today have much more of their wealth invested in paper assets. Property taxes—a flat rate—thus cost the poor (if they can buy a home) and the middle class a larger share of their wealth than they cost the wealthiest people. Some economists suggest contemporary property taxes are highly regressive.[14]

Property Taxes and Tax Rebellions This may explain why property taxes are consistently rated as the most unpopular tax by Americans.[15] Voters are particularly sensitive to property taxes. With sales and income taxes, marginal changes in rates don't tend to translate into increased hostility to the tax. Unlike the sales tax, property tax payments are made in a lump sum (unless built into monthly mortgage bills), which may add to the sting of the tax. One of the biggest political liabilities of the tax is that inflation in home values can drive up a person's tax burden much faster than any increase in their income. In booming housing markets, home prices may increased by 15–30 percent per year. Local governments are often required by law to reassess home values frequently, leading some homeowners to find steep increases in their property tax bills virtually overnight. Tax bills increased dramatically, not because elected officials raised the rates but because market demand increased home values.

This dynamic of rising home prices driving tax bills higher fueled a rebellion against property taxes in California (Proposition 13 in 1978) and Massachusetts (Proposition 2 1/2 in 1980) and led to an anti-tax movement[16] that has consequences to this day. Populist anti-tax advocates became fixtures in many states: Howard Jarvis (California), Bill Sizemore (Oregon), Tim Eyman (Washington), and Douglas Bruce (Colorado) rallied the public around anti-tax proposals they promoted via ballot measures. Policies that cut the property tax proved among their most popular proposals.

The success of ballot measures in several states and general demands for "tax relief" pressured legislatures across the nation to enact various laws that exempted property owners from new tax burdens resulting from rapid increases in the value of their homes and land. Exemptions date back to the 1930s, when states allowed poor homesteaders protections from foreclosure during the Great Depression. Today, many states make various exemptions for low-income households, veterans, and the elderly. Exemptions for agricultural land allow owners to resist pressures of selling to developers in order to avoid a growing tax burden. Exemptions, although popular, come at a cost of lost tax revenues for each level of government that collects property tax. Some states, such as Ohio, reimburse local governments for property tax revenues lost due to exemptions granted by the state.

Property tax revolts are not limited to the nation's hottest real estate markets and persisted long beyond the 1980s. In 2006, activists in 20 states were pushing for new property tax limits. Becky and Don Fagg of Lexington, South Carolina, saw their property taxes double in just five years as out-of-state buyers drove up local real estate prices and property assessments. The increased tax burden threatened their retirement plans, motivating Mrs. Fagg to form a group dedicated to abolishing taxes on a person's primary residence.[17] On the Olympic Peninsula in Washington that same year, Shelly Taylor and Jill Wilnauer reacted to rapid increases in their property taxes—increases produced by the heated local real estate market—by forming a group to press their state legislature to limit increases in the assessed value of homes to 1 percent per year. Hundreds of people crammed into a hall to attend the groups meeting where they announced their proposed constitutional amendment. The Washington amendment had not advanced as of 2007, but South Carolina used higher than expected sales tax revenues to reduce what homeowners would pay in property taxes in 2008.[18]

Other Revenue Sources

Given the political difficulties of relying on traditional tax sources, such as income, property, and general sales taxes, states and communities also generate revenues from taxes that are more narrowly targeted as well as direct charges for services. Over the last two decades, state and local governments are relying more heavily on some of these "other" sources of revenues and have been using them more than ever before.

Selective Sales Taxes

General sales taxes, discussed above, apply to most common purchases. Additional sales taxes are often levied on select items, such as fuel, alcohol, tobacco products, and public utilities. Sometimes, these taxes are referred to as excise taxes, or **sin taxes,** because they target behavior—such as drinking or smoking—that many people believe should be discouraged. If higher taxes actually cause people to consume less of the targeted item, the state may benefit. If demand for the item is **elastic** and responds to increases in prices, higher taxation will lead to less consumption of the item targeted with the tax. But if the tax applies to something that has **inelastic demand**—that is, something people must have regardless of the cost—a higher sin tax might not lower consumption.

Motor Vehicle Fuel Most of the revenues collected in this category come from state taxes on gasoline and diesel. Gas taxes are charged per gallon, with a state rate added on top of the $0.18 per gallon in tax going to the federal government. Most states add about another $0.20 per gallon—Alaska has the lowest ($0.08 per gallon), with Pennsylvania, Rhode Island, and Wisconsin having the highest (over $0.30 per gallon). The political acceptability of gas taxes may be enhanced by the fact that these funds are often dedicated to transportation expenses.[19] Gas taxes, as a share of a state's personal income, were lower in 2000 than they were in the 1960s and 1970s.[20]

Tobacco Products The proportion of state revenues from cigarette and tobacco taxes has been increasing recently. In several states that experienced tax rebellions in recent decades, citizens have actually voted to raise their state taxes. Or, at least, they voted to raise taxes on people who smoke.

On average, cigarette taxes have increased from $0.21 per pack in 1996 to $0.77 by 2006. Cigarette taxes have proved popular in part because they target an unpopular minority (smokers), with increases often linked to spending on public health programs. Voters in Washington and California, for example, approved cigarette tax increases that earmarked funds for health care (and antitobacco education). As a result of these taxes, cigarette prices now vary substantially across states. As of 2006, Rhode Island charged the most: $2.46 in state taxes per pack. New Jersey ($2.40), Washington, ($2.02), Michigan ($2.00), Maine ($2.00), and Montana ($1.70) were the next highest, respectively. It seems that proximity to Canada—where tobacco taxes are high—gives states greater ability to raise these taxes without fear that residents can buy their smokes elsewhere. Smoking is a much more affordable habit in the South, particularly in tobacco-producing states. South Carolina ($0.07), Missouri ($0.17), Mississippi (0.18), Tennessee ($0.20), and Kentucky, North Carolina, and Virginia (all three at $0.30) have the nation's lowest cigarette taxes.[21]

Alcoholic Beverages On average, states charge $0.24 in tax on a gallon of beer. Hawaii, which has no neighboring state to buy from, has the highest rate ($0.93 per gallon) and the nation's most expensive beer. Some of the cheapest beer in the United States can be found in Missouri (the home of Anheuser-Busch/Budweiser—which controls 45 percent of U.S. beer sales), Colorado (the home of Coors—which controls 10 percent of U.S. beer sales), Oregon (center of the U.S. microbrewing industry), and Wisconsin (the home of many thirsty Green Bay Packer fans, Miller, Pabst, and Stroh's Brewing—the latter three control 33 percent of U.S. beer sales). Beer taxes in each of these states, and in Wyoming, are under $0.08 per gallon. The distribution of beer taxes suggests that industries are able to avoid sin taxes in states where the industry is a key part of the economy. Wine taxes are also lowest in California ($0.20 per gallon), the nation's largest wine-producing state, and highest in Alaska and Florida, where wine should probably not be produced.

Although Rhode Island may seem like a leviathan when it comes to taxing smokes, the state is relatively libertarian when it comes to beer, taxing it at just $0.10 per gallon. Conversely, some states with low cigarette taxes have relatively high alcohol taxes (for example, South Carolina, Mississippi, and Virginia). Overall, the tax bite on smoking and drinking appears to be hardest in Alaska, Florida, and Hawaii (where tourists bear much of the costs) and lowest in Missouri, Kentucky, and Colorado.[22]

Direct Charges

Some of what state and local governments do can be funded by direct charges to the people who use a service, also know as **user fees.** For every $3.60 that state and local governments collect in taxes, another $1.00 is collected in user charges and fees. States generate billions in revenue by charging users of hospitals, highways, higher education, and other services. User charges for hospitals, sewers, garbage collection, airports, and parks contribute tens of billions of dollars to local government revenues. For the most part, none of these services are fully funded by charges to users, but fees reduce the amount of revenue from general taxes that would otherwise be used as funding.

Despite the names, user fees and charges are a source of revenue, just like any other tax. States and local governments have come to rely more heavily on fees and charges in recent years because they make it possible to avoid increasing visible taxes, such as sales or income tax. Critics of direct charges and fees argue that they can be highly regressive because people at all income levels often pay the same flat fee.

Estate Tax

Estate taxes are levied on savings and properties that a deceased person passes on to heirs. Critics of estate taxes argue that they force "family farms" to be broken up upon the death of a property owner and that they amount to double taxation because the property taxes are already paid by the person accumulating the wealth. Political opponents of estate taxes have successfully rebranded these as "death taxes," although they can be levied on the living person inheriting a person's wealth (rather than the dead person). Federal and state estate tax programs typically made exemptions for family farms, and as of 2005, the minimum value for an estate to owe the tax ranged from $670,000 to $1.5 million. This meant that the vast majority of people inheriting money are not affected by the tax.[23] Advocates of the estate tax—including Bill Gates Sr., father of one of the world's richest men—note that the estate tax is fair because it taxes wealth that was not earned by the person receiving it. Estate taxes may also be a way to tax accumulated wealth that has avoided taxation during a person's lifetime. The estate tax is also one of the few instruments of progressive taxation available to government. Gates estimates that the repeal of the estate tax would largely benefit future heirs of the United States' wealthiest estates—several of whom have funded the successful anti–estate tax lobbying effort.[24]

Critics of the estate tax have had the upper hand in national politics. In 2001, President George W. Bush signed a bill to repeal the federal estate tax until 2011. Until recently, most states didn't impose their own estate or inheritance taxes but collected an amount based on the federal estate tax. Because most states' estate taxes were linked to the federal tax, these taxes ended with the repeal of the federal estate tax, costing states several billion dollars per year. As of 2006, about half the states had instituted their own independent estate taxes to recapture some of this revenue.

Lotteries

Lotteries are seen by some as a form of voluntary taxation and have been popular enough to be approved by voters in many states. Lotteries were common in the 19th century, and lottery advocates point out they were used in 1776 to raise money for the Colonial Army.[25] Widespread corruption and strong opposition on moral grounds led to the elimination of government lotteries. No states had public lotteries again until 1964, when New Hampshire adopted a state lottery. Seven more states had lotteries by the 1973, but the lottery swept the nation after the tax revolts of the late 1970s and 1980s. Modern lotteries were promoted to state legislators and voters (by a corporation that prints the tickets and sells lottery equipment) as a politically painless way to raise revenues that could be earmarked for public education.[26] Although they are classified as a regressive tax[27], most tickets are purchased by middle- and upper-income people.[28]

Forty-one states now have lotteries, with North Carolina adopting a lottery in 2006. Most states have their lottery funds earmarked for education. North Carolina's gambling revenues—estimated at over $1 billion through 2010—are earmarked for education, but this allowed the state to reduce general revenues spent on education.[29] The North Carolina case suggests that lottery funds may simply replace general revenue funds spent on education, resulting in no net gain for schools. However, one national study found that earmarking rules matter. Every dollar of lottery profit earmarked for education increased state education spending by more than would be the case if the funds were not pre-dedicated to education.[30]

In 2004, 15 states had lottery sales well over $1 billion each, with nearly $50 billion in sales nationally.[31] However, only $14 billion of that was profit that contributed to state revenues. Most states dedicate their lottery revenues to education. However, because only a fraction of ticket sales end up as revenues, lotteries contribute a very small percentage to state funds, even to education budgets. One estimate is that states receive only 30 cents in revenue for every dollar wagered and that the yield has been in decline since the 1990s. In California, where profits are dedicated to education, the lottery provides less than 2 percent of all funds for the state's K–12 system.[32] Some evidence reveals that the market for the lottery is saturated: with so many states now running lotteries, and with competition from the growing tribal gambling industries, more places now exist for a limited number of gamblers to risk their money. States respond to declining sales by increasing payouts, which can result in modest revenues.

Gambling

All but two states (Hawaii and Utah) have dropped their prohibitions against all forms of gambling. The recent expansion of legal gambling facilities means that taxes on gross receipts from casino gambling are one of the faster-growing sources of state revenues. Indian nations are major players in expanding the American gambling industry (the industry prefers to refer to the business as *gaming*, not gambling). A tribe negotiates a compact with its state government about the scope of casino operations allowed in exchange for a certain share of the casino revenues. As tribes and states become more dependent on each other in this way, tribes have become some of the largest campaign donor for legislators in some states. For Nevada, gambling revenues are a method to export the state's tax burden to people from out of state.

Severance Taxes

Some states are blessed with valuable natural resources that provide a major source of revenues. Severance taxes are levied on resources "severed" from the earth or sea and are applied to resource extraction industries, such as fishing, mining, and oil and natural gas production. Taxes are levied on the volume of the resource extracted. When market prices for the resource are up, these revenues boom. If prices collapse, so do revenues. High energy prices as of 2007 meant that severance revenues were booming in resource-rich states. Alaska generated over 50 percent of state revenues from severance taxes, and Wyoming collected 45 percent. Three more states (New Mexico, North Dakota, and Oklahoma) collected at least 10 percent of state revenues from severance taxes. Texas collected more than twice as much as any state ($1.9 billion), but given Texas' diverse revenue system, this is only about 6 percent of the state's total tax collections. Most states lack the natural resources that make severance taxes a significant source of revenues.

Tax and Expenditure Limits

Property tax revolts of the 1970s were followed by more anti-tax and spending-limit ballot measures in many states. Elected officials in still more states embraced various policies designed to curb the growth of taxation and government spending. Known collectively as **tax and expenditure limitations (or TELs)**, these policies set formulas that determine by how much revenue and spending can grow. These formulas typically limit growth in spending or future revenues collected from existing sources to some level that keeps pace with inflation or population growth (or some combination). By 2005, 30 states had adopted some form of TELs: 23 had spending limits, four had tax revenue limits, and three had both.[33] Sixteen states also required legislative supermajority votes in order to pass a tax increase.

TELs are particularly attractive to people who accept the leviathan model of fiscal policy. However, substantial academic debate continues over whether TELs actually limit the growth of government expenditure over the long term. Several observers blame (or credit) California's Proposition 13 of 1978 with a dramatic reduction in revenue available for public services, particularly schools.[34] Others note that although property tax limits and spending limits affected which level of government raised revenues (shifting taxation from one level of government to another), overall spending was largely unaffected.[35] The first generation of TELs —particularly those enacted by legislators rather than via ballot initiatives—may not have had much effect on limiting the growth in taxation and spending.[36] It is difficult to evaluate the effects of these policies because the same formula limiting revenue growth (for example, a limit tied to population growth) might have quite different effects in a state with rapid population growth than in a state with no population growth.[37]

A second generation of TELs adopted in the 1990s and more recently may have more teeth than those adopted in the 1970s and 1980s.[38] Colorado's Taxpayer Bill of Rights (or TABOR) serves as an example. In addition to strict formulas limiting revenue growth, TABOR required a public referendum to approve any tax increase proposed in the legislature. One critical case study of TABOR suggests that it resulted in substantially reduced levels of government spending, with education and health care suffering.[39]

Effects of State Tax and Expenditure Limits

Although we noted that some debate ensues about whether TELs have systematic effects on reducing how much states tax and spend, it seems clear these policies do have effects—even some that may have been unintended. TELs may have adverse effects on a state's credit rating because they limit the government's discretion in raising funds needed to service debt.[40] In particular, strict tax limits may lead to higher borrowing costs for states because limits can make it hard to raise revenue needed to make debt payments.[41] States may avoid TELs by shifting spending authority to new programs and different jurisdictions. One study found that TELs enacted via the initiative led to the formation of new "special service districts" that operate park, library, fire, and other services—a way to tax and spend "off budget" by jurisdictions beyond the reach of state TELs.[42] Special districts can also provide a more direct method to ensure that beneficiaries of a public service are the ones who pay taxes for it.

REFORM CAN HAPPEN

COLORADO'S TABOR

Colorado voters approved a constitutional amendment in 1992, known as the "Tax Payers' Bill of Rights," or TABOR. Whereas many state TELs attempt to limit the growth of government with rules about spending growth, Colorado's TABOR focuses on limiting revenue growth. When writing a new budget, revenues from all sources (other than the federal government) cannot exceed the previous year's revenues by more than the rate of population growth, plus inflation. If the state's economy is booming, and tax collections are higher than that growth rate, any excess revenues must be returned to voters unless voters vote to spend the money. If the state's economy is in recession and revenues decrease, funds for the next year's budget are based on the recession year revenues, plus the allowed rate of growth. TABOR thus prolonged the effects of recessions on Colorado's budget by ratcheting down revenues for future, non recession years. In 2005, Colorado voters elected to suspend some of TABOR's provisions to allow the state to retain $3.7 billion in revenue growth that would otherwise have had to been returned to taxpayers.[1]

Notes

1. Tax Foundation, http://www.taxfoundation.org/research/show/283.html.

A comprehensive study of the general effects of direct democracy on state and local fiscal policy found that states with the ballot initiative process have more tax cuts, rely more on fees for revenues, and have shifted spending from the state to local levels. These state and local fiscal policies may reflect popular opinion in these states.[43]

Fiscal Federalism

State and local governments receive substantial money from the federal government to promote the federal government's goals in areas such as health care, urban renewal, education, and transportation. The relative power of the federal government and the states is often measured in dollars, with the efforts of federal and state governments to exert control over policies limited by their willingness to pay for such authority.

During the 1960s, the expansive social welfare programs under the Lyndon B. Johnson administration's Great Society led the federal government to become involved in virtually every state and local governmental activity. Between 1960 and 1968 (during which time

John F. Kennedy and Johnson, respectively, were president), the number of new federal grant programs available to state and local governments almost tripled, from 132 to 379, with federal aid to states and localities more than tripling, from $7 billion in 1960 to $24 billion in 1970.[44] In 2006, with a steady increase over time since the 1930s, the amount of annual transfers from the federal government to states and localities was more than $427 billion, including $62 billion in capital investments.[45]

The federal role in financing state and local government activity abated after the election of Ronald Reagan in 1980. Reagan's annual budgets eliminated or reduced funding for many programs established in the 1960s and 1970s. Welfare reform legislation, passed by President Bill Clinton in August 1996, also changed the federal role in funding state spending. Federal funds made up roughly 40 percent of state and local expenditures in 1980, but by 2006, they made up roughly 34 percent.[46]

The federal government's largess in aid to the states and their localities does not come free. The federal government uses a number of mechanisms to compel the states to spend the money according to the wishes of Congress. The federal government provides **grant-in-aid** to state and local governments. There are two general types of grants that the federal government uses to distributed funds to subnational governments.

Categorical grants limit how much discretion state and local governments have in using federal money. State and local governments apply for federal categorical grants that provide money for specific purposes, such as Head Start (a federally sponsored preschool program), urban forestry programs, flood mitigation assistance, or historic battlefield preservation. Some categorical grants have matching requirements, whereby the state or local government must pay part of the program's costs. Today, Congress provides about 600 different categorical grants to state and local governments. Since the 1980s, substantial federal dollars come to states and local governments through **block grants**. These were created to consolidate categorical grants, and are allocated by broad functional area (such as community development) rather than specific purposes. Block grants allow state and local governments more discretion over how, where, and on whom to spend the grants.

General Funds versus Non–General Funds

All of these various revenues may end up in different budgets before they are spent. Revenues collected from the general sales tax, income tax, and property tax often end up in a state or local government's general fund budget. Some states may also put their lottery revenues and other miscellaneous funds in their general budget. General fund revenues can typically be used for any purpose, so politicians have substantial discretion over how such revenues might be spent. Budget battles in the legislature, or between the legislature and the governor, largely center on what should be done with general fund revenues.

Revenues that are collected for a specific purpose or transferred to a state or community for a specific program often end up in a non–general fund budget. As example, most money that comes as transfers from the federal government is allocated to fund health and welfare programs and cannot be spent on other things. Likewise, tuition and fees collected by universities are dedicated to fund universities and cannot be spent on other programs. Gas taxes are often dedicated to road construction and transportation only, and most states earmark their lottery funds for education. This means that budget writers often have very little discretion over how non–general fund revenues can be spent. Over half of a state's total revenues may end up in a non–general fund budget. In Virginia's 2004–2006 budget, for example, 53 percent of all state revenues went into the non–general fund.

Adding It All Up: Variation in State Revenue Packages

Every state and local government has its own unique combination of revenue sources. When state revenue sources are displayed graphically, it's often in the form of a pie, with larger slices depicting the major revenue sources. Unfortunately, there's not one single pie to consider, as the overall mixture of state or local revenue can be expressed at least three ways. The first is to think in terms of the tax revenues a government generates on its own. But state and local taxes are only part of the story—governments also generate substantial revenues by charging for services. This means we must also consider these additional non-tax revenues as part of a government's revenue package. Finally, much of what state and local governments spend comes from funds transferred from other, higher levels of government, so a third way to express a government's revenue mix is to include all "own-source" revenues (taxes and other sources) plus transfers from other levels of government.

The Mix of State Revenues

The 50 states combined had nearly $1.3 trillion in annual revenue in 2005. To put that amount in perspective, the federal government collected about $1.5 trillion in annual revenue the same year (excluding Social Security).[47] Figure 10.1 illustrates the sources of all funds available to state governments. Of the $1.3 trillion available, about $874 billion were generated by states. This includes about $648 billion collected via state taxes, $123 billion in direct charges and fees collected by states, and about $103 billion from miscellaneous state revenue sources. Federal funds and direct charges allow states to spend about twice what they collect in taxes. Direct charges apply to users of state services and include college tuition, road tolls, park fees, and the like. As noted in Chapter 2, the federal gov-

ernment redistributes substantial funds back to the states each year—over $400 billion, mostly to fund health and welfare expenses shared between the state and federal governments.

About 74 percent of all state-generated (or own-source) revenues come from taxation, with another 14 percent from direct charges for services and 12 percent from interest earned on investments and other miscellaneous sources. Most revenue from direct charges for public services (paid only by those who use the services) comes in the form of tuition for higher education. This is one of the fastest-growing sources of funds for state governments.

Figure 10.2 focuses more narrowly on what the average state's mix of *tax* revenues might look like: about one-third coming from general sales tax (plus another 15 percent from "selective" sales taxes on things like gas, cigarettes, and alcohol), about one-third from individual income taxes (plus another 6 percent from corporate income taxes), 6 percent from license fees (mostly on vehicles), and the rest from miscellaneous taxes. Taxes bring in most, but by no means all, the revenues that states generate.

States vary tremendously in the mix of revenues they use to fund public services. A balanced package of revenues—just like a balanced stock portfolio—helps bring stability to a state's budget process through periods of economic recession. But can states thrive without having both an income and sales tax, the two main pillars of revenue systems? A few states endowed with natural resources or specialized industries avoid having to rely on one of the major taxes (income and sales). Alaska and Texas have generated tremendous revenue from oil and gas. Wyoming has profited from mining, Nevada from gambling, and Florida from tourism. These revenue sources export the burden of state taxes to people in other states, and allow these states to get by without income taxes. However, they may face budget crises when prices of their key commodity crash or if the tourist industry crashes (as Florida and Nevada learned after September 11, 2001).

Absent major tourism or natural resources, few states have the luxury of funding their

---

| Figure 10.1 |

Sources of All State Revenues, 2005

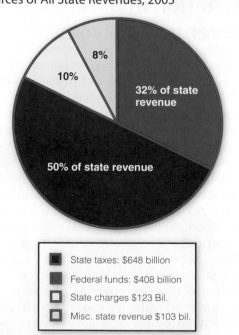

32% of state revenue

50% of state revenue

10%   8%

- ■ State taxes: $648 billion
- ■ Federal funds: $408 billion
- ☐ State charges $123 Bil.
- ☐ Misc. state revenue $103 bil.

Note: Total state revenues from all sources = $1.282 trillion. Total excludes $335 billion generated from insurance trust funds.

Source: U.S. Census Bureau, "Census of Governments 2005," http://www.census.gov/govs/state/0500usst.html.

operations without sales and income taxes—which, as just mentioned, are the two main pillars of state revenue. Those that have only one must rely heavily on it. Oregon lacks a sales tax, so it collects 70 percent of state revenues from the income tax. Washington lacks an income tax, so it must collect 60 percent of its revenues from the sales tax. New Hampshire has neither a general sales nor a general income tax and manages to balance its budget via frugality and having local governments fund many services. Although no state is average, most have revenue packages that look less like Washington, Oregon, Alaska, or New Hampshire and more like what is shown in Figure 10.2.

The Mix of Local Revenues

When transfers from higher levels of government are factored in, local governments collect about $1.16 trillion in revenues. Local governments, including cities, counties, school districts, and other special districts, collect just over $700 billion in locally generated taxes and charges, with the majority of this coming from the property tax.

Figure 10.3 illustrates that local governments collect 39 percent of this $1.16 trillion from local taxes, with a similar proportion of funds coming from transfers (mostly from their states). Most of these transfers are state funds dedicated to school districts and to cities and counties to cover their costs of running health programs. Another 16 percent of local funds

Figure 10.2

Sources of Tax Revenue Generated by State Governments, 2005

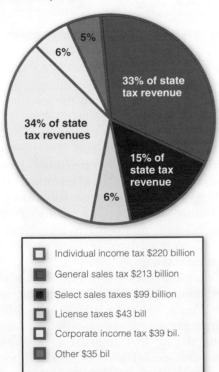

Individual income tax $220 billion
General sales tax $213 billion
Select sales taxes $99 billion
License taxes $43 bill
Corporate income tax $39 bil.
Other $35 bil

Note: Total state revenues generated by state taxes = $648 billion.

Source: U.S. Census Bureau, "Census of Governments 2005," http://www.census.gov/govs/state/0500usst.html.

Figure 10.3

Sources of All Local Government General Revenues, 2005

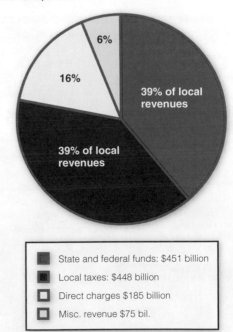

State and federal funds: $451 billion
Local taxes: $448 billion
Direct charges $185 billion
Misc. revenue $75 bil.

Note: Total local revenues = $1.160 trillion. Excludes $47 billion in revenues from insurance trusts and $99 billion from utilities.

Source: U.S. Census Bureau, http://www.census.gov/govs/estimate/0500ussl_1.html.

COMPARISONS HELP US UNDERSTAND

THIS RHODE ISLAND: A "SIN TAX" REVENUE MODEL TO EMULATE?

Concerns about social costs have limited the expansion of state-regulated gambling in some states. Others earn substantial revenues from gambling—from both Indian tribe operations and from other state-regulated games. Rhode Island collects a whopping $1,300 per capita in lottery and Video Lottery Terminal (VLT) sales.[1] Revenues from gambling made the tiny state 12th overall in the United States for *total* lottery revenues. The state lottery program was established in 1974, and thousands of VLTs have been located at racetracks since 1995. Over 11 percent of the state's general revenues came from gambling one year, whereas the U.S. average for states with a lottery is just 2 percent of revenues. Delaware, South Dakota, and West Virginia, which also make heavy use of VLTs, are the only states that rival Rhode Island in how much lottery and VLT revenue is generated per capita. Rhode Island also collects another 4 percent of all revenues from cigarette taxes. Rhode Island collects more from smoking and gambling than it does from inheritance taxes and general business taxes combined. Of course, size and location matter. Hardly any place in Rhode Island is more than 10 miles from Connecticut or Massachusetts. Many people from other states pass through Rhode Island, which might make it easy for the state to export its tax burden by selling them lottery tickets and cigarettes.

Notes

1. State of Rhode Island and Providence Plantations. 2005. Revenue Estimating Conference Memorandum. December 19.

"Money to Burn," an Oregon Video Lottery game that features a "5 cent firehouse-themed spinning reel game." Other games include "Rakin' It In," "Flush Fever," "Super Aces Bonus," and "Enchanted Unicorn," a "fantasy themed" game.

come from direct charges, mostly for hospitals and utilities.

When we focus only on the revenues that local governments collect themselves, we find that a local government's revenue package looks quite different from a state's revenues. Although most locally generated revenues come from local taxes, local governments rely much more on charges and fees than states do. Twenty-six percent of locally generated revenues come from user fees and charges for services, compared to 14 percent for state-generated revenues.

Figure 10.4 breaks down the sources of the $448 billion in taxes generated by local governments. Again, we see a substantially different picture when we compare locally generated tax revenue (Figure 10.4) to tax revenue generated at the state level (Figure 10.2). Local governments have a much less diversified tax portfolio compared to states, and they rely heavily on the property tax. School districts and special districts (districts that provide services such as fire protection or libraries) rely almost exclusively on property taxes.

Figure 10.4

Local Tax Revenues by Source, 2005

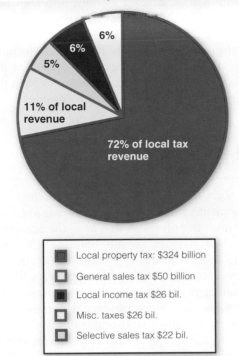

72% of local tax revenue

11% of local revenue

5%

6%

6%

- ■ Local property tax: $324 billion
- □ General sales tax $50 billion
- ■ Local income tax $26 bil.
- □ Misc. taxes $26 bil.
- □ Selective sales tax $22 bil.

Note: Total local tax revenues = $448 billion.
Source: U.S. Census Bureau, 2005, http://www.census.gov/govs/estimate/0500ussl_1.html.

Who Bears the Burden of State and Local Taxes?

Other than the income tax, most revenues that states and communities rely on are relatively regressive, compared to the federal tax structure. That is, those who earn less income pay more of their income in state and local taxes. At the same time, the wealthiest people, having far more income, pay more of the total dollars collected. Just as states and cities differ in the revenue packages they use, they also differ in terms of how regressive their taxes are. As Table 10.2 illustrates, the poorest 20 percent of a state's population can pay 12 to 18 percent of their income in state and local taxes, whereas the richest residents in the same state pay as little as 2 or 3 percent of their income in

state taxes. In some states (Delaware, Hawaii, Minnesota, and Montana), all income groups pay about the same share of their income in state taxes.

Why such differences? States that adopted the income tax early tend to rely on it more heavily, making their tax systems more progressive. A state's economy matters as well. States with larger manufacturing sectors and with wealthier people have more progressive revenue systems. Taxation may also be more progressive in states with strong competition between parties. A party out of power trying to win support from a broad base of voters may have an incentive to propose increased government spending for the poor and middle class, financed by taxes on the rich.[48] Economic growth and Democratic governors are also associated with more progressive taxation.[49] States that never adopted the income tax tend to have the most regressive overall revenue systems.

Since the tax revolt of the late 1970s, states and local governments have begun to rely more heavily on user fees (particularly direct democracy states) and specific sales taxes,

Table 10.2

The 10 Most Regressive State Tax Systems (taxes as shares of income for non-elderly residents)

	Taxes as a % of Income		
	Poorest 20%	Middle Poorest 20%	Top 1%
Washington	17.6	11.2	3.3
Florida	14.4	9.8	3.0
Tennessee	11.7	8.9	3.4
South Dakota	10.0	8.4	2.3
Texas	11.4	8.4	3.5
Illinois	13.1	10.5	5.8
Michigan	13.3	11.2	6.7
Pennsylvania	11.4	9.0	4.8
Nevada	8.3	6.5	2.0
Alabama	10.6	9.6	4.9

These states have no income tax.

such as cigarette taxes—trends that may make revenues more regressive over time.

When Do Taxes Go Up or Down?

Tax "innovation," or the adoption of new taxes, is a function of need and political opportunity. Factors that increase the need for new revenues also increase the likelihood that a government might adopt a new tax or raise an old one. Perhaps the most important thing motivating a state to adopt new taxes is, not surprisingly, fiscal hardship. States have not typically adopted new sales and income taxes during prosperous years. Although such taxes are unpopular, a fiscal crisis may make tax increases more palatable for voters and reduce the risk elected officials face when they increase taxes.[50]

Some research suggests that politicians also wait until after an election year to raise unpopular taxes, but the frequency of tax increases the year after a general election also reflects that some states budget for two years (a biennial budget). Budget that might reflect promises from the previous election are drawn in the first year of the biennium, after a new governor and legislature may have been elected. Less unpopular revenue sources—like the lottery or targeted user fees—may be more likely to be adopted in an election year as politicians try to avoid highly unpopular tax increases. New taxes adopted in one state may also be more likely if a neighboring state has already adopted the tax.[51] One prominent study suggests new taxes are more likely when the same party controls both the legislature and governor's office,[52] but others find evidence that this is not the case.[53] Similarly, politicians are more likely to increase existing taxes when the political costs are lowest; that is, when the next election is far away and the economy is bad.[54]

Taxes also go down. States often implement tax cuts when the economy is strong and revenues are growing. During the boom of the mid- to late 1990s, 44 states enacted tax cuts. Tax cuts are often packaged as a means to stimulate a state's economy, although one think-tank report suggests that states with the largest tax cuts of the 1990s had the biggest fiscal problems and were more likely to have their credit rating downgraded in the next decade. Between 2001 and 2006, states with the largest tax cuts had weaker job growth.[55]

What Are the Effects of Taxes?

Do taxes help or hurt long-run economic development? This is one of the more contentious questions in politics as well as in the academic world of economists and political scientists. Some economic theory assumes that growth depends on the development of physical and human capital; that is, on the amount that machines and people can produce. Human capital includes education, skill, and training. Physical capital can be seen in factories, tools, roads, and equipment. Traditional models of growth assume that taxes are just part of some equilibrium level of capital and that economic growth results from technical changes that increase productivity.

But things are more complex than this. There are different types of taxes—some might discourage the formation of human and physical capital, some might have fewer effects, and other taxes might actually encourage capital formation. And different taxes have different effects on how people spend their money and invest. In other words, the relationship between taxes and economic growth depends on how the money is raised and what it is spent on. Taxes that are spent on education, for example, can generate positive effects on the formation of human capital—effects that a private market might not produce.[56] However, the personal income tax might also discourage entrepreneurial activity.[57] Taxes on corporate earnings, on the other hand, might discourage economic growth,[58] but when corporate taxes are low relative to high personal income taxes, entrepreneurial activity might be encouraging because people have greater incentives to incorporate businesses.[59]

Some studies show positive effects of state taxation on state economic growth, and some studies find negative effects.[60] Results are sensitive to the statistical methods used, the time period examined, and the tax or spending patterns that are examined. Studies of state taxing and spending from the 1950s found no relationship between taxes and growth.[61] Some studies from the 1970s and early 1980s found a negative relationship, with one noting that welfare spending harmed economic growth, whereas business taxes increased growth.[62] Further evidence shows that state tax increases used to fund welfare payments depress economic growth;[63] however, state taxes spent on education, highways, and public health and safety have been shown to have favorable impacts on the location decisions of businesses.[64]

One overview of these studies concluded that most found "a weak or insignificant relationship between taxes and economic performance" because they failed to account for what taxes were spent on. Taxes dedicated to health, education, and highways were found to have a positive effect on private investment and employment in a state, but welfare spending had a negative effect. The authors concluded that their findings should not be interpreted as a prescription for curtailing welfare spending. They noted, rather, that states face a "vicious cycle" in a prolonged economic slump. They risk crowding out public investment in health, education, streets, and highways if they increase welfare spending alone, but raising taxes to fund public investment *and* welfare may further depress the economy.[65]

The Growth of State Governments

The size of government can be thought of in terms of the proportion of the total economy that is taxed and spent by government. Whatever the effects of taxing and spending, state governments are now much larger than they were 50 years ago. When the size of the economy is measured as the sum of everyone's personal income, state governments spent about $0.04 of each dollar of personal income in 1950. Today, they spend about $0.16 of each dollar.[66]

Nearly all of this growth in the size of state government occurred from 1950 to 1970. Growth was driven by massive state investments in education and highways during this period. Prior to the 1950s, the federal highway system was nonexistent, and states spent much less on infrastructure. This growth period was also when many states were building new public universities. California, for example, spent heavily on public investment in the 1950s and 1960s, building multibillion-dollar water projects, five new University of California campuses, eight new California State University campuses, and dozens of community colleges.

With highway construction on the wane by the late 1960s and the political revolts against taxation taking effect in the late 1970s, the size of state government peaked around 1978 and then declined through the 1980s. After the federal government shifted responsibility for welfare to the states in the 1990s, the size of state government began a steady increase back to levels seen in the late 1970s.[67]

Trends in State and Local Revenues

Governments have grown in size since the 1950s. With this growth and with changes in the economy, the mix of revenues that now fund state governments has changed. Federal revenues sent to the states increased sharply from 1955 through 1975 and now play a larger role in state budgets than they did 50 years ago. States now collect about twice as much of their overall revenues from income taxes than they did 50 years before and have been relying more on fees and charges (tuition) to fill out their revenue portfolios since the 1980s. Although states have increased their reliance on federal funds, income taxes, and fees, a much smaller proportion of state revenues is now generated by selective sales taxes on gasoline.[68]

As states struggle to recover from the 2002 recession, they appear to be relying on ways to raise revenues that present the least political challenges. An overview of budget proposals from the state's governors for 2006–2007 found that the largest increase in revenues would be coming from cigarette taxes (nearly $1 billion in new revenues). The next largest source of new funds was from fees (tuition). Governors proposed much more modest increases in state sales taxes while reducing net revenues collected via the personal income tax.[69] If these choices mark a trend, state revenue sources may grow more regressive over time.

Where Does the Money Go? Government Spending

Discussing state and local revenue sources before examining what government spends the money on is a bit like putting the cart before the horse. Revenues are generated in large measure to satisfy public demands for programs and services and to fund budget drivers—the major programs that state and local governments operate.

Figures 10.5 and 10.6 illustrate the major program spending areas for state and local governments, respectively. State and local governments combine to spend about $2.6 trillion: $1.3 trillion by the 50 states and $1.3 trillion by local governments.

Social Services: Health Care

Thirty-six percent of money spent by states funds social services. Social service spending, the largest and fastest-growing component of state budgets, is dominated by health care. When looking at Figure 10.5, it is important to remember that a large part of overall state spending is financed by the federal government. Most of the federal dollars going to states are from the **Medicaid** program (see Chapter 14). Medicaid accounts for most of state social service spending—about 20 percent of *all* state

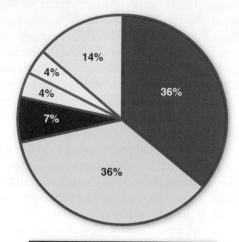

Figure 10.5

Major State Government Spending Programs, 2005

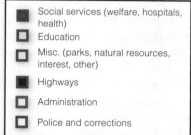

- ■ Social services (welfare, hospitals, health)
- □ Education
- □ Misc. (parks, natural resources, interest, other)
- ■ Highways
- □ Administration
- □ Police and corrections

Note: Total direct state expenditures = $1.281 trillion. Excludes $167 billion in insurance trust and pension payments.
Source: U.S. Census Bureau. 2005. State and Local Government Finances by Level of Government and by State: 2005. http://www.census.gov/govs/state/0500usst.html.

expenditures.[70] Given the absence of national health care insurance and the high costs for private health insurance, states are left with much of the responsibility for providing health care to the 47 million Americans who are uninsured. Federal funds come with standards that define minimal levels of service the states must provide, and federal dollars are given to match state spending on Medicaid. If states want to provide additional health care beyond the minimal standards—for example, offering prenatal care or providing basic health care insurance for the working poor—they must spend more.

Figure 10.6

Major Local Government Spending Programs

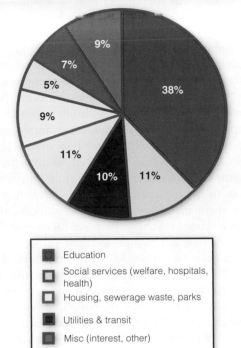

- ■ Education
- □ Social services (welfare, hospitals, health)
- □ Housing, sewerage waste, parks
- ▨ Utilities & transit
- ■ Misc (interest, other)
- □ Police, fire, corrections
- ■ Admin
- □ Highways, airports

Note: Total direct local government expenditures = $1.3 trillion. Excludes $27 billion in insurance trust expenditures.

Source: U.S. Census Bureau, Census of Governments. http://www.census.gov/govs/estimate/0500ussl_1.html.

A growing proportion of social service spending is used to fund prescription drug purchases.

Because spending on hospitals, long-term care for the elderly, mental health, and other health care–related services comprise the single-largest part of a state's budget, health care spending is the largest target for cuts in times of economic downturn. Given the size of health care in the overall state budget, it is nearly impossible to reduce spending without rolling back reimbursement rates paid to health care providers (doctors, hospitals, and nursing homes), freezing reimbursement levels, or cutting back on the number of people eligible for benefits. In times of fiscal crunch, states will cut back on health care, even if it means losing federal Medicaid matching dollars.[71] Nonetheless, the proportion of state spending on health care has been growing. Local governments, in contrast, spend much less on social services, as these programs are largely administered by the states.

Social Services: Aid to the Poor

Assistance to the poor, or welfare programs, works in a similar manner as medical benefit programs. Federal government funds are sent to the states and topped up by a state if it expands services offered or people who are eligible. Cash assistance to the poor represents a much smaller proportion of state spending on social services than health care: less than 20 percent of all social service spending. Social welfare programs include transferring cash to individuals and providing services. In 1996, Congress passed the Temporary Assistance to Needy Families (TANF) block grant program and shifted much of the responsibility for welfare assistance programs from the national government to the states. The TANF program also represented a contraction of total welfare benefits. By 1998, states and communities were spending 20 percent less on cash assistance to the poor than they were in 1992.[72]

Education

The second-largest area of direct state spending illustrated in Figure 10.5 is education—35.6 percent of total spending by the states. But if we consider state money spent by local school districts, education would be the single-largest area of state spending. The amount of state funds spent on education is actually much larger than what is suggested by Figure 10.5 because states transfer hundreds of billions of dollars to local governments to fund K–12 schools. Local schools have their own revenue source (local property taxes), but state funds are used to supplement what schools raise in local taxes. Because these funds are actually spent at the local level, they are included in our picture of the local government spending mix (Figure 10.6). If we had illustrated state spending just as a percentage of state-generated funds (excluding federal funds for social programs), education would be the largest area of state expenditure. Figure 10.5 illustrates funds that are spent directly by the state, and omits state funds spent by local school districts.

Unlike local K–12 schools, state colleges and universities have no local tax revenues and are totally reliant on state funds and tuition they collect from students. The majority of direct state spending on education (80 percent) goes to operate universities and colleges. The National Association of State Budget Officials notes that "when the state fiscal picture darkens, higher education often is the first category of spending to cut." Colleges and universities are an easy target because they are one of the largest state services that allow costs, however painful, to be transferred to users (students or their parents). Many states responded to the 2002 fiscal crisis by accelerating the shift toward financing higher education with higher direct charges (fees and tuition), while reducing general fund revenues spent. Over the decade that ended in 2004, tuition and fees increased 47 percent at public four-year universities.[73]

Figure 10.6 illustrates that education is the largest component of local government spending— 38 percent of all local expenditures, 94 percent of which is spent on elementary and secondary education (K–12 schools). Most of this money is raised by local property taxes or provided by the states and is spent by local school districts. The largest cost of education is labor: paying salaries for teachers, counselors, school administrators, technology staff, cooks, and so on.

Pensions and Unemployment

A major component of state expenditures is payments from insurance and trust funds. States spend about as much on these programs as on higher education, but they are considered "off budget" because they have their own funding sources. States maintain various trust funds to provide unemployment coverage for state residents or to provide compensation to residents who cannot work because they were injured on the job. States also maintain pension funds to cover their own employees' retirement payments, some of which provide rather generous benefits. In theory, these can be "pay as you go" programs. Workers pay weekly or monthly contributions into an unemployment insurance fund, for example, and are eligible for benefits if they lose work. Likewise, the state, as an employer, matches public employees' contributions to public pension funds to create a pool of money to cover future retirement benefit costs for state workers and public school teachers. Pension funds may be invested in order to increase their value.

In practice, things do not always work this way. When revenues are low, some states and cities forgo contributing to trust funds or borrow from the funds in order to make it appear that their budgets balance. In 2002, state and local employee pension funds were $30 billion in deficit. States have full responsibility for workers' comp and unemployment programs, so these programs do not factor into the local spending mix. For many state governments and some local governments, obligations to fully fund public employee retirement pension accounts may be a looming crisis. It is easy to forgo collecting revenues to cover the costs of pension funds, but if the deficits in such accounts grow over time, it may be harder to make up lost ground. A 2004 survey of cities found 79 percent reporting that their pension funds' fiscal health was eroding. San Diego's public employee pension fund was nearly $2 billion in deficit in 2004. The city had been providing lavish benefits while reducing payments into the fund. When a stock market crash reduced the value of the fund, the city faced bankruptcy.[74]

Transportation and Highways

About 7 percent of state spending and 5 percent of local spending are for transportation. Most state expenditures on transportation are funded by earmarked revenues placed in special non–general fund accounts, usually from gasoline taxes. Federal funds are also directed to the states for highway construction and cover about 30 percent of transportation spending. States also finance highways with bonds. Transportation represents the largest part of state spending in capital budgets. States spend more on transportation infrastructure than they do on building prisons, universities, housing, and all other infrastructure combined.

Government Administration and Debt Interest

Four percent of state and 7 percent of local expenditure are used to operate public buildings, run court systems (including paying public defenders, judges, and prosecutors), and fund general administrative costs.

Public Safety, Police, and Prisons

Four percent of state spending and 9 percent of local spending finance public safety programs. At the state level, 66 percent of public safety costs fund corrections operations (mostly salaries for prison guards and other staff); most of the remainder pays for state troopers (highway patrols). The operation of prisons is a growing part of state budgets. At the local level, most spending in this area supports local police forces.

Do State and Local Spending Actually Reflect What People Want?

Much of governing involves responding to the popular demands for spending. Thus, if a state's population consistently tells politicians they want more spent on schools and playgrounds, we might expect more spent on schools and playgrounds. Likewise, if voters routinely approve taxes and bonds for parklands, we might expect legislators to interpret this as a signal to spend money on recreation amenities. But there are other factors that might drive spending away from what most voters (or the average voter) might want. This raises at least two questions: How much do state and local spending reflect what people really want? And how much *should* they reflect what most people want?

In addition to trying to determine the preferences of the general public, elected officials hear from many different interest groups who each want some unique benefit just for themselves: a tax break here, a new road there, higher salaries for prison guards or professors, more spending on somebody's favorite program—public funds to help all sorts of relatively narrow concerns. In many legislative hearings, representatives of rather narrow constituencies may outnumber everyone else.

Governing involves the need to balance these demands and the ability to anticipate other things that also need to be done. These may include things the public might not be paying much attention to or that they might not want to spend much money on. Courts' interpretations of state and federal constitutions often force states to spend millions to reduce prison crowding. The business climate in part of a state may be threatened by traffic gridlock, forcing politicians to find ways to fund transportation options in that area. Even lightly used bridges, levees, and tunnels will eventually need maintenance or modernization to meet new safety or seismic standards. The fact that these matters may require public investment does not necessarily mean that the public supports such spending.

Part of writing a public budget, then, includes spending on some things many people do not want. Furthermore, critics of government spending suggest politicians and bureaucrats inflate public spending for their own purposes and that **fiscal illusion** allows them to hide much of what they spend from the public's eyes by using revenue sources that are hard to notice.[75] Finally, some studies found that state spending levels had nothing to do with whether Democrats or Republicans were in office.[76] All of this has been used to argue that elections, public opinion, and politics generally have little, if anything, to do with how much a government spends.

Why Is Spending Higher in Some States?

It might come as little surprise that states with more wealth tend to spend more.[77] Wealthy states have a greater tax base, and they also have more complex economies that create demands for rules and regulations—the basic stuff of government. Federal funds, rather than replacing state money, also seem to increase state spending. States that receive more money from the federal government also spend more of their own funds for public services.[78]

One of the primary determinants of spending, however, is political. States where people have more liberal opinions tend to elect liberals, who, regardless of party, spend more on public services. States where people have more conservative opinions tend to elect conservatives, who spend less. Even after accounting for a state's income, liberal states spend more per pupil on education and have more expansive Medicaid and welfare programs.[79] States also spend more on welfare when less affluent voters turn out in higher proportions in state elections.[80]

Budgeting

Deficits and Balanced Budget Requirements

If the federal government decides it wants to spend more than it is collecting in taxes, it can. The federal government can finance its operations by selling long-term U.S. Treasury bonds. Investors buy the bonds and earn interest on their investment over time. This allows for long-term borrowing to finance the annual operations of the federal government. In recent decades the federal budget has been in deficit more

years than not, which means a large percentage of each federal budget includes funds to pay interest on bonds that are outstanding. Critics of chronic federal deficits look to state **balanced budget rules** as a model for fiscal reform.

Borrowing

State governments cannot run deficits—at least not in the same way the federal government does. Virtually all states—Vermont is the only exception—have constitutional rules that require annual (or biannual) spending to not exceed revenues. Many states actually write two budgets, with balanced budget rules applying to the state's **operating budget.** Operating funds cover spending on services, salaries, and purchases of supplies. States might borrow funds in the short term to manage cash flow problems during the year (some tax collections peak in certain months, but government expenses, such as paying salaries, are more constant). Short-term debts are supposed to be repaid by the end of the budget cycle. **Capital budgets** can be a separate matter; states and local governments issue long-term bonds to finance capital investment in roads, bridges, buildings, and other infrastructure. Capital budgets may be funded with long-term borrowing, which is a form of deficit spending. Borrowing, rather than paying costs up front, can be seen as a fair way of paying for infrastructure that will be in use for years. Paying for a road, a bridge, or a sports arena all at once means that some of those who paid for it will die or move away before the project is completed and thus never benefit from it.

In addition to having balanced budget rules, some states require that voters approve the sale of any bonds that will be used to finance long-term borrowing. Some also require a supermajority vote in the legislature before the proposal can go to voters for approval.

Do Budgeting Rules Matter?

But do these budgeting rules really make any difference? Some balanced budget rules have weak provisions for enforcement. Most studies suggest that tough rules do work at preventing deficits when they are combined with limits on government borrowing, but weak rules do not.[81] Some rules simply require the governor to submit a balanced budget to the legislature or require the legislature to enact a balanced budget at the start of the fiscal year. But a state with such rules may still be allowed to run a deficit if revenue or spending estimates end up wrong.[82] Rules that simply require the budget to be balanced when written may be less effective than rules that require it to be balanced at the end of the year. Likewise, constitutional rules may be more effective than regular laws that politicians can easily amend. Finally, balanced budget rules may be more effective when enforced by an independently elected state supreme court than when enforcement depends on a court appointed by the politicians who write the budget.[83] One study noted that balanced budget rules were more effective when Republicans were in office.[84]

Some rules regulating long-term capital borrowing don't necessarily lead to less state indebtedness. Requiring a **supermajority vote** in the legislature for transportation infrastructure bills, for example, may create incentives to place a transportation project in every representative's district.[85] Even voters seem more likely to approve state-level borrowing if a project is proposed for their local area.[86]

Budget Surpluses

Independent of whatever these balanced budget rules may produce, states have a fairly predictable record of not only balancing their budgets but also ending with a surplus. In many years, states maintain a surplus "rainy day fund" to be used in times of crisis. When 50 state budges were considered across a 40-year period starting in 1961 (that is, 2,000 different budgets), 83 percent produced surpluses. Texas and New Mexico ran in the black every single year. Although Massachusetts (52 percent of budgets had a surplus), Hawaii (55 percent), and Rhode Island (60 percent) were least likely to run surpluses, they usually did.[87] With state governments usually running surpluses, they

soften the effects that federal deficits might have on the national economy. States and communities run deficits at their own peril. Lenders charge states more in interest if they have more debt (relative to the size of their economies).[88]

There may be a political risk, however, in maintaining a large "rainy day fund." A large surplus can become a target for anti-tax activists, as it illustrates that government is collecting more revenue than it needs to spend. California's tax revolt of the 1970s occurred when the state was running a multibillion-dollar surplus. Washington voters also slashed their motor vehicle tax in the late 1990s when the state was running a surplus.

Boom to Bust Budgeting

When the national economy was booming in the 1990s and tax revenues were rising in nearly every state, it was relatively easy to adopt new spending programs while also balancing budgets or running a surplus. When the national economy cooled after 2001, however, most states had difficulty balancing their budgets. By the 2003–2004 budget cycle, 44 states faced deficits when they began to draft their budgets. Many were left with spending commitments made during a period of unprecedented (and unsustainable) revenue growth. Several (Alaska, Kansas, New Jersey, New York, Oregon, and Washington) had deficits projected at more than 20 percent of available revenues if they were to simply maintain spending at the previous year's levels.

Budgeting in recession years, however, can encourage great creativity. In addition to cutting spending and raising taxes, states responded by delaying payments they owed, raising tuition, offering early retirement programs to lower salary costs, expanding gambling, raiding transportation and pension funds, mortgaging funds awarded in a settlement with tobacco companies, and borrowing money to fund operations. Only two states managed to use rainy day funds to help balance their budget (Louisiana and Mississippi). Smokers helped at least half-a-dozen states balance their books by paying higher cigarette taxes.

The most dramatic case of boom to bust budgeting resulting from the 2001–2002 recession was in California, where income tax revenues exploded in the 1990s as people cashed in on stock options in the superheated tech industry. During the 1990s, the state increased spending on K–12 education, expanded medical care eligibility, froze tuition, and cut taxes while balancing its budget. A recession began in March 2001, the tech bubble burst, and tax revenues from stock options and capital gains taxes fell from $17 billion to $6 billion between 2001 and 2002. By 2003, California faced a $38 billion deficit if it was to maintain its previous year's spending—a deficit equal to 40 percent of projected spending.[89] To put that in perspective, that was a deficit larger than the entire biennial (two-year) budget for Virginia. In 2004, California voters approved the sale of $15 billion in bonds to cover part of their deficit, but interest payments on these bonds are projected to consume 7.5 percent of general fund spending by 2009.

California's sustained fiscal crisis, although an extreme case, was not unique. The 2001–2002 economic downturn was one of the mildest recessions since World War II. Despite this, the effect of this recession on state revenues was deeper and more enduring than any other recession in the post–World War II period. California was not alone in expanding spending while cutting taxes in the boom years of the 1990s.[90] The net tax revenues collected by all states combined, in dollar amounts, was cut every year from 1995 to 2002.[91] Many are still recovering from these decisions. The total deficit for all states reached $80 billion by 2004. Despite an improving economy, deficit forecasts reemerged in California and other states for 2007.

Summary

In surveys of state and local fiscal politics from previous decades, the taxing and spending patterns of states and communities were often explained largely in terms of "environmental" factors. That is, wealthy states were said to spend more because they had more. Political factors, such as public opinion, budgeting rules, and other partisan and institutional forces, were largely dismissed because most studies found little effect of politics on fiscal policy.

The dismissal of political and institutional forces was probably a mistake resulting from flawed measures of political influence and from a lack of investigation. We now have detailed measures of state public opinion and decades of research examining the effects that taxing and spending limits (TELs), balanced budgeting rules, direct democracy, and popular opinion have on taxation and spending. Although some debate the magnitude of the effects of such rules, or of public opinion, it is clear that politics matters, perhaps more than anything else, in determining who gets what from government via fiscal policy.

Keywords

Balanced budget rules	Fiscal illusion	Regressive tax
Block grants	Flat rate tax	Sin tax
Capital budget	Inelastic demand	Supermajority vote requirement
Categorical grants	Leviathan	
Cost of living allowances (COLAs)	Medicaid	Tax equity
Elastic demand	Operating budget	Tax and expenditure limits (TELS)
Elasticity	Progressive tax	User fees

Suggested Readings

Beamer, Glenn. 1999. *Creative politics: Taxes and public goods in a federal system.* Ann Arbor: University of Michigan Press.

Briffault, Richard. 1996. *Balancing acts: The reality behind state balanced budgets.* New York: Twentieth Century Fund Press.

Brunori, David. 2005. *State tax policy: A political perspective*, 2nd ed. Washington, DC: Urban Institute Press.

Crain, W. Mark. 2003. *Volatile states: Institutions, policy, and state economies.* Ann Arbor: University of Michigan Press.

Forsythe, Dall W. 2004. *Memos to the governor: An introduction to state budgeting*, 2nd ed. Washington, DC: Georgetown University Press.

Garand, James, and Kyle Baudoin. 2004. Fiscal policy in the American states. In *politics in the American states: A comparative analysis*, 8th ed., edited by V. Gray and R Hanson. Washington, DC: CQ Press.

Smith, Daniel A. 1998. *Tax crusaders and the politics of direct democracy.* New York: Routledge.

Thurmaier, Kurt M., and Katherine G. Willoughby. 2001. *Policy and politics in state budgeting.* Armonk, NY: M. E. Sharpe.

Websites

Cato Institute (http://www.cato.org): A conservative organization that provides policy analysis "based on individual liberty, limited government, free markets and peaceful international relations."

Center for Budget Policy Priorities (http://www.cbpp.org): A liberal organization that conducts research on the needs of low-income families and the impact of policies on state budgets. Works with states and nonprofit groups to advocate for the needs of low-income families. Provides analysis of state fiscal policy.

Federation of Tax Administrators (http://www.taxadmin.org): Comparative information on state tax rates and state tax agencies.

National Association of State and Provincial Lotteries (http://www.naspl.org): Represents lottery organizations and provides reports about revenues from state lotteries.

National Association of State Budget Officers (http://www.nasbo.org): Professional organization for all state budget officers. An independent association with membership consisting of the heads of state budget offices and state finance departments. Provides reports on trends in the fiscal condition of the states.

National Council of State Legislators (http://www.ncsl.org): An organization that provides research, technical assistance, and other information to state legislators. Provides reports on state and federal relations and on key policy issues.

U.S. Census Bureau, Census of Governments (http://www.census.gov/govs/www/): Detailed data on state and local expenditures and revenues.

Jon Arnold/Danita Delimont

The Structure of Local Governments

OUTLINE

Introductory Vignette

Introduction

Forms of Local Government

The Rise of Urban America

Urban Party Machines

Who Benefited from the Machines?

The Urban Reform Movement

Consequences of Municipal Reforms

Summary

Who Is in Charge? Weak and Strong Mayors

In March 1991, the Los Angeles Police Department's brutal beating of African-American motorist Rodney King was captured on video. The tape was played repeatedly on television news, leading many to view the LAPD as a racist organization. The LAPD already had a strained relationship with the black community in south Los Angeles after aggressive responses to gang violence in the area. The LAPD's chief, Daryl Gates, also had a reputation for being arrogant and racially insensitive. He had been quoted as saying that African-American suspects occasionally died while in choke holds "because their veins or arteries don't open up like normal people" and for saying drug users should be "taken out and shot." After the King beating, local politicians, community organizations, and national figures, such as Jesse Jackson and Al Sharpton, called for Gates to be dismissed.

Mayor Tom Bradley, however, had no power to hire or fire his city's police chief. Those decisions were controlled by an independent, five-member Police Commission designed to function like a corporate board of directors. Although the mayor appointed the police commissioners, he could not control the commission's decisions. Political control of the police chief was further limited because the Los Angeles City Charter gave the Police Commission little power to discharge the chief. The charter granted the chief "substantial property right" to his job. The intent of the LA Charter, drafted in 1925, was to remove political control of city affairs from "politicians" and place it in the hands of professional managers. Architects of the city charter expected that city departments would be corrupted if politicians had direct control over them.[1]

Mayor Bradley asked Gates to resign on April 2, 1991, but Gates refused. The Police Commission also tried to suspend Gates but could not due to Gates's status as a civil servant. Gates remained in office. On April 29, 1992, the officers involved in the beatings were acquitted of all charges by a California jury. Violent riots began in Los Angeles shortly after the verdict was announced. On the first evening of the rioting, Gates attended a fundraising dinner and announced that the situation would soon be under control. Rioting lasted for three days and left 53 dead. Gates remained in office until late June 1992, when he finally resigned.

Mayors in some other cities, in contrast, have far more power to hire and fire city employees. When New York City mayor Michael Bloomberg saw a city employee playing solitaire on a city computer in 2006, he fired the man on the spot with no warning or severance pay. In 2001, the mayor of St. Petersburg, Florida, fired that city's chief of police for racial insensitivity after the chief compared a black motorist's appearance to that of an orangutan.[2] The mayor of Baltimore fired the head of the city's police force after the chief was accused of beating his girlfriend.[3] In this chapter, we learn why the powers of these local elected officials vary so widely and learn why some public employees are more insulated from political control than others. Politics in Los Angeles, and similar cities, is shaped heavily by institutional reforms designed to limit political control of municipal functions. Cities like Baltimore and New York City, in contrast, have traditions of unfettered political control of the administration of city departments.

Mayors of America's two largest cities differ in the powers they have to control city departments. New York's charter grants Mayor Michael Bloomberg substantial power to hire and fire personnel. Former Los Angeles Mayor Tom Bradley is shown here with Chief Willie Williams in 1993. Williams was hired by the LA Police Commission after Chief Daryl Gates resigned.

Introduction

The structure of American local governments today is the product of reforms that redesigned political institutions at the beginning of the 20th century. Some of these reforms have been discussed briefly in other parts of this book: nonpartisan local elections and direct democracy, for example. These are part of a larger package of institutional changes that fundamentally redefined how state and local politics work in much of the United States. Local political party organizations, or "party machines" that controlled public offices in many American cities in the 19th century, were the primary target of these reforms. We begin with a brief description of the major forms of local governments in the United States today and then examine the "machine" origins of American cities in order to understand how these local institutions have evolved into what they are today.

Many Americans might take for granted—or resent—the vast array of local governments in the United States. Local governments, including municipalities, counties, school districts (these are discussed in Chapter 15), and numerous special service districts, provide a wide array of public services. Many Americans today reside in a town or city that is part of a larger county. Scattered across those two levels of government are school districts and various special districts that provide services to your place of residence. Given all these different types of local governments, your place of residence is likely located in several local governments simultaneously.

Forms of Local Government

Municipalities

Each state has its own unique rules about how municipal governments (cities, towns, and villages) are structured and how new municipalities are incorporated. Municipalities, like all local governments, are limited to doing only what their state says they may do. This concept, commonly known as **Dillon's rule**, means that a state legislature can make different rules about how various municipalities in a state might function. Many states have one set of rules for large cities (or special rules that affect only one city) and other rules for smaller municipalities. As we see below, these rules define what these places do and how they may do it. Larger, older cities often provide a wide range of general services—including police, fire protection, building inspections, water service, and many others. As we see in Chapter 12, new cities may provide fewer services.

Counties

States are divided into geographic areas that perform some of the same functions as municipalities. Most states refer to these as *counties*, although they are known as *boroughs* in Alaska and *parishes* in Louisiana. Municipalities exist within counties,[4] and counties provide general services to portions of the county that are unincorporated (that is, outside city or town boundaries). Some counties contract with smaller cities and towns to provide a service the municipality does not offer. The range of public services provided varies substantially across the 3,000 counties in the United States. Counties are, traditionally, administrative and record-keeping jurisdictions for their states. County governments are thus often responsible for recording property records, conducting property tax assessments, administering elections, law enforcement, running jails, running courts, maintaining roads, and processing birth and death records.

Modern county governments have assumed many of the same responsibilities as large municipalities. In some ways, counties do even more than many large cities. Much of the federal and state money for health programs is spent in county hospitals and through county-administered health programs. Some states rely heavily on counties to regulate land use and development.

Special Districts

Special districts, or *single-purpose governments*, typically provide one particular service for an area. School districts may be the best-known single-purpose governments, but special districts supply dozens of different services (e.g., flood control, soil conservation, fire protection, and libraries). As of 2002, there were over 35,000 special districts in the United States. The geographic footprint of a special district may cut across city or county lines. As we see in the next chapter, a high density of special districts in an area can reduce the number of functions that a municipality might be engaged in.

The Rise of the Urban United States

Despite the huge number of cities, counties, and special districts that exist today, the United States began as a largely rural nation with little need for the public services that local governments provide today. In 1787, just 5 percent of its population resided in cities. It was, according to Thomas Jefferson, "a mass of cultivators." The Jeffersonian vision of proper democracy was one of local government in small, rural communities centered on agriculture. Democracy would survive in the United States only if its citizens were able to govern themselves directly at the local level by participating in local affairs.[5] Jefferson promoted the **Land Ordinance of 1785** as a way for the new U.S. Congress to raise money and to guarantee room for agrarian growth. The Jeffersonian vision of local agrarianism was further institutionalized by his 1803 **Louisiana Purchase.** Ample land supply ensured that the United States remained largely a rural nation of small towns throughout the 19th century. As Figure 11.1 illustrates, few people lived in large, densely populated cities. As late as 1890, barely one-third of Americans lived in places with a population greater than 2,500. Cities continued to be viewed by many as a threat to democracy, whereas agrarian communities were seen as the soul of pure democracy. Yet, despite Jefferson's misgivings, the United States became a nation of large cities as immigration and industrialization fueled their growth after the Civil War.

Figure 11.1

Percentage of Americans Living in Urban Places, 1790–2000

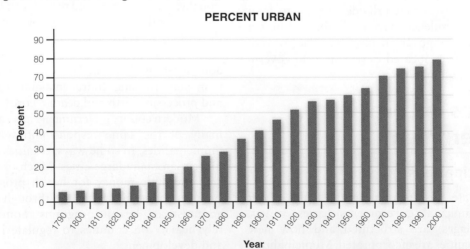

PERCENT URBAN

Source: U.S. Census Bureau data. *Urban areas* are defined as places with a population of over 2,500.

In 1850, there was only one U.S. city with a population over 500,000 (New York) and just five others with more than 100,000 residents: Baltimore, Boston, Philadelphia, New Orleans, and Cincinnati. Each of these had less than 200,000 inhabitants. By 1870—just 20 years later—there were 14 U.S. cities with over 100,000 people; seven had more than 250,000 people. Chicago grew tenfold between 1850 and 1870, to 299,000. By 1890, America had 28 cities with a population of 100,000 or more, with New York, Chicago, and Philadelphia each having over 1,000,000 people. By 1910, cities like Louisville, Minneapolis, Denver, Seattle, and Portland were all much larger than the second-largest American city was in 1850.[6]

Immigration

Although the United States largely remained a nation of small communities throughout the 19th century, its large cities were magnets for European immigrants. Immigrants were pushed from Europe by social transformations that moved peasants from their traditional lands by poverty and, for the Irish, by famine. They were pulled to the United States by the prospect of jobs associated with booming industrialization, by opportunities to farm, and by the prospect of political and religious liberties.

As Figure 11.2 illustrates, millions of Irish and Germans emigrated from their native counties to the United States from 1850 to 1910. In 1890, there were nearly 2 million foreign-born Irish living in the United States, primarily in cities (this was equal to more than half the population of Ireland at the time). The social transformation produced by this immigration was profound. Prior to the 1840s, there was a limited measure of ethnic and religious heterogeneity in the United States. There were few Catholics or Jews and a limited range of Protestant denominations, for example. In 1850, Catholics made up just 5 percent of the U.S. population. With mass emigration from Ireland, Germany, central Europe, Scandinavia, Russia, Italy, and elsewhere, ethnic and religious diversity increased dramatically. Millions of Catholics emigrated from Germany and Ireland from 1850 to 1910. Millions more emigrated from Italy, Russia, Poland, and Austria in the first decade of the 20th century. By 1906, 17 percent of Americans were Catholic, making Catholics the single-largest religious group in the nation.[7]

Figure 11.2

Immigration to the United States, in Millions, by Country of Origin

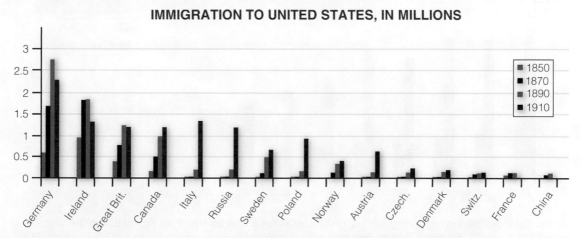

IMMIGRATION TO UNITED STATES, IN MILLIONS

Source: U.S. Census Bureau.

Note: Each bar represents the number of immigrants from a nation over the course of one decade.

Dens of Death. New York City's crowded shanties and tenements, circa 1880s; photo by Jacob Riis. Riis's muckraking photography turned public attention toward the problems of crowded, unsanitary housing and urban poverty and helped drive support for reforming city governments.

Figure 11.3

Percentage Foreign Born: Large Cities and Rural Areas, 1870–2000

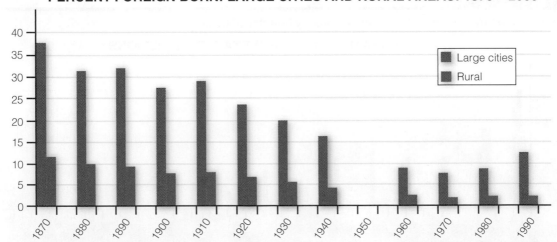

PERCENT FOREIGN BORN: LARGE CITIES AND RURAL AREAS: 1870 – 2000

Source: Campbell Gibson and Emily Lennon, "Historical Census on the Foreign Born Population of the United States: 1850–1990," U.S. Census Bureau, Population Division Working Paper no. 29, February (Washington, D.C.: U.S. Census Bureau. Population Division, 1999).

Note: Bars represent the percentage of residents who are foreign born, for each decade. Large cities are defined as places over 100,000.

Millions of Jews also immigrated to American cities between 1880 and 1915—primarily from Eastern Europe (Poland, Latvia, Lithuania, and the Ukraine) and Russia. In 1910, there were 13.5 million people who were foreign born living in the United States, mostly in cities (see Figure 11.3).

The Need for Municipal Government

Multiple governments providing many public services are a relatively modern phenomenon. Governments played little role in providing social services or public services for much of

AP Photo/John Bazemore

Firefighting is one of the oldest and most dangerous services provided by local governments. In June 2007, nine firefighters were killed battling a warehouse fire in Charleston, South Carolina, the largest loss of life since the September 11, 2001, attacks. Charleston has one of the oldest professional fire departments in the United States.

the 19th century. No Social Security, no Food Stamps, no Medicaid, and no Environmental Protection Agency of the federal government existed at that time. The rapid urbanization of the United States largely outpaced the bare minimal levels of basic public services, such as sewerage, street lighting, and garbage collection, as well as any publicly provided social welfare. As cities grew, the need for basic services also grew. **Urbanization** meant increased fire risks. Cities required sanitation (for humans and horses alike). The growth of manufacturing industries meant more people were crowded into polluted cities.

The provision of public services in this context was minimal and haphazard. Public and private police forces patrolled cities simultaneously. Fire departments were largely organized by volunteer groups, which often operated as private entities. Although Boston employed paid firefighters as early as 1678, few other U.S. cities followed Boston's lead over the next 200 years. New York City did not have paid firefighters until 1865.[8] A large city could have had multiple neighborhood-based fire brigades that did not cooperate with each other. Nineteenth-century local governments had developed with only minimal powers to regulate building standards, business practices, or public health. As there had never been much need for a public sector prior to the 1870s or for public employees, there were few regulations regarding who city officials could hire or fire. In short, the need for effective local government outpaced the urbanization and development of U.S. cities.

Origins of Urban Party Machines

Urbanization created new demands for public services and also created new forms of politics. As Figure 11.3 illustrates, immigration built U.S. cities. Many of the new immigrants settled in cities and raised their families in cities. By 1870, 44 percent of New York City's residents were born outside of the United States; 48 percent in Chicago were foreign born, as were 49 percent in San Francisco. The population of the 25 largest U.S. cities outside the South was at least one-quarter to one-third foreign born in 1890.[9]

Growth of the Voting Population

At the same time, the use of elections was expanding, although to a much more limited extent than what exists today. In the early 1800s, states placed substantial limits on who could vote. The number of voters in the United States increased dramatically after 1824. Several states began extending the right to vote to most white men in the 1820s, and all but one state moved to allow direct voting in presidential elections by 1832. By 1828, when Andrew Jackson was elected, the number of people voting tripled over what it had been in 1824. The size of the voting population continued to grow after the 1820s. Massachusetts and New York eliminated property requirements for voting in 1821, followed by Tennessee (in 1834), New Jersey (in 1844), and Virginia (in 1850). Connecticut removed the taxpaying requirement in 1845; Ohio did so in 1851.[10] In the spirit of **Jacksonian Democracy,** states were also expanding the range of offices subject to popular election. The first mayor of Chicago was elected in 1837 (he served one year). The first popular election of a Philadelphia mayor was held in 1840. With mass participation in federal, state, and local elections just emerging in the 1830s, there was a need for new methods to recruit candidates, communicate with voters, and earn voter loyalties. Out of this context, modern political parties were born—as institutions designed to meet the challenges of mobilizing regular people who had never before been allowed to play a role in elections.[11]

Early Political Parties

A political group (in some cities, they were know as "clubs" before being called *parties*) seeking to control a city would need to organize support of enough people in enough neighborhoods so they could win elections. Volunteer firehouses provided one base for organizing, as they were distributed in various neighborhoods across a city. Firehouses served as a sort of social center, as

Harper's Weekly, August 19, 1871 Page 764

Thomas Nast cartoon of Boss Tweed and Tammany Hall politicians. The upper panel refers to a *New York Times* story uncovering $5.6 million paid to a Tammany-controlled firm (Ingersoll's Co.) that supposedly supplied carpets for the County Court House. *The Times* reported on numerous contracts that showed the city paid tens of millions of dollars to contractors selected by Tammany and to a firm owned by Tweed himself, with no evidence of any benefits for the city.

Table 11.1	

Great Party Machine Politician Names and Nicknames

Name	City and Position
James Michael "Mayor of the Poor" Curley	Boston mayor, 4 terms between 1914 and 1949
John "Bathhouse" Coughlin	Chicago First Ward alderman, 1893–1938
Michael "Hinky Dink" Kenna	Chicago First Ward alderman, 1897–1923
"King" James McManes	Philadelphia Republican Machine, 1866–1880s
"Iz" Durham	Philadelphia Republican Machine, early 1900s
"Sunny Jim" McNichol	Philadelphia Republican Machine
William "Boss" Tweed	New York Tammany Hall boss, 1860s–1872
Abraham "OK" Hall	New York Tammany Hall, 1870s
"Slippery Dick" Connolly	New York city comptroller, 1870s
George Washington Plunkitt	New York state senator, Tammany Hall, 1880s
"Silent" Charlie Murphy	New York Tammany Hall boss, 1902–1924
John Francis "Red Mike" Hylan	New York mayor, 1918–1925

Sources: Clarence Stone, "Urban Political Machines: Taking Stock," *PS: Political Science and Politics* 29, no. 3 (1996): 446–50; and Peter McCaffery. *When Bosses Ruled Philadelphia* (University Park: Penn State University Press, 1993).

did local pubs. By the 1850s, volunteer fire departments were becoming more Irish and more Catholic.[12] Political clubs found the firehouse and pubs places to organize and recruit loyalists, and volunteer fire departments became political forces in large cities like New York, Baltimore, and St. Louis. Firehouses weren't simply a means that parties used to organize support but also provided "an arena in which those who wished to exercise political leadership could win men's loyalty by demonstrating their ability."[13] Machine politicians in several large cities came up through the ranks of firefighters, as did one of the nation's greatest political operatives, William "Boss" Tweed of New York City's **Tammany Hall** machine.[14]

Urban Party Machines

Urban political party organizations—known as **machines**—were born out of this 19th-century environment of industrialization, urbanization, rapid immigration, expanding democracy, and the absence of basic public services. These local party organizations gained and maintained control of cities by organizing neighborhoods to deliver votes for machine candidates on Election Day. One observer described machines as "quasi-feudal" because they were very hierarchical. At the top of the hierarchy sat the boss or the core group of leaders. The local boss and local party leaders might control the machine from the position of an elected office, but not every boss held local office. Below the boss and other organization leaders, a city was divided into districts (or **wards**), and each of these was divided into smaller units. Local neighborhoods, divided into **precincts,** were at the bottom of the hierarchy. Voters in neighborhoods remained loyal to the machine leaders when leaders provided them with favors or services. In immigrant neighborhoods where few residents had any political power or English language skills, relatively small favors might be mutually beneficial to party leaders and machine supporters alike. Irish Catholics were the backbone of machines in several, but not all, cities.

Favors that a machine organization provided to supporters could include help with finding a place to live, or assistance with food (a turkey on Christmas), or help with home-heating fuel in winter. Services could include help with the police, help with finding a job, or help with making contacts in business.[15] Machines may have also helped immigrants obtain citizenship (so they could vote). Some machine organizations offered illicit businesses protection from law enforcement, thus earning the support of tavern owners, prostitution businesses, and gambling operations. A few city machines did have reformist intentions, establishing municipally owned utilities to improve water, sewer, and street-lighting services.

These 19th-century urban party machines operated as **clientele parties:** that is, the party machine (acting as a sort of patron) served working-class and immigrant voters (the clients) by providing personal favors in exchange for votes. Machine politics was most notable in large cities, but this style of local politics also operated in small towns and rural areas.[16] Support for a party machine organization was not based on ideology but on the leaders' personalities, ethnic solidarity, and/or neighborhood loyalties.[17] This being the case, a machine could operate with a Democratic Party label or a Republican Party label. Most were Democrat, yet the Philadelphia machine of 1867–1933 was Republican.[18]

Patronage

Clientele politics involves providing something of value in exchange for political support. Prior to the late 19th century, appointment to most government jobs was controlled by elected officials. Winning politicians had the power to fire government employees and replace them with their supporters. For urban party machines, public sector jobs were one of the more lucrative perks that they could use to reward the people who helped keep the machine running. This patronage system occasionally had a high cost for politicians. Carter Harrison Sr., the mayor of Chicago, was assassinated in his home in 1893 by a "disappointed office seeker."

Precinct-Based Politics

A political machine's ability to organize a city politically depended on its ability to maintain support at the neighborhood level. Many precincts had workers loyal to the party—perhaps led by a **precinct captain**—who provided information about residents' needs and their voting habits to people higher up the party machine hierarchy. Voters might support the machine in response to the patronage and favors it provided or as the result of friendship with party loyalists in neighborhoods or some common social bond with a precinct worker. Party organizations maintained contacts in neighborhoods by sponsoring picnics, sporting events, dances, and other social events "to keep people in the orbit of the machine."[19] Service as a precinct captain was a potential means for career advancement within the party organization.

District Elections, Large Councils

Given the concentration of different ethnic groups in distinct parts of a city, and given neighborhood-based political loyalties that flowed from this, it was easier for a machine to organize a city on ethnic loyalties when representation on the city council was based on small geographic units. Local councils where each member was elected from a small geographic district helped to transfer ethnic-based neighborhood loyalties into political representation. City councils (or boards of aldermen) with a large number of districts allowed distinct, homogeneous neighborhoods to form the basis of an individual district. A smaller district would be more likely to be ethnically homogenous and thus be easier to organize on the basis of common social bonds or patronage. This helped machine organizations reach out to various ethnic groups concentrated in different parts of a city. As an example, in 1900, the Chicago City Council had 70 members, with two aldermen from each district, elected to two-year terms in partisan elections.

Partisan Elections, Party Ballot Machine control of a city required electing as many machine loyalists as possible to local councils and local offices. The "Democrat" or "Republican" name attached to a party organization provided a banner, or easily communicated brand label, under which the organization's local candidates sought office. Some parties also controlled a newspaper in a city to promote the organization and its candidates.[20] Early American elections were largely unregulated affairs, and secrecy was not always expected in voting. In some places, party organizations printed their own ballots to distribute to voters. Parties gave voters preprinted ballots listing the party's local candidates, with ballots listing only candidates preferred by the local party organization leaders. This helped the machine control who sought office, and it allowed party poll watchers to observe who voters were supporting. Party ballots printed in party newspapers could be clipped by voters to be cast when they arrived at the polling place. Party-printed ballots meant that there was little secrecy in voting, but it also provided a means of voting for new immigrants and others who were not literate enough to read a ballot and fill in without assistance the names of candidates they preferred. With much of the electorate having limited literacy, party-printed ballots made it possible for parties to communicate easily with voters and made it easier for many voters to participate in elections.

Timing of Elections Local party machines could have substantial influence on state and federal races if local elections were held at the same time as state or national contests. Local party organizations had incentives to bring their supporters to the polls in order to maintain control of the city. When local elections were contested in conjunction with state and federal races using **straight-ticket ballots,** machine organizations could deliver votes for the party's

candidates seeking state and congressional offices, and they could have influence over presidential elections. High profile state and national races, combined on the ballot with local contests, made it easier for machine organizations to mobilize a larger number of voters. Voter turnout in local elections is higher when local elections are held at the same time as national elections.[21] A local party machine's influence in the state or national party organizations as well as in state capitols and Washington, D.C., was enhanced by the local organization's ability to demonstrate that it could deliver votes for the party's candidates for higher office.

Corruption

Machines maintained voter support with patronage and favors and by building social bonds with their supporters. But some machine organizations also paid their supporters to show up to vote, and in parts of a city where support was weak, they could boost their vote share through electoral fraud—hence the classic machine-inspired slogan "Vote early, and vote often." Stuffing ballot boxes and bribing people for votes were not uncommon, and they were not something limited to big cities.[22] Support at elections—whether earned or bought—was not always enough for a party machine to maintain control of a city. Kickback schemes required people who were given public jobs or awarded lucrative city contracts to pay back part of their salary or revenues to the machine organization. Bribes were offered to judges and other officials who needed to be brought on board. Bribes could also be used to control who won contracts to build city facilities. Alliances with business leaders were important to machine politicians, as business provided resources (money and jobs) for the machine, but machine politicians and machine loyalists also had personal financial interests in private real estate and development businesses and benefited from inside information about where their cities would need to buy land or build bridges and roads.

Who Benefited from the Machines?

It is clear that machines often aided illicit businesses and that many machine leaders enriched themselves personally through their corrupt political activities. Machines also operated cities inefficiently, as they needed an inflated number of public employees to boost their opportunities for handing out jobs as patronage. This inflated public sector came at a cost that was borne by taxpayers. When factors like these are considered, it might seem hard to conclude that urban machines provided benefits to anyone but the machine leaders. Machine bosses, like Tammany Hall's George Washington Plunkitt and Richard Croker, made it no secret that they got rich off of politics. As Plunkitt famously stated, "I seen my opportunities, and I took 'em."[23] Likewise, Croker claimed, "I work for my own pocket all of the time."[24]

Despite overt corruption and inefficiencies, however, some argue that machines acted as a humanizing force, making life better for masses of immigrants arriving to the United States.[25] For one thing, the level of corruption, although shocking by contemporary American standards, was not debilitating to local economies. As Chicago mayor Carter Harrison Sr. noted in the late 1890s, the two major desires of machine politicians and regular Chicagoans were to make money and spend it. Machine corruption and **graft**—skimming from local contracts and insider trading in real estate markets—probably encouraged machine politicians to boost local economic development and pursue pro-growth strategies. More growth meant more graft, but it also meant more jobs. And because some key businesses could leave a city and move elsewhere if graft and corruption got too bad (see Chapter 12), there were limits to what machines could extract from businesses.[26]

Whatever their corrupt practices were, machines needed to win elections, and the greater the legitimate voter support they had, the better were their chances of winning. This meant they had to deliver *something* to voters—although contemporary studies suggest that machines had few decent-paying jobs to offer supporters.[27] Machines needed far more votes than they had city jobs to be filled. Machines were able to transfer real political power in many cities away from a minority of relatively affluent Protestants to the new Catholic majority. Others credit machines with contributing to the peaceful development of the United States by promoting personality-based and patronage-based politics rather than divisive ideological or radical class-based political divisions.[28] Although urban party machines championed "the little guy," workers, and the immigrant, they rarely flirted with socialist ideology. They also frequently opposed union efforts at organizing workers.[29]

But these latter points open urban party machines to further criticism. By emphasizing personal loyalties and patronage, and by opposing the emergence of organized labor (unions) in the late 19th century and early 20th century, machines may have hampered the upward mobility of the United States' less affluent urban immigrants.[30]

Demise of the Machines

Regardless of whether or not urban machines served their supporters well, the era of machines came to an end in the 20th century. Machines thrived when there were large masses of immigrants with limited language skills who lacked economic opportunities and political influence. As immigrants became more educated and affluent over time, the political base of urban machines weakened. Eventually, as immigrants earned better livings, the relative value of the favors provided by the machines declined. Changes in federal laws produced a dramatic decline in immigration after 1910, further eroding the machine's base of support. Organized labor also became more influential in the early decades of the 20th century and competed directly with machines for the loyalty (and votes) of working-class people. And as a result of the Great Depression of the 1930s, the federal government became much more active in providing for the basic needs of the poor. All these forces worked to dilute the influence of urban party machines.

REFORM CAN HAPPEN

Tammany Hall and Boss Tweed

Tammany Hall was a social organization that came to control New York City politics through much of the 19th century. In its early years, the Tammany Society was organized by Aaron Burr to build support for delivering New York's Electoral College votes to Thomas Jefferson in the 1800 presidential election. By the 1840s, Tammany was a de facto branch of the Democratic Party. Large numbers of Irish immigrants began arriving in New York in the late 1840s; Tammany sped their naturalization in exchange for vote support, and Irish Americans became the base of the Tammany organization. Tammany used its vote strength to dominate state and local elections. Around 1870, Tammany politicians defrauded the city of hundreds of millions of dollars in public funds. Boss William Marcy Tweed attempted to maintain popular support at the time with patronage and by diverting funds to buy coal for the city's poor during a severe winter in 1871. *The New York Times* and *Harper's Weekly* focused public attention on Tammany's corruption in the early 1870s. Both featured cartoons by Thomas Nast savagely lampooning Tweed and his cronies. This media scrutiny helped reformers defeat Tammany candidates in the election of 1871. Tweed fled to California but soon returned and was jailed for one year in 1874, then released. He was soon arrested again for his part in stealing public funds but fled to Spain. Someone there recognized him from a Nast cartoon, and he was arrested and returned to a New York jail, where he died in 1878. Nonetheless, the Tammany organization continued to play a strong role in New York long after Tweed's demise.[1]

Notes

1. Gustavus Myers, History of Tammany Hall (New York, 1917).

Some big-city machines—but not all—can also be faulted for failing to respond adequately to the problems facing cities at the end of the 19th century. Many did a poor job of providing public services. Basic functions, such as streetcar service, street lighting, and sewers, were contracted to underfinanced private operators. Some party machines awarded lucrative utility monopolies to their business allies, instead of having the city provide the service or contracting with a firm best suited to providing a service. These private contractors often went bankrupt or defrauded local governments of their investments, leaving cities in debt and with inadequate public services.[31] Public health was also severely neglected. Basic services, such as municipal garbage removal, were sporadic.

The Urban Reform Movement

One reason for the demise of the urban party machines, then, is functional. Machines functioned poorly on several levels. Some functions that they had performed well, such as maintaining personal, ethnic-based loyalties and providing token material rewards for their supporters, also became less important as society gradually changed. The shortcomings of urban life grew more apparent. Sporadic epidemics made thousands ill, and by the late 1880s, people had knowledge that germs were spread more rapidly in crowded places. **Muckraking journalists** rallied the public against the dangers of crowded, inadequate urban housing and the exploitation of child labor in urban factories and publicized the dangers of slaughterhouses and mass-produced food sources.

But a major reason for the demise of the machines is that rules defining how cities were governed were changed to make it far more difficult for popular political organizations to control city affairs. Industrialization and urbanization happened quite rapidly in the later part of the 19th century. By the early 1900s, several social movements were forming in both the United States and Canada to combat the ill effects of industrialization and urban life. In this environment, reformers of various stripes battled party machines to restructure the organization of city governments.

Many reform proposals were attempts to systematically change the rules about how cities could function—to replace the 19th-century personal-based style of clientelism with a more impersonal bureaucracy. Urban reformers believed that raw politics as a method for governing cities could be improved with efficient public administration.[32] Efficient administration included depersonalizing politics and replacing party loyalists in city departments with people who served because they had merit and specific job qualifications. Reformers wanted to insulate the functions of local governments from the influence of politicians who ruled because they could win elections.

Who Were the Reformers?

The various groups that worked to redefine local political institutions in the first two decades of the 20th century are loosely known as the **Progressive era** reformers. They should not be confused with the **Populist** reform movement discussed in previous chapters, although the goals of these groups often overlapped. The Populist movement of the late 19th century was largely centered in rural and agricultural areas and in western mining regions. Populists believed that government and business were dominated by elites conspiring against common people—particularly against farmers. Populists emphasized reforms that broke up concentrations of political and economic power and favored new rules that nationalized ownership of key industries and empowered common citizens (see Chapter 4). Populists are characterized as having disdain for experts and elites[33] and believed in strengthening the power of popular majorities (voters).

Progressives, in contrast, recognized that the concentration of political and economic power could be dangerous. Their targets of concentrated economic and political power included monopolistic trusts that controlled major industries, including beef, sugar, and oil. Party machines were targeted as concentrations of political power that dominated politics in many cities. Progressives also had a different vision for reform than Populists. Many Progressives believed that society could be improved through scientific study and better administrative practices and by limiting the power that wealthy corporations had in politics. As Wisconsin governor Robert M. Lafollette Sr. said, "My goal is not to smash corporations, but to drive them out of politics."

Progressives, as their name suggests, embraced what they viewed as the positive aspects of progress associated with the modern era: science, technology, and efficiency. Progressives believed that efficiency in business and government could be improved if the proper information was available and the best people were charged with implementing policy.[34] For example, Progressives believed that federal government agencies were needed to regulate private business practices and that local public health agencies were needed to collect data, such as vital statistics, that could be used to improve living conditions. Many Progressives embraced the idea that scientific management practices and practical expertise could replace politics in the administration of local government. They were not antidemocratic, but some Progressives found that popular partisan control of local governments could be a barrier to efficient administration.

Many Different Reform Groups

Many different reform groups emerged in the early 20th century, with very distinct agendas. Although they are now lumped together under the *Progressive* label, there was no single Progressive organization or overarching Progressive movement. There were Progressive, reformist wings in both the Republican and Democratic parties. While serving as the Democratic governor of New Jersey from 1911 to 1913, Woodrow Wilson fought local Democratic Party machines in his state by promoting direct primaries (see Chapter 3 and Chapter 5) and campaign finance regulations. At the same time, Teddy Roosevelt's wing of the Republican Party was promoting antitrust reforms to reign in the power of huge corporations. The Progressive era also corresponded with the rise of the modern conservation movement, which was dedicated to preserving natural resources and establishing national forests and parks. During this time, numerous other reform groups advocated for expanding the scope of public education, regulating investments in stocks and bonds, passing food safety laws, eliminating the exploitation of child labor, and improving working conditions. Religious groups and others also promoted the prohibition of alcohol as a remedy to many of the era's social ills (see Chapter 14).

Women as a Force for Social Reform

Women's groups were active in promoting Progressive reforms early in the 20th century. Lacking the power to vote, many politically engaged women sought to improve society and change policy by organizing groups that promoted reform goals.[35] In Chicago, the City Club and Women's City Club of Chicago conducted investigations of urban ills and published recommendations for reforms.[36] The Boston Women's Municipal League performed a similar role in that city. Influential women's clubs organized in most major cities. One study estimates that over 1,000,000 women participated directly in the reform movement under the banner of "municipal housekeeping"—championing reforms that improved sanitation, education, and public health.[37] Women's clubs united under the General Federation of Women's Clubs. Ellen Swallow Richards, an MIT-educated scientist, demonstrated the need for food safety laws. Jane Addams worked with the City of Chicago to improve garbage cleanup, sewers, drinking water, medical care, and street lighting.[38] In the early years of the 20th century, women also organized the backbone of the women's suffrage movement, and women played a major role in promoting reforms to legalize birth control.

Changing the Design of Local Institutions

The urban reform movement was born in this environment as a reaction against party machine dominance of local government. Groups advocating for new political arrangements formed in many American cities in the early years of the 20th century, and national organizations, including the U.S. Chamber of Commerce and the National Municipal League, provided urban reformers with ideas for reshaping local politics and the administration of local government. Many of these reforms, detailed below, linked improvements in administration with weakening the power of local party machines and made it more difficult for elected officials to affect how cities work.

Class Conflict and Institutional Reform

One influential interpretation of the Progressive era is that reformers were motivated not so much by the goal of fixing the ills of industrialization and urbanization as they were by a reaction to the "status revolution" brought about by industrialism, immigration, and the expansion of mass democracy. Several studies suggest that reform advocates came from the ranks of the wealthy, educated, Protestant classes who had lost political influence to immigrant and working-class groups represented by the machines.[39] Historian Richard Hofstadter notes that industrialization created a new social class of superrich (e.g., Andrew Carnegie, John D. Rockefeller, and Leland Stanford) who dominated business and government with their wealth.[40] At the same time, urban party machines increased the political clout of urban immigrants. Both of those trends shifted power away from the descendants of established, upper-class, patrician Protestant families. These upper-status people may have promoted reforms to reassert their social and political clout over the new superrich "robber barons" and the new, largely Catholic immigrant working class.[41]

Another interpretation argues that the Progressives were largely drawn from a new middle class that was emerging from industrialization: a class of managers, business professionals, and administrators who sought to apply new business models to local politics.[42] Observers have noted that attempts at getting the politics out of city administration with a business model of government meant gutting the representation of lower-status minorities.[43] Some Progressives promoted southern-style Jim Crow laws in order to limit the political influence of racial and ethnic minorities.[44]

How Did Local Institutions Change?

One prominent national advocacy group, the National Municipal League, offered reformers a blueprint for how to rebuild local political institutions so that the influence of mass-based political parties would be weakened and the influence of unelected experts would be increased. The National Municipal League publicized its ideas for reform in a **model city charter.** The first model charter was drafted after several years of conferencing among urban reform groups, including the City Club of New York and the Municipal League of Philadelphia.[45] The model charter was an attempt to bring national attention to how various local experiments with new political arrangements "worked" (or "failed") in various cities. Elements of the model city charter were (and continue to be) updated periodically,

and the earliest model charters embodied the Progressive reformers' ideal of how local government should function.

Because state laws define how charters for local governments are to be drawn, reform advocates had to lobby state legislatures to change state rules about local government arrangements. Progressive reformers were also able to define (or redefine) rules shaping local charters by electing sympathetic candidates as state legislators and governors. Some states had Progressive wings in both the Democratic or Republican parties, but Progressives were more often associated with the liberal wing of the Republican Party.

In many parts of the United States, there was wide public support for Democrats and Republicans who promoted Progressive reforms. Candidates who adhered to the Progressive reform agenda were elected governor in several states, including Robert M. Lafollette Sr. of Wisconsin (first elected as a Republican, 1901–1905, and latter as an Independent Progressive), John A. Johnson of Minnesota (a Democrat, 1905–1909), Edward Hoch of Kansas (a Republican, 1905–1909), Charles Evans Hughes of New York (a Republican, 1907–1910; Hughes

REFORM CAN HAPPEN

SEWER SOCIALISM

Not every city's politics was dominated by major party machines at the end of the 19th century. Milwaukee elected the first Socialist mayor in the United States in 1910, and Socialists briefly held a majority of seats on the city council.[1] Socialist Daniel Webster Hoan served as mayor from 1916 to 1940. Whereas Progressive reformers of the same era sought to improve living conditions and reduce corruption, Milwaukee Socialists also emphasized public ownership. Victor Berger, a Milwaukee newspaper editor, built the Socialists into a powerful local organization—a sort of political machine—by emphasizing reform goals. Milwaukee Socialists cleaned up neighborhoods with municipally owned sewage systems, street lighting, water systems, power systems, housing, bus system, and parks. As New York City mayor Fiorello La Guardia once said, there is no Republican, no Democratic, no Socialist way to clean a street or build a sewer; there's merely a right way or a wrong way.[2] At least 18 Socialist mayors were elected during the Progressive era.

Notes

1. Wisconsin Historical Society, "Milwaukee Sewer Socialism" (Madison: Wisconsin Historical Society, 2006).
2. Kevin Baker, "Hizzoners," *The New York Times,* May 2, 1999.

defeated Tammany-linked Democrat William Randolph Hearst), Hiram Johnson of California (1910–1920, first elected as a Republican under the Lincoln–Roosevelt Party label, then as a Progressive), Simon Bamberger of Utah (a Democrat, 1917–1921), Charles Hillman Brough of Arkansas (a Democrat, 1917–1921), and Gifford Pinchot of Pennsylvania (a Republican, 1923–1927 and 1931–1935).

Although all these governors are often classified as Progressives, some emphasized social reforms (e.g., public health and improved public education) and economic reforms (e.g., regulating monopolies) when in office more than changes to political institutions. Reformers committed to changing the nature of local political institutions also lobbied state governments to grant cities **home rule charters.**

A Menu of Reforms

Prior to the Reform era (another name for the Progressive era), mayors in most large cities had few formal powers, with major decisions controlled by large city councils. Machine organizations exercised their influence over a city by controlling council elections. Some of these institutional arrangements were characterized as **weak mayor–council systems.** Voters elected the mayor and council separately, but weak mayors often had little formal influence over city budgets, city departments, or what the city council did. By the middle of the 1800s, most U.S. cities had a city council and mayor who shared legislative and administrative powers.[46]

This does not mean that American mayors had little influence over city affairs prior to the adoption of the reforms discussed below. Table 11.2 lists the results of a survey of historians that ranks the best and worst mayors in the United States from 1820 to 1990. The rankings here are probably biased toward overrepresenting better-known mayors, particularly from large eastern cities. There may have been several lesser-known mayors (terrible or excellent) from the South or West that these historians ignored. Nonetheless, most of the worst-rated mayors were machine

operatives whose political influence stemmed not as much from the formal powers granted them in a city's charter but from their links with the party machine and their skill with clientele politics. At the top of the list of "worst" mayors is "Kaiser Bill" Thompson, who served three terms as mayor of Chicago. Thompson, a pro-German during World War I, fought against anticorruption reforms and allowed Chicago's gangsters to run unchecked (organized crime supplied the city with beer, wine, and liquor during the Prohibition era). After being defeated and investigated for fraud, he beat a reformist Prohibitionist incumbent to win a third term by promising to reopen the city's taverns.[47] Thompson died a rich man.

Other notorious pre–Reform era mayors include Frank Hague of Jersey City, whose influence in the national Democratic Party helped Franklin D. Roosevelt win the Democratic Party's nomination for president in 1932. Hague started as a precinct captain, earned a job as a city janitor, and 10 years later was mayor. The Hague machine's skill at stuffing ballot boxes and other modes of voter fraud allowed Hague to dominate politics in his state for years. Hague also became a millionaire, despite a salary of $8,000 per year.[48] Conversely, the best-rated mayors are those who worked to reform city institutions.

It is important to consider that in the early decades of the 20th century, there were many ideas for changing how local political institutions operated and that these ideas have had a tremendous effect on defining how local governments work today.

Mayor–Council Government Progressives had conflicting views about how powerful a city's mayor should be and what the relationship between the mayor and council should be. Some early reformers believed that strong mayors were needed so that a reformist leader could take firm control of government and check the actions of the city council.[49] And by concentrating control of city administration in one institution (the mayor's office) and legislative and policy-making power in another

Table 11.2

Scholars' Rankings of the Best and Worst Mayors in American History

Worst

1. William H. "Kaiser Bill" Thompson	Chicago, 1915–1923, 1927–1931
2. Frank Hague	Jersey City, 1917–1947
3. James "Jimmy" Walker	New York, 1926–1932
4. James Michael Curley	Boston, 1914–1917, 1922–1925, 1930–1933, 1946–1949
5. Frank Rizzo	Philadelphia, 1972–1980
6. A. Oakley Hall	New York, 1869–1872
7. Dennis Kucinich	Cleveland, 1977–1979
8. Fernando Wood	New York, 1855–1858, 1860–1862
9. Sam Yorty	Los Angeles, 1961–1973
10. Jane Byrne	Chicago, 1979–1983

Other "Worst"

"Diamond Joe" Quimby	Springfield, 1989–current
Michael Bilandic	Chicago, 1976–1979
Wilson Goode	Philadelphia, 1984–1992
John V. Lindsay	New York, 1966–1973

Best

1. Fiorello La Guardia	New York, 1934–1945
2. Tom L. Johnson	Cleveland, 1901–1909
3. David Lawrence	Pittsburgh, 1946–1959
4. Hazen Pingree	Detroit, 1890–1897
5. Samuel "Golden Rule" Jones	Toledo, 1897–1904
6. Richard J. Daley	Chicago, 1955–1976
7. Frank Murphy	Detroit, 1930–1933
8. Daniel W. Hoan	Milwaukee, 1916–1940
9. Tom Bradley	Los Angeles 1973–1993
10. Josiah "Great Mayor" Quincy	Boston, 1823–1828

Other Best

Andrew Young	Atlanta, 1982–1990

Source: Melvin G. Holli, *The American Mayor: The Best and the Worst Big City Leaders* (University Park: Penn State University Press, 1999). These results are taken from surveys of 120 experts about mayors of the largest U.S. cities between 1820 and 1990.

institution (the city council), reformers hoped that the separation of powers would produce better governance. A mayor with strong powers who was directly elected by the voters could also be held accountable at the ballot box. This idea of a strong, accountable mayor also reflected a business model of government. In a business corporation, for example, shareholders and a board of directors give a chief executive strong authority over the day-to-day operations of a business, and shareholders or the board can remove an executive if they are dissatisfied with the performance of the corporation. At the end of the 1890s, a strong mayor was seen as a cure to municipal corruption.[50]

The National Municipal League's first Model City Charter (of 1900) recommended that mayors be given strong executive powers. Under a **strong mayor–council system,** mayors are directly elected by the voters at the same time that the city council is. Depending on how many powers a city grants its mayor, a strong mayor may interact with a city council in a manner similar to how a governor interacts with a state legislature. A strong mayor can be given executive powers that include hiring and firing heads of city departments (and other staff), drafting budgets, and vetoing acts of the city council. Mayors may have even stronger powers if they are elected to long terms (four years rather than two), if they are not limited in how often they can seek re-election, if they don't have to share budget powers with the council, and if they have control over city schools. Figures 11.4 and 11.5 illustrate two versions of mayor council government.

The second edition of the Model City Charter, published in 1915, gave up on the strong mayor plan. Since then, subsequent Model City Charters in 1928, 1933, 1941, 1964, and 1989 advocated a council–manager system with an appointed city executive (see below). About one-third of U.S. cities had mayor–council forms of government as of 2002, but many have mayors who have limits on their formal executive powers. About 40 percent of mayor–council cities have mayors with strong powers to affect budgets and appointments of city staff.[51] Most American cities that have a mayor today, particularly in smaller cities, have mayors with weak executive powers. Just 12 percent of U.S. mayors have the responsibility for developing budgets, and just 17 percent of mayors have the power to appoint department heads. Less than 30 percent of U.S. mayors have the power to veto acts of their city's council. Eighty-five percent of American mayors' jobs are considered part-time positions.[52] As Table 11.3 illustrates, many of the United States' largest cities have mayor–council systems of government today. These cities vary in how the mayor shares power with the city council.

Council–Manager Government After 1915, the National Municipal League began advocating for a **council–manager** form of government.[53]

Figure 11.4

Weak Mayor–Council System

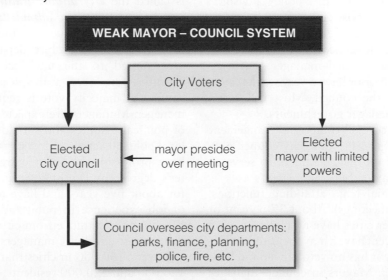

Figure 11.5

Strong Mayor–Council System

The council–manager system is the epitome of the business model of local government. Under this system, a small (five- to seven-member) council hires a professional administrator to implement its policies. The appointed executive is responsible for preparing the budget, directing day-to-day operations of city departments, overseeing personnel management, and serving as the council's chief policy advisor.[54] City managers supervise city staff, and they recruit, hire, and fire city employees within the boundaries of civil service rules. Cities with a pure form of the council–manager system either have no mayor or have a very weak mayor who serves on the council. Most U.S. cities have council–manager governments.[55]

Under the council–manager arrangement illustrated in Figure 11.6, the city council may appoint one of its own members to serve as a part-time mayor, but the mayor's role is largely ceremonial (e.g., attending functions, presiding over meetings). About 37 percent of council–manager cities have no elected mayor. Another 47 percent have a mayor elected by voters, but the mayor has no veto power and little executive power. Mayors in council–manager systems may nonetheless act as spokespersons for their community and, despite their limited executive power, may be the most visible representative of the community.

A council–manager system gives executive powers and administrative control to the council-appointed administrator, known as a *city manager* (in some places, the position is called the *city administrator*, *chief executive officer*, or *chief administrative officer*). Executive powers, such as the authority to prepare a budget or hire department heads, are granted to the unelected, professional executive who serves at the pleasure of the city council. A majority vote is required to fire a manager. Managers are expected to stay clear of political disputes and should not engage in local political activity. Most city managers now have professional academic training (a master's degree), and most serve in their position for about five years and have about 17 years of job experience in public administration.[56] Many managers move from city to city during their careers, and city managers' salaries average over $160,000 in cities that have between 120,000 and 220,000 residents.[57]

Table 11.3

Largest U.S. Cities with Mayor–Council Systems of Government

City	Population	Population Rank	Grade	Council Elections
New York, NY	8,143,000	1st	B	51 districts
Los Angeles, CA	3,844,000	2nd	C	15 districts
Chicago, IL	2,842,000	3rd	B–	50 districts (wards)
Houston, TX	2,016,000	4th	C+	9 districts and 4 at-large
Philadelphia, PA	1,463,000	5th	B	10 districts and 7 at-large
Detroit, MI	886,000	11th	B–	9 at-large
Indianapolis, IN	784,000	12th	B+	25 districts and 4 at-large
Jacksonville, FL	782,000	13th	B–	14 districts and 5 at-large
San Francisco, CA	739,000	14th	C	11 at-large
Columbus, OH	730,000	15th	C	7 at-large
Memphis, TN	762,000	17th	C+	13 districts
Baltimore, MD	635,000	18th	B–	18 districts
Milwaukee, WI	578,000	22nd	B	17 districts
Seattle, WA	573,000	23rd	B	9 at-large
Boston, MA	559,000	24th	B–	9 districts and 4 at-large
Denver, CO	557,000	25th	B–	11 districts and 2 at-large
Louisville, KY	556,000	26th	n/a	26 districts
Nashville, TN	549,000	28th	C+	35 districts and 5 at-large
Albuquerque, NM	494,000	33rd	n/a	9 districts
Atlanta, GA	470,000	35th	C+	12 districts and 3 at-large
Fresno, CA	461,000	36th	n/a	7 districts
New Orleans, LA	454,000	38th	C–	5 districts and 2 at-large
Cleveland, OH	454,000	39th	C	21 districts (wards)
Oakland, CA	409,300	43rd	n/a	7 districts and 1 at-large
Omaha, NE	390,000	44th	n/a	7 districts
Tulsa, OK	387,000	46th	n/a	9 districts
Honolulu, HI	381,000	47th	B	9 districts
Minneapolis, MN	373,000	48th	B+	13 districts (wards)
St. Louis, MO	344,000	52nd	n/a	28 districts (wards)
Tampa, FL	325,000	56th	n/a	4 districts and 3 at-large
Pittsburgh, PA	316,000	57th	n/a	9 districts
Toledo, OH	301,000	59th	n/a	6 districts and 6 at-large

Note: Grade is the overall performance rating for the cities rated by the Government Performance Project, *Governing Magazine* (2000).

Figure 11.6

Council–Manager System

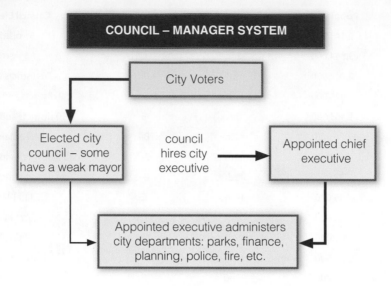

COUNCIL – MANAGER SYSTEM

City Voters

Elected city council – some have a weak mayor

council hires city executive

Appointed chief executive

Appointed executive administers city departments: parks, finance, planning, police, fire, etc.

Adoption of the council–manager reform was rapid and widespread. In 1908, Staunton, Virginia, became the first city to pass an ordinance that defined the authority of an appointed executive. In 1912, Sumter, South Carolina, was the first city to define a council–manager system in its charter, and Dayton, Ohio, became the first large city to adopt the council–manager system in 1913.[58] By 1915, 82 cities had adopted the system, and twice as many more had by 1920.[59] The council–manager plan was subsequently adopted throughout the United States and is also used in Australia, Canada, the Netherlands, and New Zealand. Most U.S. cities and towns—particularly smaller places—now operate with some version of a council–manager system, often with the councils elected in nonpartisan elections. Of the 247 American cities with a population over 100,000, 144 (58 percent) use a council–manager system. Some of the largest cities using this system include Cincinnati, Dallas, Kansas City, Phoenix, and Las Vegas. Over 92 million Americans live in cities governed with a council–manager system.[60]

Table 11.4 lists the largest American cities that use the council–manager system of government today.

Council–Manager and Mayor–Council Blends Cities continue to alter their charters to redefine the separation of powers between councils, mayors, and appointed city executives. Some mayor–councils adopted rules that borrowed features of the council–manager system in order to increase the autonomy of professional administrators. As an example, San Francisco became the first mayor–council city to hire a professional administrator in 1931, yet it remained a relatively strong mayor–council system.[61]

More recently, some council–manager systems have adopted features from mayor–council systems to increase direct political control by voters.[62] Surveys of cities suggest that over the last 25 years, a large number of cities have been switching from mayor–council systems.[63] In larger cities, however, there may be greater public pressure to have political institutions that make it easier for citizens to hold elected officials directly accountable for how a city operates. This has led some council–manager cities

Table 11.4				

Largest U.S. Cities with Council–Manager Systems of Government

City	Population	Population Rank	Grade	Council Elections
Phoenix, AZ	1,461,000	6th	A	8 districts
San Antonio, TX	1,256,000	7th	B	10 districts
San Diego, CA*	1,255,000	8th	B	8 districts
Dallas, TX	1,213,000	9th	C+	14 districts
San Jose, CA	912,000	10th	B–	10 districts
Austin, TX	690,000	16th	A–	6 at-large
Ft. Worth, TX	624,000	19th	n/a	9 districts
Charlotte, NC	611,000	20th	n/a	7 districts and 4 at-large
El Paso, TX	598,000	21st	n/a	8 districts
Las Vegas, NV	545,147	29th	n/a	6 districts (wards)
Oklahoma City, OK	531,000	31st	n/a	8 districts (wards)
Tucson, AZ	515,000	32nd	n/a	7 at-large
Long Beach, CA	474,000	34th	B	9 districts
Sacramento, CA	456,000	37th	n/a	8 districts
Kansas City, MO	445.000	40th	B–	6 districts and 6 at-large
Mesa, AZ	443,000	41st	n/a	6 districts
Virginia Beach, VA	438,000	42nd	B+	7 districts and 4 at-large
Colorado Springs, CO	369,000	49th	n/a	4 districts and 5 at-large
Arlington, TX	362,000	50th	n/a	5 districts and 4 at-large
Wichita, KS	354,000	51st	n/a	7 at-large
Raleigh, NC	341,000	53rd	n/a	5 districts and 2 at-large
Santa Ana, CA	340,000	54th	n/a	7 at-large
Anaheim, CA	331,000	55th	n/a	5 at-large
Cincinnati, OH	331,000	58th	n/a	9 at-large
Aurora, CO	297,000	60th	n/a	6 districts and 4 at-large
Richmond, VA	197,000	97th	C+	9 districts

Note: Grade is the overall performance rating for the cities as rated by the Government Performance Project, *Governing Magazine* (2000).

to adopt some of the features of mayor–council systems, such as directly elected mayors, as well as mayors with veto powers over councils.

Other council–manager cities have abandoned their council–manager systems. As examples, in 1999, Cincinnati voters approved a charter amendment that added a directly elected mayor to their council–manager system. The Cincinnati mayor has some elements of "strong mayor" powers, can veto the council, and has a role in selecting the city manager, but a city manager remains in charge of administering Cincinnati's city departments and implementing policies approved by the council. Voters in

San Diego, a council–manager city, approved a referendum in 2004 to have a four-year experiment with a strong mayor–council system. The experiment began in 2006. Oakland, California, voters approved a similar experiment in 1998 at the request of then-mayor Jerry Brown. Four years later, they voted to make the strong-mayor system permanent. In contrast, Dallas voters rejected referendums in 2005 that would have replaced their council–manager system with a stronger mayor.

Commission System The National Municipal League was initially enthusiastic about a third form of local government: the commission system. The commission system was another attempt to isolate the administration of government from politics. Under this system, voters would select people, rather than a city council, to run city departments. A commission of these elected administrators shared executive and legislative powers.

In some early versions of the commission system, voters elected commissioners who would head specific city departments—for example, a finance commissioner, a public works commissioner, and a public safety (police and fire) commissioner. These commissioners would meet together as a council to pass city budgets (a legislative function), but each individual would be in charge of administering his or her own city department (an executive function). Most of these commission systems soon proved unworkable, as commissioners would promote the interests of their own departments over the general needs of the city, and it was difficult for anyone to coordinate city policy across rival city departments. Portland, Oregon, the 32nd largest U.S. city, is the only remaining large city to use the commission form of government. In Portland, voters elect a nonpartisan mayor and four nonpartisan commissioners, who serve together as a council. The mayor is in charge of assigning the administration of various departments to the four commissioners. Tulsa, Oklahoma, was one of the last remaining commission systems in a large city. Tulsa abandoned its commission

form of government in 1989, switching to a mayor–council system.

At-Large Elections In addition to altering the powers of mayors and city councils, many of the Progressive reforms from the early 1900s were aimed at changing how councils represented a city and how local elections were conducted.

Councils elected by individual districts increase opportunities for a political group or candidate to win support based on the social or ethnic bonds of specific neighborhoods. In district elections, only voters in the district vote for their representative. This meant that various ethnic minority groups concentrated in distinct neighborhoods could win council seats. Racial and ethnic minorities are more likely to win seats via districts than under citywide elections (known as *at-large elections*).[65]

In the early 1900s, Progressive reformers argued that at-large elections would make it more difficult for machines to organize cities from the precinct level up based on ethnic loyalties. In at-large elections, everyone in the city votes for each "position" on the city council. This allows a cohesive majority to sweep every council seat. At-large elections may also produce council representation with more of a citywide focus, whereas representatives elected by districts may have more parochial concerns. Most American cities now have at-large elections, although classic strong-mayor cities, and the 60 largest U.S. cities, are more likely to use district elections (see Tables 11.3 and 11.4). Some cities have representatives on their council elected partly by districts and partly citywide.

Since the 1970s, the U.S. Supreme Court has ruled that at-large elections may illegally dilute the influence of minority groups, and as a result, many larger cities (which have more minorities) have switched from at-large to district elections and other alternative election systems in recent decades (see Chapter 3).

Smaller Councils Large councils elected by district made it easier to organize a city on ethnic and neighborhood lines, as more seats on the council allowed the city to be divided into many distinctive council districts. Reformers promoted smaller councils elected at large as a means to create governments that had a more "citywide" focus.

Nonpartisan Elections Party labels allowed the machines an easy way to inform their supporters whom they should vote for. All they needed to do was select the candidates nominated by the machine organization listed as a Democrat (or Republican) candidate (depending on the city). Progressives and the National Municipal League promoted the idea that elections for local offices did not require partisan labels. This made it more difficult for low-literacy voters to support a party organization's candidate. Most U.S. cities now have nonpartisan elections, especially cities with council–manager forms of government.[66]

Australian Ballot The urban party machine's ability to communicate with its supporters was also eroded with the introduction of the Australian Ballot (also known as the *secret ballot*). Unofficial, party-printed ballots were favored by machines because they listed only one party's candidates (that of the machine organization). The government-printed Australian ballot, in contrast, listed candidates from all parties and required voters to pick and choose among them in a private voting booth without assistance. Australian ballots also allowed voters to "split their ticket" and vote for candidates from different political parties and weakened the influence of local precinct captains who had printed and distributed ballots.[67] New York adopted the Australian ballot throughout the state in 1890.[68]

In the southern and western regions of the United States, Australian ballots were adopted for different reasons. They made it difficult for third parties, such as the Populists, to win support from illiterate working-class voters who required party-printed, straight-ticket ballots.[69] Nonpartisan elections, contested with Australian ballots, likely made it much more difficult for party organizations to get their supporters to vote for machine candidates.

Off-Year Elections Elections happen in cycles. When local elections are held on separate dates than other elections (presidential, congressional, or gubernatorial), fewer people are likely to take notice. A study of cities in California found that when local elections were held jointly with presidential elections, turnout was 36 percent higher than when elections were held at times when there were not any higher-level offices up for election. Local elections held in synch with a gubernatorial race had 21 percent higher turnout than a "local-only" election, and similar increases in turnout occur when local races are on the same ballot as candidates in a presidential primary.[70]

Voter Registration Prior to the late 1890s, there was little regulation of who could vote. Before then, a voter who arrived at the polls was automatically registered for the next election,[71] and party machines are reported to have created ways to offer immigrants "instant citizenship" to make them eligible for voting.[72] Repeat voting also inflated vote totals. One New York City election produced a reported turnout of 8 percent more than the total city voting population.[73]

By the early 1900s, many states attempted to combat electoral fraud by requiring that voters personally apply for registration before each election. Many early registration statutes applied only to the state's largest cities.[74] In 1908, the New York State Legislature passed regulations on voting, requiring that all voters in cities of over 1,000,000 people produce personal identification when voting and sign in when voting. Signatures could be matched to registration applications, and poll workers could query voters. Districts in New York City suspected of fraud-inflated vote totals in 1906 had substantially less voting in 1908.[75] As voter registration spread to other states, voter turnout in American elections fell sharply.[76]

Civil Service–Merit System Many federal government jobs became protected by civil service rules only after President James A. Garfield was assassinated in 1881 by a party activist who did not receive the patronage appointment he expected. The **Pendleton Act** of 1883 established a Civil Service Commission that began to depoliticize (or bureaucratize) the hiring and firing of many federal employees. The modern **civil service** system requires that public employees should be hired only on the basis of merit (that is, based on job-specific qualifications) and that they should not be fired unless employers can prove just cause for doing so. However, the federal civil service system does not apply to state and local governments. States and cities have adopted their own civil service systems, but differences exist across places in how many public jobs are classified as civil service and in terms of how many public employees serve at the pleasure of elected officials. Public jobs that do not fall under state or local civil service rules can still be awarded by political appointments.

Federal civil service rules did not apply to state and local government employees. Progressive reformers promoted the adoption of civil service rules on a city-by-city basis after 1900. By 1935, at least 450 U.S. cities had adopted some form of a civil service system. At least 200 more had adopted a civil service–merit system by 1938, including 80 percent of cities over 100,000.[77] This transferred the routine, day-to-day tasks of city governments from political loyalists to bureaucrats. By 1939, federal law required that states adopt some form of civil service for state workers, and in the 1960s, many states began requiring that their cities develop civil service–merit systems to depoliticize the hiring and firing of public employees. By the 1990s, most (but not all) states required their cities to adopt merit-based civil services.[78]

Today, cities vary in terms of how many city positions are classified as political appointments or civil service. In most places, only a few "policy advisor" positions are left for elected officials to appoint. In less-reformed cities, a strong mayor may still control numerous appointments to numerous city jobs and boards. A contemporary mayor of Chicago is estimated to control the appointment of 900 to 1,200 city positions.[79]

Corrupt Practices Acts After 1900, several states adopted laws to make it illegal to use bribes in elections and illegal to impersonate someone else when voting. An Oregon Corrupt Practices Act passed by voter initiative in 1908 designated as corrupt "the unlawful expenditure of money for election purposes; which covers the giving of cigars and tobacco; undue influence, including the threat of even a 'spiritual injury,' [im]personation; bribery; betting by a candidate on any pending election, or furnishing money therefore; seeking nomination for a venal motive, and not in good faith." Some states also attempted to regulate elections by limiting campaign expenditures.[80]

Strict Rules for Public Contracts Most states also now require cities to abide by strict rules when spending public money. These rules are designed to limit the ability of public officials to use public funds for their own benefit (or for the benefit of their supporters). These rules govern how public employees can make routine purchases and how contracts for public work shall be put to bid (most require sealed bids that conceal the identity of the firm bidding for the job). Other rules require detailed public records of expenditures and that city departments be subjected to external audits.

Local Direct Democracy Many reform advocates also promoted the adoption of the direct initiative, referendum, and recall for use in cities and counties. We discussed these institutions in Chapter 4. Initiatives were seen as a way to advance reform goals that might not be approved by a city council. In 1893, California changed its law to allow the initiative in every county. Nebraska granted residents of all its cities the right to use initiatives in 1897. By 1911, state laws were changed to allow initiatives in cities in 11 states, mostly in the West.[81]

Municipal Reforms as a Continuum and Constant Process

Research suggests that municipal reform efforts had greater success in places where there were fewer working-class and immigrant voters, as these voters were the major supporters of the urban party machines. This means that some of the reforms discussed above were less likely to end up being adopted in older cities and were more likely to be adopted in smaller communities and in places outside the northeastern states.[82] Cities with high percentages of Irish immigrants were particularly resistant to adopting reforms during the Progressive era, as were northern cities that had a machine presence during the Reform era (e.g., Albany, New York; Baltimore; Boston; Chicago; Cleveland; Hartford, Connecticut; Jersey City, New Jersey; New Haven, Connecticut; Indianapolis; Philadelphia; Toledo, Ohio; and Youngstown, Ohio). Western cities, and cities without established machines, were more likely to adopt several of these reforms during the Progressive era (e.g., Colorado Springs, Colorado; Pasadena, Sacramento, and San Jose, California; and Wichita, Kansas).[83]

The structure of any city's political institutions today can be categorized in terms of a continuum, with cities employing fewer of these reforms at one end of the continuum and many reforms at the other. Cities now show limited variation regarding whether or not they have corrupt practices rules, civil service systems, or strict rules about public spending. But a large amount of variation still exists across cities in terms of how these rules work and in who ultimately administers the city. These rules mean that cities also vary in terms of how much direct control elected officials ultimately have on how their city is administered.

This brings us back to the opening vignette of this chapter. The structure of political institutions that existed in Los Angeles when the Rodney King beating was videotaped placed that city much farther toward the reform end of continuum than New York. Cities like Los Angeles that adopted their charters during or after the Progressive reforms employ a large number of the reforms listed above. Rigid civil service rules, and relatively weak executive authority granted to the mayor, meant that Chief Gates could not be fired, despite overwhelming political pressure to do so. A classic reformed city would likely have a council–manager system employing a professional city manager and a weak mayor (or no mayor). The council would be elected at large in nonpartisan elections scheduled when no higher-profile partisan races are being contested.

Larger cities, particularly those in eastern states where political institutions were more firmly established before the Progressive Reform era began, are more likely to be located on the less reformed end of the continuum: that is, they are more likely to have partisan elections, council elections by district, large city councils, and nearly all city affairs controlled by elected officials. This does not mean that former machine cities, such as Chicago and New York, have been insulated from the reform movement: both of these mayor–council cities now have some reform institutions (such as civil service). As Table 11.3 illustrates, cities with mayor–council systems are still "less reformed" in that they are more likely to have larger councils (even when population is accounted for), with a high proportion of the council representing individual districts. Mayor–council cities listed in Table 11.3 average 15 seats in size, with 83 percent of seats elected from districts. In contrast, council–manager city councils listed in Table 11.4 average nine seats in size, with 68 percent elected by district.

It is important to remember that city institutions are flexible and change frequently in response to crises and public demands for reform. The reform of municipal institutions is a continuing process. After the Rodney King incident, Los Angeles went through a process of re-evaluating its charter, and proposals for stronger mayoral power emerged. And, as noted above, larger council–manager cities, including some listed in Table 11.4, are also considering changing their institutions to provide for greater political accountability in the form of a strong, directly elected mayor.

Consequences of Municipal Reforms

One thing that occurred after the Reform era was that reformed cities became more efficient and had less political corruption. The cumulative effect of many of these reforms may be efficient, professional, modern city administration that is more capable of managing the "housekeeping" functions of cities. Building codes and public health standards are now much more likely to be implemented and administered by civil servants following standard operating procedures. Business licenses and lucrative contracts to provide services to a city are more likely to be granted on the basis of standard operating procedures rather than political favoritism. Public works projects are now far more likely to be constructed by qualified contractors who offer the lowest bid. Well-regulated public utilities now provide many cities with water, power, street lighting, and sewerage. Police enforce laws with greater objectivity, and politicians cannot easily enrich themselves by directing the police to "selectively" enforce laws. Of course, it is difficult to prove that reforms themselves made cites more efficient and less corrupt. Since the early 1900s, all U.S. cities, reformed and unreformed alike, are probably governed better today.

Nonpolitical Administration?

The discussion of party machines in this chapter suggests that patronage, corruption, and other inefficiencies may have inflated public spending in unreformed cities. We also might expect public spending to be higher in unreformed cities because classic machines were designed to be responsive to many different groups that might demand city services. Reforms such as at-large, nonpartisan elections and council–manager systems could insulate city officials from such demands. One influential study did find less taxing and spending in reformed cities,[84] but subsequent research found few differences in city finances in reformed versus unreformed cities.[85] Council–manager systems may limit how much direct influence elected officials have on how city money is spent, but this need not mean that these cities spend less or

that their appointed managers are insulated from political pressures. Modern city managers face pressure from elected officials for changes in how (and to whom) services are delivered and for changes in how cities are managed.[86]

Efficiency–Accountability Trade-Off?

Some observers suggest that gains in administrative efficiency may come at the price of less direct control of city government by citizens. With so many administrative functions now supervised by appointed city managers and public employees protected against being fired for political reasons, it may be more difficult for a majority of voters to hold their government accountable at the ballot box for unpopular actions. Rigid bureaucratic rules, civil service protections, and "red tape" may make it difficult for elected officials to put political pressure on city administrators, but these rules ensure that politicians can't use their position to enrich themselves and their friends. A study of nonpartisan city council members also found that unlike machine politicians, nonpartisan elected officials may care little about getting re-elected and thus have little regard for public opinion.[87]

Another side exists to the efficiency–accountability trade-off, however. Cross-national studies show that high levels of political corruption increase cynicism about politics and depress respect for the rule of law.[88] Public corruption causes people to retreat from conventional politics. In contrast, reforms that root out political corruption may increase public confidence in democracy.

Barriers to Mass Participation

Several studies find that the combined effects of reforms, such as off-year elections and nonpartisan elections, act to depress voter participation in reform cities.[89] These reforms make local elections less visible to many people and make it more

INSTITUTIONS MATTER

HOME RULE CHARTER

The U.S. Constitution does not mention local governments or specify anything about the powers of local governments (the 10th Amendment does state that powers not delegated to the federal government via the U.S. Constitution are "reserved" to the states). After the American Revolution and after the ratification of the U.S. Constitution, the states assumed the role of defining what local governments would do, just as colonial governments had done before. Today, states and cities outline the powers of governments in **municipal charters.** A local government's charter defines how it will be governed by listing rules about the powers of local officials and the conduct of elections. Each state government may define the powers of local government as it sees fit. Within any one state, state law may allow large cities and counties different charter arrangements than smaller places. State constitutions and laws thus define what the role of towns, cities, villages, counties, and other local governments will be.

One class of local government charter is the **home rule** charter. Home rule is when the state government delegates power about setting up local political arrangements to a local government. A home rule charter can give local governments—or a specific local government—substantial discretion to decide how it will arrange its government, how it will conduct elections, what services it will provide, how it will raise and spend revenues, and how it will hire and fire employees. Home rule charters could grant a local government the autonomy to decide how to operate across all these areas. A more limited home rule charter could let local governments make their own decisions in some areas but not others. If powers are not delegated to the local government, then state laws define how things will operate locally. During the Progressive Reform era, some reformers believed it was better to let each city have home rule to best identify how it should restructure its political institutions.

difficult for many people to evaluate candidates. We provide more discussion of this in Chapter 3. For much of the 20th century, turnout for local elections was higher in large machine cities than in large reform cities.[90] Lower turnout may lead to substantial reductions in the representation of Latinos and Asian Americans on city councils and in mayors' offices. African Americans win office less often when turnout is depressed by off-year elections.

Class and Racial Bias

Scholars also note that politics and elections in reform cities such as Houston and San Jose became dominated by powerful nonpartisan "slating groups" that promoted the election of white professionals, business owners, and land developers.[91] Some of these groups were just as dominant in local politics in reform

cities as party organizations were in machine cities.[92] Class and racial bias in local politics may be affected by low turnout, itself a product of some reforms. Turnout can be lower than 10 percent in some off-year, nonpartisan local elections. Although there may not be large differences in who votes and who does not vote in high-turnout national elections, very low turnout in local elections may increase the class and racial differences between voters and nonvoters.[93] This may distort democracy because elected officials may be more attentive to the interests of voters than nonvoters. Low turnout rates also result in less representation of Latinos and Asian Americans as mayors and on city councils than they might receive when turnout is higher. At-large elections can further increase the influence of middle-class and upper-class groups in local politics by reducing opportunities for representation of African Americans and ethnic minorities (see Chapter 3). Maintaining lower levels of minority officeholders has consequences for who gets what from city government. Fewer minorities in offices mean fewer minority citizens holding city jobs.[94]

At-large elections may also change how council members do their jobs. One study concluded that districted, partisan elections were more likely to produce representation that mirrors the community and that partisan elections made it easier for voters to hold elected officials accountable.[95] At-large elections have also been found to be used, intentionally, to disenfranchise blacks in southern cities and counties.[96] Council–manager governments are also seen as being slower in their responsiveness to the demands of emerging political groups in a city.[97] Another study found that mayor–council cities were more responsive than council–manager cities in responding to social and racial cleavages in a city[98] and incorporating minorities into city jobs.[99] Minority mayors may have more ability to affect what government does, and serve their constituents, in mayor–council systems.[100]

Summary

In this chapter, we examine how the United States began as a rural nation but experienced rapid urbanization in the mid-1800s. The growth of cities outpaced the growth of effective government, and urban machines emerged in this context with a style of politics that thrived for decades. The machine style emphasized personal bonds over substantive government services. The style is well-represented by a machine politician quoted as saying that he wanted to be sure that there has to be someone in every ward of his city that "any bloke can come to—no matter what he's done—and get help. Help, you understand; none of your law and justice, but help."[101] The personal touch of machine politicians might have helped some people find jobs or fix problems with the law, but it could not assure that all people were treated equally before the law. The absence of law, justice, and effective municipal services made machines a target for reforms that redesigned local political institutions. The modern bureaucratic city, for all its cold impersonal character, is designed to have routine standards that public employees must follow if everyone is going to be treated the same.

This chapter also illustrates how changes in political institutions can affect who gets what from local government. The reforms adopted during the Progressive era altered how people become engaged with local politics. Some reforms were clearly designed to limit which sort of people would be mobilized. Many of these reforms survive to this day, but others, such as at-large elections, are often challenged and rejected. Overall, the municipal reforms discussed here may have subtle effects on how a modern city is governed. Elected officials in reformed cities have less direct influence over some administrative matters than their counterparts in cities that adopted few reforms. The opening vignette in this chapter provides a dramatic example of this. But for all their supposed separation of politics and administration, highly reformed cities may differ from contemporary "unreformed cities" not so much in how efficiently they are governed but in who governs. Institutions that increase participation, increase diversity in representation, and guarantee electoral competition—such as partisan local elections, local elections held during presidential contests, and representation by district—may create a more pluralist form of local politics. By *pluralist*, we mean a form of politics where more voices are heard and where it is difficult for any single group to consolidate power.

Keywords

Civil service	Model city charter	Straight-ticket ballot
Clientele politics	Muckraking journalists	Strong mayor–council system
Council–manager system	Municipal charters	Tammany Hall
Dillon's rule	Patronage	Urbanization
Home rule	Pendleton Act	Ward
Jacksonian democracy	Populist era	Weak mayor–council systems
Land Ordinance of 1785	Precinct	
Louisiana Purchase	Precinct captain	
Machines	Progressive era	

Suggested Readings

Bridges, Amy. 1984. *A city in the republic: Antebellum New York and the origins of machine politics*. Ithaca, NY: Cornell University Press.

———. 1997. *Morning glories: Municipal reform in the Southwest*. Princeton, NJ: Princeton University Press.

Elkins, Steven. 1987. *City and regime in the American republic*. Chicago: University of Chicago Press.

Erie, Steven. *Rainbow's end: Irish Americans and the dilemmas of urban machine politics, 1840–1985*. Berkeley: University of California Press.

Riordan, William L. 1993. *Plunkitt of Tammany Hall: A series of very plain talks on very practical politics*. New York: Bedford Books, St. Martin's (Originally published in 1905).

Spain, Daphne. 2000. *How women saved the city*. Minneapolis: University of Minnesota Press.

Websites

International City Manager Association (ICMA; http://www.icma.org): The professional and educational organization for appointed city managers, administrators, and assistants. ICMA provides technical assistance, training, and information resources to its members and the local governments. Also publishes the city manager code of ethics. Founded in 1914.

National Civic League (http://www.ncl.org): A nonprofit, nonpartisan group founded in 1894 by Teddy Roosevelt and others to promote municipal reform and community democracy. NCSL serves as a resource for anyone interested in cutting-edge community-building practices. The group was originally known as the National Municipal League and periodically publishes recommendations for government structures (the Model City Charter).

National League of Cities (http://www.nlc.org): Lobby groups for local government interests in Washington, D.C. The oldest and largest national organization representing municipal governments throughout the United States.

12

The Politics of Place

Competition over Growth and Development

V ernon, California, was incorporated in 1905 just south of downtown Los Angeles by John B. Leonis, a savvy business-man, and two ranchers who owned land near railroad lines. Upon **incorporation,** they ensured that their five square miles of land would be zoned "exclusively industrial." That is the town's motto today. As of 2000, Vernon had a population of only 91 (with 60 registered voters), but it is also home to 1,200 businesses that employs 44,000 people. Given this sparse population and huge commercial and industrial base, Vernon generated over $300 million in annual revenues from taxes and by selling bonds and electricity. It generates large annual surpluses after funding infra-structure and public services.[1] Most residents are well-paid city employees or relatives of city workers who live in homes owned by the city (this helps city officials control who can vote in local elections—but elections are a rare event). Among other services Vernon funds (including police, fire, and many services for indus-tries), the city spends about $164 per person each year on a library. Directly across the Los Angeles River, Vernon's neighbor, Com-merce, is similarly situated. The City of Commerce was incorpo-rated in 1960 to prevent Vernon and Los Angeles from annexing valuable commercial land. It generates substantial tax revenues from industry, trucking distribution businesses, shopping malls, and a casino. Commerce provides its 13,000 residents free bus service, pays Los Angeles County to provide them fire and police services, and spends $184 per person on libraries—four times the library funds for an average California city and not much less than what Beverly Hills spends.

Several cities were also established to the south and east of downtown Los Angeles and Vernon that would serve as residen-tial suburbs for the families of people who worked in factories in other cities. Within a few miles of Commerce and Vernon are Hun-tington Park, Bell, Maywood, South Gate, and others. Working-class populations in these towns boomed during World War II to serve defense industries, and for much of the 20th century, racial segregation ensured the cities were overwhelmingly white. Times have changed. Race riots in nearby Watts in 1965, the collapse of high-wage manufacturing jobs, the demise of defense spending, and immigration contributed to a flight of white residents to more affluent communities during the 1970s and 1980s. These cities still serve as bedroom communities for people who work in Vernon and Commerce, but they can't compete with their indus-trial and commercial neighbors when it comes to generating tax

OUTLINE

Introductory Vignette

Introduction

Land Use: The Key Power of American Counties and Cities

Metropolitan Fragmentation

Race and the Rise of the Suburbs

Regulating Land Use: Zoning and Eminent Domain

The Enduring Role of Pro-Growth Forces in Local Politics

Are We Better Off without Zoning?

State and Regional Planning Alternatives

Competition for Local Economic Development

The Consequences of Metropolitan Fragmentation

Regional and Metropolitan Government?

Summary

revenues needed to fund public services. Poverty rates are higher, and tax revenues and home values are lower in these immigrant bedroom cities. Whereas Vernon and Commerce spend rather lavishly on libraries, Bell, South Gate, and Maywood spend nothing. Huntington Park managed just $0.23 spending per person on books. This chapter discusses why life is different in these places. We demonstrate how and why communities use local land use powers to compete for businesses and residents that help them financially and how they have used rules to keep people out of places. These rules shaped the United States' metropolitan regions and continue to affect who gets what from government.

Fred Greaves/Reuters/Corbis

The power to incorporate as a city comes with the ability to control land use, and greater control over local revenues. The City of Vernon, California(population 90) earns millions of dollars per year from industries and a power plant located inside its border. These revenues allow Vernon to spend lavishly on public services.

Scott Tucker/Alamy

Introduction

As noted in the previous chapter, local governments are creatures of their state governments. They exist, in a sense, at the pleasure of their state. The range of services they provide, the discretion they have for making independent decisions, the range of powers granted to local elected officials, the jurisdiction of municipal courts, and the form of local elections—all these structural features of local governments are regulated by state laws.

We have also detailed the dominant role that states and the federal government have in setting the agenda for fiscal policy, health and welfare policy, transportation, and higher education. Local governments do retain a key role in controlling much of primary and secondary education policy and financing (see Chapter 15), but this power mostly lies in the hands of school districts.

So, what is left for **general purpose local governments?** What are the primary political functions of cities and counties? What do they "do" that is distinct from the powers and functions of state governments and school districts? Our first thought might be of traditional local services: fire protection, police, and sanitation. These are important services that many cities and counties do provide, but as we suggest below, this isn't really what being a city or county is all about. Many cities and counties have no police force, no fire department, and no garbage collection, and they provide no water service. So, what, then, is the key feature of local politics?

Land Use: The Key Power of American Counties and Cities

Although cities and counties are formally legal creatures of their state governments, states have traditionally granted local governments (counties and cities) substantial power over land use decisions. *Land use* refers to a broad set of policies we discuss below. Some of these policies are often referred to as *zoning*. Zoning involves decisions about where different sorts of things are allowed to be built and how much of various things get to be built. *Land use policy*, defined more broadly, involves attempts to influence the character of development that occurs in a jurisdiction's borders. These policies might work to keep certain types of people and industries out, while making it easier for other types of people and businesses to move in.

We suggest that the politics of many American local governments, and the historical development of American communities, can be best understood in terms of land use politics. Much of the politics of American places involves conflicts inside communities over the uses of land and conflicts between communities over development. The importance of land is best understood when considered in the environment that American communities find themselves in. First, we must understand that cities and counties keep much of the revenue they collect locally, and they need revenues to thrive. Second, we must recognize that the revenues they collect depend, in large part, on who (or what) ends up locating within the county or city's borders. Third, it is important to remember that people and businesses have some level of mobility.

Local Governments and Demands for Public Services

Consider how these three forces might interact. Any government needs revenues to provide services. Demands for local services, such as parks, roads, streetlights, libraries, police protection, or social services, depend in part on who (or what) locates in a city. Families with lots of kids produce demands for schools, parks, and children's libraries. A manufacturing plant might want a place that provides industrial infrastructure or cheap water and power. Land use policies can affect who locates in a place and thus affect demands for services. Zoning that allows one type of duplex, apartment buildings, or single-family housing might attract more kids. Zoning that allows only high-end condominiums or very few houses per acre might attract people with fewer kids. Zoning that allows for heavy manufacturing uses might yield demands for infrastructure like water and power. Zoning allowing light industry might produce different service requirements for cities and counties. Zoning affects and reflects the services that a place needs to provide.

Land Use and Local Revenues

Just as different land uses are associated with different service needs, they also produce different revenues. Recall from Chapter 10 that local governments depend heavily on property and sales taxes for their locally generated revenues. Some forms of land use offer tremendous potential local revenues, whereas others do not. Expensive homes might generate more property tax revenues than less expensive homes or apartments. Charges and fees applied to each new home constructed in a jurisdiction are another potential source of revenues. Commercial activity generates sales tax revenues and jobs. Car dealerships may generate limited property tax revenues but add greatly to a community's share of sales tax collections.

Location Decisions of Businesses and Firms

At any point in time, people and businesses are trying to decide where to locate. Probably dozens of factors—many somewhat random—enter into their location decisions. People move where they can afford to live or move to be near their jobs or families. They move to get away from somewhere or someone or to enjoy a different lifestyle. But some people looking to buy homes might also make their location decision, in part, after considering the quality of local schools, parks, public safety, and other public services. At the same time, they might consider what their taxes would be if they locate in one city versus another or in an unincorporated part of a county.

The same goes for business firms. When moving operations or opening a new facility, a business likely has dozens of things to consider when choosing where to locate. Businesses need to consider the local labor pool, their access to people who supply them their raw materials, and their access to those who buy their goods. But the places they have to choose between may also offer different mixes of public services at different tax levels.

The Competitive Local Environment

This is the environment that American cities and counties find themselves in. Cities and counties provide services and the cost of providing these services requires that they generate revenues. They can try to affect both demands for services, and the flow of revenue with land use decisions. One theory predicts that places will make land use decisions with an eye toward "net fiscal gain"; that is, by encouraging development that brings in more revenues than service cost while discouraging development that costs more to service than the revenues it generates.[2] Another theory proposes that residents and businesses keep a keen eye on their local tax costs and service benefits and that they pack up and move when their costs exceed the benefits they receive from their local government.[3] Local governments must compete, then, to keep spending efficient and taxes low if they are to retain the firms and residents who contribute the most revenues.

One way to think of the political environment of American local governments, then, is to think of cities and counties as businesses in a competitive marketplace. As a "business," one place might offer a unique mix of public services, maybe providing publicly owned water and power, plus its own unique location, its unique opportunities for access to nice areas, and some particular opportunities for access to transportation. All of this comes at a price: the taxes and fees charged by that jurisdiction. A neighboring community might offer a different mix of services, perhaps leaving water and power service to the private market. It might also have a different "price" (or tax level) for locating there. As general purpose local governments, cities and counties are somewhat like supermarkets, grocery stores, or a little corner shop from this perspective. Different stores cater to different types of customers. One store might emphasize bargain prices over service (and have you bag your own groceries). Another store down the road might charge more but offer more customer service and expensive gourmet items. If a store offers the wrong combination of things at too high a price, it loses customers.

In this market model of local politics, businesses and residents are like consumers in a marketplace. They are assumed to select places to locate just as they might select where they shop for groceries. If they don't like what they get for their money, they move. On its face, this assumption might seem unrealistic. Many—perhaps most—people can't tell you how much they pay in taxes for local services or for things like sewer, water, and schools, let alone know what some other local jurisdiction might be charging. Even if they could, people have roots in their communities; friends, family, jobs, and neighbors make them very hesitant to move. The poor and racial minorities who are subject to continued housing discrimination, in particular, often have little choice about where they can locate. And most businesses probably have similar roots that prevent them from packing up, even if they were keenly aware of their local tax bills.

Although the pure market model of local politics is highly unrealistic, it is a useful analogy to help understand and explain much of what local governments do, why they do it, and what they don't do. And the model is not as unrealistic as it might first seem. There is evidence that some homeowners pay attention to their mix of taxes and public services—at least for public schools—when they decide where to move.[4] There is also evidence that local taxes factor into the broad range of things businesses consider when they make their decisions about where to locate, although mainly after the range of location choices has been narrowed

to a particular metropolitan area. Moreover, if enough local officials know (or just think) that a few key residents or businesses behave as the market model suggests, then many things might work as the model predicts.

Metropolitan Fragmentation

One reason that a market model is used to describe politics of local places in the United States is because population growth occurs in highly fragmented metropolitan areas. Natural increases in population and immigration mean that the United States will add about 30 million new residents between 2000 and 2010—about the population of the State of New York. Millions of people will also move from one state to another. Table 12.1 lists America's 15-largest **metropolitan areas** and their rates of growth from 2000 to 2006. The greater Los Angeles area added over 1.3 million residents during this period and the Dallas area over 840,000 people. Estimated growth rates for the greater Atlanta, Houston, and Phoenix areas all suggest each of these regions absorbed over 700,000 additional residents in the first part of the decade. Table 12.2 illustrates that growth rates are very fast in some of the nation's smaller and midsized metropolitan regions.

Obviously, all these new residents must live somewhere. Over 80 percent of Americans reside somewhere in a metropolitan area that consists of a central city, suburbs, and **unincorporated areas** governed by a county. There are at least 300 metropolitan areas in the United States. A single metro area might be made up of multiple central cities, several dozen other incorporated cities, and several counties. Each metropolitan area in the United States is thus fragmented into dozens of different general purpose local governments providing unique location options—cities, counties, and towns, in addition to school districts and **special districts.** As we see below, many of these governments compete against each other to attract

Table 12.1			

The 15 Largest U.S. Metropolitan Areas, 2006

Rank	Metropolitan Area	Population	Growth since 2000 (%)
1	New York–Northern New Jersey–Long Island, NY–NJ–PA	18,818,536	3
2	Los Angeles–Long Beach–Santa Ana, CA	12,950,129	5
3	Chicago–Naperville–Joliet, IL–IN–WI	9,505,748	4
4	Dallas–Fort Worth–Arlington, TX	6,003,967	16
5	Philadelphia–Camden–Wilmington, PA–NJ–DE–MD	5,826,742	2
6	Houston–Sugar Land–Baytown, TX	5,539,949	17
7	Miami–Fort Lauderdale–Miami Beach, FL	5,463,857	9
8	Washington–Arlington–Alexandria, DC–VA–MD–WV	5,290,400	10
9	Atlanta–Sandy Springs–Marietta, GA	5,138,223	21
10	Detroit–Warren–Livonia, MI	4,468,966	0
11	Boston–Cambridge–Quincy, MA–NH	4,455,217	1
12	San Francisco–Oakland–Fremont, CA	4,180,027	1
13	Phoenix–Mesa–Scottsdale, AZ	4,039,182	24
14	Riverside–San Bernardino–Ontario, CA	4,026,135	24
15	Seattle–Tacoma–Bellevue, WA	3,263,497	7

Note: Growth rates from 1 April 2000 to 1 July 2006.
Source: U.S. Census Bureau.

growth that helps their place while competing to avoid growth that might not help.

The Los Angeles area is one of the largest and one of the most fragmented. Los Angeles County has 292 towns and cities, of which 88 are incorporated as legally recognized municipal governments (cities). The four counties that border Los Angeles County contain another 92 incorporated cities (34 in Orange County, 24 in Riverside County, 10 in Ventura County, and 24 in San Bernardino County).

Los Angeles is not unique. The Minneapolis–St. Paul area includes ten different counties, each with many cities and districts. There are six counties surrounding Chicago, seven in the greater Kansas City area, seven in the Denver area, eight in Indianapolis, nine around New York City, and eleven around Dallas–Fort Worth. The United States' top five most fragmented metropolitan areas—measured in terms of the number of local governments per person and the dispersion of people across

cities—are the St. Louis (MO–IL), Allentown–Bethlehem (PA–NJ), Louisville (KY–IN), and Ann Arbor (MI) metropolitan areas.[5] Within any metropolitan area, there are also dozens of special districts that supply one specific public service, such as fire protection, parks, libraries, or hospitals, as well as school districts (see Chapter 15).

Most American cities and counties exist in a sort of competitive arena, surrounded by dozens of other cities and counties that may have their own unique powers to tax, spend, and make decisions about land use inside their own borders. When people move from one metropolitan area to another, they face a range of choices about which specific place in the region they might locate to. Likewise, assuming a resident or firm in a large traditional central city like Chicago can afford to move, there are dozens of choices about where to relocate within the greater Chicago area, including suburban cities and unincorporated, semirural places.

Table 12.2

Fastest Growing U.S. Metropolitan Areas, 2006

Rank	Metropolitan Area	Population, 2006	% of Growth since 2000
1	St. George, UT	126,312	40
2	Greeley, CO	236,857	31
3	Cape Coral–Ft. Myers, FL	571,344	30
4	Bend, OR	149,140	29
5	Las Vegas–Paradise, NV	1,777,539	29
6	Provo–Orem, UT	474,180	26
7	Naples–Marco Island, FL	314,649	26
8	Raleigh–Cary, NC	994,551	25
9	Gainesville, GA	173,256	24
10	Phoenix–Mesa–Scottsdale, AZ	4,039,182	24
11	Prescott, AZ	208,014	24
12	Riverside–San Bernardino–Ontario, CA	4,026,135	24
13	McAllen–Edinburgh–Pharr, TX	700,634	23
14	Port St Lucie–Ft. Pierce, FL	392,183	23
15	Ocala, FL	316,183	22

Note: Growth rates from 1 April 2000 to 1 July 2006.
Source: U.S. Census Bureau.

Location choices are obviously constrained by many factors, but the American local environment is unique when compared to much of the developed world. American cities and counties are also granted far more control over land use and zoning powers than in many other nations. The scope of these powers varies across the states. And American cities are far more dependent on locally generated revenues than cities in Canada or Europe, for example. This means that in the United States, location decisions of residents and firms have tremendous consequences for the places they move to as well as the places they leave. If a large firm exits a place, it takes its contribution to that jurisdiction's tax base with it. So, too, when wealthy residents move away. This, combined with the fragmentation of the United States' metropolitan regions, means that there are some places that win big and others that lose big when people and businesses move.

What's a City?

The discussion thus far begs two important questions: what's a city, and what are the differences between city and county control over land use? We typically think of a metropolitan area as having a central city, surrounded by **suburbs.** Los Angeles, New York, and Chicago are our traditional ideas of what *cities* are. But what about suburban places like Lawndale (near Los Angeles), Levittown (near New York), and Lincolnshire (near Chicago)? Some of these are actual incorporated cities; some are not. Ninety-eight percent of incorporated American cities are relatively small places with populations of less than 100,000 people. Nearly two-thirds are places with less than 25,000 residents. Today, most Americans live in suburban cities that lack the scale, density, and social diversity of a larger, central city. A suburb is a city when, following state law, it incorporates as a municipality.

In most states, places often have strong incentives to become cities. If a place incorporates and becomes a formal city, it can have many or all the powers to tax, spend, and control land use as a traditional central city. If a place remains unincorporated, the larger county government it is located in may have substantial control over such matters. State laws determine the range of powers that incorporated cites have. Once incorporated, cities have some latitude in deciding what sort of services they will offer—or if they will offer any at all.

New Cities versus Traditional Cities

These newer suburban places where most Americans now live are much different than older, traditional American central cities, such as Detroit, Philadelphia, or San Francisco. Some observers use phrases like *exurbs* (for extra-urban) and *edge cities* to refer to newer, non–central city places that initially developed far from a central place. Edge cities can be seen as different than standard suburbs because they include job opportunities in addition to housing and shopping. However, growth and sprawl may eventually fill in any space between central cities, suburbs, and edge cities. Furthermore, it is not always so easy to identity a central city. Houston, Phoenix, and Los Angeles are sprawling megacities surrounded by many suburbs, but they look and feel much different than traditional cities like Boston or Chicago. Regardless of what we call these places, more Americans now live in suburbs of all sorts than live in rural places or central cities. Many of these suburban places hardly existed 50 years ago. Consider the Washington, D.C.–Arlington, Virginia, region as an example. Arlington and Washington, D.C., are somewhat traditional, neighboring cities with a mix of residential neighborhoods, cultural precincts, and economic activity that employs more than just city residents. Many people who work in those cities now live in the booming suburbs of North Virginia's Fairfax County, some in incorporated cities, such as Falls Church and Fairfax, and many in unincorporated suburban places, like McLean and Annandale. More than twice as many people live in Fairfax County than Washington, D.C. Farther out from these Virginia suburbs, but within commuting distance of D.C., lie relatively isolated places with rapidly growing populations and their own economies (that is, exurbs or edge cities), such as Manassas or Tyson's Corner.

There is often much less that is public in newer cities than in older ones, as traditional cities typically do much more in the way of providing public utilities, public services, parks, and other amenities. Progressive reformers of the early 20th century (discussed in Chapter 11) sought to improve urban living conditions by granting cities monopoly powers to supply local services that were in short supply, including street lighting, drinking water, electricity, sewerage, and waste collection. Earlier in the 19th century, local governments had granted monopolies to private firms for such services or waited for the private market to supply them. But this often led to inadequate private investment in such services, bankruptcies, and political corruption in the awarding of contracts.[6]

The Progressives' idea was to use the authority of the city to do something that the free market was failing to do. Cities began to act as nonprofit organizations that amassed enough capital (by borrowing or taxing) to supply infrastructure and services at a fair price to residents. Many older, traditional cities still reflect this Progressive ideal and provide a wide range of public services.

The Lakewood Plan

The United States experienced dramatic changes in the 1950s because millions of families were suddenly able to purchase new homes in new communities. At least three forces interacted to create a booming market for single-family homes. First, after World War II, the federal government began expanding subsidies that lowered the cost of financing a home loan. Second,

National Archives and Records Administration

Aerial photograph of Levittown, New York. Built in the 1950s, Levittown was one of the United States' first modern suburbs. Prices for new homes were relatively low because developer William J. Levitt built on cheap land beyond the central city and standardized much of the construction process.

at the same time soldiers were returning from Europe and the Pacific to buy homes, innovations in mass production of homes by builders, such as William J. Levitt, lowered building costs. Third, massive federal subsidies built a highway system that made it possible to build on cheap land far from the traditional city at the center of a metropolitan area.

Many cities that incorporated after this suburban boom did so with no intention of offering the full range of public services that older cities did. The role that cities play in the provision of local public services profoundly changed in the later half of the 20th century as existing cities shifted away from the tradition of providing a broad mix of public services, while new cities formed that provided very little in the way of services.[7] **Privatization** of city services and **contracting for services** began

to replace the tradition of cities being a single level of government that provided residents with local services, such as libraries, parks, health services, and fire protection.

In 1953, the community of Lakewood, California, developed a contract with Los Angeles County that became a model for how many new suburban cities would deal with providing services. At the time, Lakewood was the largest private land development in the United States—a massive 17,500-home development 10 miles from Los Angeles. Developers and residents had little interest in collecting Lakewood city taxes to pay for police, firefighters, road maintenance, building inspections, sewer service, or libraries. When Lakewood was unincorporated, these services were supplied by the county. The Lakewood Plan involved a detailed contract with Los Angeles County that allowed municipal incorporation for Lakewood, with the county continuing to provide the new City of Lakewood with some of the services it received when it was an unincorporated area.

Lakewood, and similar places that incorporate like this, might not seem to get much out of the deal if we simply consider cities as places designed to provide services for residents. These newer cities can avoid providing traditional municipal services (and avoid the higher taxes needed to fund services) if they **contract for services** with other governments, with **special districts,** or with private firms (for things like garbage collection). But these cities acquire two key powers when they incorporate: the power to control land use and the power to collect their own taxes. Control of these powers proved very popular for many places after the Lakewood plan innovation. Other places in Los Angeles County incorporated as cities with hardly any residents but with control over zoning and access to huge tax revenues. Local industries incorporated prime commercial land (as the City of Commerce) and prime industrial land (as the City of Industry).[8]

Local governments have also been privatizing services more rapidly since the 1970s, as cities sell off publicly owned utilities and private firms have expanded their offerings of services, like garbage collection and sewage treatment.[9] A 1995 survey of the 100-largest cities in the United States found that only three had not privatized some of their services. But most larger cities "had not fully embraced the privatization approach in a broad-based manner." The most commonly privatized services were towing, garbage collection, building security, street repair, and ambulance services.[10]

The Lakewood model for cities spread across American metropolitan regions during the post–World War II suburbanization boom. Newer cities and unincorporated places can now choose to offer little in public services, but they have a wide range of options when it comes to contracting for services. As Table 12.3 illustrates, over 20,000 new special districts were formed since 1952 to provide a particular service for a specific geographic area. Their district boundaries can include many incorporated cities as well as unincorporated areas. These districts have their own appointed or elected boards that oversee operations. Many have the power to raise taxes, issue bonds, build facilities, and employ people who provide a service. Table 12.4 shows that the most common of these are districts that manage natural resources (land management, soil conservation, water quality protection, and similar programs), fire protection, water supply, housing, and sewage treatment. The most rapidly growing categories of special districts are library districts (91 percent more since 1987), districts that provide multiple services (56 percent more), and districts designed to protect public health (53 percent more). The latter do everything from mosquito abatement to immunization and AIDS education outreach.

Table 12.3							
Number of Local Governments in the United States							
Year	1942	1952	1962	1972	1982	1992	2002
County	3,050	3,052	3,043	3,044	3,041	3,043	3,034
City (municipality)	16,220	16,807	17,997	18,517	19,076	19,296	19,431
Town (unincorporated)	18,919	17,202	17,114	16,991	16,734	16,666	16,506
Special district	8,299	12,340	18,323	23,885	28,078	33,131	35,356

Source: U.S. Census of Governments.

Table 12.4			

Special District Functions

District Type	Number of Districts	% of All Districts	Change since 1987 (%)
Natural resources	7,026	20	+10
Fire protection	5,743	16	+13
Water supply	3,423	10	+12
Housing and community development	3,413	10	−1
Sewerage	2,020	6	+26
Cemeteries	1,670	5	+3
Libraries	1,582	4	+91
Parks and recreation	1,314	4	+31
Highways	767	2	+24
Health	743	2	+53
Hospitals	735	2	−6
School building authorities	530	2	−27
Airports	512	1	+39
Other utilities	485	1	n/a
Other	2,194	6	+47
Multiple function districts	3,199	9	+56

Source: U.S. Census of Governments.

What Do Cities Do?

In addition to providing police, traditional city services may include water, public transit, sewers, nursing homes, libraries, hospitals, stadiums, natural gas, electricity, landfills, and airports. American cities that were formed in the 1800s provide many of these, with over 70 percent offering fire, water, and sewer service.[11] But special districts, contracting, and privatization have changed what it means to be a city. Over 10 percent of American cities do not provide a single municipal service other than police. Another 12 percent offer just one municipal service from the list above. Most cities formed after the 1950s don't provide fire protection, water service, sewerage, or public transit.[12]

With contracting and privatization, places can incorporate strategically and become cities that are very limited in what they do. What many do is use their public land use and tax powers to attract and assist private business. The example of Vernon, California, in the opening of this chapter may be a bit extreme, but it illuminates this. The strategy of forming cities for specialized economic purposes is not new. Oil companies incorporated an oil field as a city (Signal Hill) in Los Angeles County in the 1920s to prevent the City of Long Beach from annexing the area and gaining the tax revenues. Dennis Judd, a keen observer of American cities, demonstrates that through American history, cities were founded for economic purposes. The American colonies were chartered by England as mercantile corporations. Major American cities, such as Denver, Chicago, Pittsburgh, and Kansas City, developed because local boosters in those places were able to outcompete rival communities in recruiting residents and businesses and securing access to railways.[13]

INSTITUTIONS MATTER

THE POWER OF MUNICIPAL INCORPORATION

After making a fortune in pizza, Thomas S. Monaghan, the founder of Domino's Pizza, attracted head-lines when he entered the real estate business in 2006. Monaghan announced he was spending $250 million to buy 5,000 acres of land near Naples in southwest Florida to establish a new city, Ave Maria. His initial announcement noted plans to build 11,000 homes, a large cathedral, a new Catholic University, and the largest crucifix in the nation. The giant crucifix symbolized Monaghan's vision for his city: it would follow strict Catholic principles. Abortion, birth control, and pornography would be banned.

The Florida attorney general said it would be "up to the courts" to decide if the plan was legal. Monaghan later claimed Catholic rules would apply only to the university,[1] but his intentions were clear. As we see in this chapter, the powers of local government grant communities substantial influence over who moves to a place and over what life might be like there. Ave Maria cannot formally exclude residents based on their religion, but the idea of writing rules to ensure that only certain people live in a city is hardly new. Many property deeds in the United States still include "covenants" that prevent the sale of land to nonwhites. Many cities also had laws that forbade blacks from being around after sundown. Explicitly racially motivated rules have been struck down by the Supreme Court, so such rules are no longer legally enforceable, but some forms of exclusion are still permitted. Many American retirement communities have binding rules prohibiting home sales to people under 55. These age rules solve the political dilemma of having to raise tax revenue to fund playgrounds and schools.

Note

1. "No Abortion, No Pornography, No Contraceptives in New Town," *North Country Gazette*, 3 March 2006, http://www.northcountrygazette.org/articles/030306NewTown.html; Melissa McNamara, "Bloggers Feed on Pizza Man's Plans," CBS News Blogophile, March 8, 2006, http://www.cbsnews.com/stories/2006/03/06/blogophile/main1374192.shtml.

But the United States' larger, older cities evolved before the spread of Lakewood-style suburbs. Over time, their metropolitan areas evolved—fragmenting as more and more places incorporate to assume control of their own land use and tax powers. Of course, traditional cities try to grow by annexing outlying areas that might add to their tax base. But **annexation** is often resisted by residents in the targeted area, and older central cities can run out of adjacent unincorporated places to annex. One major study of municipal incorporation concluded that most incorporation attempts were motivated by a desire to maintain control of taxation and by fears of annexation by another city.[14] Another study suggests that incorporation of new cities in Michigan, Texas, and Florida in the 1950s and 1960s was motivated by manufacturers and white residents seeking to form exclusive communities that walled themselves off from less-affluent African Americans.[15]

Race and the Rise of the Suburbs

The rise of new suburban cities did not occur by accident. Homeownership started to become something accessible to average Americans in the 1930s, when the federal government began underwriting part of the cost of home loans. In addition to the federal highway system, two public housing programs were instrumental in the creation of the suburbs: the Federal Housing Administration (FHA), created by the National Housing Act of 1934; and the Veterans Administration (VA) loan program, created by the Servicemen's Readjustment Act of 1944. Before the FHA program, a homebuyer would need a cash down payment of no less than 33 percent of a home's value in order to secure a home loan. The FHA insured the risk of the loan

Figure 12.1

Percent of Homebuyers with FHA and/or VA Loans, 1950–2000

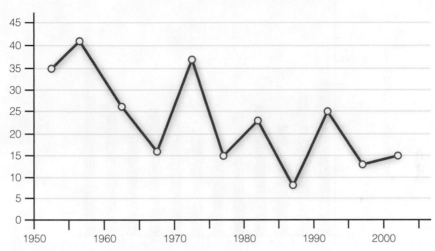

PERCENT OF HOMEBUYERS WITH
FHA/VA LOANS, 1950-2000

Sources: U.S. Department of Housing and Urban Development, "U.S. Housing Market Conditions," http://www.huduser.org/periodicals/USHMC/fall2001/summary-2.html; and Dennis R. Judd, *City Politics: Private Power and Public Policy* (Upper Saddle River, N.J.: Pearson Longman, 2004).

for a bank, which allowed banks to require a much lower down payment (10 percent of the home's value). The VA program worked in a similar manner for veterans.[16]

As Figure 12.1 illustrates, during the period between 1950 and 1970, at some points, as much as 40 percent of all private new home construction was financed with FHA and VA loans. Figure 12.2 illustrates that the 1950s was a period of incredible levels of new home construction. More homes were built in 1950, for example, than in any year during the 1980s and 1990s. Millions of Americans were able to purchase their first home because of the FHA and VA programs, and the vast majority of these were new homes being built in new communities.[17]

The original FHA lending criteria relied on real estate and banking industry preferences for racially segregated neighborhoods. From 1946 to 1959, less than 2 percent of FHA loans went to African Americans.[18] The FHA removed race as a formal criterion for lend-

ing in 1950, but banks, developers, and real estate agencies continued to enforce de facto segregation of housing, legally, because mixed-race areas were perceived as a bad investment. The Federal Housing Act of 1968 finally made it illegal for banks, developers, and realtors to discriminate in the housing market on the basis of race. In the meantime, over 30 million new homes were constructed, mostly in all-white suburbs, and over 1,200 new American cities were incorporated (see Table 12.3).

Both the VA and FHA programs also used lending criteria that favored new, detached, single-family housing construction over the higher-density, multifamily housing more common in older cities.[19] As a result, some suggest that the FHA and VA programs should be seen as a massive federal subsidy that locked racial and ethnic minorities in older cities while moving middle-class whites out of established central cities and into new suburbs.[20] Kenneth Jackson estimates that suburban St. Louis received more than six times as much FHA

Figure 12.2

Annual Construction of New Private Housing in the United States, 1950–2005 (thousands of units built)

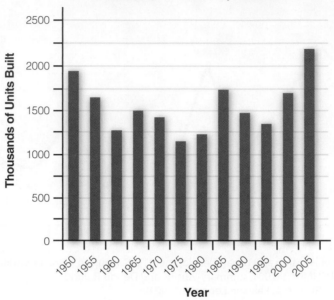

ANNUAL CONSTRUCTION OF NEW PRIVATE HOUSING IN THE US, 1950-2005

Source: U.S. Census Bureau, *Statistical Abstract of the United States: National Data Book*, 723, table 1199, http://www.census.gov/indicator/www/newresconst.pdf.

money per capita than the City of St. Louis. Long Island (a suburban area adjacent to New York City) received 60 times more FHA money per resident than Bronx County (an older, urban part of New York City).[21]

The rise of the suburbs meant that older cities were locked into a spiral of decline, encouraged by federal housing policies.[22] Prior to the suburban boom, traditional cities became home to a growing portion of the United States' African-American population. African-American migration from southern farms to northern cities increased in the early 1900s, as industrial jobs motivated hundreds of thousands to move north to find work in factories. This migration was accelerated by both world wars, when emigration from Europe slowed and demand for industrial labor increased. These events transformed the demographics of northern cities during the 20th century. Working-class blacks

entered older cities in large numbers (having few location options), whereas middle-class whites fled to newer suburbs—taking their tax revenues with them.

Regulating Land Use: Zoning and Eminent Domain

Land use powers—that is, the power to determine permissible and impermissible land uses—were originally given to state governments. Over time, however, local governments assumed more control of what went on inside their borders. There are at least four major legal powers that cities have to affect land use. Taxing and spending are two.[23] Our discussion of the market model of the city introduced the idea that a city's mix of taxing and spending might affect who locates where. We will return to this idea in a moment. Zoning and eminent domain are two additional powers cities may use to affect who gets to locate where.

American cities have traditionally been granted the authority to regulate public health, safety, and welfare. These are known as a local government's **police powers.** When state legislatures charter cities and counties, they grant them wide authority to exercise police powers. The exercise of these powers extends far beyond maintaining a police force; it also includes the ability to regulate building design, the quality of food in restaurants, and what can be built in flood zones as well as the ability to operate immunization programs. The police powers are perhaps the most important tool cities have to affect land use.

City governments were relatively passive actors in the 1800s. By the late 1800s, after decades of industrialization and immigration, American cities were overcrowded, much of their housing was dangerous and unregulated, and sanitation was lacking. Use of local police powers to regulate public health and safety accelerated in the early 20th century, as Progressive reformers, muckraker journalists, and others targeted the dangerous living conditions of cities (see Chapter 9).

Zoning Powers

Land use **zoning** was one of the chief innovations of local police powers during the Progressive era. During the period of rapid industrialization, factories and housing in cities were at times built shoulder to shoulder. The development of cars and trucks suddenly allowed a more rapid dispersion of people and industries between 1910 to 1920, creating new conflicts over land use.[24] Zoning had its origins in New York City, where wealthy Fifth Avenue residents organized to protect their exclusive residential and commercial shopping area from encroachment by the city's textile industry. The city passed the first zoning ordinance in the United States in 1916, specifying specific land uses that could be isolated in distinct areas: residential, commercial business, warehouse, and industrial. Many cities copied New York City's policy, and by the late 1920s, 60 percent of the nation's urban areas had zoning laws.[25]

Zoning was promoted as a way to prevent incompatible land uses from being in the same place. With zoning, slaughterhouses could be forced to locate far from schools or housing; factories and residential areas could be kept apart. Contemporary zoning plans often have land divided into agricultural, residential, and industrial areas.[26] Of course, someone's land may have more value if zoned one particular way. For example, vacant land near a growing city may have much more value if it is zoned to allow residential or commercial use rather than agricultural. If a local government zones land one particular way, then the landowner might not profit as much when selling or developing the land. This was the challenge to local zoning facing the U.S. Supreme Court in 1926. In a landmark case, *Village of Euclid v. Ambler Realty Company,* the Ambler Company argued that Euclid, Ohio, had unfairly devalued its land by "down zoning" its use from commercial to residential and that they had done so without due process or just compensation.

The Court sided with Euclid, ruling that zoning was a logical extension of the city's police powers that existed to protect public health and safety. Traditional police powers allow local governments to close unhealthy restaurants or require that building designs meet safety standards. These regulations create costs for property owners, but because they serve a public purpose, local governments are not required to compensate property owners for inconvenience or loss of profit. The Court ruled that cities can likewise use zoning, and affect the value of land, without having to require compensation. The Court went as far in the *Euclid* case as to state that zoning could be used to prevent incompatible residential developments from overlapping. The "residential character" of single-family home neighborhoods could be "utterly destroyed" by large apartment buildings, and, thus, it was legitimate to use zoning to separate such neighborhoods from high-density housing.[27]

Zoning powers are a powerful, popular, and often controversial tool to affect land use. It is "far and away the most widely employed land use control technique today."[28] It is powerful and popular because it allows communities to shape their character and destiny by defining land values, usually without having to compensate property owners for their losses when the permissible use of the land is changed.[29] When a new city takes shape in raw, undeveloped land, zoning is the tool that can be used to make a place "exclusively industrial," exclusively commercial, exclusively residential, or some mix of these.

Zoning allows a city to plan its development. Very low-density zoning is used to control the pace of development by regulating when an area can be built up, and low-density zoning can be used to protect watersheds used for drinking supplies, to preserve agricultural lands, to force development out of erosion-prone areas, and to preserve scenic areas. Higher-density zoning can be used to encourage construction in specific areas. Zoning maps can also be used to exclude land uses that people don't want in their community—by requiring relatively large and uniform lot sizes and forbidding the construction of duplexes and apartments, zoning can be used to ensure that only expensive housing is available in a place.

Zoning: Taking or Regulating? Zoning is controversial for at least two reasons. First, local politics in most American cities centers around land use issues, and zoning determines how land will be used. Great profits are to be made if land is zoned to allow development; greater profits are to be made if the land is zoned for whatever use is in greatest demand. It is not surprising, then, to find developers, large landowners, building industry officials, and representatives of real estate firms attending planning commission meetings to lobby city officials for particular zoning policies. Pro-development forces may oppose some of the regulations that local governments employ to control land use. To some people denied unfettered use of their land, zoning is seen as an unfair **regulatory taking**.

Critics of land use regulations refer to them as *regulatory takings* because they lower property value, via regulation, without requiring any compensation to the owner. The Fifth Amendment to the U.S. Constitution stipulates, "[N]or shall private property be taken for public use without just compensation." Historically, this was seen as limiting what the federal government could do, not states and their cities, because the original Bill of Rights was designed to limit the power of the federal government. In 1833, the Supreme Court ruled the Fifth Amendment placed no overt requirements for compensation by state and local governments. In the landmark case *Barron vs. Baltimore,* the Court ruled that the Fifth Amendment did not require the City of Baltimore to compensate the owner of a wharf for damages caused by a public project that lowered the wharf's value.[30] However, when a government physically takes property from someone, it must pay compensation.

How far can local governments go with regulations that lower the value of someone's property? Generally, the regulation must forward some "public use" and should not cause a particular owner to bear the burden of the regulation's cost. But *public use* and *burden* have been interpreted broadly. In 1992, the Supreme Court let stand an Escondido, California, **rent control** ordinance that froze rents charged on the pads of land that mobile home owners rent to park their houses. Additional rules prevented landowners from raising land rents on mobile home pads when a mobile home was sold to a new owner and prevented them from evicting people who continued to pay their rent. Owners of mobile home parks argued this was an unfair taking. They claimed the rules prevented them from profiting from rising land values and that the rules forced them to subsidize low rents for mobile home residents. The Court said this was not an actual "taking" and required no compensation to landowners because the city did not physically occupy the land or force the land-owners to rent mobile homes.[31]

In another case, David Lucas bought beachfront property in South Carolina, where he planned to build vacation homes. The state then passed the Beachfront Management Act, a law designed to protect the state's fragile barrier islands ecosystem. The law prevented Lucas from developing his barrier island property. Lucas argued the state law rendered his property valueless and hence was an unfair taking. The Supreme Court ruled in favor of Lucas in 1992 but held that compensation by governments would be required only if a law made a property totally valueless by depriving the owner of "all economically beneficial uses." Regulations that still allow at least some minimal economic use of land do not require compensation.[32] In earlier cases, however, the Court has required a local government to pay compensation for "partial takings," for example, when a county-built airport made it impossible to use neighboring land for residential (but not commercial) use.[33]

Eminent Domain

The Fifth Amendment has been interpreted as granting state and local governments the power to take property for public use but requiring that government pay compensation. This is referred to as **eminent domain.** In general, if a state or local government acts to promote some clear public use (for example, an airport, coastal preservation, or highway construction), compensation is usually required if land is physically taken from someone. In theory, governments can't take land from one person just to give it to another.[34] In practice, however, there may be few limits on a local government's ability to forcibly seize to private property that will remain in private hands, as long as it is willing to pay compensation.

In 1998, a private nonprofit redevelopment group was established in New London, Connecticut, to revitalize an industrial section of the city that contained several homes. The city hoped that new manufacturing firms and new businesses would generate more tax revenues than the existing homes. Using the power of eminent domain, the city told dozens of homeowners they had to sell in 2000 so the land underneath them could be transferred to the developer. Seven homeowners refused, arguing that it was unconstitutional for the city to take their property in order to promote private economic development.[35] Opponents of the New London action argued the city violated the "takings" clause of the Fifth Amendment and worried that it opened the way for cities to boost their tax revenues by transferring any low-revenue-generating residential property to shopping-mall developers offering more in tax revenues. In 2005, the Supreme Court ruled 5–4 against the homeowners and allowed New London's redevelopment plans to move forward. The Court held (in *Kelo v. City of New London*) that taking private property from one owner to give to another private owner was a legitimate use of eminent domain because economic growth from the new development was a permissible "public use." The decision sparked a reaction across the nation. A number of states passed ballot initiatives barring "takings" for economic development, and several state legislatures considered similar legislation.

Much Is at Stake

In rapidly growing suburban areas, the stakes of local politics surrounding land use control issues, and the potential for conflict, can be quite high. If developers succeed in preventing regulations on local land use, residents may experience a major change in the pace of growth in their community. Open spaces can be lost, traffic may become unbearable, new housing may outstrip available services, and schools may become increasingly overcrowded.

Yet, if slow-growth forces succeed in promoting local regulations that prohibit building in certain areas, developers (and owners of rural, agricultural, or forestry land in the path of growth) stand to lose tremendous profits they hoped to realize. Landowners may be an easier target for regulations than businesses. Critics of local zoning rules suggest that the "fear of exit" limits how far local governments can regulate how businesses operate. If a city places too many costly rules on businesses, then businesses might move away. But landowners can't take their property away when local governments regulate how it can be used.[36] Rather than exit, then, landowners must remain organized and active in the local political arena. Political controversy over land use regulations have fanned a "property rights" movement dedicated to limiting government's use of its police powers in land use control.

Zoning Controversy: Exclusion by Race and Income

Another major controversy surrounding zoning involves how it might be used to exclude people from a community. Zoning may be very neutral in intent but nonetheless have unintended class and racial implications. It is clear that some forms of zoning can increase home prices. If rules require larger lots and bigger homes and exclude high-density apartment buildings, housing costs more. Some suggest that zoning had its origins in attempts to exclude minorities and the poor from newer suburban areas.[37] From this perspective, zoning is seen as a public tool used to exclude minorities and the less affluent, just as private sector lending and real estate practices once did (discussed above).[38]

A survey of the 25-largest metropolitan areas in the United States found that zoning rules that allow nothing but low-density zoning are associated with places that have fewer black and Hispanic residents.[39] Low-density zoning (allowing no more than eight homes per acre) means there is less rental housing, which likely squeezes out housing opportunities for the less affluent. About 15 percent of cities in the nation were found using low-density-only zoning that allowed nothing but expensive, low-density housing. Use of this policy varies widely by region. It occurred disproportionately in regions with the highest segregation between black and white populations: Boston, New York, Philadelphia, Pittsburgh, and Cleveland. Almost half of the suburban communities around Boston used low-density-only zoning.[40]

Minority populations may be shrinking in places using low-density-only zoning. In 1990, black and Hispanic populations were relatively smaller than in 1980 in such places, despite growing movement of minorities to the suburbs.[41] There is no question that blacks had greater access to suburbs after the 1980s than during the 1950s and 1960s, but there is evidence they were being channeled into relatively few suburbs.[42] Other commonly used local land use controls—requiring adequate public facilities where growth will occur or using "urban growth boundaries" to concentrate growth in designated areas—were not found to have racially exclusionary effects.[43] But cities have other tools that can be used to exclude less-affluent residents. Some states—including Illinois and California—give their cities the power to let local voters decide if publicly subsidized housing for low-income residents can be built in their jurisdiction.[44] It is difficult to convince affluent voters that they need low-income housing in their town.

Evidence of exclusionary effects of land use regulations has produced calls for limiting local control over zoning. In 1971, the National Committee Against Discrimination in Housing (NCADH), a civil rights group, stated that "there can be no effective progress in halting the trend toward predominantly black cities surrounded by almost entirely white suburbs . . . until local governments have been deprived of the power to exclude subsidized housing and to manipulate zoning and other controls to screen out families on the basis of income, and, implicitly, of race."[45] Although some progress has occurred in integrating U.S. suburbs, it has not resulted from limiting local power to control land use.

In fact, the federal courts continue to allow cities to ban the construction of rental housing, unless state laws say otherwise or there is clear evidence of the *intent* to discriminate on the basis of race. The NCADH critique against zoning came the same year that a case involving the city of Black Jack, Missouri, reached the U.S. Supreme Court. Black Jack, a suburb of St. Louis, incorporated in 1970 to take control of zoning from St. Louis County. Area residents moved to incorporate immediately after a nonprofit group announced plans to use federal subsidies to construct low-income housing in Black Jack. The new city of Black Jack quickly adopted zoning rules that banned apartment buildings before the subsidized housing was built. Some observers noted that there was evidence that the city founders' explicit intent was to keep less-affluent blacks out of Black Jack.[46]

For a brief period, a federal court ruling suggested that it would be unconstitutional for a city to ban apartments if the effect was exclusionary, regardless of what the intent of the ban was (in other words, zoning could be seen as de facto segregation). However, in 1977, the court upheld a Chicago suburb's ban on subsidized,

racially integrated apartments for low- and moderate-income residents. The court ruled that the policy of Arlington Heights, Illinois (a city of 64,000 people with only 27 African Americans in 1970), could not be challenged with evidence showing the policy effectively excluded African Americans.[47] Rather, challenges to such zoning must establish there was an intent to exclude based on race. Because it is nearly impossible to prove a racially motivated *intent* in courts, local zoning ordinances are largely immune to challenges over their exclusionary effects.

The Enduring Role of Pro-Growth Forces in Local Politics

Whatever the exclusionary effects of zoning might be, much contemporary zoning is motivated by demands to regulate the pace and

Aerial view of a McMansions under construction in cul de sac near Houston Texas.

1980s, growth control policies were adopted by hundreds of additional jurisdictions in states, including California, Colorado, Florida, New Jersey, and New York. Several states adopted statewide growth management plans that attempted to regulate where suburban growth could occur.[59]

Slow-growth forces had their earliest influence in university communities and relatively affluent places where threats to scenic resources (for example, beaches, coastal access, and mountainsides) mobilized residents against local development. As the public mood in more communities became less supportive of growth, the range of cities adopting growth controls expanded. Support for growth control policies did not appear to have a clear ideological or partisan color[60] nor were growth control policies more prevalent among higher-income, higher-social-status suburbs.[61] They were more likely to be found in middle-class suburban cities with higher proportions of residents who were white-collar professionals. Although born out of disaffection with growth, there maybe a fairly long lag between when a city experiences rapid growth and when citizens finally mobilize against development.[62] This means that the public's reaction to the potential ill effects of growth, such as crowding and traffic, likely occurs after a place has already experienced substantial development.

Do Growth Controls Work?

Critics of growth controls argue that they restrict the supply of housing in the face of strong demand and thus increase the price of housing. Others claim that growth controls are an "environmental protection hustle" that defends privileged homeowners[63] and reflects attempts by homeowner "cartels" to create housing scarcity in order to increase home values.[64] Some studies have found that restrictive local zoning led to less housing density and less multifamily housing. Economists point out that the cumulative effects of certain policies, such as zoning for low-density housing, requiring environmental impact statements, and requiring developers to pay infrastructure costs and fees for school construction, do increase the cost of homes—but this effect may be limited to California and some eastern cities.[65] One California city requires a fee of $16,000 paid to the city per each new home—more than the cost of building new public facilities to serve each home.[66]

Economists note that there may also be benefits to land use regulations that are built into higher home prices.[67] It is hard to isolate the effect of regulations on housing prices, as growth controls are common in areas that are quite desirable to live. San Diego and Cleveland, for example, have about the same amount of land available per household. San Diego has extensive land use regulations compared to Cleveland, and land and homes are much more expensive in San Diego.[68] San Diego's housing may be much more expensive as a result of regulations or the fact that there is greater demand to live near the warm Pacific Coast beaches than the frigid shores of Lake Erie. San Diego's regulations may also reflect greater political pressure to preserve highly valued scenic amenities. Housing costs in San Diego may also be driven up by people who value the scenic areas that growth regulations have preserved.

Land use regulations can have at least two major economic effects: they can attempt to restrict housing growth (supply) or they can attempt to make new growth pay for its true costs (on infrastructure, schools, parks, and the local environment). There is no clear evidence that local growth controls actually slow growth,[69] but there is evidence that growth controls may help cities better manage their finances.[70] This suggests these policies may be aiming more for making growth pay its own way than actually stopping new growth. One study found growth restrictions associated with faster population growth because many regulations don't actually limit housing supply, and those that do may trigger building booms before they take effect.[71] Local population ceilings and caps on housing permits have also been easily circumvented in many places.[72]

INSTITUTIONS MATTER

REASONS FOR SPRAWL

The pace of growth of developed land in American metropolitan expands much faster than population growth. Why? (1) Federal, state, and local policies have subsidized the expansion of housing into undeveloped, raw land; (2) Americans like single-family homes with big backyards; (3) because families are getting smaller and there are fewer people per housing unit, we are building more homes per person than ever before; and (4) we also build much bigger homes than before.

Table 12.5 lists North American (U.S. and Canadian) metropolitan regions in terms of one indicator of sprawl: the number of people per square mile of developed land. Fewer people per square mile suggest that single-family homes are being built on large lots. The least dense places are U.S. regions that experienced much of their development after the rise of modern freeway-oriented suburbs. The list of places with the greatest population densities includes older U.S. regions where substantial development took place before the 1950s and regions in states with longer-standing state growth management laws (Hawaii and Florida). Density in Honolulu, Miami, and Ft. Lauderdale may have as much to do with state rules as physical geography, however. The effect of land use rules can be seen in the number of Canadian metropolitan regions that have higher population density. These Canadian regions have room to sprawl, but provincial governments in Canada have more control of land use than municipal governments. Provincial or state-level planning may thus constrain some sprawl. Table 12.6 provides another illustration of sprawl at the state level by ranking states in terms of growth in land used for development and the decline in population density. All these measures show that land use in the American South is growing fastest and that new growth there is more spread out than before.

There may be a positive side of sprawl, however. Sprawl can represent access to land that is cheaper to build and thus access to lower-cost housing. Low-density construction can mean more privacy than what exists in many cities. Lower-cost housing may also provide more opportunities for the less affluent to find quality housing. In this sense, there is something democratic and egalitarian about sprawl,[1] but it comes at a price. Access to cheap land requires freeways that must be paid for. New suburbs require new schools, roads, parks, and traffic lights and costly extensions of water mains and sewers. Developers won't usually pay for this unless rules force them to, but if they are forced to internalize the costs of sprawl, their new homes are less affordable.

Note

1. Robert Bruegmann, *Sprawl: A Compact History* (Chicago: University of Chicago Press, 2005).

Are We Better Off Without Zoning?

Advocates of the private market argue that land use regulations are more trouble than they are worth. Local, regional, and state rules limit how land can be used and require the "heavy hand" of government in planning. Market forces, they argue, will lead to more competition and the construction of what people really want, at a lower price.[73] If it were not for zoning and land use rules, low-cost mobile homes and high-density apartments might be more common in affluent areas. If land has scenic value, people will pay more to live there and free up space for others elsewhere. Taken farther, the anti-regulation argument might allow people to run businesses from their homes to help cover housing costs. In many places, zoning prevents this. Anti-zoning critics point to the relatively unregulated land markets of Houston, Texas, as a model. In Houston, commercial businesses, like gas stations and stores, are allowed to locate

Table 12.5

North America's 10 Least Densely Population Metropolitan Regions

Metropolitan Region	Population per Square Kilometer
Nashville, TN	457
Oklahoma City, OK	468
Mobile, AL	507
Knoxville, TN	537
Little Rock, AR	592
Tulsa, OK	602
Birmingham, AL	602
Kansas City, MO–KS	646
Greensville, SC	647
Youngstown, OH	834

North America's 10 Most Densely Population Metropolitan Regions

Metropolitan Region	Population per Square Kilometer
Toronto, Ontario, Canada	2,469
Los Angeles, CA	2,240
Miami, FL	2,096
New York City–North New Jersey	2,088
Montreal, Quebec, Canada	2,061
Honolulu, HI	1,761
Chicago, IL–Gary, IN	1,655
San Francisco–Oakland, CA	1,603
Ottawa, Ontario–Hull, Quebec	1,572
Ft. Lauderdale, FL	1,461

Source: Eran Razin and Mark Rosentraub, "Are Fragmentation and Sprawl Linked?" *Urban Affairs Quarterly* 35 (2000): 830.

next to residences. And Houston has some of the nation's cheapest housing. Zoning, they might add, can be unfair, and if it allows only low-density housing, it can encourage sprawl.

Defenders of land use regulations argue that the private market fails to really deal with the true costs of growth and development. If there were no rules, they argue, wetlands would be paved and beaches would be closed off; and if developers built parks, they would have no incentives to open them to the public. There would be no guarantee that quiet residential neighborhoods would be spared the pressure of busy shops, crowded apartments, or access to adequate parking. A private market, further-

more, can't plan ahead for the consequences of growth, including sprawl, traffic, and the need for school construction. Cities, further-more, are in competition with each other. If a city opens itself up to any sort of develop-ment, residential property values might drop, residents may exit, and tax revenues decline. Zoning, they argue, may have costs, but it also has more in the way of benefits.

Regardless of who is correct in this argu-ment, advocates of land use controls have the upper hand, as most people appear to support regulations on what can be built where,[74] and zoning is well-established as a power of local governments.

Table 12.6		

The Most Rapidly Sprawling States

States with the Greatest Sprawl from 1982 to 1997	Increase in Urban Land (%)	Decrease in Population Density (%)
Georgia	+75	−20
North Carolina	+70	−20
Tennessee	+68	−29
New Hampshire	+66	−28
West Virginia	+65	−45
New Mexico	+64	−17
Florida	+63	−7
South Carolina	+63	−25
National average	+39	−13

Source: Jerry Anthony, "Do State Growth Management Regulations Reduce Sprawl?" *Urban Affairs Review* 39 (2004): 376–97.

The Local Land Use Dilemma

Rather than asking if zoning is good or bad, it might be better to consider which levels of government are best suited to deal with land use questions.

As we have illustrated in this chapter, land use policy is largely controlled by county and city governments, and land use policy can reflect the competition between localities. When considered at the local level, zoning and various land use regulations can be quite effective in helping a city's fiscal bottom line: excluding multifamily units might lower service pressures on schools, encouraging large-lot single-family homes might bring in more tax revenues than apartments, and rules making developers "pay as they go" can keep taxes down. Without aggressive land use controls, a city may shoot itself in the foot.

But cities usually exist in a larger region, and many of the problems that citizens have to deal with—traffic, pollution, habitat loss, loss of open space, gross disparities in the quality of local schools, the segregation of the poor, and long distances between where people live and work—are problems of regional significance. These regional problems can't be solved with local control of land use, and local control of land use might act to make some problems—

such as segregation of the poor and separation of housing from employment—worse.

State and Regional Planning Alternatives

Some states and regions have adopted policies that change their local government's control over land use. As of 2004, several states had adopted laws that mandate or place strong pressures on local governments to plan for growth with an eye toward some long-term comprehensive plan. Although many states have established commissions to study sprawl or enhanced incentives for developers to preserve open space, few actually mandate that local land use plans conform with regional or state goals, such as containing sprawl.

State Growth Management Laws

States with mandatory, comprehensive growth laws may require that local governments define fixed **urban growth areas (UGAs)** to concentrate development while also requiring that local land use plans be approved by a regional or state authority. Some require the state approve major changes in local zoning plans. Florida's law prohibits local governments from issuing building permits unless adequate public services (transportation, water, sewer, and parks) are available. Washington requires that counties adopt comprehensive plans with UGAs that preserve rural areas. Oregon's law also restricts development to areas inside UGAs.

There is evidence that Florida's state growth management plan slowed development in targeted areas.[75] Population density, an indicator of sprawl, declined in Florida by 7 percent and Oregon by 2 percent, much lower rates than the national average during a period of rapid housing growth; and population density increased under Washington's growth management law.[76]

Regional Revenue Sharing

Local control of land use and local control of tax revenues combine to create incentives for places to attract businesses or residents who produce a high tax yield. It also means that some cities enjoy a large share of the benefits of development without having to pay for the costs. As an extreme example, tens of thousands of people commute to jobs in cities like Vernon, Industry, and Commerce in southern California. Those cities generate huge tax revenues, but other cities with fewer resources have to provide the parks, libraries, neighborhoods, and schools for the people who work in tax-rich commercial cities.

Some regions have implemented regional tax base sharing to reduce competition among cities for development and to create a fairer distribution of tax benefits. The idea is most advanced in the Twin Cities region of Minnesota, where 60 percent of the tax base created by new properties is taxed by the city it locates in, whereas the other 40 percent is placed in a pool that is shared by all communities. Since 1975, this tax base sharing has led to a large decrease in the disparities in tax bases across cities in the region. There are variants of this policy in the Rochester, New York; Dayton Ohio; and Hackensack, New Jersey regions.

Competition for Local Economic Development

Much of the discussion thus far centers on the politics surrounding residential development. We have shown that zoning and other land use policies may have effects on how a city develops and on who lives where.

Cities have another set of tools they use in the competition to attract business and industry, which we refer to broadly as *economic development policies*. Although some cities may actively use zoning and land use regulations to shape or limit residential development, nearly all make active use of economic development policy to attract businesses and firms. Many cities do both—they regulate residential growth while promoting economic development that brings jobs and tax revenues. One study found that most cities that make active use of residential growth controls also had moderate to active use of economic development policies at the same time. State governments are also active in working to attract business to their state, often partnering with cities and counties to do so.

States and cities compete against each other to attract businesses that might add a positive contribution to local revenues and bring local jobs. Sometimes, this competition is highly visible, for example, when a giant manufacturer like Saturn, Toyota, Intel, or Boeing announces that it is going to move thousands of jobs and billions of dollars in investment to a new location. These firms entertain competing offers from communities across the nation—offers that might include tax breaks, discounted utility service, subsidies for roads and other infrastructure, and worker training programs.

The Logic of State and Local Economic Development Policy

At some point, the location decisions of any business involve an assessment of costs: how much does it cost, say, to locate in Chicago, Dallas, or Seattle? The logic behind state and local economic development policies is to try to lower a firm's cost of locating in a particular place, thus making that place more attractive than rival locations.

There are many factors that might go into a firm's decision to move to a particular part of the country. These include climate, easy access to the people who buy their product, access to raw materials, access to a particular labor pool, transportation, availability of buildings and land, and many other factors. The decision about where to locate inside a particular region might be based on a different set of factors: the cost of property, taxes, construction, room for expansion, and many other things.[77] Managers might also consider quality-of-life issues. Many things associated with location can affect a firm's cost of production (or what economists call the *supply side* of what drives their behavior). Some of the things associated with the cost of production, such as land prices, tax rates, the costs of buildings, the price of utilities, and even the cost of training workers, might be affected by state and local economic development policies. The logic of many state and local economic development policies, then, is to offer a firm an attractive mix of things that makes it cheaper (or more profitable) to locate in one place versus another.[78]

How Does It Work?

Competition to recruit and retain sports franchises and car manufacturers represents some of the most visible examples of the economic development policy game. By threatening, either subtly or explicitly, to move a team or a plant from one place to another or by dangling thousands of new manufacturing jobs in front of different communities, these businesses hope to extract something from a host city. A state or local government is motivated to pay something to attract or retain the business if it knows the business has real options about where to locate or if it values what the business contributes to the local economy.

For example, as much as New York officials might want to think George Steinbrenner

could never take his Yankees baseball team out of New York City or the Empire State, he has a credible threat of exit. The current Los Angeles Dodgers and San Francisco Giants baseball teams moved away from New York in the 1950s. Both "New York" football teams, the Giants and the Jets, now play in New Jersey. Given this context, and Steinbrenner's threat of exit, New York officials opted to pay over $300 million in 2005 to help Steinbrenner to build a new Yankee Stadium in New York.[79]

Cities may work together with their county and state governments to craft a list of incentives to attract (or retain) a business, particularly with high-profile cases like sports teams and huge manufacturing plants. Although the Yankees or a Kia/Hyundai plant (see Sidebar 12.3) are some of the highest-profile cases in which communities compete for investment, this competition extends to smaller cities as well. Many cities, both large and small, have offices staffed with experts whose jobs are to attract business to the community. Suburban cities compete for economic development, as do rural places and big cities.

A survey of all U.S. cities with a population between 10,000 and 250,000 asked city planners about 64 different "development tactics" that places might use to attract and retain private investment. One striking finding was that only 13 of 938 cities reported doing nothing to attract economic development. On average, these small to midsized cities used about 18 different economic development policies. The most common included efforts at improving city infrastructure (78 percent of cities reported they improved their water, sewer, parking, and streets for businesses), promotional activities (79 percent reported advertising the community to prospective new businesses), land management (62 percent reported such activities as consolidating lots, condemning or acquiring land, or leasing or donating land to developers), and offering financial incentives (52 percent reported using policies such as issuing tax-exempt bonds, giving cash contributions to projects, or deferring tax payments on projects).[80] Local governments can also issue **industrial development revenue bonds**

Murry Lee/Superstock

State and local governments in Tennessee competed against other regions by providing GM with incentives to locate the Saturn assembly plant in Spring Hill. Saturn employs about 6,000 workers at the plant.

to pay the cost of new buildings, industrial parks, and other facilities that might attract businesses.

Who Uses Local Economic Development Policies?

Not all cities are aggressively seeking economic development, but many do. Some places try to offer more to businesses than other places care to or need to. Several studies have found that cities with less affluent residents and higher poverty levels offer businesses more incentives to locate, probably because officials feel keen pressure to attract jobs to such cities. There is also evidence that places with greater fiscal stress tend to be most likely to offer businesses incentives to locate in their community, and newer suburban residential cities are less likely to.[81] It seems that cities most in need of extra tax revenues and jobs that might come with economic development give away the most cash to try to get it.[82] Competition

also increases how much cities offer to attract development. Some cities appear to be locked in a sort of economic development policy arms race: a city offers more to attract firms when it is surrounded by other cities that are also active in offering incentives to business.[83]

Effects of Local Economic Development Policies

This raises two fundamental questions: do these policies work to bring businesses and jobs to the cities that offer incentives, and do public giveaways to businesses generate more gains for the city than what they cost it? There is no easy answer to either question. There are success stories about state and local giveaways generating substantial benefits. In the Kia example, (see Sidebar 12.3), the worker at the West Point, Georgia, plant is estimated to earn over $50,000 annually. If the plant

INSTITUTIONS MATTER

COMPETITION FOR KIA INVESTMENT

In early 2006, the Korean manufacturer Hyundai was searching for a place in the southern United States to locate a new American assembly plant to build its Kia line of cars. State labor laws that create a nonunion environment have made the South an attractive location for new car factories. The Kia plant could amount to a $1.2 billion investment and 5,000 jobs, the largest automaker investment in the South since Saturn located a plant in Spring Hill, Tennessee, in 1990.

Kia was reported to have looked at Meridian, Mississippi; Chattanooga, Tennessee; Decatur, Alabama; Aiken, South Carolina; and Hopkinsville, Kentucky, before settling on West Point, Georgia, a place near the border with Alabama. Hyundai already had an existing location in Montgomery, Alabama—about 140 miles from Meridian, Mississippi, and about 80 miles from West Point, Georgia. This placed the company in an excellent position to get these states into a bidding war to win the investment that would bring jobs.

In 2005, the governor of Mississippi had been touting Kia's interest in his state. But Georgia was keen to compete, having lost out to South Carolina in the 2002 bidding to attract a new Daimler Chrysler plant and having suffered Ford and General Motors decisions to shut plants there. Georgia crafted a package of tax breaks and subsidies in 2006 that proved attractive to Kia. A Korean newspaper reported that Georgia was sure to get the plant unless other states offered more and noted that Kia would receive more "incentives" from the State of Georgia than from other states in the region.[1] In March 2006, the governor of Georgia flew to South Korea to sign a $300 million package to bring the Kia plant to West Point, Georgia. The incentive package included a new freeway interchange for US 85, $76 million in state tax credits, $20 million for state-funded job training, $60 million for the state to purchase the land for Kia, and $130 million in local property tax abatement.[2]

Notes

1. Robert Bruegmann, *Sprawl: A Compact History* (Chicago: University of Chicago Press, 2005).
2. Walter Woods, "Ga. Reported Front Runner for Kia Plant," *Atlanta Journal-Constitution*, 27 February 2006.

---

stays in operation for several years, the state's investment is likely to be returned in the form of new jobs, new tax revenues generated by the facility, and taxes from well-paid workers. But there are also many attempts that yield questionable gains, particularly when a city fights to retain an existing business. There is substantial debate about whether concessions paid to retain sports franchises can ever pay for themselves.[84]

There are also reasons to expect only modest effects of policies that lower the location costs of businesses. Things that local governments can actually affect are not the primary factors affecting a business's location decision because there are larger factors (climate, the local labor pool, and access to markets) that

are largely beyond the control of state and local governments. Lower state-level taxation may attract more private investment, but if states cut taxes too low, they risk cutting public services (for example, schools, roads, and public safety) that make the state attractive.[85] At the local level, there is evidence that giveaways to businesses will attract new investment and bring in new employers, but their new jobs don't go to residents of the city hosting the business.[86] It is difficult for the city paying to attract a business to force that business to hire people from the host city, particularly in a metropolitan region with many other cities nearby.

The worst-case scenario for the effects of competition for economic development is that it may create a sort of arms race, or a "beggar thy neighbor" race to the bottom, where local governments compete against each other and give away so much that they have little to show for it in the end. Consider the situation when a firm is certain to locate in a specific region. Regardless of whether cities in the region were in competition, one will get the firm. If there is no competition, a city might get the firm without having to give up much in subsidies and tax breaks. But if there is fierce competition, one city will get the firm but at a higher cost in incentives to the business. The business is better off with this sort of competition and maybe the city that wins the competition is also, but the region may be worse off. If the firm was going to locate there anyway, cities bid against each other to lower the public benefits of having the business. Regional revenue-sharing plans (discussed above) are attempts to allow all cities in the region to share in the benefits of business location and mute cutthroat competition among neighboring cities.

The Consequences of Metropolitan Fragmentation

By now, it should be clear that the fragmentation of U.S. metropolitan regions has a great effect on what cities do. Local control of land use and local tax powers create incentives for cities to compete. They use land use controls in attempts to affect who lives where, and they use economic development policies to try to affect which firms locate where.

Some argue that it is a good thing to have dozens and dozens of independent cities in the same area, locked into this sort of competition. To them, more fragmentation means residents and businesses have more location choices, which increases competition between places to keep them happy. Places compete because of the threat of exit or because residents in fragmented regions might know if someone else in the area is getting a better deal on services

and thus pressure city hall for a similar deal.[87] One net result of this competition is supposed to be **efficiency gains.** But efficiency is a hard thing to define when talking about the places where people live and their reasons for living there. One benchmark for efficiency is the size of local government, measured in terms of municipal spending per resident. Cities in places with more competition—that is, with more surrounding suburbs and municipalities—spend less.[88] Competition might make cities less likely to provide a wide range of services or to provide services at less cost than it would be otherwise.

The trade-off for these efficiency gains may be **intermunicipal inequality.** Suburbanization since the 1950s corresponded with a growing gap in income inequality between the United States' central cities and their suburbs. A study of 55 metropolitan areas found suburbs growing wealthier, with inequality greater in regions having more reliance on local property taxes to pay for services. Local dependence on property taxes may increase the pressure on a city to exclude less-affluent residents (in order to boost the tax base) and thus increase income inequality in the region. A substantial minority presence in a region also corresponds with growing inequality, suggesting that the presence of racial minorities leads suburbs to adopt exclusionary land use policies.[89] Fragmentation is also associated with more sprawl.[90]

In addition to the efficiency and inequality consequences, fragmentation of metro areas may make it quite difficult for people to understand who is responsible for the services they receive (or don't receive). People living in areas where cities, counties, and special districts are all providing different services across traditional city boundaries find it difficult to identify who provides what.[91] This may make them less likely to be engaged with local politics. People may have stronger psychological attachments to a single political jurisdiction that provides a consolidated package of services—a traditional city—than they have to a place that receives services from several different types of local governments.[92]

The Isolation of the Poor in the United States' Major Cities

For decades, growth in U.S. metropolitan regions has been defined by a patchwork of competition and policies that exclude the poor from sharing in the fruits of economic prosperity.[93] Some suggest that fragmented metropolitan regions are designed to ensure that resources are separated from needs.[94] The United States' major cities, and many of its poorer suburbs, face a dilemma. Decades of incorporation leave large central cities, such as Los Angeles, Detroit, New York, Chicago, and Milwaukee, as well as older suburbs surrounded by neighboring communities that are rich in resources and in their tax base. Suburbs are by no means universally affluent. Many older, "inner-ring" suburbs closest to the center city have high poverty rates. Residents from newer suburbs, however, may enjoy suburban affluence *and* the amenities of their neighboring large city and may even work there, but they don't pay taxes as full-time city residents do. A history of racial segregation, federal subsidies, and rigid zoning laws in newer suburbs also leaves the older communities with a greater share of the region's poor residents—residents who have greater needs for public services. But metropolitan fragmentation means that many businesses and industries generating tax revenues are outside the traditional city's reach.

Big central cities are not the only losers in the competition among local governments. Suburban cities where the less affluent do reside spend more per person to serve their populations, but they have less valuable property to tax. This means people in poor suburbs have to pay much more in taxes per dollar value of property. Poor suburbs spend more per person than rich suburbs on health, hospitals, and public housing but less per person on police, fire, parks, and sanitation. They are also more heavily in debt.[95] With lots of valuable property, rich places generate more tax revenues per dollar value of property and thus can tax property at a lower rate. Wealthy suburbs can also provide their residents more total services at a lower tax rate.

Commenting on the unfairness effects of U.S. suburbanization, Anthony Downs, a prominent critic, notes that "the non-poor majority has rigged the game so that the poor are not represented" in the suburbs and, "The non poor cannot vote against . . . their own exclusion. This unjust situation is not likely to change until non-poor suburbanites suffer an intense shortage of under skilled labor that costs them much more dearly than it does now."[96]

Regional and Metropolitan Government?

Fragmentation of political authority over taxes and land use is the norm in U.S. metropolitan regions. But there have been proposals to deal with the effects of fragmentation by having cities and counties share some of their local powers with **regional governments.** Early in the 20th century, Progressive reformers advocated the consolidation of local governments to create more efficient administration and **economies of scale** in the delivery of services. The assumption behind metropolitan government was that it would be cheaper and more efficient to provide services like fire protection, sanitation, or public transportation from a large, centralized bureaucracy than from several competing jurisdictions.[97]

However, research suggests that consolidation does not necessarily lead to increased efficiencies for many public services.[98] Competition, it seems, generally produces more efficiency than consolidation. With some things that governments do, such as regional mass transit and air quality management, regional governments may have distinct advantages, however. Problems of sprawl and income inequality may be less severe when government is consolidated.[99] "Efficiency" gains may arise in regions where places compete to provide local services, but people living in fragmented regions who supposedly experience efficient service provision (or less service) are not happier about their public services than people who live in areas with consolidated government.[100]

Summary

Even with the rise of statewide land use rules and attempts at regionalism with programs such as revenue sharing and metropolitan government, it is unlikely that local control over land use and taxes will change substantially in the next decade. The concept of *home rule*—where cities and counties have substantial political control over their affairs—is firmly rooted in American political institutions. Nonetheless, population growth will continue to create pressure for the development of more land and for local control over who gets to build and what they get to build. This has consequences for who lives where. Population growth will likely create further pressure on some communities to regulate growth. Competition among places under the current institutional structures—fragmented authority over land use and local control over tax revenues—will continue to create places that are winners and losers: cities and towns for the wealthy, cities and towns for the middle class, and cities and towns for the less affluent.

If sprawl continues to elicit popular discontent, however, and if future development is associated with growing social inequalities between places, many states may face decisions in years to come about whether local control of land use and tax authority may have to be limited in some ways. These institutional arrangements are fundamentally important to who gets what from government.

Keywords

Annexation

Contracting for services

Economies of scale

Efficiency gains

Eminent domain

General purpose local government

Growth controls

Growth machine

Incorporation

Industrial development revenue bonds

Intermunicipal inequality

Metropolitan areas

Police powers

Privatization

Regional-metropolitan government

Regional revenue sharing

Regulatory takings

Rent control

Special districts

Sprawl

Suburb

Unincorporated area

Urban growth areas

Village of Euclid v. Ambler Realty Company

Zoning

Suggested Readings

Bruegmann, Robert. 2005. *Sprawl: A compact history.* Chicago: University of Chicago Press.

Burcell, Robert, Anthony Downs, and Sahan Mukherji. 2005. *Sprawl costs.* Washington, DC: Island Press.

Burns, Nancy. 1994. *The formation of American local governments: Private values in public institutions.* Oxford: Oxford University Press.

Downs, Anthony. 2004. *Still stuck in traffic.* Washington, DC: Brookings Institution.

Garreau, Joel. 1991. *Edge cities: Life on the new American frontier.* New York: Anchor.

Judd, Dennis R. 2004. *City politics: Private power and public policy.* Upper Saddle River, NJ: Pearson Longman.

Kemmis, Daniel. 1990. *Community and the politics of place.* Norman: University of Oklahoma Press.

Logan, John, and Harvey Molotch. 1987. *Urban fortunes: The political economy of place.* Berkeley: University of California Press.

McGinnis, Michael, ed. 1999. *Polycentric governance and development: Readings from the workshop in political theory and policy analysis.* Ann Arbor: University of Michigan Press.

Rusk, David. 1993. *Cities without suburbs.* Baltimore: Woodrow Wilson Center Special Studies, Johns Hopkins University Press.

Turner, Margery Austin, and Lynette Rawlings. 2005. *Overcoming concentrated poverty and isolation.* Washington, DC: Urban Institute.

Websites

AnthonyDowns.com (http://www.anthonydowns.com): According to his website, Downs is "the world's leading authority on real estate and urban affairs." A senior fellow at the Brookings Institution, Downs is probably the world's leading authority on suburban sprawl in the United States.

Defenders of Property Rights (http://www.yourpropertyrights.org): The only national public interest legal foundation dedicated exclusively to the protection of constitutionally guaranteed property rights. The group "works with victims of over-zealous regulations to find justice in court."

Land Use Law Center (http://www.law.pace.edu/landuse): The Land Use Law Center is "dedicated to fostering the development of sustainable communities in New York State."

Smart Growth (http://www.smartgrowth.org): A group challenging policies that facilitate sprawl. Dedicated to a range of housing options, walkable neighborhoods, mixed land uses, preservation of critical areas and open space, attractive communities, and "a sense of place."

Urban Futures (http://www.urbanfutures.org): A program of the conservative Reason Foundation devoted to providing market-oriented analysis of land use and economic development issues.

Urban Institute (http://www.urban.org): Think tank that conducts and publishes studies on urban issues, including housing issues and poverty in urban communities, gentrification, and homelessness.

13

© Scherl/SV-Bilderdienst/ The Image Works

Morality Policy

The Strange Politics of Morality Policy

In April 2000, counter to majority public opinion in the state, the Vermont General Assembly passed a bill establishing "civil unions." Then governor Howard Dean quickly signed the bill into law, giving same-sex couples legal status on par with married heterosexual couples for the first time in the United States. Analysts predicted a political backlash against those who supported the measure, and, indeed, in the fall general election, the civil union bill was a primary motivator for many who voted against these policy makers.[2] Sixteen legislators who voted for the measure lost their re-election bids; the popular Dean was re-elected but with the smallest majority of any of his 10 races in the state.

In September 2000, in response to the U.S. Food and Drug Administration's approval of the abortion pill, RU-486, Father John Earl, a 32-year-old Roman Catholic priest, smashed his car into the lobby of the Northern Illinois Women's Center, an abortion clinic in Rockford, Illinois. He then attacked the building with an ax, stopping only when confronted by the shotgun-wielding owner of the building. Although his bishop and other church officials condemned the act of violence, some anti-abortion activists and commentators called the priest a hero.[1]

OUTLINE

Introductory Vignette

Introduction

What Is Morality Policy?

The Politics of Morality Policy: Issue Evolution

Examples of Morality Policy Politics in the States and Communities: Abortion Regulation and Same-Sex Marriage

Summary

Rick Friedman/Corbis

Introduction

In these last three chapters we consolidate our discussion of the politics and institutions of state and local government to consider the outputs of government—public policy. Policy is what government does and why and how it does it. Throughout this book, we have talked about public of policy in various contexts, but in these last chapters we tackle three broad areas of policy head-on, exploring how institutions affect them, how and why reform occurs in them, and how comparisons of different policies across the states and communities can help us understand politics and government better.

The two stories in the opening vignette for this chapter are about unusual political events. Rarely do American politicians support policy that threatens their political careers, and priests hardly ever attack buildings as an act of political protest. But some policies—like same-sex marriage and abortion regulation and perhaps sex education, pornography regulation, alcohol regulation, and legalized gambling, among others—have inspired extraordinary political acts in the American states and communities, not only in recent years but also throughout our history. Most of our standard theories of political behavior and policy making suggest that people act politically in ways that enhance their own well-being. But these **morality policies** generate debate over the basic values that define our personal identities rather than debate over such tawdry and transient values as political or economic advantage. These are debates about what is right and wrong rather than about who gets what. And because of the unique debate that morality policy stirs up, the politics surrounding it have been thought to be quite different than that surrounding more run-of-the-mill policy, such as transportation or criminal justice policy.[3]

In this chapter, we examine morality policies in the states and communities, trying to understand how the institutions of government deal with them, how reform comes about on them, and how and why they differ throughout the country. Morality policies are very much in the news these days, even though they are probably much less significant in your daily life than are the policies we will discuss in the following two chapters—policies about health care, social welfare, and education. Unlike these other types of policy, morality policies are classified by the politics they generate rather than by their subject matter. And because of the unique nature of the debate surrounding these issues, their politics have unique characteristics that political scientists are just beginning to understand.

But perhaps, if thought of broadly, the politics of morality policy are not that much different than those of other types of policy. The institutions of American state and local government limit how different the politics of one type of policy can be from another. Morality policies do differ from those policies that these institutions are accustomed to handling. But these institutions channel these policies into the typical patterns of policy making and politics for which these institutions were designed. And indeed, in the end, the characteristic patterns of issue evolution and reform that state and local government institutions encourage are followed even for these unique policies—at least for the most part.

What Is Morality Policy?

We hear a lot about morality in politics these days—"culture wars," "sin taxes," and religious leaders making pronouncements on public issues like abortion, same-sex marriage, and the like. Some pundits even claimed that President George W. Bush was re-elected in 2004 because voters liked his stance on "moral issues."[4] But what makes a policy a "morality policy"?

First, it is important to understand that a deep streak of morality has run through American policy debate ever since the Pilgrims landed at Plymouth Rock in 1620 with the goal of establishing an ideal commonwealth—a "city on a hill"[5] that would serve as a model of good government for the world. To be sure, the Pilgrims' ideal included some goals of traditional, nonmorality policy, such as that government should treat its citizens fairly and provide for their common good. But always lurking in the political discussion of the Pilgrims and their genetic and philosophical descendants was the idea that public policy ought to reflect the basic moral values of their Protestant Christianity.[6] In particular, they believed that public policy ought to outlaw—or at least discourage—"sin," or certain violations of their basic religious principles or values.

Astute foreign observers of American politics have long noted the importance of morality in our political life, for good or ill. Before the Civil War, the French commentator Alexis de Tocqueville wrote that although "religion never intervenes directly in the government of American society . . . it should be considered the first of their political institutions." Later in the 19th century, the British writer G. K. Chesterton wrote

that the United States was a nation "with the soul of a church." In the 20th century, the Swedish sociologist Gunnar Myrdal argued that this country was the most "moralistic and moral[ly] conscious . . . branch of Western Civilization."[7] In short, this country has long been a "hellfire nation,"[8] where moral arguments regularly find their way into political discourse.

In the past 20 years, political scientists have begun to look systematically at American morality policy and its politics, focusing especially on the states and communities. Federalism has allowed states and communities to dominate this area of policy (see Sidebar below). One such scholar stated that morality policy exists when "one segment of society attempts by governmental fiat to impose its values on the rest of society."[9] This is a good place to start our search for a definition of *morality policy*. Although most law, especially criminal law, imposes values on society by defining right

INSTITUTIONS MATTER

FEDERALISM, HOME RULE, AND MORALITY POLICY VARIATION

The institution of federalism has allowed state and local governments to express their values through their morality policies. Although these laws must respect the values expressed in the U.S. Constitution and federal law, within those broad guidelines, states' morality policies vary greatly across the country. Consider two neighboring states—Nevada and Utah. Back in 1930, long before it became legal in any other state, Nevada embraced casino gambling as a way to generate state revenue and promote economic development. Utah, on the other hand, is one of only two states (along with Hawaii) that have a blanket ban on gambling—not even bingo in the church basement is legal. Furthermore, the sale of alcohol is very strictly regulated in Utah, whereas in Nevada, it flows much more freely. Even prostitution is legal in some parts of Nevada—but certainly not in Utah. Clearly, Nevada is not Utah, and the institution of federalism allows these states to express the different values of their citizens on these and other morality policies.

The states also recognize the importance of allowing morality policy to reflect variation of values even within their borders. For example, institutions like state home rule laws typically give communities the authority to set local decency, which is why the variation of pornography and strip clubs varies so much within states. Many states also allow for local units of government to ban alcohol sales. Some cities, including even politically rough-and-tumble Chicago, also have ordinances that allow neighborhoods to vote themselves dry (alcohol-free) or ban adult bookstores if they violate the values of their residents. These institutions—federalism, home rule, local options, and neighborhood control—allow policy makers to fine-tune public policy to fit the values of citizens, thereby avoiding conflict and controversy on these visible and electorally dangerous morality issues.

and wrong behavior, these values are usually not controversial. For example, because almost everyone agrees that it is wrong to break into someone's house and steal their TV, no conflict ensues over the values of burglary laws. But when a state allows men to marry one another, it generates disagreement with some people's deep-seated moral values. Some believe that homosexuality is fundamentally, morally wrong and that it is wrong for the state to sanction it. By recognizing same-sex marriage, the state is supporting the union, both symbolically, by issuing a marriage license, and financially, by giving the couple the various rights, privileges, obligations, and duties accorded to married couples. Americans hold a clear consensus that the government ought to support heterosexual marriage, so such a policy doesn't raise major conflicts of basic values. But a significant number of Americans do have a moral objection to same-sex marriage, and they do not want to support it, even if only through public policy.

This example highlights the many ways in which morality policy is different from nonmorality policy. First, whereas most public policy is primarily about distributing economic costs and benefits, morality policy often has little economic impact. Morality policy is about the role of government in supporting one set of values at the expense of another set of values. For example, even in a big state like Illinois, the number of abortions that Medicaid funds for poor women each year is very small. But when Governor George Ryan—a conservative Republican—vetoed a bill to ban such payments in 2001, he came under intense criticism from those in the right wing of his own party.[10] The criticism did not hinge on the amount of money these abortions would cost the state or even on the veto's impact on the number of abortions performed each year. Rather, the controversy was about whether state tax dollars—any state tax dollars—should be used to pay for a procedure that its opponents found morally repugnant.

Furthermore, morality policy debates are often about a policy's ultimate goal rather than the means to achieve it. On the other hand, some degree of consensus usually exists about the policy goal of nonmorality policy, and any debate centers around how best to reach it. For example, although everyone agrees that public health policy ought to improve the general health of a state's or community's residents, people debate about whether encouraging HMOs or empowering individual doctors is the best way to do this. But in morality policy debate, the fundamental policy goals are often under discussion because they represent different basic moral values. And these moral divisions are so basic to the debaters' identities that they cannot in any way agree to disagree on them. The differences are just too deep and too important to the debaters.

Thus, perhaps the fundamental difference between morality policy and nonmorality policy is that the latter is defined by the substance with which the policy deals and the former is defined by the style of debate surrounding it. One set of scholars makes the apt analogy that just as science is defined by the application of the scientific method rather than the thing to which the method is applied, morality policy is defined by the terms of the debate, not by what is debated.[11] *Thus, morality policies are those on which at least one side of the debate—and usually only one side—makes its arguments in morally based language.* That is, one side argues that its opponent's position is just morally wrong. In this way, morality policies are those where the most basic normative questions of right and wrong are put on the table for the government to decide. Thus, a policy dealing with any topic could be a morality policy if one of the relevant voices in the debate uses moral arguments.

Moral arguments are assertions that a behavior is banned or required by some basic and unquestionable authority. The most common sources of such assertions are the basic religious documents that adherents believe to be the fonts of God-given truth. The Christian Bible, the Islamic Koran, and the Jewish Talmud are examples of such documents. Although their interpretation is often disputed, those debating public policy often find useful basic moral arguments in these documents. Moral arguments may also come from other sources, like the U.S. Constitution or ideas about "natural rights." But the most dominant moral arguments in American policy debates have a religious basis.

Although it is not clear why certain advocates are able to make their moral arguments relevant in a policy debate when others are not, part of the story seems to be that successful advocates are able to convince significantly large numbers of people that the policy violates their basic values and, therefore, threatens their core identity. For example, advocates may convince some people that pornography denigrates women, so when the town liquor board licenses a strip club to open, the values of those who believe people ought not to be treated as objects are violated. The values of those who believe that homosexuality is sinful are violated when the government sanctions same-sex marriage. The values of those who believe that life begins at conception are violated when the government allows abortion. If an advocate can convince enough people to care about such a violation of their values, then that advocate's moral argument becomes relevant to the debate, and the policy will take on the qualities of a morality policy.

Usually, only one side of a morality policy debate makes moral arguments. Conflicting moral arguments rarely have enough support in a state or community to make them equally useful in a policy debate. Typically, those on the other side make non-morality-based arguments. For example, whereas the death penalty opponents argue that it is morally wrong for the state to kill, the other side argues that the threat of execution deters murder, a practical, not moral, argument.

Morality policy has two other characteristics that help determine its unique politics.[12] First, morality policy debate tends to be less technical than other policies, at least for those making the moral argument. The question is not whether a policy will "work" but, rather, whether it is right or wrong based on the advocates' interpretation of some religious document or some other text or belief system that they feel is authoritative. Second, the simplicity of the argument and its clear relationship to certain peoples basic values lead to the final significant characteristic of morality policy—some people can get very excited about it. Or, more precisely, interest groups can easily encourage a significant segment of the public to become very excited about it.[13] Public participation in state and local policy making is usually very limited because the average citizen is too busy with work and family to know or care much about it. But morality policy's simple arguments allow anyone to be well-informed, and advocates can use the "attack on our basic values" argument as motivation for people to pay attention and even to become vocal and active on these issues. These characteristics have led to an increase in the use of initiatives and referendums on morality policies in the last quarter century.[14]

The Politics of Morality Policy: Issue Evolution

Understanding the characteristics of morality policy allows us to explain better the politics surrounding it. Bizarre and unusual political behavior (like a priest attacking a building with a car and an axe) may become more understandable if seen in the context of morality policy. But like with other types of policy, we can also understand morality policy politics better by following its characteristic **issue evolution,** a fairly predictable pattern of how issues come onto the public agenda, how their politics develop, and how they then recede from active debate.[15] State and local government institutions largely define this process, and even though morality policy is quite distinct from run-of-the-mill nonmorality policy in some ways, these institutions force morality policy politics to follow some of the same basic patterns as other policies' politics.

Policy Equilibrium: Reflecting the Values of the Majority

For the vast majority of all potential moral questions, state and local public policies are in sync with the opinion of the majority of the general public. As such, policy makers have little incentive to change them or even discuss them. This **policy equilibrium** exists because policy makers have a strong incentive to reflect the preferences of their constituents on morality policy.[16] Because these issues affect individuals' basic values and are simple to understand, they make ideal material for campaign ads attacking incumbents. For example, if a state legislator from a conservative rural district votes to allow same-sex marriage, that single vote on an opponent's campaign brochure may be the only thing that catches voters' attention and sticks in their minds on Election Day. As you know, most people know very little about their state legislator. If the one thing they do know is that lawmaker voted for a bill that conflicts with their basic moral values, that legislator will not be re-elected. Politicians understand this dynamic very well. Although they try to represent their constituents' interests whenever they can, policy makers make a special effort to do so on these simple, visible morality issues. Thus, it is not surprising that most potential morality policy issues are not on the active **political agenda** at any given time. Only when the values of a significant portion of the population are threatened do morality issues begin to generate political activity.[17]

Let the Politics Begin: The Policy Shock

But from time to time, something happens to change either public opinion or public policy, thus upsetting the happy equilibrium between them. Such a **policy shock** can be caused by a variety of things, such as a social change (perhaps a burst of immigration or a war), a technological innovation (such as when embryonic stem cell research became feasible), or even an unusual political event (such as a state or federal supreme court unilaterally changing morality policy by declaring a law unconstitutional).[18] By disrupting the equilibrium, a policy shock gives policy makers, interest groups, and other **policy entrepreneurs** the incentive and opportunity to place the morality policy in question on the active political agenda.[19] Whether out of a deep concern for moral values or sheer political opportunism—or a little of both—a morality policy entrepreneur can stir up general public sentiment far more easily than can someone advocating a nonmorality policy. The advocate only needs to point out the threat to the moral values of the state or community—in the entrepreneur's opinion—to excite the public interest. Once a significant segment of the population thinks about the issue in moral terms, it is easy to get it on the political agenda because policy makers always want to bring morality policy into balance with their constituents' values. But sometimes, a state or community cannot reach a consensus on the moral value in question. In these cases, the policy shock and ensuing political activity make this abundantly clear. Under these conditions, morality policy politics really kicks into high gear.

Morality Policy Politics

Morality policy politics is characterized by unique interest group activity, political frustration, and enforcement problems.

Interest Groups and Morality Policy: Altruism, Grassroots, and Activism Interest groups are central to morality policy making, but their activities differ in important ways from those in nonmorality policy making. First, recall that most groups consist of people or businesses seeking economic benefits from public policy. Forming and maintaining a group require time and money, and the primary reason most people are willing to make such an effort is that they expect some sort of financial gain from it. But people who form and join groups advocating morality policy do so mainly for noneconomic reasons. Of course, the liquor industry fights restrictions on alcohol sales for economic reasons, and companies that run casinos lobby legislatures and join groups to make their businesses more profitable. But these groups do not make moral arguments in policy debates. Groups working to ban abortion, gambling, or teaching evolution in schools will gain no economic benefit from the political victory of their causes. Sure, these groups' leaders benefit economically from the political battle because it brings in donations and dues to pay their salaries, but the vast majority of these groups' members contribute their time and money solely to advance a moral cause for which they will not gain a penny. These groups' members are motivated by a sense of **altruism,** a rare motive in American politics.

Who are these rare birds in American political life—these altruistic policy activists? And why are they so motivated by altruism on morality issues? The answers lay in what these issues mean to these activists. Some people hold certain moral values very deeply, and when these values are threatened, these people are motivated to act politically, regardless of economic incentives. In fact, these people will even use their economic resources—time, money, and more—in the pursuit of what they believe to be an important moral cause. In American politics, these people tend to be those who hold a deep religious faith. Liberal or conservative, religious leaders and activists have been at the forefront of morality policy crusades from the beginning of the republic, fighting against everything from slavery, the sale of alcohol, and gambling to capital punishment, abortion, and the use of embryonic stem cells in research. In recent years, those who belong to traditional conservative religious denominations seem to be more easily motivated by a threat to their values and faith than those whose religion is either less important to them or of a less dogmatic nature.[20] In particular, those who take their religious texts literally, believing them to be the direct word of God, can be motivated to act politically by a policy entrepreneur who interprets such a text to argue that their values are threatened by government action. The United States is a very religious country,[21] and more people are motivated by a direct threat to their religious values than of by a threat to their political values. The same moral and religious fervor that motivates an Islamic militant to strap dynamite to his body in a Tel Aviv market can motivate an American to plant a pipe bomb at a Planned Parenthood clinic or burn down a new subdivision that he or she feels has ruined an important ecosystem.[22]

Furthermore, although religious people and groups are not the only ones active in morality policy making, they tend to be the only ones making moral arguments; those who define the debate in nonmoral terms tend not to be religious. For example, many anti-abortion groups are closely associated with fundamentalist Protestant denominations or the Roman Catholic Church, and they make morality arguments based on their interpretation of the Christian Bible. But their opponents who work to limit abortion restrictions, such as Planned Parenthood, tend to be secular. These opponents make arguments about women's health care, control over their own bodies, and the financial and psychological burden of unwanted pregnancies.

Two other things characterize typical morality policy interest group activity. First, due to the intense, values-charged issues involved, morality policy politics attracts many groups with a narrower focus, or "single-issue groups."[23] Groups like the Hemlock Society (advocating the right to die) and the People for the Ethical Treatment of Animals (advocating the rights of animals) usually start out with a very narrow agenda, even if they broaden their interests over time. And second, to an extent not seen in most nonmorality policy making, morality-based interest groups tend to mobilize their highly motivated members to work directly in the political arena. Often, these are not simply groups whose members write checks and let their dark-suited lobbyists do the work. First, these groups organize lots of traditional **grassroots activities,** such as rallies and marches at the state capitol during the legislative session, letter-writing and telephone-calling campaigns, and the like. Given the deep commitment that these people have to the values reflected in their policy positions, it is relatively easy for their leaders to get them involved in these activities.

But beyond these traditional grassroots and protest activities, these highly motivated activists may do extraordinary things in the pursuit of their policy goals. In the 1990s, for example, the anti-abortion group Operation Rescue staged extensive and intensive protests at abortion clinics in cities around the country.[24] These advocates sacrificed their social and family lives, and some of them even gave up their jobs so they could pursue this direct political action. Political violence can result when highly motivated (some might say unbalanced) morality policy activists take direct political action to an extreme.[25] Such morality policy advocates have committed murder, blown up buildings, and committed other forms of political terrorism. When some individuals' deeply held moral values are sufficiently threatened, they may decide that even sacrificing their lives or freedom may be justified.

Lawmaking: Political Frustration and Success

Of course, political violence is rare in the United States, even in morality policy making. But the source of this violence—frustration with the political process—is common in morality politics. Because morality policy activists typically espouse a black-and-white, right-or-wrong view of public policy, working within the normal state and local policy-making processes almost guarantees that they will be frustrated and angry with the process. How can people who believe that their policy position is dictated by God listen calmly to someone arguing for a position that they feel is morally repugnant? How can

they agree to a compromise or graciously accept losing in the legislative process on some arcane procedural maneuver that they don't understand? If the definition of *frustration* is "needing to do something but being kept from doing it," then the routine policy-making process in the states and communities is simply a recipe for frustration for highly motivated morality policy activists.

This clash of perspectives, values, and cultures—even between policy makers and activists who are political allies—typically leaves morality policy advocates on the losing end of the process, at least at first. But when these advocates can sustain their energy, interest, and motivation; when they can gather resources and learn both how the policy-making process works and the value of that process; and when their views actually reflect those of a significant segment of the state or community, they can make a significant impact on public

Colin Archer/Getty Images News

The prohibition of alcoholic beverages (1919-1933) was a "noble experiment" that was very difficult to enforce because the moral values of most Americans were not threatened by social drinking. Note the wistful look on the postman's face as these law enforcement officers destroy barrels of beer in a futile attempt to implement this morality policy.

policy. Policy makers really want to set policy that reflects their constituents' values, and if a group accurately represents those values, policy makers will agree to their proposals. Legislators, council members, governors, and mayors all have to face the electorate to keep their jobs, and they sure don't want to be on the wrong side of their constituents on these highly visible and relatively simple morality policy questions.

Implementation: The Problem of Unenforceable Laws

Another characteristic of morality policy politics is that when a strong morality policy does become law, it is often difficult to enforce. This is especially true for **vice laws**—bans on an activity that some see as sinful. Over the course of American history, state and local governments have passed many such laws, banning such things as alcohol, pornography, sodomy, prostitution, and even interracial marriage.[26] When morality policy advocates can get policy makers to accept their definition of an activity as sinful, such laws can be enacted with ease because—as one morality policy scholar argues—"no one is willing to stand up for sin."[27] But the police or regulatory agency charged with implementing such bans often has a hard time enforcing them because—as the same scholar said—for some people, "sin is fun."[28]

One reason that morality policy is difficult to implement is that these laws are written to express basic moral values rather than to solve a public problem, so policy makers simply give less thought to how they will work in practice.[29] But perhaps more fundamentally, the law may not be able to have much impact on certain simply human behaviors. Think about these bans as attempts to discourage people from engaging in certain activities by increasing the cost of doing so.[30] Even without a ban, using recreational drugs or employing or being a prostitute has significant costs, including the health risks, social stigma, and money involved. Banning these activities increases these costs by adding fines, jail time, and even greater social stigma. These additional costs may dissuade some additional people. But for those people who really want to engage in them,

the relatively minor cost increases that state and local governments can impose—especially after factoring in the often small probabilities of arrest and conviction—may not be enough to stop these people from continuing to "sin."[31]

Just as important, those charged with enforcing these laws may not share their advocates' zeal for them.[32] The police may not think that pursuing recreational drug users or those in the sex industry is a good use of their time and energy; they might rather focus on enforcing laws against violent crime or traffic safety. In fact, the police may even have a certain amount of compassion for those violating some of these laws because they encounter them so frequently.

Whether a morality policy is poorly crafted, too weak to discourage a behavior, or simply ignored by those enforcing it or those engaged in the activity, the result is the same: morality policies are often not implemented effectively. Although some may decry this situation and demand more stringent enforcement, in one important sense, implementation may be irrelevant to many morality policy advocates. Morality policy can be as much about symbolism and affirming values as it is about changing behavior.[33] State or local law asserts the official values of the government and its citizens, whether or not those values are always expressed in the behavior of those citizens, and this can be very satisfying to some of the most ardent morality policy advocates.

Fitting a Square Peg in a Round Hole: The Return to Policy Equilibrium

If and when morality policy advocates come to understand that success in state and local policy making requires compromise and patience, they can chip away at the most egregious problems they see and move slowly toward their ideal policy goals. In the American policy-making process, advocates who demand everything at once usually achieve only failure. But they often can achieve small, incremental successes. The degree to which public opinion supports their policy positions determines how far they can advance toward them in the long run.

For example, consider how opponents of the death penalty were able to restrict its use over the course of U.S. history. Following the bloody English legal tradition of the time, our first criminal justice systems executed a lot of criminals. Indeed, in 18th-century New York, about 25 percent of those convicted of crimes—any crimes—were hanged.[34] Anti–death penalty reformers used, among other considerations, the moral argument that a government had no right to kill a convict, regardless of what crime he or she may have committed.[35] But these advocates ran up against public opinion that distinctly favored execution as a form of punishment for criminals. As a result, by 1880, executions were banned in only five states—all with predominantly moralistic political cultures (Michigan, Rhode Island, Wisconsin, Iowa, and Maine).

But when these reformers shifted from trying to ban the death penalty to simply trying to limit it in certain specific ways, they had tremendous political success. They began by arguing that executing innocent people was wrong. Although that may be a moral argument, it was certainly not a contentious one. They then argued that fewer crimes merited the death penalty, with prison being an acceptable punishment for many crimes. Again, that was reasonable enough. Next, reformers objected to public and painful executions as humiliating, inhumane, and unnecessary. Many people could buy those moral arguments too—we are not barbarians, after all. For each of these arguments, death penalty reformers suggested specific, incremental policy changes like strict due process rules for trials, limiting the penalty to only first-degree murder, and "humane" execution methods (like the electric chair and the gas chamber), most of which have been widely adopted in the states. So, although death penalty reformers have not succeeded in the clear, black-and-white, symbolic victory of banning all executions in the United States, in practice, they have dramatically reduced the number of actual executions here (see Figure 13.1).

Figure 13.1

Executions in the United States: The Incremental Success of Death Penalty Reformers

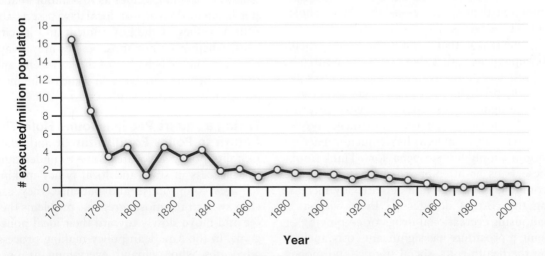

Note: This figure shows the sharp decline in the number of executions per million residents in the United States since 1770.

Sources: Death Penalty Information Center, http://deathpenaltyinfo.org/article.php?scid=8&did=269; U.S. Department of Justice, Office of Justice Programs, Bureau of Justice Statistics, http://www.ojp.usdoj.gov/bjs/glance/tables/exetab.htm; and Ken Parks, ed. 2005. *World Almanac and Book of Facts 2006.* New York: World Almanac Books, 477.

Thus, when morality policy advocates make their arguments less about absolute moral values and more about incremental, instrumental problems, they can be very successful in reforming policy. Policy makers sympathetic to their cause encourage this change of tactics because doing so changes the politics of morality policy into something more routine and familiar. Policy makers are more comfortable when basic policy goals and values are agreed upon, with only the specific ways to reach these goals being debated. Such policy debate is less threatening to elected officials because it reduces the chances that opponents will use their positions on these highly visible and contentious issues against them in the next election. Incremental, instrumental policy change is also more comfortable for executive branch officials and legislative staff because it plays to their strengths in analytical skill and experience. Thus, all the institutions of the regular policy-making system push morality policy advocates to shift from using moral arguments to using instrumental ones and from advocating major changes to advocating incremental ones. These reformers are then rewarded for doing so by seeing their policy goals advance.

As morality policy reformers learn the institutions of the policy-making process and adjust their tactics accordingly, the terms of the debate change. Morality arguments are purged and replaced by those that are less contentious. So, the gambling policy debate shifts from being about gambling's immorality to being about "gaming" and its impacts on tax revenue and tourism and, perhaps, about how to help those few people who are gambling addicts.[36] And prostitution is now banned, not because it is sinful but because of the sexually transmitted diseases, exploitation of women, and drug abuse associated with it. And the censorship debate is no longer about banning those films that no one should be allowed to see; instead, it is about labeling films so that adults can make an informed decision about just how much sex and violence they want to see.[37]

Another American political institution that helps reduce morality policy rhetoric and conflict is federalism. Americans share many basic values but there are some regional differences in the extent to which people think it is appropriate for moral values to influence a policy debate.[38] Furthermore, those who hold traditional religious values and various political ideologies are not evenly distributed across the country.[39] Federalism lets states and communities shape policy to reflect the public's moral views, allowing for a closer congruence of public opinion and policy than if we had a unitary system of government.[40] Because any disconnect between public opinion and morality policy is especially likely to ignite political activism and strife, this general characteristic of federalism is particularly important for morality policy.[41]

Thus, the institutional and political forces of state and local government push morality policy making into the mold of run-of-the-mill, nonmorality policy making. By doing so, they "de-moralize" it, discouraging the political discussion of moral values, focusing on minor changes rather than major ones, and closely matching policy to public opinion so as to reduce the aggravation that any discontinuity could cause. As this process moves on, a morality issue returns to equilibrium and again moves off the policy agenda—at least until the next external shock starts the entire process again.

Examples of Morality Policy Politics in the States and Communities: Abortion Regulation and Same-Sex Marriage

Now that we have described the typical pattern of morality policy politics, let's consider two extended examples of how the American states and communities have dealt with such policy questions. Although neither of these issues has completed the full cycle by returning to an entirely stable equilibrium—both issues are very much on the political agenda today—they illustrate well how the policy-making process works when basic moral conflict enters into the political debate. First, we describe the politics of the morality policy that has figured most prominently in American politics in recent decades—abortion regulation. Abortion politics has arguably had an impact on the current American political system as deep and long lasting as that of the Cold War or the globalization of the economy. Second, we look at a relatively new morality issue—same-sex marriage. The intensity and fast-changing terms of this issue provide a good example of a policy debate at the height of moral controversy.

Abortion Regulation

A few morality policies have generated some of the most important political battles in American history. Because morality issues are technically simple, highly visible, and touch on many people's basic values, they can motivate social movements with political impacts far beyond the immediate issue at hand. The fights to abolish slavery in the 19th century and to ban alcohol in the early 20th century were two such issues. As we begin the 21st century, we are living in a political environment shaped in large part by the debate over another such momentous morality policy—the regulation of abortion.

The battle over abortion regulation is a significant contributing factor to—if not the major cause—of many of the fundamental characteristics of American politics today, from our polarized political parties to the rise of the Christian Right to the importance and political respectability of archconservative political thought. In 1964, Republican Barry Goldwater lost the presidential race in one of the most lopsided landslides ever in what was widely attributed to his "extreme" (his own word) conservative politics. At that time, Ronald Reagan was a Democrat, and quite a few conservative Democrats and moderate—and even liberal—Republicans were in Congress. The Catholic Church was not involved in politics (except on taxation and education issues that involved its own economic self-interest), and TV evangelists talked almost exclusively about saving souls, not about politics.[42] Of course,

today, Goldwater and Reagan are mainstream Republican legends, the congressional parties are much more ideologically pure, and the Catholic Church and evangelical fundamentalists are among the most powerful political forces in the country. What happened to change American politics so fundamentally in the last 40 years? Abortion politics is a big part of the answer.

Equilibrium Before the Civil War, technical problems with surgery rendered moot most political questions about artificial abortion.[43] After the Civil War, the American Medical Association (AMA), a fledgling interest group and professional association of medical doctors, argued that as a medical procedure, questions about when an abortion was appropriate should be settled by doctors. Largely to keep those who weren't medical doctors (such as homeopaths and midwives) from performing abortions, the AMA pushed successfully to outlaw abortions that weren't "medically necessary"; that is, those that were not ordered by one of its members. Thus, in the late 19th and early 20th centuries, abortion regulation was largely not a morality policy. What little policy discussion there was regarding it was couched in technical terms.

Cracks in the long abortion policy equilibrium began to appear in the 1960s. In 1962, Sherri Finkbine, a popular Phoenix television personality, took Thalidomide for anxiety during her pregnancy.[44] The drug did severe and irreparable damage to the fetus she was carrying, and her doctor recommended an abortion. But when Finkbine's local hospital refused to perform the abortion, arguing that it was not medically necessary, she made a well-publicized appeal to change the hospital's policy. When her appeal was denied, she had the abortion in Sweden. Reports of thousands of "Thalidomide babies" born without arms or legs in Europe and outbreaks of birth-defect-causing German measles in the United States at this time made Finkbine's case representative of a situation faced by many women and a **cause célèbre**—that is, an issue causing heated controversy and widespread notoriety.

As a result of the Finkbine case and others like it, in the 1960s, some states began to reform their abortion laws to allow the procedure when the life or the health of the pregnant woman was at risk (see Table 13.1). Advocates, primarily medical groups, argued that this was strictly a health issue. In fact, the reform had so little moral opposition that conservative icon Ronald Reagan, as the Republican governor of California, signed one of the most liked abortion regulations into law in 1967.[45]

But there were rumblings of moral arguments swirling around these early reforms, even if they did not dominate the debate. The nascent women's movement, including groups such as the National Organization for Women (NOW), organized in 1966, latched onto abortion reform as a central issue, and some Catholic and evangelical Protestant leaders made moral arguments against it. Indeed, only 18 states loosened their abortion regulations between 1966 and 1972, and these states had fewer Catholics and fundamentalist Protestants and more women in the workforce, a pattern foreshadowing the future morality politics of the issue.[46] The issue that began to raise moral concerns about abortion regulation was whether the procedure should be available *on demand*, for any reason, to a pregnant woman. As of January 1973, only four states (Alaska, Hawaii, New York, and Washington) allowed abortion on demand.

The Shock: *Roe v. Wade* (1973) That month, January 1973, the U.S. Supreme Court shocked both proponents and opponents of abortion regulation reform by striking down all state abortion laws in *Roe v. Wade*.[47] This decision thrust the question of abortion on demand squarely into public debate, with all its moral implications. Based on its earlier finding[48] that the Bill of Rights implied a right to privacy, the Court held that states could not limit a woman's right to abortion on demand in the **first trimester** of her pregnancy, although they could regulate abortion in the second and third trimesters.

Few on either side of the issue felt that the Supreme Court would go this far in deregulating abortion.[49] Anti-abortion groups had largely ignored the case, not even filing any **amicus curiae briefs** with the Court on it. But in reaction to the decision in *Roe*, these groups were energized dramatically and organized permanently. On the other hand, those groups advocating for a woman's right to abortion on demand actually became less active immediately after the *Roe* decision. They thought they had won, so they celebrated and moved on.

The Morality Politics of Abortion Regulation The political shock of *Roe v. Wade* cannot be overestimated, setting off a firestorm of morality politics that has helped define

Table 13.1

State Abortion Regulation Reforms before Roe v. Wade (1973)

State	Year of Reform
Mississippi	1966
California	1967
Colorado	1967
North Carolina	1967
Georgia	1968
Maryland	1968
Arkansas	1969
Delaware	1969
Kansas	1969
New Mexico	1969
Oregon	1969
Alaska	1970
Hawaii	1970
New York	1970
South Carolina	1970
Virginia	1970
Washington	1970
Florida	1972

Source: Christopher Z. Mooney and Mei-Hsien Lee, "Legislating Morality in the American States: The Case of Pre-*Roe* Abortion Regulation Reform," *American Journal of Political Science* 39 (1995): 599–627.

American politics ever since. Those who felt that their basic moral values were threatened by legalized, on-demand abortion soon got very busy in the political arena. The first major group to do so was the Roman Catholic Church, which had the advantages of being well-organized in a hierarchical structure and of having a clear, long-standing doctrine opposing any artificial interference with conception and birth. Indeed, abortion on demand threatened the basic values of the Catholic Church so deeply that it was the first morality issue in which it got politically involved in the United States.[50] Its anti-abortion activities in the 1970s included directives from bishops to priests and from priests to parishioners to oppose abortion regulation reform, messages on the subject from the pulpit, posters in church halls, and the use of existing church groups and organizations to organize rallies, send letters to politicians, compose **Op-Ed articles** for newspapers, and so forth.

Roe v. Wade also threatened the basic moral values of many American evangelical Protestants, but they took longer to organize for political action than did the Catholics, mainly due to the less rigid organizational structures of their denominations. But by the early 1980s, conservative Protestants had established such groups as the American Christian Cause, Concerned Women for America, and the Moral Majority. These groups were both well-organized and politically potent, working effectively through both grassroots political action and their efforts to take over the Republican Party organizations in many states.[51]

Groups opposed to abortion on demand used basic moral arguments in their political rhetoric. Although they also raised some technical medical issues (such as when a fetus feels pain), their basic arguments came down simply to their fundamental belief that life begins at conception. Thus, they argued, anything that stops fetal development artificially is, effectively, murder. Because most of these anti-abortion groups were religiously based, it was quite natural for them to back their arguments with religious authority, primarily the Christian Bible for Protestant groups and papal pronouncements for Catholic groups. As the 1970s wore on, these groups adopted the positive moniker **"pro-life"** based on their moral argument. And the moral implication that their opponents were somehow "anti-life" or "pro-death" was not accidental.

Groups on the other side of the abortion battle did not make religious moral arguments. Rather, they backed their position with arguments about women's civil rights[52] and the practical implications of unwanted pregnancies. These groups tended not to be religiously based (although many liberal Protestant churches supported them) but rather were secular women's and medical groups. The positive name these groups adopted for themselves highlights the nonmoral nature of their arguments: **"pro-choice."**

Post-*Roe* abortion politics began with pro-life forces trying to ban the procedure outright in their state legislatures. Indeed, they were successful in getting anti-abortion legislation passed in many states, particularly where individuals' religious and ideological views matched those of these groups.[53] Legislators and governors in such states eagerly tried to bring public policy back into line with their constituents' views. Indeed, many states even passed new abortion bans, reaffirming their pre-*Roe* policies. These **expressive actions** allowed policy makers to demonstrate that they shared their constituents' views, but they had no practical effects because they were obviously unconstitutional, given *Roe*.

As the 1970s progressed, pro-life reformers grew less satisfied with symbolic victories, and they modified their strategies and policy agenda to work better with state and local institutions and policy-making processes. These highly motivated advocates not only continued to expand their political base by appealing to their supporters' sense of moral outrage about abortion but they also learned how to use this political clout to influence policy makers through direct lobbying, campaign contributions, and political endorsements. Just as important, they shifted their short-term policy goals from the immediate black-and-white banning of all abortions to chipping away incrementally on their availability, with the hope that such reforms would reduce the number of abortions that were actually performed. Their basic strategy became to make getting an abortion as difficult as possible so that more women contemplating the procedure would be discouraged and choose another way to deal with their unwanted pregnancies.[54]

Pro-life groups took a shotgun approach to this incremental reform strategy, working to pass a variety of abortion restrictions in many states and communities, hoping that the federal courts would not strike them all down. In a major early decision in 1976,[55] the Supreme Court ruled that four out of seven restrictions in a Missouri law were unconstitutional. But more important for the emerging incremental pro-life strategy, the Court let three of these restrictions stand. These restrictions were rather minor, requiring some medical recordkeeping, defining the "viability" of a fetus, and requiring a woman's "informed consent" before she could have an abortion. But they encouraged other states to pass more restrictions, continually testing the limits of their constitutionality. As the 1970s and 1980s progressed, the federal courts responded more and more favorably to the pro-life legal arguments.[56] Restrictions adopted by various states were tested in the courts and found to pass constitutional muster. These reforms included waiting periods, bans on public funding of abortions for poor women, various regulations of facilities and doctors providing abortions, and spousal and parental consent. Finally, in their decisions in *Webster vs. Reproductive Health Services*

Colin Archer/Getty Images News

Operation Rescue, a fundamentalist Christian pro-life advocacy group, promoted its political cause by conducting massive civil disobediance protests at abortion clinics throughout the country in the 1990's. At one point, 10,000 people per year were arrested at Operation Rescue demonstrations.

(1989)[57] and *Planned Parenthood v. Casey* (1992),[58] the Supreme Court went about as far as it could in allowing the states to regulate abortion restrictively without overturning the basic right to a first trimester abortion that was enunciated in *Roe vs. Wade*.[59]

Complementing their strategy of working incrementally through the legislative and judicial processes, in the 1980s and 1990s, pro-life groups tapped into their sympathizers' moral outrage by engaging in extensive direct political action to stop abortions, often one abortion at a time. For example, pro-life groups staged demonstrations outside abortion clinics, both to allow their members to express their opinions publicly and to try to influence the personal decisions of pregnant women entering the building. The strong views of these pro-life advocates, the emotional state of the pregnant women, and the strong views of the pro-choice advocates who often set up counterdemonstrations at these sites often made these situations very tense, resulting in much emotional trauma and sometimes physical and verbal violence and arrests. Local government officials—mayors, city councils, and the police—were dragged into many of these morality policy debates when they were forced to weigh the free speech rights of advocates on both sides against public order ordinances.[60]

Even at the height of this grassroots political activity in the late 1980s and early 1990s, some pro-life activists, filled with the zeal of the morally righteous, felt intense frustration at not being able to ban abortion quickly and completely, even though pro-life groups continued to succeed in their incremental policy-making strategy in most states. This frustration even led to several well-publicized acts of terrorism and assassination, including the bombing and vandalism of abortion clinics and the killing of doctors who performed abortions.[61]

Return to Equilibrium? In the first decade of the 21st century, the amount and intensity of grassroots political activity on abortion politics have waned. Does this mean that political equilibrium on the issue has returned?

Perhaps—but if so, probably only for a limited time. Pro-life groups continue to pursue their incremental strategy successfully in the states.[62] Today, although women still have the legal right to a first trimester abortion on demand, the ability to exercise that right is severely limited in much of the country, especially by the availability of doctors willing to perform them. For example, in the entire State of Mississippi, only one abortion clinic is currently operating.[63] Pro-life reformers also continue to adopt new tactics as they learn to work within the regular political institutions of the state and local governments. For example, staunch pro-life reformer Phil Kline has used his powers as Kansas's attorney general to subpoena abortion clinics' records extensively. Kline says this is to check for regulation violations and prosecute child rapists, but pro-choice Kansans claim that it is simply harassment designed to shut down these clinics.[64] Pro-life reformers have even begun the significant use of non-morality-based arguments, claiming, for example, that abortion harms a woman's health.[65]

Further evidence of policy equilibrium is seen in that although many abortion policy bills are still introduced every year in every state legislature, the only ones that receive serious attention tend to be those that make only small changes and have limited practical impacts. For example, in Texas in 2005, there was a heated debate over a bill to require parental *permission* for a minor to have an abortion—an incremental step from the existing law requiring only parental *notification*. In that same session, Texas lawmakers also gave a lot of attention to a bill that would have slightly strengthened restrictions on third trimester abortions, even though of the almost 80,000 abortions performed in Texas each year, fewer than 50 are on women in their third trimesters.[66]

Currently, the restrictiveness of abortion regulation varies substantially from state to state (see Table 13.2), and just like before *Roe*, a state's abortion regulations largely reflect the basic values of those who live there.[67] Abortion is more strictly regulated in conservative,

Table 13.2

Selected State Abortion Regulations, 2006

State	Parental Consent or Notification[a]	Reporting Required[b]	Counseling[c]	Waiting Period[d]	"Choose Life" Plates[e]	Clinic Access Protection[f]	Overall Abortion Regulation Restrictiveness[g]
MS	X	X	X	X	X		5
OH	X	X	X	X	X		5
OK	X	X	X	X	X		5
SD	X	X	X	X	X		5
AL	X		X	X	X		4
AR	X		X	X	X		4
IN	X	X	X	X			4
KY	X	X	X	X			4
LA	X		X	X	X		4
ND	X	X	X	X			4
NE	X	X	X	X			4
PA	X	X	X	X			4
SC	X	X	X	X			4
TX	X	X	X	X			4
UT	X	X	X	X			4
VA	X	X	X	X			4
WV	X	X	X	X			4
DE	X	X	X				3
GA	X		X	X			3
KS	X	X	X	X		X	3
MI	X	X	X	X		X	3
MN	X	X	X	X		X	3
MO	X	X		X			3
RI	X	X	X				3
WI	X	X	X	X		X	3
AK		X	X				2
CT		X			X		2
FL	X				X		2
IA	X	X					2
ID		X		X			2
TN	X		X				2
WY	X	X					2
AZ	X						1
CO	X	X				X	1
HI					X		1

Table 13.2

Selected State Abortion Regulations, 2006 (continued)

State	Parental Consent or Notification[a]	Reporting Required[b]	Counseling[c]	Waiting Period[d]	"Choose Life" Plates[e]	Clinic Access Protection[f]	Overall Abortion Regulation Restrictiveness[g]
MA	X	X				X	1
MD	X				X	X	1
NC	X	X				X	1
NM		X					1
VT	X	X					1
IL							0
ME	X	X				X	0
MT					X	X	0
NH							0
NJ							0
NV			X			X	0
NY		X				X	0
OR		X				X	0
WA		X				X	0
CA						X	−1

Note: This table indicates the abortion regulations in force in these states as of 1 December 2006. Laws enjoined by the courts are not included. Each of the regulations is a pro-life policy, except the protection of abortion clinic access, which is a pro-choice policy. The policies are as follows:

  [a] Minors must have parental notification or consent to have an abortion.

  [b] All nonsurgical abortions must be reported to a state authority.

  [c] Counseling is required before a woman can have an abortion.

  [d] A waiting period is required before a woman can have an abortion.

  [e] Automobile owners can purchase "Choose Life" license plates, with the proceeds going to pro-life causes.

  [f] A prohibition exists against blocking abortion clinic entries.

  [g] This is the number of a state's pro-life abortion regulations, minus 1 if it prohibits the blocking of access to abortion clinics.

Source: Alan Guttmacher Institute, "State Policies in Brief," 2006, http://www.guttmacher.org/statecenter/spibs/spib_OAL.pdf; and Alan Guttmacher Institute, "State Policies in Brief," 2005, http://www.agi-usa.org/statecenter/spibs/index.html.

rural states with many Evangelical Protestants. And although Catholics are more likely to live in cities, all things being equal, the more Catholics who live in a state, the more restrictive its abortion policy is. Recent research has also demonstrated that as time has passed since *Roe,* a state's abortion regulations have reflected the values of its citizens even more closely than those of its political leaders.[68] Even

members of Congress vote on abortion issues to represent their constituents' values.[69] Thus, although the fit isn't perfect, abortion policy today reflects the state-to-state distribution of citizens' values very well.

Even if abortion policy has reached some sort of policy equilibrium, it certainly has a different tone than the equilibrium before *Roe v. Wade.* It is a very uneasy equilibrium—at best, more like an armed cease-fire than a reconciliation. The pro-life forces maintain their morality-based policy goals, still hoping to ban the procedure outright nationwide. Both sides know that a single Supreme Court decision could shock the system again, starting another round of intense morality politics in the states and communities. This is why the abortion views of John Roberts and Samuel Alito figured so prominently in the U.S. Senate hearings for their Supreme Court nominations in 2005.[70] Indeed, the retirement of Justice Sandra Day O'Connor and her replacement by Justice Alito appears to have shifted the balance on the Court significantly with respect to abortion law. The first evidence of this was in *Gonzales v. Carhart,* the case handed down in April 2007 that upheld a 2003 federal law banning "partial-birth abortion" (or "intact dilation and extraction" to the medical community and pro-choice forces).[71] In a challenge to a very similar Nebraska law in 2000,[72] Justice O'Connor voted with the 5–4 majority that the law was unconstitutionally vague, but in *Gonzales,* Justice Alito's vote created a majority that approved such a ban. Will this decision be the shock that sets off a new round of morality policy making in the states and communities, as many have speculated?[73] Only time will tell.

Even before *Gonzales,* several states had been scrambling to be the first to pass a complete ban on abortion, hoping to generate the most serious challenge to *Roe* since *Planned Parenthood v. Casey* in 1992. South Dakota's legislature passed such a law in 2006, but it was defeated in a popular referendum just six months after the governor signed it.[74] The soundness of that ban's electoral defeat—even in rural, conservative South Dakota (56 percent opposed to 44 percent in favor)—and the defeat the same year in Oregon and California of two other pro-life ballot measures suggest that it will not be easy for the anti-abortion forces to succeed in passing a state abortion ban to challenge *Roe* head-to-head. But a conservative legislature in a state without the popular referendum—perhaps Mississippi or Louisiana—may well do so soon.[75] If

so, a major new abortion policy shock could occur at any time, making *Gonzales* look like a minor tremor.

The overall impact of this generation-long morality policy struggle over abortion regulation has fundamentally changed the American political landscape. The debate caused religious conservatives to become an active, organized, and permanent political force in states and communities across the country for the first time since World War II. Catholic and fundamentalist Protestant groups found their political voice and developed the institutions needed to keep them in the thick of state and local politics for decades to come. The intensity and breadth of this morality policy debate even realigned our political parties, causing greater ideological polarization in them than at any time since the Civil War.[76] And as policy makers' and the public's views have hardened and sharpened, the relatively close division of public opinion on the issue suggests that there may be no long-term equilibrium on this morality policy in our lifetimes.

Same-Sex Marriage

Same-sex marriage has only recently exploded onto the American policy agenda, but it already exhibits many of the key characteristics of morality policy. Although we can't predict the progress of this issue in coming years—or—even a few months from now—its prominence suggests that it will generate active morality politics in the states and communities for the foreseeable future.

Equilibrium The legal and social status of homosexuals in the United States has improved dramatically since the Gay Rights movement began in the late 1960s.[77] But placing same-sex couples on a legal status equal to that of as married heterosexual couples was virtually unthinkable until very recently—even among gay rights activists. Indeed, sexual relations between members of the same sex were illegal in some states even into the 21st century (see Figure 13.2). In 2003, the U.S. Supreme Court overturned all state and local anti-**sodomy**

| Figure 13.2 |

States with Anti-Sodomy Laws before *Lawrence v. Texas* (2003)

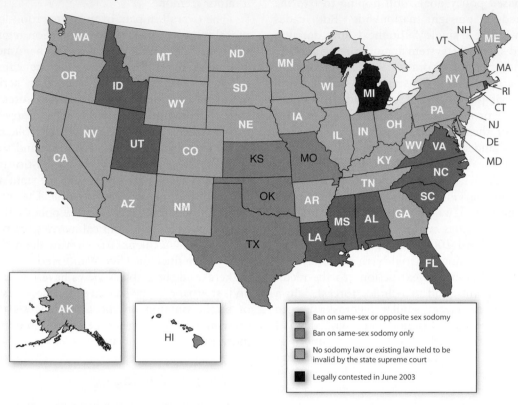

Ban on same-sex or opposite sex sodomy

Ban on same-sex sodomy only

No sodomy law or existing law held to be invalid by the state supreme court

Legally contested in June 2003

Note: These laws were in effect in June 2003, when the U.S. Supreme Court decision in *Lawrence v. Texas* invalidated all state anti-sodomy laws.

Source: Policy Institute, National Gay and Lesbian Task Force, http://www.thetaskforce.org/downloads/sodomymap0603.pdf.

laws, having upheld their constitutionality as recently as 1986.[78] Gay rights issues had been on many state and local government agendas since the 1970s, but only with such relatively incremental measures as efforts to eliminate discrimination against gays in employment, housing, adoption, and the like. Gay rights groups made steady, but largely quiet, political headway by arguing that sexual orientation, like race and gender, is simply a condition of life into which people are born, and, therefore, it is unfair to discriminate against people based on it.[79] Variation in these gay rights laws around the country typically reflected the ideology and values of the citizens of the states and communities.[80]

The Shock: Court Action in Hawaii Same-sex marriage was not even on the agenda of the Human Rights Campaign, the National Gay and Lesbian Task Force, or any of the other major gay rights advocacy groups before the early 1990s. The leaders of these groups were taken as much by surprise as were their opponents by the events that thrust the issue into the limelight.[81] As with abortion regulation, court action set off the morality politics of same-sex marriage. But in this case, courts gave not just one but a series of three increasingly significant political shocks.

While gay rights groups had pursued incremental change in state and local law, the occasional same-sex couple challenged the implicit ban on same-sex marriage simply by applying for a marriage license at their local courthouse and suing the relevant local official when they were denied one.[82] These couples routinely lost their suits, as the courts failed to accept their arguments about equal protection and equal rights under the state and federal constitutions.

But in Hawaii in 1993, something unusual happened. Three same-sex couples sued the state for the right to marry and they won. The Hawaii Supreme Court held that limiting marriage to heterosexual couples constituted sex discrimination, which violated the Hawaii Constitution.[83] This decision shocked people, policy makers, and groups—both in favor of and opposed to gay rights—across the country, instantly stirring the political pot on the issue.

Why should someone in Idaho or New York care whether Hawaii lets same-sex couples marry? For many people, both pro and con, a general moral principle is at stake. But the more practical reason for the nationwide interest in the Hawaiian court decision is that a state's marriage laws have implications beyond its boundaries. The **Full Faith and Credit Clause** of the U.S. Constitution encourages each state to recognize, honor, and enforce other states' actions, especially in the areas of civil and family law. Such reciprocity is what makes a couple's marriage in one state legally binding in another state. Thus, the reason both proponents and opponents of same-sex marriage became extraordinarily interested in the Hawaii case was the idea—although not a tested legal fact—that if one state allowed same-sex marriage, then every other state would have to recognize those same-sex marriages performed in that state. So, with this decision, the morality politics of same-sex marriage began in earnest.

The Morality Politics of Same-Sex Marriage The 1993 Hawaii decision, combined with the Constitution's Full Faith and Credit Clause, threatened some individuals' deeply held moral values about family, sexuality, and natural law, especially those for whom homosexuality itself threatened these values. By recognizing same-sex marriage as a legally binding relationship, the government would not only be condoning homosexuality but also be placing it on a par with heterosexuality. Groups who were offended by this tended to be associated with traditionalistic religions, such as fundamentalist Protestant denominations and the Roman Catholic Church.[84] In fact, many of the most active groups opposing same-sex marriage—groups like Focus on the Family and the Christian Coalition—cut their political teeth fighting for stricter abortion regulation.[85] Their arguments against same-sex marriage, like their arguments against abortion, were morally based and supported by their interpretation of biblical passages. Grassroots veterans of the abortion wars were easily motivated by such arguments.

One lesson the leaders of these groups took from their abortion experiences was the importance of defining the issue to appeal simply to many individuals' basic values. Given the growing tolerance of homosexuality in the United States, as symbolized by the passage of many state and local gay rights laws in the 1970s and 1980s, arguing that homosexuals themselves were immoral would not likely attract the broad public support they needed.[86] Instead, they argued that same-sex *marriage* threatened that "sacred institution"—traditional heterosexual marriage.[87] Indeed, this threat to heterosexual marriage was argued to be a threat to our entire society, "undermining its moral foundation," leading to polygamy and incest, and destabilizing society in general.[88] Symbolizing this argument, these groups assumed the positive moniker, *pro-family.* This was an excellent political choice—after all, who could be anti-family?

On the other hand, advocates of same-sex marriage made arguments about civil rights and equal protection, paralleling arguments made by pro-choice and racial civil rights groups.[89] Their argument was one of fairness: because homosexuality is a condition of nature, like being a woman or being black, rather than a moral failing, it is unfair to deny homosexuals the right to participate fully in society, including by getting married. Thus, pro-same-sex marriage arguments were based less on an appeal to basic moral values than on an appeal to justice.

After the Hawaii decision, advocates on both sides of the issue made their cases in the states and in Washington, D.C. But in doing so, there were at least two significant differences between the politics of same-sex marriage and the politics of abortion regulation. First, the morality-based argument of the groups opposing same-sex marriage resonated well with a clear majority of people in the country. Even if people were increasingly tolerant of homosexuality, same-sex marriage was just too far for many people. And second, the Hawaii Supreme Court (and later, courts in Massachusetts and Vermont) found that a ban on same-sex marriage violated the state's constitution, and state constitutions are far easier to amend than the federal constitution, which the U.S. Supreme Court found was violated in *Roe v. Wade*. These two features of the political landscape caused the politics of same-sex marriage to take a very different path than that of abortion regulation.

Soon after the Hawaii decision, conservatives in Congress, sensing a disjuncture between public opinion and the potential legalization of same-sex marriage, put the federal **Defense of Marriage Act (DOMA)** on a fast track, with President Bill Clinton signing it on September 21, 1996. DOMA did two things for reformers opposing same-sex marriage. First, it explicitly allowed an exception to the Full Faith and Credit Clause, allowing states not to recognize same-sex marriages sanctioned in other states. And second, it defined marriage for purposes of federal law (such as for determining eligibility for Social Security survivor's benefits) as being "a union of one man and one woman as husband and wife."

COMPARISONS HELP US UNDERSTAND

SAME-SEX MARRIAGE LAWS IN THE STATES

Since the Hawaiian court cases shocked marriage law equilibrium in 1993, the states have passed considerable legislation to regulate same-sex marriage explicitly. In 1995, Utah was the first to ban same-sex marriage by statute, and since then, all but five states have legislated on the subject through the normal legislative process or the initiative (or both) by changing their statutes or constitutions (or both) to ban marriage or other forms of legal recognition, such as civil unions, (or both), with several states acting on the subject more than once. The result has been great variation in same-sex marriage law among the states, reflecting both the values of the states' citizens on the subject and the lawmaking institutions of each state. In Figure 13.3, we map this variation on a scale that differentiates states' same-sex marriage policy by coding the following levels from darkest to lightest:

- Explicit legal recognition of same-sex unions (CT, NJ, NH, MA, and VT)

- No explicit statutory or constitutional recognition or restriction of same-sex unions (MD, NM, NY, RI, and WY)

- Statutory ban on same-sex marriage (AZ, CA, DE, IL, IN, IA, ME, MN, NC, PA, WA, and WV)

- Constitutional ban on same-sex marriage (CO, HI, MS, MO, NV, OR, and TN)

  Statutory or

- Constitutional ban on same-sex marriage, civil unions, or any other legal recognition (AL, AK, AR, FL, GA, ID, KS, KY, LA, MI, MT, NE, ND, OH, OK, SC, SD, TX, UT, VA, and WI)

What factors might explain this great variation in same-sex marriage policy? Think about those influences on morality policy discussed in this chapter, and test your hypotheses by comparing the states on Figure 13.3.

Figure 13.3

Statutory and Constitutional Restrictions on Same-Sex Marriage

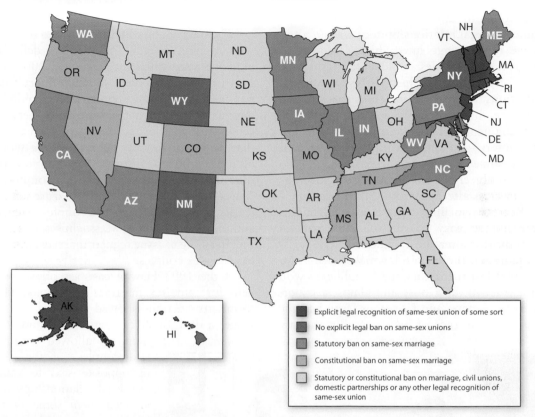

Legend:
- Explicit legal recognition of same-sex union of some sort
- No explicit legal ban on same-sex unions
- Statutory ban on same-sex marriage
- Constitutional ban on same-sex marriage
- Statutory or constitutional ban on marriage, civil unions, domestic partnerships or any other legal recognition of same-sex union

Note: Correct as of 16 November 2007. Some states may have both statutory and constitutional restrictions in which case they are scored as having a constitutional ban, which is more restrictive.

Source: Adapted from the Policy Institute, National Gay and Lesbian Task Force, http://www.thetaskforce.org/downloads/MarriageMap_06_Nov.pdf; updated by the authors.

By 2000, 34 states had adopted "little DOMAs," likewise defining marriage and banning the recognition of same-sex marriages from other states, and five more states have done so since then. The unusual speed with which both the federal and state governments acted in response to this Hawaiian case demonstrates the ability of anti-same-sex marriage groups to mobilize their members and sympathetic policy makers as well as the potent moral threat that same-sex marriage represents to many people's basic values.

In 1998, before its Supreme Court could judge appeals in the case, Hawaii's voters adopted a state constitutional amendment that explicitly outlawed same-sex marriage, making the original case moot. But by this time, the genie was out of the bottle, with pro-same-sex marriage advocates having seen the success of the judicial route that could bypass more majoritarian policy-making approaches. Sure enough, in 1999, a same-sex couple in Vermont won their marriage license lawsuit.[90] But what made the Vermont case different than the Hawaii case was that in Vermont, policy makers did not fight the decision but rather embraced it by passing legislation in 2000 that established **civil unions,** a legal relationship that was an alternative to marriage into which same-sex or opposite-sex couples could enter. Using the term "civil union" helped diffuse the moral objections that moderates had to same-sex marriage. But because the state would still be recognizing and sanctioning homosexuality, conservative activists fought it. In recent years, some gay rights activists have also come to object to civil unions, seeing them as second-class alternatives to full marriage.[91]

But even in liberal Vermont, civil unions were not an easy sell. In the 2000 general election, just after the Democratic state legislature passed the bill, 16 lawmakers who supported it lost their seats, the Republicans won a majority in the House and almost a majority in the Senate, and Governor Dean had the toughest state race of his career. But the law was not repealed, making Vermont the first state to establish for same-sex couples a legal relationship with all the legal trappings of marriage, if not the name.

The next chapter in this story had the most wide-ranging effects. In decisions delivered in November 2003 and February 2004, the Massachusetts Supreme Judicial Court ruled not only that the state's constitution prohibited any marriage law that discriminated between same- and opposite-sex couples but also that anything short of *true marriage* would establish an "unconstitutional, inferior, and discriminatory status for same-sex couples."[92] The court directed the state legislature to craft legislation allowing same-sex couples to marry, and on May 17, 2004, Massachusetts became the first state to issue regular marriage licenses to same-sex couples.

If the 1993 Hawaii case set off warning bells for same-sex marriage opponents, Massachusetts's actions showed that this was no longer a drill. By 2004, many states and communities allowed nonmarried couples (of the same or opposite sex) to establish legal relationships that allowed them some of the benefits of married couples, such as hospital visitation rights, inheritance rights, and the like. But here was the real thing—same-sex marriage, plain and simple. And what's more, immediately after the Massachusetts decision, in February and March 2004, same-sex couples all across the country began asking their city, town, and county clerks for marriage licenses, and in several places, they got them.[93] San Francisco, California, and Multnomah County, Oregon, made front-page news nationwide for granting marriage licenses for thousands of same-sex

"*I'm sorry, Jim. I love you, but I hate Vermont.*"

couples, but local government officials in such places as New Paltz, New York, Asbury Park, New Jersey, and Sandoval County, New Mexico, also issued marriage licenses to same-sex couples during this heady period.

But as it turned out, public opinion in most American states and communities would not stand for such a sharp change in this morality policy. Outside of Massachusetts, courts and governors quickly ruled that any same-sex marriage licenses issued by local governments were null and void and that no more would be forthcoming.[94] But perhaps more important—and emblematic of morality politics—in a burst of energy that demonstrated the severity of the threat to their moral values, opposition groups qualified and won ballot measures outlawing same-sex marriage in thirteen states in 2004, two more states in 2005, and another eight in 2006. One other state—Arizona—also voted on the issue in 2006, but it was defeated there in a close election. This far outstripped the only one or two such measures passed in each of the three preceding election cycles. Thus, almost one-half of the states voted on and banned same-sex marriage within one election cycle of the Massachusetts court decision establishing same-sex marriage there. This was certainly one of the fastest reform movements ever to sweep the country.

Why was direct democracy used so extensively and successfully in this anti-same-sex-marriage reform movement? First, the court decisions in Hawaii, Vermont, and Massachusetts were based on those states' constitutions, so to avoid more such decisions, groups opposed to same-sex marriage sought reforms in state constitutions directly, a move that typically requires a referendum or initiative. But more important, the politics of this morality policy made ballot measures the preferred political tactic for these opposition groups. Opponents of same-sex marriage were able to explain their arguments simply and convincingly: traditional marriage is important and same-sex marriage threatens it—just see your Bible. Even though Americans have grown increasingly tolerant of homosexuals, they are still in the minority, and

bias against them is still common.[95] Deep-seated prejudices die hard, and even socially unacceptable discrimination can be expressed discreetly in the ballot box. For example, in 1996, over 30 percent of Kentucky voters chose to keep an archaic state requirement for racial segregation in schools, and in 2000, over 40 percent of Alabama voters voted to keep a state ban on interracial marriage.[96] And it is likely that today in the United States, racial prejudice is far less socially acceptable than prejudice against homosexuals.

Table 13.3 shows the results of ballot measures to ban same-sex marriage since 1998. These figures show, first, that these bans had no difficulty passing in almost any of these states. Clearly, the general American public does not favor same-sex marriage. The average opposition vote was 69 percent—a solid majority. But also note tremendous state-to-state variation in the support for these measures, from 48 percent in Arizona to 86 percent in Mississippi. Furthermore, the reform got somewhat less support in the 2006 election than it had previously received. In addition to the defeat in Arizona, the average support for the year was only 64 percent, down from a stable annual average in previous years of about 70 percent. Five of the nine states voting in 2006 gave the measure less than 60 percent of their support, something that only two of the nineteen states voting on it from 1998 to 2005 had done. These changes may be only the result of the more supportive states adopting the measure first. But the wide variation in support suggests that in the future, like with other morality policies, we will see same-sex marriage policy vary among the states to reflect the different values of their residents.

Return to Equilibrium? The politics of same-sex marriage has not returned to equilibrium. This very new morality policy has just recently come onto the policy agenda of most states, and there will be considerable political activity on it for the foreseeable future. What this activity will be is unclear. But based on the typical pattern of morality politics, we can make an educated guess.

| Table 13.3 |

Voting Results for Anti-Same-Sex Marriage Ballot Measures, 1998–2006

State	Vote (% Yes–% No)	Ban on All Civil Unions (Same- or Opposite-Sex)?
1998		
Alaska	68–32	N
Hawaii	69–29	N
1998 average	69–31	
2000		
Nebraska*	70–30	Y
2000 average	70–30	
2002		
Nevada	67–33	N
2002 average	67–33	
2004		
Arkansas	75–25	Y
Georgia	76–24	Y
Kentucky	75–25	Y
Louisiana	78–22	Y
Michigan	59–41	Y
Mississippi	86–14	N
Missouri	71–29	N
Montana	66–34	N
North Dakota	73–27	Y
Ohio	62–38	Y
Oklahoma	76–24	Y
Oregon	57–43	N
Utah	66–34	Y
2004 average	71–29	
2005		
Kansas	70–30	Y
Texas	76–24	Y
2005 average	73–27	
2006		
Alabama	81–19	N
Arizona	48–52	Y
Colorado	55–45	N
Idaho	63–37	Y
South Carolina	78–22	Y
South Dakota	52–48	Y
Tennessee	84–16	N
Virginia	57–43	Y
Wisconsin	59–41	Y
2006 average	64–36	
Overall Average	69–31	

Note: Nebraska's 2000 anti-same-sex marriage amendment was overturned by a federal district court in May 2005 for being too broad.

Source: Policy Institute, National Gay and Lesbian Task Force, http://www.thetaskforce.org/downloads/StateBallotPolling Data2005.pdf; and National Conference of State Legislatures, http://www.ncsl.org/statevote/samesex_06.htm.

The passage of the federal DOMA law in 1996 fixed the breach in the federalism firewall caused by the Constitution's Full Faith and Credit Clause, thereby isolating the direct effects of any individual state's actions on same-sex marriage. Now each state can develop the policy that reflects the values of its own citizens without threatening the values of those in other states. Thus, we will likely see a national patchwork of same-sex marriage policies, just as we see now with abortion regulation.

Furthermore, to facilitate the fit between public opinion and same-sex marriage policy, gay rights advocates will likely pursue incremental changes in policy rather than simply demanding complete parity between same- and opposite-sex marriages. Indeed, we are beginning to see just this pattern in the states today. Although most states have banned any form of legal same-sex relationship, some states have begun to allow same-sex couples various legal rights, even to the extent of sanctioning civil unions or **domestic partnership** arrangements. In addition to Vermont, these include New Jersey, Connecticut, and New Hampshire. A handful of other states—California, Hawaii, Maine, Washington, and Oregon—have established various sorts of such arrangements that, while falling short of full civil unions, offer same-sex couples some rights.

REFORM CAN HAPPEN

OTHER MORALITY POLICIES: NOW AND IN THE FUTURE

What other morality policies are the states and communities dealing with these days? What does the future hold for morality policy politics? Although we can expect that the old, established patterns of morality politics will continue to be seen in the states and communities in the coming years, it is harder to predict exactly which issues will spark major morality policy debates. For example, 20 years ago, no one expected same-sex marriage to be the major issue that it is today. It's a safe bet that abortion regulation will continue to simmer with at least a low level of morality politics in years to come, and a Supreme Court action could set off a full-blown morality policy conflagration at any time. The following issues are also being discussed by some state and local policy makers and interest groups, and they may spark significant morality politics in the next decade:

- Embryonic stem cell research
- Teaching evolution and intelligent design in public schools
- Teaching birth control and supplying various sexual health supplies in public schools
- Animal rights and animal cruelty

One thing we haven't yet seen much of in the politics of same-sex marriage is moral outrage and frustration leading to political violence. Perhaps it is simply too early in this process for such activity. Let's hope that this will be one morality policy that can be debated civilly, allowing us to avoid the political violence that has characterized other morality policies.

Summary

Morality policies are those that invoke strong moral arguments from one side of the policy debate. At various times in the United States, these have dealt with alcohol prohibition, slavery, recreational drug use, gambling, censorship, and prostitution, among many others. People and groups advocate morality policy reforms because of a threat to their basic moral and religious values rather than to seek some economic gain. Policy makers have great incentive to keep such policy consistent with the values of their constituents, and they are usually successful at doing so. But sometimes, a policy shock, such as a court decision or a technological breakthrough, upsets the morality policy equilibrium and instigates a cycle of morality policy politics. Because morality policies tend to be technically simple, highly visible, and hard to find compromise on, their politics can be especially intense and bitter. The U.S. Constitution reserves the setting of most of these policies to the state and local governments, so that is where these battles are usually fought. The most important morality policy debate in the states and communities in recent decades has been over abortion regulation. Morality policy debates that may become important in shaping our politics in the future include same-sex marriage, research with embryonic stem cells, animal rights, and the teaching of evolution and sex education in public schools.

Keywords

Altruism

Amicus curiae brief

Cause célèbre

Civil union

Defense of Marriage Act (DOMA)

Domestic partnership

Expressive act

First trimester

Full Faith and Credit Clause

Grassroots activities

Issue evolution

Morality policy

OP-ED article

Policy entrepreneur

Policy equilibrium

Policy shock

Political agenda

Pro-life

Pro-choice

Sodomy

Vice laws

Suggested Readings

Cocca, Carolyn E. 2004. *Jailbait: The politics of statutory rape laws in the United States.* Albany: State University of New York Press.

Epstein, Lee, and Joseph F. Kobylka. 1992. *The Supreme Court and legal change: Abortion and the death penalty.* Chapel Hill: University of North Carolina Press.

Fiorina, Morris P. 2005. Culture war? *The myth of a polarized America.* New York: Pearson Longman.

Hunter, James Davison. 1991. *Culture wars.* New York: Basic Books.

Meier, Kenneth J. 1994. *The politics of sin: Drugs, alcohol, and public policy.* Armonk, NY: M. E. Sharpe.

Mooney, Christopher Z., ed. 2001. *The public clash of private values: The politics of morality policy.* New York: Chatham House.

Morone, James A. 2003. Hellfire nation: *The politics of sin in American history.* New Haven, CT: Yale University Press.

Pierce, Patrick A., and Donald E. Miller. 2004. *Gambling politics: State government and the business of betting.* Boulder, CO: Lynne Rienner.

Pinello, Daniel R. 2006. *America's struggle for same-sex marriage.* New York: Cambridge University Press.

Sharp, Elaine B., ed. 1999. *Culture wars and local politics.* Lawrence: University Press of Kansas.

Smith, T. Alexander, and Raymond Tatalovich. 2003. *Cultures at war: Moral conflicts in western democracies.* Peterborough, ON: Broadview Press.

Tatalovich, Raymond, and Byron W. Daynes, eds. 2004. *Moral controversies in American politics.* Armonk, NY: M. E. Sharpe.

Websites

Abortion Regulation

Alan Guttmacher Institute (http://www.agi-usa.org): The Guttmacher Institute is a research and advocacy organization working in the field of sexual health and for the availability of abortion services for women.

American Family Association (http://www.afa.net): The AFA is a conservative, fundamentalist Christian group dedicated to advocating public policy that reflects their interpretation of the Bible, including a complete ban on abortion.

Same-Sex Marriage

Focus on the Family (http://www.family.org): FOF is a leading conservative Christian group working on various morality policy issues, including advocating the legal definition of marriage as a relationship between one man and one woman.

National Gay and Lesbian Task Force (http://thetaskforce.org): The NGLTF is a research and advocacy group promoting gay rights, including same-sex marriage.

14

Social Welfare
and Health Care Policy

Running against Welfare

OUTLINE

Introductory Vignette

Introduction

America's Poor

Domestic Policy Making in a Federal System

Social Welfare Policy

Health Care Policy

Summary

When running for president in 1980, Ronald Reagan enjoyed telling a story about a glitzy "welfare queen" who would cruise the streets of Chicago in her Cadillac. The woman, the affable Republican recounted, had some 80 aliases, 30 addresses, and a dozen Social Security cards. By gaming the system, Reagan claimed she was able to defraud Illinois and the federal government of some $150,000 in bogus claims. After some digging by the press, it was revealed that Reagan's story was really a figment of his imagination. No such woman existed. (Reporters did manage to find a Chicago woman who had four aliases and who had bilked Social Security out of $8,000 one year.) But the former governor of California wasn't hurt by his half-truths; rather, by demonizing welfare recipients, he tapped into a growing public sentiment against social welfare programs. In the 1980s, an increasing number of people were viewing the U.S. welfare state as morally bankrupt. As journalist William Greider writes, Reagan's "famous metaphor—the 'welfare queen' who rode around in her Cadillac collecting Food Stamps—was perfectly pitched to the smoldering social resentments but also a clever fit with his broader economic objectives. Stop wasting our money on those lazy, shiftless (and, always unspoken, black) people. Get government off our backs, encourage the strong, forget the weak."[1]

Reagan's metaphor also signaled a general return to the acceptance of states' rights. His administration stressed the need to defer judgments on matters of domestic policy to state and local governments. Although it took more than 15 years from the time he was first elected president, much of Reagan's vision of reducing the role of the federal government was realized in 1996 when President Bill Clinton, a Democrat, signed into law a bill "ending welfare as we know it." No longer would governors have to "go to Washington and kiss somebody's ring to do what everybody wants us to do and that is to change welfare in our society and give people jobs and hope and optimism," as Wisconsin governor Tommy Thompson said in 1995 after abolishing his state's welfare department. The states would have broad discretion to determine how to run their welfare programs but at a cost. In exchange for giving the states more autonomy, the states would also have to pick up a greater share of paying for their programs.[2]

Introduction

Who controls social welfare and health care public policy in the United States, and who pays for it? Why is there such diversity across the states when it comes to these programs? Why are some states more innovative when it comes to reforming their health care and welfare systems? Underlying these questions is a deeper question: why should states and communities provide any welfare or health care benefits to their citizens?

Although many of you are likely too young to remember President Reagan, the social welfare revolution he set into motion endures today, especially at the subnational level. At times coerced by the federal government and at other times proactive, states and local governments have proven themselves to be adept policy entrepreneurs. They have advanced and adopted competing policy solutions to an array of social welfare and health care problems, duplicating and discarding policies along the way. Due to their own tight budgets, and compiled by cuts in domestic spending by the federal government, state and local governments have often had to come up with creative solutions when dealing with health care and social welfare issues.

We begin our inquiry with some background on America's poor. We then ask who—the states or the federal government—should provide and pay for social welfare and health care policies. After providing an overview of the diffusion of public policies across the states, we conclude by discussing an array of social welfare and health care policies, some of which are financed and administered by, or jointly with, the federal government. As with morality politics, a variety of factors can cause states and localities to adopt new social welfare and health care policies, thereby disrupting the policy equilibrium. After the initial shock, politics and policy tend to return to equilibrium. Due to the number of public policies discussed, however, we do not provide detailed case studies of the policy equilibrium dynamic in play as we did with abortion and same-sex marriage in Chapter 13.

America's Poor

The poverty rate in the United States has been relatively stable since the early 1970s. In 2006, the U.S. Census Bureau reported that 36.5 million Americans lived below the poverty line, or nearly 13 percent of the country's total population. Yet, if you put 100 economists and sociologists in a room and asked each one to define *poverty*, you would likely hear 100 different answers. Defining who is poor and what constitutes poverty is not a science. Rather, it is very impressionistic and contingent on changing economic conditions and social norms. As such, our official government measure of poverty has changed over time, depending on what standards and measurements are used in the calculation. According to the U.S. Census Bureau, the 2007 federal poverty guideline for a family of four is a household income of $20,650 or less.[3]

Who Are America's Poor?

As Table 14.1 shows in some detail, children, women, and minorities are disproportionately likely to be poor in this country. More than 3 million Americans aged 65 and older live in poverty, or nearly one of every 10 seniors. The proportion of elderly who are impoverished, though, has been dropping over the past 30 years. In contrast, the percentage of children living in poverty has increased since 2000. Over 13 million children under the age of 18, nearly one in five, live in poverty. Although millions of white, non-Hispanic children live in poverty, as a percentage, the rate is lower than it is for other racial and ethnic groups. One out of every four African-American and Native American children lives in impoverished households; one out of every five Hispanic children resides in poverty.

Women, more so than men, bear the brunt of poverty in the United States. Of the 25.5 million

Table 14.1

Who Are America's Poor?

Subject	Population	Number Below Poverty Level	% Below Poverty Level
Total Population	**284,577,956**	**37,161,510**	**13.1**
Age			
Under 18 years	71,810,759	13,245,202	18.4
18 to 64 years	178,561,896	20,703,460	11.6
65 years and over	34,205,301	3,212,848	9.4
Sex			
Male	139,214,726	16,084,141	11.6
Female	145,363,230	21,077,369	14.5
Household			
Female-headed household (with related children under 18 years), no husband present	25,519,356	9,595,278	37.6
Race and Hispanic or Latino Origin			
White	215,298,360	22,125,391	10.3
Black or African American	34,576,665	8,864,708	25.6
American Indian and Alaska Native	2,137,754	526,023	24.6
Asian	12,076,732	1,419,799	11.8
Native Hawaiian and Other Pacific Islander	401,425	72,513	18.1
Some other race	14,733,087	3,233,964	22.0
Hispanic or Latino origin (of any race)	40,219,766	8,846,742	22.0
White alone, not Hispanic or Latino	191,754,948	16,949,390	8.8
Educational Attainment (25 years and over)			
Less than high school graduate	29,976,049	6,821,205	22.8
High school graduate (includes equivalency)	55,055,121	5,852,559	10.6
Some college, associate's degree	51,091,603	3,791,685	7.4
Bachelor's degree or higher	50,411,404	1,856,925	3.7
Employment Status (16 years and over)			
Employed male	72,033,317	3,696,377	5.1
Employed female	62,226,143	4,291,326	6.9
Unemployed	10,460,849	2,898,489	27.7
Work Experience (16 years and over)			
Worked full time year-round in the past 12 months	90,870,551	2,124,809	2.3
Worked part time or part-year in the past 12 months	63,815,792	9,299,971	14.6
Did not work	66,107,970	13,785,223	20.9

Source: U.S. Census Bureau, "Poverty," 2006, http://www.census.gov/hhes/www/poverty/poverty.html.

female heads of households in 2004, nearly 38 percent fell below the poverty line. Roughly 5 million more women than men live in poverty. Scholars have advanced several explanations for the **feminization of poverty,** a phrase coined in the late 1970s. Some argue that the fragmented welfare state and paltry benefits have contributed to the rise in poverty of female-headed households. Others contend that it is changing family structures—including higher divorce rates and more children being born out of wedlock—that have led to more women being impoverished. Still others point to the significant wage gap and earning power between men and women.[4]

Where Are America's Poor?

Considerable variation exists across the states, and even within states, in terms of the level of poverty, as Figure 14.1 reveals. Connecticut and New Hampshire, each with a rate of 7.6 percent in 2004, have the lowest poverty levels of any state. Six other states (Minnesota,

---

Figure 14.1

Where Are America's Poor? Poverty Levels, by County

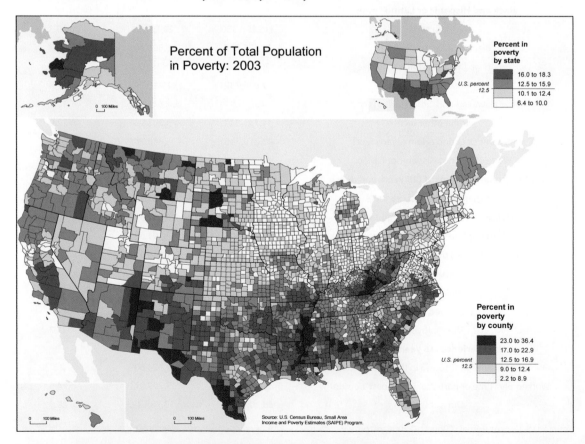

Source: U.S. Census Bureau, "Small Area Income and Poverty Estimates Program," 2006, http://www.census.gov/hhes/www/saipe/maps/iy2003/Tot_Pct_Poor2003.pdf.

Vermont, Massachusetts, New Jersey, Maryland, and Virginia) have poverty levels lower than 9.5 percent. Even in these relatively well-off states, though, pockets of acute poverty persist. At the other end of the spectrum, New Mexico, Arkansas, Louisiana, Mississippi, Kentucky, and West Virginia all have poverty levels exceeding 17.4 percent. As it has in the past, Mississippi leads the way, with some 2.8 million residents—21.6 percent of its population—living below the poverty line. In Mississippi, New Mexico, and Louisiana, more than one quarter of all children live in impoverished homes.

Despite these figures, America's poor often remain hidden, out of plain sight of most Americans. Hurricane Katrina, which ravished the Gulf Coast in late August 2005, abruptly changed the situation. One of the most lasting images left in the wake of the Category 5 storm was the mass of impoverished people desperately trying to flee their city on foot. Kanye West, a Grammy-winning rapper appearing live in *A Concert for Hurricane Relief,* criticized the federal government for not responding fast enough. Riffing on how the federal government is designed "to help the poor, the black people, the less well-off as slow as possible," West directly criticized President George W. Bush, saying he "doesn't care about black people."[5] Former First Lady Barbara Bush did herself little good when she unwittingly spoke callously of the Katrina refugees who had taken temporary shelter in the Houston Astrodome. "What I'm hearing, which is sort of scary, is they all want to stay in Texas," Mrs. Bush quipped. "Everyone is so overwhelmed by the hospitality," she continued, "and so many of the people in the arena here, you know, were underprivileged anyway, so this—this is working very well for them."[6]

Whatever one thinks of Katrina's victims—or the caustic comments of Kanye West or Barbara Bush—the hurricane exposed New Orleans' impoverished underbelly in graphic color. Televised images brought the plight of poor Americans, many of them

minorities, into homes across the country. The destruction wrought by Katrina also stirred a national debate on the root causes of poverty in America.

Social commentators have long tapped into the tradition in America of blaming the victim. In his controversial 1971 book, *The Unheavenly City,* Edward Banfield, a political scientist and advisor to President Richard Nixon, once argued that America's urban poor were inculcated with a "lower-class culture." According to Banfield, youths who grow up in a lower-class culture are driven by a self-gratifying, "live-in-the-moment" ethos, which destines many of them to remain poor.[7] Banfield's psychological analysis of the causes of urban poverty has been roundly criticized by social scientists who stress instead that the sometimes violent and even self-destructive behavior of some urban poor is in part an adaptive response to living in a stressful environment. For many scholars, those belonging to America's **underclass,** a term popularized by sociologist William Julius Wilson, are seen largely as a product of their environment. Joblessness, social isolation, and impoverished neighborhoods are all symptoms of the urban underclass, which Wilson claims is caused by low levels of education, few economic opportunities, and lack of community safeguards and resources.[8] It is perhaps worth noting that America's underclass is not isolated only in cities; many rural areas are also plagued by high rates of unemployment and low levels of education and social capital.[9]

Domestic Policy Making in a Federal System

With the exception of "providing for the safety and welfare of citizens," you will have a hard time finding anything else concerning people's health or welfare in the U.S. Constitution. In theory, the crafting, implementation, and costs of our health care and social welfare policies are to be devolved to the states and their

Thousands of Hurricane Katrina Survivors Sit Outside the Superdome in New Orleans, 4 September 2005.

communities. It should not come as a surprise, then, that health care and welfare policies can be considerably different across the states. Indeed, we might expect such differentiation. Federalist systems of government inherently encourage policy experimentation among semi-autonomous, subnational governments. The American states, U.S. Supreme Court justice Louis Brandeis noted in 1932, should serve as "laboratories of democracy," as they can try "novel social and economic experiments without risk to the rest of the country."[10]

This experimentation often leads to competition among states and localities in the provision of public policy. Competition is often understood as a healthy process, as it can possibly lead to states and localities providing better services to their citizens at a lower cost.[11] Allowing states and localities to experiment with and compete in the provision

of public policies, according to public administration gurus David Osborne and Ted Gaebler, can also help foster and develop a set of "best practices" for other jurisdictions to emulate.[12] But competition may also lead to what some call a "race to the bottom." States and localities might cut social welfare and health care services in an effort to tighten their budgets and deter individuals seeking social services from migrating to a locale where benefits are higher.[13] Still others argue that the debate is moot, as the differences in benefits among the states are relatively insignificant.[14]

Sharing Responsibility for Policy Making

Most social welfare programs are administered in partnership by the federal government and the states through a system of grants. As discussed in Chapter 10, federal grant programs are available—most notably, categorical and block grants. Since the 1930s, Congress has used federal grants to influence and even control state and local social welfare programs. Martha Derthick, an astute observer of domestic policy making and federalism, argues that the federal grant system allows the national government to force state governments to enact policies they may not have otherwise, and in doing so, the state creates a constituency within the state that supports these federal programs.[15] At the same time, the federal government rarely implements social welfare programs itself. State and local governments, and increasingly nonprofit organizations and other agencies, serve as implementing organizations. This allows for some autonomy from the federal government when it comes to shaping programs at the "street-level."[16]

Compared with other advanced industrial countries, policy making in the United States is quite fragmented. Prior to the 1930s, states and communities were almost entirely responsible for providing their own health care and social welfare programs, with the federal government playing a limited role in all three domestic policy areas. During the New Deal, however, the federal government began to provide a safety net for people in need. During the height of the Great Depression, under the administration of Franklin D. Roosevelt, the country's growing indigent population overwhelmed many state governments. In 1933, the year Roosevelt took office, the national unemployment rate was nearly 25 percent; many states had considerably higher numbers of jobless people. Under the leadership of Roosevelt, the Democratic-controlled Congress passed the **Social Security Act of 1935,** which created several programs, including Social Security and what would become known as Aid to Families with Dependent Children (AFDC), or welfare. It would become the cornerstone of the federal government's effort to alleviate poverty among a growing underclass.

Since the 1930s, Congress has continued to exert its authority in domestic policy arenas traditionally left up to the states. During the Great Society programs of the 1960s, Congress greatly expanded America's welfare state, creating federal programs dealing with access to health care (Medicaid and Medicare), public housing, hunger and poverty relief, and local community action programs. More recently, a Republican-led Congress preempted state programs in 2003 by creating a prescription drug benefit program under Medicare (but required the states to pay for the benefit).[17] Thus, to characterize the making of health care and social welfare policy as a robust competition among the states and localities, with best practices rising to the top, would be a mistake. Despite its limited constitutional authority, the federal government plays a major role in the provision of an array of public policies. It often shares with the states the administration and costs of social welfare and health care programs. From income maintenance, to legal aid, to funds for family planning, to subsidized day care, to vouchers for food, to public housing, a host of federal agencies are heavily involved in policy making.

Paying for Programs

Despite the inherent bias of federalism favoring decentralized decision making, Congress frequently has flexed its muscle, often meddling in what have traditionally been state and local affairs. Although the federal government does not always foot the bill for its involvement in subnational policy matters, in fiscal year 2006, Congress authorized transfer payments totaling more than $300 billion to help defray the costs of health, welfare, and education policies in the states.[18]

This sizeable sum flowing from the federal government is roughly equivalent to the tab picked up by state and local governments each year. According to one recent study, state and local governments also spend more than $300 billion a year on health care and welfare policies, to say nothing about the billions they spend for primary, secondary, and higher education (which we discuss in the following chapter).[19] Much of this spending by states and localities is mandated by the federal government. States, for instance, are required to provide cash assistance to needy individuals and make direct payments to health care vendors for medical assistance for the poor in accordance with federal guidelines. But state and local governments also spend billions on social welfare programs of their own design, such as providing for emergency medical and housing relief following natural disasters, refugee assistance, and constructing and maintaining nursing homes, orphanages, and hospitals.

Compounding the costs of state and local governments, Congress has recently cut back on the amount it sends to the states to pay for these programs.[20] In 2006, Congress reduced spending on social services over the following five years by some $40 billion; and it reduced aid for child support administrative and enforcement programs in the states and payments for Medicaid, a joint federal-state health care insurance program for individuals falling below the poverty level.[21]

Diffusion of Policies

Why do some states and localities adopt a set of policies, whereas others do not? The concept of **policy diffusion** has a rich tradition in political science. Diffusion of public policies occurs across time and space when one state or community adopts or emulates another jurisdiction's policies.[22] Nearly 40 years ago, Jack Walker observed that "some states act as pioneers by adopting new programs more readily than others," and that once a few programs have been adopted, "new forms of service or regulation spread among the American states."[23] He characterized the diffusion of public policies in the states as an "S-curve," with adoption of new polices starting slowly with a few entrepreneurial pioneers, then rapidly taking off across the nation, and then slowing down once again as a few remaining states refuse to follow suit. Another political

scientist, Virginia Gray, found that diffusion is often determined by such factors as the level of federal intervention in the policy area, the level of interparty competition, the economic prosperity of a community, and other time-specific factors.[24] Still others have found diffusion rates to be faster when federal incentives encourage the states to adopt the programs.[25]

To many observers, it often appears as though policy diffusion is influenced by geographic proximity. This perception is indeed often the case. Perhaps it is because "policymakers and citizens share the human cognitive bias of accept[ing] the familiar and being reassured by those things closest to them."[26] In their search to find solutions to their problems, policy makers often look first to their neighbors. Furthermore, because they are often found in competition with one another, states and localities in close proximity with one another have an economic incentive to emulate their next-door neighbors in an effort to not allow their citizens to exit. This logic can lead to programs that both enhance as well as harm the social welfare of a given state or community. For instance, a state may emulate its neighbor and adopt a lottery system of its own to bring in additional education dollars, doing so primarily to discourage its own residents from crossing over the border and playing a neighboring state's lottery. Conversely, a state may depress its level of assistance to welfare recipients so as to discourage poor people in a neighboring state from moving.

Adoption of Policies

Of course, although they are influenced by what kinds of policies are going on outside their borders, we should not expect states to blindly adopt their neighbors' policies without elected officials and policy makers in a state first assessing the economic and political conditions of their home state.[27] As we saw with morality policies, diffusion not only occurs due to a state's or community's proximity to its neighbors. With technological advances as well as policy clearinghouses, such as the National Conference of State Legislatures, American Legislative Exchange Council, Center for Budget Priorities, and Urban Institute, state and local policy makers are exposed to an array of public policy options that have been adopted across the country. One recent study examining the diffusion of state-sponsored health insurance programs for children from 1998 to 2001 found that the diffusion of policy innovations was not limited to a geographic proximity; rather, states adopted the successful programs of other states because of their political, demographic, and budgetary similarities.[28] Another has found that the diffusion of policies—such as bans on smoking in public facilities—is able to percolate upward from local governments to state governments.[29]

Social welfare and health care policies also tend to map fairly closely with public opinion along a liberal–conservative spectrum in the states.[30] In other words, state and local policy makers tend to be fairly good at responding to what their citizens so desire. But many other factors besides public attitudes lead to different social welfare and healthcare policies being adopted. A state's relative level of importance in the federalist system shapes how much federal aid the state will receive. Shifts in the amount of federal aid and federal intervention into policy domains often lie outside of the control of state and local governments. The dynamism, size, and diversity of a state's economy can affect the type of policies a state and its localities will adopt,[31] as too can the relative strength of political parties and the density and diversity of interest groups.[32]

Finally, there may be a class or racial bias in the provision of social welfare and healthcare services across the states. A state electorate with a disproportionate proportion of higher-class citizens tends to be rewarded with public policies that favor its economic interests, which come at the expense of lower-class citizens. Where the degree of economic and racial inequality is higher, social welfare spending in the states tends to be lower.[33] Scholars have also shown that the generosity of a state's welfare policies is inversely related to the

level of conservatism in the state as well as the caseload composition of racial minorities.

All these factors have been shown to help set the agenda in states and communities. As with morality policies, the stability of the policy equilibrium of health care and social welfare programs can abruptly change. More often than not, though, they tend to emerge sporadically, in a disjointed, incremental fashion.[34] Social changes and focusing events give policy entrepreneurs and other political actors the opportunity to alter the status quo. Disturbances such as the shift to a service sector, low-wage economy or rising health care costs can alter the political agenda of state and local governments. Yet, changing entrenched social welfare and health care programs often proves to be more difficult than preserving them.

Social Welfare Policy

What is welfare? When discussing social welfare programs, we often lump together two distinct types of programs: those providing social insurance and those providing public assistance. In the strict sense, **social insurance** is not welfare, as the programs are not means-tested. Rather, they are created by government to socialize risk. Social insurance programs provide economic assistance in the form of cash payments to the elderly, the disabled, and the unemployed—regardless of financial need—as long as the individual has financially contributed to the system. Social insurance programs are financed by compulsory contributions made by the beneficiaries and their employers. Although states do offer some social insurance programs, the federal government pays for and administers most of the programs in the United States.[35]

In contrast, **public assistance** programs provide aid—both cash and in-kind services—to the poor. The services and financial aid that government provides are **means-tested,** available only to individuals falling below the government's predetermined level of income or assets, and they are taxpayer financed.

Assistance, sometimes provided in the form of cash and other times as services, is provided to those who are in need, which governments determine using a calculation of a person's income and assets. Public assistance programs are administered by either federal or state governments or, in some cases, jointly by both.

As you might suspect, the term **welfare** has many connotations. In the context of state and local government, it refers to a range of public assistance services provided by government to aid and protect the most vulnerable individuals in society. Social welfare policies in the United States are also often ad hoc (that is, piecemeal and without an overarching plan). The provision of social welfare in this country is provided through a patchwork of government programs at the national, state, and local levels, combined with services and aid provided by charities operating in the private sector. As we shall see, vulnerable populations are often eligible for public assistance as well as social insurance programs. Aged and disabled persons, children and their parents, and the unemployed are eligible for a variety of social welfare programs. It is fair to say, though, that public assistance programs—compared with those of other advanced industrial countries—are neither universal nor highly coordinated between the layers of government.[36]

Social Security

Social Security—formally known as the Old Age, Survivors and Disability Insurance program (OASDI)—is a social insurance program run by the federal government. Created during the Great Depression in the 1930s, Social Security provides a safety net to workers who do not have their own. Today, more than half the private sector workforce does not accrue a private pension. One out of three workers has no dedicated retirement savings. Nearly three-quarters of the private sector workforce is without long-term disability insurance.

Social Security is an **entitlement** program. The New Deal program is self-financed, with workers contributing 6.2 percent of their gross payroll (but capped in 2006 at $94,000) into the fund, which is then matched by their employers. Approximately 161 million workers in 2006, roughly 96 percent of the workforce, had Federal Insurance Contribution Act (FICA) withholdings deducted automatically from their paychecks—a mandated contribution into the Social Security trust fund. The Social Security Administration in 2006 provided upward of $539 billion to more than 48 million Americans eligible to collect their benefits. Most payments go to retirees. Nine out of every 10 individuals ages 65 and over receive Social Security checks. These monthly payments, on average, account for nearly 40 percent of a recipient's income. For roughly one-fifth of the elderly, a Social Security check is their only source of income. Of the 48 million beneficiaries, approximately 30 million are retired workers who receive an average of $1,002 in monthly benefits. Another 3 million recipients of Social Security are dependents of workers vested in the system. Payments to these beneficiaries amounted to roughly $1.5 billion in 2005.[37]

In addition to Social Security, the federal government funds a program jointly with the states that provides payments to some disabled workers. Social Security Disability Insurance (SSDI), which is funded by a payroll tax on all documented employees, provides benefits to individuals (and certain family members) vested in the program. State governments determine whether or not a claimant is disabled under the rules in the first stage of the disability determination process.[38] The purpose of the program is to provide income to people unable to work because of a disability. In 2006, every month, some 8.3 million beneficiaries, including disabled workers, their spouses, and their dependent children, received SSDI payments.[39]

Unemployment Compensation and Workers' Compensation

Millions of Americans also benefit from two other social insurance programs. The Social

Security Act of 1935 also established the Unemployment Insurance Program, which temporarily helps workers who have involuntarily lost their jobs. The federally funded program, which was modeled after Wisconsin's unemployment compensation legislation enacted three years earlier, is overseen by the Department of Labor but is administered and regulated by the states.[40] Qualifying employers are required to pay a federal tax based on the amount of wages they pay their workforce. The tax is deposited into a federal unemployment trust fund, with each state having its own account. Because states largely determine employer contribution requirements, eligibility, and benefit levels, the benefit packages available to unemployed workers vary considerably across the states. Today, the maximum allotted time a qualified beneficiary may receive unemployment payments is 26 weeks. In order to receive benefits, recipients must be seeking work; part-time earnings are deducted from unemployment benefits.[41]

Each state also administers its own Workers' Compensation program, which requires certain employers to pay into a fund that compensates employees who are injured or disabled on the job. Eligible beneficiaries are provided with monetary awards or health care coverage. If a worker is killed on the job, the fund compensates dependents of the deceased if he or she worked for a participating employer. The program also protects the liability of employers and employees, as it limits the amount a worker may be able to recover in a lawsuit over a work-related accident.[42] Many states have created labor-management councils or commissions made up of business, labor, and state officials who work to reform and provide oversight of their workers' compensation and unemployment insurance programs.[43]

Public Assistance: From AFDC to TANF

A major change to social welfare policy in the American states occurred in 1996, when Congress passed the Personal Responsibility and Work Opportunity Reconciliation Act of 1996 (PRWORA), which created the Temporary Assistance for Needy Families (TANF) program. Although the primary goal of TANF is to move recipients off welfare and into the workforce, Congress included other goals, including caring for needy children; promoting preparation for jobs, work, and marriage; preventing and reducing out-of-wedlock pregnancies; and encouraging the formation and preservation of two-parent families.[44]

TANF is partially funded by the states and by the federal government through a series of block grants made to the states. It replaced a long-standing program also known for its acronym, AFDC, or Aid to Families with Dependent Children. Created in 1935 to provide financial assistance to widows, single mothers, and their children, AFDC was part of the Social Security Act. Originally, the joint federal-state categorical grant program was conceived as an income support program to provide cash payments to needy mothers with children. Over the years, though, its aim shifted to rehabilitating women, moving them from being dependent on welfare to having more self-sufficient lives sustained by work.[45] Having to abide by federal guidelines, the states were required to provide financial assistance to eligible individuals but were able to craft their own definition of need, establish their own benefit levels, administer their own programs, and set their own income thresholds for eligibility. The states were then reimbursed, on a matching basis, for the benefits they paid to recipients.

TANF has shifted the responsibility of providing welfare assistance to the poor from the federal government to the states. Not surprisingly, the increased flexibility among the states in regulating the eligibility requirements and administering TANF has led to a variety of welfare assistance programs across the states. Instead of doling out direct cash assistance, as provided under AFDC, TANF allows the states to substitute noncash services, such as work preparation programs, vocational training, child care assistance, transportation credits, pregnancy counseling, and job training.

REFORM CAN HAPPEN

WISCONSIN'S WELFARE EXPERIMENT

During the 1990s, many states requested waivers from the Department of Health and Human Services (DHHS) to experiment further with the provision of AFDC benefits. In Wisconsin, Tommy Thompson, the Republican governor of Wisconsin, led the charge to reform welfare. In the late 1980s, Thompson pushed through the state legislature a series of major changes to Wisconsin's AFDC program, placing increased responsibilities on welfare recipients. Hearing rumors that poor people were driving up Interstate 90 to Milwaukee to take advantage of Wisconsin's program, leaving Chicago in their rear-view mirrors, Thompson's administration cracked down on Wisconsin's relatively generous welfare benefits.

Wisconsin's Learnfare program, which received a waiver from the DHHS in 1987, cut welfare payments made to parents of school-age children if their kids were found to be regularly truant. Thompson even went so far as to try to provide financial incentives for unmarried welfare moms to become married, a policy recommendation that was widely criticized by the Catholic Church, among others in the social welfare community. Despite the criticism, several other states considered similar proposals. In 1995, Wisconsin implemented Thompson's "Work Not Welfare" program, requiring welfare recipients to work in order to receive the remainder of their benefits. The program also placed time limits on how long recipients could receive benefits, previewing the changes adopted by Congress in 1996. In part as recognition for his innovative approach to welfare reform, in 2001, Thompson was appointed secretary of the DHHS by President Bush.[1]

Notes

1. Lawrence M. Mead, "The Politics of Welfare Reform in Wisconsin," *Polity* 32 (2000): 533–59.

For example, Wisconsin in 1997 adopted "Wisconsin Works" (known as W-2), which Governor Thompson characterized as an "employment" program. W-2 requires all eligible recipients to work or further their education. In 1997, Maine created its "Parents as Scholars" project, which provides tuition assistance to low-income parents to help them return to college. TANF also provides states with some flexibility in how they administer aid and services to recipients with special needs, including individuals with mental illness and physical disabilities as well as those with drug and alcohol dependencies. To help pay for these programs, in 1998, Congress authorized the Welfare-to-Work grants program, whereby the U.S. Department of Labor provides supplemental aid to state and local agencies to coordinate their TANF activities with employment-related services.

Cutting the Welfare Rolls under TANF

When examining the raw number of individuals receiving aid under AFDC versus TANF, it appears that the program has been a success. In 1996, an average of 12.6 million women and children were receiving AFDC payments every month. By 2003, only 5.5 million women and children were receiving TANF benefits, a 56 percent drop over the seven-year period. As a percentage of all individuals in a state receiving aid, the decrease was equally impressive, dropping from 4.6 percent in 1996 to only 1.9 percent in 2003, a 60 percent drop. Nationally, less than 2 percent of the population receives welfare assistance under TANF. It bears mentioning, of course, that although many have applauded the reduction in the number of recipients receiving welfare benefits, the income levels of many of these former recipients have not improved much.

The drop in welfare cases can be attributed to four factors. First, the federal government required the states to clamp down on serial welfare recipients—those who never left AFDC or those who were repeatedly on and off AFDC—by forcing most recipients off welfare after two years. Second, the states were required to place most TANF recipients into work programs, pushing recipients to take jobs in the private sector, whatever the hourly wage. Third, in the late 1990s, when the new TANF regulations were first being implemented, states were assisted in moving individuals off their welfare rolls by the booming economy. Finally, TANF's strict eligibility guidelines helped to lower the participation rates: in 2000, only 50 percent of eligible families participated in TANF, compared to an 85 percent participation rate under AFDC in 1994.[46]

Since TANF was adopted, there has been considerable variation across the states in the number of individuals who have been removed from the welfare rolls, as Table 14.2 shows. Five states—Wyoming, Idaho, Illinois, Florida, and Louisiana—have led the way in moving AFDC recipients off welfare under TANF. All five states were led by Republican governors during the late 1990s, when the TANF reforms were being implemented. In 1996, Wyoming was tied for the fewest number (13,000) of monthly AFDC recipients; by 2003, Wyoming had slashed its welfare rolls to just 1,000 recipients, a remarkable decrease of 94 percent. Only one-tenth of 1 percent of Wyoming's population received welfare in 2003. Some large states, like Illinois and Florida, also downsized their welfare ranks under TANF. Illinois reduced its welfare recipients from an average of 655,000 a month in 1996 to just 99,000 in 2006, an 86 percent drop in the caseload. Florida reduced its caseload by some 433,000 recipients a month over the same seven years, a drop of 77 percent. In 2003, less than 1 percent of residents of Illinois and Florida received benefits under TANF.

Other states have had more difficulty moving their recipients off their welfare rolls. North Dakota, which was tied with Wyoming for the fewest welfare recipients in 1996,

Table 14.2

Average Monthly TANF Recipients and Percentage of Population Receiving Benefits in 2003, by State

State	Number of Recipients (in thousands)	% of Population
District of Columbia	43	7.7
Rhode Island	41	3.8
California	1,303	3.7
Hawaii	41	3.3
Tennessee	186	3.2
New York	501	2.6
Indiana	155	2.5
Maine	32	2.5
New Mexico	44	2.4
Washington	149	2.4
Alaska	15	2.3
Minnesota	117	2.3
Vermont	14	2.2
West Virginia	41	2.2
Missouri	121	2.1
Arizona	113	2
Michigan	201	2
Kentucky	77	1.9
Montana	17	1.9
Iowa	54	1.8
Nebraska	31	1.8
Massachusetts	109	1.7
Pennsylvania	210	1.7
Connecticut	56	1.6
Delaware	13	1.6
Georgia	136	1.6
Mississippi	46	1.6
Ohio	188	1.6
Texas	363	1.6
Kansas	40	1.5
North Dakota	9	1.4
Louisiana	58	1.3
Maryland	71	1.3
Nevada	28	1.3
New Jersey	110	1.3

State	Number of Recipients (in thousands)	% of Population
New Hampshire	15	1.2
Oregon	43	1.2
South Carolina	51	1.2
Alabama	46	1
North Carolina	84	1
Oklahoma	37	1
Virginia	75	1
Arkansas	25	0.9
Utah	22	0.9
Wisconsin	50	0.9
Colorado	35	0.8
Florida	128	0.8
Illinois	99	0.8
South Dakota	6	0.8
Idaho	3	0.2
Wyoming	1	0.1
United States	5,517	1.9

Source: U.S. Department of Health and Human Services, Administration for Children and Families, Office of Family Assistance, *2003 TANF Report to Congress,* http://www.acf.hhs.gov/programs/ofa/annual-report5/index.htm.

only reduced the number of monthly welfare recipients by 4,000 between 1996 and 2003, a marginal drop of 35 percent. Arizona, Minnesota, Rhode Island, Tennessee, Nevada, and Nebraska also had difficulty lowering the number of TANF beneficiaries on the rolls over the seven-year period. None of the states were able to cut more than 35 percent of their recipients off the rolls. Indiana, which had some 148,000 AFDC recipients in 1996, actually had an increase of 7,000 welfare recipients over the time frame, a 5 percent jump. In 2003, some 41,000 people in Rhode Island—3.8 percent of the state's population—received TANF benefits. California, with the largest number of TANF beneficiaries in the country with more than 1.3 million individuals in 2003, reduced its caseload by half over seven years, lowering

the percentage of its population receiving benefits to less than 4 percent.[47]

Cutting Benefits under TANF Perhaps more significantly, especially for those individuals and their families who are either receiving or eligible for welfare benefits, TANF allowed the states to reduce their expenditures on welfare benefits. With permission from the Department of Health and Human Services (DHHS), TANF also allows states to remove recipients from the welfare rolls sooner than the five-year maximum time limit. States may also petition the DHHS to extend welfare assistance beyond 60 months but for no more than 20 percent of their caseload. Just two years after President Clinton signed TANF into law, welfare spending by the states and communities was reduced by some 20 percent. Less than one in five dollars spent by the states on social services is disbursed in the form of cash transfers.[48]

By most standards, cash transfers to welfare beneficiaries are minimal. In 2004, the average monthly cash benefit to a single parent (usually a mother) with two dependent children was $347 a month. Table 14.3 documents the cash benefits in 2003 paid to a family of three (including the single parent). Two-fifths of the states cap their temporary cash benefits, regardless of the size of the family. In Idaho, a TANF family—regardless of its size—received a maximum benefit of $309 a month. In Wisconsin, payments are based on the amount and type of work activity of the adult in the family. Southern states provide much less in temporary welfare assistance under TANF than other states. All seven states that provide less than $200 a month to a mother with two dependent children are located in the South—Tennessee ($142), Mississippi ($146), Arkansas ($162), South Carolina ($163), Louisiana and Texas ($188 each), and Alabama ($190). Annual TANF cash benefits in Tennessee and Mississippi amount to $1,700 a year. In contrast, all eight states that provide temporary cash benefits in excess of $500 a month are located in the North, with the exception of California. Alaska leads the way, providing $821 in

Table 14.3

Maximum Monthly TANF Benefit for a Family of Three in 2004, by State

State	Family of Three	Family Cap
Alaska	$923	No
Vermont	709	No
California	704	Yes
New York	691	No
Wisconsin	673	n/a
Connecticut	636	Yes
New Hampshire	625	No
Massachusetts	618	Yes
Hawaii	570	No
Rhode Island	554	No
Washington	546	No
Minnesota	532	Yes
South Dakota	493	No
Maine	485	No
Maryland	477	No
North Dakota	477	Yes
Utah	474	No
Oregon	460	No
Michigan	459	No
West Virginia	453	No
Kansas	429	No
Iowa	426	No
New Jersey	424	Yes
Pennsylvania	421	No
Illinois	396	No
New Mexico	389	No
Virginia	389	Yes
Washington, D.C.	379	No
Montana	375	No
Ohio	373	No
Nebraska	364	Yes
Colorado	356	No
Nevada	348	No
Arizona	347	Yes
Wyoming	340	Yes
Delaware	338	Yes
Idaho	309	n/a
Florida	303	Yes
Missouri	292	No
Oklahoma	292	Yes
Kentucky	289	No
Indiana	288	Yes
Georgia	280	Yes
North Carolina	272	Yes
Louisiana	240	No
Texas	217	No
Alabama	215	No
South Carolina	205	Yes
Arkansas	204	Yes
Tennessee	185	Yes
Mississippi	170	Yes

Source: U.S. Department of Health and Human Services, Administration for Children and Families, Office of Family Assistance, *2003 TANF Report to Congress,* http://www.acf.hhs.gov/programs/ofa/annual-report5/index.htm.

monthly cash assistance to a family of three. Perennial welfare innovator Wisconsin still provides $673 a month to a family of three.[49]

As it is periodically required to do, Congress reauthorized the funding for TANF in 2006 for another five years. But in doing so, Congress not only cut the amount of funding going to the states but also asserted its federal authority over the social welfare programs by imposing more rigorous work requirements for their welfare recipients. The states are now required to have a 90 percent work participation rate for all two-parent families and a 50 percent work participation rate for all single-parent families receiving aid. In 2004, all but 12 states failed to meet the 50 percent work participation cutoff. According to one close observer, the 2006 reauthorization "basically takes the 'block' out of the block grant concept."[50] The 1996 law had originally given the states considerable discretion to design programs to move poor families off welfare.[51] The federally imposed mandates in 2006 come with even sharper teeth. States failing to implement the work participation standards—which Michael Bird of the National Conference of State Legislatures sees as "virtually guarantee[ing] that every state will incur penalties"—will be forced to forfeit roughly $23 million in federal penalties over a five-year period.[52] In addition, several innovative programs may be in jeopardy following Congress's 2006 reauthorization, as federal aid may not be used for educational programs that do not meet work participation requirements.

According to a study commissioned by the DHHS, cash assistance provided by the states declined in the mid-1990s, with expenditures on public assistance programs growing only slightly between 1997 and 2000 after TANF was enacted. When looking across states, those with weaker fiscal capacity spend less per capita on social welfare than wealthier states. Compounding this relative inequality, federal grants for social welfare programs were higher to states with greater fiscal capacity than to those with lower capacity, although the intergovernmental grants comprised a larger share of poorer states' social welfare budgets. The difference in spending between rich and poor states was most pronounced in the areas of non-health social services, including child welfare, energy assistance, child care, transportation assistance, and programs for the homeless.[53]

Food Stamps

Try living on $3 a day in grocery money. Oregon's Democratic governor, Theodore "Ted" Kulongoski, took a "Food Stamps Challenge" in the spring of 2007 as a way to raise awareness about low-income people going hungry in his state and threats to cut Food Stamps benefits. The U.S. Food Stamps Program is a federal program funded through the U.S. Department of Agriculture and jointly administered by the states. The states pick up roughly half the administrative costs of the program. Created in the 1930s during the Great Depression, in part as an agricultural price support system to keep food costs low, 26 million Americans received Food Stamps in 2005, down from a high of 28 million in 1994. The program, which was revamped in the 1960s and 1970s, augments the food-purchasing power of low-income households. In fiscal year 2003, the program cost the federal government nearly $24 billion to operate. On average, a Food Stamps recipient receives $92.69 a month, or roughly $0.90 a meal in benefits.[54]

The program imposes nationally uniform standards, so unlike TANF, little variation is seen across the states. It serves a diverse population, but all applicants are personally interviewed prior to becoming enrolled. Eligibility for the program is largely determined by income levels, and recipients do not have to have children or be disabled to qualify. Citizens, children who are legal immigrants, disabled legal immigrants, and legal immigrants who have lived in the country for at least five years are all eligible for the program. Applicants must register and search for work, and able-bodied adults under the age of 60 without dependents are only eligible for three months of assistance over a three-year period, unless a city receives a federal waiver because of high unemployment rates. Beneficiaries are issued electronic debit cards, which they may use to purchase food from participating retailers. Illegal immigrants are not eligible for Food Stamps nor are many legal immigrants who have resided in the country for less than five years. In addition, students, institutionalized individuals, and striking workers are not eligible for the program.[55]

Many people who otherwise are eligible for Food Stamps don't participate; many do not even realize they may be eligible for the benefits. As with other welfare programs, some eligible individuals may shy away from the program because of the perceived negative stigma attached to the program.[56] Still others may find it difficult to navigate the bureaucratic maze that some states have created to apply for the program.[57] Some states have made it extremely difficult for people living in their states to participate in the federally funded program. New York, for example, is

Thomas Patterson/Statesman Journal, via Associated Press, http://graphics8.nytimes.com/images/2007/05/01/us/0 stamps.600

Governor Ted Kulongoski of Oregon Shops for a Week's Worth of Food on $21, the Average for Oregonians Receiving Food Stamps.

one of four states that requires participants be fingerprinted. Along with a few other states, New York has been found to have illegally denied Food Stamps applications to eligible recipients. Only 61.5 percent of eligible individuals across the country actually participated in the program in 2003. Five states—Florida, Nevada, Massachusetts, New Jersey, and California—have participation rates lower than 50 percent of the estimated population eligible to receive Food Stamps.

Housing Programs

Like Food Stamps, the federal government provides grants and aid to the states and localities to provide low-income housing. The Community Development Block Grant (CDBG) pro-

gram, created by Congress in 1974, provides localities with funds to stimulate community development and improve housing. In the 1980s, under the Reagan administration, the program was decentralized, allowing states and communities to have broad discretion in determining what projects should be funded and how they should be implemented. Most CDBGs are allocated using a set of formulas and are made annually to eligible metropolitan areas and counties. Designated communities receive 70 percent of CDBG funds, with the states receiving the remaining 30 percent. In the 2006 fiscal year, the Department of Housing and Urban Development (HUD) transferred some $4.7 billion in CDBG funds.[58] Although municipalities and counties use CDBG funds for a wide variety of purposes, they must use them to benefit individuals with low or moderate incomes, prevent or eliminate slums or blighted areas, or meet the urgent needs of community development.

In addition to these entitlement CDBG funds, states also receive federal aid for housing and development projects. States may use the money to improve public facilities and housing that serve mostly low- and moderate-income persons, expand economic opportunities, and help eliminate hazardous conditions that may jeopardize the public health of a community. Like other states, Kentucky receives additional non-entitlement CDBG to aid its small cities and communities. In 2005, the state received supplementary grants from HUD that totaled more than $26 million.[59] Texas received more than $82 million in non-entitlement grants in 2005. Its state Office of Rural Community Affairs administers the grants, which serve more than 1,000 rural communities and 245 rural counties, helping some 375,000 low-income Texans each year.[60]

States and communities also receive federal assistance from the Federal Housing Administration (FHA), as we discussed in Chapter 12. In 2005, after Hurricanes Katrina and Rita ravished the Gulf Coast, the FHA was thrust into the national spotlight. Responding to the needs of the millions of people living in the parts of Louisiana, Mississippi, Alabama, Florida, and Texas declared to be disaster areas by President Bush, the FHA embarked on a program to guarantee mortgage financing with no down payment for any individual who was displaced during the storms. The new program applies equally to individuals who either owned or rented homes that were damaged or destroyed and allows victims of nature's wrath to buy homes anywhere in the country.[61]

Minimum Wage Laws

Critics of cutbacks to public assistance programs and the effort to downsize welfare dependency in the states often highlight the low wages that exist for many jobs in many states. Low wages can strain public assistance programs. Workers earning minimum wage, or even more, are known as **the working poor.** They often rely on public assistance—or the beneficence of charities—to make ends meet.

Individuals who otherwise work hard and play by the rules must often rely on subsidized child care programs and housing, reduced or free school lunches for their children, food stamps and soup kitchens, and public health care to get by month to month. Increasingly, critics are making a moral argument that employers ought to pay a **living wage;** that is, a wage (and benefits package) that allows working members of a community to live decently.

Since 1938, Congress has mandated that certain employers pay their employees a minimum wage. The federal minimum wage in 1938 was $0.25 per hour. In 2007, the Democratic-controlled Congress voted to raise the federal minimum wage to $7.25 per hour by the summer of 2009, bumping it up incrementally from $5.25 per hour. It was the first raise in the federal minimum wage since 1997. In real dollars, the minimum wage in 2007 was the lowest it had been in the previous 50 years.[62] Some economists

COMPARISONS HELP US UNDERSTAND

WORKING AT MINIMUM WAGE

States may set minimum wages that are higher than the national rate. In addition to the District of Columbia, 28 states in the spring of 2007 had minimum wage laws requiring employers to pay their workers more than the federal minimum wage of $5.15 an hour. The State of Washington's minimum wage led the nation at $7.93 per hour. In Washington as well as California, Oregon, Florida, Nevada, and Vermont, the state minimum wage is indexed to the rate of inflation. This guarantees that the minimum wage will continue to increase when the cost of living rises. In every state with the minimum wage indexed to inflation (except Vermont), the legislature did not vote to raise the minimum wage. Rather, activists placed initiatives on the ballot to take the issue directly to the people.

The federal minimum wage does not apply to all jobs. Some agricultural workers, employees under the age of 20 during their first 90 calendar days of employment, some full-time students, apprentices, and some workers with disabilities are not covered.[1] For these job classifications, employees are covered by *state* minimum wage laws. As Figure 14.2 shows, Kansas, Georgia, New Mexico, and Wyoming have an official minimum wage that is lower than the federal level, and five states (Alabama, Louisiana, Mississippi, South Carolina, and Tennessee) have no state minimum wage.

Notes

1. Economic Policy Institute, "Minimum Wage: Frequently Asked Questions," 2006. Available: http://www.epinet.org/content.cfm/issueguides_minwage_minwagefaq.

estimated that over 7 million Americans, or 6 percent of the workforce, would benefit by the increase in the minimum wage. Who are minimum wage workers? Nearly three-quarters are adults, 61 percent are women, and almost half are full-time workers. Nearly a million are single mothers working to stay off welfare.[63]

Not all employees are covered by the minimum wage under the Fair Labor Standards Act, as Figure 14.2 reveals. All companies with revenues of at least $500,000 a year must pay the federal minimum wage. The low-cost retailer Wal-Mart, for example, has been singled out for its aggressive anti-union labor practices and for forcing workers to work hours off the clock.[64] Although the mega-chain store created over 125,000 jobs across the county in 2005, many of the jobs were low paying and lacking health benefits. The annual wage for an average Wal-Mart "associate" that year was only $13,861, which fell well below the poverty line for a family of four.[65]

Undocumented Workers

Welfare reform has also been tied to the debate over immigration reform. Estimates place the number of undocumented immigrants living in the United States in 2007 at more than 11 million. Nearly one-third of all immigrants in the United States are likely in the country illegally.

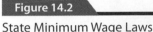

Figure 14.2

State Minimum Wage Laws

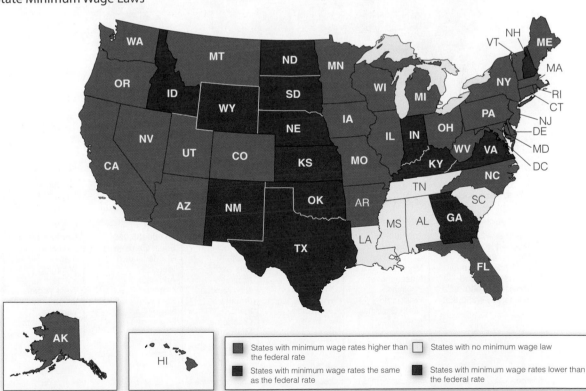

States with minimum wage rates higher than the federal rate

States with minimum wage rates the same as the federal rate

States with no minimum wage law

States with minimum wage rates lower than the federal rate

Source: U.S. Department of Labor, "Minimum Wage Laws in the States," November 2007, http://www.dol.gov/esa/minwage/america.htm.

According to a national household survey conducted in 2005, most illegal immigrants are from Latin America—particularly Mexico—which alone accounts for over half of all immigrants in the country without proper documentation. Many of these undocumented immigrants work in the service sector. Between one-fifth and one-third of all cooks, construction laborers, maids and housekeepers, grounds maintenance, and agricultural workers are estimated to be illegal aliens.[66]

The number and density of undocumented persons living across the states are uneven. As Figure 14.3 shows, some states—Maine, Vermont, New Hampshire, West Virginia, Montana, Wyoming, Alaska, and the Dakotas—had less than 10,000 illegal immigrants in 2004. In contrast, California had an estimated 2.4 million

Figure 14.3

Undocumented Immigrants

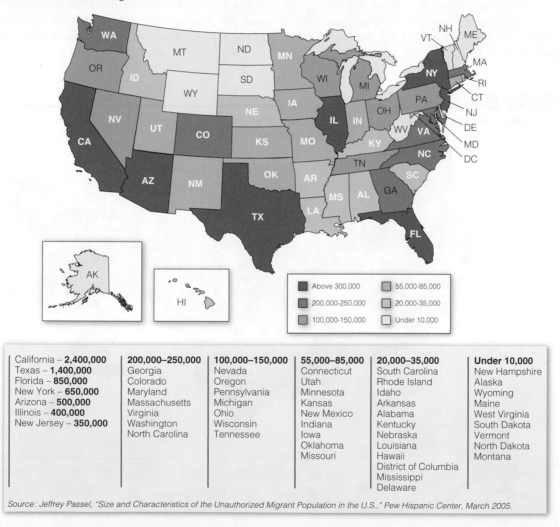

Legend:
- Above 300,000
- 200,000-250,000
- 100,000-150,000
- 55,000-85,000
- 20,000-35,000
- Under 10,000

California – 2,400,000	200,000–250,000	100,000–150,000	55,000–85,000	20,000–35,000	Under 10,000
Texas – 1,400,000	Georgia	Nevada	Connecticut	South Carolina	New Hampshire
Florida – 850,000	Colorado	Oregon	Utah	Rhode Island	Alaska
New York – 650,000	Maryland	Pennsylvania	Minnesota	Idaho	Wyoming
Arizona – 500,000	Massachusetts	Michigan	Kansas	Arkansas	Maine
Illinois – 400,000	Virginia	Ohio	New Mexico	Alabama	West Virginia
New Jersey – 350,000	Washington	Wisconsin	Indiana	Kentucky	South Dakota
	North Carolina	Tennessee	Iowa	Nebraska	Vermont
			Oklahoma	Louisiana	North Dakota
			Missouri	Hawaii	Montana
				District of Columbia	
				Mississippi	
				Delaware	

Source: Jeffrey Passel, "Size and Characteristics of the Unauthorized Migrant Population in the U.S.," Pew Hispanic Center, March 2005.

Source: Jeffrey Passel, "Size and Characteristics of the Unauthorized Migrant Population in the U.S.," Pew Hispanic Center, March 2005, http://pewhispanic.org/reports/report.php?ReportID=61.

illegal immigrants in 2004, and Texas had 1.4 million. Florida, New York, and Arizona all had more than half-a-million undocumented immigrants that year. As a proportion of its state population, Arizona leads the nation, with an estimated 8.7 percent of its residents living in the state illegally. Other states with high proportions of residents who are in the country illegally are California, Texas, Nevada, Florida, and Colorado.

Critics of illegal immigration often claim that undocumented workers take low-paying jobs away from less-educated citizens and keep wages artificially depressed. The evidence for this claim, however, is mixed. Nationally, between 1980 and 2004, millions of illegal aliens migrated to California. In 2004, nearly 7 percent of the state's population was comprised of undocumented immigrants. The wages for high school dropouts in the state fell 17 percent over the period. In Ohio, a state with only 1 percent illegal immigrants, the decline in wages for high school dropouts dropped 31 percent over the same time period. In Nevada, where 7.5 percent of the population is comprised of illegal immigrants, the median hourly wage is over $10 for high school dropouts, a dollar more than in Nebraska, Kentucky, and Ohio, three states with low percentages of undocumented workers.[67]

Not surprisingly, states facing the largest influx of undocumented immigrants have gone the furthest in enacting public policies to crack down on the situation. Despite many in the business community who have praised the work ethic of illegal aliens and their willingness to work in low-paying or socially undesirable jobs, others have blamed them for the rising costs of public assistance and services. In 1994, for example, Californians passed a ballot initiative—Proposition 187—that effectively barred social welfare services to illegal immigrants and their children. Although the measure was subsequently nullified by a federal district court, other states have emulated the California measure, with some going even beyond it. In 2004, the citizens of Arizona passed Proposition 200, a statutory initiative requiring all public agencies to verify the immigration status of individuals seeking benefits by showing proof of citizenship. After the November election, a federal district judge in Tucson upheld the law. State and local public employees face possible criminal prosecution if they do not report undocumented immigrants or if they fail to verify the immigration status of those applying for public assistance.[68]

Health Care Policy

According to the U.S. Census, in 2006 more than 47 million Americans (15.8 percent of the population) lacked health insurance. Another 30 million are estimated to have inadequate health insurance. Between 2000 and 2003 alone, more than 5 million Americans lost their health insurance.[69] The lack of health insurance and affordable health care has real costs for millions of Americans. By one calculation, more than 18,000 Americans die prematurely each year because they don't have access to or cannot afford adequate health care.[70] Medical bills are now the main reason for half of all personal bankruptcies.[71] Also, the costs of health care are not only borne by those without insurance. Health care facilities spend nearly $100 billion in services and treatment each year caring for America's uninsured and underinsured. Covering their uncompensated costs, health care providers and insurance companies pass along nearly $40 billion a year to individuals who do have insurance—in the form of higher health care fees and higher insurance premiums.[72]

Unlike most advanced industrial countries, including neighboring Canada, the United States does not have a universal, **single-payer health care** system whereby doctors and other private health care professionals have their fees paid by the government at a fixed rate. Rather, health care in the United States is largely a private affair, regulated largely by market forces. Involvement in health care by the states and the federal government has been limited and largely piecemeal, although a few states and

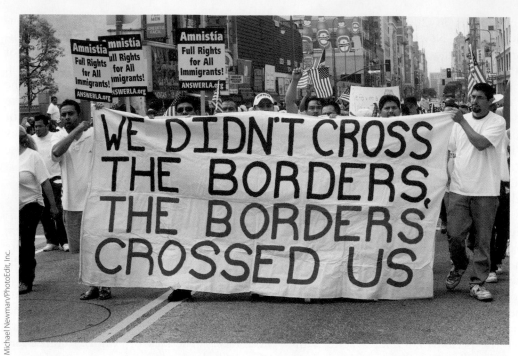

Michael Newman/PhotoEdit, Inc.

Immigration Supporters Rally in Los Angeles.

AP Photo/Ty Russell

Counter Immigration Demonstration in Oklahoma City.

communities have expanded their health care programs. It also tends to be means-tested, whereby the government determines if recipients are eligible for benefits based on their income or assets. Those who fail to qualify for government programs—which likely occurs because they earn more than the federal poverty level—are left on their own.

Why Do Americans Lack Health Insurance?

The cost of health care in the United States has skyrocketed. In 2006, over 16 percent of the country's gross domestic product (GDP) was spent on health care; in 1960, it was only 5.2 percent. Today, Americans spend more on health care than we do on food.[73] Besides the escalating costs of health care, a major reason Americans do not have health insurance is that fewer employers include health coverage in their basic employment packages.[74] Only three out of every five workers have employer-based health coverage, leaving some 36 million working Americans who do not receive health care insurance from their employers.[75] Others who remain in the ranks of the uninsured are largely unable to afford the cost of private health insurance premiums. A disproportionate number of those without employer-based coverage are minorities. Whereas 71 percent of white employees have health coverage included in their job package, only 51 percent of African Americans and 40 percent of Latinos have employer-based health insurance.[76] Some states have tried to expand health care coverage by encouraging employers to provide health care benefits. In Maine, for instance, individuals and smaller companies are able to receive bulk discounts on insurance.

Who lacks health insurance, and who should be responsible for providing it? Issues of public health, including both the protection of and improvement in the health of the public, have traditionally fallen to the states and their localities. In the 1960s the federal government ventured into the realm of public health, partnering with the states. But even today, states and their localities provide the bulk of health care assistance to citizens and noncitizens alike.

Who Are the Uninsured?

Most of the uninsured are elderly. Besides the elderly, who are by far the largest segment of the uninsured population, America's uninsured are *low income* (defined as earning below slightly less than $30,000, which is 200 percent of the federal poverty level for a family of three). Among this non-elderly population, low-income parents, their children, and low-income adults without children accounted for 65 percent of all the uninsured in 2003. The remaining 35 percent of the uninsured were workers (and their dependents) who earned at least twice the federal poverty level but were not covered by an employer's insurance or could not afford private insurance. In terms of race and ethnicity, minorities are considerably less likely to be covered by employer-provided health insurance than whites. According to the U.S. Census Bureau, a quarter of all African Americans do not have health care coverage, and 33 percent of Hispanics lack coverage.[77]

Considerable variation exists across the states when it comes to the number of non-elderly adults lacking health insurance. According to recent figures, Texas has the most dubious record, with 27 percent of its residents lacking health insurance. Mississippi, California, and Florida all had rates topping 20 percent. At the other end of the spectrum, Minnesota (9 percent) and Wisconsin (10 percent) lead the nation with the fewest residents lacking health insurance.

Medicaid

The largest public health program in the United States is **Medicaid,** which covers some 55 million low-income and disabled people and costs the federal and state governments more than $338 billion (in 2006) a year to run. A joint federal–state program created by Congress in 1965, Medicaid provides health care insurance to low-income individuals and their families. The federal agency that works with the states to administer the program is the Centers for Medicare and Medicaid Services (CMS), which has 10 regional offices spread across the country. Although most states have an agency that administers the program, some devolve the responsibility to their county or municipal governments.

Medicaid is means-tested; eligibility is determined by whether an individual (and his or her family) falls below a floor set by the federal government. The program requires the states to provide health care coverage to several categories of individuals, including those who qualify for welfare. States must also cover Supplemental Security Income (SSI) recipients—a federal cash assistance program for low-income aged, disabled, and blind persons—and all children born into families earning less than the poverty level. The states may also opt to provide additional health care for "medically needy" individuals and create programs assisting poor pregnant women and infants, institutionalized individuals, disabled children, and adopted children with special needs. In most cases, federal matching funds are available for these elective programs.[78]

Medicaid is jointly funded by the federal government and the states. The states pick up roughly 40 percent of the tab, with the federal government providing the balance of funding for the program. State expenditures on Medicaid automatically increase or decrease according to formulas set by the federal government. Under a rule implemented by the George W. Bush administration, states may require Medicaid recipients with household incomes greater than $24,900 (for a family of three) to make co-payments on doctor and hospital visits while giving patients more control over their health care options.[79]

State spending on Medicaid has expanded exponentially in recent years, despite the fact that every state has adopted cost-containment policies over the past two decades. Medicaid costs have increased nearly 10 percent every year since 2000, even though states are either freezing or reducing payments to health care providers, tightening eligibility requirements, restricting benefits, and increasing co-payments.[80] Growth in state tax revenue lags far behind that of Medicaid costs, with expenditures growing the greatest in the nation's poorest states.[81] According to the most recent data available, the average expenditure on Medicaid by the federal government and the 50 states (and the District of Columbia) amounted to $3,947 a year per enrollee. Adults covered by Medicaid received on average $1,782 in yearly benefits, and children received $1,400. Year in and year out, the greatest cost per recipient is for the elderly and the blind and disabled who are covered under Medicaid. The combined federal and state costs in 2002 averaged $10,971 per elderly enrollee and $11,547 per blind and/or disabled enrollee.

Across the states, one can see a tremendous range in per capita Medicaid costs. Detailing federal and state payments for Medicaid, Table 14.4 shows the average level of payments in 2002 across all types of Medicaid enrollees. In terms of overall Medicaid expenditures, nearly half the states spend $4,000 or less a year per beneficiary, whereas five states spend more than $6,000 per capita. New York leads the way, spending an average of $7,506 on each Medicaid recipient, whereas California spends only $2,472 per capita. One study reveals that states with more "comprehensive" health care programs tend to have more expansive Medicaid programs.[82]

In every state, more Medicaid dollars are spent on the elderly than on children and non-disabled adults, but these categories of spending still vary widely. On average, Alabama and Tennessee spent less than $6,000 a year on each blind and disabled Medicaid beneficiary, whereas Alaska, Minnesota, Connecticut, and New York all spent in excess of $20,000 per recipient. In 2002, the average Medicaid expenditures for adults ranged from $813 a year in California to $3,984 a year in Maryland, and on children from a low of $971 in Michigan to $3,570 in Maine. Although Maine is generous in its average payments to

| Table 14.4 |

Average Medicaid Payments per Enrollee by Enrollment Group, 2002, by State

	Children	Adults	Elderly	Blind and Disabled	Total
Alabama	$1,480	$1,021	$7,372	$5,154	$2,983
Alaska	$2,927	$3,861	$15,154	$20,766	$5,568
Arizona	$1,425	$1,429	$9,692	$10,503	$2,723
Arkansas	$1,426	$925	$9,397	$8,604	$3,276
California	$1,179	$813	$7,635	$11,214	$2,472
Colorado	$1,694	$2,148	$12,055	$13,265	$4,653
Connecticut	$1,859	$1,967	$21,105	$21,274	$6,740
Delaware	$1,569	$2,589	$13,753	$13,909	$4,333
District of Columbia	$2,085	$1,975	$10,164	$10,698	$4,436
Florida	$1,061	$1,579	$7,889	$9,143	$3,337
Georgia	$1,220	$2,460	$8,488	$8,070	$3,079
Hawaii	$1,232	$1,933	$9,447	$9,905	$3,241
Idaho	$1,106	$2,592	$14,181	$14,373	$3,996
Illinois	$1,399	$2,312	$11,277	$13,733	$4,153
Indiana	$1,400	$2,172	$13,580	$13,363	$4,199
Iowa	$1,531	$2,327	$12,713	$13,901	$5,078
Kansas	$1,445	$1,963	$13,844	$13,383	$4,846
Kentucky	$1,808	$2,631	$9,552	$8,131	$4,349
Louisiana	$996	$2,492	$7,552	$8,506	$3,204
Maine	$3,570	$3,073	$4,731	$7,099	$4,910
Maryland	$2,327	$3,984	$14,345	$17,053	$5,870
Massachusetts	$1,547	$1,744	$13,762	$13,664	$5,240
Michigan	$971	$1,865	$10,551	$6,234	$2,877
Minnesota	$2,264	$2,214	$13,786	$20,929	$6,345
Mississippi	$1,196	$2,805	$8,254	$7,148	$3,505
Missouri	$1,530	$1,490	$11,464	$10,862	$3,694
Montana	$2,022	$2,729	$12,997	$11,472	$4,810
Nebraska	$1,637	$2,286	$15,288	$15,644	$4,551
Nevada	$1,247	$1,752	$6,969	$9,011	$3,133
New Hampshire	$2,354	$2,512	$19,339	$19,661	$6,432
New Jersey	$1,499	$2,222	$13,957	$15,138	$5,516
New Mexico	$1,623	$1,699	$9,675	$11,294	$3,501
New York	$1,835	$3,215	$20,726	$22,773	$7,506
North Carolina	$1,410	$2,686	$9,410	$11,043	$4,312
North Dakota	$1,473	$1,719	$16,419	$16,764	$5,761
Ohio	$1,295	$2,239	$20,495	$14,631	$5,211
Oklahoma	$1,208	$1,274	$9,346	$10,266	$3,071

	Children	Adults	Elderly	Blind and Disabled	Total
Oregon	$1,505	$2,128	$10,386	$10,188	$3,326
Pennsylvania	$1,670	$2,213	$13,938	$9,107	$4,965
Rhode Island	$2,106	$2,202	$16,509	$15,582	$6,072
South Carolina	$1,372	$1,387	$7,885	$9,149	$3,009
South Dakota	$1,661	$2,395	$11,841	$13,265	$4,329
Tennessee	$1,067	$2,304	$5,344	$5,631	$2,624
Texas	$1,459	$2,393	$7,675	$10,502	$3,428
Utah	$1,751	$2,149	$10,707	$15,211	$3,918
Vermont	$2,071	$1,653	$7,447	$12,470	$3,839
Virginia	$1,351	$2,198	$8,673	$10,025	$4,110
Washington	$1,039	$2,026	$8,527	$7,357	$2,650
West Virginia	$1,458	$1,937	$11,954	$7,808	$4,013
Wisconsin	$1,156	$1,921	$10,983	$12,886	$4,614
Wyoming	$1,275	$2,271	$12,682	$14,420	$4,000
United States	$1,400	$1,782	$10,971	$11,547	$3,947

Source: Urban Institute and Kaiser Commission on Medicaid and the Uninsured, 2006, http://www.statehealthfacts.org.

children, it is quite miserly when it comes to elderly receiving Medicaid. In 2002, Maine's average Medicaid payment to the elderly was only $4,731; by comparison, Ohio, New York, and Connecticut all spent more than $20,000 per capita caring for elderly recipients of Medicaid.[83] Per capita Medicaid spending on the elderly varies widely across the states due to the level of reimbursement a state provides the owners of nursing homes that care for Medicaid patients. In some states, nursing home owners constitute a powerful lobby and place tremendous pressure on state legislatures to reimburse them at a substantial rate.

Federal Cuts in Medicaid Funding The woes of escalating Medicaid costs in the states have been compounded by decisions in Washington. In its 2007 federal budget, the Bush administration proposed a net cut of nearly $14 billion over five years in federal funds for Medicaid. Most of the proposed federal cuts in spending came in the form of fewer dollars being transferred to the states to pay for and

administer the joint program. U.S. Health and Human Services secretary Mike Leavitt said in 2006 that the federal government "is not in a position to help out states as much as before."[84] Perhaps making up for the decrease in federal funding, the Bush administration gave the states the option—if one can call it that—of reducing their own expenditures on Medicaid by either reducing the eligibility of those receiving Medicaid or reducing the range of benefits of the recipients. Alternatively, of course, the states have the politically difficult option of increasing taxes to offset their increased share for the program.

Not surprisingly, none of these solutions sit well with the states, especially governors, many of whom have their own budget problems to deal with. The rising costs of health care continue to comprise one of the most pressing issues facing governors and state policy makers. As more and more Americans lose or cannot afford health care coverage, states are expected to pick up those who fall through the cracks. Despite budgetary constraints of their own, all states, including those with low fiscal capacity and high social needs, have had to increase their expenditures on Medicaid after the economic downturn in 2001 while making cuts in other health-related public assistance programs or increasing premiums and required co-payments for doctor visits. Bill Richardson, the Democratic governor of New Mexico, has criticized the Bush administration's slashing of Medicaid funding, saying it places undue burdens on the states to provide health care to the poor. According to Richardson, "[S]tates will now become the true laboratories of innovation because the federal budget is not particularly helpful."[85]

State Experimentation with Medicaid

States carry out their Medicaid programs in ways that vary tremendously. Over half require at least some of their Medicaid recipients to belong to managed care plans, and some spend more than four times as much as others on discretionary state Medicaid expenditures. Since 1974, Hawaii has used its federal Medicaid dollars, in tandem with a requirement that employers offer health care coverage for their regular employees, to offer universal access to health care. In 1994, Tennessee launched TennCare, an innovative managed care model of health insurance, but less than 10 years later, the state was forced to deny coverage to hundreds of thousands of recipients after operational costs threatened to bankrupt the state budget. Maine passed a law in 2003 that provides a broad health care network financed by Medicaid and employer contributions. Arizona, on the other hand, did not even implement its Medicaid program until 1982. Unfortunately, only a smattering of scholarly research tries to explain why states have different types of health care coverage. Some scholars have found that state demographic and economic conditions help to explain cross-state variation in health-related expenditures, but others have found that political forces, such as party control of state legislatures and the power of interest groups, are the main determinants.[86]

Recently, Republican governors have been pushing market reforms to address the health care crisis. In Florida, for example, the state has cut back on its program by privatizing its health insurance program. Rather than providing a set menu of services under Medicaid, as other states do, in 2005 former Florida governor Jeb Bush quietly pushed through the state legislature a program that instead provides recipients with a lump sum of money with which they are expected to purchase their own private insurance. The Republican claimed the program he established "empowers" low-income families by giving them more choice in obtaining health care coverage. Under his watch, Bush—who had for years tried to keep Terri Schiavo's feeding tube inserted despite her persistent vegetative state and apparent wishes to the contrary—also allowed his state to cut Medicaid coverage for disabled and chronically ill children in need of nutritional supplements. Florida's administrative changes ended the financial assistance received by more than 1,000 children infected by AIDS and suffering from "wasting syndrome" as well as those unable to digest solid food because of cystic fibrosis.[87]

Several states under the control of Republican governors have led the way in cutting Medicaid costs. In South Carolina, Governor Mark Sanford pushed for federal approval of a program that allows Medicaid recipients to establish health savings accounts. The tax-free accounts can be used by individuals to pay for their medical expenses or purchase health insurance. In Arkansas, former governor Mike Huckabee received federal approval for a plan subsidizing small businesses that provided minimal health care insurance for their employees and making patients more accountable for the costs of their own health care. "One of the reasons we have a health-care crisis is because, as a consumer, I don't have that much skin in the game," Huckabee reasoned.[88] In 2005, Mississippi eliminated its Medicaid coverage of 65,000 elderly and disabled who had earnings between 100 percent and 133 percent of the federal poverty level, and Colorado passed a law in 2003 removing legal immigrants from Medicaid coverage. Georgia in 2005 raised the eligibility income limit for low-income pregnant women and those with children, affecting some 7,500 people.[89]

Democratic governors and state legislatures, in contrast, have pushed for extended coverage under their state plans even in times of tight budgetary constraints. Illinois, New Mexico, and California (under former Democrat governor Gray Davis) all made strides during the past 10 years to expand their health care coverage for children. In Illinois, the state in 2005 guaranteed that all children—regardless of their citizenship or income—would have access to health care coverage. After signing the legislation into law, Governor Rod Blagojevich announced, "We have now done for kids what 40 years ago Medicare did for seniors." The state plan provides universal health care coverage using a sliding scale based on income to determine the premiums.[90]

There have also been some bipartisan reform successes. In Massachusetts, the Democratic-controlled state legislature—with support from former Republican governor Mitt Romney—passed legislation in 2006 requiring all uninsured residents to purchase relatively inexpensive health insurance by July 1, 2007, or risk paying a fine. The innovative universal system of health care coverage requires the estimated 550,000 state residents without insurance to pay up to $250 a month for a basic policy. The program is underwritten in large part by some $385 million in federal Medicaid dollars (which the federal government threatened to eliminate if the state didn't reduce its number of uninsured), additional appropriations from the state, and an annual $295 per employee fee levied on businesses with 11 or more employees.[91]

State Children's Health Insurance Programs (SCHIPs)

In 1997, the federal government began providing over $24 billion in federal matching funds over a period of five years to the states to encourage them to create their own State Children's Health Insurance Programs (SCHIPs). Congress's intent was to encourage the states to expand their health care coverage for the nation's more than 6.1 million uninsured children whose parents do not qualify for Medicaid. Jointly funded by the federal and state governments and administered by the states, the state-run insurance programs have been heralded as successes. Although the federal Department of Health and Human Services has final approval over the 50 state plans, the states have retained considerable discretion, operating within broad federal guidelines, to create their own health insurance programs for children, including eligibility requirements, the package of benefits, the level of coverage, and how the programs are to be administrated.

There has been tremendous diffusion of SCHIPs across the states. Between 1998 and 2001, the states that were perceived as having successful SCHIPs—that is, the ones that were able to lower the rate of not having insurance among poor children at the same time they lowered costs—were emulated by other states. One study found that states adopting other states' successful SCHIPs have "similar partisan and ideological leanings" as well as similar budgetary constraints and that the decisions to adopt new policies were more likely to be carried out by legislators, as opposed to bureaucrats.[92] Despite the overwhelming success of SCHIPs, in 2007 President Bush vetoed a bipartisan bill that would have increased federal funding for SCHIPs by $35 billion over five years to cover an addition 4 million uninsured children. An increase in the federal tobacco tax would have paid for the increased spending.

Medicare

Medicare is a social insurance program wholly administered by the federal government. Signed into law in 1965 by President Lyndon B. Johnson, the program today serves some 42 million beneficiaries. The program, which serves primarily the elderly but also certain younger people with disabilities and those with chronic

INSTITUTIONS MATTER

HAMMERING WAL-MART ON HEALTH CARE

The State of Maryland has tried to take an aggressive tack to lower the number of working poor without health insurance and who qualify for Medicaid. In 2006, the Democratic-controlled legislature overrode the veto of former Republican governor Robert Ehrlich, establishing the state's Fair Share Health Care Fund. The law, which has been held up by the courts, requires firms with over 10,000 employees to set aside 8 percent of their payroll cost to pay their workers' health care. If a firm refuses to do so, it has to pay the same amount into the state's Medicaid program for low-income families. The sole target of the Maryland law was Wal-Mart, the state's largest private employer (with 17,000 employees) and the only private employer with more than 10,000 workers. With some $256 billion in profits in 2005, Wal-Mart generates some $13 million in tax revenue for Maryland's state and local governments every year and is a major purchaser of goods and services from businesses in the state.

Nationally, a frontal attack on Wal-Mart led by organized labor and other progressive groups has been going on for years. In addition to coming under withering criticism for not providing health care to more than 600,000 of its 1.3 million U.S.-based employees, a recent report conducted by the AFL-CIO found that in 19 states, Wal-Mart topped every firm for the number of employees receiving government health care assistance. Even in states such as Iowa, New Jersey, and Utah, where Wal-Mart is not the state's largest private sector employer, more employees of Wal-Mart receive health care aid from the state than any other company.

Should the states provide health care for private employers in exchange for low-wage jobs? Maryland lawmakers have made it clear to the retailing giant that it cannot free-ride on the backs of taxpayers. Depending on how the courts rule, Maryland's bold first step might lead to large companies in other states being required to pay for their employees' health care, as similar legislation has been introduced in more than 30 states.[1]

Notes

1. Peter Szekely, "Union Cites Wal-Mart Worker Reliance on State Aid," *The New York Times*, 14 March 2006; Lee Scott, "Wal-Mart is in Maryland to Stay," *The Washington Post*, 9 February 2006, A23.

---

kidney disease, does not focus on the poor. Individuals are eligible for hospitalization coverage under Medicare if they (or their spouse) worked for at least 10 years and made required contributions paying into the Hospital Insurance Trust Fund. Employees and their employers pay a 1.45 percent payroll tax (along with Social Security) to fund the trust fund (commonly referred to as Medicare Part A). Part A of Medicare generally covers all costs for the first 20 days of hospitalization (after an inpatient hospital deductible of $952 is met), and it is pro-rated thereafter. Those individuals who are eligible for hospital insurance may voluntarily apply for Supplementary Medical Insurance, known widely as Medicare Part B. Part B covers 80 percent of the costs for a range of

in-patient care, including physician bills, out-patient diagnoses, and physical therapy, after recipients have met the annual $124 deductible. The premium is $88.50 a month, and it is deducted directly from a recipient's Social Security, Railroad Retirement, or Civil Service retirement check.

In 2003, President Bush signed into law the Medicare Modernization Act, which was seen by many as a bonanza for pharmaceutical companies.[93] Americans spend more than $200 billion on prescription drugs annually, and the amount is growing by roughly 12 percent each year. The law provides a seemingly endless array of prescription drug plans from which eligible seniors are able to choose from to receive discounts on their medication. The drug coverage benefit, known as Part D of Medicare, immediately shifted more than 6 million poor Medicaid recipients over to the plan. The plan also covers seniors earning less than $19,000 a year, allowing these low-income seniors to purchase their prescription drugs with only $5 co-payments. By 2006, however, only 1.4 of the 8 million eligible seniors had signed up for the drug coverage.[94] Seniors who are financially better off are also permitted to participate in the Medicare drug benefit plan, paying monthly premiums and standard co-payments for any prescription drugs they purchase.[95]

Summary

States and their local communities often face major challenges when it comes to the provision of social welfare and health care services. Compared to unitary systems of government, our federalist system demands a lot from our subnational levels of government. When it comes to social ills and inequalities, such as inadequate health care, poverty, unemployment, and homelessness, they are the first (and sometimes only) line of defense. Time and again, though, state and local governments have shown their resilience and entrepreneurial spirit. They are truly "laboratories of democracy." At times competitors but always learning from one another, many states and communities have come up with innovative solutions to the many societal problems facing them. Despite the sometimes heavy hand of the federal government, health and welfare public policies are devolving considerably across the states.

Some critics contend that it is possible that we're witnessing the gradual dismantling of America's welfare state.[96] Fiscal constraints at both the state and federal levels have hampered the provision of social welfare and health care benefits to the most vulnerable members of society. In particular, the ever-expanding federal budget deficit has placed pressure on members of Congress and the president to reduce their financial commitment in funding many joint federal-state domestic programs. Many states have curtailed their experimentations with alternative health and welfare programs because of budgetary constraints or, alternatively, because of federal mandates directing them how to spend joint aid on TANF, Food Stamps, and Medicaid. States and their communities will not be afraid to do battle with the federal government when trying to protect their social welfare and health care policies but will cooperate with the federal government when it is to their advantage. What is certain is that states and their communities will continue to respond to policy shocks differently, drawing on a range of institutions to reform their policies to meet the demands of their diverse populations.

Keywords

Entitlement

Feminization of poverty

Living wage

Means-tested

Medicaid

Medicare

Policy diffusion

Public assistance

Single-payer health care

Social insurance

Social Security Act

Temporary Assistance for Needy Families (TANF)

Underclass

Welfare

Working poor

Suggested Readings

Daniels, Mark, ed. 1998. *Medicaid reform and the American states: Case studies on the politics of managed care.* Westport, CT: Greenwood Press.

Mittelstadt, Jennifer. 2005. *From welfare to workfare: The unintended consequences of liberal reform, 1945–1965.* Chapel Hill: University of North Carolina Press.

Osborne, David, and Ted Gaebler. 1992. *Reinventing government.* New York: Penguin.

Peterson, Paul, and Mark Rom. 1990. *Welfare magnets: A new case for a national welfare standard.* Washington, DC: Brookings Institution.

Pierson, Paul. 1994. *Dismantling the welfare state: Reagan, Thatcher, and the politics of retrenchment.* New York: Cambridge University Press.

Riccucci, Norma. 2005. *How management matters: Street-level bureaucrats and welfare reform.* Washington, DC: Georgetown University Press.

Schram, Sanford, Joe Soss, and Richard Fording, eds. 2003. *Race and the politics of welfare reform.* Ann Arbor: University of Michigan Press.

Websites

Council of State Governments (http://www.csg.org): CSG provides policy information for all 50 states and publishes annually the indispensable *Book of the States*.

Governing (http://www.governing.com): *Governing* is a monthly magazine whose primary audience is state and local government officials.

National Conference of State Legislatures (http://www.ncsl.org): NCSL provides a wealth of information to state legislators and the general public about state politics and policy.

National Governors' Association (http://www.nga.org): The NGA breaks down issues that are important to all 50 states, including welfare, education, health care, and budgets. It also contains the latest press releases and policy statements from various governors.

Stateline (http://www.stateline.org): *Stateline,* which is funded by the Pew Charitable Trusts, is staffed by professional journalists. In addition to original reporting on the news, Stateline provides links to other state and local news stories.

State Net (http://www.statenet.com): State Net is a full-service government relations firm that provides data, legislative intelligence, regulations, and in-depth reporting to companies concerned about the actions of state government.

Stateside Associates (http://www.stateside.com): Stateside Associates is a full-service government relations firm that provides information on issues, regulations, and legislative monitoring.

Urban Institute (http://www.urban.org): The Urban Institute provides independent nonpartisan analysis on issues dealing with community development and economic and social policy.

15

Education Policy

Who's Getting Schooled?

OUTLINE

Opening Vignette

Introduction

Issue Evolution of Education Policy

Organizational Control and Responsiveness of Public Schools

Financing Public Education

Experimenting with Public Education

The Federal Role in Public Education

Summary

As public school systems go, they are worlds apart. First, consider the Chappaqua Central School District, located in tony Westchester County, New York, home to Martha Stewart, Bill and Hillary Clinton, Vanessa Williams, and Kiss lead guitarist, Ace Frehley. Chappaqua has an exceptional system of public education, serving 4,000 kindergarten through high school students, 90 percent of whom are white. The district's total revenue for academic year 2003–2004 approached $78 million, the bulk of it generated from local property taxes, allowing the district to spend more than $17,000 per student. Much of this expense was driven by its low 12:1 student–teacher ratio. And Chappaqua's heavy investment in education seems to be paying off: 96 percent of students attending its single high school, Horace Greeley, were proficient or better in math and reading in 2004, and its graduation rate was 99 percent.

In the other world, consider the Detroit City School District in Wayne County, Michigan. By most standards, the Detroit school system is an abysmal failure. This urban district, whose residents are mainly African American, serves more than 150,000 students attending more than 250 schools. In the 2003–2004 academic year, there was an average of only one teacher for every 23 students in the district, and less than $11,000 was spent on each child per year. Fewer than half of the system's high school students were proficient at reading, and only one in five satisfied minimal requirements in math. In the end, only 22 percent of the freshmen attending Detroit's high schools in 1999 received a diploma by 2003. According to guidelines set by the federal Department of Education, the Detroit school district has continually failed to make adequate yearly progress.

Some might say that the residents of the Chappaqua Central School District place a higher value on public education than those living in Detroit. But probably more to the point, those living in Chappaqua can more easily afford to pay for quality public schools. Median household income in the district in 2005 was $184,300, with the value of the median home approaching $1 million. Over 80 percent of Chappaqua residents aged 25 and older hold at least a bachelor's degree, and unemployment is under 2 percent. Residents of Detroit probably value public education just as much as those of Chappaqua; the problem is that residents cannot afford to pay for it. In 2004, nearly 70 percent of all students there were from economically disadvantaged families, qualifying them to receive a free lunch financed by the federal government. Nearly 50 percent of households in the district had annual incomes under $30,000, and only 17 percent of adults had earned a bachelor's degree. Unemployment in Detroit hovers at nearly 15 percent, roughly twice the national rate, and property values have plummeted, with the average home now being worth less than $100,000. Resources for public education are scarce in the Motor City, and the educational results reflect that reality.[1]

Students at Guyton Elementary School in Detroit

High School students graduating from Croton-on-Hudson

Introduction

In contrast to our social welfare and health care systems, the United States does have a comprehensive, universal public education system—although many of the standards are set at the state and school district levels. Free, quality public education is a core societal value that is deeply held by most Americans. Starting in 1647, when English Calvinists passed a law in the Massachusetts Bay Colony requiring all townships to establish public schools funded through local property taxes, and spreading throughout the land in the 19th century, the concept of free-of-charge and universal public education has long been a hallmark of this country. Today, public education is viewed by many Americans as a fundamental right, although the U.S. Supreme Court has ruled otherwise.[2] Besides providing students with the knowledge and skills to find a job or pursue their education and training in college or technical school, public schools—from kindergarten through college—inculcate students with civic responsibility. Public education also has many social side effects that can lead to better quality of life and economic development for everyone in a community, even beyond the students themselves.[3] Some states and communities have even explicitly emphasized delivering high-quality public education in order to cultivate a "creative class" of residents.[4]

And yet, as the opening vignette suggests, many of the nation's public schools are failing. Microsoft founder and social philanthropist Bill Gates has recently called America's high schools "obsolete." "By obsolete," Gates continued at a February 2005 National Summit on High Schools, "I don't just mean they're broken, flawed or underfunded, though a case could be made for every one of those points. By obsolete, I mean our high schools—even when they're working as designed—cannot teach all of our students what they need to know today."[5] Although some students and education systems succeed, tens of thousands of students, especially those in urban America, are falling through the cracks of the educational

system each year. In 2003, the most recent year that national data are available, less than half of the students attending big-city high schools received their diplomas. In addition to Detroit, high school graduation rates in Cleveland, Dallas, Denver, Fort Lauderdale, Fort Worth, Houston, Los Angeles, Miami, Memphis, Milwaukee, and St. Petersburg all fell below 50 percent; less than 40 percent of high school students in Baltimore and New York City graduated on time. And for members of some racial and ethnic minority groups, the story is especially bad. Although there is considerable disagreement among experts on how to measure graduation rates, one study finds that roughly three-quarters of white and Asian-American students graduated on time, but the rate was just over 50 percent for African Americans, Hispanics, and Native Americans.[6] Overall, roughly three-quarters of all high school students scheduled to graduate in 2003 did so on time. That means that of the estimated 4 million students who should have graduated that year, about 1 million dropped out. By one calculation, that is approximately 7,000 students dropping out of school each day.[7]

Of course, as our opening vignette shows, educational outcomes vary dramatically across districts, but in many places, and for many students, the American public school system is failing. In this chapter, we look both at why and where American public schools are doing well and doing poorly. We use both a historical analysis of public education in this country and a comparison of districts in the 21st century to understand what works and what does not work and why. Although economics has much to do with today's problems in public education, some argue that educational institutions can at least have some impact on these problems.

First, we examine how American education policy has evolved over time, highlighting what has become a regular crisis of confidence in public education each generation. These periodic crises—whether based in educational reality or calculated fear-mongering by politicians—disrupt the education policy equilibrium and lead to reform and policy change. Central to this discussion of American education policy evolution is a tension that exists between the states, their school districts, and the federal government that is rooted in questions of federalism and public finance. This segues easily into our discussion of the ways states and school districts struggle to finance public education and our assessment of the equity and fairness of how school finances are allocated. Finally, we turn to questions concerning the organization and control of public education; that is, issues of educational institutions. In this section, we profile several innovations developed by states and school districts to deliver public education, including school vouchers, education management organizations, and charter schools.

Issue Evolution of Education Policy

For much of this country's history, local governments have taken the lead in providing elementary and secondary education to our nation's children. Left to their own devices to design, fund, and administer schools themselves, the local **school district** has traditionally had much autonomy from state government, to say noth-

ing of the federal government. But states and the federal government are increasingly playing a considerable role in the provision of public education. Under the administration of President George W. Bush, the federal government increased its involvement in public education by tying federal funding to programmatic and outcome-based educational policies. And that funding has been shrinking; in 2006, Congress cut spending on social services over five years by some $40 billion, including a reduction in funding for student aid for college students. As a result, several states have tried to make higher education more affordable for their residents—including, in some cases, those who are undocumented immigrants.

Prior to the 1930s, states and their communities were almost entirely responsible for providing public education to schoolchildren, with the federal government playing a limited role. It made sense, then, that there would be considerable diversity in the type and quality of public education children received when attending public schools. Since the 1930s and the New Deal, however, Congress has at times exerted its authority—albeit much less than in health care and social welfare policies. During the Great Society programs of the 1960s, for example, Congress passed several laws providing more than $1 billion in federal aid for elementary and secondary public schools with high concentrations of low-income students, funds for summer programs, categorical grants to fund bilingual education for children with limited English, and scholarships and low-interest loans for college students. A generation later, President Bill Clinton signed into law a Democrat-sponsored bill in 1994, Goals 2000: Educate America Act, which reauthorized all federal education programs, developed a voluntary national system of skill standards and certifications, and created midnight basketball leagues in public housing projects.

With regard to curriculum, local and state control over public education has become even more constrained in the

Daniel A. Smith

Public School children Attending Portable Classroom in Florida.

21st century, largely due to increasing national educational standards. There is considerable irony with respect to new federal standards concerning public education, as much of the increase in federal constraints placed on states has come on the watch of a Republican president, George W. Bush. Flying in the face of Ronald Reagan's 1980 campaign promise that he would abolish the Department of Education if he were elected—he didn't—the federal government's presence in education policy is perhaps as great as in any time in American history. Under President Bush, the federal government became much more heavily involved in overseeing K–12 public education than at any other time in the nation's history. Thus, to characterize the making of education policy as a robust competition among the states and school districts, with little intervention from the federal government, would be a major mischaracterization. Despite its limited constitutional authority—and its minimal financial expenditures—the federal government plays a major role today in the formulation of education policy in the states and communities. From subsidized day care, to vouchers for school, to school lunches, to testing children's educational progress, the federal government is heavily involved in education policy making.

Public Education in Crisis

The politicization of education policy is not new. With seemingly cyclical regularity, America's education system comes under a barrage of criticism every generation or so, at the federal, state, and local levels. Policy shocks have become a regular occurrence. In 1957, after the former Soviet Union successfully launched Sputnik, the first satellite to orbit Earth, federal officials decried the failure of the American education system to keep up with communist Russia. The following year, Congress passed the National Defense Education Act of 1958, which provided federal grants-in-aid to public and private schools (K–12 through universities) to stimulate the teaching of science, math, foreign languages, and area studies. It also provided low-interest loans to college students.[8]

A generation later, the policy equilibrium was again upset. State and federal officials—upon hearing the distress of parents and teachers at the local level—once again pulled the education alarm bell. In 1983, President Reagan's blue ribbon panel, the National Commission on Excellence in Education, issued a devastating report, "A Nation at Risk." Among its other scandalous findings, the commission found that for the first time in American history, the average high school graduate was less well-educated than those who received their diplomas a generation earlier, and American public school students were not as well-educated as their counterparts in other industrialized nations. In Cold War rhetoric matching that brought about by the Sputnik crisis, the commission claimed that American society was being eroded "by a rising tide of mediocrity that threatens our very future.... If an unfriendly foreign power had attempted to impose on America the mediocre educational performance that exists today, we might well have viewed it as an act of war.... We have, in effect, been committing an act of unthinking, unilateral educational disarmament."[9]

More recently, during the 2000 presidential campaign, the generational crisis in education was again invoked, this time by George W. Bush. Highlighting the poor achievement of many children attending public schools, and the so-called **achievement gap** between rich and poor and white and minority students, Bush touted the free market as providing the solution for what ailed public schools. Downplaying issues of inadequate and inequitable funding of schools, the then Texas governor pushed for greater school choice, including the privatization of public schools, the creation of charter schools unrestrained by state regulations, and school vouchers as possible solutions. Holding public schools accountable—which included withholding federal funds for schools that failed to perform—was seen as his solution. After winning office, with much public fanfare and the bipartisan backing of Congress, President Bush signed the **No Child Left Behind Act (NCLB)** into law in 2002. The implementation

Jason Reed/Reuters/Landov

President Bush with Education Secretary Margaret Spellings in Greensboro, North Carolina.

of the law, however, which has been accompanied by the heavy hand of the U.S. Department of Education, has caused great consternation among both liberals and conservatives in numerous states and communities.

Growth in Public Education

America's system of public education continues to expand. Between 1985 and 2004, enrollment in K–12 public schools grew by 22 percent, with the fastest growth occurring at the elementary school level. Over the same period, private school growth, by comparison, grew by only 14 percent. During the 2004–2005 school year, some 48.3 million children attended public elementary and secondary schools. An additional 13 million students matriculated at public postsecondary, degree-granting institutions (colleges, universities, and trade schools). Enrollment for grades K–12 is expected to continue to grow until 2014.[10]

Every state requires children up to a certain age to be educated, either in public or private schools or through homeschooling. In 1852, Massachusetts became the first state to require children to attend school, and by 1918, every state had a compulsory education law on the books. Today, over half of the states (32) require students to begin their schooling by age six; others, such as Pennsylvania and Washington, allow students to begin school as late as age eight. Twenty-six states allow students to quit their studies at age 16, with the remaining requiring students to stay enrolled until they are at least 17 or 18 years of age.[11]

Accompanying the growth in K–12 enrollment has been an increase in the cost of public education. In the 2004 school year, expenditures by all K–12 institutions exceeded $514 billion, with colleges and universities (public and private) expending an additional $351 billion. Nearly 5 percent of the country's gross domestic product (GDP) goes toward K–12 education alone. Adjusting for inflation, total spending on K–12 education has increased every year since 1955 in terms of total government spending or as a percentage of the national GDP. Back in 1955, total spending on primary and secondary education was $71 billion, only 2.6 percent of the GDP. Public elementary and secondary schools now employ more than 3.1 million teachers, up 27 percent from 1990. Although the average salary for public school teachers for the 2002–2003 academic year was $45,822, it was only 2 percent higher than in 1992–1993, after controlling for inflation. For example, teachers make up slightly more than half of all public school staff, but there is a wide deviation across the states. For example, teachers comprise 65 percent of all public school staff in South Carolina but only 43 percent in Kentucky.[12]

Organizational Control and Responsiveness of Public Schools

There is a strong tradition of deferring to local school boards to carry out public education decisions. Yet, state governments ultimately exercise broad authority over school districts. As discussed in Chapter 11, school districts are creations of state government. Not surprisingly, there is considerable variation across the states when it comes to how public school systems are organized.

Organizational Control of Public Schools

Nationwide, over 90 percent of all public schools are run by locally elected school boards. Three states—Hawaii, Alaska, and Maine—are outliers in that the state government has a heavier role in administering public schools. Hawaii is unique in that it has a unitary, state-run system for public education. In North Carolina and Virginia, counties are charged with running public schools. In some cases, cities—including Boston, Chicago, and New York—have taken over the administration of public schools that fall within their municipal jurisdiction. Although not going to the degree of state control over education as in Hawaii, Alaska, and Maine, some states have usurped local control over certain school districts. In the mid-1990s, for example, New Jersey's state Department of Education took over Newark's public schools because of failing schools. Since that time, though, the performance of the 43,000 students attending Newark's public schools has not improved much. In 2004, over 70 percent of all 11th graders failed the comprehensive math test given by the state—twice the statewide failure rate. Two-thirds of Newark's 8th graders also failed the state math tests, and over half failed the language test.[13]

In most states, the local school board appoints a superintendent, hires staff and teachers, helps to determine the curriculum, and sets school calendars and attendance requirements. Perhaps most importantly, local school boards determine the annual tax levies for operating expenses and the capital construction budget of school districts. However, in most states, the rate of local tax levies to fund public schools as

well as the ability to float school construction bonds are limited by the state constitution. By 1940, 27 states had placed constitutional limits on the bonding authority of local school districts, and 15 limited local tax levies of school districts.[14] Today, nearly all the states place these limits on school districts. In addition, most states now also require tax levy increases and bond measures to be put to a public vote via a referendum.

Some states even require a supermajority vote at the local level on such fiscal measures. Between 1942 and 2007, for example, local school levies in Washington had to receive a popular vote of at least 60 percent (and have at least 40 percent turnout of the last election) in order to be approved. Critics claimed that the state's anti-majoritarian requirement allowed a minority to thwart the building of a better education system by making it difficult for local school districts to fund new school programs and build new facilities. Although the success rate of local referendums is quite high (in part because they are placed on the ballot in desynchronized, off-year, and even special elections, all with very low turnout), the state legislature placed a successful constitutional amendment on the ballot in 2007 that lowered the threshold to a simple majority.[15] In Oregon, which has similar supermajority requirements for the passage of levy and bond measures, some school districts have had to close public schools early and issue layoff notices to teachers and administrators following the defeat of operating expense referendums. In 1986, the Estacada school district (southeast of Portland) shut down its schools twice after voters rejected requests to increase its budget.[16]

Local school boards are also legally constrained in all pedagogical and substantive areas set by the state legislature and state constitution. Every state has a secretary or commissioner who oversees the statewide Department of Education (or a similar agency, such as a Department of Public Instruction). Figure 15.1 displays a flowchart of Massachusetts's public education administration, which is typical for many states. The top public school administrator in 36 states

Figure 15.1

Administrative Flowchart for Massachusetts Public Schools

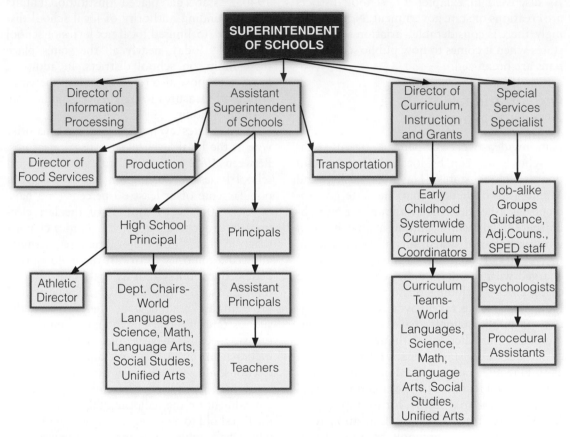

Source: Walpole Public Schools, "Public Schools Administrative Flowchart," 2006, http://www.walpole.ma.us/
District_Home_page/flowchart.htm.

is appointed; in the remaining 14 states, the education chief is elected statewide. These officials are in charge of supervising their state's public education system but usually work in tandem with a statewide board of education. All but two states (Minnesota and Wisconsin) have a state Board of Education. These semiautonomous bodies generally have six functions:

1. Establish certification standards for teachers and administrators.
2. Create standards for accreditation of school districts and teacher and administrator preparation programs.
3. Set high school graduation requirements.
4. Create state testing programs.
5. Review and approve the budget of the state education agency.
6. Develop rules and regulations for the administration of state education programs.

Currently, 32 states have statewide education boards that are appointed (usually by the governor), 11 have elected boards, and five states have boards that have both appointed and elected members. In the South, state control over education policy tends to be greater. In the North, especially in the New England region, local school districts tend to have more autonomy over their curriculum and other staffing decisions.[17]

Beginning in the 1950s, many states began drastically cutting their number of school districts. Taking advantage of economies of scale, proponents argued that by consolidating and centralizing districts, states could achieve increased cost savings in delivering educational programs. In 1932, there were over 127,000 independent school districts; today, there are roughly 14,000. As Table 15.1 shows, there are still thousands of very small school districts. Nearly 44 percent of all school districts serve populations of less than 5,000 people, amounting to 2.4 million school-age children. Only 1,487 school districts (10.4 percent) serve populations with greater than 40,000 people. Yet, large school districts account for 62.2 percent of the country's school-age population—some 33 million children under the age of 18.[18]

School District Responsiveness

Scholars are giving increased attention to how responsive school districts are to local public opinion. Although advocates of local control argue that school districts that devolve authority and decentralize decision making are more accountable, recent scholarship suggests this is not necessarily the case. Somewhat counterintuitively, a recent major study finds that of the more than "Ten Thousand Democracies,"

appointed school boards tend to be at least as responsive as elected ones. The structure of school boards, it appears, does not necessarily impact the educational policies a school board adopts. School boards that are closest to the people—those run in New England–style town meetings, for example—tend not to reflect local public opinion any better than school boards appointed by other elected officials or even those folded within a city or county government. Local public opinion toward public education, especially of minorities, tends to be represented quite well by school boards that are unelected. This is perhaps due to the fact that other elected officials may be more apt to listen to and respond to public opinion and to place pressure on their appointees than school board members who are elected in low-information contests.[19]

More broadly, school boards generally do a good job reflecting local public opinion. Perhaps surprisingly, school boards that are integrated with other governmental bodies (such as counties or cities) have policies that are more reflective of the population being served. For example, a school district that is consolidated with a local government tends to have minority representation that is more reflective of the population being served. With respect to public support for school funding, as we

---

Table 15.1

Number of School Districts and Distribution of the School-Age Population, 2000

School District Population	Number of School Districts	% of School Districts	Total School-Age Population	% of Total School-Age Population
Less than 5,000	6,252	43.7	2,406,420	4.5
5,000 to 9,999	2,550	17.8	3,446,217	6.5
10,000 to 19,999	2,377	16.6	6,177,845	11.6
20,000 to 39,999	1,637	11.4	8,058,266	15.2
40,000 or more	1,487	10.4	33,007,255	62.2
Totals	14,310	100.0	53,096,003	100.0

Source: U.S. Census Bureau, Population Division, June 2004, http://www.census.gov/population/www/documentation/twps0074/tab10.pdf.

discuss in more detail in the following section, the level of school district financing also tends to map fairly closely to local public opinion. African-American communities tend to support more spending on education than other racial and ethnic groups. Even communities with well-established elderly populations living on fixed incomes and with no school-aged children, who intuitively might seem likely to oppose the financing of public schools, generally support the use of property taxes to support quality public education.[20]

Financing Public Education

As you know from Chapter 1's opening vignette, which compared the costs of a public education at the flagship universities in Florida and Pennsylvania, there are considerable differences across the states when it comes to the subsidization of higher education. There are also considerable differences across states and school districts regarding how much is spent per pupil on K–12 public education. Although some states and school districts are striving to privatize public education, others are trying to bolster funding and enhance public schools.

Comparing K–12 Public Education Finance across the States

The financing of K–12 public education has undergone a major restructuring since the 1950s. Public financing of schools has been wholly reformed, with less reliance on local revenue sources to fund local schools. Public education has gradually become one of the largest budgetary items for state and local governments. On average, the states spend 21 percent of their annual budgets on K–12 education. As Table 15.2 shows, the total revenue needed to provide K–12 education has increased steadily over the years, even when factoring in inflation. In 1919–1920, local school districts provided 83.2 percent of the revenue for K–12 education, with the states

Table 15.2

Sources of Revenue for K–12 Public Schools, 1919–1920 to 2001–2002

School year	Total (in 1,000s)	Federal (in 1,000s)	State (in 1,000s)	Local (in 1,000s)	% Federal	% State	% Local
1919–1920	$970,121	$2,475	$160,085	$807,561	0.3	16.5	83.2
1929–1930	$2,088,557	$7,334	$353,670	$1,727,553	0.4	16.9	82.7
1939–1940	$2,260,527	$39,810	$684,354	$1,536,363	1.8	30.3	68.0
1949–1950	$5,437,044	$155,848	$2,165,689	$3,115,507	2.9	39.8	57.3
1959–1960	$14,746,618	$651,639	$5,768,047	$8,326,932	4.4	39.1	56.5
1969–1970	$40,266,923	$3,219,557	$16,062,776	$20,984,589	8.0	39.9	52.1
1979–1980	$96,881,165	$9,503,537	$45,348,814	$42,028,813	9.8	46.8	43.4
1989–1990	$208,547,573	$12,700,784	$98,238,633	$97,608,157	6.1	47.1	46.8
1999–2000	$372,943,802	$27,097,866	$184,613,352	$161,232,584	7.3	49.5	43.2
2001–2002	$419,501,976	$33,144,633	$206,541,793	$179,815,551	7.9	49.2	42.9

Source: U.S. Department of Education, National Center for Education Statistics, Common Core of Data, "CCD Data File: National Public Education Financial Survey FY 2003 Preliminary," 2005, http://nces.ed.gov/pubsearch/pubsinfo.asp?pubid=2005358.

providing 16.5 percent and the federal government less than 1 percent.

The states now play a major role in funding K–12 education. Since the 1920s, state governments have increasingly provided a greater proportion of the financing of public education. Accordingly, the proportion financed by local government has decreased over time. The 1978 school year was the first in which state governments collectively provided more revenue than local governments for K–12 education. Today, state and local governments foot most of the bill for K–12 education: for every dollar spent on primary and secondary education, roughly 92 cents flow from state and local governments. In 2001–2002, state governments accounted for 49.2 percent of total K–12 education revenue, and local governments accounted for 42.9 percent. The federal government accounted for slightly less than 8 percent of total revenues for public education.

When looking comparatively across the states, northeastern states tend to fund their public education systems to a far greater extent with local property taxes than do southern and western states. In 2002, well over 40 percent of all financing for public schools in northeastern states was generated by local property taxes. Local property taxes accounted for roughly 35 percent of revenue in southern states and only 33 percent in western states. Local property taxes in midwestern states accounted for slightly less than 40 percent of total public school revenues in 2002. Western and southern states make up for the lack of property taxes by relying much more heavily on state funding. They also fund their systems of public education with a great share of federal dollars. There are, of course, exceptions to these general trends. In New Hampshire, 87 percent of K–12 funding is derived from local revenue sources, with only 9 percent flowing from the state, which does not have either a general sales tax or an income tax. In New Mexico, the state provides 72 percent of the funding for K–12 education. In Hawaii, the state provides 89 percent of the financing for its unitary system of public education. Table 15.3 provides the percentages

Table 15.3

Percent of Total Public K–12 Revenues across Sources, by State, 2004

State	Local	State	Federal
District of Columbia	84.8	—	15.2
Nevada	63.1	29.6	7.4
Connecticut	58.6	36.3	5.1
Nebraska	58.2	32.8	9.0
Missouri	57.1	34.3	8.6
Pennsylvania	56.0	35.8	8.3
Maryland	55.4	38.1	6.5
Virginia	54.2	38.8	7.0
Massachusetts	52.9	40.4	6.7
New Jersey	52.1	43.4	4.5
Rhode Island	51.4	41.2	7.4
Texas	50.6	38.6	10.8
South Dakota	50.0	34.4	15.7
Colorado	49.9	43.3	6.8
Maine	49.1	42.2	8.7
New York	49.1	43.2	7.6
New Hampshire	48.5	45.8	5.7
Ohio	47.9	44.9	7.2
North Dakota	46.5	38.1	15.4
Tennessee	46.4	42.9	10.7
Iowa	45.9	8.6	8.6
Florida	45.8	43.7	10.6
Georgia	45.2	45.9	8.9
South Carolina	43.3	46.1	10.6
Indiana	42.3	51.0	6.8
Wisconsin	41.3	52.2	6.5
Arizona	40.3	47.8	11.9
Montana	40.0	44.6	15.4
Kansas	39.8	51.1	9.1
Oregon	38.9	52.0	9.1
Wyoming	38.1	52.2	9.7
Louisiana	37.7	48.7	13.5
Utah	34.5	55.7	9.9
Arkansas	34.0	53.3	12.7
California	33.5	55.6	10.9
Illinois	33.4	33.4	8.4
Oklahoma	32.7	54.4	12.9

Percent of Total Public K–12 Revenues across Sources, by State, 2004 (continued)

State	Local	State	Federal
Alabama	32.2	55.6	12.2
Idaho	31.6	58.1	10.4
Kentucky	30.6	57.3	12.2
Michigan	30.1	61.8	8.0
Mississippi	29.8	54.8	15.4
Washington	29.5	61.2	9.3
Delaware	29.0	62.0	9.0
West Virginia	27.9	60.7	11.5
North Carolina	26.7	62.9	10.5
Vermont	25.9	66.3	7.8
Alaska	24.8	56.7	18.5
Minnesota	24.3	69.5	6.2
New Mexico	13.2	69.2	17.6
Hawaii	2.4	86.6	11.0
United States (average)	43.9	47.1	9.1

Source: U.S. Department of Education, National Center for Education Statistics, Common Core of Data, "Overview of Public Elementary and Secondary Students, Staff, Schools, School Districts, Revenues, and Expenditures: School Year 2004–2005 and Fiscal Year 2004," table 6, http://nces.ed.gov/pubs2007/2007309.pdf.

of local, state, and federal funding for K–12 education for the 50 states and the District of Columbia.

The states have used several methods to ensure the funding of public schools. In the past, states would make fixed grants that went directly to school districts. These grants were usually based on the number of pupils per district, irrespective of the relative wealth of the district. Today, most states use a combination of two funding strategies to finance K–12 education. Some states use categorical grants, targeting revenue to support programs and facilities in property-poor districts that have maxed out their local taxing revenues. The state is able to equalize school funding across school districts by using a formula that combines state dollars with local taxes

as well as federal funds. Other states attempt to centralize school financing by using general funds to provide funding to all schools equally, avoiding inequalities across property-rich and property-poor districts. Figure 15.2 shows the very complex system of funding public education in Colorado, which, among other sources, finances its schools with a mixture of property taxes, lottery funds, and school trust lands as well as income taxes, sales taxes, and other taxes that flow into its general fund.

There is considerable variation across states in terms of the amount of per pupil funding for K–12 public education. Per pupil spending has traditionally been the highest in northeastern states and the lowest in southern and western states, as Table 15.4 shows. New York leads the country in K–12 education spending per pupil. In the 2003–2004 academic year, the state spent an average of $12,059 on each elementary and secondary school student. Higher per pupil spending by a state, however, does not mean that students are guaranteed achieving higher academic performance. Only 62 percent of New York State's 9th graders in 2000–2001 graduated on time in 2004. Utah, which allocated only $5,091 per K–12 pupil, had a graduation rate exceeding 82 percent in 2004, one of the highest rates in the country. South Carolina, spending $7,559 per student, had the lowest graduation rate of any state, just 49 percent.

Financing K–12 Public Education

Dissatisfied with the inequities in public education, many parents in the 1970s began pursuing legal avenues to challenge the reliance on local property taxes to fund public education. During the decade, numerous lawsuits were filed by public interest groups that challenged the dependence on local property taxes to finance public school systems. The lawsuits were filed on behalf of poor school districts or minority children in poorly funded schools. They questioned the funding

Figure 15.2

Colorado Sources of School Funding

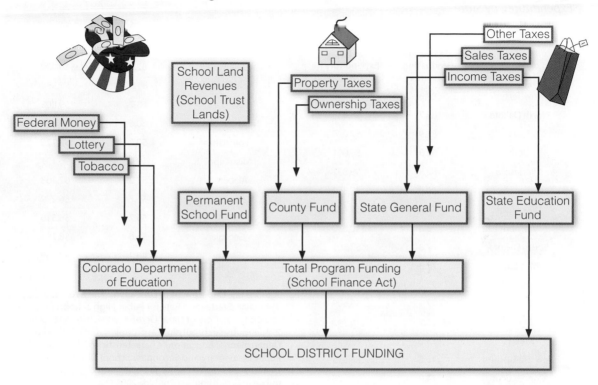

Source: Donnell-Kay Foundation, "Amendment 23 and Public School Financing in Colorado," March 2003, http://www.headfirstcolorado.org/A23FINAL.pdf.

formulas for public education, claiming they violated the equity or adequacy of public education clauses found in most state constitutions. Between 1968 and 1998, hundreds of lawsuits were filed in state courts across the country. In more than 25 of the lawsuits, state supreme courts ruled that state funding formulas based on the property tax were unconstitutional.

California's Superior Court was the first in the country to find that its state's heavy reliance on local property taxes was unconstitutional because it caused gross disparities and inequities in the funding of public schools. Evidence introduced by the plaintiffs, the Western Center on Law and Poverty, showed wide disparities in funding existed across school districts, with districts raising over half of their revenue through local property taxes. The school funding in two Los Angeles County unified school districts—Baldwin Park and Beverly Hills—was particularly egregious, with the former spending only $577 per pupil in the 1968–1969 school year and the latter spending $1,232 per pupil. In its decision, the court found that the quality of public education for a child could not be a condition of his or her parents, or neighbors' property values. In its 1971 decision *Serrano v. Priest,* the court required the state to equalize local property tax bases by using statewide tax revenue and to provide poorer districts with funding to bring their per pupil spending up to the mean. Along with subsequent rulings,

Table 15.4

2004 High School Graduation Rates and per Pupil Expenditures, by State

State	% of Ninth Graders in 2000–2001 Graduating on Time	Per Pupil Expenditures, 2003–2004
New Jersey	89.8	$11,390
North Dakota	83.7	$6,835
Iowa	82.9	$7,098
Utah	82.5	$5,091
Minnesota	82.3	$8,821
Nebraska	80.0	$7,352
Wisconsin	79.0	$9,483
Vermont	78.6	$10,630
South Dakota	77.8	$7,300
Montana	77.3	$7,688
Idaho	77.2	$6,372
Pennsylvania	77.1	$8,609
Maine	75.7	$10,145
Kansas	75.2	$7,622
New Hampshire	75.2	$8,915
Connecticut	74.9	$11,773
Arkansas	74.2	$6,005
Maryland	74.1	$9,186
Massachusetts	74.0	$10,772
Virginia	73.7	$6,441
Missouri	73.6	$6,947
Oklahoma	73.2	$6,429
Wyoming	72.7	$9,756
Ohio	72.3	$9,136
Illinois	72.2	$9,839
Rhode Island	72.0	$10,258
Michigan	71.5	$8,671
West Virginia	71.2	$9,169
Nevada	70.2	$6,230
Colorado	70.0	$8,023
Arizona	69.9	$5,347
California	69.6	$7,692
Oregon	68.8	$7,587
Indiana	68.6	$8,414
Washington	68.5	$7,446
Kentucky	64.9	$7,474
Hawaii	64.8	$8,220
Texas	64.2	$7,335
New York	62.1	$12,059
Delaware	62.0	$10,470
New Mexico	61.5	$7,370
Alaska	60.7	$9,808
North Carolina	60.6	$6,727
Louisiana	59.2	$7,179
Mississippi	59.1	$6,137
Alabama	57.2	$7,163
Tennessee	56.7	$6,279
Florida	55.7	$6,516
Georgia	53.6	$8,703
South Carolina	49.2	$7,559

Sources: U.S. Department of Education, "The Averaged Freshman Graduation Rate for Public High Schools from the Common Core of Data," October 2005, http://165.224.221.98/pubsearch/pubsinfo.asp?pubid=2006601; and U.S. Department of Education, "Characteristics of the 100 Largest Public Elementary and Secondary School Districts in the United States: 2002–03," August 2005, http://165.224.221.98/pubsearch/pubsinfo.asp?pubid=2005312.

the state was forced to decouple school district expenditures from local property taxes, essentially making California's K–12 education system a unitary system, financed out of Sacramento.[21] California's system of financing public education was further centralized with the passage of Proposition 13 in 1978, which directed property tax revenues to the state. In 1996, voters continued the centralization of school financing when they passed Proposition 98, which guaranteed a minimum level of statefunding for each school district.[22]

Advocates wanting to reform public school financing were dealt a blow in 1973 when the U.S. Supreme Court ruled that there was nothing in the U.S. Constitution guaranteeing citizens a right to equal per pupil funding. In its 5–4 ruling, *San Antonio Independent School District v. Rodriguez* (1973), the court found that the 14th Amendment's Equal Protection Clause did not establish a right to equal per student funding. The court's decision left future questions of educational equity up to the states.

Notwithstanding the high court's ruling, many states were forced to alter their systems of school financing that were grounded in local property taxes after successful legal action. In the late 1980s, the school financing systems in Montana, Texas, and Kentucky—which were based solely on property tax revenues—were all struck down by state courts. The Texas legislature, for example, finally responded in 1994 with what became known as the "Robin Hood Plan." The plan, which set up regional taxing authorities and then shared local revenues across rich and poor districts, successfully reduced by $500 per pupil the gap in expenditures between property-poor and property-rich districts. However, it drastically reduced the total amount of property wealth that could be taxed to finance public schools.[23]

Financing Higher Education

State and local governments have invested considerable sums to build a world-class system of higher education. In fiscal year 2006, subnational governments spent some $77.7 billion on direct support for the general operating expenses of public and independent colleges and universities. This was up from just $21 billion in 1981. State sources fund roughly 90 percent of the higher education bill, with local appropriations filling in the balance. The funding of public colleges and universities, however, is not always stable. The recession that hampered the nation's economy between 2001 and 2005 had long-term repercussions for the funding levels of higher education systems. Indeed, fiscal year 2006 was the first year since 2001 that per student

constant dollar state funding for higher education actually increased. The reason for the slight increase in 2006 was twofold: college and university student enrollment tapered off and state and local government spending increased by 7.6 percent.[24]

Whether or not the recent increase in funding for higher education should be interpreted as a harbinger for better times for colleges and universities is not so clear, however. Future fiscal solvency of institutions of higher learning remains uneven across the states. Between 1991 and 2006, for example, 21 states experienced enrollment growth that was above the national mean. Only a third of those states—Arkansas, Georgia, Kentucky, Louisiana, Nevada, New Mexico, and Texas—increased per student state educational appropriations, with Georgia leading the way. In terms of state wealth (measured by the per capita total taxable resources of a state), 17 states exceed the national average for their per capita taxable resources. Of these states, only seven—Connecticut, California, Minnesota, New Jersey, New York, Rhode Island, and Wyoming—exceeded the national average for per capita spending on higher education. Nationally, support for higher education from state and local governments fell nearly 6 percent from 1995 to 2005, dropping to just $260 annually per capita. In 2006, the state of New Hampshire spent only $88 per capita to finance higher education.

Other states, relatively speaking, are pouring significant resources into higher education. Wyoming, not normally considered a leader in higher education, led the nation by spending more than $629 per capita in 2006 in funding its colleges and universities.[25] One of the reasons for Wyoming's relatively greater commitment to funding higher education has to do with the fact that nearly 20 percent of the appropriations for colleges and universities in the state are generated through fees and lease agreements with oil and mineral extraction companies. Furthermore, in 2006, Wyoming voters approved the creation of a $500 million endowment paid for by state mineral taxes to create academic scholarships for all Wyoming students attending state universities and colleges as well as to pay for endowed chairs and research funds for state-school faculty.

Not all state higher education systems are doing so well. When compared with the billion-dollar endowments of Harvard, Yale, Stanford, and other prestigious private universities, many state colleges and universities are struggling to make ends meet. A recent scenario in Florida, for instance, may well become the norm in other states. After the Republican-controlled legislature in 2007 authorized a 5 percent increase in state appropriations for higher education, newly elected Republican governor Charlie Crist—a self-styled populist—vetoed the bill, saying he wanted to keep education costs affordable for Florida's families. Keep in mind that the State of Florida has arguably the least expensive tuition for in-state students in the country. But keeping tuition low has other costs for students. The 11 state universities in the Sunshine State have one of the worst student–faculty ratios in the country—some 30 students for every tenured or tenure-track professor, five more than the national average—and required courses are often very difficult to get into. Faced with another round of budget cuts, the president of Florida State University—T. K. Wetherell, a former Republican speaker of the Florida House of Representatives—decided to take matters into his own hands. In 2007, following Governor Crist's veto of higher education appropriations, Wetherell announced that Florida State University (FSU) would freeze enrollment in 2007–2008 and would make substantial reductions in undergraduate admissions the following academic year. "Something's got to give," Wetherell said, noting that one of his secretaries pays almost $9,500 a year in daycare, nearly three times the amount of FSU's annual tuition. "I don't think you can find anybody in America that can run a

world-class university on one-third of what a daycare center costs—it can't be done."[26] Governor Crist eventually relented, agreeing to a modest tuition increase.

In an effort to keep tuition down but maintain the quality of their institutions of higher education, several states are relying on Americans' penchant for gambling to help. Nontax appropriations, such as proceeds generated from state lotteries, casinos, and other forms of gaming, have grown rapidly in some states since the 1990s. Revenue from these sources now accounts for nearly $2 billion of all state expenditures on higher education. In three states—Georgia, South Carolina, and West Virginia—more than 15 percent of state appropriations for higher education are derived from gaming revenues. Another 15 states generate at least some of their revenues through effective "sin taxes" on these activities. Most of these states use revenues generated from these activities to provide need-based scholarships. Modeled after Georgia's HOPE (Helping Outstanding Pupils Educationally) Scholarship Program, which was established in 1993 and has awarded more than $3.6 billion to over 1 million in-state students attending Georgia's universities, colleges, and technical schools, several other state programs—including New Mexico's Student Success Scholarships, Oklahoma's Higher Learning Access Program, West Virginia's PROMISE Program, and South Carolina's HOPE Scholarship Program—have all had notable success making higher education more affordable to qualified students. Georgia's HOPE Program is a merit-based program financed by state lottery revenues. In 2006, 20 percent of the state's $2.5 billion higher education budget was derived from funds generated by the lottery, and 99 percent of in-state freshmen at the University of Georgia were scholarship recipients. The scholarship pays a student's full-time tuition and fees (about $2,500 a semester), plus an additional $150 for books.[27]

Experimenting with Public Education

Embodying the entrepreneurial spirit, most states and school districts have experimented with new policies to try to reform the public school system and ensure that children receive a quality education. From public school choice within a school district, to vouchers for private education, to charter schools, to public-private partnerships, to tying teacher pay to student performance in the classroom or on state achievement tests, states and their respective school districts have pursued many market-oriented and outcome-based solutions to try to make students, teachers, and schools more accountable. Some programs have met with more favorable results than others.[28] We discuss four public elementary and secondary educational programs: school vouchers,

educational management organizations, charter schools, and homeschooling.

School Vouchers

Many states and their school districts have turned to the private sector to try to revamp public education. The driving force behind the privatization of public education is the idea that the private sector, through competition and school choice, can be more efficient in providing a higher-quality education for students than existing public schools. The idea behind **school vouchers,** first floated by the late economist Milton Friedman in the 1950s, is to eliminate the education "monopoly" held by the public sector and teachers' unions. By providing financial assistance in the form of vouchers to parents who have children in poor-performing public schools, Friedman argued parents should be able to transfer their children to private

REFORM CAN HAPPEN

WASHINGTON, D.C.'S SCHOOL VOUCHER EXPERIMENT

Although Milwaukee's school voucher program—established in 1990—is the nation's longest-standing school choice program, Washington, D.C.'s is quickly becoming one of the most extensive. In addition to the 58,000 students who go to public schools in the district, some 1,700 low-income, largely minority children use taxpayer-funded vouchers to attend 58 private (both secular and parochial) schools in the area. Funded by grants by the federal Department of Education, the school choice pilot program was established in 2005. Mayor Anthony Williams, the district's former mayor, endorsed the program, saying that it allowed poor parents to exercise their choice to move children out of failing schools. Critics, such as the National Education Association, the largest teachers' union in the country, countered by saying the program was "exploiting the frustration of these minority parents to push for a political agenda" that seeks to chip away at public schools. In addition to the voucher program, roughly a quarter of the district's students attend charter schools. Hundreds of thousands of students in other school districts across the country—such as those attending public schools in Houston, New York City, Oakland, and Dayton, Ohio—have also opted for charter schools. But charter schools, unlike the voucher system in D.C. that allows students to attend private schools, are still financed by the school district, even though they are privately operated.[1]

Note

1. Diana Jean Schemo, "Federal Program on Vouchers Draws Strong Minority Support," *The New York Times*, 6 April 2006, A1.

schools, where—so the theory goes—incentives that drive the private sector will produce the same or better schools at a lower cost. Vouchers not only give parents more of a choice in their children's educational opportunities, supporters claim, but also force public schools to compete with private schools in order to retain students and public funding.[29] Critics charge that vouchers siphon funding from public schools, weakening them for the children who remain there and diverting dollars to schools that often do not have the same accountability standards that public schools must meet.[30]

Voucher programs—which, broadly defined, include not only tuition subsidies paid for by state (or federal) governments but also benefits through tax deductions—are permissible under the U.S. Constitution. In its 5–4 decision in *Zelman v. Simmons-Harris,* the U.S. Supreme Court in 2002 ruled that a Cleveland, Ohio, voucher program did not violate the establishment clause of the U.S. Constitution, even though vouchers could be used to send children to nonsectarian as well as religious private schools. A dozen states, as well as Washington, D.C., have adopted some form of voucher or tax credit school choice program, in which a total of 130,000 students participated in 2006. Milwaukee's Parental Choice Program, established in 1990, was the first voucher program of its kind.[31] Although the court's ruling upheld the city's school voucher program, school voucher programs have not been extensively replicated in other school districts or states, as some state constitutions expressly forbid the practice.

Many state educational voucher programs have run into legal roadblocks. Recently, voucher programs in Florida, Vermont, and Washington have been struck down by state courts. Florida's Opportunity Scholarship Program, touted by former governor Jeb Bush and enacted by the state legislature in 2000, provided tuition vouchers for public school students to attend private schools. But in 2006, the Florida Supreme Court nixed the program, ruling that it violated the state constitution's "uniform public education" clause. Similarly, the Colorado Supreme Court struck down a

2003 law passed by the state legislature that created a tax-funded voucher program that would have allowed students to attend private schools, including religious ones. The Colorado high court ruled that the law, which would have forced the state's 11 school districts to participate in the voucher program, violated a provision in the state constitution that local districts retain control over education funds that are raised locally. Other states have faced not only legal barriers but also political ones when trying to create voucher programs. Voucher programs have faced stiff public opposition. Statewide public opinion is not particularly warm toward the programs (every voucher proposal placed on a statewide ballot via the initiative process has been defeated at the polls), and teachers unions have wielded considerable political clout to thwart the programs.[32] Most recently, in a 2007 popular referendum, Utah voters soundly rejected the state legislature's bid to permit school vouchers.

Education Management Organizations

Other states have permitted their school districts to hire for-profit companies—called *education management organizations* (EMOs)—to run some of their public schools. In 2001, the Pennsylvania Department of Education hired a private firm, Edison Schools, Inc., to assess Philadelphia's public schools, with some 200,000 students. The school district was in serious financial trouble, running up a $215 million debt. The state ended up taking over the district in December 2001, creating a five-member Philadelphia School Reform Commission to run the schools. The commission then contracted with seven different entities—Chancellor Beacon, Foundations, Inc., Universal Companies, Victory Schools, the University of Pennsylvania, Temple University, and Edison Schools—to administer 45 low-performing elementary and middle schools, with Edison receiving a five-year, $60 million contract to manage 20 schools. In 2005, the commission awarded Edison contracts to administer two more schools.[33]

INSTITUTIONS MATTER

"BABY BLAINE" AND THE PROHIBITION OF VOUCHERS

James Blaine, a Republican U.S. representative from Maine, advanced an amendment to the U.S. Constitution in 1875 that would have prohibited states from using any public funds or lands to support private schools "under the control of any religious sect." Nearly a century earlier, during the formative period of the nation, it was common for many communities, and even some states, to support with public funds religious institutions affiliated with the Protestant Church. Playing off the anti-Catholic sentiments and the nativist fear of "popery" that were quite prevalent among some Protestants in the 19th century, Blaine wanted to preempt efforts by immigrant communities to use their growing political clout to have public treasuries fund parochial schools tied to the Catholic Church. Although Blaine's effort proved unsuccessful at the national level, many states went on to adopt their own "Baby Blaine" constitutional amendments. Congress even passed a law requiring Blaine provisions to be included in the constitutions of all new states entering the union. Today, over 30 states have Blaine-like amendments in their constitutions, banning state aid to religious organizations, or private entities more generally. For example, in Nevada, "No public funds of any kind or character whatever, State, County, or Municipal, shall be used for a sectarian purpose." Alaska's constitution plainly states, "No money shall be paid from public funds for the direct benefit of any religious or other private educational institution." Arizona's is just as clear: "No tax shall be laid or appropriation of public money made in aid of any church, or private or sectarian school." Because of these institutional barriers, it is unlikely that education reformers will have much success pushing vouchers in these states. Blaine's legacy, questionable because of its bigoted underpinnings, continues to resonate in many of the states.[1]

Note

1. "Beware of the Ghost of James G. Blaine," *New York Sun*, 20 January 2006. Available: http://www.nysun.com/article/26224; David Akerman, "Education Vouchers: Constitutional Issues and Cases," Report for Congress, Congressional Research Service, The Library of Congress, 20 May 2003. Available: http://www.firstamendmentcenter.org/pdf/CRS.voucher1.pdf.

Edison is the largest EMO in the country. In 2004, it managed over 150 schools with over 84,000 students in 24 states as well as several schools in Washington, D.C. Although some have praised the revamping of public schools in Philadelphia and other school districts, there is substantial evidence that students attending these for-profit companies do not outperform those attending traditional public schools.[34] Citing dissatisfaction with results, school districts in Georgia, Kansas, and Texas recently terminated their five-year contracts with Edison.[35]

Charter Schools

Publicly funded and operated by a school district, **charter schools** are freed from many of the administrative, staffing, and peda-gogical constraints facing traditional public schools. Charter schools usually have narrow missions, allowing them to focus on certain types of students and use alternative teaching and assessment methods. Because they have a semiautonomous status and are not bound by district- or statewide regulations, charter schools are able to utilize innovative pedagogies and creative methods of learning beyond what is being done in standard public schools. Charter schools are sometimes affiliated with a local business or institution of higher learning. Although exempt from many state and school district requirements, charter schools remain under the control of the local school board and may not promote a particular religious denomination, charge tuition, or use selective criteria for admissions.[36]

In 1991, Minnesota became the first state to allow school districts to establish charter schools, with California doing so the following year. Today, over 40 states have authorized local school districts to create charter schools. Most public school charters are granted for three to five years. In 2006, over 3,600 charter schools were in operation, serving more than 1 million K–12 students.[37] Unlike school voucher and privatization programs, charter school programs tend to have bipartisan legislative support.[38] Indeed, the president of the American Federation of Teachers, a union representing thousands of public school teachers, called on school districts to create charter schools in the 1980s, partly as a way to stave off the push for private school vouchers and the creation of privately run EMOs.

Although supporters tout the flexibility charter schools provide public school educators, the schools have not been a universal success. Some critics charge that charter schools do not improve student achievement, whereas others decry the lack of information available to parents to make good choices regarding the merits of charter schools. Some criticize state governments for failing to provide adequate oversight of charter schools. Scholars complain that state education departments often do not collect enough student-level data from charter schools, making it impossible to gauge the individual progress of students. And many charter schools have been held up to public scrutiny for their curricula, such as integrating religious themes that are inappropriate for publicly funded schools.[39]

Homeschooling

One of the fastest growing reforms in K–12 education has been homeschooling. Tracking the number of children being homeschooled is difficult; records on homeschooling kept by school districts and the states are often not complete, and many homeschooled children return to the ranks of the public schools. One scholar has estimated the number of children who were homeschooled in the 1960s at upward of 15,000.[40] As recently as a decade ago, national data on the number of children being homeschooled were still difficult to obtain. One estimate placed the figure at 850,000 nationwide in 1999, roughly 1.7 percent of all school-aged children in grades K–12. By 2003, a national study revealed that over 1.1 million (or 2.2 percent of all school-aged children) were being homeschooled. Every state, as well as the District of Columbia, permits parents to homeschool their children, but a great degree of variation exists across the states concerning the laws regulating homeschooling. Most state legislatures passed statutes regulating homeschooling in the 1980s and 1990s, although Oklahoma has protected the right of parents to homeschool their children since statehood. Some states require the primary parent who is doing the homeschooling to have certain educational requirements, and others do not. A few states require certain subjects to be taught, whereas others are more vague. And some states mandate that homeschooled students be tested along the same lines as those educated

Courtesy, US Department of Education

Former U.S. Education Secretary Rod Paige visits the Community Academy Public Charter School in Washington, D.C., during National Charter Schools Week

COMPARISONS HELP US UNDERSTAND

INITIATING EDUCATION POLICY

Do voters want something for nothing? Over the past several election cycles, voters living in several states allowing the initiative have passed ballot measures that increase spending on public education. The ballot measures have not, however, earmarked dedicated revenue streams to fund these additional appropriations for K–12 education. In 2002, voters in the state of Washington approved class size reduction ballot measures (Initiative 728) and cost-of-living increases for teachers (Initiative 732) that did not create new revenue sources.[1] That same year, voters in Florida passed their own class size reduction measure (Amendment 9), a measure opposed by former Republican governor Jeb Bush. The younger brother of President Bush was overheard by the press saying he had "devious plans" to kill the initiative because he thought it would cost the state some $27 billion spread over seven years, yet some four years after the measure passed, the state had only spent $3.7 billion on class size reduction.[2] In 2000, voters in Colorado passed a constitutional initiative (Amendment 23) that provides increased funding for K–12 public education in the state.[3] More than a decade earlier, Californians adopted Proposition 98, a constitutional amendment sponsored by the California Teachers Association that mandated that K–14 education (which includes the first two years of college) receive roughly 35 percent of the budget from the state's annual general fund.[4] All of these initiatives—which were, and still are, quite popular with the electorate—have effectively earmarked a portion of the state budget for public education.

Notes

1. Washington Research Council, "Governor's Budget Sets Priorities, Lives within Means," Policy Brief 01–16, 20 December 2002. Available: http://www.researchcouncil.org/Briefs/2002/PB02–16/BudgetLives.pdf.
2. Mary Ellen Klas, "Class-size amendment may finally get funding," *Miami Herald*, 17 April 2006. Available: http://www.miami.com/mld/miamiherald/news/state/14358383.htm.
3. Donnell-Kay Foundation, "Amendment 23 and Public School Financing in Colorado," March 2003. Available: http://www.headfirstcolorado.org/A23FINAL.pdf.
4. Lisa Snell, "California's 2005 K–12 Education Primer," Policy Brief 40, *Reason*, May 2005. Available: http://www.reason.org/pb40_california_education_reform.pdf.

in the public schools, whereas others do not require any formal assessments.[41]

The demographics of children who are homeschooled are quite different from those found in traditional public schools. Homeschooled children are disproportionately white and are members of lower- to middle-income families. Caucasian children are twice as likely as African-American children to be homeschooled, and nearly four times as likely to be taught at home as Hispanic children. Children living in larger, two-parent families, with one parent not participating in the labor force, are far more likely to be homeschooled than other school-aged children. Most parents who opt out of the public school system cite concerns with the social environment of public schools and their desire to impart moral and religious teachings as reasons why they decided to engage in homeschooling. Voluminous pedagogical materials are available for parents of homeschoolers. According to a national survey conducted by the U.S. Department of Education in 2003, slightly less than half of all homeschooled children rely on some form of distance learning to supplement their studies. Over three-quarters of homeschooled students are instructed with curriculum materials obtained at a public library or from a private vendor. Over one-third of all homeschooling is done using materials obtained from a church, synagogue, or other religious organization.[42]

Critics of homeschooling have voiced numerous concerns. One of the chief complaints of homeschooling is whether the parent doing the teaching is qualified to do so and has the requisite skills necessary to educate his or her children. Their concerns have some empirical backing. Roughly one-quarter of all parents who teach their own children have a high school diploma or less, with only 20 percent having education beyond a bachelor's degree. Other critics cite the lack of socialization of homeschooled children with their peers and the diminished likelihood that children will be exposed to viewpoints differing from those of their parents, which can hinder the development of critical-thinking skills.[43] Despite these and other concerns, homeschooling is only likely to grow, as Americans have increasingly come to accept this alternative method of parents self-educating their children.

The Federal Role in Public Education

Even though it has no constitutional role, the federal government has increasingly become involved in the financing and administration of public education. Following the landmark 1954 decision *Brown v. Board of Education,* in which the U.S. Supreme Court used the equal protection under the laws language of the 14th Amendment to find segregation in public schools unconstitutional, the federal government frequently, if at times reluctantly, has intervened in the effort to desegregate public schools. In 1957, President Dwight D. Eisenhower went so far as to federalize the Arkansas National Guard to ensure the integration of Little Rock High School after Arkansas governor Orval Faubus had used the troops to prevent nine African American students from entering the school. The 1964 Civil Rights Act solidified *Brown,* mandating that no federal

funding could be used by schools if racial discrimination existed.

The following year, Congress enacted the Elementary and Secondary Education Act of 1965 (ESEA). ESEA provides federal funding in the form of categorical and block grants to the states and school districts with substantial levels of low-income families. Most of the federal government's aid for K–12 education goes directly to school districts. Title I of ESEA today provides more than $13 billion a year in aid to school districts with the aim of improving the academic achievement of students who come from families with substantial levels of poverty. Nearly every elementary school receives Title I funding, although only one-tenth of high schools receive such funding. Additional federal funding under ESEA goes toward incentive grants to the states to improve teacher quality, English language instruction, community learning centers, aid to schools that service children whose parents live on military bases, and after-school programs. The federal government also provides over $10 billion in aid through Part B of the Individuals with Disabilities Education Act (IDEA), which assists states and schools to educate children with disabilities. In the wake of Hurricane Katrina in 2005, which displaced thousands of public school students, the U.S. Department of Education provided vouchers amounting up to $7,500 per pupil that allowed students to attend private, sectarian schools.

The No Child Left Behind Act of 2002 (NCLB)

Touted as the most significant piece of domestic legislation during his first term in office, President Bush signed NCLB into law with much bipartisan fanfare in January 2002. Bush heralded the law as necessary for the nation's schools to narrow the educational **achievement gap** that separates students across the dimensions of race, ethnicity, income, English proficiency, and disability.[44] NCLB, which is driven ideologically by libertarian, market-driven, school choice models of education reform,[45] relies on standardized testing of students to weed out and penalize poorly performing schools.

NCLB affects school funding and education policy at both the elementary and secondary levels for all states and public schools receiving any federal funding under Title I of ESEA. Federal appropriations for K–12 education under NCLB increased from $22 billion in 2002 to $24.4 billion in 2005. The law mandates that the states administer reading and math examinations to students in third through eighth grades as well as for high school students at least once. States are required to develop standards of proficiency and then track the progress toward proficiency of all their students. Students are then placed in eight subcategories—five are racial–ethnic (Caucasian, Asian, African American, Hispanic, and Native American) and three are based on need (special education, limited English proficiency, and free and reduced price meals). At least 95 percent of students in each subcategory must take the exams, and students in every subcategory are supposed to achieve close to 100 percent proficiency on the tests by the 2013–2014 academic year.

The law, some 670 pages long and containing 588 federal mandates, is a mixed bag of carrots and sticks.[46] As for incentives, NCLB provides an array of federal resources to the states and their school districts. The law gives increased flexibility to the states and school districts in allocating their federal dollars, provides grants for free tutoring to students in schools that are designated as "failing," and finances after-school learning programs. There are federal funds available for school districts to establish charter schools as well as grants to schools with heavy populations of American Indians, Alaska Natives, and students of migrant workers. NCLB assists parents who wish to transfer their children out of low-performing schools to other public schools, including charter schools. NCLB also provides funding for K–3 reading programs and grants for professional development as well as training for teachers and math and science curriculums.

As for punishments, the law packs a severe wallop for school districts whose students fail to measure up to federal standards. Specifically, the law places harsh sanctions on states and school districts whose students do not meet certain achievement goals. If any one of a school's eight student subcategories fails to attain **adequate yearly progress (AYP),** which is based on its performances on annual achievement tests, the whole school receives a failing grade. The first time a school fails to meet AYP, the law stipulates that the school must notify parents that it is a "failing" school and allow students to transfer to a passing school in the district. If the school does not achieve AYP in all of the subcategories the following year, it must provide tutoring to students who performed poorly on the exam. If in the third year the school fails to meet AYP, it must introduce a new curriculum, extend the school day or year, or even replace school teachers and administrators. If after the fourth year the school still does not achieve AYP, the school may be closed down, taken over by the state, or transformed into an independent charter school.[47]

Is NCLB Working?

NCLB, which was up for reauthorization by Congress in 2007, has clearly identified that children in thousands of public schools are not achieving the academic standards set by the U.S. Department of Education (DOE). In the 2004–2005 academic year, 24,470 public schools—some 27 percent of all schools—failed to meet AYP requirements. Only 28 percent of all public schools in Florida improved their AYP scores in 2005 compared to the previous year, the worst percentage in the country. Two-thirds of Hawaii's public schools failed to show any improvement, as did over half in Washington, D.C., and Nevada.[48] The federal law exempts students in private K–12 schools from taking the annual standardized examinations.

Critics have charged Congress of failing to adequately appropriate funding for NCLB. A handful of Republican and Democratic governors, and many state legislators and state education chiefs, have criticized Congress for mandating education standards that should be under the purview of state and local officials. As such, they claim NCLB amounts to an unfunded federal mandate on states and school districts: they must abide by the various requirements of the legislation, but they also incur increased costs to carry out the federal programs. Some state and school officials claim that this is especially true regarding the standardized testing the NCLB requires for most elementary and secondary students attending public schools. In 2005, Connecticut sued the DOE for requiring the state to pay for more than $50 million in programs but not providing any financial assistance. Conservatives have charged that NCLB allows the federal government too much power to meddle in what should be the domain of state and local governments. Recently, several Republican-dominated state legislatures, including Utah and Virginia, have considered legislation to allow their state to opt out of NCLB or refuse to appropriate state funds to pay for programs mandated by the federal government. Concerned that it intrudes on local control of education, Jim Dillard, the Republican chairman of Virginia's House Education Committee, said NCLB was a "massive federal intrusion" and was "simply unworkable" and "utopian nonsense." Vermont passed legislation prohibiting the state to spend money to implement NCLB, and over 20 more states have requested that Congress appropriate more money to change or increase funding for the program.[49]

Other state and local education policy officials have criticized the law for not being stringent enough. The law allows the states to set their own benchmarks for AYP as well as adjust the standards on the achievement tests and formulas used to calculate AYP. Critics claim this allows states to manipulate actual progress levels of their schools. Oklahoma, for instance, showed improbable improvement when the percentage of the state's "failing" schools fell from 25 percent to just 3 percent in one year. Diane Ravitch, an education professor at New York University and a former assistant secretary of education under President George H. W. Bush, claims that the "stats are meaningless in the absence of a common test and common standards."[50]

For its part, the DOE claims that states do not have to participate in NCLB programs. Of course, if a state voluntarily opts out of the program the state is cut off from federal funding associated with the program, which in some cases is not an insignificant amount. Maryland, for example, risked losing millions of dollars in federal funding if it did not take over "failing" junior high and high schools in Baltimore. Wielding its stick, the federal agency has also threatened to withhold future funding earmarked to schools not meeting AYP if a state does not inform students in "failing" schools about their educational options. A 2006 report issued by the DOE found that over half of all school districts with subpar schools did not inform parents that their children attending "failing" schools could attend other public or private schools or that they could receive free tutoring. Only 17 percent of eligible students signed up for the free tutoring in 2005, and only 38,000 students transferred to other schools, less than 1 percent of the 4 million who were eligible. Margaret Spellings, President Bush's DOE secretary, has said that "there are a number of steps we can take to enforce these provisions, including withholding federal funds."[51] Critics of the NCLB, though, have claimed that the tutoring programs, which cost upward of $1,800 per student, are of such poor quality that they are not worth the effort. Furthermore, the tutoring programs are not available in many of the poorest, and poorest-performing, schools.

Summary

The power of local school districts and even the states to determine education policy has eroded considerably over the past decade. Although the federal government has increased K–12 and higher education appropriations, Congress has attached many strings to these disbursements. The ability of states and school districts to be innovative and experimental has become circumscribed due to increased federal intervention in education policy. Specifically, states and their school districts have felt the heavy hand of the federal government since the passage of NCLB by Congress in 2002. The multitude of federal standards and requirements that public schools and students must meet has preempted the authority of states and local school districts to devise their own strategies and solutions to deal with local educational problems. Furthermore, the implicit effort by the federal government to privatize public education—through the encouragement of school choice voucher programs, EMOs, charter schools, and homeschooling, combined with the closing of underperforming public schools—has limited the range of options traditionally left to state and local education officials.

Yet, you should not expect states and local school districts to take the recent federal usurpation of power over education policy lightly. As in past battles, they will swing back when the time and partisan alignments are right. Rest assured, education policy will continue to be one of the most hotly contested policy areas in the coming years and is likely to be a central hub of the perennial power struggle between state and local governments and the federal government.

Keywords

Achievement gap	**Charter school**	**School districts**
Adequate yearly progress (AYP)	**No Child Left Behind Act (NCLB)**	**School voucher**

Suggested Readings

Fiske, Edward, and Helen Ladd. 2000. *When schools compete: A cautionary tale.* Washington, DC: Brookings Institution.

Mintrom, Michael. 2000. *Policy entrepreneurs and school choice.* Washington, DC: Georgetown University Press.

Schrag, Peter. 2003. *Final test: The battle for adequacy in America's schools.* New York: New Press.

Whittle, Chris. 2005. *Crash course: Imagining a better future for public education.* New York: Riverhead Hardcover.

Witte, John F. 2001. *The market approach to education: An analysis of America's first voucher program.* Princeton, NJ: Princeton University Press.

Websites

American Federation of Teachers (http://www.aft.org)**:** With over 3,000 local affiliates, 43 state affiliates, and 1.3 million members, the AFT union provides a treasure trove of information advocating public education and its educators.

Friedman Foundation (http://www.friedmanfoundation.org)**:** Founded to promote the ideals and theories of economists Milton and Rose Friedman, the foundation provides information on school choice and privatization efforts.

National Charter School Research Project (http://www.ncsrp.org)**:** Based at the University of Washington, the NCSRP offers a wealth of scholarly research on the charter school debate.

National Conference of State Legislatures (http://www.ncsl.org)**:** NCSL provides nonpartisan information on education legislation in the states, including data on education finance, voucher programs, and teacher quality.

National Education Association (http://www.nea.org)**:** The NEA, with over 3.2 million members, offers a wealth of research and data on education reforms in the states and communities.

National Governors' Association (http://www.nga.org)**:** The NGA provides nonpartisan information on education issues in the states.

U.S. Department of Education, National Center for Education Statistics (http://nces.ed.gov)**:** The indispensable federal repository for data and analysis on education policy in the United States.

Chapter 1

[1] "National Universities: Top Schools," *U.S. News and World Report,* 2008, http://colleges.usnews.rankingsandreviews.com/usnews/edu/college/rankings/ranknatudoc_brief.php.

[2] Ironically, over the past several years, as the cost of the Bright Futures program has skyrocketed, many Republican lawmakers in Tallahassee have tried unsuccessfully to cap the scholarship amounts and reduce the number of eligible students receiving the awards. "What we need to do is get a better handle on how to control the cost of Bright Futures," said Representative David Mealor in 2003, the chairman of the Florida House Subcommittee on Higher Education. "We are trying to honor our commitment and, at the same time, address the financial dilemma we're facing." Every year, the state legislature receives tremendous pressure from public colleges and universities to increase the funding for higher education. Simultaneously, it encounters tremendous public pressure not to alter the scholarship program and not allow the state Board of Governors, which oversees higher education, to raise tuition. As with many other entitlement programs, Floridians like Bright Futures. See Anita Kumar, "Bright Futures Cuts Tuition for Too Many, Lawmakers Say," *St. Petersburg Times,* online ed., March 31, 2003.

[3] Graham B. Spanier, "The Privatization of American Public Higher Education," Spring 2004, http://president.psu.edu/presentations/privatization_031604.pdf.

[4] Spanier, "The Privatization of American Public Higher Education," 9.

[5] Michael B. Berkman and Eric Plutzer, *Ten Thousand Democracies: Politics and Public Opinion in America's School Districts* (Washington, D.C.: Georgetown University Press, 2005).

[6] As you will see in Chapter 7, because of various court decisions and legislative action in 6 of these states, only 15 states have state legislative term limits today.

[7] Charles Barrilleaux, Thomas Holbrook, and Laura Langer, "Electoral Competition, Legislative Balance, and American State Welfare Policy," *American Journal of Political Science* 46 (2002): 415–27.

[8] U.S. Census Bureau. 2002. Census of Governments. GC02-1(P). Washington, D.C.: U.S. Government Printing Office.

[9] For many years, only some counties of Indiana would use daylight-saving time, whereas other parts would stay on standard time for the entire year. But in 2005, after a painful political process, Hoosier policy makers adopted legislation to move the entire state back and forth between daylight-saving and standard times with the rest of the country. See Joseph Popiolkowski, "Daylight-Savings Time Dawns in Indiana," *Stateline.org,* online ed., September 20, 2005.

[10] John F. Camobreco and Michelle A. Barnello, "Post-materialism and Post-Industrialism: Cultural Influences on Female Representation in State Legislatures," *State Politics and Policy Quarterly* 3 (2003): 117–38; Kevin Arceneaux, "The 'Gender Gap' in State Legislative Representation: New Data to Tackle an Old Question," *Political Research Quarterly* 54 (2001): 143–60; and Kira Sanbonmatsu, *Where Women Run: Gender and Party in the American States* (Ann Arbor: University of Michigan Press, 2006).

[11] James D. King, "Single-Member Districts and the Representation of Women in American State Legislatures: The Effects of Electoral System Change," *State Politics and Policy Quarterly* 2 (2002): 161–75; and Peverill Squire, "Legislative Professionalization and Membership Diversity in State Legislatures," *Legislative Studies Quarterly* 17 (1992): 69–79.

[12] Richard L. Fox and Jennifer L. Lawless, "Entering the Arena? Gender and the Decision to Run for Office," *American Journal of Political Science* 48 (2004): 264–80.

[13] Malcolm E. Jewell and Sarah M. Morehouse, *Political Parties and Elections in American States*, 4th ed. (Washington, D.C.: CQ Press, 2001).

[14] Because states vary so greatly in population size, the only fair way to compare state spending is via per capita measures: that is, the amount spent per person living in a state.

[15] Thomas E. Dye, *Politics, Economics, and the Public: Policy Outcomes in the American States* (Chicago: Rand McNally, 1966).

[16] The 11 states that made up the Confederacy were Virginia, North Carolina, South Carolina, Georgia, Florida, Tennessee, Alabama, Mississippi, Louisiana, Arkansas, and Texas. Missouri, Kentucky, Delaware and Maryland were known as *border states.* Although many of their citizens were sympathetic to the Confederacy, they never seceded from the Union. Also, West Virginia was a section of Virginia at the beginning of the war, but in 1863, in a move that rankled Virginia for over 100 years, it split off to become a separate state supporting the Union.

[17] V. O. Key Jr., *Southern Politics* (New York: Knopf, 1949).

[18] Raymond Tatalovich, *Nativism Reborn? The Official English Language Movement and the American States* (Lexington: University Press of Kentucky, 1995).

[19] Rodney E. Hero, *Faces of Inequality: Social Diversity in American Politics* (Oxford: Oxford University Press, 1998); Rodney E. Hero and Caroline J. Tolbert, "A Racial/Ethnic Diversity Interpretation of Politics and Policy in the States of the U.S.," *American Journal of Political Science* 40 (1996): 851–71; and Kenneth Meier, Joseph Stewart Jr., and Robert England, *Race, Class, and Education: The Politics of Second Generation Discrimination* (Madison: University of Wisconsin Press, 1989).

[20] Hero, *Faces of Inequality.*

[21] Hero, *Faces of Inequality.*

[22] State legislative sessions also tend to begin after harvest time and end before planting, for the same outdated reason.

[23] In these systems, students usually get just as much time off school, but it is distributed more evenly throughout the year. See Cynthia Opheim, Kristine Hopkins Mohajer, and Robert W. Read Jr., "Evaluating Year-Round Schools in Texas," *Education* 116 (1995): 115–26.

[24] Laura Langer, "Measuring Income Distribution across Space and Time in the American States," *Social Science Quarterly* 80 (1999): 55–67.

[25] Robert S. Erikson, Gerald C. Wright, and John P. McIver, *Statehouse Democracy: Public Opinion and Policy in the American States* (New York: Cambridge University Press, 1993); and Robert S. Erikson, Gerald C. Wright, and John P. McIver, "Public Opinion in the States: A Quarter Century of Change and Stability," in *Public Opinion in State Politics*, ed. Jeffrey E. Cohen (Stanford, Calif.: Stanford University Press, 2006).

[26] Erikson, Wright, and McIver, *Statehouse Democracy;* and Erikson, Wright, and McIver, "Public Opinion in the States." The role of ideology is so important in many political theories that several groups of political scientists have tried to measure it in the states in a variety of ways. For examples, see William D. Berry, Evan J. Ringquist, Richard C. Fording, and Russell L. Hanson, "Measuring Citizen and Government Ideology in the American States, 1960–93," *American Journal of Political Science* 41 (1998): 327–48; Paul Brace, Kevin Arceneaux, Martin Johnson, and Stacy Ulbig, "Does State Political Ideology Change over Time?" *Political Research Quarterly* 57 (2004): 529–40; Paul Brace, Kellie Sims-Butler, Kevin Arceneaux, and Martin

Johnson, "Public Opinion in the American States: New Perspectives Using National Survey Data," *American Journal of Political Science* 46 (2002): 173–89; Ronald E. Weber and William R. Shaffer, "Public Opinion and American State Policy Making," *Midwest Journal of Political Science* 16 (1972): 633–49; William D. Berry, Evan J. Ringquist, Richard C. Fording, and Russell L. Hanson, "The Measurement and Stability of State Citizen Ideology," *State Politics and Policy Quarterly* 7 (2007): 111–32; and *Cohen, Public Opinion in State Politics.*

[27] Erikson, Wright, and McIver, *Statehouse Democracy;* and Erikson, Wright, and McIver, "Public Opinion in the States."

[28] Barrilleaux, Holbrook, and Langer, "Electoral Competition."

[29] Daniel J. Elazar, *American Federalism: A View from the States,* 3rd ed. (New York: Harper and Row, 1984).

[30] For an example of a political cultural argument informed by Elazar's framework, see Joel Lieske, "Regional Subcultures of the United States," *Journal of Politics* 55 (1993): 888–913.

[31] Barbara Norrander, "Measuring State Public Opinion with the Senate National Election Study," *State Politics and Policy Quarterly* 1 (2001): 111–25.

[32] E. E. Schattschneider, *The Semisovereign People* (New York: Harcourt Brace Jovanovich, 1960).

[33] Christopher Z. Mooney, "'Why Do They Tax Dogs in West Virginia?' Teaching Political Science through Comparative State Politics," *PS: Political Science & Politics* 31 (1998): 199–203.

[34] Janet Buttolph Johnson and H. T. Reynolds, *Political Science Research Methods,* 5th ed. (Washington, D.C.: CQ Press, 2005), 113–23.

[35] Daniel A. Smith and Caroline Tolbert, *Educated by Initiative: The Effects of Direct Democracy on Citizens and Political Organizations* (Ann Arbor: University of Michigan Press, 2004).

Chapter 2

[1] Susan Llewelyn Leach, "A Driver's License as National ID?" *Christian Science Monitor* (January 24, 2005). Available: http://www.csmonitor.com/2005/0124/p11s02-ussc.html; Eric Kelderman, "States' Rebellion at Real ID Echoes in Congress," Stateline.org (May 9, 2007). Available: http://www.stateline.org/live/details/story?contentId=206433.

[2] Ronald Watts, "Federalism, Federal Political Systems, and Federations," *Annual Review of Political Science* 1 (1998): 117–37.

[3] Paul Peterson, *City Limits*. Chicago: University of Chicago Press, 1981, p. 67.

[4] David Walker, *The Rebirth of Federalism*. Chatham, NJ: Chatham House, 1995.

[5] Samuel Beer, *To Make a Nation: The Rediscovery of American Federalism*. Cambridge, MA: Harvard University Press, 1993, pp. 1–2.

[6] James Madison, "The Federalist No. 39: Conformity of the Plan to Republican Principles," *Independent Journal*, Wednesday, January 16, 1788. Available: http://www.constitution.org/fed/federa39.htm.

[7] Morton Grodzins, *The American System*, in Robert Goldwin, ed., *A Nation of States*, Chicago: Rand McNally, 1969; and Morton Grodzins, *The American System*. Chicago: Rand McNally and Company, 1966.

[8] "Democracy Denied: The Racial History and Impact of Disenfranchisement Laws in the United States," *Demos*, April 2003. Available: http://www.demos-usa.org/pubs/FD_-_Brief.pdf.

[9] Christopher Hammons, "Was James Madison Wrong? Rethinking the American Preference for Short, Framework-Oriented Constitutions, *American Political Science Review*, 93 (1999): 837–49.

[10] "Facts about the Death Penalty," *Death Penalty Information Center*, May 25, 2005. Available: http://www.deathpenaltyinfo.org.

[11] Thomas Anton, *American Federalism and Public Policy*, New York: Random House, 1989, p. 3; and Virginia Gray and Peter Eisinger, *American States & Cities*, 2nd ed. New York: Longman, 1997, p. 26.

[12] Michael Goldsmith, "Central Control Over Local Government—A Western European Comparison," *Local Government Studies* 28 (2002): 91–112.

[13] Europa, "Activities of the European Union," Available (June 2005): http://europa.eu.int/pol/index_en.htm.

[14] Daniel Elazar, *American Federalism: A View from the States*. 3rd ed. New York: Harper & Row, 1984; Daniel Elazar, "Contrasting unitary and federal systems," *International Political Science Review* 18 (1997): 237–52.

[15] World Bank, *World Development Report*, Washington, D.C. 1999/2000. Available: http://www.worldbank.org/wdr/2000/.

[16] Charles Tarlton, "Symmetry and Asymmetry as Elements of Federalism: A Theoretical Speculation," *Journal of Politics* 27 (1965): 861–74.

[17] Martha Derthick, "American Federalism: Half-Full or Half-Empty," *The Brookings Review* 18 (2000): 24–7.

[18] Jack Rakove, *Original Meanings: Politics and Ideas in the Making of the Constitution*. New York: Knopf, 1997, p. 168.

[19] Over a span of a few years, a series of Parliamentary acts were handed down from London, including the 1765 Stamp Act, which required the colonies to place revenue stamps on all official documents, the 1767 Townshend Acts, which placed duties on colonial imports, and the 1773 Tea Act, which granted the East India Company a monopoly over export of tea from Britain.

[20] The Articles effectively served for nearly 12 years as the country's first constitution, despite the fact that it was not ratified until March 1781. Merrill Jensen, *The New Nation: A History of the United States during the Confederation: 1781–1789*. New York: Vintage Books, 1950, 18–27.

[21] Letter from George Washington to David Humphreys, October 22, 1786. The George Washington Papers at the Library of Congress, 1741–1799. Available: http://lcweb2.loc.gov/cgi-bin/query/r?ammem/mgw:@field(DOCID+@lit(gw290023)).

[22] David Brian Robertson, "Madison's Opponents and Constitutional Design," *American Political Science Review* 99 (2005): 225–43.

[23] Joseph Ellis, *Founding Brothers: The Revolutionary Generation*. New York: Knopf, 2001.

[24] David Epstein, *The Political Theory of the Federalist*. Chicago: University of Chicago Press, 1984; Frederic Stimson, *The American Constitution as It Protects Private Rights*. New York: Charles Scribner's Sons, 1923.

[25] Jack Rakove, *Original Meanings: Politics and Ideas in the Making of the Constitution*. New York: Knopf, 1997.

[26] Institute of Governmental Studies, "Indian Gaming in California," University of California at Berkeley, 2006. Available: http://www.igs.berkeley.edu/library/htIndianGaming.htm.

[27] David Bogen, *Privileges and Immunities: A Reference Guide to the United States Constitution*. Westport, CT: Praeger, 2003.

[28] Herbert Storing, ed. *The Anti-Federalist: Writings by the Opponents of the Constitution*. Chicago: University of Chicago Press, 1985, p. 1.

[29] Joseph Zimmerman, *Contemporary American Federalism*. Westport, CT: Praeger, 1992.

[30] Joseph Zimmerman, *Congressional Preemption: Regulatory Federalism*. Albany: State University of New York Press, 2005.

[31] Raymond Scheppach, "Federal Preemption: A Serious Threat," August 17, 2004. Available: http://www.Stateline.org.

[32] Quoted in Kenneth Vines, "The Federal Setting of State Politics," in Herbert Jacob and Kenneth Vines, eds., *Politics in the American States*, 3rd ed. Boston: Little, Brown and Company, 1976.

[33] Thomas Dye, *American Federalism: Competition among Governments*. Lexington, MA: Lexington Books Heath, 1990; and D. Kenyon and John Kincaid, eds., *Competition among States and Local Governments: Efficiency and Equity in American Federalism*, Washington, D.C.: The Urban Institute, 1991. See also, William Riker. 1987. *The Development of American Federalism*. Boston: Kluwer Academic Publishers.

[34] Zimmerman, *Contemporary American Federalism*, 1992.

[35] Alexis de Tocqueville, *Democracy in America*. Book 1, chapter 5. Available: http://xroads.virginia.edu/~HYPER/DETOC/home.html.

[36] See Stephen Skowronek, *Building a New American State: The Expansion of National Administrative Capacities, 1877–1920*. Cambridge: Cambridge University Press, 1982.

[37] Daniel J. Elazar, *The American Partnership: Intergovernmental Co-operation in the Nineteenth-Century United States*. Chicago: University of Chicago Press, 1962.

[38] Martha Derthick, "Wither Federalism?" *The Urban Institute*, 2 (1996). Available: http://www.urban.org/UploadedPDF/derthick.pdf.

[39] William E. Leuchtenberg, *Franklin D. Roosevelt and the New Deal, 1932–1940*. Princeton: Princeton University Press, 1963; and Alan Brinkley, *The End of Reform: New Deal Liberalism in Recession and War*. New York: Knopf, 1995.

[40] Elazar, *The American Partnership*, 1962.

[41] Walker, *The Rebirth of Federalism*, 1995.

[42] John Kincaid, "From Dual to Coercive Federalism in American Intergovernmental Relations," in John Jun and Deil Wright, eds., *Globalization and Decentralization*. Washington, D.C.: Georgetown University Press, 1996, pp. 29–47.

[43] Walker, *The Rebirth of Federalism*, 1995, p. 25.

[44] Timothy Conlan, *New Federalism: Intergovernmental Reform from Nixon to Reagan*. Washington, D.C.: Brookings, 1988.

[45] Michael Katz, *The Undeserving Poor: From the War on Poverty to the War on Welfare*. New York: Pantheon, 1989; and James Patterson, *America's Struggle Against Poverty, 1900–1980*. Cambridge: Harvard University Press, 1981.

[46] John Schwarz, *America's Hidden Success: A Reassessment of Public Policy from Kennedy to Reagan*. Revised ed. New York: W.W. Norton 1988, pp. 68–9.

[47] Peter Eisinger, *The Rise of the Entrepreneurial States*. Madison: University of Wisconsin Press, 1988; and David Osborne, *Laboratories of Democracy*, Boston: Harvard Business School Press, 1988.

[48] Alice Rivlin, "The Federal Government in a Federal System: Current Intergovernmental Programs and Options for Change," *Congressional Budget Office*, August 1983. Available: http://www.cbo.gov/showdoc.cfm?index=5067&sequence=0.

[49] Samuel Beer, *To Make a Nation: The Rediscovery of American Federalism*. Cambridge, MA: Harvard University Press, 1993, p. xiii.

[50] Timothy Conlan, *From New Federalism to Devolution: Twenty-Five Years of Intergovernmental Reform*. Washington, D.C.: Brookings, 1998.

[51] American Bar Association Report, "The Federalization of Criminal Law," (February 16, 1999), Available: http://www.abanet.org/crimjust/fedreport.html.

[52] Ann Bowman and George Krause, "Power Shift: Measuring Policy Centralization in U.S. Intergovernmental Relations, 1947–1998," *American Politics Research* 31 (2005): 301–25.

[53] E.J. Dionne and William Kristol, *Bush v. Gore: The Court Cases and the Commentary*. Washington, D.C.: Brookings Institution Press, 2001.

[54] Harry Scheiber, "Federalism and the American Economic Order, 1789–1910," *Law & Society Review* 10 (1975): 57–118.

[55] Carl Swidorski, "The Courts, the Labor Movement and the Struggle for Freedom of Expression and Association, 1919–1940," *Labor History* 45 (2004): 61–84.

[56] James Bryce, *The American Commonwealth* (vol. 2). New York: Macmillian, 1893, pp. 358–59.

[57] Gerald Rosenberg, *The Hollow Hope: Can Courts Bring about Social Change?* Chicago: University of Chicago Press, 1991.

[58] Jean Cohen, "Democracy, Difference and the Right of Privacy," in Seyla Benhabib, *Democracy and Difference: Contesting the Boundaries of the Political.* Princeton, N.J.: Princeton University Press, pp. 187–217.

[59] John Kincaid, "The State and Federal Bills of Rights: Partners and Rivals in Liberty," *Intergovernmental Perspective* 17 (1991): 31–4.

[60] John Pittenger, "Garcia and the Political Safeguards of Federalism: Is There a Better Solution to the Conundrum of the Tenth Amendment?" *Publius* 22 (1992): 1–19.

[61] Cornell Clayton and Howard Gillman, eds., *Supreme Court Decision-Making: New Institutional Approaches.* Chicago: University of Chicago Press, 1999.

[62] Mark Tushnet, *Taking the Constitution Away from the Courts.* Princeton, N.J.: Princeton University Press, 1999.

[63] Sanford Schram and Carol Weissert, "The State of U.S. Federalism: 1998–1999," *Publius: The Journal of Federalism* 29 (1999): 1–34.

[64] Linda Greenhouse, "The Rehnquist Court and Its Imperiled States' Right Legacy," *The New York Times*, June 13, 2005: A3.

[65] Greenhouse, "The Rehnquist Court and Its Imperiled States' Right Legacy," 2005.

[66] Charles Lane, "Court Hears Case on Suicide Law," *The Washington Post*, October 6, 2005: A4.

[67] Charles Lane, "Justices Uphold Oregon Assisted-Suicide Law," *The Washington Post*, January 18, 2006: A1.

[68] Bill of Rights Defense Committee, "Resolutions Passed and Efforts Underway, By State," 2005. Available: http://www.bordc.org/index.php.

[69] Robert Preiss, "The National Guard and Homeland Defense," *Joint Forces Quarterly*, 36 (2005): 72–78. Available: http://www.ngb.army.mil/media/transcripts/Preiss_JFQ_36_article.pdf.

[70] Lawrence Kapp, "Reserve Component Personnel Issues: Questions and Answers," *Congressional Research Service, Library of Congress*, January 10, 2005. Available: http://us.gallerywatch.com/docs/php/US/CRS/RL30802.pdf.

[71] Kavan Peterson, "Governors Lose in Power Struggle over National Guard," *Stateline*, January 12, 2007. Available: http://www.stateline.org/live/details/story?contentId=170453.

[72] Joseph Zimmerman, "Federal Preemption under Reagan's New Federalism," *Publius* 21 (1991): 7–28.

[73] U.S. Office of Management and Budget, "The Budget of the United States Government, Fiscal Year 2006, Historical Tables." Available: http://www.gpoaccess.gov/usbudget/fy06/pdf/hist.pdf.

[74] Karen Mossberger, *The Politics of Ideas and the Spread of Enterprise Zones.* Washington, D.C.: Georgetown University Press, 2000.

[75] Karl Van Horn, *The State of the States.* Washington, D.C.: CQ Press, 1989.

Chapter 3

[1] *BBC News,* "U.S. Mass Protest for Immigrants," 11 April 2006.

[2] See Thomas Jefferson, *Notes on the State of Virginia* (1785); see also John Winthrop, "A Model of Christian Charity" (1630).

[3] See Alexis de Tocqueville, *Democracy in America,* 2 vols. (1835–40). See also Robert Dahl, "The City and the Future of Democracy," *American Political Science Review* 61 (1967).

[4] Participation in local elections is also lower than in national elections elsewhere. For Britain, see Collin Rallings and Michael Thrasher, "Local Electoral Participation in Britain," *Parliamentary Affairs* 65 (2003): 700–15. In the Netherlands, see Henl van de Kolk, "Turnout in Local Elections: Explanations of Individual and Municipal Turnout Differences" (paper presented at the European Consortium for Political Research Joint Workshops, 2003).

[5] Esther Fuchs, Lorraine Minnite, and Robert Shapiro, "Political Capital and Political Participation" (unpublished manuscript).

[6] In 2004, turnout was 56 percent of voting-age population and 60 percent of voting-eligible population. This was the highest level of participation in the United States since 1992.

[7] Stephen Macedo et al., *Democracy at Risk: How Political Choices Undermine Citizen Participation, and What We Can Do about It* (Washington, D.C.: Brookings Institution, 2005).

[8] See, for example, Sidney Verba, Kay Schlozman, and Henry E. Brady, *Voice and Equality: Civic Voluntarism in American Politics* (Cambridge, Mass.: Harvard University Press, 1995).

[9] Verba, Schlozman, and Brady, *Voice and Equality.*

[10] Jan Leighley and Jonathan Nagler, "Socioeconomic Class Bias in Turnout, 1964–1988: The Voters Remain the Same," *American Political Science Review* 86, no. 3 (1992): 725–36; and Jan Leighley and Jonathan Nagler, "Individual and Systemic Influences on Turnout: Who Votes?" *Journal of Politics* 54, no. 3 (1992): 718–40.

[11] Verba, Schlozman, and Brady, *Voice and Equality.*

[12] Zoltan Hanjal and Paul Lewis, "Municipal Institutions and Voter Turnout in Local Elections," *Urban Affairs Quarterly* 38, no. 5 (2003): 654–68.

[13] Eric Plutzer, "Voter Turnout and the Life Cycle: A Latent Growth Curve Analysis" (paper presented at the Midwest Political Science Association meeting, 1997).

[14] Verba, Schlozman, and Brady, *Voice and Equality.*

[15] Elaine Sharp, "Citizen Initiated Contacting of Local Officials and Socio-Economic Status," *American Political Science Review* 76 (1982): 109–15; but see Rodney Hero, "Explaining Citizen-Initiated Contacting of Government Officials," *Social Science Quarterly* 67 (1986): 626–35; and Michael Hirlinger, "Citizen-Initiated Contacting of Local Officials," *Journal of Politics* 54 (1992): 553–64.

[16] Mancur Olson, *The Logic of Collective Action* (1965).

[17] As of January 2000. See Federal Elections Commission, http://www.fec.gov/press/pacchart.htm.

[18] John Logan and Gordana Rabrenovic, "Neighborhood Associations: Their Issues, Their Allies," *Urban Affairs Quarterly* (1990): 2668–94.

[19] Theda Skocpol, Christopher Howard, and Susan Goodrich Lehmann, "Women's Associations and the Enactment of Mothers' Pensions in the United States," *American Political Science Review* 87, no. 3 (1993): 686–701.

[20] Ada Davis, "The Evolution of the Institutions of Mothers Pensions in the United States," *American Journal of Sociology* 35 (1937): 573–87.

[21] National Advisory Commission on Civil Disorders Kerner Commission Report; and Edward Banfield, *Rioting for Fun and Profit.*

[22] There were 20 such riots in 1919 alone. Dennis R. Judd and Todd Swanstrom, *City Politics* (2004).

[23] T. David Mason and Jerry Murtagh, "Who Riots? An Empirical Examination of the 'New Urban Black' versus Social Marginality Thesis," *Political Behavior* 7, no. 4 (2004): 352:73. Also *Social Science Quarterly,* special issue (1969).

[24] Social Benchmark Survey.

[25] Verba, Schlozman, and Brady, *Voice and Equality,* 72.

[26] See Alexander Keyssar, *The Right to Vote: The Contested History of Democracy in the United States* (New York. Basic Books, 2000).

[27] U.S. Department of Justice, http://www.usdoj.gov/crt/voting/intro/intro_c.htm.

[28] Bernard Grofman, Lisa Handley, and Richard G. Niemi, *Minority Representation and the Quest for Voting Equality* (New York: Cambridge Press, 1992).

[29] Chandler Davidson, "The Evolution of Voting Rights Law," in Grofman, Handley, and Niemi, *Minority Representation.*

[30] In *Oregon v. Mitchell* (1970), the U.S. Supreme Court upheld a temporary five-year federal ban on the tests. The ban was made permanent in 1975.

[31] Chandler Davidson and Bernard Grofman, eds., *Quiet Revolution in the South: The Impact of Voting Rights Act 1965–1990* (Princeton, N.J.: Princeton University Press, 1994).

[32] Kim Q. Hill and Jan Leighley, "Racial Diversity, Voter Turnout, and Mobilizing Institutions in the United States," *American Politics Quarterly* 27, no. 3 (1999): 275–95; and Shaun Bowler and Todd Donovan, "State-Level Barriers to Participation" (paper presented at the American Political Science Association meeting, September 2005).

[33] Bowler and Donovan, "State-Level Barriers to Participation."

[34] Leighley and Nagler 1992; Jan Leighley, and Jonathan Nagler. 1992. "Individual and Systemic Influences on Turnout: Who Votes?" *Journal of Politics,* 54, 718–741 and Rosenstone and Wolfinger 1978. "The effect of registration laws on voter turnout" American Political Science Review. 72: 22–45

[35] William Riker, "The Two-Party System and Duverger's Law: An Essay on the History of Political Science," *American Political Science Review* 76, no. 4 (1982): 753–66.

[36] Rob Ritchie, *Monopoly Politics*; and Center for Voting and Democracy.

[37] NCSL report.

[38] Todd Donovan and Shaun Bowler, *Reforming the Republic: Democratic Institutions for the New America* (Upper Saddle River, N.J.: Prentice Hall, 2004).

[39] Over 1 percent of the Texas adult population are felons or ex-felons. The U.S. average is 0.67 percent. See Michael

McDonald, Voter Turnout Project, George Mason University). Ex-felons may vote in Texas but parolees, inmates, and probationers may not. Mississippi and Florida also prevent ex-felons from voting.

[40] See Jeff Manza and Christopher Uggen, *Locked Out: Felon Disenfranchisement and American Democracy* (New York: Oxford University Press, 2005).

[41] Angela Behrens, Christopher Uggen, and Jeff Manza, "Ballot Manipulation and the 'Menace of Negro Domination': Racial Threat and Felon Disenfranchisement in the United States, 1850–2002," *American Journal of Sociology* 109 (2003): 559–605.

[42] Michael P. McDonald and Sam Popkin, "The Myth of the Vanishing Voter," *American Political Science Review* 95 (2000): 963–74.

[43] Analysis from Bowler and Donovan, "State-Level Barriers to Participation."

[44] Walter Dean Burnham, *Critical Elections and the Mainsprings of American Politics* (New York: Norton, 1970), chs. 4–5.

[45] Tari Renner, "The Municipal Election Process: The Impact on Minority Representation," in *The Municipal Yearbook,* ed. International City Managers Association (Washington, D.C.: International City Managers Association, 2005).

[46] Amy Bridges, *Morning Glories* (Princeton, N.J.: Princeton University Press, 1999); and Burnham, *Critical Elections.*

[47] Steven Rosenstone and John Mark Hansen, *Mobilization, Participation and Democracy in America* (New York: Longman, 2003).

[48] Alan S. Gerber and Donald P. Green, "The Effects of Personal Canvassing, Telephone Calls and Direct Mail on Voter Turnout: A Field Experiment," *American Political Science Review* 94, no. 3 (1993): 658.

[49] Robert Putnam, *Bowling Alone* (New York: Simon and Schuster, 2000).

[50] *The New York Times,* 21 September 2003. p. 30.

[51] Amy Bridges, *Morning Glories;* Samuel P. Hays. 1961 "The Politics of Municipal Reform in the Progressive Era." *Pacific Northwest Quarterly;* and Chandler Davidson and George Korbel, "At-Large Elections and Minority Group Representation," *Journal of Politics* 43 (1981): 982–1005.

[52] Paul Kleppner, *Chicago Divided: The Making of a Black Mayor* (DeKalb: Northern Illinois Press, 1985). For a thorough review of the literature and critical analysis of this proposition, see Keith Reeves, *Voting Hopes or Fears: White Voters, Black Candidates and Racial Politics in America* (New York: Oxford University Press, 1997).

[53] Davidson and Grofman, *Quiet Revolution in the South;* 1992; and Richard Engstrom and Michael D. McDonald, "The Election of Blacks to City Councils," *American Political Science Review* 75 (1981): 344–54.

[54] Eric Oliver, "City Size and Civic Involvement in Metropolitan America," *American Political Science Review* 94, no. 2 (2000): 362–63; also see Robert Dahl and Edward Tufte, *Size and Democracy* (1973).

[55] Hanjal and Lewis, "Municipal Institutions and Voter Turnout." Also see Stephen Hansen, Thomas Palfrey, and Howard Rosenthal, "The Downsian Model of Electoral Participation: Formal Theory and Empirical Analysis of the Constituency Size Effect," *Public Choice* 52 (1987): 15–33.

[56] Frank Bryan, *Real Democracy: The New England Town Meeting and How It Works* (Chicago: University of Chicago Press, 2003).

[57] James Coleman, *Foundations of Social Theory* (Cambridge, Mass.: Belknap, 1990); and Putnam, *Bowling Alone.*

[58] Wendy Rahn and Thomas Rudolph, "A Tale of Political Trust in American Cities," *Public Opinion Quarterly* 69 (2005): 530–60.

[59] Putman, *Bowling Alone.*

[60] Social Capital Benchmark Survey; and author's calculations.

[61] James Gimpel and J. E. Schuknecht, "Political Participation and the Accessibility of the Ballot Box," *Political Geography* 22 (2003): 471–88.

[62] Daniel Patrick Moynihan, *Maximum Feasible Misunderstanding: Community Action in the War on Poverty* (New York: Basic Books, 1969).

[63] When the effects of income and education on participation are accounted for, African Americans vote at higher rates than whites. Leighley and Nagler, "Individual and Systemic Influences."

[64] Jeffrey Karp and Susan Banducci, "Absentee Voting, Participation, and Mobilization," *American Politics Research* 29 (2001): 183–95.

[65] J. Eric Oliver, "The Effects of Eligibility Restrictions and Party Activity on Absentee Voting and Overall Turnout," *American Journal of Political Science* 40 (1996): 498–513; and Jeff Karp and Susan Banducci, "Going Postal: How

All Mail Elections Influence Turnout," *Political Behavior* 22 (2000): 223–39. On Internet voting, see R. Michael Alvarez and Jonathan Nagler, "The Likely Consequences of Internet Voting for Political Representation," *Loyola of Los Angeles Law Review* 34:1115–52.

[66] A full extension of this argument can be found in Adam Berinsky, "The Perverse Consequences of Electoral Reform in the United States," *American Politics Research* 33, no. 4 (2005): 471–91.

[67] Andre Blais and Ken Carty, "Does Proportional Representation Foster Voter Turnout?" *European Journal of Political Research* 18. (1990): pp 167–81; and Shaun Bowler, Todd Donovan, and David Brockington, *Election Reform and Minority Representation* (2003).

[68] For a discussion, see Gary Cox and Michael Munger, "Closeness, Expenditures and Turnout in the 1982 US House Election," *American Political Science Review* 83 (1989): 217–31.

[69] V. O. Key Jr., *Southern Politics: In the State and Nation* (New York: Knopf, 1949).

[70] Bowler, Donovan, and Brockington, *Election Reform.*

[71] Lonna Atkeson and Randal Partin, "Economic and Referendum Voting," *American Political Science Review* 89 (1995): 99–107.

[72] Robert Stein, "Economic Voting for Governor and US Senator," *Journal of Politics* 52 (1990): 29–53.

[73] Chandler Davidson and Luis Fraga, "Slating Groups as Parties in a 'Nonpartisan' Setting," *Western Political Quarterly* 41 (1988): 373–390.

[74] Key, *Southern Politics.*

[75] Shaun Bowler, Todd Donovan, and Joseph Snipp, "Local Sources of Information and Voter Choice in State Elections: Micro-Level Foundations of the Friends and Neighbors Effect," *American Politics Quarterly* 21 (1993): 473–89.

[76] Shaun Bowler, Todd Donovan, and Jeffrey Karp, "Why Politicians Like Electoral Institutions: Self-Interest, Values or Ideology," *Journal of Politics* 68, no. 2 (2006): 454.

[77] U.S. Census Bureau, press release, 18 September 2003; and Public Policy Institute of California, "California Voter and Party Profile," June 2004, http://www.naleo.org/press_releases/CA_Profile_02-04_fin.pdf.

[78] Alexandra Marks, "Should Non Citizens Vote?" *Christian Science Monitor,* 27 April 2004.

[79] Robert Erikson, Gerald Wright, and John P. McIver, *Statehouse Democracy: Public Opinion and Policy in the American States* (New York: Cambridge University Press, 1993).

[80] Key, *Southern Politics,* ch. 14, 307. Evidence from the contemporary era suggests the poor get more when Democrats are in power rather than when their party is losing in close competition against Republicans.

[81] Elisabeth Gerber and Rebecca Morton, "Primary Election Systems and Representation," *Journal of Law, Economics and Organizations* 14, no. 2 (1998): 304–24

[82] Elisabeth Gerber, *The Populist Paradox* (Princeton, N.J.: Princeton University Press, 1999); also see John Matsusaka, *For the Many or the Few* (Chicago: University of Chicago Press, 2004).

[83] Raymond Wolfinger and Steven Rosenstone, *Who Votes* (New Haven, Conn.: Yale University Press, 1980); and Sidney Verba, Kay Schlozman, Henry Brady, and Norman Nie, "Citizen Activity: Who Participates? What Do They Say?" *American Political Science Review* (1993): 303–18.

[84] Adam Berinsky, "Silent Voices: Opinion Polls, Social Welfare Policy and Political Equality in America," *American Journal of Political Science* 46 (2002): 276–87.

[85] Frances Fox Piven and Richard A. Cloward, *Why Americans Don't Vote* (New York: Pantheon, 1989); and Walter Dean Burnham, "The Turnout Problem," in *Elections American Style,* ed. A. James Reichley (1987).

[86] Kim Q. Hill and Jan Leighley, "The Policy Consequences of Class Bias in State Electorates," *American Journal of Political Science* 36, no. 2 (1992): 351–65.

[87] Kim Q. Hill, Jan Leighley, and Angela Hinton-Andersson, "Lower-Class Mobilization and Policy Linkages in the U.S. States," *American Journal of Political Science* 39, no. 1 (1998): 75–86.

[88] Coleen Grogan, "Political-Economic Factors Influencing State Medicaid Policy," *Political Research Quarterly* 47, no. 3 (1994): 589–623.

[89] Brian Knight, "Supermajority Vote Requirements for Tax Increases: Evidence from the States," *Journal of Public Economics* 67, no. 1 (2000): 41–67.

[90] Rogers and Rogers 2000; and Timothy Besley and Anne Case, "Political Institutions and Policy Choices: Evidence from the United States," *Journal of Economic Literature* 41, no. 1 (2002): 7–73.

[91] Maurice Klain, "A New Look at the Constituencies: The Need for a Recount and Reappraisal," *American Political Science Review* 49 (1955): 1105–19.

[92] *Baker v. Carr,* 1962; *Reynolds v. Sims,* 1964; and *Wesberry v. Sanders,* 1964.

[93] Malcolm E. Jewell, *Representation in State Legislatures* (Lexington: University of Kentucky Press, 1982); and Gary Moncrief and Joel Thompson, "Electoral Structure and State Legislative Representation," *Journal of Politics* 54 (1992): 246–56.

[94] Lilliard Richardson and Christopher Cooper, "The Mismeasure of MMD: Reassessing the Impact of Multi-Member Districts on the Representation on Descriptive Representation in the United States" (2003).

[95] Engstrom and McDonald, "The Election of Blacks to City Councils."

[96] Anthony Downs, *An Economic Theory of Democracy* (1957); and Gary Cox, "Centripetal and Centrifugal Incentives in Electoral Systems," *American Journal of Political Science* 34 (1990): 903–35.

[97] Lilliard Richardson, Brian Russell, and Christopher Cooper, "Legislative Representation in Single Member versus Multi Member District Systems: The Arizona State Legislature," *Political Research Quarterly* 57 (2004): 337–44.

[98] Greg Adams, "Legislative Effects of Single-Member vs. Multi-Member Districts," *American Journal of Political Science* 40 (1996): 129–44.

[99] Peter Francia and Paul Herrnson, "Begging for Bucks," *Campaigns and Elections,* April 2001.

[100] Kedron Bardwell, "Campaign Finance Laws and the Competition for Spending in Gubernatorial Elections," *Social Science Quarterly* 84, no. 4 (2003): 811–25; and Robert K. Goidel, Donald A. Gross, and Todd G. Shields, *Money Matters: Consequences of Campaign Finance Reform in U.S. House Elections* (Lanham, Md.: Rowman & Littlefield, 1999).

[101] Gary Jacobson, "The Effects of Campaign Spending in House Elections: New Evidence for Old Arguments," *American Journal of Political Science* 34 (1990): 334–62; and Donald Philip Green and Jonathan S. Krasno, "Rebuttal to Jacobson's 'New Evidence for Old Arguments,'" *American Journal of Political Science* 34 (1990): 363–72.

[102] Todd Donovan, Shaun Bowler, and David McCuan, "Political Consultants and the Initiative Industrial Complex," in *Dangerous Democracy?* eds. Sabato, Ernst, and Larson (Lanham, Md.: Rowman & Littlefield, 2001), 127.

[103] Shaun Bowler and Todd Donovan, *Demanding Choices* (Ann Arbor: University of Michigan Press, 1998), 152.

[104] Robert Hogan, "Campaign and Contextual Influences on Voter Participation in State Legislative Elections," *American Politics Review* 27, no. 4 (1999): 403–33.

[105] Francia and Herrnson, "Begging for Bucks."

[106] John Pippen, Shaun Bowler, and Todd Donovan, "Election Reform and Direct Democracy: Campaign Finance Regulation in the American States," *American Politics Quarterly* 30, no. 6 (2002): 559–82.

[107] Donald Gross, Robert Goidel, and Todd Shields, "State Campaign Finance Regulations and Electoral Competition," *American Politics Research* 30, no. 2 (2002): 143–65.

[108] Peter Francia and Paul S. Herrnson, "The Impact of Public Finance Laws on State Legislative Elections," *American Politics Research* 31, no. 5 (2003): 520–39.

[109] Depending on the year, about one-third of Americans fail to identify with either major party, and less than 40 percent of Americans support the idea of maintaining the two-party system (NES data, 2000–02).

[110] Howard J. Gold, "Explaining Third-Party Success in Gubernatorial Elections," *Social Science Journal* 42 (2005): 523–40.

[111] National Conference of State Legislatures, "2006 Partisan Composition of State Legislatures," http://www.ncsl.org/statevote/partycomptable2007.htm.

[112] Wilma Rule and Joseph F. Zimmerman, *United States Electoral Systems: Their Impact on Women and Minorities* (Westport, Conn.: Greenwood Press, 1992).

[113] Miki Caul, "Women's Representation in Parliament: The Role of Political Parties," *Party Politics* 5 (1999): 79–98.

[114] Samantha Sanchez, "Money and Diversity in State Legislatures, 2003" (Helena, Mont.: Institute on Money in State Politics, 2005).

[115] Engstrom and McDonald, "The Election of Blacks to City Councils."

[116] Douglas Massey and Nancy Denton, "Trends in Residential Segregation of Blacks, Hispanics and Asians," *American Sociological Review* 52 (1987): 802–25.

[117] Jerry Polinard, Robert Wrinkle, and Tomas Longoria, "The Impact of District Elections on the Mexican American Community," *Social Science Quarterly* 17, no. 3 (1991): 608–14; Delbert Taebel. 1978. "Minority Representation on City Councils: The Impact of Structure on Blacks and Hispanics." *Social Science Quarterly.* 59: 142-52; A. Velditz and C. Johnson. 1982. "Community Segregation, Electoral

Structure and Minority Representation." *Social Science Quarterly* 67: 729–36.

[118] David Leal, Ken Meier, and Valerie Martinez–Ebers, "The Politics of Latino Education: The Biases of At-Large Elections," *Journal of Politics* 66, no. 4 (2004): 1224.

[119] J. L. Polinard, Robert Wrinkle, Tomas Longoria, and Norman Binder, *Electoral Structure and Urban Policy: The Impact of Mexican American Communities* (New York: M. E. Sharpe, 1994); and Kenneth J. Meier, Eric Gonzalez Juenke, Robert Wrinkle, and J. L. Polinard, "Structural Choices and Representation Biases: The Post-Election Color of Representation," *American Journal of Political Science* 49, no. 4 (2005): pp. 748–749.

[120] Lawrence Bobo and Frank Gilliam Jr., "Race, Sociopolitical Participation and Black Empowerment," *American Political Science Review* (1990): 377–93; Adrian Pantoja and Gary Segura, "Does Ethnicity Matter? Descriptive Representation in Legislatures," *Social Science Quarterly* 84 (2003): 441–60; and Susan Banducci, Todd Donovan, and Jeffrey Karp, "Minority Representation, Empowerment and Participation," *Journal of Politics* 66 (2004): 534.

[121] David Lublin, *The Paradox of Representation: Racial Gerrymandering and Minority Interests in Congress* (Princeton, N.J.: Princeton University Press, 1997).

[122] Sanchez, "Money and Diversity in State Legislatures, 2003," 6.

Chapter 4

[1] Elizabeth Garrett, "Democracy in the Wake of the California Recall," *University of Pennsylvania Law Review* 153 (2004): 239–84; Daniel A. Smith, "Initiatives and Referendums: The Effects of Direct Democracy on Candidate Elections," in *The Electoral Challenge: Theory Meets Practice,* ed. Steven Craig (Washington, D.C.: CQ Press, 2006); and Richard Hasen, "Rethinking the Unconstitutionality of Contribution and Expenditure Limits in Ballot Measure Campaigns," *Southern California Law Review* 78 (2005): 885–926.

[2] John Matsusaka, *For the Many or the Few: The Initiative, Public Policy, and American Democracy* (Chicago: University of Chicago Press, 2004).

[3] David Butler and Austin Ranney, eds., *Referendums around the World: The Growing Use of Direct Democracy* (Washington, D.C.: AEI Press, 1994).

[4] David Magleby, *Direct Legislation: Voting on Ballot Propositions in the United States* (Baltimore: Johns Hopkins University Press, 1984).

[5] A simple majority is usually required for approval, although some states require more. See Richard Ellis, *Democratic Delusions: The Initiative Process in America* (Lawrence: University Press of Kansas, 2002).

[6] Shaun Bowler and Bruce Cain, eds., *Clicker Politics: Essays on the California Recall* (Englewood Cliffs, N.J.: Prentice Hall, 2005).

[7] Magleby, *Direct Legislation.*

[8] Todd Donovan and Shaun Bowler, "Responsible and Representative?" in *Citizens as Legislators: Direct Democracy in the United States,* ed. Shaun Bowler, Todd Donovan, and Caroline Tolbert (Columbus: Ohio State University Press, 1998).

[9] David Schuman, "The Origin of State Constitutional Direct Democracy: William Simon Uren and the Oregon System," *Temple Law Review* 67 (1994); 947–63, 949.

[10] Daniel A. Smith and Caroline J. Tolbert, *Educated by Initiative: The Effects of Direct Democracy on Citizens and Political Organizations in the American States* (Ann Arbor: University of Michigan Press, 2004).

[11] Steven Piott, *Giving Voters a Voice: The Origins of the Initiative and Referendum in America* (Columbia: University of Missouri Press, 2003).

[12] Shaun Bowler, Todd Donovan, and Eric D. Lawrence, "Introducing Direct Democracy" (paper presented at the annual meeting of the American Political Science Association, Washington, D.C., August 2005).

[13] Bruce Cain and Kenneth Miller, "The Populist Legacy: Initiatives and the Undermining of Representative Government," in *Dangerous Democracy? The Battle over Ballot Initiatives in America,* ed. Larry Sabato, Bruce Larson, and Howard Ernst (Lanham, Md.: Rowman & Littlefield, 2002).

[14] Daniel A. Smith, *Tax Crusaders and the Politics of Direct Democracy* (New York: Routledge, 1998); Todd Donovan, Shaun Bowler, David McCuan, and Ken Fernandez, "Contending Players and Strategies: Opposition Advantages in Initiative Elections," in Bowler, Donovan, and Tolbert, *Citizens as Legislators.*

[15] Ellis, *Democratic Delusions.*

[16] David Magleby, "Direct Legislation in America," in Butler and Ranney, *Referendums around the World.*

[17] Caroline J. Tolbert, "Cycles of Democracy: Direct Democracy and Institutional Realignment in the American States," *Political Science Quarterly* 118 (2003): 467–89.

[18] Russell Dalton, Wilhelm Burklin, and Andrew Drummond, "Public Attitudes toward Direct Democracy," *Journal*

of Democracy 12 (2001): 141–53; and Ian Budge, "Political Parties in Direct Democracy," in *Referendum Democracy: Citizens, Elites and Deliberation in Referendum Campaigns,* ed. Matthew Mendelsohn and Andrew Parkin (New York: Palgrave, 2002).

[19] David Magleby, "Direct Legislation in America," in Butler and Ranney, *Referendums around the World.*

[20] David Broder, *Democracy Derailed: Initiative Campaigns and the Power of Money* (New York: Harcourt Brace, 2000); and Sabato, Larson, and Ernst, *Dangerous Democracy?*

[21] Smith, *Tax Crusaders and the Politics of Direct Democracy.*

[22] Gregory B. Lewis, "Same-Sex Marriage and the 2004 Presidential Election," *PS: Political Science and Politics* 38 (2005): 195–200; Daniel A. Smith, Matthew DeSantis, and Jason Kassel, "Same-Sex Marriage Ballot Measures and the 2004 Presidential Election," *State and Local Government Review* 38, no. 2 (2006): 77–90; Alan Abramowitz, "Terrorism, Gay Marriage, and Incumbency: Explaining the Republican Victory in the 2004 Presidential Election," *Forum* 2 (2004): art. 3, http://www.bepress.com/forum/vol2/iss4/art3; Barry Burden, "An Alternative Account of the 2004 Presidential Election," *Forum* 2 (2004): art. 2, http://www.bepress.com/forum/vol2/iss4/art2; and David Campbell and J. Quinn Monson, "The Case of Bush's Re-Election: Did Gay Marriage Do It?" (paper presented at the annual meeting of the Midwest Political Science Association, Chicago, 2005).

[23] Steven P. Nicholson, *Voting the Agenda: Candidates Elections and Ballot Propositions* (Princeton, N.J.: Princeton University Press, 2005).

[24] Daniel A. Smith and Caroline Tolbert, "The Initiative to Party: Partisanship and Ballot Initiatives in California," *Party Politics* 7 (2001): 781–99; and Richard Hasen, "Parties Take the Initiative (and Vice Versa)," *Columbian Law Review* 100 (2001): 731–52.

[25] Jeanne Cummings, "Wedge Issue: Minimum Wage," *Wall Street Journal,* 1 May 2006, p. A4.

[26] Ellis, *Democratic Delusions.*

[27] Shaun Bowler and Todd Donovan, *Demanding Choices: Opinion, Voting, and Direct Democracy* (Ann Arbor: University of Michigan Press, 1998).

[28] Smith and Tolbert, *Educated by Initiative.*

[29] Ballot Initiative Strategy Center, "Election Results 2004," December 2004, http://ballot.org

Shaun Bowler and Todd Donovan, "Measuring the Effect of Direct Democracy on State Policy: Not All Initiatives Are Created Equal," *State Politics and Policy Quarterly* 4 (2004): 345–63.

[31] Caroline Tolbert, Daniel Lowenstein, and Todd Donovan, "Election Law and Rules for Using Initiatives," in Bowler, Donovan, and Tolbert, *Citizens as Legislators.*

[32] Ballot Initiative Strategy Center, "Election Results 2004."

[33] National Conference of State Legislatures, *Initiative and Referendum in the 21st Century: Final Report and Recommendations of the NCSL I&R Task Force,* Denver, Colo., 2000, http://www.ncsl.org/programs/legman/irtaskfc/IandR_report.pdf.

[34] Winston Crouch, *The Initiative and Referendum in California* (Los Angeles: Haynes Foundation, 1950).

[35] Daniel Lowenstein, *Election Law: Cases and Materials* (Durham, N.C.: Carolina Academic Press, 1995), 282.

[36] Ellis, *Democratic Delusions,* 144–46.

[37] For a more detailed discussion of California's initiative process, see California Secretary of State, http://www.ss.ca.gov/elections/elections.htm.

[38] Susan Banducci, "Direct Legislation: When Is It Used and When Does It Pass?" in Bowler, Donovan, and Tolbert, *Citizens as Legislators.*

[39] Charles Beard and Birl Shultz, eds., *Documents on the State-Wide Initiative, Referendum and Recall* (New York: Macmillan, 1912); and David McCuan, Shaun Bowler, Todd Donovan, and Ken Fernandez, "California's Political Warriors: Campaign Professionals and the Initiative Process," in Bowler, Donovan, and Tolbert, *Citizens as Legislators.*

[40] Daniel A. Smith and Joseph Lubinski, "Direct Democracy during the Progressive Era: A Crack in the Populist Veneer?" *Journal of Policy History* 14, no. 4 (2002): 349–83.

[41] Broder, *Democracy Derailed;* Peter Schrag, *Paradise Lost: California's Experience, America's Future* (New York: New Press, 1998); John Haskell, *Direct Democracy or Representative Government? Dispelling the Populist Myth* (Boulder, Colo.: Westview, 2001); and Ellis, *Democratic Delusions.*

[42] National Conference of State Legislatures, *Initiative and Referendum in the 21st Century.*

[43] *Meyer v. Grant* 486 U.S. 414 (1988).

[44] Daniel A. Smith, "Special Interests and Direct Democracy: An Historical Glance," in *The Battle over Citizen*

Lawmaking, ed. M. Dane Waters (Durham: University Press of North Carolina, 2001).

[45] Schrag, *Paradise Lost;* and David Magleby and Kelly Patterson, "Consultants and Direct Democracy," *PS: Political Science and Politics* 31 (1998): 160–62.

[46] Shaun Bowler, Todd Donovan, Max Neiman, and Johnny Peel, "Institutional Threat and Partisan Outcomes: Legislative Candidates' Attitudes toward Direct Democracy," *State Politics & Policy Quarterly* 1 (2001): 364–79.

[47] Smith, "Initiatives and Referendums."

[48] Magleby and Patterson, "Consultants and Direct Democracy."

[49] Schrag, *Paradise Lost,* 16.

[50] Todd Donovan, Shaun Bowler, and Dave McCuan, "Political Consultants and the Initiative Industrial Complex." [In S. Bowler, T. Donovan, and C. Tolbert (eds.) Citizens as Legislators. Columbus, OH: Ohio State University Press]

[51] Daniel A. Smith, "Money Talks: Ballot Initiative Spending in 2004," Ballot Initiative Strategy Center Foundation, Washington, D.C., May 2006, http://www.ballot.org.

[52] Smith, "Money Talks."

[53] *Buckley v. Valeo* 424 U.S. 1 (1976).

[54] *First National Bank of Boston v. Bellotti* 435 U.S. 765 (1978); and Daniel A. Smith, "Campaign Financing of Ballot Initiatives in the American States," in Sabato, Larson, and Ernst, *Dangerous Democracy?*

[55] Tolbert, Lowenstein, and Donovan, "Election Law and Rules for Using Initiatives."

[56] For variants of this argument, David Broder, *Democracy Derailed;* Schrag, *Paradise Lost;* and Smith, *Tax Crusaders and the Politics of Direct Democracy.*

[57] Elizabeth Gerber, *The Populist Paradox: Interest Group Influence and the Promise of Direct Legislation* (Princeton, N.J.: Princeton University Press, 1999), 69–71.

[58] Gerber, *The Populist Paradox,* 110.

[59] Elizabeth Gerber, "Interest Group Influence in the California Initiative Process," Public Policy Institute of California Report, November 1998, http://www.ppic.org/content/pubs/R_1198EGR.pdf.

[60] Arthur Lupia, "Shortcuts versus Encyclopedias: Information and Voting Behavior in California Insurance Reform Elections," *American Political Science Review* 88 (1994): 63–76.

[61] Smith, "Money Talks."

[62] Banducci, "Direct Legislation."

[63] Magleby, *Direct Legislation;* and Bowler and Donovan, *Demanding Choices.*

[64] Gerber, *The Populist Paradox,* 18–19; and Donovan, Bowler, McCuan, and Fernandez, "Contending Players and Strategies," 90.

[65] Bowler and Donovan, *Demanding Choices.*

[66] Arthur Lupia, "Dumber than Chimps? An Assessment of Direct Democracy Voters," in Sabato, Larson, and Ernst, *Dangerous Democracy?*

[67] Arthur Lupia and Matthew McCubbins, *The Democratic Dilemma: Can Citizens Learn What They Need to Know?* (New York: Cambridge University Press, 1998); Lupia, "Shortcuts versus Encyclopedias"; and Bowler and Donovan, *Demanding Choices.*

[68] Smith and Tolbert, "The Initiative to Party"; and Regina Branton, "Examining Individual-Level Voting Behavior on State Ballot Propositions," *Political Research Quarterly* 56 (2003): 367–77.

[69] Bowler, Donovan, Neiman, and Peel, "Institutional Threat and Partisan Outcomes," 370.

[70] Shaun Bowler and Todd Donovan, "Do Voters Have a Cue? TV Ads as a Source of Information in Referendum Voting," *European Journal of Political Research* 41 (2002): 777–93.

[71] Bowler and Donovan, "Do Voters Have a Cue?"

[72] Mark Smith, "Ballot Initiatives and the Democratic Citizen," *Journal of Politics* 64 (2002): 892–903.

[73] Bowler and Donovan, *Demanding Choices.*

[74] Smith and Tolbert, *Educated by Initiative.*

[75] Smith, "Initiatives and Referendums."

[76] Smith and Tolbert, "The Initiative to Party."

[77] Caroline J. Tolbert, John Grummel, and Daniel A. Smith, "The Effect of Ballot Initiatives on Voter Turnout in the American States," *American Politics Research* 29 (2001): 625–48.

[78] John Allswang, *The Initiative and Referendum in California, 1898–1998* (Stanford, Calif.: Stanford University Press, 2000): 125–26.

[79] Steven P. Nicholson, *Voting the Agenda: Candidates Elections and Ballot Propositions* (Princeton, N.J.: Princeton University Press, 2005), 111, 124.

[80] Jame Dao, "Flush with Victory, Grass-Roots Crusader against Same-Sex Marriage Thinks Big," *The New York Times,* 26 November 2004, p. A28.

[81] Todd Donovan, Caroline Tolbert, and Daniel Smith, "Do State-Level Ballot Measures Affect Presidential Elections?" (paper presented at the annual meeting of the American Political Science Association, Washington, D.C., August 2005); Sunshine Hillygus and Todd Shields, "Moral Issues and Voter Decision Making in the 2004 Presidential Election," *PS: Political Science and Politics* 38 (2005): 201–10; Smith, DeSantis, and Kassel, "Same-Sex Marriage Ballot Measures"; Burden, "An Alternative Account of the 2004 Presidential Election"; and Abramowitz, "Terrorism, Gay Marriage, and Incumbency."

[82] Magleby, *Direct Legislation,* 197.

[83] Tolbert, Grummel, and Smith, "The Effect of Ballot Initiatives on Voter Turnout in the American States."

[84] Mark Smith, "The Contingent Effects of Ballot Initiatives and Candidate Races on Turnout," *American Journal of Political Science* 45 (2001): 700–6.

[85] Zoltan Hajnal and Paul Lewis, "Municipal Institutions and Voter Turnout in Local Elections," *Urban Affairs Review* 35 (2003): 645–68.

[86] Smith and Tolbert, "The Initiative to Party."

[87] Smith and Tolbert, *Educated by Initiative.*

[88] Frederick Boehmke, "The Effect of Direct Democracy on the Size and Diversity of State Interest Group Populations," *Journal of Politics* 64 (2002): 827–44.

[89] Smith and Tolbert, *Educated by Initiative.*

[90] Smith, "Ballot Initiatives and the Democratic Citizen."

[91] Caroline J. Tolbert, Ramona McNeal, and Daniel A. Smith, "Enhancing Civic Engagement: The Effect of Direct Democracy on Political Participation and Knowledge," *State Politics and Policy Quarterly* 3 (2003): 23–41.

[92] Shaun Bowler and Todd Donovan, "Democracy, Institutions and Attitudes about Citizen Influence on Government," *British Journal of Political Science* 32 (2002): 371–90.

[93] Bruno Frey and L. Goette, "Does the Popular Vote Destroy Civil Rights?" *American Journal of Political Science* 41 (1998): 245–69; and Matthias Benz and Alois Stutzer, "Are Voters Better Informed When They Have a Larger Say in Politics?" *Public Choice* 119 (2004): 31–59.

[94] See, for example, Lydia Chavez, *The Color Bind: California's Battle to End Affirmative Action* (Berkeley: University of California Press, 1998); Barbara Gamble, "Putting Civil Rights to a Popular Vote," *American Journal of Political Science* 41 (1998): 245–69; and Rodney Hero and Caroline Tolbert, "A Racial/Ethnic Diversity In-

terpretation of Politics and Policy in the States of the U.S.," *American Journal of Political Science* 40 (1996): 851–71.

[95] Chavez, *The Color Bind.*

[96] Jack Citrin, Beth Reingold, Evelyn Walters, and Donald Green, "The 'Official English' Movement and the Symbolic Politics of Language in the United States," *Western Political Quarterly* 43 (1990): 535–60.

[97] Donald Haider-Markel, "AIDS and Gay Civil Rights: Politics and Policy at the Ballot Box," *American Review of Politics* 20 (1999): 349–75; and Todd Donovan, James Wenzel, and Shaun Bowler, "Direct Democracy Initiatives after *Romer,*" in *The Politics of Gay Rights,* eds. Craig Zimmerman, Ken Wald, and Clyde Wilcox (Chicago: University of Chicago Press, 2000).

[98] Roger Caves, *Land Use Planning: The Ballot Box Revolution* (Newbury Park, Calif.: Sage, 1992).

[99] Cain and Miller, "The Populist Legacy," in Sabato, Larson, and Ernst, *Dangerous Democracy?* 52.

[100] Zoltan Hajnal, Elisabeth Gerber, and H. Louch, "Minorities and Direct Legislation: Evidence from California Ballot Proposition Elections," *Journal of Politics* 64 (2002): 154–77.

[101] Donovan, Wenzel, and Bowler, "Direct Democracy Initiatives after *Romer.*"

[102] *Romer v. Evans* 517 U.S. 620 (1996).

[103] Kenneth Miller, "Constraining Populism: The Real Challenge of Initiative Reform," *Santa Clara Law Review* 41 (2001): 1037–84; and Bowler and Donovan, *Demanding Choices.*

[104] Donovan, Wenzel, and Bowler, "Direct Democracy and Minorities."

[105] The exception is Louisiana. Caroline Tolbert, "Changing Rules for State Legislatures: Direct Democracy and Governance Policies," in Bowler, Donovan, and Tolbert, *Citizens as Legislators;* and Bowler and Donovan, "Measuring the Effect of Direct Democracy on State Policy."

[106] Gerber, *The Populist Paradox.*

[107] Thomas Romer and Howard Rosenthal, "Bureaucrats versus Voters: On the Political Economy of Resource Allocation by Direct Democracy," *Quarterly Journal of Economics* 93 (1979): 563–87.

[108] Kevin Arceneaux, "Direct Democracy and the Link between Public Opinion and State Abortion Policy," *State Politics and Policy Quarterly* 2 (2002): 372–87; Elisabeth Gerber, "Legislative Response to the Threat of Popular Initiatives," *American Journal of Political Science* 40

(1996): 99–128; Gerber, *The Populist Paradox;* Matsusaka, *For the Many or the Few;* and Bowler and Donovan, "Measuring the Effect of Direct Democracy on State Policy."

[109] Michael Hagen, Edward Lascher, and John Camobreco, "Response to Matsusaka: Estimating the Effect of Ballot Initiatives on Policy Responsiveness," *Journal of Politics* 63 (2001): 1257–63; and John Camobreco, "Preferences, Fiscal Policies, and the Initiative Process," *Journal of Politics* 60 (1998): 819–29.

[110] Tolbert, "Changing Rules for State Legislatures."

[111.] John Pippen, Shaun Bowler, and Todd Donovan, "Election Reform and Direct Democracy: The Case of Campaign Finance Regulations in the American States," *American Politics Research* 30 (2002): 559–82.

[112] Elisabeth Gerber, Arthur Lupia, Mathew McCubbins, and Roderick Kiewiet, *Stealing the Initiative* (Upper Saddle River, N.J.: Prentice Hall, 2001), 110.

[113] Miller, "Constraining Populism."

[114] Alan Rosenthal, *The Decline of Representative Government* (Washington D.C.: CQ Press, 1998).

[115] Broder, *Democracy Derailed;* also see Schrag, *Paradise Lost.*

[116] Shaun Bowler and Todd Donovan, "Reasoning about Institutional Change: Winners, Losers and Support for Electoral Reform," *British Journal of Political Science* (forthcoming).

[117] Bowler, Donovan, Neiman, and Peel, "Institutional Threat and Partisan Outcomes."

[118] Craig Holman, "An Assessment of New Jersey's Proposed Limited Initiative Process," Brennan Center for Justice at New York University School of Law, 2002, http://www.iandrinstitute.org/New%20IRI%20Website%20Info/I&R%20Research%20and%20History/I&R%20Studies/Holman%20-%20Review%20of%20Proposed%20NJ%20Initiative%20Process%20IRI.pdf.

[119] For a summary of these arguments, see Smith and Tolbert, *Educated by Initiative.*

[120] Gamble, "Putting Civil Rights to a Popular Vote."

[121] Schrag, *Paradise Lost,* 226.

[122] Smith, *Tax Crusaders and the Politics of Direct Democracy.*

[123] Bowler, Donovan, Neiman, and Peel, "Institutional Threat and Partisan Outcomes."

[124] Waters, *The Battle over Citizen Lawmaking.*

[125] *Meyer v. Grant* 486 U.S. 414 (1988).

[126] Smith, "Campaign Financing of Ballot Initiatives in the American States."

[127] National Conference of State Legislatures, *Initiative and Referendum in the 21st Century.*

[128] Elisabeth Gerber and Arthur Lupia, "Campaign Competition and Policy Responsiveness in Direct Political Behavior," *Political Behavior* 17 (1995): 287–306.

[129] Holman, "An Assessment of New Jersey's Proposed Limited Initiative Process."

[130] Shaun Bowler, Todd Donovan, and Jeffrey Karp, "Why Politicians Like Electoral Institutions: Self-Interest, Values, or Ideology?" *Journal of Politics* 68 (2006): 434–46.

Chapter 5

[1] Gary Robertson, "Legislative Candidates Run Unopposed," *Sacramento Bee,* 27 October 2006, http://dwb.sacbee.com/24hour/politics/election/state_local/story/3404323p-12511215c.html.

[2] Sarah Morehouse and Malcolm Jewell, *State Politics, Parties, and Policy,* 2nd ed. (Boulder, Colo.: Rowman & Littlefield, 2003), 15.

[3] David Hedge, *Governance and the Changing American States* (Boulder, Colo.: Westview, 1998).

[4] John Bibby and Thomas Holbrook, "Parties and Elections," in *Politics in the American States: A Comparative Analysis,* 8th ed., eds. Virginia Gray and Russell Hanson (Washington, D.C.: CQ Press, 2004).

[5] John Coleman, "Responsible, Functional, or Both? American Political Parties and the APSA Report after Fifty Years," in *The State of the Parties: The Changing Role of Contemporary American Parties,* 4th ed., eds. John Green and Rick Farmer (Lanham, Md.: Rowman & Littlefield, 2003).

[6] Edmund Burke, *Select Works of Edmund Burke: A New Imprint of the Payne Edition,* vol. 1 (Indianapolis, Ind.: Liberty Fund, 1999), 150.

[7] Richard Hofstadter, *The Idea of a Party System: The Rise of Legitimate Opposition in the United States, 1780–1840* (Berkeley: University of California Press, 1969).

[8] John Gerring, *Party Ideologies in America, 1828–1996* (Cambridge: Cambridge University Press, 2001).

[9] Geoffrey C. Layman, Thomas M. Carsey, and Juliana Menasce Horowitz, "Party Polarization in American Politics: Characteristics, Causes, and Consequences," *Annual Review of Political Science* 9 (June 2006): 67–81; and Gary Miller and Norman Schofield, "Activists and Partisan Realignment in the United States," *American Political Science Review* 97 (May 2003): 245–60.

[10] Anson Morse, "What Is a Party?" *Political Science Quarterly* 11 (1896): 68–81, 74.

[11] Anthony Downs, *An Economic Theory of Democracy* (New York: Harper, 1957): 25.

[12] Leon Epstein, *Political Parties in Western Democracies* (New York: Praeger, 1967).

[13] Leon Epstein, *Political Parties in the American Mold* (Madison: University of Wisconsin Press, 1986): 25.

[14] Sandy Maisel, "Political Parties at the Century's End," in *The Parties Respond,* 2nd ed., ed. Sandy Maisel (Boulder, Colo.: Westview, 1994): 383.

[15] E. E. Schattschneider, *Party Government* (New York: Holt, Rinehart & Winston, 1942): 1.

[16] Walter Dean Burnham, *Critical Elections and the Mainsprings of American Politics* (New York: Norton, 1970); and Seymour Martin Lipset, "The Indispensability of Political Parties," *Journal of Democracy* 11 (2000): 48–55.

[17] George Washington, "Farewell Address," 1796, http://usinfo.state.gov/usa/infousa/facts/democrac/49htm.

[18] Joseph Schlesinger, "The New American Political Party," *American Political Science Review* 79 (1985): 1152–69; and John Aldrich, *Why Parties? The Origin and Transformation of Party Politics in America* (Chicago: University of Chicago Press, 1995).

[19] Epstein, *Political Parties in the American Mold,* 155–99.

[20] V. O. Key, *Southern Politics in the State and Nation* (New York: Knopf, 1949).

[21] Bibby and Holbrook, "Parties and Elections."

[22] David Ryden, *The Constitution, Interest Groups, and Political Parties* (Albany: State University of New York Press, 1996).

[23] Sandy Maisel and John Bibby, "Power, Money, and Responsibility in the Major American Parties," in *Responsible Partisanship? The Evolution of American Political Parties since 1950,* eds. John Green and Paul Herrnson (Lawrence: University Press of Kansas, 2002).

[24] Lisa Disch, *The Tyranny of the Two-Party System* (New York: Columbia University Press, 2002).

[25] Bruce Cain and Megan Mullin, "Competing for Attention and Votes: The Role of State Parties in Setting Presidential Nomination Rules," in Maisel, *The Parties Respond.*

[26] National Conference of State Legislatures, "Presidential Primaries," http://ncsl.org/programs/legman/elect/Changing-EliminatingPP.htm.

[27] Rebecca Morton, *Analyzing Elections* (New York: Norton, 2006).

[28] Morehouse and Jewell, *State Politics, Parties and Policy,* 113.

[29] Argersinger, "A Place at the Table'," *American Historical Review* 85 (1980): 287–306.

[30] Joel Rodgers, "Pull the Plug," *Administrative Law Review* 52 (2000): 743–68; and David Dulio and James Thurber, "America's Two-Party System: Friend or Foe?" *Administrative Law Review* 52 (2000): 769–92.

[31] Richard Winger, "The Importance of Ballot Access," 1994, http://www.ballot-access.org/winger/iba.html.

[32] Richard Winger, "What Are Ballots For?" 1988, http://www.ballot-access.org/winger/wabf.html.

[33] Todd Donovan, Janine Parry, and Shaun Bowler, "O Other, Where Art Thou: Support for Multi-Party Politics in the US," *Social Science Quarterly* 86 (2005): 147–59.

[34] Elisabeth Gerber and Rebecca Morton, "Primary Election Systems and Representation," *Journal of Law, Economics, and Organization* 14 (1998): 304–24.

[35] V. O. Key, *Politics, Parties, and Pressure Groups,* 5th ed. (New York: Thomas Y. Crowell, 1964): 163–65.

[36] J. P. Monroe, *The Political Party Matrix: The Resistance of Organization* (Albany: State University of New York Press, 2001).

[37] Donald Green, Bradley Palmquest, and Eric Schickler, *Partisan Hearts and Minds: Political Parties and the Social Identities of Voters* (New Haven, Conn.: Yale University Press, 2002).

[38] Morris Fiorina, *Retrospective Voting in American National Elections* (New Haven, Conn.: Yale University Press, 1981).

[39] Robert Erikson, Michael MacKuen, and James Stimson, *The Macro Polity* (New York: Cambridge University Press, 2002); and Alan Abramowitz and Kyle Saunders, "Ideological Realignment in the U.S. Electorate," *Journal of Politics* 60 (1998): 634–52.

[40] See William Berry et al., "Measuring Citizen and Government Ideology in the American States," *American Jour-*

nal of Political Science 42 (1998): 327–48; Gerald Wright, Robert Erikson, and John McIver, "Measuring State Partisanship and Ideology with Survey Data," *Journal of Politics* 47 (1985): 469–89; Barbara Norrander, "Measuring State Public Opinion with the Senate National Election Study," *State Politics and Policy Quarterly* 1 (2001): 111–25; Paul Brace et al., "Public Opinion in the American States: New Perspectives Using National Data," *American Journal of Political Science* 46 (2002): 173–89; and Thomas Carsey and Geoffrey Layman, "Party Polarization and 'Conflict Extension' in the American Electorate," *American Journal of Political Science* 46 (2002): 786–802.

[41] Wright, Erikson, and McIver, "Measuring State Partisanship and Ideology."

[42] Downs, *An Economic Theory of Democracy*; and Thomas Dye, "Party and Policy in the States," *Journal of Politics* 46 (1984): 1097–116.

[43] Martin Wattenberg, *Where Have All the Voters Gone?* (Cambridge, Mass.: Harvard University Press, 2002); and Thomas Patterson, *The Vanishing Voter: Public Involvement in an Age of Uncertainty* (New York: Knopf, 2002).

[44] Kim Hill and Jan Leighley, "Party Ideology, Organization, and Competitiveness as Mobilizing Forces in American Democracy," *American Journal of Political Science* 37 (1993): 1158–78.

[45] Matthew Crenson and Benjamin Ginsberg, *Downsizing Democracy: How America Sidelined Its Citizens and Privatized Its Public* (Baltimore: Johns Hopkins University Press, 2002); and Peter Francia et al., "The Battle for the Legislature: Party Campaigning in State House and State Senate Elections," in Green and Farmer, *The State of the Parties.*

[46] Francis Fox Piven and Richard Cloward, *Why Americans Still Don't Vote: And Why Politicians Want It That Way* (Boston: Beacon Press, 2000); and Steven Schier, *By Invitation Only: The Rise of Exclusive Politics in the United States* (Pittsburgh, Pa.: University of Pittsburgh Press, 2000).

[47] John Bibby, "Party Networks: National-State Integration, Allied Groups, and Issue Activists," in *The State of the Parties: The Changing Role of Contemporary Parties,* 3rd ed., eds. John Green and Daniel Shea (New York: Rowman & Littlefield, 1999).

[48] Schlesinger, "The New American Political Party."

[49] Raymond La Raja, "State Political Parties after BCRA," in *Life after Reform,* ed. Michael Malbin (Boulder, Colo.: Rowman & Littlefield, 2003).

[50] J. P. Monroe, *The Political Party Matrix* (Albany: State University of New York Press, 2001).

[51] Anthony Corrado, "Money and Politics: A History of Federal Campaign Finance Law," in *A New Campaign Finance Sourcebook,* ed. Anthony Corrado et al. (Washington, D.C.: Brookings Institution, 2003).

[52] Joel Silbey, "Beyond Realignment and Realignment Theory: American Political Eras, 1789–1989," in *The End of Realignment? Interpreting American Electoral Eras,* ed. Byron Shafer (Madison: University of Wisconsin Press, 1991).

[53] David Broder, *The Party's Over: The Failure of Politics in America* (New York: Harper & Row, 1972); and Wattenberg, *Where Have All the Voters Gone?*

[54] Joel Silbey, *The American Political Nation, 1838–1893* (Stanford, Calif.: Stanford University Press, 1991).

[55] Cornelius Cotter, James L. Gibson, John F. Bibby, and Robert J. Huckshorn, *Party Organizations in American Politics* (New Brunswick, N.J.: Eagleton Institute of Politics, Rutgers University, 1984).

[56] Paul Herrnson, "Do Parties Make a Difference? The Role of Party Organizations in Congressional Elections," *Journal of Politics* 48 (1986): 589–613; and Xandra Kayden and Eddie Mahe, *The Party Goes On: The Persistence of the Two Party System in the United States* (New York: Basic Books, 1985).

[57] John Aldrich et al., "Challenges to the American Two-Party System: Evidence from the 1968, 1980, 1992, and 1996 Presidential Elections," *Political Research Quarterly* 53 (2000): 495–522; and Morehouse and Jewell, *State Politics, Parties, and Policy.*

[58] David Mayhew, *Placing Parties in American Politics: Organization, Electoral Settings, and Government Activity in the Twentieth Century* (Princeton, N.J.: Princeton University Press, 1986), 19–20.

[59] Sarah Morehouse, *The Governor as Party Leader: Campaigning and Governing* (Ann Arbor: University of Michigan Press, 1998).

[60] See, for example, James Gibson et al., "Assessing Party Organizational Strength," *American Journal of Political Science* 27 (1983): 193–222; James Gibson, John Frendreis, and Laura Vertz, "Party Dynamics in the 1980s: Changes in County Party Organizational Strength 1980–1984," *American Journal of Political Science* 33 (1989): 67–90; and Robert Huckshorn et al., "Party Integration and Party Organizational Strength," *Journal of Politics* 48 (1986): 976–91.

[61] Daniel Coffey, "Measuring Gubernatorial Ideology: A Content Analysis of State of the State Speeches," *State Politics and Policy Quarterly* 5 (2005): 88–103. See also

John Coleman, "Party Organizational Strength and Public Support for Parties," *American Journal of Political Science* 40 (1996): 805–24.

[62] Center for Responsive Government, "Contributions Limits on State Party Committees," 2002, http://www.publicintegrity.org/partylines/overview.aspx?act=cl.

[63] Raymond La Raja, Susan Orr, and Daniel Smith, "Surviving BCRA: State Party Finance in 2004," in *The State of the Parties,* 5th ed., eds. John Green and Daniel Coffey (Boulder, Colo.: Rowman & Littlefield, 2006).

[64] *McConnell v. Federal Election Commission,* 540 U.S., 2003 U.S. Lexis 9195 (2003).

[65] The term *soft money* was originally used in 1983 to describe "largely unregulated and unlimited nonfederal money raised by political parties that fall outside FECA limitations"; Diane Dwyre and Robin Kolodny, "Throwing out the Rule Book: Party Financing of the 2000 Elections," in *Financing the 2000 Election,* ed. David B. Magleby (Washington, D.C.: Brookings Institution Press, 2002): 142.

[66] Bibby and Holbrook, "Parties and Elections."

[67] Ruth Jones, "State Public Campaign Finance: Implications for Partisan Politics," *American Journal of Political Science* 25 (1981): 342–61; Ray La Raja, "Political Parties in the Era of Soft Money," in Maisel, *The Parties Respond;* Ray La Raja, "State Parties and Soft Money: How Much Party Building?" in Green and Farmer, *The State of the Parties;* and Sarah Morehouse and Malcolm Jewell, "State Parties: Independent Partners in the Money Relationship," in Green and Farmer, *The State of the Parties.*

[68] La Raja, Orr, and Smith, "Surviving BCRA."

[69] Theodore Lowi and Joseph Romance, *A Republic of Parties? Debating the Two-Party System?* (Lanham, Md.: Rowman & Littlefield, 1998).

[70] V. O. Key, *The Responsible Electorate: Rationality in Presidential Voting, 1936–1960* (Cambridge, Mass.: Harvard University Press, 1966).

[71] Schattschneider, *Party Government.*

[72] National Conference of State Legislatures, "2006 Partisan Composition of State Legislatures," http://www.ncsl.org/statevote/partycomptable2007htm.

[73] Austin Ranney, "Parties in State Politics," in *Politics in the American States,* eds. Herbert Jacobs and Kenneth N. Vines (Boston: Little, Brown, 1965). See also James King, "Inter-Party Competition in the American States: An Examination of Index Components," *Western Political Quarterly* 42 (1989): 83–92; and Thomas Holbrook and Emily Van Dunk, "Electoral Competition in the American States," *American Political Science Review* 87 (1993): 955–62.

[74] Morehouse and Jewell, *State Politics, Parties, and Policy,* 109.

[75] Bibby and Holbrook, "Parties and Elections."

[76] James Garand, "Partisan Change and Shifting Expenditure Priorities in the American States, 1945–1978," *American Politics Quarterly* (October 1985): 355–91; and Morehouse and Jewell, *State Politics, Parties, and Policy,* 50.

[77] Holbrook and Van Dunk, "Electoral Competition in the American States"; Charles Barrilleux, "Party Strength, Party Change, and Policymaking in the American States," *Party Politics* 6 (2000): 61–73; Charles Barrilleux, "A Test of the Independent Influences of Inter-Party Electoral Competition and Party Strength on State Policy," *American Journal of Political Science* 41 (1997): 1462–66; Charles Barrilleux, Thomas Holbrook, and Laura Langer, "Electoral Competition, Legislative Balance, and American State Welfare Policy," *American Journal of Political Science* 46 (2002): 415–27; and James Alt and Robert Lowry, "Divided Government, Fiscal Institutions and Budget Deficits: Evidence from the States," *American Political Science Review* 88 (1994): 811–28.

[78] Calculations derived from Morehouse and Jewell, *State Politics, Parties, and Policy,* table 2.1.

[79] Daniel Smith, "Initiatives and Referendums: The Effects of Direct Democracy on Candidate Elections," in *The Electoral Challenge: Theory Meets Practice,* ed. Steven Craig (Washington, D.C.: CQ Press, 2006).

[80] Peter Schrag, *Paradise Lost: California's Experience, America's Future* (New York: New Press, 1998), 226

[81] Daniel Smith and Caroline Tolbert, "The Initiative to Party: Partisanship and Ballot Initiatives in California," *Party Politics* 7 (2001): 739–57.

[82] John Bibby and Sandy Maisel, *Two Parties—or More?* 2nd ed. (Boulder, Colo.: Westview, 2002).

[83] Richard Niemi and Paul Herrnson, "Beyond the Butterfly: The Complexity of U.S. Ballots," *Perspectives on Politics* 1 (2003): 317–26.

[84] David Kimball, Chris T. Owens, and Katherine M. Keeney, "Residual Votes and Political Representation," in *Counting Votes: Lessons from the 2000 Presidential Election in Florida,* ed. Robert Watson (Gainesville: University Press of Florida, 2004).

[85] Steven Rosenstone, Roy Behr, and Edward Lazarus, *Third Parties in America: Citizen Response to Major Party*

Failure, 2nd ed. (Princeton, N.J.: Princeton University Press, 1996).

Chapter 6

[1] Michael Shear, "Va. Growth Bolstered by Well-Funded Voting Bloc," *Washington Post,* 30 January 2006, p. B1.

[2] Jeffrey Berry, *The New Liberalism: The Rising Power of Citizen Groups* (Washington, D.C.: Brookings Institution Press, 1997), 19.

[3] Alexis de Tocqueville, *Democracy in America,* vol. 2, bk. 2 (1835–40).

[4] Robert Dahl, *Who Governs?* (New Haven, Conn.: Yale University Press, 1961).

[5] Peter Bachrach and Morton S. Baratz, "Two Faces of Power," *American Political Science Review* 56 (1962): 947–52.

[6] James Madison, *The Federalist No. 10,* 1788, http://www.constitution.org/fed/federa10.htm.

[7] David Truman, *The Governmental Process* (New York: Alfred A. Knopf, 1951), 502–11. For a formal model showing how unorganized interests may be afforded representation, see Arthur T. Denzau and Michael C. Munger, "Legislators and Interest Groups: How Unorganized Interests Get Represented," American Political Science Review 80 (1986): 89–106.

[8] See David Lowery and Holly Brasher, *Organized Interests and American Government* (Boston: McGraw Hill, 2003). Lowery and Brasher argue that a neopluralist approach provides a "middle ground" and that "under specific conditions, the world of interest organization politics might appear consistent with either [of the] other two perspectives." For a classic neopluralist approach to interest groups, see John P. Heinz, Edward Laumann, Robert L. Nelson, and Robert Salisbury, *The Hollow Core* (Cambridge, Mass.: Harvard University Press, 1993).

[9] E. E. Schattschneider, *The Semisovereign People* (New York: Holt, Rinehart & Winston, 1960).

[10] Charles Lindblom, "Market as Prison," *Journal of Politics* 44 (1982): 324–36.

[11] Madison, *The Federalist No. 10.*

[12] David Lowery and Virginia Gray, "Bias in the Heavenly Chorus: Interests in Society and before Government," *Journal of Theoretical Politics* 16 (2004): 5–30, 6.

[13] Truman, *The Governmental Process.*

[14] Mancur Olson, *The Logic of Collective Action* (Cambridge, Mass.: Harvard University Press, 1965).

[15] James Q. Wilson, *Political Organizations* (New York: Basic Books, 1973).

[16] Robert Salisbury, "An Exchange Theory of Interest Groups," *Midwest Journal of Political Science* 13 (1969): 1–32; and Robert Salisbury, "The Paradox of Interest in Washington: More Groups, Less Clout," in *The New American Political System,* ed. Anthony King (Washington, D.C.: American Enterprise Institute, 1978).

[17] Jack Walker, "The Origins and Maintenance of Interest Groups," *American Political Science Review* 77 (1983): 390–406.

[18] Kay Lehman Schlozman, Sidney Verba, and Henry Brady, "Civic Participation and the Equality Problem," in *Civic Engagement in American Democracy,* ed. Theda Skocpol and Morris P. Fiorian (Washington, D.C.: Brookings Institution Press, 1999); see also Lawrence Rothenberg, "Organizational Maintenance and the Retention Decision in Groups," *American Political Science Review* 82 (1988): 1129–52.

[19] Kay Lehman Schlozman and John Tierney, *Organized Interests and American Democracy* (New York: Harper & Row, 1986); Thomas Gais, *Improper Influence: Campaign Finance Law, Political Interest Groups, and the Problem of Equality* (Ann Arbor: University of Michigan Press, 1986); and Ken Kollman, *Outside Lobbying: Public Opinion and Interest Groups Strategies* (Princeton, N.J.: Princeton University Press, 1998).

[20] Anthony Nownes and Patricia Freeman, "Interest Group Activity in the States," *Journal of Politics* 60 (1998): 86–112.

[21] Christopher Cooper and Anthony Nownes, "Citizen Groups in Big City Politics," *State and Local Government Review* 35 (2003): 102–11. We examine local power structures and land-based growth coalitions in more detail in Chapters 11 and 12.

[22] Alan Rosenthal, *The Third House: Lobbyists and Lobbying in the States* (Washington, D.C.: CQ Press, 1993), 5.

[23] Richard Witmer and Fredrick Boehmke, "American Indian Political Incorporation in the Post–Indian Gaming Regulatory Act Era," *Social Science Journal* 44 (2007): 127–45.

[24] Martin Dyckman, "It's Fla. Voters vs. the True Constituency," *St. Petersburg (Fla.) Times,* 3 April 2005.

[25] Anthony Nownes, *Pressure and Power: Organized Interests in American Politics* (Boston: Houghton Mifflin, 2001).

[26] Rosenthal, *The Third House.*

[27] Clive Thomas and Ronald Hrebenar, "Interest Groups in the States," in *Politics in the American States: A Comparative Analysis,* 8th ed., ed. Virginia Gray and Russell Hanson (Washington, D.C.: CQ Press, 2004).

[28] Nownes and Freeman, "Interest Group Activity in the States."

[29] Thomas and Hrebenar, "Interest Groups in the States."

[30] Nownes and Freeman, "Interest Group Activity in the States."

[31] Center for Lobbying in the Public Interest, "Ten Immutable Paradoxes of Public Interest Lobbying," http://clpi.org/tips_facts.html#.

[32] Jennifer Anderson et al., "Mayflies and Old Bulls: Organization Persistence in State Interest Communities," *State Politics and Policy Quarterly* 4 (2004): 140–60.

[33] John Broder, "Amid Scandals, States Overhaul Lobbying Laws," *The New York Times,* 24 January 2006.

[34] Anderson et al., "Mayflies and Old Bulls."

[35] Rosenthal, *The Third House;* and Beth Rosenson, "Against Their Apparent Self-Interest: The Authorization of Independent State Legislative Ethics Commissions, 1973–1996," *State Politics and Policy Quarterly* 3 (2003): 42–66.

[36] Peggy Kerns and Ginger Sampson, "Do Ethics Laws Work?" *State Legislatures* (July/August 2003): 40–43.

[37] Adam Newmark, "Measuring State Legislative Lobbying Regulation," *State Politics and Policy Quarterly* 5 (2005): 182–91.

[38] Broder, "Amid Scandals, States Overhaul Lobbying Laws."

[39] John Carey, Richard Niemi, and Lynda Powell, *Term Limits in State Legislatures* (Ann Arbor: University of Michigan Press, 2000); and Marjorie Sarbaugh-Thompson et al., *The Political and Institutional Effects of Term Limits* (New York: Palgrave Macmillan, 2004).

[40] Christopher Mooney, "The Impact of State Legislative Term Limits on Lobbyists and Interest Groups" (paper presented at the Fifth Annual State Politics and Policy Conference, East Lansing, Mich., May 2005).

[41] Elisabeth S. Clemens, *The People's Lobby: Organizational Innovation and the Rise of Interest Group Politics in the United States, 1890–1925* (Chicago: University of Chicago Press, 1997).

[42] Alexa Bluth, "Thousands Protest Governor's Plans," *Sacramento Bee,* 26 May 2005, http://www.sacbee.com/content/politics/v-pring/story/1295653p-13803679c.html.

[43] Kenneth Goldstein, *Interest Groups, Lobbying, and Participation in America* (Cambridge: Cambridge University Press, 1999); and Jack Walker, *Mobilizing Interest Groups in America: Patrons, Professionals, and Social Movements* (Ann Arbor: University of Michigan, 1991).

[44] Rosenthal, *The Third House,* 155.

[45] Nownes and Freeman, "Interest Group Activity in the States."

[46] Frederick Boehmke, *The Indirect Effect of Direct Legislation: How Institutions Shape Interest Group Systems* (Columbus: Ohio State University Press, 2005).

[47] Elisabeth Gerber, *The Populist Paradox: Interest Group Influence and the Promise of Direct Legislation* (Princeton, N.J.: Princeton University Press, 1999); and Daniel Smith, *Tax Crusaders and the Politics of Direct Democracy* (New York: Routledge, 1998).

[48] Daniel Smith and Joseph Lubinski, "Direct Democracy during the Progressive Era: A Crack in the Populist Veneer?" *Journal of Policy History* 14 (2002): 349–83.

[49] Daniel Smith, "Special Interests and Direct Democracy: An Historical Glance," in *The Battle over Citizen Lawmaking: A Collection of Essays,* ed. M. Dane Waters (Durham, N.C.: Carolina Academic Press, 2001).

[50] Joseph G. Lapalombara and Charles B. Hagan, "Direct Legislation: An Appraisal and a Suggestion," *American Political Science Review* 45 (June 1951): 400–21; Shaun Bowler and Todd Donovan, *Demanding Choices: Opinion, Voting, and Direct Democracy* (Ann Arbor: University of Michigan Press, 1998): 118–28.

[51] Kate Folmar and Aaron Davis, "Fall Ballot Campaign Set Record for Expenses," *San Jose Mercury News,* 1 February 2006.

[52] Ballot Initiative Strategy Center, "PhRMA Breaks National Fundraising Record for Ballot Campaigns," 9 August 2005, http://ballot.org.

[53] Elisabeth Garrett and Daniel Smith, "Veiled Political Actors and Campaign Disclosure Laws in Direct Democracy," *Election Law Journal* 4 (2005): 295–328.

[54] *Nixon v. Shrink Missouri Government PAC* (2000); but see the Supreme Court's decision, Sorrell, *Vermont Republican State Committee, et al.* (2006), for limits on expenditures and how low states can regulate contributions to candidates.

55 Edward Feigenbaum and James Palmer, *Campaign Finance Law 2002* (Washington, D.C.: Federal Election Commission, 2003).

56 Edwin Bender, "Energy Companies Build Power Base in Statehouses," Institute on Money in State Politics, http://www.followthemoney.org/press/Reports/200410061.pdf.

57 Bender, "Energy Companies Build Power Base in Statehouses."

58 Institute on Money in State Politics, "State Elections Overview, 2004," http://www.followthemoney.org/press/Reports/200601041.pdf.

59 "Make Your Voice Heard," *Realtor Magazine Online,* 1 March 2005, http://www.realtor.org/rmomag.nsf/0/c265e4d06795d2a986256fa9005ec7aa?OpenDocument.

60 Denise Roth Barber, "Names in the News: The NRA," Institute on Money in State Politics, 13 July 2004, http://www.followthemoney.org/press/Reports/200407131.pdf.

61 Robert Hogan, "State Campaign Finance Laws and Interest Group Electioneering Activities," *Journal of Politics* 67 (2005): 887–906.

62 Nownes and Freeman, "Interest Group Activity in the States."

63 *Brown v. Board of Education of Topeka* 347 U.S. 483 (1954).

64 Andrew Koshner, *Solving the Puzzle of Interest Group Litigation* (Westport, Conn.: Greenwood Press, 1998).

65 Donald R. Songer and Ashlyn Kuersten, "The Success of Amici in State Supreme Courts," *Political Research Quarterly* 48 (1995): 31–42; Melinda Gann Hall, "Constituent Influence in State Supreme Courts: Conceptual Notes and a Case Study," *Journal of Politics* 49 (1987): 1117–24; and Lee Epstein and C. K. Rowland, "Debunking the Myth of Interest Group Invincibility in the Courts," *American Political Science Review* 58 (1991): 206–17.

66 Nownes, *Pressure and Power.*

67 Darrell West, *Checkbook Democracy* (Boston: Northeastern University Press, 2000).

68 Theda Skocpol, "Associations without Members," *American Prospect* 45 (1999): 66–73.

69 Jeffrey Berry, *The Interest Group Society,* 3rd ed. (New York: Longman, 1997).

70 Anderson et al., "Mayflies and Old Bulls."

71 Theda Skocpol, Marshall Ganz, and Ziad Munson, "A Nation of Organizers: The Institutional Origins of Civic Voluntarism in the United States," *American Political Science Review* 94 (2000): 527–46.

72 David Lowery and Virginia Gray, "The Density of State Interest Group Systems," *Journal of Politics* 55 (1993): 191–206.

73 Virginia Gray and David Lowery, *The Population Ecology of Interest Representation: Lobbying Communities in the American States* (Ann Arbor: University of Michigan Press, 1996).

74 Virginia Gray and David Lowery, "The Expression of Density Dependence in State Communities of Organized Interests," *American Politics Research* 29 (2001): 374–91; and Virginia Gray and David Lowery, "The Institutionalization of State Communities of Organized Interests," *Political Research Quarterly* 54 (2001): 265–84.

75 Frederick Boehmke, "The Effect of Direct Democracy on the Size and Diversity of State Interest Group Populations," *Journal of Politics* 64 (2002): 827–44.

76 Daniel Smith and Caroline Tolbert, *Educated by Initiative: The Effects of Direct Democracy on Citizens and Political Organizations in the American States* (Ann Arbor: University of Michigan Press, 2004).

77 Sarah Morehouse and Malcolm Jewell, *State Politics, Parties and Policy,* 2nd ed. (New York: Rowman & Littlefield, 2003).

78 Gray and Lowery, *The Population Ecology of Interest Representation.*

79 Anderson et al., "Mayflies and Old Bulls."

80. John Gaventa, *Power and Powerlessness: Quiescence and Rebellion in an Appalachian Valley* (Champaign-Urbana: University of Illinois Press, 1980).

81 Clive Thomas and Ron Hrebenar, "Who's Got Clout?" *State Legislatures* (April 1999): 30–34; Kevin Hula, *Lobbying Together: Interest Group Coalitions in Legislative Politics* (Washington, D.C.: Georgetown University Press, 1999); and Michael T. Heaney, "Outside the Issue Niche: The Multidimensionality of Interest Group Identity," *American Politics Research* 32 (2004): 1–41.

82 Belle Zeller, *American State Legislatures,* 2nd ed. (New York: Thomas Y. Crowell, 1954).

83 Anderson et al., "Mayflies and Old Bulls."

84 Lowery and Gray, "Bias in the Heavenly Chorus."

85 Schattschneider, *The Semisovereign People;* and Schlozman and Tierney, *Organized Interests and American Democracy.*

[86] John Heinz et al., *The Hollow Core* (Cambridge, Mass.: Harvard University Press, 1993); and Thomas and Hrebenar, "Interest Groups in the States."

[87] Heinz et al., *The Hollow Core*; and Mark Smith, *American Business and Political Power* (Chicago: University of Chicago Press, 2000).

[88] Thomas and Hrebenar, "Interest Groups in the States."

[89] Morehouse and Jewell, *State Politics, Parties and Policy*.

Chapter 7

[1] C. Lynwood Smith Jr., *Strengthening the Florida Legislature* (New Brunswick, N.J.: Rutgers University Press, 1970), 227.

[2] Smith, *Strengthening the Florida Legislature*.

[3] James Button, "Blacks," in *Florida Politics and Government*, ed. Manning J. Dauer (Gainesville: University Press of Florida, 1980); and Joan Carver, "Women in Florida," in Dauer, *Florida Politics and Government*.

[4] Council of State Governments, *The Book of the States 2006*, vol. 38 (Lexington, KY: Council of State Governments, 2006), 84.

[5] Data retrieved from the clerk of the Florida House of Representatives and the secretary of the Florida Senate.

[6] Alan Rosenthal, "The Legislative Institution: In Transition and at Risk," in *The State of the States*, ed. Carl E. Van Horn, 2nd ed. (Washington, D.C.: CQ Press, 1993), 115.

[7] Alan Rosenthal, *Heavy Lifting: The Job of the American Legislature* (Washington, D.C.: CQ Press, 2004).

[8] Michael B. Berkman, "State Legislators in Congress: Strategic Politicians, Professional Legislatures, and the Party Nexus," *American Journal of Political Science* 38 (1994): 1025–55.

[9] Center for American Women and Politics, "Women State Legislators: Leadership Positions and Committee Chairs 2005," fact sheet (New Brunswick, N.J.: Rutgers University, 2005).

[10] Bernard Grofman and Lisa Handley, "The Impact of the Voting Rights Act on Black Representation in Southern State Legislatures," *Legislative Studies Quarterly* 16 (1991): 111–28.

[11] All these legislators were elected to their seats except for those few at any one time who have been appointed to serve out the remainder of a term for a legislator who died or resigned.

[12] Richard G. Niemi, Lynda W. Powell, William D. Berry, Thomas M. Carsey, and James M. Snyder Jr., "Competition in State Legislative Elections, 1992–2002," in *The Marketplace of Democracy*, ed. Michael P. McDonald and John Samples (Washington, D.C.: Brookings Institution, 2006); and Robert E. Hogan, "Institutional and District-Level Sources of Competition in State Legislative Elections," *Social Science Quarterly* 84 (2003): 543–60.

[13] John McGlennon and Cory Kaufman, "Expanding the Playing Field: Competition Rises for State Legislative Seats in 2006," report from the Thomas Jefferson Program in Public Policy (Williamsburg, VA: College of William and Mary, 2006); and National Conference of State Legislatures, http://www.ncsl.org/programs/press/2004/unopposed_2004.htm.

[14] Richard G. Niemi and Lynda W. Powell, "Limited Citizenship? Knowing and Contacting State Legislators after Term Limits," in *The Test of Time*, ed. Rick Farmer, John David Rausch Jr., and John C. Green (Lanham, MD: Lexington, 2003).

[15] Gary F. Moncrief, Peverill Squire, and Malcolm E. Jewell, *Who Runs for the Legislature?* (Upper Saddle River, N.J.: Prentice Hall, 2001), ch. 4.

[16] Jeff Venezuela, "Midwest Local TV Newscasts Average 36 Seconds of Election Coverage in Typical 30-Minute Broadcast," press release (Madison: UW NewsLab, University of Wisconsin–Madison, 2006).

[17] Charles Layton and Mary Walton, "The State of the American Newspaper: Missing the Story at the Statehouse," *American Journalism Review* (July/August 1998): 42–63.

[18] Malcolm E. Jewell and Sarah M. Morehouse, *Political Parties and Elections in American States*, 4th ed. (Washington, D.C.: CQ Press, 2001), 201.

[19] Except Nebraska, where state legislative elections are nonpartisan.

[20] Tom Loftus, *The Art of Legislative Politics* (Washington, D.C.: CQ Press, 1994); Moncrief, Squire, and Jewell, *Who Runs for the Legislature?*; and Ralph G. Wright, *Inside the Statehouse: Lessons from the Speaker* (Washington, D.C.: CQ Press, 2005).

[21] R. W. Lariscy, S. F. Tinkham, H. H. Edwards, and K. O. Jones, "The 'Ground War' of Political Campaigns: Nonpaid Activities in U.S. State Legislative Races,"

Journalism and Mass Communication Quarterly 81 (2004): 477–97.

22 Anthony Gierzynski and David Breaux, "Legislative Elections and the Importance of Money," *Legislative Studies Quarterly* 21 (1996): 337–57.

23 Robert E. Hogan, "Challenger Emergence, Incumbent Success, and Electoral Accountability in State Legislative Elections," *Journal of Politics* 66 (2004): 1283–303; David Breaux, "Specifying the Impact of Incumbency on State Legislative Elections," *American Politics Quarterly* 18 (1990): 270–86; and William D. Berry, Michael B. Berkman, and Stuart Schneiderman, "Explaining Incumbency Re-Election," *American Political Science Review* 94 (2000): 859–74.

24 Alan Greenblatt, "Perks That Kill," *Governing* (July 2006): 18.

25 Robert G. Boatright, "Static Ambition in a Changing World: Legislators' Preparations for, and Responses to, Redistricting," *State Politics and Policy Quarterly* 4 (2004): 436–54.

26 Richard K. Scher, Jon L. Mills, and John J. Hotaling, *Voting Rights and Democracy* (Chicago: Nelson-Hall, 1997).

27 Stephen Ansolabehere and James M. Snyder Jr. "Reapportionment and Party Realignment in the American States," *University of Pennsylvania Law Review* 153 (2004): 433–57.

28 This principle of equal-population districts applies only within a given chamber. So, for example, Texas House districts may have more people in them than North Carolina House districts, but all Texas House districts must be equal in population.

29 The key cases on state legislative redistricting in this period were *Baker v. Carr* 369 U.S. 186 (1962), *Reynolds v. Sims* 377 U.S. 533 (1964), and *Lucas v. 44th General Assembly of Colorado* 377 U.S. 713 (1964).

30 At the time, the principle was referred to as "one man, one vote," but we prefer the less sexist phrasing.

31 Gordon E. Baker, *The Reapportionment Revolution* (New York: Random House, 1966).

32 Jack R. Van der Slik and Kent D. Redfield, *Lawmaking in Illinois* (Springfield, IL: Sangamon State University, 1989).

33 Ansolabehere and Snyder, "Reapportionment and Party Realignment."

34 Layla Copelin, "DeLay and His Legacy Are Both on Trial," *Austin (Tex.) American-Statesman,* 18 December 2005, p. A1; David Espo, "Top Court Rules States Free to Redistrict," *Sacramento Bee,* online ed., 28 June 2006; and

Tim Storey, "Supreme Court Tackles Texas," *State Legislatures,* April 2006, 22–24.

35 *League of Latin American Citizens v. Perry* 548 U.S. XXX (2006).

36 For example, it was largely during this political battle that DeLay allegedly committed the acts for which he was later indicted and had to resign from Congress.

37 Michael P. McDonald, "A Comparative Analysis of Redistricting Institutions in the United States, 2001–02," *State Politics and Politics Quarterly* 4 (2004): 371–95.

38 The U.S. Supreme Court allows the largest and smallest districts in a state legislative chamber to vary by as much as 10 percent.

39 Jason Barabas and Jennifer Jerit, "Redistricting Principles and Racial Representation," *State Politics and Policy Quarterly* 4 (2004): 415–36.

40 Brian F. Schaffner, Michael W. Wagner, and Jonathon Winburn, "Incumbents Out, Party In? Term Limits and Partisan Redistricting in State Legislatures," *State Politics and Policy Quarterly* 4 (2004): 396–414; and David Butler and Bruce Cain, *Congressional Redistricting: Comparative and Theoretical Perspectives* (New York: Macmillan, 1992).

41 Grofman and Handley, "The Impact of the Voting Rights Act."

42 *Thornburg v. Gingles* 478 U.S. 30 (1986).

43 *Easley v. Cromartie* 532 U.S. 234 (2001).

44 *Easley v. Cromartie.*

45 McDonald, "A Comparative Analysis."

46 Carolyn J. Tolbert, Daniel A. Smith, and John C. Green, "Support for and the Mobilizing Effects of Election Reform Ballot Propositions" (paper presented at the annual meeting of the American Political Science Association, Philadelphia, September 2006).

47 Alan Ehrenhalt, "Party Lines," *Governing* (January 2007): 11–12.

48 Schaffner, Wagner, and Winburn, "Incumbents Out, Party In?"

49 Barabas and Jerit, "Redistricting Principles and Racial Representation"; and Jonathon Winburn, "The Realities of Redistricting: Political Control and Partisan Consequences" (Ph.D. diss., Indiana University, Bloomington, 2005).

50 Alan Greenblatt, "Monster Maps: Has Devious District-Making Killed Electoral Competition?" *Governing,* (January 2006): 46–50.

[51] National Conference of State Legislatures, "Legislator Demographics," 2006, http://www.ncsl.org/programs/legman/about/demographic_overview.htm.

[52] U.S. Census Bureau, *The Statistical Abstract of the United States, 2005*, http://www.census.gov/statab/www/.

[53] Susan J. Carroll, "Women in State Government: Historical Overview and Trends," in *The Book of the States 2004*, vol. 36 (Lexington, KY: Council of State Governments, 2004).

[54] Robert Darcy, "Women in the State Legislative Power Structure: Committee Chairs," *Social Science Quarterly* 77 (1996): 888–98.

[55] Center for American Women and Politics, "Women State Legislators"; and Robert Tanner, "Female State Leaders Double since 2000," *Chicago Sun-Times*, online ed., 3 April 2007.

[56] In 2007, the percentage climbed to 23.5 percent.

[57] James D. King, "Single-Member Districts and the Representation of Women in American State Legislatures: The Effects of Electoral System Change," *State Politics and Policy Quarterly* 2 (2002): 161–75; and Peverill Squire, "Legislative Professionalization and Membership Diversity in State Legislatures," *Legislative Studies Quarterly* 17 (1992): 69–79.

[58] Kevin Arseneaux, "The 'Gender Gap' in State Legislative Representation: New Data to Tackle an Old Question," *Political Research Quarterly* 54 (2001): 143–60; John F. Camobreco and Michelle A. Barnello, "Postmaterialism and Post-Industrialism: Cultural Influences on Female Representation in State Legislatures," *State Politics and Policy Quarterly* 3 (2003): 117–38; and Kira Sanbonmatsu, *Where Women Run: Gender and Party in the American States* (Ann Arbor: University of Michigan Press, 2006).

[59] Richard L. Fox and Jennifer L. Lawless, "Entering the Arena? Gender and the Decision to Run for Office," *American Journal of Political Science* 48 (2004): 264–80.

[60] Samantha Sanchez, *Money and Diversity in State Legislatures, 2003* (Helena, MT: Institute on Money in State Politics, 2005).

[61] Grofman and Handley, "The Impact of the Voting Rights Act"; and Janine A. Parry and William H. Miller, "'The Great Negro State of the Country?' Black Legislators in Arkansas, 1973–2000," *Journal of Black Studies* 36 (2006): 833–72.

[62] Rodney Hero, F. C. Garcia, J. Garcia, and H. Pachon, "Latino Participation, Partisanship, and Office

Holding," *PS: Politics and Political Science* 33 (2000): 529–34.

[63] "Indians Gain Percentage in Next Legislature," *Daily Oklahoman*, online ed., 16 November 2006.

[64] David Lublin, *The Paradox of Representation* (Princeton, N.J.: Princeton University Press, 1999).

[65] Rodney E. Hero and Carolyn J. Tolbert, "Latinos and Substantive Representation in the U.S. House of Representatives: Direct, Indirect, or Nonexistent?" *American Journal of Political Science* 39 (1995): 640–52.

[66] Kathleen A. Bratton and Kerry L. Haynie, "Agenda Setting and Legislative Success in State Legislatures: The Effects of Gender and Race," *Journal of Politics* 61 (1999): 658–79.

[67] C. T. Owens, "Black Substantive Representation in State Legislatures from 1971–1994," *Social Science Quarterly* 86 (2005): 779–91; and Robert R. Preuhs, "The Conditional Effects of Minority Descriptive Representation: Black Legislators and Policy Influence in the American States," *Journal of Politics* 68 (2006): 585–99.

[68] Caroline J. Tolbert and Gertrude A. Steuernagel, "Women Lawmakers, State Mandate, and Women's Health," *Women and Politics* 22 (2001): 1–39.

[69] James Button and David Hedge, "Legislative Life in the 1900s: A Comparison of Black and White State Legislators," *Legislative Studies Quarterly* 21 (1996): 199–218.

[70] Kerry L. Haynie, *African American Legislators in the American States* (New York: Columbia University Press, 2001).

[71] Anne Marie Camissa and Beth Reingold, "Women in State Legislatures and State Legislative Research: Beyond Sameness and Difference," *State Politics and Policy Quarterly* 4 (2004): 181–210.

[72] Sarah Pogionne, "Exploring Gender Differences in State Legislators' Policy Preferences," *Political Research Quarterly* 57 (2004): 305–14.

[73] Lyn Kathlene, "Power and Influence in State Legislative Policy-Making: The Interaction of Gender and Position in Committee Hearing Debates," *American Political Science Review* 88 (1994): 560–76.

[74] Robert R. Preuhs, "Descriptive Representation, Legislative Leadership, and Direct Democracy: Latino Influence on English Only Laws in the States, 1984–2002," *State Politics and Policy Quarterly* 5 (2005): 203–24; and Cindy S. Rosenthal, *When Women Lead: Integrative Leadership*

in State Legislatures (New York: Oxford University Press, 1998).

[75] Darcy, "Women in the State Legislative Power Structure"; Byron D'Andra Orey, L. Marvin Overby, and Christopher W. Larimer, "African-American Committee Chairs in American State Legislatures" (University of Nebraska–Lincoln, 2006).

[76] Tracy Osborn, "Women Representing Women: Pursuing a Women's Agenda in the States" (Ph.D. diss., Indiana University, 2004).

[77] This is true except for those relatively very few laws that are passed through the initiative process.

[78] See the Michigan Legislature's excellent website to examine their laws, bills, committee reports, and other legislative documents: http://www.legislature.mi.gov. Today, most state legislatures have websites like this that allow you to search for various legislative documents and laws.

[79] Tommy Neal, *Learning the Game: How the Legislative Process Works* (Denver, CO: National Conference of State Legislatures, 2005), 33.

[80] This varies quite a bit, with Colorado passing more than 50 percent of its bills and Massachusetts passing less than 5 percent in a typical year; see Council of State Governments, *The Book of the States 2006*.

[81] Wayne Francis, *The Legislative Committee Game: A Comparative Analysis of Fifty States* (Columbus: Ohio State University Press, 1989).

[82] Council of State Governments, *The Book of the States 2006*, 178–80.

[83] A few states, like Colorado, limit the ability of the majority leader to screen out bills from floor consideration, requiring a floor vote on every bill that is reported out of committee. This reduces both the power of the majority leader and the amount of deliberation any given bill can have on the floor.

[84] This is except for special types of bills that require a supermajority vote, such as bills for borrowing money or votes to override a governor's veto.

[85] This process is best described in the context of congressional roll call voting in John W. Kingdon, *Congressmen's Voting Decisions*, 3rd ed. (Ann Arbor: University of Michigan Press, 1989).

[86] Vicky M. Wilkins and Garry Young, "The Influence of Governors on Veto Override Attempts: A Test of Pivotal Politics," *Legislative Studies Quarterly* 27 (2002): 557–76.

[87] Richard F. Fenno, *The Power of the Purse: Appropriations Politics in Congress* (Boston: Little, Brown, 1966).

[88] Council of State Governments, *The Book of the States 2006*.

[89] In some states, the budget is a single bill, whereas in others, it is split into several bills. This discussion of the legislative budget process is relevant to either approach.

[90] John A. Hird, *Power, Knowledge, and Politics: Policy Analysis in the States* (Washington, D.C.: Georgetown University Press, 2005).

[91] Because of the budget's importance, several legislatures use joint budget committees. Joint committees have members of both the senate and the house, like conference committees do.

[92] John D. Huber, Charles R. Shipan, and Madelaine Pfahler, "Legislatures and Statutory Control of Bureaucracy," *American Journal of Political Science* 45 (2001): 330–45; and Craig Volden, "A Formal Model of the Politics of Delegation in a Separation of Powers System," *American Journal of Political Science* 46 (2002): 111–33.

[93] Mathew D. McCubbins and Thomas Schwartz, "Congressional Oversight Overlooked: Police Patrols versus Fire Alarms," *American Journal of Political Science* 28 (1984): 165–79.

[94] Brian J. Gerber, Cherie Maestas, and Nelson C. Dometrius, "State Legislative Influence over Agency Rulemaking: The Utility of ex Ante Review," *State Politics and Policy Quarterly* 5 (2005): 24–46.

[95] W. Daniel Ebersole, "Trends in State Government Accounting, Auditing and Treasury," in Council of State Governments, *The Book of the States 2005*, vol. 37 (Lexington, KY: Council of State Governments, 2005).

[96] Christopher Reenock and Sarah Poggione, "Agency Design as an Ongoing Tool of Bureaucratic Influence," *Legislative Studies Quarterly* 29 (2004): 383–406.

[97] Malcolm E. Jewell, *Representation in State Legislatures* (Lexington: University Press of Kentucky, 1982); Michael A. Smith, *Bringing Representation Home: State Legislators among Their Constituencies* (Columbia: University of Missouri Press, 2003); and Ronald E. Weber, "The Quality of State Legislative Representation: A Critical Assessment," *Journal of Politics* 61 (1999): 609–27.

[98] Shannon Jenkins, "The Impact of Party and Ideology on Roll-Call Voting in State Legislatures," *Legislative Studies Quarterly* 31 (2006): 235–57.

[99] Robert S. Erikson, Gerald C. Wright, and John P. Mc-Iver, *Statehouse Democracy: Public Opinion and Policy in the American States* (New York: Cambridge University Press, 1993).

[100] Joel A. Thompson and Gary F. Moncrief, "Pursuing the Pork in a State Legislature: A Research Note," *Legislative Studies Quarterly* 13 (1988): 393–401.

[101] Michael C. Herron and Brett A. Theodos, "Government Redistribution in the Shadow of Legislative Elections: A Study of the Illinois Member Initiative Grants Program," *Legislative Studies Quarterly* 39 (2004): 287–312.

[102] Camissa and Reingold, "Women in State Legislatures and State Legislative Research"; and Haynie, *African American Legislators.*

[103] Most legislatures have methods by which under very unusual circumstances—usually involving legislators convicted of crime—they can expel members, but such actions are extremely rare.

[104] Lawrence Becker, *Doing the Right Thing: Collective Action and Procedural Choice in the New Legislative Process* (Columbus: Ohio State University Press, 2005).

[105] James Coleman Battista, "Re-Examining Legislative Committee Representativeness in the States," *State Politics and Policy Quarterly* 4 (2004): 135–57; L. Marvin Overby and Thomas A. Kazee, "Outlying Committees in the Statehouse: An Examination of the Prevalence of Committee Outliers in State Legislatures," *Journal of Politics* 62 (2000): 701–28; and Nancy Martorano, "Balancing Power: Committee System Autonomy and Legislative Organization," *Legislative Studies Quarterly* 31 (2006): 205–34.

[106] Richard Clucas, "Improving the Harvest of State Legislative Research," *State Politics and Policy Quarterly* 3 (2003): 387–419.

[107] Twelve state legislators in 2007 had not been elected as either a Democrat or Republican: six Progressives and one independent in Vermont, two independents in Maine, one independent in Kentucky, one Constitution Party member in Montana, and one write-in candidate in Massachusetts who was a Democrat but not the nominee of that party in the 2006 election. See Council of State Governments, *The Book of the States 2006.*

[108] Jenkins, "The Impact of Party and Ideology"; and Gerald C. Wright and Brian F. Schaffner, "The Influence of Party: Evidence from the State Legislatures," *American Political Science Review* 96 (2002): 367–80.

[109] Nancy Martorano, "Cohesion or Reciprocity? Majority Party Strength and Minority Party Procedural Rights in the Legislative Process," *State Politics and Policy Quarterly* 4 (2004): 55–73.

[110] V. O. Key Jr., *Southern Politics* (New York: Vintage, 1949).

[111] Charles S. Bullock III and Mark J. Rozell, eds., *The New Politics of the Old South: An Introduction to Southern Politics* (Lanham, MD: Rowman & Littlefield, 2006).

[112] Keith E. Hamm and Gary F. Moncrief, "Legislative Politics in the States," in *Politics in the American State,* eds. Virginia Gray and Russell L. Hanson, 8th ed. (Washington, D.C.: CQ Press, 2004). Note that in certain very rare political circumstances, a minority party member may become a chamber's presiding officer, as is currently the case in the Pennsylvania House. See Eric Kelderman, "Battles for Gavels Kick off 2007 Sessions," *Statelines.org,* online ed., 11 January 2007.

[113] Kent D. Redfield, "What Keeps the 4 Tops on Top? Leadership Power in the Illinois General Assembly," in *Almanac of Illinois Politics: 1998,* eds. David A. Joens and Paul Kleppner (Springfield, IL: Institute of Public Affairs, 1998); and Andy Furillo, "'Big 5' Put a Range of Issues on the Table," *Sacramento Bee,* online ed., 25 August 2005.

[114] Richard A. Clucas, "Principal-Agent Theory and the Power of State House Speakers," *Legislative Studies Quarterly* 26 (2001): 319–38.

[115] Clucas, "Principal-Agent Theory."

[116] Richard A. Clucas, *The Speaker's Electoral Connection: Willie Brown and the California Assembly* (Berkeley: IGS Press, University of California, Berkeley, 1995); Anthony Gierzynski, *Legislative Party Campaign Committees in the American States* (Lexington: University Press of Kentucky, 1992); Loftus, *The Art of Legislative Politics;* and Wright, *Inside the Statehouse.*

[117] Thad Kousser, *Term Limits and the Dismantling of State Legislative Professionalism* (New York: Cambridge University Press, 2005).

[118] Peverill Squire, "Historical Evolution of Legislatures in the United States," *Annual Review of Political Science* 9 (2006): 19–44; Alexander Heard, ed., *State Legislatures in American Politics* (Englewood Cliffs, N.J.: Prentice Hall, 1966); and James Nathan Miller, "Hamstrung Legislatures," *National Civic Review* 54 (1965): 178–87.

[119] Citizens Conference on State Legislatures, *The Sometime Governments* (New York: Bantam, 1971).

[120] H. W. Jerome Maddox, "Opportunity Costs and Outside Careers in U.S. State Legislatures," *Legislative Studies Quarterly* 20 (2004): 517–44.

[121] Neil Malhorta, "Government Growth and Professionalism in U.S. State Legislatures," *Legislative Studies Quarterly* 31 (2006): 563–84; James D. King, "Changes in Professionalism in U.S. State Legislatures," *Legislative Studies Quarterly* 25 (2000): 327–44; and Christopher Z. Mooney, "Citizens, Structures, and Sister States: Influences on State Legislative Reform," *Legislative Studies Quarterly* 20 (1995): 47–68.

[122] Peverill Squire, "Measuring Legislative Professionalism," *State Politics and Policy Quarterly* 7 (2007): 211-27.

[123] Christopher Z. Mooney, "Measuring U.S. State Legislative Professionalism: An Evaluation of Five Indices," *State and Local Government Review* 26 (1994): 70–78, 74; see also Ann O'M. Bowman and Richard C. Kearney, *The Resurgence of the States* (Englewood Cliffs, N.J.: Prentice Hall, 1986).

[124] Rosenthal "The Legislative Institution."

[125] Morris P. Fiorina, *Divided Government,* 2nd ed. (New York: Longman, 2002).

[126] S. Owings and R. Borck, "Legislative Professionalism and Government Spending: Do Citizen Legislators Really Spend Less?" *Public Finance Review* 28 (2000): 210–25.

[127] Neil Malhorta, "Selection Effects and the Impact of Legislative Professionalism on Government Spending" (Department of Political Science, Stanford University, 2007).

[128] Berry, Berkman, and Schneiderman, "Explaining Incumbency Re-Election."

[129] Peverill Squire, "Uncontested Seats in State Legislative Elections," *Legislative Studies Quarterly* 25 (2000): 131–46.

[130] Cherie Maestas, "The Incentive to Listen: Progressive Ambition, Resources and Opinion Monitoring among State Legislators," *Journal of Politics* 65 (2003): 439–56.

[131] Peverill Squire, "Professionalization and Public Opinion of State Legislatures," *Journal of Politics* 55 (1993): 479–91.

[132] For example, see George F. Will, *Restoration: Congress, Term Limits, and the Recovery of Deliberative Democracy* (New York: Free Press, 1993).

[133] In 1995, the U.S. Supreme Court held that a state cannot limit the terms of its members of Congress (*U.S. Term Limits, Inc. v. Thornton* 514 U.S. 779).

[134] Kousser, *Term Limits.*

[135] Alaska and Illinois also have a form of the initiative, but these states have not voted on term limits.

[136] Karl T. Kurtz, Bruce Cain, and Richard G. Niemi, eds., *Institutional Change in American Politics: The Case of Term Limits* (Ann Arbor: University of Michigan Press, 2007); John M. Carey, Richard G. Niemi, and Lynda W. Powell, *Term Limits in the State Legislatures* (Ann Arbor: University of Michigan Press, 2000); and Marjorie Sarbaugh-Thompson, Lyke Thompson, Charles D. Elder, John Strate, and Richard C. Elling, *The Political and Institutional Effects of Term Limits* (New York: Palgrave-Macmillan, 2004).

[137] John H. Fund, "Term Limitation: An Idea Whose Time Has Come," in *Limiting Legislative Terms,* eds. Gerald Benjamin and Michael J. Malbin (Washington, D.C.: Congressional Quarterly Press, 1992); Mark P. Petracca, "The Poison of Professional Politics," *Policy Analysis,* online ed., 151 (1991); and Will, *Restoration.*

[138] Amihai Glazer and Martin P. Wattenberg, "How Will Term Limits Affect Legislative Work?" in *Legislative Term Limits: Public Choice Perspectives,* ed. Bernard Grofman (Boston: Kluwer, 1996); and Nelson Polsby, "Limiting Terms Won't Curb Special Interests, Improve the Legislature, or Enhance Democracy," *Public Affairs Report* 31 (Spring 1990): 9. Note that these same arguments arose again in the short-lived attempt by Pennsylvania governor Ed Rendell to adopt term limits in the Keystone State in 2007; see Daylin Leach, "Don't Dumb Down the Legislature," *Philadelphia Daily News,* online ed., 27 April 2007.

[139] Daniel A. Smith, "Overturning Term Limits: The Legislature's Own Private Idaho?" *PS: Political Science and Politics* 36 (2003): 215–20.

[140] Kermit Daniel and John R. Lott Jr., "Term Limits and Electoral Competition: Evidence from California's State Legislative Races," *Public Choice* 90 (1997): 165–84.

[141] Sarbaugh-Thompson et al., *The Political and Institutional Effects of Term Limits;* Scot Schraufnagel and Karen Halperin, "Term Limits, Electoral Competition, and Representational Diversity: The Case of Florida," *State Politics and Policy Quarterly* 6 (2006): 448–62; and Seth Masket and Jeffrey B. Lewis, "A Return to Normalcy? Revisiting the Effects of Term Limits on Competitiveness and Spending in California Assembly Elections," *State Politics and Policy Quarterly* 7 (2007): 20–38.

[142] Kousser, *Term Limits.*

[143] Christopher Z. Mooney, "The Effects of Term Limits in Professionalized State Legislatures," in *Legislating without Experience: Case Studies in State Legislative Term Limits,* eds. Rick Farmer, Christopher Z. Mooney, Richard Powell, and John Green (Lanham, MD: Lexington Books, 2008);

Richard J. Powell, "The Impact of Term Limits on the Candidacy Decisions of State Legislators in U.S. House Elections," *Legislative Studies Quarterly* 25 (2000): 645–61; Rebecca A. Tothero, "The Impact of Term Limits on State Legislators' Ambition for Local Office: The Case of Michigan's House," *Publius* 33 (2003): 111–22; Jeffrey Lazarus, "Term Limits' Multiple Effects on State Legislators' Career Decisions," *State Politics and Policy Quarterly* 6 (2006): 357–83; and Jennifer A. Steen, "The Impact of State Legislative Term Limits on the Supply of Congressional Candidates," *State Politics and Policy Quarterly* 6 (2006): 430–47.

[144] Gary Moncrief, Lynda Powell, and Tim Storey, "Composition of Legislatures," in Kurtz, Niemi, and Cain, *Institutional Change in American Politics;* and Schraufnagel and Halperin, "Term Limits."

[145] Gary F. Moncrief, Richard G. Niemi, and Linda W. Powell, "Time, Term Limits, and Trends in Membership Stability in U.S. State Legislatures," *Legislative Studies Quarterly* 29 (2004): 357–81.

[146] Christopher Z. Mooney, Jason Wood, and Gerald C. Wright, "Out with the Old-Heads and in with the Young Turks: The Effects of Term Limits in Semi-Professional State Legislatures," in Farmer et al., *Legislating without Experience: Case Studies in State Legislative Term Limits.*

[147] Art English and Brian Weberg, "Term Limits in the Arkansas General Assembly: A Citizen Legislature Responds," Joint Project on Term Limits case study report (Denver, CO: National Conference of State Legislatures, 2004), http://www.ncsl.org/jptl/casestudies/Arkansasv2.pdf.

[148] Thad Kousser and John Straayer, "Budgets and the Policy Process," in Kurtz, Niemi, and Cain, *Institutional Change in American Politics;* Schaffner, Wagner, and Winburn, "Incumbents Out, Party In?"; and Marjorie Sarbaugh-Thompson, Lyke Thompson, Charles D. Elder, Meg Comins, Richard C. Elling, and John Strate, "Democracy among Strangers: Term Limits' Effects on Relationships between State Legislators in Michigan," *State Politics and Policy Quarterly* 6 (2006): 384–409.

[149] John M. Carey, Richard Niemi, Lynda W. Powell, and Gary F. Moncrief, "The Effects of Term Limits on State Legislatures: A New Survey of the 50 States," *Legislative Studies Quarterly* 31 (2006): 105–34; and Lynda W. Powell, Richard G. Niemi, and Michael Smith, "Constituent Attention and Interest Representation," in Kurtz, Niemi, and Cain, *Institutional Change in American Politics.*

[150] Steve Law, "Lawmaking Talent Lost through Revolving Door," *Statesman Journal Online,* 13 February 2000, 9.

[151] Sarbaugh-Thompson et al., "Democracy among Strangers."

[152] Alan Greenblatt, "The Truth about Term Limits," *Governing* (January 2006): 24–28.

[153] Kousser and Straayer, "Budgets and the Policy Process."

[154] Law, "Lawmaking Talent Lost," 15.

[155] Carey et al., "The Effects of Term Limits"; and Carey, Niemi, and Powell, *Term Limits in the State Legislatures.*

[156] Kousser and Straayer, "Budgets and the Policy Process."

[157] Eric Kelderman, "Term Limits Take out Legislative Leaders," *Stateline.org,* online ed., 25 April 2006.

[158] Sarbaugh-Thompson et al., "Democracy among Strangers."

[159] Mooney 2007, op. cit.

[160] Mooney 2007, op. cit.

Chapter 8

[1] Jennifer Bayot, "Pataki Rules out 4th Term but Not a Run for the White House," *The New York Times,* online ed., 27 July 2005.

[2] Marc Humbert, "New York Governor's Race Could Be a Battle," *Sacramento Bee,* online ed., 19 August 2005.

[3] Marc Humbert, "N.Y. Governor's Speech Looks beyond State," *Sacramento Bee,* online ed., 4 January 2006; and Marc Humbert, "Pataki Takes 2008 Ambitions on the Road," *Sacramento Bee,* online ed., 4 August 2006.

[4] Peverill Squire and Christina Fastnow, "Comparing Gubernatorial and Senatorial Elections," *Political Research Quarterly* 47 (1994): 705–20.

[5] Roxana Hegeman, "Rescuers Comb through Rubble," Springfield, Ill., *State Journal-Register,* 7 May 2007, 2.

[6] "Gov. Minner to Meet with DaimlerChrysler, AstraZeneca in Germany and Italy Next Week," press release, Office of the Governor, State of Delaware, 31 March 2005.

[7] Thad Beyle, "Governors," in *Politics in the American States,* 8th ed., ed. Virginia Gray and Russell L. Hanson (Washington, D.C.: CQ Press, 2004).

[8] Leslie Lipson, *The American Governor: From Figurehead to Leader* (New York:, 1968).

[9] Coleman B. Ransone Jr., *The American Governorship* (Westport, Conn.: Greenwood, 1982); and Nelson C.

Dometrius, "Governors: Their Heritage and Future," in *American State and Local Politics,* ed. Ronald E. Weber and Paul Brace (New York: Chatham House, 1999).

[10] Council of State Governments, *The Book of the States: 2006,* vol. 38 (Lexington, Ky.: Council of State Governments, 2006), table 4.1.

[11] Randall W. Partin, "Campaign Intensity and Voter Information: A Look at Gubernatorial Contests," *American Politics Research* 29 (2001): 115–40.

[12] E. Freedman and F. Fico, "Whither the Experts? Newspaper Use of Horse Race and Issue Experts in Coverage of Open Governors' Races in 2002," *Journalism and Mass Communication Quarterly* 81 (2004): 498–510.

[13] James D. King, "Incumbent Popularity and Vote Choice in Gubernatorial Elections," *Journal of Politics* 63 (2001): 585–97.

[14] John E. Chubb, "Institutions, the Economy, and the Dynamics of State Elections," *American Political Science Review* 82 (1988): 133–54; and Lonna Rae Atkeson and Randall W. Partin, "Economic and Referendum Voting: A Comparison of Gubernatorial and Senatorial Elections," *American Political Science Review* 89 (1995): 99–107.

[15] Kevin M. Leyden and Stephen A. Borrelli, "The Effect of State Economic Conditions on Gubernatorial Elections: Does a Unified Government Make a Difference?" *Western Political Quarterly* 48 (1995): 275–90.

[16] Jason A. MacDonald and Lee Sigelman, "Public Assessments of Gubernatorial Performance," *American Politics Quarterly* 27 (1999): 201–15.

[17] Eric R. A. N. Smith, *The Unchanging American Voter* (Berkeley: University of California Press, 1989).

[18] Chubb, "Institutions, the Economy, and the Dynamics of State Elections."

[19] Robert Tanner, "GOP Governors Say Bush's Missteps Hurting," *Sacramento Bee,* online ed., 27 February 2006; Adam Nagourney, "Democrats See Hope of Winning Governors' Seats," *The New York Times,* online ed., 26 February 2006; and Laura Mecoy, "Bush Visits: Governor's Not in Sight," *Sacramento Bee,* online ed., 21 October 2005.

[20] Stephen A. Salamore and Barbara G. Salamore, "The Transformation of State Electoral Politics," in *The State of the States,* 2nd ed., ed. Carl E. Van Horn (Washington, D.C.: CQ Press, 1993).

[21] Thomas M. Carsey, *Campaign Dynamics: The Race for Governor* (Ann Arbor: University of Michigan Press, 2000).

[22] Thad Beyle, "Governors: Elections, Campaign Costs and Powers," in *The Book of the States: 2005,* vol. 38 (Lexington, Ky.: Council of State Governments, 2006).

[23] Malcolm E. Jewell and Sarah M. Morehouse, *Political Parties and Elections in American States,* 4th ed. (Washington, D.C.: CQ Press, 2001), 163–66; and Thad Beyle, "Governors: The Middlemen and Women in Our Political System," in *Politics in the American States,* 6th ed., ed. Virginia Gray and Herbert Jacob (Washington, D.C.: CQ Press, 1996).

[24] Kent D. Redfield, *Money Counts: How Dollars Dominate Illinois Politics and What We Can Do about It* (Springfield, Ill.: Institute for Public Affairs, 2001).

[25] Kedron Bardwell, "Campaign Finance Laws and the Competition for Spending in Gubernatorial Elections," *Social Science Quarterly* 84 (2003): 811–25; and Donald A. Gross and Robert K. Goidel, "The Impact of State Campaign Finance Laws," *State Politics and Policy Quarterly* 1 (2001): 180–95.

[26] Gary Delsohn, "3-State Swing to Raise Funds," *Sacramento Bee,* online ed., 20 May 2005.

[27] Robert Tanner, "Governors' Groups Lead in Raising Campaign Dollars," *State Journal-Register,* 6 August 2006, p. 8.

[28] Jennifer A. Steen, *Self-Financed Candidates in Congressional Elections* (Ann Arbor: University of Michigan Press, 2006).

[29] Robert Tanner, "Democrats Win 2 Governorships," *State Journal-Register,* 9 November 2005, p. 8.

[30] Bruce Cain, quoted in Aaron C. Davis, "Only Rich Need Apply," San Jose, Calif., *Mercury News,* online ed., 5 April 2006.

[31] Dan Walters, "This Is the Week the Race for Governor Shifted into High Gear," *Sacramento Bee,* online ed., 24 March 2006.

[32] Salamore and Salamore, "The Transformation of State Electoral Politics."

[33] Sarah McCally Morehouse, *The Governor as Party Leader: Campaigning and Governing* (Ann Arbor: University of Michigan Press, 1998).

[34] Kenneth Dautrich and David A. Yalof, "The State of State Elections," in *The State of the States,* 4th ed., ed. Carl E. Van Horn (Washington, D.C.: CQ Press, 2006).

[35] Dan Seligson, "Home State Blues: Republicans Face Tough Foes in Red State Democratic Governors," *Campaigns & Elections,* online ed., 2005.

[36] Beyle, "Governors."

[37] David R. Mayhew, *Congress: The Electoral Connection* (New Haven, Conn.: Yale University Press, 1974).

[38] Larry Sabato, *Good-Bye to Good-Time Charlie: The American Governorship Transformed,* 2nd ed. (Washington, D.C.: CQ Press, 1983).

[39] Beyle, "Governors."

[40] Andrew Pollack, David Carr, and Carolyn Marshall, "Schwarzenegger Is Drawing Fire for an Ad Deal," *The New York Times,* 15 July 2005, p. A1; and Tom Chorneau, "Schwarzenegger Contract Raises Question," *Sacramento Bee,* online ed., 1 August 2005.

[41] Alisha Davis and Ali Lorraine "'The Body' Fumbles," *Newsweek* 136, no. 22 (2000): 88.

[42] John O'Neil and Avi Salzman, "Ex-Governor of Connecticut Pleads Guilty to Corruption," *The New York Times,* online ed., 23 December 2004; and Stevenson Swanson, "New Jersey Governor to Quit over Gay Affair," *Chicago Tribune,* online ed., 13 August 2004.

[43] Presidents Richard Nixon and Gerald Ford had also been vice president.

[44] Barry Massey, "N. M. Gov.'s Critics Fault His Ambition," *Sacramento Bee,* online ed., 9 October 2006.

[45] Glen Johnson, "Gov. Romney's Future May Hinge on Big Dig," *Sacramento Bee,* online ed., 18 July 2006.

[46] As to sexual orientation, no openly gay person has ever been elected governor of a U.S. state. New Jersey's former governor Jim McGreevey announced that he was gay when he resigned in 2004. His resignation was prompted by ethical and legal questions regarding having sexual relations with an aide and improprieties in the awarding of contracts, not his sexual orientation.

[47] Quoted in Susan J. Carroll, "Women in State Government: Historical Overview and Current Trends," in *The State of the States,* vol. 36 (Lexington, Ky.: Council of State Governments, 2004).

[48] Grasso was re-elected in 1978 but resigned in 1980 for health reasons, dying soon after.

[49] The first African American to serve as governor took office over 100 years before Wilder. In 1872, during the Reconstruction era after the Civil War, as the president pro tem of the Louisiana state senate, P. B. S. Pinchback became governor upon the death of the sitting governor, Oscar Dunn.

[50] Richard E. Neustadt, *Presidential Power and the Modern Presidents* (New York: Free Press, 1990).

[51] For those few states that still do biennial budgeting, it must pass through the legislature every two years.

[52] Dall W. Forsythe, *Memos to the Governor: An Introduction to State Budgeting,* 2nd ed. (Washington, D.C.: Georgetown University Press, 2004); Charles Barrilleaux and Michael Berkman, "Do Governors Matter? Budgeting and the Politics of State Policymaking," *Political Research Quarterly* 56 (2003): 409–17; Thad L. Beyle, "The Governor's Formal Powers: A View from the Governor's Chair," *Public Administration Review* 28 (1968): 540–45; and E. Lee. Bernick, "Gubernatorial Tools: Formal and Informal," *Journal of Politics* 41 (1979): 656–65.

[53] Vicky M. Wilkins and Garry Young, "The Influence of Governors on Veto Override Attempts: A Test of Pivotal Politics," *Legislative Studies Quarterly* 27 (2002): 557–76.

[54] Steven Walters, "Thompson's Legacy," *Milwaukee (Wisc.) Journal-Sentinel,* 24 December 2000, pp. 1A and 10A.

[55] This is also called a "package veto."

[56] Daniel C. Vock, "Govs Enjoy Quirky Veto Power," *Stateline.org,* online ed., 24 April 2007.

[57] Deb Reichman, "Bush Urges Senate to Pass Line-Item Veto," *Sacramento Bee,* online ed., 27 June 2006.

[58] In 1996, Congress tried to give the president an item veto through legislation, but the Supreme Court held that this was unconstitutional. See *Clinton v. City of New York* 524 U.S. 417 (1998).

[59] In addition to Alabama, Illinois, Massachusetts, Montana, New Jersey, and Virginia, South Dakota gives its governor the amendatory veto when the legislature is in session, and Wisconsin does so on budget bills; Vock, "Govs Enjoy Quirky Veto Power."

[60] J. A. Dearden and T. A. Husted, "Do Governors Get What They Want? An Alternative Examination of the Line-Item Veto," *Public Choice* 77 (1993): 707–23.

[61] Thad Beyle, "Being Governor," in *The State of the States,* 4th ed., ed. Carl E. Van Horn (Washington, D.C.: CQ Press, 2006).

[62] Beyle, "Being Governor."

[63] The length of time a governor may actually serve also depends on voters (and, in some cases, federal prosecutors), but term limits and term length are the institutional aspects of tenure potential.

[64] See *The Book of the States 2006,* vol. 38 (Lexington, Ky.: Council of State Governments, 2006), table 4.1.

[65] Rob Gurwitt, "The Last One-Term Statehouse," *Governing* (October 2005): 36–42.

[66] Robert J. Dilger, "A Comparative Analysis of Gubernatorial Enabling Resources," *State and Local Government Review* 26 (1995): 118–26.

[67] Margaret R. Ferguson, *The Executive Branch of State Government* (Santa Barbara, Calif.: ABC-CLIO, 2006): 176–79.

[68] Forsythe, *Memos to the Governor.*

[69] Margaret R. Ferguson, "Gubernatorial Policy Leadership in the Fifty States" (Ph.D. diss., University of North Carolina at Chapel Hill, 1996).

[70] Legislators usually receive expense money for these special sessions to cover their meals, hotels, and so on, but they do not receive extra salary for them.

[71] "Perry Expands Call," *Austin (Texas) American-Statesman,* online ed., 11 May 2006; and Andy Furillo, "Governor Wants Special Session on Prisons," *Sacramento Bee,* online ed., 26 June 2006.

[72] Doug Finke. "Under Pressure: Groups Push Jones on Budget Cuts Vote," (Springfield, IL) *State Journal Register,* 4 October 2007, p.1

[73] Cynthia J. Bowling, Margaret R. Ferguson, and Colleen Clemons, "Executive Orders in the American States" (paper presented at the 6th Annual State Politics and Policy Conference, Lubbock, Texas, 2006).

[74] Council of State Governments 2005, op. cit., 222–24.

[75] Tom Hester Jr., "Gov. Jon Corzine Shuts Down New Jersey Government," *State Journal-Register,* 2 July 2006, p. 7; and "Corzine's Cuts: Hard to Some, Soft to GOP," *Philadelphia Inquirer,* online ed., 11 July 2006.

[76] Prisons, hospitals, and other services deemed essential continued to operate.

[77] Beyle, "Governors."

[78] Charles Barrilleaux, "Governors, Bureaus, and Policymaking," *State and Local Government Review* 31 (1999): 53–59.

[79] The role of head of state is actually a formal gubernatorial duty in the sense that it derives from state statutes and constitutional provisions. But the political and policy importance of the role is derived from a governor's choices about the use of this duty. In this sense, the head of state role is an informal power.

[80] Thad E. Hall, "Changes in Legislative Support for the Governor's Program over Time," *Legislative Studies Quarterly* 27 (2002): 107–22.

[81] Michael Lewis, "The Personal Is the Antipolitical," *The New York Times Magazine* 153 (2003): 40–130.

[82] Philip J. Roberts, *A Penny for the Governor, a Dollar for Uncle Sam: Income Taxation in Washington* (Seattle: University of Washington Press, 2002).

[83] Richard G. Niemi, Thad Beyle, and Lee Sigelman, "Gubernatorial, Senatorial, and State-Level Presidential Job Approval: The U.S. Officials Job Approval Ratings (JAR) Collection," *State Politics and Policy Quarterly* 2 (2002): 215–29.

[84] Gary Delsohn, "Governor Embarks on Image Change," *Sacramento Bee,* online ed., 26 July 2005.

[85] Bernard Schoenburg, "Senior CMS Workers Urged to Push Education Plan," *Springfield, Ill., State Journal-Register*, 15 April 2005, p. 11.

[86] James D. King and Jeffrey E. Cohen, "What Determines a Governor's Popularity?" *State Politics and Policy Quarterly* 5 (2005): 225–47.

[87] Jeffrey E. Cohen and James D. King, "Relative Unemployment and Gubernatorial Popularity," *Journal of Politics* 66 (2004): 1267–82.

[88] Squire and Fastnow, "Comparing Gubernatorial and Senatorial Elections."

[89] G. Patrick Lynch, "The Media in State and Local Politics," in *Media Power, Media Politics,* ed. Mark J. Rozell (Lanham, Md.: Rowman & Littlefield, 2003).

[90] Dometrius, "Governors."

[91] Malcolm E. Jewell and Marcia Lynn Wicker, *Legislative Leadership in the American States* (Ann Arbor: University of Michigan Press, 1994).

[92] V. O. Key Jr., *Southern Politics in the State and Nation* (New York: Knopf, 1949).

[93] Gurwitt, "The Last One-Term Statehouse."

[94] Morris P. Fiorina, *Divided Government,* 2nd ed. (Boston: Allyn & Bacon, 1996).

[95] Dometrius, "Governors."

[96] Alan Rosenthal, *Heavy Lifting: The Job of the American Legislature* (Washington, D.C.: CQ Press, 2004), ch. 9.

[97] John W. Kingdon, *Agendas, Alternatives, and Public Policies* (Glenview, Ill.: Scott, Foresman, 1984).

[98] Rosenthal, *Heavy Lifting.*

[99] The discussion in this section is based on a variety of newspaper articles published in the *Sacramento Bee,*

including Daniel Weintraub, "Pushing Broad Agenda, Governor Will Go Both Ways," 22 March 2005; Tom Chorneau, "Governor Says Special Election Would Return Power 'to the People,'" 19 May 2005; Dan Walters, "Jackson Upstages Schwarzenegger—Portent for Governor's Crusade?" 14 June 2005; Gary Delsohn, "Governor Cites Prop 13 to Open Election Drive," 15 June 2005; Gary Delsohn, "Field Poll: Special Election Turns off Voters," 21 June 2005; Jim Sanders, "Flawed Measure Ignites New Flap," 15 July 2005; Gary Delsohn, "Governor, Allies Spent $23 Million," 2 August 2005; Beth Fouhy, "So Close, yet So Far: How Election Compromise Talks Fell Through," 29 August 2005; Gary Delsohn and Laura Mecoy, "Governor's 'Reforms' Get Cold Shoulder," 9 November 2005; and Steve Lawrence, "Senate Likely to Revisit Redistricting Issue This Week," 18 June 2006.

[100] Quoted in Delsohn and Mecoy, "Governor's 'Reforms' Get Cold Shoulder."

[101] Margaret Robertson Ferguson, "Chief Executive Success in the Legislative Arena," *State Politics and Policy Quarterly* 3 (2003): 158–82.

[102] Quoted in Delsohn and Mecoy, "Governor's 'Reforms' Get Cold Shoulder."

[103] Peter Hecht, "Governor's Decisive U-Turn," *Sacramento Bee*, online ed., 10 November 2006.

[104] Kendra A. Hovey and Harold A. Hovey, *CQ's State Fact Finder* (Washington, D.C.: CQ Press, 2007), 114.

[105] Norma M. Riccucci, *How Management Works: Street-Level Bureaucrats and Welfare Reform* (Washington, D.C.: Georgetown University Press, 2005).

[106] George A. Krause, David E. Lewis, and James W. Douglas, "Political Appointments, Civil Service Systems, and Bureaucratic Competence: Organizational Balancing and Executive Branch Revenue Forecasts in the American States," *American Journal of Political Science* 50 (2006): 770–87.

[107] Charles Barrilleaux, "Statehouse Bureaucracy: Institutional Consistency in a Changing Environment," in *American State and Local Politics: Directions for the 21st Century,* ed. Ronald E. Weber and Paul Brace (New York: Chatham House, 1999).

[108] The discussion in this section is based on a variety of newspaper articles, including Diane Rado and Ray Long, "Blagojevich Sets School Power Grab," *Chicago Tribune,* 14 January 2004, p. 1; Stephanie Banchero and Tracy Dell'Angela, "Educators Jabbing at Governor's School Fix," *Chicago Tribune,* 18 January 2004, p. 1; Diane Rado and Ray Long, "Schools Could Get $2.2 Billion but Blagojevich Doesn't Want State Education Panel Handling It," *Chicago Tribune,* 23 March 2004, p. 1; Ray Long and Christi Parsons, "Madigan Condemns Governor's School Plan," *Chicago Tribune,* 6 May 2004, p. 1; Adriana Colindres, "Lawmakers Give Governor Power to Remake Education Board," *Springfield, Ill., State Journal-Register,* 23 July 2004, p. 1; Adriana Colindres, "Governor Shakes up State Education Board with New Appointees," *Springfield, Ill., State Journal-Register,* 14 September 2004, p. 1; and Diane Rado, "Junk-Food Ban Faces School Board Critics: State Panel Questions Governor's Proposal," *Chicago Tribune,* 16 March 2006, p. 3.

[109] Alan Greenblatt, "A Rage to Reorganize," *Governing* (March 2005): 30–35.

[110] Todd Milburn, "Governor Agrees to New Casino Deal with Tribe," *Sacramento Bee,* online ed., 8 August 2006; and Kevin Yamamura, "Schwarzenegger Slams House Republicans for Immigration Reform Plan Delays," *Sacramento Bee,* online ed., 21 June 2006.

[111] Beyle, "Governors: The Middlemen and Women."

[112] Peter Hecht, "Blair, Schwarzenegger Make Global Warming Deal," *Sacramento Bee,* online ed., 31 July 2006.

[113] Joachim Blatter, "Beyond Hierarchies and Networks: Institutional Logics and Change in Transboundary Spaces," *Governance* 16 (2003): 503–26.

[114] The discussion in this section is based on a variety of newspaper articles, including Ralph Blumenthal, "Citing Border Violence, 2 States Declare a Crisis," *The New York Times,* 17 August 2005, p. 14; Arthur H. Rotstein, "Napolitano Checks out Border Safety in Statewide Tour," *Associated Press State and Local Wire,* online ed., 2 November 2005; Jacques Billeaud, "Arizona Governor Four Months ahead of Bush on Border Troops," *Associated Press State and Local Wire,* online ed., 16 May 2006; Lara Jakes Jordan, "Homeland Security to Probe Border Strategy," *Associated Press Online,* online ed., 23 August 2005; John Pomfret, "At Front Line of Immigration Debate; Ariz. Governor Favors Tough Enforcement but Humane Treatment," *The Washington Post,* 31 May 2006, p. A03; Blake Schmidt, "Utah Governor Visits Guardsmen," Yuma, Ariz., *Sun,* online ed., 13 June 2006; Paul Davenport, "Napolitano Signs Pact for National Guard Border Duty," *Associated Press State and Local Wire,* online ed., 2 June 2006; Jacques Billeaud, "Governor Vetoes Bill to Pay for Sending Troops to the Border," *Associated Press State and Local Wire,* online ed., 10 March 2006; Robert Tanner, "Swamped with Illegal Immigrants at Home,

Governors Pushing for Action in Washington," *Associated Press,* online ed., 27 February 2006; Arthur H. Rotstein, "Illegal Immigration Top Story of 2005 in Arizona," *Associated Press State and Local Wire,* online ed., 31 December 2005; Lisa Riley Roche, "Huntsman Hopes to Rally Western Governors," *Deseret (Utah) Morning News,* online ed., 8 November 2005; "Governors Announce Steps on Cross-Border Safety," *Associated Press State and Local Wire,* online ed., 21 June 2005; Scott Baldauf, "Border States Forge Their Own Foreign Policy," *Christian Science Monitor,* 10 July 2000, 2; and Jacques Billeaud, "Ariz. Gov. Vetoes Criminal Immigrant Bill," *Sacramento Bee,* online ed., 18 April 2006.

[115] James A. Barnes, "Wedge Issue Could Splinter GOP Base," *National Journal* 37 (2005): 3006–8.

[116] Edgar Ruiz, "Regional Cooperation: The Border Legislative Conference," *Spectrum* (Fall 2004): 20–21.

Chapter 9

[1] These figures are for cases that were concluded in 2002, the most recent year for which complete data are available; see the National Center for State Courts, http://www.ncsconline.org; and the Bureau of Justice Statistics, http://www.bjs.gov.

[2] Lawrence Baum, *American Courts: Process and Policy,* 5th ed. (Boston: Houghton Mifflin, 2001), ch. 7.

[3] Shauna M. Strickland, *State Court Caseload Statistics, 2003* (Williamsburg, Va.: National Center for State Courts, 2004).

[4] Eric Helland and Alexander Tabarrok, "Runaway Judges? Selection Effects and the Jury," *Journal of Law, Economics, and Organization* 16 (2000): 306–33.

[5] Henry R. Glick, "Courts: Politics and the Judicial Process," in *Politics in the American States,* 8th ed., ed. Virginia Gray and Russell L. Hanson (Washington, D.C.: CQ Press, 2004).

[6] Mamie Till-Mobley and Christopher Benson, *The Death of Innocence: The Story of the Hate Crime That Changed America* (New York: Random House, 2003).

[7] Glick, "Courts."

[8] George Fisher, *Plea Bargaining's Triumph: A History of Plea Bargaining in America* (Stanford, Calif.: Stanford University Press, 2003).

[9] James G. Lakely, "Bush Hits 'Frivolous Lawsuits,'" *Washington Times,* online ed., 16 December 2004; Joel B.

Grossman, Herbert M. Kritzer, and S. Macauley, "Do the 'Haves' Still Come out Ahead?" *Law and Society Review* 33 (1999): 803–10; W. F. Samuelson, "Settlements out of Court: Efficiency and Equity," *Group Decision and Negotiation* 7 (1998): 157–77; and Herbert M. Kritzer, "Contingent-Fee Lawyers and Their Clients: Settlement Expectations, Settlement Realities, and Issues of Control in the Lawyer-Client Relationship," *Law and Social Inquiry* 23 (1998): 795–821.

[10] Even an interest group is organized to fight this problem, as they see it. They have a telling name: the Lawsuit Abuse Reform Coalition. See Lawsuit Abuse Reform Coalition, http://www.lawsuitabusereform.org.

[11] Jeff Yates, Belinda Creel Davis, and Henry R. Glick, "The Politics of Torts: Explaining Litigation Rates in the American States," *State Politics and Policy Quarterly* 1 (2001): 127–43.

[12] Gregory A. Huber and Sanford C. Gordon, "Accountability and Coercion: Is Justice Blind When It Runs for Office?" *American Journal of Political Science* 48 (2004): 247–63.

[13] Donald R. Songer and Kelly A. Crews-Meyer, "Does Gender Matter?" *Social Science Quarterly* 81 (2000): 750–62; and Donald R. Songer and Susan J. Tabrizi, "The Religious Right on the Court," *Journal of Politics* 61 (1999): 506–26.

[14] C. West Huddleston III, "Drug Courts: An Effective Strategy for Communities Facing Methamphetamine," in *Bureau of Justice Assistance Bulletin* (Washington, D.C.: U.S. Department of Justice, 2005).

[15] Madelynn Herman, "The Mental Health Concept," typescript (Williamsburg, Va.: Knowledge and Information Services, National Center for State Courts, 2000).

[16] National Center for State Courts, *Examining the Work of State Courts, 2003* (Williamsburg, Va.: National Center for State Courts, 2004).

[17] Roger A. Hanson, *Appellate Court Performance Standards and Measures* (Williamsburg, Va.: National Center for State Courts, 1999).

[18] Shirley S. Abrahamson, "Homegrown Justice: The State Constitutions," in *Developments in State Constitutional Law,* ed. Bradley D. McGraw (St. Paul, Minn.: West, 1985): 315.

[19] The U.S. Supreme Court may overturn a state supreme court's decision but only based on some aspect of the U.S. Constitution, not state law.

[20] "Iowa Court Decision a Victory for State Legislatures," *NCSL News,* online ed., 17 June 2004, http:www.ncsl.org/programs/press/2004/pr040617.htm.

[21] Fred Cheesman, Roger A. Hanson, and Brian J. Ostrom, "Caseload and Timeliness in State Supreme Courts," *Caseload Highlights: Examining the Work of State Courts* 7, no. 2 (2001): 1–6.

[22] National Center for State Courts, *Examining the Work of State Courts.*

[23] National Center for State Courts, *Examining the Work of State Courts.*

[24] Texas and Oklahoma each have two supreme courts, one for civil cases and one for criminal cases, but each of these has the last word for the cases it hears.

[25] Victor E. Flango and Ann L. Keith, "How Useful Is the New Aggressive Driving Legislation?" *Court Review* 40, nos. 3–4 (2004): 34–43.

[26] Related to this example, consider the way the legal definition of *parent* evolved in the following cases before the California Supreme Court: *In re Nicholas H.* (6 June 2002) 28 Cal. 4th 56; *In re Jesusa V.* (16 April 2004) 97 Cal.App. 4th 878; and *Elisa B. v. Superior Court* (22 August 2005) 118 Cal.App. 4th 966.

[27] Paul Brace and Melinda Gann Hall, "Neo-Institutionalism and Dissent on State Supreme Courts," *Journal of Politics* 52 (1990): 54–70; and Paul Brace and Melinda Gann Hall, "Integrated Models of Judicial Dissent," *Journal of Politics* 55 (1993): 914–35.

[28] For example, consider the different opinions of two groups over the Massachusetts Supreme Judicial Court's decision that the state cannot ban same-sex marriage: Andrea Lafferty, "Massachusetts Supreme Judicial Court Legalizes Same-Sex Marriage!" Traditional Values Coalition, 2004, http://www.traditionalvalues.org/modules.php?sid=1323; and National Organization for Women (NOW), "NOW Leaders Applaud Massachusetts Supreme Court Ruling Favoring Same-Sex Marriage Rights," 2004, http://www.now.org/issues/lgbi/020604marriage.html.

[29] Paul Brace and Melinda Gann Hall, "The Interplay of Preferences, Case Facts, Context, and Structure in the Politics of Judicial Choice," *Journal of Politics* 59 (1997): 1206–31.

[30] Craig A. Traut and Carol F. Emmert, "Expanding the Integrated Model of Judicial Decision Making: The California Justices and Capital Punishment," *Journal of Politics* 60 (1998): 1166–80.

[31] Philip Dubois, *From Ballot to Bench* (Austin: University of Texas Press, 1980).

[32] Maldavi McCall, "Gender, Judicial Dissent, and Issue Salience: The Voting Behavior of State Supreme Court Justices in Sexual Harassment Cases, 1980–1998," *Social Science Journal* 40 (2003): 79–97; and Songer and Crews-Meyers, "Does Gender Matter?"

[33] Songer and Tabrizi, "The Religious Right on the Court."

[34] Laura Langer, *Judicial Review in State Supreme Courts: A Comparative Study* (Albany: State University of New York Press, 1999).

[35] Craig F. Emmert, "An Integrated Case-Related Model of Judicial Decisionmaking: Explaining State Supreme Court Decisions in Judicial Review Cases," *Journal of Politics* 54 (1992): 543–52.

[36] Charles H. Sheldon, "Judicial Review and the Supreme Court of Washington, 1890–1986," *Publius* 17 (1987): 69–89.

[37] Lee Epstein, "Exploring the Participation of Organized Interests in State Court Litigation," *Political Research Quarterly* 47 (1994): 335–51.

[38] Glick, op. cit.

[39] Glendon A. Schubert, *The Judicial Mind: The Attitudes and Ideologies of Supreme Court Justices, 1946–1963* (Evanston, Ill.: Northwestern University Press, 1965).

[40] Charles H. Sheldon and Linda S. Maule, *Choosing Justice: The Recruitment of State and Federal Judges* (Pullman: Washington State University Press, 1997).

[41] Donald A. Downs, *Nazis in Skokie: Freedom, Community and the First Amendment* (South Bend, Ind.: University of Notre Dame Press, 1985).

[42] F. Andrew Hanssen, "Learning about Judicial Independence: Institutional Change in the State Courts," *Journal of Legal Studies* 33 (2004): 431–73.

[43] Kermit L. Hall, "Progressive Reform and the Decline of Democratic Accountability: The Popular Election of State Supreme Court Judges, 1850–1920," *American Bar Foundation Research Journal* 2 (1984): 345–63.

[44] Of course, because all federal judges are appointed by the president, the same argument could be made about the federal judiciary.

[45] For example, see American Bar Association, "Independence of the Judiciary: Judicial Elections Are Becoming More Politicized," 2006, http://www.abanet.org/publiced/lawday/talking/judicialelections.html.

[46] David Klein and Lawrence Baum, "Ballot Information and Voting Decisions in Judicial Elections," *Political Research Quarterly* 54 (2001): 709–28. On the other hand, recent research has shown that American voters may actually cast a more informed vote in judicial elections than had previously been thought; see Melinda Gann Hall and Chris W. Bonneau, "Predicting Challengers in State Supreme Court Elections: Context and the Politics of Institutional Design," *Political Research Quarterly* 56 (2003): 337–49; and Melinda Gann Hall and Chris W. Bonneau, "Does Quality Matter? Challengers in State Supreme Court Elections," *American Journal of Political Science* 50 (2006): 20–33.

[47] "The Sins of Justice Yarbrough," *Time,* online ed., 18 July 1977.

[48] Chris W. Bonneau, "What Price Justice(s)? Understanding Campaign Spending in State Supreme Court Elections," *State Politics and Policy Quarterly* 5 (2005): 107–25; and Eric Velasco, "Bids for State Court Carry High Price Tags," *Birmingham (Ala.) News,* online ed., 12 June 2006.

[49] Robert Lenzner and Matthew Miller, "Buying Justice," *Forbes,* 21 July 2003, 64; Zach Patton, "Robe Warriors," in *State and Local Government, 2007 Edition,* ed. Kevin B. Smith (Washington, D.C.: CQ Press, 2006); and Illinois Campaign for Political Reform, "Downstate Judicial Races Leave Records in the Dust," press release, 2006, http://www.ilcampaign.org/blog/2006/11/downstate-judicial-races-leave-records.html.

[50] Matthew Manweller, "The 'Angriest Crocodile': Information Costs, Direct Democracy Activists, and the Politicization of State Judicial Elections," *State and Local Government Review* 37 (2005): 86–102.

[51] James Eisenstein, "Financing Pennsylvania's Supreme Court Candidates," *Judicature* 84 (2000): 10–19; and Michael J. Goodman and William C. Rempel, "In Las Vegas, They're Playing with a Stacked Judicial Deck," *Los Angeles Times,* online ed., 8 June 2006.

[52] Adam Liptak, "Justice Bemoans 'Seat-Buying,'" *State Journal-Register,* 1 October 2006, p. 4.

[53] Nevada Judge Gene T. Porter, quoted in Goodman and Rempel, "In Las Vegas, They're Playing with a Stacked Judicial Deck."

[54] Damon M. Cann, "Justice for Sale? Campaign Contributions and Judicial Decisionmaking," *State Politics and Policy Quarterly* 7 (2007): 281–97.

[55] *Republican Party of Minnesota v. White,* 536 US 765 (2002).

[56] *U.S. Eighth Circuit Court, Dimick v. Republican Party of Minnesota* (No. 05–566).

[57] Doug Bend, "North Carolina's Public Financing of Judicial Campaigns: A Preliminary Analysis," *Georgetown Journal of Legal Ethics,* online ed. (Summer 2005).

[58] Patton, "Robe Warriors."

[59] R. L. Dudley, "Turnover and Tenure on State High Courts: Does Method of Selection Make a Difference?" *Justice System Journal* 19 (1997): 1–16.

[60] James P. Wenzel, Shaun Bowler, and David J. Lanoue, "The Sources of Public Confidence in State Courts: Experience and Institutions," *American Politics Research* 31 (2003): 191–211; and Sara C. Benesh, "Understanding Public Confidence in America Courts," *Journal of Politics* 68 (2006): 697–707.

[61] Barbara L. Graham, "Do Judicial Selection Systems Matter? A Study of Black Representation on State Courts," *American Politics Quarterly* 18 (1990): 316–36; and Mark S. Hurwitz and Drew Noble Lanier, "Explaining Judicial Diversity: The Differential Ability of Women and Minorities to Attain Seats on State Supreme and Appellate Courts," *State Politics and Policy Quarterly* 3 (2003): 329–52.

[62] Nicholas O. Alozie, "Selection Methods and the Recruitment of Women to State Courts of Last Resort," *Social Science Quarterly* 77 (1996): 110–26; Kathleen A. Bratton and Rorie L. Spill, "Existing Diversity and Judicial Selection: The Role of the Appointment Method in Establishing Gender Diversity in State Supreme Courts," *Social Science Quarterly* 83 (2002): 504–18; and Hurwitz and Lanier, "Explaining Judicial Diversity."

[63] Henry R. Glick and Craig F. Emmert, "Selection Systems and Judicial Characteristics: The Recruitment of State Supreme Court Justices," *Judicature* 70 (1987): 228–35.

[64] Brace and Hall, "The Interplay of Preferences, Case Facts, Context, and Structure."

[65] Traut and Emmert, "Expanding the Integrated Model of Judicial Decision Making."

[66] Melinda Gann Hall, "Constituent Influence in State Supreme Courts: Conceptual Notes and a Case Study," *Journal of Politics* 49 (1987): 1117–24; and Melinda Gann Hall, "Electoral Politics and Strategic Voting in State Supreme Courts," *Journal of Politics* 54 (1992): 427–46.

[67] Huber and Gordon, "Accountability and Coercion."

[68] Harold W. Elder, "Property Rights Structures and Criminal Courts: An Analysis of State Criminal Courts," *International Review of Law and Economics* 7 (1987): 21–32.

[69] Melinda Gann Hall, "State Supreme Courts in American Democracy: Probing the Myths of Judicial Reform," *American Political Science Review* 95 (2001): 315–30.

[70] Paul Brace and Melinda Gann Hall, "Justices' Response to Case Facts," *American Politics Quarterly* 24 (1996): 237–61; and Stuart S. Nagel, *Comparing Elected and Appointed Judicial Systems* (Beverly Hills, Calif.: Sage, 1973).

[71] Alexander Tabarrok and Eric Helland, "Court Politics: The Political Economy of Tort Awards," *Journal of Law and Economics* 42 (1999): 157–88.

[72] Hall, "State Supreme Courts in American Democracy."

[73] Zach Patton, "Judging the Judges," *Governing* (October 2006): 41–3.

[74] "Congress and Court-Stripping: Just Keep Your Shirts On," *Church and State,* online ed., May 2004.

[75] Nancy McCarthy, "South Dakota Measures Puts Judges on Edge," *California Law Journal,* online ed., November 2006.

Chapter 10

[1] William Niskanen, *Bureaucracy and Representative Government* (Chicago: Aldine-Atherton, 1971), "Revenue Structure, Fiscal Illusion and Budgetary Choice," *Public Choice* (1976): 45–61; James Buchanan and Richard E. Wagner, *Democracy in Deficit* (New York: Academic Press, 1977); and Robert Higgs, *Crisis and Leviathan: Critical Episodes in the Growth of American Government* (New York: Oxford, 1987).

[2] South Dakota does levy a tax on bank income.

[3] http://www.taxadmin.org/fta/rate/ind_inc.html.

[4] James Garand and Kyle Baudoin, "Fiscal Policy in the American States," in *Politics in the American States: A Comparative Analysis,* 8th ed., ed. V. Gray and R Hanson (Washington, D.C.: CQ Press, 2004).

[5] 1996 Center for Tax Justice Report: Michael P. Ettlinger, John F. O'Hare, Robert S. McIntyre, Julie King, Neil Miransky, and Elizabeth A. Fray. 1996 "Who Pays? A Distributional Analysis of the Tax Systems of the 50 States." Citizens for Tax Justice. http://www.ctj.org/html/whopay.htm.

[6] Shaun Bowler and Todd Donovan, "Public Responsiveness to Taxation," *Political Research Quarterly* (1995): Vol. 48: 79–99.

[7] Susan Hansen, *The Politics of Taxation: Revenue without Representation* (New York: Praeger, 1983).

[8] Richard Winters, "The Politics of Taxing and Spending," in *Politics in the American States: A Comparative Analysis.* 7th ed., ed. V. Gray and R Hanson (Washington, D.C.: CQ Press, 1999).

[9] Hansen, *The Politics of Taxation.*

[10] Winters, "The Politics of Taxing and Spending."

[11] W. Duncombe, "Economic Change and the Evolving State Tax Structure: The Case of the Sales Tax," *National Tax Journal* (1992): 308.

[12] State laws also determine what percentage of the assessed value of property is subject to the tax.

[13] National Council of State Legislators, *A Guide to Property Tax: Property Tax Relief,* report on property tax (Denver, CO: National Council of State Legislators, 2002).

[14] Daniel B. Suits, "Measurement of Tax Progressivity," *American Economic Review* 67, no. 4 (1977): 747.

[15] Bowler and Donovan, "Public Responsiveness to Taxation."

[16] David O. Sears and Jack Citrin, *Something for Nothing in California* (Berkeley: University of California Press, 1982); David Lowery and Lee Sigelman, "Understanding the Tax Revolt: Eight Explanations," *American Political Science Review* (1981): 963–74; and Daniel A. Smith, *Tax Crusaders and the Politics of Direct Democracy* (New York: Routledge, 1999).

[17] Rafel Gerena-Morales, "Across U.S., Rising Property Taxes Spark Revolts," *Wall Street Journal,* February 1, 2006, p. B4.

[18] Data in this section are from the Federation of Tax Administrators, http://www.taxadmin.org.

[19] Garand and Baudoin, "Fiscal Policy in the American States."

[20] Cigarette tax information is from the Federation of Tax Administrators, http://www.taxadmin.org. Rates are as of January 1, 2006.

[21] Based on ranking states in terms of the sum of their wine, spirits, beer, and cigarette taxes. This ranking excludes states with government-operated liquor stores.

[22] Elizabeth McNichol, Center for Budget and Policy Priorities, 2004, http://www.cbpp.org/2–18–04sfp.htm#_ftn1.

[23] William Gates Sr. and Chuck Collins, "Tax the Wealthy: Why America Needs the Estate Tax," *American Prospect,* June 17, 2002.

[24] National Association of State and Provincial Lotteries, http://www.naspl.org/history.html.

[25] David Broder, *Democracy Derailed: Initiative Campaigns and the Power of Money* (San Diego, Calif.: Harcourt, 2000): 83–84.

[26] Daniel B. Suits, "Gambling Taxes: Regressivity and Revenue Potential," *National Tax Journal* 30 (1977): 25–33.

[27] John Mikesell and C. Kurt Zorn, "State Lotteries as Fiscal Saviors or Fiscal Fraud," *Public Administration Review* 46 (1986): 311–20.

[28] Mosi Secret, "Lottery Will Replace $1B in State Money: Bill Was Changed after Passage," *Independent Weekly,* February 8, 2006, http://indyweek.com/gyrobase/Content? oid=oid%3A27511.

[29] Neva Kerbeshian Novarro, "Does Earmarking Matter? The Case of State Lottery Profits and Educational Spending," Stanford Institute for Economic Policy Research Discussion Paper no. 02–19 (Stanford, Calif.: Stanford Institute for Economic Policy Research, 2002).

[30] http://www.naspl.org/ranksales.html.

[31] California Department of Education, *State Lottery Fact Book 2004* (Sacramento: California Department of Education, 2004).

[32] National Council of State Legislators, http://www.ncsl.org/programs/fiscal/tels2005.htm.

[33] Peter Schrag, *Paradise Lost: California's Experience, America's Future* (Berkeley: University of California Press, 2004).

[34] Elisabeth Gerber, Arthur Lupia, Mathew McCubbins, and D. R. Kiewiet, *Stealing the Initiative: How State Government Responds to Direct Democracy* (Upper Saddle River, N.J.: Prentice Hall, 2001).

[35] Shaun Bowler and Todd Donovan, "Evolution in State Governance Structures," *Political Research Quarterly* (2004): 189–196; and James Alt and Robert Lowry, "Divided Government, Fiscal Institutions, and Budget Deficits: Evidence from the States," *American Political Science Review* 88 (1994): 811–28.

[36] Ronald Shadbegian, "Do Tax and Expenditure Limitations Affect the Size and Growth of Government?" *Contemporary Economic Policy* (January 1996): pp 22–35.

[37] Michael New, *Limiting Government through Direct Democracy: The Case of State Tax and Expenditure Limitations,* Cato Policy Analysis no. 420 (Washington, D.C.: Cato Institute, 2001).

[38] Bell Policy Center, "Ten Years of TABOR: A Study of Colorado's Taxpayer's Bill of Rights" (Denver, CO: Bell Policy Center, 2003).

[39] Todd Donovan and Shaun Bowler, "Responsive or Responsible Government," in *Citizens as Legislators,* ed. S. Bowler, T. Donovan, and C. Tolbert (Columbus: Ohio State University Press, 1998); and James Clingermayer and B. D. Wood, "Disentangling Patterns of State Debt Financing," *American Political Science Review* (1995): pp. 108–120. In contrast, see D. R. Kiewiet and K. Szakaly, "Constitutional Limitations of Borrowing: An Analysis of State Bonded Indebtedness," *Journal of Law, Economics and Organizations* (1996): 62–97.

[40] James Poterba and Kim Rueben, *Fiscal Rules and State Borrowing Costs* (San Francisco: Public Policy Institute of California, 1999).

[41] Bowler and Donovan, Evolution in State Governance Structures."

[42] John Matsusaka, *For the Many or the Few: The Initiative, Public Policy and American Democracy* (Chicago: University of Chicago Press, 2004).

[43] Timothy Conlan, *New Federalism: Intergovernmental Reform from Nixon to Reagan* (Washington, D.C.: Brookings Institution, 1988): 6.

[44] U.S. Office of Management and Budget, "The Budget of the United States Government, Fiscal Year 2006, Historical Tables," 2006, http://a255.g.akamaitech.net/7/255/2422/23feb20050900/www.gpoaccess.gov/usbudget/fy06/pdf/hist.pdf.

[45] U.S. Census Bureau, http://www.census.gov/prod/2004pubs/04statab/stlocgov.pdf.

[46] These are expressed in 2002 dollars; see White House, "Summary of Receipts, Outlays, and Surpluses or Deficits (-): 1789–2008," http://www.whitehouse.gov/omb/budget/fy2004/hist.html, Table 1.

[47] David Lowery, "The Distribution of Tax Burdens in the American States: The Determinants of Fiscal Incidence," *Western Political Quarterly* (1986): 137–58; and V. O. Key, *Southern Politics in the State and Nation* (New York: Knopf, 1949). This effect may depend on the period being studied. See B. R. Fry and R. D. Winters, "The Politics of Redistribution," *American Political Science Review* 70 (1970): 508–22.

[48] Neil Berch, "Explaining the Changes in Tax Incidence in the States," *Political Research Quarterly* 48 (1995): 629–41.

[49] Hansen, *The Politics of Taxation.*

[50] Francis Berry and William D. Berry, "State Lottery Adoptions as Policy Innovations," *American Political Science Review* (1990): 395–415.

[51] Hansen, *The Politics of Taxation.*

[52] Francis Berry and William D. Berry, "Tax Innovation in the States: Capitalizing on Political Opportunity," *American Journal of Political Science* (1992): 715–42.

[53] Francis Berry and William D. Berry, "The Politics of Tax Increases in the States," *American Journal of Political Science* (1994): 855–99.

[54] Nicholas Johnson and Brian Filipowich, *Tax Cuts and Continued Consequences* (Washington, D.C.: Center for Budget and Policy Priorities, 2006).

[55] Robert Lucas, "On the Mechanics of Economic Development," *Journal of Monetary Economics* (1988): 3–42; and Enrico Moretti, "Estimating the External Return to Higher Education, *Journal of Econometrics* (2003): 175–202.

[56] William M. Gentry and R. Glenn Hubbard. 2000. "Tax Policy and Entrepreneurial Entry." *American Economic Review.* 283–87.

[57] Young Lee and Roger H Gordon, "Tax Structure and Economic Growth," *Journal of Public Economics* (2005).

[58] J. B. Cullen and Robert H. Gordon, "Taxes and Entrepreneurial Activity: Theory and Evidence for the U.S.," NBER Working Paper No. 9015 (New York: National Bureau of Economic Research, 2002).

[59] Heckman 1976 James Heckman "A Life-Cycle Model of Earnings, Learning, and Consumption," *Journal of Political Economy,* University of Chicago Press, vol. 84(4), pages S11–44; in contrast, see P. A. Trostel, "The Effect of Taxation on Human Capital," *Journal of Political Economy* (1993): 327–350.

[60] Clark C. Bloom. 1955. *State and Local Tax Differentials and the Location of Manufacturing.* Iowa City: Bureau of Business and Economic Research; Wilbur Thompson and John M. Mattilla. 1959. *An Econometric Model of Postwar State Economic Development.* Wayne State University Press.; Dennis W. Carlton 1979. "Why New Firms Locate Where they Do. In W. Wheaton (ed.) Interregional Movements and Regional Growth. Washington, D.C.: The Urban Institute.

[61] Thomas Romans and Ganti Subrahmanyam, 1979. "State and Local Taxes, Transfers, and Regional Economic Growth," *Southern Economic Journal.* 435–444; Robert J. Newman. 1983. "Industry Migration and Growth in the South. *Review of Economics and Statistics.* 76–86.

[62] Romans and Subrahmanyam, "State and Local Taxes"; and L. Jay Helms, "The Effect of State and Local Taxes on Economic Growth: A Time Series–Cross Sectional Approach," *Review of Economics and Statistics* 67 (1985): 574–82.

[63] Helms, "The Effect of State and Local Taxes on Economic Growth."

[64] Alaeddin Mofidi and Joe A. Stone, "Do State and Local Taxes Affect Economic Growth?" *Review of Economics and Statistics* (1990): 686–91.

[65] Garand and Baudoin, "Fiscal Policy in the American States," 293.

[66] Garand and Baudoin, "Fiscal Policy in the American States."

[67] Winters, "The Politics of Taxing and Spending."

[68] Fiscal Survey of the States 2005 National Association of State Government Budget Officers. http://www.nasbo.org/Publications/fiscalsurvey/fsfall2005.pdf.

[69] Kenneth Feingold et al., "Social Program Spending and State Fiscal Crisis," Urban Institute Occasional Paper no. 70 (Washington, D.C.: Urban Institute, 2003).

[70] Feingold et al., "Social Program Spending and State Fiscal Crisis."

[71] Mark Rom, "Transforming State Health and Welfare Programs," in *Politics in the American States: A Comparative Analysis* (Washington, D.C.: CQ Press, 2004)

[72] National Association of State Budget Officers, *State Expenditure Report* (Washington, D.C.: NASBO, 2003).

[73] John Ritter, "San Diego Now Enron by the Sea," *USA Today,* 24 October 2004.

[74] Wagner 1976 *Democracy in Deficit,* 1977.

[75] Thomas Dye, *Politics Economics, and the Public* (Chicago: Rand McNally, 1966); and James Garand, "Explaining Government Growth in the US States," *American Political Science Review* (1988): 837–49.

[76] Dye, *Politics Economics, and the Public;* and Richard Hofferbert. 1966. "The Relationship Between Public Policy and Some Structural and Environmental Variables in the American States." *American Political Science Review.* 73–82.

[77] Garand, "Explaining Government Growth in the US States."

[78] Robert S. Erikson, Gerald C. Wright, and John P. McIver, *Statehouse Democracy: Public Opinion and Policy in the American States* (Cambridge: Cambridge University Press, 1993): 85.

[79] Kim Q. Hill and Jan Leighley, "The Policy Consequences of Class Bias in State Electorates," *American Journal of Political Science* (1992): 351–65.

[80] James Poterba, "Budget Institutions and Fiscal Policy in the U.S. States," *American Economic Review* 86, no. 2 (Papers and Proceedings; 1996): 395–400.

[81] James Poterba, "Balanced Budget Rules and Fiscal Policy: Evidence from the States," *National Tax Journal* (1995): 329–327.

[82] Hening Bohn and Robert P. Inman, "Balanced Budget Rules and Public Deficits: Evidence from the U.S. States," NBER Working Paper no. W5533, 1996, http://ssrn.com/abstract=4069.

[83] James Alt and Robert Lowry, "Divided Government, Fiscal Institutions, and Budget Deficits: Evidence from the States," *American Political Science Review* 88 (1994): 811–28.

[84] Kiewiet and Szakaly, "Constitutional Limitations of Borrowing."

[85] Shaun Bowler and Todd Donovan, *Demanding Choices: Opinion, Voting, and Direct Democracy* (Ann Arbor: University of Michigan Press, 1998).

[86] Garand and Baudoin, "Fiscal Policy in the American States."

[87] Tamim Bayoumi, Morris Goldstein, and Geoffrey Woglom, "Do Credit Markets Discipline Sovereign Borrowers?" *Journal of Money, Credit and Banking* 27 (1995): 1046–59.

[88] Reports from 2003 place the deficit for 2004 at $31 billion (2003; see American Legislative Exchange Council, "Budget Deficit Chart" http://www.alec.org/meSWFiles/pdf/Deficits.pdf); to $38 billion (2005; see Public Policy Institute of California, "Just the Facts: California's State Budget," January [Sacramento: Public Policy Institute of California, 2005]).

[89] Feingold et al., "Social Program Spending and State Fiscal Crisis."

[90] Elaine Magg and David Merriman, *Tax Policy Response to Revenue Shortfall* (Washington, D.C.: Urban Institute, 2003).

[91] Garand, "Explaining Government Growth in the US States."

Chapter 11

[1] *Report of the Independent Commission on the Los Angeles Police Department* (Los Angeles: Independent Commission on the Los Angeles Police Department, 1991), ch. 10.

[2] National Briefing, "South Florida: Mayor Fires Police Chief," *The New York Times*, 20 December 2001.

[3] National Briefing, "Mid Atlantic: Maryland: Mayor Fires Police Commissioner," *The New York Times*, 11 November 2004.

[4] In Virginia, municipalities are jurisdictions independent from the counties they are located in. In Connecticut and Rhode Island, county governments play no functional role.

[5] Herbert Storing, *What the Antifederalists Were For* (Chicago: University of Chicago Press, 1981).

[6] Data from Campbell Gibson, "Population of the 100 Largest Cities and Other Urban Places in the United States: 1790–1990," U.S. Census Bureau. Population Division Working Paper no. 27, June (Washington, D.C.: U.S. Census Bureau. Population Division, 1998).

[7] Julie Byrne, *Roman Catholics and Immigration in Nineteenth Century America* (National Humanities Center November 2000. Research Triangle Park, N.C.)

[8] Terry Golway, "Firefighters," *American Heritage Magazine* 56, no. 6 (November/December 2005).

[9] Campbell Gibson and Emily Lennon, "Historical Census on the Foreign Born Population of the United States: 1850–1990," U.S. Census Bureau, Population Division Working Paper no. 29, February (Washington, D.C.: U.S. Census Bureau, Population Division, 1999).

[10] Alexander Keysar, *The Right to Vote: The Contested History of Democracy in the United States* (New York: Basic Books, 2000), table A.2

[11] Richard Gunther and Larry Diamond, "Species of Political Parties," *Party Politics* 9 (2003): 167–99.

[12] Golway, "Firefighters."

[13] Amy Bridges, *A City in the Republic: Antebellum New York and the Origins of Machine Politics* (Ithaca, N.Y.: Cornell University Press, 1984).

[14] Amy Greenberg, *Cause for Alarm: The Volunteer Fire Department in the Nineteenth Century City* (Cambridge, Mass.: Harvard University Press, 1998).

[15] Steven P. Erie, *Rainbow's End: Irish Americans and the Dilemmas of Urban Machine Politics, 1840–1985* (Berkeley: University of California Press, 1988).

[16] Erie, *Rainbow's End.*

[17] Gunther and Diamond, "Species of Political Parties."

[18] Peter McCaffery, *When Bosses Ruled Philadelphia* (University Park: Pennsylvania State University Press, 1993).

[19] Clarence Stone, "Urban Political Machines: Taking Stock," *PS: Political Science and Politics* 29, no. 3 (1996): 446–50.

[20] Robert McChesney, *Corporate Media as a Threat to Democracy* (New York: Seven Stories Press, 1997).

[21] Zoltan Hajnal and Paul Lewis, "Municipal Institutions and Voter Turnout in Local Elections," *Urban Affairs Quarterly* 5 (2003): 645–68.

[22] Loomis Mayfield, "Voting Fraud in Early Twentieth-Century Pittsburgh," *Journal of Interdisciplinary History* 24, no. 1 (1993): 59–84; and Genevive Gist, "Progressive Reform in a Rural Community: The Adams County Vote Fraud Case," *Mississippi Valley Historical Review* 48 (1961): 60–78.

[23] William L. Riordan, *Plunkitt of Tammany Hall: A Series of Very Plain Talks on Very Practical Politics* (1905; reprint, New York: Bedford Books, St. Martin's, 1993).

[24] Lincoln Steffens, *The Autobiography of Lincoln Steffens* (New York: Harcourt, 1968).

[25] Clarence Stone, "Urban Machines: Taking Stock," *PS: Political Science and Politics* 29 (1996): 450; and Steffens, *The Autobiography of Lincoln Steffens.*

[26] Rebecca Menes, "Corruption in Cities: Graft and Politics in American Cities at the Turn of the Twentieth Century," NBER Working Paper no. 9990, September (New York: National Bureau of Economic Research, 2003).

[27] Erie, *Rainbow's End.*

[28] Edward Banfield and James Q. Wilson, *City Politics* (New York: Vintage, 1963).

[29] Dennis R. Judd and Todd Swanstrom. *City Politics: Private Power and Public Policy.* 2004. Pearson Longman. New York.

[30] Martin Shefter, "The Emergence of the Political Machine," in *Theoretical Perspectives on Urban Politics,* ed. W. Hawley and M. Lipsky (Englewood Cliffs, N.J.: Prentice Hall, 1976); Bridges, *A City in the Republic;* and McCaffery, *When Bosses Ruled Philadelphia.*

[31] Amy Bridges, *Morning Glories: Municipal Reform in the Southwest* (Princeton, N.J.: Princeton University Press, 1997).

[32] Kenneth Feingold, *Experts and Politicians: Reform Challenges to Machine Politics in New York, Cleveland and Chicago* (Princeton, N.J.: Princeton University Press, 1995).

[33] Richard Hofstadter, *The Age of Reform* (New York: Knopf, 1955).

[34] Samuel Haber, *Efficiency and Uplift: Scientific Management in the Progressive Era: 1885–1930* (Chicago: University of Chicago Press, 1964).

[35] Daphne Spain, *How Women Saved the City* (Minneapolis: University of Minnesota Press, 2000).

[36] Maureen A. Flanagan, "Gender and Urban Political Reform: The City Club and the Woman's City Club of Chicago in the Progressive Era," *American Historical Review* 95 (1990): 1032–50.

[37] Flanagan, "Gender and Urban Political Reform."

[38] Jane Addams, *Twenty Years at Hull House* (Chicago, 1910).

[39] Samuel P. Hays, *The Politics of Reform in Municipal Government in the Progressive Era* (Indianapolis, Ind.: Bobbs-Merrill, 1972).

[40] Hofstadter, *The Age of Reform.*

[41] David Morgan and Robert England, *Managing Urban America* (Chatham, N.J.: Chatham House, 1999).

[42] Robert H. Weibe, *Businessmen and Reform: A Study of Progressive Movements* (Chicago: Quadrangle, 1968).

[43] Banfield and Wilson, *City Politics,* 170–71.

[44] Glenda Elizabeth Gilmore, ed., *Who Were the Progressives?* (New Haven, Conn.: Yale University Press, 2002).

[45] National Municipal League, *Municipal Program* (New York: Macmillan, 1900).

[46] Charles Adrian, "Forms of City Government in American History," *Municipal Yearbook* (Washington DC: International City Manager's Association.1988).

[47] Melvin G. Holli, *The American Mayor: The Best and Worst Big City Leaders* (University Park: Pennsylvania State University Press, 1999).

[48] John Fund, "How to Steal an Election," *City Journal,* 2004, http://www.city-journal.org/printable.php?id=1701.

[49] Charles Adrian and Charles Press, *Governing Urban America* (New York: McGraw Hill, 1977): 160.

[50] Victor S. Desantis and Tari Renner, "City Government Structures: An Attempt at Clarification," *State and Local Government Review* 324 (2002): 95–104.

[51] International City Managers Association, "2001–2002 Survey," Washington, D.C.: International City Managers Association.

[52] http://www.ncl.org/publications/index.html.

[53] International City Managers Association, *The Council-Manager Form of Government* (Washington, D.C.: ICMA, 2006).

[54] International City Managers Association, *Form of Government Survey* (Washington, D.C.: ICMA, 2001).

[55] Robert Salisbury Source should be: David Morgan, Robert England and John Pellissero. 2006. Managing Urban America. CQ Press. Washington DC.

[56] ICMA salary survey Worcester Regional Research Board. Oh Manager, Where Art Thou? Best Practices for Selecting a City Manager. Worcester, MA 2004.

[57] International City Managers Association, *The Council-Manager Form of Government.*

[58] http://www.ncl.org/npp/charter/process.html.

[59] International City Managers Association, *The Council-Manager Form of Government.*

[60] Adrian, "Forms of City Government in American History."

[61] H. George Frederickson, G. A. Johnson, and C. Wood, "The Changing Structure of American Cities," *Public Administration Review* 64 (May 2004).

[62] Desantis and Renner, "City Government Structures."

[63] Frederickson, Johnson, and Wood, "The Changing Structure of American Cities."

[64] Richard Engstrom and Michael D. McDonald, "The Election of Blacks to City Councils," *American Political Science Review* 72 (1981): 344–54.

[65] Ninety percent of council manager cities have nonpartisan elections; Desantis and Renner, "City Government Structures."

[66] Some elite party officials may have allied with reformers in support of the Australian ballot to limit the influence of local precinct captains. John Reynolds and Richard McCormick, "'Outlawing 'Treachery': Split Tickets and Ballot Laws in New York and New Jersey, 1880–1910," *Journal of American History* 72 (1986): 835–58.

[67] Gary Cox and Morgan Kousser, "Turnout and Rural Corruption: New York as a Test Case," *American Journal of Political Science* 25 (1981): 646.

[68] J. Morgan Kousser, *The Shaping of Southern Politics* (New Haven, Conn.: Yale University Press, 1974).

[69] Zoltan Hajnal, Paul Lewis, and Hugh Louch, *Municipal Elections in California: Turnout, Timing and Competition* (San Francisco: Public Policy Institute of California, 2002).

[70] Cox and Kousser, "Turnout and Rural Corruption."

[71] See Fund, "How to Steal an Election"; Kevin Phillips and Paul Blackman, *Electoral Reform and Voter Participation* (Washington, DC: AEI Press, 1975); Gist, "Progressive Reform in a Rural Community"; and Mayfield, "Voting Fraud in Early Twentieth-Century Pittsburgh," for dates on introduction of these reforms across states.

[72] Fund, "How to Steal an Election."

[73] Walter Dean Burnham, *Critical Elections and the Mainsprings of American Politics* (New York: Norton, 1970): 81.

[74] John Lapp, "Election: Identification of Voters," *American Political Science Review* 3, no. 1 (1909): 62–3.

[75] Jerrod Rusk, "Communications," *American Political Science Review* 65 (1971): 1152–57; Jerrod Rusk, "Comment: The American Electoral Universe," *American Political Science Review* 68 (1974): 1028–49.

[76] Pamela Tolbert and Lynne Zucker, "Institutional Sources of Change in the Formal Structure of Organizations: The Diffusion of Civil Service Reform, 1880–1935," *Administrative Science Quarterly* 28 (1983): 22. Also see H. George Frederickson, Bret Logan, and Curtis Wood, "Municipal Reform: A Well Kept Secret," *State and Local Government Review* 35, no. 1 (2003): 7–14.

[77] Frederickson, Logan, and Wood, "Municipal Reform."

[78] Author's personal communication with Ron Michaelson, former Executive Director of the Illinois State Board of Elections.

[79] Leon E. Aylsworth, "Corrupt Practices," *American Political Science Review* 65 (1909): 50–56.

[80] John Matsusaka, *For the Many or the Few* (Chicago: University of Chicago Press, 2004).

[81] James Weinstein, *Corporate Ideal in the Liberal State, 1900–1918* (Boston: Beacon Press, 1968).

[82] James Gimpel, "Reform Resistant and Reform Adopting Machines: The Electoral Foundations of Urban Politics," *Political Research Quarterly* 46, no. 2 (1993): 371–82.

[83] Robert Lineberry and Edmond Fowler "Reformism and Public Policies in American Cities," *American Political Science Review* (1967): 701–16.

[84] David Morgan and John Pelissero, "Urban Policy: Does Political Structure Matter?" *American Political Science Review* 74 (1980): 999–1006.

[85] James H. Svara, "The Politics-Administration Dichotomy Model as Aberration," *Public Administration Review* 58 (1998): 51.

[86] Kenneth Prewitt, "Political Ambitions, Volunteerism, and Electoral Accountability," *American Political Science Review* (1970): 5–17.

[87] Todd Donovan, David Denemark, and Shaun Bowler, "Trust, Citizenship and Participation: Australia in Comparative Perspective." In *Australian Social Attitudes: The 2nd Report*, ed. David Denemark et al. (Sydney: University of New South Wales Press, 2007).

[88] Albert Karing and B. Oliver Walter, "Decline in Municipal Voter Turnout: A Function of Changing Structure," *American Politics Quarterly* 11 (1983): 491–505; and Hajnal and Lewis, "Municipal Institutions and Voter Turnout in Local Elections."

[89] Jessica Trounstine, "Dominant Regimes and the Demise of Urban Democracy," *Journal of Politics* (2006): 879–93.

[90] Chandler Davidson and Luis Fraga, "Slating Groups as Parties in a 'Nonpartisan' Setting," *Western Political Quarterly* 41 (1988): 373–90; and Bridges, *Morning Glories.*

[91] Trounstine, "Dominant Regimes and the Demise of Urban Democracy."

[92] Albert Karing and B. Oliver Walter, "Decline in Municipal Voter Turnout: A Function of Changing Structure," *American Politics Quarterly* 11 (1983): 491–505.

[93] Peter K. Eisenger, "Black Employment in Municipal Jobs: The Impact of Black Political Power," *American Political Science Review* 76 (1982): 380–90; Lana Stein, "Representative Local Government: Minorities in the Municipal Workforce," *Journal of Politics* 48 (1986): 694–713; and Thomas Dye and James Renick, "Political Power and City Jobs: Determinants of Minority Employment," *Social Science Quarterly* 62 (1981): 457–86.

[94] Susan Welch and Timothy Bledsoe, *Urban Reform and Its Consequences* (Chicago: University of Chicago Press, 1988).

[95] Chandler Davidson and George Korbel, "At-Large Elections and Minority Group Representation: A Re-examination of Historical and Contemporary Evidence," *Journal of Politics* 43 (1981): 982.

[96] Charles H. Levine, Irene S. Rubin, and George Wolohojian, "Resource Scarcity and the Reform Model: The Management of Retrenchment in Cincinnati and Oakland," *Public Administration Review* 41 (1981): 627.

[97] Lineberry and Fowler, "Reformism and Public Policies in American Cities."

[98] Stein, "Representative Local Government."

[99] Albert Karing and Susan Welch, *Black Representation and Urban Policy* (Chicago: University of Chicago Press, 1980).

[100] Martin Lomansy, quoted in Steffens, *The Autobiography of Lincoln Steffens.*

[101] Gustavus Myers, *History of Tammany Hall* (New York, 1917).

Chapter 12

[1] Hector Becerra, "Vernon Shoo-Ins Shoo Outsiders," *Los Angeles Times,* 12 February 2006, http://www.latimes.com/news/local/la-me-vernon12feb12,0,6053598, full .story?coll=la-home-headlines.

[2] James M. Buchanan, "Principles of Urban Fiscal Strategy," *Public Choice* (1971).

[3] Charles Tiebout, "A Pure Theory of Municipal Expenditures," *Journal of Political Economy* (1956).

[4] Paul Teske, Mark Schneider, Michael Mintrom, and Samuel Best, "Establishing the Microfoundations of a Macro Theory," *American Political Science Review* (1993); and Stephen Percy and Brett Hawkins, "Further in Tests of the Individual-Level Propositions from the Tiebout Model," *Journal of Politics* 54 (1992): 1149–57.

[5] Eran Razin and Mark Rosentraub, "Are Fragmentation and Sprawl Linked?" *Urban Affairs Quarterly* 35 (2000): 830.

[6] Amy Bridges, *Morning Glories: Municipal Reform in the Southwest* (Princeton, N.J.: Princeton University Press, 1997).

[7] David Lowery, "Consumer Sovereignty and Quasi Market Failure," *Journal of Public Administration Research and Theory* 8 (1998).

[8] Gary Miller, *Cities by Contract: The Politics of Municipal Incorporation* (Cambridge, Mass.: MIT Press, 1981).

[9] E. S. Savas, *Privatization: The Key to Better Government* (Chatham, N.J.: Chatham House, 1987).

[10] Robert Jay Dilger, Randolph R. Moffett, and Linda Struyk, "Privatization of Municipal Services in American's Largest Cities," *Public Administration Review* 57 (1997): 21.

[11] Nancy Burns, *The Formation of American Local Governments: Private Values in Public Institutions* (Oxford: Oxford University Press, 1994).

[12] Burns, *The Formation of American Local Governments,* 9.

[13] Dennis R. Judd, *City Politics: Private Power and Public Policy* (Upper Saddle River, N.J.: Pearson Longman, 2004).

[14] Miller, *Cities by contract.*

[15] Burns, *The Formation of American Local Governments.*

[16] Kenneth T. Jackson, *Crabgrass Frontier: The Suburbanization of the United States* (Oxford: Oxford University Press, 1985).

[17] Judd, *City Politics,* 147.

[18] Mark Gefland, *A Nation of Cities: The Federal Government and Urban America* (Oxford: Oxford University Press, 1975).

[19] Jackson, *Crabgrass Frontier.*

[20] Douglass Massey and Nancy Denton, *American Apartheid: Segregation and the Making of the Underclass* (Cambridge, Mass.: Harvard University Press, 1993).

[21] Jackson, *Crabgrass Frontier,* 208.

[22] Massey and Denton, *American Apartheid,* 55.

[23] T. W. Patterson, *Land Use Planning: Techniques of Implementation* (Malbar, FL: Kreiger Publishing, 1988); and Roger W. Caves, *Land Use Planning: The Ballot Box Revolution* (Beverly Hills, CA: Sage, 1992).

[24] William A. Fishel, "An Economic History of Zoning and a Cure for Its Exclusionary Effects," *Urban Studies* 41 (2004): 317–40.

[25] Seymour Toll, *Zoned America* (New York: Crossman, 1969).

[26] Caves, *Land Use Planning.*

[27] *Village of Euclid v. Ambler Realty Co.,* 272 US 365 (1926); cited in Judd, *City Politics.*

[28] Caves, *Land Use Planning,* 30.

[29] J. R. Levy, *Contemporary Urban Planning* (Englewood Cliffs, N.J.: Prentice Hall, 1988.

[30] *Barron v. Baltimore* (1833).

[31] *Yee v. City of Escondido* (1992).

[32] *Lucas v. South Carolina Coastal Commission* (1992).

[33] *Griggs v. Allegheny County* (1962).

[34] James G. Durhan, "Efficient Just Compensation as a Limit on Eminent Domain," *Minnesota Law Review* 69 (1985).

[35] *Kelo v. City of New London* (2005).

[36] William Fischel, *Regulatory Takings: Law, Economics and Politics* (Cambridge, Mass.: Harvard University Press, 1998).

[37] Michael N. Danielson, "The Politics of Exclusionary Zoning in Suburbia," *Political Science Quarterly* (1976).

[38] Richard F. Babcock and Fred Bosselman, *Exclusionary Zoning: Land Use Regulation and Housing in the 1970s* (New York: Praeger, 1973).

[39] Rolf Pendall, "Local Land Use Regulation and the Chain of Exclusion," *Journal of the American Planning Association* 66 (2000): 125–42.

[40] Pendall, "Local Land Use Regulation," 138.

[41] Pendall, "Local Land Use Regulation."

[42] Mark Schneider and Thomas Phelan, "Black Suburbanization in the 1980s," *Demography* 30 (1993): 278.

[43] Pendall, "Local Land Use Regulation"; but see Todd Donovan and Max Neiman, "Local Growth Control Policies and Changes in Community Characteristics," *Social Science Quarterly* 76 (1995): 780–93.

[44] Normal D. Peel, Garthe E. Pickett, and Stephen T. Buehl, "Racial Discrimination in Public Housing Site Selection," *Stanford Law Review* 23 (1970): 63–147; and *James v. Valtierra* 420 U.S. 137 (1971) upheld the constitutionality of such rules.

[45] Cited by Danielson, "The Politics of Exclusionary Zoning in Suburbia," 1.

[46] Judd, *City Politics,* 281; and Donald Kirby et al., *Residential Zoning and Equal Housing Opportunities* (Washington, D.C.: Urban Institute, 1972).

[47] *Arlington Heights v. Metropolitan Housing Corp.,* 429 U.S. 252 (1977).

[48] The following draws ideas from John Logan and Harvey Molotch, *The Political Economy of Place* (Berkeley: University of California Press, 1987).

[49] Harvey Molotch, "The City as a Growth Machine," *American Journal of Sociology* (1976).

[50] Paul Peterson, *City Limits* (Chicago: University of Chicago Press, 1981).

51 Todd Donovan, "Community Controversy and Adoption of Local Economic Development Policies," *Social Science Quarterly* 74 (1995): 386.

52 Mark Baldassare and Georgjeanna Wilson, "Changing Sources of Suburban Support for Local Growth Controls," *Urban Studies* 33 (1996): 459–471.

53 Roland Anglin, "Diminishing Utility: The Effect of Citizen Preferences for Local Growth," *Urban Affairs Quarterly* 25 (1990): 684–96.

54 Mark Baldassare, "Predicting Local Concern about Growth: The Roots of Citizen Discontent," *Journal of Urban Affairs* 6 (1985): 39–49; Scott Bollens, "Constituents for Regionalism: Approaches to Growth Management," *Urban Affairs Quarterly* 26 (1990): 46–67.

55 John Logan and Gordana Rabrenovic, "Neighborhood Associations: Their Issues, Their Allies and Their Opponents," *Urban Affairs Quarterly* 26 (1990): 68–94.

56 Mark Schneider and Paul Teske, "The Anti-Growth Entrepreneur: Challenging the Equilibrium of the Growth Machine," *Journal of Politics* 55 (1993): 720–36.

57 Todd Donovan and Max Neiman, "Citizen Mobilization and the Adoption of Local Growth Control," *Western Political Quarterly* (1992): 651–75.

58 D. Dowall, *Suburban Squeeze* (Berkeley, CA: University of California Press, 1984).

59 Scott Bollens, "State Growth Management Acts: Intergovernmental Frameworks and Policy Objectives," *Journal of the American Planning Association* 58 (1992): 454.

60 Max Neiman and Mark Gottinder, "Characteristics of Support for Local Growth Control," *Urban Affairs Quarterly* (1981).

61 Marc Baldassare and William Protash, "Growth Controls, Population Growth and Community Satisfaction," *American Sociological Review* 47 (1982): 339–46.

62 Todd Donovan and Max Neiman, "Community Social Status, Suburban Growth and Restrictions on Residential Development," *Urban Affairs Quarterly* 28 (1992): 323–36. Another study found no relationship between growth rates and the adoption of regulations on development. John Logan and Min Zhou, "The Adoption of Growth Controls in Suburban Communities," *Social Science Quarterly* 71 (1990): 118–29.

63 Bernard Freiden, *The Environmental Protection Hustle* (Cambridge, Mass.: MIT Press, 1979).

64 R. Ellickson, "Suburban Growth Controls: An Economic and Legal Analysis," *Yale Law Review* 86 (1977): 389–511.

65 Edward Glaeser and Joseph Gyourko, "The Impact of Zoning on Housing Affordability," National Bureau of Economic Research Working Paper no. 8835 (New York: NBER, 2002).

66 Anthony Downs, "The Real Problem with Suburban Anti-Growth Policies," *Brookings Review* (Spring 1988): 26.

67 Glaeser and Gyourko, "The Impact of Zoning on Housing Affordability"; Henry O. Pallakowski and Susan Wachter, "Private Markets, Public Decisions: An Assessment of Local Land Use Controls for the 1990s," *Land Economics* 66 (1990): 315–24; J. Black and J. Hoblen, "Land Price Inflation and Affordable Housing," *Urban Geography* 6 (1985): 27–47; and Anne B. Shlay and Peter Rossi, "Keeping Up the Neighborhood: Estimating the Net Effects of Zoning," *American Sociological Review* 46 (1981): 703–19.

68 Glaeser and Gyourko, "The Impact of Zoning on Housing Affordability," 23.

69 John Logan and Min Zhou, "Do Suburban Growth Controls Control Growth?" *American Sociological Review* 54 (1989): 461–71; and John Landis, "Do Growth Controls Work? A New Assessment," *Journal of the American Planning Association* 58 (1992): 489.

70 Landis, "Do Growth Controls Work?" 502.

71 Todd Donovan and Max Neiman, "Local Growth Controls and Changes in Community Characteristics," *Social Science Quarterly* 76 (1995): 780.

72 Landis, "Do Growth Controls Work?" 502.

73 William Fischel, *The Economics of Zoning Laws: A Property Rights Approach to American Land Use Controls* (Johns Hopkins University Press, 1985); B. Frieden, *The Environmental Hustle* (Cambridge, Mass.: MIT Press, 1979).

74 Baldassare and Wilson, "Changing Sources."

75 Richard Feiock, "The Political Economy of Growth Management," *American Politics Quarterly* 22 (1994): 208–20.

76 Jerry Anthony, "Do State Growth Management Regulations Reduce Sprawl?" *Urban Affairs Review* 39 (2004): 376–97.

77 Peter Eisinger, *The Rise of the Entrepreneurial State: State and Local Economic Development Policies* (Madison: University of Wisconsin Press, 1988): 221.

[78] Eisinger, *The Rise of the Entrepreneurial State.*

[79] Allen Barra, "Stadium Cheating, Wild Pitch: Why Does George Steinbrenner Want to Tear Down the House That Ruth Built," *Village Voice,* 9 May 2005.

[80] Arnold Fleishman, Gary P. Green, and Tsz Man Kwong, "What's a City to Do? Explaining Differences in Local Economic Development Policies," *Western Political Quarterly* (1992): 678–99.

[81] Todd Donovan, Max Neiman, and Susan Brumbaugh, "Two Dimensions of Local Growth Strategies," In Mark Baldassare, ed., *Studies in Community Sociology* 4 (JJAI Press, 1992): 153–169.

[82] Irene S. Rubin and Herbert J. Rubin, "Economic Development Incentives: The Poor (Cities) Pay More," *Urban Affairs Quarterly* 23 (1987): 37–62.

[83] Fleishmann, Green, and Kwong, "What's a City to Do?" See also Ann O'M. Bowman, "Competition for Economic Development among Southeastern Cities," *Urban Affairs Quarterly* 23 (1988): 511–27.

[84] Charles C. Euchner, *Playing the Field: Why Sports Teams Move and Cities Fight to Keep Them* (Baltimore: Johns Hopkins University Press, 1994).

[85] Eisinger, *The Rise of the Entrepreneurial State,* 220.

[86] Richard Feiock, "The Effects of Economic Development Policy on Local Economic Development," *American Journal of Political Science* 35 (1991): 643–55.

[87] Roger Parks and Elinor Ostrom, "Complex Models of Urban Service Delivery Systems," *Urban Policy Analysis,* TN Clarck, ed., 21. (Beverly Hills, CA: Sage, 1981).

[88] Mark Schneider, "Inter-Municipal Competition, Budget-Maximizing Bureaucrats, and the Level of Suburban Competition," *American Journal of Political Science* 33, no. 3 (1989): 612.

[89] John R. Logan and Mark Schneider, "Governmental Organization and City/Suburb Income Inequality, 1960–1970," *Urban Affairs Quarterly* 17 (1982): 303–18.

[90] E. Razin and M. Rosentraub, "Are Fragmentation and Sprawl Interlinked? North American Evidence," *Urban Affairs Review,* 35 (2000): 821.

[91] William E. Lyons, David Lowery, and Ruth Hoogland DeHoog, "Institutional-Induced Attribution Errors: Their Composition and Impact of Citizen Satisfaction with Local Governmental Services," *American Politics Quarterly* 18 (1990): 169–96.

[92] David Lowery, William Lyons, and Ruth Hoogland De-Hoog, "Citizenship and Community Attachment in the Empowered Locality," *Urban Affairs Quarterly* 28 (1992): 69–103.

[93] Downs, "The Real Problem with Suburban Anti-Growth Policies."

[94] Max Neiman, "Social Stratification and Governmental Inequality," *American Political Science Review* 53 (1976): 474–93; and Richard Child Hill, "Separate and Unequal: Governmental Inequality in the Metropolis," *American Political Science Review* 68 (1974): 1557–86.

[95] Mark Schneider and John Logan, "Fiscal Implications of Class Segregation: Inequalities in the Distribution of Public Good and Services in Suburban Municipalities, *Urban Affairs Quarterly* 17 (1981): 23–36.

[96] Downs, "The Real Problem with Suburban Anti-Growth Policies," 29.

[97] Nelson Wikstrom and G. Ross Stephens, *Metropolitan Government and Governance: Theoretical Perspectives, Empirical Analysis, and the Future* (Oxford: Oxford University Press, 1999).

[98] Gordon Tullock. 1981. Federalism and Problems of Scale in G. Brennan, R.L. Matthews and B. Grewal (eds.) The Economics of Federalism. Canberra: Australian National University Press and David Lowery, "Answering the Public Choice Challenge to Progressive Reform Institutions: A Neoprogressive Research Agenda," *Governance* 12 (1999): 29–56.

[99] David Rusk, *Cities without Suburbs* (Baltimore: Woodrow Wilson Center Special Studies, Johns Hopkins University Press, 1995); and Anthony Downs, *New Visions for Metropolitan America* (Washington, D.C.: Brookings Institution, 1994).

[100] William E. Lyons and David Lowery, "Governmental Fragmentation versus Consolidation: Five Public Choice Myths about How to Create Informed, Happy Citizens," *Public Administration Review* 49 (1989): 533–43.

Chapter 13

[1] Andrew Greeley, "The Charade Goes On," *Beliefnet.com,* November 23, 2000.

[2] D. A. Saucier and A. J. Cawman, "Civil Unions in Vermont: Political Attitudes, Religious Fundamentalism, and Sexual Prejudice," *Journal of Homosexuality* 48 (2004): 1–18.

3 Christopher Z. Mooney, "The Public Clash of Private Values: The Politics of Morality Policy," in *The Public Clash of Private Values: The Politics of Morality Policy,* ed. Christopher Z. Mooney (New York: Chatham House, 2001).

4 This is the sort of analysis you read in the newspapers just after the election, for example in "Election 2004: Religious Vote Fuels Victory for GOP," *Atlanta Journal-Constitution,* November 4, 2004, p. A19. But for social scientists' more reasoned views, see Morris P. Fiorina, *Culture War? The Myth of a Polarized America* (New York: Pearson Longman, 2005); D. Sunshine Hillygus and Todd G. Shields, "Moral Issues and Voter Decision Making in the 2004 Presidential Election," *PS: Political Science & Politics* 38 (2005): 201–9; and Gary Langer and Jon Cohen, "Voters and Values in the 2004 Election," *Public Opinion Quarterly* 69 (2005): 744–61.

5 John Winthrop, "A Modell of Christian Charity" ([1630] 1867), in *Life and Letters of John Winthrop,* ed. Robert C. Winthrop, quoted in Bartleby.com, http://www.bartleby.com/73/1611.html.

6 James A. Morone, *Hellfire Nation: The Politics of Sin in American History* (New Haven, Conn.: Yale University Press, 2003).

7 All quoted in Morone, *Hellfire Nation,* 4.

8 Morone, *Hellfire Nation,* 4.

9 Kenneth J. Meier, *The Politics of Sin* (Armonk, N.Y.: M. E. Sharpe, 1994), 4. Meier is the godfather of morality policy scholarship, and his *The Politics of Sin* is the place to start reading on this subject.

10 Dave McKinney, "In a Classic Tragedy, the Protagonist's Character Always Prefigures His Fall," *Illinois Issues,* online ed., November 2002.

11 David C. Leege, Kenneth D. Wald, Brian S. Krueger, and Paul D. Mueller, *The Politics of Cultural Differences: Social Change and Voter Mobilization in the Post–New Deal Period* (Princeton, N.J.: Princeton University Press, 2002).

12 Meier, *The Politics of Sin;* Donald P. Haider-Markel and Kenneth J. Meier, "The Politics of Gay and Lesbian Rights: Expanding the Scope of the Conflict," *Journal of Politics* 58 (1996): 332–49; Mooney, "The Public Clash of Private Values."

13 Christopher Z. Mooney and Richard G. Schuldt, "Does Morality Policy Exist? Testing a Basic Assumption" (paper presented at the annual meeting of the American Political Science Association, Philadelphia, September 2006).

14 T. Alexander Smith and Raymond Tatalovich, *Cultures at War: Moral Conflicts in Western Democracies* (Peterborough, ON: Broadview Press, 2003), ch. 7.

15 Our discussion of morality policy evolution draws much from the more general pattern of punctuated equilibrium in policy development discussed in Frank R. Baumgartner and Bryan D. Jones, *Agendas and Instability in American Politics* (Chicago: University of Chicago Press, 1993).

16 Christopher Z. Mooney and Mei-Hsien Lee, "Legislating Morality in the American States: The Case of Pre-*Roe* Abortion Regulation Reform," *American Journal of Political Science* 39 (1995): 599–627; and Christopher Z. Mooney and Mei-Hsien Lee, "The Influence of Values on Consensus and Contentious Morality Policy: U.S. Death Penalty Reform, 1956–82," *Journal of Politics* 62 (2000): 223–39.

17 Donley T. Studlar, "What Constitutes Morality Policy? A Cross-National Analysis," in Mooney, *The Public Clash of Private Values.*

18 Baumgartner and Jones, *Agendas and Instability in American Politics.*

19 John W. Kingdon, *Agendas, Alternatives, and Public Policies,* 2nd ed. (New York: HarperCollins, 1995); and Mark Schneider and Paul Teske, "Toward a Theory of the Political Entrepreneur: Evidence from Local Government," *American Political Science Review* 36 (1992): 737–47.

20 Geoffrey Layman, *The Great Divide: Religious and Cultural Conflict in American Party Politics* (New York: Columbia University Press, 2001).

21 Pippa Norris and Ronald Inglehart, *Sacred and Secular: Religion and Politics Worldwide* (New York: Cambridge University Press, 2004).

22 Still, a threat to a person's economic interests is probably a far more significant political motivator than either of these two altruistic motives.

23 Smith and Tatalovich, *Cultures at War,* 78–80.

24 Susan E. Clarke, "Ideas, Interests, and Institutions: Shaping Abortion Politics in Denver," in *Culture Wars and Local Politics,* ed. Elaine B. Sharp (Lawrence: University Press of Kansas, 1999).

25 James Davidson Hunter, *Before the Shooting Begins: Searching for Democracy in America's Culture Wars* (New York: Free Press, 1994).

26 In 1967, the U.S. Supreme Court found that banning interracial marriage violated the 14th Amendment to the U.S. Constitution, thus overturning such laws (*Loving v. Virginia* 388 U.S. 1, 395 [1967]).

[27] Kenneth J. Meier, "Drugs, Sex, and Rock and Roll: A Theory of Morality Politics," in Mooney, *The Public Clash of Private Values.*

[28] Meier, "Drugs, Sex, and Rock and Roll."

[29] Malcolm L. Goggin and Christopher Z. Mooney, "Congressional Use of Policy Information on Fact and Value Issues," in Mooney, *The Public Clash of Private Values;* and Meier, "Drugs, Sex, and Rock and Roll."

[30] Meier, "Drugs, Sex, and Rock and Roll."

[31] Tom R. Tyler, *Why People Obey the Law* (New Haven, Conn.: Yale University Press, 1990).

[32] Smith and Tatalovich, *Cultures at War.*

[33] Murray Edelman, *The Symbolic Uses of Politics,* 2nd ed. (Urbana: University of Illinois Press, 1985).

[34] Walter Berns, *For Capital Punishment: Crime and the Morality of the Death Penalty* (New York: Basic Books, 1979), p. 43–44.

[35] Christopher Z. Mooney and Mei-Hsien Lee, "Morality Policy Re-Invention: State Death Penalties," *Annals of the American Academy of Political and Social Science* 566 (1999): 80–92.

[36] Patrick A. Pierce and Donald E. Miller, *Gambling Politics: State Government and the Business of Betting* (Boulder, Colo.: Lynne Rienner, 2004).

[37] Richard A. Brisbin Jr., "From Censorship to Ratings: Substantive Rationality, Political Entrepreneurship, and Sex in the Movies," in Mooney, *The Public Clash of Private Values.*

[38] Daniel J. Elazar, *Cities of the Prairie: The Metropolitan Frontier and American Politics* (New York: Basic Books, 1970).

[39] Robert S. Erikson, Gerald C. Wright, and John P. McIver, *Statehouse Democracy* (New York: Cambridge University Press, 1993); and Layman, *The Great Divide.*

[40] Christopher Z. Mooney, "The Decline of Federalism and the Rise of Morality Policy Conflict in the United States," *Publius* 30 (2000): 171–88.

[41] Mooney and Lee, "Legislating Morality in the American States"; and Mooney and Lee, "The Influence of Values on Consensus and Contentious Morality Policy."

[42] But consider Billie James Hargis, who in the 1940s and 1950s was the godfather of conservative radio and television evangelists. See James Reichley and A. James Reichley, *Faith in Politics* (Washington, D.C.: Brookings Institution, 2002).

[43] James C. Mohr, *Abortion in America: The Origins and Evolution of National Policy, 1800–1900* (New York: Oxford University Press, 1979); Laurence H. Tribe. 1992. *Abortion: The Clash of Absolutes.* New York: W.W. Norton; Luker, Kristin 1984. *Abortion and the Politics of Motherhood.* Berkeley, CA: University of California Press

[44] Raymond Tatalovich, *The Politics of Abortion in the United States and Canada* (Armonk, N.Y.: M. E. Sharpe, 1997).

[45] John Culver and April Smailes, "Abortion Politics and Policies in California" (paper presented at the annual meeting of the Western Political Science Association, Seattle, Wash., 1999).

[46] Mooney and Lee, "Legislating Morality in the American States."

[47] *Roe v. Wade* 410 U.S. 113 (1973).

[48] *Griswold v. Connecticut* 381 U.S. 479 (1965).

[49] Marian Faux, *Roe v. Wade* (New York: Macmillan, 1988).

[50] Paul J. Fabrizio, "Evolving into Morality Politics: U.S. Catholic Bishops' Statements on U.S. Politics from 1792 to the Present," in Mooney, *The Public Clash of Private Values.*

[51] Matthew Moen, *The Transformation of the Christian Right* (Tuscaloosa: University of Alabama Press, 1993).

[52] Some might argue that arguments based on an appeal to basic rights in the U.S. Constitution are themselves moral arguments. See Smith and Tatalovich, *Cultures at War.*

[53] Lee Epstein and Joseph F. Kobylka, *The Supreme Court and Legal Change* (Chapel Hill: University of North Carolina Press, 1992); and Glen Halva-Neubauer, "Abortion Policy in the Post-Webster Age," *Publius* 20 (1990): 27–44.

[54] Epstein and Kobylka, *The Supreme Court and Legal Change.*

[55] *Planned Parenthood of Central Missouri v. Danforth* 428 U.S. 52 (1976).

[56] Epstein and Kobylka, *The Supreme Court and Legal Change.*

[57] *Webster v. Reproductive Health Services* 492 U.S. 490 (1989).

[58] *Planned Parenthood v. Casey* 505 U.S. 833 (1992).

[59] Barbara Hinkson Craig and David M. O'Brien, *Abortion and American Politics* (Chatham, N.J.: Chatham House, 1993).

[60] Clarke, Op. cit.

[61] Jennifer Gonnerman, "The Terrorist Campaign against Abortion," *Village Voice,* online ed., November 3–9, 1998; and Hunter, *Before the Shooting Begins.*

[62] Kirk Johnson, "New Push Likely for Restrictions over Abortion," *New York Times,* online ed., April 20, 2007.

[63] Margaret Talev, "Abortion Foes Split on Strategy," *Sacramento (CA) Bee,* online ed., March 6, 2006.

[64] John Hanna, "Kan. AG Alarms Abortion-Rights Groups," *Sacramento (CA) Bee,* online ed., September 27, 2006.

[65] David Crary, "South Dakota Voters to Weigh Abortion Ban," *(Springfield,IL) State Journal-Register,* November 3, 2006, 8.

[66] Michelle M. Martinez, "House Passes Abortion Measures," *Austin (Tx.) American-Statesman,* online ed., May 17, 2005.

[67] M. H. Medhoff, "The Determinants and Impact of State Abortion Restrictions," *American Journal of Economics and Sociology* 61 (2002): 481–93.

[68] John F. Camobreco and Michelle A. Barnello, "Democratic Responsiveness and Policy Shock: The Case of Abortion," *State Politics and Policy Quarterly* 8 (2008): XX-XXX.

[69] Elizabeth A. Oldmixon, "Culture Wars in the Congressional Theater: How the U.S. House of Representatives Legislates Morality, 1993–1998," *Social Science Quarterly* 83 (2002): 775–88.

[70] Jan Crawford Greenburg, "How Focus on *Roe* Pushes aside Other Court Issues," *Chicago Tribune,* online ed., December 29, 2005.

[71] *Gonzales v. Carhart* 550 U.S. (2007).

[72] *Stenberg v. Carhart* 530 U.S. 914 (2000).

[73] Jess Bravin, "Ruling to Shift Abortion Fight," *Wall Street Journal,* online ed., April 19, 2007; and Christine Vestel, "Abortion Ruling Sets New State Battle Lines," *Stateline.org,* online ed., April 30, 2007.

[74] Associated Press, "Social Issues at the Polls," (Springfield, IL) *State Journal-Register,* November 9, 2006, p. 3.

[75] Associated Press, "La. Senate Sends Abortion Ban to Gov.," *Sacramento (CA) Bee,* online ed., June 6, 2006; and Associated Press, "Miss. House Advances Bill to Ban Abortion," *Chicago Tribune,* online ed., March 1, 2006.

[76] Layman, *The Great Divide.*

[77] Eric Marcus, *Making Gay History: The Half-Century Fight for Gay and Lesbian Equal Rights* (New York: Harper, 2002).

[78] *Lawrence and Garner v. Texas* 539 U.S. 558 (2003); and *Bowers v. Hardwick.* 478 U.S. 186 (1986).

[79] Martin Dupuis, *Same-Sex Marriage, Legal Mobilization, and the Politics of Rights* (New York: Peter Lang, 2002).

[80] Haider-Markel and Meier, "The Politics of Gay and Lesbian Rights"; S. A. Soule, "Going to the Chapel? Same-Sex Marriage Bans in the United States, 1973–2000," *Social Problems* 51 (2004): 453–77; and Kenneth D. Wald, James W. Button, and Barbara A. Rienzo, "The Politics of Gay Rights in American Communities: Explaining Anti-Discrimination Ordinances and Policies," *American Journal of Political Science* 40 (1996): 1152–78.

[81] Patrick J. Egan and Kenneth Sherrill, "Marriage and the Shifting Priorities of a New Generation of Lesbians and Gays," *PS: Political Science and Politics* 38 (2005): 229–33.

[82] Daniel R. Pinello, *America's Struggle for Same-Sex Marriage* (New York: Cambridge University Press, 2006)

[83] *Baehr v. Lewin* 852 P.2d 44 (Ha.Sup.Ct. 1993).

[84] Donald P. Haider-Markel, "Policy Diffusion as a Geographical Expansion of the Scope of Political Conflict: Same-Sex Marriage Bans in the 1990s," *State Politics and Policy Quarterly* 1 (2001): 5–26.

[85] John Russell, *Funding the Culture Wars: Philanthropy, Church and State* (Washington, D.C.: National Committee for Responsive Philanthropy, 2005).

[86] Fredrick Liu and Stephen Macedo, "The Federal Marriage Amendment and the Strange Evolution of the Conservative Case against Gay Marriage," *PS: Political Science and Politics* 38 (2005): 211–17.

[87] Christian Worldview Concepts, "A Case against 'Gay Marriage,'" *Christian Worldview Concepts* 1 (2004): 1–4.

[88] Christian Worldview Concepts, "A Case against 'Gay Marriage.'"

[89] Dupuis, *Same-Sex Marriage, Legal Mobilization, and the Politics of Rights.*

[90] *Baker v. State* 744 A.2d 864 (Vt. 1999).

[91] Geoff Mulvihill, "N.J. Court Opens the Door to Gay Marriage," (Springfield, IL) *State Journal-Register,* October 26, 2006, 3.

[92] Pinello, *America's Struggle for Same-Sex Marriage.*

[93] Pinello, *America's Struggle for Same-Sex Marriage.*

[94] Pinello, *America's Struggle for Same-Sex Marriage.*

[95] A. S. Yang, "The Polls—Trends: Attitudes toward Homosexuality," *Public Opinion Quarterly* 61 (1997): 477–507.

[96] Voter error could explain a portion of this shocking level of support for these racist policies. One study estimated that only 6.4 percent of these Kentucky voters actually intended to vote for school segregation (the others were apparently confused by the ballot language)—but this still demonstrates substantial support for a policy that had been found unconstitutional over 40 years before the vote. See: D. Stephen Voss and Penny Miller, "Following a False Trail: The Hunt for Backlash in Kentucky's 1996 Desegregation Vote," *State Politics and Policy Quarterly* 1 (2001): 62–80.

Chapter 14

[1] William Greider, "The Gipper's Economy," *The Nation,* 28 June 2004; and Ange-Marie Hancock, *The Politics of Disgust: The Public Identity of the Welfare Queen* (New York: New York University Press, 2004).

[2] Frances Fox Piven and Richard Cloward, *The New Class War: Reagan's Attack on the Welfare State and Its Consequences* (New York: Pantheon, 1982); R. Kent Weaver, *Ending Welfare as We Know It* (Washington, D.C.: Brookings Institution, 2000); and United We Stand America, *Preparing Our Country for the 21st Century: The Official Transcript of the United We Stand America Conference* (New York: HarperCollins, 1995), 207–08.

[3] U.S. Bureau of the Census, "Current Population Survey, Annual Social and Economic Supplements," 2005, http://factfinder.census.gov/servlet/STTable?_bm=y&-geo_id=01000US&-qr_name=ACS_2004_EST_G00_S1701&-ds_name=ACS_2004_EST_G00_; Kathleen Short, John Iceland, and Joseph Dalaker, "Defining and Redefining Poverty" (paper presented at the annual meetings of the American Sociological Association of America, Chicago, 16–19 August 2002), http://www.census.gov/hhes/poverty/povmeas/papers/define.pdf; and U.S. Department of Health and Human Services, "Computations for the 2007 Annual Update of the HHS Poverty Guidelines," 2007, http://aspe.hhs.gov/poverty/07computations.shtml. Several other definitions of *poverty* exist: see U.S. Census Bureau, "American Community Survey 2004 Subject Definitions," http://www.census.gov/acs/www/Downloads/2004/usedata/ Subject_Definitions.pdf.

[4] Diana Pearce, "The Feminization of Poverty: Women, Work, and Welfare," *Urban and Social Change Review* 11 (1978): 28–36.

[5] "Kanye West Rips Bush during NBC Telethon," *Billboard,* September 3, 2005, http://www.billboard.com/bbcom/news/article_display.jsp?vnu_content_id=1001054572.

[6] "Houston, We May Have a Problem," *Marketplace,* September 5, 2005, http://marketplace.publicradio.org/shows/2005/09/05/PM200509051.html.

[7] Edward C. Banfield, *The Unheavenly City: The Nature and Future of Our Urban Crisis* (Boston: Little, Brown, 1970).

[8] William Julius Wilson, *The Truly Disadvantaged* (Chicago: University of Chicago Press, 1987).

[9] Sharon Austin, *The Transformation of Plantation Politics: Black Politics, Concentrated Poverty, and Social Capital in the Mississippi Delta* (Albany: State University of New York Press, 2006).

[10] Louis Brandeis, *New State Ice Company v. Liebmann,* 285 U.S. 262, 311 (1932).

[11] Charles Tiebout, "A Pure Theory of Local Expenditures," *Journal of Political Economy* 64 (1956): 416–24.

[12] David Osborne and Ted Gaebler, *Reinventing Government* (New York: Penguin, 1992).

[13] Paul Peterson and Mark Rom, *Welfare Magnets: A New Case for a National Welfare Standard* (Washington, D.C.: Brookings Institution, 1990); but see Craig Volden, "The Politics of Competitive Federalism: A Race to the Bottom in Welfare Benefits?" *American Journal of Political Science* 46 (2002): 352–63; and Mark Rom, Paul Peterson, and Kenneth Scheve, "Interstate Competition and Welfare Policy," *Publius* 28 (1998): 17–38.

[14] Sanford Schram and Joe Soss, "The Real Value of Welfare: Why There Is No Welfare Migration," *Politics & Society* 27 (1998): 39–66.

[15] Martha Derthick, "Ways of Achieving Federal Objectives," in *American Intergovernmental Relations,* ed. Laurence O'Toole, 3rd ed. (Washington, D.C.: Congressional Quarterly Press, 2000).

[16] Michael Lipsky, ed., *Street Level Bureaucrats* (New York: Russell Sage Foundation, 1980). See also Lael Keiser, "Street-Level Bureaucrats, Administrative Power and the Manipulation of Federal Social Security Disability Programs," *State Politics and Policy Quarterly* 1 (2001): 144–64.

[17] Daniel C. Vock, "States Suing Feds over Seniors' Rx Costs," *Stateline,* 20 May 2006, http://www.Stateline.org.

[18] U.S. Office of Management and Budget, "The Budget of the United States Government, Fiscal Year 2006, Historical Tables," http://a255.g.akamaitech.net/7/255/2422/23feb20050900/www.gpoaccess.gov/usbudget/fy06/pdf/hist.pdf.

[19] Richard Toikka et al., "Spending on Social Welfare Programs in Rich and Poor States," U.S. Department of Health and Human Services, 30 June 2004, http://aspe.hhs.gov/hsp/social-welfare-spending04/.

[20] U.S. Office of Management and Budget, "The Budget of the United States Government, Fiscal Year 2006, Historical Tables," http://a255.g.akamaitech.net/7/255/2422/23feb20050900/www.gpoaccess.gov/usbudget/fy06/pdf/hist.pdf.

[21] Christine Vestal, "Feds Pinch State Welfare Programs," *Stateline,* 3 February 2006, http://www.Stateline.org.

[22] Jack Walker, "The Diffusion of Innovations among the American States," *American Political Science Review* 63 (1969): 880–99; Virginia Gray, "Innovation in the States: A Diffusion Study," *American Political Science Review* 67 (1973): 1174–85; Frances Stokes Berry and William Berry, "State Lottery Adoptions as Policy Innovations: An Event History Analysis," *American Political Science Review* 84 (1990): 395–415; Frances Stokes Berry and William Berry, "Innovation and Diffusion Models in Policy Research," in *Theories of the Policy Process,* ed. Paul Sabatier (Boulder, Colo.: Westview, 1999); Christopher Mooney and Mei-Hsien Lee, "Legislative Morality in the American States: The Case of Pre-*Roe* Abortion Regulation Reform," *American Journal of Political Science* 39 (1995): 599–627; and Donald Haider-Markel, "Policy Diffusion as a Geographical Expansion of the Scope of Political Conflict: Same-Sex Marriage Bans in the 1990s," *State Politics and Policy Quarterly* 1 (2001): 5–26.

[23] Jack Walker, "The Diffusion of Innovations among the American States," *American Political Science Review* 63 (1969): 880–99.

[24] Gray, "Innovation in the States."

[25] Susan Welch and Kay Thompson, "The Impact of Federal Incentives on State Policy Innovation," *American Journal of Political Science* 24 (1980): 715–26.

[26] Christopher Mooney, "Modeling Regional Effects on State Policy Diffusion," *Political Research Quarterly* 54 (2001): 103–24.

[27] Berry and Berry, "State Lottery Adoptions as Policy Innovations"; and Lawrence J. Grossback, Sean Nicholson-Crotty, and David A. M. Peterson, "Ideology and Learning in Policy Diffusion," *American Politics Research* 32 (2004): 521–45.

[28] Craig Volden, "States as Policy Laboratories: Emulating Success in the Children's Health Insurance Program," *American Journal of Political Science* 50 (2006): 294–312.

[29] Charles Shipan and Craig Volden, "Bottom-Up Federalism: The Diffusion of Antismoking Policies from U.S. Cities to States," *American Journal of Political Science* 50 (2006): 294–312.

[30] Gerald Wright, Robert Erikson, and John McIver, "Public Opinion and Policy Liberalism in the American States," *American Journal of Political Science* 31 (1987): 980–1001.

[31] Thomas Dye, *Politics, Economics, and the Public: Policy Outcomes in the American States* (Chicago: Rand McNally, 1966); Frederick Boehmke and Richard Witmer, "Disentangling Diffusion: The Effects of Social Learning and Economic Competition on State Policy Innovation and Expansion," *Political Research Quarterly* 57 (2004): 39–51; and Toikka et al., "Spending on Social Welfare Programs in Rich and Poor States."

[32] V. O. Key, *Southern Politics* (New York: Knopf, 1949); and Thad Kousser, "Politics, Economics, and State Policy: Discretionary Medicaid Spending, 1980–1993," *Journal of Health Politics, Policy and Law* 27 (2002): 639–71.

[33] Kim Quaile Hill and Jan Leighley, "The Policy Consequences of Class Bias in State Electorates," *American Journal of Political Science* 36 (1992): 351–65.

[34] John Kingdon, *Agendas, Alternatives and Public Policies* (Boston: Little, Brown, 1984), 76.

[35] See Christopher Howard, *The Hidden Welfare State: Tax Expenditures and Social Policy in the United States* (Princeton, N.J.: Princeton University Press, 1997), for a discussion of how Americans define welfare and the implications that different definitions have for policy making and policy outcomes.

[36] Gøsta Esping-Andersen, *The Three Worlds of Welfare Capitalism* (Princeton, N.J.: Princeton University Press, 1990); and Joe Soss and Lael Keiser, "The Political Roots of Disability Claims: How State Environments and Polices Shape Citizen Demands," *Political Research Quarterly* 59 (2006): 133–48.

[37] Social Security Administration, "Social Security Basic Facts," 2 February 2006, http://www.ssa.gov/pressoffice/basicfact.htm. For several decades, questions have abounded over the entitlement program's solvency. Some economists have estimated that the Social Security Trust Fund will dry up by 2040, leaving many workers who are college-aged and younger high and dry come their retirement. In 2031, it is estimated that there will be 71 million eligible seniors over the age of 65, nearly twice the number today. More daunting is that by 2031, there will only be

2.1 workers for every Social Security beneficiary receiving payments; today, the ratio is a much healthier 3.3 workers for every beneficiary.

[38] Keiser, "Street-Level Bureaucrats, Administrative Power and the Manipulation of Federal Social Security Disability Programs."

[39] Social Security Administration, "Press Office," http://www.ssa.gov/pressoffice/factsfig.htm. The Social Security Administration also administers the Social Security Income (SSI) program, a public assistance program that uses general funds to provide monthly payments to impoverished elderly, blind, and disabled individuals on the basis of their financial need.

[40] Wisconsin Department of Workforce Development, "Timeline History: 1883–2004," http://www.dwd.state.wi.us/dwd/DWDHistory/default.htm.

[41] Cornell University Law School, Legal Information Institute, "Unemployment Compensation," http://www.law.cornell.edu/wex/index.php/Unemployment_compensation; and Economic Policy Institute, "Workers Compensation," http://www.epinet.org/content.cfm/datazone_uicalc_index.

[42] Cornell University Law School, Legal Information Institute, "Workers Compensation," http://www.law.cornell.edu/wex/index.php/Workers_compensation.

[43] Daniel Smith, "Removing the Pluralist Blinders: Labor-Management Councils and Industrial Policy in the American States," *Economic Development Quarterly* 7 (1993): 373–89.

[44] Committee on Ways and Means, U.S. House of Representatives, *2005 Green Book,* Government Printing Office, http://www.gpoaccess.gov/wmprints/green/2004.html.

[45] Jennifer Mittelstadt, *From Welfare to Workfare: The Unintended Consequences of Liberal Reform, 1945–1965* (Chapel Hill: University of North Carolina Press, 2005).

[46] Olivia Golden, "Assessing the New Federalism: Eight Years Later," Urban Institute, 2005, http://www.urban.org/url.cfm?ID=311198.

[47] U.S. Department of Health and Human Services, "Indicators of Welfare Dependence: Annual Report to Congress," 2005, http://aspe.hhs.gov/hsp/indicators05/index.htm.

[48] U.S. Department of Health and Human Services, "Fact Sheet," March 2006, http://www.acf.hhs.gov/opa/fact_sheets/tanf_factsheet.html.

[49] Meridith Walters, Gene Falk, and Vee Burke, "CRS Report for Congress: TANF Cash Benefits as of January 1, 2004," updated 12 September 2005, http://www.nationalaglawcenter.org/assets/crs/RL32598.pdf.

[50] Vestal, "Feds Pinch State Welfare Programs."

[51] Norma Riccucci, *How Management Matters: Street-Level Bureaucrats and Welfare Reform* (Washington, D.C.: Georgetown University Press, 2005).

[52] Vestal, "Feds Pinch State Welfare Programs."

[53] Toikka et al., "Spending on Social Welfare Programs in Rich and Poor States."

[54] U.S. Department of Agriculture, "A Short History of the Food Stamp Program," 2007, http://www.fns.usda.gov/fsp/rules/Legislation/history.htm.

[55] U.S. Department of Health and Human Services, "Indicators of Welfare Dependence"; and Food Research and Action Center, "Food Stamps Program," March 2006, http://www.frac.org/html/federal_food_programs/programs/fsp.html.

[56] Joe Soss, "Lessons of Welfare: Policy Design, Political Learning, and Political Action," *American Political Science Review* 93 (1999): 363–80.

[57] Sanford Schram, Joe Soss, and Richard Fording, eds., *Race and the Politics of Welfare Reform* (Ann Arbor: University of Michigan Press, 2003); and Lael Keiser and Joe Soss, "With Good Cause: Bureaucratic Discretion and the Politics of Child Support Enforcement," *American Journal of Political Science* 42 (1998): 1133–56.

[58] Council of State Community Development Agencies, "COSCDA Federal Advocacy Priorities, Fiscal Year 2006," March 2006, http://www.coscda.org/membersonly/06legpriorities.pdf.

[59] Governor's Office for Local Development, "Kentucky Small Cities Community Development Block Grant (CDBG) Program," http://www.gold.ky.gov/grants/cdbg.htm.

[60] Office of Rural Community Affairs, "Texas Community Development Block Grant Program." March 2006, http://www.orca.state.tx.us/index.php/Community+Development/CDBG+General+Info.

[61] U.S. Department of Housing and Urban Development, "HUD Announces No Down Payment Mortgages for Hurricane Disaster Victims," 2005, http://www.hud.gov/news/release.cfm?content=pr05-143.cfm.

[62] Jared Bernstein, Elizabeth McNichol, and Karen Lyons, "Pulling Apart: A State-by-State Analysis of Income

Trends," Center on Budget and Policy Priorities, January 2006, http://www.cbpp.org/1–26–06sfp.pdf.

[63] Center for Policy Alternatives, "Living Wage," 2006, http://www.stateaction.org/issues/issue.cfm/issue/Living-Wage.xml; and Economic Policy Institute, "Minimum Wage: Frequently Asked Questions," 2006, http://www.epi.org/content.cfm/issueguides_minwage_minwagefaq.

[64] WakeupWalMart.com, "The Real Facts about Wal-Mart," 2006, http://www.wakeupwalmart.com/facts/.

[65] U.S. Department of Labor, "History of Federal Minimum Wage Rates under the Fair Labor Standards Act, 1938–1996," 2006, http://www.dol.gov/esa/minwage/chart.htm.

[66] Jeffrey Passel, "Size and Characteristics of the Unauthorized Migrant Population in the U.S.," Pew Hispanic Center, March 2005, http://pewhispanic.org/reports/report.php?ReportID=61.

[67] Eduardo Porter, "Cost of Illegal Immigration May Be Less Than Meets the Eye," *The New York Times,* 16 April 2006, p. BU3.

[68] Susan Carroll and Yvonne Wingett, "Prop. 200 Now Law in Arizona," *(Phoenix) Arizona Republic,* 23 December 2004, http://www.azcentral.com/specials/special29/articles/1223prop200hearing23.html.

[69] U.S. Census Bureau, "Income, Poverty and Health Insurance Coverage in the United States: 2003," August 2004, http://www.census.gov/prod/2004pubs/p60–226.pdf.

[70] Institute of Medicine, "Hidden Costs, Value Lost: Uninsurance in America," National Academy of Sciences, 2003, http://www.iom.edu/CMS/3809/4660/12313.aspx.

[71] Families USA, "Health Care: Are You Better Off Today Than You Were Four Years Ago?" September 2004, http://www.familiesusa.org/assets/pdfs/Are_You_Better_Off_rev20053139.pdf.

[72] Institute of Medicine, "Hidden Costs, Value Lost."

[73] Paul Krugman and Robin Wells, "The Health Care Crisis and What to Do about It," *New York Review of Books,* 23 March 2006, http://www.nybooks.com/articles/18802.

[74] Sara Collins, Karen Davis, and Alice Ho, "A Shared Responsibility: U.S. Employers and the Provision of Health Insurance to Employees," *Inquiry* 41 (2005): 6–15.

[75] Kaiser Family Foundation/Health Research and Educational Trust, "Employer Health Benefits: 2005 Summary of Findings," 14 September 2005, http://www.kff.org/insurance/7315/sections/upload/7316.pdf.

[76] Bradley Shrunk and James Reschovsky, "Trends in U.S. Health Insurance Coverage, 2001–2003," Tracking Report no. 9, Center for Health Systems Change, August 2004, http://www.hschange.org/CONTENT/694/.

[77] Carmen DeNavas-Walt, Bernadette Proctor, and Cheryl Lee, "Income, Poverty, and Health Insurance Coverage in the United States: 2004," U.S. Bureau of the Census, August 2005, http://www.census.gov/prod/2005pubs/p60–229.pdf.

[78] Health Care Financing Administration, *The spDATA Book: Characteristics of Medicaid State Programs* (Washington, D.C.: Government Printing Office, 1993).

[79] Daniel Vock, "Medicaid Cuts, Welfare Reform Target Poor," *Stateline,* 2 February 2006, http://www.Stateline.org.

[80] Vernon Smith et al., "The Continuing Medicaid Budget Challenge: State Medicaid Spending Growth and Cost Containment in Fiscal Years 2004 and 2005," Kaiser Commission on Medicaid and the Uninsured, October 2004, http://www.kff.org/medicaid/7190.cfm.

[81] Toikka et al., "Spending on Social Welfare Programs in Rich and Poor States"; and Donald Boyd, "The State Fiscal Crisis and Its Aftermath," Kaiser Commission on Medicaid and the Uninsured, September 2003, http://www.kff.org/medicaid/loader.cfm?url=/commonspot/security/getfile.cfm&PageID=22130.

[82] Shruti Rajan, "Publicly Subsidized Health Insurance: A Typology of State Approaches," *Health Affairs* (May–June 1998): 101–17.

[83] Kaiser Family Foundation, "State Health Facts," 2006, http://www.statehealthfacts.org.

[84] Kathleen Hunter, "Bush Budget Short on State Aid," *Stateline,* 6 February 2006, http://www.Stateline.org.

[85] Hunter, "Bush Budget Short on State Aid."

[86] Mark Daniels, ed., *Medicaid Reform and the American States: Case Studies on the Politics of Managed Care* (Westport, Conn.: Greenwood, 1998); Charles Barrilleaux and M. E. Miller, "The Political Economy of State Medicaid Policy," *American Political Science Review* 82 (1988): 1089–1106; Dye, *Politics, Economics, and the Public;* Richard Winters, "Party Control and Policy Change," *American Journal of Political Science* 20 (1976): 597–636; and Kousser, "Politics, Economics, and State Policy."

[87] Carol Miller, "Policy Denies Nutrients to 1,000," *Miami Herald,* 24 March 2006, http://www.miami.com/mld/miamiherald/14173441.htm.

[88] Ronald Brownstein, "Governors on Divergent Paths to Control Health Costs," *Los Angeles Times,* 14 March 2006.

[89] Smith et al., "The Continuing Medicaid Budget Challenge."

[90] Brownstein, "Governors on Divergent Paths to Control Health Costs."

[91] David Fahrenthold, "Mass. Bill Requires Health Coverage," *The Washington Post,* 5 April 2006, p. A1; and John Hechinger and David Armstrong, "Massachusetts Seeks to Mandate Health Coverage: Bill Would Penalize Citizens Who Don't Buy Insurance; Business Fears Higher Costs," *Wall Street Journal,* 5 April 2006, p. A1.

[92] Volden, *States as Policy Laboratories,* 295.

[93] Marcia Angell, "The Truth about the Drug Companies," *New York Review of Books,* 15 July 2004, http://www.nybooks.com/articles/17244.

[94] Ceci Connolly, "Millions Not Joining Medicare Drug Plan," *The Washington Post,* 21 February 2006, p. A1.

[95] U.S. Department of Health and Human Services, "Prescription Drug Services," http://www.medicare.gov/pdphome.asp.

[96] Neil Gilbert, *Transformation of the Welfare State: The Silent Surrender of Public Responsibility* (New York: Oxford University Press, 2002); but see Paul Pierson, *Dismantling the Welfare State: Reagan, Thatcher, and the Politics of Retrenchment* (New York: Cambridge University Press, 1994).

[97] Lawrence M. Mead, "The Politics of Welfare Reform in Wisconsin," *Polity* 32 (2000): 533–59.

[98] Economic Policy Institute, "Minimum Wage: Frequently Asked Questions," 2006, http://www.epinet.org/content.cfm/issueguides_minwage_minwagefaq.

[99] Peter Szekely, "Union Cites Wal-Mart Worker Reliance on State Aid," *The New York Times,* 14 March 2006; and Lee Scott, "Wal-Mart Is in Maryland to Stay," *The Washington Post,* 9 February 2006, p. A23.

Chapter 15

[1] School district and demographic statistics for Chappaqua and Detroit are calculated from the National Center for Education Statistics (NCES), U.S. Department of Education, 2007, http://nces.ed.gov/edfin/; and City-Data.com, 2007, http://www.city-data.com.

[2] Loucas Petronicolos and William New, "Anti-Immigrant Legislation, Social Justice, and the Right to Equal Educational Opportunity," *American Educational Research Journal* 36 (1999): 373–408.

[3] Thomas Hungerford and Robert Wassmer, "K–12 Education in the U.S. Economy," National Education Association Research Working Paper, April 2004, http://www.nea.org/edstats/images/economy.pdf.

[4] Richard Florida, *The Rise of the Creative Class* (New York: Basic Books, 2002).

[5] Bill Gates, cofounder, Bill and Melinda Gates Foundation, prepared remarks, National Education Summit on High Schools, February 26, 2005, http://www.gatesfoundation.org/MediaCenter/Speeches/BillgSpeeches/BGSpeechNGA-050226.htm.

[6] Christopher B. Swanson, "Who Graduates? Who Doesn't? A Statistical Portrait of Public High School Graduation, Class of 2001," Urban Institute's Education Policy Center, 2004, http://www.urban.org/UploadedPDF/410934_WhoGraduates.pdf. See also Lawrence Michel and Joydeep Roy, "Rethinking High School Graduation Rates and Trends," Economic Policy Institute, 2006. http://www.epi.org/books/rethinking_hs_grad_rates/rethinking_hs_grad_rates-FULL_TEXT.pdf.

[7] Greg Toppo, "Big-City Schools Struggle with Graduation Rates," *USA Today,* 20 June 2006, http://www.usatoday.com/news/education/2006–06–20-dropout-rates_x.htm.

[8] Barbara Clowse, *Brainpower for the Cold War: The Sputnik Crisis and National Defense Education Act of 1958* (Westport, Conn.: Greenwood, 1981).

[9] National Commission on Excellence in Education, "A Nation at Risk: The Imperative for Educational Reform," April 1983, http://www.ed.gov/pubs/NatAtRisk/index.html.

[10] U.S. Department of Education, National Center for Education Statistics, "Digest of Education Statistics, 2004," April 2005, http://nces.ed.gov/programs/digest/d04/tables/dt04_001.asp.

[11] National Conference of State Legislatures, "Compulsory Education," March 2006, http://www.ncsl.org/programs/educ/CompulsoryEd.htm.

[12] U.S. Department of Education, Center for Education Statistics, "Digest of Education Statistics, 2004."

[13] Damien Cave and Josh Benson, "Voucher Issue a Touchy Topic in Newark Race," *The New York Times,* 17 April 2006, p. A20.

[14] R. L. Johns, "Regulation and Limitation of Credit to Boards of Education," *Review of Educational Research* 11 (1941): 190–96.

[15] Eric Stevick, "New Legislature Brings New Hope for Levy Bill: Education Boosters See Good Prospects for a Bill to Let Levies Pass with a Simple Majority," *(Everett, Wash.) Daily Herald,* 5 January 2007, http://www.heraldnet.com/stories/07/01/05/100loc_a1levy001.cfm.

[16] Oregon Education Association, "150 Years of Public Service to Education," 2006, http://www.oregoned.org.

[17] Education Commission of the States, "State Boards/Chiefs/Agencies," 2006, http://ecs.org/html/issue.asp?issueID=192.

[18] U.S. Department of Education, Center for Education Statistics, "School District Demographics," June 2004, http://nces.ed.gov/surveys/sdds/.

[19] Michael B. Berkman and Eric Plutzer, *Ten Thousand Democracies: Politics and Public Opinion in America's School Districts* (Washington, D.C.: Georgetown University Press, 2005).

[20] Berkman and Plutzer, *Ten Thousand Democracies.*

[21] Peter Schrag, *Final Test: The Battle for Adequacy in America's Schools* (New York: New Press, 2003); William Fischel, "How *Serrano* Caused Proposition 13," *Journal of Law and Politics* 12 (1996): 607–45; and D. Roderick Kiewiet, "Californians Can't Blame Everything on Proposition 13," *Public Affairs Report* 40 (November 1999), http://www.igs.berkeley.edu/publications/par/Nov1999/Kiewiet.html.

[22] Jon Sonstelie, Eric Brunner, and Kenneth Ardon, "For Better or for Worse? School Finance Reform in California," Public Policy Institute of California, 2000, http://www.ppic.org/content/pubs/report/R_200JSR.pdf.

[23] Caroline Hoxby and Ilyana Kuziemko, "Robin Hood and His Not-So-Merry Plan: Capitalization and the Self-Destruction of Texas' School Finance Equalization Plan," NBER Working Paper no. 10722, September (New York: National Bureau of Economic Research, 2004), http://www.nber.org/papers/w10722; and Ralph Blumenthal, "No Easy Solution as Texas Must Revisit School Financing," *The New York Times,* 28 March 2006, p. A15.

[24] State Higher Education Executive Officers, "State Higher Education Finance, FY 2006," 2007, http://www.sheeo.org/Finance/shef_fy06.pdf.

[25] State Higher Education Executive Officers, "State Higher Education Finance, FY 2006."

[26] Brent Kallestad, "University President Announces Enrollment Freeze," *Daytona Beach (Fla.) News-Journal,* 15 June 2007.

[27] Georgia Lottery, "HOPE Scholarships," 2007, http://www.galottery.com/gen/education/hopeScholarship.jsp.

[28] John F. Witte, "Private School versus Public School Achievement: Are There Findings That Should Affect the Educational Choice Debate?" *Economics of Education Review* 11 (1992): 371–94.

[29] Milton Friedman, "The Role of Government in Education," in *Economics and the Public Interest,* ed. Robert A. Solo (New Brunswick, N.J.: Rutgers University Press, 1955); and Alliance for School Choice, "School Choice around the Nation," 2006, http://www.allianceforschoolchoice.org/school_choice_states.aspx.

[30] National Education Association, "Privatization," 2006, http://www.nea.org/privatization/index.html.

[31] John F. Witte, *The Market Approach to Education: An Analysis of America's First Voucher Program* (Princeton, N.J.: Princeton University Press, 2001); John F. Witte, "Who Benefits from the Milwaukee Choice Program?" in *Who Chooses? Who Loses? Culture, Institutions and the Unequal Effects of School Choice,* ed. B. Fuller and R. Elmore (New York: Teachers College Press, 1996); and National Conference of State Legislatures, "Vouchers, Tax Credits and Deductions," 2006, http://www.ncsl.org/programs/educ/VoucherMain.htm.

[32] National Education Association, "Privatization of Public Education: From Vouchers to Outsourcing," September 2004, http://www.nea.org/neatodayextra/0409extra.html.

[33] Robert Strauss, "Edison Awarded 2 More Philadelphia Schools," *The Washington Post,* 16 May 2005, p. A3; and Chris Whittle, *Crash Course: Imagining a Better Future for Public Education* (New York: Riverhead Hardcover, 2005).

[34] U.S. General Accounting Office, "Public Schools: Comparison of Achievement Results for Students Attending Privately Managed and Traditional Schools in Six Cities," October 2003, http://www.asu.edu/educ/epsl/EPRU/documents/EPRU-0310-45-OWI.pdf.

[35] "School Reform in Philadelphia," *Online Newshour,* 2005, http://www.pbs.org/newshour/bb/education/reform/schools.html.

[36] Ray Budde, "The Evolution of the Charter Concept," *Phi Delta Kappan* 78 (1996): 72–3; Michael Mintrom, *Policy Entrepreneurs and School Choice* (Washington,

D.C.: Georgetown University Press, 2000); and Michael Mintrom, "Policy Entrepreneurs and the Diffusion of Innovation," *American Journal of Political Science* 41 (1997): 738–65.

[37] Jonathon Christensen, "Charter School Data: What States Collect," National Charter School Research Project, 2006, http://www.ncsrp.org/downloads/hfr06/hfr06_briefweb.pdf.

[38] National Conference of State Legislatures, "Charter Schools," 2006, http://www.ncsl.org/programs/educ/CharterMain.htm.

[39] Robin Lake and Paul Hill, eds., *Hopes, Fears, and Reality: A Balanced Look at American Charter Schools in 2006* (Seattle, Wash.: National Charter School Research Project, 2006), http://www.ncsrp.org/cs/csr/download/csr_files/hfrdec1_web.pdf.

[40] Patricia Lines, "Homeschooling," ERIC Digest Series no. 151, 2001, http://eric.uoregon.edu/publications/digests/digest151.html.

[41] Peter Wielhouwer, Gregory Rathje, and Jamie Dye, "Before the Spelling Bee: Accounting for Variation in State Home School Regulations" (paper presented at the annual meeting of the State Politics and Policy Quarterly Conference, Austin, Texas, February 2007).

[42] Daniel Princiotta, Stacey Bielick, and Christopher Chapman, "Homeschooling in the United States: 2003," U.S. Department of Education, National Center for Education Statistics, 2003, http://nces.ed.gov/pubs2006/2006042.pdf.

[43] Rob Reich, "The Civic Perils of Homeschooling," *Educational Leadership* 59 (2002): 56–9.

[44] National Conference of State Legislatures, "The No Child Left Behind Act and High School Reform," 2005, http://www.ncsl.org.

[45] See, for example, John Chubb and Terry Moe, *Politics, Markets and America's Schools* (Washington, D.C.: Brookings Institution, 1990; for a critique of this ideology, see Kevin Smith and Kenneth Meier, *The Case against School Choice: Politics, Markets, and Fools* (Armonk, N.Y.: M. E. Sharpe, 1995).

[46] Paul Basken, "Parts of Education Law Are Ignored," *The Washington Post,* 11 April 2006, p. A4, http://www.washingtonpost.com/wp-dyn/content/article/2006/04/10/AR2006041001294.html.

[47] Jay Mathews, "No Reader Left Behind: A Guide to the Law," *The Washington Post,* 12 March 2006, p. B4.

[48] Paul Basken, "States Have More Schools Falling Behind," *The Washington Post,* 29 March 2006, p. A17.

[49] Greg Toppo, "States Fight No Child Left Behind, Calling It Intrusive," *USA Today,* 11 February 2004, http://www.usatoday.com/news/education/2004-02-11-no-child-usat_x.htm.

[50] Basken, "States Have More Schools Falling Behind."

[51] Susan Saulny, "Few Students Seek Free Tutoring or Transfers from Failing Schools," *The New York Times,* 6 April 2006, p. A16.

[52] Diana Jean Schemo, "Federal Program on Vouchers Draws Strong Minority Support," *The New York Times,* 6 April 2006, p. A1.

[53] "Beware of the Ghost of James G. Blaine," *New York Sun,* 20 January 2006, http://www.nysun.com/article/26224; and David Akerman, "Education Vouchers: Constitutional Issues and Cases," Report for Congress, Congressional Research Service, Library of Congress, 20 May 2003, http://www.firstamendmentcenter.org/pdf/CRS.voucher1.pdf.

[54] Washington Research Council, "Governor's Budget Sets Priorities, Lives within Means," Policy Brief 01–16, 20 December 2002, http://www.researchcouncil.org/Briefs/2002/PB02–16/BudgetLives.pdf.

[55] Mary Ellen Klas, "Class-Size Amendment May Finally Get Funding," *Miami Herald,* 17 April 2006, http://www.miami.com/mld/miamiherald/news/state/14358383.htm.

[56] Donnell-Kay Foundation, "Amendment 23 and Public School Financing in Colorado," March 2003, http://www.headfirstcolorado.org/A23FINAL.pdf.

[57] Lisa Snell, "California's 2005 K–12 Education Primer," Policy Brief 40, *Reason,* May 2005, http://www.reason.org/pb40_california_education_reform.pdf.

Achievement gap: The gulf in performance and educational attainment between rich and poor and white and minority students.

Adequate yearly progress (AYP): Mandated by the No Child Left Behind Act (NCLB) of 2002, it is a statewide accountability system requiring each state to ensure that every one of its schools and districts is meeting specified achievement goals.

Adjudication: To settle a dispute by judicial procedure.

Adjudicator: Legal professional trained in resolving disputes between parties outside of the courtroom.

Administrative rules: Regulations, restrictions, and requirements written by executive agencies and used to implement public policy enacted through the legislature, the courts, or the governor.

Administrative rules review committee: The state legislative committee whose job it is to check whether the thousands of rules that a state's executive agencies propose each year follow the intent of the legislation that authorized that agency to establish those rules.

Adversarial argument: As in a courtroom, when two parties to a dispute make their best arguments to a neutral third party, who then decides the dispute. This is as opposed to a negotiated settlement where the parties work back and forth between themselves to resolve the dispute.

Altruism: The motivation to act out of a desire to help others, rather than out of a desire for personal benefit.

Amend: To modify a bill in the lawmaking process.

Amendatory veto: The power of some states' governors to send a passed bill back to the legislature asking for specific changes in it before he or she will sign it.

Amicus curiae brief: Latin for a "friend of the court" brief, a legal argument offered by a person or group that is not a party to a case but would like to influence its outcome.

Annexation: The legal process of adding unincorporated land and/or residents beyond a political jurisdiction's boundary, to make it part of the incorporated jurisdiction. Annexation may be done to provide services to outlying areas, or to increase tax revenues for the jurisdiction annexing the land.

Appropriations bill: A bill that authorizes a state agency to spend money in specific ways.

Articles of Confederation: The country's first constitution, ratified in March 1781.

Astroturf campaign: An artificial campaign orchestrated by an interest group to appear as though it is growing naturally from the grassroots.

At-large elections: Many elections for local government such as city or county councils (or commissions) are often contested such that every voter in the jurisdiction votes on every council position up for election. Voters cast one vote per position being contested. Rather than representing a specific geographic area within the jurisdiction, elected officials represent the entire jurisdiction. At-large elections can allow a cohesive majority group to sweep every position.

Balanced budget rules: A requirement that a state's budget has revenues equal to spending. Rules may apply to projected revenues and spending, or to actual levels.

Bench trial: Trial with no jury, where the judge or judges alone decide the outcome.

Bicameral: Having two chambers, such as in 49 state legislatures and Congress, which have a house of representatives (called by another name in some states) and a senate.

Bill: A proposed law that is formally introduced by a legislator for consideration by his or her chamber.

Bill of Rights: Ratified in December 1791, the first 10 amendments to the U.S. Constitution ensure the protection of individuals and the states from the national government.

Bill sponsor: The legislator who proposes that a bill be considered by his or her chamber.

Bipartisan Campaign Reform Act of 2002: Also known as BCRA, this act not only banned federal political parties from using soft money for federal election activity but also restricted some activities of state and local parties.

Blanket primary: Primary elections nominate candidates for the general election. In a blanket primary election, candidates from all parties are listed on the same ballot. Voters participate regardless of their party affiliation, and are able to select candidates of different parties for different offices.

Block grants: Fixed-sum federal grants allocated by formula giving state and local governments broad leeway in designing and implementing designated programs.

Bureaucracy: The administrative structure of any large, complex organization, like a government, that is characterized by hierarchical control and fixed rules of procedure.

Campaign finance regulations: Rules and statutes regulating the ways in which money can be gathered and spent by political campaigns, defining what is required, permissible, and impermissible.

Capital budget: The portion of state spending on infrastructure such as buildings, bridges, and roads. Capital budgets may be exempt from balanced budget rules.

Casework: The activities of a legislator and his or her staff in helping constituents with specific problems, usually with state government. For example, a legislator may help a constituent solve a problem with getting a driver's license or adjusting a state tax bill.

Categorical grants: Grants from the federal government to states and cities that are for specific purposes defined by Congress.

Caucus: Used by parties to nominate candidates, with party members informally meeting, deliberating, and casting a vote for their preferred candidate.

Cause célèbre: French for a "famous legal case," denoting an issue causing heated controversy.

Centralization: Empowering a national governing authority with unitary control and authority.

Chamber floor: Where and when the members of one chamber (the house or senate) meet as a group to debate and vote on legislation.

Charter school: A public school that is operated by a school district, but is freed from the administrative, staffing, and pedagogical constraints of traditional public schools and usually has a narrow mission.

Citizen legislature: A state legislature that is largely a part-time body, whose members are paid a modest salary, have little staff, meet infrequently, and are expected to have careers and interests other than the state legislature.

Civil service: Appointed administrators and public employees. Civil service jobs are usually awarded based on merit exams and qualifications, rather than political connections.

Civil service system: A system of hiring, promoting, and firing government workers based on job-related criteria rather than on political connections or other biases.

Civil union: A relationship between two people (whether an opposite- or same-sex couple) with much of the legal rights and obligations of marriage, but without the title of *marriage*.

Class action lawsuit: A lawsuit brought by one party on behalf of a group of individuals all having the same grievance.

Clean money and public financing of campaigns: Some states provide public funds for candidates seeking political office if they agree to limits on the contributions they receive from private sources.

Clientele politics: A style of politics where the people in control of government provide something of value in exchange for political support. Support for clientele parties is based on what sort of favors a party can supply, or the personal contacts that the party builds with supporters.

Closed primary: A primary nomination election in which voters registered with a political party are permitted to vote only for candidates of the party with whom they are registered.

Coercive federalism: A federalist arrangement whereby the federal government spearheads and funds programs; also referred to as *creative federalism.*

Collective action problem: The problem of coordinating a group of people to achieve a common goal.

Commerce Clause: Gives Congress the power "to regulate Commerce with foreign Nations, and among the several States, and with the Indian Tribes." Used by Congress to expand its power vis-à-vis the states.

Committee jurisdiction: The policy area and bills that a legislative committee has the responsibility to consider in its deliberations.

Common law: The system of laws originated and developed in England, based on court decisions, the doctrines implicit in those decisions, and customs and usages rather than on codified written laws.

Commutation: The power of some governors unilaterally to reduce the sentence of a person convicted of a crime.

Comparative method: An approach to political analysis that entails comparing units of analysis (such as states or communities) on more than one characteristic to help understand the relationships among those characteristics.

Confederal system: Also known as a *confederacy,* a system of governance whereby the national government is subject to the control of subnational, autonomous governments.

Conference committee: A temporary legislative committee made up of equal members of the senate and house who meet to reconcile the differences between the versions of a bill passed by the two chambers and to propose a single version for both chambers to consider.

Conflict of interest: A situation in which a government decision maker may personally benefit from his or her official actions, or a judge has a personal interest in the outcome of a case that may bias his or her actions in that case.

Constitutional initiative: An initiative measure that amends a state's constitution, or adds new language to a constitution. Constitutional measures can alter rules about a state's political process. If approved by voters, constitutional measures are typically more difficult for elected officials to amend or repeal than statutory initiatives.

Contiguous: Areas of land that touch (except for islands).

Contract lobbyist: A professional lobbyist who temporarily works on behalf of a client.

Contracting for services: A community or political jurisdiction entering a contract with another to provide services. Cities or unincorporated areas may contract with counties, other cities, or special districts for services such as fire, police, sanitation, and libraries.

Cooperative federalism: A federalism arrangement whereby responsibilities for most governmental functions are interdependent, shared between the federal and state governments.

Cost of living allowances (COLAs): A pay increase that matches the rate of inflation. COLAs maintain a fixed level of purchasing power, not an increase in purchasing power.

Council–manager system: Form of city government in which an elected council acts as a legislature, with no mayor. An appointed, professional city manager is hired to oversee executive functions. Some council–manager systems have one council member serve as a ceremonial mayor with no formal powers.

Court of last resort: Those courts whose decisions cannot be appealed to another court; these courts have the final word on a given set of laws. Typically called the *supreme court* (or something similar).

Cracking: Dispersing a party's voters among many districts so it will win fewer district races.

Cumulative voting: A form of voting in at-large elections for city councils and other bodies. Voters are given as many votes as positions up for election on the council. Rather than casting one vote per council position, voters can, if they want, give one candidate multiple votes. This makes it less likely that a cohesive majority will sweep all positions up for election.

Decentralization: Devolving to citizens or their elected representatives more power to make decisions, including the formation and implementation of public policies.

Defendant: The person or institution against whom an action is brought in a court of law; the person being sued or accused of a crime.

Defense of Marriage Act (DOMA): Federal law enacted in 1996 that (1) defined *marriage* for the purposes of federal law as a relationship between one man and one woman, and (2) allowed the states not to recognize same-sex marriages sanctioned in other states.

Descriptive representation: The idea that a representative should reflect the characteristics of the people (the constituents) who she (or he) represents. Characteristics could include race, ethnicity, gender, and other traits related to the identity of the representative's constituents.

Devolution: The decentralization of power and authority from a central government to state or local governments.

Dillon's rule: Concept about the nature of local government powers (or "municipal corporations") from John F. Dillon, scholar and

judge, circa 1872. Whereas states may be seen as having powers beyond those listed in the U.S. Constitution, local governments have only those powers explicitly granted to them by a state. Cities, counties, school districts, and "special districts" are thus legal entities created by their states.

Direct initiative: A measure proposed by a citizen or group. If the proposal qualifies with sufficient signatures, it is voted on directly by the public, and becomes law if approved.

Direct primary: An election in which voters select one candidate affiliated with a political party for each elected office; the party nominees later face one another in a general election.

Director of state courts: Administrator hired by a court system to handle the bureaucratic chores of the system, including personnel and budget issues.

District magnitude: The number of people elected to represent a political jurisdiction. In most American legislative races, district magnitude equals one. In at-large races, in multimember districts, and in most proportional representation systems, district magnitude is greater than one.

Disturbance theory: A macro-level theory that assumes groups emerge in response to societal changes.

Divided government: When two of the three legs of the legislative process (the governor, the house, and the senate) are controlled by different parties.

Docket: A calendar of the cases awaiting action in a court.

Domestic partnership: A relationship similar to a civil union, but usually with somewhat fewer legal rights and obligations.

Double jeopardy: The prosecution of a defendant for a criminal offense for which he or she has already been acquitted; this is prohibited by the Fifth Amendment to the U.S. Constitution.

Drug courts: Trial courts of limited jurisdiction used in some states and localities to prosecute certain minor drug and related offenses, with a focus on reducing recidivism and drug abuse treatment. Judges and lawyers working in these courts specialize in the issues surrounding drug abuse and addiction.

Dual federalism: A system of federalism whereby governmental functions are apportioned so that the national and subnational governments are accorded sovereign power within their respective spheres; sometimes referred to as "layer cake" federalism.

Earmark: In the context of government budgeting, the reservation of the revenue from a certain fee or tax into its own fund to be spent only for a specified purpose.

Earned media: Generating newsworthy events or stories for free publicity.

Economies of scale: Savings that may be achieved in the cost of production or service delivery by larger enterprises. Savings may be due to lower cost per unit of providing some service, or due to investment in expensive equipment that might be underutilized in a smaller setting.

Efficacy: The sense that one's effort at something can make a difference. *Personal efficacy* is the sense that you are able to understand politics. *External efficacy* is the belief that public officials will respond to your political acts.

Efficiency gains: Providing services or goods at a lower cost per unit of service or per unit of the good supplied.

Elastic demand: Demand for something is said to be elastic if it responds to changes in price. If a tax raises the price of something that has elastic demand, such as travel or some luxury items, the tax may reduce consumption of the good.

Elasticity: The responsiveness of something to a change in price.

Electioneering: Explicitly supporting or opposing candidates or political parties, including recruiting and endorsing candidates, fundraising, phone banking, canvassing, and advertising.

Eminent domain: The power of the state and local governments to appropriate private property, typically for a public purpose. Some states also delegate this power to private entities, such as utility companies.

Entitlement: A government program guaranteeing a level of benefits to participating individuals or entities.

Ex post oversight: When the legislature investigates how well an agency is carrying out the intent of a law.

Executive budget: A reform of the Progressive era under which the first proposal of the budget for a government's next fiscal year is put together by the chief executive, whether it is the president, governor, or mayor.

Expressive act: Action taken for its symbolic meaning, rather than to have a practical effect.

Federal preemption: Federal government taking regulatory action that overrides state laws.

Federalism: The structural relationship between a national government and its constitutive states.

Feminization of poverty: The gap between women and men who are caught in the cycle of poverty, which is caused by occupational segregation, poor wages and lower pay than men, bearing the bulk of child care costs, and other structural conditions.

First trimester: The first three months of pregnancy, because a normal full pregnancy is nine months long.

Fiscal illusion: One explanation of government growth is fiscal illusion. The idea is that when states collect revenues by withholding taxes from paychecks or by taxing corporations, taxes are hidden. People might thus underestimate the true cost of public services, causing them to support more spending. James C. Garand, in "Explaining Government Growth in the U.S. States," contends that little empirical evidence supports this explanation.

Flat rate tax: A flat rate income tax applies the same tax rate to everyone, regardless of their income levels.

Free-rider problem: When the benefit of some valuable good or service cannot be restricted to those who pay for it.

Full Faith and Credit Clause: Article 4, Section 1, of the U.S. Constitution, which stipulates that the states must mutually accept one another's public acts, records, and judicial proceedings.

Full veto: The power of the chief executive to block the passage of an entire passed bill, subject to override by a supermajority vote of the legislature.

Functional party model: A theory that parties are pragmatic, self-interested organizations, striving to maximize votes in order to win elections and control political office.

Gatekeeping: Determining which questions and decisions will and will not be considered.

General jurisdiction: Referring to courts that deal with virtually any type of case.

General purpose local government: Cities and counties are general purpose governments, as they typically provide a range of services and functions; some provide much more than others.

General Revenue Sharing (GRS): A federal grant-in-aid program that provides financial aid to subnational units, but does not prescribe how those units are to allocate the funding.

Gerrymander: The process of drawing governmental district boundaries for political advantage.

Good-time Charlie: Some state governors in the mid-20th century who were less active in attacking public policy problems, less educated, older, and less qualified than most governors serving since that time; the term was coined by political scientist Larry Sabato.

Grandfather clause: Exemptions to post–Civil War rules granted to whites, based on the fact that they had a father or grandfather who was a citizen prior to the Civil War. As slaves (noncitizens), blacks were excluded by grandfather clauses.

Grassroots activities: Political activities undertaken by a group's members, rather than by its leaders, typically involving direct political action, like writing letters to policy makers and attending political rallies.

Growth controls: Various land use regulations that attempt to manage the pace and location of residential development.

Growth machine: A coalition of people active in local politics, united by a preference for policies that encourage population growth in their community.

Gubernatorial powers: Institutional and informal tools that a governor can use to develop and promote public policy, manage the state bureaucracy, and act as intergovernmental relations (IGR) manager, among other duties.

Head of state: The main public representative of a government.

Home rule: The delegation of power from a state government to local governments. Home rule charters define the boundaries of local government autonomy, and result in less state control over local government affairs.

Hypothesis: A potential answer to a research question that is based on theory and that will be tested by observing data in the world.

Implementation: The execution by government agencies of laws passed by the legislature.

Incorporation: State laws define the process of municipal incorporation. This is required for a city or town to have greater autonomy from its county and state governments.

Incorporation of the Bill of Rights: A legal doctrine whereby parts of the U.S. Bill of Rights are applied to the states through the Fourteenth Amendment's Due Process Clause.

Incumbent: The person currently holding a position.

Incumbent-protection district: A governmental district drawn to give electoral advantage to the incumbent.

Indirect initiative: A measure proposed by a citizen or group. If the proposal qualifies, it is directed to the state legislature. The legislature can vote to approve the measure as written, or refer it to the voters for approval. The legislature may also refer an alternate proposal along with the initiative proposal.

Individualistic political culture: The general and informal set of beliefs and attitudes that politics in a state or community is a place where individuals can work to advance their personal economic and social interests largely the same as they would do in private business.

Industrial development revenue bonds: Debt issued by local governments on behalf of a private company for the purpose of building facilities or acquiring land. Interest payments on revenue bonds are financed by revenues from the project the bonds are issued for.

Inelastic demand: Demand for something is said to be inelastic if it does not respond to changes in price. If a tax raises the price of something that has inelastic demand, such as basic foods, medical care, or things that people are addicted to, the tax may not reduce consumption of the good.

In-house lobbyist: A professional lobbyist who is a permanent employee of an interest group.

Injunction: A court order prohibiting someone from taking some action.

Interest group: A formally organized body of individuals, organizations, or public or private enterprises sharing common goals and joining in a collective attempt to influence the electoral and policy-making processes.

Interest group system density: The number of functioning groups relative to the size of a state's economy.

Interest group system diversity: The spread of groups in a state across social and economic realms.

Intergovernmental relations: The interactions among the federal government, the states, and local governments.

Intermediate courts of appeal: Courts that hear appeals of trial decisions and are concerned with whether the trial was fair and conducted with proper procedures. ICAs were developed as a way to take the burden of routine appeals off of supreme courts so that supreme courts can focus on the most important cases.

Intermunicipal inequality: Differences between communities in the social status and wealth of community residents.

Issue advocacy: A form of political speech focusing on issues of public concern that mentions issues and the positions taken on those issues by elected officials or candidates, but stops short of expressly advocating the support or defeat of those elected officials or candidates.

Issue evolution: The process by which the definition and politics of a public policy issue change over time.

Jacksonian democracy: A broad philosophy of government, associated with the era when Andrew Jackson was president (1829–1837), that emphasized executive power, broad suffrage (for white males), the election of many public officials, laissez-faire economics, and patronage appointments for government employment.

Judicial review: The power of a supreme court to judge whether a law is in violation of the state constitution and, if so, to nullify that law.

Jurisdiction: Geographical or topical area over which a court, institution, or official has power and authority.

Jury: A randomly selected group of citizens who are sworn by a court to hear and render a verdict and/or set a penalty in a trial.

Lame duck: An elected official who will not or cannot run for his or her current office in the next election; also, any official who has been voted out of office and is serving in the last days of a term before the new official is sworn in.

Land Ordinance of 1785: An act of Congress that set a process to sell land west of the Appalachian Mountains, north of the Ohio River, and east of the Mississippi River for $1.00 per acre. The act set rules for the creation of townships in the area.

Legal brief: A document stating legal facts and arguments.

Legislative intent: What the legislature meant for a piece of legislation to do when it passed it.

Legislative professionalism: When a legislature is established to be largely a full-time body, with members who are paid a living wage, have plenty of staff, and believe that legislating is their primary job.

Legislative referendum: Legislation approved by the legislature, but referred to the voters for final approval. Some legislation, like constitutional amendments (in most states) or bond issues (in some states and communities), must be referred to voters for final approval.

Legislative turnover: The degree to which the membership of a legislature changes after an election.

Leviathan: The model of government as an entity that seeks to increase revenues beyond even what the public might demand.

Limited jurisdiction: Referring to courts that handle cases on only certain topics, such as traffic courts or probate courts.

Line-item veto: The power of some governors to block only parts of passed appropriations bills from becoming law, subject to override by a supermajority vote of the legislature.

Literacy tests: Post–Civil War rules that denied blacks the vote; literacy tests included tests designed to be too difficult for most people to pass. The test could ask people to interpret passages from the U.S. Constitution, and allowed local officials the discretion to judge if answers were right or wrong. Whites who would fail the tests could vote based on a grandfather clause.

Living wage: An area-specific level of income and benefits needed for working individuals to subsist at a basic or decent level that takes into consideration cost of living factors.

Lobbying: Communicating with elected officials in general, as well as the systematic effort to shape public policy by pressuring governmental officials to make decisions in line with the goals of an organized interest. The term *lobbying* comes from the fact that representatives were often approached in the lobby of legislative buildings.

Louisiana Purchase: The purchase of the French Territory of Louisiana (more than 500 million acres of land) from France in 1803. The purchase included land that is now Arkansas, Kansas, Missouri, Iowa, Nebraska, and Oklahoma, as well as much of what is now Louisiana, Colorado, Minnesota, Montana, North and South Dakota, and Wyoming.

Machines: A term for local political party organizations that used patronage and clientele politics to control elections in many U.S. cities.

Majority-minority district: Legislative districts where district lines are drawn so that people from a specific minority group comprise a majority of voters in the district.

Malapportionment: When the districts in a legislative chamber are not equal in population.

Means-tested: The provision of need-based public assistance and financial aid by government that is available only to individuals falling below a predetermined level of income or assets.

Media market: Region where the population is exposed to the same (or similar) media offerings, including the same television and radio stations and newspapers.

Medicaid: Created by Congress in 1965, a joint federal- and state-financed public assistance program administered by the states that provides payments directly to health care providers for medical services rendered to means-tested low-income individuals and families.

Medicare: Created by Congress in 1965, a federally financed social insurance health care program for people 65 or older and people of all ages with certain disabilities.

Mental health courts: Trial courts of limited jurisdiction used in some states and localities to prosecute certain offenses by those who have a mental illness, with a focus on reducing recidivism by treating the mental illness. Judges and lawyers working in these courts specialize in the issues surrounding mental health.

Merit Plan: A method used to select at least some judges in 24 states whereby (1) a panel of experts recommends a few candidates for a judicial opening to the governor, (2) who then appoints one person to that position for a trial period, and (3) after which the judge faces a retention election to see whether he or she will earn a full term.

Metropolitan areas: Regions of mostly contiguous population centers, as defined by the U.S. Census Bureau. A large area, such as New York, can include several metropolitan areas (northern New Jersey, Long Island, and Connecticut) consolidated into a larger metropolitan area. Smaller regions, such as Pocatello, Idaho, may include cities and towns in a single county.

Meyer v. Grant: A 1988 U.S. Supreme Court ruling against a Colorado law that made it a felony to pay for the collection of signatures on initiative and referendum petitions. The Court ruled that spending to collect signatures was "core political speech" and that no state could ban campaign spending on signature collection. Since 2005, however, two federal appellate courts (the 8th Circuit and 9th Circuit) have permitted states to ban payment per signature, thus requiring that paid petitioners receive a salary or an hourly wage.

Mobilization of bias: The benefiting of private, organized interests in an interest group system.

Model city charter: Recommendations for how city political institutions should be arranged.

Model charters published by the National Municipal League (now called the National Civic League) have been published since 1900.

Moralistic political culture: The general and informal set of beliefs and attitudes that politics in a state or community is intended to enhance the public good and for the uplifting of the have-nots of society.

Morality policy: A policy on which at least one side of the debate (and often only one side) bases its arguments on basic moral values, often supported by religious beliefs.

Muckraking journalists: Journalists and authors who exposed issues of political corruption, public health dangers, and child labor practices. The writing of muckrakers was featured in newspapers and magazines such as *Cosmopolitan, Harper's Weekly,* and *McClure's.* Some famous muckrakers included Thomas Nast, Lincoln Stephens, and Upton Sinclair.

Multimember district (MMD): Legislative districts that elect more than one representative. Some state legislative districts, and many local councils, have more than one representative elected per district.

Multiparty politics: Political systems where three or more parties are able to win office. The United States, in contrast, is dominated by two-party politics.

Municipal charters: The set of rules that define how cities are structured, what the powers of local officials are, and how local elections shall be conducted.

National Governors Conference: Bipartisan association of the 55 state and territorial governors, supported by research and training staff.

National Supremacy Clause: Stipulates that the U.S. Constitution and national laws and treaties "shall be the supreme law of the land."

Necessary and Proper Clause: Known also as the *Elastic Clause,* it grants Congress the power to make all laws that shall be "necessary and proper for carrying into execution the foregoing powers," that is, the other congressional powers listed in Article I, Section 8 of the Constitution.

Neutral competence: The value that a government agency should implement policy based only on original legislative intent and its workers' professional norms and training rather than by nonlegislative political pressure.

No Child Left Behind Act (NCLB): Signed into law by President George W. Bush in January 2002, the bipartisan act greatly expanded the role of the federal government in K–12 public education. The law requires annual assessments of student performance, requiring that children and schools attain adequate yearly progress (AYP).

Nonpartisan blanket primary: All candidates, regardless of their party, face off in the same primary election, with a candidate winning the election outright if he or she wins more than 50 percent of the vote.

Nonpartisan primary: An election to nominate candidates for the general election where candidates have no party labels, and all voters can participate. Used in many local elections, and at the state level in Nebraska.

Nullification: A constitutional theory, advanced most notably by John C. Calhoun and other advocates of states' rights, espousing the right of a state to declare null and void a law passed by the U.S. Congress that the state found to be unconstitutional or disagreeable.

Office-block ballot: Groups together all candidates running for a single political office by the political office rather than by their party.

OP-ED article: Newspaper article written to advocate a point of view, usually found opposite the editorial page (hence the name *OP-ED*).

Open primary: A primary nomination election. Any registered voter, including independents, can participate. Voters must decide which party's primary they will participate in, and can choose only among that party's candidates.

Operating budget: The part of a state's budget dedicated to paying for current operations, such as public services and public employee salaries.

Original jurisdiction: The right of a court to be the first to hear a case; where a case must begin its path through the judicial system.

Out-of-court settlement: An agreement made privately between the parties to a civil suit before a trial court decision.

Outsider gubernatorial candidates: Candidates for governor who are not traditional politicians but who have achieved success in other ways, such as in business or as entertainers.

Override: When the legislature passes a law despite a gubernatorial veto, usually by a supermajority vote in each chamber.

Packing: Concentrating one party's voters into a few districts so as to "waste" those votes over 50 percent, allowing the other party to win more district races.

Pardon: The power of some governors to throw out the conviction of a person convicted of a crime.

Participation bias: The difference between the general population of eligible voters and the people who actually participate in elections. Bias in participation exists if participants are substantially different than nonparticipants.

Partisan dealignment: The weakening of the attachment that voters have to a political party.

Partisan primary: A primary election to decide a party's nominee for the general election ballot.

Party boss: The head of an urban or state party machine who controls elections and the disbursement of patronage.

Party caucus: All the legislators in a given chamber from a given party, such as the house Democrats or the senate Republicans.

Party fusion: Permits two or more parties to nominate the same candidate for office, with the candidate's name appearing on the ballot alongside the name of each party by which he or she is cross-endorsed.

Party identification: Also known as PID, it is the strength of an individual's attachment to a political party.

Party-column ballot: Groups together all candidates running for different political offices by their party affiliation, making straight-ticket voting possible.

Patronage: Favors and benefits that elected officials provide their supporters. Nineteenth-century party machines used city jobs as one source of patronage to reward loyal supporters.

Patronage appointments: The rewarding of government offices to loyal supporters in exchange for their political support.

Patronage job: A government job obtained at least in part through political connections rather than entirely by personal merit; used by elected officials to reward their political supporters and secure loyalty from the bureaucracy.

Pendleton Act: The Civil Service Reform Act of 1883, which created a modern civil service for the federal government. This made it more difficult for politicians to place their supporters in federal government jobs.

Petition: To make a formal request.

Plaintiff: The party that starts a lawsuit in a court of law.

Plea bargaining: A deal in which the defendant in a criminal case agrees to plead guilty to a lesser charge if the prosecutor agrees to drop a more serious charge.

Pluralism: A political theory that assumes conflict is at the heart of politics and that the diversity of interests will lead to consensual outcomes through discussion and debate.

Police powers: Local government power to provide for the common health, safety, and welfare of a community. The broad exercise of such power can be seen in setting public health, building, and food safety codes, and preventing construction in flood zones.

Policy agenda: The public problems and solutions that are discussed and addressed by policy makers at a given time.

Policy diffusion: The transfer or emulation of an idea, institution, or policy of one political jurisdiction by another.

Policy entrepreneur: A person who identifies a public need and works to motivate citizens and policy makers to change policy to satisfy that need.

Policy equilibrium: When policy-making forces (such as the current policy, interest group preferences, public opinion, and the issue environment) are balanced, so that little policy debate or change occurs.

Policy shock: An event that changes an issue's political environment, disrupts the policy equilibrium, and starts active policy making.

Political accountability: The value that government agencies should implement law following closely the wishes of current elected officials.

Political action committee (PAC): A legal entity that allows like-minded individuals who belong to a corporation, labor union, or virtually any other organization to bundle their contributions and give them to candidates or political parties.

Political agenda: The public problems and policy solutions under discussion by policy makers and the public at any given time.

Political capital: The intangible goodwill or support for an elected official that can be used to influence the actions of other officials informally.

Political ideology: A relatively coherent and consistent set of beliefs about who ought to rule, what principles ought to be used to govern, and what policies rulers ought to pursue.

Political institution: The rules, laws, and organizations through which and by which government functions.

Poll tax: A tax or fee that must be paid in order to secure the right to register or to vote.

Popular referendum: Legislation approved by the legislature (or a local government) that is put to a popular vote as a result of a successful petition for a referendum. It allows voters to have the final decision on legislation written by elected officials.

Populist era: The 1890s, during which time the Populist political movement was influential, particularly in the West. Populists advocated greater popular democracy, government control of key industries, and a national income tax.

Populist Party: A "third" American political party that had its greatest success in the 1890s. Populists were elected to state legislatures as well as to the U.S. House and Senate. The party called for political reforms including direct democracy, direct election of the U.S. Senate, and direct election of the president.

Pork barrel: A derogatory and subjective term referring to government spending that is focused on a single geographic area, such as a bridge or a park, suggesting that such spending is wasteful and politically motivated.

Potential interest: An interest that is yet to be organized but has some latent acceptance in society.

Precinct: One of the smallest geographic units in a town, city, or county. Precincts comprise several city blocks. A neighborhood might consist of several precincts.

Precinct captain: A party machine operative who worked to organize a city neighborhood on behalf of the party machine.

Primary election: An election to decide which candidates will be able to be listed on the general election (November) ballot.

Privatization: When a city transfers the authority to supply a service to a private firm.

Privileges and Immunities Clause: Ensures that residents of one state cannot be discriminated against by another state when it comes to fundamental matters, such as pursuing one's professional occupation or gaining access to the courts.

Problem-solving courts: Trial courts of limited jurisdiction whose focus is less on prosecuting crimes or settling lawsuits than on helping the parties in the case work out certain types of especially difficult problems; for example, family court, drug court, and mental health courts can be thought of as problem-solving courts.

Progressive era: A period of political change and reform during the early decades of the 20th century. Some Progressives hoped to reform politics by limiting the power of corporations and political parties.

Progressive tax: A progressive tax has wealthier people pay a larger proportion of their income to cover the tax. The less affluent pay a lower share of their income toward the tax.

Progressives: Members of the political party and social movement of the early 20th century whose aim was to improve government and public policy through rationality and broadening political participation.

Pro-life and pro-choice: Positive, self-identifying labels for groups opposing abortion (pro-life) and supporting the availability of legal abortion (pro-choice).

Proposition 13: A constitutional initiative approved by California voters in 1978. One of the first major antitax initiatives, Proposition 13 froze property values at 1977 levels, limited future increases in property taxes, and is credited with setting an antitax mood that helped propel Ronald Reagan to the White House.

Public assistance: A means-tested program that provides aid—both cash and in-kind services—to the poor.

Public goods: Policies or actions providing broad benefits, rather than narrow benefits to a specific group.

Racial gerrymandering: Drawing boundaries for legislative districts on the basis of race.

Rank-and-file legislator: Legislator who does not hold a leadership position in his or her chamber.

Reapportionment revolution: The political upheaval in the states in the 1960s following the U.S. Supreme Court's mandate that they redraw their legislative and congressional districts to be equal in size in each chamber.

Recall: A vote to remove an elected official from public office. Recall proposals qualify if sufficient signatures are collected.

Recidivism: The tendency to relapse into a previous pattern of behavior, especially criminal behavior.

Reconstruction. The post–Civil War era (1865–1877) when government and public policy in the 11 states of the former Confederacy were dominated by the federal government, immigrants from the northern states ("carpetbaggers"), and freed slaves, and where those sympathetic with the Confederacy were shut out of the political process.

Recuse: To disqualify from participation in a decision on grounds such as prejudice, personal involvement, or conflict of interest.

Redistricting: The redrawing of political districts, as required after each census to keep them equal in population.

Reduction veto: The power of some state governors to reduce the level of spending authorized in an appropriations bill passed by the legislature, subject to an override by a supermajority vote of the legislature.

Regional-metropolitan government: Governing structures that united various local governments, often for a single purpose, such as managing airports, protecting air quality, running parks, or providing public transportation. A few large cities consolidated with their counties to form a single government (for example, Nashville and San Francisco).

Regional revenue sharing: Several local jurisdictions in an area can pool revenues from a tax source, or from new development, and then distribute the revenue across all jurisdictions.

Regressive tax: A regressive tax is one in which the less affluent pay a greater share of their income to cover the tax. The wealthy pay a lower share of their income toward the tax.

Regulatory takings: Government actions that deny a property owner fair use of property without adequate compensation.

Rent control: Local policies that attempt to limit the amount that landowners may increase rents each year on existing tenants.

Responsible party model: A theory advanced by 18th-century Irish philosopher Edmund Burke that parties should be ideologically consistent, presenting voters with a clear platform and set of policies that are principled and distinctive. Elected officials are expected to be held responsible for implementing the party's program and policies.

Retention election: An election in which the issue on the ballot is whether an incumbent should be kept in office (yes or no), rather than one that offers a choice between two or more competing candidates.

Roll call: When legislators are required to cast a recorded vote on a bill or motion, whether in a committee or on the chamber floor.

Runaway jury: A subjective and pejorative term used to describe a jury whose verdict, in the judgment of the describer, goes against the obvious facts in the case.

School districts: A form of a special-purpose local government that operates public schools; differing in autonomy, their geographic boundaries, taxing authority, and policy recommendations are broadly set (and limited) by state officials.

School voucher: The use of public funds to cover the costs of private education, whereby financial aid in the form of a voucher is provided to parents to transfer their children from public schools to private schools.

Selective benefit: The provision by a group of some material, purposive, or solidarity incentive that can be enjoyed only by members of the group.

Self-financing candidates: Candidates for office who mainly use their own money for their campaign expenses.

Semiclosed primary: Voting in a party's primary is permitted for voters who are registered with the party or as independents.

Semiopen primary: Registered voters may vote in any party's primary, but they must publicly declare for which party's primary they choose to vote.

Sin tax: A tax on an item or behavior that is unpopular, or a tax on a product that the state seeks to reduce consumption of.

Single-member district (SMD): Legislative district in which only one legislator from the same chamber serves.

Single-payer health care: A health system financed by one source—usually the federal government—in which doctors and other private health care professionals provide basic services to every person, with their fees paid by the government at a fixed rate.

Single-subject rule: Rules that require that an initiative address only one question or issue. Twelve states have such rules for their initiative process. The definition of a *single subject* varies widely, as does how courts interpret them. Some courts have become more assertive in rejecting initiatives on the grounds that this rule is violated.

Small claims courts: A trial court of limited jurisdiction that deals only with civil suits of less than a specified amount of claimed damages (e.g., $5,000) and in which the plaintiff and defendant are not represented by legal counsel.

Social capital: Networks of trust and reciprocity built from participation in voluntary social groups.

Social insurance: Rather than means-tested, a government-created program (such as Social Security) that socializes risk by forcing the compulsory contributions of participants.

Social Security Act: Technically known as the Old Age, Survivors and Disability Insurance program (OASDI), a federal social insurance program created in 1935 providing economic assistance mainly to retired workers and their families.

Sodomy: Any sexual act other than coitus between a man and a woman, often referring to homosexual activity.

Soft money: Campaign funds not regulated by federal election laws, originally intended to be used for party building and for state and local general electioneering activities.

Special districts: Local governments that are established (under state laws) for limited purposes, such as providing a single public service.

Special session: An extraordinary meeting of the legislature after its regular session has adjourned, usually called by the governor to consider a very limited policy agenda.

Spoils system: An informal system in which political appointments are rewarded on the basis of political considerations, rather than fitness for office.

Sprawl: Sprawl is typically characterized by excessive land use. This includes low-density housing, limited options for transportation (other than cars), gaps between developed and undeveloped areas, high levels of pavement for parking spaces, and uniformity of housing type.

Standing committee: An at least semipermanent legislative committee that evaluates legislation in a particular area of policy.

State of the State address: In most states, the annual address by the governor to the state legislature at the beginning of its session in which he or she describes the condition of the state and presents a policy agenda for the coming legislative session.

Statutory initiative: An initiative measure that amends a regular law, or adds a new law to the statute books. If approved by voters, statutory initiative measures have the status of laws passed through the regular legislative process. Statutory initiative laws are thus typically easier for elected officials to amend (or repeal) than constitutional initiative laws.

Stay of execution: The power of governors in most states with capital punishment to delay temporarily executing a condemned person.

Straight-ticket ballot: A type of ballot that allows (or requires) voters to cast their votes for candidates of a single political party.

Street-level bureaucrats: Government workers who have direct contact with the public, such as police officers, teachers, and driver's license examiners.

Strong mayor–council system: Form of city government where an elected mayor holds many executive functions, including influence over budgeting, appointment of department heads, and veto powers. Sometimes referred to as a mayor–council system.

Suburb: A community separate and distinct from an established central city. Suburbs can be incorporated cities or towns, as well as unincorporated places.

Supermajority: A portion of a vote that is greater than one-half, such as two-thirds or three-fifths.

Supermajority vote requirement: A rule that requires more than a simple majority vote to approve a budget, for example, 60 percent or a two-thirds majority.

Supreme court: The highest court in a judicial system, with final appellate jurisdiction over cases of law in that system.

Tammany Hall: A machine that controlled New York City politics during the late 1800s.

Targeting electoral strategy: Focusing campaign resources where they will be most effective, especially by supplying more resources to close races and fewer to those in which a candidate will likely either lose or win.

Tax and expenditure limits (TELS): Rules that limit how much a state legislature may increase revenues or spending in an annual budget.

Tax equity: Tax equity refers to which income groups bear the burden of a tax.

Temporary Assistance for Needy Families (TANF): Created by Congress in 1996 to replace AFDC (Aid to Families with Dependent Children), a social welfare program that provides monthly cash assistance (up to four years) to means-tested poor families with children under the age of 18; it requires recipients to participate in a work activity.

Term limits: The requirement that a person can be elected to a certain office only for a specified number of terms or years.

Top-two primary: Allows eligible voters, irrespective of their party affiliation, to vote in a primary for any candidate running on any party ticket, with the top candidates from each political party squaring off in the general election.

Tort: Damage, injury, or a wrongful act to person or property—whether done willfully or negligently— for which a civil suit can be brought.

Traditionalistic political culture: The general and informal set of beliefs and attitudes that politics in a state or community is the domain of social and economic elites and that the have-nots ought not to get involved in politics.

Trial court: A court before which issues of fact and law are tried and determined for a legal case.

Trial transcript: The official, verbatim, and written record of what was said during a trial.

Two-party contestation: When both major parties have a general election nominee in a race for a given office.

Underclass: The least privileged social stratum, characterized by joblessness, social isolation, and impoverished and unsafe neighborhoods.

Unfunded mandate: A public policy that requires a subnational government to pay for an activity or project established by the federal government.

Unicameral: Having only one chamber, such as the Nebraska Legislature, which has a senate but no house.

Unified government: When all three legs of the legislative process (the governor, the house, and the senate) are controlled by the same party.

Unincorporated area: Areas of a county that have not formally incorporated as a municipality (city, town, and village). Unincorporated areas are typically administered by county governments, and may receive services from counties and special districts.

Unitary system: A system of governance with a strong central government that controls virtually all aspects of its constitutive subnational governments.

Urban growth areas: Areas adjacent to existing development that is slated for future growth. Some state land use plans attempt to increase housing density within designated urban growth area boundaries before allowing development in outlying areas.

Urbanization: The sociologist Louis Wirth defined urbanization as a process where a city grows in size, density, and heterogeneity.

User fees: A direct charge for use of a service, charged to the user of the service. Examples include tuition and hospital charges.

Veto-proof majority: When the legislative majority party has a supermajority of members large enough to override a gubernatorial veto, if all majority party members vote to do so.

Vice laws: Laws banning certain activities thought to be sinful, particularly gambling, prostitution, pornography, sodomy, and drug use.

Village of Euclid v. Ambler Realty Company: A U.S. Supreme Court decision from 1926 that established that local government police powers include zoning power.

Voting cue: A simple signal about how to vote, in lieu of more detailed information; for example, a candidate's political party.

Voting Rights Act: A law passed by Congress in 1965 designed to remove racial barriers to voting. The original law gave the federal government authority over local voter registration procedures in several southern states. It has been amended and reauthorized by Congress several times since 1965.

Voting-age population: All U.S. residents age 18 and over.

Voting-eligible population: All U.S. citizens age 18 and over who are not excluded from voter eligibility due to criminal status (felony convictions, incarceration, or parole) or due to being declared incompetent to vote.

Ward: Also known as a *district*. Districts and wards elect their own representatives to a city council.

Watchdog: A group that monitors and publicizes the actions of government officials and agencies, and pulls a public alarm when something is awry.

Weak mayor–council systems: Form of city government where a mayor has limited formal power. In the machine era, a city council in weak mayor systems had influence over executive and administrative functions such as hiring and purchasing. Sometimes referred to as a council–mayor system.

Wedge issues: Controversial issues placed for a public vote via the initiative or referendum process by one political party or group, with the goal of dividing candidates and supporters of a rival party or group.

Welfare: A range of public assistance services provided by government to aid and protect the most vulnerable individuals in society; includes both social insurance and public assistance programs.

Winner-take-all: Also known as *plurality* election rules. When a single person represents a jurisdiction or just one person can win an elected position, the candidate with the most votes (the first to win, so to speak) is elected.

Working poor: A social stratum comprised of individuals who are gainfully employed, but who earn too little to subsist, thereby relying on public assistance and charities to make ends meet.

Writ of certiorari: The discretionary review of a lower court's ruling.

Zoning: The power of local governments to regulate land use. A zoning map divides a community into areas where specific types of land use are allowed (for example, residential, commercial, industrial, or agricultural). Zoning ordinances provide detailed standards for allowable building designs, lot sizes, building heights, landscaping requirements, and yard size, and how far buildings must be set back from the road.

A

Abrahamson, Shirley S. 298
Abramowitz, Alan 105, 117, 142
Adams, Greg 91
Adrian, Charles 367
Aldrich, John 134, 147
Allswang, John 117
Alozie, Nicholas O. 313
Alt, James 155, 333, 347
Alvarez, R. Michael 85-86
Anderson, Jennifer 172, 184, 187, 190
Anglin, Roland 403
Ansolabehere, Stephen 203, 204
Anthony, Jerry 408
Anton, Thomas 40
Arceneaux, Kevin 26, 101
Atkeson, Lonna Rae 87, 246
Austin, Sharon 451
Aylsworth, Leon E. 376

B

Babcock, Richard F. 400
Bachrach, Peter 162
Baker, Gordon E. 203
Baldassare, Mark 403, 404, 406
Banducci, Susan 85, 95, 109, 118
Banfield, Edward 76, 362, 366, 451
Barabas, Jason 205, 210
Baratz, Morton S. 162
Barber, Denise Roth 181
Bardwell, Kedron 91, 249
Barnello, Michelle A. 11, 212, 434
Barnes, James A. 279
Barrilleaux, Charles 6, 26, 258, 264, 275, 475
Baudoin, Kyle 325, 341, 347
Baum, Lawrence 286, 310
Bayoumi, Tamim 347
Beard, Charles 109-110
Becerra, Hector 383
Beer, Samuel 39, 52
Behr, Roy 156
Behrens, Angela 82
Bend, Doug 312
Bender, Edwin 180
Benesh, Sara C. 313
Benjamin, Gerald 235
Benson, Christopher 293
Benz, Matthias 118
Berch, Neil 339
Berinsky, Adam 86, 89
Berkman, Michael B. 5, 195, 202, 233, 258, 487, 488
Berns, Walter 426
Berry, Frances Stokes 340, 454
Berry, Jeffrey 162, 183-184
Berry, William D. 26, 142, 198, 202, 340, 454

Besley, Timothy 90
Best, Samuel 387
Beyle, Thad 245, 248, 251, 258, 261, 264, 266, 277
Bibby, John 132, 135, 144, 146, 148, 155-156
Bielick, Stacey 499-500
Binder, Norman 94
Black, J. 404
Blackman, Paul 375
Blais, Andre 86
Blatter, Joachim 278
Bledsoe, Timothy 380
Bluth, Alexa 176
Boatright, Robert G. 203
Bobo, Lawrence 95
Boehmke, Frederick 118, 169, 178, 186, 455
Bogen, David 45
Bohn, Hening 347
Bollens, Scott 403, 404
Bonneau, Chris W. 310
Borck, R. 233
Borrelli, Stephen A. 246
Bosselman, Fred 400
Bowler, Shaun 80, 81, 86, 86-87, 87, 88, 92, 100, 101, 104, 105, 109-110, 111, 114, 115, 119, 121, 123, 123-124, 125, 126, 141, 313, 325, 333, 347, 378
Bowling, Cynthia J. 264
Bowman, Ann O'M 54, 233, 410
Brace, Paul 26, 142, 302, 303, 314
Brady, Henry E. 71, 73, 74, 77, 89
Brandeis, Louis 452
Brasher, Holly 165
Bratton, Kathleen A. 216, 313
Breaux, David 202
Bridges, Amy 83, 84, 359, 362, 363, 379, 390
Brisbin, Jr., Richard A. 247
Brockington, David 86, 87
Broder, David 105, 110, 111, 123, 146, 332
Broder, John 172, 174
Brumbaugh, Susan 410
Bryan, Frank 84
Bryce, James 57
Buchanan, James M. 320, 386
Budge, Ian 105
Buehl, Stephen T. 400
Bullock, III, Charles S. 228
Burden, Barry 117, 396
Burklin, Wilhelm 105
Burnham, Walter Dean 82, 134, 175
Burns, Nancy 393, 394
Butler, David 99
Button, James 193, 216

Byrne, Julie 355

C

Cain, Bruce 100, 104, 119, 135, 235, 236
Camissa, Anne Marie 217, 226
Camobreco, John F. 11, 121, 212, 434
Campbell, David 105
Cann, Damon M. 312
Carey, John F. 174, 235, 236, 237
Carroll, Susan J. 211, 255
Carsey, Thomas M. 132, 142, 198, 248
Carty, Ken 86
Case, Anne 90
Caul, Miki 93
Caves, Roger 119, 397
Cawman, A.J. 418
Chapman, Christopher 499-500
Chavez, Lydia 119
Cheesman, Fred 299
Chubb, John E. 246, 248, 500-501
Citrin, Jack 119, 329
Clarke, Susan E. 424
Clayton, Connell 59
Clemens, Elisabeth S. 175
Clemons, Colleen 264
Clingermayer, James 333
Cloward, Richard A. 89, 144, 447
Clowse, Barbara 483
Clucas, Richard A. 229, 230
Coffey, Daniel 147, 148
Cohen, Jean 58
Cohen, Jeffrey E. 267
Coleman, James 84
Coleman, John 142, 147
Collins, Sara 469
Comins, Meg 236
Conlan, Timothy 51, 52, 334
Connolly, Ceci 476
Cooper, Christopher 91, 168
Copelin, Layla 204
Corrado, Anthony 146
Cotter, Cornelius 146
Cox, Gary 86, 91, 375
Craig, Barbara Hinkson 432
Craig, Steven 97
Crenson, Matthew 144
Crews-Meyer, Kelly A. 295
Crouch, Winston 108
Cullen, J.B. 340
Culver, John 129
Cummings, Jeanne 105

D

Dahl, Robert 162
Dalaker, Joseph 448
Dalton, Russell 105

Daniel, Kermit 235
Daniels, Mark 473
Danielson, Michael N. 400
Dao, Jame 117
Darcy, Robert 211-212
Dautrich, Kenneth 250
Davidson, Chandler 79, 80, 84, 87, 379, 380
Davis, Aaron 179
Davis, Ada 75
Davis, Belinda Creel 294
Davis, Karen 469
Dearden, J.A. 259
DeHoog, Ruth Hoogland 412
Delsohn, Gary 272
Denemark, David 378
Denton, Nancy 93, 395, 396
Denzan, Arthur T. 164
Derthick, Martha 41
DeSantis, Matthew 105, 117
Desantis, Victor S. 369
Diamond, Larry 358, 360
Dilger, Robert Jay 262, 392
Dionne, E.J. 54
Disch, Lisa 135
Dometrius, Nelson C. 225, 245, 269, 271
Douglas, James W. 274
Dowall, D. 403
Downs, Anthony 91, 133, 143, 404, 413, 308
Downs, Donald A. 308
Drummond, Andrew 105
Dubois, Philip 303
Dudley, R.L. 313
Duncombe, W. 326
Dupuis, Martin 436, 437
Durham, James G. 399
Dwyre, Diane 148
Dyckman, Martin 169
Dye, Jamie 498-499
Dye, Thomas E. 15, 48, 143, 345, 346, 379, 455, 473

E

Ebersole, W. Daniel 225
Edelman, Murray 425
Edwards, H.H. 202
Egan, Patrick J. 436
Ehrenhalt, Alan 206
Eisenger, Peter K. 40, 52, 379, 409, 411
Eisenstein, James 311
Elazar, Daniel J. 26, 40, 49, 50, 427
Elder, Charles D. 235, 236
Elder, Harold W. 314
Ellickson, R. 404
Elling, Richard C. 235, 236
Ellis, Joseph 43
Ellis, Richard 100, 104, 105, 109, 110
Emmert, Carol F. 303, 304, 313

England, Robert 365, 370
English, Art 236
Engstrom, Richard 84, 91, 94, 374

Epstein, David 43
Epstein, Lee 183, 304, 430, 431
Epstein, Leon 133, 134
Erie, Steven P. 360
Erikson, Robert S. 26, 88, 142, 346, 427, 455
Ernst, Howard 104, 115
Esping-Andersen, Gosta 456
Euchner, Charles C. 411

F

Fabrizio, Paul J. 430
Farmer, Rick 236
Fastnow, Christina 245, 267
Faux, Marian 429
Feigenbaum, Edward 180
Feingold, Kenneth 342, 348, 364
Feiock, Richard 408, 411
Fenno, Richard F. 222-223
Ferguson, Margaret R. 263, 264, 272
Fernandez, Ken 104, 109, 110, 114
Fico, F. 246
Filipowich, Brian 340
Fiorina, Morris 142, 167, 233, 270
Fischel, William 491-492
Fishel, William A. 397, 400, 405
Fisher, George 294
Flanagan, Maureen A. 365
Flango, Victor F. 300
Fleishman, Arnold 409, 410
Florida, Richard 481
Folmar, Kate 179
Fording, Richard C. 26, 462
Forsythe, Dall W. 258, 263
Fouhy, Beth 272
Fowler, Edmond 377
Fox, Richard L. 12, 212-213
Fraga, Luis 87, 379
Francia, Peter 91, 92, 93
Francis, Wayne 220
Frederickson, H. George 372, 375
Freedman, E. 246
Freeman, Patricia 168, 171, 176, 182
Freidan, Bernard 404, 405
Frey, Bruno 118
Fry, B.R. 336
Fuchs, Esther 71
Fund, John H. 235, 375

G

Gaebler, Ted 452
Gais, Thomas 167-168
Gamble, Barbara 119, 124
Garand, James 154, 325, 341, 345, 346, 347, 348
Garcia, F.C. 214
Garcia, J. 214
Garrett, Elizabeth 97
Gaventa, John 187
Gefland, Mark 395
Gentry, William M. 340
Gerber, Alan S. 83
Gerber, Brian J. 225
Gerber, Elisabeth R. 89, 113, 114, 119, 121, 122, 125, 142, 178, 333

Gerring, John 132
Gibson, Campbell 357-358
Gibson, James L. 146, 147
Gierzynski, Anthony 202
Gilbert, Neil 476
Gilliam, Jr., Frank 95
Gillman, Howard 59
Gilmore, Glenda Elizabeth 366
Gimpel, James 84
Ginsberg, Benjamin 144
Glaeser, Edward 404
Glazer, Amihai 235
Glick, Henry R. 293, 294, 304, 313
Goette, L. 118
Goggin, Malcolm L. 425
Goidel, Robert K. 91, 92, 249
Gold, Howard J. 93
Golden, Olivia 459
Goldsmith, Michael 40
Goldstein, Kenneth 176
Goldstein, Morris 347
Goodman, Michael J. 311
Gordon, Roger H. 340
Gordon, Sanford C. 295, 314
Gottinder, Mark 404
Graham, Barbara L. 313
Gray, Virginia 165, 184, 187, 190, 245, 248, 293, 454
Greeley, Andrew 417
Green, Donald P. 83, 92, 119, 135, 142, 144
Green, Gary P. 409, 410
Green, John 236
Greenberg, Amy 359
Greenblatt, Alan 202
Greenhouse, Linda 59, 60
Greider, William 447
Grofman, Bernard 79, 80, 84, 197, 205, 214, 236
Grogan, Coleen 90
Gross, Donald A. 91, 92, 249
Grossback, Lawrence J. 454
Grossman, Joel B. 294
Gunther, Richard 358, 360
Gurwitt, Rob 262, 270
Gyourko, Joseph 404

H

Haber, Samuel 364
Hagan, Michael 121
Haider-Markel, Donald 119, 421, 436, 437, 454
Hall, Kermit L. 310
Hall, Melinda Gann 183, 302, 303, 310, 314
Hall, Thad E. 266
Halperin, Karen 235
Hamm, Keith E. 229
Hammons, Christopher 40
Hancock, Ange-Marie 447
Handley, Lisa 78-79, 197, 2
Hanjal, Zoltan 74, 84
Hansen, John Mark 83
Hansen, Susan 325, 326, 339, 340

Hanson, Roger A. 297, 299
Hanson, Russell L. 26, 245, 293
Hanssen, F. Andrew 308
Hasen, Richard 97
Haskell, John 110
Haynie, Kerry L. 216, 217, 226
Hays, Samuel P. 84, 365
Heckman, James 340-341
Hedge, David 132, 216
Hegeman, Roxana 245
Heinz, John P. 165, 190
Helland, Eric 314
Helms, L. Jay 341
Hero, Rodney E. 19, 20, 74, 119, 198, 216
Herrnson, Paul 91, 92, 93, 135, 146-147, 156
Higgs, Robert 320
Hill, Kim Quaile 80, 90, 143, 346, 455
Hill, Paul 498
Hillygus, Sunshine 117
Hinton-Andersson, Angela 90
Hird, John A. 223
Ho, Alice 469
Hoblen, J. 404
Hofstadter, Richard 132, 364, 365
Hogan, Robert E. 92, 182, 198, 202
Holbrook, Thomas 6, 26, 132, 135, 148, 152
Holli, Melvin G. 367
Holman, Craig 124, 126
Horowitz, Juliana Menasce 132
Hotaling, John J. 203
Hovey, Harold A. 274
Hovey, Kendra A. 274
Howard, Christopher 75, 455
Hoxby, Caroline 493
Hrebenar, Ronald 171, 187
Hubbard, R. Glenn 340
Huber, Gregory A. 295, 314
Huber, John D. 224
Huckshorn, Robert J. 146
Huddleston III, C. West 296
Hungerford, Thomas 481
Hunter, James Davidson 424
Hurwitz, Mark S. 313
Husted, T.A. 259

I
Iceland, John 448
Inglehart, Ronald 423
Inman, Robert P. 347

J
Jackson, Kenneth T. 395, 396
Jacobs, Herbert 152, 248
Jacobson, Gary 395, 396
Jenkins, Shannon 225
Jensen, Merrill 41
Jerit, Jennifer 205, 210
Jewell, Malcolm E. 12, 91, 132, 139, 147, 150, 186, 190, 199, 201, 202, 225, 248, 270
Johns, R.L. 485

Johnson, G.A. 372
Johnson, Janet Buttolph 32
Johnson, Martin 26
Johnson, Nicholas 340
Jones, Bryan D. 421, 422
Jones, K.O. 202
Jones, Ruth 150
Judd, Dennis R. 77, 362, 393, 395
Juenke, Eric Gonzalez 94

K
KKapp, Lawrence 62
Karing, Albert 378, 379, 380
Karp, Jeffrey 85, 86, 88, 95, 126
Kassel, Jason 105, 117
Kathlene, Lyn 218
Katz, Michael 51
Kaufman, Cory 198
Kayden, Xandra 146-147
Keeney, Katherine M. 156
Keiser, Lael 456, 462
Keith, Ann L. 300
Kelderman, Eric 229, 237
Kerns, Peggy 172
Key, Jr., V.O. 16, 86, 87, 89, 134, 142, 150, 228, 270, 336, 455
Keyssar, Alexander 78, 358
Kiewiet, D. Roderick 122, 333, 347, 491-492
Kimball, David 156
Kincaid, John 51, 58
King, James D. 12, 152, 212, 232, 246, 267
Kingdon, John W. 221, 271, 422, 455
Klain, Maurice 90
Klein, David 310
Kleppner, Paul 84
Knight, Brian 90
Kobylka, Joseph F. 430, 431
Kollman, Ken 167-168
Kolodny, Robin 148
Korbel, George 84, 380
Koshmner, Andrew 182
Kousser, Morgan 375
Kousser, Thad 231, 233, 236, 237
Krasno, Jonathan S. 92
Krause, George A. 54
Kritzer, Herbert M. 294
Krueger, Brian S. 420
Kuersten, Ashlyn 183
Kumar, Anita 3
Kurtz, Karl T. 235, 236
Kuziemko, Ilyana 493
Kwong, Tsz Man 409, 410

L
La Raja, Raymond 144, 148, 150
Lake, Robin 498
Landis, John 404
Langer, Laura 6, 25, 26, 155, 303
Lanier, Drew Noble 313
Lanoue, David J. 313
Lapalombara, Joseph 179
Lapp, John 375
Larimer, Christopher 218

Larisey, R.W. 202
Larson, Bruce 104, 115
Laschler, Edward 121
Laumann, Edward 165
Law, Steve 236, 237
Lawless, Jennifer L. 12, 212-213
Lawrence, Eric D. 104
Lawrence, Steve 272
Layman, Geoffrey C. 132, 142, 423
Layton, Charles 201
Lazarus, Edward 156
Lazarus, Jeffrey 236
Leach, Daylin 235
Leal, David 94
Lee, Mei-Hsien 422, 426, 454
Lee, Young 340
Leege, David C. 420
Lehmann, Susan Goodrich 75
Leighley, Jan 74, 80, 85, 90, 143, 346, 455
Lennon, Emily 357-358
Lenzner, Robert 311
Leuchtenberg, William E. 50
Levine, Charles H. 380
Levy, J.R. 398
Lewis, David E. 274
Lewis, Gregory B. 105
Lewis, Paul 74, 84, 118, 361, 375, 378
Leyden, Kevin M. 246
Lieske, Joel 28
Lindblom, Charles 165
Lineberry, Robert 377
Lipset, Seymour Martin 134
Lipsky, Michael 453
Lipson, Leslie 245
Liptak, Adam 311
Liu, Fredrick 437
Loftus, Tom 202
Logan, Bret 375
Logan, John 74, 402, 403, 404, 412, 413
Longoria, Tomas 94
Lott, Jr., John R. 235
Louch, Hugh 375
Lowenstein, Daniel 109, 111
Lowery, David 165, 184, 187, 190, 329, 336, 391, 412, 413
Lowi, Theodore 150
Lowry, Robert 154-155, 347
Lubinski, Joseph 110, 178
Lublin, David 95, 214
Lucas, Robert 340
Luker, Kristin 428
Lupia, Arthur 113, 115, 122, 125, 333
Lynch, G. Patrick 267
Lyons, William E. 412, 413

M
Macauley, S. 294
MacDonald, Jason A. 247
Macedo, Stephen 71, 437
MacKuen, Michael 142

Maddox, H.W. Jerome 232
Maestas, Cherie 225, 233
Magg, Elaine 348
Magleby, David 99, 104, 105, 110-111, 111,113-114, 148
Mahe, Eddie 146-147,
Maisel, Sandy 134, 135, 155-156
Malbin, Michael J. 235
Malhorta, Neil 232, 233
Manweller, Matthew 311
Manza, Jeff 82
Marks, Alexandra 88
Martinez-Ebers, Valerie 94
Martorano, Nancy 228
Masket, Seth 235
Mason, T. David 77
Massey, Douglass 395, 396
Matsuzaka, John 98, 333, 376
Maule, Linda S. 307
Mayfield, Loomis 361, 375
Mayhew, David R. 147, 251
McCaffery, Peter 360
McCall, Maldavi 303
McCarthy, Nancy 315
McChesney, Robert 361
McCormick, Richard 375
McCuan, David 92, 104, 109-110, 111, 114
McCubbins, Matthew 115, 122, 224, 333
McDonald, Michael 82, 91, 94, 204, 374
McGlennon, John 198
McIver, John P. 26, 88, 142, 142-143, 346, 427, 455
McKinney, Dave 420
McNeal, Ramona 118
Mead, Lawrence M. 476
Mecoy, Laura 272
Medhoff, M. H. 432
Meier, Kenneth 419, 421, 425, 436, 500-501
Menes, Rebecca 362
Merriman, David 348
Mikesell, John 332
Miller, Donald E. 427
Miller, Gary 132, 392, 394
Miller, James Nathan 231
Miller, Kenneth 104, 119, 122
Miller, Matthew 311
Miller, William H. 214
Mills, Jon L. 203
Minnite, Lorraine 71
Mintrom, Michael 387
Mittelstadt, Jennifer 457
Moe, Terry 500-501
Moen, Matthew 430
Moffett, Randolph R. 392
Mofidi, Alaeddin 341
Mohajer, Kristine Hopkins 22
Mohr, James C. 428
Molotch, Harvey 402
Moncrief, Gary F. 91, 199, 202, 226, 229, 236

Monroe, J.P. 142, 145
Monson, J. Quinn 105
Morehouse, Sarah M. 12, 132, 139, 147, 150, 186, 190, 201, 248, 250
Morgan, David 365, 370, 378
Morone, James A. 418
Morse, Anson 133
Morton, Rebecca 89, 139, 142
Mossberger, Karen 64
Mueller, Paul D. 420
Mullins, Megan 138
Munger, Michael 86, 164
Munson, Ziad 184
Murtagh, Jerry 77
Myers, Guvtavo, 363

N
Nagler, Jonathan 74, 80, 85-86
Neal, Tommy 219
Neiman, Max 111, 115, 125, 400, 403, 404, 410, 413
Nelson, Robert L. 165
Neustadt, Richard E. 257
New, Michael 333
New, William 481
Newmark, Adam 173
Nicholson, Steven P. 105, 117
Nicholson-Crotty, Sean 454
Nie, Norman 89
Niemi, Richard G. 78, 79, 156, 174, 198, 199, 235, 236, 237, 266
Niskanen, William 320
Norrander, Barbara 28, 142
Norris, Pippa 423
Novarro, Neva Kerbeshian 332
Nownes, Anthony 168, 170, 171, 176, 182, 183

O
O'Brien, David M. 432
Oldmixon, Elizabeth A. 434
Oliver, J. Eric 84, 86
Olson, Mancur 74
Olson, Maurice 166
Opheim, Cynthia 22
Orey, Byron D'Andra 218
Orr, Susan 148
Osborn, Tracy 218
Osborne, David 452
Ostrom, Brian J. 299
Ostrum, Elinor 412
Overby, Marvin 218
Owens, Chris T. 156, 216
Owings, S. 233

P
Pachon, H. 214
Pallakowski, Henry O. 404
Palmer, James 180
Palmquest, Bradley 142
Pantoja, Adrian 94
Parks, Roger 412
Parry, Janine 141, 214
Partin, Randall W. 87, 246
Patterson, Kelly 110, 111
Patterson, T.W. 396

Patton, Zach 311, 312, 314
Pearce, Diana 450
Peel, Johnny 111, 115, 123-124, 125
Peel, Normal D. 400
Pellissero, John 370, 378
Pendall, Rolf 400
Peterson, David A. M. 454
Peterson, Kavan 63
Peterson, Paul 403, 452
Petracca, Mark P. 235
Petronicolos, Loucas 481
Phelan, Thomas 400
Phillips, Kevin 375
Pickett, Garthe E. 400
Pierce, Patrick A. 427
Pierson, Paul 476
Pinelo, Daniel R. 437
Piott, Steven 104
Pippen, John 92, 121
Pittenger, John 58
Piven, Frances Fox 89, 144, 447
Plutzer, Eric 5, 74, 487, 488
Pogionne, Sarah 218
Polinard, Jerry 94
Polsby, Nelson 235
Popiolkowski, Joseph 7
Popkin, Sam 82
Poterba, James 333, 346, 347
Powell, Lynda 174, 198, 199, 235, 236, 237
Powell, Richard 236
Preiss, Robert 61
Press, Charles 367
Preuhs, Robert R. 217, 218
Prewitt, Kenneth 378
Princiotta, Daniel 499-500
Protash, William 404
Putnam, Robert 84

R
Rabrenovic, Gordana 74, 403
Rahn, Wendy 84
Rakove, Jack 41, 43
Rallings, Collin 71
Ranney, Austin 99, 152
Ransone, Jr. Coleman B. 245
Rathje, Gregory 498, 499
Razin, Eran 388, 412
Read, Jr., Robert W. 22
Redfield, Kent D. 204, 229, 249
Reenock, Christopher 225
Reeves, Keith 84
Reich, Rob 500
Reingold, Beth 119, 217
Rempel, William C. 311
Renick, James 379
Renner, Tari 83, 369
Reynolds, H. T. 32
Reynolds, John 375
Riccucci, Norma 274
Richardson, Lillard 91
Riker, William 80
Ringquist, Evan J. 26
Riordan, William L. 326

Ritchie, Rob 81
Ritter, John 344
Rivlin, Alice 52
Roberts, Philip J. 266
Robertson, David Brian 43
Robertson, Larry 131
Rodgers, Joel 140
Rom, Mark 343, 452
Romance, Joseph 150
Romans, Thomas 341
Romer, Thomas 121
Rosenberg, Gerald 57
Rosenson, Beth 172
Rosenstone, Steven 83, 89, 156
Rosenthal, Alan 122, 123, 169, 171,
    83, 89, 156, 169, 195, 233, 271
Rosenthal, Cindy S. 218
Rosenthal, Howard 121
Rosentraub, Mark 388, 412
Rossi, Peter 404
Rothenberg, Lawrence 167
Rowland, C.K. 183
Rozell, Mark J. 228
Rubin, Herbert J. 410
Rubin, Irene S. 380, 410
Rudolph, Thomas 84
Rueben, Kim 333
Ruiz, Edgar 279, 280
Rule, Wilma 93
Rusk, David 413
Rusk, Jerrod 375
Russell, Brian 91
Russell, John 437
Ryden, David 135

S
Sabatier, Paul 454
Sabato, Larry 104, 115, 251
Salamore, Barbara G. 248
Salamore, Stephen A. 248
Salisbury, Robert 165
Sampson, Ginger 172
Samuelson, W.F. 294
Sanbonmatsu, Kira 11, 212
Sanchez, Samantha 94, 95, 213
Sanders, Jim 272
Sarbaugh-Thompson, Marjorie 174,
    235, , 236, 238
Saucier, D. A. 418
Saunders, Kyle 142
Savas, E.S. 392
Schaffner, Brian F. 205, 210, 228, 236
Schattschneider, E. E. 134, 150, 165,
    190
Scheiber, Harry 56
Scheppach, Raymond 48
Scher, Richard K. 203
Schickler, Eric 142
Schier, Steven 144
Schlesinger, Joseph 134, 144
Schlozman, Kay 71,73, 74, 77, 89,
    167, 190
Schneider, Mark 387, 400, 403, 412,
    413

Schneiderman, Stuart 202, 233
Schofield, Norman 132
Schrag, Peter 110, 111, 124, 133
Schram, Sanford 59, 452, 462
Schraufnagel, Scot 235
Schubert, Glendon A. 304
Schuknecht, J.E. 85
Schuldt, Richard G. 4521
Schultz, Birl 109-110
Schuman, David 101
Schwartz, Thomas 224
Schwarz, John 52
Sears, David O. 329
Segura, Gary 95
Seligson, Dan 250
Shaffer, William R. 26
Shapiro, Robert 71
Sharp, Elaine 74
Sharpe, M.E. 94, 419, 428, 501
Shea, Daniel 144
Shear, Michael 161
Sheffter, Martin 362
Sheldon, Charles H. 304, 307
Sherrill, Kenneth 436
Shields, Todd G. 91, 92, 117, 418
Shipan, Charles R. 455
Shlay, Anne B. 404
Short, Kathleen 448
Sigelman, Lee 247, 266, 329
Silbey, Joel 146
Sims-Butler 26
Skocpol, Theda 75, 167, 183, 184
Skowronek, Stephen 49
Smailes, April 429
Smith, Eric R.A.N. 247
Smith, Jr., C. Lynwood 193
Smith, Kevin 500, 501
Smith, Mark 116
Smith, Michael 225
Smith, T. Alexander 421
Snipp, Joseph 87
Snyder, Jr., James M. 198, 203, 204
Songer, Donald R. 183, 295, 303
Soss, Ide 452
Soss, Joe , 456, 462
Spain, Daphne 365
Spanier, Graham B. 4, 5
Spill, Rorie L. 313
Squire, Peverill 199, 202, 212, 231,
    233, 245, 267, 232, 233
Steen, Jennifer A. 236, 249
Steffens, Lincoln 362
Stein, Lana 379
Stein, Robert 87
Stephens, G. Ross 413
Steuernagel, Gertrude A. 216
Stevick, Eric 485
Stimson, James 142
Stone, Clarence 360, 362
Stone, Joe A. 341
Storey, Tim 236
Storing, Herbert 47
Straayer, John 235 236, 237, 236, 237

Strate, John 235 236
Strickland, Shauna M. 288
Struyk, Linda 392
Studlar, Donley T. 422
Stutzer, Alois 118
Subrahmanyam, Ganti 341
Suits, Daniel B. 329, 332
Svara, James H. 378
Swanson, Christopher B. 481
Swanstrom, Todd 77, 362
Swidorski, Carl 57
Szakaly, K. 333, 347

T
Tabarrok, Alexander 314, 292-293
Tabrizi, Susan J. 295, 303
Tanner, Robert 212, 249
Tarlton, Charles 41
Tatalovich, Raymond 19, 421, 423,
    425, 428
Teske, Paul 387, 403
Thompson, Joel 91
Thompson, Kay 454
Thompson, Lyke 235, 236
Thrasher, Michael 71
Tiebour, Charles 386, 452
Tierney, John 190, 167, 168
Till-Mobley, Mamie 293
Tinkham, S.F. 202
Tolbert, Pamela 375
Tothero, Rebecca A. 236
Traut, Craig A. 303
Tribe, Laurence H. 428
Troikka, Richard 455, 462, 453, 454
Trostel, P.A. 340, 341
Trounstine, Jessica 378, 379
Truman, David 164, 166
Tullock, Gordon 413
Tushnet, Mark 59
Tyler, Tom R. 425

U
Uggen, Christopher 82
Ulbig, Stacy 26

V
VVan der Slik, Jack R. 204
Van Dunk, Emily 152, 155
Van Horn, Carl E. 261
Van Horn, Karl 65
Venezuela, Jeff 201
Verba, Sidney 71, 73, 74, 89
Vestal, Christine 454, 461, 462
Vines, Kenneth N. 152
Vock, Daniel C. 453
Volden, Craig 455

W
Wagner, Michael W. 205, 210, 236
Wagner, Richard E. 320, 344
Wald, Ken
Wald, Kenneth D. 420
Walker, David 38, 50, 51
Walker, Jack 167, 176, 454
Walter, B. Oliver 378, 379
Walters, Dan 272

Walters, Evelyn 119
Walton, Mary 201
Wassmer, Robert 481
Waters, M. Dane 111, 125
Wattenberg, Martin 144, 235
Watts, Ronald 38
Weaver, R. Kent 447
Weber, Ronald E. 26, 225, 274, 275
Weberg, Brian 236
Weibe, Robert H. 365
Weinstein, James 376
Weintraub, Daniel 272
Weissert, Carol 59
Welch, Susan 380, 454
Wenzel, James 119, 313
Wenzel, James P.
West, Darrell 183
Wicker, Marcia Lynn 270

Wielhouwer, Peter 498-499
Wikstrom, Nelson 413
Wilcox, Clyde 119
Wilkins, Vicky M. 222, 259
Will, George F. 233
Wilson, Georgjeanna 403, 406
Wilson, James Q. 167, 362
Wilson, William Julius 451
Winburn, Jonathon 205, 210, 236
Winger, Richard 141
Winters, Richard 141, 325,326,336, 341, 474, 455
Witmer, Richard 169, 455
Witte, John F. 495
Woglom, Geoffrey 347
Wolfinger, Raymond 89
Wolohojian, George 380
Wood, B.D. 333
Wood, C. 372, 375

Wood, Jason 236
Wright, Gerald C. 26, 88, 142, 228, 236, 346, 427, 455
Wright, Ralph G. 202
Wrinkle, Robert 94

Y
Yalof, David A. 250
Yang, A.S. 441
Yates, Jeff 294
Young, Garry 222

Z
Zeller, Belle 190
Zhou, Min 404
Zimmerman, Craig 119
Zimmerman, Joseph 47, 48, 63, 93
Zorn, C. Kurt 332
Zucker, Lynne 375

Subject Index

A

abortion rights, 28, 59–60, 417, 424, 428–435
achievement gap, 483, 500
Addams, Jane, 365
adequate yearly progress (AYP), 500
adjudication, 288–289
adjudicator, 295
administration, as portion of state spending, 342
administrative rules, 274
administrative rules review committee, 225
adversarial argument, 288, 289
AFL-CIO, 188
African Americans, 16, 19
  civil rights movement, 76–77, 293, 500
  and homeschooling, 499
  ininsured, 469
  migration patterns, United States, 396
  population by state, 17, 18
  in poverty, 20, 448, 449
  representation in government, 18–19, 94, 195, 213–218
  voting rights, 18–19, 75, 78–79, 135
Age of Reform From Bryan to FDR (Hofstadter), 275
Agricultural Adjustment Act, 52
agricultural economy, 22, 24
Aid to Families with Dependent Children (AFDC), 52, 55, 75, 90, 453, 457, 458
Alabama
  abortion regulations, 433
  anti-sodomy laws, 436
  average Medicaid payment per enrollee, 471
  barriers to voting, 83
  cigarette tax, 34
  corruption, perceived level, 34
  court system, 289
  elderly population, 21
  farm income, 23
  Governor's institutional powers, 34
  governor's institutional powers, 265
  governor's political party, 14
  governor's popularity, 268
  gubernatorial election cycle, 247
  higher education spending, per capita, 14
  immigrants, undocumented, 466
  income per capita, 23
  inpact of interest groups, 189
  interest groups, by type, 185

  interparty competition, 1999–2003, 154
  jucidial selection mechanisms, 305, 309
  legislative professionalism, 232
  lobbying laws, 173
  manufacturing employment, 23
  maximum TANF benefit, 461
  minimum wage laws, 465
  minority representation, state legislature, 215, 217
  mobility of population, 21
  partisan contestation in state legislative races, 200
  partisan distribution of legislative seats, 206
  party contributions and expenditures, 149
  policy preferences, 29
  political culture, 28
  political ideology, 27
  population density, 21
  primaries, 136
  public school revenue across sources, 490
  racial and ethnic characteristics, 17
  Ranney Indices of Party Control, 153
  regressive tax system, 339
  same-sex marriage laws, 439
  school funding and high school graduation rates, 492
  state and local taxes as percentage of income, 324
  state legislature, 196
  TANF recipients, 460
  voter participation, 78
  wealth relative to other states, 25
  women in state legislature, 11
Alan Guttmacher Institute, 434
Alaska
  abortion regulations, 433
  anti-sodomy laws, 436
  average Medicaid payment per enrollee, 471
  barriers to voting, 83
  cigarette tax, 34
  corruption, perceived level, 34
  farm income, 23
  Governor's institutional powers, 34
  governor's institutional powers, 265
  governor's political party, 13
  governor's popularity, 269
  gubernatorial election cycle, 247
  higher education spending, per capita, 14

  historic use of initiative, 110
  immigrants, undocumented, 466
  income per capita, 23
  initiatives, ease of qualifying, 112
  inpact of interest groups, 189
  interest groups, by type, 185
  interparty competition, 1999–2003, 154
  lobbying laws, 173
  manufacturing employment, 23
  maximum TANF benefit, 461
  minimum wage laws, 465
  partisan contestation in state legislative races, 200
  party contributions and expenditures, 149
  policy preferences, 29
  political culture, 28
  political ideology, 27
  primaries, 136, 137
  public school revenue across sources, 490
  racial and ethnic characteristics, 17
  Ranney Indices of Party Control, 153
  same-sex marriage laws, 439
  school funding and high school graduation rates, 492
  state and local taxes as percentage of income, 324
  state legislature, 196
  TANF recipients, 459
  voter participation, 78
  wealth relative to other states, 25
  women in state legislature, 11
Alaska Hire Law, 48
alcoholic beverage taxes, 330–331
Alexander, J. D., 170
Alfred P. Purrah Federal Building, 286
Alito, Samuel, 435
Allen, Paul, 113
altruism, 423
amend, 220
amendatory vote, 220
Americal National Election Studies, 28
American Association for Justice (Association of Trial Lawyers of America), 163
American Association of Retired Persons (AARP), 166
American Enterprise Institute, 61–62
American Farm Bureau, 163
American Federation of Teachers, 163, 187, 188, 498
American Journal of Political Science, 133, 429

American Legislative Exchange
Council, 455
American Mayor, The (Holli), 368
American Medical Association
(AMA), 428
American Political Science Review,
79
American State and Local Politics
(Weber and Brace), 275
Americans With Disabilities Act, 61
amicus curiae (friend of the court),
304
Anaheim, California, 373
Anaheim/Santa Ana, California,
homeland security grants, 65
analysis methods
comparative, 32–33
Angelyne, 103
Anheuser-Busch, 188
animal rights, 178
Anti Drug Abuse Act of 1988, 54
antitrust reform, 364
appeals courts, 287
names of, by state, 289–292
Arizona
barriers to voting, 83
cigarette tax, 34
corruption, perceived level, 34
court system, 289
elderly population, 20
farm income, 23
Governor's institutional powers,
34
governor's institutional powers,
265
governor's political party, 13
governor's popularity, 268
gubernatorial election cycle, 247
historic use of initiative, 110
income per capita, 23
initiatives, ease of qualifying, 112
inpact of interest groups, 189
interest groups, by type, 186
interparty competition, 1999–
2003, 154
jucidial selection mechanisms,
305, 309
legislative professionalism, 232
lobbying laws, 173
manufacturing employment, 23
minority representation, state
legislature, 215, 217
partisan contestation in state
legislative races, 200
partisan distribution of legislative
seats, 206
party contributions and
expenditures, 149
Phoenix, homeland security
grants, 65
policy preferences, 29
political culture, 28
political ideology, 27
primaries, 136
public school revenue across
sources, 489
racial and ethnic characteristics, 17

Ranney Indices of Party Control,
153
school funding and high school
graduation rates, 492
state and local taxes as
percentage of income, 323
state legislature, 196
term limits, 234
voter participation, 78
wealth relative to other states, 25
women in state legislature, 11
Arkansas
abortion regulations, 433
anti-sodomy laws, 436
average Medicaid payment per
enrollee, 471
barriers to voting, 83
cigarette tax, 34
corruption, perceived level, 34
court system, 289
elderly population, 21
farm income, 23
Governor's institutional powers,
34
governor's institutional powers,
265
governor's political party, 13
governor's popularity, 268
gubernatorial election cycle, 247
higher education spending, per
capita, 14
historic use of initiative, 110
immigrants, undocumented, 466
income per capita, 23
initiatives, ease of qualifying, 112
inpact of interest groups, 189
interest groups, by type, 185
interparty competition, 1999–
2003, 154
jucidial selection mechanisms,
305, 309
legislative professionalism, 232
lobbying laws, 173
manufacturing employment, 23
maximum TANF benefit, 461
minimum wage laws, 465
minority representation, state
legislature, 215, 217
mobility of population, 21
partisan contestation in state
legislative races, 200, 201
partisan distribution of legislative
seats, 206
party contributions and
expenditures, 149
policy preferences, 29
political culture, 28
political ideology, 27
population density, 21
primaries, 136
public school revenue across
sources, 489
Ranney Indices of Party Control,
153
same-sex marriage laws, 439
school funding and high school
graduation rates, 492

state and local taxes as
percentage of income, 323
TANF recipients, 460
term limits, 234
voter participation, 78
wealth relative to other states, 25
women in state legislature, 13
Arlington, Texas, 373
Articles of Confederation, 43–44
Asian Americans, 16, 122
population by state, 17, 18
representation in government, 94
Asian or Pacific Islanders
representation in government, 94
Association of Washington Business,
164
at large elections, 374
Atlanta, Georgia homeland security
grants, 65
Atlanta Journal-Constitution, 411
at-large elections, 86
Aurora, Colorado, 373
Austin, Texas, 373
Austin American-Statesman, 208
Australian ballot, 156, 375

B
Baker V. Carr, 59
Baldacci, John, 269
ballot access, 156
Ballot Initiative Strategy Center, 103
Ballot Initiative Strategy Center
Foundation, 116
ballot initiatives, 101–102, 106–107.
see also initiatives
and issue advocacy, 178–179
same-sex marriage, 442
top ten most expensive
campaigns, 115
voting on, 116–117
ballots, 156, 157
Australian, 154, 375
straight-ticket, 360
Baltimore, 371
municipal government, 352
Bamberger, Simon, 367
bankers associations
influence of, 188
Barbour, Haley, 252, 268
Barkley, Charles, 250
*Barron v. Mayor and City Council
of Baltimore*, 58
*Bellotti v. First National Bank of
Boston*, 114
bench trials, 293–294, 295
Bias, Len, 54
bicameral, 195
Big Swap, of Reagan era, 54
bilingual education, 19, 482
Bill of Rights, 49, 50, 58–59
bill sponsor, 220
bills, progress to laws, 219–224
biometrics, 39
Bipartisan Campaign Reform Act of
2002, 148, 150
Blagojevich, Rod, 249, 267, 269,
276–277

Blaine, James, 497
Blanco, Kathleen, 64, 256, 267
Blandic, Michael, 368
Blanket primaries, 137–138
block grants, 335
Bloomberg, Michael, 351
Blunt, Matt, 269
Book of the States, 309
Book of the States (Council of State Governments), 196–197, 232, 247, 248, 262
borders, United States, 277–280
Boston, 371
Bours, Eduardo, 279–280
Bradley, Tom, 351, 368
Brady Bill, 55, 60
brain drain, 3
Brandeis, Louis, 452
Branti v. Finkel, 141
Bredesen, Phil, 173–174, 268
Bright Futures scholarship, 3, 5
British Journal of Political Science, 126
Brookings Institution, 199
Brough, Charles Hillman, 367
Brown, Jerry, 253
Brown v. Board of Education, 59, 500
Bruce, David, 329
Bryant, Roy, 293
Bryant, William Jennings, 106
Bryce, Lord James, 59
budget surpluses, 347
budgeting, 346–348
    boom to bust, 347–348
Buffalo, New York, homeland security grants, 65
builders and contractors
    contributions to state party committees, 181
    influence of, 188
bureacracy, 274–275
Burger, Warren, 59
Bush, Barbara, 451
Bush, George H. W., 54, 60, 61, 254, 502
Bush, George W., 55, 107, 252, 253, 254, 331, 418, 451, 458, 464, 473, 474, 482, 483, 484
Bush, Jeb, 252, 268
Bush v. Gore, 56, 57
Byrne, Jane, 368

C

California
    abortion regulations, 434
    Anaheim/Santa Ana, homeland security grants, 65
    anti-sodomy laws, 436
    average Medicaid payment per enrollee, 471
    barriers to voting, 83
    cigarette tax, 34
    corruption, perceived level, 34
    court system, 289
    farm income, 23
    Governor's institutional powers, 34

governor's institutional powers, 265
governor's political party, 13
governor's popularity, 269
gubernatorial election cycle, 247
historic use of initiative, 110
immigrants, undocumented, 466
income per capita, 23
industrial towns, 383–384
initiatives, ease of qualifying, 112
inpact of interest groups, 189
institutions of direct democracy, 101
interest groups, by type, 186
interparty competition, 1999–2003, 154
jucidial selection mechanisms, 305, 309
legislative professionalism, 232
lobbying laws, 173
manufacturing employment, 23
maximum TANF benefit, 461
minimum wage laws, 465
minority representation, state legislature, 215, 217
opinion of direct democracy, 125
partisan contestation in state legislative races, 200
partisan distribution of legislative seats, 206
party contributions and expenditures, 149
policy preferences, 29
political culture, 28
political ideology, 27
political parties, 12
primaries, 136
Proposition 13, 107, 119, 123
public school revenue across sources, 489
racial and ethnic characteristics, 17
Ranney Indices of Party Control, 153
same-sex marriage laws, 439
school funding and high school graduation rates, 492
state and local taxes as percentage of income, 323
state courts, 301
state legislature, 196
TANF recipients, 459
term limits, 234
voter participation, 78
wealth relative to other states, 25
women in state legislature, 11
California Democratic Party organizational structure, 145
California Democratic Party v. Jones, 137–138
California recall, 100–102
California recall ballot, 102
campaign finance regulation, 249
campaign spending, 91–93, 311–312
    legislative elections, 199
capital budgets, 346
capital punishment, 28, 55

executions in the United States by year, 426
Carcieri, Donald, 128, 252, 268
Carey, Mary, 102, 102, 103
Carnegie, Andrew, 365
Carter, Jimmy, 254
categorical grants, 52, 335
Cattlemen's Association, 163
caucuses, 136–137
cause célèbre, 428
CBS News Blogophile, 394
Census Bureau, United States, 18, 22, 323–324, 337, 339, 342, 343, 354, 355, 388, 392, 393, 396, 448, 449, 450, 487
Center for American Women and Politics, Rutgers University, 11, 212, 213
Center for Budget Priorities, 455
Center for Public Integrity, 149–150
centralization, 42–43, 51, 51–56
Chamber of Commerce, 163, 187, 188, 365
Chancellor Beacon, 496
Chappaqua, New York, school system, 479–480
Charlotte, North Carolina, 373
    homeland security grants, 65
charter schools, 497–498
Cherokee Nation v. Georgia, 46
Chicago, 371
Chicago homeland security grants, 65
Chicago Public Schools, 5
Chiles, Lawton "Bud", 48
Chinese Americans, 122
Christian Coalition, 437
Christian Science Monitor, 81
cigarette tax, by state, 34–35
Cincinnatti, Ohio, 373
cities
    functions of, 393–394
cities, new vs. traditional, 390
citizen legilsatures, 232
Citizens Conference on State Legislatures (CCSL), 231
city, definition, 389–390
civil liberties, and homeland security, 62–63
civil rights, 53, 59
Civil Rights Act of 1964, 53, 500
civil rights movement, 76–77, 293, 500
civil service, 376
Civil Service Commission, 376
civil unions, homosexual, 417
civil vs. criminal law, 286–287
Civil War era, 16, 44, 51, 214
    and federalism, 58
Civilian Conservation Corps (CCC), 52
class, social, and voter participation, 89–90
class action lawsuits, 315
class conflict, 365–366
    and welfare policy, 455
classrooms, portable, 482

clean money, 92–93
clean money laws, 92–93
Cleveland, Grover, 254
clientele parties, 360
Clingman v. Beaver, 136
Clinton, Bill, 55, 254, 270, 334,
    438, 447, 460, 482
clout, 187
coercive federalism, 52–53
Cold War era, 483
Coleman, Gary, 103
collective action problem, 225–226
collective action theory, 74
College of William and Mary,
    200–201, 311
college tuition, 3–4
    New Hampshire, 14
    Wyoming, 13
Collins, Martha Layne, 255
Colorado
    abortion regulations, 433
    anti-sodomy laws, 436
    average Medicaid payment per
        enrollee, 471
    barriers to voting, 83
    court system, 289
    farm income, 23
    governor's institutional powers,
        265
    governor's political party, 13
    governor's popularity, 268
    gubernatorial election
        cycle, 247
    higher education spending, per
        capita, 14
    historic use of initiative, 110
    immigrants, undocumented, 466
    initiatives, ease of qualifying, 112
    inpact of interest groups, 189
    interest groups, by type, 186
    interparty competition, 1999–
        2003, 154
    jucidial selection mechanisms,
        305, 309
    legislative professionalism, 232
    lobbying laws, 173
    manufacturing employment, 23
    maximum TANF benefit, 461
    minimum wage laws, 465
    minority representation, state
        legislature, 215, 217
    partisan contestation in state
        legislative races, 200
    partisan distribution of legislative
        seats, 206
    party contributions and
        expenditures, 149
    primaries, 136
    public school revenue across
        sources, 489
    racial and ethnic characteristics,
        17
    Ranney Indices of Party Control,
        153
    same-sex marriage laws, 439
    school funding and high school
        graduation rates, 492
    school funding sources, 491

state and local taxes as
    percentage of income, 323
state legislature, 196
TANF recipients, 460
Taxpayer's Bill of Rights
    (TABOR), 123
term limits, 234
women in state legislature, 11
Colorado Springs, Colorado, 373
Columbus, Ohio, 371
    homeland security grants, 65
Commerce, California, 383–384
Commerce Clause, 46, 47, 56, 60,
    61
Commerce Department's Bureau of
    Economic Analysis, 24
commission system, 374
committees' jurisdictions, 227
Common Cause, 163
common law, 287
Community Development Block
    Grant (CDBG), 463
comparative method of analysis,
    6–7, 32–33
Comprehensive Crime Control Act
    of 1984, 54
confederal systems, 43
conflict of interest, 253, 311–312
Connecticut
    abortion regulations, 433
    anti-sodomy laws, 436
    average Medicaid payment per
        enrollee, 471
    barriers to voting, 83
    cigarette tax, 34
    corruption, perceived level, 34
    court system, 289
    farm income, 23
    Governor's institutional powers,
        34
    governor's institutional powers,
        265
    governor's political party, 13
    governor's popularity, 268
    gubernatorial election cycle, 247
    income per capita, 23
    inpact of interest groups, 189
    interest groups, by type, 185
    interparty competition, 1999–
        2003, 154
    jucidial selection mechanisms,
        305, 309
    legislative professionalism, 232
    lobbying laws, 173
    manufacturing employment, 23
    maximum TANF benefit, 461
    minority representation, state
        legislature, 215, 217
    partisan contestation in state
        legislative races, 200
    partisan distribution of legislative
        seats, 206
    party contributions and
        expenditures, 149
    policy preferences, 29
    political culture, 28
    political ideology, 27
    primaries, 136

public school revenue across
    sources, 489
racial and ethnic characteristics,
    17
Ranney Indices of Party Control,
    153
same-sex marriage laws, 439
school funding and high school
    graduation rates, 492
state and local taxes as
    percentage of income, 323
state legislature, 196
voter participation, 78
wealth relative to other states, 25
women in state legislature, 11
Connolly, "Slippery Dick", 359
conservation movement, 364–365
conservative ideologues, 90
    and welfare policy, 455
Constitution, United States, 45–47,
    48–49, 50, 59–60
    state powers under, 48–49
constitutional initiatives, 109
contact lobbyists, 171
contiguous, 204
contracting for services, 391, 392
Coolidge, Calvin, 254
cooperative federalism, 41, 52
Cops (TV show), 285
Corrupt Practices Acts, 376
corrupt practices acts, 376
corruption, 145–146, 360
corruption, perceived, by state,
    34–35
Corzine, Jon, 268
cost of living allowances (COLAs),
    348
Coughlin, John "Bathhouse", 359
Council of State Governments, 196–
    197, 232, 247, 248, 262, 309
Council on Governmental Ethics
    Laws, 173
council-manager and mayor-council
    blends, 372, 373–374
council-manager government, 369,
    371–372
counties, 353–354
    and land use, 385
court system, 282–317
    bench vs. jury trials, 293–294, 295
    civil vs. criminal law, 286–287
    intermediate courts of appeal,
        287, 297–298
    organization of states', 287–302
    out-of-court settlements, 294
    and policy making, 303–304
    problem-solving courts, 295
    procedures, 288–289
    reform, of state, 314–315
    simple vs. complex structure,
        state, 301
    small claims courts, 295
    state courts and the federal
        system, 285–287
    structure, of state, 288
CourTools, 314
courts of limited jurisdiction,
    295–296

court-stripping, 314, 315
Cox, Edward, 244
CQ's state factfinder, 24
cracking, 206
creative federalism, 52–53
criminal vs. civil law, 286–287
Crist, Charlie, 251, 266, 494
Crist, Victor, 131
Cuban Americans, 16
cultural diffusion, 28
cumulative voting, 86, 91
Cuomo, Mario, 243
Curley, James Michael "Mayor of the Poor", 359, 368

D

Dairy Farmers of America, 163
Daley, Richard J., 368
Dallas, 373
Daniels, Mitch, 252, 269
Davis, Gray, 102, 266
Davis v. Bandermer, 142
de Tocqueville, Alexis, 71
Dean, Howard, 270, 417
death penalty, 28, 55
    executions in the United States by year, 426
Death Penalty Information Center, 426
Debs, Eugene, 106
decentralization, 43, 44
Declaration of Independence, 44
Defense of Marriage Act (DOMA), 438, 439, 442
Delaware
    abortion regulations, 433
    anti-sodomy laws, 436
    average Medicaid payment per enrollee, 471
    barriers to voting, 83
    cigarette tax, 34
    corruption, perceived level, 34
    court system, 289
    farm income, 23
    Governor's institutional powers, 34
    governor's institutional powers, 265
    governor's political party, 13
    governor's popularity, 269
    gubernatorial election cycle, 247
    higher education spending, per capita, 14
    immigrants, undocumented, 466
    income per capita, 23
    inpact of interest groups, 189
    interest groups, by type, 185
    interparty competition, 1999–2003, 154
    jucidial selection mechanisms, 305, 309
    legislative professionalism, 232
    lobbying laws, 173
    manufacturing employment, 23
    maximum TANF benefit, 461
    minimum wage laws, 465
    minority representation, state legislature, 215, 217

partisan contestation in state legislative races, 200
    partisan distribution of legislative seats, 206
    party contributions and expenditures, 149
    policy preferences, 29
    political culture, 28
    political ideology, 27
    primaries, 136
    public school revenue across sources, 490
    racial and ethnic characteristics, 17
    Ranney Indices of Party Control, 153
    same-sex marriage laws, 439
    school funding and high school graduation rates, 492
    state and local taxes as percentage of income, 324
    state legislature, 196
    TANF recipients, 459
    voter participation, 78
    wealth relative to other states, 25
    women in state legislature, 11
DeLay, Tom, 204
Democratic and Republican parties, 12–13, 16, 90. *see also* political parties
Democratic Governors Association, 249
Democratic National Committee (DNC), 138
Denver, Colorado, 371
    homeland security grants, 65
Depression era, 50, 51, 52, 453, 456, 462
de-professionalization, of state legislatures, 237
Derthick, Martha, 44
descriptive representation, 94
Detroit, 371
Detroit City School District, Wayne County, Michigan, 479–480
devolution, 51, 55–56
Dillard, Jim, 502
Dillon's rule, 353
direct democracy, 98–128, 155
    as deceptive, 117–118
    and electoral politics, 118–123
    financing, 113–116
    institutions of, 101
    local, 376
    long-term effects, 123–124
    and minorities, 119–121
    populist origins of, 105–106
    pros and cons of, 126–127
    public opinion of, 125–126
    and the Supreme Court, 114
    and voter turnout, 119–120
direct initiative, 101–102
direct primary, 136
Disabilities Education Act (DEA), 500
disabled people, 500
discrimination, 16, 18–19, 19–20, 48, 59, 135, 500

district attorney, 286
district magnitude, 90
District of Columbia
    public school revenue across sources, 489
District of Columbia, TANF recipients, 459
districts, drawing, 79, 90–91
    multimember districts, 90
disturbance theory, 166
divided government, 270
dockets, 298
Doctors without Borders, 8
domestic partnerships, 442. *see also* same-sex marriage
Donnell-Kay Foundation, 491, 499
double jeopardy, 293
Douglas, Jim, 268
Doyle, Jim, 268
Dred Scott v. Sanford, 48, 57
drug courts, 296
drug laws, 54, 55, 61–62
dual federalism, 41, 57–58, 58–59
dual-party system, 141–142
Due Process Clause, 59
Duke, David, 138
Durham, "Iz:", 359

E

earmarked, 258
earned media, 176
Easley, Michael, 268
Eastern and Southern European Americans, 16
Economic Analysis Bureau, United States Department of Commerce, 24
economic characteristics, and policy, 20
economic development policy, 408–412
Economic Opportunities Act of 1964, 53
Economic Policy Institute, 464
economies of scale, 413
economy
    agricultural, 24
    manufacturing, 22, 24
Edison Schools, 496, 497
Educate America Act, 482
Education, Department of, 484, 488, 489, 490, 492, 495, 501
education financing, 490–494
    higher education, 493–494
    higher education spending by state, 14
    K-12 public education, 490–494
education funding
    and high school graduation rates, by state, 492
    K-12 revenue, across sources by state, 489–490
    sources of revenue, K-12 public schools, 488
education interest groups, 188
education management organizations (EMOs), 496–497
education policy, 3–6, 478–504

administrative flowchart, Massachusetts public schools, 486
charter schools, 497–498
crisis, in public education, 483–484
desegregation, 59, 500
discrimination in, 59
education management organizations (EMOs), 496–497
English as a Second Language (ESL) programs, 19
federal role, in public education, 500–504
financing public schools, 488–494
growth, of public education, 483, 484
Head Start program, 53
initiating, 499
issue evolution, 482–484
No Child Left Behind Act, 55–56, 243, 482–483
organizational control, of public schools, 483–488
as portion of local spending, 343–344
as portion of state spending, 342
school districts' distribution of school-age population, 2000, 487
school vouchers, 495–496
spending, 482, 483
Edwards, Edwin, 138
efficacy, definition, 74
e-government, 87
Ehrlich, Robert, 268, 275
Eisenhower, Dwight D., 59, 254, 500
El Paso, Texas, 373
elastic demand, 330
elderly population
in poverty, 448, 449
Social Security payments to, 456
by state, 21–22
uninsured, 469
elderly populations, 20
electioneering, 179
elections
campaign spending, 91–93
financing, 148–150
gubernatorial, 246–251
judicial, 311–313
at large, 374
nonpartisan, 375
off-year, 375
partisan contestation in state legislatures, 200–201
primary election systems, 89
state legislature, 197–202
elections, noncompetitive, 83–84
electoral boundaries, 79
electoral politics, and ballot initiatives, 118–123
Elementary and Secondary Education Act, 500

Elements of Civil Government (Peterman), 157
Eleventh Amendment, 61
emergency and medical services initiative, 116
eminent domain, 399
EMOs (education management organizations), 496–497
English as a Second Language (ESL) programs, 19, 482
Enron Corporation, 174
enterprises, 164
entitlement program, 456
environmental activism, 364–365
Environmental Protection Agency (EPA), 53
estate taxes, 331
ethics laws, state, 174
Eu v. San Francisco Democratic Committee, 139
European Journal of Political Research, 118
European Union, 42
euthanasia, 62, 423
ex post oversight, 224
executive branch
oversight by leglature, 224–226
executive orders, 263
expansion of slot machines initiative, 116
Eyman, Tim, 329

F
Fagg, Becky and Donald, 329
Fair Labor Standards Act, 465
Family and Medical Leave Act, 61
farm income by state, 23–24
Faubus, Orval, 59
feder systems, 43
Federal Elections Campaign Act of 1971, 148, 150
Federal Housing Act of 1968, 395
Federal Housing Administration (FHA), 394–396, 463–464
Federal Insurance Contribution Act (FICA), 456
federal powers, under United States Constitution, 45–46
federal preemption, 49
federalism, 38–67
Calhoun's compact theory of, 50–51
and Civil War era, 58–59
coercive, 52–53
cooperative, 41, 52
creative, 52–53
definition, 40
dual, 41, 57–58, 58–59
erosion of, 49–51
and fiscal policy, 334–335
and homeland security, 62–66
major United States Supreme Court rulings, 56–57
models of, 41
and morality policy, 419
new, 53–54
opportunistic, 65
political expediency of, 54

and state diversity, 40–42
and welfare programs, 452–453
Federalist Papers, 45, 134, 164
Federalists, 45
feminization of poverty, 450
Ferguson, Mirian "Ma", 255
Fifteenth Amendment, 77, 78
Fifth Amendment, 59
Finney, Joan, 255
firefighters, 357
First Amendment, 138
fiscal federalism, 334–335
fiscal illusion, 346
fiscal policy, 318–349
borrowing, 346
budgeting, 346–348
general vs. non-general funds, 335
major revenue sources, 329–333. see also taxes
flat taxes, 324
Fletcher, Ernie, 269, 275
Flint, Larry, 103
Florida
barriers to voting, 83
Bright Futures scholarship, 3, 5
cigarette tax, 34
corruption, perceived level, 34
court system, 290
demographic changes, 193–194
elderly population, 20
farm income, 23
Governor's institutional powers, 34
governor's institutional powers, 265
governor's political party, 13
gubernatorial election cycle, 247
higher education spending, per capita, 14
historic use of initiative, 110
immigrants, undocumented, 466
income per capita, 23
initiatives, ease of qualifying, 112
inpact of interest groups, 189
interest groups, by type, 186
interparty competition, 1999–2003, 154
Jacksonville homeland security grants, 65
jucidial selection mechanisms, 305, 309
legislative professionalism, 232
lobbying laws, 173
manufacturing employment, 23
minimum wage laws, 465
minority representation, state legislature, 215, 217
partisan contestation in state legislative races, 200
partisan distribution of legislative seats, 206
party contributions and expenditures, 149
policy preferences, 29
political culture, 28
political ideology, 27
primaries, 136

public school revenue across sources, 489
racial and ethnic characteristics, 17
Ranney Indices of Party Control, 153
regressive tax system, 339
school funding and high school graduation rates, 492
state college tuition, 3–4
state and local taxes as percentage of income, 324
state legislature, 196
TANF recipients, 460
tax base, 15
term limits, 234
voter participation, 78
wealth relative to other states, 25
women in state legislature, 11
Focus on the Family, 437
food stamps, 462–463
Fort Worth, Texas, 373
Foster, Mike, 128
Fourteenth Amendment, 48, 58–59, 60, 141, 493
and *Roe v. Wade*, 59–60
Frasier, Lynn, 102
free-rider problem, 166
Freudenthal, Dave, 252, 268
Full Faith and Credit Clause, 48, 437, 442
full veto, 259
functional party model, 133–134
fusion, party, 139–140
Fusion Democrats, 106

G
gambling, 332, 427
Garcia v. San Antonio Metropolitan Transit Authority, 57, 60
Garfield, James A., 375–376
Gates, Bill, 481
Gates, Daryl, 351
GAVEL (give a vote to every legislator), 237
gay marriage, 416–417, 435–443
laws by state, 439
gay rights, 121, 122
states with sodomy laws before *Lawrence v. Texas*, 436
General Federation of Women's Clubs, 75
General Motors, 8
general purpose local governments, 385
General Revenue Sharing (GRS), 53
geography, and community variation, 15–16
George III, King of England, 44
Georgia
abortion regulations, 433
anti-sodomy laws, 436
Atlanta homeland security grants, 65
average Medicaid payment per enrollee, 471
barriers to voting, 83
cigarette tax, 34

corruption, perceived level, 34
court system, 290
farm income, 23
Governor's institutional powers, 94
governor's institutional powers, 265
governor's political party, 14
governor's popularity, 268
gubernatorial election cycle, 247
higher education spending, per capita, 14
immigrants, undocumented, 466
income per capita, 23
inpact of interest groups, 189
interest groups, by type, 185
interparty competition, 1999–2003, 154
jucidial selection mechanisms, 305, 309
legislative professionalism, 232
lobbying laws, 173
manufacturing employment, 23
maximum TANF benefit, 461
minimum wage laws, 465
minority representation, state legislature, 215, 217
partisan contestation in state legislative races, 201
partisan distribution of legislative seats, 206
party contributions and expenditures, 149
policy preferences, 29
political culture, 28
political ideology, 27
primaries, 136
racial and ethnic characteristics, 17
Ranney Indices of Party Control, 153
same-sex marriage laws, 439
state and local taxes as percentage of income, 323
state legislature, 196
TANF recipients, 459
voter participation, 78
wealth relative to other states, 25
women in state legislature, 14
Gerry, Elbridge, 208
gerrymandering, 206–210
Get Out the Vote (GOTV) drives, 85, 146
Gibbons, Jim, 251
Gibbons v. Ogden, 56
Gideon v. Wainwright, 59
Gingles v. Thornberg, 91
Gingrich, Newt, 155
Gitlow v. New York, 58–59
Goals 2000 bill, 482
Goldberg, J. C. P., 315
Golisano, Thomas, 243
Gomillion v. Lightfoot, 75
Gonzales v. Carhart, 435
Gonzales v. Oregon, 57, 62
Gonzales v. Raich, 57, 61
Goode, Wilson, 368
goodtime Charlies, 251

Governing Magazine, 210, 275, 371
government
definition, 8–9
personal impact of, 5, 7, 8
governors, 242–281
as administrators, 273–277
careers, after, 253–254
as intergovernmental relations managers, 277–280
as policy makers, 271–273
presidents who were former, 254
professional backgrounds, 251–252
three jobs of, 271–280
women and minorities as, 254–257
governor's powers
challenges to, 270
informal, 265–270
institutional, 34–35, 257–265
graft, 361
grandfather clauses, 78
Grange, 163
Granholm, Jennifer, 256
Granholm v. Heald, 47
grants, 52, 335
Grasso, Ella, 255
grassroots mobilization, 176, 178
grassroots political activity, 75–77, 423–424
Great Society programs, 51–56, 52–53, 334, 453, 482
Green Party, 156
Greenhouse, Linda, 61
Gregoire, Christine, 256, 268
Greve, Michael, 61–62
Griswold v. Connecticut, 59
gubernatorial elections, 246–251
campaign costs, 248–250
cycles by state, 247
outcomes, 250–251
gubernatorial popularity, by state, 268–269
gubernatorial powers, 257–270
appointment power, 261
budget-making authority, 258–259
executive orders, 263
informal, 265–270
institutional, 258–264
legislative agenda-setting, 262–263
personal staff, 262–263
tenure potential, 261–262
veto, 259–260
Guinn, Kenny, 268
Guinn v. United States, 75
gun laws, 54–55
Gun-Free School Zones Act of 1990, 54–55, 60

H
Hague, Frank, 367, 368
Hall, A. Oakley, 368
Hamilton, Alexander, 45, 48
Hardin-Tammons, Renee, 283, 284
Harper v. Virginia Board of Elections, 75

Harrison, Carter, Sr., 360, 361
Harrison, William Henry, 254
Hartford Courant, 174
Harvard University, 494
Hawaii
    abortion regulations, 433
    anti-sodomy laws, 436
    average Medicaid payment per
        enrollee, 471
    barriers to voting, 83
    cigarette tax, 34
    corruption, perceived level, 34
    court system, 290
    farm income, 23
    gay rights action, 436–437
    Governor's institutional powers,
        34
    governor's institutional powers,
        265
    governor's political party, 13
    governor's popularity, 268
    gubernatorial election cycle, 247
    immigrants, undocumented, 466
    income per capita, 23
    inpact of interest groups, 189
    interest groups, by type, 185
    interparty competition, 1999–
        2003, 154
    jucidial selection mechanisms,
        305, 309
    legislative professionalism, 232
    lobbying laws, 173
    manufacturing employment, 23
    maximum TANF benefit, 461
    minimum wage laws, 465
    minority representation, state
        legislature, 215, 217
    partisan contestation in state
        legislative races, 200
    partisan distribution of legislative
        seats, 206
    party contributions and
        expenditures, 149
    policy preferences, 29
    political culture, 28
    political ideology, 27
    primaries, 136
    public school revenue across
        sources, 490
    racial and ethnic characteristics, 17
    Ranney Indices of Party Control,
        153
    same-sex marriage laws, 439
    school funding and high school
        graduation rates, 492
    state and local taxes as
        percentage of income, 323
    state legislature, 196
    TANF recipients, 459
    voter participation, 78
    wealth relative to other states, 25
    women in state legislature, 11
Hayes, Garrett Michael, 158
Hayes, Mark Taylor, 158
Hayes, Rutherford B., 254
Hays, Frank L. "Pancho", 171
Hays Hays and Wilson lobbying
    firm, 171

head of state, 245, 266
Head Start program, 53
Health and Human Services
    Department, 458, 459–460, 461,
    462
health care policy, 467, 469–476
    reform, 472–474, 475–476
    state children's health insurance
        programs (SCHIPS), 474
health care spending, 342,
    343, 469
health insurance
    uninsured population, 469
health professionals
    contributions to state party
        committees, 181
Hearst, William Randolph, 367
Help America Vote Act, 56
Hemlock Society, 423
Henry, Brad, 251, 268
Hickel, Walter J., 158
higher education, spending by state,
    13, 14
higher education spending, per
    capita, 493–494
highways, 344–345
    as portion of local spending, 343
    state spending on, 342
Hispanics. *see* Latinos
history, and community variation,
    15–16
History of Tammany Hall (Myers),
    363
Hoan, Daniel Webster, 366, 368
Hoch, Edward, 366
Hoeven, John, 252, 268
Hollister, Nancy P., 256
Home Builders Association of
    Virginia, 161
home ownership, 394–396
home rule charters, 367, 379
    and morality policy, 419
Homeland Security, 62–63
homeland security, 62–66
    grants, 64, 65
Homeland Security, Department
    of, 65
homeschooling, 498, 499–500
Homestead Act, 51
Honolulu, 371
hospital and nursing home
    association interest groups, 188
House of Representatives, 195
Housing Act of 1937, 53
housing construction, new, 1950–
    2005, 396
housing programs, 463–464
Houston, Texas, 371
Huckabee, Mike, 473
HUD (Department of Housing and
    Urban Development), 53, 463
Hughes, Charles Evans, 366–367
Hull, Jane Dee, 255, 256
Human Rights Campaign, 436
Humane Society, 178
Huntsman, Jon, 268
Hurricane Katrina, 63, 64, 267, 451,
    452, 463–464

Hylan, John Francis "Red Mike",
    359
hypothesis, 32–33

I
Idaho
    abortion regulations, 433
    anti-sodomy laws, 436
    average Medicaid payment per
        enrollee, 471
    barriers to voting, 83
    court system, 290
    farm income, 23
    governor's institutional powers,
        265
    governor's political party, 13
    governor's popularity, 268
    gubernatorial election cycle, 247
    historic use of initiative, 110
    immigrants, undocumented, 466
    initiatives, ease of qualifying, 112
    inpact of interest groups, 189
    interest groups, by type, 185
    interparty competition, 1999–
        2003, 154
    jucidial selection mechanisms,
        305, 309
    legislative professionalism, 232
    lobbying laws, 173
    manufacturing employment, 23
    maximum TANF benefit, 461
    minimum wage laws, 465
    minority representation, state
        legislature, 215, 217
    partisan contestation in state
        legislative races, 200
    partisan distribution of legislative
        seats, 206
    party contributions and
        expenditures, 149
    primaries, 136
    public school revenue across
        sources, 490
    racial and ethnic characteristics,
        17
    Ranney Indices of Party Control,
        153
    same-sex marriage laws, 439
    school funding and high school
        graduation rates, 492
    state and local taxes as
        percentage of income, 324
    state legislature, 196
    TANF recipients, 460
    term limits repealed, 236
    women in state legislature, 11
ideologies, political, 26–28
    by state, 27
Illinois
    abortion regulations, 434
    anti-sodomy laws, 436
    average Medicaid payment per
        enrollee, 471
    barriers to voting, 83
    farm income, 23
    governor's institutional powers,
        265
    governor's political party, 13

governor's popularity, 269
gubernatorial election cycle, 247
higher education spending, per
    capita, 14
historic use of initiative, 110
immigrants, undocumented, 466
initiatives, ease of qualifying, 112
inpact of interest groups, 189
interest groups, by type, 185
interparty competition, 1999–
    2003, 154
lobbying laws, 173
manufacturing employment, 23
maximum TANF benefit, 461
minimum wage laws, 465
partisan contestation in state
    legislative races, 200
party contributions and
    expenditures, 149
primaries, 136
public school revenue across
    sources, 489
racial and ethnic characteristics,
    17
Ranney Indices of Party Control,
    153
regressive tax system, 339
same-sex marriage laws, 439
school funding and high school
    graduation rates, 492
state and local taxes as
    percentage of income, 323
state legislature, 196
TANF recipients, 460
women in state legislature, 11
immigrants
    backlash against, 19
    foreign born as percentage of
        population, by year, 356
    illegal, 465–466
    number in millions, by country of
        origin, 355
    population by state, 17, 18
    voting rights, 81
immigration, 355–357
immigration laws, 69–70
implementation of laws, 224
income per capita, by state, 23–24
income tax, 324–325
    states without, 339
incorporation, 383, 394
incumbent, 202
incumbent-protection districts, 205
independent expenditures, 179
Indian Gaming Regulatory Act, 46,
    61
Indiana
    abortion regulations, 433
    anti-sodomy laws, 436
    average Medicaid payment per
        enrollee, 471
    barriers to voting, 83
    cigarette tax, 34
    corruption, perceived level, 34
    court system, 290
    farm income, 23
    Governor's institutional powers,
        34

governor's institutional powers,
    265
governor's political party, 13
governor's popularity, 269
gubernatorial election cycle, 247
higher education spending, per
    capita, 14
immigrants, undocumented, 466
income per capita, 23
inpact of interest groups, 189
interest groups, by type, 185
interparty competition, 1999–
    2003, 154
jucidial selection mechanisms,
    305, 309
legislative professionalism, 232
lobbying laws, 173
manufacturing employment, 23
maximum TANF benefit, 461
minimum wage laws, 465
minority representation, state
    legislature, 215, 217
partisan contestation in state
    legislative races, 200
partisan distribution of legislative
    seats, 206
party contributions and
    expenditures, 149
policy preferences, 29
political culture, 28
political ideology, 27
primaries, 136
public school revenue across
    sources, 489
racial and ethnic characteristics,
    17
Ranney Indices of Party Control,
    153
same-sex marriage laws, 439
school funding and high school
    graduation rates, 492
state and local taxes as
    percentage of income, 323
state legislature, 196
TANF recipients, 459
voter participation, 78
wealth relative to other states, 25
women in state legislature, 11
Indianapolis, 371
indirect initiative, 102
individualistic political culture,
    28–30
Individuals with Disabilities Act
    (IDEA), 59
industrial development revenue
    bonds, 410
inelastic demand, 330
in-house lobbyists, 171
initiatives, 100–101, 106–107
    constitutional, 109
    constitutionality, 124
    content limitations, 110–111
    differences across states, 109–114
    expanding, 127–128
    and issue advocacy, 178–179
    qualifying for ballot, 111
    restricting, 127
    role of the media, 117–118

and special interests, 114–115, 120
    statutory, 109
    top ten most expensive
        campaigns, 116
Institute on Money in State Politics,
    94, 181
insurance, health. see health
    insurance
insurance industry
    contributions to state party
        committees, 181
    influence of, 188
Insurrection Act, 64
interest group competition, 187–190
interest group system density, 184,
    186–187
interest group system diversity, 184
interest group techniques, 167–183
    insider and outsider, percentage
        of groups using, 169
    litigation, 182–183
    lobbying, 167–174
interest groups, 160–191
    and ballot initiatives, 114–115,
        120, 178–179
    definition, 163
    dynamics of state systems,
        183–190
    formation, 166–167
    functions of, 162
    members, 167
    and morality policy, 422–424
    most influential, 187–189
    overall impact, by state, 189
    types of, 163–164
intergovernmental relations (IGR),
    40, 276–280
intermediate courts of appeal, 287,
    297
    names of, by state, 289–292
intermunicipal inequality, 412
Internet
    and sales tax, 327
interparty competition
    state legislatures, 150–155
Iowa
    court system, 290
    farm income, 23
    governor's institutional powers,
        265
    governor's political party, 13
    governor's popularity, 268
    gubernatorial election cycle, 247
    higher education spending, per
        capita, 14
    immigrants, undocumented, 466
    inpact of interest groups, 189
    interest groups, by type, 186
    interparty competition, 1999–
        2003, 154
    jucidial selection mechanisms,
        305, 309
    legislative professionalism, 232
    lobbying laws, 173
    manufacturing employment, 23
    minimum wage laws, 465
    minority representation, state
        legislature, 215, 217

partisan contestation in state
legislative races, 200
partisan distribution of legislative
seats, 206
party contributions and
expenditures, 149
public school revenue across
sources, 489
racial and ethnic characteristics,
17
Ranney Indices of Party Control,
153
school funding and high school
graduation rates, 492
state and local taxes as
percentage of income, 323
state legislature, 196, 210
TANF recipients, 459
women in state legislature, 11
issue advocacy, 174–176
and ballot initiatives, 178–179
definition, 174
and earned media, 176
and grassroots mobilization, 176,
178

J

Jackson, Andrew, 254, 275, 358
Jacksonian democracy, 262, 358
Jacksonian Era, The, 1882–1848
(Van Deusen), 275
Jacksonville, Florida, 371
homeland security grants, 65
Japanese Americans, 18, 122
Jarvis, Howard, 329
Jay, John, 45
Jefferson, Thomas, 71, 254
Jersey City/Newark, New Jersey,
homeland security grants, 65
Jim Crow laws, 16, 135
Johanns, Mike, 253
John C. Calhoun: A Biography,
50–51
John Marshall School of Law, 311
Johnson, Andrew, 254
Johnson, Hiram, 367
Johnson, John A., 366
Johnson, Lyndon B., 84, 334, 474
Johnson, Tom L., 368
Joint Center for Political and
Economic Studies, 215–216
Jones, Emil, 195
Jones, Samuel "Golden Rule", 368
Journal of Politics, 169
jucidial selection mechanisms, 305
Judge Brown (TV show), 285
Judge Judy (TV show), 287
judges
bench trials, 293–295, 294, 295
role of, 308
State Supreme Court, 283–284
Judicial Accountability Initiative
laws (JAIL), 315
judicial selection mechanisms,
304–314
consequences of, 310–314
mechanisms of, 305–307, 307
juries, 289, 292–293, 295

jurisdiction, 9, 31
jury nullification, 293
Justice Department, 62, 426

K

Kaine, Timothy, 161, 245, 268
Kaiser Commission on Medicaid and
the Uninsured, 471–472
Kansas
abortion regulations, 433
anti-sodomy laws, 436
average Medicaid payment per
enrollee, 471
court system, 290
farm income, 23
governor's political party, 13
governor's popularity, 268
historic use of initiative, 110
immigrants, undocumented, 466
institutions of direct democracy,
101
jucidial selection mechanisms,
305, 309
legislative professionalism, 232
manufacturing employment, 23
maximum TANF benefit, 461
minimum wage laws, 465
minority representation, state
legislature, 215, 217
partisan contestation in state
legislative races, 200
partisan distribution of legislative
seats, 206
public school revenue across
sources, 489
racial and ethnic characteristics, 17
same-sex marriage laws, 439
school funding and high school
graduation rates, 492
state and local taxes as
percentage of income, 323
state legislature, 196
TANF recipients, 459
women in state legislature, 11
Kansas City, Missouri, 373
Karmeier, Lloyd, 283, 284
Katrina (hurricane), 63, 64, 267,
451, 452, 463–464
Katz, Vera, 195
Kean, Thomas, 253
Kelo v. City of New London, 399
Kenna, Michael "Hinky Dink", 359
Kennedy, John F., 52, 334
Kentucky
abortion regulations, 433
anti-sodomy laws, 436
average Medicaid payment per
enrollee, 471
barriers to voting, 83
cigarette tax, 34
corruption, perceived level, 34
court system, 290
farm income, 23
Governor's institutional powers,
34
governor's institutional powers,
265
governor's political party, 13

governor's popularity, 269
gubernatorial election cycle, 247
higher education spending, per
capita, 14
income per capita, 23
inpact of interest groups, 189
interest groups, by type, 185
interparty competition, 1999–
2003, 154
jucidial selection mechanisms,
305, 309
legislative professionalism, 232
lobbying laws, 173
Louisville, homeland security
grants, 65
manufacturing employment, 23
maximum TANF benefit, 461
minority representation, state
legislature, 215, 217
partisan contestation in state
legislative races, 201
partisan distribution of legislative
seats, 206
party contributions and
expenditures, 149
policy preferences, 29
political culture, 28
political ideology, 27
primaries, 136
public school revenue across
sources, 490
racial and ethnic characteristics,
17
Ranney Indices of Party Control,
153
same-sex marriage laws, 439
school funding and high school
graduation rates, 492
state and local taxes as
percentage of income, 323
state legislature, 196
voter participation, 78
wealth relative to other states,
25
women in state legislature, 11
Kia automobile assembly plant,
410–411
King, Angus, 93, 158
King, Martin Luther, Jr., 77, 84
King, Rodney, 63, 351, 377
Kline, Phil, 432
Kowalski, Linda, 174
Kucinich, Dennis, 368
Kulongoski, Ted, 252, 268
Kulongoski, Theodore, 462, 463
Kunin, Madeleine M., 255

L

La Guardia, Fiorello, 366, 368
Lafollette, Robert M., 366
Lakewood Plan, 390, 391–392
lame duck, 261
Land Ordinance of 1785, 354
land use, 385–387, 396–401. *see
also* zoning
and economic development,
408–412
and revenue sharing, 408

state controls, 407–408
and urban sprawl, 405, 407
Las Vegas, 373
Latinos, 16, 18
and homeschooling, 199
political representation, 213–214
population by state, 17, 18
in poverty, 448, 449
representation in government, 94, 257
Law & Order (TV show), 287
lawmaking, 219–224
and morality policy, 424–427
Lawrence, David, 368
laws. *see also* court system
criminal vs civil, 286–287
implementation of, 224, 425
lawyers interest groups
contributions to state party committees, 181
influence of, 188
League of United Latin American Citizens v. Perry, 204
Leavitt, Mike, 472
legal briefs, 297–298
legislative appointment, 305
legislative intent, 224
legislative professionalism, 231–233
legislative scorecards, 177, 178
Legislative Studies Quarterly, 199
legislative turnover, 236
legislators
rank-and-file, 223
Leonis, John B., 383
leviathans, 320
Levitt, William J., 391
Levittown, New York, 391
liberal ideologies, 26, 27, 90
and welfare policy, 455
Libertarian Party, 156, 158
Lincoln, Abraham, 58–59
Lindsay, John V., 368
line-item veto, 220
Lingle, Linda, 256, 268
liquor interest groups, 188
literacy tests, 78, 79
litigation, definition, 182
living wage, 464
lobbying, 74, 167–174
and issue advocacy, 174–176
lobbyists, 170–174
contributions to state party committees, 181
laws regulating, by state, 173–174
regulating, 172–174
types of, 171–172
work of, 170–171
lobbyists,
Statehouse corps, 172
local governments, 350–381
direct democracy and, 376
forms of, 353–354
need for, 357
number of, by form, 392
local governments, spending, 343
local revenues, 337, 338–339

Locke, Gary, 138, 244, 257
Long Beach, California, 373
Los Angeles, 371
municipal government, 351, 377
Los Angeles County, 388
Los Angeles Times, 113
lotteries, 332, 338
Louisiana
abortion regulations, 433
anti-sodomy laws, 436
average Medicaid payment per enrollee, 471
barriers to voting, 83
cigarette tax, 34
corruption, perceived level, 34
court system, 290
farm income, 23
Governor's institutional powers, 34
governor's institutional powers, 265
governor's political party, 13
governor's popularity, 269
gubernatorial election cycle, 247
higher education spending, per capita, 14
immigrants, undocumented, 466
income per capita, 23
inpact of interest groups, 189
institutions of direct democracy, 101
interest groups, by type, 185
interparty competition, 1999–2003, 154
jucidial selection mechanisms, 305, 309
legislative professionalism, 232
lobbying laws, 173
manufacturing employment, 23
maximum TANF benefit, 461
minimum wage laws, 465
minority representation, state legislature, 215, 217
New Orleans, homeland security grants, 65
partisan distribution of legislative seats, 206
party contributions and expenditures, 149
policy preferences, 29
political culture, 28
political ideology, 27
primaries, 136
public school revenue across sources, 489
racial and ethnic characteristics, 17
Ranney Indices of Party Control, 153
same-sex marriage laws, 439
school funding and high school graduation rates, 492
state and local taxes as percentage of income, 323
state legislature, 196
TANF recipients, 459
term limits, 234

voter participation, 78
wealth relative to other states, 25
women in state legislature, 11
Louisiana Purchase, 354
Louisville, Kentucky, 371
homeland security grants, 65
Lynch, John, 268

M
machines, urban party, 143–144, 359–363
beneficiaries of, 361
demise of, 361, 362
Madison, James, 41, 45, 48
Magna Carta, 223
Maine
abortion regulations, 434
anti-sodomy laws, 436
average Medicaid payment per enrollee, 471
barriers to voting, 83
cigarette tax, 34
corruption, perceived level, 34
court system, 290
farm income, 23
Governor's institutional powers, 34
governor's institutional powers, 265
governor's political party, 13
governor's popularity, 269
gubernatorial election cycle, 247
historic use of initiative, 110
immigrants, undocumented, 466
income per capita, 23
inpact of interest groups, 189
interest groups, by type, 185
interparty competition, 1999–2003, 154
jucidial selection mechanisms, 305, 309
legislative professionalism, 232
lobbying laws, 173
manufacturing employment, 23
maximum TANF benefit, 461
minimum wage laws, 465
minority representation, state legislature, 215, 217
partisan contestation in state legislative races, 200
partisan distribution of legislative seats, 207
party contributions and expenditures, 149
policy preferences, 29
political culture, 28
political ideology, 27
primaries, 136
public school revenue across sources, 489
racial and ethnic characteristics, 17
Ranney Indices of Party Control, 153
same-sex marriage laws, 439
school funding and high school graduation rates, 492

state and local taxes as
percentage of income, 323
state legislature, 196
TANF recipients, 459
term limits, 234
voter participation, 78
wealth relative to other states, 25
women in state legislature, 11
malaportionment, 203
Manchin, Joe, 267, 268
manufacturers interest groups, 188
manufacturing economy, 22, 24
marijuana for medical use, 61–62,
108–109
Marketplace of Democracy, The
(McDonald and Samples), 199
Martinez, Mel, 118
Martz, Judy, 255
Maryland
abortion regulations, 434
anti-sodomy laws, 436
average Medicaid payment per
enrollee, 471
barriers to voting, 83
cigarette tax, 34
corruption, perceived level, 34
court system, 290
farm income, 23
Governor's institutional powers,
34
governor's institutional powers,
265
gubernatorial election cycle, 247
immigrants, undocumented, 466
income per capita, 23
inpact of interest groups, 189
interest groups, by type, 185
interparty competition,
1999–2003, 154
jucidial selection mechanisms,
305, 309
legislative professionalism, 232
lobbying laws, 173
manufacturing employment,
23
maximum TANF benefit, 461
minimum wage laws, 465
minority representation, state
legislature, 215, 217
partisan contestation in state
legislative races, 201
partisan distribution of legislative
seats, 207
party contributions and
expenditures, 149
policy preferences, 29
political culture, 28
political ideology, 27
primaries, 136
public school revenue across
sources, 489
racial and ethnic characteristics,
17
Ranney Indices of Party Control,
153
same-sex marriage laws, 439
school funding and high school
graduation rates, 492

state and local taxes as
percentage of income, 323
TANF recipients, 459
voter participation, 78
wealth relative to other states, 25
women in state legislature, 11
Massachusetts
abortion regulations, 434
administrative flowchart for
public schools, 486
anti-sodomy laws, 436
average Medicaid payment per
enrollee, 471
barriers to voting, 83
cartoon map, 208
court system, 290
governor's institutional powers,
265
governor's political party, 13
governor's popularity, 268
gubernatorial election cycle, 247
higher education spending, per
capita, 14
historic use of initiative, 110
immigrants, undocumented, 466
initiatives, ease of qualifying, 112
inpact of interest groups, 189
interest groups, by type, 185
interparty competition, 1999–
2003, 154
jucidial selection mechanisms,
305, 309
legislative professionalism, 232
lobbying laws, 173
maximum TANF benefit, 461
minimum wage laws, 465
minority representation, state
legislature, 215, 217
partisan distribution of legislative
seats, 207
party contributions and
expenditures, 149
primaries, 136
public school revenue across
sources, 489
racial and ethnic characteristics,
17
Ranney Indices of Party Control,
153
same-sex marriage laws, 439,
440
school funding and high school
graduation rates, 492
state and local taxes as
percentage of income, 323
state legislature, 196
TANF recipients, 459
term limits repealed, 236
women in state legislature, 11
Massey Energy, 311
mayor-council government, 367–372
mayors, 351–352
mayors, history's best and worst,
368
McCain-Feingold Act, 148–149
McCarthy era, 141
*McConnell v. Federal Election
Commission*, 148

McCulloch v. Maryland, 56, 57
McGreevey, Jim, 253
McKinley, William, 254
McNichol, "Sunny Jim", 359
McVeigh, Timothy, 286, 287
means-tested, 455
Mecham, Evan, 253
media
court system portrayed in, 285
earned, 176
and governor's power, 267–268
and legislative elections, 199, 201
role in initiative campaigns,
117–118
and urban reform, 363
media market, 199
Medicaid, 53, 90, 342, 453, 454,
469–472
funding, 472–474
Medicaid payment, average per
enrollee by state, 471
medical interest groups, 188
medical marijuana laws, 61–62,
108–108
Medicare, 53, 453, 474, 475–476
Medicare Modernization Act,
475–476
Memphis, Tennessee, 371
mental health courts, 296
mercy killing, 62, 423
Merit Plan, 307, 309–310, 312–313
Mesa, Arizona, 373
metropolitan areas, 387
15 largest United States, 388
fastest growing United States,
389
metropolitan fragmentation,
387–394
consequences of, 412–413
Mexico-United States border,
278–280
Michigan
abortion regulations, 433
anti-sodomy laws, 436
average Medicaid payment per
enrollee, 471
barriers to voting, 83
cigarette tax, 34
corruption, perceived level, 34
court system, 290
farm income, 23
Governor's institutional powers,
34
governor's institutional powers,
265
governor's political party, 13
governor's popularity, 269
gubernatorial election cycle, 247
higher education spending, per
capita, 14
immigrants, undocumented, 466
income per capita, 23
initiatives, ease of qualifying,
112
inpact of interest groups, 189
interest groups, by type, 186
interparty competition, 1999–
2003, 154

jucidial selection mechanisms,
305, 309
legislative professionalism, 232
lobbying laws, 173
manufacturing employment, 23
maximum TANF benefit, 461
minimum wage laws, 465
minority representation, state
legislature, 215, 217
partisan contestation in state
legislative races, 200
partisan distribution of legislative
seats, 207
party contributions and
expenditures, 149
policy preferences, 29
political culture, 28
political ideology, 27
primaries, 136
public school revenue across
sources, 490
racial and ethnic characteristics,
17
Ranney Indices of Party Control,
153
regressive tax system, 339
same-sex marriage laws, 439
school funding and high school
graduation rates, 492
state and local taxes as
percentage of income, 323
state legislature, 196
TANF recipients, 459
term limits, 234
voter participation, 78
wealth relative to other states, 25
women in state legislature, 11
Michigan Beer and Wine
Wholesalers, 164
Microsoft Corporation, 481
Midwestern states
political culture, 27, 28
migration patterns, United States,
16, 19
and cultural diffusion, 28
Milam, J. W., 293
militias, and homeland security,
63–64
Milwaukee, Wisconsin, 371
homeland security grants, 65
Milwaukee Journal-Sentinel, 260
minimum wage laws, 464–465
Minneapolis, 371
Minner, Ruth Ann, 245, 256, 269
Minnesota
abortion regulations, 433
anti-sodomy laws, 436
average Medicaid payment per
enrollee, 471
barriers to voting, 83
cigarette tax, 34
corruption, perceived level, 34
court system, 290
farm income, 23
Governor's institutional powers,
34
governor's institutional powers,
265

governor's political party, 13
governor's popularity, 268
gubernatorial election cycle, 247
higher education spending, per
capita, 14
immigrants, undocumented, 466
income per capita, 23
inpact of interest groups, 189
interest groups, by type, 186
interparty competition,
1999–2003, 154
jucidial selection mechanisms,
305, 309
legislative professionalism, 232
lobbying laws, 173
manufacturing employment, 23
maximum TANF benefit, 461
minimum wage laws, 465
minority representation, state
legislature, 215, 217
partisan contestation in state
legislative races, 200
partisan distribution of legislative
seats, 207
party contributions and
expenditures, 149
policy preferences, 29
political culture, 28
political ideology, 27
primaries, 136
public school revenue across
sources, 490
racial and ethnic characteristics,
17
Ranney Indices of Party Control,
153
same-sex marriage laws, 439
school funding and high school
graduation rates, 492
state and local taxes as
percentage of income, 323
state legislature, 196
TANF recipients, 459
voter participation, 78
wealth relative to other states, 25
women in state legislature, 11
minorities
and direct democracy campaigns,
121–123
in poverty, 448
and redistricting, 205
representation in government,
93–95, 211–218, 257
uninsured, 469
Miranda v. Arizona, 59
Mississippi
barriers to voting, 83
governor's institutional powers,
265
governor's popularity, 268
gubernatorial election cycle, 247
historic use of initiative, 110
immigrants, undocumented, 466
initiatives, ease of qualifying, 112
inpact of interest groups, 189
interest groups, by type, 185
interparty competition, 1999–
2003, 154

lobbying laws, 173
minimum wage laws, 465
party contributions and
expenditures, 149
primaries, 136
public school revenue across
sources, 490
Ranney Indices of Party Control,
153
school funding and high school
graduation rates, 492
state and local taxes as
percentage of income, 323
TANF recipients, 459
Mississippi River basin, 16
Missouri
abortion regulations, 433
anti-sodomy laws, 436
average Medicaid payment per
enrollee, 471
barriers to voting, 83
court system, 290
governor's institutional powers,
265
governor's popularity, 269
gubernatorial election cycle, 247
higher education spending, per
capita, 14
historic use of initiative, 110
initiatives, ease of qualifying, 112
inpact of interest groups, 189
institutions of direct democracy,
101
interest groups, by type, 185
interparty competition,
1999–2003, 154
jucidial selection mechanisms,
305, 309
legislative professionalism, 232
lobbying laws, 173
maximum TANF benefit, 461
minority representation, state
legislature, 215, 217
partisan contestation in state
legislative races, 200
partisan distribution of legislative
seats, 207
party contributions and
expenditures, 149
primaries, 136
public school revenue across
sources, 489
racial and ethnic characteristics,
17
Ranney Indices of Party Control,
153
same-sex marriage laws, 439
school funding and high school
graduation rates, 492
St. Louis homeland security
grants, 65
state and local taxes as
percentage of income, 324
state legislature, 196
term limits, 234
women in state legislature, 11
Missouri Plan, 307, 309–310
mixed primary, 137

mobility, population, by state, 21–22
mobilization of bias, 165
Mobilizing Democracy (Levi, Johnson and Stokes), 75
model city charter, 366
Mofford, Rose, 256
Monroe, James, 254
Montana
    abortion regulations, 434
    anti-sodomy laws, 436
    average Medicaid payment per enrollee, 471
    barriers to voting, 83
    cigarette tax, 34
    corruption, perceived level, 34
    court system, 291
    farm income, 23
    Governor's institutional powers, 34
    governor's institutional powers, 265
    governor's political party, 13
    governor's popularity, 268
    gubernatorial election cycle, 247
    higher education spending, per capita, 14
    historic use of initiative, 110
    immigrants, undocumented, 466
    income per capita, 23
    initiatives, ease of qualifying, 112
    inpact of interest groups, 189
    institutions of direct democracy, 101
    interest groups, by type, 186
    interparty competition, 1999–2003, 154
    jucidial selection mechanisms, 305, 309
    legislative professionalism, 232
    lobbying laws, 173
    manufacturing employment, 23
    maximum TANF benefit, 461
    minimum wage laws, 465
    minority representation, state legislature, 215, 217
    partisan contestation in state legislative races, 200
    partisan distribution of legislative seats, 207
    party contributions and expenditures, 149
    policy preferences, 29
    political culture, 28
    political ideology, 27
    primaries, 136
    public school revenue across sources, 489
    racial and ethnic characteristics, 17
    Ranney Indices of Party Control, 153
    same-sex marriage laws, 439
    school funding and high school graduation rates, 492
    state legislature, 196
    TANF recipients, 459
    term limits, 234
    voter participation, 78

wealth relative to other states, 25
women in state legislature, 11
moralistic political culture, 26
morality policy, 416–445
    and civil rights, 437–438
    definition, 418–420
    and home rule, 419
    and interest groups, 422–424
    issue evolution, 421–427
    and lawmaking, 424–427
    and policy equilibrium, 422, 432, 434
    and religion, 420–421, 423, 428, 434, 437
    and values of the majority, 422
Morrill Acts, 51
Motor Voter Act, 80, 85
MTV's Rock the Vote, 85
muck-raking journalists, 363
multimember districts, 90, 91
multimember districts (MMDs), 197
multiparty politics, 93
municipal charters, 379
municipal governments
    land use powers, 396–398
    need for, 357
    and party machines, 359–363
    and pro- vs. slow-growth, 401–405
    and urban reform, 363–380
    variations in, 351–353
municipal incorporation, 383, 394
municipalities, 353
muntimember districts (MMD's), 197
Murkowski, Frank, 269
Murphy, Frank, 368
Murphy, "Silent" Charlie, 359

N

Nader, Ralph, 90
Napolitano, Janet, 256, 268, 277–278
National Abortion and Reproductive Rights Action League (NARAL), 180
National Association of Latino Appointed and Elected Oficials, 215–216
National Center for State Courts, 232, 296, 300
National Commission on Excellence in Education, 483
National Committee Against Discrimination in Housing (NCADH), 400–401
National Conference of State Legislatures, 151, 234, 236, 442, 455, 462
National Council of State Legislatures, 196–197
National Defense Education Act of 1958, 483
National Education Association, 187, 188
National Election Study, 72, 73
National Gay and Lesbian Task Force, 436, 439, 442

national government powers, 46
National Governor's Association, 13
National Guard, 63, 64
National Housing Act of 1934, 394
National Milk Producers Federation, 163
National Municipal League, 365, 366, 374
National Organization for the Reform of Marijuana Laws (NORML), 108
National Pork Producers Council, 163
National Review online, 315
National Rifle Association (NRA), 119, 163, 180, 181, 189
National Right to Life Committee, 182
National Summit on High Schools, 2005, 481
National Supremacy Clause, 46–47
National Voter Registration Act, 80
Native Americans, 113
    in poverty, 448, 449
    representation in government, 94
Natural Law Party, 156
Nebraska
    abortion regulations, 433
    anti-sodomy laws, 436
    average Medicaid payment per enrollee, 471
    barriers to voting, 83
    cigarette tax, 34
    corruption, perceived level, 34
    court system, 291
    farm income, 23
    Governor's institutional powers, 34
    governor's institutional powers, 265
    governor's political party, 13
    governor's popularity, 268
    gubernatorial election cycle, 247
    higher education spending, per capita, 14
    historic use of initiative, 110
    immigrants, undocumented, 466
    income per capita, 23
    initiatives, ease of qualifying, 112
    inpact of interest groups, 189
    institutions of direct democracy, 101
    interest groups, by type, 185
    interparty competition, 1999–2003, 154
    jucidial selection mechanisms, 305, 309
    legislative professionalism, 232
    lobbying laws, 173
    manufacturing employment, 23
    maximum TANF benefit, 461
    minimum wage laws, 465
    minority representation, state legislature, 215, 217
    Omaha homeland security grants, 65
    partisan distribution of legislative seats, 207

party contributions and
expenditures, 149
policy preferences, 29
political culture, 28
political ideology, 27
primaries, 136
public school revenue across
sources, 489
racial and ethnic characteristics,
17
Ranney Indices of Party Control,
153
same-sex marriage laws, 439
school funding and high school
graduation rates, 492
state and local taxes as
percentage of income, 323
state legislature, 196
TANF recipients, 459
term limits, 234
voter participation, 78
wealth relative to other states, 25
women in state legislature, 11
Necessary and Proper Clause, 47, 60
neutral competence, 274
Nevada
abortion regulations, 434
anti-sodomy laws, 436
average Medicaid payment per
enrollee, 471
barriers to voting, 83
cigarette tax, 34
corruption, perceived level, 34
court system, 291
farm income, 23
Governor's institutional powers,
34
governor's institutional powers,
265
governor's political party, 13
governor's popularity, 268
gubernatorial election cycle, 247
historic use of initiative, 110
immigrants, undocumented, 466
income per capita, 23
initiatives, ease of qualifying, 112
inpact of interest groups, 189
institutions of direct democracy,
101
interest groups, by type, 185
interparty competition, 1999–
2003, 154
jucidial selection mechanisms,
305, 309
legislative professionalism, 232
lobbying laws, 173
manufacturing employment, 23
maximum TANF benefit, 461
minimum wage laws, 465
minority representation, state
legislature, 215, 217
partisan distribution of legislative
seats, 207
party contributions and
expenditures, 149
policy preferences, 29
political culture, 28
political ideology, 27

primaries, 136
public school revenue across
sources, 489
Ranney Indices of Party Control,
153
regressive tax system, 339
same-sex marriage laws, 439
school funding and high school
graduation rates, 492
state and local taxes as
percentage of income, 324
state legislature, 196
TANF recipients, 459
term limits, 234
voter participation, 78
wealth relative to other states, 25
women in state legislature, 11
Nevada v. Hibbs, 57, 61
New Deal, 50, 51–56, 453
New England states, 16. *see
also* Connecticut; Maine;
Massachusetts; New Hampshire;
Rhode Island; Vermont
political culture, 26
New Hampshire
abortion regulations, 434
anti-sodomy laws, 436
average Medicaid payment per
enrollee, 471
barriers to voting, 83
cigarette tax, 34
college tuition, 13, 14
corruption, perceived level, 34
court system, 232
farm income, 23
Governor's institutional powers,
34
governor's institutional powers,
265
governor's political party, 13
governor's popularity, 268
gubernatorial election cycle, 247
higher education spending, per
capita, 14
immigrants, undocumented, 466
income per capita, 23
inpact of interest groups, 189
institutions of direct democracy,
101
interest groups, by type, 185
interparty competition, 1999–
2003, 154
jucidial selection mechanisms,
305, 309
legislative professionalism, 232
lobbying laws, 173
manufacturing employment, 23
maximum TANF benefit, 461
minimum wage laws, 465
minority representation, state
legislature, 215, 217
partisan contestation in state
legislative races, 200
partisan distribution of legislative
seats, 207
party contributions and
expenditures, 149
policy preferences, 29

political culture, 28
political ideology, 27
primaries, 136
public school revenue across
sources, 489
racial and ethnic characteristics,
17
Ranney Indices of Party Control,
153
same-sex marriage laws, 439
school funding and high school
graduation rates, 492
state and local taxes as
percentage of income, 324
state legislature, 196
TANF recipients, 460
voter participation, 78
wealth relative to other states, 25
women in state legislature, 11
New Jersey
abortion regulations, 434
anti-sodomy laws, 436
average Medicaid payment per
enrollee, 471
barriers to voting, 83
cigarette tax, 34
corruption, perceived level, 34
court system, 291
farm income, 23
Governor's institutional powers,
34
governor's institutional powers,
265
governor's political party, 13
governor's popularity, 268
gubernatorial election cycle, 247
higher education spending, per
capita, 14
immigrants, undocumented, 466
income per capita, 23
inpact of interest groups, 189
institutions of direct democracy,
101
interest groups, by type, 185
interparty competition, 1999–
2003, 154
Jersey City/Newark, homeland
security grants, 65
jucidial selection mechanisms,
305, 309
legislative professionalism, 232
lobbying laws, 173
manufacturing employment, 23
maximum TANF benefit, 461
minimum wage laws, 465
minority representation, state
legislature, 215, 217
partisan distribution of legislative
seats, 207
party contributions and
expenditures, 149
policy preferences, 29
political culture, 28
political ideology, 27
primaries, 136
public school revenue across
sources, 489
racial and ethnic characteristics, 17

Ranney Indices of Party Control,
153
same-sex marriage laws, 439
school funding and high school
graduation rates, 492
state and local taxes as
percentage of income, 323
state legislature, 196
TANF recipients, 459
voter participation, 78
wealth relative to other states, 25
women in state legislature, 11
New Mexico
abortion regulations, 434
anti-sodomy laws, 436
average Medicaid payment per
enrollee, 471
barriers to voting, 83
cigarette tax, 34
corruption, perceived level,
34
court system, 291
farm income, 23
Governor's institutional powers,
34
governor's institutional powers,
265
governor's political party, 13
governor's popularity, 268
gubernatorial election cycle, 247
higher education spending, per
capita, 14
immigrants, undocumented, 466
income per capita, 23
inpact of interest groups, 189
institutions of direct democracy,
101
interest groups, by type, 186
interparty competition,
1999–2003, 154
jucidial selection mechanisms,
305, 309
legislative professionalism, 232
lobbying laws, 173
manufacturing employment, 23
maximum TANF benefit, 461
minimum wage laws, 465
minority representation, state
legislature, 215, 217
partisan contestation in state
legislative races, 201
partisan distribution of legislative
seats, 207
party contributions and
expenditures, 149
policy preferences, 29
political culture, 28
political ideology, 27
primaries, 136
public school revenue across
sources, 490
racial and ethnic characteristics,
17
Ranney Indices of Party Control,
153
same-sex marriage laws, 439
school funding and high school
graduation rates, 492

state and local taxes as
percentage of income, 324
state legislature, 196
TANF recipients, 459
voter participation, 78
wealth relative to other states, 25
women in state legislature, 11
New Mexico Housing Trust Fund
(HTF), 168
New Mexico Human Needs
Coordinating Council, 168
New Orleans, Louisiana, 371
homeland security grants, 65
New State Ice Co. v Liebmann, 66
New York City, 371
homeland security grants, 65
metropolitan area, 388
municipal government, 351
New York City Democratic machine,
146
New York State
abortion regulations, 434
anti-sodomy laws, 436
average Medicaid payment per
enrollee, 471
barriers to voting, 83
Buffalo, homeland security
grants, 65
cigarette tax, 34
corruption, perceived level, 34
court system, 291
farm income, 23
Governor's institutional powers,
34
governor's institutional powers,
265
governor's political party, 13
governor's popularity, 269
gubernatorial election cycle, 247
higher education spending, per
capita, 14
immigrants, undocumented, 466
income per capita, 23
inpact of interest groups, 189
institutions of direct democracy,
101
interest groups, by type, 185
interparty competition, 1999–
2003, 154
jucidial selection mechanisms,
305, 309
legislative professionalism, 232
lobbying laws, 173
manufacturing employment, 23
maximum TANF benefit, 461
minimum wage laws, 465
minority representation, state
legislature, 215, 217
partisan contestation in state
legislative races, 200
partisan distribution of legislative
seats, 207
party contributions and
expenditures, 149
policy preferences, 29
political culture, 28
political ideology, 27
primaries, 136

public school revenue across
sources, 489
racial and ethnic characteristics,
17
Ranney Indices of Party Control,
153
same-sex marriage laws, 439
school funding and high school
graduation rates, 492
state and local taxes as
percentage of income, 323
state courts, 301
state legislature, 196
TANF recipients, 459
voter participation, 78
wealth relative to other states, 25
women in state legislature, 11
New York Sun, 497
New York Times, 47, 61, 64, 65,
119, 210, 366
New Yorkers Against Gun Violence,
177
Nichols, Terry, 286
9/11 attacks, 39, 40, 49
response to, 62–66
1984 (Orwell), 7
Ninth Amendment, 59
Nixon, Richard M., 53, 451
No Child Left Behind Act, 55–56,
243, 482–483, 483–484,
500–502
nonpartisan blanket primaries, 138
nonpartisan elections, 375
North Carolina
abortion regulations, 434
anti-sodomy laws, 436
average Medicaid payment per
enrollee, 471
barriers to voting, 83
Charlotte homeland security
grants, 65
court system, 291
governor's institutional powers,
265
governor's political party, 13
governor's popularity, 268
gubernatorial election cycle, 247
higher education spending, per
capita, 14
immigrants, undocumented, 466
inpact of interest groups, 189
institutions of direct democracy,
101
interest groups, by type, 185
interparty competition, 1999–
2003, 154
jucidial selection mechanisms,
305, 309
legislative professionalism, 232
lobbying laws, 173
maximum TANF benefit, 461
minimum wage laws, 465
minority representation, state
legislature, 215, 217
partisan contestation in state
legislative races, 200
partisan distribution of legislative
seats, 207

party contributions and
    expenditures, 149
primaries, 136
public school revenue across
    sources, 490
racial and ethnic characteristics,
    17
Ranney Indices of Party Control,
    153
same-sex marriage laws, 439
school funding and high school
    graduation rates, 492
state and local taxes as
    percentage of income, 323
state legislature, 196
TANF recipients, 460
women in state legislature, 11
North Dakota
    abortion regulations, 433
    anti-sodomy laws, 436
    average Medicaid payment per
        enrollee, 471
    barriers to voting, 83
    cigarette tax, 34
    corruption, perceived level, 34
    court system, 291
    farm income, 23
    Governor's institutional powers,
        34
    governor's institutional powers,
        265
    governor's political party, 13
    governor's popularity, 268
    gubernatorial election cycle, 247
    higher education spending, per
        capita, 14
    historic use of initiative, 110
    income per capita, 23
    initiatives, ease of qualifying, 112
    inpact of interest groups, 189
    institutions of direct democracy,
        101
    interest groups, by type, 185
    interparty competition,
        1999–2003, 154
    jucidial selection mechanisms,
        305, 309
    legislative professionalism, 232
    lobbying laws, 173
    manufacturing employment, 23
    maximum TANF benefit, 461
    minority representation, state
        legislature, 215, 217
    partisan contestation in state
        legislative races, 200
    partisan distribution of legislative
        seats, 207
    party contributions and
        expenditures, 149
    policy preferences, 29
    political culture, 28
    political ideology, 27
    primaries, 136
    public school revenue across
        sources, 489
    racial and ethnic characteristics, 17
    Ranney Indices of Party Control,
        153

same-sex marriage laws, 439
school funding and high school
    graduation rates, 492
state and local taxes as
    percentage of income, 324
state legislature, 197
voter participation, 78
wealth relative to other states, 25
women in state legislature, 11
nullification, 50, 51

O
Oakland, California, 371
Obama, Barack, 195
O'Connor, Sandra Day, 142, 435
Office of Economic Opportunity, 53
office-block ballot, 156, 157
Ohio
    abortion regulations, 433
    anti-sodomy laws, 436
    average Medicaid payment per
        enrollee, 471
    barriers to voting, 83
    cigarette tax, 34
    Columbus, homeland security
        grants, 65
    corruption, perceived level, 34
    court system, 291
    farm income, 23
    Governor's institutional powers,
        34
    governor's institutional powers,
        265
    governor's political party, 13
    governor's popularity, 269
    gubernatorial election cycle, 247
    higher education spending, per
        capita, 14
    historic use of initiative, 110
    immigrants, undocumented, 466
    income per capita, 23
    initiatives, ease of qualifying, 112
    inpact of interest groups, 189
    interest groups, by type, 185
    interparty competition,
        1999–2003, 154
    jucidial selection mechanisms,
        305, 309
    legislative professionalism, 232
    lobbying laws, 173
    manufacturing employment, 23
    maximum TANF benefit, 461
    minimum wage laws, 465
    minority representation, state
        legislature, 215, 217
    partisan contestation in state
        legislative races, 200
    partisan distribution of legislative
        seats, 207
    party contributions and
        expenditures, 149
    policy preferences, 29
    political culture, 28
    political ideology, 27
    primaries, 136
    public school revenue across
        sources, 489
    racial and ethnic characteristics, 17

Ranney Indices of Party Control,
    153
same-sex marriage laws, 439
school funding and high school
    graduation rates, 492
state and local taxes as
    percentage of income, 323
state legislature, 197
TANF recipients, 459
term limits, 234
voter participation, 78
wealth relative to other states, 25
women in state legislature, 11
Oklahoma
    abortion regulations, 433
    anti-sodomy laws, 436
    average Medicaid payment per
        enrollee, 471
    barriers to voting, 83
    cigarette tax, 34
    corruption, perceived level, 34
    court system, 291
    farm income, 23
    Governor's institutional powers,
        34
    governor's institutional powers,
        265
    governor's political party, 13
    governor's popularity, 268
    gubernatorial election cycle, 247
    higher education spending, per
        capita, 13
    historic use of initiative, 110
    immigrants, undocumented, 466
    income per capita, 23
    inpact of interest groups, 189
    interest groups, by type, 185
    interparty competition,
        1999–2003, 154
    jucidial selection mechanisms,
        305, 309
    legislative professionalism, 232
    lobbying laws, 173
    manufacturing employment, 23
    maximum TANF benefit, 461
    minimum wage laws, 465
    minority representation, state
        legislature, 216, 217
    partisan contestation in state
        legislative races, 200
    partisan distribution of legislative
        seats, 207
    party contributions and
        expenditures, 149
    policy preferences, 29
    political culture, 28
    political ideology, 27
    primaries, 136
    public school revenue across
        sources, 489
    racial and ethnic characteristics,
        17
    Ranney Indices of Party Control,
        153
    same-sex marriage laws,
        439
    school funding and high school
        graduation rates, 492

state and local taxes as
  percentage of income, 324
state legislature, 197
TANF recipients, 460
term limits, 234
voter participation, 78
wealth relative to other states, 25
women in state legislature, 11
Oklahoma City, 373
Oklahoma City bombing, 286, 287
Omaha, 371
  homeland security grants, 65
O'Neill, Tip, 54
Op-ed articles, 430
operating budget, 346
Operation Rescue, 424, 431
Oregon
  abortion regulations, 434
  anti-sodomy laws, 436
  average Medicaid payment per
    enrollee, 472
  barriers to voting, 83
  cigarette tax, 35
  corruption, perceived level, 35
  court system, 291
  farm income, 24
  Governor's institutional powers,
    35
  governor's institutional powers,
    265
  governor's political party, 13
  governor's popularity, 268
  gubernatorial election cycle, 247
  higher education spending, per
    capita, 14
  historic use of initiative, 110
  immigrants, undocumented, 466
  income per capita, 24
  initiatives, ease of qualifying, 112
  inpact of interest groups, 189
  institutions of direct democracy,
    101
  interest groups, by type, 186
  interparty competition,
    1999–2003, 154
  jucidial selection mechanisms,
    305, 309
  legislative professionalism, 232
  lobbying laws, 173
  manufacturing employment, 24
  maximum TANF benefit, 461
  minimum wage laws, 465
  minority representation, state
    legislature, 216, 217
  mobility of population, 22
  partisan distribution of legislative
    seats, 207
  party contributions and
    expenditures, 149
  policy preferences, 30
  political culture, 28
  political ideology, 27
  primaries, 136
  public school revenue across
    sources, 489
  racial and ethnic characteristics, 18
  Ranney Indices of Party Control,
    153

same-sex marriage laws, 439
school funding and high school
  graduation rates, 492
state and local taxes as
  percentage of income, 324
state legislature, 197
TANF recipients, 460
term limits repealed, 236
voter participation, 78
wealth relative to other states, 25
women in state legislature, 11
Oregon Corrupt Practices Act, 376
original jurisdiction, 298
Orr, Kay A., 255
out-of-court settlements, 294
outsider gubernatorial candidates,
  252–253
override, 259
Owens, bill, 268

P

Pacific Railroad Act, 51
packing, 206
Paige, Rod, 498
Palin, Sarah, 256
participation, political, 71–75
participation bias, 89–90
parties, political, 12–13, 16
  and voter choice, 87
parties-in-government, 150–155
parties-in-the-electorate, 142–144
partisan dealignment, 144
party boss, 146
party contributions and
  expenditures, by state, 149–150
Party era, 145–146
party fusion, 139–140, 140
party identification
  and participation, 144
  and voting, 247, 250
party identification (PID), 142
party organization, 144–150
party-column ballot, 156, 157
Pataki, George, 128, 243, 244, 269
patients rights initiative, 116
Patrick, Deval, 257
Patriot Act, 62–63
patronage, 360
patronage appointments, 145–146,
  275
Pawlenty, Tim, 251
peak associations, 164
Pendleton Act, 376
Peninsula Clarion (Alaska), 237
Penn State University, 3–4, 4, 13,
  359
Pennsylvania
  abortion regulations, 433
  anti-sodomy laws, 436
  average Medicaid payment per
    enrollee, 472
  barriers to voting, 83
  cigarette tax, 35
  corruption, perceived level, 35
  court system, 291
  farm income, 24
  Governor's institutional powers,
    35

governor's institutional powers,
  265
governor's political party, 13
governor's popularity, 268
gubernatorial election cycle, 247
higher education spending, per
  capita, 14
immigrants, undocumented, 466
income per capita, 24
inpact of interest groups, 189
institutions of direct democracy,
  101
interest groups, by type, 185
interparty competition, 1999–
  2003, 154
jucidial selection mechanisms,
  305, 309
legislative professionalism, 232
lobbying laws, 173
manufacturing employment, 24
maximum TANF benefit, 461
minimum wage laws, 465
minority representation, state
  legislature, 216, 217
mobility of population, 22
partisan contestation in state
  legislative races, 200
partisan distribution of legislative
  seats, 207
party contributions and
  expenditures, 149
Pittsburgh, homeland security
  grants, 65
policy preferences, 30
political culture, 28
political ideology, 27
primaries, 136
public school revenue across
  sources, 489
racial and ethnic characteristics,
  18
Ranney Indices of Party Control,
  153
regressive tax system, 339
same-sex marriage laws, 439
school funding and high school
  graduation rates, 492
state college tuition, 3–4
state and local taxes as
  percentage of income, 323
state legislature, 197
TANF recipients, 459
voter participation, 78
wealth relative to other states, 25
women in state legislature, 11
pensions, 344
People for the Ethical Treatment of
  Animals (PETA), 423
People's Party, 158
Perdue, Sonny, 158, 268
Perry, Rick, 262, 269
personal barriers, to voter
  participation, 84–85
personal impact, of local
  government, 7, 8
Personal Responsibility and Work
  Opportunity Reconciliation Act
  (PRWORA), 55

Pew Hispanic Center, 466
pharmaceutical industry association
    (PhRMA), 179
Philadelphia, 371
Philip Morris Company, 114, 171
Phoenix, Arizona, 373
    homeland security grants, 65
PID (party identification), 142
Pinchot, Gifford, 367
Pingree, Hazen, 368
Pittsburgh, Pennsylvania, 371
    homeland security grants, 65
Planned Parenthood, 423
Planned Parenthood v. Casey, 432,
    435
plea bargains, 294
Pluralism, 164–165
police and corrections
    as portion of local spending, 343,
        345
    as portion of state spending, 342,
        345
police powers, 360, 397
policy agenda, 271
Policy Center, 323–324
policy diffusion, 454
policy entrepreneurs, 422
policy equilibrium, 422
    and morality policy, 425–427,
        432, 434
policy reform, 15
policy shock, 422
political accountability, 274
political action committees (PACs),
    74, 148, 161, 180, 181–182
political activism, 75–77, 423–424
political capital, 266
political culture, 26–28
    by state, 28
political ideology, 26–28, 142
    and party, 142–144
    and party identification, by state,
        143–144
political institutions, 5–6
    definition, 8
    reform, 30–32
political participation, 71–75
    grassroots, 75–77
    levels of, 77
    perceived impact, 72, 73
political parties, 12–13, 16, 130–159
    anti-party sentiments, 134
    balance, in state legislature, 270
    ballot access, 140–141, 360
    control of legislative seats, 1940–
        2004, 151
    corruption, 145–146
    early, 358, 359
    endorsement of candidates, 139
    factions within, 133
    financing, 147–148, 149
    functions of, 134
    governor's by state, 13
    interparty competition, 131,
        150–155
    issue-oriented, 140
    organizational strength,
        measuring, 147

presidential party nominations,
    138
Progressive era, 146
    rebirth of, 147–147
    regulating, 133–142
    theories of, 132–134
    third parties, 140, 141, 155–158
    two-party duopoly, 140–141
Political Research Quarterly, 122,
    185–186
Political Science and Politics, 359
politics
    definition, 9
Politics in the American States
    (Thomas and Hrebenar),
    188, 189
politics of place, 382–415
Polk, James K., 254
poll tax, 75
poor people, 448–451
    demographics, 448–451
population density
    least- and most-populated
        regions, 406
    by state, 21–22
    United States, 402
population density, and policy, 20
population growth, 401–405
Population Reference Bureau, 22
Populist movement, 103, 364
Populist Party, 105–106
pork barrel, 223
potential interests, 164
poverty. see also social welfare
    policy
    in cities, 413
    federal income guidelines, 448
    levels, by county, 450
    and racism, 20, 448
    rate, 448
Powell, Lewis, 141
power
    centralized, 42–43
    decentralized, 43, 44
precedents, legal, 299
precinct captain, 360
prejudice, 16
presidential party nominations, 138
primary election systems, 89,
    136–137
    effect on representation, 138–139
Princeton University, 252
Printz v. United States, 57, 60
privatization, 391
Privileges and Immunities Clause, 48
problem-solving courts, 295
professionalism
    de-professionalization, 237
Progressive era, 84, 106–107, 364–
    365, 397
    parties during, 146
    reforms of, 258
Progressive movement, 101
Progressive Party, 367
pro-life groups, 424, 430
property taxes, 325, 326–329
Proposition 13, California, 107, 119,
    123

protection from medical malpractice
    initiative, 116
public assistance. see also welfare
    programs
    vs. social insurance, 455–456
public goods, 9, 164
public opinion, and governor's
    power, 266–267
Public Opinion in State Politics
    (Cohen), 27
public policy
    definition, 9–10
    and direct democracy, 123–124
public services, demand for,
    385–386

Q
Querze, Alana, 122
Quimby, "Diamond Joe", 368
Quincy, Josiah "Great Mayor", 368

R
race
    and community variation, 16–20
    populations, by state, 17, 18
racial gerrymandering, 78
racism, 16, 18–19, 19–20, 48, 59,
    135, 293
    and federal housing programs,
        395–396
    in municipal government,
        379–380
    and poverty, 20, 448
    and voting rights, 80. see
        also voting rights, African
        Americans
    and welfare policy, 455
    and zoning regulations,
        400–401
rank-and-file legislators, 223
Ranney Index, 151–153
Ravitch, Diane, 502
Ray, Dixie Lee, 255
Reagan, Ronald, 252, 254, 334,
    429, 447, 448, 483
Reagan, Ronald, era, 53–54, 60
Real ID law, 39
realtors' interest groups, 188
recall, 101–102
recidivism, 296
recuse, 312
Red Cross, 8
Red Scare, 141
redistricting, 81, 195, 202–210
referendum, 100–103. see also
    initiatives
reform, 15, 30–32
Reform era. see Progressive era
reform movements, 364–380
    social, 364
reforms, municipal, 363–380
regional governments, 413
regressive taxes, 339
regulatory functions, of government,
    7
Rehnquist, William H., 60, 61,
    139–140
Reiner, Rob, 113, 250

religion
  and morality policy, 420–421,
    423, 428, 434, 437
religion, of immigrants, 355
Rell, Jodi, 255, 256, 268
Rendell, Ed, 246, 268
representation
  as function of legislature,
    225–227
representation in government
  African Americans, 18–19
  minorities, 91, 93–95
  and multimember districts, 91
  state legislatures, 225–226
  women, 11–12, 93
Republican and Democratic parties,
  12–13, 16, 90. see also political
  parties
Reserve Clause, 49
responsible party model, 130–134
Restoration (Will), 199
retail sales industry
  contributions to state party
    committees, 181
retention election, 305, 307
retirees, 20
revenue packages, by state, 335–339
  sources of all state revenues, 336
revenue sharing, 408
revenue sources, 329–333. see also
  taxes
  direct charges, 331
  gambling, 332
  local, 337, 338–339
  tax and expenditure limits
    (TELs), 333–334
  and zoning, 386–387
Rhode Island
  abortion regulations, 433
  anti-sodomy laws, 436
  average Medicaid payment per
    enrollee, 472
  barriers to voting, 83
  cigarette tax, 35
  corruption, perceived level, 35
  court system, 291
  farm income, 24
  Governor's institutional powers,
    35
  governor's institutional powers,
    265
  governor's political party, 13
  governor's popularity, 268
  gubernatorial election cycle, 247
  immigrants, undocumented, 466
  income per capita, 24
  inpact of interest groups, 189
  interest groups, by type, 186
  interparty competition,
    1999–2003, 154
  jucidial selection mechanisms,
    305, 309
  legislative professionalism,
    232
  lobbying laws, 173
  manufacturing employment, 24
  maximum TANF benefit, 461
  minimum wage laws, 465

minority representation, state
  legislature, 216, 217
mobility of population, 22
partisan contestation in state
  legislative races, 201
partisan distribution of legislative
  seats, 207
party contributions and
  expenditures, 149
policy preferences, 30
political culture, 28
political ideology, 27
primaries, 136
public school revenue across
  sources, 489
racial and ethnic characteristics,
  18
Ranney Indices of Party Control,
  153
same-sex marriage laws, 439
school funding and high school
  graduation
  rates, 492
sin taxes, 338
state and local taxes as
  percentage of income, 323
state legislature, 197
TANF recipients, 459
voter participation, 78
wealth relative to other states, 25
women in state legislature, 11
Richards, Ann, 255
Richards, Ellen Swallow, 365
Richardson, Bill, 257, 268, 270
Richmond, Virginia, 373
right to die, 62, 423
Riley, Bob, 268
rioting, 76–77
Risch, Jim, 268
Rizzo, Frank, 368
Roberts, Barbaba, 255
Roberts, John, 61, 62, 435
Rockefeller, John D., 365
Roe v. Wade, 59–60, 429–430, 432
Romer, Roy, 253
Romney, George, 252
Romney, Mitt, 252, 254, 268
Roosevelt, Franklin D., 52, 367, 453
Roosevelt, Theodore, 254, 364
Ross, Nellie Taylor, 255
Rounds, Mike, 268
Rowland, John, 174, 253
Roy, Vesta M., 256
RU-486 (abortion pill), 417
runaway juries, 292–293
Russell Sage Foundation, 75
*Rutan v. Republican Party of
  Illinois*, 142, 275
Rutgers University
  Center for American Women and
    Politics, 212, 213
Center for American Women and
  Politics, Rutgers
  University, 11

S
Sacramento, California, 373
  homeland security grants, 65

Sacramento Bee, 210
sales tax, 266, 327
same-sex marriage, 416–417,
  435–443
  ballot initiativevs, 442
  laws by state, 439
*San Antonio Independent School
  District v. Rodriguez*, 493
San Antonio, Texas, 373
San Diego, 373
San Francisco, 371
San Jose, 373
Sanford, Mark, 268, 473
Santa Ana, California, 373
Saturn automobile assembly plant,
  410
Scalia, Antonin, 141–142
Schiavo, Terry, 473
school desegregation, 59, 500
school districts, 485–487
school shootings, 245
school voucher programs, 495–496
schools. see education policy
Schwartenegger, Arnold, 12,
  99–100, 102, 113, 118, 176,
  179, 249, 252, 253, 262, 267,
  269, 271–273
Schweitzer, Brian, 268
Seattle, 371
Sebelius, Kathleen, 245, 256, 268
secret ballot, 156, 375
securities and investment industry
  contributions to state party
  committees, 181
selective benefit, 166
self-financing candidates, 249
Selma, Alabama, civil rights march,
  76
Seminole Tribe v. State of Florida,
  57, 61
semi-open primary, 136
Senate, 195
senators, 195, 197
September 11, 2001, 39, 40, 49
  response to, 62–66
severance taxes, 332
Shaheen, Jeanne, 255
Sharpton, Al, 351
shortcuts, voters', 117, 247
Sierra Club, 163
sin taxes, 330–331, 338
single-member districts (SMD's), 90,
  91, 197
single-payer health care, 467
single-purpose governments, 354
Sixteenth Amendment, 51
Sixth Amendment, 59
Sizemore, Bill, 329
Slaughterhouse Cases, 48
slavery, 48
small claims courts, 295
social capital, 84
Social Capital Benchmark Survey,
  73, 85
social insurance, 455
social movements, 76
social reform movements, 365
Social Science Quarterly, 25, 199

Social Security, 456
Social Security Act of 1935, 453, 456–457, 457
Social Security Administration, 456
Social Security Disability Insurance (SSDI), 456
social services. see welfare programs
social welfare policy, 446–477
  and class conflict, 455
  diffusion, 454
  funding, 453–454
  minimum wage laws, 464–465
  and racism, 455
  reform, 457–462
social welfare programs
  housing, 463–464
Socialist Party, 366
soft money, 148, 150
Soros, George, 113
South Carolina
  abortion regulations, 433
  anti-sodomy laws, 436
  average Medicaid payment per enrollee, 472
  barriers to voting, 83
  cigarette tax, 35
  corruption, perceived level, 35
  court system, 291
  farm income, 24
  Governor's institutional powers, 35
  governor's institutional powers, 265
  governor's political party, 13
  governor's popularity, 268
  gubernatorial election cycle, 247
  immigrants, undocumented, 466
  income per capita, 24
  inpact of interest groups, 189
  institutions of direct democracy, 101
  interest groups, by type, 185
  interparty competition, 1999–2003, 154
  jucidial selection mechanisms, 305, 309
  legislative professionalism, 232
  lobbying laws, 173
  manufacturing employment, 24
  maximum TANF benefit, 461
  minimum wage laws, 465
  minority representation, state legislature, 216, 217
  mobility of population, 22
  partisan contestation in state legislative races, 201
  partisan distribution of legislative seats, 207
  party contributions and expenditures, 149
  policy preferences, 30
  political culture, 28
  political ideology, 27
  primaries, 136
  racial and ethnic characteristics, 18
  Ranney Indices of Party Control, 153
  same-sex marriage laws, 439

state and local taxes as percentage of income, 323
  state legislature, 197
  TANF recipients, 460
  voter participation, 78
  wealth relative to other states, 25
  women in state legislature, 13
South Dakota
  abortion regulations, 433
  anti-sodomy laws, 436
  average Medicaid payment per enrollee, 472
  barriers to voting, 83
  cigarette tax, 35
  corruption, perceived level, 35
  court system, 291
  farm income, 24
  Governor's institutional powers, 35
  governor's institutional powers, 265
  governor's political party, 13
  governor's popularity, 268
  gubernatorial election cycle, 247
  higher education spending, per capita, 14
  historic use of initiative, 110
  immigrants, undocumented, 466
  income per capita, 24
  initiatives, ease of qualifying, 112
  inpact of interest groups, 189
  institutions of direct democracy, 101
  interest groups, by type, 186
  interparty competition, 1999–2003, 154
  jucidial selection mechanisms, 305, 309
  legislative professionalism, 232
  lobbying laws, 173
  manufacturing employment, 24
  maximum TANF benefit, 461
  minimum wage laws, 465
  minority representation, state legislature, 216, 217
  mobility of population, 22
  partisan contestation in state legislative races, 200
  partisan distribution of legislative seats, 207
  party contributions and expenditures, 149
  policy preferences, 30
  political culture, 28
  political ideology, 27
  primaries, 136
  public school revenue across sources, 489
  racial and ethnic characteristics, 18
  Ranney Indices of Party Control, 153
  regressive tax system, 339
  same-sex marriage laws, 439
  school funding and high school graduation rates, 492
  state and local taxes as percentage of income, 324

  state legislature, 197
  TANF recipients, 460
  term limits, 234
  voter participation, 78
  wealth relative to other states, 25
  women in state legislature, 11
Southern Politics in the State and Nation (Key), 154
Southern states, 12–13, 16, 18–19.
  see also individual states
  political culture, 27
special districts, 354, 387, 388, 392
  functions of, 393
Spellings, Margaret, 484, 502
Spitzer, Eliot, 251
spoils system, 145–146
sportsmen's interest groups, 188
sprawl, urban, 405, 407, 412
Sprawl: A Compact History (Bruegmann), 411
St. Louis, Missouri, 371
standing committee, 220
Stanford, Leland, 365
state courts
  in the federal system, 285–287
State Daryman's Association, 163
State Farm Insurance, 311
state government independently elected executives, 262
state government powers, 46, 48–49
  expanding, 60–61
state governments
  expenditures, 342–348
state legislators, 211–218
  minorities, 211, 213–218
  women, 211–213, 217–218
state legislature
  partisan distribution of seats, 206–207
  redistricting, 202–210
state legislatures, 193–241
  collective action problem, 225–226
  committees, 227
  duties of, 218–231
  elections, 197–202
  interparty competition, 150–155
  leadership, 229–231
  minority representation, 11–12, 93, 195
  partisan control, by state, 151
  party caucuses, 227–228
  professionalism, 231–233
  redistricting, 195
  reform, 231–238
  structures, 195–198
State of the State address, 262
State of the States, The, 256
State Politics and Policy Quarterly, 29–30, 79, 125, 210
State Politics, Parties, and Policy (Morehouse and Jewell), 133
Stateline.org, 275
state's attorney, 286
Statistical Abstract of the United States, 215–216
statutory initiatives, 109

stem cell research initiatives, 116
straight-ticket ballots, 360
street-level bureaucrats, 274
Strickland, Ted, 251
strong mayor-council system, 369, 370
suburbs, rise of, 394–396
suffrage
  African Americans, 18–19, 78–79, 135, 254
  women, 16, 78, 254
suicide, physician-assisted, 62
supermajority vote, 259, 347
supreme court, state, 287, 298–302
  administrative duties of, 302
  jucidial selection mechanisms, 308–310
  names of, by state, 289–292
Supreme Court, United States, 56–62, 57, 59–60
  and abortion rights, 59–60, 429–430, 431–432, 435
  and direct democracy campaigns, 114
  and dual federalism, 57
  and education policy, 492–493, 500
  and election regulations, 135–136, 139, 141–142, 148, 179–180, 204
  and voting rights, 136
  and zoning regulations, 397, 399
Survey USA, 269
Swift, Jane, 256
Symington, Fife, 102, 253

T

Taft, Bob, 267, 269
Tammany Hall, 146, 358, 359, 363
Tampa, Florida, 371
targeting electoral strategy, 230
Tashijian v. Republican Party of Connecticut, 135–136
tax and expenditure limits (TELs), 333–334
Tax Foundation, 323–324
tax rebellions, 329
taxes, 321–334
  antitax initiatives, 107, 333–334
  cigarette tax, by state, 34–35
  criteria for evaluating, 321
  effects of, 340–341
  estate, 331
  flat rate, 324
  and government power, 320
  income tax, 324–325
  increasing and decreasing, 340
  motor vehicle, 330
  poll tax, 75, 78
  property, 325, 326–329
  regressive, states with ten most, 339
  sales tax, 266, 327
  severance, 332
  sin, 330–331, 338
  sources of state tax revenue, 337
  state and local as percentage of income, 323–324

tax base of diverse regions, 15–16
tobacco products, 330
Taxpayer's Bill of Rights (TABOR), 121, 237, 333, 334
Taylor, Shelly, 329
Taylor, Zachary, 131
teen courts, 296
Temple University, 496
Temporary Assistance for Needy Families (TANF), 55, 343, 457–462
  benefits, cut, 460–461
  maximum benefit by state, 461
  recipients, by state, 459–460
Tennessee
  abortion regulations, 433
  anti-sodomy laws, 436
  average Medicaid payment per enrollee, 472
  barriers to voting, 83
  cigarette tax, 35
  corruption, perceived level, 35
  court system, 291
  farm income, 24
  geography, and community variation, 16
  Governor's institutional powers, 35
  governor's institutional powers, 265
  governor's political party, 13
  governor's popularity, 268
  gubernatorial election cycle, 247
  higher education spending, per capita, 14
  income per capita, 24
  inpact of interest groups, 189
  interest groups, by type, 185
  interparty competition, 1999–2003, 154
  jucidial selection mechanisms, 305, 309
  legislative professionalism, 232
  lobbying laws, 173
  manufacturing employment, 24
  maximum TANF benefit, 461
  minority representation, state legislature, 216, 217
  mobility of population, 22
  partisan contestation in state legislative races, 201
  partisan distribution of legislative seats, 207
  party contributions and expenditures, 149
  policy preferences, 30
  political culture, 28
  political ideology, 27
  primaries, 136
  public school revenue across sources, 489
  racial and ethnic characteristics, 18
  Ranney Indices of Party Control, 153
  regressive tax system, 339
  same-sex marriage laws, 439

school funding and high school graduation rates, 492
state and local taxes as percentage of income, 324
state legislature, 197
voter participation, 78
wealth relative to other states, 25
women in state legislature, 11
Tennessee v. Lane, 57, 61
Tenth Amendment, 49
term limits, 199, 234–238
  impact of, 235–238
  repeals, 236
Term Limits and the Dismantling of State Legislative Professionalism (Kousser), 237
terrorism
  and federal powers, 62–66
Texas
  abortion regulations, 433
  anti-sodomy laws, 436
  average Medicaid payment per enrollee, 472
  barriers to voting, 83
  cigarette tax, 35
  corruption, perceived level, 35
  court system, 291
  farm income, 24
  Governor's institutional powers, 35
  governor's institutional powers, 265
  governor's political party, 13
  governor's popularity, 269
  gubernatorial election cycle, 247
  higher education spending, per capita, 14
  immigrants, undocumented, 466
  income per capita, 24
  inpact of interest groups, 189
  interest groups, by type, 185
  interparty competition, 1999–2003, 154
  jucidial selection mechanisms, 305, 309
  legislative professionalism, 232
  lobbying laws, 173
  manufacturing employment, 24
  maximum TANF benefit, 461
  minimum wage laws, 465
  minority representation, state legislature, 216, 217
  mobility of population, 22
  partisan contestation in state legislative races, 201
  partisan distribution of legislative seats, 207
  party contributions and expenditures, 149
  policy preferences, 30
  political culture, 28
  political ideology, 27
  primaries, 136
  public school revenue across sources, 489
  racial and ethnic characteristics, 18
  Ranney Indices of Party Control, 153

redistricting, 208–209
regressive tax system, 339
same-sex marriage laws, 439
school funding and high school
    graduation rates, 492
state and local taxes as
    percentage of income, 324
state legislature, 197
TANF recipients, 459
tax base, 15
voter participation, 78
wealth relative to other states, 25
women in state legislature, 11
Texas Petroleum Marketers and
    Convenience Store Association,
    164
third parties, 140, 141, 155–156
Thirteenth Amendment, 48
Thomas Jefferson Program in Public
    Policy, William and Mary,
    200–201
Thompson, "Kaiser Bill", 367, 368
Thompson, Tommy, 447, 458
Thoughts on the Present Discontents
    (Burke), 132, 133
Till, Emmett, 293
Timmons v. Twin Cities Area New
    Party, 139
tobacco taxes, 330
Tocqueville, Alexis de, 162
Toledo, 371
top-two primaries, 137–138
tort reform, 315
tort reform initiative, 116
traditional party organization (TPO),
    147
traditionalistic political culture,
    27–28
transportation, 344–345
Transportation, Department of, 39
trial courts, 287, 292–295
    names of, by state, 289–292
trial transcript, 297
tribal gaming compact initiative, 116
tribal gaming compact renegotiation
    initiative, 115
tribal governments
    contributions to state party
        committees, 181
truckers and transport interest
    groups, 188
trust, in government, 73
tuition, college, 3–4
Tulsa, Oklahoma, 371
Tweed, William Marcy "Boss", 146,
    358, 359, 363
two-party contestation, 199
two-party duopoly, 141–142

U

underclass, 451
Unemployment Insurance Program,
    457
unfair business competition
    initiative, 116
unfunded mandate, 55
Unheavenly City, The (Banfield), 451
unicameral, 195, 228

unified executive budget, 258
unified government, 270
unincorporated areas, 387
unions, 180
    contributions to state party
        committees, 181
    influence of, 188
    public sector, 175, 176, 181, 188
unitary systems, 42–43, 43
United States, founding of, 44–45
United States Term Limits
    (organization), 233–234
United States v. Lopez, 57
United States v. Morrison, 57, 60
Universal Companies, 496
University of Alabama v. Garrett, 57
University of California, 341
University of Florida, 3–4
University of Maryland, 54
University of New Hampshire, 14
University of Pennsylvania, 496
University of Tennessee, 327
Unz, Ron, 113
Urban Affairs Quarterly, 406
Urban Affairs Review, 407
urban growth areas (UGAs), 407
Urban Institute, 455, 471–472
urban population, percentage of
    United States, 315
urban reform movement, 363–380
    and class conflict, 365–366,
        379–380
    consequences of, 377–380
    efficiency and accountability, 378
    mechanisms of, 366–370
    and racism, 379–380
    and voter participation,
        378–379
urban sprawl, 405, 407, 412
urbanization, 354–357
USA Patriot Act, 62–63
Utah
    abortion regulations, 433
    anti-sodomy laws, 436
    average Medicaid payment per
        enrollee, 472
    barriers to voting, 83
    cigarette tax, 35
    corruption, perceived level, 35
    court system, 291
    farm income, 24
    Governor's institutional powers,
        35
    governor's institutional powers,
        265
    governor's political party, 13f
    governor's popularity, 268
    gubernatorial election cycle, 247
    higher education spending, per
        capita, 14
    historic use of initiative, 110
    immigrants, undocumented, 466
    income per capita, 24
    initiatives, ease of qualifying, 112
    inpact of interest groups, 189
    institutions of direct democracy,
        101
    interest groups, by type, 185

interparty competition,
    1999–2003, 154
jucidial selection mechanisms,
    305, 309
legislative professionalism, 232
lobbying laws, 173
manufacturing employment, 24
maximum TANF benefit, 461
minimum wage laws, 465
minority representation, state
    legislature, 216, 217
mobility of population, 22
partisan contestation in state
    legislative races, 200
partisan distribution of legislative
    seats, 207
party contributions and
    expenditures, 149
policy preferences, 30
political culture, 28
political ideology, 27
primaries, 136
public school revenue across
    sources, 489
racial and ethnic characteristics,
    18
Ranney Indices of Party Control,
    153
same-sex marriage laws, 439
school funding and high school
    graduation rates, 492
state and local taxes as
    percentage of income, 323
state legislature, 197
TANF recipients, 460
term limits repealed, 236
voter participation, 78
wealth relative to other states, 25
women in state legislature, 11
utility companies
influence of, 188

V

Van Buren, Martin, 145, 254
Van de Kamp, John, 119
Vanna White Veto, 260
Ventura, Jesse, 93, 128, 158, 252,
    253
Vermont
    abortion regulations, 434
    anti-sodomy laws, 436
    average Medicaid payment per
        enrollee, 472
    barriers to voting, 83
    cigarette tax, 35
    corruption, perceived level, 35
    court system, 291
    farm income, 24
    Governor's institutional powers,
        35
    governor's institutional powers,
        265
    governor's political party, 13
    governor's popularity, 268
    gubernatorial election cycle, 247
    higher education spending, per
        capita, 14
    immigrants, undocumented, 466
    income per capita, 24

inpact of interest groups, 189
interest groups, by type, 185
interparty competition,
    1999–2003, 154
jucidial selection mechanisms,
    305, 309
legislative professionalism, 232
lobbying laws, 173
manufacturing employment, 24
maximum TANF benefit, 461
minimum wage laws, 465
minority representation, state
    legislature, 216, 217
mobility of population, 22
partisan contestation in state
    legislative races, 200
partisan distribution of legislative
    seats, 207
party contributions and
    expenditures, 149
policy preferences, 30
political culture, 28
political ideology, 27
primaries, 136
public school revenue across
    sources, 490
racial and ethnic characteristics,
    18
Ranney Indices of Party Control,
    153
same-sex marriage laws, 439,
    439–440
school funding and high school
    graduation rates, 492
state and local taxes as
    percentage of income, 323
state legislature, 197
TANF recipients, 459
voter participation, 78
wealth relative to other states, 25
women in state legislature, 11
Vernon, California, 383–384
Veteran's Administration (VA) loans,
    394–396
veto, line-item, 220
veto power, 259–260
veto-proof majority, 259
vice laws, 425
Victory Schools, 496
*Village of Euclid v. Ambler Realty
    Company*, 397
Vilsack, Tom, 268
Virginia
    barriers to voting, 83
    governor's institutional powers,
        265
    governor's political party, 13
    governor's popularity, 268
    gubernatorial election cycle, 247
    higher education spending, per
        capita, 14
    immigrants, undocumented, 466
    inpact of interest groups, 189
    institutions of direct democracy,
        101
    interest groups, by type, 185
    interparty competition, 1999–
        2003, 154

lobbying laws, 173
minimum wage laws, 465
mobility of population, 22
party contributions and
    expenditures, 149
primaries, 136
public school revenue across
    sources, 489
racial and ethnic characteristics,
    18
Ranney Indices of Party Control,
    153
school funding and high school
    graduation rates, 492
state and local taxes as
    percentage of income, 324
state legislature, 197
TANF recipients, 460
women in state legislature, 11
Virginia Tech shootings, 245
voluntary associations. *see* interest
    groups
voter approval for gambling
    initiative, 116
voter participation, 71–74, 73–74
    attitudes toward barriers, 85
    barriers, breaking down, 85–87
    barriers to, by state, 83
    districting barriers, 80–81
    effects, on public policy, 87–88
    levels of, 77, 78
    participation bias, 89–90
    party system barriers, 82, 83
    and public opinion, 88–89
    registration barriers, 80
    and urban reform, 378–379
    and voter choice, 87
    and voting reforms, 85–86
voter registration, 375
voting
    decisionmaking process, 198,
        199, 201–202
    and electoral boundaries, 79
voting cue, 201
voting population, increase in, 358
voting rights, 75–80
    African Americans, 18–19, 135,
        254
    barriers to participation, 75–80,
        80–87. *see also* racism, and
        voting rights
    ineligibility, 81–82
    and noncitizens, 81
    regulating, 135–136
    women, 254
    womens, 16, 78
Voting Rights Act, 79
Voting Rights Act of 1964, 53, 75
Voting Rights Act of 1965, 78, 84,
    85, 205, 214
voting shortcuts, 115, 247
voting-age population, 77
voting-elibible population, 77

W
Walker, James "Jimmy", 368
Walker, Olene, 256
Wallace, George, 90
Wallace, Lurleen, 255

Wal-Mart, 187, 294, 465, 475
War on Poverty, 49, 51–56, 52–53
wards, 359
Warner, Mark, 270
Warren, Earl, 59
Washington, George, 45
Washington Post, 64, 327, 475
Washington Research Council, 499
Washington State
    abortion regulations, 433, 434
    anti-sodomy laws, 436
    average Medicaid payment per
        enrollee, 472
    barriers to voting, 83
    cigarette tax, 35
    corruption, perceived level, 35
    court system, 291
    farm income, 24
    Governor's institutional powers,
        35
    governor's institutional powers,
        265
    governor's political party, 13
    governor's popularity, 268
    gubernatorial election cycle, 247
    higher education spending, per
        capita, 14
    historic use of initiative, 110
    immigrants, undocumented, 466
    income per capita, 24
    initiatives, ease of qualifying, 112
    inpact of interest groups, 189
    institutions of direct democracy,
        101
    interest groups, by type, 185
    interparty competition, 1999–
        2003, 154
    jucidial selection mechanisms,
        305, 309
    legislative professionalism, 232
    lobbying laws, 173
    manufacturing employment, 24
    maximum TANF benefit, 461
    minimum wage laws, 465
    minority representation, state
        legislature, 216, 217
    mobility of population, 22
    opinion of direct democracy, 125
    partisan distribution of legislative
        seats, 207
    party contributions and
        expenditures, 149
    policy preferences, 30
    political culture, 28
    political ideology, 27
    primaries, 136
    public school revenue across
        sources, 490
    racial and ethnic characteristics,
        18
    Ranney Indices of Party Control,
        153
    regressive tax system, 339
    same-sex marriage laws, 439
    school funding and high school
        graduation rates, 492
    state and local taxes as
        percentage of income, 323

state legislature, 197
TANF recipients, 459
term limits repealed, 236
voter participation, 78
wealth relative to other states, 25
women in state legislature, 11
watchdogs, 162
weak mayor-council system, 367, 369
wealth, distribution of, 24–25
Webster v. Reproductive Health Services, 60, 431–432
wedge issues, 118
Weicker, Lowell P., Jr., 158
welfare, 456
welfare programs, 52–53, 55, 75, 90, 334
   Aid to Families with Dependent Children (AFDC). *see* Aid to Families with Dependent Children (AFDC)
   food stamps, 462–463
   funding, 453–454
   and political ideology, 455
   as portion of local spending, 343
   as portion of state spending, 342–343
   vs. social insurance, 455–456
   Temporary Assistance for Needy Families (TANF). *see* Temporary Assistance for Needy Families (TANF)
welfare reform, 447–448
Welfare-to-Work grants, 458
West, Kanye, 451
West Virginia
   barriers to voting, 83
   cigarette tax, 35
   corruption, perceived level, 35
   court system, 291
   farm income, 24
   Governor's institutional powers, 35
   governor's institutional powers, 265
   governor's political party, 13
   governor's popularity, 268
   gubernatorial election cycle, 247
   higher education spending, per capita, 14
   immigrants, undocumented, 466
   income per capita, 24
   inpact of interest groups, 189
   interest groups, by type, 185
   interparty competition, 1999–2003, 154
   jucidial selection mechanisms, 305, 309
   legislative professionalism, 232
   lobbying laws, 173
   manufacturing employment, 24
   minimum wage laws, 465
   minority representation, state legislature, 216, 217
   mobility of population, 22
   partisan contestation in state legislative races, 200

partisan distribution of legislative seats, 207
party contributions and expenditures, 149
policy preferences, 30
political culture, 28
political ideology, 27
primaries, 136
public school revenue across sources, 490
racial and ethnic characteristics, 18
Ranney Indices of Party Control, 153
school funding and high school graduation rates, 492
state and local taxes as percentage of income, 323
state legislature, 197
TANF recipients, 459
voter participation, 78
wealth relative to other states, 25
women in state legislature, 11
Western Center on Law and Poverty, 491
Western states, 16, 18. *see also* individual states
Wetherell, T. K., 494
wetlands, 406
Whites
   population by state, 17, 18
Whitman, Christine Todd, 255
Wichita, Kansas, 373
Wilder, Virginia L. Douglas, 253
Williams v. Rhodes, 141
Wilnauer, Jill, 329
Wilson, Pete, 119, 155
Wilson, Woodrow, 103, 252, 364
wine sales, Internet, 47
winner-take-all basis, 93
Wisconsin, 200
   barriers to voting, 83
   cigarette tax, 35
   corruption, perceived level, 35
   court system, 291
   farm income, 24
   Governor's institutional powers, 35
   governor's institutional powers, 265
   governor's political party, 13
   governor's popularity, 268
   gubernatorial election cycle, 247
   gubernatorial veto power, 259, 260
   higher education spending, per capita, 14
   immigrants, undocumented, 466
   income per capita, 24
   inpact of interest groups, 189
   interest groups, by type, 185
   interparty competition, 1999–2003, 154
   jucidial selection mechanisms, 305, 309
   legislative professionalism, 232
   lobbying laws, 173
   manufacturing employment, 24

Milwaukee, homeland security grants, 65
minimum wage laws, 465
minority representation, state legislature, 216, 217
mobility of population, 22
partisan distribution of legislative seats, 207
party contributions and expenditures, 149
policy preferences, 30
political culture, 28
political ideology, 27
primaries, 136
public school revenue across sources, 489
racial and ethnic characteristics, 18
Ranney Indices of Party Control, 153
school funding and high school graduation rates, 492
state and local taxes as percentage of income, 323
state legislature, 197
TANF recipients, 460
voter participation, 78
wealth relative to other states, 25
welfare programs, 458
women in state legislature, 11
Wisconsin Dairy Business Association, 163
Wisconsin Historical Society, 366
Wise, Bob, 244
women
   in poverty, 448, 449, 450
   and social reform movements, 365
   in state legislatures, 217–218
women in government
   as governors, 254–257
   in state legislatures, 11–12, 93, 195, 211–213
   Western states, 16
women's suffrage, 78
Wood, Fernando, 368
Worcester v. Georgia, 46
workers, undocumented, 465–466
Workers' Compensation program, 457
working poor, 464
Works Progress Administration (WPA), 52
World Almanac, 426
World Bank, 43, 44
World Socialist Web Site, 315
World Trade Center attacks, 39, 40, 49
   response to, 62–66
World War II era
   post-, 233
writ, 299
Wyoming
   abortion regulations, 433
   anti-sodomy laws, 436
   average Medicaid payment per enrollee, 472
   barriers to voting, 83

cigarette tax, 35
college tuition, 13, 14
corruption, perceived level, 35
court system, 291
Governor's institutional powers, 35
governor's institutional powers, 265
governor's political party, 13
governor's popularity, 268
gubernatorial election cycle, 247
higher education spending, per capita, 14
historic use of initiative, 110
immigrants, undocumented, 466
income per capita, 24
initiatives, ease of qualifying, 112
inpact of interest groups, 189
institutions of direct democracy, 101
interest groups, by type, 186
interparty competition, 1999–2003, 154
jucidial selection mechanisms, 305, 309
legislative professionalism, 232

lobbying laws, 173
manufacturing employment, 24
maximum TANF benefit, 461
minimum wage laws, 465
minority representation, state legislature, 216, 217
mobility of population, 22
partisan contestation in state legislative races, 201
partisan distribution of legislative seats, 207
party contributions and expenditures, 149
policy preferences, 30
political culture, 28
political ideology, 27
primaries, 136
public school revenue across sources, 489
racial and ethnic characteristics, 18
Ranney Indices of Party Control, 153
same-sex marriage laws, 439
school funding and high school graduation rates, 492

state and local taxes as percentage of income, 324
state legislature, 197
TANF recipients, 460
term limits repealed, 236
voter participation, 78
wealth relative to other states, 25
women in state legislature, 13
women's suffrage, 16

Y
Yale Law Journal, 315
Yale University, 494
Yorty, Sam, 368
Young, Andrew, 368

Z
zoning, 397–401. *see also* land use
definition, 385
opposition to, 405, 406, 407
and racism, 400–401
and revenues, 386–387

Governor's Institutional Powers

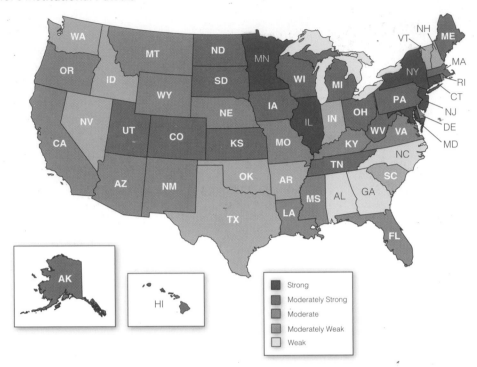

Strong
Moderately Strong
Moderate
Moderately Weak
Weak

Note: This is a modification for Beyle's index of governors' institutional power, based on appointments, independently elected executives, tenure potential, the state budget, and the veto.

Source: Beyle, Thad. 2004. "Governors." In *Politics in the American States*, eds. Virginia Gray and Russell L. Hanson. Washington, DC: CQ Press.

★★★

State Legislative Term Limits

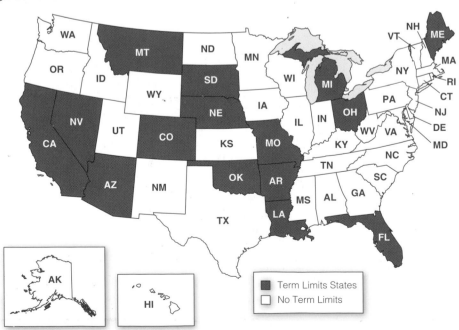

Term Limits States
No Term Limits